HTML, XHTML, and CSS

Comprehensive

Sixth Edition

HTML, XHTML, and CSS

Comprehensive
Sixth Edition

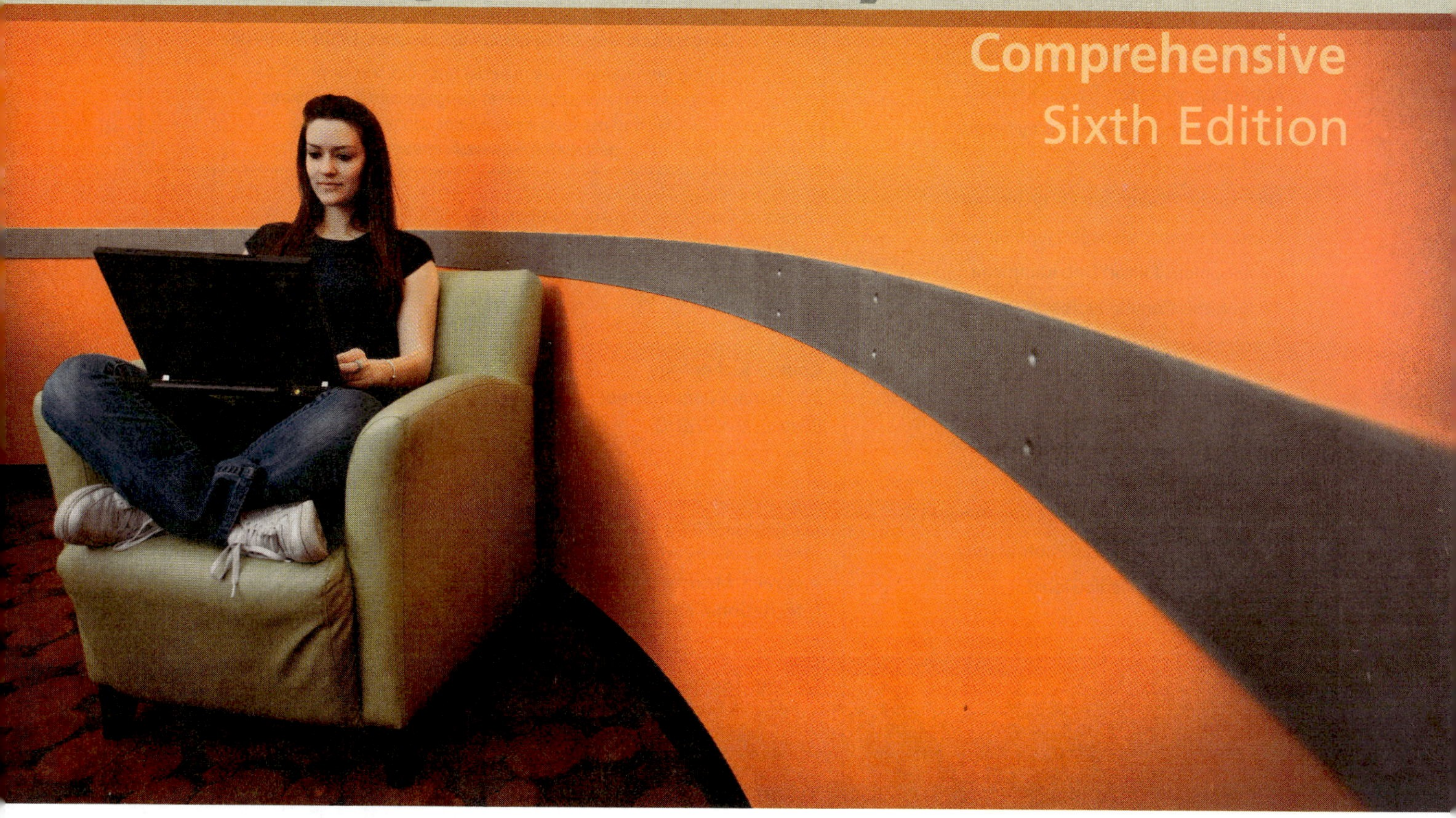

Gary B. Shelly
Denise M. Woods
William J. Dorin

Australia • Brazil • Japan • Korea • Mexico • Singapore • Spain • United Kingdom • United States

HTML, XHTML, and CSS Comprehensive, Sixth Edition
Gary B. Shelly, Denise M. Woods, William J. Dorin

Vice President, Publisher: Nicole Pinard
Executive Editor: Kathleen McMahon
Product Manager: Crystal Parenteau
Associate Product Manager: Aimee Poirier
Editorial Assistant: Lauren Brody
Director of Marketing: Cheryl Costantini
Marketing Manager: Tristen Kendall
Marketing Coordinator: Stacey Leasca
Print Buyer: Julio Esperas
Director of Production: Patty Stephan
Content Project Manager: Jennifer Feltri
Development Editor: Deb Kaufmann
Copyeditor: Camille Kiolbasa
Proofreader: Christine Clark
Indexer: Ken Hassman
QA Manuscript Reviewers: John Freitas, Serge Palladino, and Susan Whalen
Art Director: Marissa Falco
Cover Designer: Lisa Kuhn, Curio Press, LLC
Cover Photo: Tom Kates Photography
Compositor: PreMediaGlobal

Library of Congress Control Number: 2010929584

ISBN-13: 978-0-538-74754-7

ISBN-10: 0-538-74754-4

Course Technology
20 Channel Center Street
Boston, MA 02210
USA

Cengage Learning is a leading provider of customized learning solutions with office locations around the globe, including Singapore, the United Kingdom, Australia, Mexico, Brazil, and Japan. Locate your local office at: **international.cengage.com/region**

Cengage Learning products are represented in Canada by Nelson Education, Ltd.

For your course and learning solutions, visit **www.cengage.com**

To learn more about Course Technology, visit **www.cengage.com/coursetechnology**

Purchase any of our products at your local collage bookstore or at our preferred online store at **www.CengageBrain.com**

Printed in the United States of America
2 3 4 5 6 15 14 13 12 11

HTML, XHTML, and CSS

Comprehensive
Sixth Edition

Contents

SPECIAL FEATURE 1
Attracting Visitors to Your Web Site

CHAPTER FIVE
Creating an Image Map

CHAPTER NINE
Integrating JavaScript and HTML

CHAPTER TEN
Creating Pop-Up Windows, Adding Scrolling Messages, and Validating Forms

Appendices

APPENDIX A
HTML Quick Reference

APPENDIX B
Browser-Safe Color Palette

APPENDIX C
Accessibility Standards and the Web

APPENDIX D
CSS Properties and Values

Preface

The Shelly Cashman Series® offers the finest textbooks in computer education. We are proud of the fact that our previous HTML books have been so well received. With each new edition of our HTML books, we have made significant improvements based on the comments made by instructors and students. The *HTML, XHTML, and CSS, Sixth Edition* books continue with the innovation, quality, and reliability you have come to expect from the Shelly Cashman Series.

In 2006 and 2007, the Shelly Cashman Series development team carefully reviewed our pedagogy and analyzed its effectiveness in teaching today's student. An extensive customer survey produced results confirming what the series is best known for: its step-by-step, screen-by-screen instructions, its project-oriented approach, and the quality of its content.

We learned, though, that students entering computer courses today are different than students taking these classes just a few years ago. Students today read less, but need to retain more. They need not only to be able to perform skills, but to retain those skills and know how to apply them to different settings. Today's students need to be continually engaged and challenged to retain what they're learning.

As a result, we've renewed our commitment to focusing on the user and how they learn best. This commitment is reflected in every change we've made to our HTML book.

Objectives of This Textbook

HTML, XHTML, and CSS: Comprehensive, Sixth Edition is intended for use in a three-unit course that presents an in-depth coverage of HTML and basic Web design techniques. No experience with Web page development or computer programming is required. Specific objectives of this book are as follows:

- To teach the fundamentals of developing Web pages using a comprehensive Web development life cycle
- To acquaint students with the HTML and CSS languages and creating Web pages suitable for course work, professional purposes, and personal use
- To expose students to common Web page formats and functions
- To promote curiosity and independent exploration of World Wide Web resources
- To develop an exercise-oriented approach that allows students to learn by example
- To encourage independent study and help those who are learning how to create Web pages in a distance education environment
- To acquaint students with the XHTML guidelines
- To illustrate how to create dynamic Web pages and add functionality using JavaScript and the Document Object Model (DOM)
- To show the benefits of XML

Distinguishing Features

A Proven Pedagogy with an Emphasis on Project Planning Each chapter presents a practical problem to be solved, within a project planning framework. The project orientation is strengthened by the use of Plan Ahead boxes that encourage critical thinking about how to proceed at various points in the project. Step-by-step instructions with supporting screens guide students through the steps. Instructional steps are supported by the Q&A, Experimental Step, and BTW features.

A Visually Engaging Book that Maintains Student Interest The step-by-step tasks, with supporting figures, provide a rich visual experience for the student. Call-outs on the screens that present both explanatory and navigational information provide students with information they need when they need to know it.

Supporting Reference Materials (Appendices) The appendices provide additional information about HTML, XHTML, and CSS topics, with appendices such as the HTML Quick Reference, CSS Properties and Values, and Publishing Web Pages to a Web Server.

Integration of the World Wide Web The World Wide Web is integrated into the HTML, XHTML, and CSS learning experience by (1) BTW annotations; and (2) the Learn It Online section for each chapter.

End-of-Chapter Student Activities Extensive end-of-chapter activities provide a variety of reinforcement opportunities for students where they can apply and expand their skills through individual and group work.

Organization of This Textbook

HTML, XHTML, and CSS: Comprehensive, Sixth Edition consists of twelve chapters and two Special Features on HTML, XHTML, and CSS, and eight appendices. The Chapters and Appendices are organized as follows:

Chapter 1 – Introduction to HTML This introductory chapter provides students with an overview of the Internet, World Wide Web, Web pages, HTML, and Web development. Topics include the types and purposes of Web sites, Web browsers, HTML standards, and Document Object Model (DOM) and Extensible Hypertext Markup Language (XHTML) and their relationship to HTML. Additionally, Web editors, the five phases of the Web development life cycle, and the importance of validating and testing Web pages for usability are defined.

Chapter 2 – Creating and Editing a Web Page Using Inline Styles In Chapter 2, students are introduced to basic HTML tags and the various parts of a Web page. Topics include starting and quitting Notepad++ and a browser, entering headings and text into an HTML file, creating a bulleted list with HTML using Cascading Style Sheets and inline styles, adding an image and a horizontal rule, saving the HTML file and viewing it in the browser, validating the HTML code, viewing the HTML source code for a Web page, printing the HTML file and the Web page, and Web page design.

Chapter 3 – Creating Web pages with Links, Images, and Embedded Style Sheets In Chapter 3, students are introduced to linking terms and definitions. Topics include adding an e-mail link, linking to another page on the same Web site, linking to another Web site, setting link targets within a page, linking to targets, using absolute and relative paths, using different types of image files, specifying alternative text for images, defining image size, wrapping text around an image, inserting images onto Web pages, and using embedded style sheets.

Chapter 4 – Creating Tables in a Web Site Using an External Style Sheet In Chapter 4, students learn how to create tables using HTML tags. First, students assess table needs and then plan the table. Topics include table definitions and terms, table uses, creating borderless tables; inserting images into tables; vertical and horizontal alignment within a table, adding color to a cell, adding links to another page, adding an e-mail link, using the rowspan and colspan attributes, adding captions, spacing within and between cells, and creating and using an external style sheet.

Special Feature 1 – Attracting Visitors to Your Web Site In this feature, students learn how to advertise their Web pages. Topics include using meta tags and keywords, submitting Web pages to a search engine, publicizing Web pages, and finding Web site hosting sites.

Chapter 5 – Creating an Image Map In Chapter 5, students learn how to use an image map to create more advanced Web page navigation. Topics include image mapping purpose and considerations, selecting appropriate images for mapping, dividing an image into hotspots, creating links from those hotspots, and using text links in conjunction with image links.

Chapter 6 – Creating a Form on a Web Page In Chapter 6, students create a form for collecting user input. Topics include form basics, adding controls such as check boxes, radio buttons, text boxes, and other controls on a form, creating Submit and Reset buttons, and creating an e-mail link to submit the form information back to the Web page data collector. Students also are introduced to using advanced selection menus and fieldset tags to segregate groups of information.

Chapter 7 – Using Advanced Cascading Style Sheets In Chapter 7, students are introduced to some more advanced uses of Cascading Style Sheets (CSS). Topics include adding a drop-down menu for navigation, adding pop-up image effects, and using CSS for tables instead of using HTML table tags.

Chapter 8 – Adding Multimedia Content to Web Pages In Chapter 8, students learn how to add audio and video clips to a Web page. Topics include the benefits and limitations of multimedia content for Web pages, audio and video formats, and commonly used parameters for embedded multimedia.

Special Feature 2 – Converting Frames on Your Web Site In this feature, students learn ways to convert a Web site with a frame layout to one without frames. Topics include the frame definition file, different frame layouts, and converting frames to a traditional Web page.

Chapter 10 – Creating Pop-up Windows, Adding Scrolling Messages, and Validating Forms In Chapter 10, three common uses of JavaScript are presented; creating pop-up windows, adding scrolling messages, and validating forms. Topics include using JavaScript to conduct data entry validation on the client computer; working with the Document Object Model (DOM), forms, string lengths, and the Math object pow() method; using the if...else control structure with the parseInt(), is NaN(), and parseFloat() built-in functions to validate user input forms; and writing user-defined functions called by event handlers.

Chapter 11 – Using DOM to Enhance Web Pages In Chapter 11, students use DHTML in Web page development. Topics include defining the Document Object Model (DOM); creating layers using divisions (<div>tag); writing the code to make text or image objects scroll across or down a Web page; using the JavaScript setTimeout() and clearTimeout() methods to start and stop scrolling; using JavaScript to create rotating banners on a Web page; using onmouseover and onmouseout event handlers to execute pop-up ScreenTips; using the <span> tag as a container for embedded style sheet code to format Web pages text and the ScreenTips; and calling user-defined functions directly with the JavaScript command.

Chapter 12 – Creating and Using XML Documents In Chapter 12, students develop an understanding of XML documents, the W3C design goals for creating XML tags, and real-world uses for XML. Topics include learning the syntax rules for well-formed and valid XML documents; defining the document prolog, document instance, and recordset; describing the purpose of processing instructions; creating Document Type Definitions (DTD) and XML Schemas; binding an XSL style sheet to an XML document, and an XML document to an HTML Web page; using the built-in table element methods; and creating a JavaScript user-defined function to search for specific data items in an XML document.

Appendix A – HTML Quick Reference Appendix A includes an HTML quick reference that contains the most frequently used tags and their associated attributes.

Appendix B – Browser-Safe Color Palette Appendix B summarizes the 216 browser-safe colors that appear equally well on different monitors, operating systems, and browsers.

Appendix C – Accessibility Standards for the Web Appendix C provides an overview of Web accessibility issues and the Section 508 Web accessibility guidelines used by developers to create accessible Web sites.

Appendix D – CSS Properties and Values Appendix D provides a listing of Cascading Style Sheet (CSS) properties and values together with a description of use.

Appendix E – Publishing Your Web Site Appendix E provides a quick overview of how to publish Web pages to a Web host and also discusses how to choose a Web host and how to upload your Web files via FTP.

Appendix F – Symbols and Characters Quick Reference Appendix F shows the entity characters used to represent special symbols and characters in HTML and XHTML.

Appendix G – JavaScript Quick Reference Appendix G is a JavaScript quick reference of statements, objects, properties, methods, and event handlers.

Appendix H – XML Quick Reference Appendix H is an XML quick reference that contains syntax rules, XML applications, element definitions and attributes, coding examples, and a brief summary of XML Schema and XLS style sheet notation.

End-of-Chapter Student Activities

A notable strength of the Shelly Cashman Series HTML, XHTML, and CSS books is the extensive student activities at the end of each chapter. Well-structured student activities can make the difference between students merely participating in a class and students retaining the information they learn. The activities in the Shelly Cashman Series books include the following.

CHAPTER SUMMARY A concluding paragraph, followed by a listing of the tasks completed within a chapter together with the pages on which the step-by-step, screen-by-screen explanations appear.

LEARN IT ONLINE Every chapter features a Learn It Online section that is comprised of six exercises. These exercises include True/False, Multiple Choice, Short Answer, Flash Cards, Practice Test, and Learning Games.

APPLY YOUR KNOWLEDGE This exercise usually requires students to open and manipulate a file from the Data Files that parallels the activities learned in the chapter. To obtain a copy of the Data Files for Students, follow the instructions on the inside back cover of this text.

EXTEND YOUR KNOWLEDGE This exercise allows students to extend and expand on the skills learned within the chapter.

MAKE IT RIGHT This exercise requires students to analyze a document, identify errors and issues, and correct those errors and issues using skills learned in the chapter.

IN THE LAB Three in-depth assignments per chapter require students to utilize the chapter concepts and techniques to solve problems on a computer.

CASES AND PLACES Five unique real-world case-study situations, including Make It Personal, an open-ended project that relates to student's personal lives, and one small-group activity.

Instructor Resources CD-ROM

The Instructor Resources include both teaching and testing aids.

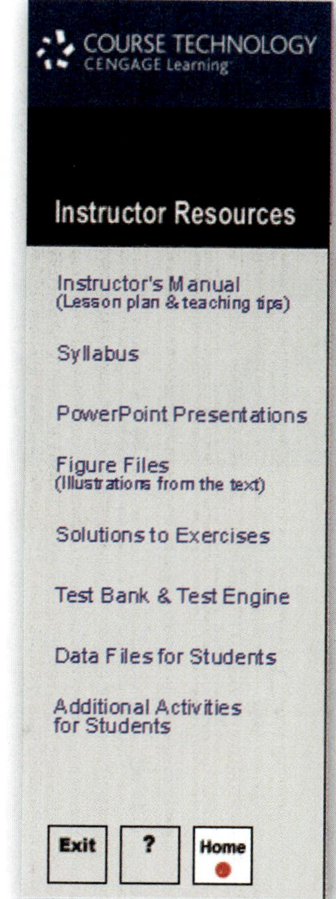

INSTRUCTOR'S MANUAL Includes lecture notes summarizing the chapter sections, figures and boxed elements found in every chapter, teacher tips, classroom activities, lab activities, and quick quizzes in Microsoft Word files.

SYLLABUS Easily customizable sample syllabi that cover policies, assignments, exams, and other course information.

FIGURE FILES Illustrations for every figure in the textbook in electronic form.

POWERPOINT PRESENTATIONS A multimedia lecture presentation system that provides slides for each chapter. Presentations are based on chapter objectives.

SOLUTIONS TO EXERCISES Includes solutions for all end-of-chapter and chapter reinforcement exercises.

TEST BANK & TEST ENGINE Test Banks include 112 questions for every chapter, featuring objective-based and critical thinking question types, and including page number references. Also included is the test engine, ExamView, the ultimate tool for your objective-based testing needs.

DATA FILES FOR STUDENTS Includes all the files that are required by students to complete the exercises.

ADDITIONAL ACTIVITIES FOR STUDENTS Consists of Chapter Reinforcement Exercises, which are true/false, multiple-choice, and short answer questions that help students gain confidence in the material learned.

Content for Online Learning

Course Technology has partnered with the leading distance learning solution providers and class-management platforms today. To access this material, Instructors will visit our password-protected instructor resources available at www.cengage.com/coursetechnology. Instructor resources include the following: additional case projects, sample syllabi, PowerPoint presentations per chapter, and more. For additional information or for an instructor username and password, please contact your sales representative. For students to access this material, they must have purchased a WebTutor PIN-code specific to this title and your campus platform. The resources for students may include (based on instructor preferences), but not limited to: topic review, review questions and practice tests.

CourseNotes

Course Technology's CourseNotes are six-panel quick reference cards that reinforce the most important concepts and features of a software application in a visual and user-friendly format. CourseNotes serve as a great reference tool during and after the student completes the course. CourseNotes are available for software applications such as Microsoft Office 2007, Word 2007, Excel 2007, Access 2007, PowerPoint 2007, and Windows 7. There are also topic-based CourseNotes available for Best Practices in Social Networking, Hot Topics in Technology, and Web 2.0. Visit www.cengage.com/ct/coursenotes to learn more!

Guided Tours

Add excitement and interactivity to your classroom with "*A Guided Tour*" product line. Play one of the brief mini-movies to spice up your lecture and spark classroom discussion. Or, assign a movie for homework and ask students to complete the correlated assignment that accompanies each topic. "*A Guided Tour*" product line takes the prep-work out of providing your students with information on new technologies and software applications and helps keep students engaged with content relevant to their lives; all in under an hour!

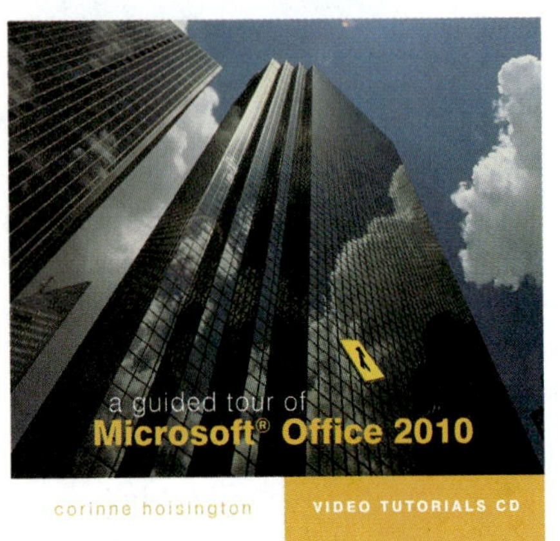

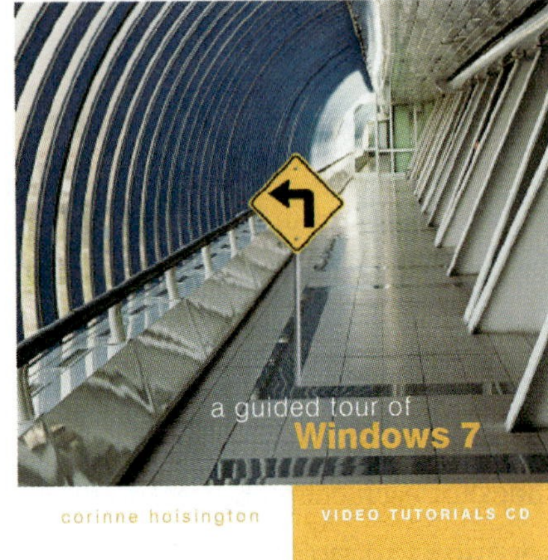

About Our Covers

The Shelly Cashman Series is continually updating our approach and content to reflect the way today's students learn and experience new technology. This focus on student success is reflected on our covers, which feature real students from Westfield State College using the Shelly Cashman Series in their courses, and reflect the varied ages and backgrounds of the students learning with our books. When you use the Shelly Cashman Series, you can be assured that you are learning computer skills using the most effective courseware available.

Textbook Walk-Through

The Shelly Cashman Series Pedagogy: Project-Based — Step-by-Step — Variety of Assessments

Plan Ahead boxes prepare students to create successful projects by encouraging them to think strategically about what they are trying to accomplish before they begin working.

Step-by-Step instructions now provide a context beyond the point-and-click. Each step provides information on why students are performing each task, or what will occur as a result.

Plan Ahead

General Project Guidelines

When creating a Web page, the actions you perform and decisions you make will affect the appearance and characteristics of the finished page. As you create a Web page, such as the project shown in Figure 2–1 on the previous page, you should follow these general guidelines:

1. **Complete Web page planning.** Before developing a Web page, you must know the purpose of the Web site, identify the users of the site and their computing environments, and decide who owns the information on the Web page.
2. **Analyze the need for the Web page.** In the analysis phase of the Web development life cycle, you should analyze what content to include on the Web page. In this phase, you determine the tasks and the information that the users need. Refer to Table 1–4 on page HTML 15 for information on the phases of the Web development life cycle.
3. **Choose the content for the Web page.** Once you have completed the analysis, you need to determine what content to include on the Web page. Follow the *less is more* principle. The less text, the more likely the Web page will be read. Use as few words as possible to make a point.
4. **Determine the file naming convention that you will use for this Web page.** Before you start creating and saving files, you should decide on a standard way of naming your files. Should you use the .htm or .html extension? As explained later in the chapter, you use the .htm extension when the host Web server only allows short file names. You use .html when the host Web server allows long file names. What name should you give your file to indicate the file's content or purpose? For instance, naming a Web page page1.html does not describe what that Web page is; a more descriptive name is helpful in development of the Web site.
5. **Determine where to save the Web page.** You can store a Web page permanently, or **save** it, on a variety of storage media, including a hard disk, USB flash drive, CD, or DVD. Your instructor or the company for whom you are developing the Web page may have specific storage media requirements.
6. **Determine what folder structure to use on your storage device.** Once you have determined the storage media to use, you should also determine folder location, structure, and names on which to save the Web page. This should be done before you start to save any of your files.

...**ormat various elements of the Web page.** The overall appearance of a ...cantly affects its ability to communicate clearly. Examples of how you ...ppearance, or **format**, of the Web page include adding an image, color ...horizontal rules.

...**graphical images.** Eye-catching graphical images help convey the Web ...ssage and add visual interest. Graphics can be used to show a product, ...benefit, or visually convey a message that is not expressed easily

...**o position and how to format the graphical images.** The position and ...phical images should grab the attention of passersby and draw them ...Web page.

...**e for XHTML compliance.** An important part of Web development is ...that your Web page follows XHTML standards. The World Wide Web ...) has an online validator that allows you to test your Web page and ...ny errors.

...ore specific details concerning the above guidelines are presented ...in the chapter. The chapter also will identify the actions performed ...egarding these guidelines during the creation of the Web page shown

To Save an HTML File

You have performed many steps in creating this project and do not want to risk losing the work you have done so far. Also, to view HTML in a browser, you must save the file. The following steps show how to save an HTML file.

1

- With a USB flash drive connected to one of the computer's USB ports, click File on the Notepad++ menu bar (Figure 2–15).

File menu name

Save As command

File menu choices

Figure 2–15

2

- Click Save As on the File menu to display the Save As dialog box (Figure 2–16).

Q&A Do I have to save to a USB flash drive?

No. You can save to any device or folder. A folder is a specific location on a storage medium. Use the same process, but select your device or folder.

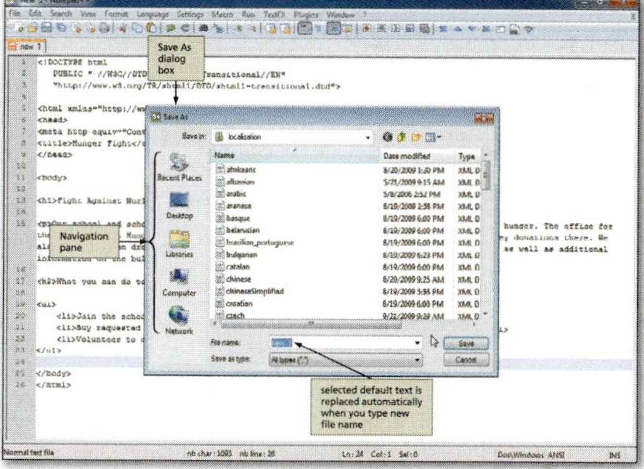

Figure 2–16

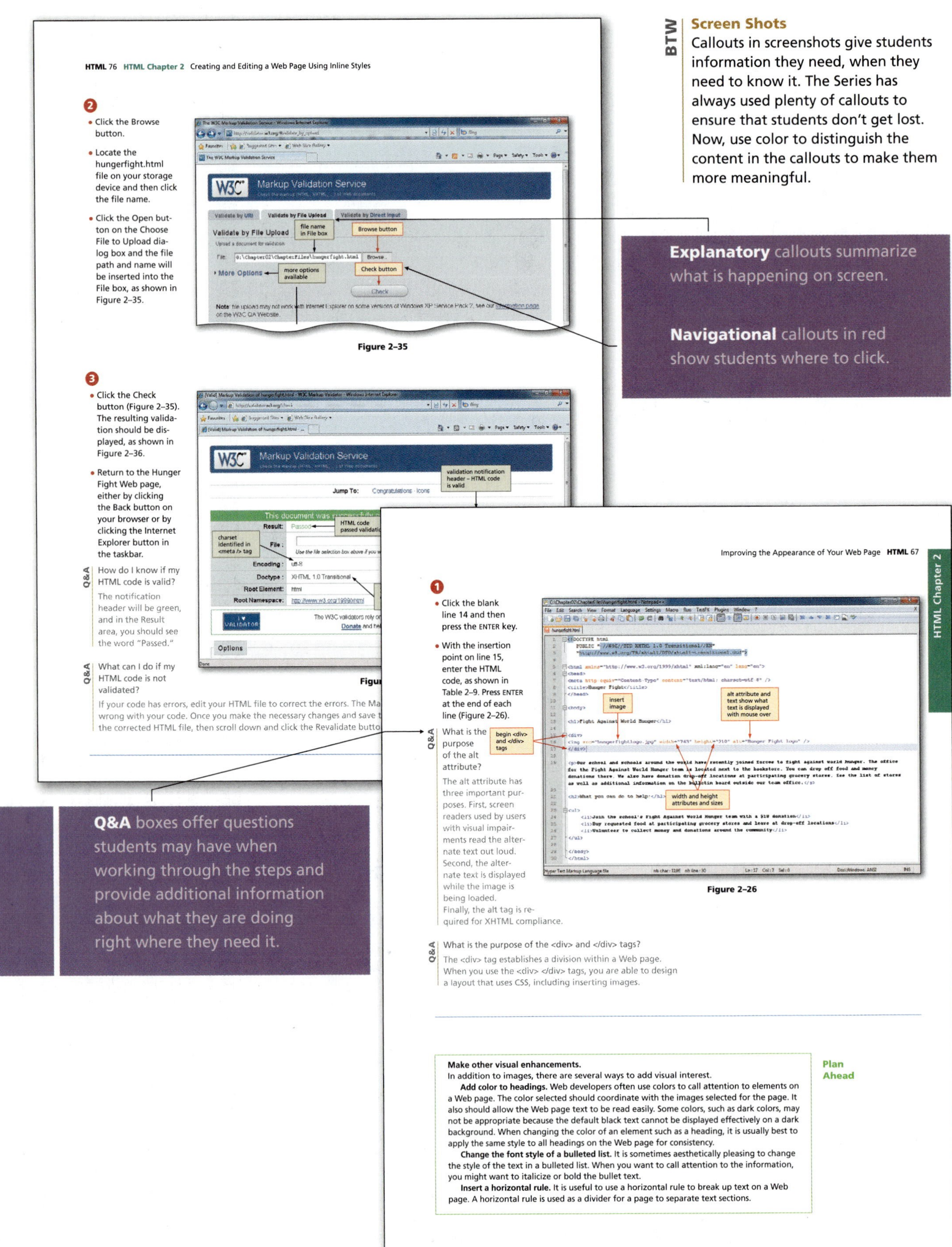

BTW

Screen Shots

Callouts in screenshots give students information they need, when they need to know it. The Series has always used plenty of callouts to ensure that students don't get lost. Now, use color to distinguish the content in the callouts to make them more meaningful.

Explanatory callouts summarize what is happening on screen.

Navigational callouts in red show students where to click.

Q&A boxes offer questions students may have when working through the steps and provide additional information about what they are doing right where they need it.

HTML 76 HTML Chapter 2 Creating and Editing a Web Page Using Inline Styles

2

- Click the Browse button.
- Locate the hungerfight.html file on your storage device and then click the file name.
- Click the Open button on the Choose File to Upload dialog box and the file path and name will be inserted into the File box, as shown in Figure 2–35.

Figure 2–35

3

- Click the Check button (Figure 2–35). The resulting validation should be displayed, as shown in Figure 2–36.
- Return to the Hunger Fight Web page, either by clicking the Back button on your browser or by clicking the Internet Explorer button in the taskbar.

Q&A How do I know if my HTML code is valid?

The notification header will be green, and in the Result area, you should see the word "Passed."

Q&A What can I do if my HTML code is not validated?

If your code has errors, edit your HTML file to correct the errors. The Ma... wrong with your code. Once you make the necessary changes and save t... the corrected HTML file, then scroll down and click the Revalidate butto...

Improving the Appearance of Your Web Page HTML 67

HTML Chapter 2

1

- Click the blank line 14 and then press the ENTER key.
- With the insertion point on line 15, enter the HTML code, as shown in Table 2–9. Press ENTER at the end of each line (Figure 2–26).

Q&A What is the purpose of the alt attribute?

The alt attribute has three important purposes. First, screen readers used by users with visual impairments read the alternate text out loud. Second, the alternate text is displayed while the image is being loaded. Finally, the alt tag is required for XHTML compliance.

Figure 2–26

Q&A What is the purpose of the <div> and </div> tags?

The <div> tag establishes a division within a Web page. When you use the <div> </div> tags, you are able to design a layout that uses CSS, including inserting images.

Plan Ahead

Make other visual enhancements.

In addition to images, there are several ways to add visual interest.

Add color to headings. Web developers often use colors to call attention to elements on a Web page. The color selected should coordinate with the images selected for the page. It also should allow the Web page text to be read easily. Some colors, such as dark colors, may not be appropriate because the default black text cannot be displayed effectively on a dark background. When changing the color of an element such as a heading, it is usually best to apply the same style to all headings on the Web page for consistency.

Change the font style of a bulleted list. It is sometimes aesthetically pleasing to change the style of the text in a bulleted list. When you want to call attention to the information, you might want to italicize or bold the bullet text.

Insert a horizontal rule. It is useful to use a horizontal rule to break up text on a Web page. A horizontal rule is used as a divider for a page to separate text sections.

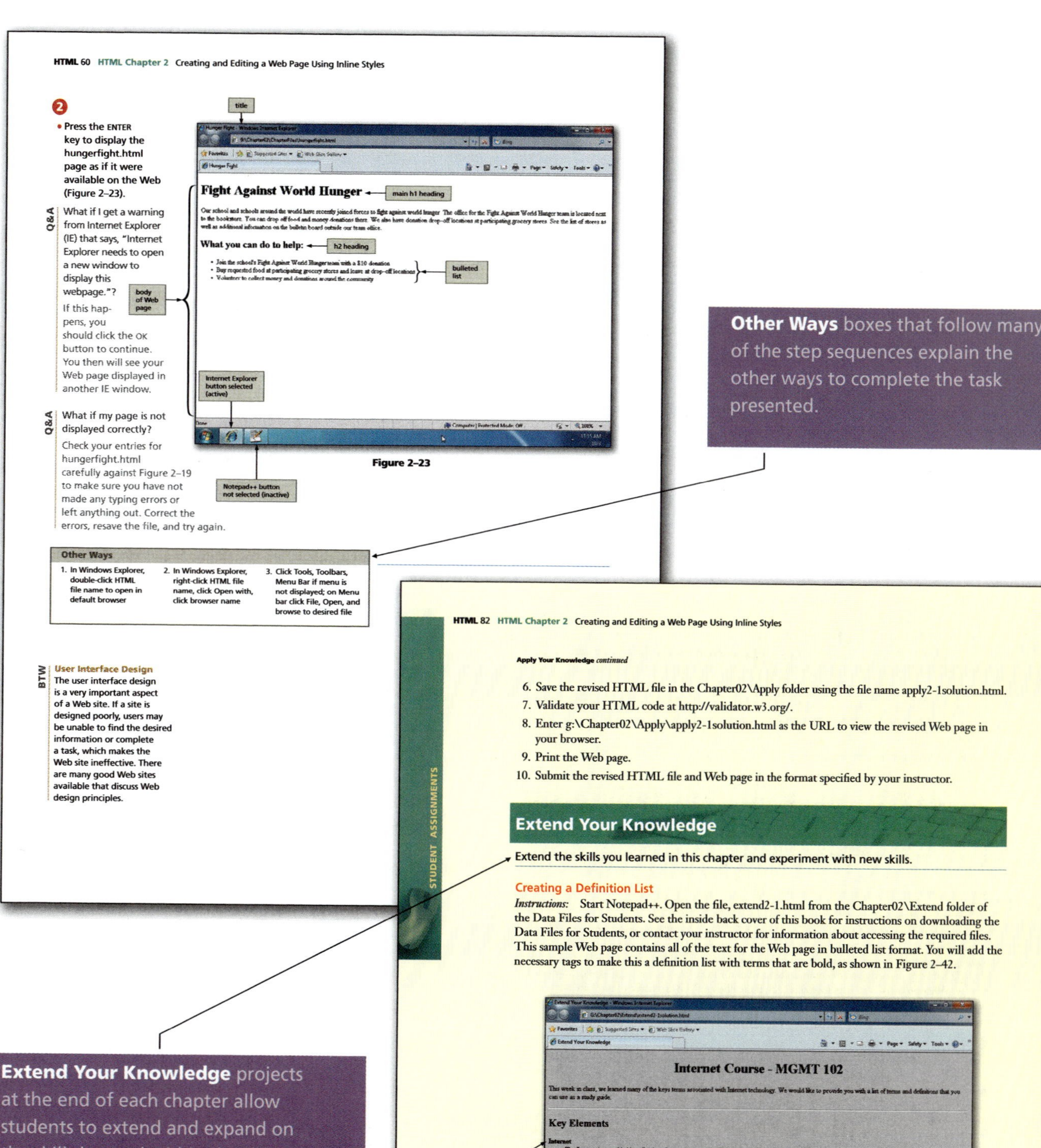

HTML 60 HTML Chapter 2 Creating and Editing a Web Page Using Inline Styles

2

- Press the ENTER key to display the hungerfight.html page as if it were available on the Web (Figure 2–23).

Q&A What if I get a warning from Internet Explorer (IE) that says, "Internet Explorer needs to open a new window to display this webpage."?

If this happens, you should click the OK button to continue. You then will see your Web page displayed in another IE window.

Q&A What if my page is not displayed correctly?

Check your entries for hungerfight.html carefully against Figure 2–19 to make sure you have not made any typing errors or left anything out. Correct the errors, resave the file, and try again.

Figure 2–23

Other Ways

1. In Windows Explorer, double-click HTML file name to open in default browser
2. In Windows Explorer, right-click HTML file name, click Open with, click browser name
3. Click Tools, Toolbars, Menu Bar if menu is not displayed; on Menu bar click File, Open, and browse to desired file

BTW **User Interface Design**

The user interface design is a very important aspect of a Web site. If a site is designed poorly, users may be unable to find the desired information or complete a task, which makes the Web site ineffective. There are many good Web sites available that discuss Web design principles.

Other Ways boxes that follow many of the step sequences explain the other ways to complete the task presented.

HTML 82 HTML Chapter 2 Creating and Editing a Web Page Using Inline Styles

STUDENT ASSIGNMENTS

Apply Your Knowledge *continued*

6. Save the revised HTML file in the Chapter02\Apply folder using the file name apply2-1solution.html.
7. Validate your HTML code at http://validator.w3.org/.
8. Enter g:\Chapter02\Apply\apply2-1solution.html as the URL to view the revised Web page in your browser.
9. Print the Web page.
10. Submit the revised HTML file and Web page in the format specified by your instructor.

Extend Your Knowledge

Extend the skills you learned in this chapter and experiment with new skills.

Creating a Definition List

Instructions: Start Notepad++. Open the file, extend2-1.html from the Chapter02\Extend folder of the Data Files for Students. See the inside back cover of this book for instructions on downloading the Data Files for Students, or contact your instructor for information about accessing the required files. This sample Web page contains all of the text for the Web page in bulleted list format. You will add the necessary tags to make this a definition list with terms that are bold, as shown in Figure 2–42.

Figure 2–42

Perform the following tasks:

1. Using the text given in the file extend2-1.html, make changes to the HTML code to change the Web page from a bulleted list to a definition list by following the definition list code shown in Figure 2–14 on page HTML 52.

Extend Your Knowledge projects at the end of each chapter allow students to extend and expand on the skills learned within the chapter. Students use critical thinking to experiment with new skills to complete each project.

2. Add the additional HTML code necessary to make the terms bold (see font-weight for style in Appendix D) and a background color of #e0e0e0 (see background-color in Appendix D).
3. Save the revised document in the Chapter02\Extend folder with the file name extend2-1solution.html, validate the Web page, and then submit it in the format specified by your instructor.

Make It Right

Analyze a document and correct all errors and/or improve the design.

Correcting the Friendly Reminder Web Page

Instructions: Start Notepad++. Open the file makeitright2-1.html from the Chapter02\MakeItRight folder of the Data Files for Students. See the inside back cover of this book for instructions on downloading the Data Files for Students, or contact your instructor for information about accessing the required files. The Web page is a modified version of what you see in Figure 2–43. Make the necessary corrections to the Web page to make it look like Figure 2–43. Format the heading to use the Heading 1 style center-aligned on the Web page (see the text-align property in Appendix D to center a heading). Add two size-10px horizontal rules, as shown in Figure 2–43. Save the file in the Chapter02\MakeItRight folder as makeitright2-1solution.html, validate the Web page, and then submit it in the format specified by your instructor.

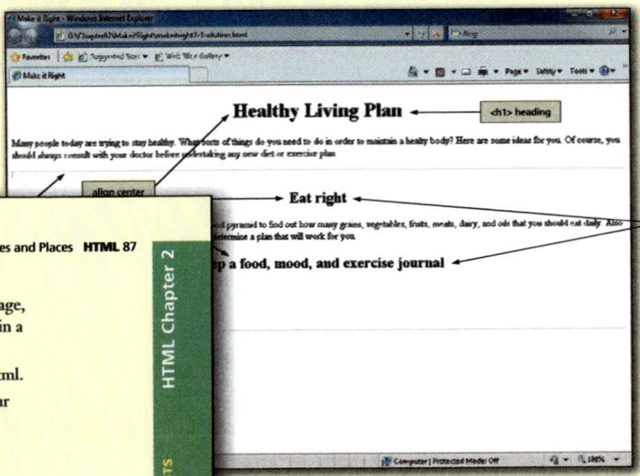

Healthy Living Plan

<h1> heading

align center

Eat right

<h2> headings

...p a food, mood, and exercise journal

Figure 2–43

Make It Right projects call on students to analyze a file, discover errors in it, and fix them using the skills they learned in the chapter.

3. Insert the image file cloudy.jpg, stored in the Chapter02\IntheLab folder. Right-click the image, click Properties, and then click the Details tab to find out the image's dimensions, or open it in a graphics program. Note that the bullets used for the list are square in shape.
4. Save the HTML file in the Chapter02\IntheLab folder using the file name lab2-3solution.html.
5. Enter g:\Chapter02\IntheLab\lab2-3solution.html as the URL to view the Web page in your browser.
6. Print the Web page from your browser.
7. Submit the revised HTML file and Web page in the format specified by your instructor.

Cases and Places

Apply your creative thinking and problem-solving skills to design and implement a solution.

• Easier •• More Difficult

• 1: Add to the Food Drive Web Page

Mr. Wattigney, the director of the Community Food Bank, likes the Web page you created for Lab 2-1. Now that the Food Drive is over, he would like you to update the Web page with new information on upcoming community events. Before updating the page, search the Web to review the Web pages at other food banks or departments of community services for ideas on content to include or formatting to change. What do their Web sites look like? Are there changes you can make to the Lab 2-1 Web page that reflect what other places have done? Using the concepts presented in this chapter, include additional information or change the formatting to make the page more interesting and timely.

• 2: Create an Artist Web Site

You are creating a new Web site for a local photographer. The photographer has asked that you use descriptive alt attributes for images on the Web page, because many of the viewers of his Web page have very slow Internet connections and images often do not load quickly. Search the Web for information on adding useful, descriptive alt attributes for images. Also find information on using thumbnail images. Give suggestions for loading images faster. Create a document with a brief paragraph explaining the information that you found in your research. Make suggestions about how the photographer's Web site can be made more effective.

•• 3: Create a Web Page of CSS Properties

You have learned a lot about using Cascading Style Sheets (CSS) so far in the class. You still have some questions, though, about how to insert certain styles. Research information on the Web (don't forget to look at the W3.org site) to find Web sites that list CSS properties and values that complement Appendix D. In a Word document, add the URLs that you found to be very helpful. Under each URL write a brief paragraph that describes why you thought the site could be useful for new Web developers. Share your list of URLs with fellow students.

•• 4: Create a Personal Web Page

Make It Personal

Your class instructor wants to post all of the students' Web pages on the school server to show what his or her students are interested in. Create a Web page of personal information, listing items such as your school major, jobs that you have had in the past, and your hobbies and interests. To make your personal

Continued >

Found within the Cases & Places exercises, the **Make It Personal** exercises call on students to create an open-ended project that relates to their personal lives.

HTML, XHTML, and CSS

Comprehensive

Sixth Edition

1 Introduction to HTML, XHTML, and CSS

Objectives

You will have mastered the material in this chapter when you can:

- Describe the Internet and its associated key terms
- Describe the World Wide Web and its associated key terms
- Describe the types and purposes of Web sites
- Discuss Web browsers and identify their purpose
- Define Hypertext Markup Language (HTML) and its associated standards used for Web development
- Discuss the use of Cascading Style Sheets (CSS) in Web development
- Define the Document Object Model (DOM) and describe its relationship to HTML
- Define Extensible Hypertext Markup Language (XHTML) and describe its relationship to HTML
- Identify tools used to create HTML documents
- Describe the five phases of the Web development life cycle
- Describe the different methods of Web site design and the purpose of each Web site structure
- Discuss the importance of testing throughout the Web development life cycle
- Explain the importance of being an observant Web user

1 Introduction to HTML, XHTML, and CSS

Introduction

Before diving into the details of creating Web pages with HTML, XHTML, and CSS, it is useful to look at how these technologies relate to the development of the Internet and the World Wide Web. The Internet began with the connection of computers and computer networks. This connectivity has had a huge impact on our daily lives. Today, millions of people worldwide have access to the Internet, the world's largest network. Billions of Web pages, providing information on any subject you can imagine, are currently available on the World Wide Web. People use the Internet to search for information, to communicate with others around the world, and to seek entertainment. Students register for classes, pay tuition, and find out final grades via this computer network. Stores and individuals sell their products using computer connectivity, and most industries rely on the Internet and the World Wide Web for business transactions.

Hypertext Markup Language (HTML) and more recently Extensible Hypertext Markup Language (XHTML) and Cascading Style Sheets (CSS) allow the World Wide Web to exist. In order to utilize these technologies effectively, you need to understand the main concepts behind the Internet and HTML. In this chapter, you learn some basics about the Internet, the World Wide Web, intranets, and extranets. You are introduced to Web browsers, definitions of HTML and associated key terms, the five phases of the Web development life cycle, and the tasks that are involved in each phase.

What Is the Internet?

Most people today have had exposure to the Internet at school, in their homes, at their jobs, or at their local library. The **Internet** is a worldwide collection of computers and computer networks that links billions of computers used by businesses, government, educational institutions, organizations, and individuals using modems, phone lines, television cables, satellite links, fiber-optic connections, and other communications devices and media (Figure 1–1).

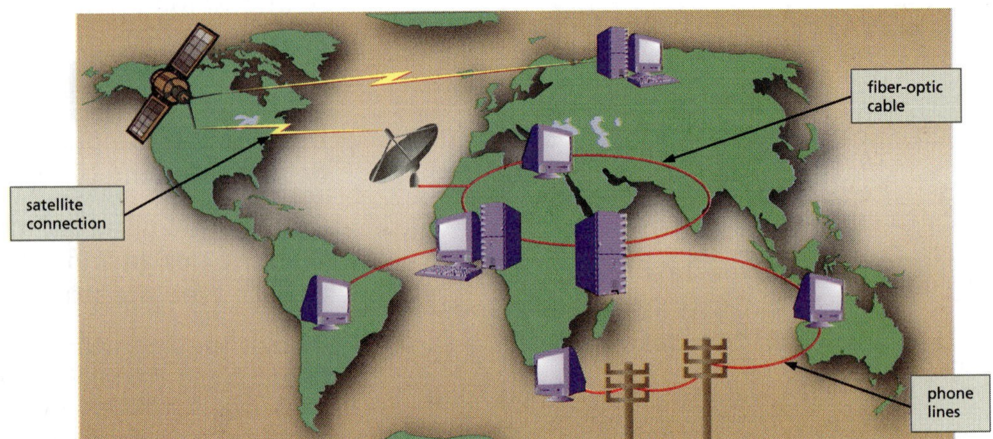

Figure 1–1 The Internet is a worldwide collection of computer networks.

A **network** is a collection of two or more computers that are connected to share resources and information. Today, high-, medium-, and low-speed data lines connect networks. These data lines allow data (including text, graphical images, and audio and video data) to move from one computer to another. The **Internet backbone** is a collection of high-speed data lines that connect major computer systems located around the world. An **Internet service provider (ISP)** is a company that has a permanent connection to the Internet backbone. ISPs utilize high- or medium-speed data lines to allow individuals and companies to connect to the backbone for access to the Internet. An Internet connection at home generally is a DSL or cable data line that connects to an ISP.

Millions of people in most countries around the world connect to the Internet using computers in their homes, offices, schools, and public locations such as libraries. Users with computers connected to the Internet can access a variety of services, including e-mail, social networking, online shopping, and the World Wide Web (Figure 1–2).

Figure 1–2 The Internet makes available a variety of services such as e-mail and the World Wide Web.

What Is the World Wide Web?

The **World Wide Web**, also called the **Web**, is the part of the Internet that supports multimedia and consists of a collection of linked documents. To support multimedia, the Web relies on the **Hypertext Transfer Protocol (HTTP)**, which is a set of rules for exchanging text, graphic, sound, video, and other multimedia files. The linked documents, or pages of information, on the Web are known as **Web pages**. Because the Web supports text, graphics, sound, and video, a Web page can include any of these multimedia elements. The Web is ever-changing and consists of billions of Web pages. Because of the ease of creating Web pages, more are being added all the time.

Internet and WWW History

The World Wide Web Consortium (W3C or w3.org), the de facto organization that governs HTML, provides a particularly rich history of the Internet and the World Wide Web. Search on "Internet history" or "WWW history" in your browser for many additional sources.

A **Web site** is a related collection of Web pages that is created and maintained by an individual, company, educational institution, or other organization. For example, as shown in Figure 1–3, many organizations, such as the Museum of Science and Industry in Chicago, publish and maintain Web sites. Each Web site contains a **home page**, which is the first document users see when they access the Web site. The home page often serves as an index or table of contents to other documents and files displayed on the site.

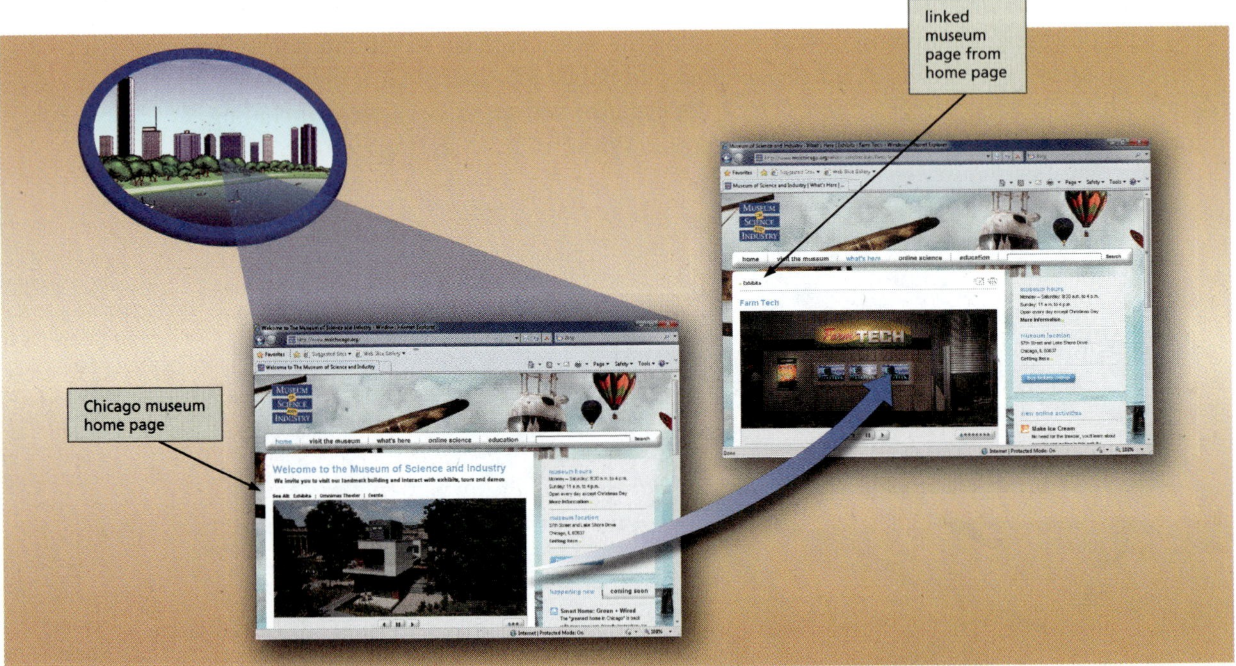

Figure 1–3 A Web site is a related collection of Web pages that is created and maintained by an individual, company, educational institution, or other organization.

Web Servers

Web pages are stored on a **Web server**, or **host**, which is a computer that stores and sends (serves) requested Web pages and other files. Any computer that has Web server software installed and is connected to the Internet can act as a Web server. Every Web site is stored on, and runs from, one or more Web servers. A large Web site may be spread over several servers in different geographic locations.

In order to make the Web pages that you have developed available to your audience, you have to publish those pages. **Publishing** is copying the Web pages and associated files such as graphics and audio to a Web server. Once a Web page is published, anyone who has access to the Internet can view it, regardless of where the Web server is located. For example, although the Chicago Museum of Science and Industry Web site is stored on a Web server somewhere in the United States, it is available for viewing by anyone in the world. Once a Web page is published, it can be read by almost any computer: whether you use the Mac, Windows, or Linux operating system, with a variety of computer hardware, you have access to billions of published Web pages.

Web Site Types and Purposes

The three general types of Web sites are Internet, intranet, and extranet. Table 1–1 lists characteristics of each of these three types of Web sites.

Table 1–1 Types of Web Sites

Type	Users	Access	Applications
Internet	Anyone	Public	Used to share information such as personal information, product catalogs, course information with the public
intranet	Employees or members	Private	Used to share information such as forms, manuals, organization schedules with employees or members
extranet	Select business partners	Private	Used to share information such as inventory updates, product specifications, financial information with business partners and customers

An **Internet site**, also known as a **Web site**, is a site generally available to the public. Individuals, groups, companies, and educational institutions use Web sites for a variety of purposes. Intranets and extranets also use Internet technology, but access is limited to specified groups. An **intranet** is a private network that uses Internet technologies to share company information among employees. An intranet is contained within a company or organization's network, which makes it private and only available to those who need access. Policy and procedure manuals usually are found on an intranet. Other documents such as employee directories, company newsletters, product catalogs, and training manuals often are distributed through an intranet.

An **extranet** is a private network that uses Internet technologies to share business information with select corporate partners or key customers. Companies and organizations can use an extranet to share product manuals, training modules, inventory status, and order information. An extranet also might allow retailers to purchase inventory directly or to pay bills online.

Companies use Web sites to advertise or sell their products and services worldwide, as well as to provide technical and product support for their customers. Many company Web sites also support **electronic commerce (e-commerce)**, which is the buying and selling of goods and services on the Internet. Using e-commerce technologies, these Web sites allow customers to browse product catalogs, comparison shop, and order products online. Figure 1–4 shows Amazon.com, which is a company that sells products only online. Many company Web sites also provide job postings and announcements, a frequently asked questions (FAQs) section, customer feedback links to solicit comments from their customers, and searchable technical support databases.

BTW

Intranets and Extranets

There are many Web sites that discuss ideas for intranets and extranets. Many companies are already using these technologies and share their "best practice" techniques. The CIO Intranet/Extranet Research Center provides valuable information on building and maintaining an intranet or extranet, along with additional resources.

BTW

E-Commerce

Today, e-commerce is a standard part of doing business. E-commerce technologies, however, continue to change, offering new applications and potential uses. Several online magazines are dedicated to providing an in-depth look at e-commerce. Many print magazines also provide useful information about this important way to do business.

Figure 1–4 Amazon.com is a company that operates online only.

Colleges, universities, and other schools use Web sites to distribute information about areas of study, provide course information, or register students for classes online. Instructors use their Web sites to issue announcements, post questions on reading material, list contact information, and provide easy access to lecture notes and slides. Many instructors today use the course management software adopted by their respective schools to upload course content. Using a standard course management product across a university makes it easier for students to find information relative to their various courses. Many course management tools allow instructors to write their own Web content for courses. With many systems, instructors can use Web pages to provide further information for their students within the structure of the course management tool provided by the school. In addition to keeping in contact with current students via the Web, universities also utilize the Web to keep in touch with their alumni, as shown in Figure 1–5.

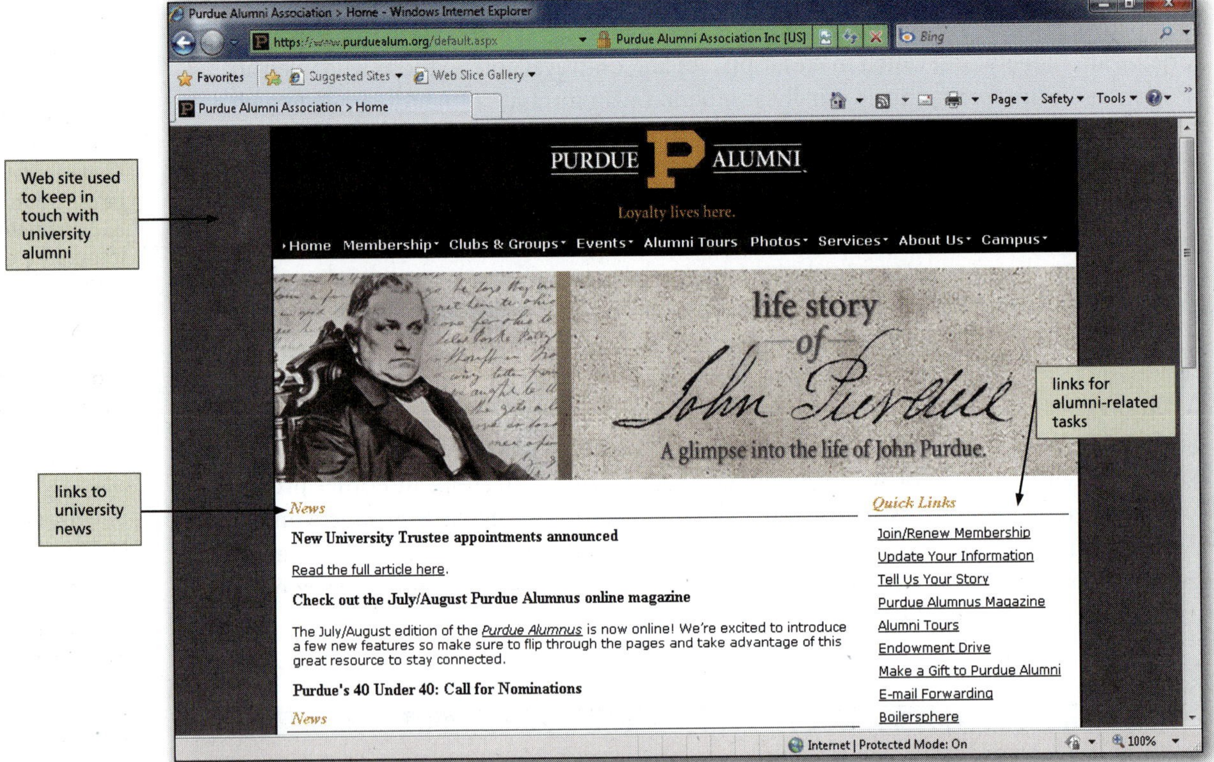

Figure 1–5 Many universities have alumni Web sites.

In addition to the use of the Internet by companies and educational institutions, individuals might create personal Web sites that include their résumés to make them easily accessible to any interested employers. Families can share photographs, video and audio clips, stories, schedules, or other information through Web sites (Figure 1–6). Many individual Web sites allow password protection, which makes a safer environment for sharing information.

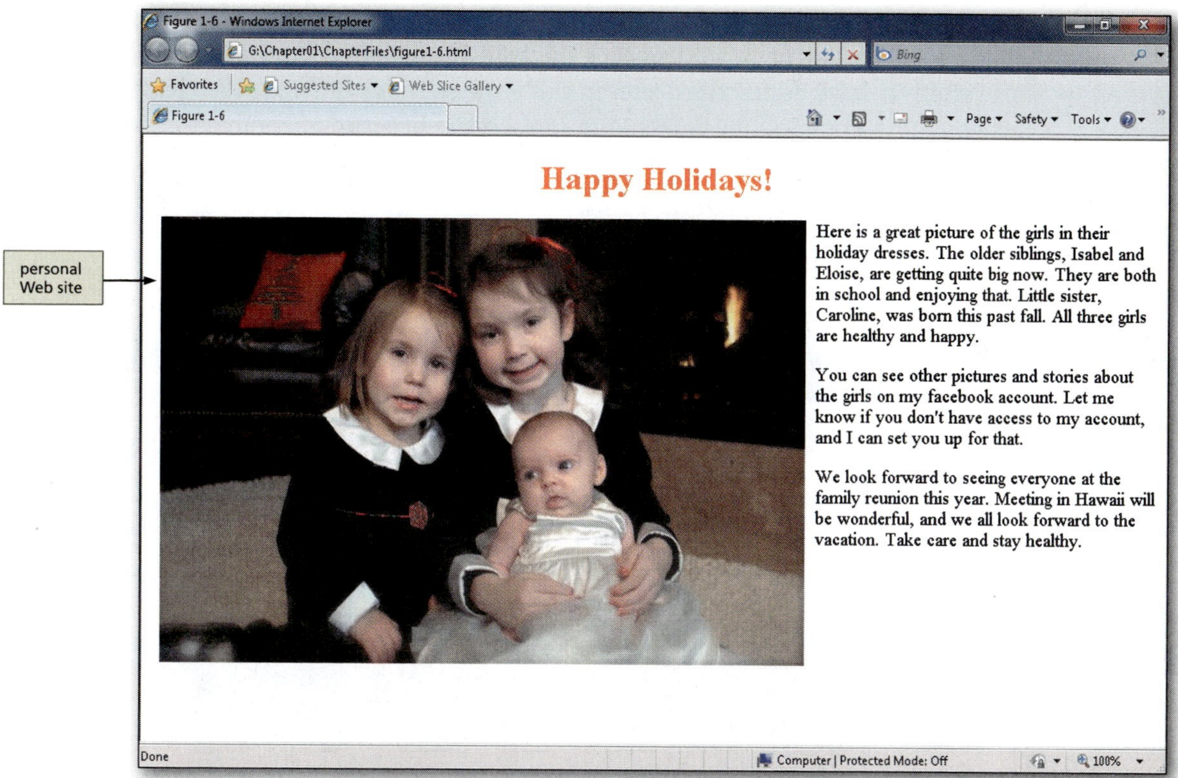

Figure 1–6 Personal Web sites are used to communicate with family and friends.

Web Browsers

To display a Web page on any type of Web site, a computer needs to have a Web browser installed. A **Web browser**, also called a **browser**, is a program that interprets and displays Web pages and enables you to view and interact with a Web page. Microsoft Internet Explorer, Mozilla Firefox, and Apple Safari are popular browsers today. Browsers provide a variety of features, including the capability to locate Web pages, to link forward and backward among Web pages, to add a favorite or bookmark a Web page, and to choose security settings.

To locate a Web page using a browser, you type the Web page's Uniform Resource Locator (URL) in the browser's Address or Location bar. A **Uniform Resource Locator (URL)** is the address of a document or other file accessible on the Internet. An example of a URL on the Web is:

http://www.scsite.com/html6e/index.html

The URL indicates to the browser to use the HTTP communications protocol to locate the index.html Web page in the html6e folder on the scsite.com Web server. Web page URLs can be found in a wide range of places, including school catalogs, business cards, product packaging, and advertisements.

Hyperlinks are an essential part of the World Wide Web. A **hyperlink**, also called a **link**, is an element used to connect one Web page to another Web page that's located on the same server or used to link Web pages located on a different Web server located anywhere in the world. Clicking a hyperlink allows you to move quickly from one Web page to another, and the user does not have to be concerned about where the Web pages reside. You also can click hyperlinks to move to a different section of the same Web page.

With hyperlinks, a Web site user does not necessarily have to view information in a linear way. Instead, he or she can click the available hyperlinks to view the information in a variety of ways, as described later in this chapter. Many different Web page elements, including text, graphics, and animations, can serve as hyperlinks. Figure 1–7 shows examples of several different Web page elements used as hyperlinks.

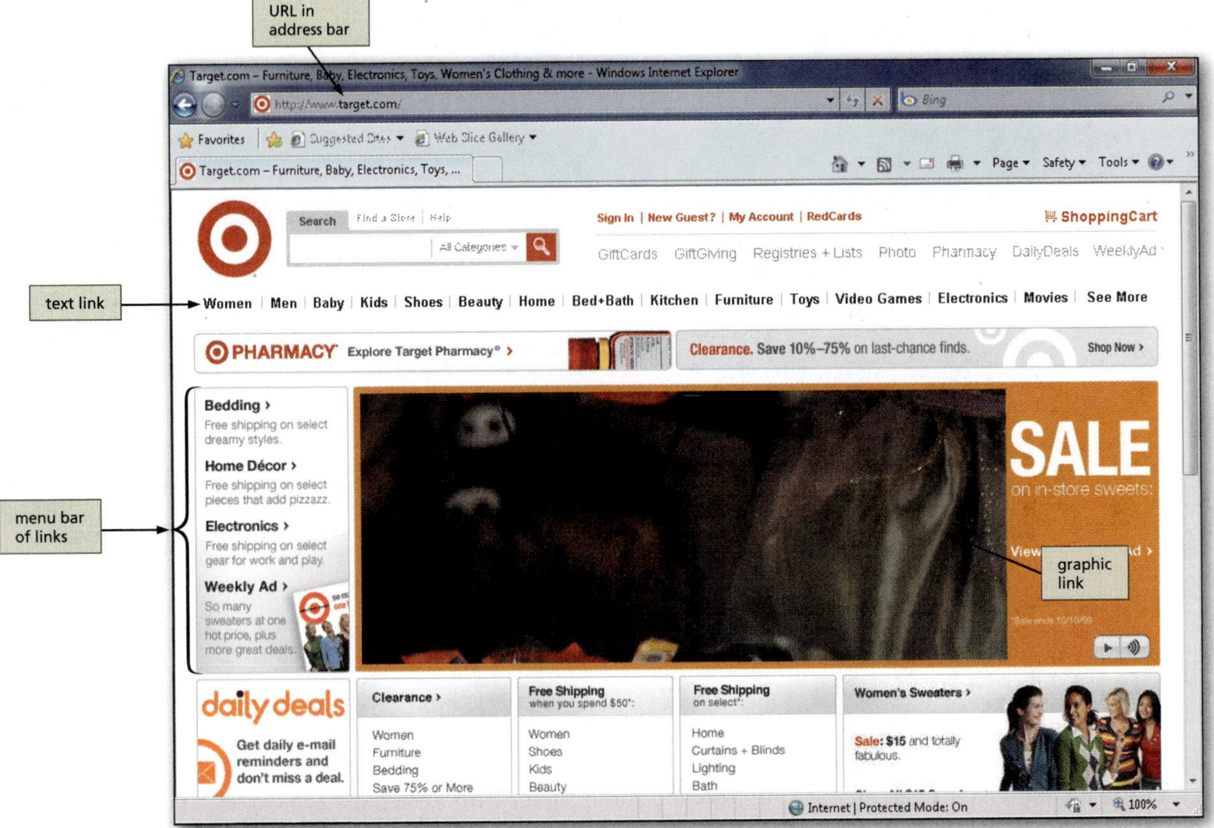

Figure 1–7 A Web page can use many different Web page elements as hyperlinks.

What Is Hypertext Markup Language?

Web pages are created using **Hypertext Markup Language** (**HTML**), which is an authoring language used to create documents for the World Wide Web. HTML uses a set of special instructions called **tags** or **markup** to define the structure and layout of a Web document and specify how the page is displayed in a browser.

A Web page is a file that contains both text and HTML tags. HTML tags mark the text to define how it should appear when viewed as a page on the Web. HTML includes hundreds of tags used to format Web pages and create hyperlinks to other documents or Web pages. For instance, the HTML tags <p> and </p> are used to indicate a new paragraph with a blank line above it, <table> and </table> are used to indicate the start and end of a table, and <hr /> is used to display a horizontal rule across the page. Figure 1–8a shows the HTML tags needed to create the Web page shown in Figure 1–8b. You also can enhance HTML tags by using attributes, as shown in Figure 1–8a. **Attributes** define additional characteristics such as font weight or style for the HTML tag.

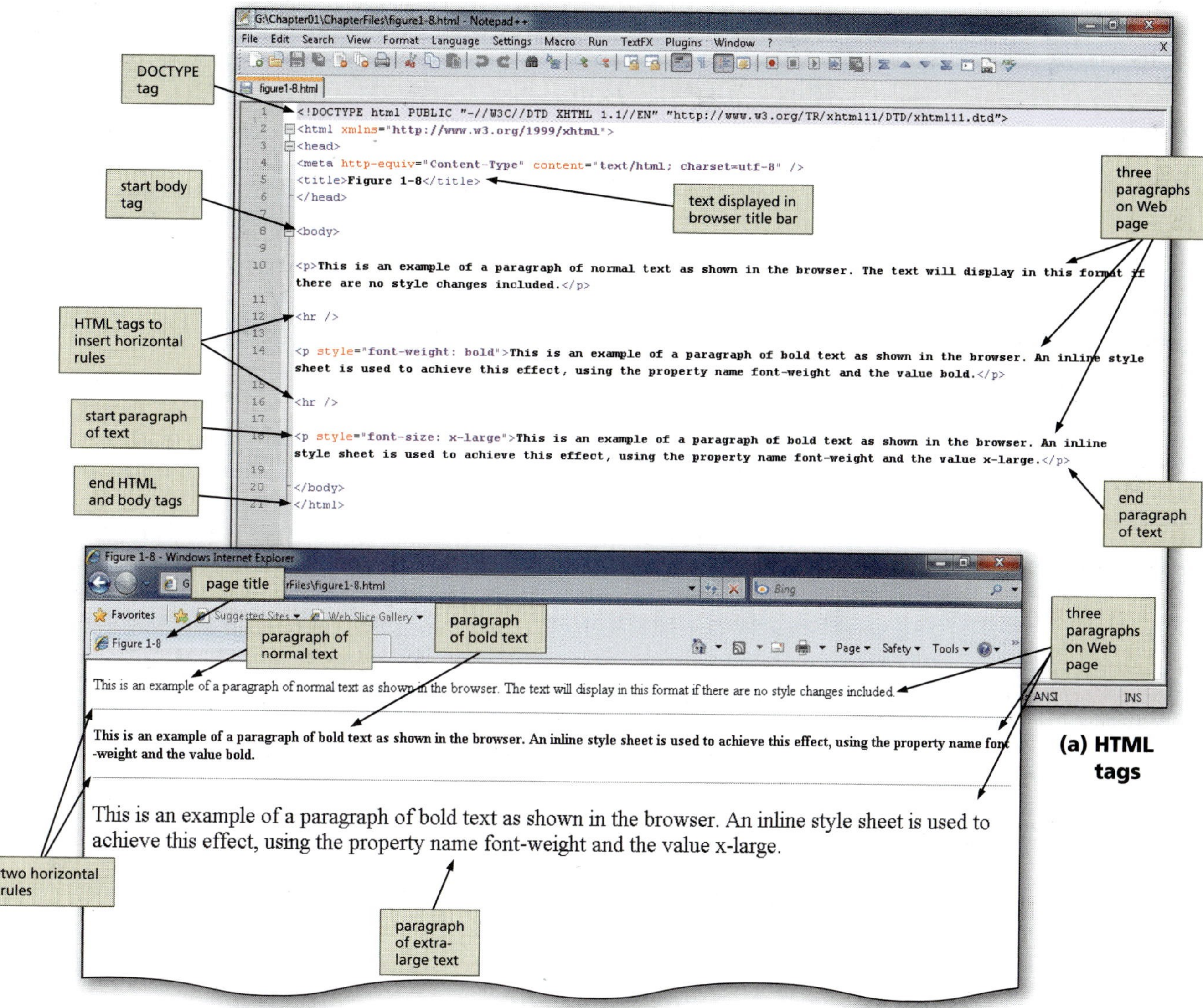

(b) Resulting Web page

Figure 1–8 A Web page is a file that contains both text and HTML tags.

HTML is **platform independent**, meaning you can create, or code, an HTML file on one type of computer and then use a browser on another type of computer to view that file as a Web page. The page looks the same regardless of what platform you are using. One of the greatest benefits of Web technology is that the same Web page can be viewed on many different types of digital hardware, including mobile devices like smart phones.

HTML Elements

HTML combines descriptive tags with special tags that denote how a document should appear in a Web browser. HTML elements include headings, paragraphs, hyperlinks, lists, images, and more. Most HTML elements consist of three parts: a start tag, content, and an end tag. For example, to specify that certain text should appear bold in a Web page, you would enter the following HTML code:

```
<bold>this is bold text</bold>
```

where <bold> is the start bold code and </bold> is the end bold code. Table 1–2 on the next page shows examples of some HTML elements.

Table 1–2 HTML Elements

Element	Tag	Purpose
Title	<title>...</title>	Indicates title to appear on the title bar in the browser
Body	<body>...</body>	Specifies what appears on the Web page; all Web page content is inserted within the start <body> tag and end </body> tag
Paragraph	<p>...</p>	Inserts a blank line before paragraph text
Line Break	 	Inserts a line break before the next element without a blank line

BTW

HTML Elements
Numerous sources of information about HTML elements are available. The World Wide Web Consortium (w3.org) provides the most comprehensive list of tags and attributes together with examples of their use. One of the main goals of the W3C is to help those building Web sites understand and utilize standards that make the Web accessible to all.

HTML Coding Practices

Similar to all programming languages, HTML has a set of coding practices designed to simplify the process of creating and editing HTML files and ensure that Web pages appear correctly in different browsers.

When creating an HTML file, you should separate sections of the HTML code with spaces and by using the Tab key. Adding space between sections, either with blank lines or by tabbing, gives you an immediate view of the sections of code that relate to one another and helps you view the HTML elements in your document more clearly. HTML browsers ignore spaces that exist between the tags in your HTML document, so the spaces and indentations inserted within the code will not appear on the Web page. Figure 1–9 shows an example of an HTML file with code sections separated by blank lines and code section indentations. Another developer looking at this code can see immediately where the specific sections are located in the code.

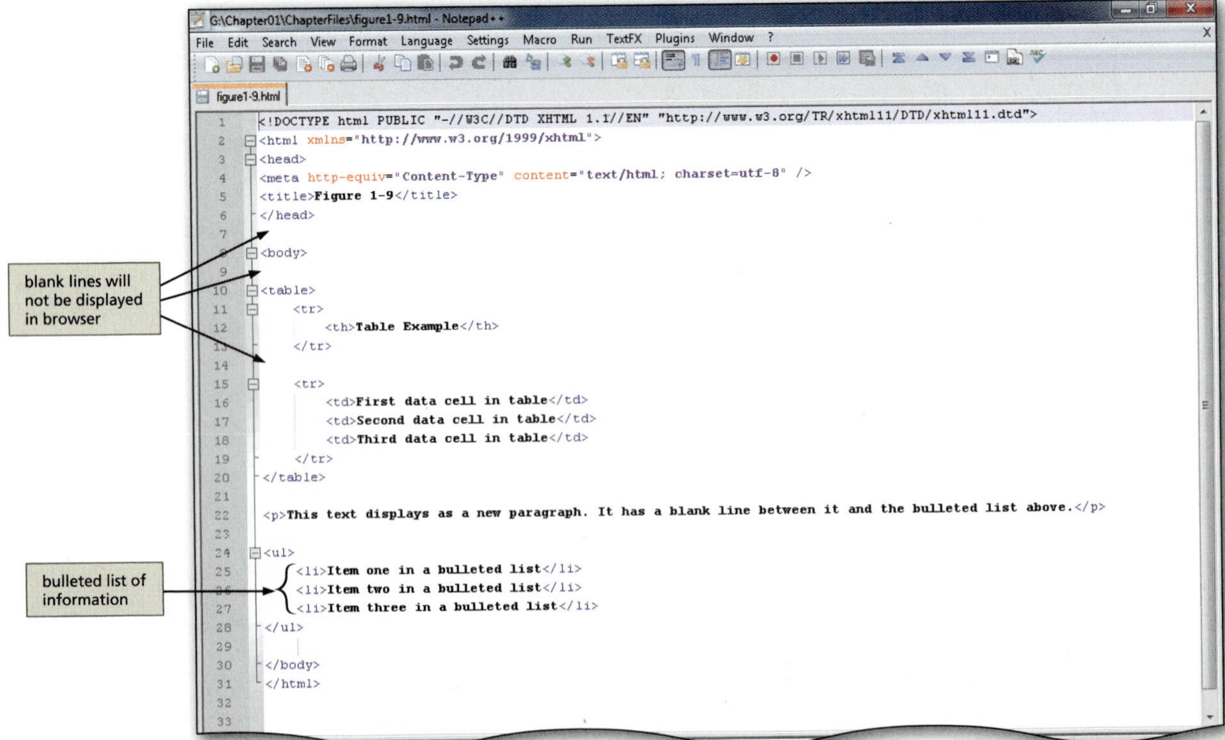

Figure 1–9 Adding spaces to HTML code separates sections to make reading easier.

HTML Versions

HTML has gone through several versions, each of which expands the capabilities of HTML. Although HTML version 5.0 is under development, it has not yet been released. The most recent version of HTML is HTML 4.01, although most browsers still support HTML versions 3.2 and 2.0. To ensure that browsers can interpret each new version of HTML, the World Wide Web Consortium (W3C) maintains HTML standards, or specifications, which are publicly available on its Web site. As described later in this chapter, it is important to verify that Web pages are displayed as intended in a variety of browsers during the testing phase of development.

Cascading Style Sheets

This book has taken a new direction with the 6th edition by eliminating deprecated tags and attributes. **Deprecated** tags and attributes are tags and attributes that are no longer recommended in the latest W3C standard. In Appendix A, deprecated tags and attributes are highlighted with an asterisk. In an effort to eliminate deprecated HTML tags, the chapter projects utilize Cascading Style Sheets (CSS) to alter the style (or look) of a Web page. Although HTML allows Web developers to make changes to the structure, design, and content of a Web page, it is limited in its ability to define the appearance, or style, across one or more Web pages. **Cascading Style Sheets (CSS)** allow you to specify styles for various Web page elements. A **style** is a rule that defines the appearance of a Web page element. A **style sheet** is a series of rules that defines the style for a Web page or an entire Web site. With a style sheet, you can alter the appearance of a Web page or pages by changing characteristics such as font family, font size, margins, and link specifications, as well as visual elements such as colors and borders. CSS is not used to add any content to your Web site; it just makes your content look more stylish.

With CSS you can specify the style for an element within a single Web page or throughout an entire Web site. For example, if you want all text paragraphs on a Web page to be indented by five spaces, you can use a style sheet to handle the indenting, rather than coding each paragraph with an indentation. And, if you decided you wanted to change the indent to three spaces, you would change just one style sheet line rather than changing the coding for each paragraph. So you can see that using CSS saves a lot of time and makes it much easier to make style changes.

CSS is not HTML; it is a separate language used to enhance the display capabilities of HTML. The World Wide Web Consortium (W3C), the same organization that defines HTML standards, defines the specifications for CSS. Appendix A at the back of this book and available online provides a list of HTML tags and corresponding attributes that will allow you to alter the Web page elements as needed, and Appendix D has complete information on the properties and values associated with different CSS elements.

BTW

CSS, DHTML, and XHTML
The w3.org Web site has an extensive amount of information and tutorials about Cascading Style Sheets (CSS), Dynamic HTML (DHTML), and Extensible HTML (XHTML). The standards suggested in the W3C Web site are the ones that most Web developers follow.

Document Object Model (DOM)

HTML can be used with other Web technologies to provide additional Web page functionality. For example, the term **Document Object Model (DOM)** describes a combination of HTML tags, CSS, and a scripting language such as JavaScript. DOM allows JavaScript and other languages to manipulate the structure of the underlying document to create interactive, animated Web pages. This is a model in which the Web page (or document) contains objects (elements, links, etc.) that can be manipulated. This allows a Web developer to add, delete, or change an element or attribute. Web pages enhanced with

DOM can be more responsive to visitor interaction than basic HTML Web pages. Not all interactive Web pages require DOM, but if you have a need for extensive interactivity, then this might be a model to consider. CSS, JavaScript, and DOM are covered in later chapters in the Comprehensive (12-chapter) version of this book.

Extensible Hypertext Markup Language (XHTML)

As you have learned, HTML uses tags to describe how a document should appear in a Web browser, or the Web page format. **Extensible Markup Language (XML)** is a markup language that uses tags to describe the structure and content of a document, not the format. **Extensible Hypertext Markup Language (XHTML)** is a reformulation of HTML formatting so it conforms to XML structure and content rules. By combining HTML and XML, XHTML combines the display features of HTML and the stricter coding standards required by XML.

If you create a Web page in HTML and do not follow XHTML coding standards exactly (for example, by not using an end </p> tag), the Web browser on your computer can still interpret and display the Web page correctly. However, newer types of browsers, such as those for mobile phones or handheld computers, cannot interpret HTML code that does not meet XHTML standards. Because XHTML has such strict coding standards, it helps ensure that Web pages created in XHTML will be readable by many different types of applications. An important step in Web development is to check that your Web pages are XHTML compliant. You will validate your Web pages starting in Chapter 2 and continue that process throughout the book.

Table 1–3 lists some of the XHTML coding rules that Web developers should follow to ensure that their HTML code conforms to XHTML standards. All of the projects in this book follow XHTML standards (as discussed in Chapter 2) and adhere to the rules outlined in Table 1–3. The specifics of each rule are explained in detail when used in a project.

Table 1–3 XHTML Coding Practices

Practice	Invalid Example	Valid Example
HTML file must include a DOCTYPE statement	<html> <head><title>sample Web page</title>	<!DOCTYPE html PUBLIC "-//W3C//DTD XHTML 1.0 Transitional//EN" "http://www.w3.org/TR/xhtml1/DTD/xhtml1-transitional.dtd"> <html> <head><title>sample Web page</title> </head>
All tags and attributes must be written in lowercase	<TABLE WIDTH="100%">	<table width="100%">
All attribute values must be enclosed by single or double quotation marks	<table width=100%>	<table width="100%">
All tags must be closed, including tags such as img, hr, and br, which do not have end tags, but which must be closed as a matter of practice	 <hr> <p>This is another paragraph	 <hr /> <p>This is another paragraph</p>
All elements must be nested properly	<p><strong>This is a bold paragraph</p></strong>	<p><strong>This is a bold paragraph</strong></p>

Tools for Creating HTML Documents

You can create Web pages using HTML with a simple text editor, such as Notepad++, Notepad, TextPad, or SimpleText. A **text editor** is a program that allows a user to enter, change, save, and print text, such as HTML. Text editors do not have many advanced features, but they do allow you to develop HTML documents easily. For instance, if you want to insert the DOCTYPE tags into the Web page file, type the necessary text into any of the text editors, as shown in Figure 1–10a and Figure 1–10b. Although Notepad (Figure 1–10b) is an adequate text editor for Web development, note its differences from Notepad++. Notepad++ is a more robust text editor that uses color schemes for HTML code as it is entered.

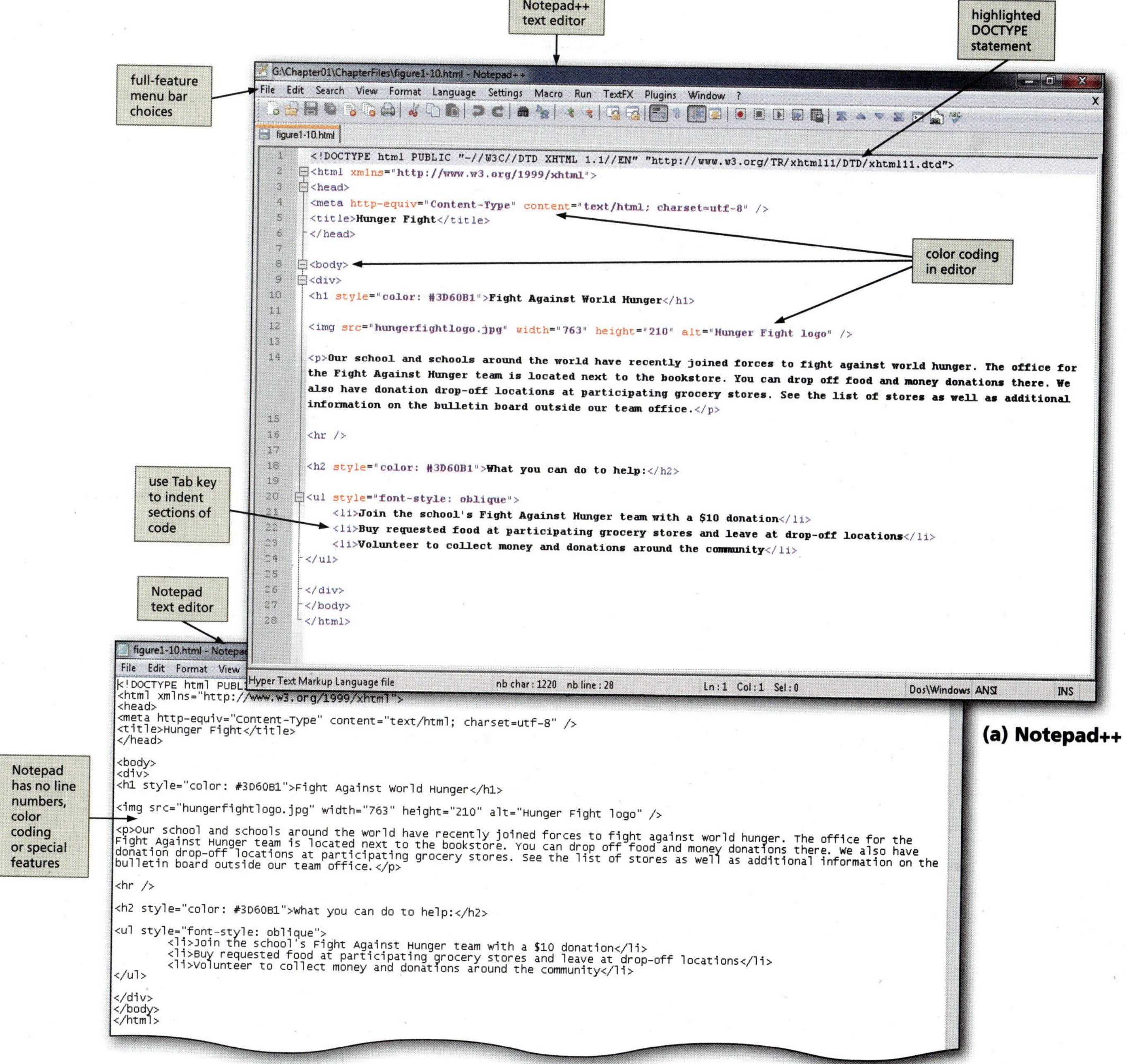

(a) Notepad++

(b) Notepad

Figure 1–10 With a text editor such as Notepad++ or Notepad, you enter HTML tags and text that create a Web page.

You also can create Web pages using an HTML text editor, such as EditPlus or BBEdit (for Macintosh). An **HTML text editor** is a program that provides basic text-editing functions, as well as more advanced features such as color-coding for various HTML tags, menus to insert HTML tags, and spell checkers. An **HTML object editor**, such as Eiffel Software object editor, provides the additional functionality of an outline editor that allows you to expand and collapse HTML objects and properties, edit parameters, and view graphics attached to the expanded objects.

Many popular software applications also provide features that enable you to develop Web pages easily. Microsoft Word, Excel, and PowerPoint, for example, have a Save as Web Page feature that converts a document into an HTML file by automatically adding HTML tags to the document. Using Microsoft Access, you can create a Web page that allows you to view data in a database. Adobe Acrobat also has an export feature that creates HTML files. Each of these applications also allows you to add hyperlinks, drop-down boxes, option buttons, or scrolling text to the Web page.

These advanced Web features make it simple to save any document, spreadsheet, database, or presentation to display as a Web page. Corporate policy and procedures manuals and PowerPoint presentations, for example, easily can be saved as Web pages and published to the company's intranet. Extranet users can be given access to Web pages that allow them to view or update information stored in a database.

BTW

Free HTML WYSIWYG Editors

There are a number of popular WYSIWYG editors that are being used by many novice Web developers to create well-designed, interactive Web sites. You can find these by searching for "WYSIWYG HTML editor" in most search engines.

You also can create Web pages using a WYSIWYG editor such as Adobe Dreamweaver, Amaya, or CoffeeCup HTML Editor. A **WYSIWYG editor** is a program that provides a graphical user interface that allows a developer to preview the Web page during its development. WYSIWYG (pronounced wizzy-wig) is an acronym for What You See Is What You Get. A WYSIWYG editor creates the HTML code for you as you add elements to the Web page, which means that you do not have to enter HTML tags directly. The main problem with WYSIWYG editors is that they often create "puffed-up" HTML code (HTML tags with many lines of unnecessary additional code surrounding them).

Regardless of which type of program you use to create Web pages, it is important to understand the specifics of HTML so you can make changes outside of the editor. For instance, you may be able to create a Web page with Dreamweaver, but if you want to make some minor changes, it is very helpful to know the HTML tags themselves. It also is important to understand the Web development life cycle so the Web pages in your Web site are consistent and complete.

Web Development Life Cycle

For years, university and college information technology courses have stressed the importance of following the Systems Development Life Cycle when designing and implementing new software to ensure consistency and completeness. The Web development process should follow a similar cycle. Comprehensive planning and analysis ensure that developers will provide what the users want. If you start to code your Web pages without thorough planning and analysis, you run the risk of missing pertinent information. It is much less expensive to make corrections to a Web site in the early phases of project development than it is to alter Web pages that are completed.

The Web development life cycle outlined in this section is one that can be utilized for any type or size of Web development project. The **Web development life cycle** is a process that can be used for developing Web pages at any level of complexity. The Web development life cycle includes the following phases: planning, analysis, design and development, testing, and implementation and maintenance. Table 1–4 lists several questions that should be asked during each phase in the Web development life cycle. Throughout this book, you will follow this systematic cycle as you develop your Web pages.

Table 1–4 Web Development Phases and Questions

Web Development Phase	Questions to Ask
Planning	• What is the purpose of this Web site? • Who will use this Web site? • What are the users' computing environments? • Who owns and authors the information on the Web site? • Who decides if/where the information goes on the Web site?
Analysis	• What tasks do the users need to perform? • What information is useful to the users? • What process considerations must be made?
Design and Development	• How many Web pages will be included in the Web site? • How will the Web pages be organized? • What type of Web site structure is appropriate for the content? • How can I best present the content for ease of use? • What file naming convention will be employed for this Web site? • What folder structure will be used for the Web page files? • How do I apply XHTML standards throughout the development process? • What forms of multimedia contribute positively to the Web site? • How can accessibility issues be addressed without limiting usability? • Will there be an international audience?
Testing	• Do the Web pages pass the World Wide Web Consortium (W3C) validation process as XHTML compliant? • Is the Web site content correct? • Does the Web site function correctly? • Are users able to find the information they need to complete desired tasks? • Is navigation clear and easy to use?
Implementation and Maintenance	• How is the Web site published? • How can users be attracted to visit and revisit the Web site? • How is the Web site updated? • Who is responsible for content updates? • Who is responsible for structure updates? • How will users be notified about updates to the Web site? • Will the Web site be monitored?

Web Site Planning

Web site planning, which is the first phase of the Web development life cycle, involves identifying the goals or purpose of the Web site. The first step in the Web site planning phase is to answer the question "What is the purpose of this Web site?" As you have learned, individuals and groups design and publish Web sites for a variety of purposes. Individuals develop Web sites to share their hobbies, to post résumés, or just to share ideas on personal interests. Organizations create Web sites to keep members informed of upcoming events or to recruit new members. Businesses create Web sites to advertise and sell products or to give their customers 24-hour online support. Instructors publish Web sites, or add information to their courses using the school's online course management software, to inform students of course policies, assignments, and due dates, as well as course requirements. Until you adequately can identify the intended purpose of the Web site, you should not proceed with the Web development project.

In addition to understanding the Web site's purpose, you also should understand who will use the Web site and the computing environments of most of the users. Knowing the makeup of your target audience — including age, gender, general demographic background, and level of computer literacy — will help you design a Web site appropriate for all users. Understanding users' computing environments will determine what types of Web technologies to use. For example, if most users have low-speed Internet connections, you would not want to create pages with large graphics or multimedia elements.

A final aspect to the Web site planning phase is to identify the content owners and authors. To determine this, you need to ask the questions:

- Who owns and authors the information on the Web site?
- Who decides if/where the information goes on the Web site?

Once you have identified who will provide and authorize the Web site content, you can include those individuals in all aspects of the Web development project.

Web Site Analysis

During the analysis phase, you make decisions about the Web site content and functionality. To help define the appropriate Web site content and functionality, you first should identify the tasks that users need to perform. Answering that question allows you to define necessary content to facilitate those tasks and determine useful information for the users. Extraneous content should be eliminated from the Web site because it does not serve any purpose.

In the analysis phase, it also is important to consider the processes required to support Web site features. For example, if you determine that users should be able to order products through the Web site, then you also need to define the processes or actions to be taken each time an order is submitted. For instance, after an order is submitted, how will that order be processed throughout the back-office business applications such as inventory control and accounts payable? Will users receive e-mail confirmations with details about their orders? The analysis phase is one of the more important phases in the Web development life cycle. Clearly understanding and defining the desired content and functionality of the Web site will direct the type of Web site that you design and reduce changes during Web site development.

BTW

Accessibility Standards
Creating a Web site that is accessible to all users allows your Web site to reach the widest audience. Further, under Section 508 law, any Web site or technology used by a U.S. federal agency must be usable by people with disabilities. See Appendix C for Section 508 guidelines.

Web Site Design and Development

After determining the purpose of the Web site and defining the content and functionality, you need to consider the Web site's design. Some key considerations in Web site design are defining how to organize Web page content, selecting the appropriate Web site structure, determining how to use multimedia, addressing accessibility issues, and designing pages for an international audience. One of the most important aspects of Web site design is determining the best way to provide navigation on the Web site. If users cannot easily find the information that they are seeking, they will not return to your Web site.

Many ways to organize a Web page exist, just as many ways to organize a report or paper exist. Table 1–5 lists some organizational standards for creating a Web page that is easy to read and navigate.

Table 1–5 Web Page Organizational Standards

Element	Organizational Standard	Reason
Titles	Use simple titles that clearly explain the purpose of the page	Titles help users understand the purpose of the page; a good title explains the page in the search engine results lists
Headings	Use headings to separate main topics	Headings make a Web page easier to read; simple headlines clearly explain the purpose of the page

Table 1–5 Web Page Organizational Standards (continued)

Element	Organizational Standard	Reason
Horizontal Rules	Insert horizontal rules to separate main topics	Horizontal rules provide graphical elements to break up Web page content
Paragraphs	Use paragraphs to help divide large amounts of text	Paragraphs provide shorter, more readable sections of text
Lists	Utilize bulleted or numbered lists when appropriate	Lists provide organized, easy-to-read text that readers can scan
Page Length	Maintain suitable Web page lengths	Web users do not always scroll to view information on longer pages; appropriate page lengths increase the likelihood that users will view key information
Information	Emphasize the most important information by placing it at the top of a Web page	Web users are quick to peruse a page; placing critical information at the top of the page increases the likelihood that users will view key information
Other	Incorporate a contact e-mail address; include the date of the last modification	E-mail addresses and dates give users a way to contact a Web site developer with questions; the date last modified helps users determine the timeliness of the site information

Web sites can use several different types of structures, including linear, hierarchical, and webbed. Each structure links, or connects, the Web pages in a different way to define how users navigate the site and view the Web pages. You should select a structure for the Web site based on how users will navigate the site and view the Web site content.

A **linear** Web site structure connects Web pages in a straight line, as shown in Figure 1–11. A linear Web site structure is appropriate if the information on the Web pages should be read in a specific order. For example, if the information on the first Web page, Module 1, is necessary for understanding information on the second Web page, Module 2, you should use a linear structure. Each page would have links from one Web page to the next, as well as a link back to the previous Web page. There are many cases in which Web pages need to be read one after the other.

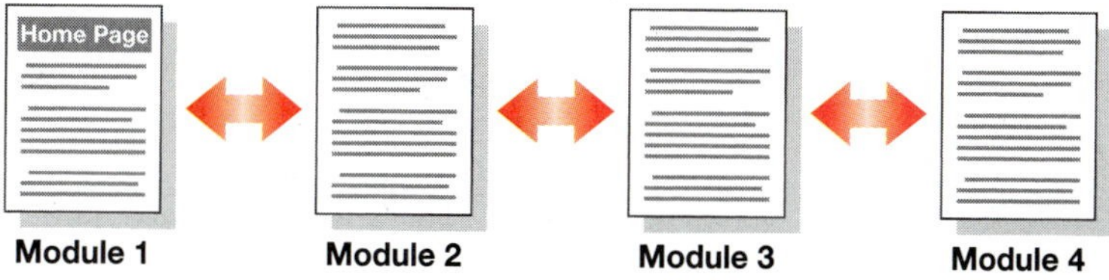

Figure 1–11 Linear Web site structure.

A variation of a linear Web site structure includes the addition of a link to the home page of the Web site, as shown in Figure 1–12. For some Web sites, moving from one

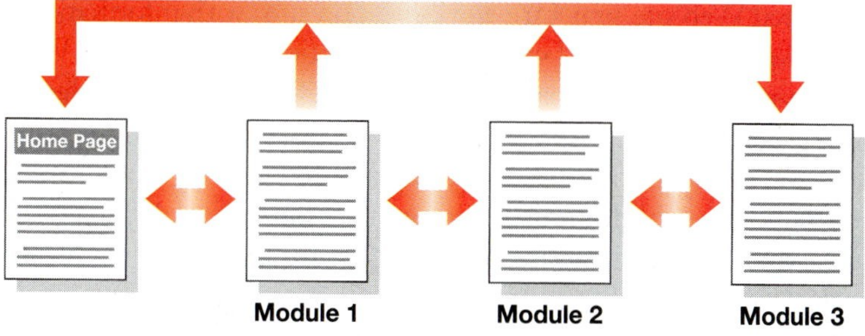

Figure 1–12 Linear Web site structure with links to home page.

module to the next module is still important, but you also want to provide users with easy access to the home page at any time. In this case, you would still provide links from the module Web pages to the previous and next module, but each Web page would also have a link back to the home page. In this way, the user does not have to click the previous link multiple times in order to get back to the home page.

BTW

User Interface Design
The user interface design is an important aspect of a Web site. If a site is designed poorly, users may be unable to find the desired information or complete a task, which makes the Web site ineffective.

A **hierarchical** Web site structure connects Web pages in a treelike structure, as shown in Figure 1–13. A hierarchical Web site structure works well on a site with a main index or table of contents page that links to all other Web pages. With this structure, the main index page would display general information, and secondary pages would include more detailed information. Notice how logically the information in Figure 1–13 is organized. A Web page visitor can easily go from the home page to any of the three modules. In addition, the visitor can easily get to the Module 3 Quiz by way of the Module 3 link. One of the inherent problems with this structure, though, is the inability to move easily from one section of pages to another. As an example, to move from Module 1 Page 2 to the Module 3 Summary, the visitor would have to use the Back button to get to the Home Page and then click the Module 3 link. This is moderately annoying for a site with two Web pages, but think what it would be like if Module 1 had 100 Web pages!

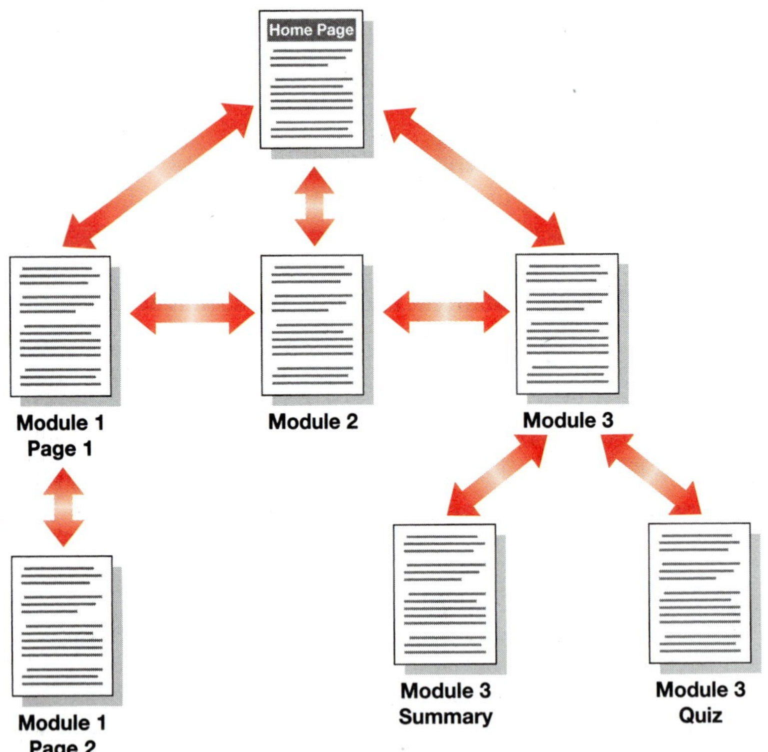

Figure 1–13 Hierarchical Web site structure.

To circumvent the problems with the hierarchical model, you can use a webbed model (Figure 1-14). A **webbed** Web site structure has no set organization, as shown in Figure 1–14. A webbed Web site structure works best on sites with information that does not need to be read in a specific order and with many navigation options. The World Wide Web uses a webbed structure, so users can navigate among Web pages in any order they choose. Notice how the Web site visitor can more easily move between modules or module summaries with this structure. With this model, you most often provide a link to the Home Page from each page, resulting in an additional arrow going from each individual Web page back to the home page (which is difficult to depict in these small figures). Many Web sites today utilize a graphical image (usually the company or institutional logo) in the top-left corner of each Web page as a link to the home page. You will use that technique later in the book.

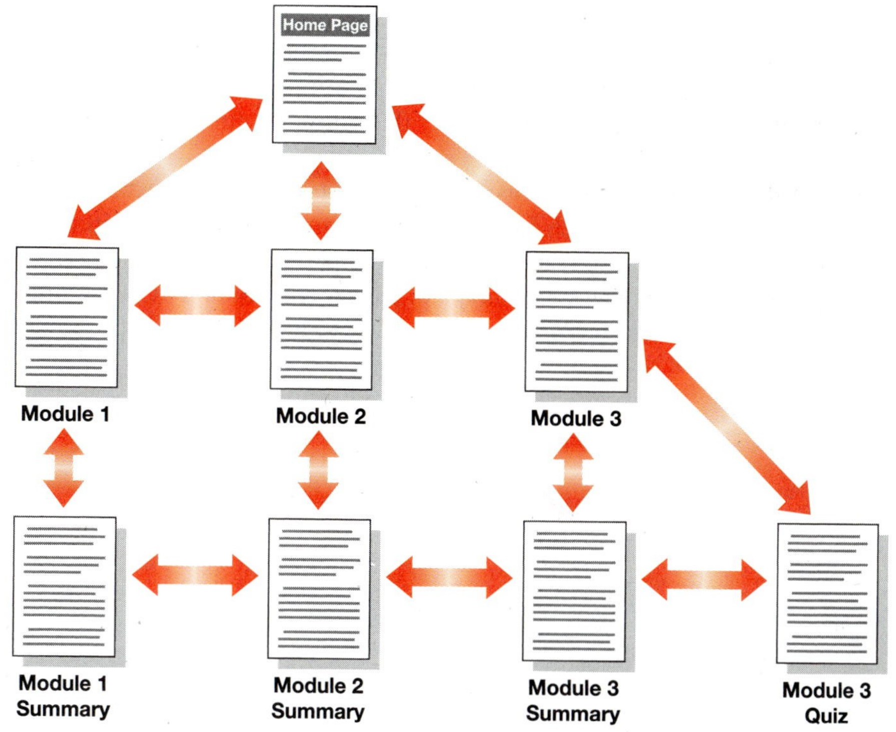

Figure 1–14 Webbed Web site structure.

Most Web sites are a combination of the linear, hierarchical, and webbed structures. Some information on the Web site might be organized hierarchically from an index page, other information might be accessible from all areas of the site, and still other information might be organized linearly to be read in a specific order. Using a combination of the three structures is appropriate if it helps users navigate the site easily. The key is to get the right information to the users in the most efficient way possible.

Regardless of the structure or structures that you use, you should balance the narrowness and depth of the Web site. A **broad Web site** is one in which the home page is the main index page, and all other Web pages are linked individually to the home page (Figure 1–15).

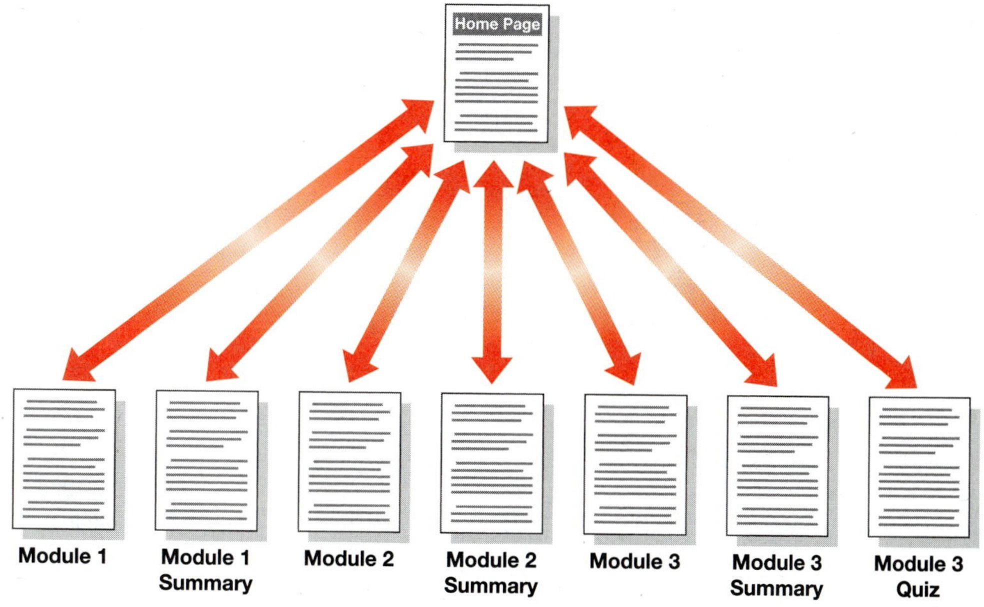

Figure 1–15 Broad Web site.

By making the other Web pages accessible only through the home page, a broad Web site forces the user to return to the home page to move from one Web page to another. The structure makes navigation time-consuming and limiting for users. A better structure would present a user with navigation alternatives that allow for direct movement between Web pages.

A **deep Web site** is one that has many levels of pages, requiring the user to click many times to reach a particular Web page (Figure 1–16). By requiring a visitor to move through several Web pages before reaching the desired page, a deep Web site forces a user to spend time viewing interim pages that may not have useful content. As an example, note the difference between finding the Module 3 Summary in Figure 1–13 on page HTML 18

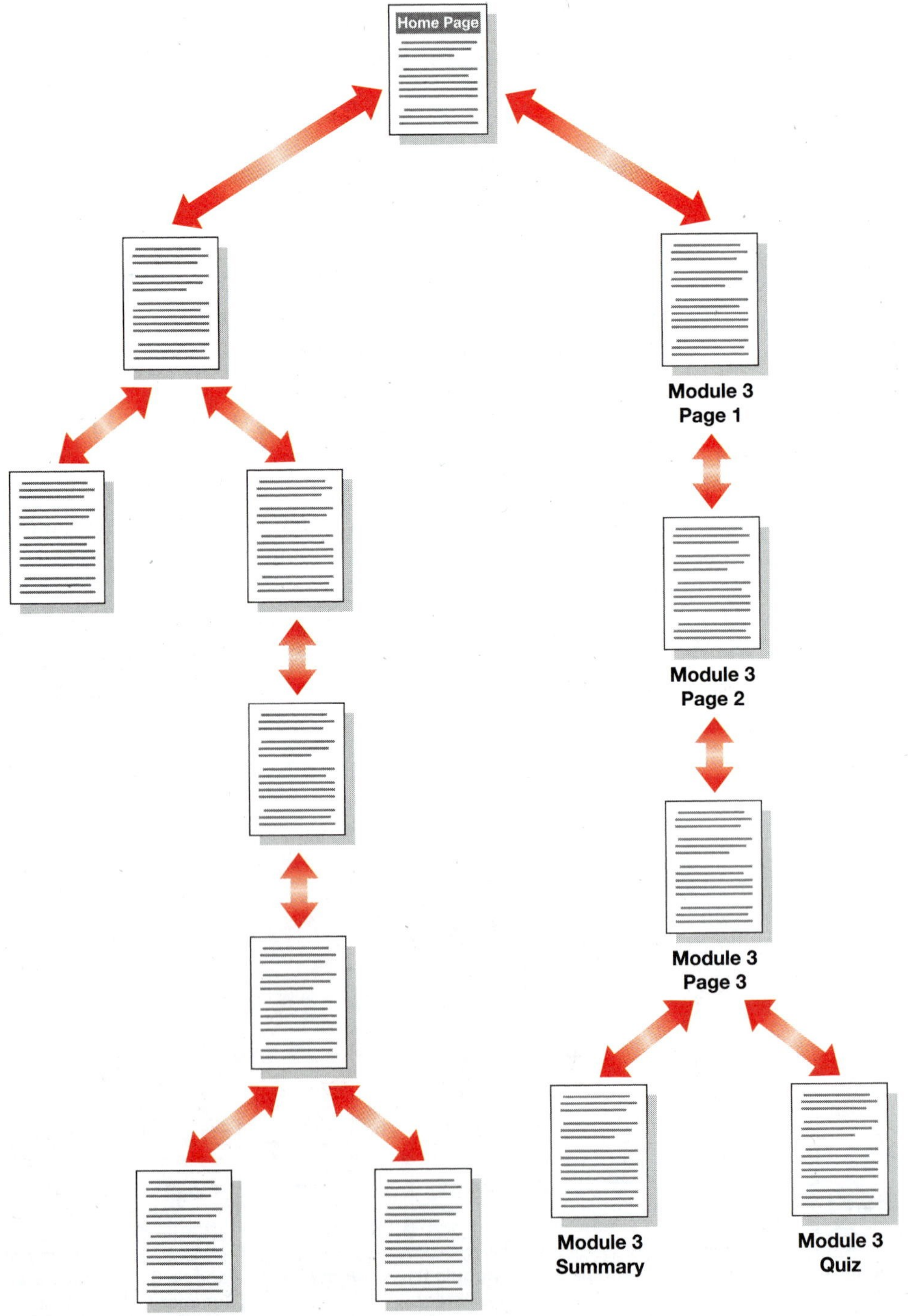

Figure 1–16 Deep Web site.

as compared to finding the same Web page (Module 3 Summary) in Figure 1–16. Assume that the user went through the Figure 1–13 Web site once to study the Module 3 material. When the user returns to the Web site using the Figure 1–16 structure, however, to review the Module 3 Summary Web page and then take the Module 3 Quiz, the user would have to go completely through the Module 3 material, Web page by Web page, in order to get to the Module 3 Summary page. You probably want to give users easier access to that Web page.

As a Web developer, you must select an appropriate structure for the Web site and work to balance breadth and depth. Users go to a Web site looking for information to complete a task. Good design provides ease of navigation, allowing users to find content quickly and easily. In addition to planning the design of the Web site itself, a Web developer should always plan the specifics of the file naming and storage conventions early on in the design phase. Once you determine the structure of the Web site and the approximate number of pages necessary to fulfill the site purpose, then you need to identify what standards to use with file naming and the folder structure. For instance, saving your Web pages with names such as page1.html and page2.html does not tell you the purpose of those Web pages. A better option would be to name the Sabatina Pizza Web site's home page sabatinahome.html or sabatinas.html, and the Web page with the user order form could be named orderform.html. Those file names tell the developer, as well as future developers maintaining the Web site, the purpose of those Web pages.

The same principle applies to the folder structure that you use in your Web development. The projects in this book have so few Web page files and graphic files that all content (Web pages and graphics) is stored together in one folder. With a large Web site, however, you may want to put the Web page files in a separate folder from the graphics files. Larger, more complex Web sites might also require a folder just to store video or audio clips. Where you store the files will affect how you access those files in your HTML code. Determining a good folder structure in the planning phase of the Web development life cycle is important. You'll learn more about effective folder structures in Chapter 3.

> **BTW**
> **Web Page Structure**
> There are many resources available on the Web that further discuss Web site structures. In addition to general design information, there are a number of tools available for sale or free download that can help you design your Web sites. Enter the phrase "Web site structure" into a search engine to find many valuable design sources.

During the design and development phase, you also should consider what, if any, types of multimedia could contribute positively to the Web site experience. For instance, adding a video message from the company CEO might be useful, but if the computing environment of your users cannot accommodate video playback, then the video serves no purpose. In general, do not use advanced multimedia technologies in a Web site unless they make a positive contribution to the Web site experience. Today, more Web sites are using audio and video content. These new additions sometimes enhance the overall purpose of the Web site, but they sometimes detract from the message.

Finally, consider accessibility issues and internationalization. A Web developer should always design for viewing by a diverse audience, including physically impaired and global users. A key consideration is that the software used by physically impaired individuals does not work with some Web features. For instance, if you use graphics on the Web site, always include alternative text for each graphic. To support an international audience, use generic icons that can be understood globally, avoid slang expressions in the content, and build simple pages that load quickly over lower-speed connections.

The design issues just discussed are only a few of the basic Web page design issues that you need to consider. Throughout this book, design issues will be addressed as they relate to each project. Many excellent Web page design resources also are available on the Internet.

Once the design of the Web site is determined, Web development can begin. The rest of the chapters in this book discuss good Web page standards, in addition to the actual development of Web pages. You will learn many development techniques, including links, tables, graphics, image maps, and Web forms. The umbrella that covers all of the development techniques taught in this book is the use of Cascading Style Sheets (CSS).

BTW

Web Site Testing
Testing should be done on all pages in a Web site. You should also test the links within the Web page, to other Web pages in the Web site, and to external Web sites. Testing is an important part of Web development and assures that your Web pages work as intended.

Web Site Testing

A Web site should be tested at various stages of the Web design and development processes. The testing process should be comprehensive and include a review of Web page content, functionality, and usability. Web sites with broken links, missing graphics, and incorrect content create a poor impression. You want to attract users to your Web site and maintain their interest. If visitors find that your Web site is poorly tested and maintained, they will be less likely to return. You cannot get your message out if users don't frequently visit the Web site. Some basic steps to test content and functionality include:

- Validating each Web page by running it through the W3C markup validation service
- Proofreading page content and titles to review for accurate spelling and grammar
- Checking links to ensure they are not broken and are linked correctly
- Checking graphics to confirm they appear properly and are linked correctly
- Ensuring that accessibility and internationalization issues are addressed
- Testing forms and other interactive page elements
- Testing pages to make sure they load quickly, even over lower-speed connections
- Printing each page to check how printed pages look

Usability is the measure of how well a product, such as a Web site, allows a user to accomplish his or her goals. **Usability testing** is a method by which users of a Web site or other product are asked to perform certain tasks in an effort to measure the product's ease-of-use and the user's perception of the experience. Usability testing for a Web site should focus on three key aspects: content, navigation, and presentation.

Usability testing can be conducted in several ways; one effective way is to directly observe users interfacing with (or using) the Web site. As you observe users, you can track the links they click and record their actions and comments. You even can ask the users to explain what tasks they were trying to accomplish while navigating the site. The information gained by observing users can be invaluable in helping identify potential problem areas in the Web site. For example, if you observe that users have difficulty finding the Web page that lists store locations and hours of operation, you may want to clarify the link descriptions or make the links more prominent on the home page.

Another way to conduct usability testing is to give users a specific task to complete (such as finding a product price list) and then observe how they navigate the site to complete the task. If possible, ask them to explain why they selected certain links. Both of these observation methods are extremely valuable, but require access to users.

Usability testing also can be completed using a questionnaire or survey. When writing a questionnaire or survey, be sure to write open-ended questions that can give you valuable information. For instance, asking the yes/no question "Is the Web site visually appealing?" will not gather useful information. If you change that question to use a scaled response, such as, "Rate the visual appeal of this Web site, using a scale of 1 for low and 5 for high," you can get more valuable input from the users. Make sure, however, that the scale itself is clear and understandable to the users. If you intend that a selection of 1 equates to a "low" rating, but the users think a 1 means "high," then your survey results are questionable. A usability testing questionnaire always should include space for users to write additional explanatory comments.

Figure 1–17 shows some examples of types of questions and organization that you might include in a Web site usability testing questionnaire.

In addition to content, functionality, and usability testing, there are other types of testing. For a newly implemented or maintained Web site, two other types of tests should be conducted: compatibility testing and stress testing. **Compatibility testing** is done to verify that the Web site works with a variety of browsers and browser versions. Initially, test using the browsers that your audience is most likely to use. Different browsers display some

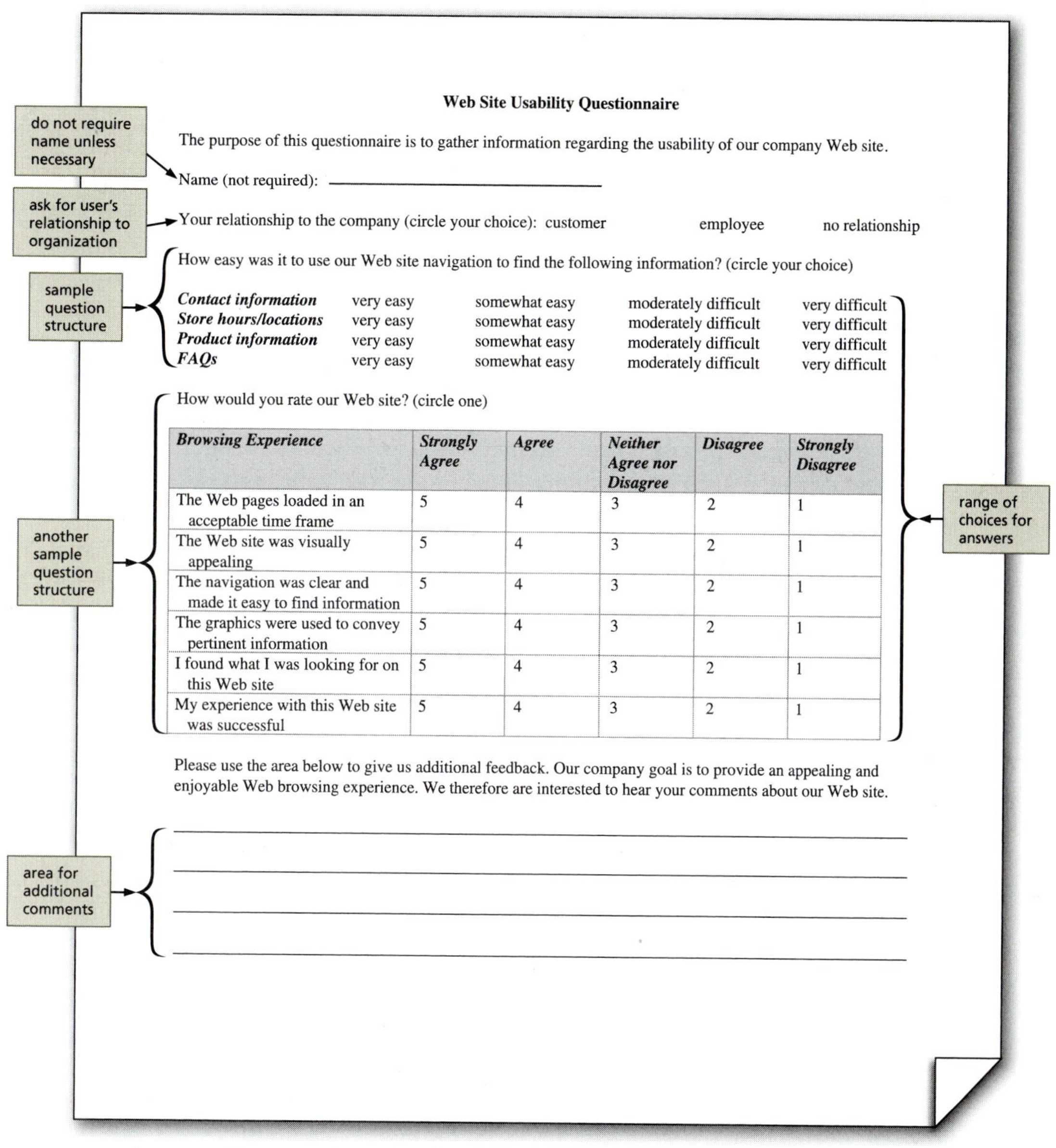
Web Site Usability Questionnaire

The purpose of this questionnaire is to gather information regarding the usability of our company Web site.

Name (not required): ____________________

Your relationship to the company (circle your choice): customer employee no relationship

How easy was it to use our Web site navigation to find the following information? (circle your choice)

Contact information	very easy	somewhat easy	moderately difficult	very difficult
Store hours/locations	very easy	somewhat easy	moderately difficult	very difficult
Product information	very easy	somewhat easy	moderately difficult	very difficult
FAQs	very easy	somewhat easy	moderately difficult	very difficult

How would you rate our Web site? (circle one)

Browsing Experience	*Strongly Agree*	*Agree*	*Neither Agree nor Disagree*	*Disagree*	*Strongly Disagree*
The Web pages loaded in an acceptable time frame	5	4	3	2	1
The Web site was visually appealing	5	4	3	2	1
The navigation was clear and made it easy to find information	5	4	3	2	1
The graphics were used to convey pertinent information	5	4	3	2	1
I found what I was looking for on this Web site	5	4	3	2	1
My experience with this Web site was successful	5	4	3	2	1

Please use the area below to give us additional feedback. Our company goal is to provide an appealing and enjoyable Web browsing experience. We therefore are interested to hear your comments about our Web site.

Figure 1–17 Web site usability testing questionnaire.

aspects of Web pages differently, so it is important to test Web pages in several different browsers to verify they appear correctly in each browser. If you have used technologies that are not supported by older browsers or that require plug-ins, consider changing the content or providing alternative Web pages for viewing in older browsers. If your audience uses both PC and Macintosh computers, you need to test the Web pages using browsers on both platforms. You also may want to test the Web pages in several versions of the same browser (usually the two most recent versions), in the event users have not yet upgraded.

Stress testing determines what happens on your Web site when greater numbers of users access the site. A Web site with 10 users accessing it simultaneously may be fine. When 100 users use the Web site at once, it may operate at an unacceptably slow speed. Stress testing verifies that a Web site runs at an acceptable speed with many users. There are many cases in which companies did not effectively stress test their Web sites. The results of this lack of testing have been disastrous, with Web sites locking up when too many users tried to access the same Web site function. Especially in the case of Web sites used for e-commerce, it is imperative for the Web site to stay online. A crashed or locked-up Web site will not sell products or services, and the company stands to lose a lot of money.

Web Site Implementation and Maintenance

Once Web site testing is complete and any required changes have been made, the Web site can be implemented. Implementation of a Web site involves the actual publishing of the Web pages to a Web server. Many HTML editors and WYSIWYG editors provide publishing capabilities. You also can use FTP software, such as WS_FTP or CuteFTP, to publish your Web pages to a Web server. After you publish a Web site, you should test the Web pages again to confirm no obvious errors exist such as broken links or missing graphics.

After a site is tested and implemented, you need to develop a process to maintain the Web site; users will undoubtedly request changes and timely content will require updates. You need to ensure, however, that updates to the Web site do not compromise the site's integrity and consistency. For example, if you have several different people updating various Web pages on a large Web site, you might find it difficult to maintain a consistent look on pages across the Web site. You should plan to update your Web site on a regular basis to keep content up-to-date. This could mean hourly, daily, weekly, or less often, depending on the site's purpose. Do not allow your content to become stale, outdated, or include broken links to Web pages that no longer exist. As a user looking for information related to a specific topic, how likely are you to believe the information found on a Web site that says "Last update on December 10, 1998" comes from a reliable source?

To help manage the task of Web site maintenance, first determine who is responsible for updates to content, structure, functionality, and so on. Then, limit update responsibilities to specific users. Be sure the implementation is controlled by one or more Web developers who can verify that the Web pages are tested thoroughly before they are published.

As updates and changes are made to a Web site, consider notifying users with a graphic banner or a "What's New" announcement, explaining any new features and how the features will benefit them. This technique not only keeps users informed, but also encourages them to come back to the Web site to see what is new.

Finally, Web site monitoring is another key aspect of maintaining a Web site. Usually, the Web servers that host Web sites keep logs of information about Web site usage. A **log** is the file that lists all of the Web pages that have been requested from the Web site. Web site logs are an invaluable source of information for a Web developer. Obtaining and analyzing the logs allow you to determine such things as the number of visitors, browser types and versions, connection speeds, pages most commonly requested, and usage patterns. With this information, you can design a Web site that is effective for your targeted audience, providing visitors with a rich and rewarding experience.

BTW

Quick Reference
For a list of HTML tags and their associated attributes, see the HTML Quick Reference (Appendix A) at the back of this book, or visit the HTML Quick Reference Web page (scsite.com/HTML6e/qr).

Be an Observant Web User

As you embark on this course, and perhaps start your Web development career, one useful practice is to be an observant Web user. Most of us use the Web several times a day (or more often) to complete our daily tasks. As a Web developer, you should review the Web pages that you access with an eye on functionality and design. As described in the first In the Lab exercise at the end of the chapter, you can bookmark Web sites you think are effective and ineffective, good and bad, and use them as references for your own Web development efforts. Watch for trends on the Web as you search for information or make online purchases. For example, running banners used to be very popular on the Web, but now other design techniques have taken over. Being an observant Web user can help you become a more effective Web developer.

Chapter Summary

In this chapter, you have learned about the Internet, the World Wide Web, and associated technologies, including Web servers and Web browsers. You learned the essential role of HTML in creating Web pages and reviewed tools used to create HTML documents. You also learned that most Web development projects follow a five-phase life cycle. The items listed below include all the new concepts you have learned in this chapter.

1. Describe the Internet (HTML 2)
2. Describe the World Wide Web (HTML 3)
3. Define Web servers (HTML 4)
4. Describe the Internet, intranets, and extranets (HTML 5)
5. Discuss Web browsers (HTML 7)
6. Define Hypertext Markup Language (HTML 8)
7. Describe HTML elements (HTML 9)
8. List HTML coding practices (HTML 10)
9. Explain HTML versions (HTML 11)
10. Describe Cascading Style Sheets (HTML 11)
11. Define the Document Object Model (HTML 11)
12. Define Extensible Hypertext Markup Language (XHTML) (HTML 12)
13. Describe tools for creating HTML documents (HTML 13)
14. Discuss the Web development life cycle (HTML 14)
15. Describe steps in the Web development planning phase (HTML 15)
16. Explain the Web development analysis phase (HTML 16)
17. Discuss Web design and development (HTML 16)
18. Describe various Web site structures (HTML 17)
19. Discuss the importance of Web site testing, including usability testing, compatibility testing, and stress testing (HTML 22)
20. Discuss Web site implementation and maintenance (HTML 24)
21. Explain the importance of being an observant Web user (HTML 24)

Learn It Online

Test your knowledge of chapter content and key terms.

Instructions: To complete the Learn It Online exercises, start your browser, click the Address bar, and then enter the Web address `scsite.com/html6e/learn`. When the HTML Learn It Online page is displayed, click the link for the exercise you want to complete and read the instructions.

Chapter Reinforcement TF, MC, and SA

A series of true/false, multiple choice, and short answer questions that test your knowledge of the chapter content.

Flash Cards

An interactive learning environment where you identify chapter key terms associated with displayed definitions.

Practice Test

A series of multiple choice questions that test your knowledge of chapter content and key terms.

Who Wants to Be a Computer Genius?

An interactive game that challenges your knowledge of chapter content in the style of a television quiz show.

Wheel of Terms

An interactive game that challenges your knowledge of chapter key terms in the style of the television show *Wheel of Fortune*.

Crossword Puzzle Challenge

A crossword puzzle that challenges your knowledge of key terms presented in the chapter.

STUDENT ASSIGNMENTS

Apply Your Knowledge

Reinforce the skills and apply the concepts you learned in this chapter.

Understanding Web Page Structures

Instructions: Figure 1–18 shows the Web site of a popular retailer, Costco. As you learned in this chapter, three common Web site structures include linear, hierarchical, and webbed. Based on that information, determine the structure used in the Costco.com Web site. Review other similar Web sites and determine which Web site design features are beneficial to a user. Incorporate those ideas into a new Web site design for Costco.com. Use paper to sketch the new Web site design for the Costco.com Web site.

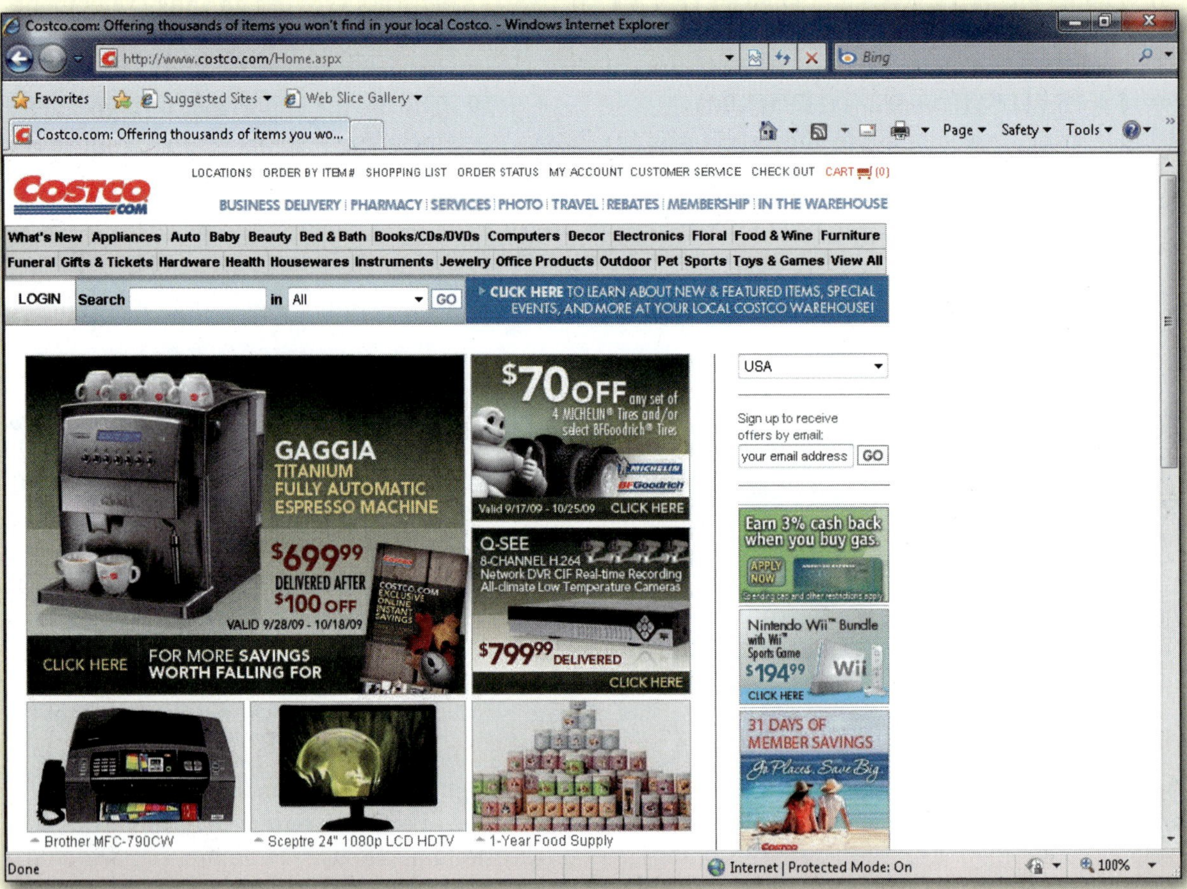

Figure 1–18

Perform the following tasks:

1. Start your browser. Open the Costco.com Web site in your browser. Print the home page by clicking Print on the File menu or by clicking the Print icon.
2. Explore the Costco.com Web site, determine the structure that the Web site utilizes (linear, hierarchical, or webbed), and then write that on the printout.
3. Find two other online retail store Web sites. Print the home pages for each of those sites. Navigate these Web sites to identify any design features that are beneficial to a user.
4. Using ideas from the online retail Web sites that you found in Step 3, sketch a new Web site structure and design for the Costco.com site on paper.
5. Write your name on the printouts and the sketch and hand them in to your instructor.

Extend Your Knowledge

Extend the skills you learned in this chapter and experiment with new skills.

Evaluating a User Survey

Instructions: Start your word-processing program. Open the document extend1-1.doc from the Chapter01\Extend folder of the Data Files for Students. See the inside back cover of this book for instructions on downloading the Data Files for Students, or contact your instructor for information about accessing the required files. This sample Web site survey shows various questions that could be asked in gathering feedback on Web site usability. It is important to assess the usability of your Web site, as mentioned in the chapter.

You will evaluate the user survey and modify the questions or add new questions that apply to the Web site that you have chosen. You then will ask five people to take your survey.

Perform the following tasks:

1. Connect to the Internet and identify one Web site that you think is confusing, difficult to use, or unattractive.
2. Make changes to the user survey by following some of the guidelines provided in Figure 1–17 on page HTML 20 and save the file as extend1-1solution.doc. Add questions to the survey that will help you determine a user's opinion of the selected Web site. Remember that the purpose of using surveys is to improve a Web site. Your questions therefore have to provide you with information that can help you achieve that goal.
3. Print five copies of your edited survey and distribute those printed copies to at least five family members or friends. Have them complete the survey relative to the Web site that you chose in Step 1. Collect their survey responses.
4. Determine what you learned from the results of the surveys. How helpful was the survey in determining needed improvements to the selected Web site? Were there other questions or other types of questions that you could ask that could have provided more valuable information about the Web site?
5. Identify what you can do to improve your Web site survey. Using a word processor, type your analysis at the bottom of your extend1-1solution.doc document, and then submit it in the format specified by your instructor.

Make It Right

Analyze a document and correct all errors and/or improve the design.

Correcting the Web Site Type Table

Instructions: Start your word-processing program. Open the file makeitright1-1.doc from the Chapter01\MakeItRight folder of the Data Files for Students. See the inside back cover of this book for instructions on downloading the Data Files for Students, or contact your instructor for information about accessing the required files. The document, shown in Table 1–7 on the next page, is a modified version of Table 1–5 (on page HTML 17). The table, which intentionally contains errors, lists the Web page organizational standards discussed in Chapter 1. Without referring to Table 1–5, make the necessary corrections to Table 1–7 by identifying the correct organizational standard and reason for each of the seven elements listed. Save the revised document as makeitright1-1solution.doc and then submit it in the form specified by your instructor.

Continued >

STUDENT ASSIGNMENTS

Make It Right *continued*

Table 1–7 Types of Web Sites

Element	Organizational Standard	Reason
Titles	Use these to separate main topics	These provide graphical elements to break up Web page content
Headings	Use simple ones that clearly explain the purpose of the page	These provide shorter, more-readable sections of text
Horizontal Rules	Utilize these in bulleted or numbered format when appropriate	Web users do not always scroll to view information on longer pages; appropriate page lengths increase the likelihood that users will view key information
Paragraphs	Maintain suitable Web page lengths	Web users are quick to peruse a page; placing critical information at the top of the page increases the likelihood that users will view key information
Lists	Insert these graphical elements to separate main topics	These provide organized, easy-to-read text that readers can scan
Page Length	Use these to help divide large amounts of text	Titles help users understand the purpose of the page; a good title explains the page in the search engine results lists
Information	Emphasize the most important information by placing it at the top of a Web page	These make a Web page easier to read; simple headlines clearly explain the purpose of the page

In the Lab

Design and/or create a document using the guidelines, concepts, and skills presented in this chapter. Labs are listed in order of increasing difficulty.

Lab 1: Evaluating Web Sites

Problem: In Chapter 1, you learned the importance of being an observant Web user, which can help you become a more effective Web developer. To further develop that concept, find and then discuss "good" and "bad" ("effective" and "ineffective") Web sites. Start your browser and your word-processing program. Open the file lab1-1.doc from the Chapter01\IntheLab folder of the Data Files for Students. See the inside back cover of this book for instructions for downloading the Data Files for Students, or contact your instructor for information on accessing the required files for this book.

Instructions: Perform the following steps using your browser and the file listed.

1. Browse the Internet and find one "good" (i.e., effective) or one "bad" (i.e., ineffective) Web site. Determine, based on your own opinion, what is "good" and what is "bad" in these Web sites. You will identify the specific reason for your opinion in Step 2 below.
2. Using the lab1-1.doc file, rate the usability of the good and bad Web sites that you selected. Be sure to add additional comments in the survey to specifically identify your positive or negative feelings about the Web site. Save the documents using the file names lab1-1goodsolution.doc and lab1-1badsolution.doc.
3. Team up with one other student and discuss your survey results while reviewing the Web sites that you selected. Also review your student partner's Web site and surveys.
4. Open the word-processing document named lab1-1comparison.doc and note any differences of opinion in your survey results and the opinion of your student partner. Make sure to include the

URLs of the four Web sites that you and your partner reviewed in this new document. Save the document using the file name lab1-1comparison.doc.

5. Submit your own solutions (lab1-1goodsolution.doc and lab1-1badsolution.doc) and the team document (lab1-1comparison.doc) in the format specified by your instructor.

In the Lab

Lab 2: Designing a Web Site for the School Counselors

Problem: Your school's counseling department wants you to design a Web site to link to/from the school's main Web site. To do this, you must complete the planning and analysis phases by answering such questions as:

- What tasks do students want to complete on the Web site?
- What tasks will the school counselors want to complete on the Web site?
- What types of information should be included?
- Who will provide information on the Web site content?

Interview several students of the school and determine the answers to these questions. Based on that information, you will draw a sketch of a design for the home page of the counseling department's Web site, such as the design shown in Figure 1–19.

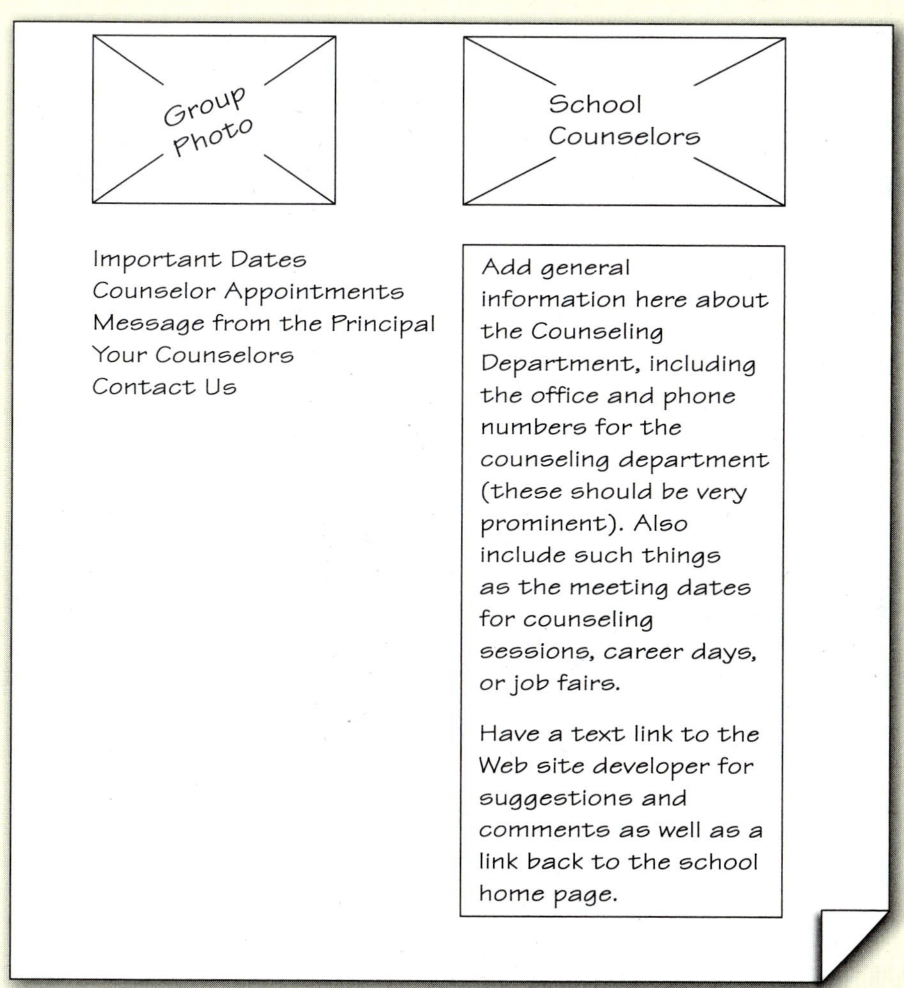

Figure 1–19

Continued >

STUDENT ASSIGNMENTS

In the Lab *continued*

Instructions: Perform the following tasks using your word-processing program and paper.

1. Review the questions in the planning and analysis phases of the Web development life cycle, as shown in Table 1–4 on page HTML 15.
2. Assess the value of those questions listed in the table. Add other questions that you think are relevant to the planning and analysis of a counseling department Web site.
3. Start your word-processing program. If necessary, open a new document. Enter the questions you will use for planning and analysis. Save the document using the file name lab1-2solution.doc. Print the document.
4. Using the questions that you developed, interview school counselors to determine what information should be included in the Web site, who will provide the information, and so on.
5. After gathering the required information, sketch a design for the home page of the Web site on paper.
6. Share your design sketch with students of the school and some of the counselors to get their opinions on your design.
7. Redraw the design on paper, making any changes based on the input from the students and counselors.
8. Write Original Design on the first design sketch.
9. Write Second Design on the second design sketch.
10. Write your name on the lab1-2solution printout and sketches and hand them in to your instructor.

In the Lab

Lab 3: Asking Planning Phase Questions: Internet, Intranet, and Extranet Designs

Problem: Three different types of Web sites were discussed in this chapter — Internet, intranet, and extranet. Each type of Web site is designed for a different target audience. Think of a business (for example, a restaurant, library, or card store) that you frequently visit and how that business might use an Internet, intranet, and extranet site. The Planning phase questions found in Table 1–4 on page HTML 15 have been reproduced in Table 1–8. Determine the answers to these questions and enter your ideas in the table. If there are questions that are difficult/impossible to answer directly (for example, What are users' computing environments?), list ways that you can find the answers to those questions.

Table 1–8 Planning Phase Questions

Type Of Business			
Planning Question	**Internet**	**Intranet**	**Extranet**
What is the purpose of this Web site?			
Who will use this Web site?			
What are users' computing environments?			
Who owns and authors the information on the Web site?			
Who decides if/where the information goes on the Web site?			

Instructions: Start your word-processing program. Open the file lab1-3.doc from the Chapter01\IntheLab folder of the Data Files for Students. See the inside back cover of this book for instructions for downloading the Data Files for Students, or contact your instructor for information on accessing the required files. Perform the following tasks using your word-processing program.

1. Enter the type of business in the first row of the table. Determine the answers to the first question for all three types of Web sites and then enter the answers in the appropriate table cells. If the business you choose has no reason to maintain one of the three types of Web sites (Internet, intranet, or extranet), thoroughly identify in your answer why they would not need it.
2. Continue answering the other four questions.
3. Save the file using the file name lab1-3solution.doc and then submit it in the format specified by your instructor.

Cases and Places

Apply your creative thinking and problem-solving skills to design and implement a solution.

• Easier •• More Difficult

• 1: Learn More About Web Access Issues

Your company wants to offer online courses to employees. Several employees have physical challenges, and it is imperative that the online courses be accessible to everyone. Your manager has asked you to learn more about accessibility guidelines to determine what changes are needed to make the company's online courses accessible to those with physical challenges. Research accessibility issues on the Web and determine what needs should be considered to satisfy accessibility requirements. Make sure to visit the W3.org Web site. Consider the following questions when doing your research: What types of physical challenges do you have to consider when developing Web pages? What recommendations do the Web sites make for accessibility? Why is this important to you as a Web developer?

• 2: Determine Web Site Structure

You have recently started a job as a Web developer at Triple-Tom Design. In your new job, you often are asked to restructure clients' existing Web sites to make them more user friendly and easier to navigate. Find a Web site that utilizes more than one Web site structure (linear, hierarchical, and/or webbed). Is the information conveyed on the Web site displayed in the appropriate structure? Does the structure effectively support the information communicated? Print the home page of the Web site that you found. On a blank sheet of paper, sketch a design that you think might be more appropriate for the message. Use a word-processing program to create a document that explains why your new design is more effective.

•• 3: Learn More About CSS

This chapter introduced the use of Cascading Style Sheets (CSS) in Web development. You will utilize CSS throughout this book, so it is important that you become familiar with it. Visit the W3Schools Web site (*w3schools.com*) to learn more about CSS. Find three other sources of information about CSS on other Web sites. Using a word-processing program, create a document that briefly describes CSS and how you can best utilize it for Web development.

Continued >

Cases and Places *continued*

•• 4: Design a Web Site for Your Sister

Make It Personal

Your sister would like to sell the jewelry that she makes online. You would like to develop a Web site for her that can display her jewelry and be a means for sales transactions. Thoroughly investigate the Web sites of other online jewelers and print home pages from three of them. Before starting on the design, you decide to create a list of Web design principles to which the Web site will adhere. Search the Web for more information about Web site design. Find three Web sites that give information about Web design principles. In a word-processing document, take the ideas presented in this chapter together with the ideas presented in the other Web sites and make a comprehensive list of Web design principles. Determine whether or not the Web sites that you printed comply with good design principles. Where appropriate, identify any conflicting design principles discussed in the Web sites.

•• 5: Create a Usability Survey

Working Together

Your school recently updated its Web site. The school administration has selected a team to develop a usability survey or questionnaire that you can give to a group of users (including students, parents, and teachers) to evaluate the new Web site. What types of information do you hope to gain by distributing this survey or questionnaire? How can you convey information on the survey or questionnaire so it clearly identifies what you are asking? Create a usability survey using your word-processing program. Give the survey or questionnaire to at least five people, including at least one from each group identified above. Allow participants to complete the survey or questionnaire and then look at the results. If possible, ask the users what they thought the various questions conveyed. Is that what you wanted to convey? If not, think of clearer, more relevant questions and redistribute the survey to another group of participants.

2 Creating and Editing a Web Page Using Inline Styles

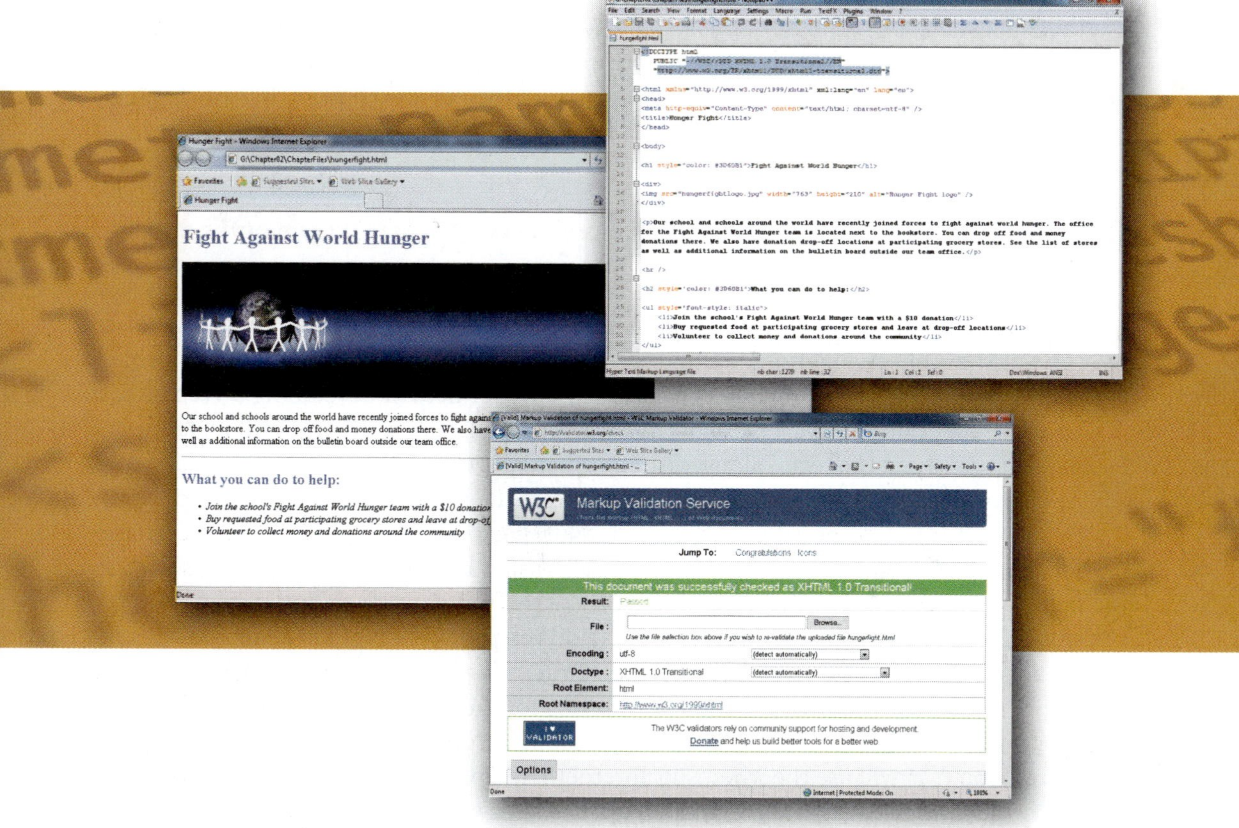

Objectives

You will have mastered the material in this chapter when you can:

- Identify elements of a Web page
- Start Notepad++ and describe the Notepad++ window
- Enable word wrap in Notepad++
- Enter HTML tags
- Enter a centered heading and a paragraph of text
- Create an unordered, ordered, or definition list
- Save an HTML file
- Use a browser to view a Web page
- Activate Notepad++
- Identify Web page image types and attributes
- Add an image, change the color of headings on a Web page, change bulleted list style, and add a horizontal rule using inline styles
- View the HTML source code in a browser
- Print a Web page and an HTML file
- Quit Notepad++ and a browser

2 Creating and Editing a Web Page Using Inline Styles

Introduction

With an understanding of the Web development life cycle, you should have a good idea about the importance of proper Web site planning, analysis, and design. After completing these phases, the next phase is the actual development of a Web page using HTML. As discussed in Chapter 1, Web pages are created employing HTML, which uses a set of special tags to define the structure, layout, and appearance of a Web page. In this chapter, you create and edit a Web page using basic HTML tags.

Project — Fight Against World Hunger Web Page

Chapter 2 illustrates how to use HTML to create a Web page for the school's Fight Against World Hunger team, as shown in Figure 2–1a. The team is joining other students around the world to collect donations and money. Because you are the only Web development major in the group, team members have asked for your help in developing a Web page to advertise the team's cause. The Fight Against World Hunger Web page will include general information about the team, along with information on how to donate and participate.

To enter text and HTML tags used to create the Web page, you will use a program called Notepad++, as shown in Figure 2–1b. **Notepad++** is a basic text editor you can use for simple documents or for creating Web pages using HTML. Previous editions of this book used Notepad, a text editor that is a part of the Windows operating system. Notepad worked well to enter the HTML elements and Web page content, but Notepad++ is a more sophisticated text editor with more features. Notepad++ has line numbering, which is very helpful when reading code. It also is color-coded for the text that is entered, as you will see later in the chapter. Because of this added versatility, Notepad++ is the chosen text editor for this edition. You will use the Microsoft Internet Explorer browser to view your Web page as you create it. By default, Internet Explorer is installed with Windows, and Notepad++ can be downloaded for free on the Web. If you do not have Notepad++ or Internet Explorer available on your computer, other text editor or browser programs will work.

Overview

As you read this chapter, you will learn how to create the Web page shown in Figure 2–1 by performing these general tasks:

- Enter HTML code into the Notepad++ window.
- Save the file as an HTML file.
- Enter basic HTML tags and add text to the file.
- Organize the text by adding headings and creating a bulleted list.
- Enhance the Web page's appearance with inline styles.
- View the Web page and HTML code in your browser.
- Validate the Web page.
- Print the Web page.

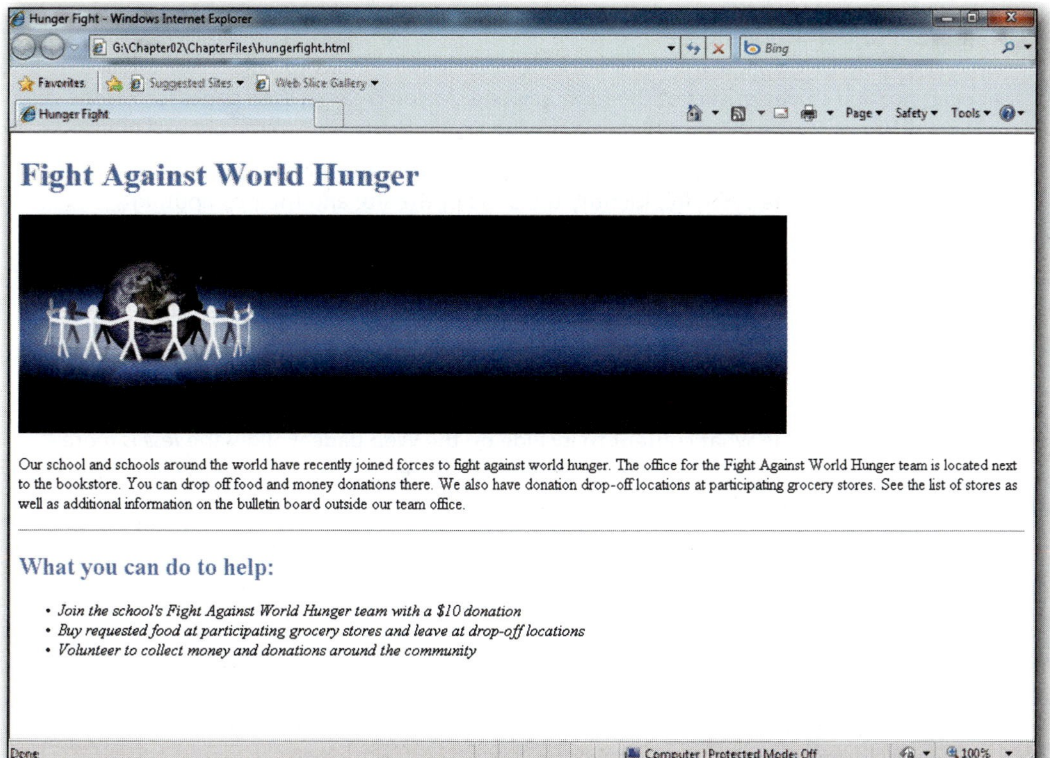

(a) Fight Against World Hunger Web page.

G:\Chapter02\ChapterFiles\hungerfight.html - Notepad++

```
<!DOCTYPE html
    PUBLIC "-//W3C//DTD XHTML 1.0 Transitional//EN"
    "http://www.w3.org/TR/xhtml1/DTD/xhtml1-transitional.dtd">

<html xmlns="http://www.w3.org/1999/xhtml" xml:lang="en" lang="en">
<head>
<meta http-equiv="Content-Type" content="text/html; charset=utf-8" />
<title>Hunger Fight</title>
</head>

<body>

<h1 style="color: #3D60B1">Fight Against World Hunger</h1>

<div>
<img src="hungerfightlogo.jpg" width="763" height="210" alt="Hunger Fight logo" />
</div>

<p>Our school and schools around the world have recently joined forces to fight against world hunger. The office
for the Fight Against World Hunger team is located next to the bookstore. You can drop off food and money
donations there. We also have donation drop-off locations at participating grocery stores. See the list of stores
as well as additional information on the bulletin board outside our team office.</p>

<hr />

<h2 style="color: #3D60B1">What you can do to help:</h2>

<ul style="font-style: italic">
    <li>Join the school's Fight Against World Hunger team with a $10 donation</li>
    <li>Buy requested food at participating grocery stores and leave at drop-off locations</li>
    <li>Volunteer to collect money and donations around the community</li>
</ul>
```

Hyper Text Markup Language file | nb char : 1279 | nb line : 32 | Ln : 1 Col : 1 Sel : 0 | Dos\Windows ANSI | INS

(b) HTML code used to create the Web page.

Figure 2–1

Plan Ahead

General Project Guidelines

When creating a Web page, the actions you perform and decisions you make will affect the appearance and characteristics of the finished page. As you create a Web page, such as the project shown in Figure 2–1 on the previous page, you should follow these general guidelines:

1. **Complete Web page planning.** Before developing a Web page, you must know the purpose of the Web site, identify the users of the site and their computing environments, and decide who owns the information on the Web page.
2. **Analyze the need for the Web page.** In the analysis phase of the Web development life cycle, you should analyze what content to include on the Web page. In this phase, you determine the tasks and the information that the users need. Refer to Table 1–4 on page HTML 15 for information on the phases of the Web development life cycle.
3. **Choose the content for the Web page.** Once you have completed the analysis, you need to determine what content to include on the Web page. Follow the *less is more* principle. The less text, the more likely the Web page will be read. Use as few words as possible to make a point.
4. **Determine the file naming convention that you will use for this Web page.** Before you start creating and saving files, you should decide on a standard way of naming your files. Should you use the .htm or .html extension? As explained later in the chapter, you use the .htm extension when the host Web server only allows short file names. You use .html when the host Web server allows long file names. What name should you give your file to indicate the file's content or purpose? For instance, naming a Web page page1.html does not describe what that Web page is; a more descriptive name is helpful in development of the Web site.
5. **Determine where to save the Web page.** You can store a Web page permanently, or **save** it, on a variety of storage media, including a hard disk, USB flash drive, CD, or DVD. Your instructor or the company for whom you are developing the Web page may have specific storage media requirements.
6. **Determine what folder structure to use on your storage device.** Once you have determined the storage media to use, you should also determine folder location, structure, and names on which to save the Web page. This should be done before you start to save any of your files.
7. **Identify how to format various elements of the Web page.** The overall appearance of a Web page significantly affects its ability to communicate clearly. Examples of how you can modify the appearance, or **format**, of the Web page include adding an image, color to headings, and horizontal rules.
8. **Find appropriate graphical images.** Eye-catching graphical images help convey the Web page's overall message and add visual interest. Graphics can be used to show a product, service, result, or benefit, or visually convey a message that is not expressed easily with words.
9. **Establish where to position and how to format the graphical images.** The position and format of the graphical images should grab the attention of passersby and draw them into reading the Web page.
10. **Test the Web page for XHTML compliance.** An important part of Web development is testing to assure that your Web page follows XHTML standards. The World Wide Web Consortium (W3C) has an online validator that allows you to test your Web page and clearly explains any errors.

When necessary, more specific details concerning the above guidelines are presented at appropriate points in the chapter. The chapter also will identify the actions performed and decisions made regarding these guidelines during the creation of the Web page shown in Figure 2–1a.

Elements of a Web Page

Today, many people — individuals, students, teachers, business executives, Web developers, and others — are developing Web pages for personal or professional reasons. Each person has his or her own style and the resulting Web pages are as diverse as the people who create them. Most Web pages, however, include several basic features, or elements, as shown in Figure 2–2.

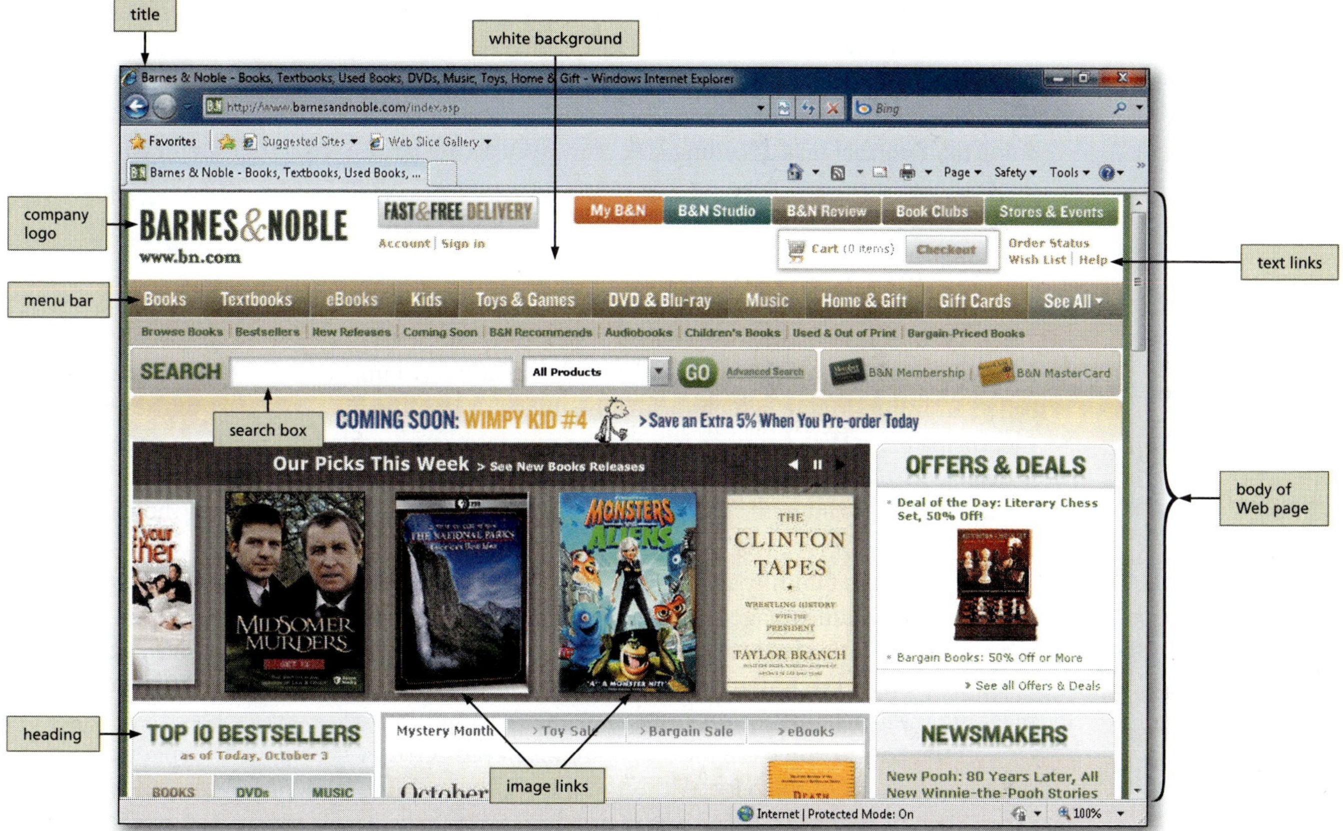

Figure 2–2 Elements of a Web page.

Window Elements

The **title** of a Web page is the text that appears on the title bar and taskbar of the browser window when the Web page appears. The title also is the name assigned to the page if a user adds the page to the browser's list of **favorites**, or **bookmarks**. Because of its importance, you always should include a title on your Web page. The title, which usually is the first element you see, should identify the subject or purpose of the page. The title should be concise, yet descriptive, and briefly explain the page's content or purpose to the visitor.

The **body** of the Web page contains the information that is displayed in the browser window. The body can include text, graphics, and other elements. The Web page displays anything that is contained within the <body> (start body) and </body> (end body) tags. The **background** of a Web page is a solid color, a picture, or a graphic against which the other elements on the Web page appear. When choosing your background, be sure it does not overpower the information on the Web page. As you surf the Web, watch for background colors or images that do not allow the content of the Web page to show through. This is certainly a "what not to do" guideline for Web developers.

BTW

Favorites and Bookmarks

Internet Explorer and Mozilla Firefox have a feature that allows you to add Web pages to a list so you quickly can access them in the future. Internet Explorer refers to these as Favorites, while Firefox calls them Bookmarks. Web developers need to make sure that they include a descriptive title on their Web pages because that is the title that is shown in the bookmark or favorite.

BTW

HTML Resources
The Web has many wonderful sources of information on HTML and Web page development. One of the better sources is the HTML Goodies Web site, which has primers and tutorials on a variety of topics as well as free downloads and discussion areas. To learn more about this Web site, search for the term "HTML Goodies" in a search engine.

Text Elements

Normal text is the default text format used for the main content of a Web page. Normal text can be used in a standard paragraph or formatted to appear as: bold, italic, or underlined; in different colors; and so on. You can also use inline cascading style sheets (CSS) to alter the format of the text, an approach used throughout this book. Normal text also can be used in a series of text items called a **list**. Typically, lists are bulleted or numbered. Various attributes of lists can be altered. For example, you might want to have square bullets rather than the default round bullets, or to have your list text in italic or bold.

Headings are used to set off paragraphs of text or different sections of a page. Headings are a larger font size than normal text and often are bold or italic or a different color than normal text. Heading sizes run from 1 (the largest) to 6 (the smallest). You generally go from one heading size to the next smallest when setting up a Web page.

Image Elements

Web pages typically use several different types of graphics, or images, such as an icon, bullet, line, photo, illustration, or other picture. An image used in a Web page also is called an **inline image**, which means the image or graphic file is not part of the HTML file. Instead, the Web browser merges the separate graphic file into the Web page as it is displayed in the browser window. The HTML file contains <img> tags that tell the browser which graphic file to request from the server, where to insert it on the page, and how to display it.

Web pages typically use several different types of inline images. An **image map** is a special type of inline image in which you define one or more areas as hotspots. A **hotspot** is an area of an image that activates a function when selected. For example, each hotspot in an image map can link to a different Web page. Some inline images are **animated**, meaning they include motion and can change in appearance.

Horizontal rules are lines that are displayed across a Web page to separate different sections of the page. Although the appearance of a horizontal rule can vary, many Web pages use an inline image as a horizontal rule. Alternatively, you can use the horizontal rule tag (<hr />) to add a simple horizontal rule, such as the one used in this chapter project.

Hyperlink Elements

One of the more important elements of a Web page is a hyperlink, or link. A **link** is text, an image, or another Web page element that you click to instruct the browser to go to a location in a file or to request a file from a server. On the Web, links are the primary way to navigate between Web pages and among Web sites. Links point not only to Web pages, but also to graphics, sound, video, program files, e-mail addresses, and parts of the same Web page. Text links, also called hypertext links, are the most commonly used hyperlinks. For example, the text "Order Status" in Figure 2–2 links to the status of the user's orders. When text identifies a hyperlink, it usually appears as underlined text, in a color different from the rest of the Web page text. Image links are also very common. For example, there are two image links identified in Figure 2–2. Clicking either of those image links sends (or links) the user to another Web page that contains further information about those items. A company logo often serves as an image link to a home page or corporate information.

Defining Web Page Structure

To create an HTML document, you use a text editor to enter information about the structure of the Web page, the content of the Web page, and instructions for how that content should be displayed. This book uses the Notepad++ text editor to enter the HTML elements and content for all projects and exercises.

Before you begin entering the content for this project, you must start by entering tags that define the overall structure of the Web page. You do this by inserting a <!DOCTYPE> tag and five tags (<html>, <head>, <meta />, <title>, and <body>) together with the closing tags (</html>, </head>, </title>, and </body>). These tags define the structure of a standard Web page and divide the HTML file into its basic sections: header information and the body of the page that contains text and graphics.

The **<!DOCTYPE>** tag is used to tell the browser which HTML or XHTML version and type the document uses. The World Wide Web Consortium (W3C) supports three document types for HTML or XHTML: strict, transitional, and frameset. The **strict** document type is specified when you want to prohibit the use of deprecated tags. **Deprecated tags** are tags that the W3C has earmarked for eventual removal from their specifications, because those tags have been replaced with newer, more functional tags. The **transitional** document type allows the use of deprecated tags. The **frameset** document type, which is used to support frames on a Web page, also allows the use of deprecated tags. The <!DOCTYPE> tag includes a URL that references a Document Type Definition found on the w3.org Web site. Although this book does not use deprecated tags, the projects do use the XHTML 1.0 transitional document type, because the projects use a few tags (e.g., name) that are not supported by the XHTML 1.1 standard. A **Document Type Definition (DTD)** is a file containing definitions of tags and instructions for how they should be used in a Web page. The project in this chapter uses the transitional document type.

BTW
The DOCTYPE Tag
The W3Schools Web site provides additional information about the DOCTYPE tags used for the strict, transitional, and frameset document types. To learn more about the DOCTYPE tag, visit the W3C Web site. It provides a wealth of information on this and other HTML tags.

Defining the HTML Document

The first set of tags beyond the <!DOCTYPE> tag, **<html>** and **</html>**, indicates the start and end of an HTML document. This set of tags contains all of the content of the Web page, the tags that format that content, and the tags that define the different parts of the document. Software tools, such as browsers, use these tags to determine where the HTML code in a file begins and ends.

The Header The next set of tags, **<head>** and **</head>**, contains the Web page title and other document header information. One of the tags inserted into the <head> </head> container is the meta tag. The **<meta />** tag has several functions. In this chapter, it is used to declare the character encoding UTF-8. The **Unicode Transformation Format (UTF)** is a compressed format that allows computers to display and manipulate text. When the browser encounters this meta tag, it will display the Web page properly, based on the particular UTF-8 encoding embedded in the tag. UTF-8 is the preferred encoding standard for Web pages, e-mail, and other applications. The encoding chosen also is important when validating the Web page. The meta tag has other purposes that are described in subsequent chapters of the book. The <title> tag is another tag inserted into the <head> </head> container. The **<title>** and **</title>** tags indicate the title of the Web page, which appears on the browser title bar and taskbar when the Web page is displayed in the browser window. The title also is the name given to the page when a user adds the page to a favorites or bookmarks list.

BTW
XHTML Compliance
To make your HTML files compliant with XHTML standards, always enter tags in lowercase (with the exception of the <!DOCTYPE> tag, which is always uppercase). Throughout this book, the project directions follow these standards to help you learn good HTML and XHTML coding practices.

The Body The final set of tags, **<body>** and **</body>**, contains the main content of the Web page. All text, images, links, and other content are contained within this final set of tags. Table 2–1 on the next page lists the functions of the tags described so far, as well as other tags that you use in this chapter.

Table 2–1 Basic HTML Tags and Their Functions

HTML Tag	Function
<!DOCTYPE>	Indicates the version and type of HTML used; includes a URL reference to a DTD
<html> </html>	Indicates the start and end of an HTML document
<head> </head>	Indicates the start and end of a section of the document used for the title and other document header information
<meta />	Indicates hidden information about the Web page
<title> </title>	Indicates the start and end of the title. The title does not appear in the body of the Web page, but appears on the title bar of the browser.
<body> </body>	Indicates the start and end of the body of the Web page
<h*n*> </h*n*>	Indicates the start and end of the text section called a heading; sizes range from <h1> through <h6>. See Figure 2–8a on page HTML 46 for heading size samples.
<p> </p>	Indicates the start and end of a new paragraph; inserts a blank line above the new paragraph
<ul> </ul>	Indicates the start and end of an unordered (bulleted) list
<li> </li>	Indicates that the item that follows the tag is an item within a list
<hr />	Inserts a horizontal rule
 	Inserts a line break at the point where the tag appears

BTW

WordPad

WordPad is a text editor included with Windows that you can also use to create HTML files. To start WordPad, click the Start button on the taskbar, point to All Programs on the Start menu, point to Accessories on the All Programs submenu, and then click WordPad on the Accessories submenu. WordPad help provides tips on how to use the product.

Most HTML start tags, such as <html>, <head>, <title>, and <body>, have corresponding end tags, </html>, </head>, </title>, and </body>. Note that, for tags that do not have end tags, such as <meta />, <hr />, and <br />, the tag is closed using a space followed by a forward slash.

To Start Notepad++

With the planning, analysis, and design of the Web page complete, you can begin developing the Web page by entering HTML using a text editor.

The following steps, which assume Windows 7 is running and Notepad++ is installed, start Notepad++ based on a typical installation. You may need to ask your instructor how to download, install, and start Notepad++ for your computer.

- Click the Start button on the Windows taskbar to display the Start menu.
- Click All Programs at the bottom of the left pane on the Start menu to display the All Programs list.
- Click the Notepad++ folder in the All Programs list (Figure 2–3).

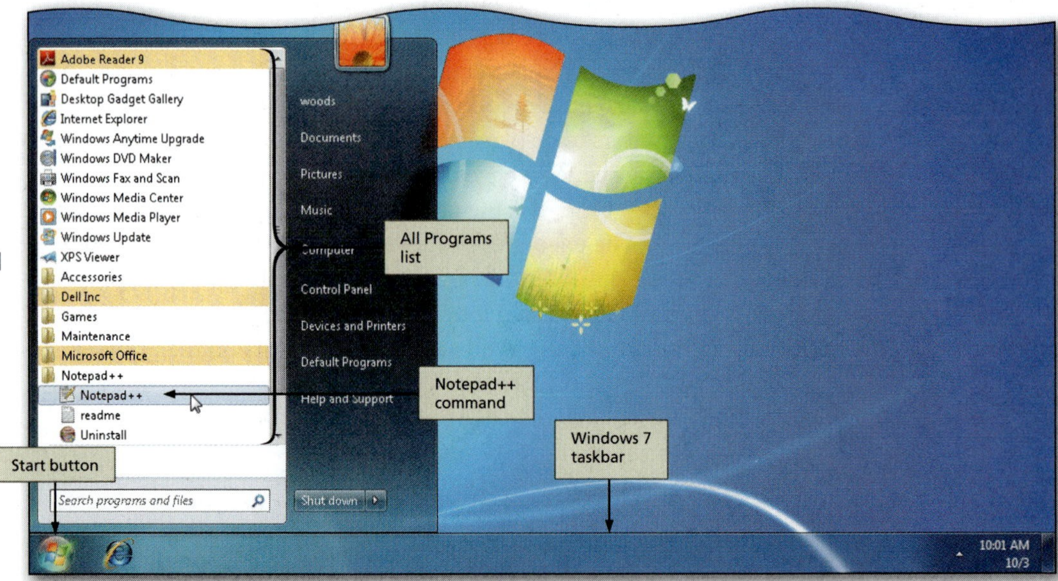

Figure 2–3

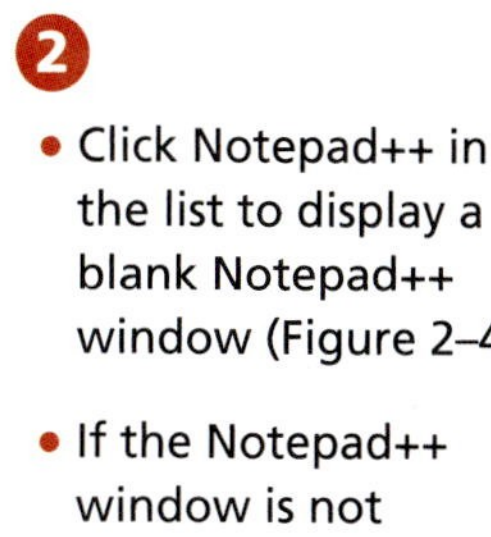

2

- Click Notepad++ in the list to display a blank Notepad++ window (Figure 2–4).
- If the Notepad++ window is not maximized, click the Maximize button on the Notepad++ title bar to maximize it.

Q&A What is a maximized window?

A maximized window fills the entire screen. When you maximize a window, the Maximize button changes to a Restore Down button.

Q&A How can I add Notepad++ to my Start menu or the taskbar?

To add Notepad++ to the Start menu or taskbar, complete Step 1 above. Right-click Notepad++, then click Pin to Start menu or Pin to taskbar.

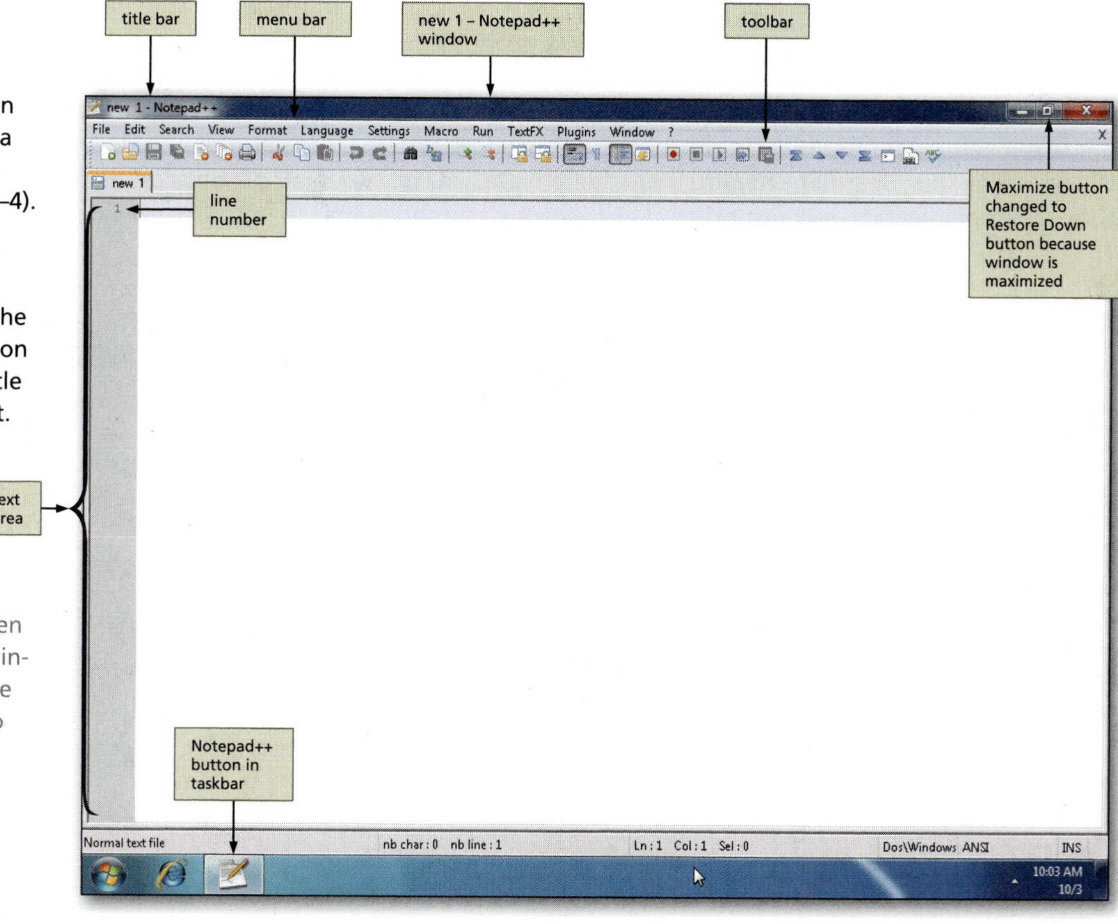

Figure 2–4

Other Ways	
1. Double-click Notepad++ icon on desktop, if one is present	2. Click Notepad++ on Start menu, if it is present

BTW

Notepad++ Help
Notepad++ has a wealth of help information available. There is Notepad++ Help internal to the program as well as help facilities online. NpWiki is the wiki for Notepad++ that you can access. The primary aim of this wiki is to be a storehouse for all information about Notepad++.

To Enable Word Wrap in Notepad++

In Notepad++, the text entered in the text area scrolls continuously to the right unless the word wrap feature is enabled, or turned on. **Word wrap** causes text lines to break at the right edge of the window and appear on a new line, so all entered text is visible in the Notepad++ window. With paragraphs of text and word wrap enabled, the text all appears on one logical line number even though it may display on multiple physical lines in Notepad++. Word wrap does not affect the way text prints. The following step shows how to enable word wrap in Notepad++.

1

- Click View on the menu bar (Figure 2–5).
- If Word wrap does not have a check mark next to it, click Word wrap.

Q&A How do I know if Word wrap is enabled?

When Word wrap is enabled, a check mark precedes the Word wrap command on the View menu, and when you type, your words remain on the screen.

Q&A What happens to the text if Word wrap is not enabled?

The text of a paragraph would appear all on one line in Notepad++ and scroll off the screen, though the Web page would still be displayed correctly in the browser. For readability in Notepad++, you should enable Word wrap.

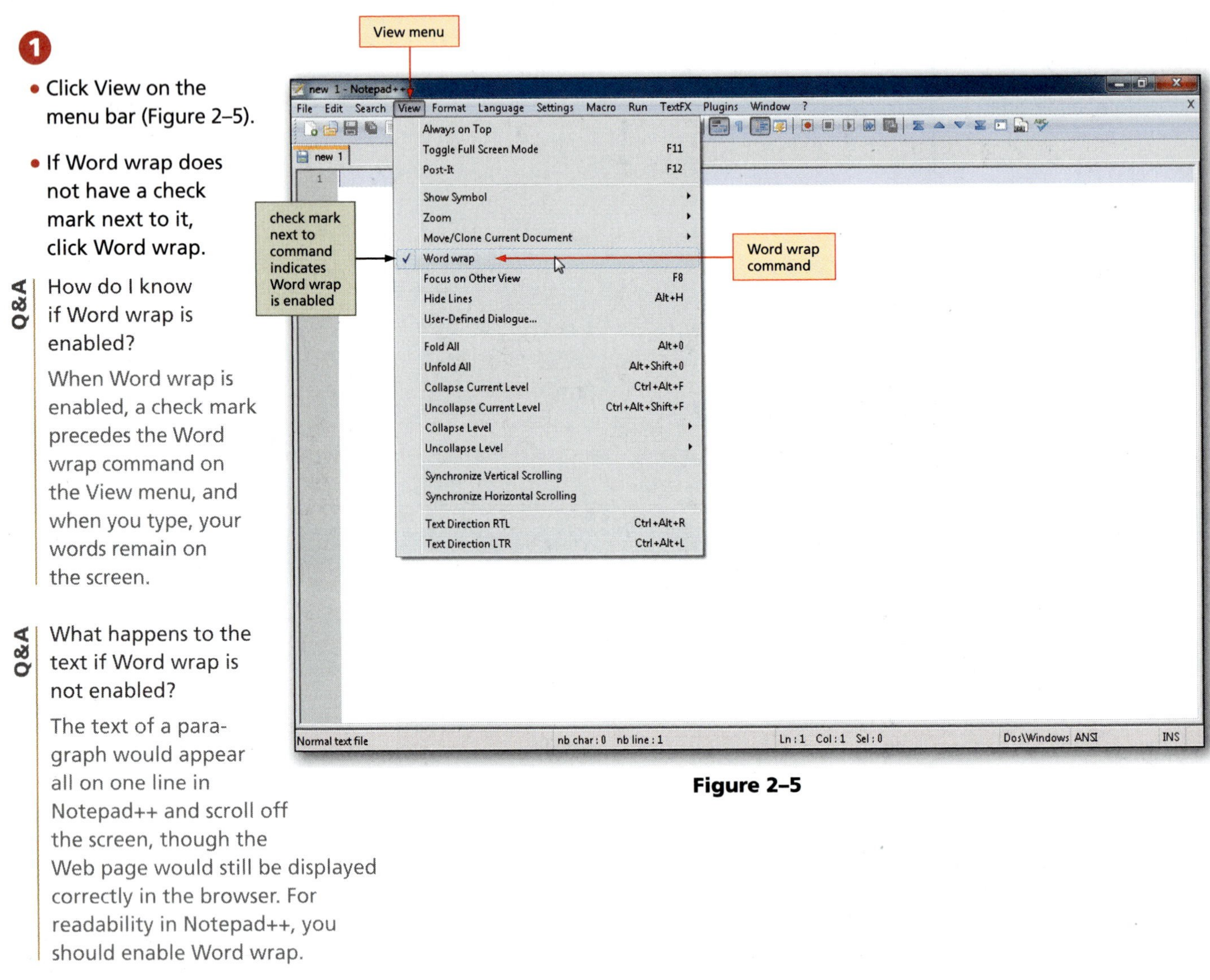

Figure 2–5

To Define the Web Page Structure Using HTML Tags

The first task is to enter the initial tags that define the Web page structure. Table 2–2 contains the HTML tags and text used to create the Web page shown in Figure 2–1a on page HTML 35. In this chapter and throughout this book, where large segments of HTML code or text are to be entered, you will find this code or text in tables with line number references, rather than within the steps. The steps will direct you to enter the text shown in the tables.

Table 2–2 Initial HTML Tags

Line	HTML Tag and Text
1	<!DOCTYPE html
2	PUBLIC "-//W3C//DTD XHTML 1.0 Transitional//EN"
3	"http://www.w3.org/TR/xhtml1/DTD/xhtml1-transitional.dtd">
4	
5	<html xmlns="http://www.w3.org/1999/xhtml" xml:lang="en" lang="en">
6	<head>
7	<meta http-equiv="Content-Type" content="text/html; charset=utf-8" />
8	<title>Hunger Fight</title>
9	</head>

The following steps illustrate how to enter the initial tags that define the structure of the Web page.

1

- Enter the HTML code shown in Table 2–2 (Figure 2–6). Press ENTER at the end of each line. If you make an error as you are typing, use the BACKSPACE key to delete all the characters back to and including the incorrect characters, and then continue typing.
- Press the ENTER key twice to start the next line of code, leaving one blank line after the </head> tag.
- Compare what you typed to Figure 2–6. If you notice errors, use your mouse pointer or arrow keys to move the insertion point to the right of each error and use the BACKSPACE key to correct the error.

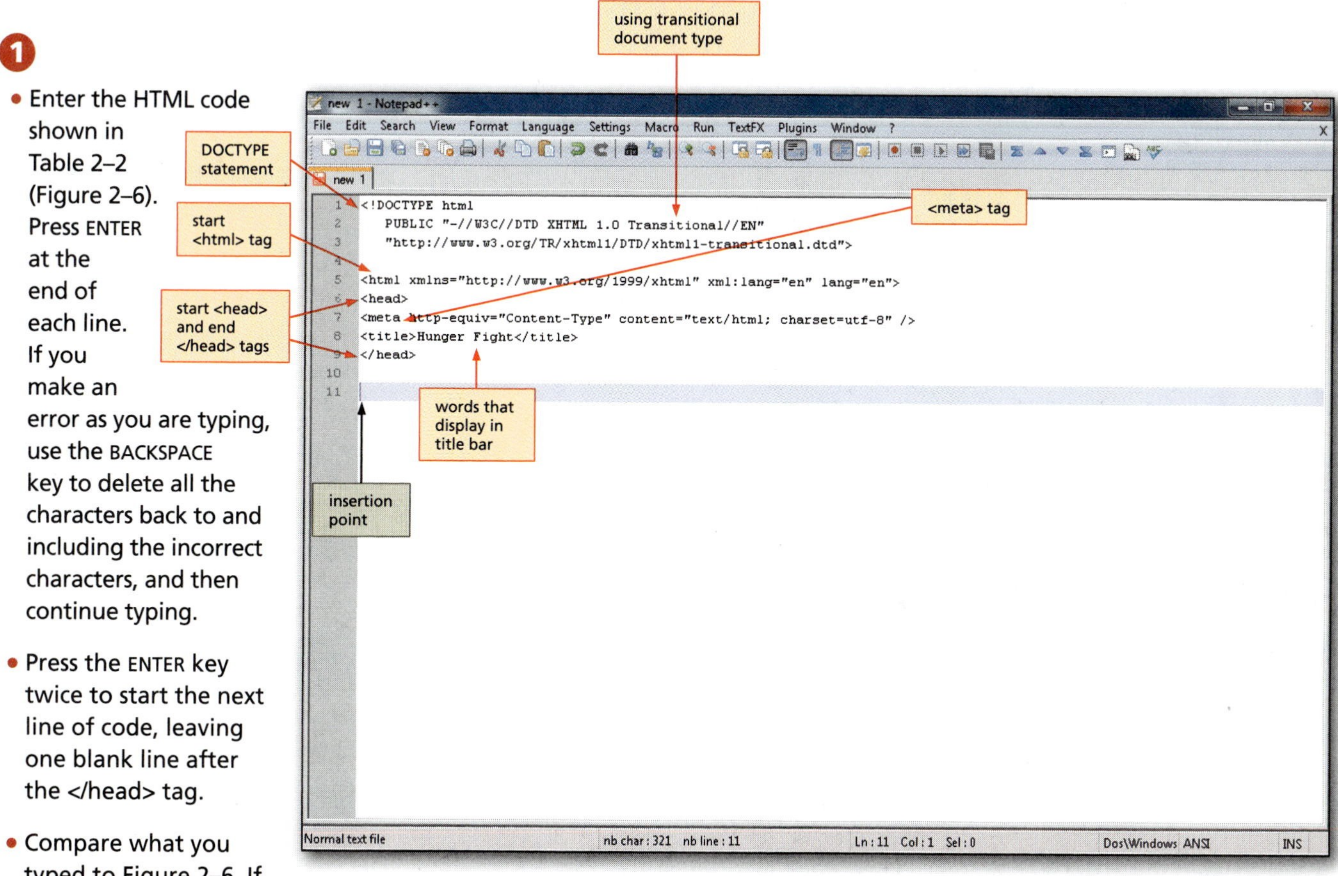

Figure 2–6

- On line 11, type <body> and then press the ENTER key twice.
- Type </body> and then press the ENTER key.
- Type </html> as the end tag (Figure 2–7).
- Compare what you typed to Figure 2–7 and correct errors in your typing if necessary.

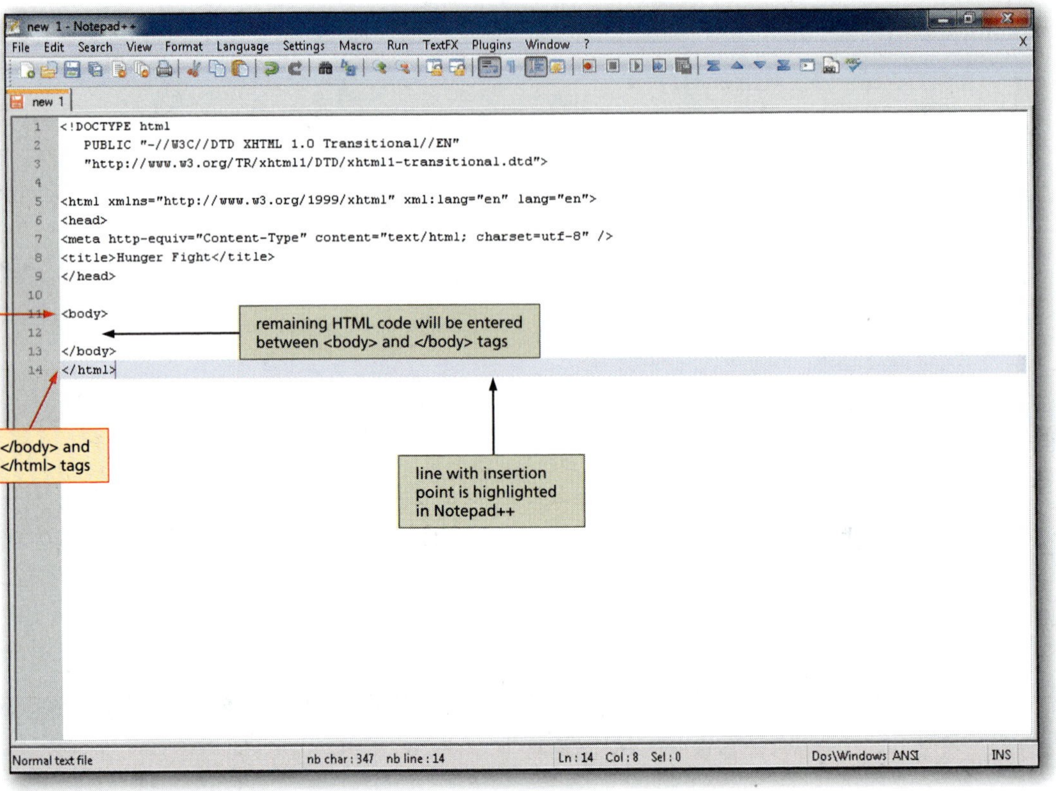

```
1  <!DOCTYPE html
2     PUBLIC "-//W3C//DTD XHTML 1.0 Transitional//EN"
3     "http://www.w3.org/TR/xhtml1/DTD/xhtml1-transitional.dtd">
4
5  <html xmlns="http://www.w3.org/1999/xhtml" xml:lang="en" lang="en">
6  <head>
7  <meta http-equiv="Content-Type" content="text/html; charset=utf-8" />
8  <title>Hunger Fight</title>
9  </head>
10
11 <body>
12
13 </body>
14 </html>
```


Figure 2–7

Q&A Why am I using the transitional document type? Doesn't that allow the use of deprecated tags?

Yes, you can use deprecated tags with a transitional document type. Some valid tags (e.g., name) cannot be used with the XHTML 1.1 standard, so this text uses XHTML 1.0 with the transitional document type.

Q&A What is the difference between the <title> and <body> tags?

The text contained within the <title> </title> tags is what appears on the browser title bar when the Web page is displayed in the browser window. The text and graphics contained within the <body> </body> tags are what is displayed in the browser window.

Q&A Do I have to type the initial HTML tags for every Web page that I develop?

The same initial HTML tags are used in many other chapters. To avoid retyping these tags, you can save the code that you just typed, and give it a new file name, something like structure.html or template.html. If you save this file at the root level of your folders, you will have easy access to it for other chapters.

Q&A Can I use either uppercase or lowercase letters for my HTML code?

To make your HTML files compliant with XHTML standards, always enter tags in lowercase (with the exception of the <!DOCTYPE> tag, which is always uppercase). In this book, the project directions follow these guidelines to help you learn acceptable HTML and XHTML coding standards.

Plan Ahead

Identify how to format various elements of the text.
By formatting the characters and paragraphs on a Web page, you can improve its overall appearance. On a Web page, consider the following formatting suggestions.

- **Effectively utilize headings.** The main heading is generally the first line of text on the Web page. It conveys the purpose of the Web page, such as asking for help with the food drive. Heading size standards should be followed, as shown in Figure 2–8 on the next page. The main heading should be size 1, and subtopics or subheadings should be size 2. It is generally not a good idea to jump from one heading size to a heading two sizes smaller. For instance, if your main heading is size 1, then the next heading down should be heading size 2, not heading size 4.
- **Use default text size when appropriate.** The body text consists of all text between the heading and the bottom of the Web page. This text highlights the key points of the message in as few words as possible. It should be easy to read and follow. While emphasizing the positive, the body text must be realistic, truthful, and believable. The default font size and style are appropriate to use for the body of text.
- **Highlight key paragraphs with bullets.** A **bullet** is a dot or other symbol positioned at the beginning of a paragraph. The bulleted list contains specific information that is more clearly identified by a list versus a paragraph of text.

Entering Web Page Content

Once you have established the Web page structure, it is time to enter the content of the Web page, including headings, informational text paragraphs, and a bulleted list.

Headings are used to separate text or add new topics on the Web page. Several styles and sizes of headings exist, indicated by the tags <h1> through <h6>, with <h1> being the largest. Generally, you use the Heading 1 style for the main heading. Figure 2–8a on the next page shows a Web page using various sizes of headings. A Web page usually has only one main heading; therefore, the HTML file for that Web page usually has only one set of <h1> </h1> tags. One method of maintaining a consistent look on a Web page is to use the same heading size for headings at the same topic level (Figure 2–8b). Notice that the paragraphs of text and the bulleted lists are all separated by size 2 headings in Figure 2–8b. This separation indicates that the text (i.e., two paragraphs plus one bulleted list) is all at the same level of importance on the Web page.

Web pages generally contain a significant amount of text. Because you turned Word wrap on (Figure 2–5 on page HTML 42) in Notepad++, you will see all of the text that you type in one Notepad++ window. Breaking the text into paragraphs helps to separate key ideas and makes the text easier to read. Paragraphs are separated with a blank line by using <p> (start paragraph) and </p> (end paragraph) tags. Putting too much text on one Web page is not a good choice. Your audience can get lost in large amounts of text. If you find that you have to press the Page Down key dozens of times to get to the bottom of the Web page, you need to think about restructuring your Web page. You can split up large pieces of information under more headings, which will be more manageable and more readable.

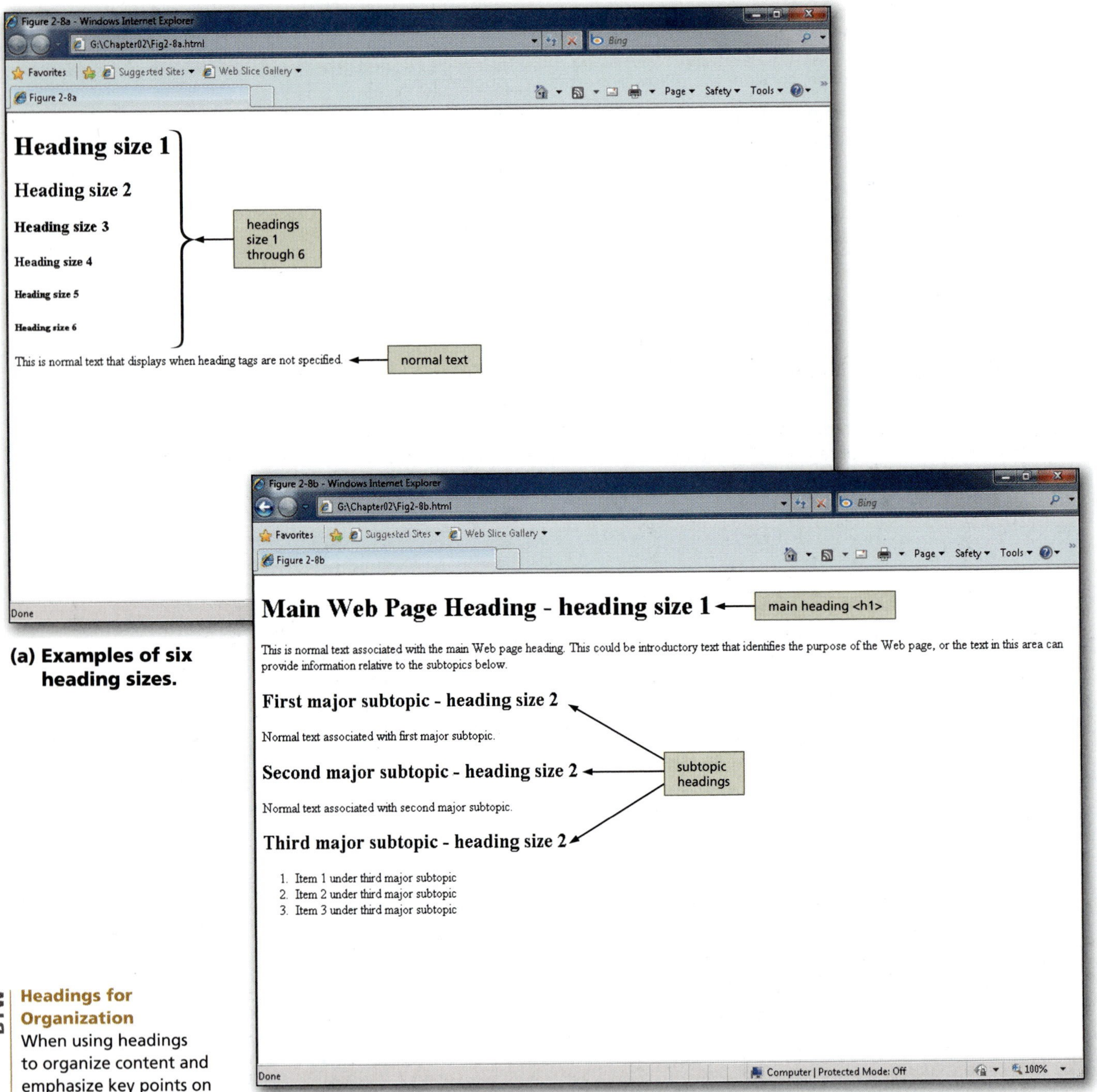

(a) Examples of six heading sizes.

(b) A consistent use of headings can help organize Web page content.

Figure 2–8

BTW

Headings for Organization

When using headings to organize content and emphasize key points on a Web page, be sure to use them consistently. That is, if you use a Heading 2 (<h2>) style for a specific level of text, you always should use a Heading 2 style to break up information at that level. Also, do not skip levels of headings in your document. For example, do not start with a Heading 1 (<h1>) style and then use a Heading 3 (<h3>) style.

Sometimes text on a Web page is easier for users to read and understand when it is formatted as a list, instead of as a paragraph. HTML provides several types of lists, but the most popular are unordered (bulleted) and ordered (numbered) lists. During the design phase of the Web development life cycle, you decide on the most effective way to structure the Web content and format the text on the Web page. Your main goal is to give Web page visitors an effective way to find the information that they need. If users cannot easily find what they need, they will not revisit your Web site.

To Enter a Heading

The heading, Fight Against World Hunger, is the main heading and indicates the main message of the Web page. To draw attention to this heading, you will use the <h1> tag for the heading. The following step illustrates how to enter a heading on the Web page.

- With the insertion point on line 12, press the ENTER key once, leaving a blank line after the <body> tag.
- Type `<h1>Fight Against World Hunger</h1>` in the text area, and then press the ENTER key twice (Figure 2–9).

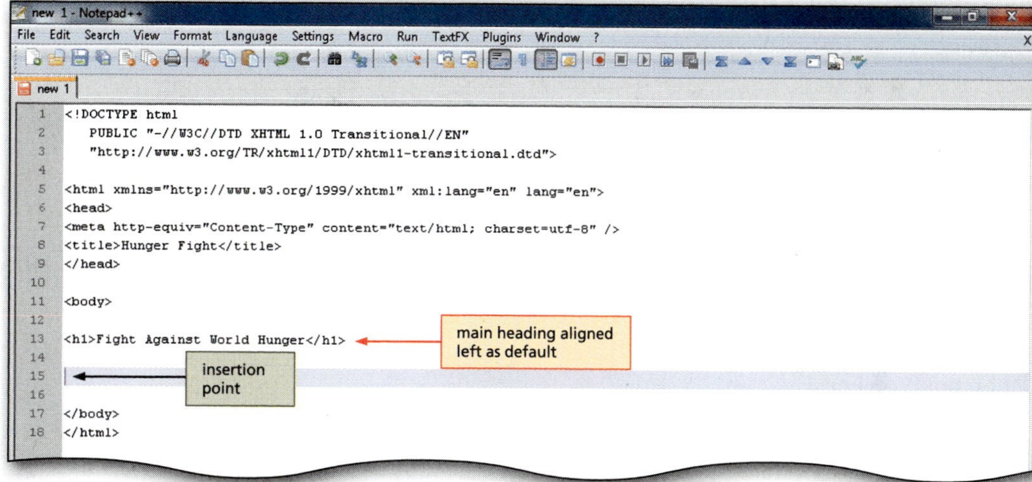

Figure 2–9

Q&A

Why did you put an additional line in the HTML code after the <body> tag and the heading?

An additional line space was inserted for readability. This blank line will not be displayed on the Web page.

To Enter a Paragraph of Text

After you enter the heading, the next step is to add a paragraph of text using the <p> tag. When the browser finds a <p> tag in an HTML file, it starts a new line and inserts a blank line above the new paragraph. The </p> end tag indicates the end of the paragraph. When you enter this paragraph of text, do not press the ENTER key at the end of each line. Because Word wrap is turned on, your text will wrap to the next line even without pressing the ENTER key. Table 2–3 contains the HTML tags and text used in the paragraph.

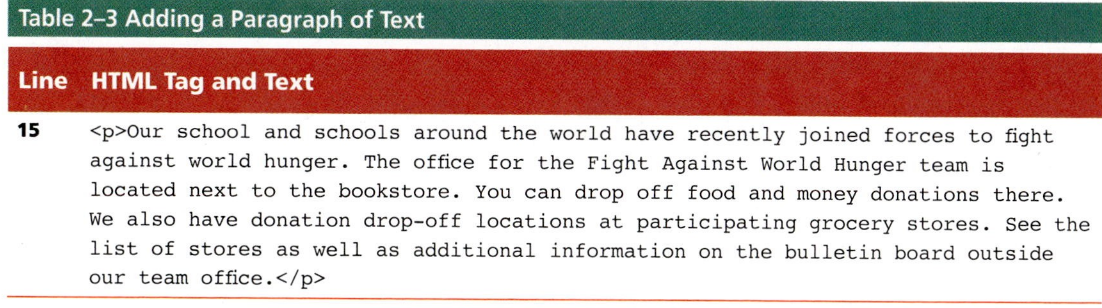

Table 2–3 Adding a Paragraph of Text

Line	HTML Tag and Text
15	`<p>Our school and schools around the world have recently joined forces to fight against world hunger. The office for the Fight Against World Hunger team is located next to the bookstore. You can drop off food and money donations there. We also have donation drop-off locations at participating grocery stores. See the list of stores as well as additional information on the bulletin board outside our team office.</p>`

The following step illustrates how to enter a paragraph of text in an HTML file.

- With the insertion point on line 15, enter the HTML code, as shown in Table 2–3 on the previous page. Do not press ENTER at the end of each line when entering this text and use only one space after periods.
- Press the ENTER key twice to position the insertion point on line 17 (Figure 2–10).

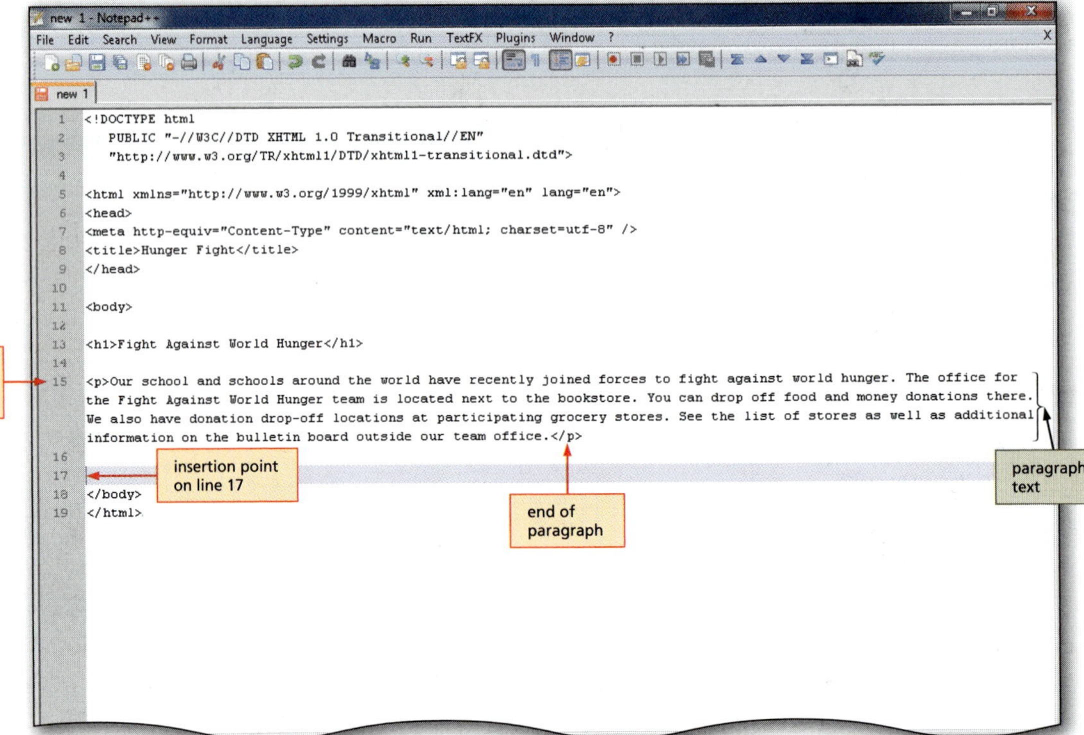

Figure 2–10

Q&A

Why do you not press the ENTER key after each line of code in Table 2–3?

Because you turned on Word wrap right after you started Notepad++, the text that you enter as the paragraph will automatically wrap to the next line. The text goes to the end of the Notepad++ window and then wraps. If you had not turned on Word wrap, your text would continue scrolling to the right as you type, and text to the left would scroll off the screen. With Word wrap on, all text remains visible in the Notepad++ window.

BTW

List Styles
It is helpful sometimes to structure the text of a Web page in a list. There are several list options that you can use. The Web page purpose determines which would be more effective. See Appendix D List Styles for style options that can be used with lists.

Using Lists to Present Content

Lists structure text into an itemized format. Typically, lists are bulleted (unordered) or numbered (ordered). An **unordered list**, which also is called a **bulleted list**, formats information using small images called bullets. Figure 2–11 shows Web page text formatted as unordered, or bulleted, lists and the HTML code used to create the lists.

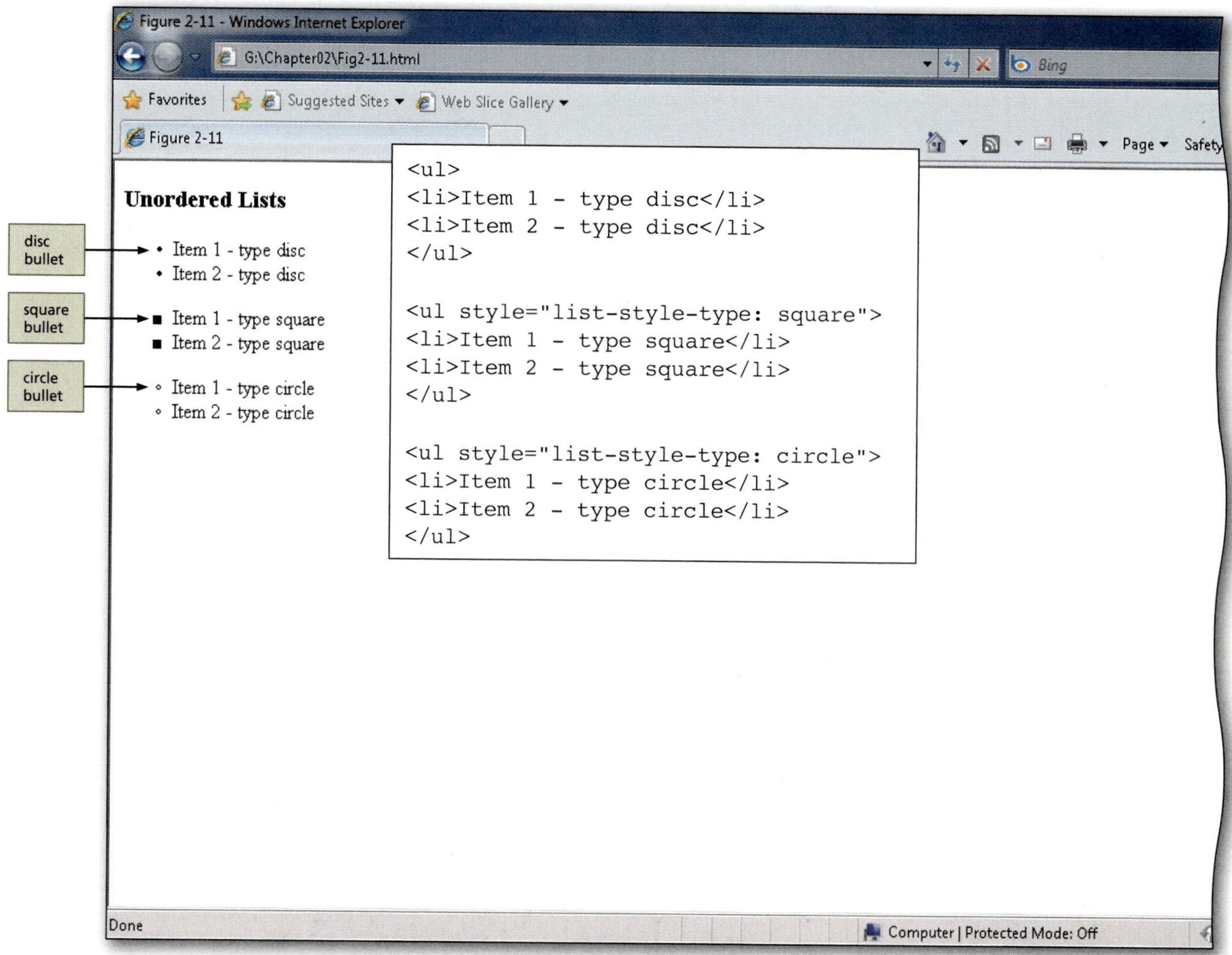

Figure 2–11

An **ordered list**, which also is called a **numbered list**, formats information in a series using numbers or letters. An ordered list works well to organize items where order must be emphasized, such as a series of steps. Figure 2–12 on the next page shows Web page text formatted as ordered, or numbered, lists and the HTML tags used to create the lists.

The **<ul>** and **</ul>** tags must be at the start and end of an unordered or bulleted list. The **<ol>** and **</ol>** tags are used at the start and end of an ordered or numbered list. Unordered and ordered lists have optional bullet and number types. As shown in Figure 2–11, an unordered list can use one of three different bullet options: disc, square, or circle. If no type is identified, the default, disc, is used. An ordered list can use numbers, letters, or Roman numerals, as shown in Figure 2–12. The default option is to use Arabic numbers, such as 1, 2, and 3.

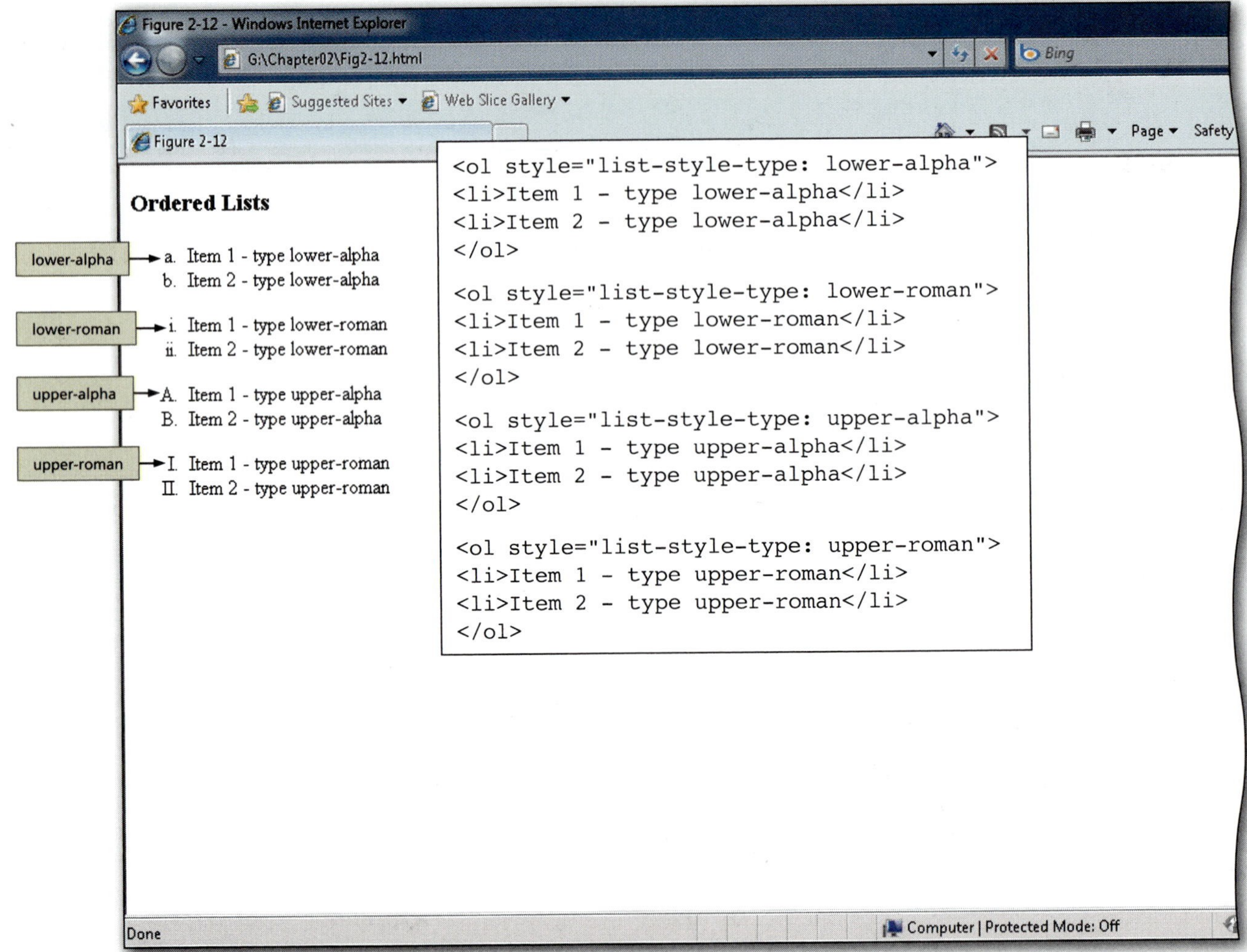

Figure 2–12

After the <ul> or <ol> tag is entered to define the type of list, the **<li>** and **</li>** tags are used to define a list item within an ordered or unordered list.

To Create an Unordered List

To highlight what Web site visitors can do to help the Fight Against World Hunger, you will create a bulleted (unordered) list using the HTML tags and text shown in Table 2–4. Remember that each list item must start with <li> and end with </li>.

Table 2–4 Adding an Unordered List

Line	HTML Tag and Text
17	`<h2>What you can do to help:</h2>`
18	
19	`<ul>`
20	`  <li>Join the school's Fight Against World Hunger team with a $10 donation</li>`
21	`  <li>Buy requested food at participating grocery stores and leave at drop-off locations</li>`
22	`  <li>Volunteer to collect money and donations around the community</li>`
23	`</ul>`

The following step illustrates how to create an unordered, or bulleted, list using the default bullet style.

1

- With the insertion point on line 17, enter the HTML code, as shown in Table 2–4. When you enter the text on lines 20, 21, and 22, make sure to press the TAB key at the start of the line, and then enter the text. Press ENTER at the end of each line.
- Press the ENTER key after typing line 23, leaving a blank line on 24 (Figure 2–13).

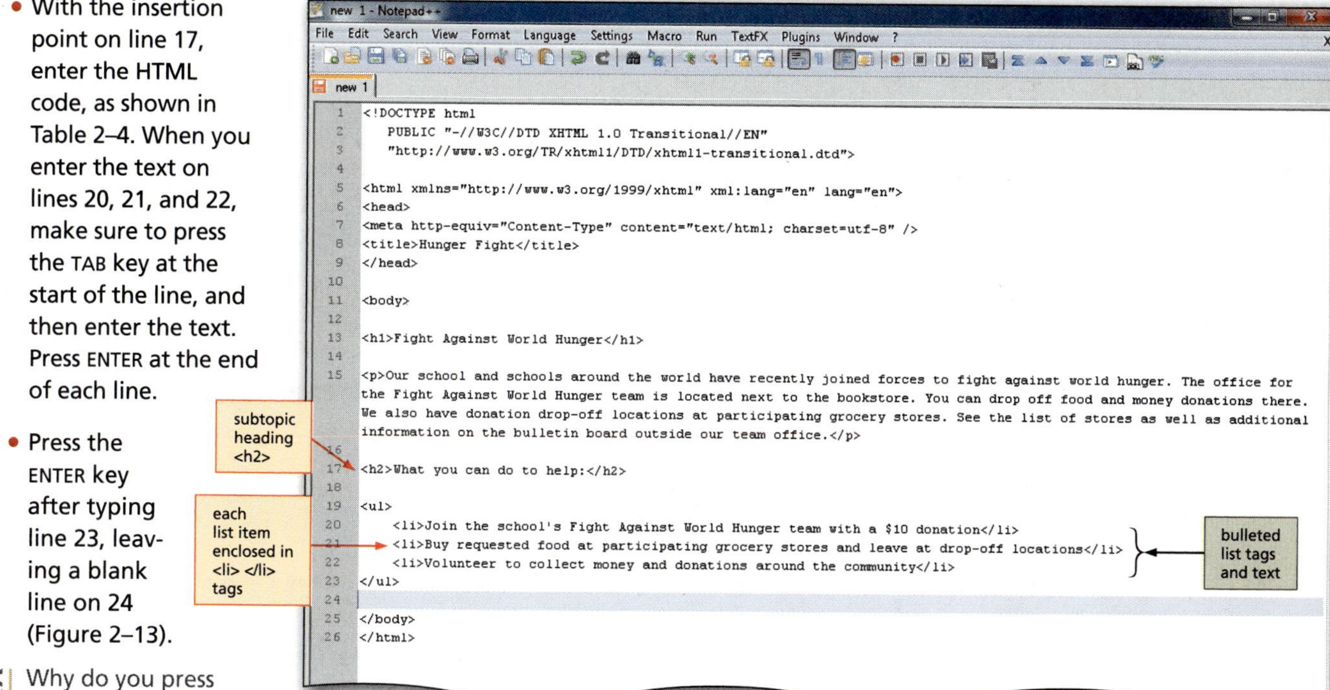

Figure 2–13

Q&A Why do you press the TAB key at the start of the lines with the <li> (list item) code?

Using the TAB key (to indent) when you enter list items helps format the text so that you can easily see that this text is different from the paragraph of text. Indenting text helps the Web developer see that certain segments of code are related to each other.

Q&A What types of bullets will this list contain?

Because the code does not specify a type attribute, the list uses the default disc bullet. Other bullet options are square, circle, numbers, letters, and Roman numerals. You can also use a graphical image as a bullet, which you will do in later chapters.

More About List Formats

If you use the <ul> or <ol> start tags without attributes, you will get the default bullet (disc) or number style (Arabic numerals). To change the bullet or number type, the **list-style-type** property is entered within the <ol> or <ul> tags. To create a list with square bullets, you would type the line

```
<ul style="list-style-type: square">
```

as the inline style (CSS) code. You can find other list style properties and values in Appendix D.

In addition to ordered and unordered lists, there is a third kind of list, called a **definition list**, which offsets information in a dictionary-like style. Although they are used less often than unordered or ordered lists, definition lists are useful to create a glossary-like list of terms and definitions, as shown in Figure 2–14a on the next page. Figure 2–14b shows the HTML code used to create the definition list.

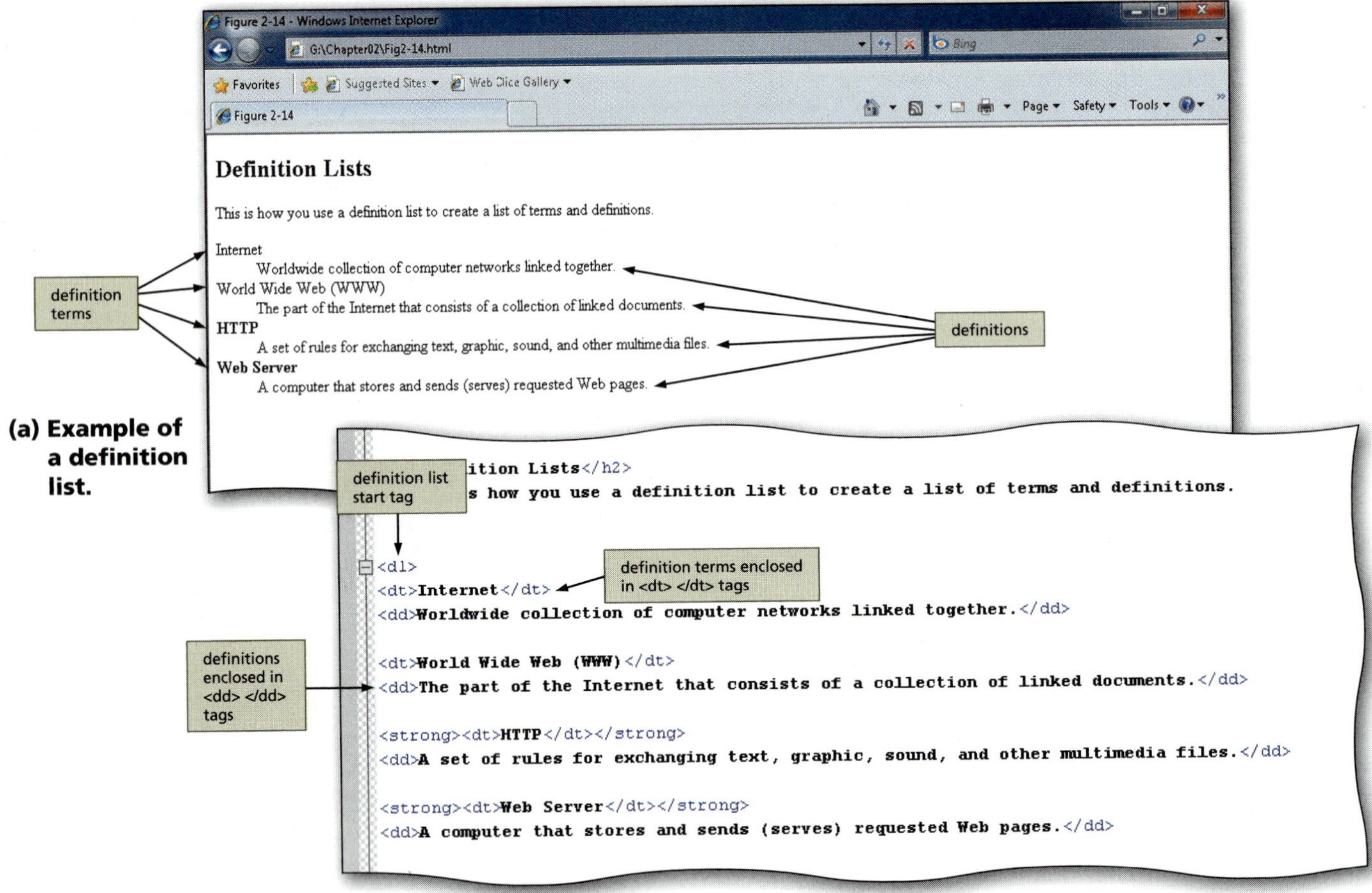

(a) Example of a definition list.

(b) HTML code used to create a definition list.

Figure 2–14

The syntax for definition lists is not as straightforward as the <ul>, <ol>, or <li> structure that is used in the unordered and ordered list styles. With definition lists, you use the **<dl>** and **</dl>** tags to start and end the list. A **<dt>** tag indicates a term, and a **<dd>** tag identifies the definition of that term by offsetting the definition from the term. Table 2–5 lists the elements of a definition list and their purposes.

Table 2–5 Definition List Elements and Purposes

Definition List Element	Purpose
<dl> </dl>	Start and end a definition list
<dt> </dt>	Identify a term
<dd> </dd>	Identify the definition of the term directly above

As shown in Figure 2–14, by default, the definition term is left-aligned on the line and the definition for each term is indented so it is easily distinguishable as the definition for the term above it. In order to more clearly identify the definition term, you may want to make the term bold, as shown in the last two definitions (HTTP and Web Server) in Figure 2–14. You could do this by using an inline style that includes the following code:

```
<dt style="font-weight: bold">
```

Saving and Organizing HTML Files

Before you can see how your HTML file looks in a Web browser, you must save it. It also is important to save your HTML file for the following reasons:

- The document in memory will be lost if the computer is turned off or you lose electrical power while the text editor is open.
- If you run out of time before completing your project, you may finish your document at a future time without starting over.

To save your file, you use the Notepad++ File, Save command. When you save a file, you give your file a name and follow that with the file extension. As mentioned earlier in the book, file names should always make sense relative to their purpose. For instance, naming a file page1 does not indicate the purpose of that file. Naming the file hungerfight immediately identifies that this file has something to do with that topic. The Web page files in this book are always named with all lowercase letters and with no spaces. This is a standard that is followed throughout the book.

HTML files must end with an extension of **.htm** or **.html**. Many older Web page servers can only display pages with the .htm extension, or short file names (i.e., file names that are only up to eight characters in length). HTML files with an extension of .html can be viewed on Web servers running an operating system that allows long file names (i.e., file names that can be up to 255 characters in length). Almost all current operating systems allow long file names, including Windows 7, Windows Vista, Windows XP, Windows Server 2003/2008, Windows 2000, Macintosh, and Linux. For Web servers that run an operating system that does not accept long file names, you need the .htm extension. In this book, all files are saved using the .html extension.

You will use a very simple folder structure with all the projects in this book. It is therefore important to organize your files in folders so that all files for a project or end-of-chapter exercise, including HTML code and graphical images, are saved in the same folder. If you correctly downloaded the files from the Data Files for Students (see the inside back cover of this book), you will have the required file structure. When you initially save the hungerfight.html file, you will save it in the ChapterFiles subfolder of the Chapter02 folder. The graphical image used in Chapter 2, hungerfightlogo.jpg, will be stored in that same folder — Chapter02\ChapterFiles. Because the chapter projects in this book are relatively simple and use few images, images and HTML code are stored in the same folder. In real-world applications, though, hundreds or thousands of files might exist in a Web site, and it is more appropriate to separate the HTML code and graphical images into different subfolders. You will learn more about organizing HTML files and folders in Chapter 3.

BTW

HTML File Names
HTML files have an extension of .html or .htm. The home page of a Web site is often called index .html, index.htm, default .html, or default.htm. Check with the service provider to find out which name they use.

BTW

Saving Your Work
It is a good idea to save your HTML file periodically as you are working to avoid the risk of losing your work completed thus far. You could get into the habit of saving your file after any large addition (i.e., a paragraph) of information. You might also want to save the file after typing in several HTML tags that would be difficult to re-do.

Plan Ahead

Determine where to save the Web page.
When saving a Web page, you must decide which storage medium to use.

- If you always work on the same computer and have no need to transport your projects to a different location, then your computer's hard drive will suffice as a storage location. It is a good idea, however, to save a backup copy of your projects on a separate medium in case the file becomes corrupted or the computer's hard disk fails.
- If you plan to work on your projects in various locations or on multiple computers, then you should save your projects on a portable medium, such as a USB flash drive or CD. The projects in this book use a USB flash drive, which saves files quickly and reliably and can be reused. CDs are easily portable and serve as good backups for the final versions of projects because they generally can save files only one time.
- The above are general guidelines about saving your files. Your instructor may give you specific instructions for saving your work that differ from the steps that follow.

To Save an HTML File

You have performed many steps in creating this project and do not want to risk losing the work you have done so far. Also, to view HTML in a browser, you must save the file. The following steps show how to save an HTML file.

1

- With a USB flash drive connected to one of the computer's USB ports, click File on the Notepad++ menu bar (Figure 2–15).

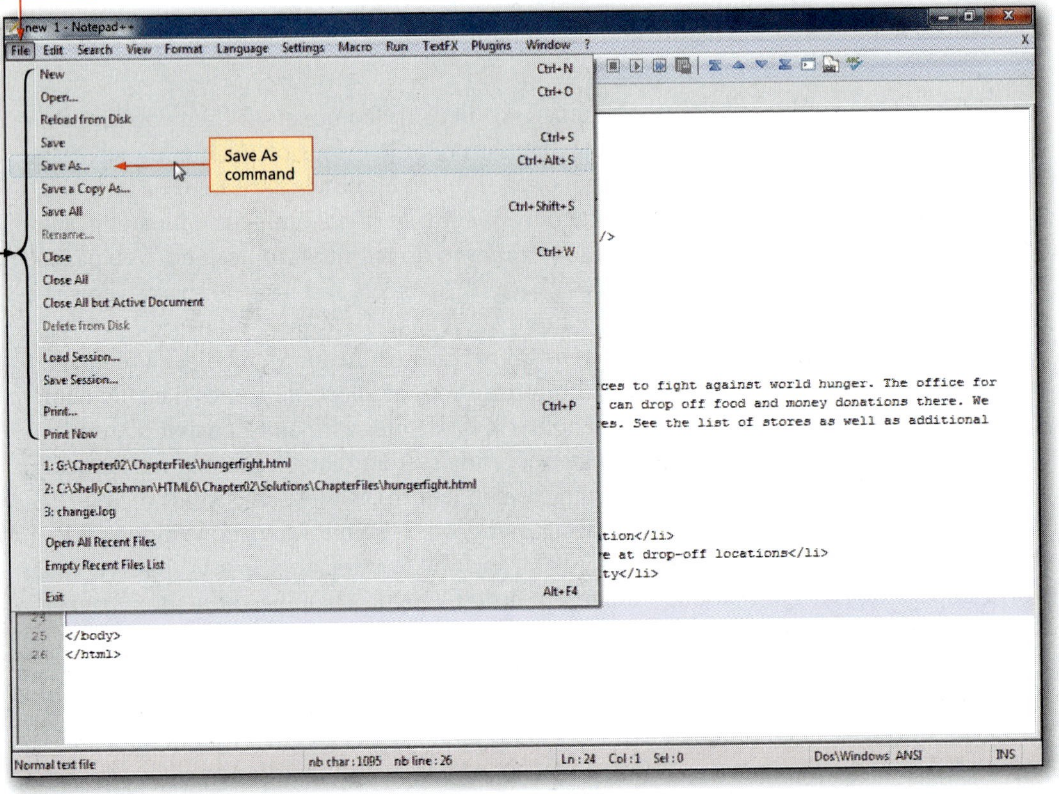

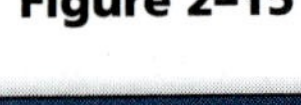

Figure 2–15

2

- Click Save As on the File menu to display the Save As dialog box (Figure 2–16).

Q&A

Do I have to save to a USB flash drive?

No. You can save to any device or folder. A folder is a specific location on a storage medium. Use the same process, but select your device or folder.

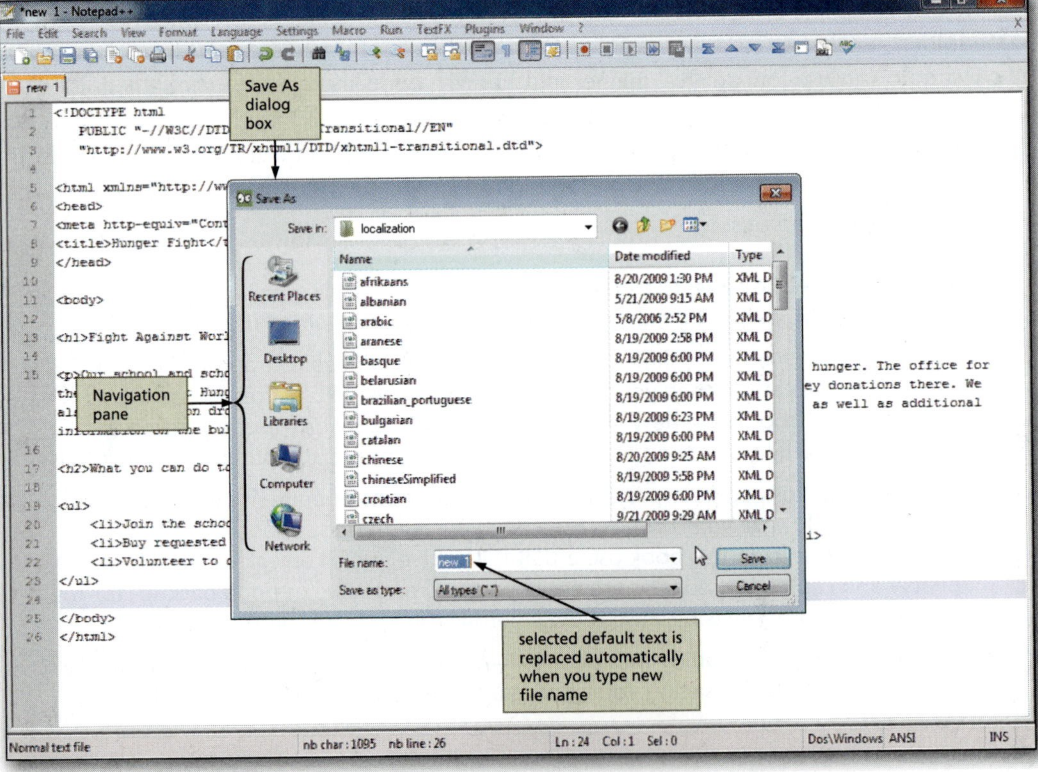

Figure 2–16

3

- Type `hungerfight.html` in the File name text box to change the file name. Do not press ENTER after typing the file name.
- Click Computer in the left side of the dialog box to display a list of available drives (Figure 2–17).
- If necessary, scroll until your USB flash drive, such as UDISK 2.0 (G:), appears in the list of available drives.

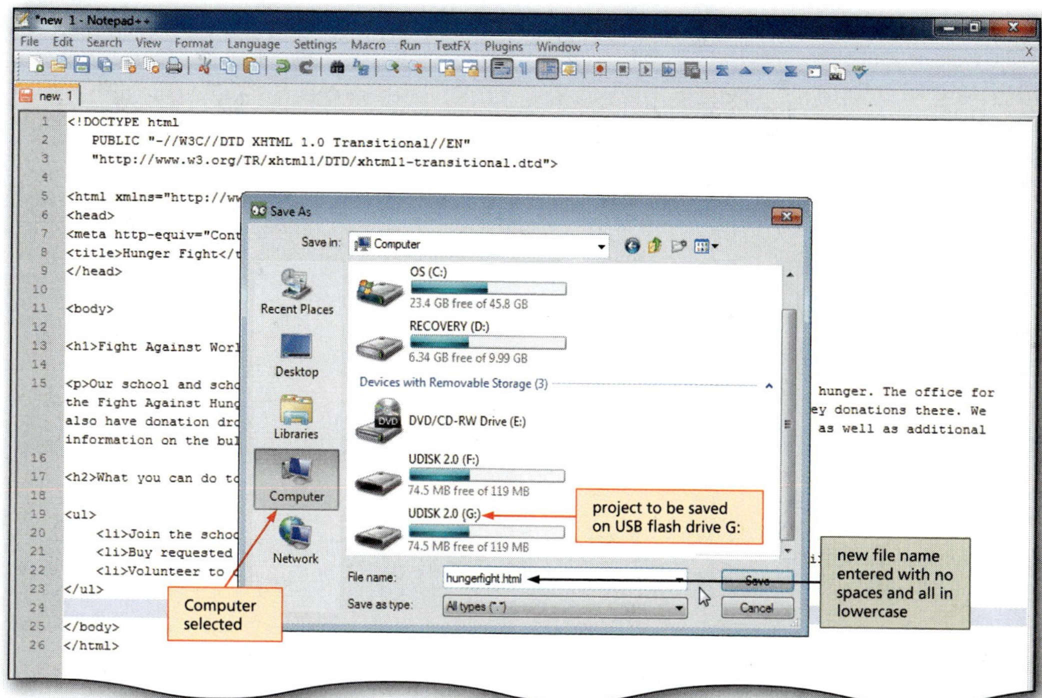

Figure 2–17

Q&A Why is my list of files, folders, and drives arranged and named differently from those shown in the figure?

Your computer's configuration determines how the list of files and folders is displayed and how drives are named.

Q&A How do I know the drive and folder in which my file will be saved?

Notepad++ displays a list of available drives and folders. You then select the drive and/or folder into which you want to save the file.

BTW

Storing Your Files

Many schools provide students with space on a Web server to store their Web pages. However, saving your Web pages to another medium (e.g., a USB flash drive) assures that you have a backup copy of the files that you created. Saving Web page files to the hard drive on a computer in a school lab runs the risk of it not being there the next time you are in that lab. Many schools delete all files other than those installed by the lab technician at the start-up of each computer.

- Double-click UDISK 2.0 (G:) (or your storage device) in the Computer list to select the USB flash drive, drive G in this case, as the new save location.

Q&A What if my USB flash drive has a different name or letter?

It is likely that your USB flash drive will have a different name and drive letter and be connected to a different port. Verify that the device in your Computer list is correct.

- If necessary, open the Chapter02\ChapterFiles folder (Figure 2–18).

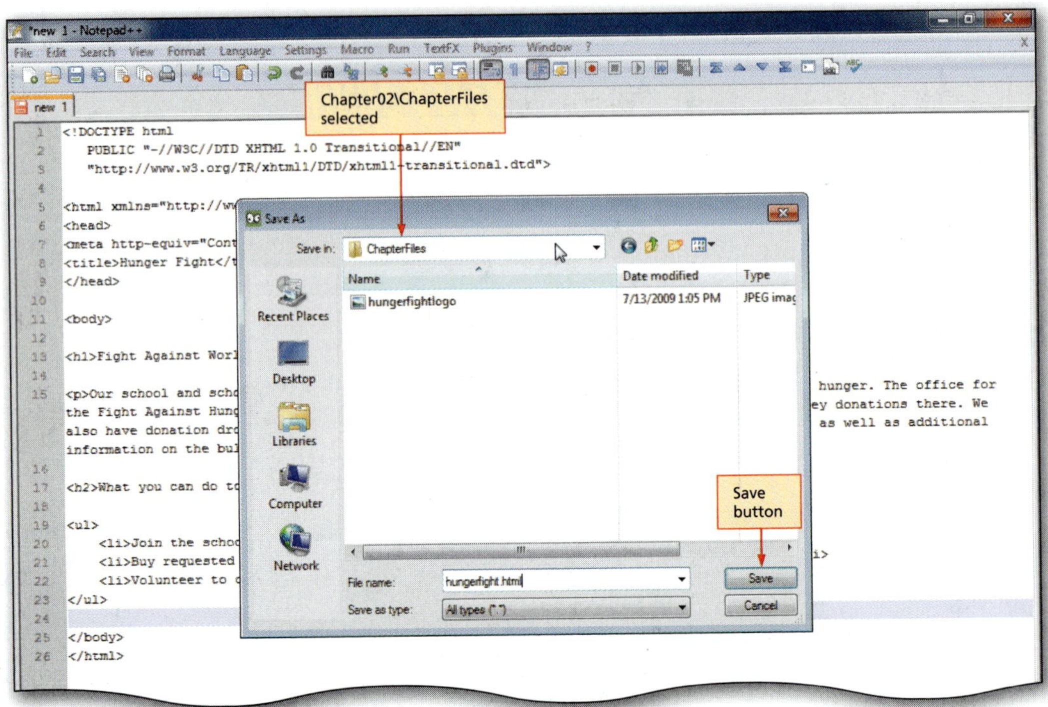

Figure 2–18

Q&A What if my USB flash drive does not have a folder named Chapter02\ChapterFiles?

If you followed the steps to download the chapter files from the Data Files for Students, you should have a folder named Chapter02\ChapterFiles. If you do not, check with your instructor.

- Click the Save button in the Save As dialog box to save the file on the USB flash drive with the name hungerfight.html (Figure 2–19).

Q&A Is my file only on the USB drive now?

No, although the HTML file is saved on a USB drive, it also remains in memory and is displayed on the screen (Figure 2–19). Notepad++ displays the new file name on the title bar and on the document tab.

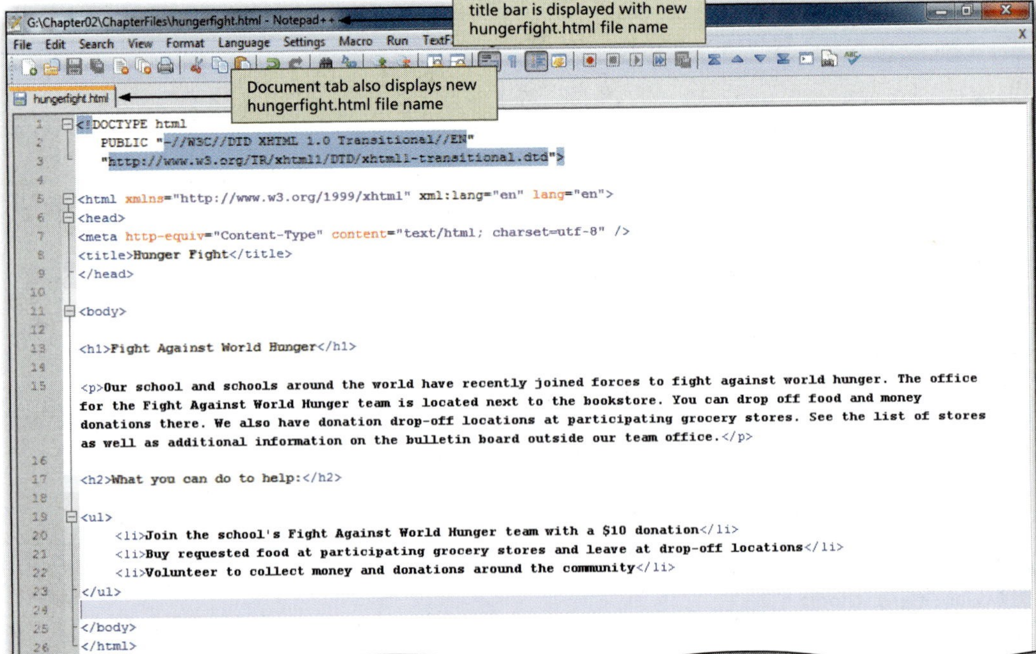

Figure 2–19

Other Ways

1. Press CTRL+ALT+S, type the file name, click Computer, select drive or folder, click the Save button

Using a Browser to View a Web Page

After entering code in the HTML file and saving it, you should view the Web page in a browser to see what the Web page looks like up to this point. The HTML file is displayed in the browser as if the file were available on the Web. In general, viewing the Web page periodically during development is good coding practice, because it allows you to see the effect of various HTML tags on the text and to check for errors in your HTML file.

If your computer is connected to the Internet when the browser window opens, it displays a **home page**, or **start page**, which is a Web page that appears each time Internet Explorer starts.

To Start a Browser

With the HTML file saved on the USB drive, the next step is to view the Web page using a browser. Because Windows is **multitasking**, you can have more than one program running at a time, such as Notepad++ and your browser. The following steps illustrate how to start a browser to view a Web page.

- Click the Internet Explorer icon on the taskbar (Figure 2–20).

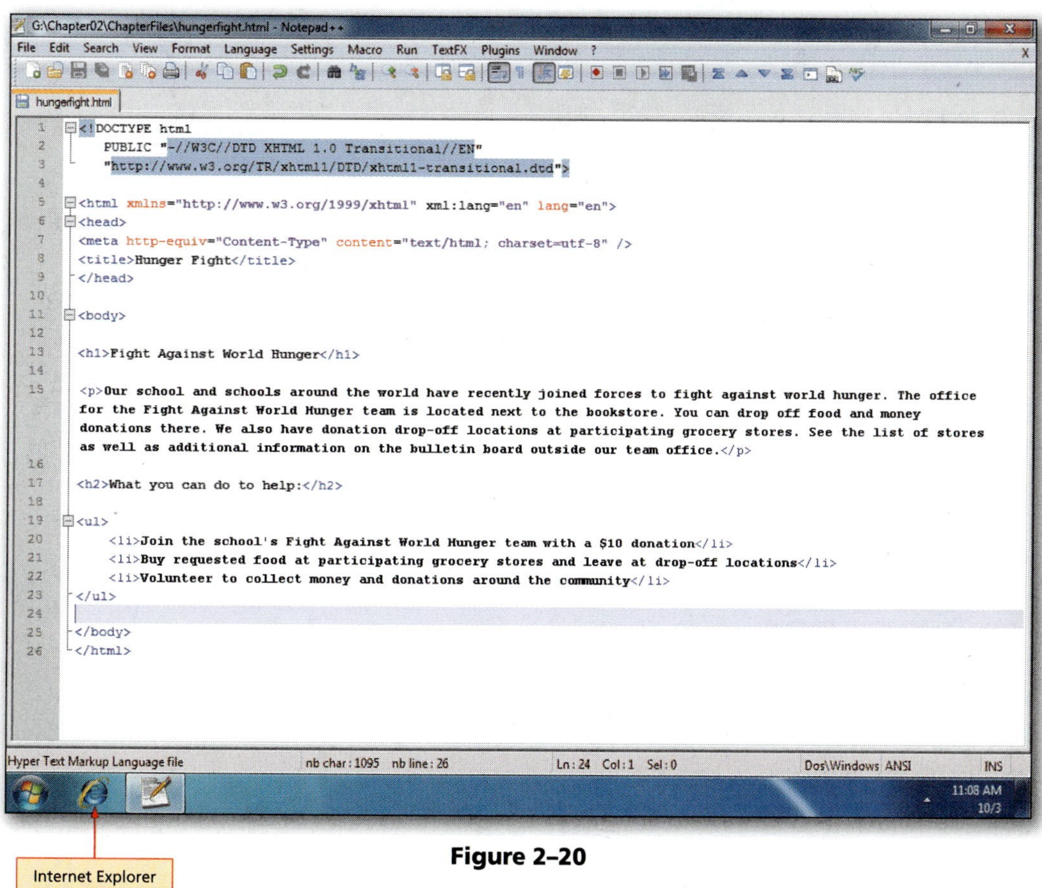

Figure 2–20

2

- If necessary, click the Maximize button to maximize the browser window (Figure 2–21).

Q&A

Why does my browser display a different window?

Because it is possible to customize browser settings to change the Web page that appears as the home page, the home page that is displayed by your browser may be different. Schools and organizations often set a main page on their Web sites as the home page for browsers installed on lab or office computers.

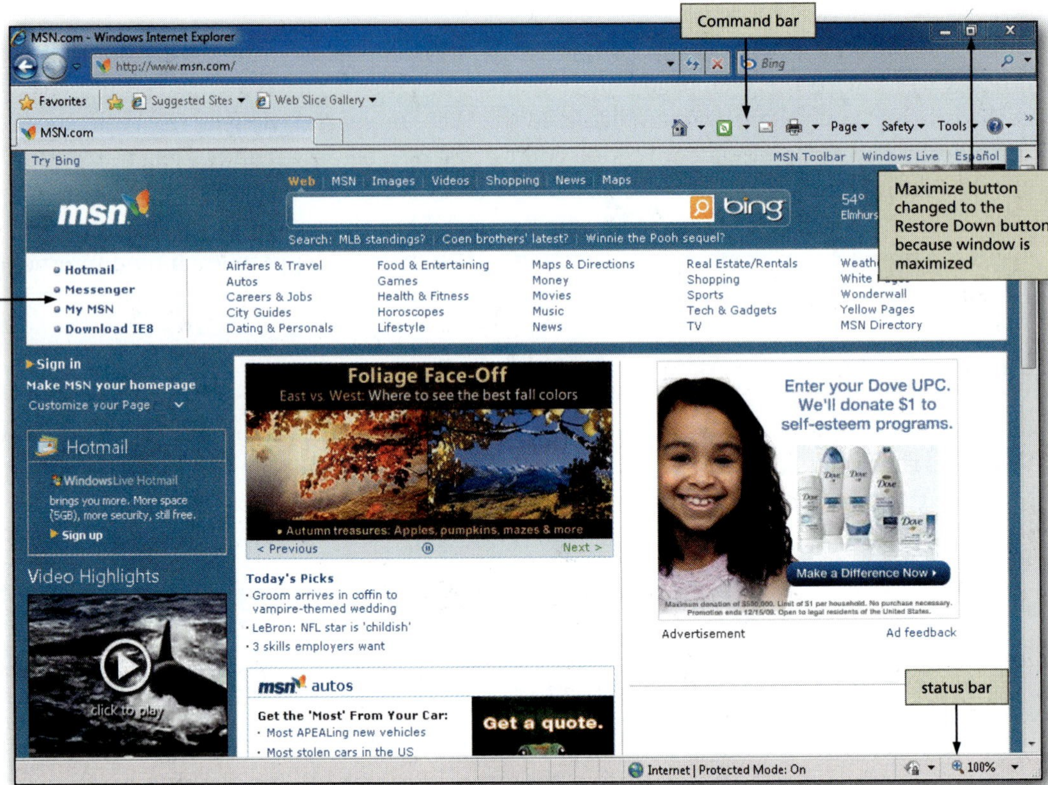

Figure 2–21

Other Ways

1. Click Start, All Programs, Internet Explorer
2. Double-click Internet Explorer icon on desktop, if one is present

BTW

Developing Web Pages for Multiple Browsers

When developing Web pages, you must consider the types of browsers visitors will use, including Internet Explorer and Mozilla Firefox for Windows or Safari or Internet Explorer for Mac OS. The Apple Web site provides suggestions for creating Web pages that will work in a wide range of browsers. Part of thorough testing includes bringing your Web pages up in different versions of different browsers.

To View a Web Page in a Browser

A browser allows you to open a Web file located on your computer and have full browsing capabilities, as if the Web page were stored on a Web server and made available on the Web. The following steps use this technique to view the HTML file, hungerfight.html, in a browser.

1

- Click the Address bar to select the URL on the Address bar.
- Type `g:\Chapter02\ChapterFiles\hungerfight.html` to display the new URL on the Address bar (Figure 2–22). The Web page is not displayed until you press the ENTER key, as shown in the next step.

Q&A How can I correct the URL on the Address bar?

The URL is displayed on the Address bar. If you type an incorrect letter or symbol on the Address bar and notice the error before moving to the next step, use the BACKSPACE key to erase all the characters back to and including the one that is incorrect, and then continue typing.

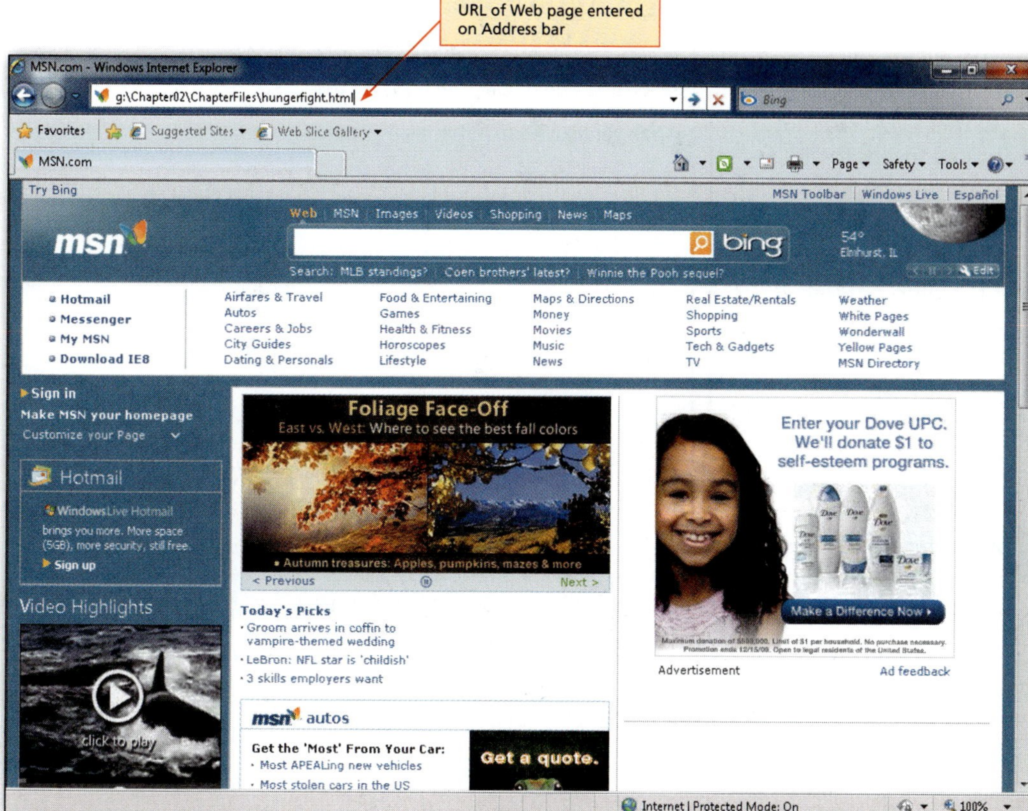

Figure 2–22

Q&A What if my file is in a different location?

You can type in the path to your file in the Address bar, or browse to your file, as shown in Other Ways on the next page.

2

- Press the ENTER key to display the hungerfight.html page as if it were available on the Web (Figure 2–23).

Q&A What if I get a warning from Internet Explorer (IE) that says, "Internet Explorer needs to open a new window to display this webpage."?

If this happens, you should click the OK button to continue. You then will see your Web page displayed in another IE window.

Q&A What if my page is not displayed correctly?

Check your entries for hungerfight.html carefully against Figure 2–19 to make sure you have not made any typing errors or left anything out. Correct the errors, resave the file, and try again.

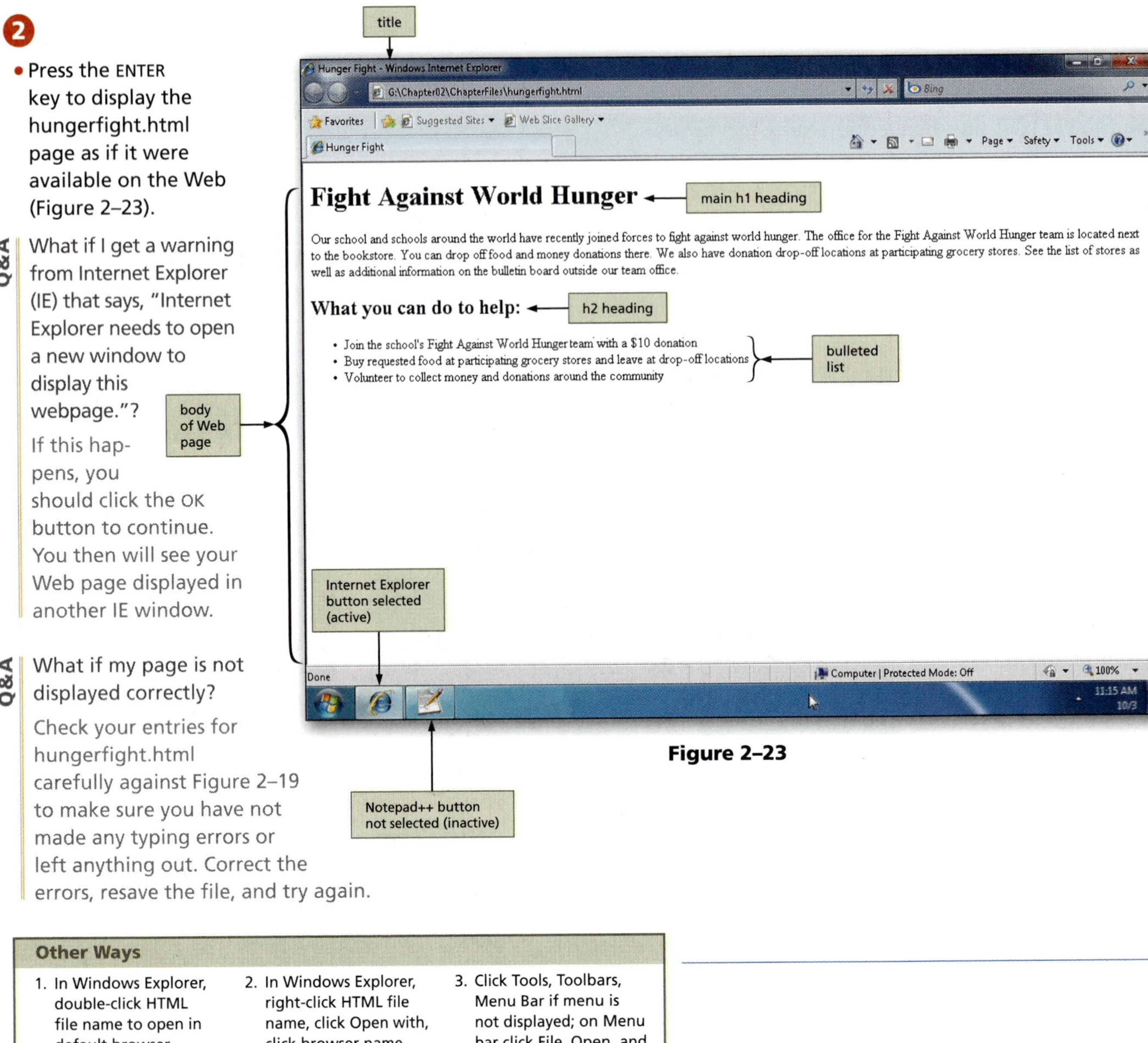

Figure 2–23

Other Ways

1. In Windows Explorer, double-click HTML file name to open in default browser
2. In Windows Explorer, right-click HTML file name, click Open with, click browser name
3. Click Tools, Toolbars, Menu Bar if menu is not displayed; on Menu bar click File, Open, and browse to desired file

BTW

User Interface Design

The user interface design is a very important aspect of a Web site. If a site is designed poorly, users may be unable to find the desired information or complete a task, which makes the Web site ineffective. There are many good Web sites available that discuss Web design principles.

To Activate Notepad++

After viewing the Web page, you can modify the Web page by adding additional tags or text to the HTML file. To continue editing, you first must return to the Notepad++ window. The following step illustrates how to activate Notepad++.

- Click the Notepad++ button on the taskbar to maximize Notepad++ and make it the active window (Figure 2–24).

Notepad++ button selected (active)

Figure 2–24

Improving the Appearance of Your Web Page

One goal in Web page development is to create a Web page that is visually appealing and maintains the interest of the visitors. The Web page developed thus far in the chapter is functional, but lacks visual appeal. In this section, you will learn how to improve the appearance of the Web page from the one shown in Figure 2–25a to the one shown in Figure 2–25b by adding an image, adding a color to the headings, adding a horizontal rule, and changing the font style of the bulleted list. Many of these tasks can be accomplished by using style sheets.

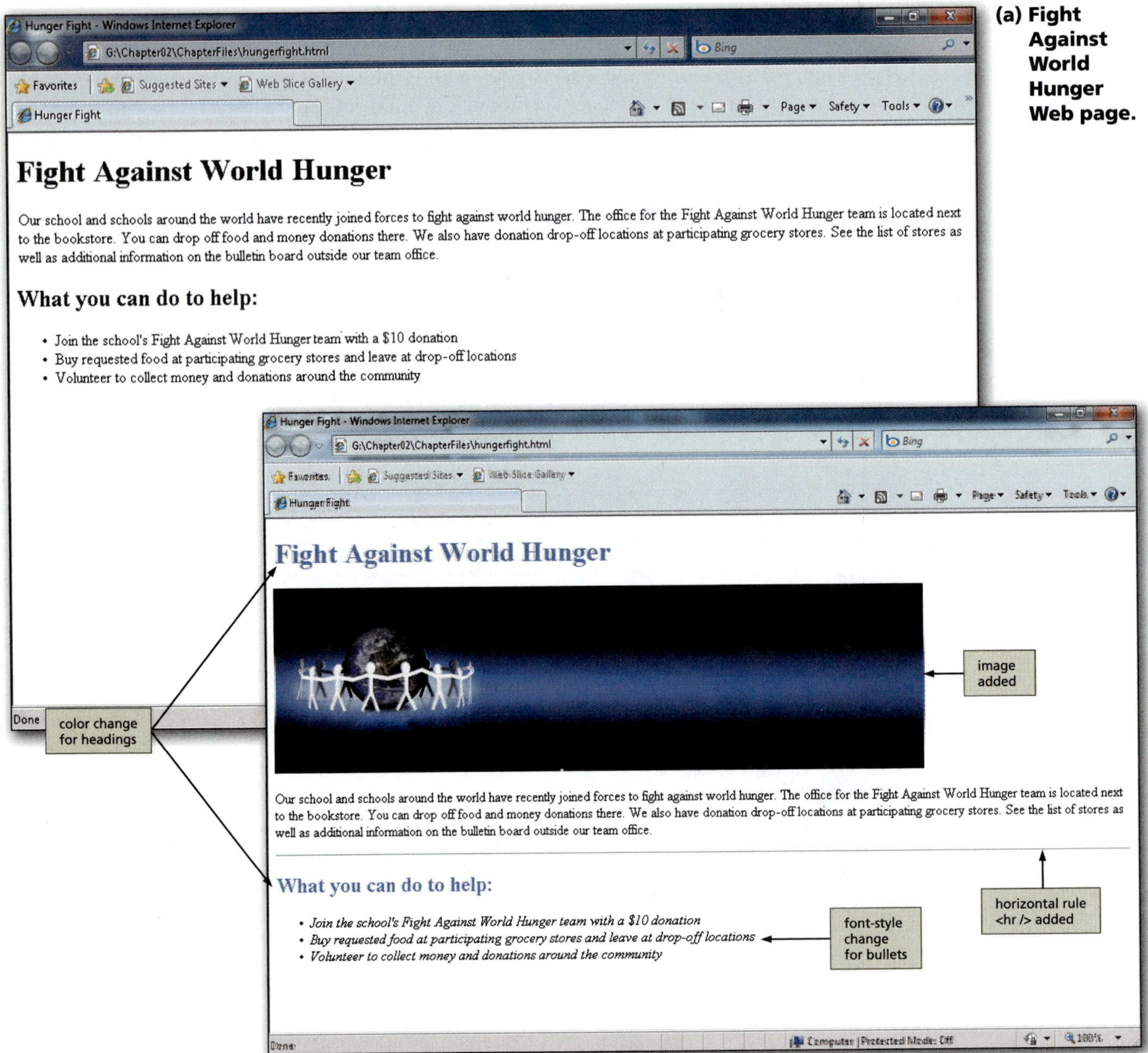

(a) Fight Against World Hunger Web page.

(b) Fight Against World Hunger Web page formatted to improve appearance.

Figure 2–25

Using Style Sheets

Although HTML allows Web developers to make changes to the structure, design, and content of a Web page, HTML is limited in its ability to define the appearance, or style, across one or more Web pages. As a result, style sheets were created.

As a review, a **style** is a rule that defines the appearance of an element on a Web page. A **style sheet** is a series of rules that defines the style for a Web page or an entire Web site. With a style sheet, you can alter the appearance of a Web page or pages by changing characteristics such as font family, font size, margins, and link specifications.

CSS supports three types of style sheets: inline, embedded, and external (or linked). With an **inline style**, you add a style to an individual HTML tag, such as a heading or paragraph. The style changes that specific tag, but does not affect other tags in the document. With an **embedded style sheet**, you add the style sheet within the <head> tags of the HTML document to define the style for an entire Web page. With a linked style sheet, or **external style sheet**, you create a text file that contains all of the styles you want to apply, and save the text file with the file extension .css. You then add a link to this external style sheet on any Web page in the Web site. External style sheets give you the most flexibility and are ideal to apply the same formats to all of the Web pages in a Web site. External style sheets also make it easy to change formats quickly across Web pages. You will use inline styles in this chapter's project to enhance the styles of the headings (change the color) and the bulleted list (change the font style).

Style Sheet Precedence As shown in Table 2–6, the three style sheets supported by CSS control the appearance of a Web page at different levels. Each style sheet type also has a different level of precedence or priority in relationship to the others. An external style sheet, for example, is used to define styles for multiple pages in a Web site. An embedded style sheet is used to change the style of one Web page, but overrides or takes precedence over any styles defined in an external style sheet. An inline style is used to control the style within an individual HTML tag and takes precedence over the styles defined in both embedded and external style sheets.

BTW

Inline Styles
Using an inline style is helpful when you want to alter the appearance (or style) of a single HTML element. Appendix D contains the Cascading Style Sheet Properties and Values supported by most browsers. The inline styles used in this chapter can be found in the appendix. For more information on inline styles, look at w3.org.

Table 2–6 Style Sheet Precedence

Type	Level and Precedence
Inline	• To change the style within an individual HTML tag • Overrides embedded and external style sheets
Embedded	• To change the style of one Web page • Overrides external style sheets
External	• To change the style of multiple pages in a Web site

Because style sheets have different levels of precedence, all three types of style sheets can be used on a single Web page. For example, you may want some elements of a Web page to match the other Web pages in the Web site, but you also may want to vary the look of certain sections of that Web page. You can do this by using the three types of style sheets.

Style Statement Format No matter what type of style sheet you use, you must use a **style statement** to define the style. The following code shows an example of a style statement used in an inline style:

```
<h1 style="font-family: Garamond; font-color: navy">
```

A style statement is made up of a selector and a declaration. The part of the style statement that identifies the page elements is called the **selector**. In this example, the selector is h1 (header size 1). The part of the style statement that identifies how the element(s) should appear is called the **declaration**. In this example, the declaration is everything between the quotation marks: the font-family and font-color properties and their values (Garamond and navy, respectively). A declaration includes at least one type of style, or **property**, to apply to the selected element. Examples of properties include color, text-indent, border-width, and font-style. For each property, the declaration includes a related **value**, which specifies the display parameters for that specific property.

Each property accepts specific values, based on the styles that property can define. The property, font-color, for example, can accept the value, navy, but cannot accept the value, 10%, because that is not a valid color value. In the next section of this chapter, you will change the heading color to blue for both the h1 and h2 headings. Using inline styles in this case is appropriate because there are only two headings to change on the Web page. If you had many headings to change, an embedded or external style sheet would be more appropriate. This will be discussed in later chapters.

Inline Styles An inline style is used to define the style of an individual HTML tag. For example, to change the style of a single paragraph, you could add an inline style with the <p> (paragraph) tag as the selector and a declaration that defines new font style and style values for that paragraph, as shown here:

```
<p style="font-style: italic; font-size: 8pt">
```

Because they take precedence over the other types of style sheets and affect the style for individual HTML tags, inline styles are helpful when one section of a Web page needs to have a style different from the rest of the Web page. In this chapter's project, an inline style is used to change the color of the headings on the Web page and to change the font style in the bulleted list.

Now that you understand how style sheets and inline styles function, it is time to think about adding an image to enhance the appearance of your Web page.

Plan Ahead

Find appropriate graphical images.
To use graphical images, also called graphics, on a Web page, the image must be stored digitally in a file. Files containing graphical images are available from a variety of sources:

- Microsoft has free digital images on the Web for use in a document. Other Web sites also have images available, some of which are free, while others require a fee.
- You can take a picture with a digital camera and **download** it, which is the process of copying the digital picture from the camera to your computer.
- With a scanner, you can convert a printed picture, drawing, or diagram to a digital file.

If you receive a picture from a source other than yourself, do not use the file until you are certain it does not contain a virus. A **virus** is a computer program that can damage files and programs on your computer. Use an antivirus program to verify that any files you use are virus free.

Establish where to position and how to format the graphical image. The content, size, shape, position, and format of a graphic should capture the interest of passersby, enticing them to stop and read the Web page. Often, the graphic is the center of attraction and visually the largest element on a page. If you use colors in the graphical image, be sure they are part of the Web page's color scheme.

Identify the width and height of the image. The width and height (measured in pixels) of an image should always be identified in the <img> tag. These dimensions are used by the browser to determine the size to display the image. If you do not identify those attributes, the browser has to determine the size. This slows the process down for the browser.

Provide alternate text for the image. Alternate text should always be used for each image. This text is especially useful to users with visual impairments who use a screen reader, which translates information on a computer screen into audio output. The length of the alternate text should be reasonable.

Web Page Images

Images are used in many ways to enhance the look of a Web page and make it more interesting and colorful. Images can be used to add background color, to help organize a Web page, to help clarify a point being made in the text, or to serve as links to other Web pages. Images also are often used to break up Web page sections (such as with a horizontal rule) or as directional elements that allow a visitor to navigate a Web site.

Using Web Page Divisions

It is sometimes helpful to break up your Web page into divisions (or sections), which allows you to apply styles to different Web page elements. Throughout this book, you always use the start <div> and end </div> division tags as a container in which to insert images. Utilizing division tags allows you to add styles such as centering your image or adding background color to your images.

Image Types

Web pages use three types of files as images: GIF, JPEG, and PNG (Table 2–7). **Graphics Interchange Format** (**GIF**) files have an extension of .gif. A graphic image saved as a GIF (pronounced *jiff* or *giff*) uses compression techniques, called LZW compression, to make it smaller for download on the Web. Standard (or noninterlaced) GIF images are displayed one line at a time when loading. Interlaced GIF images load all at once, starting with a blurry look and becoming sharper as they load. Using interlaced GIFs for large images is a good technique, because a Web page visitor can see a blurred outline of the image as it loads. GIF is a patented format, however, and therefore widespread use is limited.

A second type of image file is **Portable Network Graphics** (**PNG**), which has a .png or .ping extension. The PNG (pronounced *ping*) format also is a compressed file format that supports multiple colors and resolutions. The World Wide Web Consortium developed the PNG format as a graphics standard and patent-free alternative to the GIF format. Most newer browsers support PNG images.

Finally, **Joint Photographic Experts Group** (**JPEG**) files have an extension of .jpg, .jpe, or .jpeg. A JPEG (pronounced *JAY-peg*) is a graphic image saved using a compression technique other than LZW. JPEG files often are used for more complex images, such as photographs, because the JPEG file format supports more colors and resolutions than the other file types.

> **BTW**
> **Images**
> Images on Web pages are viewed in a variety of environments, including slow connections to the Internet and slower computers. Optimizing your images is important to increase the speed of download for all of your Web page visitors. Search the Web for more information on image optimization.

Table 2–7 Image Types and Uses

Image Type	Use
Graphics Interchange Format (GIF)	• Use for images with few colors (<256) • Allows for transparent backgrounds
Portable Network Graphics (PNG)	• Newest format for images • Use for all types of images • Allows for variation in transparency
Joint Photographic Experts Group (JPEG)	• Use for images with many colors (>256), such as photographs

If an image is not in one of these formats, you can use a paint or graphics-editing program to convert an image to a .gif, .jpg, or .png format. Some paint programs even allow you to save a GIF image as interlaced. A number of paint and graphics-editing programs, such Adobe Photoshop and Corel Paint Shop Pro, are available in the marketplace today.

BTW

Overusing Images
Be cautious about overusing images on a Web page. Using too many images may give your Web page a cluttered look or distract the visitor from the purpose of the Web page. An image should have a purpose, such as to convey content, visually organize a page, provide a hyperlink, or serve another function.

Image Attributes

You can enhance HTML tags by using attributes. **Attributes** define additional characteristics for the HTML tag. For instance, you should use the width and height attributes for all <img> tags. Table 2–8 lists the attributes that can be used with the <img> tag. In this chapter, the src and alt attributes are used in the <img> tag. Image attributes will be explained in detail, because they are used in later chapters.

Table 2–8 Image Attributes

Attribute	Function
alt	• Alternative text to display when an image is being loaded • Especially useful for screen readers, which translate information on a computer screen into audio output • Should be a brief representation of the purpose of the image • Generally should stick to 50 characters or fewer
height	• Defines the height of the image, measured in pixels • Improves loading time
hspace	• Defines the horizontal space that separates the image from the text
src	• Defines the URL of the image to be loaded
vspace	• Defines the vertical space that separates the image from the text
width	• Defines the width of the image, measured in pixels • Improves loading time

To Add an Image

In the early days when the Web was used mostly by researchers needing to share information with each other, having purely functional, text-only Web pages was the norm. Today, Web page visitors are used to a more graphically oriented world, and have come to expect Web pages to use images that provide visual interest. The following step illustrates how to add an image to a Web page by entering an <img> tag in the HTML file using the tags and text shown in Table 2–9.

Table 2–9 Adding an Image

Line	HTML Tag and Text
15	`<div>`
16	`<img src="hungerfightlogo.jpg" width="763" height="210" alt="Hunger Fight logo" />`
17	`</div>`

1

- Click the blank line 14 and then press the ENTER key.
- With the insertion point on line 15, enter the HTML code, as shown in Table 2–9. Press ENTER at the end of each line (Figure 2–26).

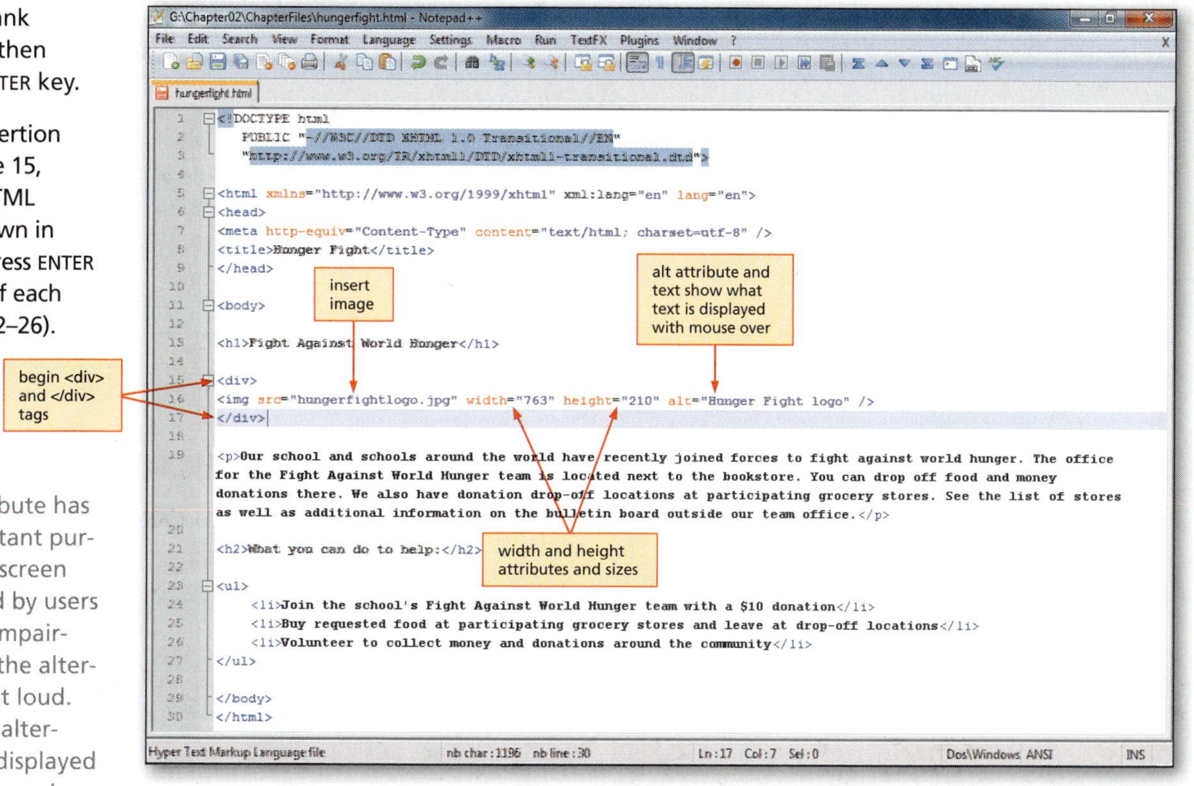

Q&A What is the purpose of the alt attribute?

The alt attribute has three important purposes. First, screen readers used by users with visual impairments read the alternate text out loud. Second, the alternate text is displayed while the image is being loaded. Finally, the alt tag is required for XHTML compliance.

G:\Chapter02\ChapterFiles\hungerfight.html - Notepad++

File Edit Search View Format Language Settings Macro Run TextFX Plugins Window ?

hungerfight.html

```
1  <!DOCTYPE html
2     PUBLIC "-//W3C//DTD XHTML 1.0 Transitional//EN"
3     "http://www.w3.org/TR/xhtml1/DTD/xhtml1-transitional.dtd">
4
5  <html xmlns="http://www.w3.org/1999/xhtml" xml:lang="en" lang="en">
6  <head>
7  <meta http-equiv="Content-Type" content="text/html; charset=utf-8" />
8  <title>Hunger Fight</title>
9  </head>
10
11 <body>
12
13 <h1>Fight Against World Hunger</h1>
14
15 <div>
16 <img src="hungerfightlogo.jpg" width="763" height="210" alt="Hunger Fight logo" />
17 </div>
18
19 <p>Our school and schools around the world have recently joined forces to fight against world hunger. The office
   for the Fight Against World Hunger team is located next to the bookstore. You can drop off food and money
   donations there. We also have donation drop-off locations at participating grocery stores. See the list of stores
   as well as additional information on the bulletin board outside our team office.</p>
20
21 <h2>What you can do to help:</h2>
22
23 <ul>
24     <li>Join the school's Fight Against World Hunger team with a $10 donation</li>
25     <li>Buy requested food at participating grocery stores and leave at drop-off locations</li>
26     <li>Volunteer to collect money and donations around the community</li>
27 </ul>
28
29 </body>
30 </html>
```

Hyper Text Markup Language file nb char : 1196 nb line : 30 Ln : 17 Col : 7 Sel : 0 Dos\Windows ANSI INS

Figure 2–26

Q&A What is the purpose of the <div> and </div> tags?

The <div> tag establishes a division within a Web page. When you use the <div> </div> tags, you are able to design a layout that uses CSS, including inserting images.

Plan Ahead

Make other visual enhancements.
In addition to images, there are several ways to add visual interest.

Add color to headings. Web developers often use colors to call attention to elements on a Web page. The color selected should coordinate with the images selected for the page. It also should allow the Web page text to be read easily. Some colors, such as dark colors, may not be appropriate because the default black text cannot be displayed effectively on a dark background. When changing the color of an element such as a heading, it is usually best to apply the same style to all headings on the Web page for consistency.

Change the font style of a bulleted list. It is sometimes aesthetically pleasing to change the style of the text in a bulleted list. When you want to call attention to the information, you might want to italicize or bold the bullet text.

Insert a horizontal rule. It is useful to use a horizontal rule to break up text on a Web page. A horizontal rule is used as a divider for a page to separate text sections.

BTW

Colors

Figure 2–27 does not list all possible Web colors. Many other colors are available that you can use for Web page backgrounds or text fonts. For more information about colors, see Appendix B or search the Web for browser colors.

Other Visual Enhancements

One way to help capture a Web page visitor's attention is to use color. Many colors are available for use as a Web page background, text, or link. Figure 2–27 shows colors often used on Web pages, with the corresponding six-digit number codes. The six-digit number codes can be used to specify a color for a background, text, or links. The headings on the Fight Against World Hunger Web page are currently black (the default color). You will spruce up the Web page by adding color to the headings using inline styles.

COLORS IN HEX

Here is a table of common colors with their hexadecimal equivalents. Use the codes to define the desired color for the background, text, or links.

#ffc6a5	#ff9473	#ff6342	#ff3118	#ff0000	#d60000	#ad0000	#840000	#630000
#ffe7c6	#ffce9c	#ffb573	#ff9c4a	#ff8429	#d66321	#ad4a18	#844d18	#632910
#ffffc6	#ffff9c	#ffff6b	#ffff42	#ffff10	#d6c610	#ad9410	#847308	#635208
#f7ffce	#efef ad	#e7f784	#def763	#d6ef39	#b5bd31	#8c9429	#6b6b21	#524a18
#de93bd	#c6ef8c	#adde63	#94d639	#7bc618	#639c18	#527b10	#425a10	#314208
#ceefbd	#a5de94	#7bc66b	#52b552	#299c39	#218429	#186321	#184a18	#103910
#c6e7de	#94d6ce	#63bdb5	#31ada5	#089494	#087b7b	#006363	#004a4a	#003139
#c6eff7	#94d6e7	#63c6de	#31b5d6	#00a5c6	#0084a5	#006b84	#005263	#00394a
#bdc6de	#949cce	#6373b5	#3152a5	#083194	#082984	#08296b	#08215a	#00184a
#c6b5de	#9c7bbd	#7b52a5	#522994	#31007b	#29006b	#21005a	#21004a	#180042
#debdde	#ce84c6	#b552ad	#9c2994	#8c007b	#730063	#5a0052	#4a0042	#390031
#f7bdde	#e78cc6	#de5aad	#d63194	#ce007b	#a50063	#840052	#6b0042	#520031
#ffffff	#e0e0e0	#bfbfbf	#a1a1a1	#808080	#616161	#404040	#212121	#000000

THE SIXTEEN PREDEFINED COLORS

(Because these colors belong to the RGB spectrum, they will look a bit different on-screen.)

silver	gray	maroon	green	navy	purple	olive	teal
white	black	red	lime	blue	magenta	yellow	cyan

Figure 2–27

BTW

Browser-safe Colors

Web developers used to have to make sure that they used browser-safe colors (Appendix B). The trend for monitors today is to display "true color" which means that any of 16 million colors can be displayed on the monitor. Few people use 8-bit monitors anymore, so you generally do not have to limit yourself to browser-safe colors.

The color codes and names shown in Figure 2–27 can be used for background, text, and link colors. The color property is used in the <h1> and <h2> tags to specify the color for these headings. The color #3D60B1 will be used for these headings because it is one of the colors found in the graphical image inserted in the steps above.

Another way to visually enhance the Web page is to change the style of some of the text. This calls attention to that particular text on the Web page. In this section, you change the text in the bulleted list to an italic style using an inline style. This change helps call attention to the three points in that bulleted list.

Finally, you add a horizontal rule to further enhance this Web page. As discussed earlier in the chapter, horizontal rules are lines that act as dividers on a Web page to provide a visual separation of sections on the page. You can use an inline image to add a horizontal rule, or you can use the horizontal rule tag (<hr />) to add a simple horizontal rule, as shown in the following steps. Figure 2–28 shows examples of a variety of horizontal rules and the HTML code used to add them. The default horizontal rule is shown in the first rule on the page. Dimension is added to a horizontal rule by increasing the number of pixels that are displayed.

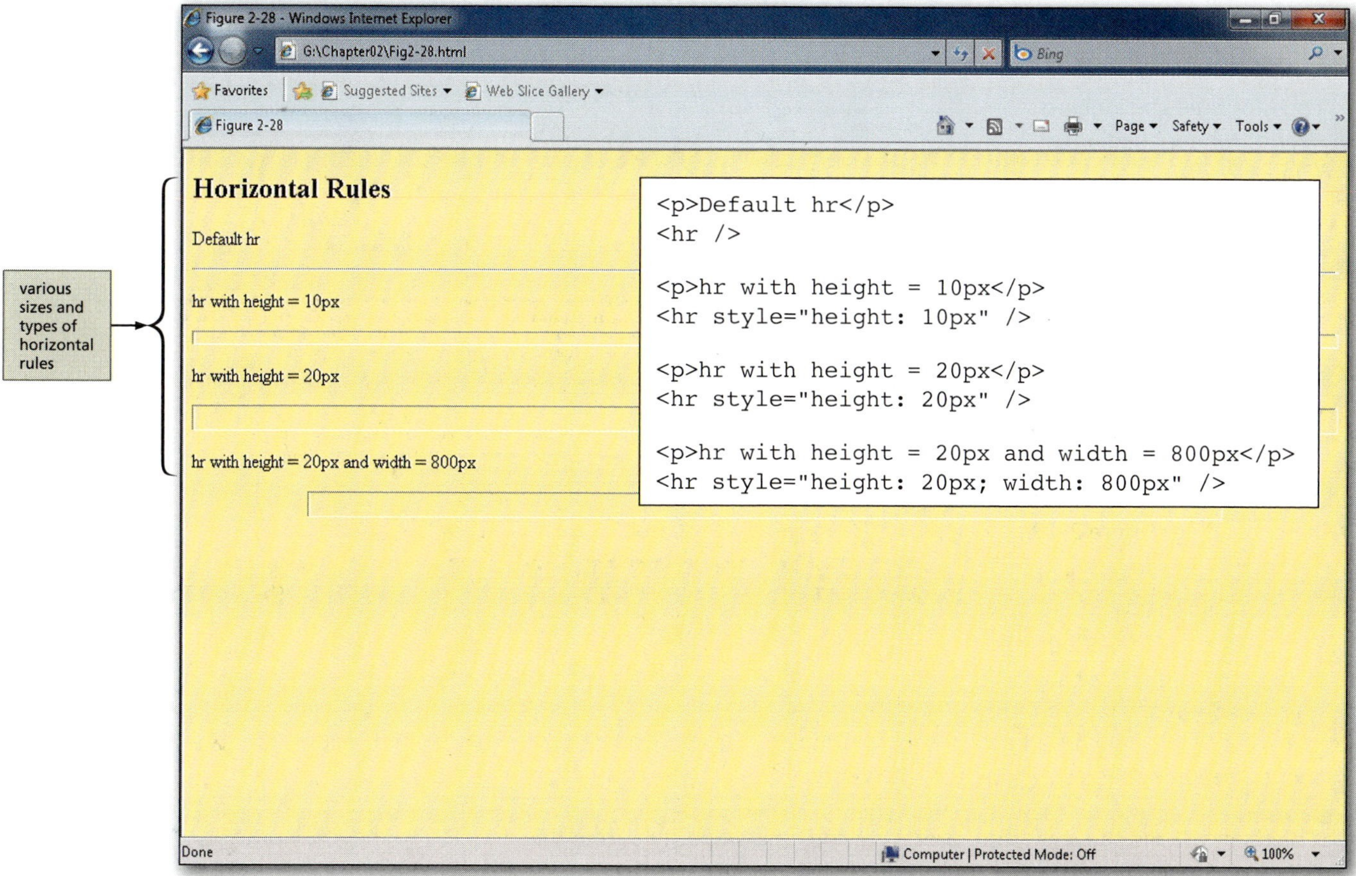

Figure 2–28

To Add Color to Web Page Headings

To change the color of headings on a Web page, the color property must be added in the <h1> and <h2> tags of the HTML file. The **color** property lets you change the color of various elements on the Web page. The following step shows how to add a color using the color property in an inline style.

- Click after the "1" but before the closing bracket in <h1> on line 13 and then press the SPACEBAR.
- Type `style="color: #3D60B1"` as the color code for the Fight Against World Hunger heading (Figure 2–29).
- Click after the "2" but before the closing bracket in <h2> on line 21 and then press the SPACEBAR.
- Type `style="color: #3D60B1"` as the color code for the What you can do to help: heading (Figure 2–29).

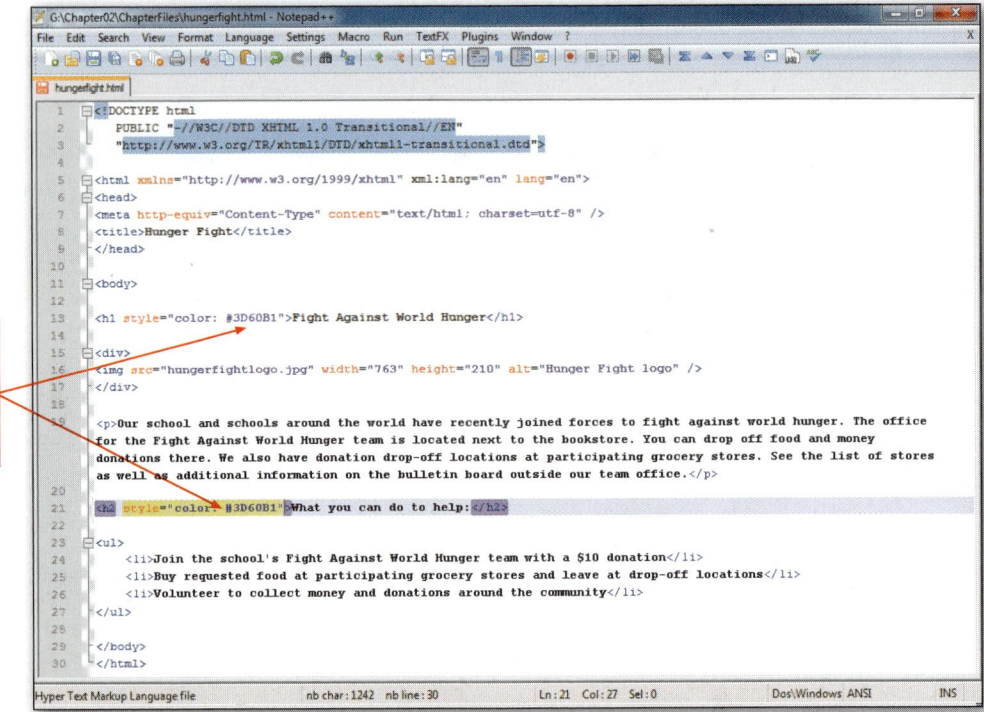

color code #3D60B1 added to headings in <h1> and <h2> tags

```
G:\Chapter02\ChapterFiles\hungerfight.html - Notepad++
File Edit Search View Format Language Settings Macro Run TextFX Plugins Window ?
hungerfight.html
1  <!DOCTYPE html
2     PUBLIC "-//W3C//DTD XHTML 1.0 Transitional//EN"
3     "http://www.w3.org/TR/xhtml1/DTD/xhtml1-transitional.dtd">
4
5  <html xmlns="http://www.w3.org/1999/xhtml" xml:lang="en" lang="en">
6  <head>
7  <meta http-equiv="Content-Type" content="text/html; charset=utf-8" />
8  <title>Hunger Fight</title>
9  </head>
10
11 <body>
12
13 <h1 style="color: #3D60B1">Fight Against World Hunger</h1>
14
15 <div>
16 <img src="hungerfightlogo.jpg" width="763" height="210" alt="Hunger Fight logo" />
17 </div>
18
19 <p>Our school and schools around the world have recently joined forces to fight against world hunger. The office
   for the Fight Against World Hunger team is located next to the bookstore. You can drop off food and money
   donations there. We also have donation drop-off locations at participating grocery stores. See the list of stores
   as well as additional information on the bulletin board outside our team office.</p>
20
21 <h2 style="color: #3D60B1">What you can do to help:</h2>
22
23 <ul>
24     <li>Join the school's Fight Against World Hunger team with a $10 donation</li>
25     <li>Buy requested food at participating grocery stores and leave at drop-off locations</li>
26     <li>Volunteer to collect money and donations around the community</li>
27 </ul>
28
29 </body>
30 </html>
Hyper Text Markup Language file    nb char : 1242   nb line : 30    Ln : 21   Col : 27   Sel : 0    Dos\Windows ANSI    INS
```

Figure 2–29

Q&A Can I use any hexadecimal code or color name to change colors of headings?

Although you may use any of the hexadecimal codes or color names available, you have to make sure that the color is appropriate for the headings of your Web page. You do not want a heading that is too light in color or otherwise diminishes the headings.

Q&A Could I have used the copy/paste process to copy the inline style from the <h1> tag to the <h2> tag?

Yes, copying/pasting would have the same result. However, if you want to copy a style to all the headings on a Web page, it is easier to use embedded or external style sheets, which you learn about in the next two chapters.

To Change the Bulleted List Style

To change the style of the bulleted list, you again use an inline style with the font-style property. The **font-style** property lets you change the style of the font, or text, selected. There are three values for the font-style, normal, italic, and oblique, although only normal and italic are widely supported by the browsers of various properties of elements on the Web page. The following step shows how to add a color using the color property in an inline style.

- Click after the "l" but before the closing bracket in <ul> on line 23 and then press the SPACEBAR.
- Type `style="font-style: italic"` as the code (Figure 2–30).

G:\Chapter02\ChapterFiles\hungerfight.html - Notepad++

File Edit Search View Format Language Settings Macro Run TextFX Plugins Window ?

hungerfight.html

```
1  <!DOCTYPE html
2     PUBLIC "-//W3C//DTD XHTML 1.0 Transitional//EN"
3     "http://www.w3.org/TR/xhtml1/DTD/xhtml1-transitional.dtd">
4
5  <html xmlns="http://www.w3.org/1999/xhtml" xml:lang="en" lang="en">
6  <head>
7  <meta http-equiv="Content-Type" content="text/html; charset=utf-8" />
8  <title>Hunger Fight</title>
9  </head>
10
11 <body>
12
13 <h1 style="color: #3D60B1">Fight Against World Hunger</h1>
14
15 <div>
16 <img src="hungerfightlogo.jpg" width="763" height="210" alt="Hunger Fight logo" />
17 </div>
18
19 <p>Our school and schools around the world have recently joined forces to fight against world hunger. The office
   for the Fight Against World Hunger team is located next to the bookstore. You can drop off food and money
   donations there. We also have donation drop-off locations at participating grocery stores. See the list of stores
   as well as additional information on the bulletin board outside our team office.</p>
20
21 <h2 style="color: #3D60B1">What you can do to help:</h2>
22
23 <ul style="font-style: italic">
24     <li>Join the school's Fight Against World Hunger team with a $10 donation</li>
25     <li>Buy requested food at participating grocery stores and leave at drop-off locations</li>
26     <li>Volunteer to collect money and donations around the community</li>
27 </ul>
28
29 </body>
30 </html>
```

change to <ul> tag to display italic text

Hyper Text Markup Language file | nb char : 1269 | nb line : 30 | Ln : 23 | Col : 31 | Sel : 0 | Dos\Windows ANSI | INS

Figure 2–30

To Add a Horizontal Rule

The following step illustrates how to add a horizontal rule to a Web page.

- Click the blank line 20 and then press the ENTER key.
- Type <hr /> as the HTML tag and then press the ENTER key (Figure 2–31).
- Click File on the menu bar and then click Save.

G:\Chapter02\ChapterFiles\hungerfight.html - Notepad++

```
1  <!DOCTYPE html
2     PUBLIC "-//W3C//DTD XHTML 1.0 Transitional//EN"
3     "http://www.w3.org/TR/xhtml1/DTD/xhtml1-transitional.dtd">
4
5  <html xmlns="http://www.w3.org/1999/xhtml" xml:lang="en" lang="en">
6  <head>
7  <meta http-equiv="Content-Type" content="text/html; charset=utf-8" />
8  <title>Hunger Fight</title>
9  </head>
10
11 <body>
12
13 <h1 style="color: #3D60B1">Fight Against World Hunger</h1>
14
15 <div>
16 <img src="hungerfightlogo.jpg" width="763" height="210" alt="Hunger Fight logo" />
17 </div>
18
19 <p>Our school and schools around the world have recently joined forces to fight against world hunger. The office
   for the Fight Against World Hunger team is located next to the bookstore. You can drop off food and money
   donations there. We also have donation drop-off locations at participating grocery stores. See the list of stores
   as well as additional information on the bulletin board outside our team office.</p>
20
21 <hr />
22
23 <h2 style="color: #3D60B1">What you can do to help:</h2>
24
25 <ul style="font-style: italic">
26    <li>Join the school's Fight Against World Hunger team with a $10 donation</li>
27    <li>Buy requested food at participating grocery stores and leave at drop-off locations</li>
28    <li>Volunteer to collect money and donations around the community</li>
29 </ul>
30
```

add horizontal rule

Hyper Text Markup Language file nb char: 1279 nb line: 32 Ln: 22 Col: 1 Sel: 0 Dos\Windows ANSI INS

Figure 2–31

BTW

HTML and XHTML Tags
The Web has excellent sources that list HTML and XHTML tags. For more information about HTML and XHTML, search for "HTML tags" or "XHTML tags" in a search engine.

To Refresh the View in a Browser

As you continue developing the HTML file in Notepad++, it is a good idea to view the file in your browser as you make modifications. Be sure to click the Refresh button when viewing the modified Web page in the browser, to ensure the latest version of the Web page is displayed. The step on the next page shows how to refresh the view of a Web page in a browser in order to view the modified Web page.

1

- Click the Internet Explorer button on the taskbar to display the home page.
- Click the Refresh button on the Address bar to display the modified Web page (Figure 2–32).

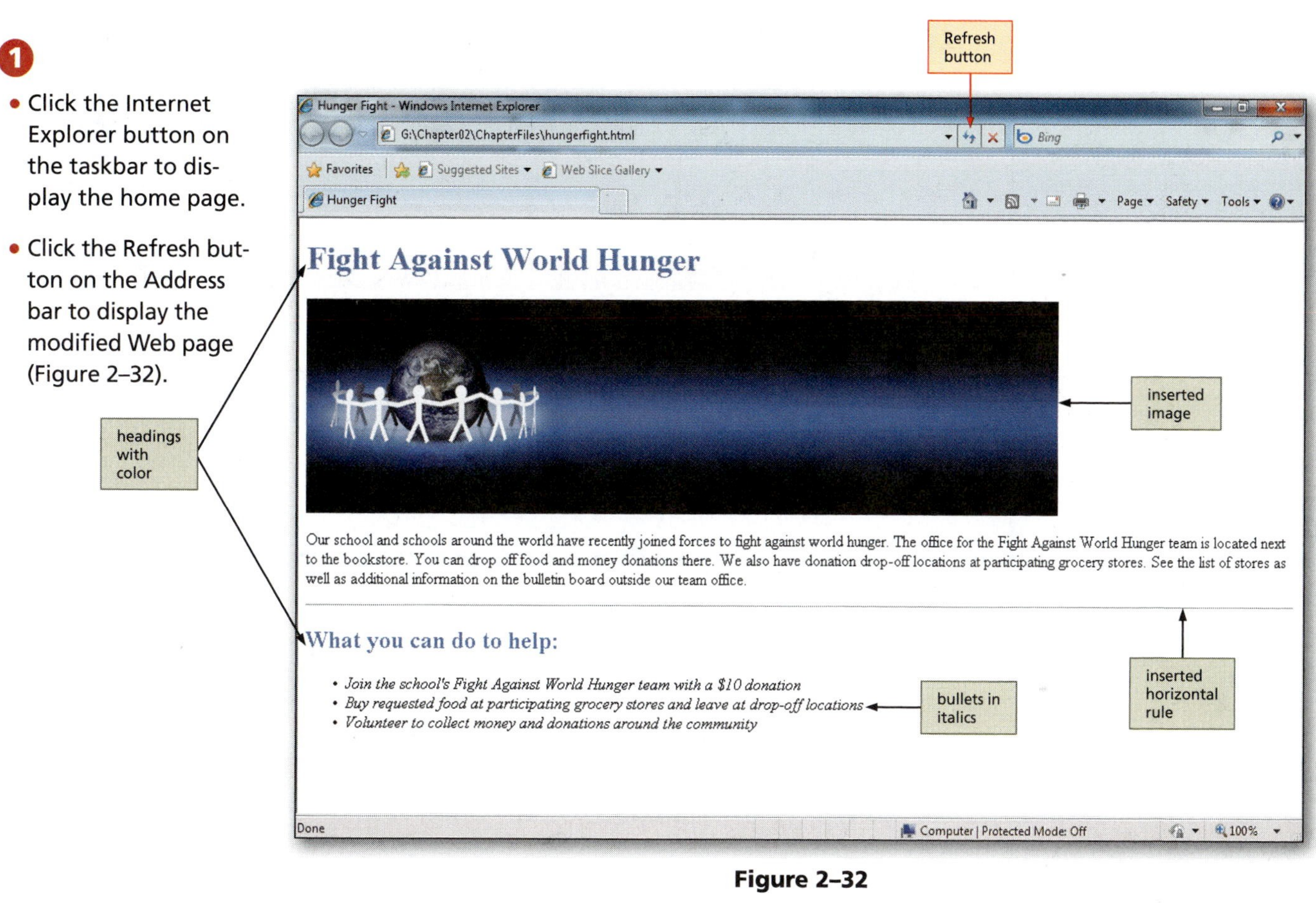

Figure 2–32

Other Ways

1. In Internet Explorer, press F5 to refresh

Validating and Viewing HTML Code

In Chapter 1, you read about validating your HTML code. Many validation services are available on the Web that can be used to assure that your HTML code follows standards. This should always be a part of your Web page testing. The validation service used in this book is the W3C Markup Validation Service (validator.w3.org). The XHTML validator looks at the DOCTYPE statement to see which version of HTML or XHTML you are using, and then checks to see if the code is valid for that version. In this chapter, the project uses Transitional code.

If validation detects an error in your HTML code, you see the warning "Errors found while checking this document as XHTML 1.0 Transitional!" in the header bar, which is red (Figure 2–33a on the next page). The Result line shows the number of errors that you have. You can scroll down the page or click the Jump To: Validation Output link to see detailed comments on each error.

It is important to note that one error can result in more errors. As an example, the <hr /> tag in the hungerfight.html file was changed to <hr> to show code with an error. Figure 2–33b shows that in this case, one initial error resulted in a total of four errors.

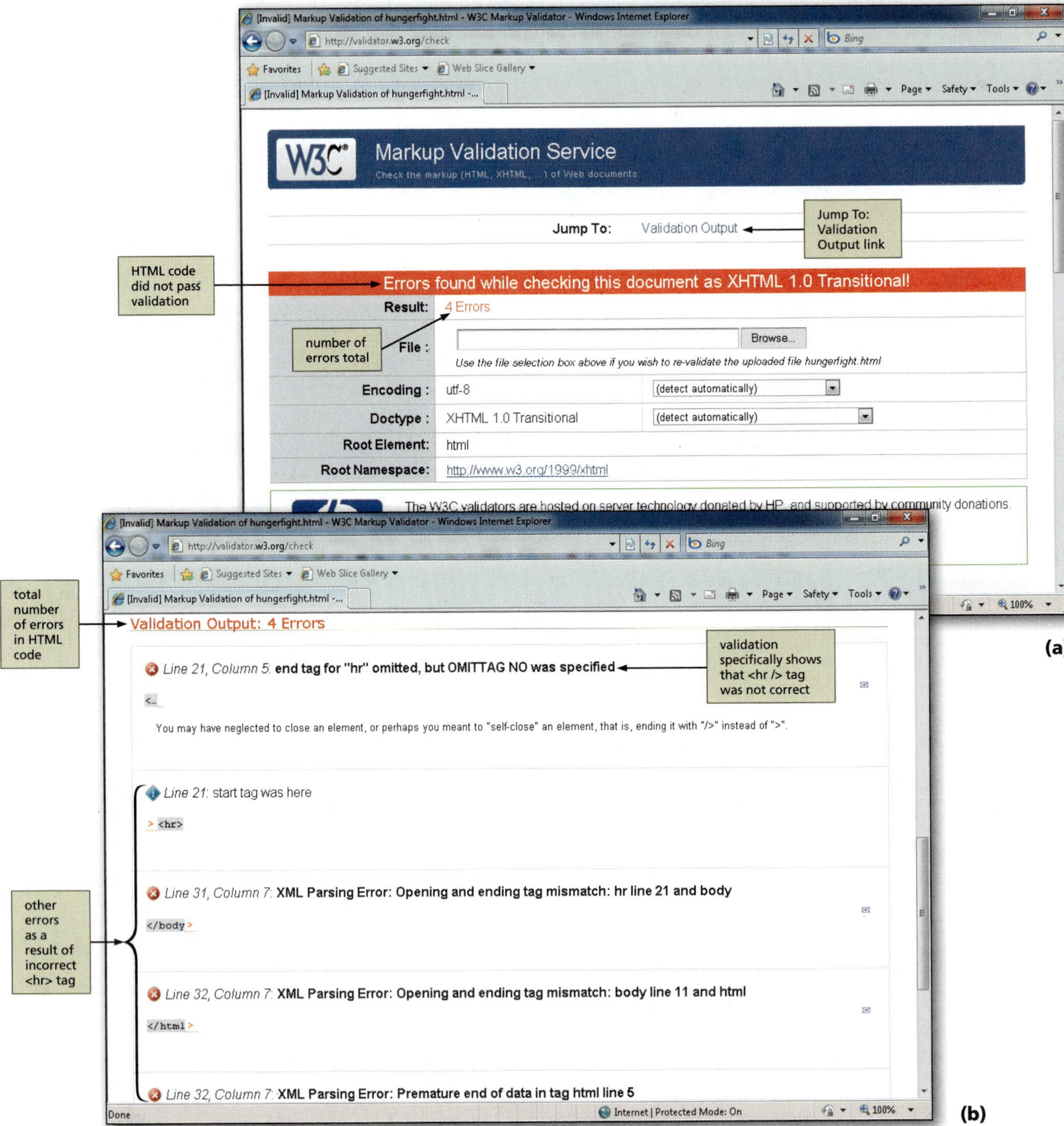

Figure 2–33

Source code is the code or instructions used to create a Web page or program. For a Web page, the source code is the HTML code, which then is translated by a browser into a graphical Web page. You can view the HTML source code for any Web page from within your browser. This feature allows you to check your own HTML source code, as well as to see the HTML code other developers used to create their Web pages. If a feature on a Web page is appropriate or appealing for your Web page, you can view the source to understand the HTML required to add that feature and then copy sections of the HTML code to put on your own Web pages.

To Validate HTML Code

Now that you have added all the basic elements to your Web page and enhanced it with images, color, italics, and rules, you need to validate your code. The following steps illustrate how to validate your HTML code using the W3 validator.

1

- Click the Address bar on the browser to highlight the current URL.
- Type `validator.w3.org` to replace the current entry, and then press the ENTER key.
- If necessary, click OK if the browser asks to open a new window.
- Click the Validate by File Upload tab (Figure 2–34).

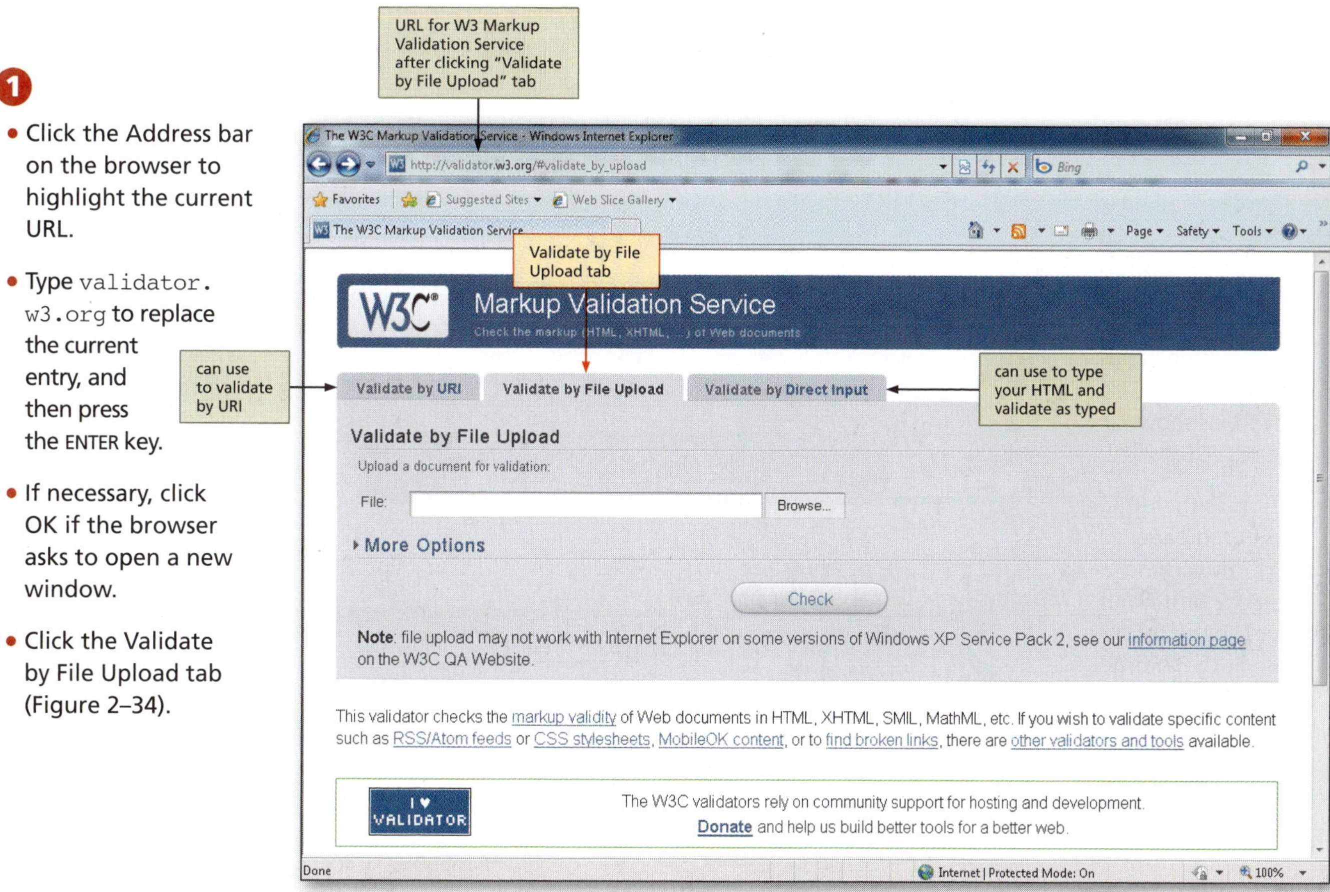

Figure 2–34

- Click the Browse button.
- Locate the hungerfight.html file on your storage device and then click the file name.
- Click the Open button on the Choose File to Upload dialog box and the file path and name will be inserted into the File box, as shown in Figure 2–35.

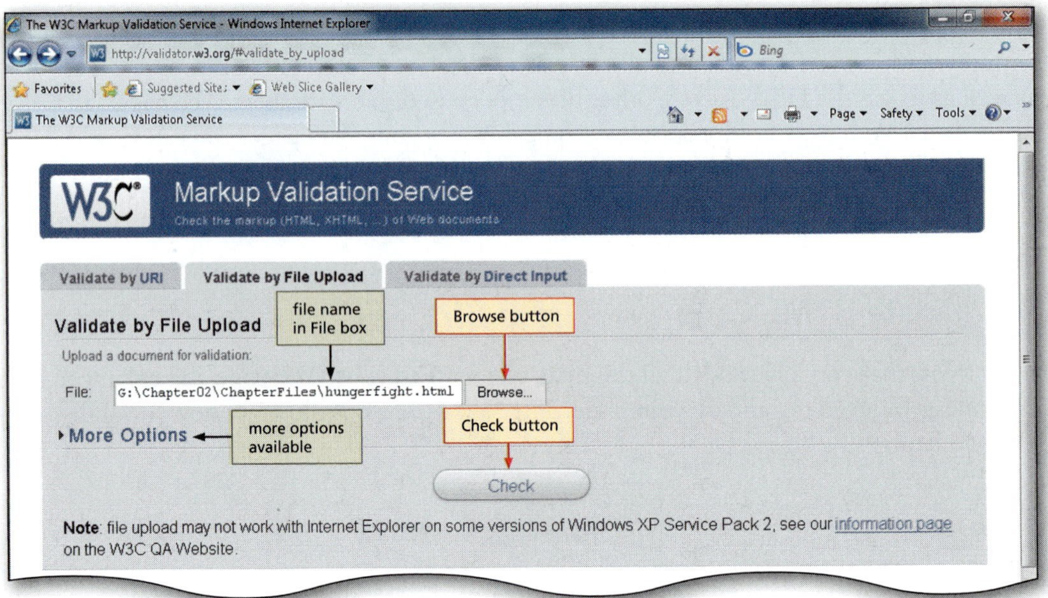

Figure 2–35

- Click the Check button (Figure 2–35). The resulting validation should be displayed, as shown in Figure 2–36.
- Return to the Hunger Fight Web page, either by clicking the Back button on your browser or by clicking the Internet Explorer button in the taskbar.

Q&A How do I know if my HTML code is valid?

The notification header will be green, and in the Result area, you should see the word "Passed."

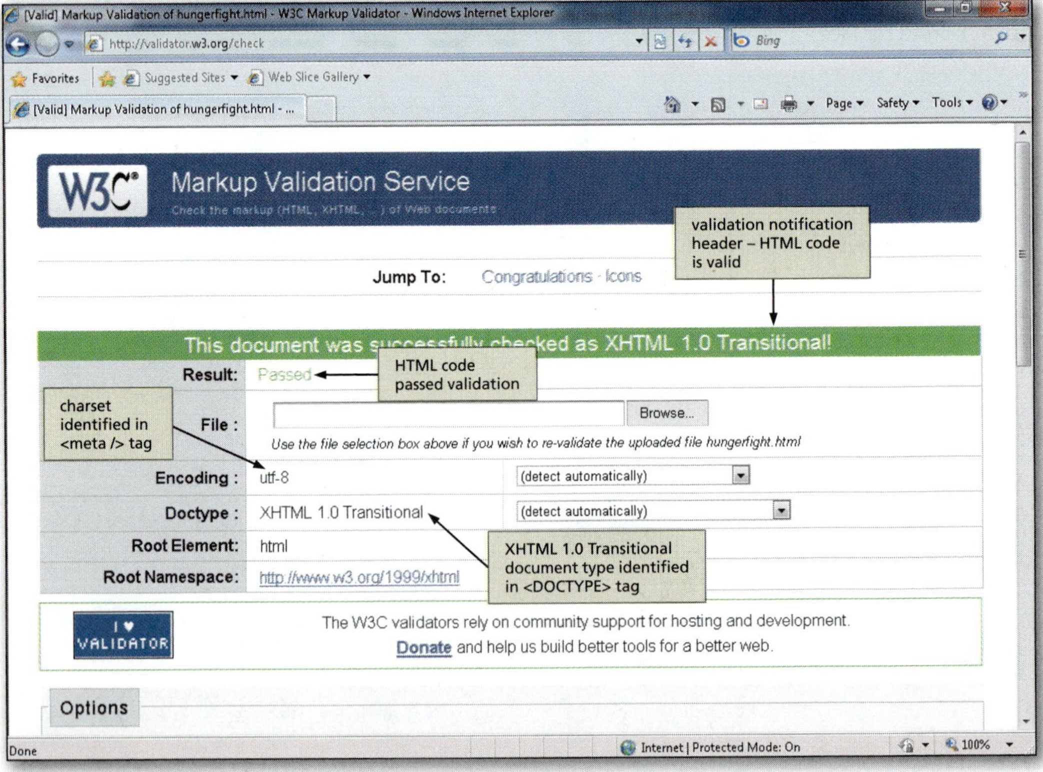

Figure 2–36

Q&A What can I do if my HTML code is not validated?

If your code has errors, edit your HTML file to correct the errors. The Markup Validation Service report lists what is wrong with your code. Once you make the necessary changes and save the file, you can use the Browse button to open the corrected HTML file, then scroll down and click the Revalidate button to validate the changed code.

To View HTML Source Code for a Web Page

You can use your browser to look at the source code for most Web pages. The following steps show how to view the HTML source code for your Web page using a browser.

1

- Click Page on the Command bar (Figure 2–37).
- Click View Source to view the HTML code in the default text editor.

Q&A Do all browsers allow me to view the HTML source code in the same way?

Browsers such as Firefox or Safari differ from Internet Explorer and might use different buttons or menu options to access source code. For instance, in Mozilla Firefox, select View and then Page Source.

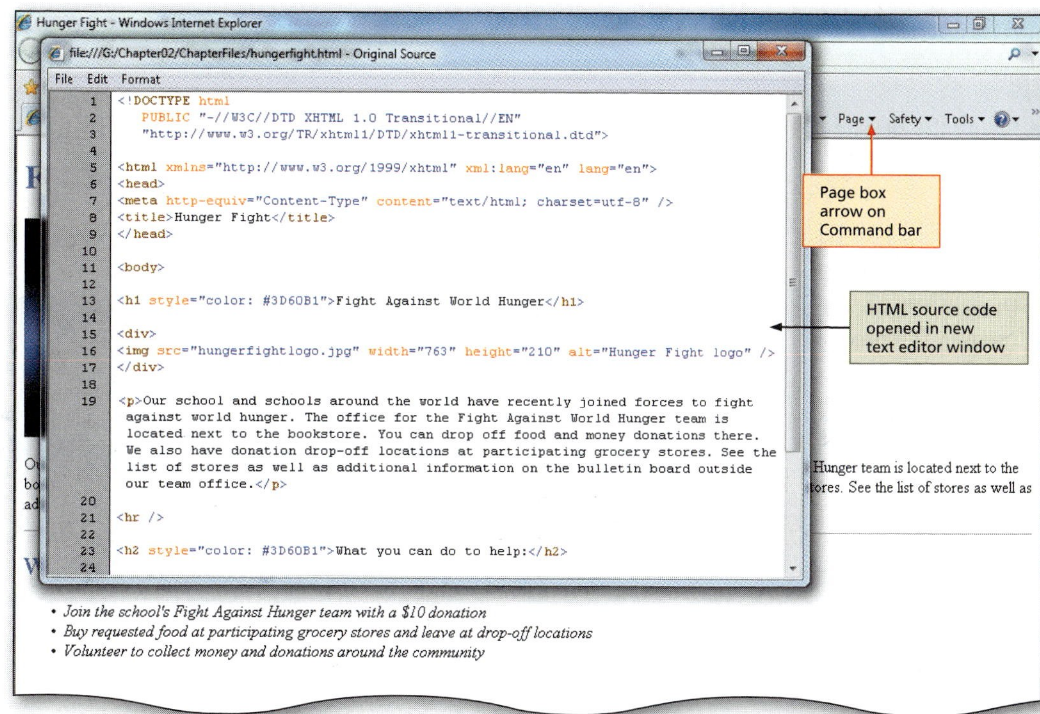

Figure 2–37

2

- Click the Close button on the text editor title bar to close the active text editor window (Figure 2–38).

Q&A What is the default text editor?

It is likely to be Notepad for Internet Explorer, but could be Notepad++ or another editor depending on your browser setup.

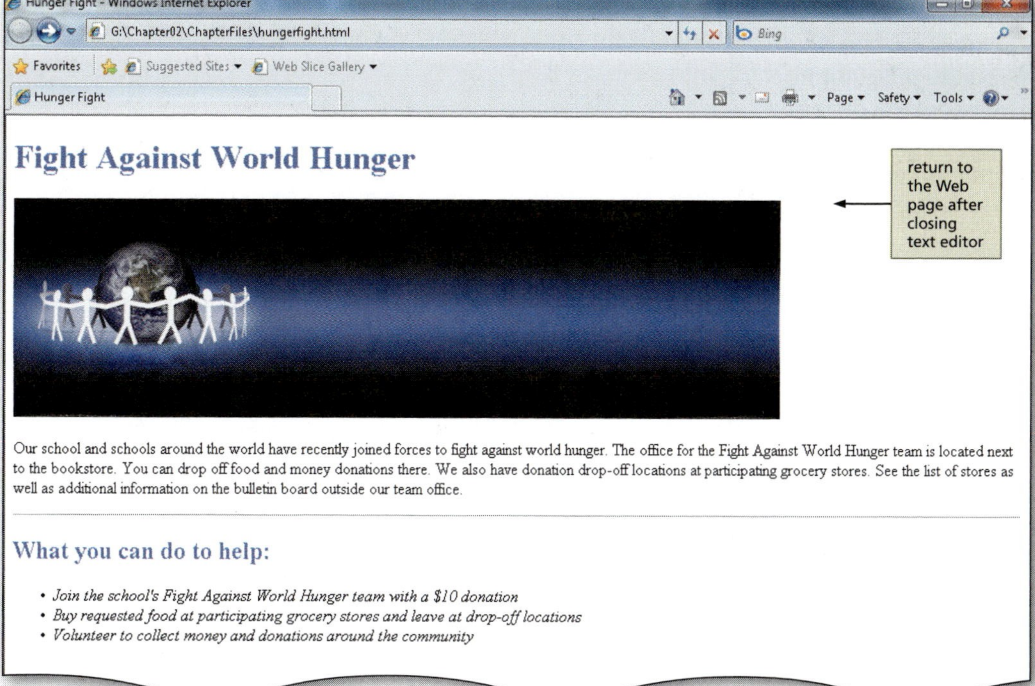

Figure 2–38

To Print a Web Page and an HTML File

After you have created the HTML file and saved it, you might want to print a copy of the HTML code and the resulting Web page. A printed version of a file, Web page, or other document is called a **hard copy** or **printout**. Printed copies of HTML files and Web pages can be kept for reference or to distribute. In many cases, HTML files and Web pages are printed and kept in binders for use by others. The following steps show how to print a Web page and its corresponding HTML file.

- Ready the printer according to the printer instructions.
- With the Fight Against World Hunger Web page open in the browser window, click the Print icon on the Command bar.
- When the Print dialog box appears, click the Print button.
- When the printer stops printing the Web page, retrieve the printout (Figure 2–39).

Q&A Are there other ways to print a Web page?

Pressing CTRL+P opens the Print dialog box, where you can select print options. You can also use the File menu, Print option.

Hunger Fight | Page 1 of 1

Fight Against World Hunger

Our school and schools around the world have recently joined forces to fight against world hunger. The office for the Fight Against World Hunger team is located next to the bookstore. You can drop off food and money donations there. We also have donation drop-off locations at participating grocery stores. See the list of stores as well as additional information on the bulletin board outside our team office.

What you can do to help:

- *Join the school's Fight Against World Hunger team with a $10 donation*
- *Buy requested food at participating grocery stores and leave at drop-off locations*
- *Volunteer to collect money and donations around the community*

Figure 2–39

- Click the Notepad++ button on the taskbar to activate the Notepad++ window.
- Click File on the menu bar, click the Print command, and then click the Print button to print a hard copy of the HTML code (Figure 2–40).

Q&A

Why do I need a printout of the HTML code?

Having a hard-copy printout is an invaluable tool for beginning developers. A printed copy can help you immediately see the relationship between the HTML tags and the Web page that you view in the browser.

```
<!DOCTYPE html
   PUBLIC "-//W3C//DTD XHTML 1.0 Transitional//EN"
   "http://www.w3.org/TR/xhtml1/DTD/xhtml1-transitional.dtd">

<html xmlns="http://www.w3.org/1999/xhtml" xml:lang="en" lang="en">
<head>
<meta http-equiv="Content-Type" content="text/html; charset=utf-8" />
<title>Hunger Fight</title>
</head>

<body>

<h1 style="color: #3D60B1">Fight Against World Hunger</h1>

<div>
<img src="hungerfightlogo.jpg" width="763" height="210" alt="Hunger Fight logo" />
</div>

<p>Our school and schools around the world have recently joined forces to fight against
world hunger. The office for the Fight Against World Hunger team is located next to the
bookstore. You can drop off food and money donations there. We also have donation
drop-off locations at participating grocery stores. See the list of stores as well as
additional information on the bulletin board outside our team office.</p>

<hr />

<h2 style="color: #3D60B1">What you can do to help:</h2>

<ul style="font-style: italic">
    <li>Join the school's Fight Against World Hunger team with a $10 donation</li>
    <li>Buy requested food at participating grocery stores and leave at drop-off
locations</li>
    <li>Volunteer to collect money and donations around the community</li>
</ul>

</body>
</html>
```

-1-

Figure 2–40

BTW

Quick Reference
For a list of HTML tags and their associated attributes, see the HTML Quick Reference (Appendix A) at the back of this book, or visit the HTML Quick Reference Web page (scsite.com/HTML6e/qr). For a list of CSS properties and values, see Appendix D.

To Quit Notepad++ and a Browser

The following step shows how to quit Notepad++ and a browser.

1. In Notepad++, click the File menu, then Close All.
2. Click the Close button on the Notepad++ title bar.
3. Click the Close button on the Hunger Fight Internet Explorer title bar.

Chapter Summary

In this chapter, you have learned how to identify the elements of a Web page, define the Web page structure, and enter Web page content using a text editor. You enhanced Web page appearance using inline styles, saved and validated your code, and viewed your Web page and source code in a browser. The items listed below include all the new HTML skills you have learned in this chapter.

1. Start Notepad++ (HTML 40)
2. Enable Word Wrap in Notepad++ (HTML 42)
3. Define the Web Page Structure Using HTML Tags (HTML 42)
4. Enter a Heading (HTML 47)
5. Enter a Paragraph of Text (HTML 47)
6. Create an Unordered List (HTML 50)
7. Save an HTML File (HTML 54)
8. Start a Browser (HTML 57)
9. View a Web Page in a Browser (HTML 59)
10. Activate Notepad++ (HTML 61)
11. Add an Image (HTML 66)
12. Add Color to Web Page Headings (HTML 70)
13. Change the Bulleted List Style (HTML 71)
14. Add a Horizontal Rule (HTML 72)
15. Refresh the View in a Browser (HTML 73)
16. Validate HTML Code (HTML 75)
17. View HTML Source Code for a Web Page (HTML 77)
18. Print a Web Page and an HTML File (HTML 78)
19. Quit Notepad++ and a Browser (HTML 80)

Learn It Online

Test your knowledge of chapter content and key terms.

Instructions: To complete the Learn It Online exercises, start your browser, click the Address bar, and then enter the Web address `scsite.com/html6e/learn`. When the HTML Learn It Online page is displayed, click the link for the exercise you want to complete and read the instructions.

Chapter Reinforcement TF, MC, and SA

A series of true/false, multiple choice, and short answer questions that test your knowledge of the chapter content.

Flash Cards

An interactive learning environment where you identify chapter key terms associated with displayed definitions.

Practice Test

A series of multiple choice questions that test your knowledge of chapter content and key terms.

Who Wants To Be a Computer Genius?

An interactive game that challenges your knowledge of chapter content in the style of a television quiz show.

Wheel of Terms

An interactive game that challenges your knowledge of chapter key terms in the style of the television show, *Wheel of Fortune*.

Crossword Puzzle Challenge

A crossword puzzle that challenges your knowledge of key terms presented in the chapter.

Apply Your Knowledge

Reinforce the skills and apply the concepts you learned in this chapter.

Editing the Apply Your Knowledge Web Page

Instructions: Start Notepad++. Open the file apply2-1.html from the Chapter02\Apply folder of the Data Files for Students. See the inside back cover of this book for instructions for downloading the Data Files for Students, or contact your instructor for information about accessing the required files for this book.

The apply2-1.html file is a partially completed HTML file that you will use for this exercise. Figure 2–41 shows the Apply Your Knowledge Web page as it should be displayed in a browser after the additional HTML tags and attributes are added.

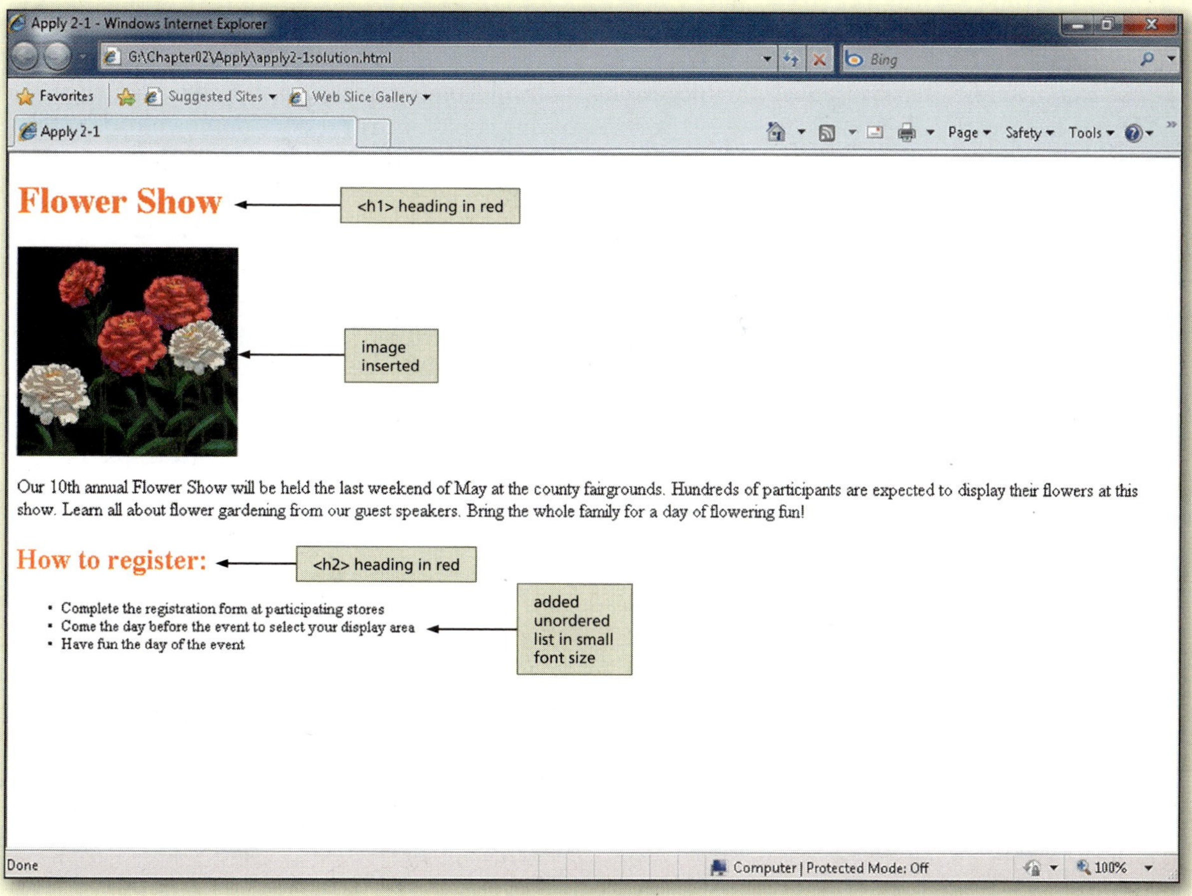

Figure 2–41

Perform the following tasks:

1. Enter g:\Chapter02\Apply\apply2-1.html as the URL to view the Web page in your browser.
2. Examine the HTML file and its appearance in the browser.
3. Using Notepad++, change the HTML code to make the Web page look similar to the one shown in Figure 2–41. Both headings are the color red. (*Hint:* Use the style="color: red" property.)
4. Add the image flowershow.jpg (in the Chapter02\Apply folder) to the Web page. It has a width of 192 pixels and a height of 175 pixels. (*Hint:* Include the image in a <div> </div> container and remember to use the alt attribute.)
5. Make the bulleted list in a small font size. (*Hint:* Use the style="font-size: small" property.)

Continued >

Apply Your Knowledge *continued*

6. Save the revised HTML file in the Chapter02\Apply folder using the file name apply2-1solution.html.
7. Validate your HTML code at http://validator.w3.org/.
8. Enter g:\Chapter02\Apply\apply2-1solution.html as the URL to view the revised Web page in your browser.
9. Print the Web page.
10. Submit the revised HTML file and Web page in the format specified by your instructor.

Extend Your Knowledge

Extend the skills you learned in this chapter and experiment with new skills.

Creating a Definition List

Instructions: Start Notepad++. Open the file, extend2-1.html from the Chapter02\Extend folder of the Data Files for Students. See the inside back cover of this book for instructions on downloading the Data Files for Students, or contact your instructor for information about accessing the required files. This sample Web page contains all of the text for the Web page in bulleted list format. You will add the necessary tags to make this a definition list with terms that are bold, as shown in Figure 2–42.

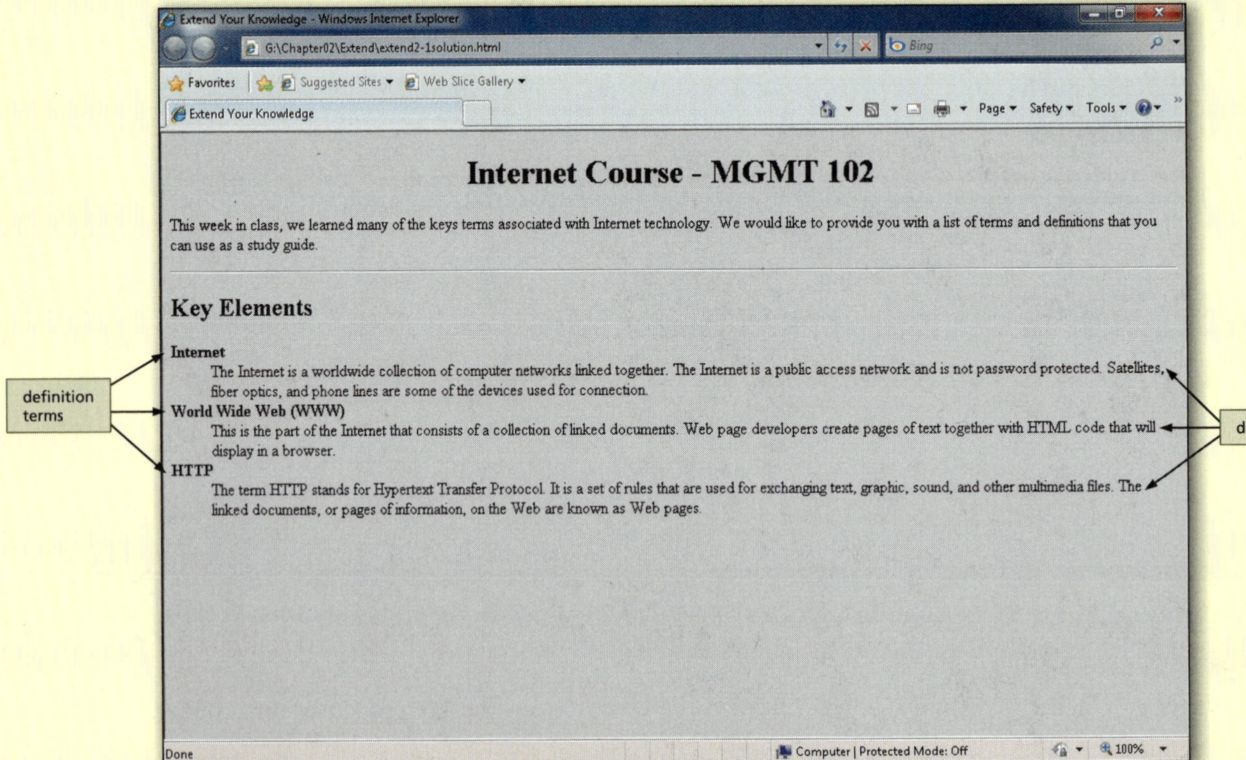

Figure 2–42

Perform the following tasks:

1. Using the text given in the file extend2-1.html, make changes to the HTML code to change the Web page from a bulleted list to a definition list by following the definition list code shown in Figure 2–14 on page HTML 52.

2. Add the additional HTML code necessary to make the terms bold (see font-weight for style in Appendix D) and a background color of #e0e0e0 (see background-color in Appendix D).
3. Save the revised document in the Chapter02\Extend folder with the file name extend2-1solution.html, validate the Web page, and then submit it in the format specified by your instructor.

Make It Right

Analyze a document and correct all errors and/or improve the design.

Correcting the Friendly Reminder Web Page

Instructions: Start Notepad++. Open the file makeitright2-1.html from the Chapter02\MakeItRight folder of the Data Files for Students. See the inside back cover of this book for instructions on downloading the Data Files for Students, or contact your instructor for information about accessing the required files. The Web page is a modified version of what you see in Figure 2–43. Make the necessary corrections to the Web page to make it look like Figure 2–43. Format the heading to use the Heading 1 style center-aligned on the Web page (see the text-align property in Appendix D to center a heading). Add two size-10px horizontal rules, as shown in Figure 2–43. Save the file in the Chapter02\MakeItRight folder as makeitright2-1solution.html, validate the Web page, and then submit it in the format specified by your instructor.

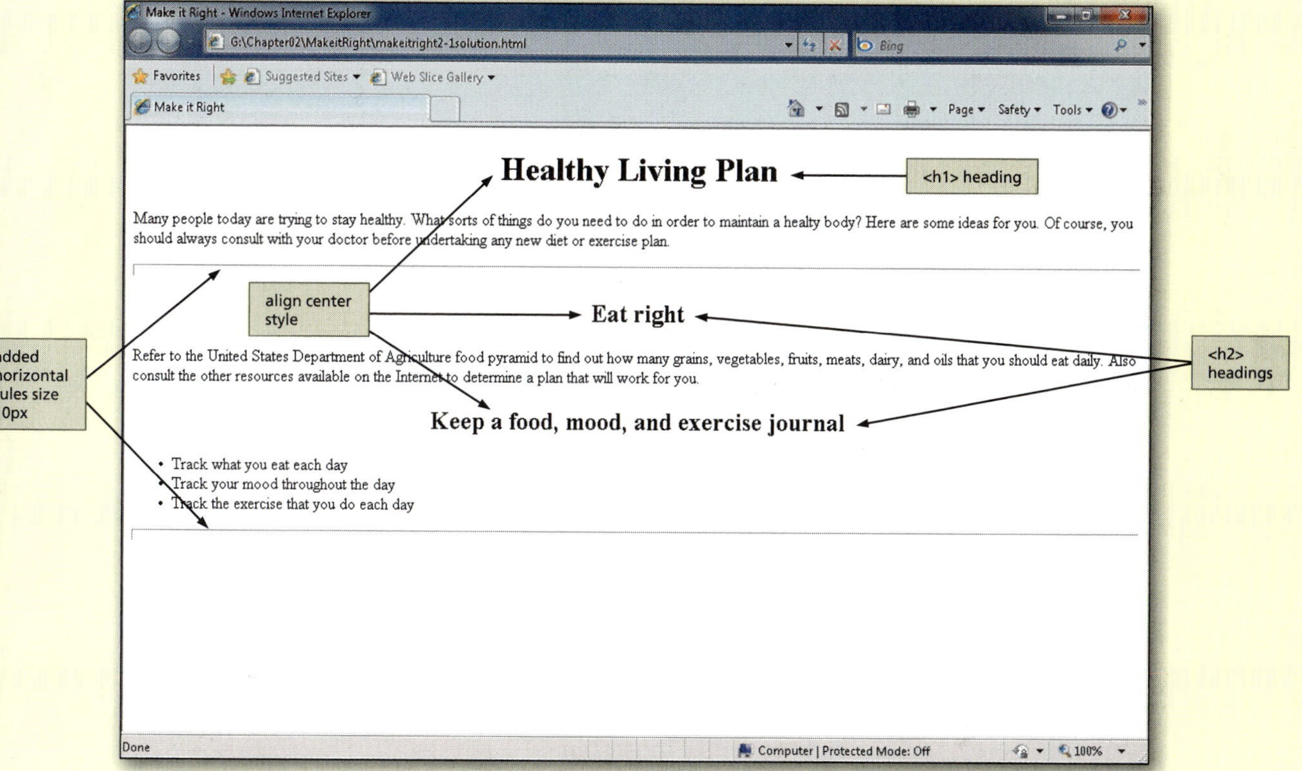

Figure 2–43

In the Lab

Lab 1: Creating a Food Drive Web Page

Problem: You did volunteer work for the Community Food Drive in your city. You would like to recruit other friends to volunteer for community service. You have been asked to create a Web page to display information about why you choose to volunteer and let people know how they also can help, as shown in Figure 2–44.

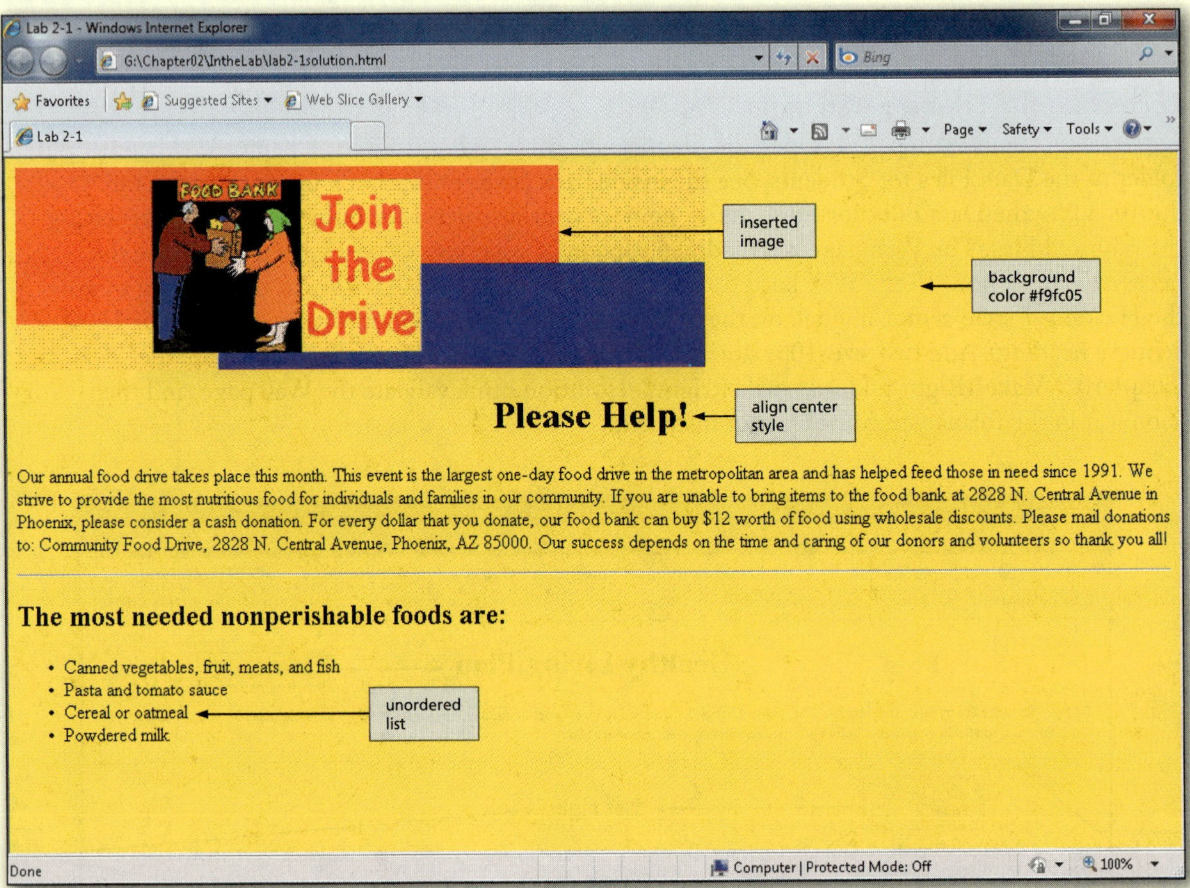

Figure 2–44

Instructions: Perform the following steps:

1. Start Notepad++ and create a new HTML file with the title, Lab 2-1, within the <title> </title> tags. For the initial HTML tags, you can use the structure.html file if you created one at the start of this chapter's project, otherwise type the initial tags.
2. Begin the body section by adding the fooddrivelogo.gif image as well as the heading, Please Help! Format the heading to use the Heading 1 style center-aligned on the Web page. (*Hint:* See the text-align property in Appendix D to center the heading.)
3. Add a left-aligned heading, as shown, using the Heading 2 style.
4. Add a background color to the Web page using the #f9fc05 color code. (*Hint:* Use the style="background-color: color number" property.)
5. Add an unordered list of nonperishable foods, as shown in Figure 2–44.
6. Save the file in the Chapter02\IntheLab folder as lab2-1solution.html.

7. Print the lab2-1.html file.
8. Enter g:\Chapter02\IntheLab\lab2-1solution.html as the URL to view the Web page in your browser.
9. Print the Web page.
10. Submit the revised HTML file and Web page in the format specified by your instructor.

In the Lab

Lab 2: Creating an Informational Web Page

Problem: You continue to enjoy volunteering and decide to prepare a Web page announcement, such as the one shown in Figure 2–45, to promote the latest food drive.

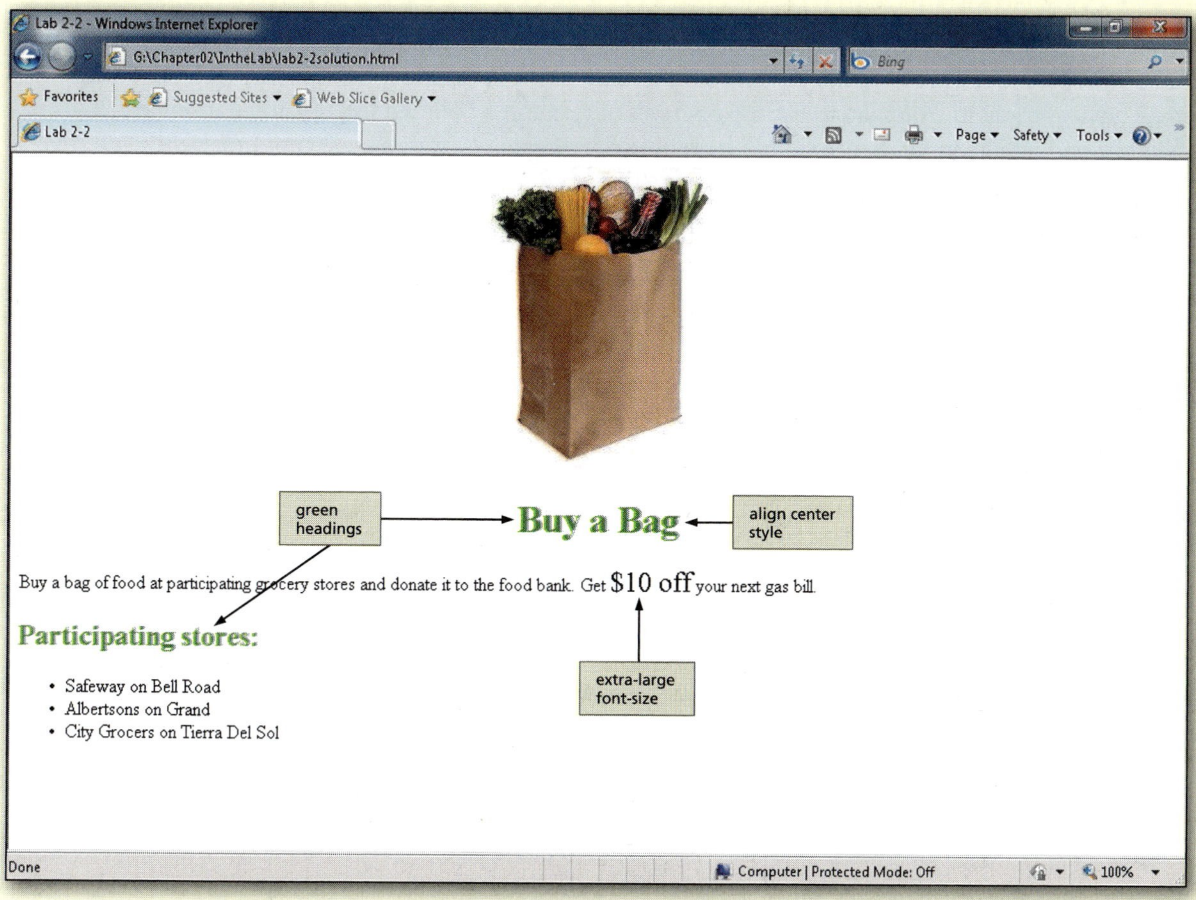

Figure 2–45

Instructions: Perform the following steps:

1. Start Notepad++ and create a new HTML file with the title Lab 2-2 within the <title> </title> tags.
2. The Web page uses the foodbag.jpg image file, which has a width of 207 and a height of 256. Center the image (see the text-align property in Appendix D). Use the color green for both headings.
3. Add the paragraph of text, as shown in Figure 2–45. Make the words "$10 off" x-large style of font (see the <span> HTML tag in Appendix A to help with that).
4. Create one bulleted list with the information shown.

Continued >

In the Lab *continued*

5. Save the file in the Chapter02\IntheLab folder using the file name lab2-2solution.html.
6. Print the lab2-2solution.html file.
7. Enter g:\Chapter02\IntheLab\lab2-2solution.html as the URL to view the Web page in your browser.
8. Print the Web page.
9. Submit the revised HTML file and Web page in the format specified by your instructor.

In the Lab

Lab 3: Composing a Personal Web Page

Problem: Your friends are concerned that they aren't able to save money. They have asked you for help, since you seem to always have money saved for a rainy day. You decide to compose a Web page with some advice for them. You plan to use a paragraph of text and a bulleted list, as shown in Figure 2–46. The text and bullets in the figure should be replaced with your own money-saving experience and tips.

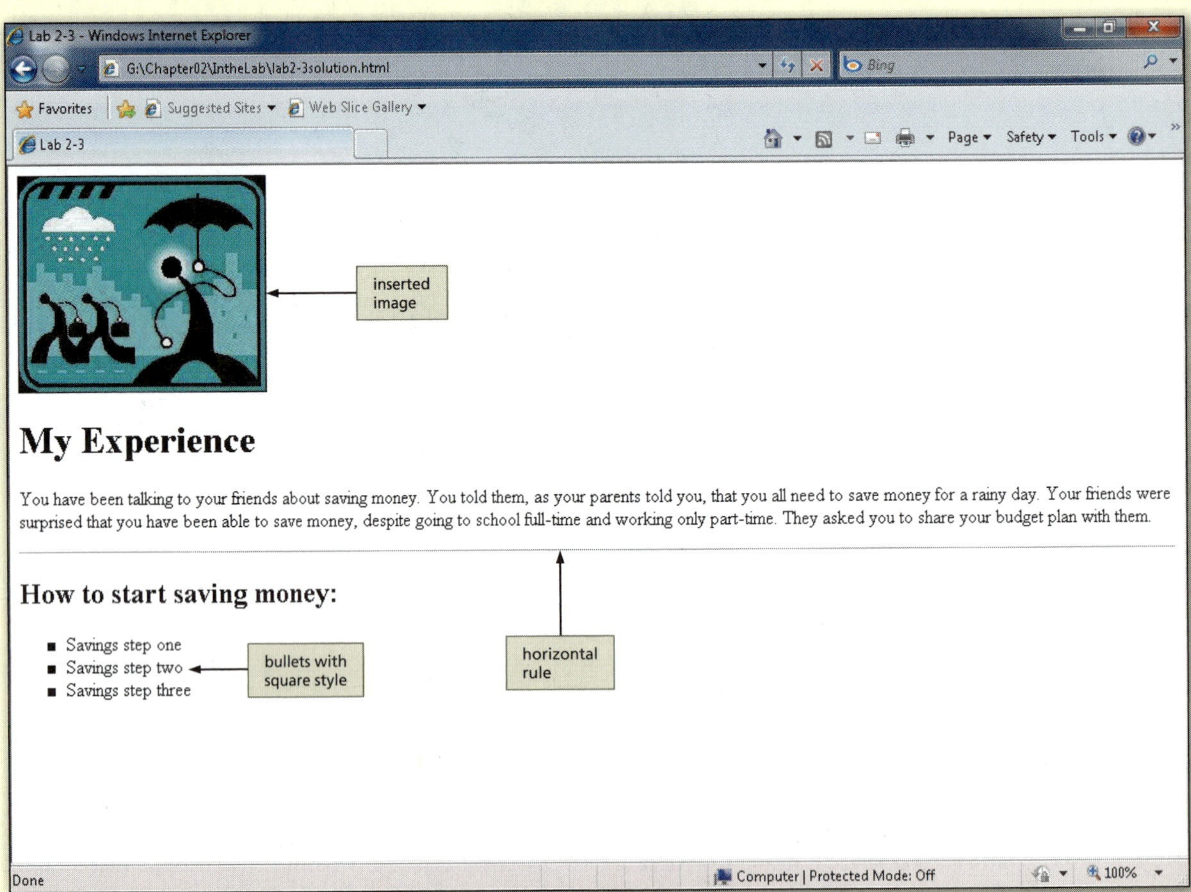

Figure 2–46

Instructions: Perform the following steps:

1. Start Notepad++ and create a new HTML file with the title Lab 2-3 within the <title> </title> tags.
2. Include a short paragraph of information and a bulleted list, using a format similar to the one shown in Figure 2–46, to provide information about your money-saving experience.

3. Insert the image file cloudy.jpg, stored in the Chapter02\IntheLab folder. Right-click the image, click Properties, and then click the Details tab to find out the image's dimensions, or open it in a graphics program. Note that the bullets used for the list are square in shape.
4. Save the HTML file in the Chapter02\IntheLab folder using the file name lab2-3solution.html.
5. Enter g:\Chapter02\IntheLab\lab2-3solution.html as the URL to view the Web page in your browser.
6. Print the Web page from your browser.
7. Submit the revised HTML file and Web page in the format specified by your instructor.

Cases and Places

Apply your creative thinking and problem-solving skills to design and implement a solution.

• Easier •• More Difficult

• 1: Add to the Food Drive Web Page

Mr. Wattigney, the director of the Community Food Bank, likes the Web page you created for Lab 2-1. Now that the Food Drive is over, he would like you to update the Web page with new information on upcoming community events. Before updating the page, search the Web to review the Web pages at other food banks or departments of community services for ideas on content to include or formatting to change. What do their Web sites look like? Are there changes you can make to the Lab 2-1 Web page that reflect what other places have done? Using the concepts presented in this chapter, include additional information or change the formatting to make the page more interesting and timely.

• 2: Create an Artist Web Site

You are creating a new Web site for a local photographer. The photographer has asked that you use descriptive alt attributes for images on the Web page, because many of the viewers of his Web page have very slow Internet connections and images often do not load quickly. Search the Web for information on adding useful, descriptive alt attributes for images. Also find information on using thumbnail images. Give suggestions for loading images faster. Create a document with a brief paragraph explaining the information that you found in your research. Make suggestions about how the photographer's Web site can be made more effective.

•• 3: Create a Web Page of CSS Properties

You have learned a lot about using Cascading Style Sheets (CSS) so far in the class. You still have some questions, though, about how to insert certain styles. Research information on the Web (don't forget to look at the W3.org site) to find Web sites that list CSS properties and values that complement Appendix D. In a Word document, add the URLs that you found to be very helpful. Under each URL write a brief paragraph that describes why you thought the site could be useful for new Web developers. Share your list of URLs with fellow students.

•• 4: Create a Personal Web Page

Make It Personal

Your class instructor wants to post all of the students' Web pages on the school server to show what his or her students are interested in. Create a Web page of personal information, listing items such as your school major, jobs that you have had in the past, and your hobbies and interests. To make your personal

Continued >

Cases and Places *continued*

Web page more visually interesting, search the Web for images that reflect your interests. (Remember that if the image is copyrighted, you cannot use it on a personal Web page unless you follow the guidelines provided with the image.) Insert an image or two onto the Web page to help explain who you are.

•• 5: Create Web Pages with Different CSS Properties

Working Together

Work with other students to review the CSS in Appendix D together with the Web sites dedicated to CSS found in Cases and Places 3. Try to find a use for some CSS properties that you have not used so far in this chapter (maybe something with margins). Plan how you can use five CSS properties not used in Chapter 2 to improve one of the Web pages you created in this chapter (either the chapter project or an end-of-chapter project). Utilize the five different CSS properties in the Web page. Explain in a Word document what CSS properties you used, why you used them, and how they improved the Web page.

3 Creating Web Pages with Links, Images, and Embedded Style Sheets

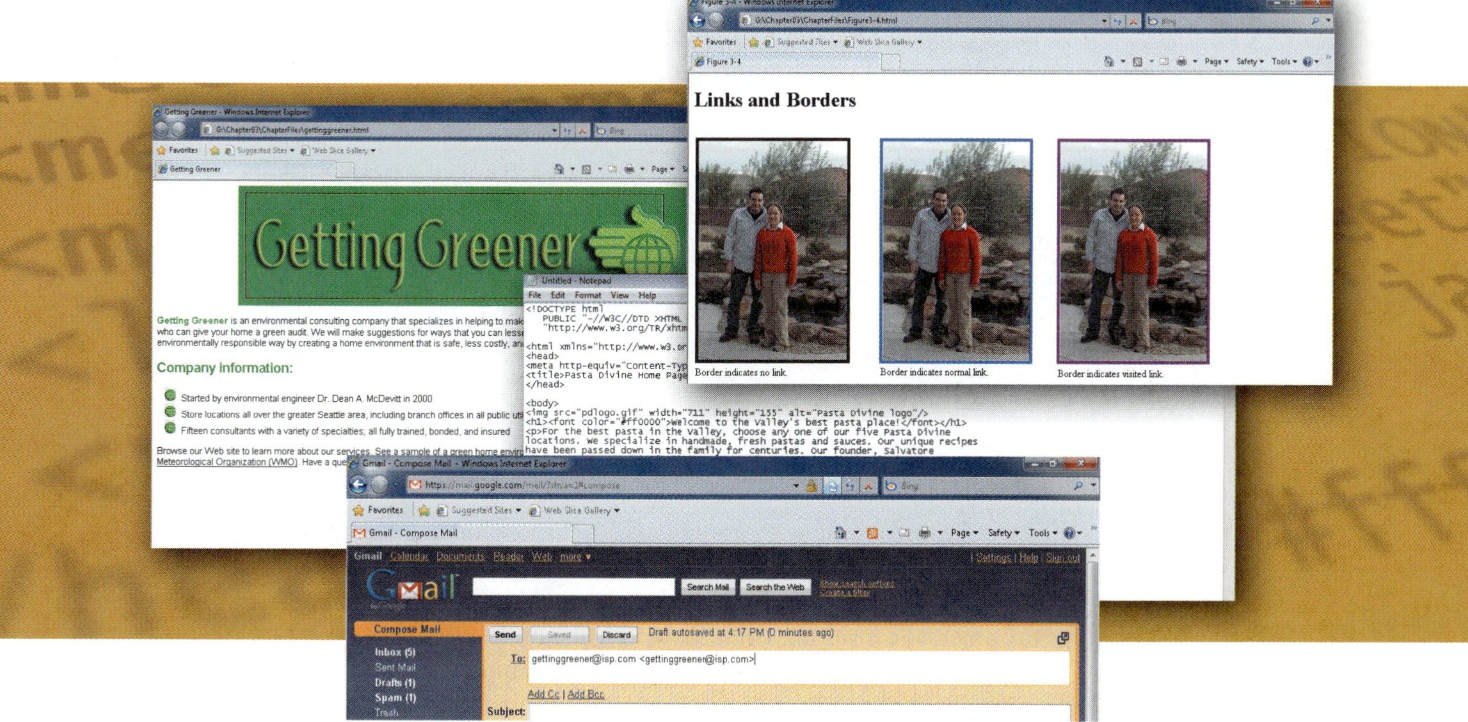

Objectives

You will have mastered the material in this chapter when you can:

- Describe linking terms and definitions
- Create a home page and enhance a Web page using images
- Change body and heading format using embedded style sheets
- Align and add color to text using embedded and inline styles
- Use an inline style to insert an image for bullets in an unordered list
- Add a text link to a Web page in the same Web site
- Add an e-mail link
- Add a text link to a Web page on another Web site
- Use absolute and relative paths
- Save, validate, and view an HTML file and test the links
- Use style classes to add an image with wrapped text
- Add links to targets within a Web page
- Copy and paste HTML code
- Add an image link to a Web page in the same Web site

3 Creating Web Pages with Links, Images, and Embedded Style Sheets

Introduction

One of the most useful and important aspects of the World Wide Web is the ability to connect (link) one Web page to other Web pages — on the same server or on different Web servers — located anywhere in the world. Using hyperlinks, a Web site visitor can move from one page to another, and view information in any order. Many different Web page elements, including text, graphics, and animations, can serve as hyperlinks. In this chapter, you will create Web pages that are linked together using both text links and image links. In the last chapter, you used inline styles to change the appearance of individual elements or HTML tags. In this chapter, you will also use embedded style sheets to set the appearance of elements such as headings and body text for the entire Web page. Before starting on this project, you would have already completed the Web site planning, analysis, and design phases of the Web Development Life Cycle.

Project — Getting Greener Web Site

Chapter 3 illustrates how to use HTML to create a home page for the Getting Greener Web site (Figure 3–1a) and to edit the existing greenhome.html Web page (Figure 3–1b) to improve its appearance and function. Your older brother, Dean, recently opened an environmental consulting company and named it Getting Greener. He would like to advertise his company on the Web and show a sample home on which he has done a green audit. He knows that you have studied Web development in college and asks you to develop two Web pages that are linked together: a home page, and a Web page with the sample home. During your analysis, you determined that there are four basic types of links to use. The first type is a link from one Web page to another in the same Web site. The second type is a link to a Web page on a different Web site. The third type is an e-mail link. The fourth type is a link within one Web page. You plan to utilize all four of these types of links for your brother's Web site.

The Getting Greener home page (Figure 3–1a) includes a logo image banner, headings, an unordered (bulleted) list with a graphic image as the bullet, an e-mail link, and a text link to a Web page on another Web site. This page also includes a link to the greenhome.html Web page. The Green Home Web page (Figure 3–1b) contains two images with text wrapped around them and internal links that allow visitors to move easily from section to section within the Web page. The Web page also has an image link back to Getting Greener's home page.

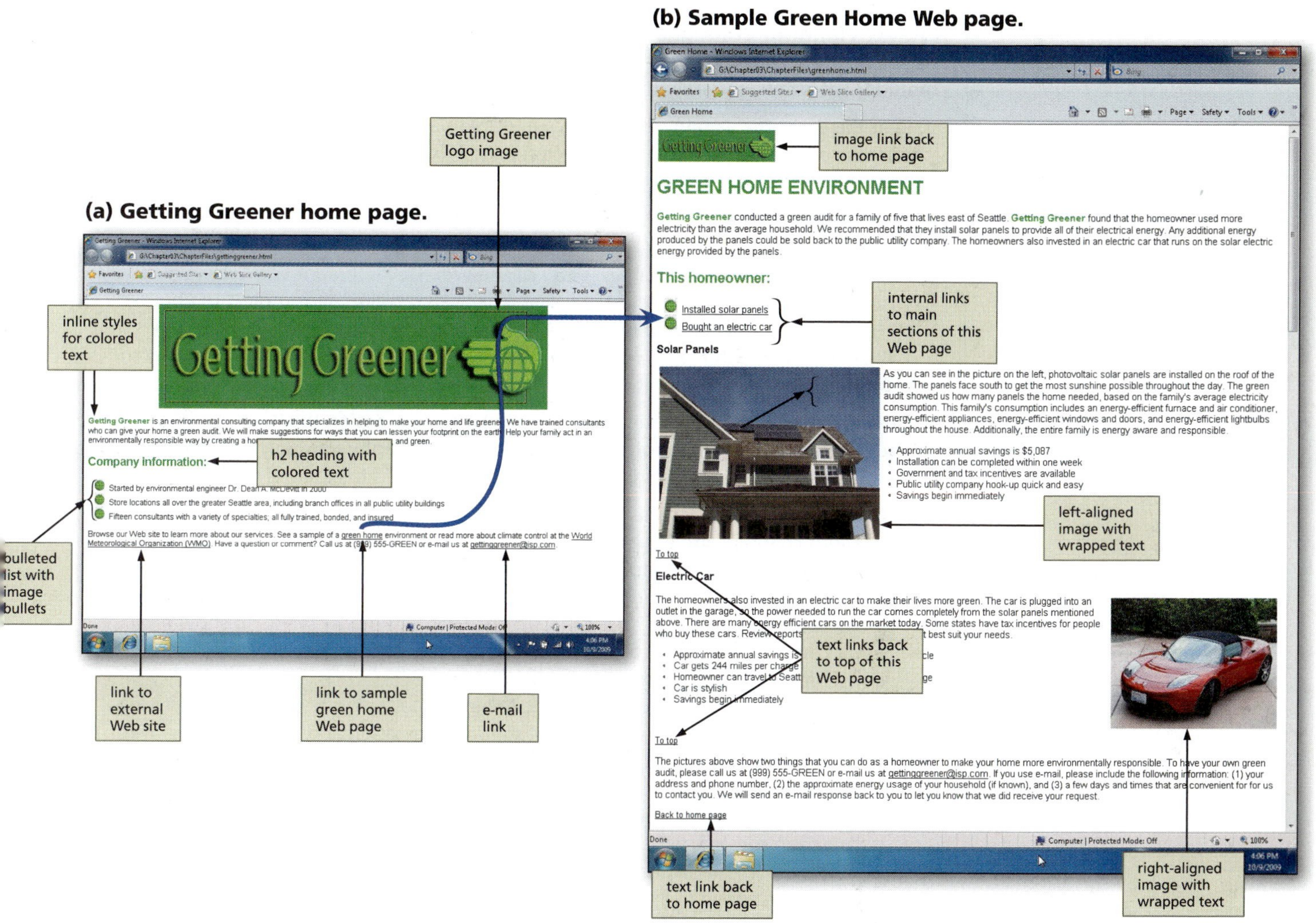

(b) Sample Green Home Web page.

(a) Getting Greener home page.

Figure 3–1

Overview

As you read this chapter, you will learn how to create the Web page shown in Figure 3–1 by performing these general tasks:

- Enter HTML code into the Notepad++ window.
- Save the file as an HTML file.
- Enter basic HTML tags and add text to the file.
- Use embedded style sheets, inline styles, and classes to change the format of text and headings.
- Use an inline style to create a bulleted list with a graphic image as the bullets.
- Add a link to another Web page in the same Web site.
- Add a link to an external Web site.
- Add an e-mail link.
- Add targets and links within the same Web page.
- View the Web pages and HTML code in your browser.
- Validate the Web pages.
- Print the Web pages.

Plan Ahead

Project Planning Guidelines

As you create Web pages, such as the project shown in Figure 3–1 on the previous page, you should follow these general guidelines:

1. **Plan the Web site**. Before developing a multiple-page Web site, you must plan the purpose of the site. Refer to Table 1–4 on page HTML 15 for information on the planning phase of the Web Development Life Cycle. In this phase, you determine the purpose of the Web site, identify the users of the site and their computing environments, and decide who owns the information on the Web page.
2. **Analyze the need**. In the analysis phase of the Web Development Life Cycle, you analyze what content to include in the Web page. The Web development project in Chapter 3 is different than the one completed in Chapter 2 because it contains two Web pages that will be linked together. Part of the analysis phase then includes determining how the multiple Web pages work together to form a Web site.
3. **Design the Web site.** Once the analysis is complete, you design the Web site. In this phase, you determine the content of the site, both text and graphics. Design steps specific to this chapter also include determining links within the site and to external Web sites.
   a. **Choose the content for the Web pages**. This part of the life cycle also differs from the previous chapter's project because all of the content does not have to appear on one Web page, as it did in Chapter 2. With a multiple-page Web site, you can distribute the content as needed throughout the Web site. Because of the nature of this Web site, pictures are a large part of the content. The Web site owner wants to show a sample of his company's work. Pictures help show what one family has done to become more environmentally responsible.
   b. **Determine the types of Cascading Style Sheets (CSS) that you will use**. You already learned how to use inline styles to best support the design and purpose of the Web site. In this chapter, you utilize both inline and embedded style sheets to alter the appearance (or style) of various Web page elements. You also incorporate classes with your embedded style sheets to further control the style of elements on the Web page. You need to consider which of these options is best suited for the styles of your Web site.
   c. **Determine how the pages will link to one another**. This Web site consists of a **home page** (the first page in a Web site) and a secondary Web page to which you will link. You need to determine how to link (e.g., with text or a graphic) from the home page to the secondary page and how to link back to the home page.
   d. **Establish what other links are necessary**. In addition to links between the home page and secondary Web page, you need an e-mail link. It is standard for Web developers to provide an e-mail link on the home page of a Web site for visitor comments or questions. Additionally, the secondary Web page (greenhome.html) is a long page that requires visitors to scroll down for navigation. Because of its length, it is important to provide easy and quick ways to navigate the Web page. You do this using links within the Web page.
4. **Develop the Web page(s) and insert all links**. Once the analysis and design is complete, the Web developer creates the Web page(s) using HTML and CSS. Good Web development standard practices should be followed in this step. Examples of good practices include utilizing the proper initial HTML tags, as shown in the previous chapter, and always identifying alt text with images.
5. **Test all Web pages within the Web site**. An important part of Web development is testing to assure that you are following XHTML standards. For the projects in this book, you will use the World Wide Web Consortium (W3C) validator that allows you to test your Web pages and clearly explains any errors it finds. When testing, you should check all content for accuracy. Also, all links (external, internal, and page to page within the same Web site) should be tested.

When necessary, more specific details concerning the above guidelines are presented at appropriate points in the chapter. The chapter also will identify the actions performed and decisions made regarding these guidelines during the creation of the Web page shown in Figure 3–1.

Using Links on a Web Page

As you have learned, many different Web page elements, including text, images, and animations, can serve as links. Text and images are the elements most widely used as links. Figure 3–2 shows examples of text and image links.

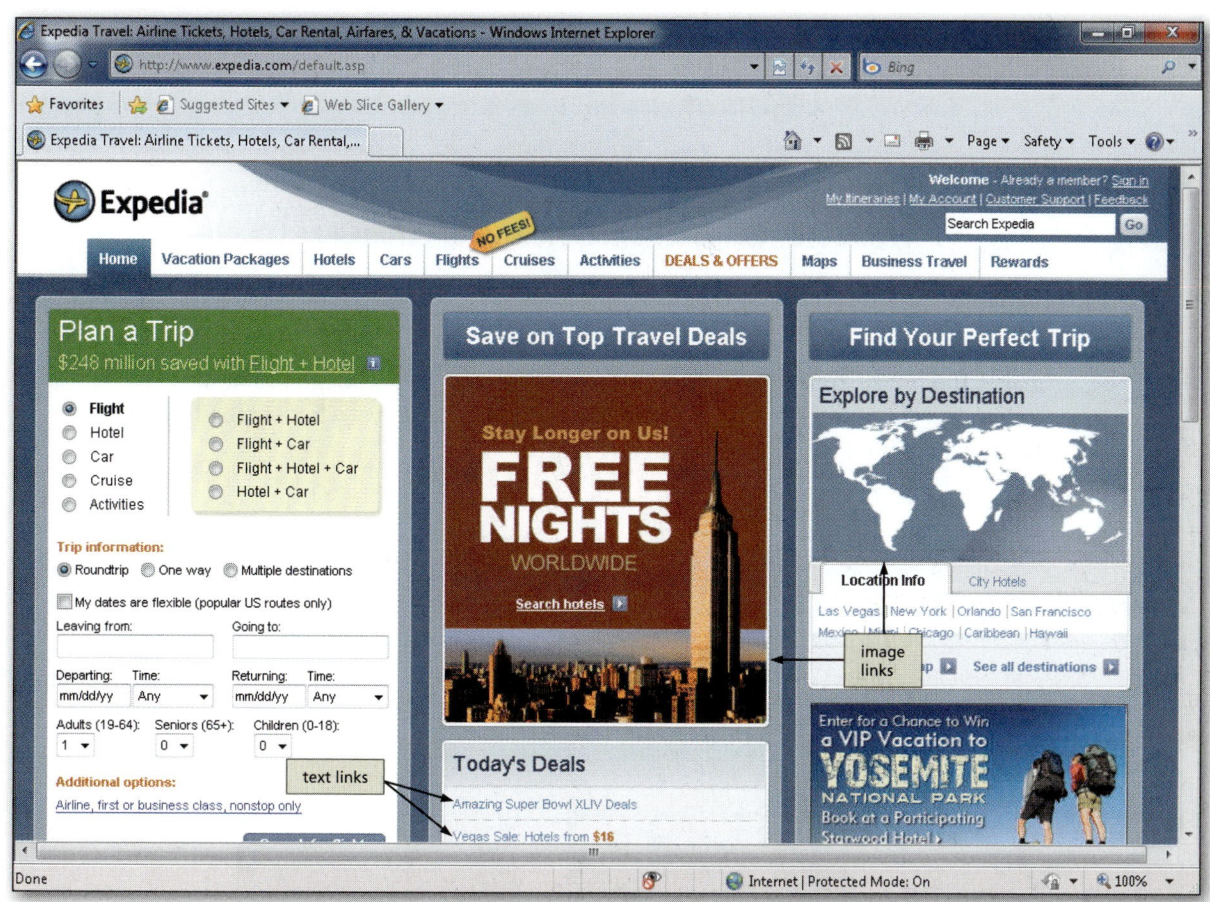

Figure 3–2 Text and image links on a Web page.

When using text links on a Web page, use descriptive text as the clickable word or phrase. For example, the phrase "Click here" does not explain the purpose of the link to the visitor. By contrast, the phrase "Save up to 40% on flights" indicates that the link connects to a Web page with discounted airline tickets.

When text identifies a link, it often appears as underlined text, in a color different from the main Web page text. Unless otherwise changed in the anchor <a> or <body> tags, the browser settings define the colors of text links throughout a Web page. For example, with Internet Explorer, the default color for a normal link that has not been clicked (or visited) is blue, a visited link is purple, and an active link (a link just clicked by a user) varies in color. Figure 3–3 on the next page shows examples of text links in all three states (normal, visited, and active). Generally, as shown in Figure 3–3, moving the mouse pointer over a link causes the mouse pointer to change to a pointing hand. This change notifies the user that a link is available from that text or image.

BTW

Link Help

Many Web sites provide help for new HTML developers. For more information about links, search for key words such as "HTML Tutorials" or "HTML Help" in any good search engine.

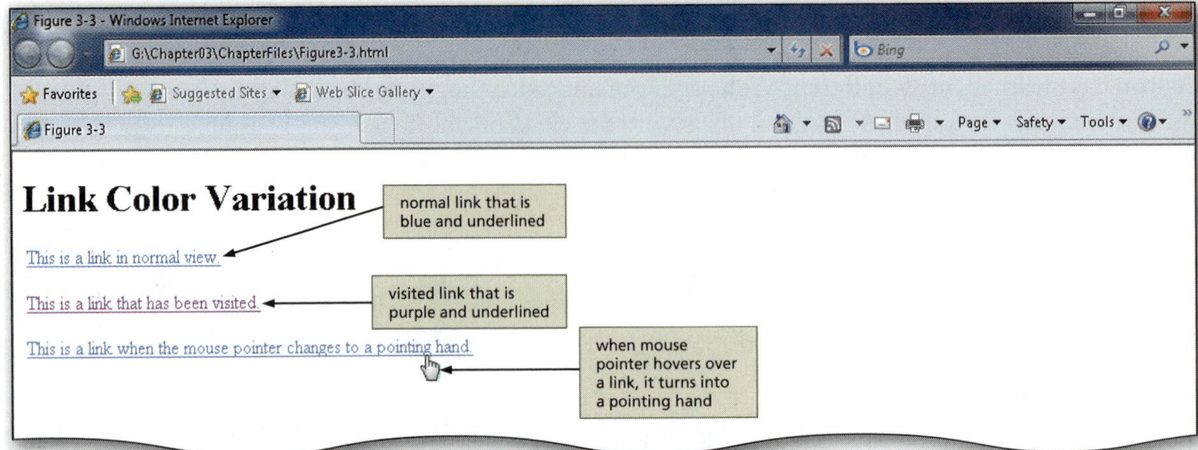

Figure 3–3 Examples of text link color variations.

The same color defaults apply to the border color around an image link. A border makes the image appear as if it has a frame around it. If the image has no border, no frame will appear around the image. The color of the border shows whether the border is a link, and whether the link has been visited (Figure 3–4).

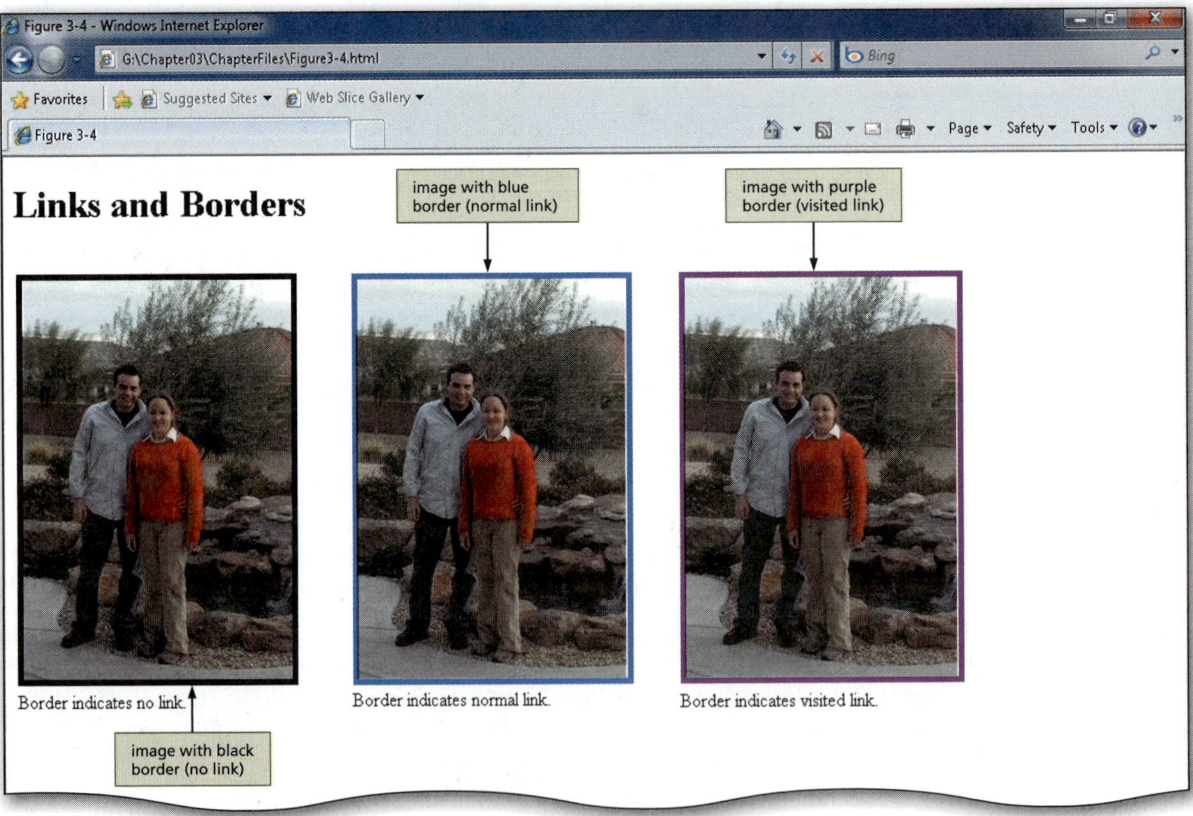

Figure 3–4

If you want to change the color of text links or image link borders to override the browser defaults, you can designate those changes in the anchor <a> or <body> elements using an embedded or external style sheet, or by using an inline style. Recall that you use an inline style to change the appearance (or style) of a single element. An embedded style sheet is used to change the styles of similar elements in one Web page. Finally, an external style sheet is contained in a separate .css document and is used to change the style in an entire Web site. (You will use an external style sheet in the next chapter.) To use an embedded or external style sheet in the anchor element to change normal, visited, and active link colors from the default, you would use the following format:

BTW

Link Colors
You can change the link colors in popular browsers. In Internet Explorer, you find color selection on the Tools menu, Internet Options. In Mozilla Firefox, click the Tools menu, Options, Content tab. In both browsers, you change colors by clicking a color grid.

```
a     {color: black}
```

where color is a designated color name, such as black, or a hexadecimal color code. To make the same change with an inline style, the tag format is:

```
<a style="color: black">
```

You can disable the underlining of a link with the text-decoration property within the anchor tag. The **text-decoration property** allows text to be "decorated" with one of five values: underline, overline, line-through, blink, or none. This property can be used in a variety of tags including the anchor tag. Links, by default, are underlined to indicate that they are links.

In the design phase you should consider carefully the benefits and detriments of any style change, especially to a default style. Be sure that users are still able to immediately see that specific text is used as a link before turning off link underlines or changing the default link color. If you determine that you can effectively turn the underline off on a link (as you do for the image link that you create later in this chapter), you can change the text-decoration attribute to none. To do this with an embedded or external style, you would enter the following code:

```
a     {text-decoration: none}
```

To change text-decoration to none with an inline style, enter:

```
<a style="text-decoration: none">
```

Linking to Another Web Page Within the Same Web Site

Web pages often include links to connect one Web page to another page within the same Web site. For example, a visitor can click a link on the home page of a Web site (Figure 3–5a on the next page) to connect and view another Web page on the same Web site (Figure 3–5b). The Web pages created in this project include links to other pages in the same Web site: (1) the Getting Greener home page includes a text link to the Green Home Web page; and (2) the Green Home Web page includes an image link back to the Getting Greener home page. To link the words "green home" on the gettinggreener.html home page to the greenhome.html Web page, you need the following HTML code:

BTW

Links on a Web Page
An anchor tag also allows visitors to move within a single Web page. Use the name attribute to allow movement from one area to another on the same page. This linking technique is useful, particularly on long pages. An index of links also can provide easy access to various areas within the Web page.

```
<a href="greenhome.html">green home</a>
```

The href in the anchor <a> tag indicates that when the words "green home" are clicked, the visitor links to the greenhome.html Web page. You end the link with the </a> tag. If you did not add the </a> tag, then all text after the words "green home" would be linked.

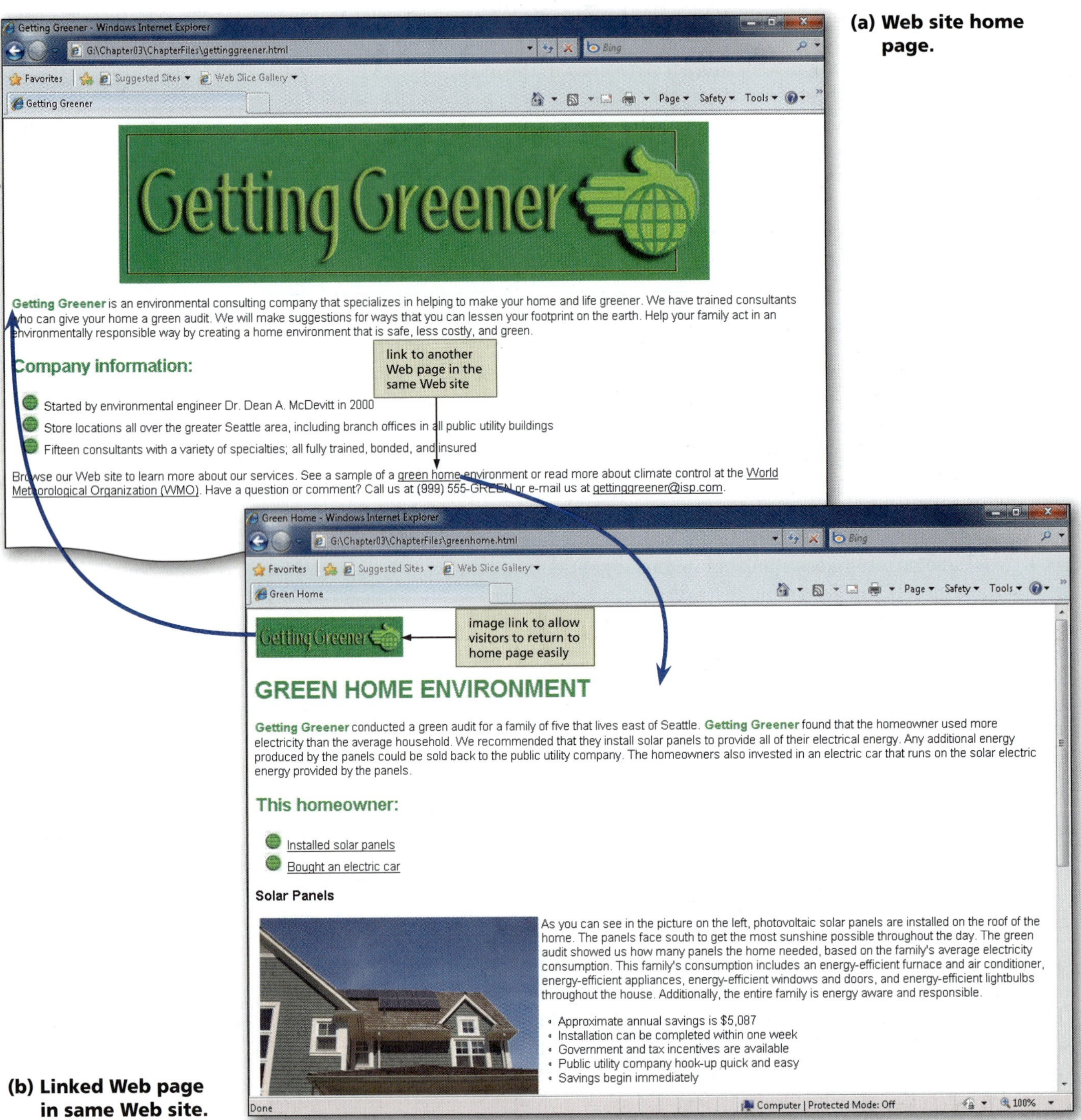

(a) Web site home page.

(b) Linked Web page in same Web site.

Figure 3–5

Linking to a Web Page in Another Web Site

One of the most powerful features of Web development is the ability to link to Web pages outside of your Web site. Web developers use these links to connect their Web pages to other Web pages with information on the same topic. The links are what give the Web its value as an interconnected resource and provide its "webbiness." In this project, the home page (Figure 3–6a) includes a link to a page on another Web site where the visitor can find additional information about climate control (Figure 3–6b). To link the words "World Meteorological Organization (WMO)" on the gettinggreener.html home page to an external Web site, you need the following HTML code:

```
<a href="http://www.wmo.int/">World Meteorological Organization
(WMO)</a>
```

Notice that the code is basically the same as that used to link to a Web page within the same Web site. However, you have to add the complete URL (http://www.wmo.int/) when you link to an external Web site.

(a) Web page with text link to external Web site.

(b) Linked Web page in external Web site.

Figure 3–6

Linking Within a Web Page

Links within a Web page allow visitors to move quickly from one section of the Web page to another. This is especially important in Web pages that are long and require a visitor to scroll down to see all of the content. Many Web pages contain a list of links like a menu or table of contents at the top of the page, with links to sections within the Web page (Figure 3–7). In this project, the Green Home Web page includes links from the top section of the Web page to other sections within the page, as well as links back to the top of the Web page. There are two steps to link within a Web page. First, you have to set a target using a name that makes sense to the purpose of the link. Then, you create a link to that target using the name given. The following HTML code shows an example of a target named solar and then the use of that target as a link. The first statement is inserted at the top of the section of the Web page to which you want to link. The second statement is inserted into the bulleted list at the top of the Web page.

```
<a name="solar"></a>
<a href="#solar">Installed solar panels</a>
```

Again, notice that you also use the anchor <a> tag for this type of link. However, with this inner-page link, you insert the # before the target name to indicate that you want to link to a specific section of the Web page, not necessarily the top of the page. Sometimes when you are browsing the Web, you might see a # used in a link address. That generally links you to a specific section of the Web page.

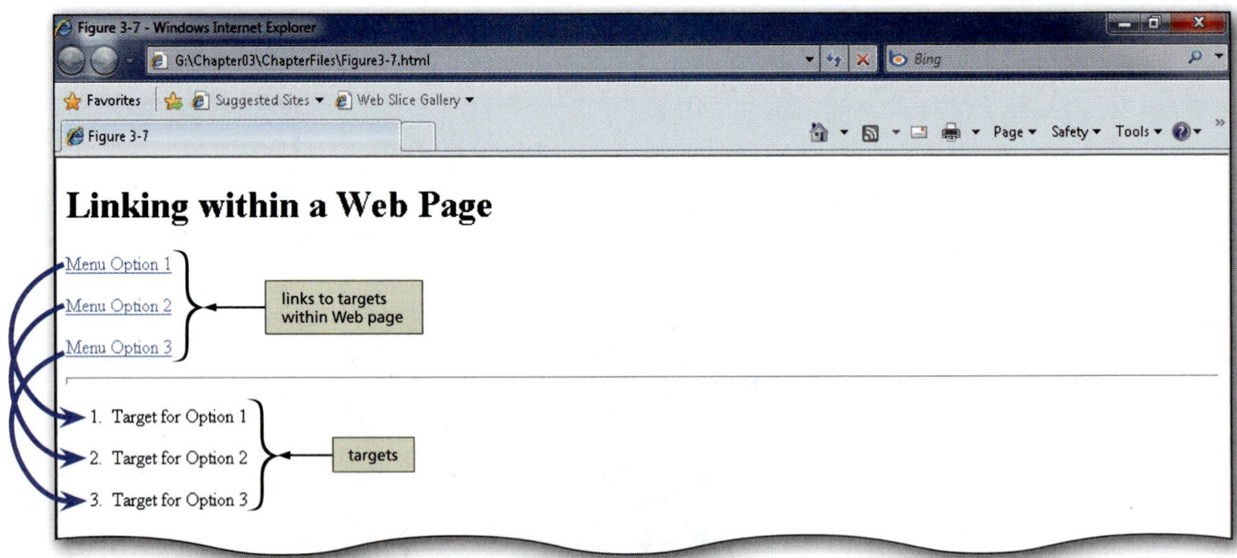

Figure 3–7 Web page with internal links.

> **BTW**
> **E-Mail Links**
> You can assign more than one e-mail address to a mailto: tag. Use the form "mailto:first@isp.com, second@isp.com" in the <a href=> tag. Some older browsers may not support this tag.

Linking to an E-Mail Address

A well-designed Web page always provides a way for visitors to contact the person at the company responsible for maintaining the Web site or addressing customer questions and comments. An easy way to provide contact information is to include an e-mail link on the Web site's home page, as well as on other pages in the Web site. As shown in Figure 3–8, when a visitor clicks the **e-mail link**, it automatically opens a new message in the default e-mail program and inserts the appropriate contact e-mail address in the To field. Visitors then can type and send an e-mail to request additional information, comment on the

Web site, or notify the company of a problem with its Web site. (*Note*: If your browser is not configured to send e-mail, the e-mail link will not work.) The following HTML code shows an example of how to link the words gettinggreener@isp.com to an e-mail link.

```
<a href="mailto:gettinggreener@isp.com">gettinggreener@isp.com</a>
```

You again use the anchor <a> tag for this type of link. In the href attribute, though, you use the mailto:e-mail address as the value. It may seem strange to have the e-mail address gettinggreener@isp.com twice in this code. The first occurrence of the e-mail address is for the link itself. The second occurrence of gettinggreener@isp.com is used for the words on the Web page that you use as the link.

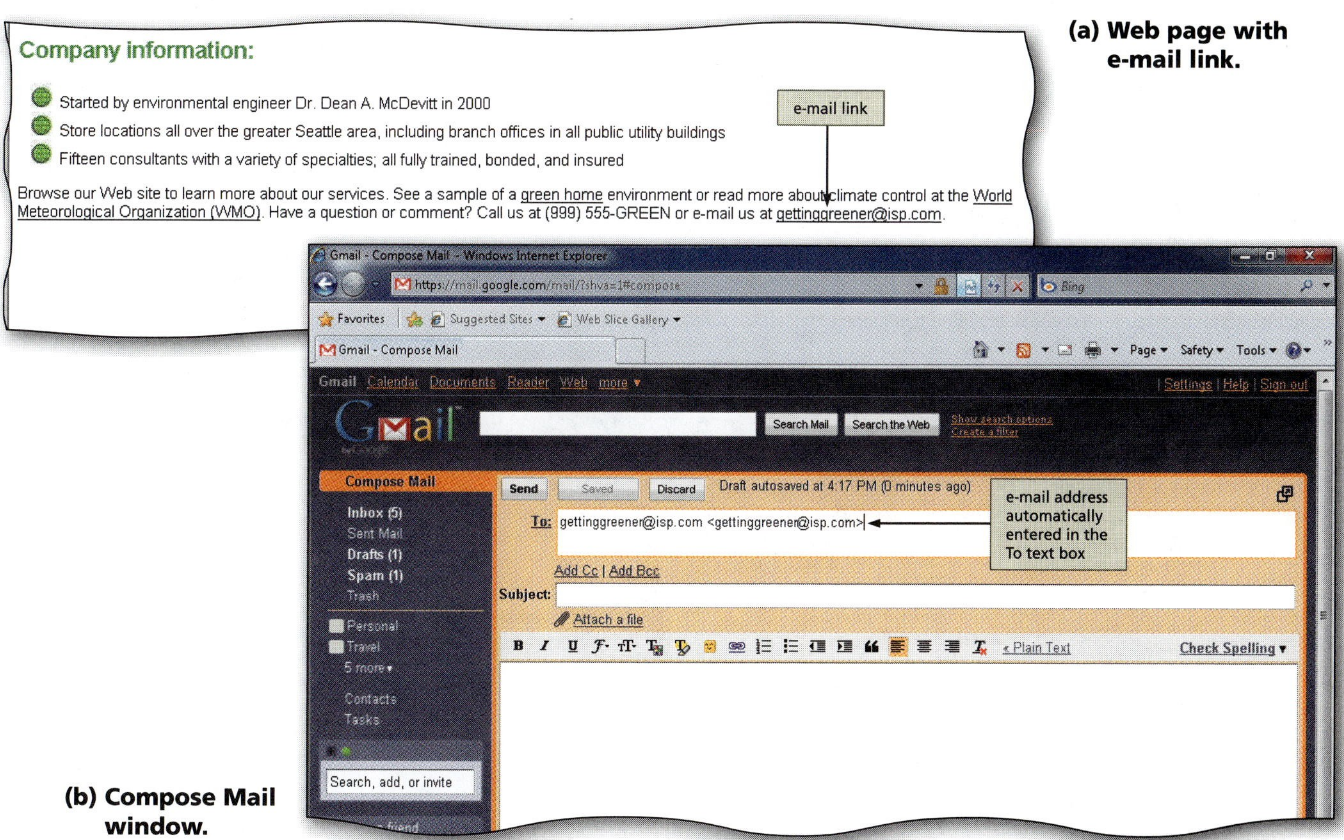

Figure 3–8

Creating a Home Page

The first Web page developed in this chapter is the home page of the Getting Greener Web site. A home page is the main page of a Web site, which visitors to a Web site generally will view first. A Web site home page should identify the purpose of the Web site by briefly stating what content, services, or features it provides. The home page also should indicate clearly what links the visitor should click to move from one page on the site to another. A Web developer should design the Web site in such a way that the links from one Web page to another are apparent and the navigation is clear. The Web site home page also should include an e-mail link, so visitors easily can find contact information for the individual or organization. Many Web sites now include an additional e-mail link to the Web development team. Users can utilize this e-mail link to notify the Web developers of any problems with the Web site or to comment on the site.

You begin creating the home page by starting Notepad++ and entering the initial HTML tags. Then you add an image, heading, text, and an unordered list to your home page. Finally, you add text and e-mail links, and then test the links.

To Start Notepad++

The following steps, which assume Windows 7 is running, start Notepad++ based on a typical installation. You may need to ask your instructor how to start Notepad++ for your computer.

1. Click the Start button on the Windows taskbar to display the Start menu.
2. Click All Programs at the bottom of the left pane on the Start menu to display the All Programs list.
3. Click Notepad++ in the All Programs list.
4. Click Notepad++ in the list to display the Notepad++ window. If there are files already open in Notepad from previous projects, close them all now by clicking the Close button on each open file.
5. If the Notepad++ window is not maximized, click the Maximize button on the Notepad++ title bar to maximize it (Figure 3–9).
6. Click View on the menu bar.
7. If the Word wrap command does not have a check mark next to it, click Word wrap.

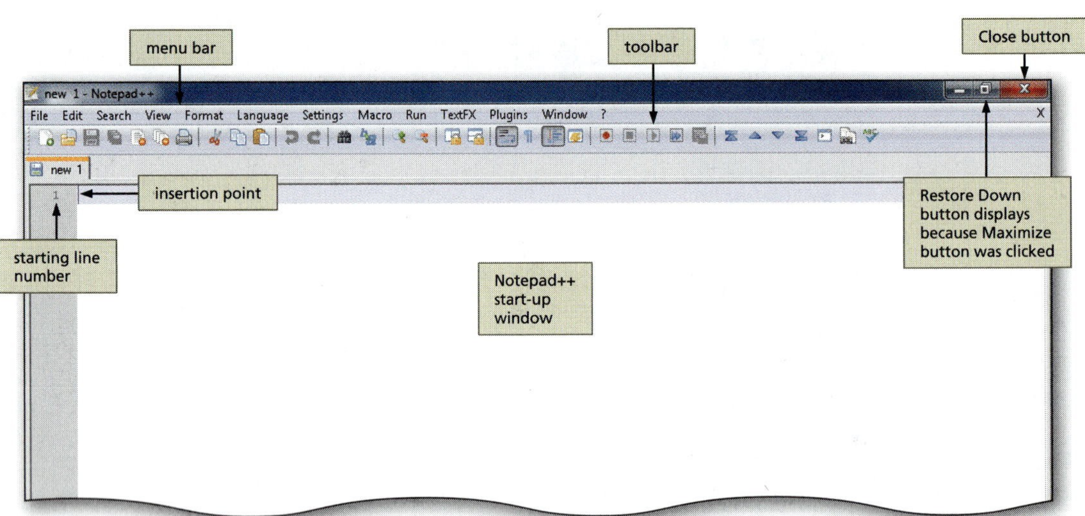

Figure 3–9

To Enter Initial HTML Tags to Define the Web Page Structure

BTW

Copy Initial Structure
Remember that you can type in the initial HTML tags and save that code in a file called structure.html, which you can then open and use as the basis for all HTML files. This eliminates the need for you to type this same code at the beginning of every HTML file. Just remember to save structure.html with a new name as soon as you open it.

Just as you did in Chapter 2, you start your file with the initial HTML tags that define the structure of the Web page. Table 3–1 contains the tags and text for this task.

Table 3–1 Initial HTML Tags

Line	HTML Tag and Text
1	<!DOCTYPE html
2	PUBLIC "-//W3C//DTD XHTML 1.0 Transitional//EN"
3	"http://www.w3.org/TR/xhtml1/DTD/xhtml1-transitional.dtd">
4	
5	<html xmlns="http://www.w3.org/1999/xhtml" xml:lang="en" lang="en">

Table 3–1 Initial HTML Tags (continued)

Line	HTML Tag and Text
6	`<head>`
7	`<meta http-equiv="Content-Type" content="text/html;charset=utf-8" />`
8	`<title>Getting Greener</title>`
9	`</head>`
10	
11	`<body>`
12	
13	`</body>`
14	`</html>`

The following steps illustrate how to enter the initial tags that define the structure of the Web page.

1. Enter the HTML code shown in Table 3–1. Press enter at the end of each line. If you make an error as you are typing, use the backspace key to delete all the characters back to and including the incorrect characters, then continue typing.
2. Position the insertion point on the blank line between the <body> and </body> tags (line 12) and press the enter key (Figure 3–10).
3. Compare what you typed to Figure 3–10. If you notice errors, use your mouse pointer or arrow keys to move the insertion point to the right of each error and use the backspace key to correct the error.

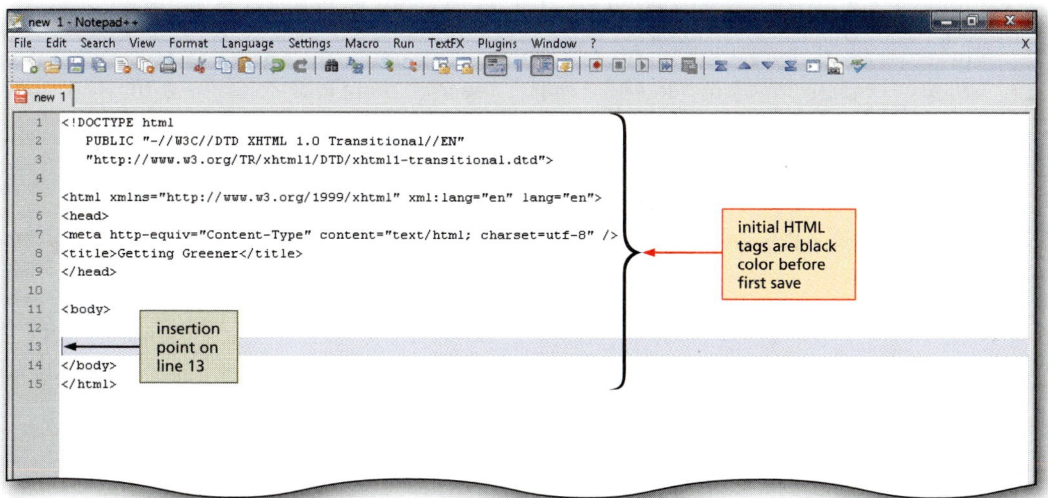

Figure 3–10

To Save an HTML File

With the initial HTML code for the Getting Greener home page entered, you should save the file. Saving the file frequently ensures you won't lose your work. Saving a file in Notepad++ also adds color to code that can help you identify different elements more easily. The following step illustrates how to save an HTML file in Notepad++.

1. With a USB flash drive connected to one of the computer's USB ports, click File on the Notepad++ menu bar and then click Save.
2. Type `gettinggreener.html` in the File name text box (do not press enter).
3. Click Computer in the left pane of the Windows Explorer window to display a list of available drives.
4. If necessary, scroll until UDISK 2.0 (G:) or the name of your storage device is displayed in the list of available drives.
5. Open the Chapter03\ChapterFiles folder.
6. Click the Save button in the Save As dialog box to save the file on the USB flash drive in the Chapter03\ChapterFiles folder with the name gettinggreener.html.

Plan Ahead

Identify how to format various elements of the text.
Before inserting the graphical and color elements on a Web page, you should plan how you want to format them. By effectively utilizing graphics and color, you can call attention to important topics on the Web page without overpowering it. Consider the following formatting suggestions.

- **Effectively utilize graphics.** An important part of Web development is the use of graphics to call attention to a Web page. Generally, companies utilize the same logo on their Web site as they use on print material associated with the company, such as business cards and letterheads. Using the same graphical image on all marketing materials, including the Web site, is a good way to provide a consistent visual and brand message to customers.
- **Utilize headings that connect to the graphics.** In many cases, companies use the logo banner as the main heading on their home page, as opposed to using an <h1> heading. It is sometimes good to coordinate the color of the headings and graphics contained on the Web page to the logo banner. This can bring attention to the company logo banner, and it makes the Web page look cohesive with coordinating colors. Heading size standards should generally be followed from h1 (the largest) to h6 (the smallest). In this project, though, you use the company logo banner as your main heading, so you have no h1 heading. You therefore start with the next smaller size heading, h2, as shown in Figure 3–1a on page HTML 91. Figure 3–1b on page HTML 91 shows the use of h1 and h2 headings in appropriate precedence.

To Add a Center-Aligned Banner Image Using an Inline Style

The Getting Greener home page includes an image logo banner to provide visual appeal, catch the visitor's interest, and promote the company's brand. The following steps illustrate how to add an image to a Web page using an inline style to center the image and an <img> tag to insert the image. To use the inline style, you need the <div> </div> tags. Remember that the <div></div> tags create a container that defines logical divisions in your Web page. The <div> tag is similar to a paragraph tag, but it allows you to divide the page into larger sections and to define the style of whole sections within your Web page. You could define a section of your page and give that section a different style from the surrounding text. When you use the <div> </div> tags, you are able to design a layout that uses CSS, including inserting images. You use the <div></div> tags in this case to center the image on the Web page. Table 3–2 contains the code for adding the centered logo banner.

Table 3–2 HTML Code for Adding a Center-Aligned Banner Image

Line	HTML Tag and Text
13	`<div style="text-align: center">`
14	`    <img src="earthlogo.jpg" width="735" height="190" alt="Green logo" />`
15	`</div>`

- With the insertion point on line 13, enter the HTML code shown in Table 3–2, pressing ENTER at the end of each line. Make sure to indent the second line of code by using the TAB key. This separates the start and end <div> tags from the <img> tag, highlighting the image insertion. Press the ENTER key twice at the end of line 15 to position the insertion point on line 17 (Figure 3–11).

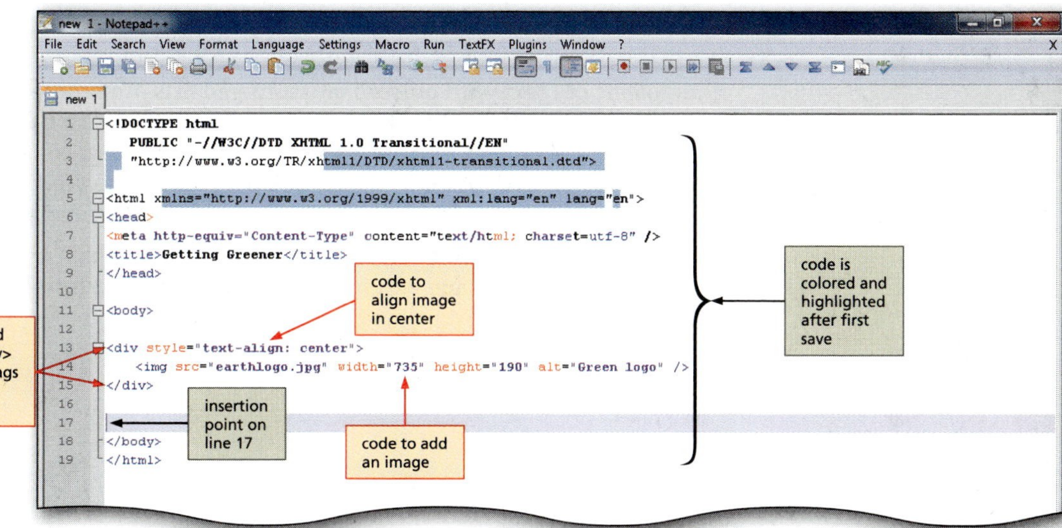

Figure 3–11

Q&A Why should I include the width, height, and alt attributes?

Adding width and height attributes can improve page loading time because the browser does not have to figure the width and height before loading the image. Never use the height and width attributes to resize an image, however. Use graphic editing software to resize it and save it with a different file name. The height and width attributes as used in the img tag should reflect the actual image size. The alt attribute provides information about the purpose of the image when the user's mouse hovers over the image and while the image is loading.

Q&A What is the purpose of the <div> </div> tags?

The <div> tag defines a division or a section in an HTML document. The <div> tag is often used to group elements to format them with styles. In this case, to center the image, you have to use the <div> </div> tags. The statement style="text-align: center" is the inline style that centers this image. An image is left-aligned by default.

Plan Ahead

Identify how to format text elements of the home page.

You should always make a plan before inserting the text elements of a Web page. By formatting the characters and paragraphs on a Web page, you can improve its overall appearance. Effectively formatting the text also makes the message or purpose of the Web page clearer to the users. On a Web page, consider the following formatting suggestions.

- **Use default text size when appropriate**. The body text consists of all text between the heading and the bottom of the Web page. This text is the main content of the Web page and should be used to highlight the key points of your message. You can vary your content by utilizing both paragraphs of text and lists.
- **Determine what text formatting to use**. In a long Web page, it may help to vary your text as a way to break information up between headings. Using bold, color, or italicized text sparingly gives the Web page a more interesting look. Make sure not to overdo the formatting of text because you can make the page look cluttered. It is more difficult to find the content for which you are searching in a cluttered Web page.
- **Determine what style sheets to use**. Consider using style sheets to vary the format of text elements. If the text varies across paragraphs, an inline style is good to use. If you want all of the text in the Web page to be the same, an embedded style sheet is appropriate. If the text is common across more than one Web page, an external style sheet (discussed in the next chapter) should be used.
- **Highlight key text with ordered or unordered lists**. An ordered or unordered list contains specific information that is more clearly identified by a list versus a paragraph of text. In this project, you use a bulleted (unordered) list but vary it by changing the type of bullet used. Using an image as a bullet gives the Web page a nice look and is different than the standard (default) disc bullet for unordered lists.
- **Determine other information suitable for the home page**. Other information that is suitable for a home page includes: the company address (often found in the logo), a phone number, and an e-mail link.

To Add Paragraphs of Text

After the earth logo image for the Getting Greener home page is inserted, you need to add two paragraphs of text introducing Getting Greener. Table 3–3 shows the tags and text to enter.

Table 3–3 HTML Code for Adding Two Paragraphs of Text

Line	HTML Tag and Text
17	<p>Getting Greener is an environmental consulting company that specializes in helping to make your home and life greener. We have trained consultants who can give your home a green audit. We will make suggestions for ways that you can lessen your footprint on the earth. Help your family act in an environmentally responsible way by creating a home environment that is safe, less costly, and green.</p>
18	
19	<p>Browse our Web site to learn more about our services. See a sample of a green home environment or read more about climate control at the World Meteorological Organization (WMO). Have a question or comment? Call us at (999) 555-GREEN or e-mail us at gettinggreener@isp.com.</p>

1 With the insertion point on line 17, enter the HTML code shown in Table 3–3. Press enter twice after the </p> tag on line 17 and once after the </p> tag on line 19. After entering the two paragraphs, the insertion point is on line 20 (Figure 3–12).

Q&A Do I have to end all paragraphs of text with the </p> tag?

A Web page without </p> tags would display in the browser correctly. This Web page would not pass validation using the W3C Markup Validation Service, however. One missed </p> tag will result in many errors during validation.

Q&A What if I wanted the second paragraph to start without a blank line above it?

If you wanted the second paragraph to move to the next line without a blank line in between, you would use the <br /> tag instead of <p> </p>.

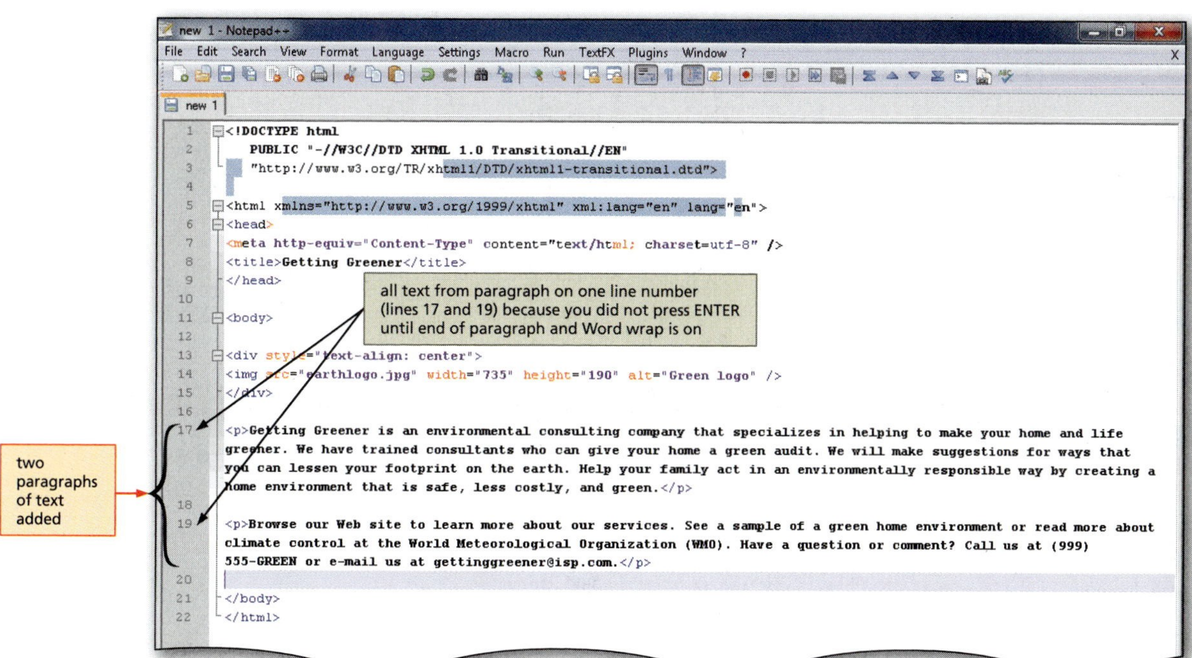

Figure 3–12

Using an Inline Style to Add Interest to a Bulleted List

You've decided to highlight company information on the home page with an unordered (bulleted) list. To integrate the list with the rest of the page, and to add interest, you want to make the bullets the same as the earth symbol in the company logo. To do this, you'll add an h2 heading above the list and use an inline style to create the bullets.

Inserting an h2 heading above the unordered list visually separates the list from other elements on the Web page and indicates what the items in the list describe. An h1 heading is normally the main heading of the Web page, but in this case, the logo (earthlogo.jpg) is used in lieu of the h1 heading. It serves the same purpose to identify the company and call attention to the top of the Web page. Using an h1 heading under the logo banner would be redundant. So you will start with an h2 heading because it is smaller and an appropriate size to set off the bulleted list.

There are a variety of list-style types (bullets and numbers) that you can use, as described in Chapter 2. You used an inline style with the list-style-type property to make square bullets for the Chapter 2 project. For this Web page, you are going to use the list-style-image property to use a small image (earthbullet.jpg) instead of a disc, circle, or square bullet. You do this by identifying the image earthbullet.jpg as the URL to display in place of a bullet.

To Create an Unordered (Bulleted) List Using Images as Bullets

Table 3–4 shows the HTML code used to add an h2 heading and create a bulleted list with “earth” image bullets for the Getting Greener home page.

Table 3–4 HTML Code for Creating an Unordered (Bulleted) List with Image Bullets

Line	HTML Tag and Text
19	`<h2>Company information:</h2>`
20	
21	`<ul style="list-style-image: url(earthbullet.jpg)">`
22	`<li>Started by environmental engineer Dr. Dean A. McDevitt in 2000</li>`
23	`<li>Store locations all over the greater Seattle area, including branch offices in all public utility buildings</li>`
24	`<li>Fifteen consultants with a variety of specialties; all fully trained, bonded, and insured</li>`
25	`</ul>`

The following step shows how to create the unordered (bulleted) list that appears on the Getting Greener home page.

- Click the blank line 18 and press the ENTER key.
- Enter the HTML code shown in Table 3–4.
- After the </ul> in line 25, press the ENTER key to insert a blank line on line 26 (Figure 3–13).

Q&A What if I wanted to use a different bullet type?

For an open circle bullet, use list-style-type: "circle". To use the default disc (filled circle) bullet, the list-style-type does not need to be included.

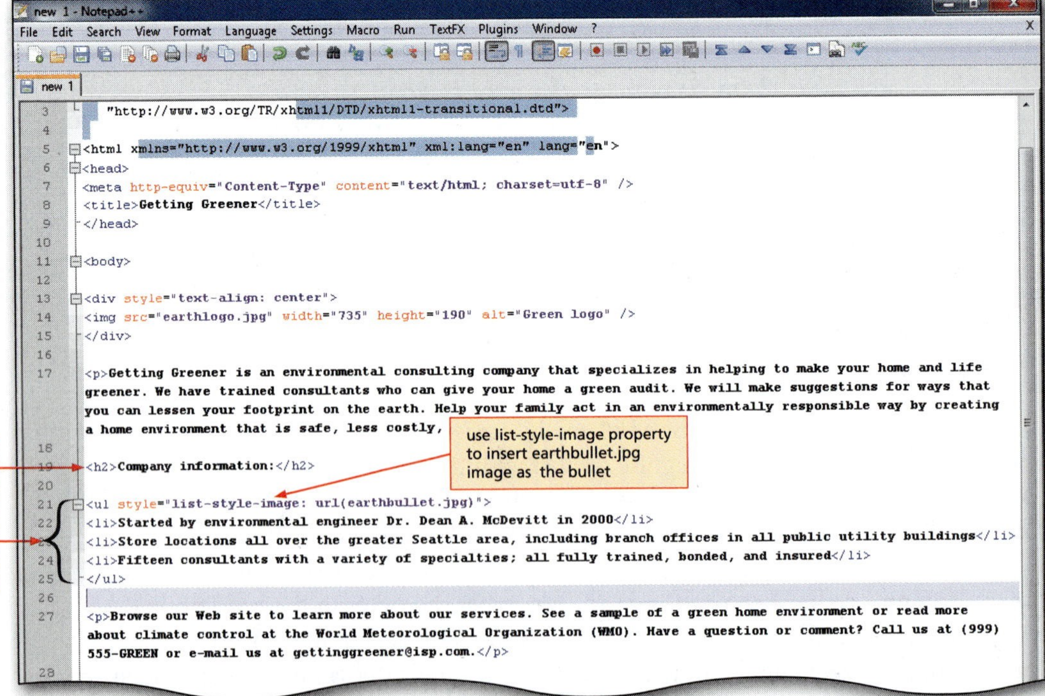

Figure 3–13

Plan how and where to use the four types of links.

- **Identify how to link from the home page to another page in the same Web site.** Linking to another Web page in the same Web site is often done with text links. When determining what words to use, make sure that the text links are clear and easy to understand. Using a phrase such as "click here" is not one that clearly identifies where the link will go. Choosing words such as "green home" tells the Web site visitor to click that link if they want to see a sample of a green home.
- **Use an e-mail link on the home page.** A good standard practice is to include an e-mail link on the home page. Again, using words such as "click here" are not as effective as using a company's actual e-mail address (gettinggreener@isp.com in this case) as the e-mail link text.
- **Determine external links for the home page.** Visitors to a Web site might want additional information on a topic, so a link also can be included on the home page. Linking to an external Web site (i.e., one that is outside of the boundaries of the current Web site) is appropriate to provide additional information. Again, it is important to select words or phrases that make sense for that link.
- **Use internal links on long Web pages.** Another good standard practice is to include links within a Web page when the page is long (i.e., when you have to press the PAGE DOWN key several times to get to the end of the Web page). Internal links help visitors navigate more easily within long Web pages. Also consider using links to help the visitor easily return back to the top of a long Web page.

Plan Ahead

Adding a Text Link to Another Web Page Within the Same Web Site

For the purpose of this Web site, the <a> and </a> tags are used to create links on a Web page. The <a> tag also is called the **anchor tag** because it is used to create anchors for links to another page in the same Web site, to a Web page in an external Web site, within the same Web page, and for e-mail links. The anchor tag can also be used to specify the base language of the target URL or to specify the media type of the link. The href attribute stands for a hyperlink reference. This is a reference (an address) to a resource on the Web. Hyperlinks can point to any resource on the Web, including an HTML page, an image, a sound file, or a video. The basic form of the tag used to create a link is:

```
<a href="URL">linktext</a>
```

where linktext is the clickable word or phrase that is displayed on the Web page and the value for href (hypertext reference) is the name or URL of the linked page or file. Table 3–5 shows some of the <a> tag attributes and their functions.

BTW

Other Links
You also can create a link to other Web pages (that is, non-http), an FTP site, and newsgroups. To link to an FTP site, type ftp://URL rather than http://URL as used in this project. For a newsgroup, type news:newsgroup name, and for any particular article within the newsgroup, type news:article name as the entry.

Table 3–5 <a> Tag Attributes and Functions

Attribute	Function
href	Specifies the URL of the linked page or file.
name	Defines a name for the current anchor so it may be the target or destination of another link. Each anchor on a Web page must use a unique name.
rel	Indicates a forward relationship from the current document to the linked document. The value of the rel attribute is a link type, such as prev, next, index, or copyright. For example, the Web page chapter3.html might include the tag <a rel="next" href="chapter4.html"> to indicate a link to the Web page for the next chapter, chapter4.html.

Table 3–5 <a> Tag Attributes and Functions (continued)

Attribute	Function
rev	Indicates a reverse (backward) relationship from the current document to the linked document. The value of the rev attribute is a link type, such as prev, next, index, or copyright. For example, the chapter3.html Web page might include the tag <a rev="prev" href="chapter2.html"> to indicate a link to the Web page for the previous chapter, chapter2.html.
type	Specifies the content type (also known as media types or MIME types) of the linked page or file to help a browser determine if it can handle the resource type. Examples of content types include text/html, image/jpeg, video/quicktime, application/java, text/css, and text/javascript.

Before creating a link, be sure you know the URL or name of the file to be linked and the text that will serve as the clickable word or phrase. The words should be descriptive and tell the Web page visitor the purpose of the link. For the Getting Greener home page, the text link is a phrase in a paragraph at the bottom of the Web page.

To Add a Text Link to Another Web Page Within the Same Web Site

The Getting Greener home page includes a text link to the Green Home Web page, which is part of the same Web site. The following step illustrates how to add a text link to another Web page within the same Web site.

1

- Click immediately to the left of the g in the word green on line 27.
- Type `<a href="greenhome.html">` to start the link, setting the Web page greenhome.html as the linked Web page.
- Click immediately to the right of the e in home on line 27. Type `</a>` to close the link (Figure 3–14).

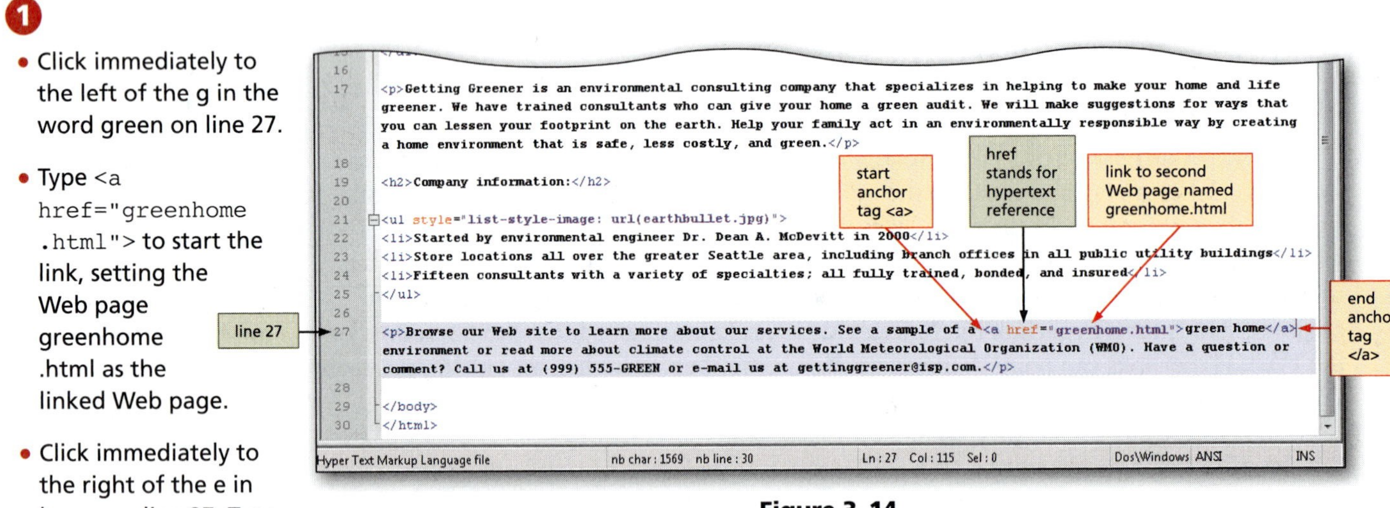

Figure 3–14

Q&A What is the href attribute for?

The href stands for "hypertext reference" and precedes the URL of the destination Web page.

Q&A How will I know if my text is a link when it is displayed in the browser?

In the browser, the mouse pointer turns into a pointing finger where there is a link. Also, as the default, text used as a link will be blue and underlined. You can change the color and style of a link, and you do that later in the chapter.

Q&A What happens if I forget to insert the </a> tag on a link?

A text link without the </a> tag will not display correctly in the browser. If you forget to use the </a> tag to end this text link, all of the text beyond the <a href=""> tag will serve as that link. In this example, all of the text that follows the g in green will link to the greenhome.html Web page, which is certainly not what you want.

Adding an E-Mail Link

Adding an e-mail link is similar to adding a text link, but instead of using a URL as the href attribute value, the href attribute value for an e-mail link uses the form:

```
<a href="mailto:address@email.com">linktext</a>
```

where the href attribute value uses the word mailto to indicate it is an e-mail link, followed by a colon and the e-mail address to which to send the e-mail message. When the browser recognizes a **mailto** URL in a clicked link, it automatically opens a new message in the default e-mail program and inserts the appropriate contact e-mail address in the To field. The clickable text used for an e-mail link typically is the e-mail address used in the e-mail link. The Web page also should provide some information before the link, so visitors know the purpose of the e-mail link.

BTW

E-Mail Links

E-Mail Links may not work in a school setting because there may not be an e-mail client installed on the school servers. You therefore may not be able to test this link.

To Add an E-Mail Link

The Getting Greener home page includes an e-mail link so customers can contact Getting Greener for additional information or to comment on the Web page. The <a> and </a> tags used to create a text link to a Web page also are used to create an e-mail link. The following step shows how to add an e-mail link to a Web page.

- Click immediately to the left of the g in the beginning of gettinggreener@isp .com on line 27. Type `<a href="mailto: gettinggreener@ isp.com">` as the start of the e-mail link. This will link to the e-mail address get-tinggreener@isp.com when the link is clicked.

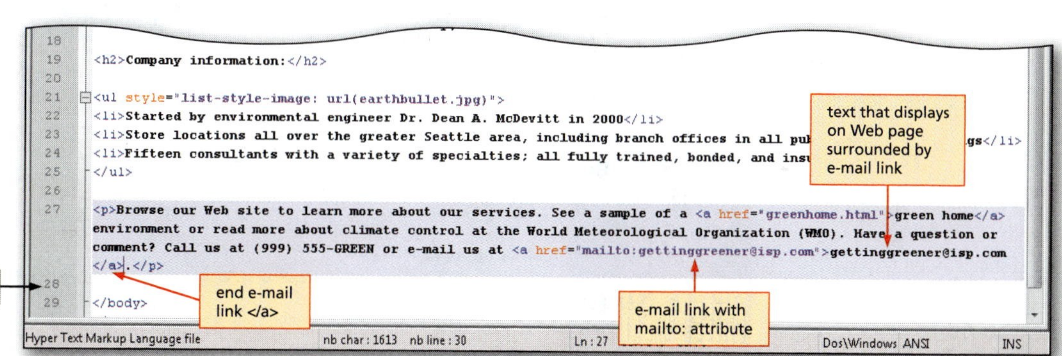

Figure 3–15

- Click immediately after the m in isp.com and before the period in the e-mail address text on line 27.
- Type `</a>` to end the e-mail link, as shown in Figure 3–15.

Q&A

I see two occurrences of gettinggreener@isp.com on line 27. Why do I need two?

The first occurrence of gettinggreener@isp.com (the one within the link <a> tag following the mailto:) is the destination of the link. The second occurrence of gettinggreener@isp.com is the text link itself that will be displayed in the browser.

Adding Other Information to an E-Mail Link

Sometimes, you need to add a message in the body of the e-mail in addition to the subject. This technique can be very helpful when more than one e-mail link is positioned on a Web page, and each link has a different purpose. For instance, one e-mail might be used for general questions, whereas another link might be used for specific information. You also can include a carbon-copy (cc) address. For instance, to include just a subject or to include a subject and body message text in the above mailto:, you would complete the following steps.

To Add a Subject to an E-Mail Link

1 Type `<a href="mailto:gettinggreener@isp.com?subject=green home">` as the tag.

Sometimes, you need to add a message in the body of the e-mail in addition to the subject. This technique can be very helpful when more than one e-mail link is positioned on a Web page, and each link has a different purpose. For instance, one e-mail might be used for general questions, whereas another link might be used for specific information. Using the subject and body attributes can be helpful for this scenario. Notice that the two attributes (subject and body) are separated by an ampersand in the following example. The following step shows how to add the subject "green home" to the e-mail together with the message text "How can I get a green audit?" as shown in Figure 3–16.

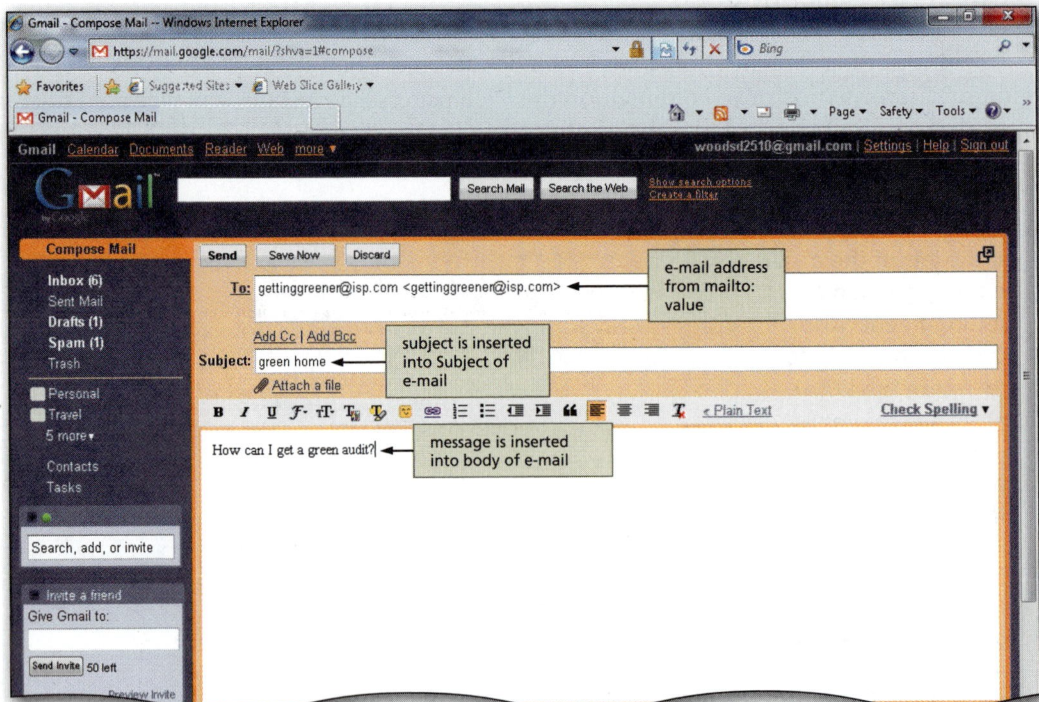

Figure 3–16

To Add a Subject Together with Body Message Text

1 Type `<a href="mailto:gettinggreener@isp.com?subject=green home;body=How can I get a green audit?">` as the tag.

To Add a Text Link to a Web Page in Another Web Site

The <a> and </a> tags used to create a text link to a Web page within the same Web site also are used to create a link to a Web page in another Web site. The following step illustrates how to add a text link on the Green Home Web page to an external Web page that describes climate control information.

- Click immediately to the left of the W in World on line 27 and type `<a href="http://www.wmo.int/">` to add the text link that will connect to the external Web site when clicked.

```
18
19  <h2>Company information:</h2>
20
21  <ul style="list-style-image: url(earthbullet.jpg)">
22  <li>Started by environmental engineer Dr. Dean A. McDevitt in 2000</l
23  <li>Store locations all over the greater Seattle area, including bran        n all public utility buildings</li>
24  <li>Fifteen consultants with a variety of specialties; all fully trai        , and insured</li>
25  </ul>
26
27  <p>Browse our Web site to learn more about our services. See a sample of a <a href="greenhome.html">green home</a>
    environment or read more about climate control at the <a href="http://www.wmo.int/">World Meteorological
    Organization (WMO)</a>. Have a question or comment? Call us at (999) 555-GREEN or e-mail us at <a href=
    "mailto:gettinggreener@isp.com">gettinggreener@isp.com</a>.</p>
28
29  </body>
```


Figure 3–17

- Click immediately to the right of the) in (WMO) on line 27 and type `</a>` to end the tag, as shown in Figure 3–17.

Q&A When I type in the URL in the Address box of my browser, I never type in the http:// part of the URL. Why do I have to add the http:// in the link?

Although you do not need to type the http:// into the URL on the browser, you always must include this as part of the href when creating external links. See the discussion on absolute and relative paths below for more information.

Q&A Why did I need the http:// part of the URL for this external link, but I did not need that for the green home link?

The Green Home Web page is stored in the same folder as the home page from which you are linking. You, therefore, do not need to include any information other than the name of the Web page file. Review the following section on absolute and relative paths for more information.

Q&A When I link to the external Web page (*www.wmo.int*), I have to use the Back button on the browser to return to my home page. Is that the only way to get back?

Yes. You have to use the Back button because this is an external Web site. There is no way to provide a link back to your home page from an external Web site. In later chapters, you will learn how to open a new window for external sites.

Using Absolute and Relative Paths

At this point, it is appropriate to revisit the overall concept of how the files are organized and saved. As noted in the last chapter, the projects in this book use a very simple folder structure. In this book, the graphical images are stored in the same folder as the HTML files, for example, in the Chapter03\ChapterFiles folder. For most real-world applications, however, it would be more appropriate to separate the HTML code and the graphical images into different folders. Figure 3–18 on the next page shows an example of a more complex file structure that could be used for this book.

To understand how to use this sort of folder structure, you need to identify the folder location, or path, to the files. A **path** describes the location (folder or external Web site) where the files can be found, beginning with the UDISK G:\ drive (or another drive

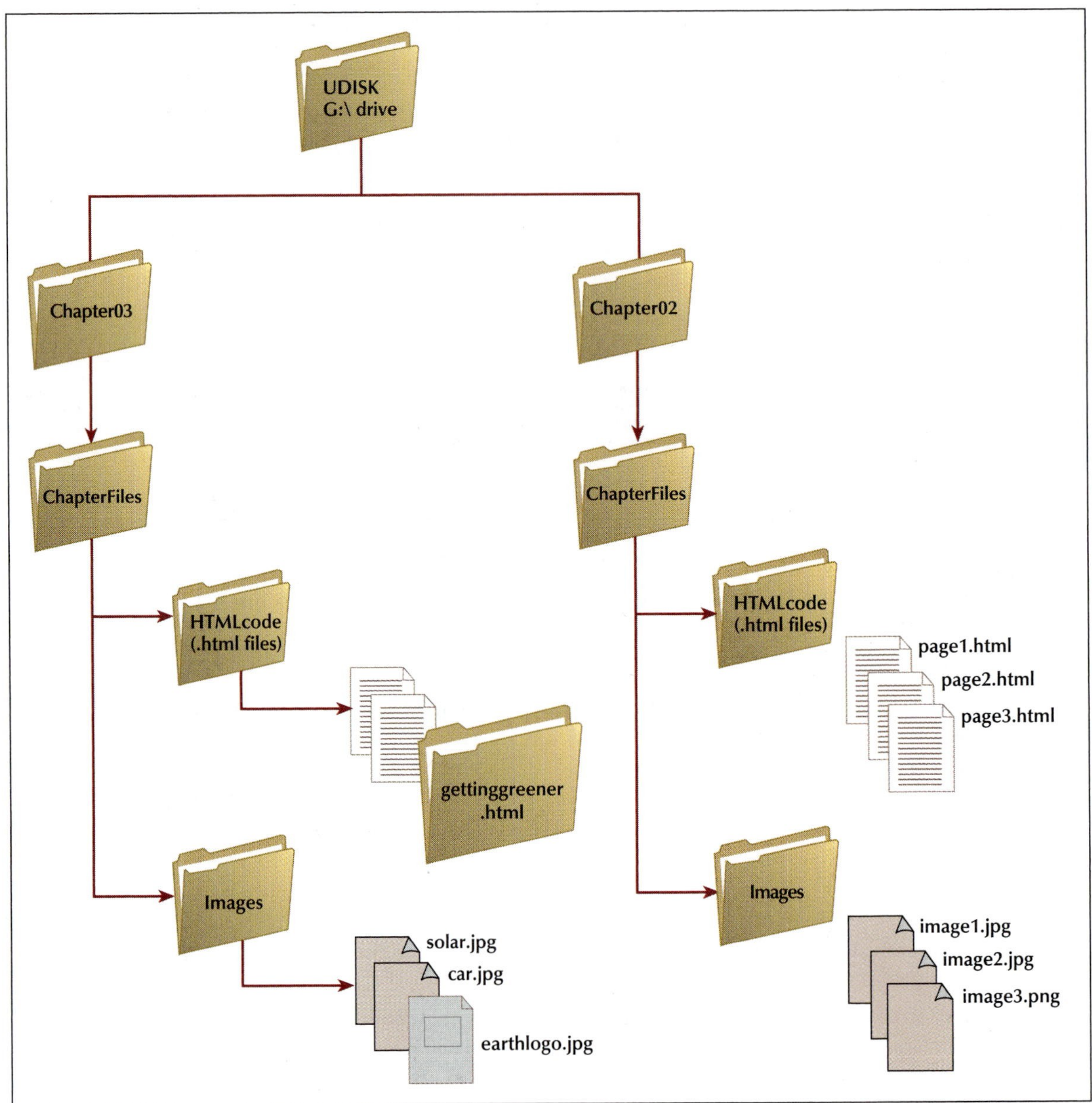

Figure 3–18

on your computer). This beginning location also is known as root. You can use either an absolute or relative path when identifying the location of the files. An **absolute path** specifies the exact address for the file to which you are linking or displaying a graphic. You can think of an absolute path as the complete address of a house, including the house number, street name, city, state, and zip. In order to use that absolute address, you would have to give the entire path (or address) to a person who wants to get to that particular house. When you are referencing a Web page from a server outside of the server on which your Web pages reside, you have to use an absolute path. In this chapter, you use the absolute path to the World Meteorological Organization (WMO). This is because that Web page is located outside of the server (or storage media) on which the Web pages created in the chapter reside. Your link statement for this external Web site is:

```
<a href="http://www.wmo.int/">World Meteorological Organization
(WMO)</a>
```

Although absolute paths indicate the specific addresses of files, they can be cumbersome. If you have to move any of the files to a different folder or a different Web server, then all absolute paths would have to change.

Relative paths specify the location of a file, relative to the location of the file that is currently in use. This is analogous to telling someone your house is located four doors down from the only gas station on that street. Your address in this case is relative to the beginning point, the gas station. Because your user has a beginning point (the gas station), you can describe the ending address (the house) relative to the beginning. A relative path allows you to move up the folder structure. So in the example in which you want to display the image earthlogo.jpg (stored in the Images subfolder) from the Web page gettinggreener.html (stored in the HTMLcode subfolder) within the Chapter03\ChapterFiles folder, you would use the following relative path structure:

```
\Images\earthlogo.jpg
```

Looking at Figure 3–18, you would store the image earthlogo.jpg in the Images folder and store the Web page itself, the gettinggreener.html file, in the HTMLcode subfolder. If you moved to the HTMLcode subfolder and viewed the gettinggreener.html file, the image earthlogo.jpg would not appear because it is not in the same subfolder. To display the gettinggreener.html file with the earthlogo.jpg image, you would use the following relative path structure:

```
<img src="Images/earthlogo.jpg" width="735" height="190"
alt="Green logo" />
```

Another example is the relative addressing that you use in this chapter to link to the second Web page from the home page, and vice versa. The HTML code to link from the home page, gettinggreener.html to the second Web page is:

```
<a href="greenhome.html">green home</a>
```

and to go from the greenhome.html Web page back to the home page, your HTML code is:

```
<a href="gettinggreener.html">home page</a>
```

For another example, let's see what the code would look like if you had two folders for this chapter project. You currently have one folder ChapterFiles in the Chapter03 folder. To have the same basic folder structure as you see in Figure 3–18, you would create a second folder named Images that is on the same folder level as ChapterFiles. So you would then have two folders in the Chapter03 folder. If you moved your images (solar.jpg and car.jpg) to that Images folder, your HTML code to access those images would look like this:

```
<p><img src="Images/solar.jpg" width="348" height="261"
alt="Solar panels" /></p>

<p><img src="Images/car.jpg" width="261" height="202"
alt="Electric car" /></p>
```

It is better to use relative paths for flexibility whenever feasible. If the root folder (i.e., the "highest" folder in the hierarchy) must change for some reason, you do not have to change all addressing if you used relative paths. As an example, if you had to change from g:\Chapter03\ to another folder, all related subfolders would automatically change. With absolute addressing, all paths would have to be individually changed.

Adding Interest and Focus with Styles

In Chapter 2, you learned how to vary the size of headings with the <h1> through <h6> tags. Any text on a Web page, including headings, can be formatted with a different color or style to make it stand out by using style properties. Table 3–6 lists some properties that can be used to enhance standard text on a Web page using styles. Remember that CSS and styles are the preferred technique to satisfy XHTML standards.

BTW

Font Properties
Refer to Appendix D for a more complete list of CSS font properties and values. You can also set font characteristics with the HTML <font> tag (see Appendix A), but this deprecated tag is not used in this project.

Table 3–6 Font Properties and Values

Property	Function
color	• Changes the font color • Can use a six-digit color code or color name
font-family	• Changes the font face or type • Values include fonts, such as Verdana or Arial; text appears using the default font if the font face is not specified
font-size	• Changes the font size. • Value can be an actual numeric size, a percentage, or values such as large, medium, small, etc.
font-style	• Changes the style of a font • Values include normal, italic, and oblique
font-weight	• Changes the weight of a font • Values include normal, bold, bolder, and lighter

Figure 3–19 shows how several of these attributes affect the appearance of text.

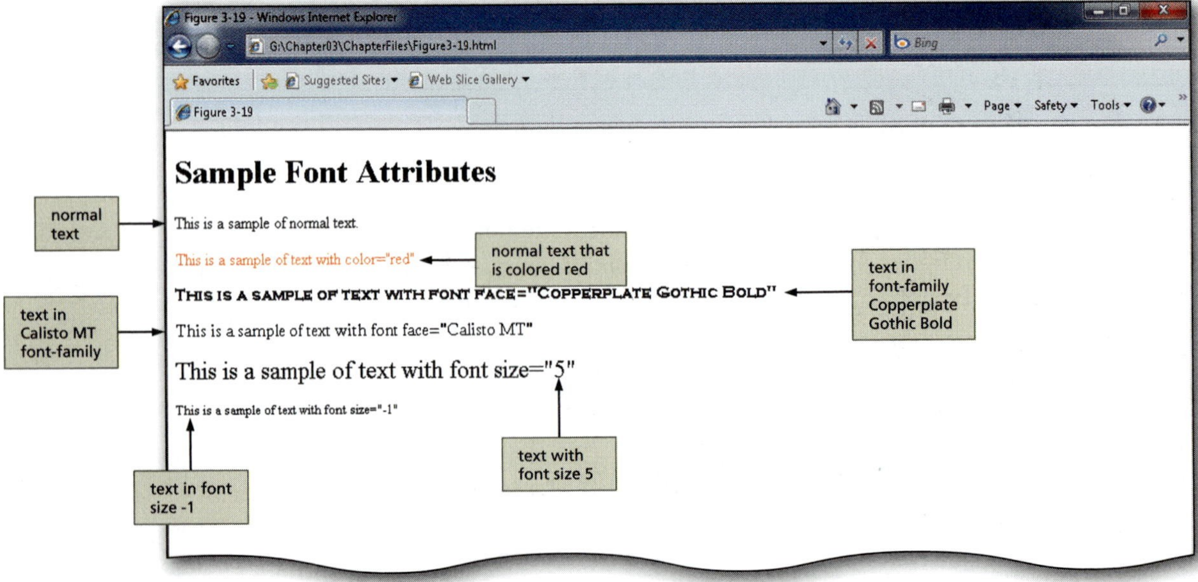

Figure 3–19 Examples of various fonts.

Adding Interest and Focus with HTML Tags

There is another way to format text that is compliant with the XHTML 1.0 Transitional standard used in this book. Web pages that use the Transitional DOCTYPE statement allow the use of deprecated tags, as explained in Chapter 2. These Web pages validate the HTML elements and attributes, including deprecated elements, successfully. Text can also be formatted using the formatting tags in HTML. Earlier in the project, you changed the font-weight of some text on the Web page using an inline style. Instead of that style sheet, you could have also used the HTML bold tags (<b> </b>) that make text bold. HTML provides a number of tags that can be used to format text, several of which are listed in Table 3–7. These cannot be used for the XHTML standard above 1.0, but they can be used for the XHTML 1.0 Transitional standard.

Table 3–7 Text Formatting Tags

HTML Tag	Function
<b> </b>	Physical style tag that displays text as bold
<big> </big>	Increases the font size in comparison to the surrounding text
<blockquote> </blockquote>	Designates a long quotation; indents margins on sections of text
<em> </em>	Logical style tag that displays text with emphasis (usually appears as italicized)
<i> </i>	Physical style tag that displays text as italicized
<pre> </pre>	Sets enclosed text as preformatted material, meaning it preserves spaces and line breaks; often used for text in column format in another document pasted into HTML code
<small> </small>	Decreases the font size in comparison to the surrounding text
<strong> </strong>	Logical style tag that displays text with strong emphasis (usually appears as bold)
	Displays text as subscript (below normal text)
	Displays text as superscript (above normal text)
<tt> </tt>	Displays text as teletype or monospace text

BTW

Deprecated and Obsolete Tags

A deprecated element or attribute is one that has been outdated. Deprecated elements may become obsolete in the future, but most browsers continue to support deprecated elements for backward compatibility. You can still use deprecated tags with a Transitional document type as used in this book. Obsolete elements and attributes have no guarantee of browser support, and they are no longer defined in the W3C specification.

Figure 3–20 shows a sample Web page with some HTML text format tags. These tags fall into two categories: logical style tags and physical style tags. **Logical style tags** allow a browser to interpret the tag based on browser settings, relative to other text on a Web page. The <h2> heading tag, for example, is a logical style that indicates the heading text should be larger than regular text but smaller than text formatted using an <h1> heading tag. The <strong> tag is another logical style, which indicates that text should have a strong emphasis, and which most browsers interpret as displaying the text in bold font. **Physical style tags** specify a particular font change that is interpreted strictly by all browsers. For example, to ensure that text appears as bold font, you would enclose it between a start <b> and end </b> tag. The <strong> tag is a better fit for XHTML standards, and it does not dictate how the browser displays the text. In practice, the <strong> and <b> tags usually have the same result when the Web page is displayed.

BTW

Logical versus Physical Styles

For more information about the differences between logical and physical styles, search the Web for the key words "HTML logical style" or "HTML physical style".

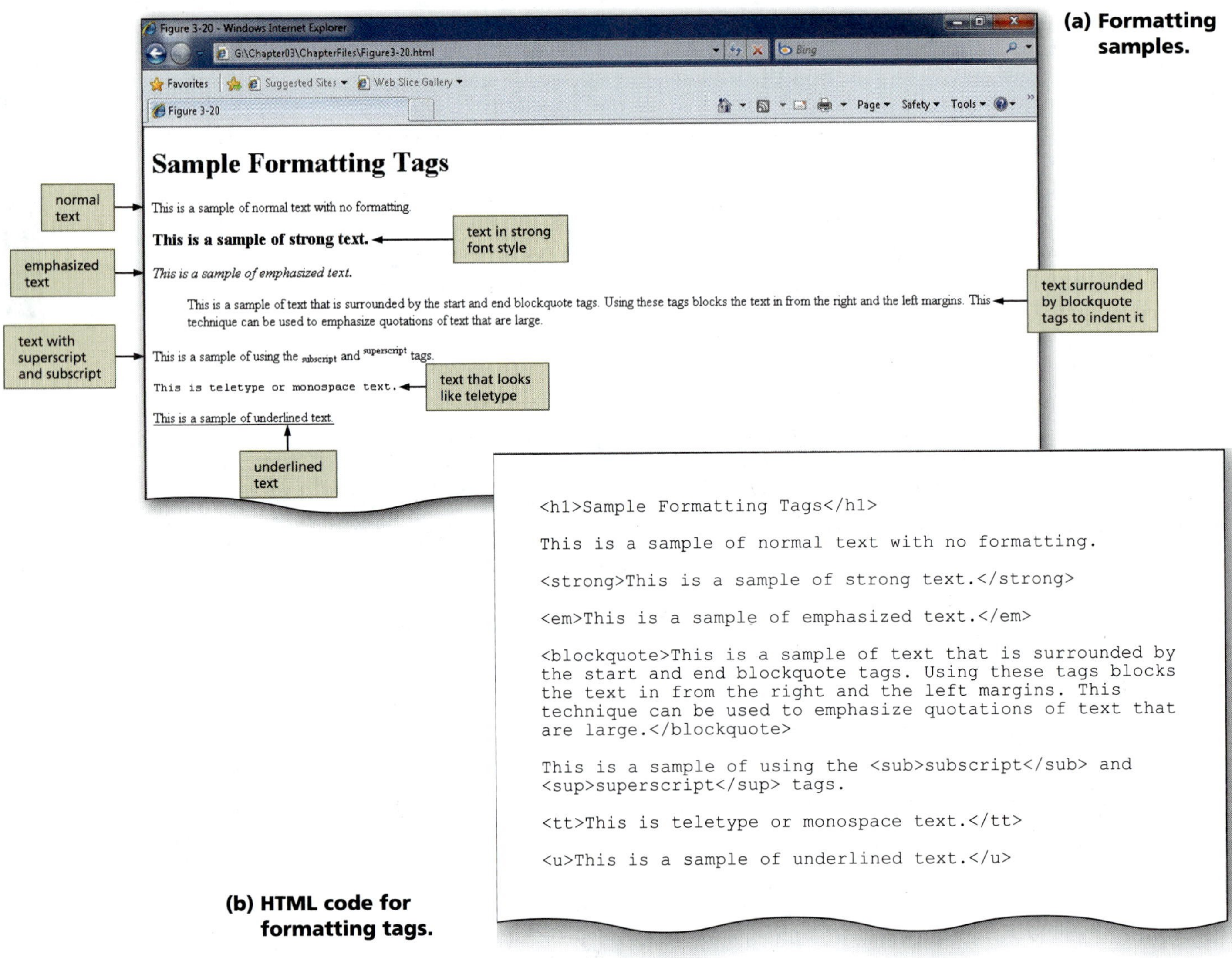

(a) Formatting samples.

```
<h1>Sample Formatting Tags</h1>

This is a sample of normal text with no formatting.

<strong>This is a sample of strong text.</strong>

<em>This is a sample of emphasized text.</em>

<blockquote>This is a sample of text that is surrounded by
the start and end blockquote tags. Using these tags blocks
the text in from the right and the left margins. This
technique can be used to emphasize quotations of text that
are large.</blockquote>

This is a sample of using the <sub>subscript</sub> and
<sup>superscript</sup> tags.

<tt>This is teletype or monospace text.</tt>

<u>This is a sample of underlined text.</u>
```

(b) HTML code for formatting tags.

Figure 3–20

> **BTW**
> **CSS Types**
> Remember that an inline style changes the style of an individual element; an embedded style sheet changes the style of an entire Web page; and an external style sheet changes the style in multiple Web pages in the same Web site. If you want to change the style of a single element, use an inline style.

Style Sheet Precedence Review

In Chapter 2, you learned how to insert an inline style. The project in this chapter also uses an inline style and introduces you to embedded style sheets. You learn about the third and final form of style, external style sheets, in Chapter 4. It will be helpful at this point to review the information from Chapter 2 on the precedence of styles (see Table 2-6 on page HTML 63). An inline style is used to control the style within an individual HTML tag and takes precedence over both embedded and external style sheets. An embedded sheet is used to change the style of an element over one Web page, but overrides or takes precedence over any styles defined in an external style sheet. An external style sheet is a separate document with a .css extension that is used to define styles for multiple pages in a Web site.

Because styles have different levels of precedence, all three types of styles can be used on a single Web page. For example, in this part of the chapter, you define body, anchor, and heading styles with embedded style sheets that are used for both the gettinggreen.html file and the greenhome.html file. You also insert a few inline styles on each Web page. Because of the precedence rules, the inline styles take precedence over the embedded style sheets. For instance, if you use an embedded style sheet to make all paragraphs Garamond font-family in normal text type and size 12, you can override that font-family, style, and size for a specific paragraph with an inline style within that paragraph's

<p> tag. Maybe there is a paragraph that you want to highlight, so you make it bold with an inline style. Or maybe there is a paragraph that you want to downplay, and you make it smaller and italic with an inline style. It is important to determine how and when to use the various styles in the design phase of Web development.

Plan Ahead

Identify which level of style or style sheet to use.
Because of precedence rules, it is generally better to look at the broadest level style first. In this chapter project, you use inline and embedded style sheets, with embedded being the broader level. In other words, an embedded style sheet is used for the entire Web page, and an inline style is used in a particular HTML tag. In Chapter 4, you will add an external style sheet (the broadest level) to your chapter project.

- **Identify what styles need to be different than the standards used across the Web site**. Sometimes you need to vary a style in order to call attention to the content or pull attention away from it. Many Web sites have a legal statement on the bottom of the home page. That is not necessarily something that needs to be the same font-size as the rest of the content on that Web page. So you may choose a smaller font-size and maybe make the text italic for that content. Two types of style sheets are used for styles that are different across a Web site, embedded and inline.
- **Use embedded style sheets to affect a single Web page**. This type of style is good to use if you want the style to affect just one (or a few) Web pages, and not all pages across the Web site.
- **Use inline styles for individual styles**. If you want to change the style of one or a few elements of one Web page, then using inline styles is the most appropriate. If a style is intended for most (or all) of the Web page, consider using an embedded or external style sheet.

Using Embedded Style Sheets

An embedded style sheet is used to control the style of a single Web page. To add an embedded style sheet to a Web page, you insert a start <style> tag at the top of the Web page within the <head> </head> tags that define the header section. After adding the desired style statements, you end the embedded style sheet by adding an end </style> tag.

The following code shows an example of an embedded style sheet to set the h1 heading to the Garamond font family, point size 32. This code would be added between the <head> and </head> tags within <style> </style> tags:

```
<style type="text/css">
h1 {font-family: Garamond;
   font-size: 32pt}
</style>
```

In this embedded style, the h1 (header size 1) element is the **selector**, and the remainder of the code is the **declaration**. The declaration sets the values for two different properties. The first property-value statement sets the h1 font family to Garamond. The second property-value statement sets the font size to 32 point. This means that the browser will display all h1 headers in 32-point Garamond font. You could use this embedded style sheet to easily change all h1 headings, in lieu of making the same change with an inline style in each individual heading tag.

The various types of Cascading Style Sheets allow you to control many different property values for various elements on a Web page. Table 3–8 lists six main properties and related options that are used in CSS. A complete list of properties and property values that can be used in CSS is included in Appendix D.

BTW

HTML/CSS Terminology

In HTML, a *tag* is a special instruction to the browser to specify how the Web page is displayed. Many tags have attributes that help to further modify what is displayed. In CSS, a style *statement* is made up of a selector and a declaration. The part of the style statement that identifies the page element(s) is called the *selector*. The part of the style statement that identifies how the element(s) should appear is called the *declaration*. A declaration includes at least one type of style, or property, to apply to the selected element.

Table 3–8 CSS Properties and Options

Property Name	Options That Can Be Controlled
background	• color • image • position
border	• color • style • width
font	• family • size • style • variant • weight
list	• image • position • type
margin	• length • percentage
text	• alignment • decoration • indentation • spacing • white space

BTW

Specifying Alternative Fonts

If a Web page font is not available on users' computers, you can create a list of fonts and the browser will determine the font to use. For example, if the Web page uses a Geneva font, but Arial or Helvetica would also work well, you create a comma-separated list of acceptable fonts, using <font face="geneva, arial,helvetica"> *your text*</font> as the code. If a Web page uses a font that Web page visitors do not have on their computers, the Web page appears using a default font (usually Times New Roman).

The following code shows an example of an embedded style sheet that you will use in the chapter project:

```
<style type="text/css">
body     {font-family: Arial, Verdana, Garamond;
         font-size: 11pt}
h1, h2   {color: #00934a}
a        {color: black}
a:hover  {background: #00934a;
         color: white}
</style>
```

This embedded style sheet defines four elements on the page: body, headings, links, and the link-hover property. The first style statement uses the **body** selector to specify that all text on the Web page should be one of the font families: Arial, Verdana, or Garamond, in 11 point size. Computers do not always have every font-family installed, so Web developers usually specify multiple font-families. If the first font-family is not available, then the next takes effect. If none of the named font-families are installed, the computer's default font is used. Separate the font-families by commas.

The second style statement defines values for the h1 and h2 properties. The value #00934a will give all h1 and h2 headings on this Web page the color green. On the home page, there is no h1 heading, but there is one on the second Web page, and later in the chapter you will use this same embedded style sheet for that Web page, which has both h1 and h2 headings.

The third style statement defines one property of the link element. The selector **a** is used to indicate the link element. The property-value statement *color: black* changes from the default blue color for links. Because the style statement uses **a** as the selector, it changes all link states (normal, visited, active) to these property values. You also can define a unique style for normal, visited, and active links by creating three separate style statements with **a:link**, **a:visited**, and **a:active** as the selectors.

The last style statement uses the **a:hover** selector to define the style of a link when the mouse pointer points to, or **hovers** over, a link. In this statement, you use a pseudo-class (hover) to have more control over the anchor (link) element. A **pseudo-class** is attached to a selector with a colon to specify a state or relation to the selector to give the Web developer more control over that selector. The format to use with a pseudo-class is entered in the form:

```
selector:pseudo-class { property: value; }
```

with a colon between the selector and the pseudo-class. There are four pseudo-classes that can be used when applied to the anchor or link selector:

- link, for an unvisited link
- visited, for a link to a page that has already been visited
- active, for a link when it gains focus (for example, when it is clicked)
- hover, for a link when the cursor is held over it.

The hover statement tells the browser to display white link text on a green (#00934a) background when the mouse hovers over the link. Adding a link hover style significantly changes the look of the links and adds a dimension of interactivity to the Web page.

The <!-- and --> code used in the embedded style sheet (just after the start style <style> and just before the end style </style> tags) are comment lines. These comment lines tell the browser to ignore whatever is between the comment lines if the browser cannot interpret the code between. So if your Web page user has a browser that is not current, it may not be able to interpret embedded style sheets. An older browser would see the start of the comment <!-- and treat anything between that line and the --> as a comment. This is a good Web development technique.

Recall that embedded style sheets have the second-highest level of precedence of the three types of styles. Although an inline style overrides the properties of an embedded style sheet, the embedded style sheet takes precedence over an external style sheet.

To Add Embedded Style Sheet Statements

Table 3–9 shows the CSS code for an embedded style sheet to specify the font and size for body text on this Web page.

Table 3–9 CSS Code for an Embedded Style Sheet

Line	CSS Selectors and Declarations
9	<style type="text/css">
10	<!--
11	
12	`body {font-family: Arial, Verdana, Garamond;`

Table 3–9 CSS Code for an Embedded Style Sheet (continued)

Line	CSS Selectors and Declarations
13	`            font-size: 11pt}`
14	
15	`h1, h2  {color: #00934a}`
16	
17	`a        {color: black}`
18	
19	`a:hover {background: #00934a;`
20	`            color: white}`
21	
22	`-->`
23	`</style>`

The following step shows how to enter the embedded style sheet code to change h1 and h2 headings to green, change all links to blank, and change the color of the link hover to green background with white text to provide visual impact.

1

- Click immediately to the right of the > in </title> on line 8 and press the ENTER key.
- Type the code in Table 3–9 but do not press the ENTER key at the end of line 23 (Figure 3–21).

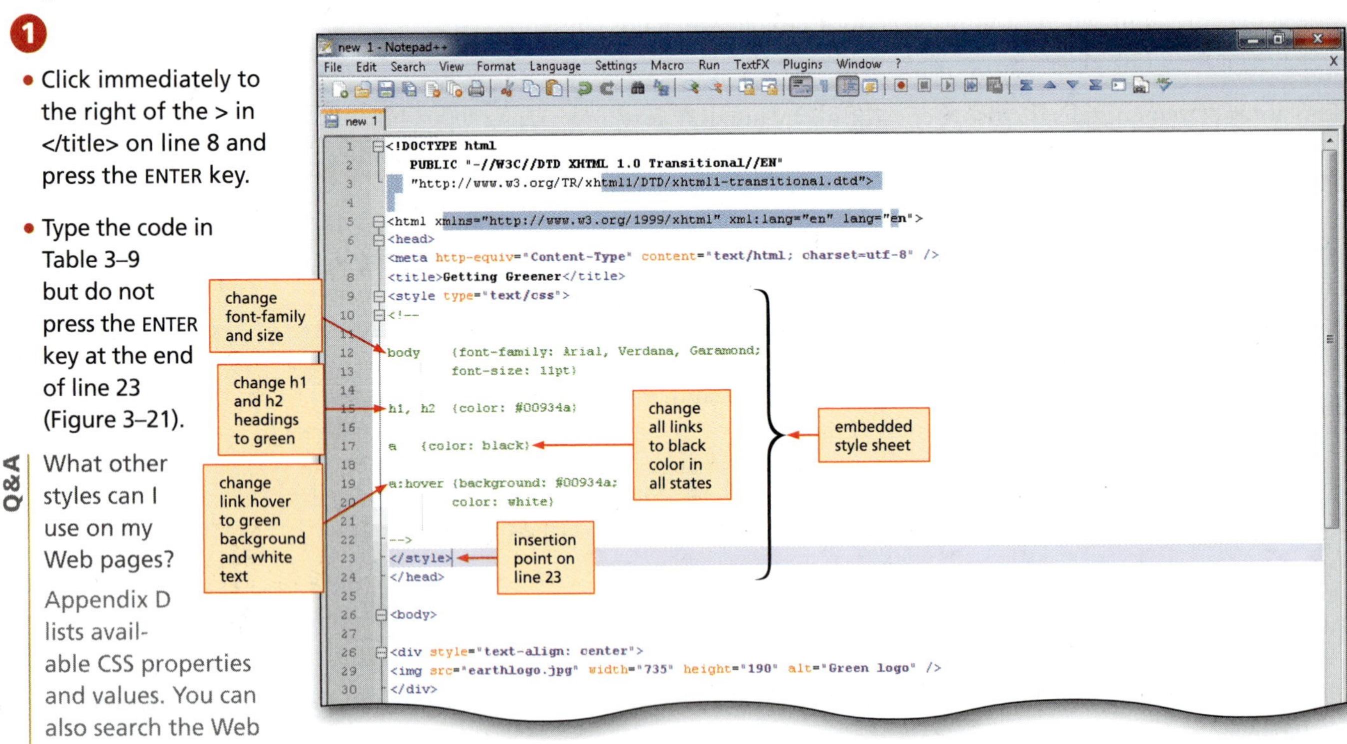

Figure 3–21

Q&A What other styles can I use on my Web pages?

Appendix D lists available CSS properties and values. You can also search the Web for examples of how CSS are used for Web development. Finally, be an active Web page visitor and review the source code on Web pages with styles that you think are particularly effective or ineffective.

Q&A Is there a way to eliminate the underline on text links altogether?

You can use a:hover text-decoration: none to eliminate the underline completely. Understand, however, that users look for underlined text when they try to find the links on a Web page, so use this cautiously.

To Add an Inline Style for Color

The following step shows how to enter an inline style to add a green color (#00934a) in a bold font-weight to provide visual impact and call attention to the company name, Getting Greener. With this inline style, you use the <span> </span> tags. The **<span> </span>** tags create a container into which a user can add an inline style. The <span> provides a finer level of control for styles, as opposed to the <div> </div> tags, which define block-level structure or division in the HTML document. The <span> tag tells the browser to apply the chosen styles to whatever is within the <span></span> container.

- With the insertion point right after the > in <p> on line 32, type `<span style="color: #00934a; font-weight: bold">` (Figure 3–22).
- With the insertion point right after the r in Greener on line 32, type `</span>` (Figure 3–22).

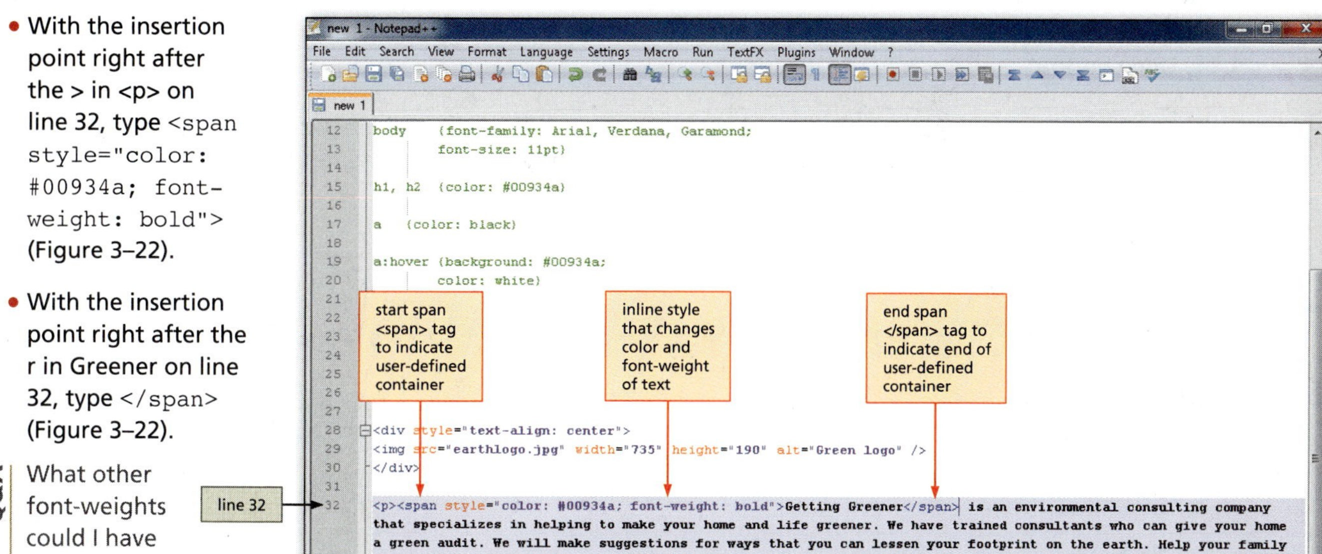

Figure 3–22

Q&A What other font-weights could I have used?

The four font-weights are normal, bold, bolder, and lighter. If you don't specify a font-weight, normal is the default.

Q&A What different colors can I use for text?

There are a variety of colors that you can use for headings, text, and backgrounds. You can name the color by color name or hexadecimal code. See Figure 2–27 on page HTML 68 for examples.

To Save an HTML File

With the HTML code for the Getting Greener home page complete, you should re-save the file. The following step shows how to save an HTML file that has been previously saved.

1. Click the Save icon on the Notepad++ toolbar to save the most recent version of gettinggreener.html on the same storage device and in the same folder as the last time you saved it.

Validating the HTML, Viewing the Web Page, and Testing Links

After you save the HTML file for the Getting Greener home page, it should be validated to ensure that it meets current XHTML standards and viewed in a browser to confirm the Web page is displayed as desired. It also is important to test the two links in the Getting Greener home page to verify that they function as expected.

To Validate HTML Code

1. Open Internet Explorer.
2. Navigate to the Web site `validator.w3.org`
3. Click the Validate by File Upload tab.
4. Click the Browse button.
5. Locate the gettinggreener.html file on your storage device and click the file name.
6. Click the Open button.
7. Click the Check button. A successful validation should be displayed, as shown in Figure 3–23a. If you have errors in your code, you may see a screen similar to Figure 3–23b. In this example, the errors relate to a missing </p> tag.

Q&A

What if my HTML code does not validate?

If your code has errors, you should edit your HTML file to correct the errors. The Markup Validation Service report lists clearly what is wrong with your code. Once you make the necessary changes and save the file, you can again use the Browse button to open the corrected HTML file. You then use the Revalidate button to validate the changed code.

Q&A

Why is the first error shown in Figure 3–23b on line 34, not line 32, where the </p> is missing?

Usually, the validator shows the exact error and line number on which the error occurs. Sometimes, however, the validator shows subsequent errors that occur as a result of the initial error. You may have to look a line prior to the first error line shown to find the initial error, as in this case.

BTW

Common Validation Errors

Common validation errors include not spelling tags, selectors, or attributes correctly; using uppercase letters (except for DOCTYPE); and not nesting tags correctly. A single coding error can cause many lines of errors during validation. For instance, Figure 3-23b shows a Web page that has seven errors caused by a single missing </p> tag on line 32.

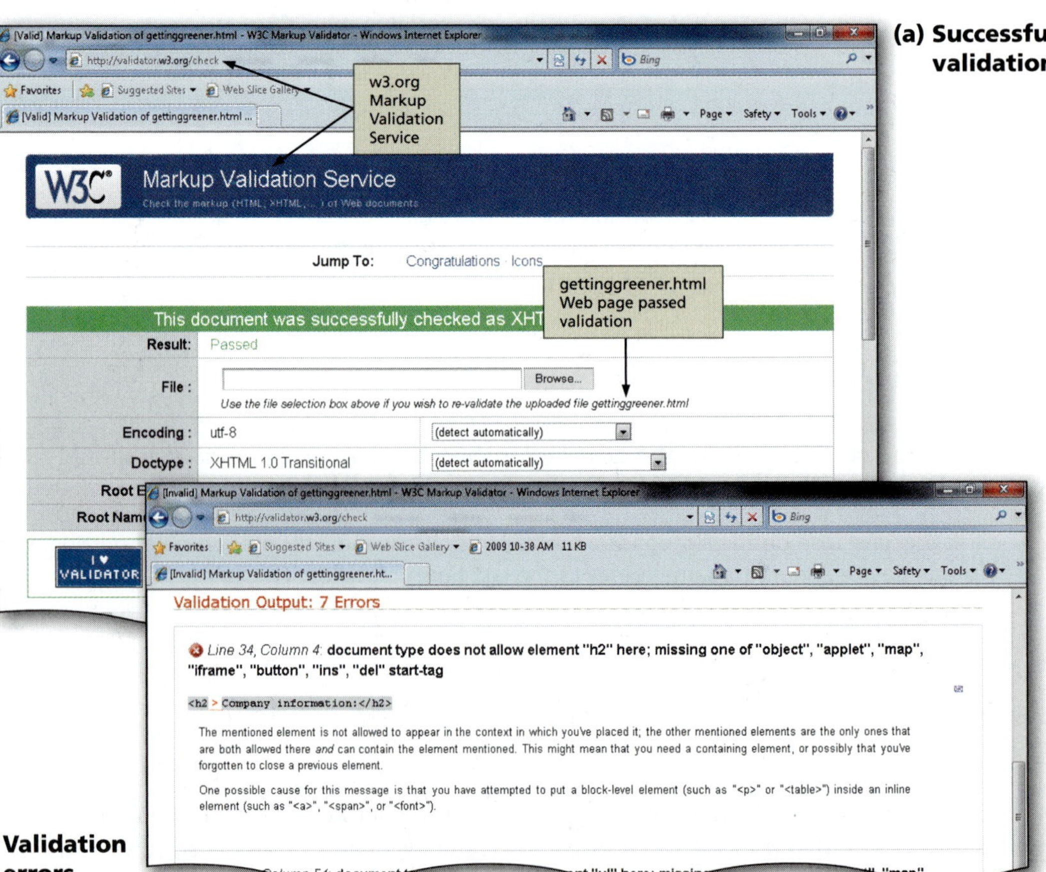

(a) Successful validation.

(b) Validation errors.

Figure 3–23

To Print an HTML File

After your HTML code has passed validation, it's a good idea to make a hard copy printout of it.

1. Click the Notepad++ button on the taskbar to activate the Notepad++ window.

2. Click File on the menu bar and then click the Print command, and then click the Print button to print a hard copy of the HTML code (Figure 3–24).

```
<!DOCTYPE html
   PUBLIC "-//W3C//DTD XHTML 1.0 Transitional//EN"
   "http://www.w3.org/TR/xhtml1/DTD/xhtml1-transitional.dtd">

<html xmlns="http://www.w3.org/1999/xhtml" xml:lang="en" lang="en">
<head>
<meta http-equiv="Content-Type" content="text/html; charset=utf-8" />
<title>Getting Greener</title>
<style type="text/css">
<!--

body    {font-family: Arial, Verdana, Garamond;
        font-size: 11pt}

h1, h2  {color: #00934a}

a    {color: black}

a:hover {background: #00934a;
        color: white}

-->
</style>
</head>

<body>

<div style="text-align: center">
    <img src="earthlogo.jpg" width="735" height="190" alt="Green logo" />
</div>

<p><span style="color: #00934a; font-weight: bold">Getting Greener</span> is an
environmental consulting company that specializes in helping to make your home and life
greener. We have trained consultants who can give your home a green audit. We will make
suggestions for ways that you can lessen your footprint on the earth. Help your family
act in an environmentally responsible way by creating a home environment that is safe,
less costly, and green.</p>

<h2>Company information:</h2>

<ul style="list-style-image: url(earthbullet.jpg)">
<li>Started by environmental engineer Dr. Dean A. McDevitt in 2000</li>
<li>Store locations all over the greater Seattle area, including branch offices in all
public utility buildings</li>
<li>Fifteen consultants with a variety of specialties; all fully trained, bonded, and
insured</li>
</ul>

<p>Browse our Web site to learn more about our services. See a sample of a <a href=
"greenhome.html">green home</a> environment or read more about climate control at the <a
 href="http://www.wmo.int/">World Meteorological Organization (WMO)</a>. Have a
question or comment? Call us at (999) 555-GREEN or e-mail us at
<a href="mailto:gettinggreener@isp.com">gettinggreener@isp.com</a>.</p>

</body>
</html>
```

Figure 3–24

To View a Web Page

The following steps illustrate how to view the HTML file in a browser.

1. Open Internet Explorer.
2. In Internet Explorer, click the Address bar to select the URL in the Address bar.
3. Type `g:\Chapter03\ChapterFiles\gettinggreener.html` (or the specific path to your file) to display the new URL in the Address bar and then press the ENTER key (Figure 3–25).

Q&A

What if my page does not display correctly?

Check your gettinggreener.html code carefully in Notepad++ to make sure you have not made any typing errors or left anything out. Correct the errors, re-save the file, and try again.

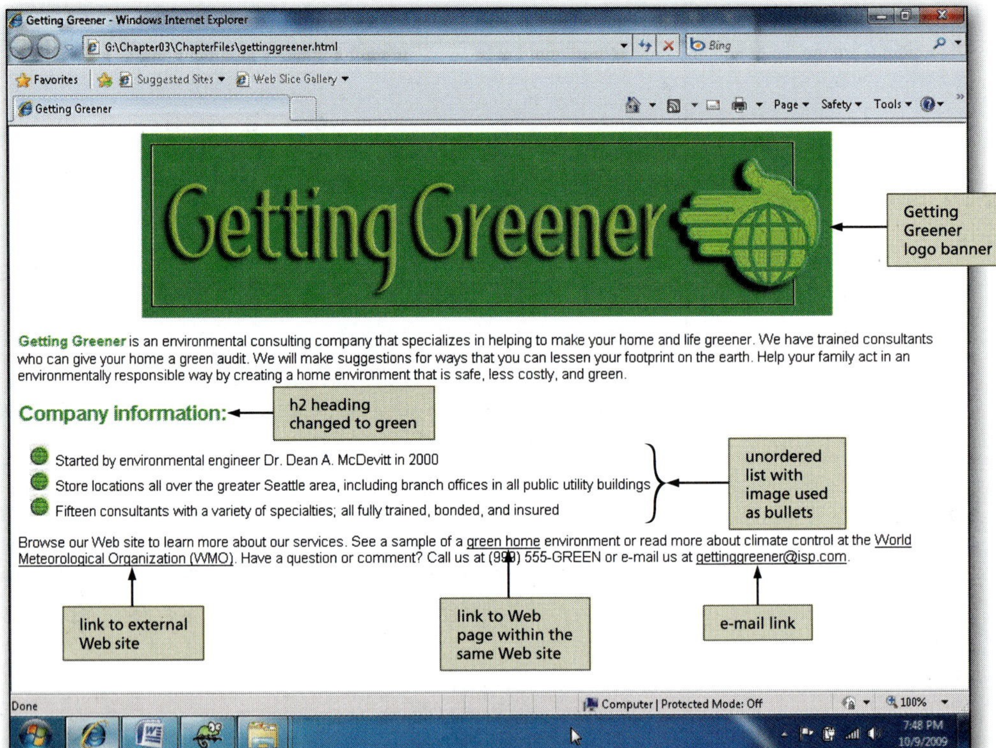

Figure 3–25

Plan Ahead

Test your Web page.

- **Determine what you need to test**. It is important to have a test plan when you test your Web pages. Planning what to test assures that all functionality of the Web page is tested. You should specifically test the display of the Web page itself and test that all of the links on the Web page work correctly.
- **Test the Web page as displayed in the browser**. Certainly the first part of testing is to verify that your Web page is displayed in the browser as intended. Ask yourself the following questions: (1) Are the images all displayed where they should be? (2) Is the text presented as intended? (3) Are the links displayed as intended?
- **Test the links**. In your testing plan, you need to address all of the links that you have inserted into the Web page. It is especially important to test external links, that is, those over which you have no control. If you need to link outside of the Web pages that you developed, then periodically test the links to make sure they are still valid. It helps to create a matrix that includes three columns for information. The first column contains information about all of the links on the Web page. The second column contains information about the intended results of those links. The third column is the one that you complete during testing. If the link tests as it should, you can note that by putting a check mark in the third column. If the link test result is not as it should be, you can note in the third column what the result is. Using a technique such as this makes it easier to do thorough testing. When you know what the results of the test should be, it helps you verify valid links. This is an excellent technique to use when there are different people developing and testing the Web pages. The matrix will notify the developers of the test results clearly.

BTW

Web Page Testing
An important part of Web page development is testing Web page links. For more information about link testing, search the Web for key words such as "HTML testing" or look at the World Wide Web Consortium (w3.org) Web site.

To Test Links on a Web Page

The following steps show how to test the links in the Getting Greener home page to verify that they work correctly.

- With the Getting Greener home page displayed in the browser, point to the e-mail link, gettinggreener@isp.com and then click the link to open the default e-mail program with the address gettinggreener@isp.com in the To: text box, as shown in Figure 3–26.
- Click the Close button in the Compose Mail window. If a dialog box asks if you want to save changes, click No.

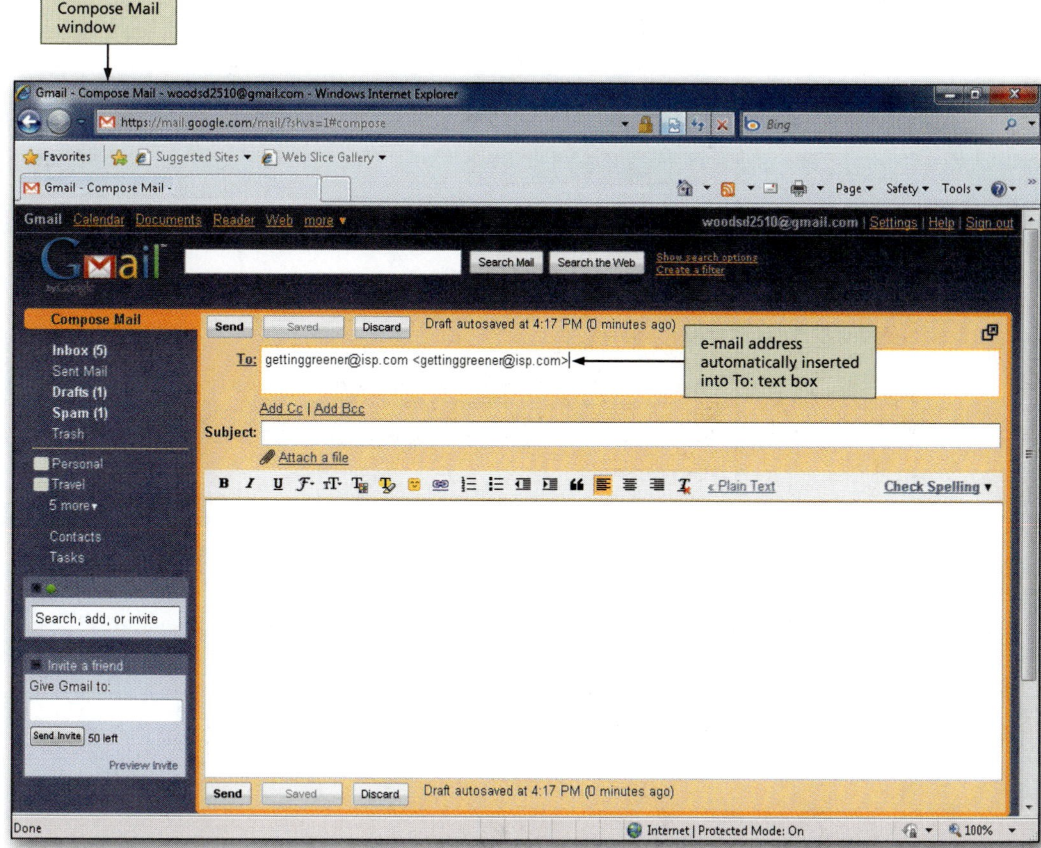

Figure 3–26

- Click the WMO link to test the external link on the Web page. Close the browser window or use the Back button to return to the Getting Greener home page.
- With the USB flash drive in drive G, point to the green home link and click the link. The secondary Web page, greenhome .html, is displayed (Figure 3–27), although it is not completed.

Q&A My e-mail does not work when I click the link. Why does that happen?

You may not have an e-mail client installed on your computer or your school's servers. You therefore may not be able to test this e-mail link.

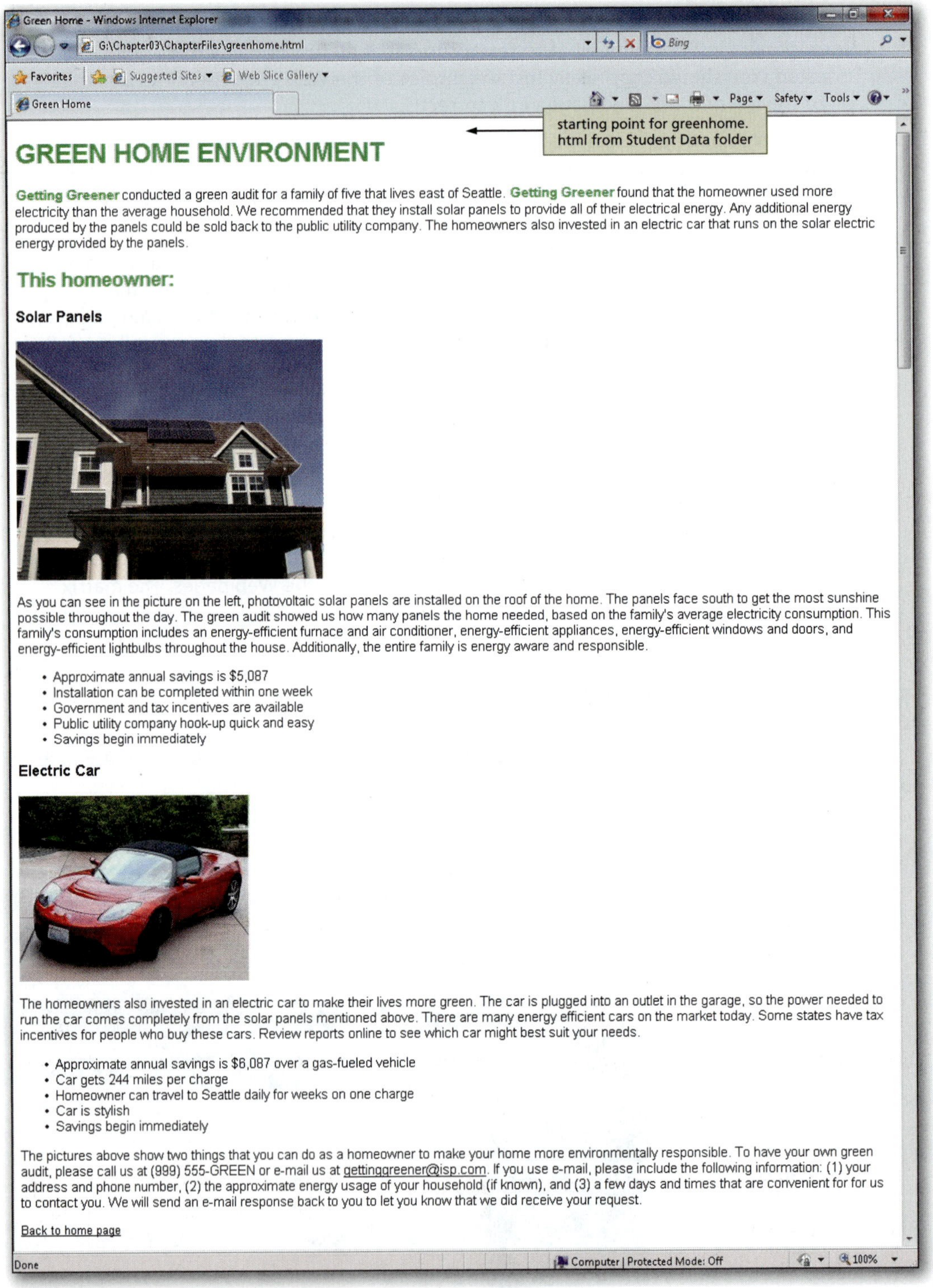

Figure 3–27

To Print a Web Page

Print the Web page for future reference.

1. Close the browser window or click the Back button on the Standard toolbar to return to the Getting Greener home page.
2. Click the Print icon on the Command bar.
3. Once the Getting Greener home page is printed (Figure 3–28), click the green home link to return to that Web page.

Q&A

I do not see the bullets when I print preview the Web page. Can I change that so I can see the bullets?

Yes. In IE, click Tools and then click Internet Options. Click the Advanced tab and scroll to the Printing section. Click the check box "Print background colors and images."

Getting Greener Page 1 of 1

Getting Greener is an environmental consulting company that specializes in helping to make your home and life greener. We have trained consultants who can give your home a green audit. We will make suggestions for ways that you can lessen your footprint on the earth. Help your family act in an environmentally responsible way by creating a home environment that is safe, less costly, and green.

Company information:

Started by environmental engineer Dr. Dean A. McDevitt in 2000

Store locations all over the greater Seattle area, including branch offices in all public utility buildings

Fifteen consultants with a variety of specialties; all fully trained, bonded, and insured

Browse our Web site to learn more about our services. See a sample of a green home environment or read more about climate control at the World Meteorological Organization (WMO). Have a question or comment? Call us at (999) 555-GREEN or e-mail us at gettinggreener@isp.com.

Figure 3–28

Editing the Second Web Page

With the home page complete, the next step is to enhance the Green Home Web page. For this part of the project, you will download an existing Web page file and edit the HTML code to create the Web page, as shown in Figure 3–29 on the next page. You will add two images and set text to wrap around the images. You also will add two additional types of links: links within the same Web page and an image link to a Web page in the same Web site.

As you have learned, the <a> tag used to create a link must specify the page, file, or location to which it links. In the case of a link within a Web page, the <a> tag specifies a **target**, or named location, in the same file. Before adding the links and targets in the Green Home Web page, you need to add an unordered (bulleted) list that uses the

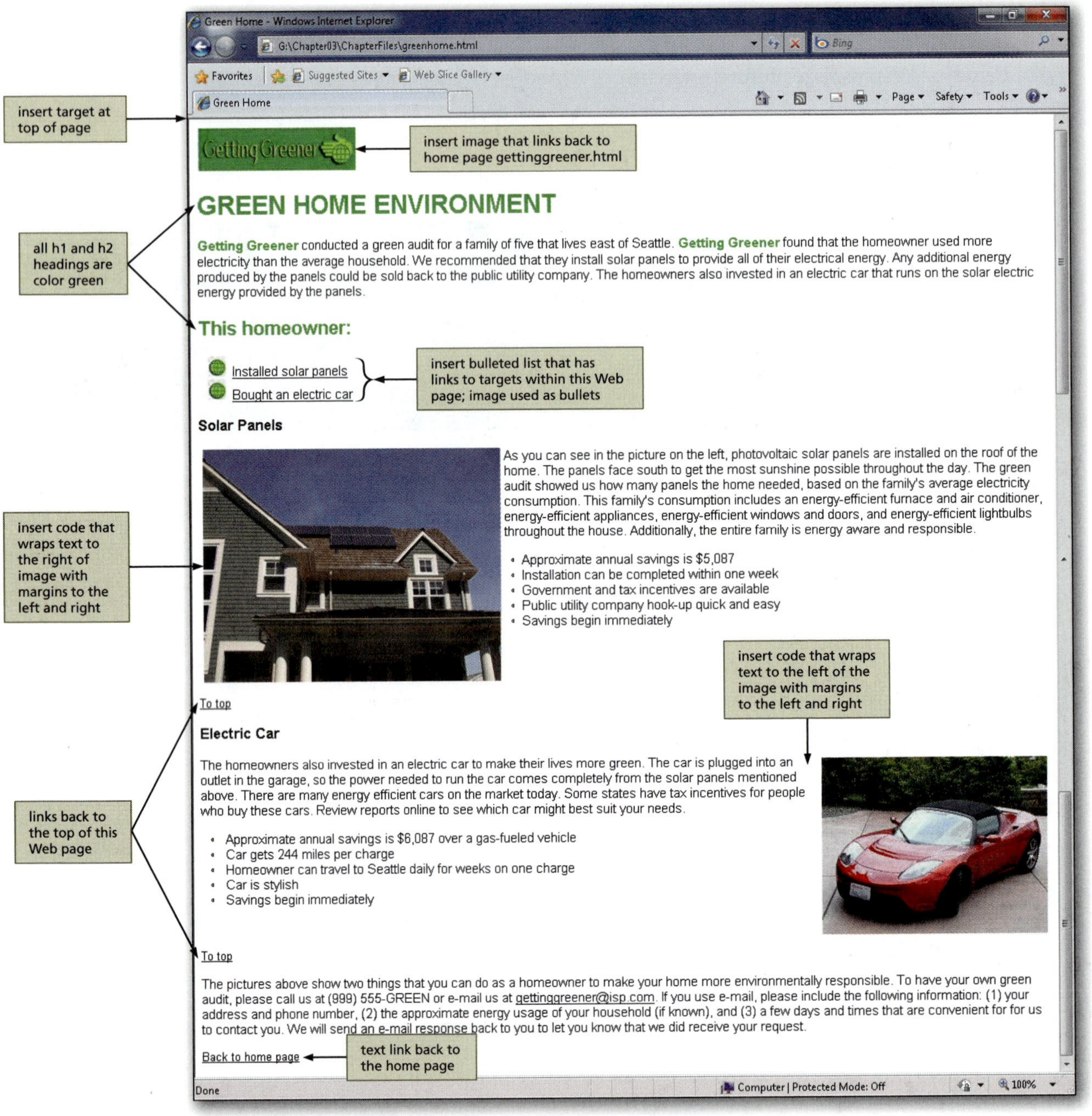

insert target at top of page

insert image that links back to home page gettinggreener.html

all h1 and h2 headings are color green

insert bulleted list that has links to targets within this Web page; image used as bullets

insert code that wraps text to the right of image with margins to the left and right

insert code that wraps text to the left of the image with margins to the left and right

links back to the top of this Web page

text link back to the home page

Figure 3–29

> **BTW**
> **Web Page Improvement**
> Web page development is an ongoing process. In Web page development, you create a Web page, view it in a browser, and then look for ways to improve the appearance of the page.

(earthbullet.jpg) image as the bullets. This list contains two items — Installed solar panels and Bought an electric car — and must be added to the page. The list items will serve as the links that are directed to the heading at the top of each major section of the Green Home Web page. When clicked, these links will move the Web page visitor to the targets, which are named solar and car, respectively.

Because the Web page is so long, it is a good design practice to provide users with a quick way to move back to the top of the Web page without scrolling back. For this purpose, the Web page includes two text links named To top. These links are located just above the Solar Panels and Electric Car headings. When clicked, any To top link takes the Web page visitor back to the top of the page.

To complete the Green Home Web page, you will create an image link, so users can click the back to home page link to return to the Getting Greener home page. There is already a text link inserted at the bottom of the Web page that can be used to return to the home page. It is always important to provide a link back to the home page from subsequent Web pages. Your visitors should not have to use the Back button on the browser to return to the home page.

To Open an HTML File

The following steps illustrate how to open the greenhome.html file in Notepad++.

1. Click the Notepad++ button on the taskbar.
2. With a USB flash drive connected to one of the computer's USB ports, click File on the menu bar and then click Open.
3. Click Computer in the navigation pane to display a list of available drives.
4. If necessary, scroll until UDISK 2.0 (G:) is displayed in the list of available drives.
5. If necessary, navigate to the USB drive (G:). Click the Chapter03 folder, and then click the ChapterFiles folder in the list of available folders.
6. Click greenhome.html in the list of files.
7. Click the Open button in the Open dialog box to display the HTML code for the greenhome.html Web page, as shown in Figure 3–30.

Q&A

If I open another file in Notepad++, will I lose the gettinggreener.html file?

The last saved version of gettinggreener.html will still be on the USB drive, even though another HTML file is open in Notepad++. Additionally, even after you open the new file in Notepad++ the other file (gettinggreener.html) remains open in another tab in Notepad++. That is one of the benefits of Notepad++; you can have more than one file open at the same time.

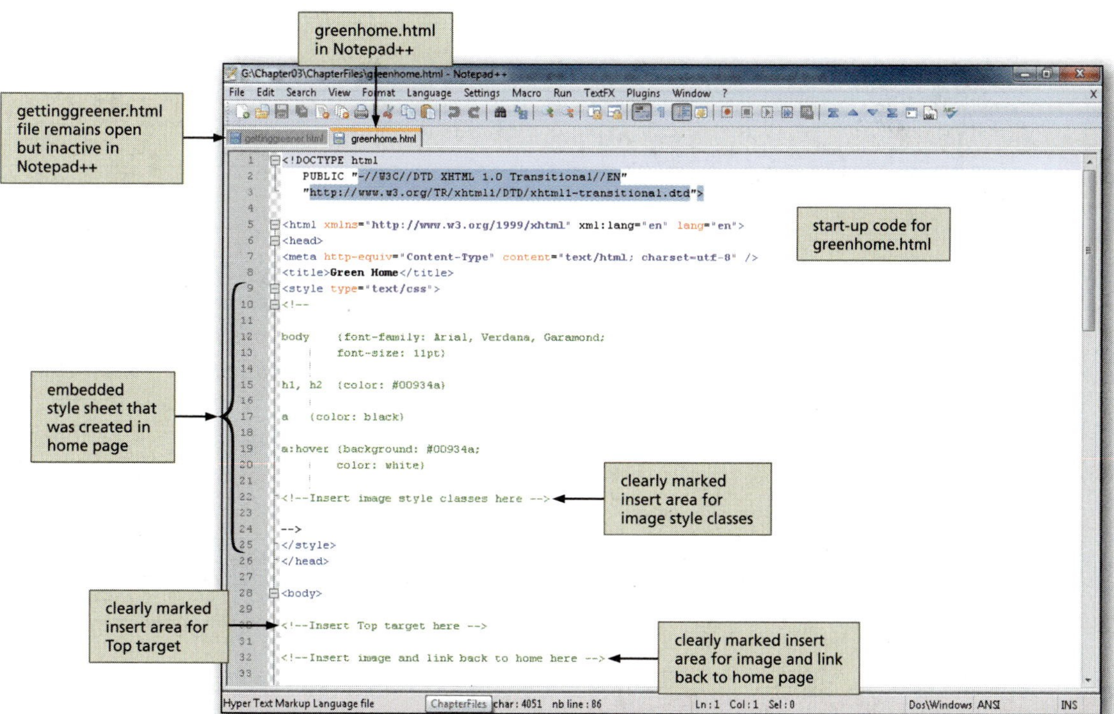

Figure 3–30

Plan Ahead

- **Determine what graphic images will be used and how to format them.** They say that a picture is worth a thousand words. In Web development, it sometimes makes your message clearer and more attractive if you use pictures. In the planning stage, you have to consider which pictures will help (and not hinder) your content. You also have to decide how to align the text relative to the pictures. Sometimes it makes sense to put the text above or below the picture. It might also be appropriate to wrap the text around the picture. You need to determine all of these specifics before you create the Web page.
- **Identify what links are needed on a long Web page.** When you have an especially long Web page (one in which the visitor has to use the PAGE DOWN key), you should provide links within the Web page for easier navigation. You need to decide where it makes sense to put page breaks. Often it is best to put a link to major topics within the Web page. Make sure that the Web page visitor can easily move to those areas by providing links toward the top of the Web page.
- **Use links back to the top of the page.** Another good technique for long Web pages is to allow visitors to link back to the top of the Web page easily from several places on the page. Providing links back to the top of a long Web page makes browsing more enjoyable.
- **Create a link back to the home page.** If possible, you should always provide a link from secondary Web pages back to the home page. Your visitors should not have to use the Back button on the browser to get back to the home page of the Web site. A common Web development practice is to use a company logo (often a smaller version) to navigate back to the home page. Again, the purpose of this image link as well as other links mentioned here is to make your Web site easy to navigate.

Working with Classes in Style Statements

Notice that the greenhome.html file contains the same embedded style sheet that you created in the gettinggreener.html file earlier in this chapter. For the second Web page, you will add one additional element (img) to the embedded style sheet. In order to utilize the image element as needed on the second Web page (greenhome.html), you need to understand the concept of classes as used with CSS. CSS classes give you more control over the style on a Web page.

Recall that a style statement is made up of a selector and a declaration. The part of the style statement that identifies the page elements is called the selector.

```
a     {color: black}
```

The example above shows a section of the embedded style sheet used in the greenhome.html Web page. The selector in the example is the a (the anchor or link). The part of the style statement that identifies how the element(s) should appear is called the declaration. In this example, the declaration is everything between the curly brackets. This includes the property named color and the value named black.

There is another level of control that you can have over the styles that display on a Web page. For example, rather than having all paragraphs of text appear in the same style, you might want the style of the first paragraph on a page to be different from the other paragraphs of text. To gain more control for these purposes, you can define specific elements of an HTML file as a category, or **class**. You then can create a specific style for each class. Using classes in CSS thus allows you to apply styles to HTML tags selectively.

Using a class, for example, you could apply one style to a beginning paragraph and a different style to a closing paragraph on the same Web page.

Defining and using classes in CSS is a two-step process. First, any elements that belong to the class are marked by adding the tag:

```
class="classname"
```

where classname is the identifier or name of the class.

Any word can be used as a class name, as long as it does not contain spaces. In general, however, you should use descriptive names that illustrate the purpose of a class (for example, beginning, legallanguage, or copyrighttext), rather than names that describe the appearance of the class (for example, bluetext, largeritalic, or boldsmallarial). Using names that describe the purpose makes the code easier to read and more flexible. For this chapter, you will use the class names align-left and align-right in the img element. This immediately tells someone reviewing this code that the styles defined by those classes are used to align images either left or right.

After you have named the classes, you can use the class names in a selector and define a specific style for the class. For example, within the <style> tags in an embedded or external style sheet, you enter a style statement in the format:

```
p.beginning {color: red;
             font: 20pt}
```

where the p indicates that the class applies to a specific category of the paragraph tag and beginning is the class name. The tag and the class name are separated by a period. Together, the tag and the class name make up the selector for the style statement. The declaration then lists the property-value statements that should be applied to elements in the class.

For instance, if you want to display the beginning paragraph text in a 20-point red font, you would add a style statement like the one shown in the sample code in Figure 3–31a on the next page and then use the tag, <p class="beginning">, to apply the style defined by the declaration associated with the p.beginning selector. If the paragraph <p> tag is used without the class name, the paragraph appears in the default format or other format as defined by a style. To use this class name in an HTML tag, you would type:

```
<p class="beginning">
```

as the code.

In addition to the style for the beginning paragraphs, Figure 3–31a shows an example of HTML code with classes defined for and applied to the middle and end paragraphs. Figure 3–31b shows how the resulting Web page appears in the browser.

You can add as many classes to your Web pages as you need. This is a very useful Web development technique that allows flexibility and variety in a Web page. One drawback is that classes can be defined for use only in embedded or external style sheets. Because the purpose of using classes is to format a group of elements, not individual elements, classes do not work in inline styles.

The example below shows another section of the embedded style sheet in the greenhome.html Web page. In this example, you use a pseudo-class to have more control over the hover state in the anchor element.

```
a:hover     {background: #00934a;
             color: white}
```

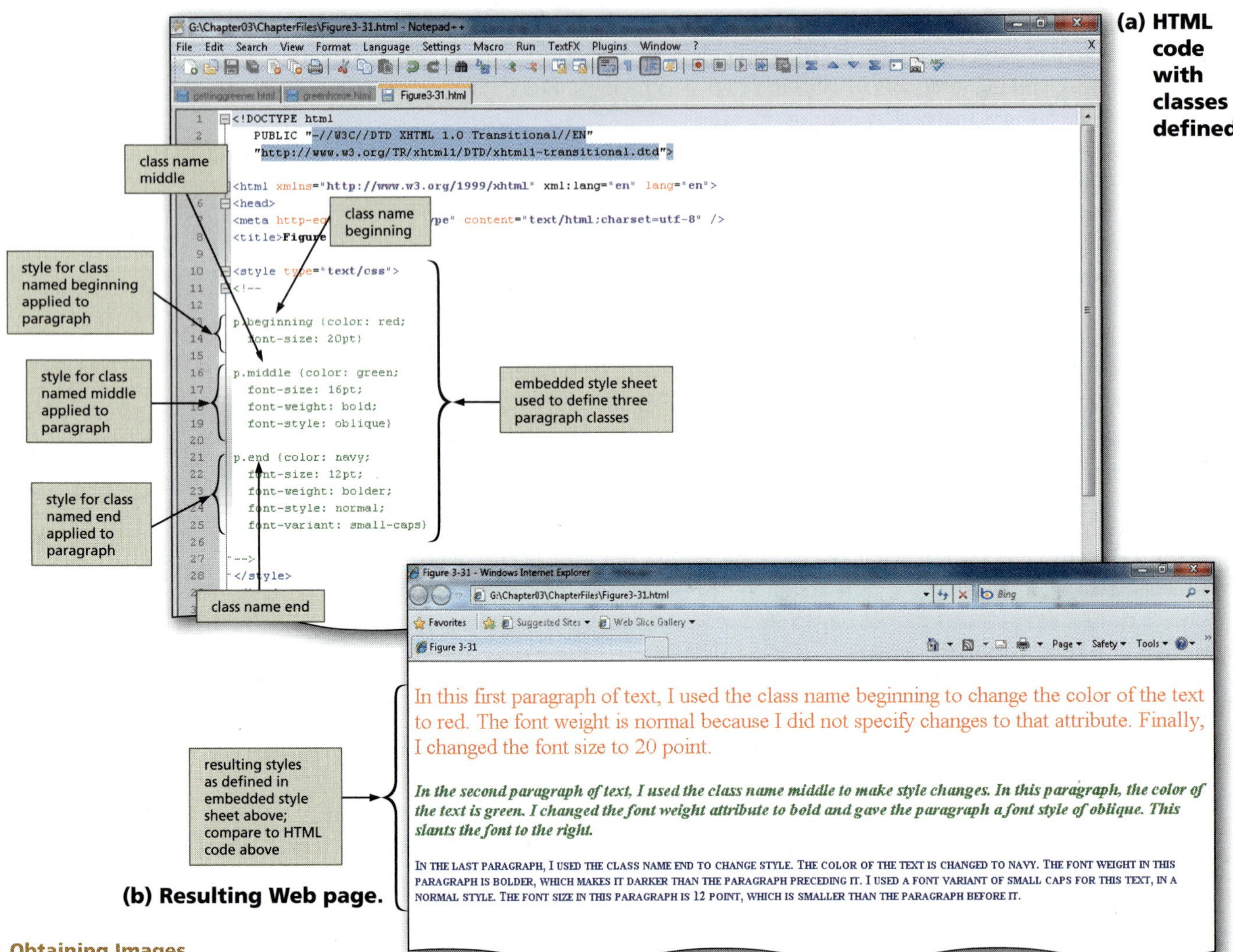

Figure 3–31

BTW

Obtaining Images

The Web contains thousands of image files that can be downloaded for free and used for noncommercial purposes. Search for "free GIFs" or "free Web images" to find images. If you find a graphic you want to use, right-click the image, click Save Picture As on the shortcut menu, and then save the image to your computer. Many applications come with clip art that can be used on Web pages. Other types of digital images, such as images scanned by a scanner or pictures taken with a digital camera, also can be included on a Web page. You also can create images using a paint or image-editing program. Regardless of where you get the images, always follow copyright rules and regulations.

Adding an Image with Wrapped Text

As shown in Appendix A, the <img> tag has many attributes, including attributes to specify height, width, and alternative text.

Alignment also is a key consideration when inserting an image. Alignment can give an image and the surrounding text completely different looks. Figure 3–32 shows two images, the first of which is left-aligned, which wraps any text to the right of the image. In this chapter, you use an embedded style sheet to align (float) the image to the left or right and wrap the text to the right or left of the positioned image. You also add some space (margins) around the image so that it is separated from the text. To accomplish these tasks, you use the float and margin properties.

The float property indicates in which direction (in this case left and right) to display (or float) an element being inserted on a Web page. **Floating** an element like an image allows the element to move to the side indicated in the float statement. As a result of that repositioning (floating), the other elements, like text, are moved up and allowed to wrap next to the floated element. When you first open the greenhome.html file in Internet Explorer (Figure 3–27 on page HTML 126), both images are left-aligned. Notice that the text is aligned beneath each image, leaving a lot of white space to the right of the images. The text does not surround the images in Figure 3–27, as it does in Figure 3–29 on page HTML 128. You achieve this text wrap by using the float property. In addition to floating the element, you should also provide some space around the image. The margin-left and margin-right properties indicate how many pixels of space to put around each element. In this case, you will have five pixels of space around the right and left of each image. Figure 3–32 shows examples of images with margin spacing.

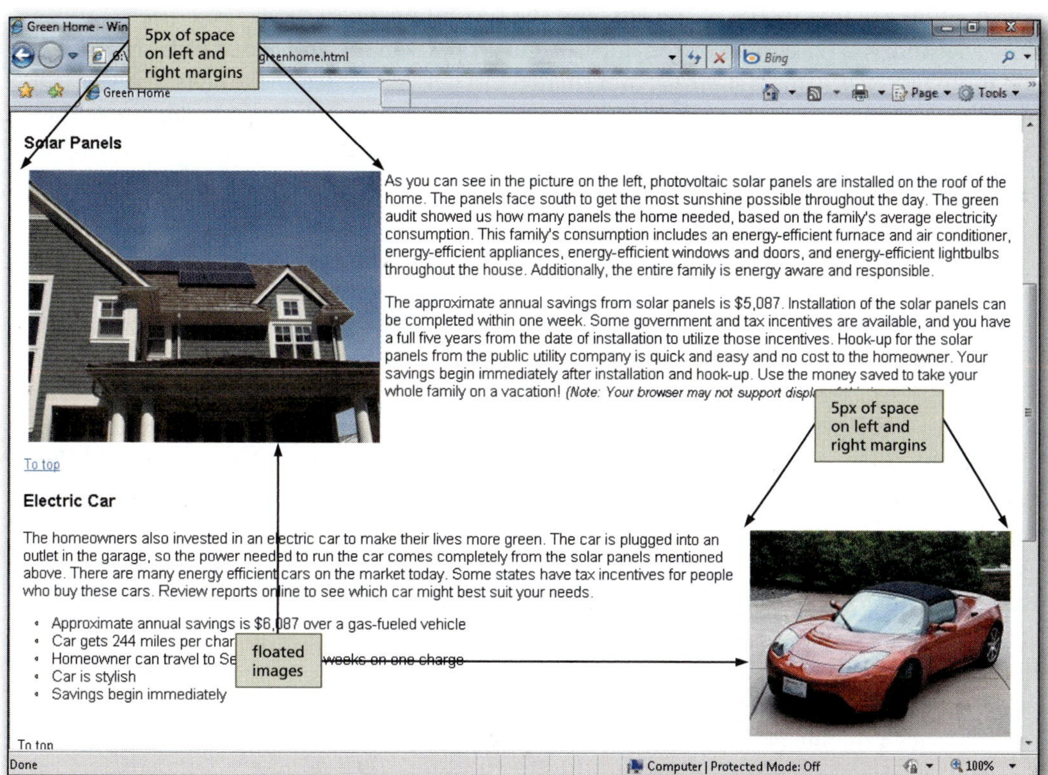
5px of space on left and right margins
Solar Panels
As you can see in the picture on the left, photovoltaic solar panels are installed on the roof of the home. The panels face south to get the most sunshine possible throughout the day. The green audit showed us how many panels the home needed, based on the family's average electricity consumption. This family's consumption includes an energy-efficient furnace and air conditioner, energy-efficient appliances, energy-efficient windows and doors, and energy-efficient lightbulbs throughout the house. Additionally, the entire family is energy aware and responsible.
The approximate annual savings from solar panels is $5,087. Installation of the solar panels can be completed within one week. Some government and tax incentives are available, and you have a full five years from the date of installation to utilize those incentives. Hook-up for the solar panels from the public utility company is quick and easy and no cost to the homeowner. Your savings begin immediately after installation and hook-up. Use the money saved to take your whole family on a vacation!
5px of space on left and right margins
To top
Electric Car
floated images
Car is stylish
Savings begin immediately
Computer | Protected Mode: Off
100%

Figure 3–32 Left- and right-aligned images.

There are several ways to align text around images using styles. You can do this with an inline style (HTML code shown below) or with an embedded style sheet. The format of the HTML code to add the left- and right-aligned images with an inline style is:

```
<img style="float: left; margin-left: 5px; margin-right:
5px" src="solar.jpg" width="349" height="261" alt="Solar
Panels" />
<img style="float: right; margin-left: 5px; margin-right:
5px" src="car.jpg" width="261" height="202" alt="Electric car"
align="right" />
```

where the float property tells the browser on which side to float the image element, and the margin properties tell the browser how much space (5 pixels) to add around the image. Using an inline style is a perfectly acceptable way to float an image element, wrap the text, and add margins of space around the image, but there may be a more efficient way to do it.

If you have numerous images to float on the page, it is better to use classes in an embedded style sheet than to use inline styles.

This project uses an embedded style sheet with a two-step approach. First, you will insert the class names align-left and align-right into the image <img> tags that will use the classes. Then, you add those class names (align-left and align-right) to an image <img> element in the embedded style sheet. To use this two-step approach, first you add the HTML code for the left-align and right-align class names in the <img> tag itself within the Web page content:

```
<img class="align-left" src="solar.jpg" width="348"
 height="261" alt="Solar panels" />
<img class="align-right" src="car.jpg" width="261" height="202"
 alt="Electric car" />
```

which aligns the first image to the left, and the second image to the right.

Second, you have to insert the img (image) property in the embedded style sheet and add those two class names (align-left and align-right) where you define the style that you will use for images. This involves the following code that is inserted into the embedded style sheet:

```
img.align-left     {float: left;
                    margin-left: 5px;
                    margin-right: 5px}
img.align-right    {float: right;
                    margin-left: 5px;
                    margin-right: 5px}
```

where img is the property element and align-right and align-left are the class names. The class names align-right and align-left are arbitrary; you could name them anything. When naming classes, use names that make sense. Notice that the class names are separated from the element img with a period.

Another way to control space around images is to use the paragraph <p> tag. Remember that a paragraph tag inserts a blank line above the next object (text or image) after the paragraph tag. Figure 3–33a shows an example of using a <p> tag before inserting the Solar image, whereas Figure 3–33b shows an example of not using a <p> tag before the <img> tag. In this project, we will use the paragraph tag before the <img> tag to give more space between the image and the heading.

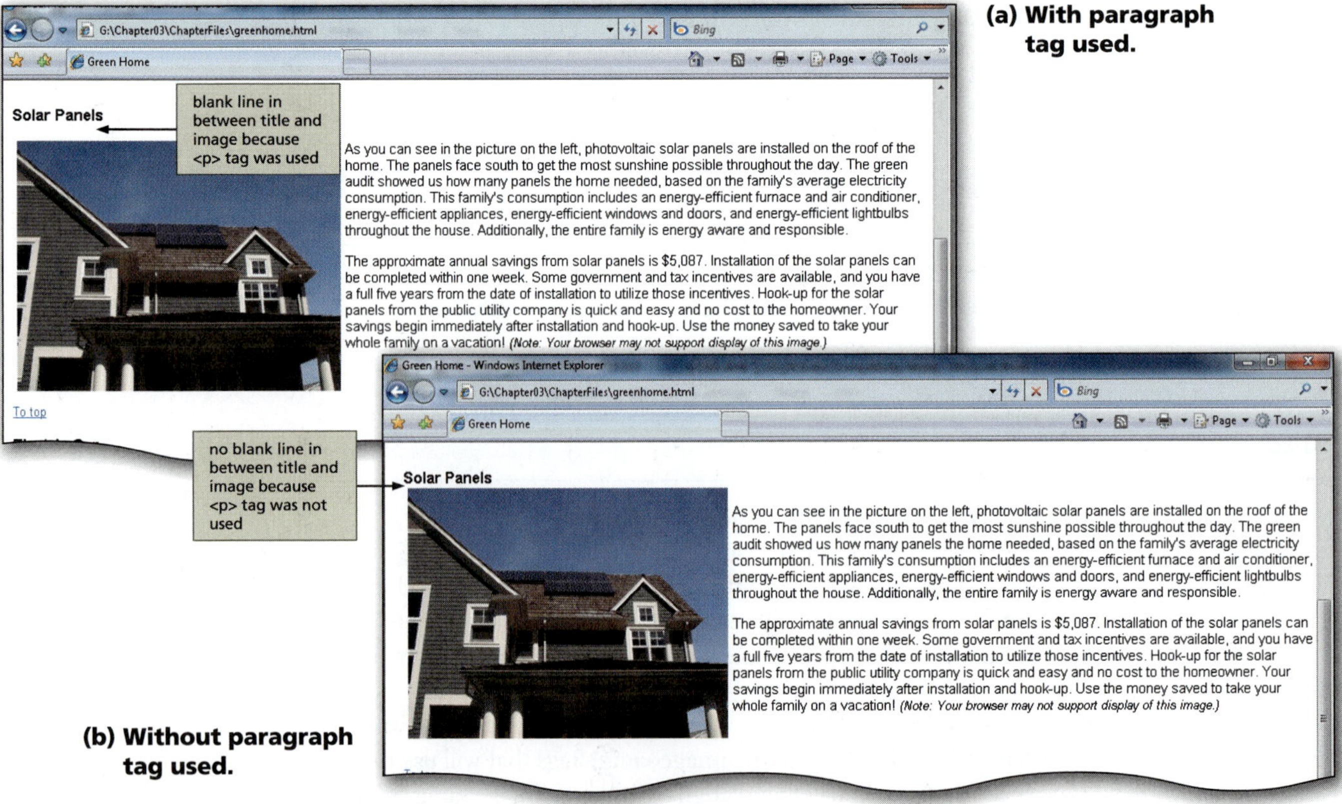

Figure 3–33

Using Thumbnail Images

Many Web developers use thumbnail images to improve page loading time. A **thumbnail image** is a smaller version of the image itself. The thumbnail is used as a link that, when clicked, will load the full-sized image. Figure 3–34a shows an example of a thumbnail image. When the image is clicked, the browser loads the full-sized image (Figure 3–34b). Loading images can take a long time, depending on the size and the complexity of the image. Using a thumbnail image gives a visitor the opportunity to decide whether to view the full-sized image.

To create a thumbnail version of an image, the image can be resized to a smaller size in a paint or image-editing program and then saved with a different file name. The thumbnail image then is added to a Web page as an image link to the larger version of the image. The HTML code to add a thumbnail image that links to a larger image takes the form:

```
<a href="largeimage.gif"><img src="thumbnail.gif" /></a>
```

where largeimage.gif is the name of the full-sized image and thumbnail.gif is the name of the smaller version of the image. In the case of this simple thumbnail example, a visitor clicks the thumbnail image to view the larger image, but there is no "return" button or link on the full-sized image Web page for the user to return to the original Web page. In this case, the visitor would have to use the Back button on the browser's Standard toolbar to return to the original Web page displaying the thumbnail image. For most Web development projects, however, you always want to provide a link for the visitors and not force them to use the Back button.

BTW

Thumbnail Size
The size of a thumbnail varies depending on the clarity of the image and its purpose. Generally a 100–150 pixel height and 100–150 pixel width is an appropriate size. If you need the visitor to see more of the image even in the small size, then a larger thumbnail is fine. If a thumbnail is easily distinguishable at a very small size (100 x 100), then that size is appropriate. Also, you should never resize an image using the height and width attributes in the HTML code. You should resize the image in an editing program and save it with a new file name.

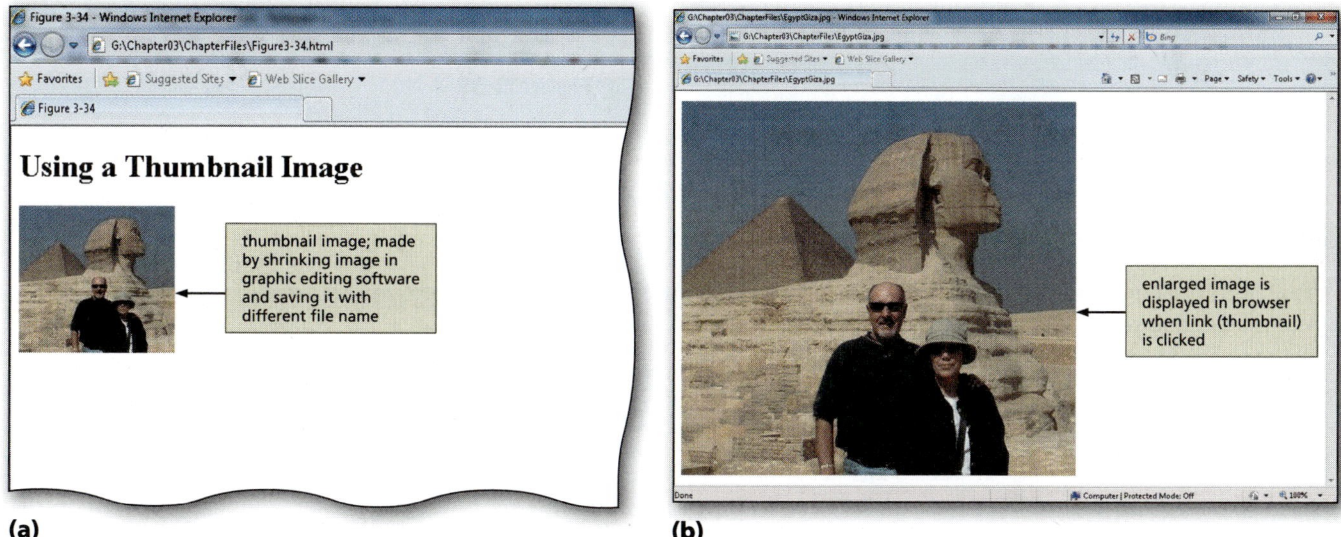

Figure 3–34

Wrap Text Around Images Using CSS Classes

Now you will use an embedded style sheet to wrap the text around the two images on the greenhome.html Web page. Remember that an embedded style sheet takes effect only for the Web page into which it is embedded. The embedded style sheet is placed within the <head> </head> container at the top of the Web page file.

The following steps show you how to insert left- and right-aligned images with wrapped text by adding class names to the img tags and then defining the classes within the embedded style sheets. Table 3–10 shows the code you'll need to define the classes in Step 3.

- With the greenhome.html file displayed in Notepad++, click immediately to the left of the s in src on line 44 to begin adding the class name to the first <img> tag.
- Type `class="align-left"` and press the SPACEBAR so that there is a space between what you just typed and src.
- Click immediately to the left of the s in src on line 62 to begin adding the class name to the second <img> tag.
- Type `class="align-right"` and press the SPACEBAR so that there is a space between what you just typed and src (Figure 3–35).

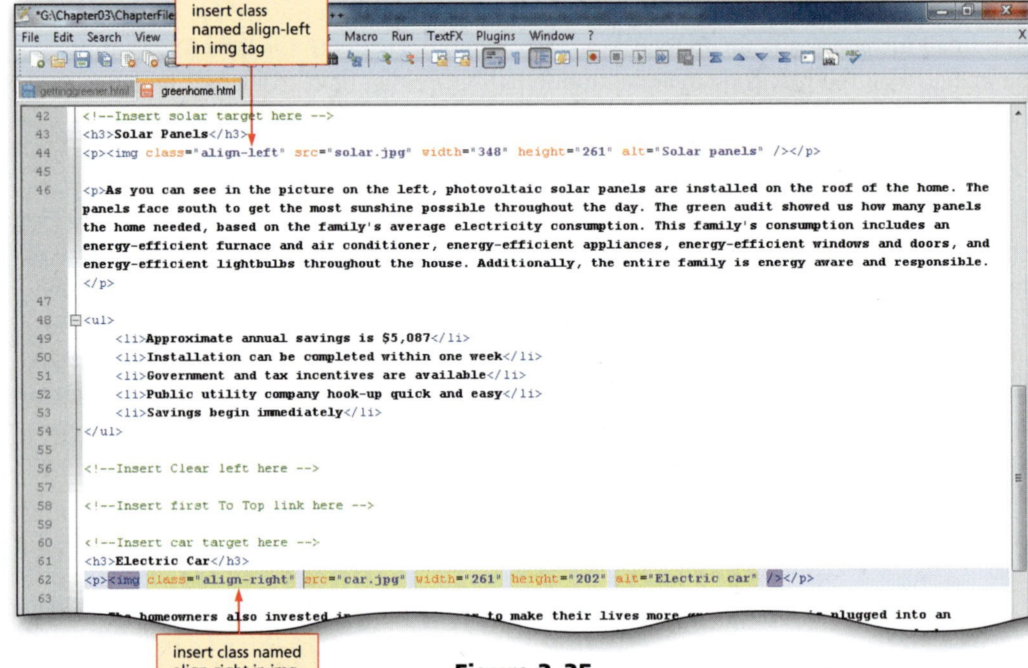

Figure 3–35

2

- Highlight the line <! Insert image style classes here --> on line 22, as shown in Figure 3–36, to begin adding image classes.

Q&A Do I have to press the DELETE key to delete the text that I highlighted in Step 2?

No, you do not have to press the DELETE key to delete the text on line 22. As long as the text is highlighted, the text is automatically deleted as soon as you start typing the HTML code in Step 3.

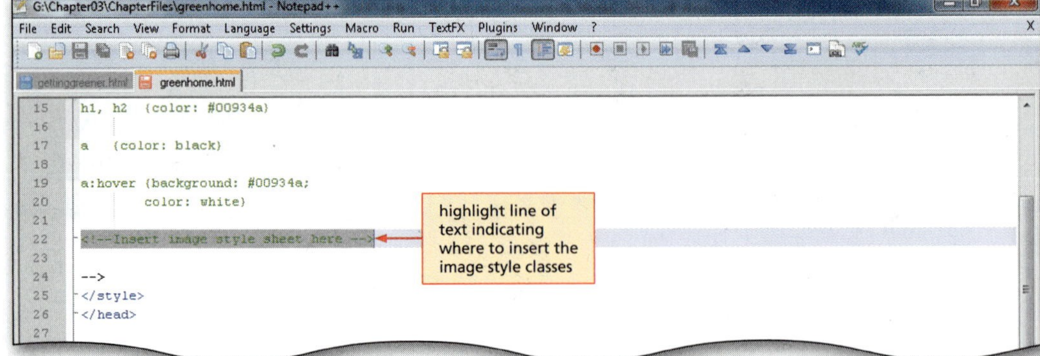

Figure 3–36

Table 3–10 CSS Code to Insert Class Definitions in Embedded Style Sheets

Line	CSS Selectors and Declarations	
22	`img.align-right`	`{float: right;`
23		`margin-left: 5px;`
24		`margin-right: 5px}`
25		
26	`img.align-left`	`{float: left;`
27		`margin-left: 5px;`
28		`margin-right: 5px}`

3

- Type the HTML code in Table 3–10 but do not press the ENTER key at the end of line 28. This HTML code inserts the embedded style sheets that will be used by the align-left and align-right class names inserted in the previous step. This will align the images left or right on the Web page, with text wrapped to the right or left and with five pixels of horizontal space around the image (Figure 3–37).

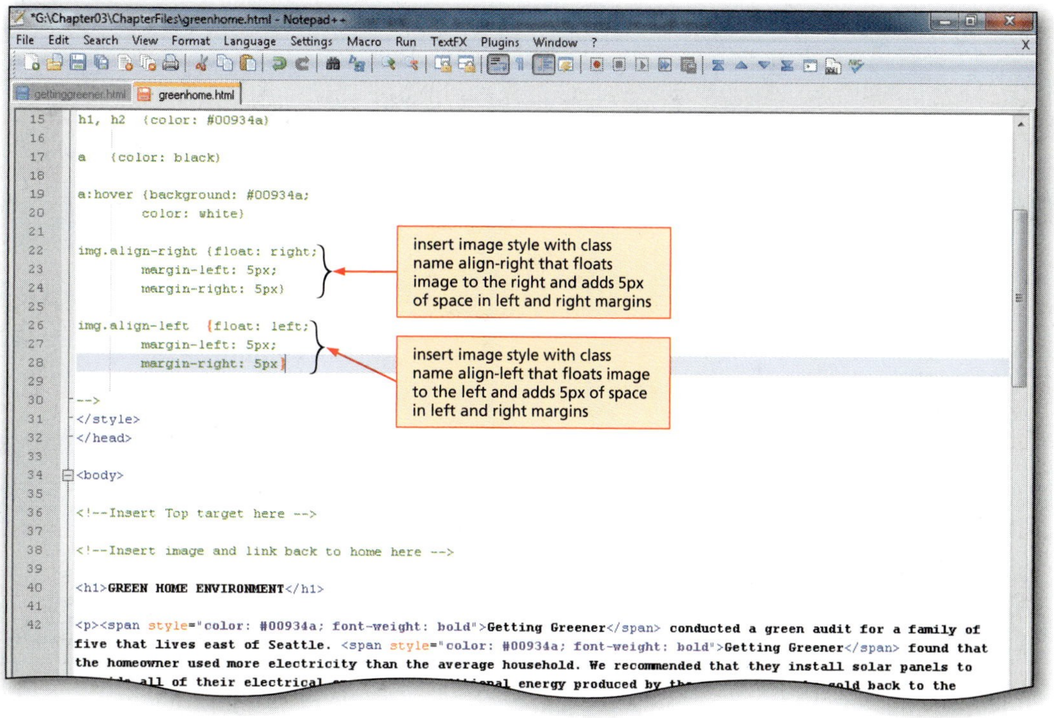

Figure 3–37

Q&A Why are we using the float property in these style sheets?

The float property allows you to position elements (in this case photographs) on the Web page.

Q&A Why do we need margin-left and margin-right properties?

These properties provide five pixels (in this case) of space around the left and right sides of the image that is being inserted. If those are not entered, then the text aligns itself right next to the image. Allowing a bit of space between these two elements makes the image and text neater.

To Clear Text Wrapping

After specifying an image alignment and defining how text wraps, you must enter a break (<br />) tag to stop the text wrapping. You use the <br style="clear: both" />, <br style="clear: left" />", or <br style="clear: right" /> tags to show where the text should stop wrapping. The following steps show how to enter code to clear the text wrapping.

- Highlight the line <Insert Clear left here --> on line 62, and then type `<br style="clear: left" />` as the tag (Figure 3–38).

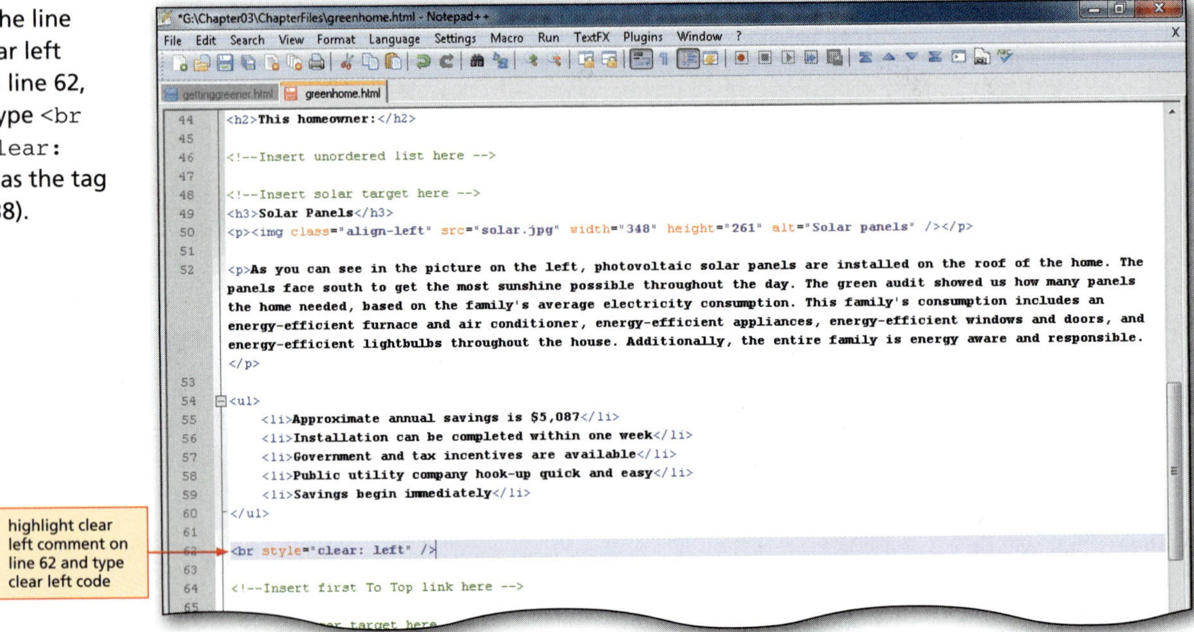

Figure 3–38

2

- Highlight the line <!--Insert Clear right here --> on line 80, and then type `<br style="clear: right" />` as the tag to clear the text wrapping for both left- and right-aligned images, as displayed in Figure 3–39.

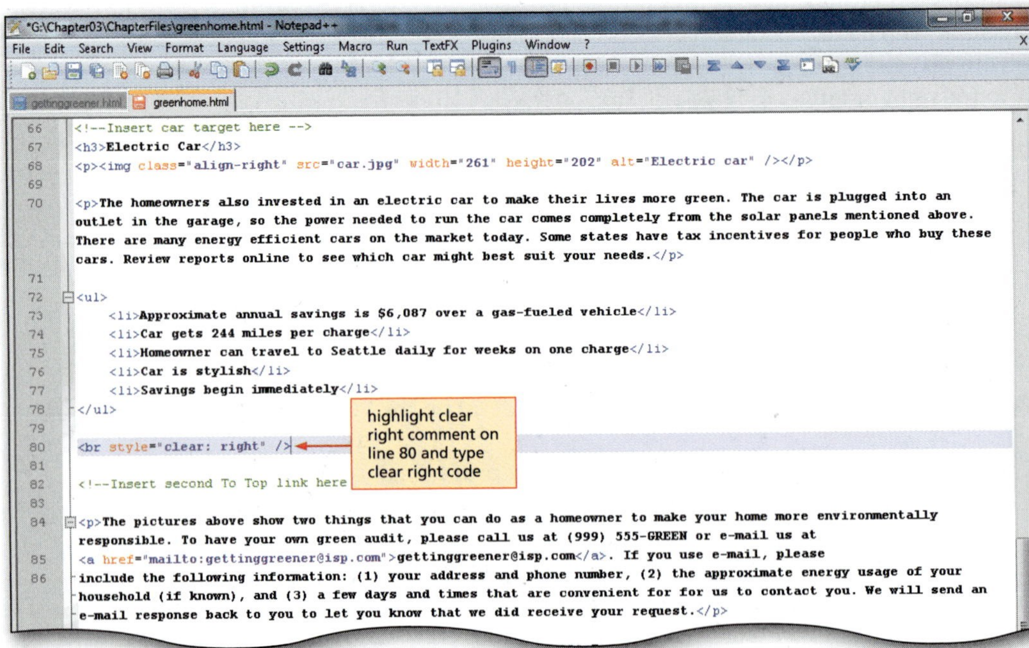

Figure 3–39

Q&A What happens if you do not use the <br style="clear: direction" /> tag?

Your text following the wrapped image will not be displayed as you intended. The following text will continue to wrap beyond the end of the text and image combination.

Q&A Is there one tag to clear all alignments?

Yes. The <br style="clear: both" /> tag clears all text alignments.

Adding Links Within a Web Page

The final links to be added in this project are links within the Green Home Web page. Because the Green Home Web page is quite long, it would be easier for visitors to have a menu or list at the top of the Web page that facilitates immediate movement to another section. Figure 3–40 shows how clicking the text link Installed solar panels in the bulleted list near the top of the page links to the Solar Panels section in another part of the Web page. When the mouse pointer is moved over the words Installed solar panels and is clicked, the browser repositions, or links, the page to the target named solar. Notice when the mouse hovers over the link, the link changes to green background and white text. That is because of the a:hover styles that are embedded on this Web page.

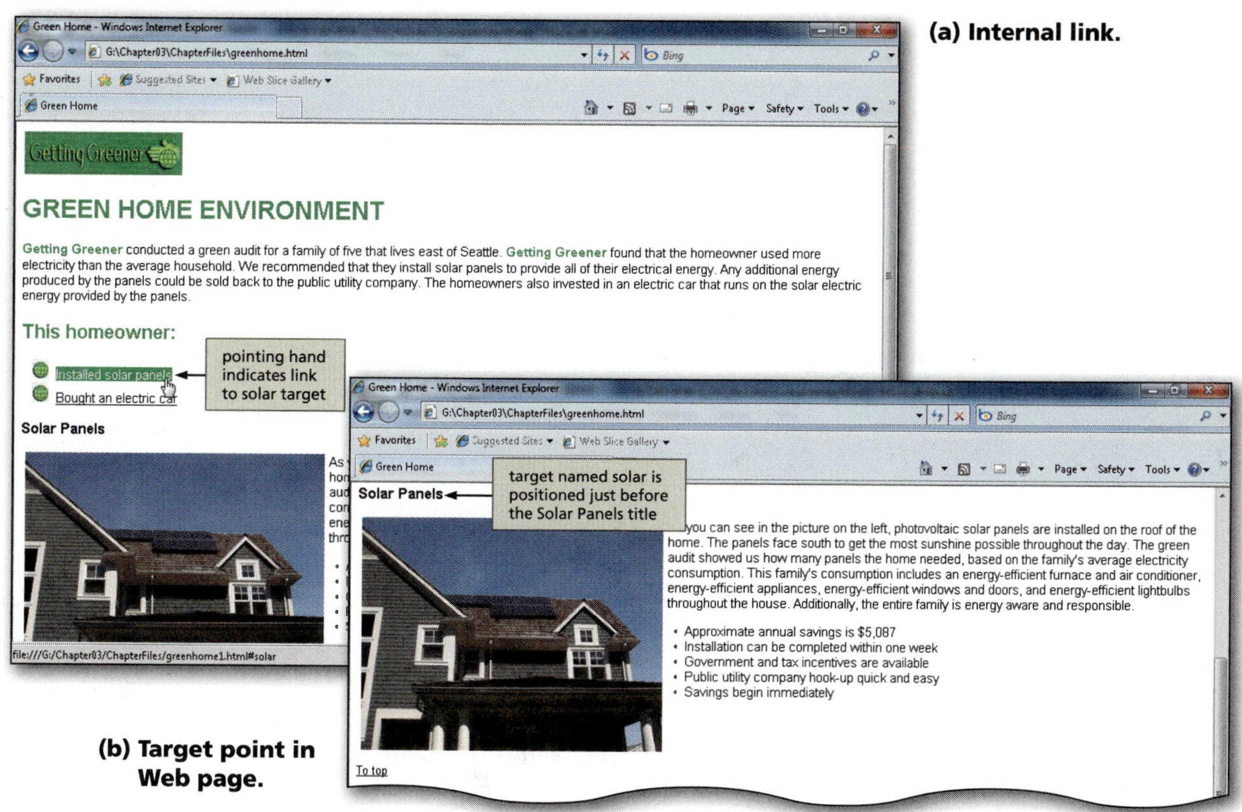

(a) Internal link.

(b) Target point in Web page.

Figure 3–40

To create links within the same Web page, the targets for the links first must be created. Link targets are created using the <a> tag with the name attribute, using the form:

```
<a name="targetname"></a>
```

where targetname is a unique name for a link target within that Web page. Notice that the tag uses the name attribute, rather than the href attribute, and that no text is included between the start <a> and end </a> tag, because the target is not intended to appear on the Web page as a clickable link. Instead, the link target is intended to mark a specific area of the Web page, to which a link can be directed.

Links to link targets are created using the <a> tag with the href attribute, using the form:

```
<a href="#targetname">
```

where targetname is the name of a link target in that Web page. Notice that the tag uses the href attribute, followed by the pound sign (#) and the target name enclosed in quotation marks.

To Set Link Targets

The next step is to set link targets to the Solar Panels and Electric Car sections of the Web page. The following steps show how to set the two link targets in the Green Home Web page.

- Highlight the line <!-- Insert solar target here --> on line 48.
- Type `<a name="solar"></a>` to create a link target named solar (Figure 3–41).

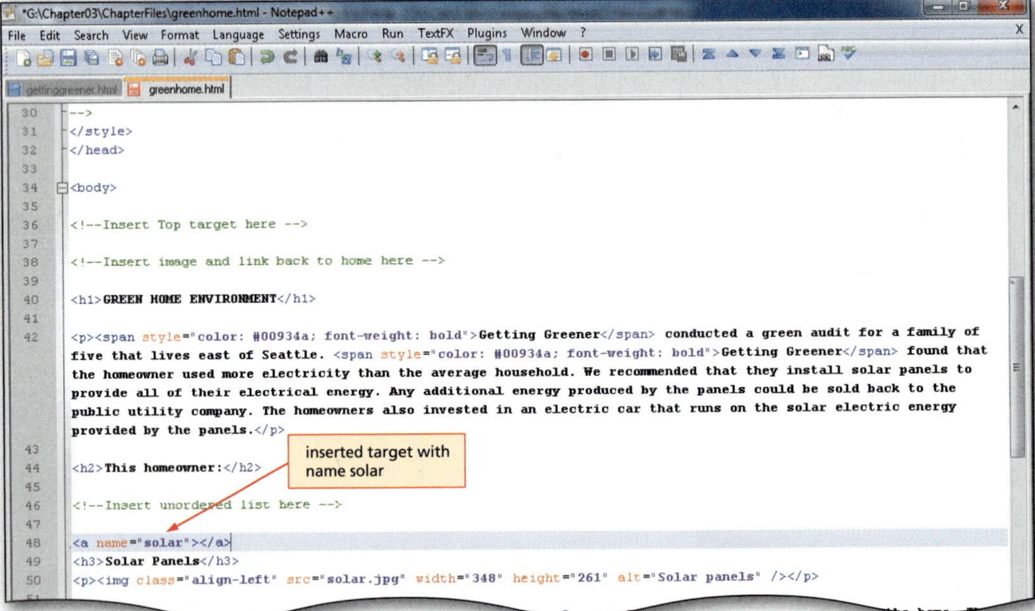

Figure 3–41

2

- Highlight the line <!--Insert car target here --> on line 66.
- Type `<a name="car"></a>` to create a link target named car (Figure 3–42).

Q&A

There is nothing between the start anchor and end anchor tags for these targets. Will they work?

These targets are just placeholders, so they do not need any words or phrases; they only need a target name, as shown in the anchor tag.

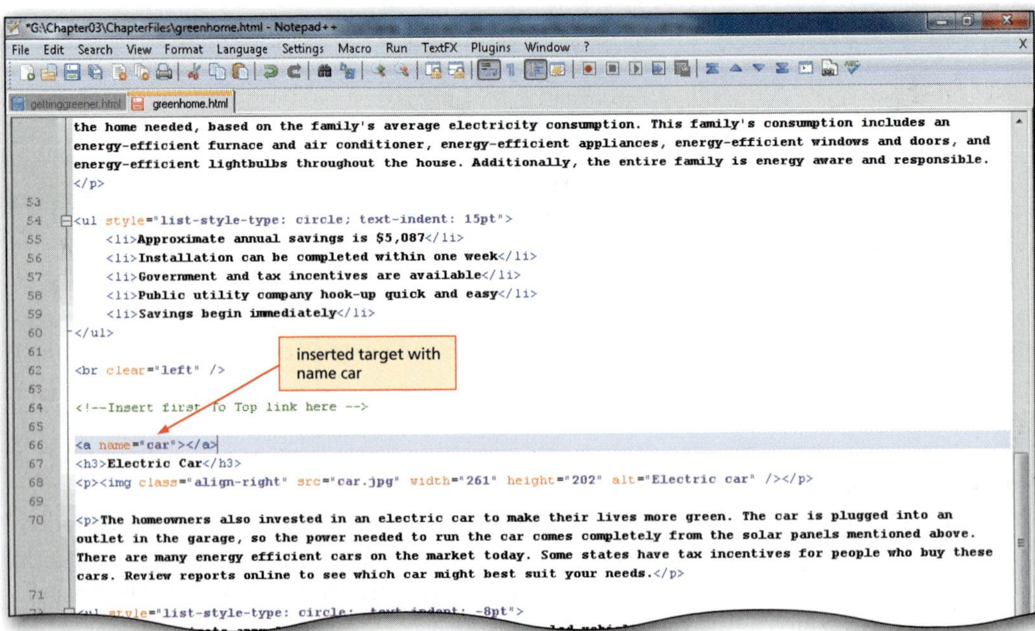

Figure 3–42

To Add Links to Link Targets Within a Web Page

The next step is to add link targets using the code shown in Table 3–11.

Table 3–11 HTML Code to Insert Bulleted List with Links to Link Targets

Line	HTML Tag and Text
46	`<ul style="list-style-image: url(earthbullet.jpg)">`
47	`<li><a href="#solar">Installed solar panels</a></li>`
48	`<li><a href="#car">Bought an electric car</a></li>`
49	`</ul>`

The following step shows how to add the code to create an unordered (bulleted) list and then to use the list items as links to link targets within the Web page.

- Highlight the line <!--Insert unordered list here --> on line 46.
- Type the HTML code in Table 3–11 but do not press the ENTER key at the end of line 49. This HTML code inserts the bulleted list that provides links to the two targets (solar and car) inserted above. Notice that you use the same earthbullet.jpg image that you used on the home page as the bullet (Figure 3–43). This helps with consistency across the Web site.

Figure 3–43

Q&A Do I have to use a bulleted list for the links?

No, you can use any text for the links to the targets created in the step above. The bulleted list makes the links easy to use and keeps the links in one area of the Web page.

To Add Links to a Target at the Top of the Page

In this step, you add two To top links to provide a quick way to move back to the top of the Web page. To make these links, you first set the target at the top of the page, and then create the links to that target. You will also use an inline style to make the link text smaller than the regular font size. The following steps illustrate how to add links to a target at the top of the page.

- Highlight the line <!--Insert Top target here --> on line 36.
- Type `<a name="top"></a>` as the tag that will create a target at the top of the Web page named top (Figure 3–44).

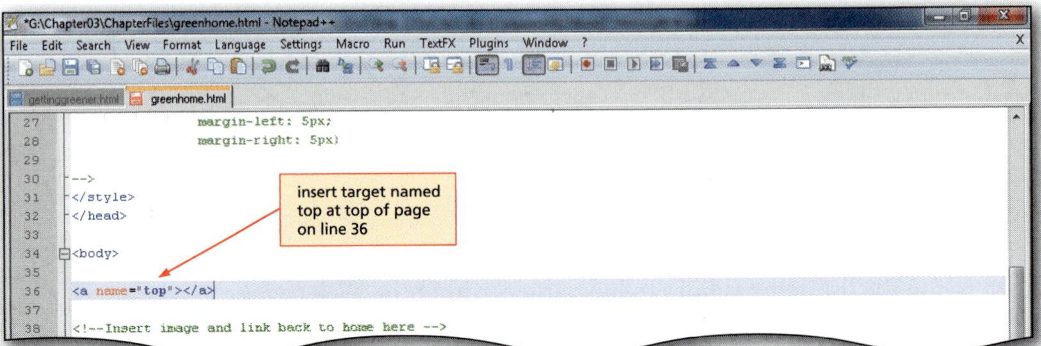

Figure 3–44

- Highlight the line <!--Insert first To top link here --> on line 67.
- Type `<p><a href="#top"><span style="font-size: small">To top</span></a></p>` as the tag (Figure 3–45).

Q&A

Why do you use a small size font for this link?

The link back to the top of the page should be subtle yet noticeable as distinguished from the other text on the page. Notice that the text link at the very bottom of the Web page to return to the home page is the same small size.

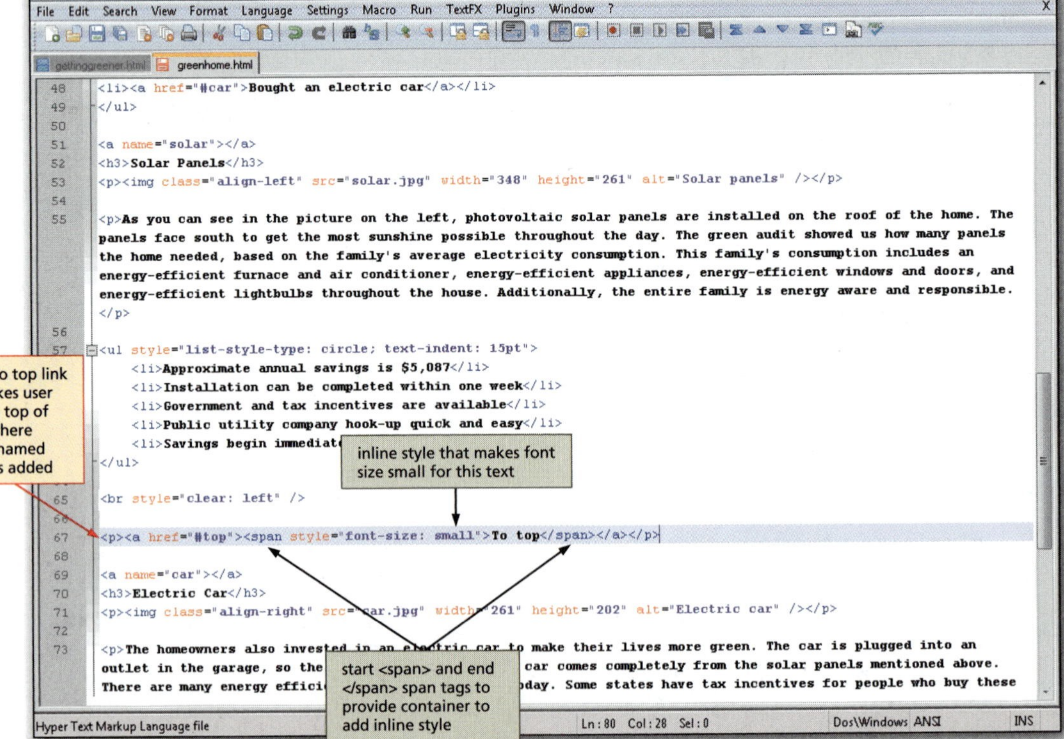

Figure 3–45

To Copy and Paste HTML Code

The copy and paste feature can be very useful for entering the same code in different places. The following step shows how to copy and paste the link code to three other lines in the HTML code.

- Highlight the HTML code `<p><a href="#top"><span style="font-size: small">To top</span></a></p>` on line 67.
- Click Edit on the menu bar and then click Copy.
- Highlight the line <!--Insert second To top link here --> on line 85 to position the pointer.
- Click Edit on the menu bar and then click Paste to paste the HTML code that you copied into line 85 (Figure 3–46).

```
69  <a name="car"></a>
70  <h3>Electric Car</h3>
71  <p><img class="align-right" src="car.jpg" width="261" height="202" alt="Electric car" /></p>
72
73  <p>The homeowners also invested in an electric car to make their lives more green. The car is plugged into an
    outlet in the garage, so the power needed to run the car comes completely from the solar panels mentioned above.
    There are many energy efficient cars on the market today. Some states have tax incentives for people who buy these
    cars. Review reports online to see which car might best suit your needs.</p>
74
75  <ul style="list-style-type: circle;  text-indent: -8pt">
76      <li>Approximate annual savings is $6,087 over a gas-fueled vehicle</li>
77      <li>Car gets 244 miles per charge</li>
78      <li>Homeowner can travel to Seattle daily for weeks on one charge</li>
79      <li>Car is stylish</li>
80      <li>Savings begin immediately</li>
81  </ul>
82
83  <br style="clear: right" />
84
85  <p><a href="#top"><span style="font-size: small">To top</span></a></p>
86
87  <p>The pictures above show two things that you can do as a homeowner to make your home more environmentally
    responsible. To have your own green audit, please call us at (999) 555-GREEN or e-mail us at
88  <a href="mailto:gettinggreener@isp.com">gettinggreener@isp.com</a>. If you use e-mail, please
89  include the following information: (1) your address and phone number, (2) the approximate energy usage of your
    household (if known), and (3) a few days and times that are convenient for for us to contact you. We will send an
    e-mail response back to you to let you know that we did receive your request.</p>
```


Figure 3–46

To Add an Image Link to a Web Page

The last step is to add an image link from the Green Home Web page back to the Getting Greener home page. The style for links that you set with an embedded style sheet earlier says that link background color is green and text is white. For an image link, however, this would not be appropriate. To override the embedded style sheet for just this one instance, you will use an inline style to set a background-color that is transparent with text-decoration of none (no underline). Remember that according to the style precedence rules, an inline style takes precedence over an embedded style sheet. These two styles (background-color: transparent; text-decoration: none) ensure that no border appears around the image and there is no line under the link image. Table 3–12 shows the code used to insert the image link.

Table 3–12 HTML Code to Insert Image Link to Home

Line	HTML Tag and Text
38	`<div>`
39	`<a href="gettinggreener.html" style="background-color: transparent; text-decoration: none">`
40	`<img style="border-color: transparent" src="earthsm.jpg" width="184" height="48" alt="Back to home page" /></a>`
41	`</div>`

The following step shows how to create an image link at the top of the Green Home Web page.

- Highlight the line <!--Insert image and link back to home here --> on line 38.
- Type the HTML code in Table 3–12 but do not press the ENTER key at the end of line 41. This HTML code inserts a link back to home from the image earthsm.jpg. This image is a smaller version of the earthlogo.jpg image that you used on the home page (Figure 3–47).

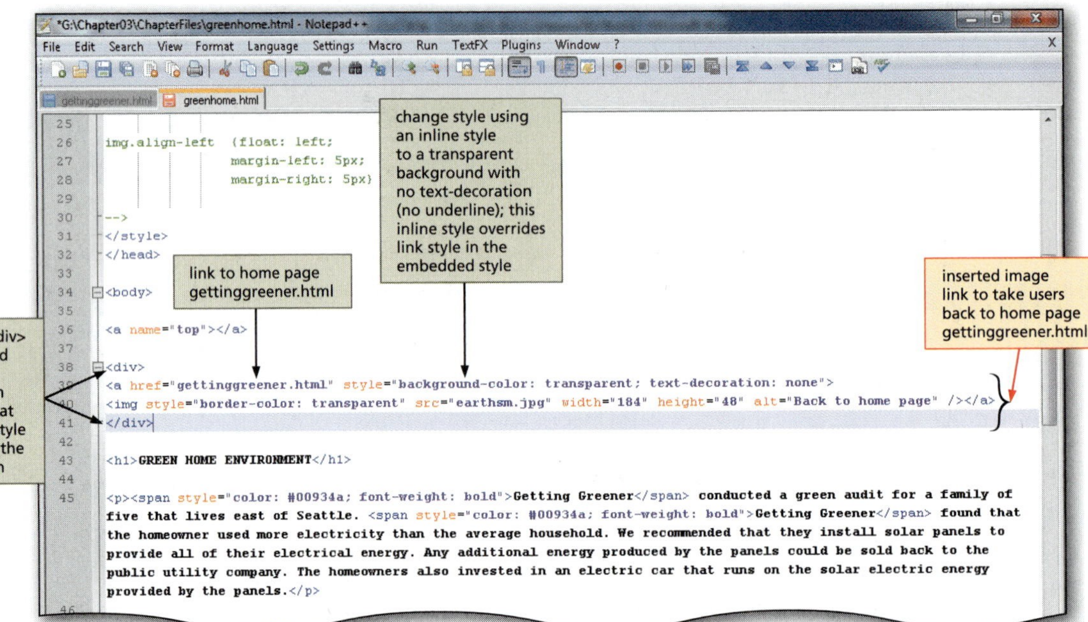

Figure 3–47

To Save, Validate, and Print the HTML File

With the HTML code for the Green Home Web page complete, the HTML file should be saved, the Web page should be validated at w3.org, and a copy of the file should be printed as a reference.

1. If necessary, activate the Notepad++ window.
2. Click File on the menu bar, and then Save on the File menu to save the HTML file as greenhome.html.
3. Open a new browser window and go to validator.w3.org.
4. Click the Validate by File Upload tab, browse to the greenhome.html Web page, and then click Open.
5. Click the Check button to determine if the Web page is valid. If the file is not valid, make corrections,
re-save, and revalidate.
6. Click the Notepad++ button on the taskbar to display the greenhome.html code. Click File on the menu bar, click Print on the File menu, and then click the Print button in the Print dialog box to print the HTML code.

To View and Test a Web Page

With the HTML code validated and saved, you should view the Web page and test the links.

1. Click the Internet Explorer button on the taskbar to view the page in your browser.

2. Click the Refresh button on the Standard toolbar to display the changes made to the Web page, which should now look like Figure 3–1b on page HTML 91.

3. Verify that all internal links work correctly by clicking the two links in the bulleted list at the top of the Web page. Also make sure to check the two To top links. Finally, verify that the image link to the home page works.

Q&A

How can I tell if internal links are working when the link and target are displayed in the same browser window?

To see movement to a link, you might need to restore down and resize the browser window so that the target is not visible, then click the link.

To Print a Web Page

1. Click the Print icon on the Command bar to print the Web page (Figure 3–48).

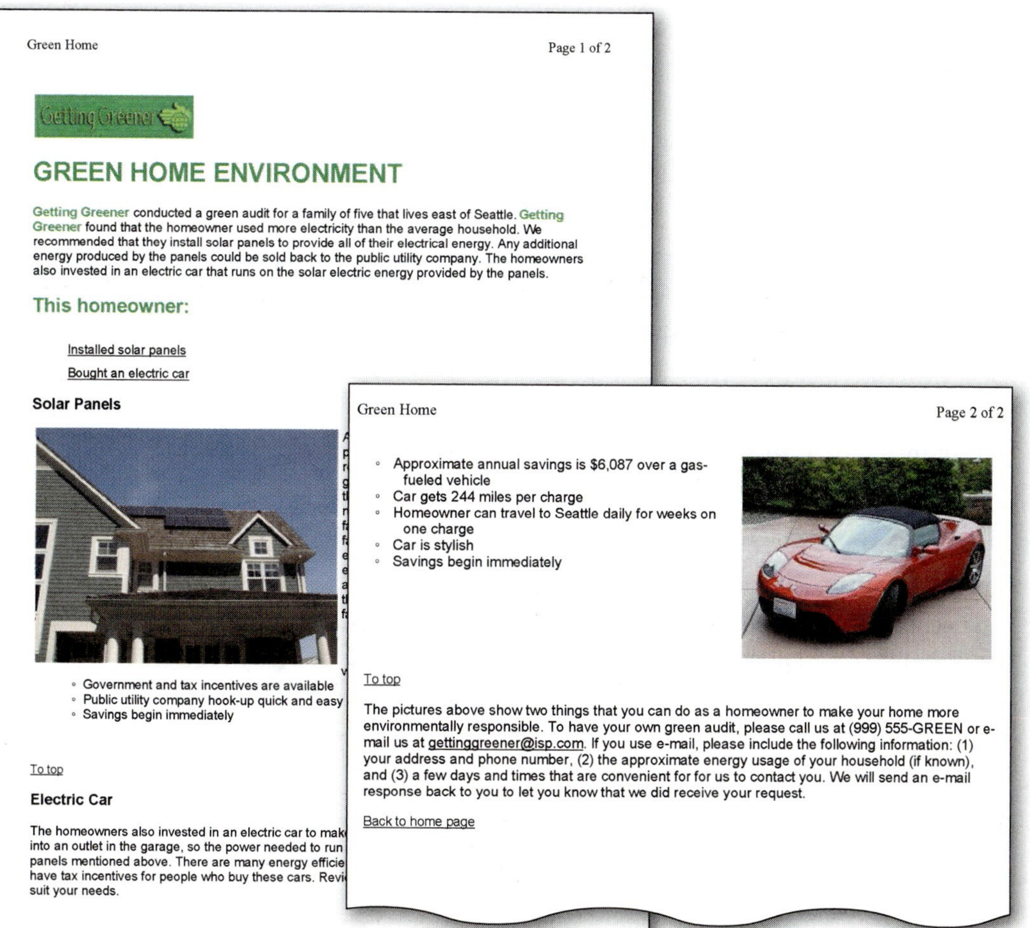

Green Home Page 1 of 2

GREEN HOME ENVIRONMENT

Getting Greener conducted a green audit for a family of five that lives east of Seattle. Getting Greener found that the homeowner used more electricity than the average household. We recommended that they install solar panels to provide all of their electrical energy. Any additional energy produced by the panels could be sold back to the public utility company. The homeowners also invested in an electric car that runs on the solar electric energy provided by the panels.

This homeowner:

Installed solar panels
Bought an electric car

Solar Panels

- Government and tax incentives are available
- Public utility company hook-up quick and easy
- Savings begin immediately

To top

Electric Car

The homeowners also invested in an electric car to mak into an outlet in the garage, so the power needed to run panels mentioned above. There are many energy efficie have tax incentives for people who buy these cars. Revi suit your needs.

Green Home Page 2 of 2

- Approximate annual savings is $6,087 over a gas-fueled vehicle
- Car gets 244 miles per charge
- Homeowner can travel to Seattle daily for weeks on one charge
- Car is stylish
- Savings begin immediately

To top

The pictures above show two things that you can do as a homeowner to make your home more environmentally responsible. To have your own green audit, please call us at (999) 555-GREEN or e-mail us at gettinggreener@isp.com. If you use e-mail, please include the following information: (1) your address and phone number, (2) the approximate energy usage of your household (if known), and (3) a few days and times that are convenient for for us to contact you. We will send an e-mail response back to you to let you know that we did receive your request.

Back to home page

Figure 3–48

BTW

Quick Reference
For a list of HTML tags and their associated attributes, see the HTML Quick Reference (Appendix A) at the back of this book, or visit the Quick Reference Web page for this book (scsite.com/HTML6e/qr). For a list of CSS properties and values, see Appendix D, or visit scsite.com/HTML6e/qr.

To Quit Notepad++ and a Browser

1. In Notepad++, click the File menu, then Close All.
2. Click the Close button on the Notepad++ title bar.
3. Click the Close button on all open browser windows.

Chapter Summary

In this chapter, you have learned how to develop a two-page Web site with links, images, and formatted text. You learned how to use inline and embedded style sheets and style classes to format elements in each Web page. The items listed below include all the new HTML and CSS skills you have learned in this chapter.

1. Add a Center-Aligned Banner Image Using an Inline Style (HTML 102)
2. Create an Unordered (Bulleted) List Using Images as Bullets (HTML 106)
3. Add a Text Link to Another Web Page Within the Same Web Site (HTML 108)
4. Add an E-Mail Link (HTML 109)
5. Add a Text Link to a Web Page in Another Web Site (HTML 111)
6. Add Embedded Style Statements (HTML 119)
7. Add an Inline Style for Color (HTML 121)
8. Test Links on a Web Page (HTML 125)
9. Wrap Text Around Images Using CSS Classes (HTML 136)
10. Clear Text Wrapping (HTML 138)
11. Set Link Targets (HTML 140)
12. Add Links to Link Targets Within a Web Page (HTML 141)
13. Add Links to a Target at the Top of the Page (HTML 142)
14. Copy and Paste HTML Code (HTML 143)
15. Add an Image Link to a Web Page (HTML 143)

Learn It Online

Test your knowledge of chapter content and key terms.

Instructions: To complete the Learn It Online exercises, start your browser, click the Address bar, and then enter the Web address `scsite.com/html6e/learn`. When the HTML Learn It Online page is displayed, click the link for the exercise you want to complete and read the instructions.

Chapter Reinforcement TF, MC, and SA

A series of true/false, multiple choice, and short answer questions that test your knowledge of the chapter content.

Flash Cards

An interactive learning environment where you identify chapter key terms associated with displayed definitions.

Practice Test

A series of multiple choice questions that test your knowledge of chapter content and key terms.

Who Wants To Be a Computer Genius?

An interactive game that challenges your knowledge of chapter content in the style of a television quiz show.

Wheel of Terms

An interactive game that challenges your knowledge of chapter key terms in the style of the television show, *Wheel of Fortune*.

Crossword Puzzle Challenge

A crossword puzzle that challenges your knowledge of key terms presented in the chapter.

Apply Your Knowledge

Reinforce the skills and apply the concepts you learned in this chapter.

Adding Text Formatting to a Web Page Using Inline Styles

Instructions: Start Notepad++. Open the file apply3-1.html from the Chapter03\Apply folder of the Data Files for Students. See the inside back cover of this book for instructions on downloading the Data Files for Students, or contact your instructor for information about accessing the required files.

The apply3-1.html file is a partially completed HTML file that you will use for this exercise. Figure 3–49 shows the Apply Your Knowledge Web page as it should be displayed in a browser after the additional HTML tags and attributes are added.

Perform the following tasks:

1. Enter g:\Chapter03\Apply\apply3-1.html as the URL to view the Web page in your browser.
2. Examine the HTML file in Notepad++ and its appearance in the browser.
3. In Notepad++, change the HTML code to make the Web page look similar to the one shown in Figure 3–49.
4. Use an inline style to create a left-aligned h1 heading, Dorm Room Doctors, and make it blue.
5. Using the <div></div> container, right-align the image garbage.jpg (width=600, height=428). Give the image a right-and left-margins of 10 pixels. (Make sure to use the alt attribute.)
6. Make the first paragraph a large font. Color the words YES red in that paragraph. (*Hint:* Use the <span> tag.)
7. The second paragraph should be normal font, but make the word sanity blue and italic.
8. In the third paragraph, make the phone number and e-mail address red and in a bolder font-weight.
9. Save the revised HTML file in the Chapter03\Apply folder using the file name apply3-1solution.html.

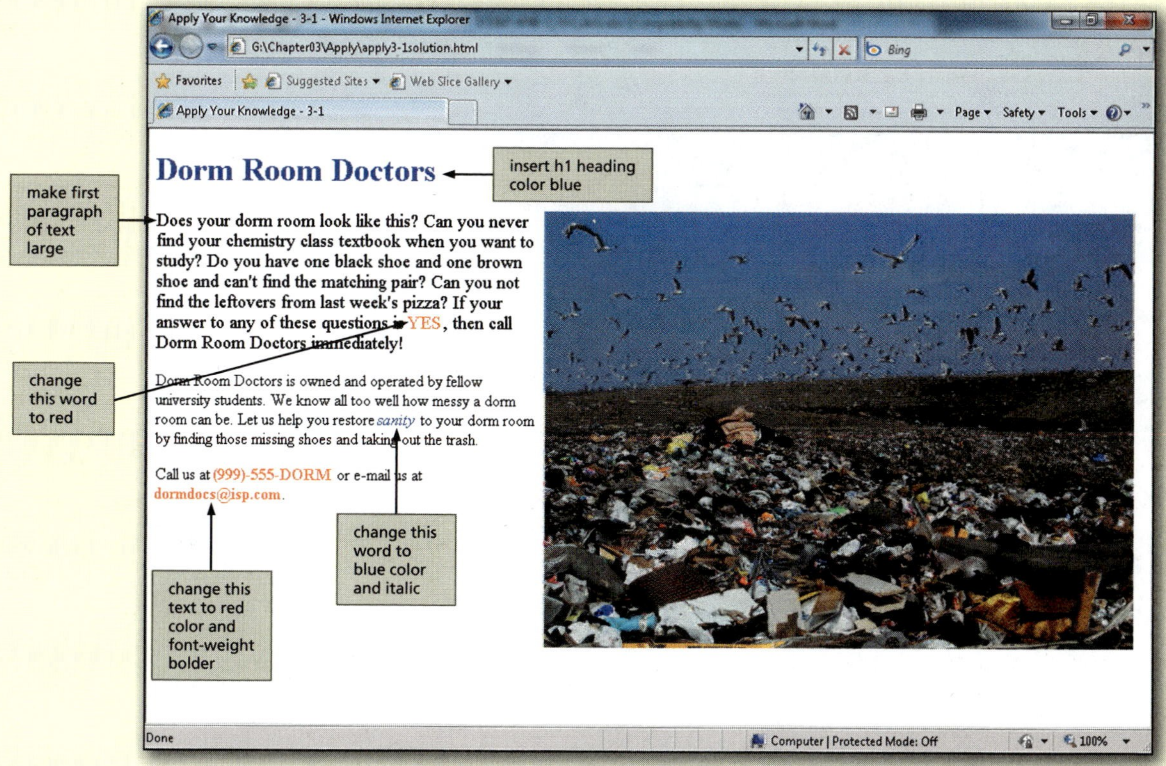

Figure 3–49

Continued >

Apply Your Knowledge *continued*

10. Validate your code.
11. Print the revised HTML file.
12. Enter g:\Chapter03\Apply\apply3-1solution.html as the URL to view the revised Web page in your browser.
13. Print the Web page.
14. Submit the revised HTML file and Web page in the format specified by your instructor.

Extend Your Knowledge

Extend the skills you learned in this chapter and experiment with new skills.

Creating Targets and Links

Instructions: Start Notepad++. Open the file extend3-1.html from the Chapter03\Extend folder of the Data Files for Students. See the inside back cover of this book for instructions on downloading the Data Files for Students, or contact your instructor for information about accessing the required files. This sample HTML file contains all of the text for the Web page shown in Figure 3–50. You will add the necessary tags to make this Web page appear with left- and right-aligned images, text formatting, and links, as shown in Figure 3–50.

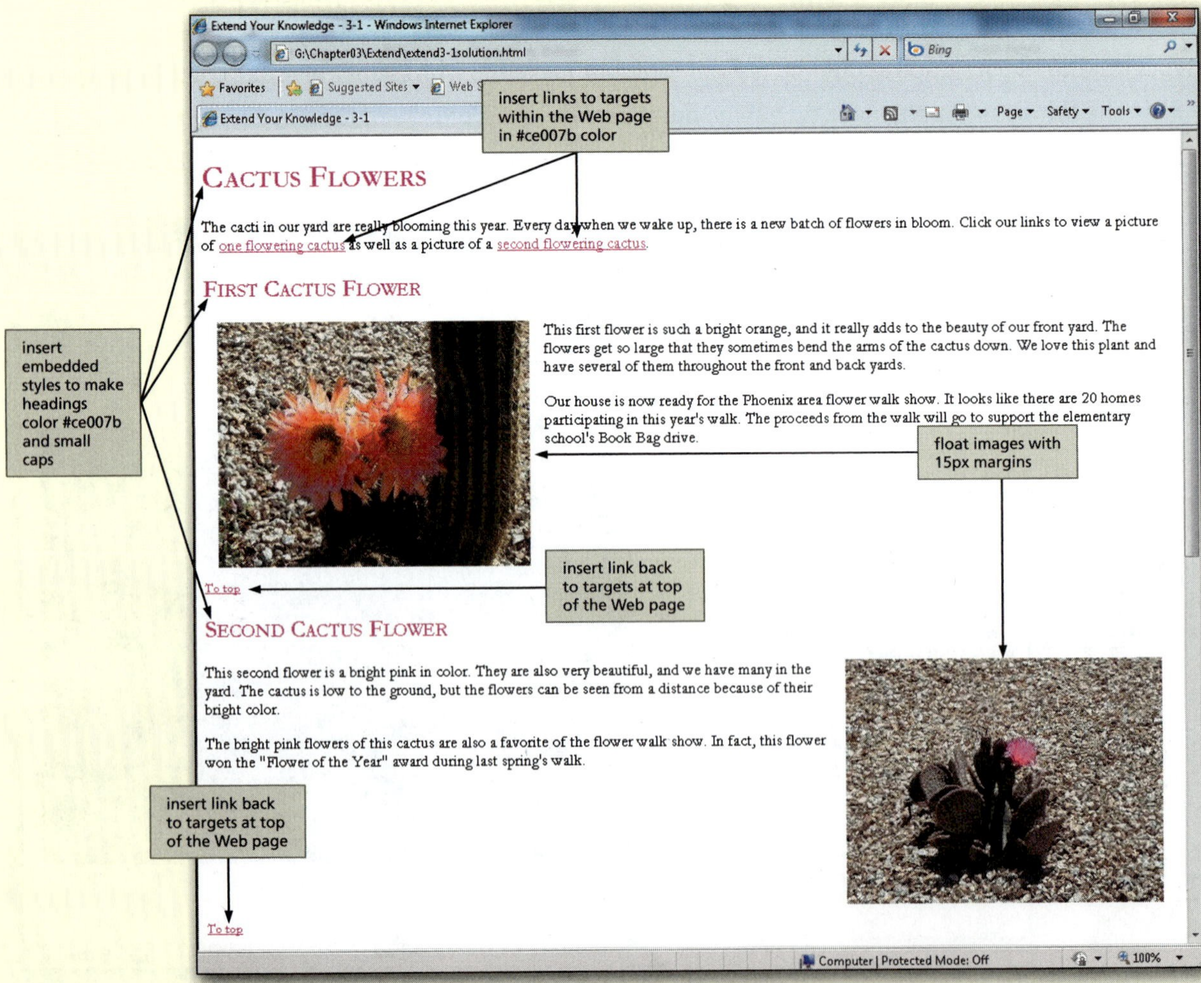

Figure 3–50

Perform the following tasks:

1. Insert the following embedded style sheets:

body	{font-family: Garamond, Arial, Verdana; font-size: 12pt}
h1, h2	{color: #ce007b; font-variant: small-caps}
img	{hspace: 20}
.align-right	{float: right; margin-left: 15px; margin-right: 15px}
.align-left	{float: left; margin-left: 15px; margin-right: 15px}
a	{text-decoration: underline; color: #ce007b}
a:hover	{background: #ce007b; color: white}

2. Make sure to use inline styles for all other styles. Add code to align the second picture on the right, also with margins of 15px. (*Hint:* Remember to clear alignment for both images.)
3. Add the HTML code to create three targets (one at the top of the Web page, one near the first h2 heading, and the last near the second h2 heading). Also create two link(s) back to the top with font size small, as shown in Figure 3–50.
4. Validate your HTML code and test all links.
5. Save the revised document as extend3-1solution.html and submit it in the format specified by your instructor.

Make It Right

Analyze a document; correct all errors and improve the design.

Correcting the Grand Canyon Web Page

Instructions: Start Notepad++. Open the file makeitright3-1.html from the Chapter03\MakeItRight folder of the Data Files for Students. See the inside back cover of this book for instructions on downloading the Data Files for Students, or contact your instructor for information about accessing the required files. The Web page is a modified version of what you see in Figure 3–51 on the next page. Make the necessary corrections to the Web page to make it look like the figure. The background color is #ffffc5 for this Web page. Use an inline style to float the images and provide margins. The Web page uses the images grandcanyon1.jpg and grandcanyon2.jpg, which have widths and heights of 346, 259, and 321, 288, respectively.

Continued >

Make It Right *continued*

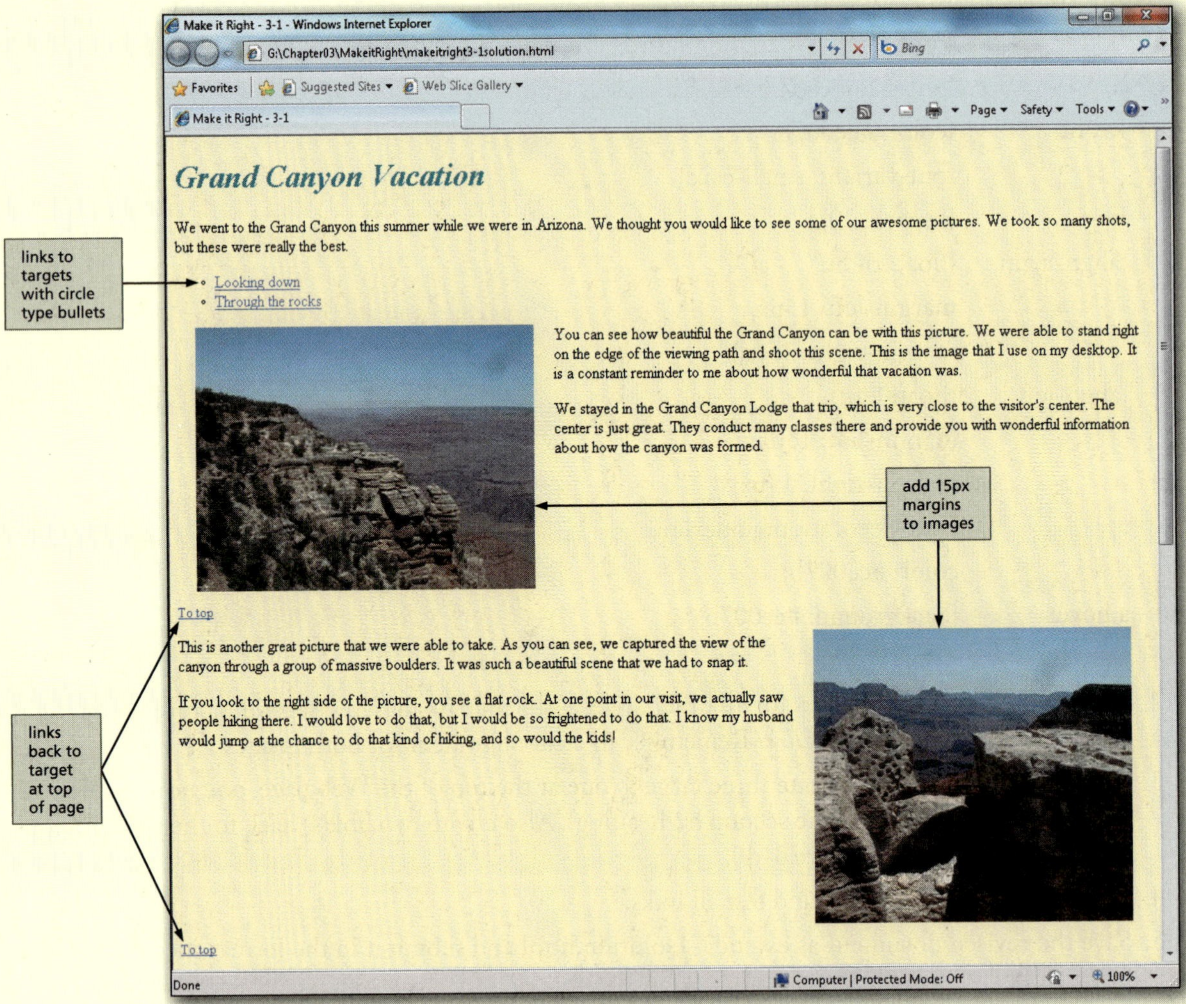

Figure 3–51

In the Lab

Lab 1: Creating a Web Page with Links

Problem: Your instructor wants you to create a Web page demonstrating your knowledge of link targets. You have been asked to create a Web page to demonstrate this technique, similar to the one shown in Figure 3–52. Use inline styles for all styles in the Web page.

Instructions: Perform the following steps:

1. Start Notepad++ and create a new HTML file with the title, Lab 3-1, in the main heading section.
2. Begin the body section by adding the image recycle.gif and aligning it to the left. Use the margin-left-and-right with values of 10 pixels.
3. Add the heading Help the Earth - Recycle. Format the heading to use the Heading 1 style, left-aligned, italic, with the font color black.
4. Add an unordered list with the three list items, as shown in Figure 3–52. These three items will be used to link to the three sections of text below them.

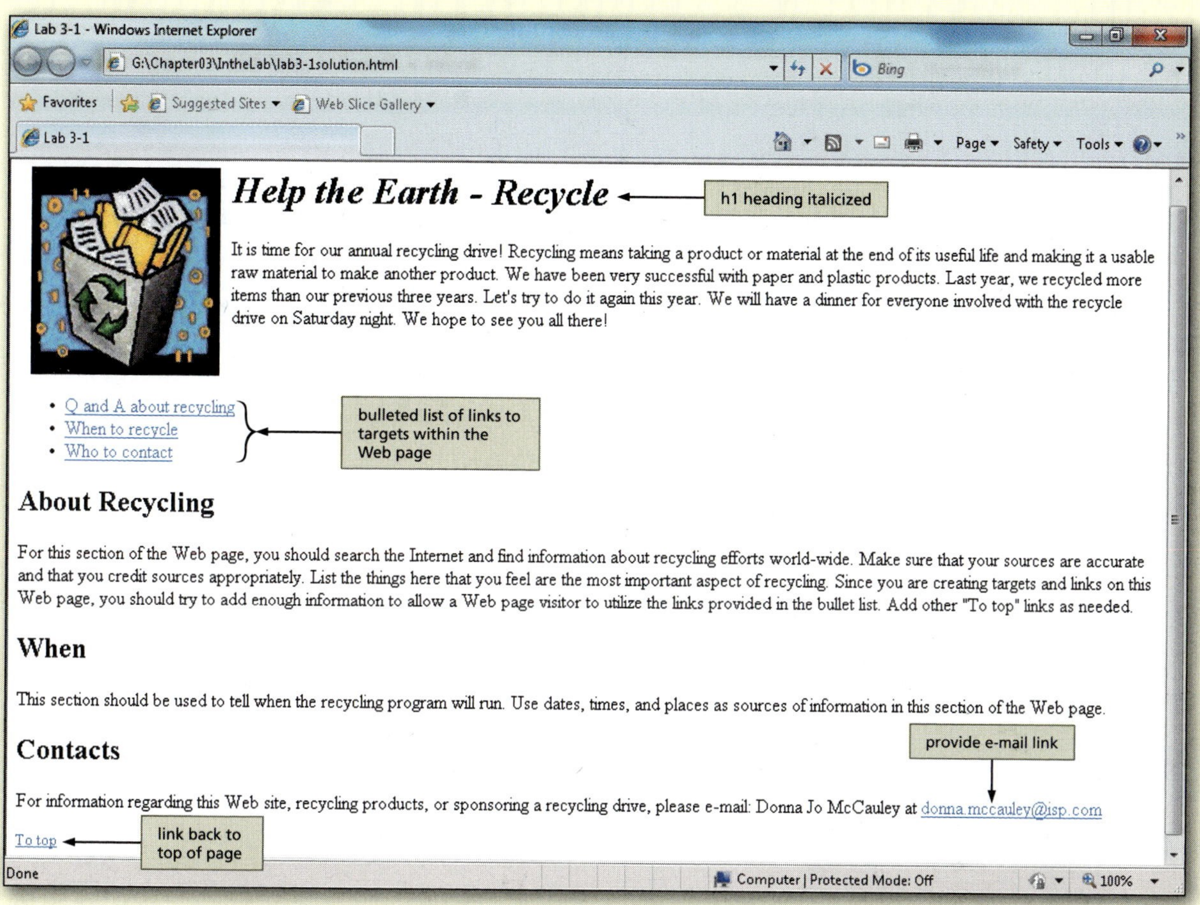

Figure 3–52

5. Add a Heading 2 style heading, About Recycling, and set a link target named about. Type a paragraph of text based on your research of the topic, as shown in Figure 3–52.
6. Add a Heading 2 style heading, When, and set a link target named when. Type a paragraph based on your research of the topic, as shown in Figure 3–52.
7. Add a Heading 2 style heading, Contacts, and set a link target named contacts. Type the paragraph, as shown in Figure 3–52.
8. Create a link target at the top of the page named top.
9. Create a top link at the bottom of the page, as shown in Figure 3–52. Set the link to direct to the top target at the top of the page.
10. Create links from the bulleted list to the three targets.
11. Create an e-mail link, as shown in Figure 3–52.
12. Save the HTML file in the Chapter03\IntheLab folder using the file name lab3-1solution.html.
13. Validate the lab-3-1solution.html file.
14. Print the lab3-1solution.html file.
15. Enter the URL `g:\Chapter03\IntheLab\lab3-1solution.html` to view the Web page in your browser.
16. Print the Web page.
17. Submit the HTML file and Web page in the format specified by your instructor.

In the Lab

2: Creating a Web Page with Links

Problem: Your instructor wants you to create a Web page demonstrating your knowledge of link targets. You have been asked to create a Web page to demonstrate this technique, similar to the one shown in Figure 3–53.

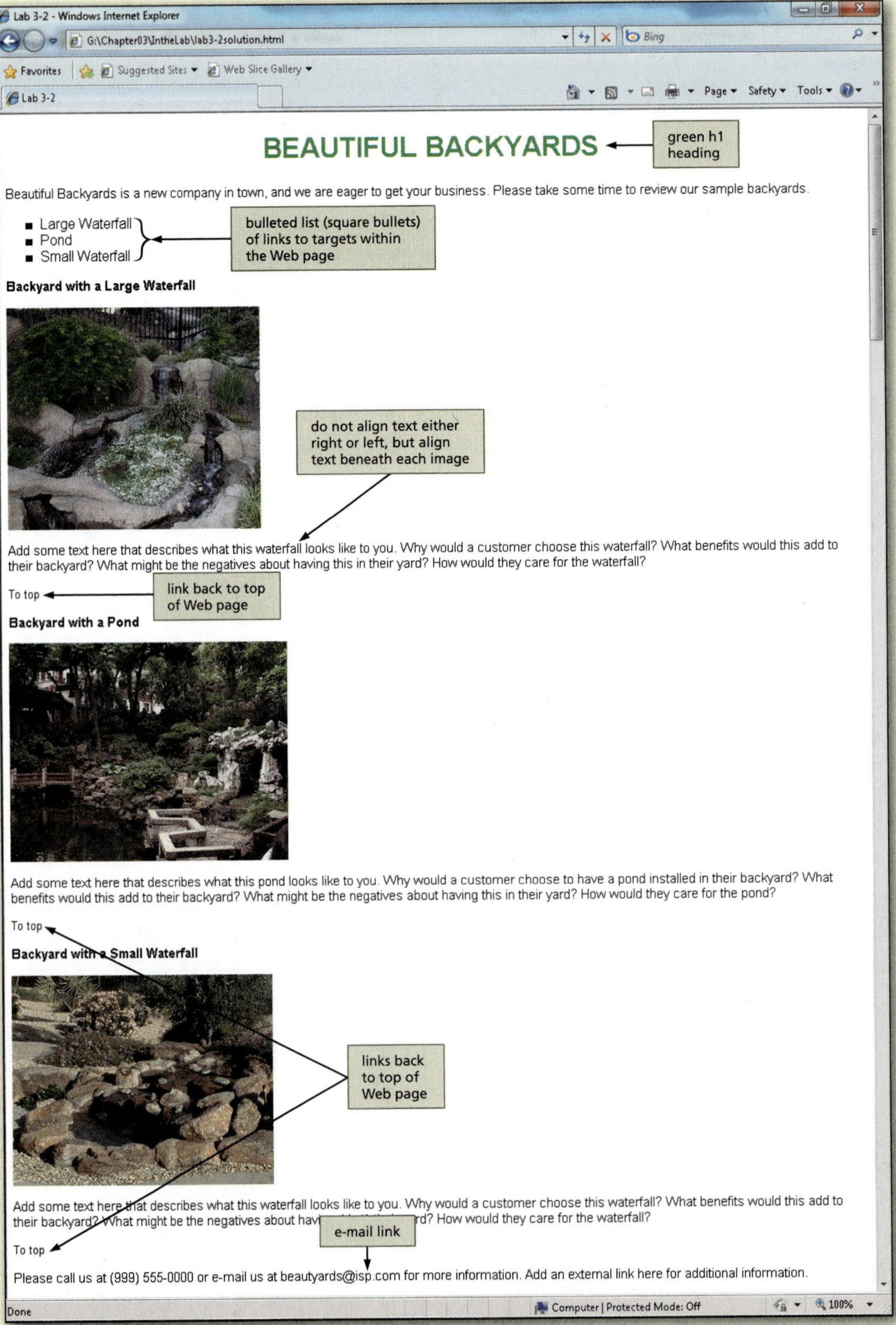

Figure 3–53

Instructions: Perform the following steps:

1. Start Notepad++ and create a new HTML file with the title, Lab 3-2, in the main heading section.
2. Begin the body section by adding an h1 heading that is centered.
3. Add the following code into an embedded style. Notice that all text links have the same background color as the h1 heading at the top of the Web page. This is because of the code that you put in the embedded style, as follows:

```
h1        {color: #00934a;
          font-family: Arial, Verdana, Garamond}
h2        {color: #00934a;
          font-family: Arial, Verdana, Garamond}
p         {font-family: Arial, Verdana, Garamond;
          font-size: 11pt}
a         {text-decoration: none;
          color: black;
          font-family: Arial, Verdana, Garamond}
a:hover   {background: #00934a;
          color: white}
ul        {font-family: Arial, Verdana, Garamond;
          list-style-type: square}
```

4. Add an unordered list with the three list items, as shown in Figure 3–53. These three items will be used to link to the three sections of text below them.
5. Add a title (not a heading) Backyard with a Large Waterfall and use a font-weight of bolder. Add the image largewaterfall.jpg that has a width of 294 and a height of 247.
6. Add a second title, Backyard with a Pond, and image pond.jpg (width=324; height=243). Set a link target named pond. Type a paragraph based on your research of the topic, as shown in Figure 3–53.
7. Add a third title, Backyard with a Small Waterfall, and image smallwaterfall.jpg (width=304; height=234).
8. Create a link target at the top of the page named top.
9. Add three To top links, one after each section, as shown in Figure 3–53. Set the link to direct to the top target at the top of the page.
10. Create links from the bulleted list to the three targets.
11. Create an e-mail link, as shown in Figure 3–53.
12. Save the HTML file in the Chapter03\IntheLab folder using the file name lab3-2solution.html.
13. Validate the lab3-2solution.html file.
14. Print the lab3-2solution.html file.
15. Enter the URL `g:\Chapter03\IntheLab\lab3-2solution.html` to view the Web page in your browser.
16. Print the Web page.
17. Submit the HTML file and Web page in the format specified by your instructor.

STUDENT ASSIGNMENTS

In the Lab

3: Creating Two Linked Web Pages

Problem: Your Communications instructor has asked each student in the class to create a two-page Web site to help students in the class get to know more about the area in which you are majoring in school. She suggested using the basic template shown in Figures 3–54a and 3–54b as a starting point. The first Web page (Figure 3–54a) is a home page that includes basic information about your major. Really try to answer the questions listed (for example, why you chose this major), as shown on the Web page. If you can, add an image related to your chosen field somewhere on the Web page. Add a link to the second Web page. The second Web page (Figure 3–54b) includes a paragraph of text and numbered lists with links.

Instructions: Perform the following steps:

1. Start Notepad++ and create a new HTML file with the title Lab 3-3 in the main heading section.
2. In the first Web page, include a Heading style 1 heading, similar to the one shown in Figure 3–54a, and a short paragraph of text. Experiment and use any color for the heading (navy is shown).
3. Create a text link to the second Web page, lab3-3specifics.html.
4. Save the HTML file in the Chapter03\IntheLab folder using the file name lab3-3solution.html. Validate the lab3-3solution.html file. Print the lab3-3solution.html file.
5. Start a new HTML file with the title Lab 3-3 Specifics in the main heading section.
6. In the second Web page, include a Heading style 1 heading, similar to the one shown in Figure 3–54b, a short paragraph of text, and two Heading style 2 headings. Use any color for the headings; navy is

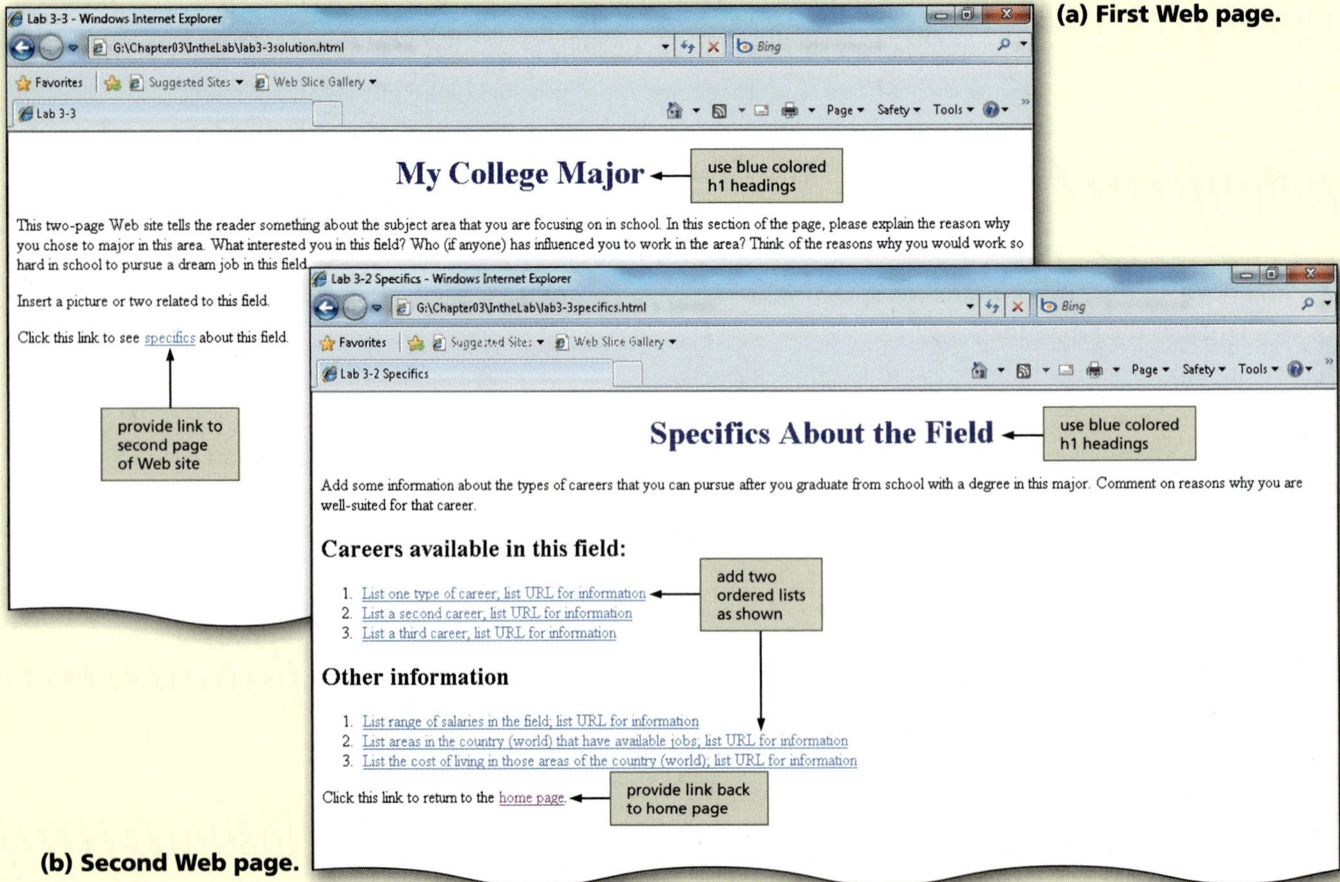

(a) First Web page.

(b) Second Web page.

Figure 3–54

shown in the h1 and black is used in the h2 headings. From the standpoint of consistency, you may want to make those headings all the same color. (*Hint:* Use an embedded style for this.)

7. Create two ordered (numbered) lists with at least two items that serve as links to Web pages on another Web site. Add a link back to the first Web page, as shown in Figure 3–54b.
8. Save the HTML file in the Chapter03\IntheLab folder using the file name lab3-3specifics.html. Validate the lab3-3specifics.html file. Print the lab3-3specifics.html file.
9. Enter the URL `g:\Chapter03\IntheLab\lab3-3solution.html` to view the Web page in your browser. Click the text link to the second Web page. Click the links in the lists to test them.
10. Print the Web pages.
11. Submit the HTML file and Web page in the format specified by your instructor.

Cases and Places

Apply your creative thinking and problem-solving skills to design and implement a solution.

• Easier ••More Difficult

• 1: Add a Web Page to the Getting Greener Site

Laquisha Carter is very impressed with the Getting Greener Web pages and now would like to add a Web page listing other "green" things that you can do to help the environment. Search the Web to find at least four Web sites that contain information about other environmentally responsible things that you can do. Create a Web page that includes a Heading 1 style heading, a brief paragraph of descriptive text, and list links to those Web sites. Modify the Getting Greener home page to include a link to the new Web page.

• 2: Create a Web Page with Text Formatting

You recently got an internship developing Web pages for Jose Sanchez Painters. Mr. Sanchez has asked you to update the home page for his Web site to make it more visually appealing. As a first step, you plan to create a Web page with sample text formats, such as the ones shown in Figure 3–20 on page HTML 116, to share with Mr. Sanchez and get his input on which types of formatting he prefers. Create such a Web page and include text formatted as bold, italic, underlined, superscript, and subscript; use different colors and sizes for each type of text. Use CSS styles for most of your styles, but also use some of the text formatting tags shown in the chapter. Determine why you would choose to use one over the other (i.e., styles versus formatting tags). Be sure to include one sample using the font-weights of bold tag and one using bolder to see how they compare when displayed together. Compare those to using <bold> or <strong> as formatting tags. Be creative and make sure that the Web page looks good but that the new styles do not distract from the content. Be prepared to explain to your client, Mr. Sanchez, why some font-families (e.g., something very cursive style) might not be appropriate.

•• 3: Add Image Links to External Sites

To update the Getting Greener Web site further, you want to add image links so the pictures on the Green Home Web page also are links to Web pages in an external Web site. Search the Web for information specific to each of the two Green Home images used in the project. Modify the Green Home Web page so each "green" image is used as a link to a Web page in an external Web site. After adding the links, you decide the text paragraphs on the page are too close to the pictures. Modify the Green Home Web page to use the properties of float together with margins in the <img> element to add space around each image. Also try two variations of other properties you can use with the <img> element in addition to float and margin. (*Hint:* See Appendix D for ideas.)

Continued >

Cases and Places *continued*

•• 4: Create a Web Page with Text Links and Define Link Colors

Make It Personal

Your sister owns a clothing store and recently had a Web site developed for her company. She is unhappy that the links on the company Web pages appear in blue when unvisited and purple when visited, because those colors do not match the company logo. She has asked you to update the Web pages. Create a Web page similar to Figure 3–4 on page HTML 94, with three text links to a Web page in an external Web site. Add the appropriate link styles to define the link colors requested by your sister. Also, explain why you might not want to change the colors of the links from the standard blue and violet but show ways that you can accommodate different colors and not confuse users.

•• 5: Create a Prototype Web Site with Five Pages

Working Together

Your manager at Uptown Enterprises has asked your team to create a simple five-page prototype of the Web pages in the new Entertainment section for the online magazine CityStuff. The home page should include headings and brief paragraphs of text for Arts, Music, Movies, and Dining. Within each paragraph of text is a link to one of the four detailed Web pages for each section (for example, the Arts link should connect to the Arts Web page). The home page also includes an e-mail link at the bottom of the page. Add a To top link that connects to a target at the top of the page. The four detailed Web pages should include links to external Web sites of interest and a link back to the home page. If possible, also find appropriate images to use as a background or in the Web page, and set text to wrap around the images. Remember to use CSS. Determine during the design phase whether it would be better to use inline or embedded style sheets or both for this Web site.

4 Creating Tables in a Web Site Using an External Style Sheet

Objectives

You will have mastered the material in this chapter when you can:

- Define table elements
- Describe the steps used to plan, design, and code a table
- Create a borderless table for a horizontal menu bar with text links
- Create an external style sheet to define styles across a Web site
- Utilize classes to give you more control over styles
- Link an external style sheet to Web pages where you want its styles applied
- Copy and paste HTML code to a new file
- Create a table with borders and insert text
- Alter the spacing between and within cells using the cellspacing and cellpadding attributes
- Utilize inline styles to alter the style of individual elements on a Web page
- Add background color to rows and cells
- Insert a caption below a table
- Create headings that span rows using the rowspan attribute

4 Creating Tables in a Web Site Using an External Style Sheet

Introduction

So far, you have learned how to make a basic Web page and how to link one Web page to another, both within the same Web site and external to the Web site. You also learned how to create inline styles and embedded style sheets to alter the appearance of Web page elements. In this chapter's project, you create an external (linked) style sheet to set the style for elements across multiple Web pages. The project also adds to your HTML knowledge by teaching you how to organize and present information on a Web page using tables with rows and columns. In this chapter, you learn about the elements used in a table and how to plan, design, and code a table. You learn how to use a table to create a horizontal menu bar with text links, and to create tables to organize text and images. You will enhance the Web site by manipulating the properties and attributes of tables and paragraphs, altering borders, colors, and spacing, and adding a table caption.

Project — Sabatina's Pizza Web Site

Having a reliable Web site makes it easier for a company's customers to find the establishment, provides a way to communicate the company's brand, and allows the company to provide additional services. As advertising director for Sabatina's Pizza, you want to enhance Sabatina's Web site to increase the company's exposure to current and new customers, and to incorporate ideas gathered from customer feedback surveys. The new site will allow customers to browse through tables of information that outline the appetizers, salads, and pizzas offered by the restaurant.

As shown in Figure 4–1a, the Sabatina's Pizza home page includes a company logo banner and a borderless table that contains a menu bar under the logo. The borderless table gives users easy access to all pages in the Web site. This table is available on every Web page in the Web site. The Appetizers, Salads, and Pizza Web pages (Figures 4–1b, 4–1c, and 4–1d) each include the company logo banner and the same borderless table at the top, as well as one table with borders that displays the contents of that particular Web page. In this project, you will create the sabatinas.html and appetizers.html Web pages. You will edit the salads.html Web page (Figure 4–1c) to add cellspacing and cellpadding attributes, thereby adjusting the spacing between cells. The pizza.html Web page file (Figure 4–1d) is also edited to add a caption with information about the table and to use the rowspan attribute to create headings that span several rows.

As you read through this chapter and work on the project, you will learn how to plan, design, and code tables to create a user-friendly Web site. You also will learn to format tables and to combine table features to make the pages more readable. In addition, you will learn to create a menu bar with text links.

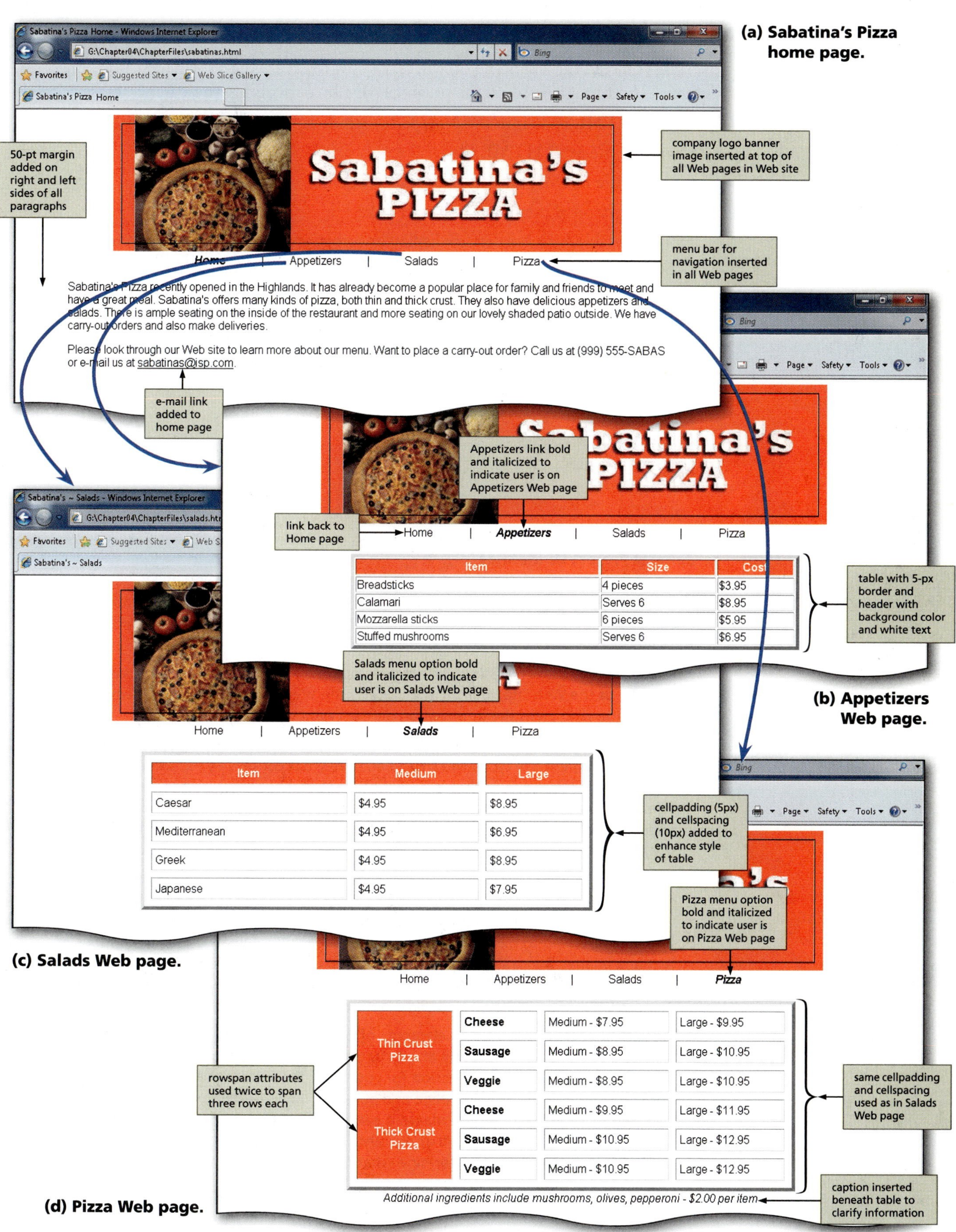
(a) Sabatina's Pizza home page.
Sabatina's Pizza Home - Windows Internet Explorer
G:\Chapter04\ChapterFiles\sabatinas.html
Sabatina's PIZZA
Home | Appetizers | Salads | Pizza
Sabatina's Pizza recently opened in the Highlands. It has already become a popular place for family and friends to meet and have a great meal. Sabatina's offers many kinds of pizza, both thin and thick crust. They also have delicious appetizers and salads. There is ample seating on the inside of the restaurant and more seating on our lovely shaded patio outside. We have carry-out orders and also make deliveries.
Please look through our Web site to learn more about our menu. Want to place a carry-out order? Call us at (999) 555-SABAS or e-mail us at sabatinas@isp.com.
50-pt margin added on right and left sides of all paragraphs
company logo banner image inserted at top of all Web pages in Web site
menu bar for navigation inserted in all Web pages
e-mail link added to home page
Appetizers link bold and italicized to indicate user is on Appetizers Web page
link back to Home page
Home | Appetizers | Salads | Pizza
Item | Size | Cost
Breadsticks | 4 pieces | $3.95
Calamari | Serves 6 | $8.95
Mozzarella sticks | 6 pieces | $5.95
Stuffed mushrooms | Serves 6 | $6.95
table with 5-px border and header with background color and white text
(b) Appetizers Web page.
Sabatina's ~ Salads - Windows Internet Explorer
G:\Chapter04\ChapterFiles\salads.htm
Salads menu option bold and italicized to indicate user is on Salads Web page
Home | Appetizers | Salads | Pizza
Item | Medium | Large
Caesar | $4.95 | $8.95
Mediterranean | $4.95 | $6.95
Greek | $4.95 | $8.95
Japanese | $4.95 | $7.95
cellpadding (5px) and cellspacing (10px) added to enhance style of table
(c) Salads Web page.
Pizza menu option bold and italicized to indicate user is on Pizza Web page
Home | Appetizers | Salads | Pizza
Thin Crust Pizza | Cheese | Medium - $7.95 | Large - $9.95
Sausage | Medium - $8.95 | Large - $10.95
Veggie | Medium - $8.95 | Large - $10.95
Thick Crust Pizza | Cheese | Medium - $9.95 | Large - $11.95
Sausage | Medium - $10.95 | Large - $12.95
Veggie | Medium - $10.95 | Large - $12.95
Additional ingredients include mushrooms, olives, pepperoni - $2.00 per item
rowspan attributes used twice to span three rows each
same cellpadding and cellspacing used as in Salads Web page
caption inserted beneath table to clarify information
(d) Pizza Web page.

Figure 4–1

Overview

As you read this chapter, you will learn how to create the Web pages shown in Figures 4–1a through 4–1d on the previous page by performing these general tasks:

- Enter HTML code into the Notepad++ window.
- Save the file as an HTML file.
- Enter basic HTML tags and add text to the file.
- Add a horizontal menu bar with text links.
- Create a table with borders to display information in an organized manner.
- Create an external style sheet to set the style for all Web pages in the Web site.
- Use classes to give more control over the styles used.
- Link an external style sheet to Web pages.
- Utilize inline styles to alter the style of individual elements on the Web page.
- Add HTML tags that enhance a table with cellpadding and cellspacing.
- Enhance a Web table with rowspanning.
- Add a caption to a table.
- Print the HTML code and Web pages

Plan Ahead

General Project Guidelines

When creating a Web page, the actions you perform and decisions you make will affect the appearance and characteristics (the styles) of the finished page. As you create Web pages, such as those shown in Figures 4–1a through 4–1d, you should follow these general guidelines:

1. **Complete Web page planning.** Before developing a Web page, you must know the purpose of the Web site, identify the users of the site and their computing environments, and decide who owns the information on the Web page.
2. **Analyze the content and organization of the Web page**. In the analysis phase of the Web development life cycle, you should analyze what content to include on the Web page and how to organize that information. In this phase, you need to determine what information you want to convey so that you can highlight that information on the Web page using different techniques. Refer to Table 1–4 on page HTML 15 for information on the phases of the Web development life cycle.
3. **Choose the content and organization for the Web page**. Once you have completed the analysis, you need to determine specifically what content to include on the Web page. With tables, you are able to display the Web page content in a very organized manner. Tables can be used to display text only, as well as graphical images or combinations of text and images. Some text is better highlighted by using different colors for column or row headings. Other information is displayed more effectively with row- and column-spanning techniques. This should all be determined before coding the Web pages.
4. **Identify how to format various elements of the Web page**. The overall appearance or style of a Web page significantly affects its ability to communicate clearly. Additionally, you want to provide easy navigation for your Web site visitors. Adding images and color helps to communicate your message and adding a menu bar with links to the other Web pages within the Web site makes it easy to navigate the Web site. Determine what style sheets to use for the overall appearance or style, including external, embedded, and inline style sheets. Also determine what formatting tag attributes need to be implemented.

Plan Ahead

(continued)

5. **Determine where to save the Web page.** You can store a Web page permanently, or save it on a variety of storage media, including a hard disk, USB flash drive, CD, or DVD. You also can indicate a specific location on the storage media for saving the Web page. Recognize the appropriate absolute and relative addressing that you will need as determined by your analysis.
6. **Create the Web page and links.** After analyzing and designing the Web site, you need to develop the individual Web pages. It is important to maintain a consistent look throughout the Web site. Use graphics and links consistently so that your Web site visitor does not become confused.
7. **Test all Web pages within the Web site.** An important part of Web development is testing to assure that you are following XHTML standards. This book uses the World Wide Web Consortium (W3C) validator that allows you to test your Web page and clearly explains any errors you have. Additionally, you should check all content for accuracy and test all links.

When necessary, more specific details concerning the above guidelines are presented at appropriate points in the chapter. The chapter also will identify the actions performed and decisions made regarding these guidelines during the creation of the Web pages shown in Figures 4–1a through 4–1d on page HTML 159.

Planning and Designing a Multipage Web Site

The Web site that you create in this chapter consists of four Web pages: sabatinas.html, appetizers.html, salads.html, and pizza.html. With a multipage Web site, you need to design the overall look of the Web site itself, as well as the individual Web pages. You will use both formatting tag attributes and style sheets to create the overall appearance (or style) of the Web site. An **external style sheet** is used to define styles for multiple pages in a Web site. With external (linked) style sheets, you create the style sheet first in a separate file saved with a .css extension. You then link this style sheet into any Web page in which you want to use it.

In Chapters 2 and 3, you learned how to insert inline and embedded style sheets into your Web pages. Recall that inline style sheets are used to change the style of an individual HTML tag. An embedded style sheet is inserted between the <head> and </head> tags of a single Web page within the style container (<style> and </style>). Embedded style sheets are used to change the style for elements on an entire Web page. For the project in this chapter, where you have a multipage Web site, you will learn how to create an external, or linked, style sheet.

Creating Web Pages with Tables

Tables allow you to organize information on a Web page using HTML tags. Tables are useful when you want to arrange text and images into rows and columns in order to make the information straightforward and clear to the Web page visitor. You can use tables to create Web pages with newspaper-type columns of text or structured lists of information. Tables can be complex, using the rowspan and colspan attributes to span rows and columns, background colors in cells, and borders to provide formatting (Figure 4–2a on the next page). Tables also can be simple, with a basic grid format and no color (Figure 4–2b). The purpose of the table helps to define what formatting is appropriate.

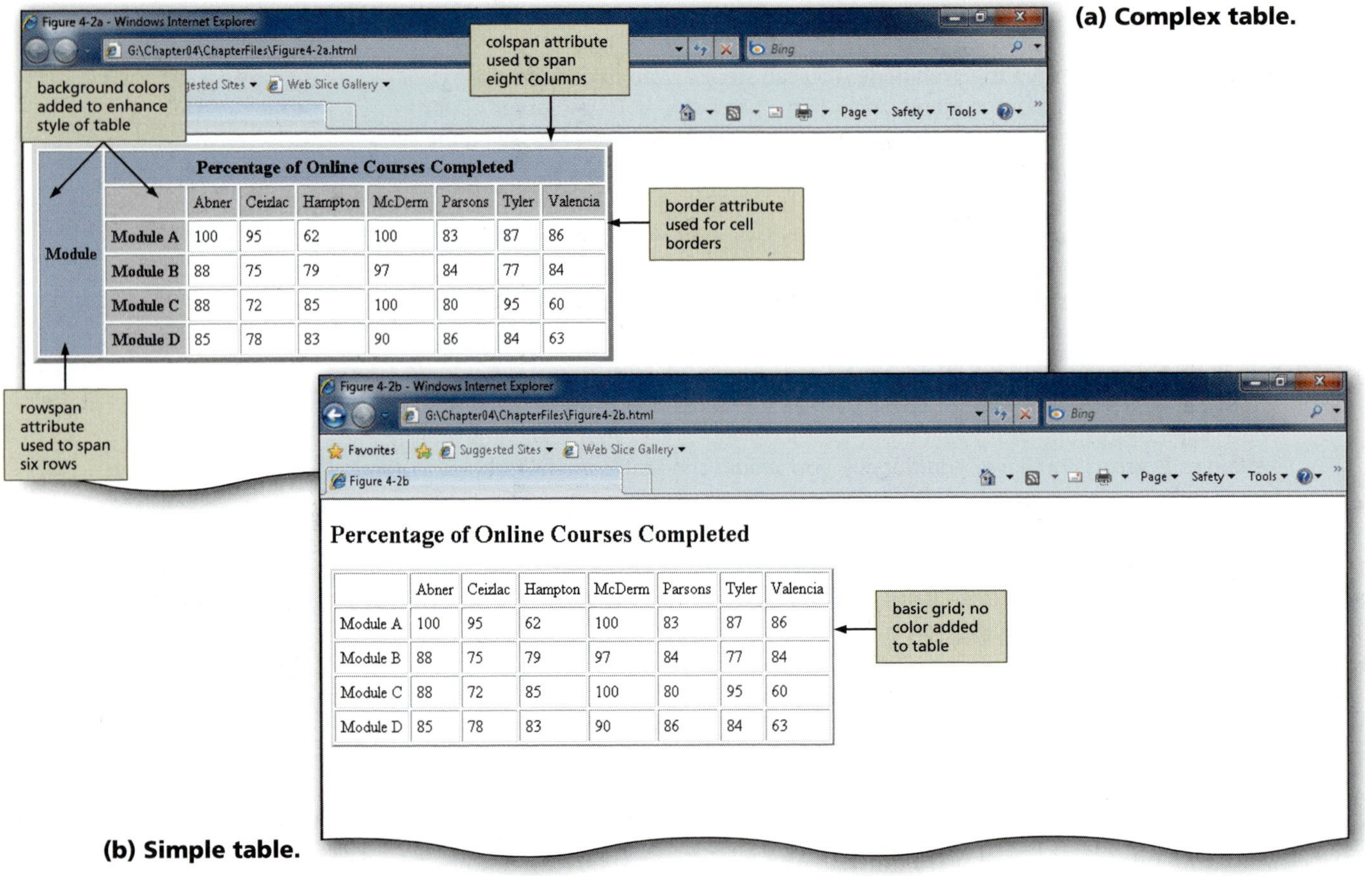

(a) Complex table.

Figure 4-2a - Windows Internet Explorer

background colors added to enhance style of table

colspan attribute used to span eight columns

Module	Percentage of Online Courses Completed							
		Abner	Ceizlac	Hampton	McDerm	Parsons	Tyler	Valencia
	Module A	100	95	62	100	83	87	86
	Module B	88	75	79	97	84	77	84
	Module C	88	72	85	100	80	95	60
	Module D	85	78	83	90	86	84	63

border attribute used for cell borders

rowspan attribute used to span six rows

Figure 4-2b - Windows Internet Explorer

Percentage of Online Courses Completed

	Abner	Ceizlac	Hampton	McDerm	Parsons	Tyler	Valencia
Module A	100	95	62	100	83	87	86
Module B	88	75	79	97	84	77	84
Module C	88	72	85	100	80	95	60
Module D	85	78	83	90	86	84	63

basic grid; no color added to table

(b) Simple table.

Figure 4–2

In Chapter 3, you learned how to wrap text around an image. You also can use tables to position text and images, such as the one shown in Figure 4–3; this is a borderless table used to position text to the left of the map images. An advantage of using a table to position text and images instead of just wrapping the text around the image is that you have greater control over the placement of the text and image.

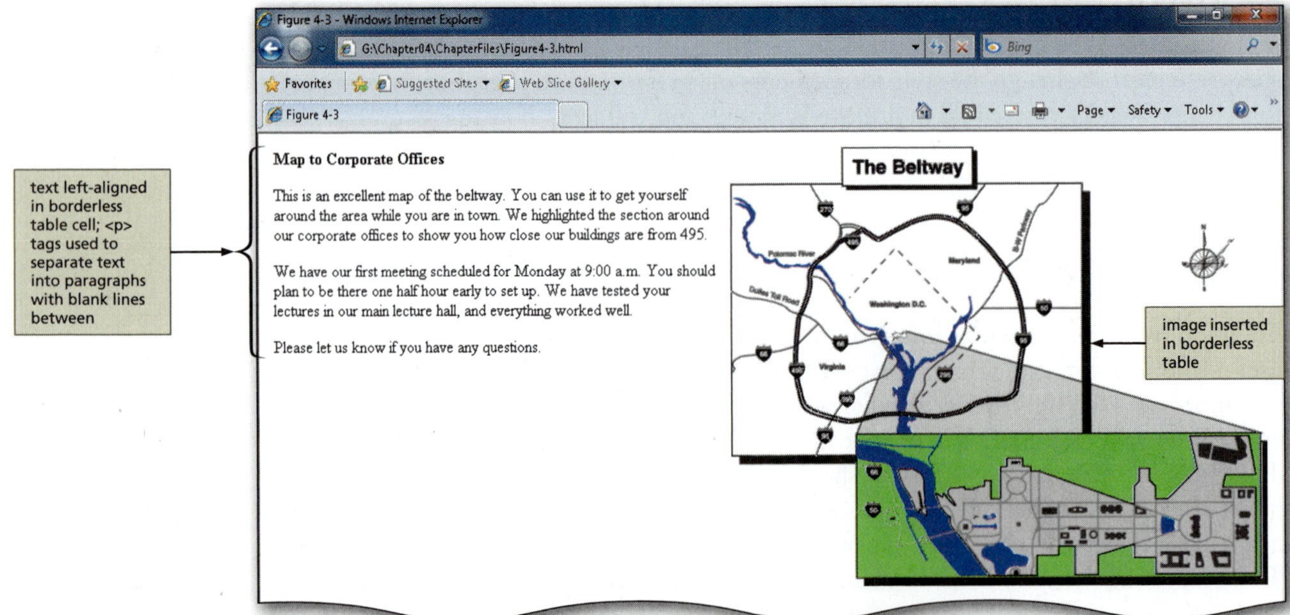

Figure 4–3 Image and text positioned in table.

Tables also can be used to create a border or frame around an image. Figure 4–4 shows a Web page with an image inserted into a table with one row and one cell. The border is set to a pixel width of 15 to create the appearance of a frame. Using a table to create a frame is a simple technique that gives an image a polished look and highlights the image.

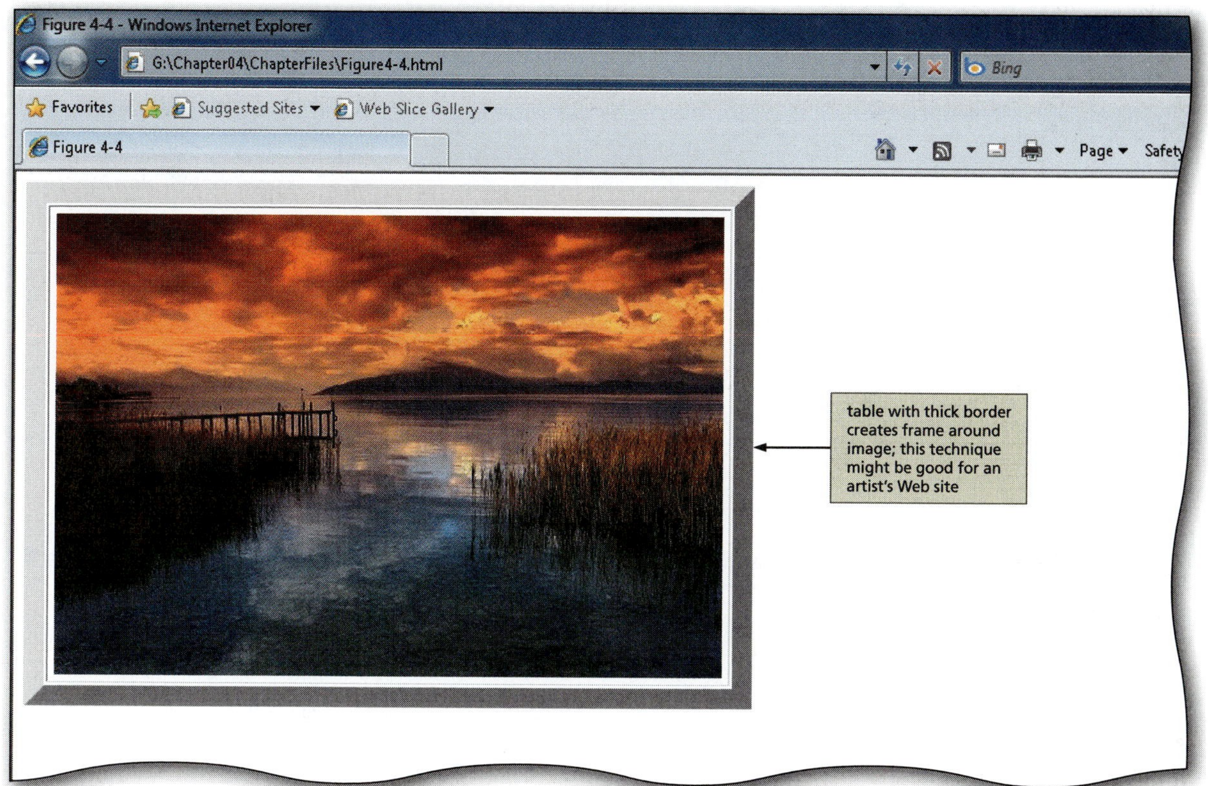

Figure 4–4 Table used as image frame.

Table Elements

Tables consist of rows, columns, and cells, much like spreadsheets. A **row** is a horizontal line of information. A **column** is a vertical line of information. A **cell** is the intersection of a row and a column. Figure 4–5 on the next page shows examples of these three elements. In Figure 4–5a, the fifth row in the table has a gray background. In Figure 4–5b, the fourth column has a peach background. In Figure 4–5c, the cell at the intersection of column 2 and row 6 has a gold background.

As shown in Figure 4–5c, a cell can be one of two types: a heading cell or a data cell. A **heading cell** displays text as bold and center-aligned. A **data cell** displays normal text that is left-aligned.

Understanding the row, column, and cell elements is important as you create a table using HTML. Properties and attributes are set relative to these table elements. For example, you can set attributes for an entire row of information, for a single cell, or for one or more cells within a row.

BTW

Tables
Tables are useful for a variety of purposes. They can store information in tabular form or create a layout on a Web page. Layouts created with tables give more flexibility to the Web developer. You have more control over the placement of information or images. Many popular Web sites use tables.

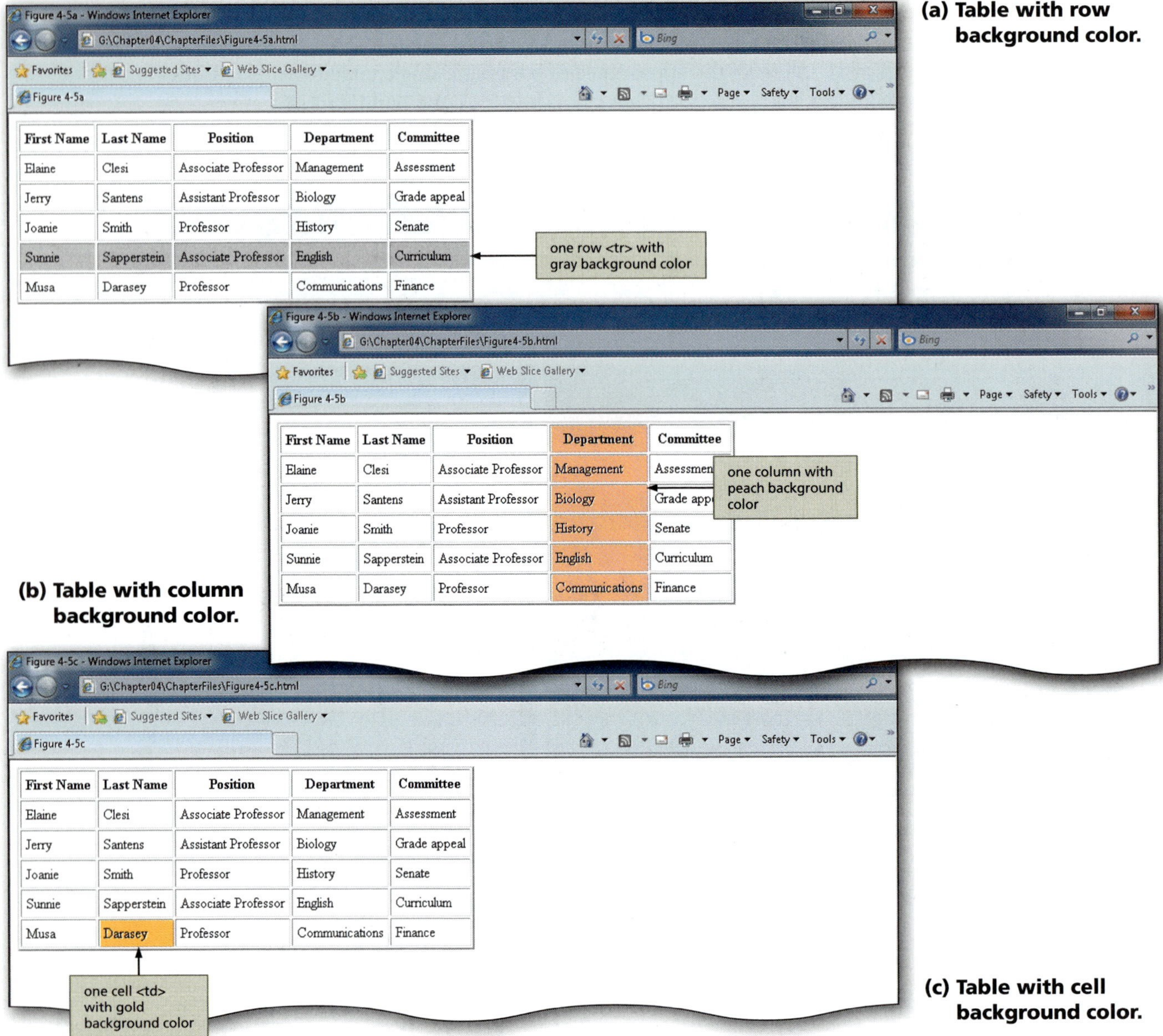

(a) Table with row background color.

(b) Table with column background color.

(c) Table with cell background color.

Figure 4–5

> **BTW**
> **Table Elements**
> Many Web sources discuss table parts, giving numerous examples and tips. For more information about HTML table parts, search the Web for key terms such as HTML Table Elements or Table Properties.

Adding Style to Table Elements

As discussed earlier, there are many ways to set the style (or appearance) of a Web page element. You can use formatting tag attributes (e.g., setting cellpadding and cellspacing on a table) to set the appearance or style. You also can use inline, embedded, or external (linked) style sheets to set the style. During the design phase of the Web development life cycle, you determine how to set the styles for the elements on your Web pages. In this chapter, you use an external (linked) style sheet to set styles for the tables across the entire Web site.

Table Borders, Headers, Captions, and Rules

Tables include features such as table borders, table headers, table captions, and rules attributes (Figure 4–6). A **table border** is the line that encloses the perimeter of the table. A **table header** is the same as a heading cell — it is any cell with bold text that indicates the purpose of the row or column. A header row is used to identify the meaning of the numbers in each column, and headings that span columns and rows are used to provide additional information. Headers also are used by non-visual browsers to identify table content. See the guidelines in Appendix C for specific information about making your Web pages available to the nearly 20% of the world population who have some sort of disability. A **table caption** is descriptive text located above or below the table that further describes the purpose of the table.

Tables can use these features individually or in combination. The purpose for the table dictates which of these features are used. For example, the table shown in Figure 4–6 lists columns of numbers. A header row is used to identify the meaning of the numbers in each column, and headings that span columns and rows are used to provide additional information. Finally, the table caption explains that each number is based on thousands (that is, the 10 listed in the table represents 10,000).

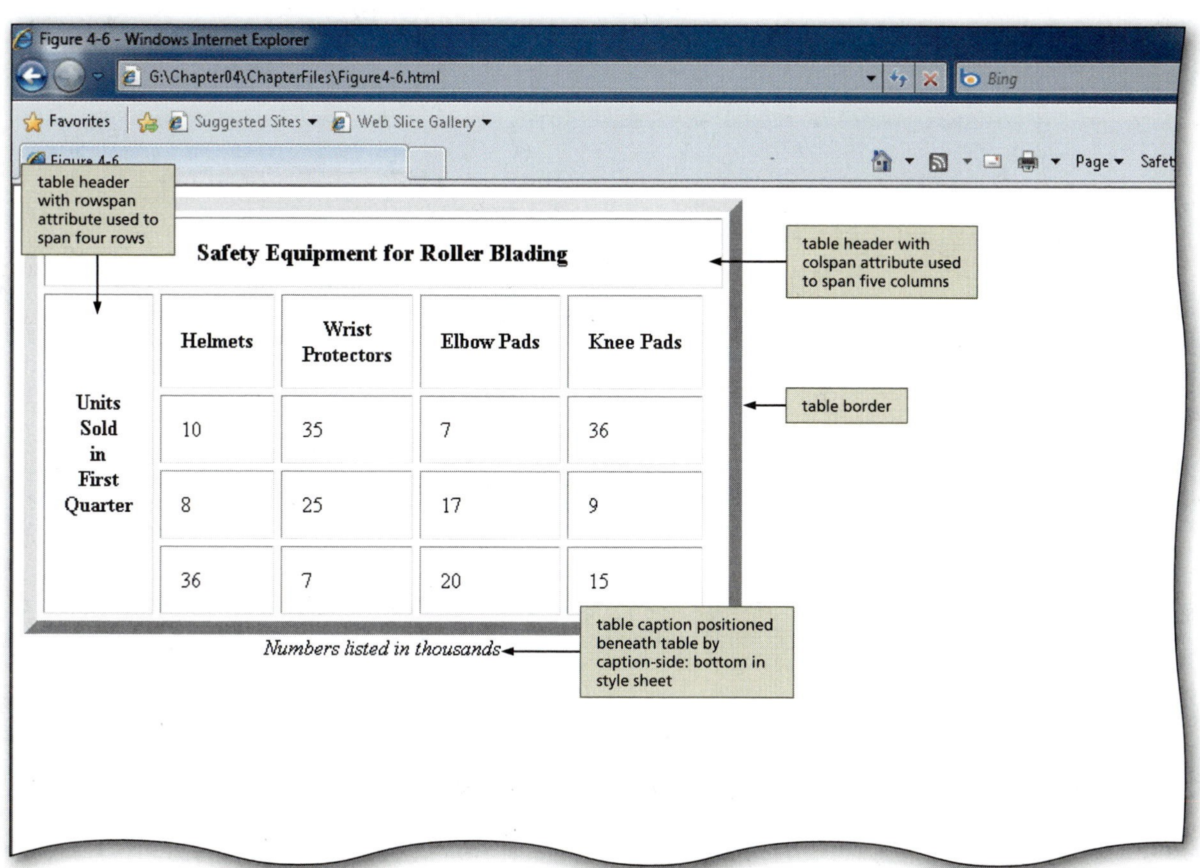

Figure 4–6 Table headers, border, and caption.

Another useful table feature is the rules attribute, which creates horizontal or vertical lines in a table. The **rules attribute** allows a Web developer to select which internal borders to show in a table. It supports several values to provide different formatting options. For example, using rules="none" creates a table with no internal rules. Using rules="cols" creates a table with vertical rules between each column in the table (Figure 4–7a), while rules="rows" creates a table with horizontal rules between each row in the table (Figure 4–7b). Appendix A provides additional information on values supported by the rules attribute.

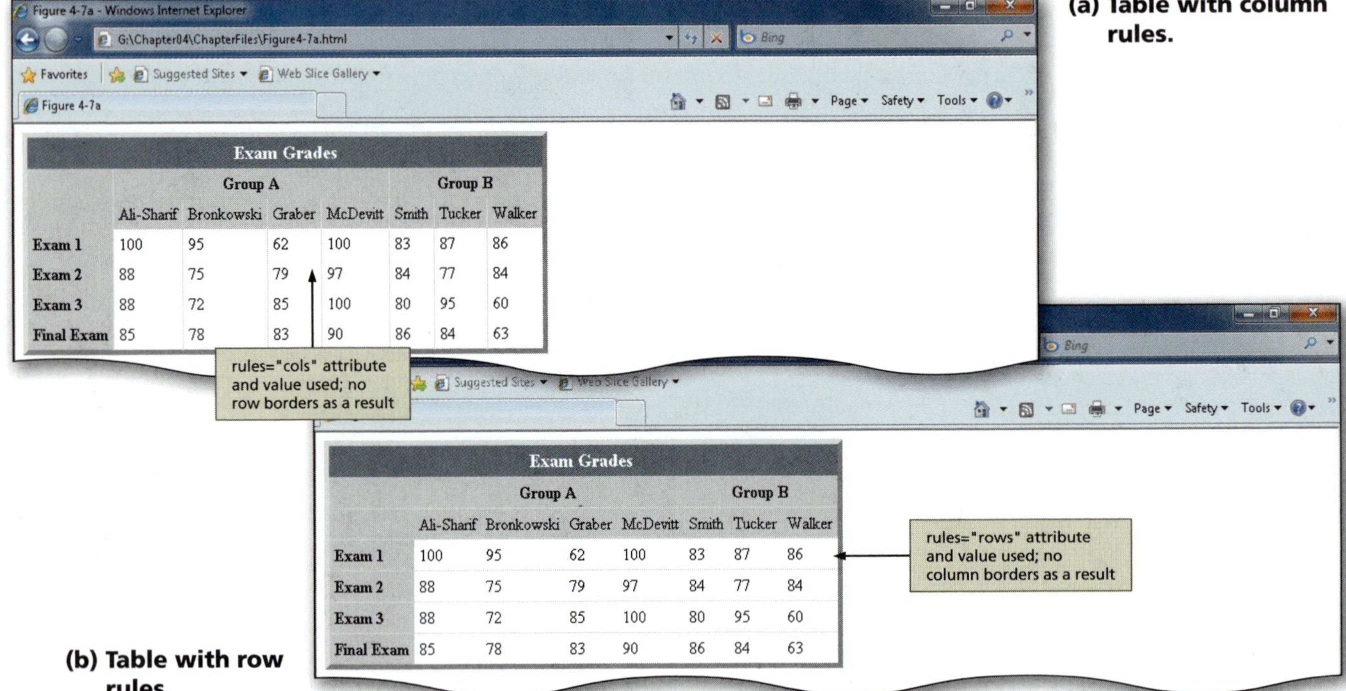

(a) Table with column rules.

(b) Table with row rules.

Figure 4–7

Determining the Need for, Planning, and Coding a Table

Creating tables for a Web page is a three-step process: (1) determining if a table is needed, (2) planning the table, and (3) coding the table. Each of these steps is discussed in detail in the following sections.

Determining If a Table Is Needed

First, you must determine whether a table is necessary. Not all Web pages require the use of tables. A general rule is that a table should be used when it will help organize information or Web page elements in such a way that it is easier for the Web page visitor to read. Tables generally are useful on a Web page if the Web page needs to display a structured, organized list of information or includes text and images that must be positioned in a very specific manner. Figures 4–8a and 4–8b show examples of information displayed as text in both a table and a bulleted list. To present this information, a table (Figure 4–8a) would be the better choice. The bulleted list (Figure 4–8b) might give the Web page an acceptable look, but the table presents the information more clearly.

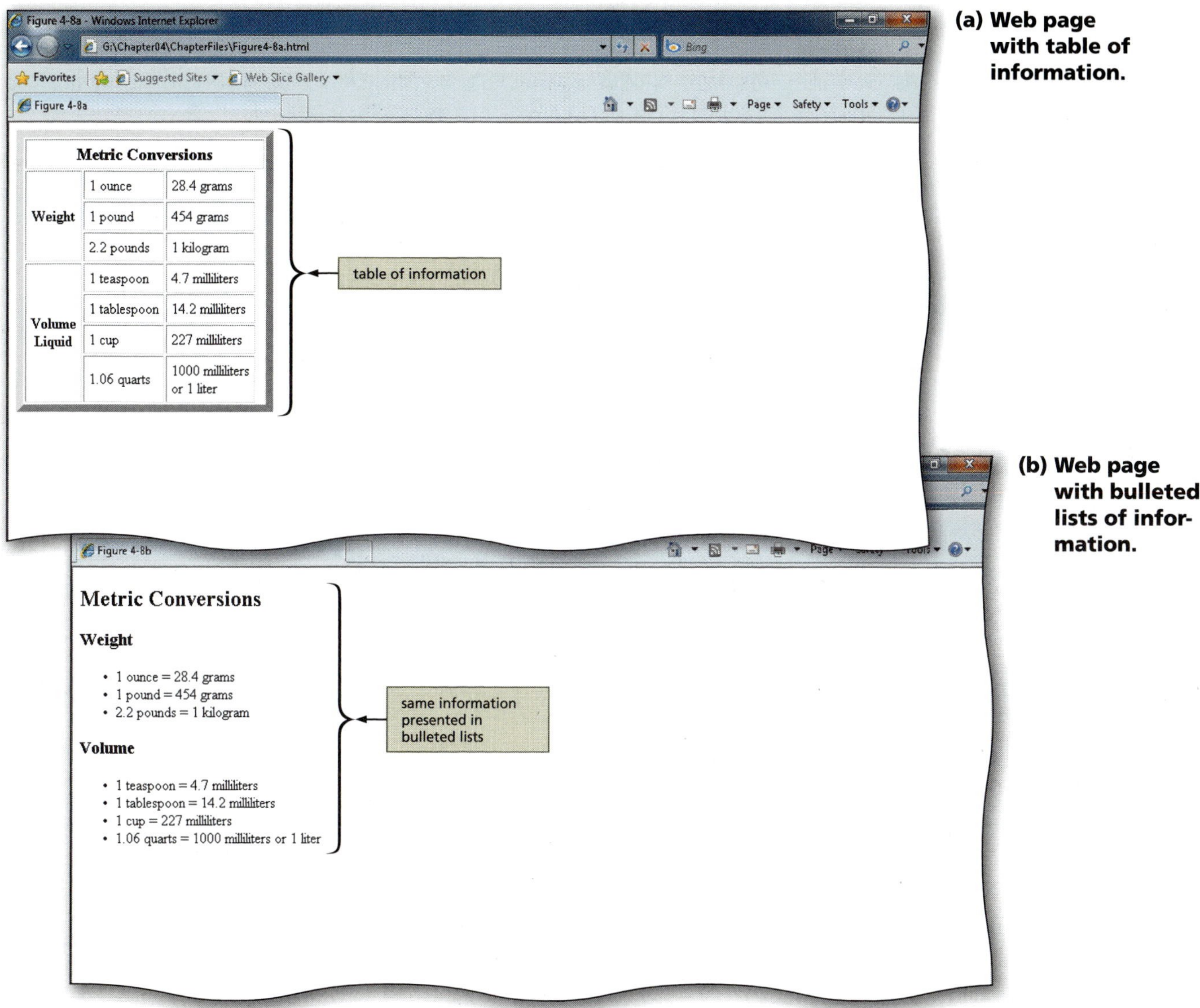

(a) Web page with table of information.

(b) Web page with bulleted lists of information.

Figure 4–8

Planning the Table

To create effective tables, you must plan how the information will appear in the table and then create a good design. Before writing any HTML code, sketch the table on paper. After the table is sketched on paper, it is easier to see how many rows and columns to create, if the table will include headings, and if any of the headings span rows or columns. Conceptualizing the table on paper first saves time when you try to determine which HTML table tags to use to create the table.

For example, to create a simple table that lists the times run by various cross-country team members, you might sketch the table shown in Figure 4–9a on the next page. If runners participate in two different race lengths, such as 5K and 10K, that information can be included in a table designed as shown in Figure 4–9b. If the table needs to include different race dates for each race length, that information can be included in a table such as the one shown in Figure 4–9c. Finally, to make the table easier for the Web page visitor to understand, the table should include headings that span rows and columns and a caption. For instance, in Figure 4–9b, the headings 5K and 10K each span two columns of data. Because column spanning is used, you can easily see which runners ran in the 5K or 10K races. In Figure 4–9c, because of row spanning, you can easily tell what date each race was run. Design issues such as these should be considered in the planning stage before any HTML code is entered. Figure 4–10 shows how the table might look after it is coded. You will use a variety of style sheets together with formatting tag attributes to create the tables for the project in this chapter.

BTW

Table Tutorial
Table tutorials are available through online sources. Tutorials take you step-by-step through the table creation process. Search the Web for the phrase HTML Table Tutorial to find excellent sources of information.

NAME1	NAME2	NAME3	NAME4
TIME	TIME	TIME	TIME

(a) Simple table.

5K		10K	
NAME1	NAME2	NAME3	NAME4
TIME	TIME	TIME	TIME

(b) Column spanning added.

		5K		10K	
		NAME1	NAME2	NAME3	NAME4
Meet Dates	MAY 5	TIME	TIME	TIME	TIME
	MAY 12	TIME	TIME	TIME	TIME
	MAY 19	TIME	TIME	TIME	TIME
	MAY 26	TIME	TIME	TIME	TIME

(c) Row spanning added.

Figure 4–9

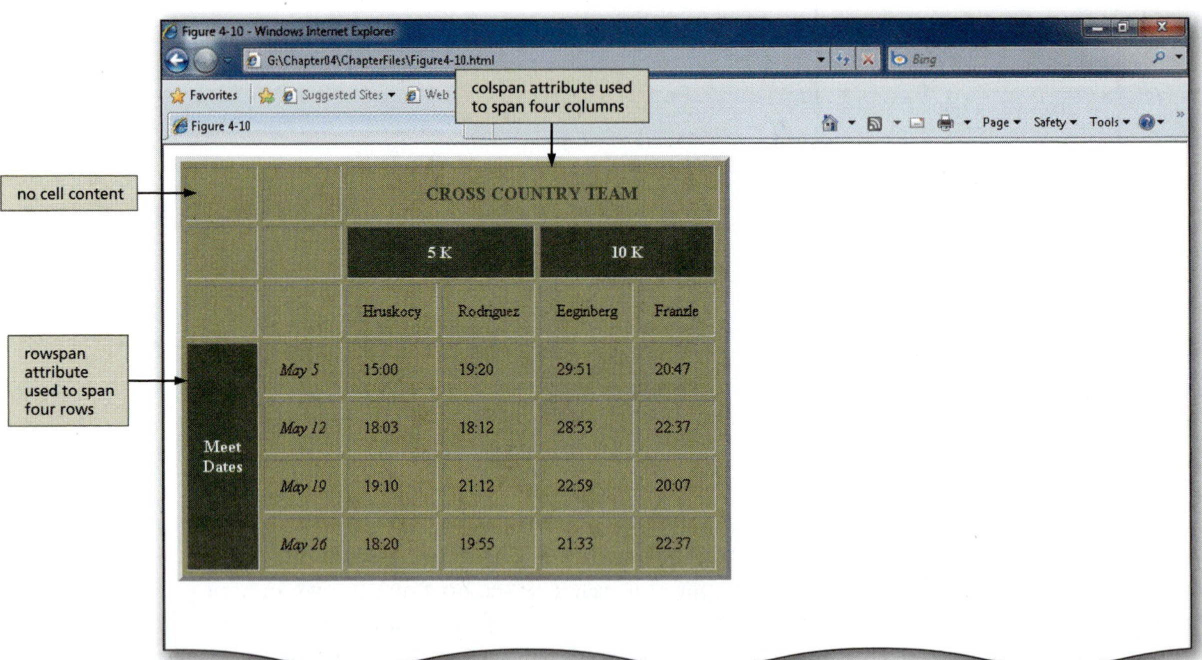

Figure 4–10 Table with row and column spanning.

Coding the Table

After you have completed the table design, you can begin coding the table using HTML tags. Table 4–1 shows the four main HTML tags used to create a table. Each of these tags has a number of attributes, which are discussed later in this chapter.

Figure 4–11a shows an example of these tags used in an HTML file, and Figure 4–11b shows the resulting Web page. As shown in Figure 4–11b, the table has four rows (a table header and three rows of data cells) and two columns. The rows are indicated in the HTML file

Table 4–1 HTML Table Tags

Tag	Function
<table></table>	• Indicates the start and end of a table • All other table tags are inserted within these tags
<tr> </tr>	• Indicates the start and end of a table row • Rows consist of heading or data cells
<th> </th>	• Indicates the start and end of a table heading (also called a heading cell) • Table headings default to bold text and center-alignment
<td> </td>	• Indicates the start and end of a data cell in a table • Data cells default to normal text and left-alignment

in Figure 4–11a by the start **<tr>** tags and the end **</tr>** tags. For this simple table, the number of columns in the table is determined based on the number of cells within each row. As shown in Figure 4–11b, each row has two cells, which results in a table with two columns. (Later in this chapter, you will learn how to indicate the number of columns within the <table> tag.)

As shown in the HTML in Figure 4–11a, the first row includes table heading cells, as indicated by the start **<th>** tag and end **</th>** tag. In the second, third, and fourth rows, the cells contain data, indicated by the start **<td>** tag and end **</td>** tag. In the resulting table, as shown in Figure 4–11b, the table header in row 1 appears as bold and centered text. The text in the data cells in rows 2 through 4 is left-aligned and normal text. The table in Figure 4–11b has a border, and cellspacing of 5 pixels was added to highlight further differences between the cells. You learn about cellspacing later in the chapter.

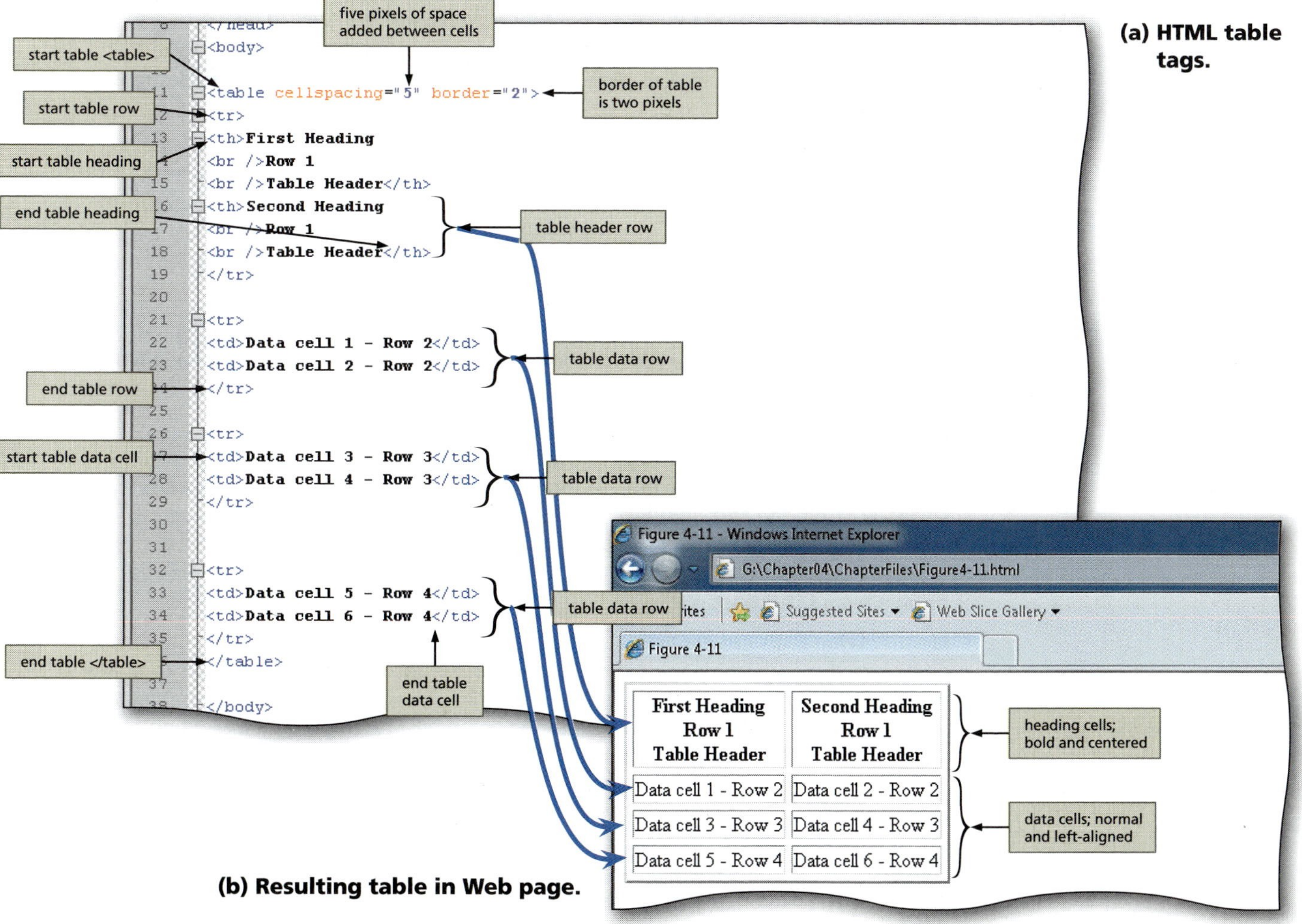

(a) HTML table tags.

(b) Resulting table in Web page.

Figure 4–11

BTW

Table Borders
Table borders frame an image. You can insert a single image into a one-row, one-column table. Using a border gives the image a 3-D appearance, making the image appear to have a frame around it. A border of 1 pixel (border="1") is too small to use as a frame, but border="25" is too large.

Table Tag Attributes

Each of the four main table tags listed in Table 4–1 on page HTML 169 has different attributes. Table 4–2 lists the table tags and the main attributes associated with each. The <th> and <td> tags, which are both used to specify the contents of a cell, have the same attributes. Many of the table tags' attributes listed in Table 4–2 are used in creating the Sabatina's Pizza Web site.

Table 4–2 Table Tag Attributes and Functions

Tag	Attribute	Function
<table> </table>	border cellspacing cellpadding cols width	• Defines width of table border in pixels • Defines space between cells in pixels • Defines space between a cell's contents and its border in pixels • Defines number of columns • Sets table width relative to window width
<tr> </tr>	valign	• Vertically aligns row (top, middle, bottom)
<th> </th> and <td> </td>	colspan rowspan valign	• Sets number of columns spanned by a cell • Sets number of rows spanned by a cell • Vertically aligns cell (top, middle, bottom)

Plan Ahead

Identify the format of various Web page elements.
Before inserting tables or graphical elements in a Web page, you should plan how you want to format them. By effectively utilizing tables and graphics, you can better organize the most important topics on the Web page. Consider the following formatting suggestions.

- **Effectively utilize graphics.** An important part of Web development is the use of graphics to call attention to a Web page. Generally, companies utilize the same logo on their Web site as they use on print material associated with the company, such as business cards and letterheads. Using the same graphical image on all marketing materials, including the Web site, is a good way to provide a consistent visual image and brand message to customers. Colorful company logos can also add an attention-grabbing element to a Web page.
- **Format tables to organize Web page content.** Sometimes it is better to have no border around the table, while other times borders enhance the look of the table, depending on the content and purpose of the table. In this chapter, you will use both bordered and borderless tables. Another consideration is where to place the table (left-, right-, or center-aligned).
- **Determine what table formatting to use**. When using a table to organize text links, it is important to first decide how to format the table. Although you may not want to distract from the text links by creating a table with a heavy border, you need to separate the text links in such a way that they are easy to find. Creating a borderless table with separators (e.g., pipe symbols) between the text links helps organize but not distract from the links.
- **Identify what links are needed**. Each Web page in a multipage Web site should have a link back to the home page of the Web site. Web developers often use the company logo to link back to the home page. In this project, the logo is also the central image of the Web pages. Because of that, a better option might be to provide a text link called Home that visitors can use to return to the home page. Each Web page should include links to the other pages on the Web site. Putting these links in a table at the top of each Web page helps visitors navigate easily, and providing the navigation menu bar across all Web pages in the Web site is also important for consistency. If a Web page is very long, it also might be a good idea to put the same text link table at the bottom of the Web page. Again, the purpose of providing links is to make it easy to navigate the Web site.

Creating a Home Page with Banner Logo and Borderless Table

The first Web page developed in this chapter's project is the home page of the Sabatina's Pizza Web site. As you have learned, the home page is the main page of a Web site and is what Web site visitors generally view first. Visitors then click links to move from the home page to the other Web pages in the site. The Sabatina's Pizza home page includes the company logo as a banner image and a borderless table that contains three links to other pages: the Appetizers Web page, the Salads Web page, and the Pizza Web page. The home page also provides an e-mail link, so visitors can contact Sabatina's Pizza easily.

To Start Notepad++

The first step in creating the Sabatina's Pizza Web site is to start Notepad++ and ensure that word wrap is enabled. The following steps, which assume Windows 7 is running, start Notepad++ based on a typical installation. You may need to ask your instructor how to start Notepad++ for your computer.

1. Click the Start button on the Windows taskbar to display the Start menu.
2. Click All Programs at the bottom of the left pane on the Start menu to display the All Programs list.
3. Click Notepad++ in the All Programs list.
4. Click Notepad++ in the list to display the Notepad++ window.
5. If the Notepad++ window is not maximized, click the Maximize button on the Notepad++ title bar to maximize it.
6. Click View on the menu bar.
7. If the Word wrap command does not have a check mark next to it, click Word wrap.

To Enter Initial HTML Tags to Define the Web Page Structure

Just as you did in Chapters 2 and 3, you start your file with the initial HTML tags that define the structure of the Web page. Table 4–3 contains the tags and text for this task.

Table 4–3 Initial HTML Tags

Line	HTML Tag and Text
1	<!DOCTYPE html
2	PUBLIC "-//W3C//DTD XHTML 1.0 Transitional//EN"
3	"http://www.w3.org/TR/xhtml1/DTD/xhtml1-transitional.dtd">
4	
5	<html xmlns="http://www.w3.org/1999/xhtml" xml:lang="en" lang="en">
6	<head>
7	<meta http-equiv="Content-Type" content="text/html; charset=utf-8" />
8	<title>Sabatina's Pizza Home</title>
9	</head>
10	

Table 4–3 Initial HTML Tags (continued)

Line	HTML Tag and Text
11	`<body>`
12	
13	`</body>`
14	`</html>`

The following steps illustrate how to enter the initial tags that define the structure of the Web page.

1. Enter the HTML code shown in Table 4-3. Press ENTER at the end of each line. If you make an error as you are typing, use the BACKSPACE key to delete all the characters back to and including the incorrect characters, then continue typing.
2. Position the insertion point on the blank line between the <body> and </body> tags (line 12) and press the ENTER key to position the insertion point on line 13 (Figure 4–12).
3. Compare what you typed to Figure 4–12. If you notice errors, use your mouse pointer or ARROW keys to move the insertion point to the right of each error and use the BACKSPACE key to correct the error.

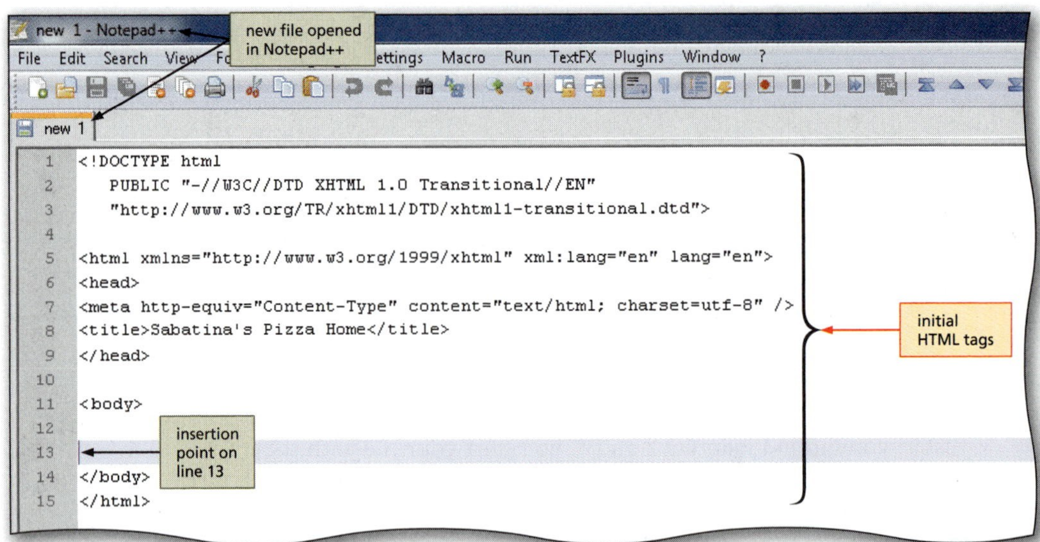

Figure 4–12

To Save an HTML File

With the initial HTML code for the Sabatina's Pizza home page entered, you should save the file. Saving the file frequently ensures you won't lose your work. Saving a file in Notepad++ also adds color to code that can help you identify different elements more easily. The following steps illustrate how to save an HTML file in Notepad++.

1. With a USB flash drive connected to one of the computer's USB ports, click File on the Notepad++ menu bar and then click Save.
2. Type `sabatinas.html` in the File name text box (do not press ENTER).
3. Click Computer in the left pane of the Save As dialog box to display a list of available drives.
4. If necessary, scroll until UDISK 2.0 (G:) or the name of your storage device is displayed in the list of available drives.

5. Open the Chapter04\ChapterFiles folder.

6. Click the Save button in the Save As dialog box to save the file on the USB flash drive in the Chapter04\ChapterFiles folder with the name sabatinas.html.

To Insert and Center an Image

The first task for the Sabatina's Pizza home page is to insert the company logo banner, sabatinaslogo.jpg. As stated earlier in the book, the company logo is generally used in all communication that represents the company, including on the Web site, on business cards, and on company letterheads. Table 4–4 contains the HTML code to add the centered logo banner image.

Table 4–4 HTML Code for Adding and Centering an Image

Line	HTML Tag and Text
13	`<div style="text-align: center">`
14	`<img src="sabatinaslogo.jpg" width="735" height="190" alt="Sabatina's logo" />`
15	`</div>`

The following step shows how to add a centered banner image.

1

- With the insertion point on line 13, enter the HTML code shown in Table 4–4, pressing ENTER at the end of each line. Make sure to indent the second line of code by using the TAB key. This separates the start and end <div> tag from the <img> tag, highlighting the image insertion. Press the ENTER key twice at the end of line 15 to position the insertion point on line 17 (Figure 4–13).

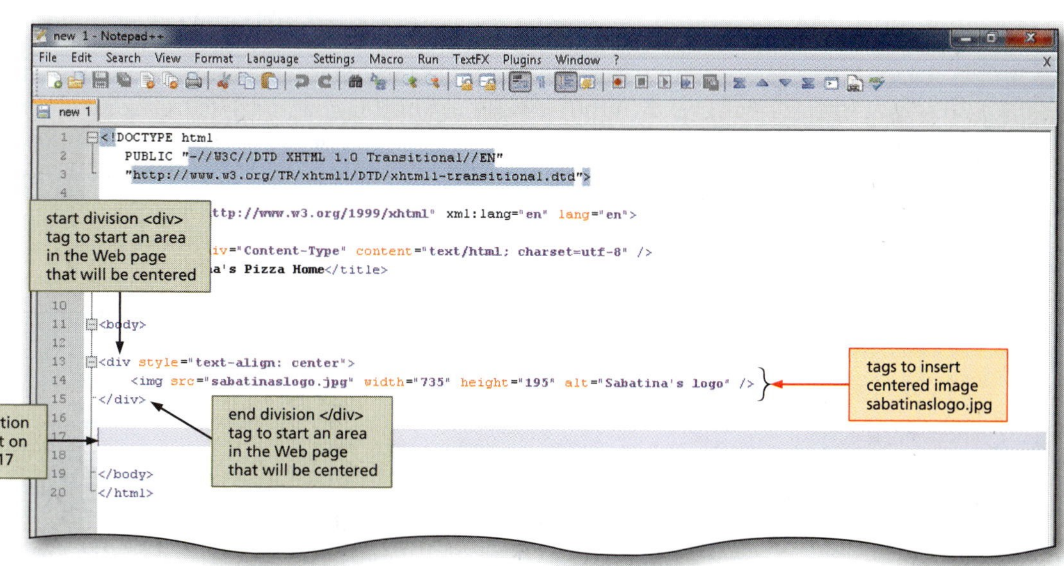

Figure 4–13

Q&A When I pressed ENTER at the end of line 14, Notepad++ indented line 15 also. How do I remove the indent?

You have to press the left arrow key or Backspace to get back to the left margin before you insert the </div> tag.

Q&A How can I determine the height and width of an image?

You can determine the height and width of an image by opening the image in a paint or image-editing program. Once you know the height and width, you also can adjust the width and height by using the width and height attributes in the <img> tag. Be aware that, in doing so, you might cause the image to look distorted on the Web page.

Q&A Why can't I just put the <img> tag within the <center></center> container to center this image?

If you look up the <center> tag in Appendix A, you see that it is deprecated. This book uses Cascading Style Sheets and the <div> </div> container rather than deprecated tags.

Using a Table to Create a Horizontal Menu Bar

The Web site created in this project consists of four Web pages. Visitors should be able to move easily from one Web page to any of the other three Web pages. Providing a menu bar prominently across the top of the Web page (Figure 4–14) gives the visitor ready access to navigation links. You will create a table to hold the menu bar links.

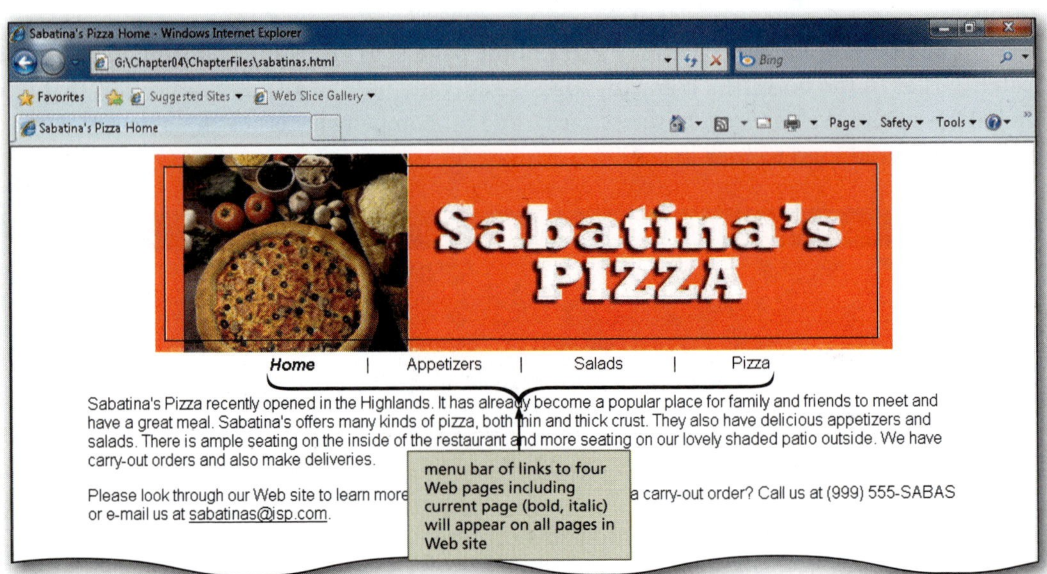

Figure 4–14

> **BTW**
> **Navigation**
> Studies have been conducted to assess the best location on a Web page to place navigation bars and lists. The research results are varied, with indications that navigation options on the top, side, and bottom of a Web page show slight differences in visitor usability. The most important aspect of Web page navigation is to make the options easy enough to locate so visitors do not have to search for them.

All of the styles for this and other tables are set in the external style sheet that you will create in the next section of this chapter. The horizontal menu bar table is borderless (no border property is used), and has one row and seven columns (each divider is a column, as well as the text links). To better align the menu bar with the Sabatina's Pizza logo, the table is set to 60% of the window's width, so that it is not as wide as the logo. The menu bar has four links — Home, Appetizers, Salads, and Pizza — that link to the Web pages sabatinas.html, appetizers.html, salads.html, and pizza.html, respectively. Each link is inserted in a single column (cell). The | (pipe) symbol is included in a column between each of the four links to separate them visually.

The width of each column (cell) in the table is specified in the external style sheet, which will be linked to the home page and all other Web pages in this Web site later in the chapter. (If you do not define the width for these cells, the width defaults to the size of the word or symbol in the cell.) Classes that are used in the home page and in the other three Web pages are also defined in the external style sheet. The menuword and menupipe classes need to be inserted in the menu bar in order to adopt the styles as defined in the external style sheet. The class menuword will be used to set each of the cells in which there are words (i.e., Home, Appetizers, Salads, and Pizza) to 23% of the width of the table. The menupipe class will be used to set each of the cells in which there are pipe symbols to 1% of the size of the table. When you specify sizes in percentages, it is generally best not to set the entire 100% width. The menuwordselect class is used to highlight the link to the page being viewed in the browser. For example, when you click the link to the Appetizers Web page, the word Appetizers in the menu bar is bold and italicized. Each Web page uses the menuwordselect class for one link word.

Just as you did in Chapter 3, you add the class names to your Web pages before you create the classes, in this case, in the external style sheet. All menu bar styles are controlled with the external style sheet. If you didn't use an external style sheet, you would have to type each style into each menu bar on each Web page in the Web site. The advantage of using external (linked) style sheets is that if you need to make a change across the entire Web site, you make that change only once — in the external style sheet. The change then takes effect in every Web page into which the external (linked) style sheet has been linked. Using an external style sheet, you create the .css file once and link it with one line of code into each Web page.

To Create a Horizontal Menu Bar with Text Links

Table 4–5 shows the HTML code for the horizontal menu bar table.

Table 4–5 HTML Code to Insert a Menu Bar

<table>
<tr><th>Line</th><th>HTML Tag and Text</th></tr>
<tr><td>17</td><td><table class="menu"></td></tr>
<tr><td>18</td><td><tr></td></tr>
<tr><td>19</td><td><td class="menuwordselect"><a href="sabatinas.html">Home</a></td></td></tr>
<tr><td>20</td><td><td class="menupipe">|</td></td></tr>
<tr><td>21</td><td><td class="menuword"><a href="appetizers.html">Appetizers</a></td></td></tr>
<tr><td>22</td><td><td class="menupipe">|</td></td></tr>
<tr><td>23</td><td><td class="menuword"><a href="salads.html">Salads</a></td></td></tr>
<tr><td>24</td><td><td class="menupipe">|</td></td></tr>
<tr><td>25</td><td><td class="menuword"><a href="pizza.html">Pizza</a></td></td></tr>
<tr><td>26</td><td></tr></td></tr>
<tr><td>27</td><td></table></td></tr>
</table>

The following step shows how to create a table that contains text links to four pages on the Web site, separated by pipe symbols. The pipe symbol is usually found above the ENTER key; it is inserted when you press Shift and the \ (backslash) key.

1

- With the insertion point on line 17, enter the HTML code, as shown in Table 4–5, pressing ENTER after each line. Use the TAB key to indent the code, as shown in the table. Press the ENTER key once more after line 28 (Figure 4–15) to position the insertion point on line 29.

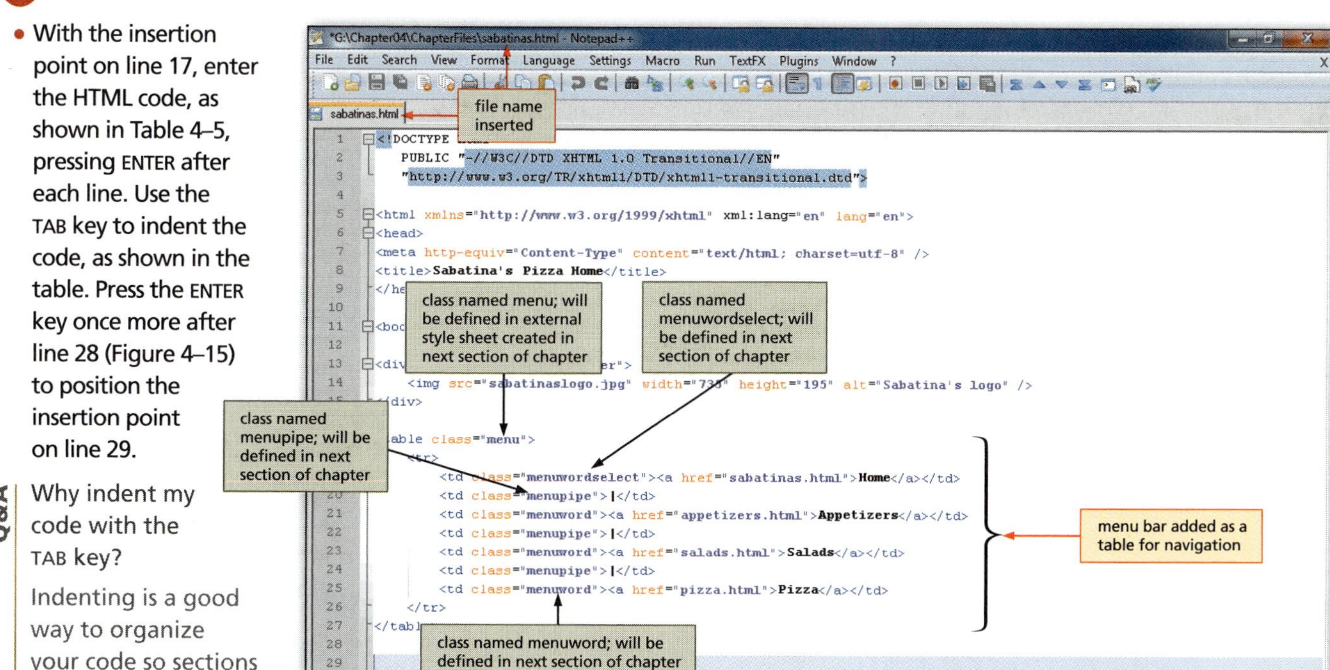

Figure 4–15

Q&A

Why indent my code with the TAB key?

Indenting is a good way to organize your code so sections are recognizable. You can immediately see what lines of code are related to a single row in the table, as contained within the indented <tr> </tr> tags. This is helpful when you have many rows in the table, as in the pizza.html file.

To Add Paragraphs of Text

Next, two paragraphs of text must be added to the Web page. The text is displayed beneath the menu bar of links you just inserted. You use a paragraph <p> tag to insert a blank line between the menu bar and the text. Table 4–6 contains the code to add the paragraphs of text.

Table 4–6 HTML Code to Add Paragraphs of Text

Line	HTML Tag and Text
29	`<p>Sabatina's Pizza recently opened in the Highlands. It has already become a popular place for family and friends to meet and have a great meal. Sabatina's offers many kinds of pizza, both thin and thick crust. They also have delicious appetizers and salads. There is ample seating on the inside of the restaurant and more seating on our lovely shaded patio outside. We have carry-out orders and also make deliveries.</p>`
30	
31	`<p>Please look through our Web site to learn more about our menu. Want to place a carry-out order? Call us at (999) 555-SABAS or e-mail us at <a href="mailto:sabatinas@isp.com"><span style="text-decoration: underline">sabatinas@isp.com</span></a>.</p>`

The following step illustrates how to add paragraphs of text.

1 With the insertion point on line 29, enter the HTML code, as shown in Table 4–6, to insert the paragraphs of text, pressing the ENTER key after each line, including line 31 (Figure 4–16).

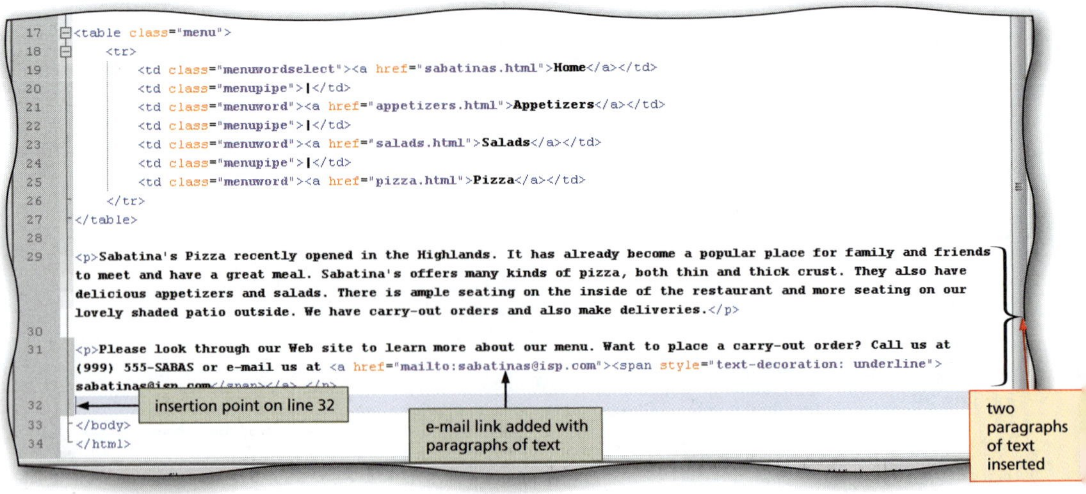

```
17 <table class="menu">
18     <tr>
19         <td class="menuwordselect"><a href="sabatinas.html">Home</a></td>
20         <td class="menupipe">|</td>
21         <td class="menuword"><a href="appetizers.html">Appetizers</a></td>
22         <td class="menupipe">|</td>
23         <td class="menuword"><a href="salads.html">Salads</a></td>
24         <td class="menupipe">|</td>
25         <td class="menuword"><a href="pizza.html">Pizza</a></td>
26     </tr>
27 </table>
28
29 <p>Sabatina's Pizza recently opened in the Highlands. It has already become a popular place for family and friends
   to meet and have a great meal. Sabatina's offers many kinds of pizza, both thin and thick crust. They also have
   delicious appetizers and salads. There is ample seating on the inside of the restaurant and more seating on our
   lovely shaded patio outside. We have carry-out orders and also make deliveries.</p>
30
31 <p>Please look through our Web site to learn more about our menu. Want to place a carry-out order? Call us at
   (999) 555-SABAS or e-mail us at <a href="mailto:sabatinas@isp.com"><span style="text-decoration: underline">
   sabatinas@isp.com</span></a>.</p>
32 
33 </body>
34 </html>
```

insertion point on line 32

e-mail link added with paragraphs of text

two paragraphs of text inserted

Figure 4–16

To Save the HTML File

With the HTML code for the Sabatina's Pizza home page complete, you should re-save the file. The following step shows how to save an HTML file that has been previously saved.

1. Click the Save icon on the Notepad++ toolbar to save the most recent version of sabatinas.html on the same storage device and in the same folder as the last time you saved it (Figure 4–17).

*G:\Chapter04\ChapterFiles\sabatinas.html - Notepad++

Save icon

completed code

```
<!DOCTYPE html
  PUBLIC "-//W3C//DTD XHTML 1.0 Transitional//EN"
  "http://www.w3.org/TR/xhtml1/DTD/xhtml1-transitional.dtd">

<html xmlns="http://www.w3.org/1999/xhtml" xml:lang="en" lang="en">
<head>
<meta http-equiv="Content-Type" content="text/html; charset=utf-8" />
<title>Sabatina's Pizza Home</title>
</head>

<body>

<div style="text-align: center">
    <img src="sabatinaslogo.jpg" width="735" height="195" alt="Sabatina's logo" />
</div>

<table class="menu">
    <tr>
        <td class="menuwordselect"><a href="sabatinas.html">Home</a></td>
        <td class="menupipe">|</td>
        <td class="menuword"><a href="appetizers.html">Appetizers</a></td>
        <td class="menupipe">|</td>
```

Figure 4–17

Viewing the Web Page and Testing Links

After you save the HTML file for the Sabatina's Pizza home page, it should be viewed in a browser to confirm the Web page appears as desired. You do not validate or print the Web page yet because you still have one statement (the link) to add to the file. It also is important to test the four links on the Sabatina's Pizza home page to verify they function as expected.

To View a Web Page

The following steps illustrate how to view the HTML file in a browser.

1. In Internet Explorer, click the Address bar to select the URL on the Address bar.
2. Type `g:\Chapter04\ChapterFiles\sabatinas.html` or the location of your file on the Address bar of your browser and press ENTER to display the Web page (Figure 4–18).

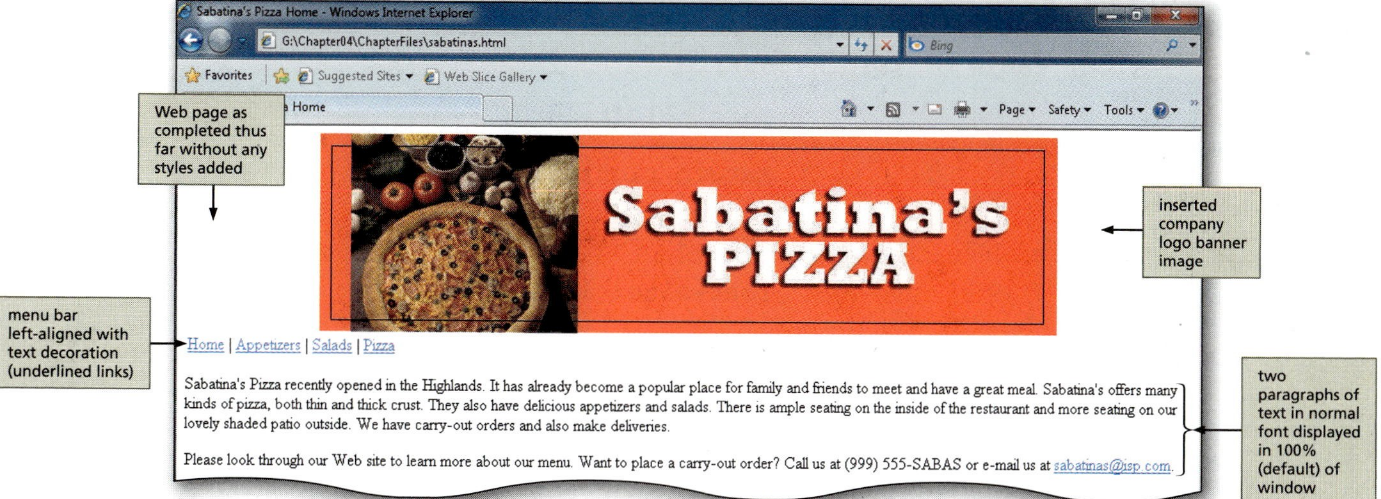

Figure 4–18

To Test Links on a Web Page

The following steps show how to test the links on Sabatina's Pizza home page to verify that they work correctly.

1. With Sabatina's home page displayed in the browser, point to the e-mail link, sabatinas@isp .com and click the link to open the default e-mail program with the address sabatinas@isp .com in the To: text box.
2. Click the Close button in the New Message window. If a dialog box asks if you want to save changes, click No.
3. With the USB flash drive in drive G, click the Salads link from the home page just created. Click back to the Home page from the Salads page. Next, click the Pizza link from the Home page. Click back to the Home page from the Pizza page. The link for the Appetizers page will not work because that Web page is not yet created; you will create it later in this chapter.

External Style Sheets

External style sheets are the most comprehensive type of style sheet and can be used to control the consistency and look of many Web pages within a Web site. Adding an external style sheet to a Web page involves a two-step process of creating an external style sheet and then linking this style sheet to the desired Web pages. The most beneficial feature of the external style sheet is that you can easily change the style (appearance) of all Web pages into which the style sheet is linked just by changing the external style sheet. For instance, the font-family and font-size for all four Web pages in this chapter's project are set in the external style sheet. If the owners of the Web site decide that they do not like the look (or style) of that font-family or font-size, you only have to make the change in one file — the external style sheet. Compare that process to having the font-family and font-size inserted into every single Web page in a Web site either with embedded style sheets or (worst case) inline styles. To make a change to all font-family and font-size styles, you would have to change those in every single place that those styles reside. External (linked) style sheets are the most efficient and powerful way to change styles for an entire Web site.

An external style sheet is a text file that contains the selectors and declarations for the styles you want to apply across the Web site. The sample code that follows shows an example of an external style sheet used to set table, paragraph, and link formatting. Note the use of classes (e.g., menu, menuword, menupipe) in this external style sheet that provides a finer level of control within a table used for navigation.

BTW

Classes
Note that the classes are named with a period (.) after the element is defined. Thus, the table .menu statement identifies a class named menu that will be used with the table elements.

```
table     {width: 65%;
                   margin-left:auto;
                   margin-right:auto;
                   font-family: Arial, Verdana, Garamond;
                   font-size: 12 pt}
          .menu    {text-align: center;
                   width: 60%}
          .menuword {width: 23%}
          .menupipe {width: 1%}
```

```
th        {color: white;
          background-color: #ff1828}
caption   {caption-side: bottom;
          font-style: italic}
p         {margin-left: 50pt;
          margin-right: 50pt;
          font-family: Arial, Verdana, Garamond;
          font-size: 12pt}
a         {text-decoration: none;
          font-family: Arial, Verdana, Garamond;
          font-size: 12pt;
          color: black}
```

The format of the external style sheet is very similar to the format of the embedded style sheet. An external style sheet, however, does not need <style> </style> tags to start and end the style sheet; it only needs the style statements.

To create an external style sheet, enter all of the style statements in a text file using Notepad++ or another text editor, and then save the text file with a .css (for Cascading Style Sheet) extension. The code shown above, for example, can be saved with the file name styles1.css and then linked onto multiple Web pages.

Remember that the <head> tag is used for a variety of purposes. The information contained within the <head></head> container of your HTML document provides information to browsers and search engines but is not displayed on the Web page itself. The following tags can be used within the <head></head> container: <base>, <link>, <meta>, <script>, <style>, and <title>. For each Web page to which you want to apply the styles in an external style sheet, a <link /> tag similar to the sample code below must be inserted within the <head></head> tags of the Web page:

```
<link rel="stylesheet" type="text/css" href="styles1.css" />
```

The <link /> tag indicates that the style sheet styles1.css should be applied to this Web page. The property-value statement rel="stylesheet" defines the relationship of the linked document (that is, it defines it as a style sheet). The property-value statement type="text/css" indicates the content and language used in the linked document. The property-value statement href="styles1.css" indicates the name and location of the linked style sheet, styles1.css. To apply this style sheet to other pages in the Web site, you would insert the same <link /> tag between the <head></head> tags of each Web page.

Plan Ahead

Determine what type of style sheets or other formatting to use in your Web pages.

- **Determine which styles will be common across the Web pages in the Web site.** Some things should be constant across Web pages in a Web site. For instance, if tables are used, their style is generally common or consistent throughout the Web site. A font-family style is also something that is generally common across all Web pages in a Web site. Consider using external (or linked) style sheets for styles that will encompass all Web pages in a multipage Web site. Because it is a four-page Web site, the project in this chapter is a perfect application for external (or linked) style sheets. You use an external style sheet in this project to set styles for the body, paragraphs, links, and some table styles.
- **Identify elements that need to differ from the style used across the Web site.**
  - Consider using embedded style sheets for Web pages in which the styles apply only to one particular Web page. You can use embedded style sheets when you want elements within one Web page to look similar to one another. In the project in Chapter 4, however, you do not use embedded style sheets.
  - Consider using inline styles for any style that is unique for a single element, such as when you want one word or paragraph on one Web page to look different than all others. In this project, you use inline styles to align images and vary some text.
  - Consider using formatting tag attributes to give style to a single element. In this project, you use the cellpadding and cellspacing attributes, and others.

BTW

Adding Comments
If your instructor wants you to add your name to the CSS code file, you can do that by adding your name within a comment line. Use /* and */ to surround the added information (e.g., your name), making it a comment.

Adding an External Style Sheet

The next step is to create an external style sheet (.css file) and link it to the Web pages where it will be used. The external (linked) style sheet will set the style for body text, paragraphs, links, and table format.

Because the font-family and font-size style is used for all text on all Web pages, you can put that style in the body element, identified on the external style sheet as body. All links (identified as *a* in the external style sheet) will be black through all states (normal, visited, and active) and use no text decoration (that is, the text links will not be underlined). Most of the tables will have a 65% width relative to the window. The exception is the menu bar table that you created earlier, which will be slightly smaller (60% width). Finally, you will use classes, as discussed in Chapter 3, to have more control over particular elements of the tables in the Web site. You use a class named menu for the menu bar links. You also want to separate the menu bar table cells with pipe symbols. To do that, you use classes named menuword and menupipe to specify the width of each of those cells. You also insert a class named menuwordselect, which is used later for the menu tables in the Web site. Note that the classes are named with a period (.) after the element is defined. Thus, the table.menu statement identifies a class named menu that will be used with the table elements.

Plan Ahead

Create and link an external style sheet.
The external style sheet is the most powerful and lowest precedence style sheet. With this style sheet, you can easily create a common look across a Web site by creating the external (.css) style sheet and linking it onto all Web pages.

- **Create the .css file.** The first step is to create the external style sheet itself. This file, which contains all of the style statements that you want, has to be saved with a file name extension of .css. Make sure to store this file in the same folder as the other Web pages.
- **Link the external style sheet onto the Web pages.** The second step is to link the external style sheet (.css file) onto the Web pages where you want the styles to be applied. The link statement is placed between the <head> and </head> tags.

To Create an External Style Sheet

Table 4–7 shows the style statements for an external style sheet for the Sabatina's Pizza Web site. To create an external style sheet, you open a new text file and enter CSS code for the style statements that define the Web page style. After coding the style statements, you save the file with the file extension .css to identify it as a CSS file.

Table 4–7 Code for an External Style Sheet

CSS Properties and Values

```
body    {font-family: Arial, Verdana, Garamond;
        font-size: 12pt}

p       {margin-left: 50pt;
        margin-right: 50pt}

a       {text-decoration: none;
        color: black}

table   {width: 65%;
        margin-left:auto;
        margin-right:auto}

        .menu   {text-align: center;
                width: 60%}

        .menuword {width: 23%}

        .menuwordselect {width: 23%;  font-weight: bolder; font-style: italic}

        .menupipe {width: 1%}

th      {color: white;
        background-color: #ff1828}

caption         {caption-side: bottom;
                font-style: italic}
```

The following steps illustrate how to create and save an external style sheet.

1

- If necessary, click the Notepad++ button on the taskbar to display sabatinas.html. Click File on the menu bar and then click New.
- Enter the CSS code, as shown in Table 4–7, using the TAB key to align text, as shown (Figure 4–19).

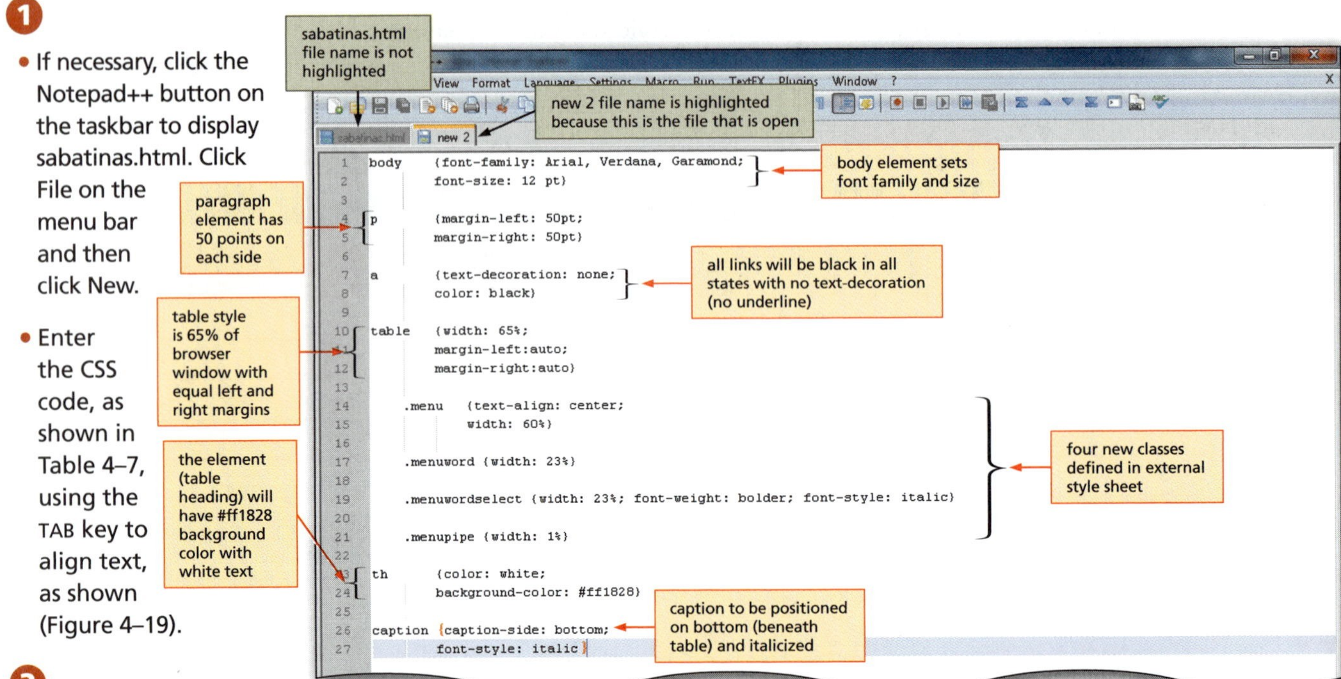

Figure 4–19

2

- With the USB drive plugged into your computer, click File on the menu bar and then click Save As. Type `styles1.css` in the File name text box. If necessary, navigate to the G:\Chapter04\ChapterFiles folder. Click the Save button in the Save As dialog box to save the file as styles1.css.
- Open Internet Explorer and navigate to jigsaw.w3.org/css-validator/#validate_by_upload.
- Validate the styles1.css file.
- Return to the styles1.css Notepad++ file and print a hard copy of the style sheet (Figure 4–20).

```
body{font-family: Arial, Verdana, Garamond;
        font-size: 12 pt}

p       {margin-left: 50pt;
        margin-right: 50pt}

a       {text-decoration: none;
        color: black}

table{width: 65%;
        margin-left:auto;
        margin-right:auto}

    .menu   {text-align: center;
            width: 60%}

    .menuword {width: 23%}

    .menuwordselect {width: 23%; font-weight: bolder; font-style: italic}

    .menupipe {width: 1%}

th      {color: white;
        background-color: #ff1828}

caption {caption-side: bottom;
        font-style: italic}
```

Figure 4–20

Examining the External Style Sheet

Because the CSS code for the external style sheet is complex, a review is necessary to learn what it does. The CSS code that you entered and is shown in Table 4-7 on page HTML 181 defines a new style for four main elements on a Web page: body, paragraphs, links, and tables. It is a good idea (but not a requirement) to insert your styles in order in the external style sheet.

The first style statement on lines 1 and 2 is entered as:

```
body    {font-family: Arial, Verdana, Garamond;
        font-size: 12 pt}
```

to change the font-family and font-size for the text throughout the Web site. You use the body element because you want these styles to apply to text across the Web site (Figure 4-19). If you wanted to apply one font-family or font-size to paragraphs of text and another font-family and font-size to the text in links, you would use the elements *p* and *a* rather than body to create those styles. This project uses three different font-family styles (Arial, Verdana, and Garamond) just in case the computer on which the Web page is viewed does not have the first (Arial) or second (Verdana) font-family. If the computer does not have any of the three font-families, then the normal (default browser) font-family is used.

The next styles are applied to the paragraph (p) element on lines 4 and 5:

```
p    {margin-left: 50pt;
     margin-right: 50pt}
```

With this style, you are adding right and left margins that are 50 points wide. This pulls the paragraph text in 50 points both from the left and right. To see what that style statement does to the look of the home page for this Web site, look at Figure 4–18 on page HTML 177 compared to Figure 4–1a on page HTML 159.

Lines 7 and 8 define the styles for all links by using the link (a) element:

```
a    {text-decoration: none;
     color: black}
```

This statement sets links to have no text-decoration (underlines) and makes all link states (normal, visited, and active) black in color. With a text-decoration setting of none, the browser will not display lines under any links. Setting the link color to black throughout eliminates the blue and purple (normal and visited) link colors that you would normally have. You can see in Figure 4–1a through 4-1d that users can tell what page they are on by the style of the link text in the menu bar; the name of the page they are visiting appears bold and italic in the menu bar. This is accomplished with the menuwordselect class that was defined in the styles1.css file that you just created. For instance, you can see that the style of the Home link (Figure 4–21 on the next page) when you are on the Home Web page is darker (bolder) and italicized. As you move from page to page, that bolder and italicized style moves to the respective page text link. For this feature, the menuwordselect class is inserted into the appropriate text link. The menuwordselect class is used once on each Web page.

BTW

Colors

To find the exact color, you can open the logo in a graphic image editing program and use one of the tools (such as the eye dropper tool) to click on the logo itself. If you then look at the color box, you should see the six-digit hexadecimal code for that color.

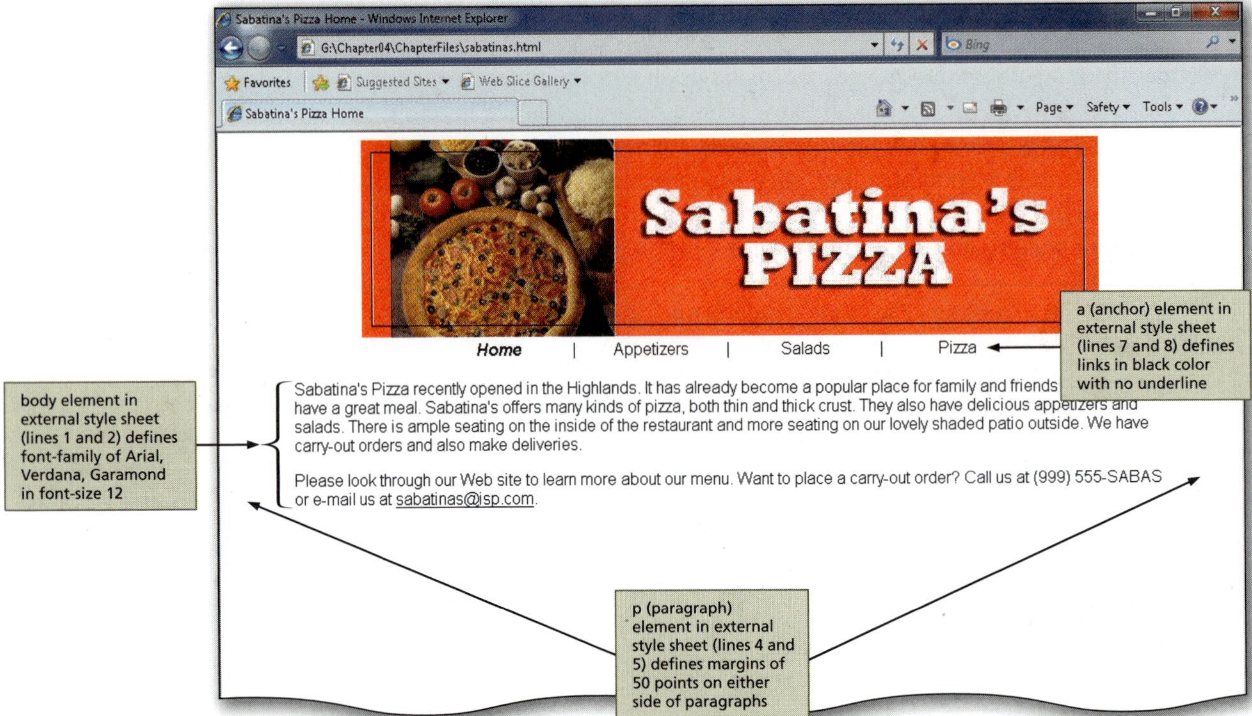

Figure 4–21

In this external style sheet, all table-related styles are inserted together from lines 10 through 27:

```
table               {width: 65%;
                    margin-left:auto;
                    margin-right:auto}
   .menu            {text-align: center;
                    width: 60%}
   .menuword        {width: 23%}
   .menuwordselect  {width: 23%;  font-weight: bolder;
                    font-style: italic}
   .menupipe        {width: 1%}
th                  {color: white;
                    background-color: #ff1828}
caption             {caption-side: bottom;
                    font-style: italic}
```

Lines 10 through 12 identify the general style for all tables on the Web pages. The width of all tables (with the exception of the menu bar) will be 65% of the browser window. You control the width of the menu bar table by naming a class called menu (remember this can be any arbitrary name), as shown in the code in the styles1.css Web page file. The margin:auto statements horizontally center the element table with respect to the edges of the window. The values used for each side are equal because of the auto designator.

On lines 14 through 21, beneath the table element, are four named classes: menu, menuword, menuwordselect, and menupipe. Those lines are indented so that you can immediately see that they are related to the table element. On line 15, the style of the menu class is designated to be 60% rather than the 65% of all other tables. Line 14 tells the browser to display the text within the cells of the table in the center. See the differences created by these styles in Figure 4–22.

The menuword class sets the width of that column to 23%. The menupipe class sets the column with the pipe symbol to 1%. The menuwordselect class specifies a word to highlight by making it bolder and italicized. In Figure 4–22, the selected word is Appetizers. See how that word in the menu bar is bolder and italicized. You can utilize these classes (menu, menuword, menuwordselect, and menupipe) with the HTML code that you just typed in the sabatinas.html file. For the Sabatina's Pizza Home page, the menuwordselect class is used for the Home link (Figure 4–19, page HTML 182). When you click the Appetizers link though, the word Appetizers will be in bold and italics because you will use the menuwordselect class for that link. See the effect of that code in Figure 4–22.

In lines 23 and 24, you identify styles for all table headers (<th>). You designate a background color of #ff1828 (which is a red) with text color that is white (Figure 4–22). The red that is used is the same red that is in the Sabatina's Pizza logo banner.

BTW

External Style Sheet Validator

For the external style sheet, be sure to use the CSS validator found at the w3.org validation service at http://jigsaw.w3.org/css-validator/#validate_by_upload.

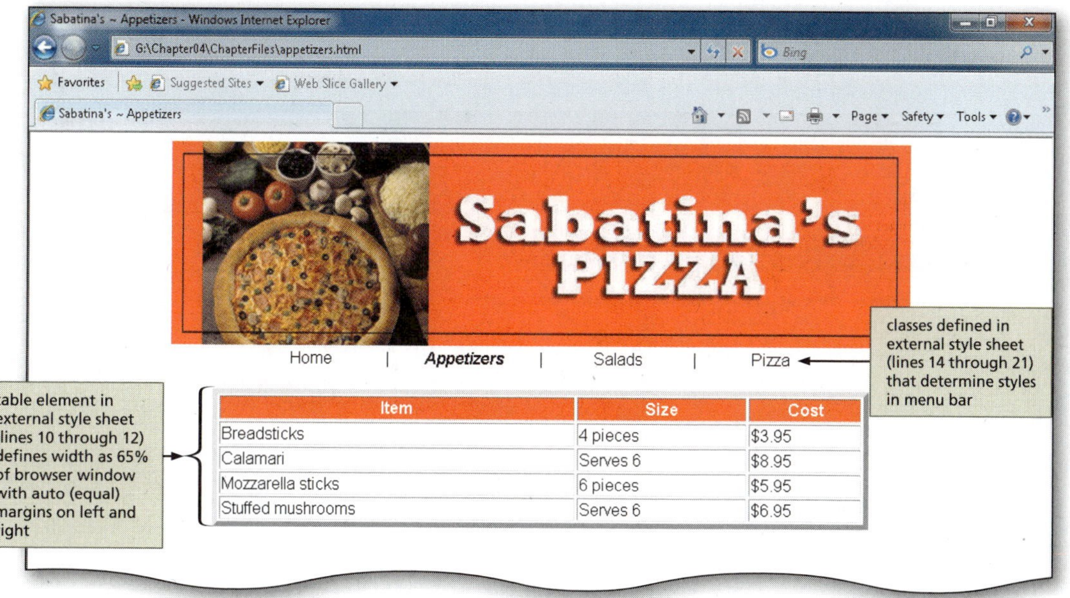

Figure 4–22

The final section of CSS code, lines 26 and 27, defines the styles to be applied to table captions. You want all captions to be aligned beneath the table and italicized.

Linking to the External Style Sheet

Four Web pages in the Sabatina's Pizza Web site require the same style: sabatinas .html, appetizers.html, salads.html, and pizza.html. Linking the external style sheet to each of these Web pages gives them the same styles for margins, paragraph text, links, and tables.

To link to the external style sheet, a <link /> tag must be inserted onto each of these four Web pages. The <link /> tag used to link an external style sheet is added within the <head></head> tag of the Web page HTML code. The general format of the <link /> tag is:

```
<link rel="stylesheet" type="text/css" href="styles1.css" />
```

where rel="stylesheet" establishes that the linked document is a style sheet, type="text/ css" indicates that the CSS language is used in the text file containing the style sheet, and href="styles1.css" provides the name and location (URL) of the linked style sheet. To link a style sheet to a Web page, the <link /> tag must use "stylesheet" as the value for the rel property and text/css as the value for the type property. The URL used as the value for the href property varies, based on the name and location of the file used as the external style sheet. The URL used here indicates that the external style sheet, styles1.css, is located in the main or root directory of the Web site.

To Link to an External Style Sheet

After creating and saving the external style sheet, .css file, you use a <link /> tag to link the external style sheet to any Web pages to which you want to apply the style. Notice that the link tag is one of those (like the <img /> tag) that does not have a separate end tag (e.g., <body> and </body>). You therefore should use the / after a space and before the > in the tag to indicate the end of the tag.

The following step illustrates how to add a link to an external style sheet using a <link /> tag and then save the HTML file.

- Click the sabatinas .html tab in Notepad++ to make it the active window.
- With the sabatinas .html file open, click the end of line 8 after the > and press the ENTER key twice. Your insertion point should be positioned on line 10.
- Type `<link rel="stylesheet" type="text/css" href="styles1 .css" />` as the HTML code and then press the ENTER key, as shown in Figure 4–23.
- Click the Save button on the Notepad++ toolbar.

G:\Chapter04\ChapterFiles\sabatinas.html - Notepad++

File Edit Search View Format Language Settings Macro Run TextFX Plugins Window ?

sabatinas.html styles1.css

```
1  <!DOCTYPE html
2     PUBLIC "-//W3C//DTD XHTML 1.0 Transitional//EN"
3     "http://www.w3.org/TR/xhtml1/DTD/xhtml1-transitional.dtd">
4
5  <html xmlns="http://www.w3.org/1999/xhtml" xml:lang="en" lang="en">
6  <head>
7  <meta http-equiv="Content-Type" content="text/html; charset=utf-8" />
8  <title>Sabatina's Pizza Home</title>
9
10 <link rel="stylesheet" type="text/css" href="styles1.css" />
11
12 </head>
13
14 <body>
15
16 <div style="text-align: center">
17     <img src="sabatinaslogo.jpg" width="735" height="195" alt="Sabatina's logo" />
18 </div>
```

link to external style sheet; because of this one line of code, all styles defined in styles1.css external style sheet will take effect on this Web page

Figure 4–23

Q&A

Is that all it takes to use an external style sheet — to insert that link statement?

Yes, that is all you need to do to use the styles identified in the external style sheet. The styles specified in the external style sheet will apply to that page, unless an embedded or inline style sheet takes precedence. Remember too that if you want to change a style, you just change it in the external (linked) style sheet itself. It automatically takes effect in any Web page that is linked to the external style sheet. (Remember to click the Refresh button if that Web page is already open in the browser.)

Q&A

Will the table styles from the styles1.css file take effect for all tables within the Web site?

As long as you insert the style sheet link statement onto the Web page, then the table styles will take effect. Remember that you can override those styles with either an embedded or an inline style sheet. You would do this if there is a table that you want to vary from all other tables in the Web site.

Q&A

Why is an external style sheet sometimes called a linked style sheet?

The style sheet that you created above is external to (as opposed to inline or embedded in) the Web page in which it is used. That's why it is called an external style sheet. The external style sheet is used by linking it into a Web page. It is called linked because you use a <link /> tag to insert it.

Validating and Printing the HTML, Viewing the Web Page, and Testing Links

After you save the HTML file for the Sabatina's Pizza home page, it should be validated to ensure that it meets current XHTML standards and viewed in a browser to confirm the Web page displays as desired. It also is important to test the links in the Sabatina's Pizza home page to verify that they function as expected.

To Validate a Web Page

The following steps illustrate how to validate an HTML file.

1. Open Internet Explorer and navigate to the Web site validator.w3.org.
2. Click the Validate by File Upload tab.
3. Click the Browse button.
4. Locate the sabatinas.html file on your storage device and click the file name.
5. Click the Open button in the Choose File to Upload dialog box and the file name will be inserted into the File box.
6. Click the Check button.

Q&A

What if my HTML code does not pass the validation process?

If your file does not pass validation, make changes to the file to correct your errors. You should then revalidate the file.

To Print an HTML File

After your HTML code has passed validation, it is a good idea to make a hard copy printout of it.

1. Click the Notepad++ button on the taskbar to activate the Notepad++ window.
2. Click File on the menu bar, click the Print command, and then click the Print button to print a hard copy of the HTML code (Figure 4–24).

C:\ShellyCashman\HTML6\Chapter04\Solutions\ChapterFiles\sabatinas.html   Monday, December 07, 2009 11:44 AM

```
<!DOCTYPE html
   PUBLIC "-//W3C//DTD XHTML 1.0 Transitional//EN"
   "http://www.w3.org/TR/xhtml1/DTD/xhtml1-transitional.dtd">

<html xmlns="http://www.w3.org/1999/xhtml" xml:lang="en" lang="en">
<head>
<meta http-equiv="Content-Type" content="text/html; charset=utf-8" />
<title>Sabatina's Pizza Home</title>

<link rel="stylesheet" type="text/css" href="styles1.css" />

</head>

<body>

<div style="text-align: center">
    <img src="sabatinaslogo.jpg" width="735" height="190" alt="Sabatina's logo" />
</div>

<table class="menu">
    <tr>
        <td class="menuwordselect"><a href="sabatinas.html">Home</a></td>
        <td class="menupipe">|</td>
        <td class="menuword"><a href="appetizers.html">Appetizers</a></td>
        <td class="menupipe">|</td>
        <td class="menuword"><a href="salads.html">Salads</a></td>
        <td class="menupipe">|</td>
        <td class="menuword"><a href="pizza.html">Pizza</a></td>
    </tr>
</table>

<p>Sabatina's Pizza recently opened in the Highlands. It has already become a popular
place for family and friends to meet and have a great meal. Sabatina's offers many
kinds of pizza, both thin and thick crust. They also have delicious appetizers and
salads. There is ample seating on the inside of the restaurant and more seating on our
lovely shaded patio outside. We have carry-out orders and also make deliveries.</p>

<p>Please look through our Web site to learn more about our menu. Want to place a
carry-out order? Call us at (999) 555-SABAS or e-mail us at <a href=
"mailto:sabatinas@isp.com"><span style="text-decoration: underline">sabatinas@isp.com
</span></a>.</p>

</body>
</html>
```

Figure 4–24

To View, Test, and Print a Web Page

1. Click the Internet Explorer button on the Windows taskbar to activate Internet Explorer.
2. In Internet Explorer, click the Address bar to select the URL in the Address bar.
3. Type `g:\Chapter04\ChapterFiles\sabatinas.html` (or the specific path to your file) to display the new URL in the Address bar and then press the ENTER key.
4. Click the Salads and Pizza links to test that they work correctly.
5. Click the Print button on the Internet Explorer Command bar to print the Web page (Figure 4–25).

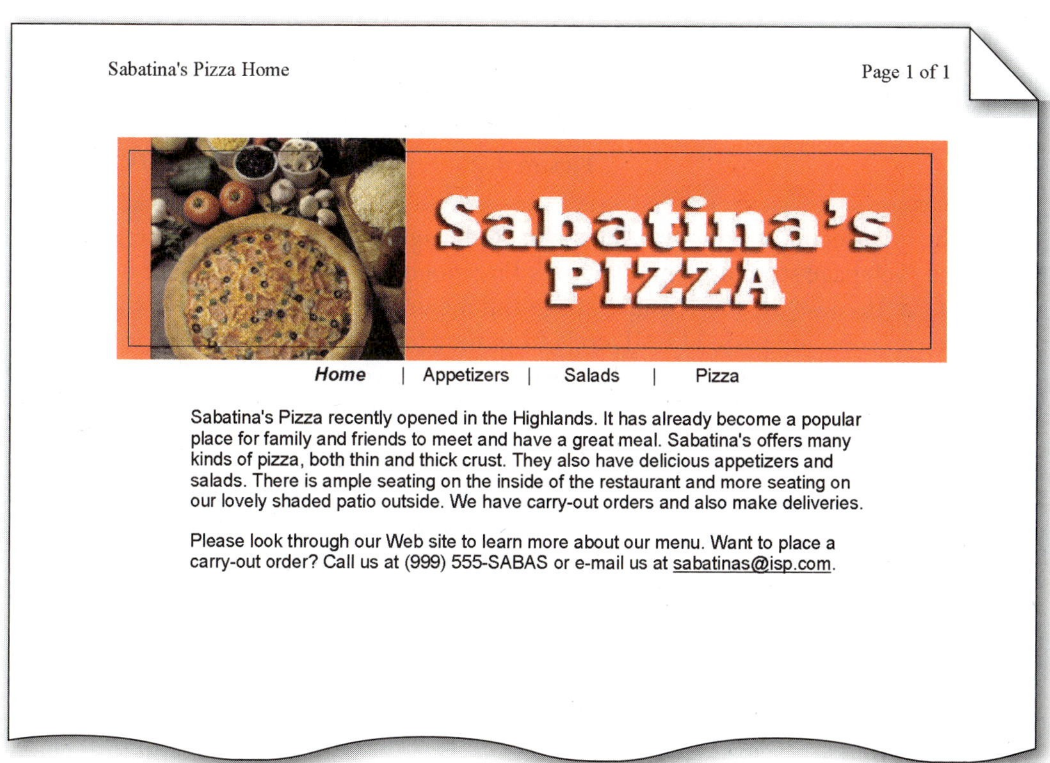

Figure 4–25

Creating a Second Web Page

You have created the Sabatina's Pizza home page with a horizontal menu bar of text links for easy navigation to other pages in the site and an external style sheet. Now it is time to create one of those linked pages — the Appetizers page (Figure 4–26 on the next page). Like the home page, the Appetizers page includes the logo image and a horizontal menu bar of text links. Having the Sabatina's Pizza logo and the horizontal menu bar at the top of each page provides consistency throughout the Web site. The menu bar lists the four Web pages — Home, Appetizers, Salads, and Pizza — with a | (pipe) symbol between links. Beneath the menu bar is a table listing the appetizers that are available at Sabatina's Pizza.

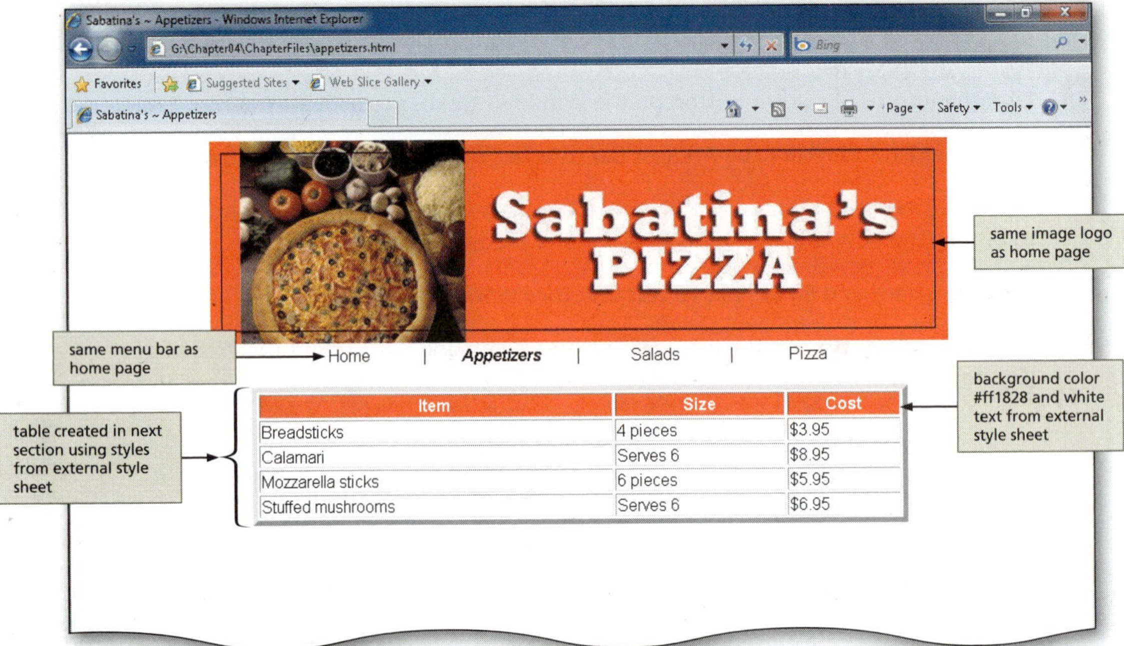

Figure 4–26

The first step in creating the Appetizers Web page is to add the HTML tags to define the Web page structure, the Sabatina's Pizza logo banner image, and the horizontal menu bar. Because the logo banner image and menu bar are the same as on the home page, you can copy and paste HTML code from the Home page and then edit it for the Appetizers page. You would copy/paste this code because you have already tested it by opening the sabatinas.html file in the browser, and you know the code works. Rather than retyping the code, and possibly getting errors, a copy/paste will assure that it is correct.

To Copy and Paste HTML Code to a New File

The following step shows how to copy the HTML tags to define the Web page structure and the horizontal menu table from the HTML file, sabatinas.html, to a new HTML file.

1. If necessary, click the Notepad++ button on the taskbar and click the sabatinas.html tab to make it the active window.
2. Click immediately to the left of the < in the <!DOCTYPE html tag on line 1.
3. Drag through the </table> tag on line 30 to highlight lines 1 through 30.
4. Press CTRL+C to copy the selected lines to the Clipboard.
5. Click File on the Notepad++ menu bar and then click New.
6. Press CTRL+V to paste the contents from the Clipboard into a new file. Press the ENTER key twice to position the insertion point on line 32.
7. Change the words Pizza Home in the <title> on line 8 to ~ Appetizers (using the tilde ~ character).
8. Change the word menuwordselect on line 22 to menuword.
9. Change the word menuword on line 24 to menuwordselect.

To Save an HTML File

With the HTML code for the structure code and menu table added, the appetizers .html file should be saved.

1. With a USB drive plugged into the computer, click File on the menu bar and then click Save As. Type `appetizers.html` in the File name text box.

2. If necessary, click USB (G:) in the Save in list. Double-click the Chapter04 folder and then double-click the ChapterFiles folder in the list of available folders. Click the Save button in the Save As dialog box (Figure 4–27).

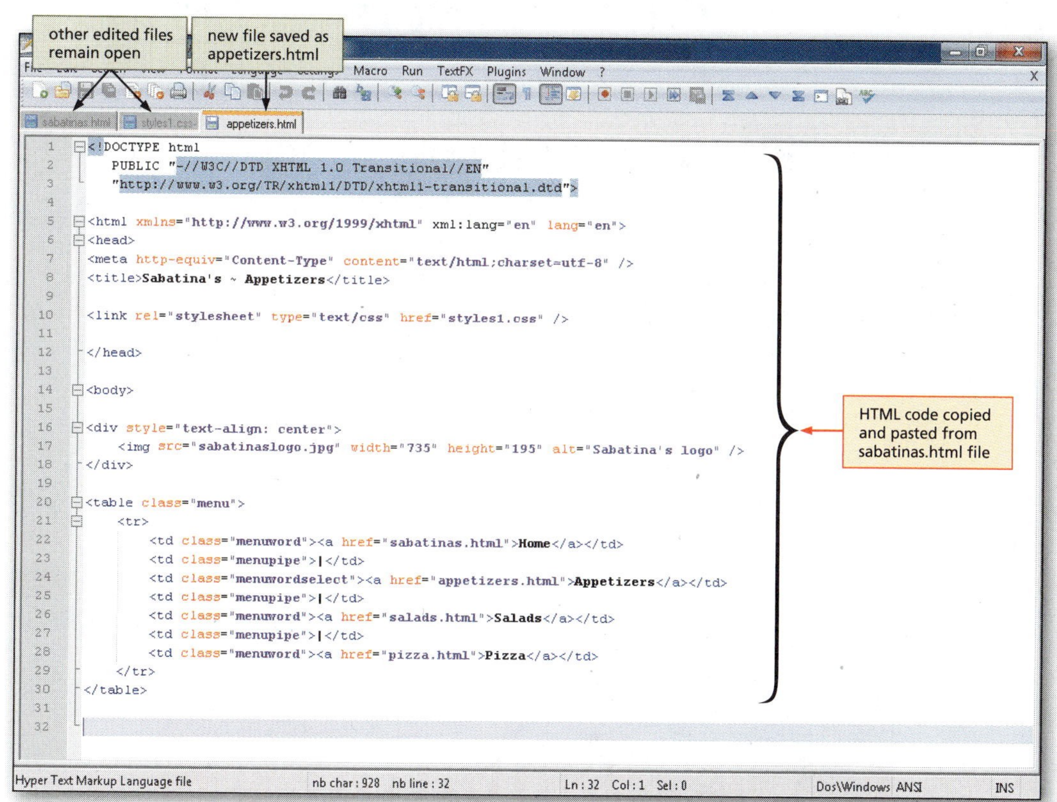

Figure 4–27

Plan Ahead

Determine what styles are needed for the second Web page.
Prior to adding more code to the Appetizers Web page, think through what styles you have defined and determine if there is anything in this Web page that needs to differ from the external style sheet. Any differences can be inserted as a formatting attribute, an inline style, or as an embedded style sheet that will override the styles defined in the external style sheet.

- **Review the table formatting in the external style sheet to see if it is appropriate for this page.** Borderless tables often are appropriate when the tables are used to position text and image elements. In other instances, such as when a table is used to structure columns and rows of information, borders are appropriate.
- **Identify any other styles that may need to be applied to tables on this page.** It is important to make your tables clear enough that users can easily identify the information that they need. You may want to start with the basic table format and add options as necessary.

Adding a Table with Borders

The borderless table style defined in the styles1.css external style sheet works well for the horizontal menu that appears on every page. However, the borderless format would be less effective in presenting the three columns and five rows of information about available appetizers at Sabatina's Pizza. Figure 4–28a shows this information in a table with borders. Figure 4–28b shows the same information in a table without borders. As shown in this figure, using a table with borders makes the information on the Appetizers Web page easier to read and provides a frame that gives the table a three-dimensional appearance.

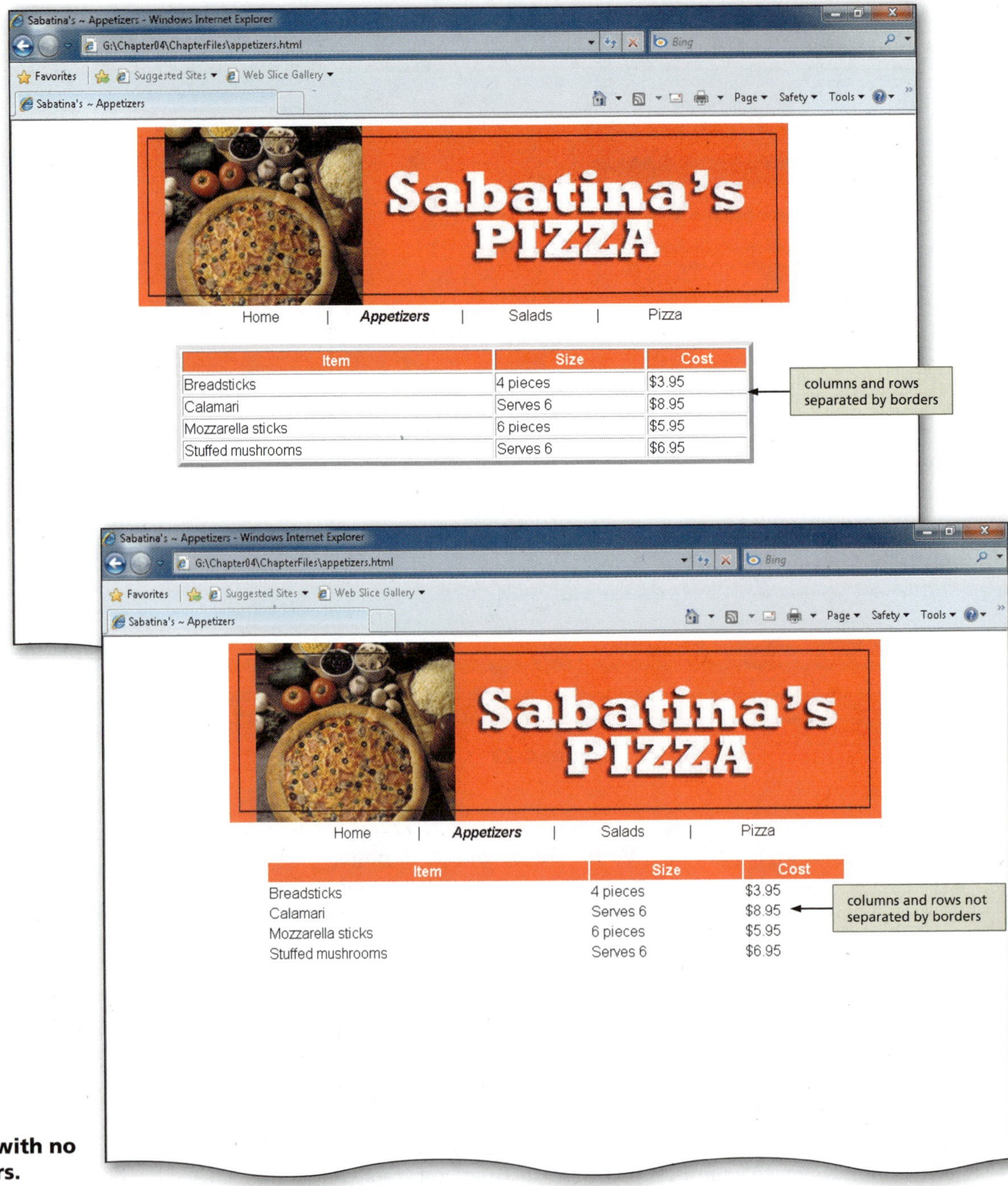

Figure 4–28

To Create a Table with Borders and Insert Text

Creating the table shown in Figure 4–28a involves first creating a table with three columns and five rows. The first row of the table is for column headings; the other rows are for data. As you have learned, table heading cells <th> differ from data cells <td> in their appearance. Text in a heading cell appears as bold and centered, while text in a data cell appears as normal and left-aligned. In the external style sheet styles1.css that you created in an earlier section of the project, you gave table header cells a background color of #ff1828 and white text. Table 4–8 contains the HTML tags and text used to create the table of appetizers on the Appetizers Web page.

Table 4–8 HTML Code to Create a Table

Line	HTML Tag and Text
32	
33	<table border="5">
34	<tr>
35	<th>Item</th>
36	<th>Size</th>
37	<th>Cost</th>
38	</tr>
39	
40	<tr>
41	<td>Breadsticks</td>
42	<td>4 pieces</td>
43	<td>$3.95</td>
44	</tr>
45	
46	<tr>
47	<td>Calamari</td>
48	<td>Serves 6</td>
49	<td>$8.95</td>
50	</tr>
51	
52	<tr>
53	<td>Mozzarella sticks</td>
54	<td>6 pieces</td>
55	<td>$5.95</td>
56	</tr>
57	
58	<tr>
59	<td>Stuffed mushrooms</td>
60	<td>Serves 6</td>
61	<td>$6.95</td>
62	</tr>
63	</table>
64	
65	</body>
66	</html>

The following step illustrates how to create a table with borders and insert text into heading and data cells.

1

- With the insertion point on line 32, enter the HTML code for the Appetizers table, as shown in Table 4–8, using TAB to create indents, and pressing ENTER after each line except the last line (Figure 4–29).

Q&A What does the number in the table border line (line 33) represent?

It represents the number of pixels that you want the border to be. The higher the number, the wider the border.

Q&A Are there other attributes that can be used in the <table>, <tr>, <th>, and <td> tags?

Many other attributes can be used in the <table> related tags (see Appendix A). The best way to review these attributes is to try them in simple tables to see the effect. Viewing tables with various attributes designated side by side on a Web page helps you to determine which attributes to use.

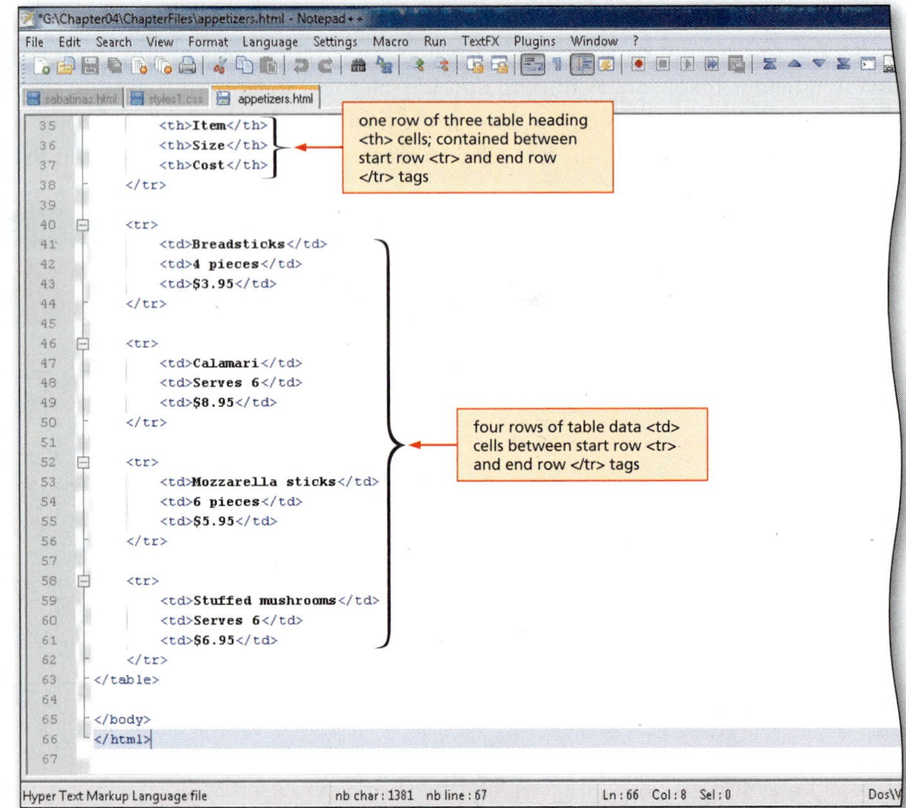

Figure 4–29

Q&A Why are we using a white font color for the headings?

Because the background color is so dark (#ff1828), you could not easily read the heading if it was the default color of black. Changing the font color to white on a dark background color makes it easier to read.

To Save, Validate, View, and Print the Web Page

After adding the remaining HTML code, perform the following steps to save, validate, view, and print the Appetizers Web page.

1. In Notepad++, click the Save icon on the toolbar to save appetizers.html.
2. Click the Internet Explorer button on the taskbar.
3. Use the W3C validator service to validate the appetizers.html Web page.
4. Click the Notepad++ button to return to Notepad++.
5. Print the appetizers.html Notepad++ file (Figure 4–30).
6. Use the Back button or Internet Explorer tabs to return to the Sabatina's home page.
7. Click the Appetizers link on the home page to show the most recent file.
8. Click the Print button on the Command bar to print the Web page, as shown in Figure 4–31.

```
<!DOCTYPE html
   PUBLIC "-//W3C//DTD XHTML 1.0 Transitional//EN"
   "http://www.w3.org/TR/xhtml1/DTD/xhtml1-transitional.dtd">

<html xmlns="http://www.w3.org/1999/xhtml" xml:lang="en" lang="en">
<head>
<meta http-equiv="Content-Type" content="text/html;charset=utf-8" />
<title>Sabatina's ~ Appetizers</title>

<link rel="stylesheet" type="text/css" href="styles1.css" />

</head>

<body>

<div style="text-align: center">
    <img src="sabatinaslogo.jpg" width="735" height="195" alt="Sabatina's logo" />
</div>

<table class="menu">
    <tr>
        <td class="menuword"><a href="sabatinas.html">Home</a></td>
        <td class="menupipe">|</td>
        <td class="menuwordselect"><a href="appetizers.html">Appetizers</a></td>
        <td class="menupipe">|</td>
        <td class="menuword"><a href="salads.html">Salads</a></td>
        <td class="menupipe">|</td>
        <td class="menuword"><a href="pizza.html">Pizza</a></td>
    </tr>
</table>

<br />
<table border="5">
    <tr>
        <th>Item</th>
        <th>Size</th>
        <th>Cost</th>
    </tr>

    <tr>
        <td>Breadsticks</td>
        <td>4 pieces</td>
        <td>$3.95</td>
    </tr>

    <tr>
        <td>Calamari</td>
        <td>Serves 6</td>
        <td>$8.95</td>
    </tr>

    <tr>
        <td>Mozzarella sticks</td>

        <td>6 pieces</td>
        <td>$5.95</td>
    </tr>

    <tr>
        <td>Stuffed mushrooms</
        <td>Serves 6</td>
        <td>$6.95</td>
    </tr>
</table>

</body>
</html>
```

Figure 4–30

Sabatina's ~ Appetizers Page 1 of 1

Sabatina's PIZZA

Home | *Appetizers* | Salads | Pizza

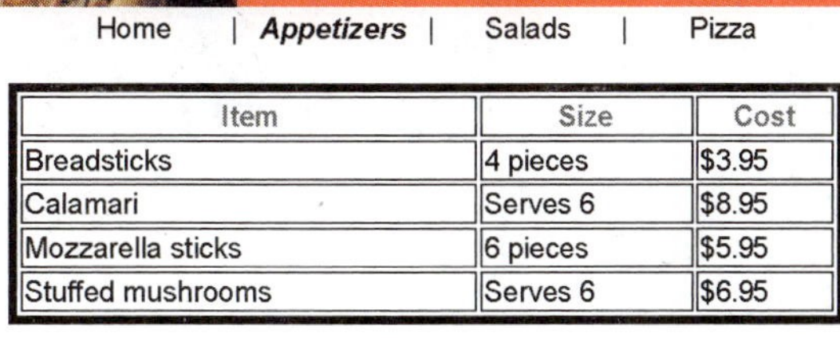

Item	Size	Cost
Breadsticks	4 pieces	$3.95
Calamari	Serves 6	$8.95
Mozzarella sticks	6 pieces	$5.95
Stuffed mushrooms	Serves 6	$6.95

Figure 4–31

To Test Links on a Web Page

After confirming that the Web page appears as desired, the four links on the horizontal menu bar should be tested to verify that they function as expected. The following steps show how to test the links on the appetizers.html Web page. Compare Figure 4–32a (the starting Web page) to Figure 4–32b (the ending Web page after the HTML code is entered in the next section).

1. Click the Home link to change to the Sabatina's Pizza home page.
2. Click the Appetizers link to return to the appetizers.html Web page.
3. Click the Pizza link. (You will add a heading to the Pizza page later in the project.)
4. Click the Salads link (Figure 4–32a).

Q&A Why isn't the Salads Web page formatted with the styles in the external style sheet?

In order for the external style sheet to take effect, you have to insert the <link> statement into the HTML code in the Salads file.

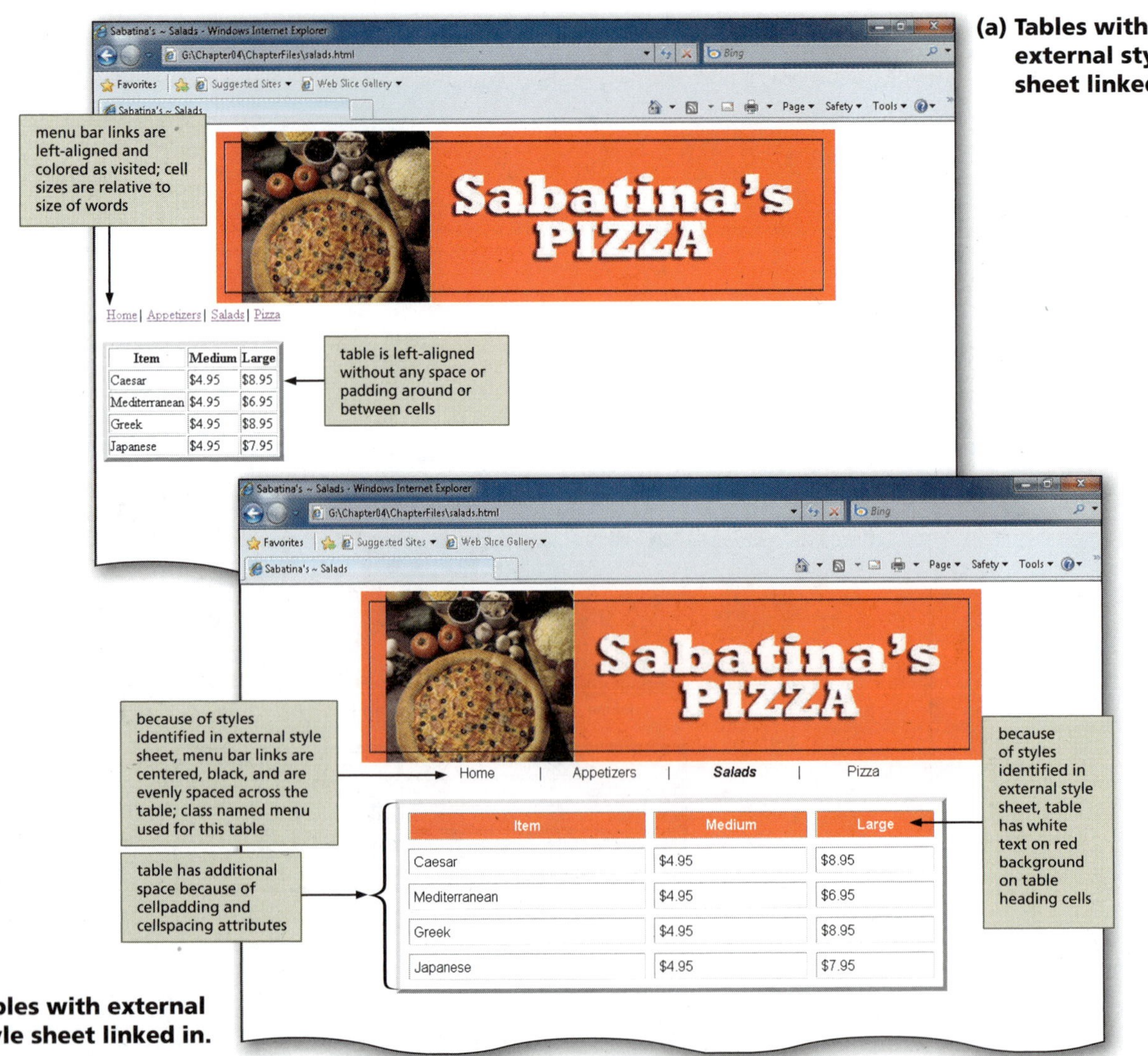

(a) Tables with no external style sheet linked in.
menu bar links are left-aligned and colored as visited; cell sizes are relative to size of words
Sabatina's PIZZA
Home | Appetizers | Salads | Pizza
Item Medium Large
Caesar $4.95 $8.95
Mediterranean $4.95 $6.95
Greek $4.95 $8.95
Japanese $4.95 $7.95
table is left-aligned without any space or padding around or between cells
because of styles identified in external style sheet, menu bar links are centered, black, and are evenly spaced across the table; class named menu used for this table
Home | Appetizers | Salads | Pizza
table has additional space because of cellpadding and cellspacing attributes
because of styles identified in external style sheet, table has white text on red background on table heading cells
(b) Tables with external style sheet linked in.

Figure 4–32

Adding a Link, Cellspacing, and Cellpadding

The table of information on the Appetizers Web page did not use the cellspacing or cellpadding attributes. The size of each data cell, therefore, automatically was set to the minimum size needed for the text inserted in the data cell. The salads.html Web page, however, should be modified to use cellspacing and cellpadding by adding the cellspacing and cellpadding attributes to the <table> tag. **Cellspacing** defines the number of pixels of space between cells in a table. Additional cellspacing makes the borders around each cell look thicker (see the thickness of the borders in Figure 4–33b versus Figure 4–33a). Although there is no official default, browsers usually use a default of 2 for cellspacing. **Cellpadding** defines the number of pixels of space between a cell's contents and the cell wall. In other words, if you add cellpadding, you give more space around the content within that cell. The default for cellpadding is 1. Figures 4–33a and 4–33b illustrate how using the cellspacing and cellpadding <table> tag attributes can affect a table's appearance.

BTW

Cellspacing
The cellspacing attribute adds pixels between cells. The purpose of cellspacing is to add additional space in the separation between the cells, whether or not a border exists. With a border, cellspacing increases the size of the border between the cells. Without a border, cellspacing increases the amount of white space between the cells.

BTW

Cellpadding
The cellpadding attribute adds pixels within a cell border. The purpose of cellpadding is to keep the content within each cell from looking like it is too close to the content of another cell. Cellpadding will set a margin for the right, left, top, and bottom of the cell all at once with the specification of one tag.

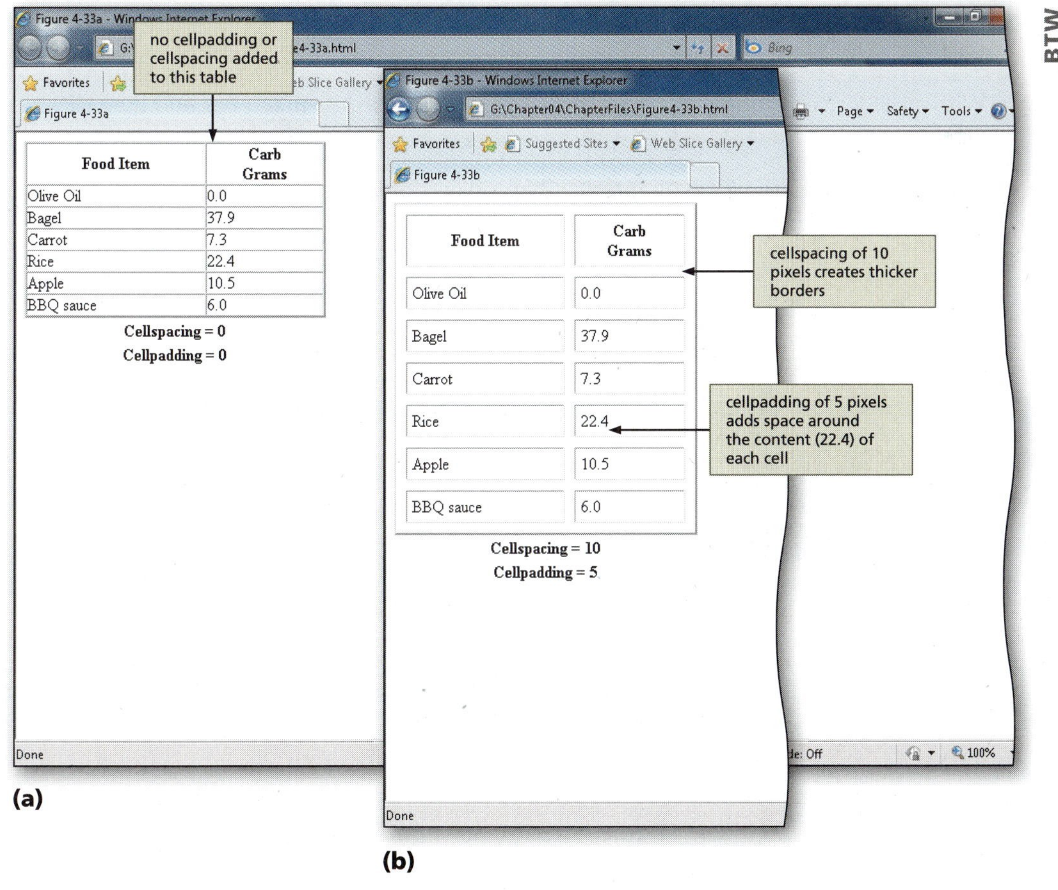

Figure 4–33 Tables with and without cellspacing and cellpadding.

Plan Ahead

- **Determine if you need to use cellpadding, cellspacing, or both.** The first thing you should consider is if you need these spacing attributes at all. If your content is getting across to the users without any modification to the spacing, then maybe you do not need to do this. Look again at the appetizers.html Web page. The information there is completely readable, and there is no cellpadding or cellspacing.
- **Determine what table spacing to use.** If you decide that you do need to insert space within or around the cells of data, then you should next consider how much space to provide within the table. Cellspacing is the space between the borders of each cell. Cellpadding is the space between a cell's content and its border. Both attributes serve the purpose of making the table of information easier to read. No rule of thumb says how much cellpadding or cellspacing should be used. Try various values to see the effect on the table.

To Open an HTML File

In the following steps, you activate Notepad++ and open the salads.html Web page file.

1. Click the - Notepad++ button on the taskbar.
2. With a USB drive plugged into your computer, click File on the menu bar and then click Open on the File menu.
3. If necessary, navigate to the Chapter04\ChapterFiles folder on the USB drive.
4. Double-click salads.html in the list of files to open the file in Notepad++ (Figure 4–34).

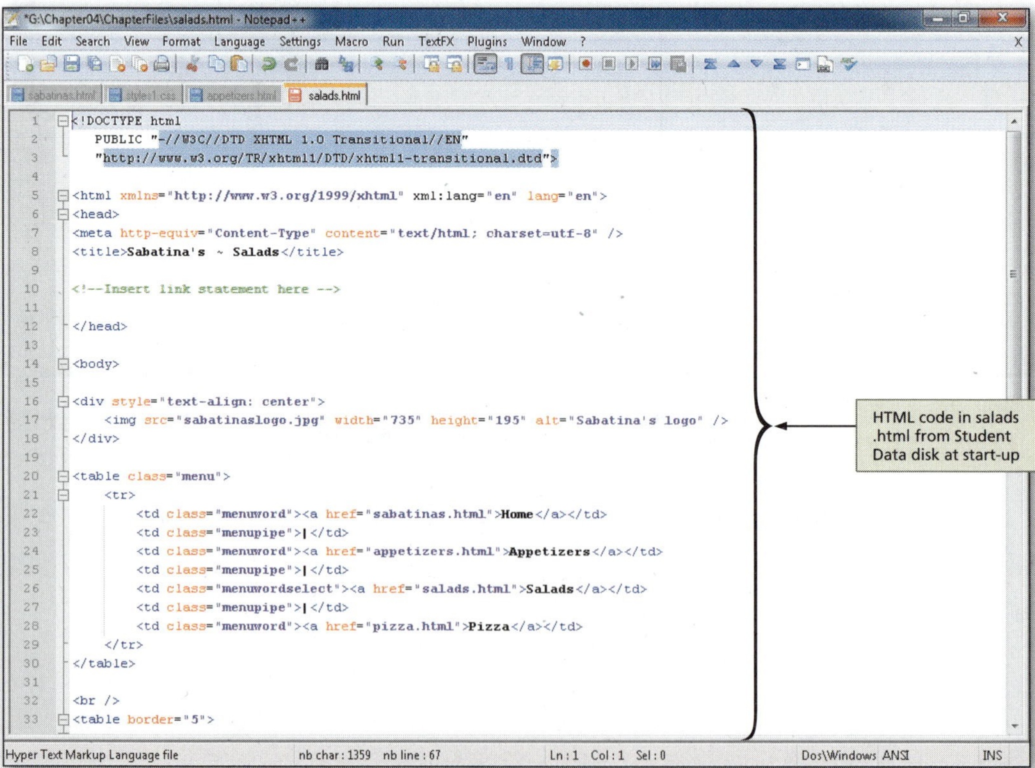

Figure 4–34

To Link to an External Style Sheet

The first thing you need to do in this Web page is link to the external style sheet that contains the overall styles you want this Web page to have.

1. Highlight the phrase <!--Insert link statement here --> on line 10.
2. Type `<link rel="stylesheet" type="text/css" href="styles1.css" />` to enter the link to the external style sheet. Do not press the ENTER key.

Q&A Remind me, what does this link statement do?

This statement links this Web page to the external style sheet that you created earlier. You need this link to the external (or linked) style sheet in order to apply those styles to the Web page.

To Add Cellspacing and Cellpadding to a Table

With the salads.html file open, the HTML code to add cellspacing and cellpadding can be added. The following step shows how to add cellspacing and cellpadding to a table.

1.

- Click immediately to the right of the second " (quotation mark) in the border="5" statement on line 33 and then press the SPACEBAR.
- Type `cellpadding="5" cellspacing="10"` as the attributes and values but do not press the ENTER key (Figure 4–35).

Experiment

- Change the values in the cellpadding and cellspacing attributes to see what that does to the table. Try values that are smaller or much larger to see the effect.

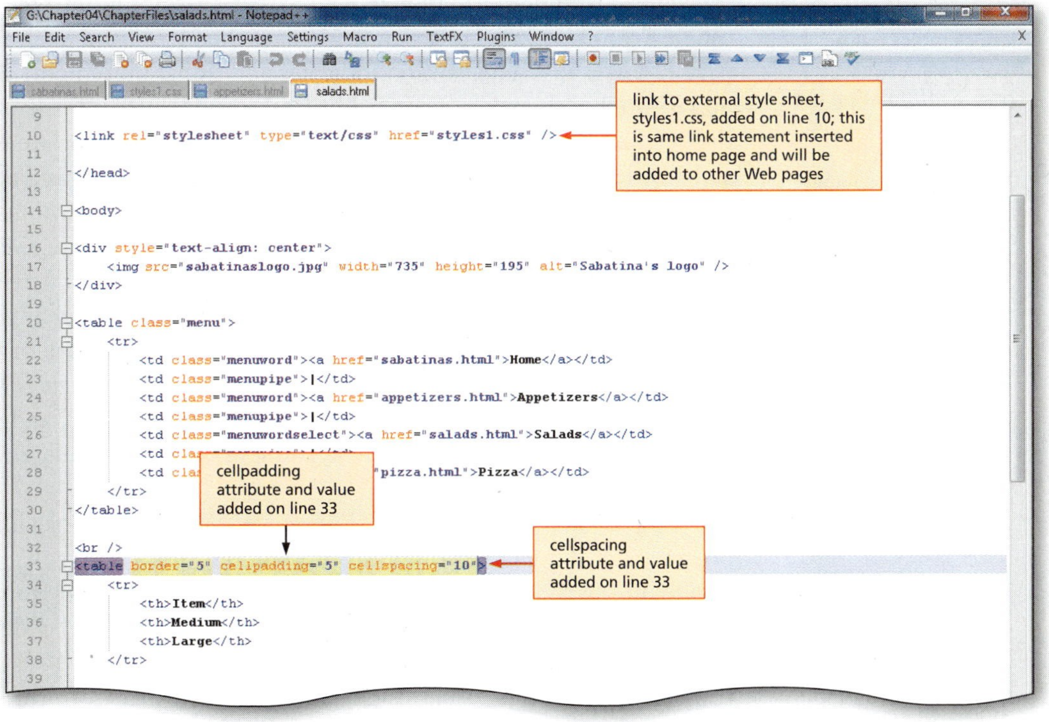

link to external style sheet, styles1.css, added on line 10; this is same link statement inserted into home page and will be added to other Web pages

cellpadding attribute and value added on line 33

cellspacing attribute and value added on line 33

Figure 4–35

Q&A What is the amount of cellpadding and cellspacing if I do not specify this in the table tag?

The default value for cellpadding is 1, while the default value for cellspacing is 2.

Q&A Can I set the cellpadding and cellspacing differently for different cells?

No, you cannot set cellpadding and cellspacing differently for various cells. This attribute is only available for the <table> (whole table) tag.

To Save, Validate, Print, and View the HTML File and Print the Web Page

1. With the USB drive plugged into your computer, click File on the menu bar and then click Save to save the salads.html file.
2. Click the Internet Explorer button on the taskbar to display the Sabatina's ~ Salads page.
3. Validate the Web page using the W3C validator service.
4. Use the Back button or Internet Explorer tabs to return to the Sabatina's ~ Salads page.
5. Click the Refresh icon on the Address bar to show the most recent file.
6. Click the Print button on the Command bar to print the Web page.
7. Click the Notepad++ button to return to Notepad++. Print the file.

BTW

Row and Column Spanning
Creating headings that span rows and columns defines tables more clearly. Many Web sites contain information about row and column spanning. For more information about row and column spanning, search the Web. Many tutorials have good suggestions for the use of column and row spanning.

Adding a Caption and Spanning Rows

If you need to add information to a table that does not fit into the table data cells, a caption can be a good option. For example, look at the pizza.html Web page in Figure 4–1d on page HTML 159. The caption indicates additional ingredients that are available for the pizzas listed in the table. That "additional ingredients" information does not fit into either the heading or data cells for the table. It is also not appropriate to have that information as an h1 or h2 heading. Putting that information in a caption is a perfect solution.

When you want to merge several cells into one, you can use row or column spanning. You can span rows or columns anywhere in a table. Generally, row and column spanning is used to create headings in tables. The **rowspan attribute** of the <th> or <td> tag sets a number of rows spanned by a cell. Although the chapter project uses only row spanning, you can also span columns. The **colspan attribute** of the <th> or <td> tag sets a number of columns spanned by a cell. Figure 4–10 on page HTML 168 shows examples of both column and row spanning. Notice that both the 5K and 10K headings span (or go across) two columns each. The heading Meet Dates spans (or goes across) four rows of information.

Figure 4–36 shows what the pizza.html Web page looks like at the start of the process. All of the table content is present, but there is no row or column spanning. You decide during the design phase that this table would benefit from row spanning, but that column spanning is unnecessary. You will enter the HTML code to complete the row spanning (Figure 4–37). In Figure 4–37, the heading Thin Crust Pizza is an example of row spanning. In this case, this heading spans three rows. In the same figure, the words Thick Crust Pizza also span three rows of information.

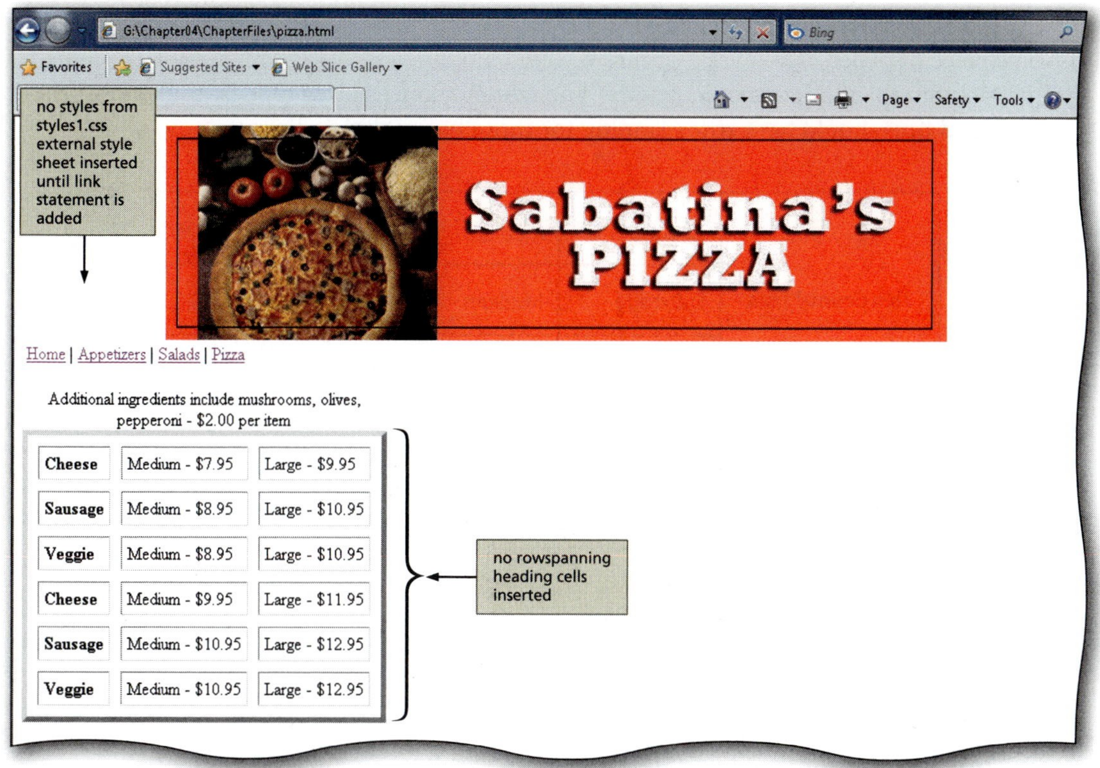

Figure 4–36 Pizza Web page before enhancements.

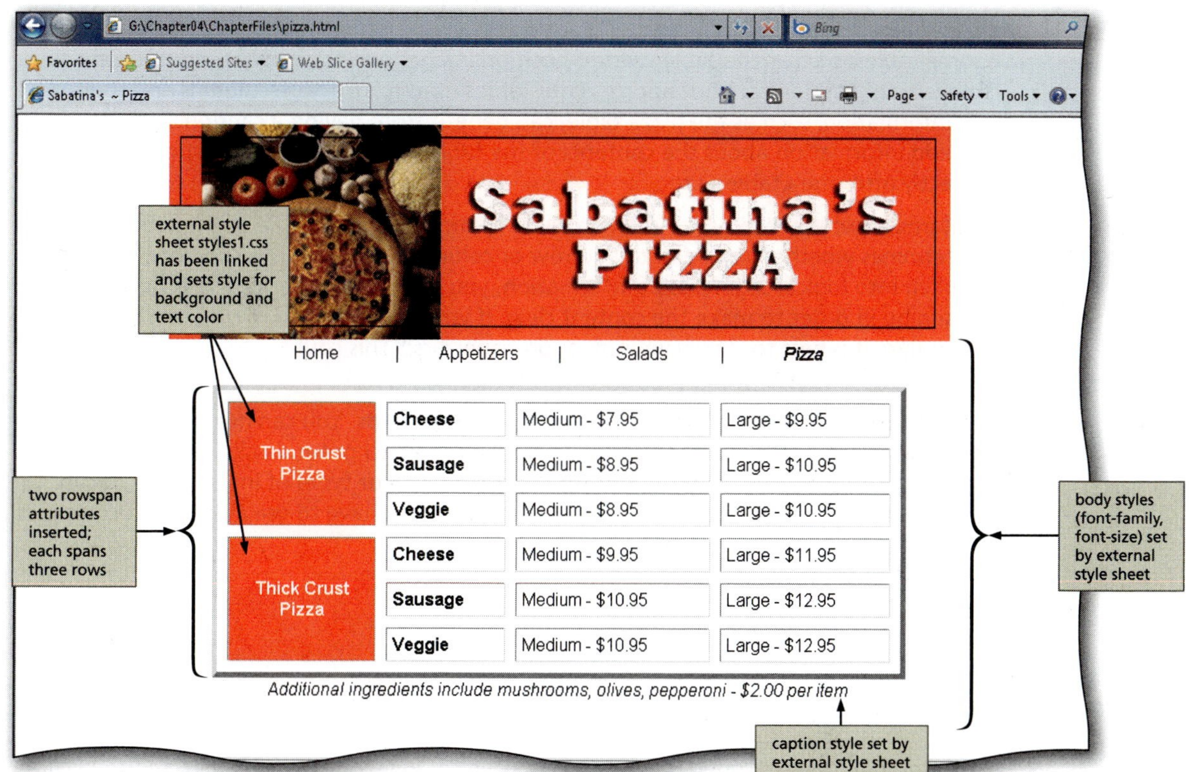

Figure 4–37 Pizza Web page after enhancements.

The first step when deciding to span rows or columns is to sketch the table design on a piece of paper, as shown in Figure 4–38. Again, for this Web page, it was determined that column spanning was unnecessary. The table organizes pizza type by thin and thick crust and thus should have row spanning for those two main headings.

Thin Crust Pizza	Cheese	Medium - $7.95	Large - $9.95
	Sausage	Medium - $8.95	Large - $10.95
	Veggie	Medium - $8.95	Large - $10.95
Thick Crust Pizza	Cheese	Medium - $9.95	Large - $11.95
	Sausage	Medium - $10.95	Large - $12.95
	Veggie	Medium - $10.95	Large - $12.95

Figure 4–38

After defining the main sections of the table, you must determine how many rows each heading should span. For example, the first heading, Thin Crust Pizza, should span three rows. The second heading for Thick Crust Pizza should span three rows as well. In the following steps, you open the file pizza.html, link the external style sheet styles1.css, and add rowspan attributes to create table headings that span rows.

Plan Ahead

- **Determine if a caption is needed.** A caption can help clarify the table's purpose. For some tables, such as the table used to position images and the tables used to create menu bars, captions are not appropriate. Tables used to structure columns and rows of information, such as the pizza table, can benefit from having a caption to clarify or add information about the contents of the table. The caption tag must be inserted directly after the <table> tag.
- **Determine whether to use row and column spanning.** The purpose of the table determines whether you need to add row or column spanning. If the content is broken into logical segments of information, you may need to include row or column spanning in order to make the content clear. If you decide to add row or column spanning, it is best to sketch your ideas on paper first. This could help you understand more clearly what tags you need to use where.
- **Determine if different colors are needed for backgrounds.** You can help visitors more easily read a table full of information by varying the background colors effectively. If you use the same color background for the same level (or type) of information, it can help visually organize the information. Again, you may have to use a light font color if the background color is very dark.

To Open an HTML File

1. Click the Notepad++ button on the taskbar.
2. With the USB drive plugged into your computer, click File on the menu bar and then click Open on the File menu.
3. If necessary, navigate to the Chapter04\ChapterFiles folder on the USB drive.
4. Double-click pizza.html in the list of files to open the file in Notepad++.

To Link the External Style Sheet

The first thing you need to do in this Web page is link to the external style sheet that contains the styles that you want for this Web page.

1 Highlight the text <!--Insert link statement here --> on line 10.

2 Type <link rel="stylesheet" type="text/css" href="styles1.css" /> to enter the link to the external style sheet. Do not press the ENTER key.

To Add a Table Caption

Captions are added to tables using the <caption> </caption> tags to enclose the caption text. The formatting to make the caption italic and align it at the bottom of the table is included in the external style sheet (styles1.css) that is now linked to this page.

The following step shows how to add a caption below the pizza table.

- Highlight the text <!--Insert caption statement here --> on line 35.
- Type <caption>Additional ingredients include mushrooms, olives, pepperoni - $2.00 per item</caption> as the tag to add the italic caption below the table (Figure 4–39).

Experiment

- Add an inline style to the caption statement that aligns the caption-side to the top (top alignment for captions is the default). The inline style will override the external style sheet. Remember to take the inline style out once you are finished with the caption so that the bottom alignment default in the external style sheet takes effect again.

Q&A Why would I use the caption tag?

The caption further explains the main purpose of the table, or adds information that doesn't fit elsewhere in the table. Other uses are to identify units of measure or to give a number or title to the table.

```
9
10  <link rel="stylesheet" type="text/css" href="styles1.css" />
11
12  </head>
13
14  <body>
15
16  <div style="text-align: center">
17      <img src="sabatinaslogo.jpg" width="735" height="195" alt="Sabatina's logo" />
18  </div>
19
20  <table class="menu">
21      <tr>
22          <td class="menuword"><a href="sabatinas.html">Home</a></td>
23          <td class="menupipe">|</td>
24          <td class="menuword"><a href="appetizers.html">Appetizers</a></td>
25          <td class="menupipe">|</td>
26          <td class="menuword"><a href="salads.html">Salads</a></td>
27          <td class="menupipe">|</td>
28          <td class="menuwordselect"><a href="pizza.html">Pizza</a></td>
29      </tr>
30  </table>
31
32  <br />
33  <table border="5" cellpadding="5" cellspacing="10">
34
35  <caption>Additional ingredients include mushrooms, olives, pepperoni - $2.00 per item</caption>
36
37      <tr>
38  <!--Insert first rowspan heading here -->
39          <td style="font-weight: bold">Cheese</td>
40          <td>Medium - $7.95</td>
41          <td>Large - $9.95</td>
```


Figure 4–39

To Create the Headings That Span Rows

The following steps illustrate how to enter HTML code to create two headings that each span three rows.

- Highlight <!--Insert first rowspan heading here --> on line 38.
- Press the TAB key twice and then type `<th rowspan="3">Thin Crust` and then press the ENTER key; the next line is automatically indented to the same level.
- Type `<br />Pizza` and then press the ENTER key.
- Type `</th>` as the HTML code but do not press the ENTER key (Figure 4–40).

Figure 4–40

Q&A What is the purpose of the <br /> tag in the steps above?

The <br /> tag moves the word Pizza to a second line so that the first column is not too much wider than the other columns in the table.

Q&A Why are we not using the colspan attribute in this table?

The colspan attribute is used to add headings that span columns in a table. In this pizza table, column spanning is not necessary or appropriate. One column of information concerns the ingredients on the pizza, and the other two columns contain the pricing for medium and large pizzas. There is no column heading that would be appropriate to span those three columns.

2

- Highlight <!--Insert second rowspan heading here --> on line 59.
- Press the TAB key twice and then type `<th rowspan="3">Thick Crust` and then press the ENTER key.
- Type `<br />Pizza` and then press the ENTER key.
- Type `</th>` as the HTML code but do not press the ENTER key (Figure 4–41).

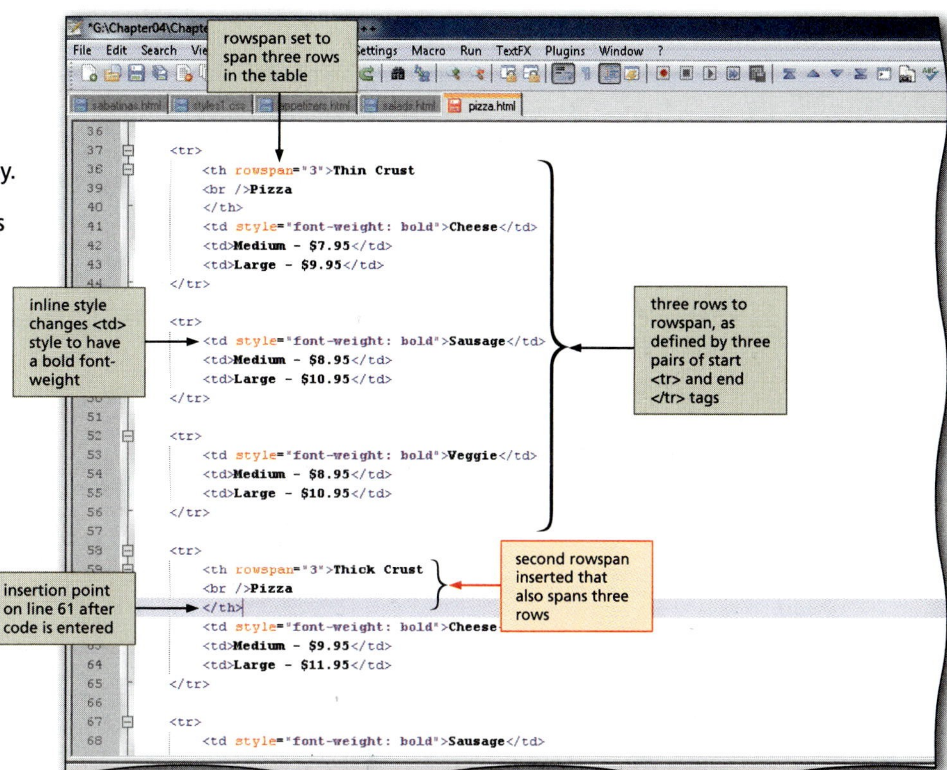

Figure 4–41

Q&A

Why isn't there an extra pair of <tr> </tr> tags between the rowspan title (Thin Crust Pizza) and the line of HTML code for data (Cheese)?

Thin Crust Pizza and Cheese are on the same row (row 1) that is being spanned. Row 2 contains the line with Sausage; row 3 is the line with Veggie. Therefore, the rowspan value is set to 3. The text that spans the rows (Thin Crust Pizza and Thick Crust Pizza) is always aligned with the first row of text.

Experiment

- Remove the <br /> tag from the HTML code that you entered on lines 39 and 60. See how this changes the look of the table.
- Change the <br /> tag on lines 39 and 60 to a <p> tag (don't forget the </p>). See what that does to the look of the table.

To Save, Validate, and Print the HTML File

1. With the USB drive plugged into your computer, click the Save icon on the Notepad++ toolbar to save the pizza.html file.
2. Validate the HTML file using the validator.w3.org Web page.
3. Print the Notepad++ file.

To View and Print the Web Page

1. Click the Internet Explorer button on the taskbar.
2. Click the Pizza link on the menu table to display the Pizza Web page.
3. Print the Web page with rowspan attributes entered (Figure 4–42).

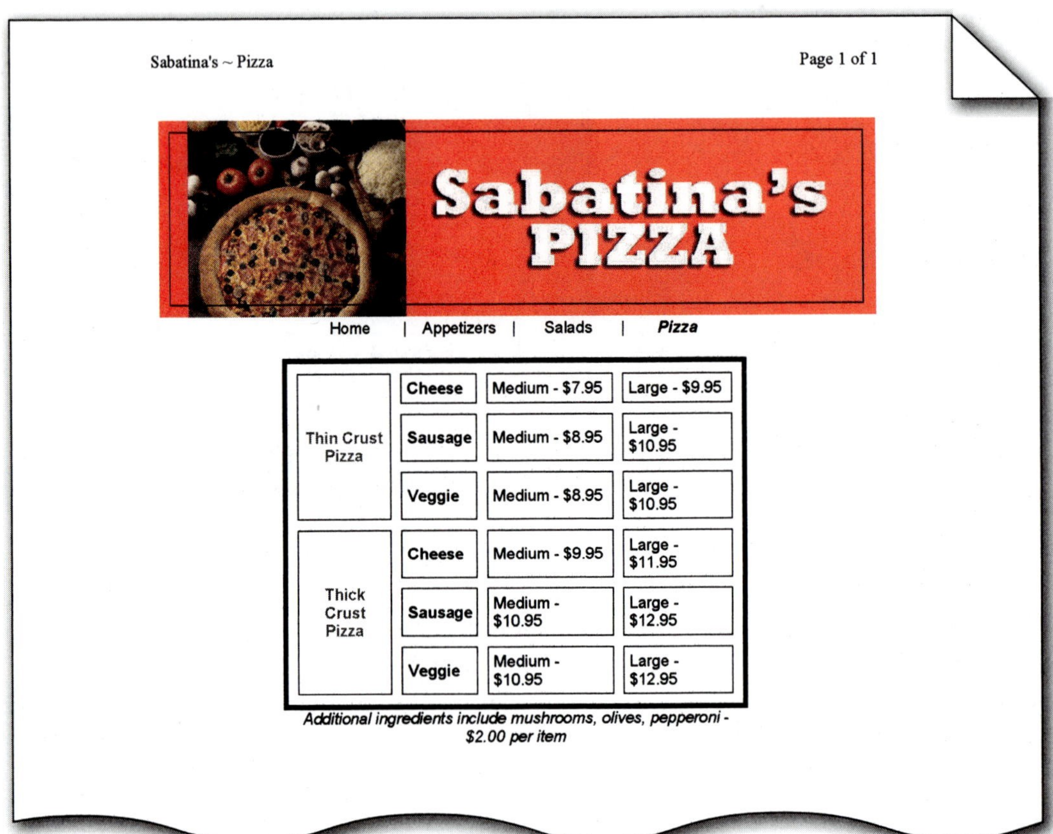

Figure 4–42

To Quit Notepad++ and a Browser

1. In Notepad++, click the File menu, then Close All.
2. Click the Close button on the Notepad++ title bar.
3. Click the Close button on the browser title bar. If necessary, click the Close all tabs button.

Chapter Summary

In this chapter, you learned how to create and link an external style sheet, about table elements, and the steps to plan, design, and code a table in HTML. You also learned to enhance a table with background color, cellspacing, cellpadding, a caption, and headers that span rows. The items listed below include all the new HTML skills you learned in this chapter.

1. Insert and Center an Image (HTML 173)
2. Create a Horizontal Menu Bar with Text Links (HTML 175)
3. Create an External Style Sheet (HTML 181)
4. Link to an External Style Sheet (HTML 186)
5. Copy and Paste HTML Code to a New File (HTML 190)
6. Create a Table with Borders and Insert Text (HTML 193)
7. Add Cellspacing and Cellpadding to a Table (HTML 199)
8. Add a Table Caption (HTML 203)
9. Create Headings that Span Rows (HTML 204)

Learn It Online

Test your knowledge of chapter content and key terms.

Instructions: To complete the Learn It Online exercises, start your browser, click the Address bar, and then enter the Web address `scsite.com/html6e/learn`. When the HTML Learn It Online page is displayed, click the link for the exercise you want to complete and read the instructions.

Chapter Reinforcement TF, MC, and SA

A series of true/false, multiple choice, and short answer questions that test your knowledge of the chapter content.

Flash Cards

An interactive learning environment where you identify chapter key terms associated with displayed definitions.

Practice Test

A series of multiple choice questions that test your knowledge of chapter content and key terms.

Who Wants To Be a Computer Genius?

An interactive game that challenges your knowledge of chapter content in the style of a television quiz show.

Wheel of Terms

An interactive game that challenges your knowledge of chapter key terms in the style of the television show, *Wheel of Fortune*.

Crossword Puzzle Challenge

A crossword puzzle that challenges your knowledge of key terms presented in the chapter.

Apply Your Knowledge

Reinforce the skills and apply the concepts you learned in this chapter.

Editing a Table on a Web Page

Instructions: Start Notepad++. Open the file apply4-1.html from the Chapter04\Apply folder of the Data Files for Students. See the inside back cover of this book for instructions on downloading the Data Files for Students, or contact your instructor for information about accessing the required files.

The apply4-1.html file is a partially completed HTML file that you will use for this exercise. Figure 4–43 shows the Apply Your Knowledge Web page as it should display in a browser after the additional HTML tags and attributes are added.

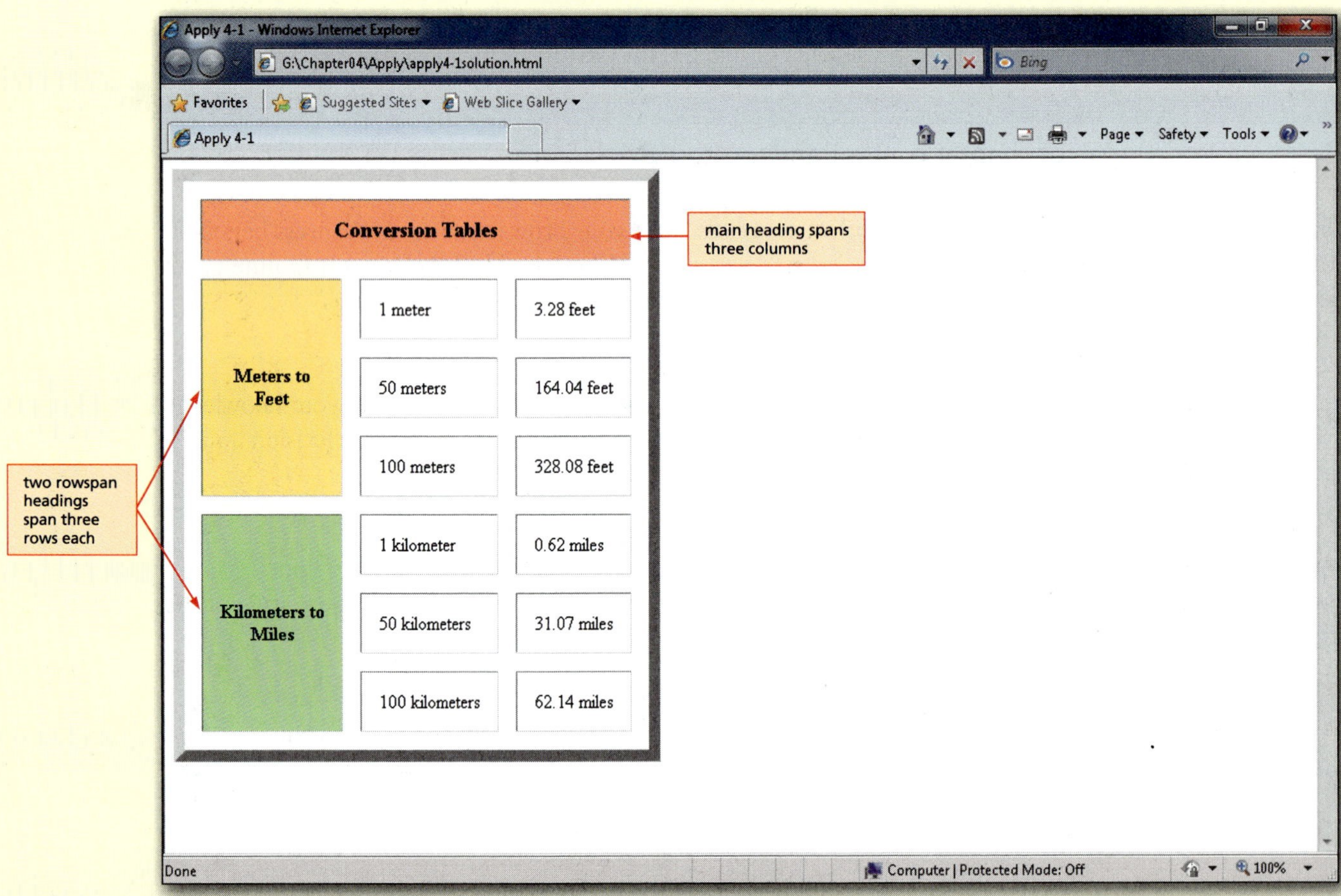

Figure 4–43

Perform the following tasks:

1. Enter the URL g:\Chapter04\Apply\apply4-1.html to view the Web page in your browser.
2. Examine the HTML file and its appearance as a Web page in the browser.
3. Add a border of 10, cellspacing of 15, and cellpadding of 15 to the table.
4. Add any HTML code necessary for additional features shown on the Web page in Figure 4–43. Your changes should include a colspan heading that spans three columns of information and two rowspan headings that span three rows each. The main heading is font-size large.
5. Colors used for the headings are colspan - #ff9473; first rowspan - #ffff6b; second rowspan - #a5de94 (experiment with the colors if you wish).
6. Save the revised file in the Chapter04\Apply folder using the file name apply4-1solution.html.
7. Validate the code using the W3C validator service.
8. Print the revised HTML file.
9. Enter the URL g:\Chapter04\Apply\apply4-1solution.html to view the Web page in your browser.
10. Print the Web page.
11. Submit the revised HTML file and Web page in the format specified by your instructor.

Extend Your Knowledge

Extend the skills you learned in this chapter and experiment with new skills.

Creating a Table with Rules

Instructions: Start Notepad++. Open the file extend4-1.html from the Chapter04\Extend folder of the Data Files for Students. See the inside back cover of this book for instructions on downloading the Data Files for Students, or contact your instructor for information about accessing the required files. This sample HTML file contains all of the text for the Web page shown in Figure 4–44. You add the necessary tags to make this Web page display the table, as shown in Figure 4–44.

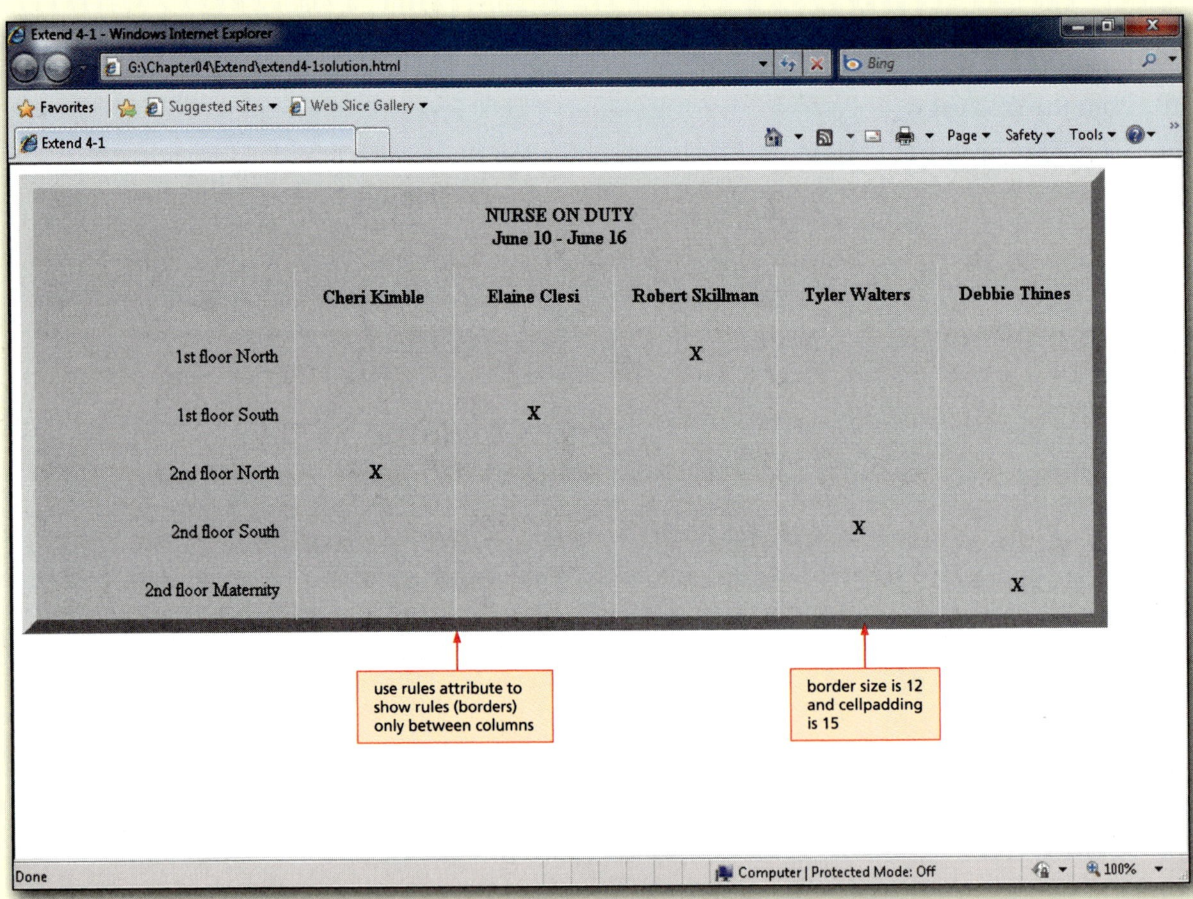

Figure 4–44

Perform the following tasks:

1. Add HTML code to align the table on the left of the Web page. Align the text in the first column to the right of the data cell. (*Hint:* Review the text-align property.) Also give it a border of 12 with cellpadding of 15.
2. Insert the additional HTML code necessary to change the rules (see Appendix A) to only display columns.
3. Color the background #e0e0e0.
4. Add other table attributes not used in this chapter to further enhance the table. (*Hint:* See Appendix A.)
5. Save the revised document as extend4-1solution.html and validate the code using the W3C validator service.
6. Create an external style sheet that contains the following styles and save it as stylesextend4-1.css.
7. Link stylesextend4-1.css into the Web page extend4-1solution.html.

```
table          {text-align: center}
.twentyfive    {width: 25%}
.fifteen       {width: 15%}
```

8. Re-save extend4-1solution.html. Print the revised HTML file and Web page and submit them in the format specified by your instructor.

Make It Right

Analyze a document and correct all errors and/or improve the design.

Correcting the Golf Course Tournament Schedule

Instructions: Start your browser. Open the file makeitright4-1.html from the Chapter04\MakeItRight folder of the Data Files for Students. See the inside back cover of this book for instructions on downloading the Data Files for Students, or contact your instructor for information about accessing the required files. The Web page is a modified version of what you see in Figure 4–45. Make the necessary corrections to the Web page to make it look like Figure 4–45, using inline styles for all styles. The Web page should include the six columns of information with a main heading that spans all six columns. The second row contains the image golf.jpg in the first cell. The second row also has a line break between the person's first and last name. (*Hint:* Use the <br /> tag.) Save the file as makeitright4-1solution.html and validate the code.

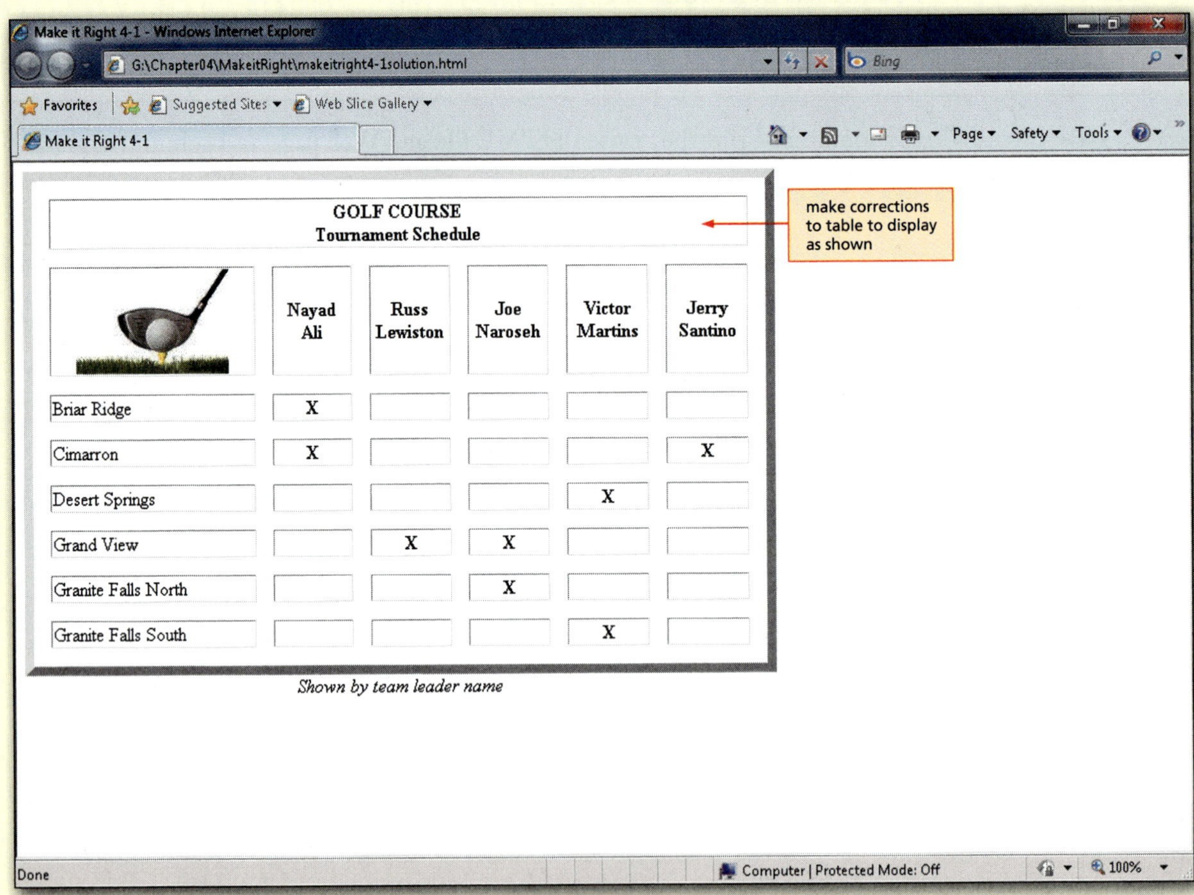

Figure 4–45

In the Lab

Lab 1: Creating a Table with Multiple Images

Problem: The owners of Beautiful Backyards (see Lab 3-2 at the end of Chapter 3) want to review the potential for the use of tables on their company home page and compare that with the Web page created in Lab 3-2. You have been asked to create a Web page that shows the two images and how tables can be used to display them and the associated text, as shown in Figure 4–46.

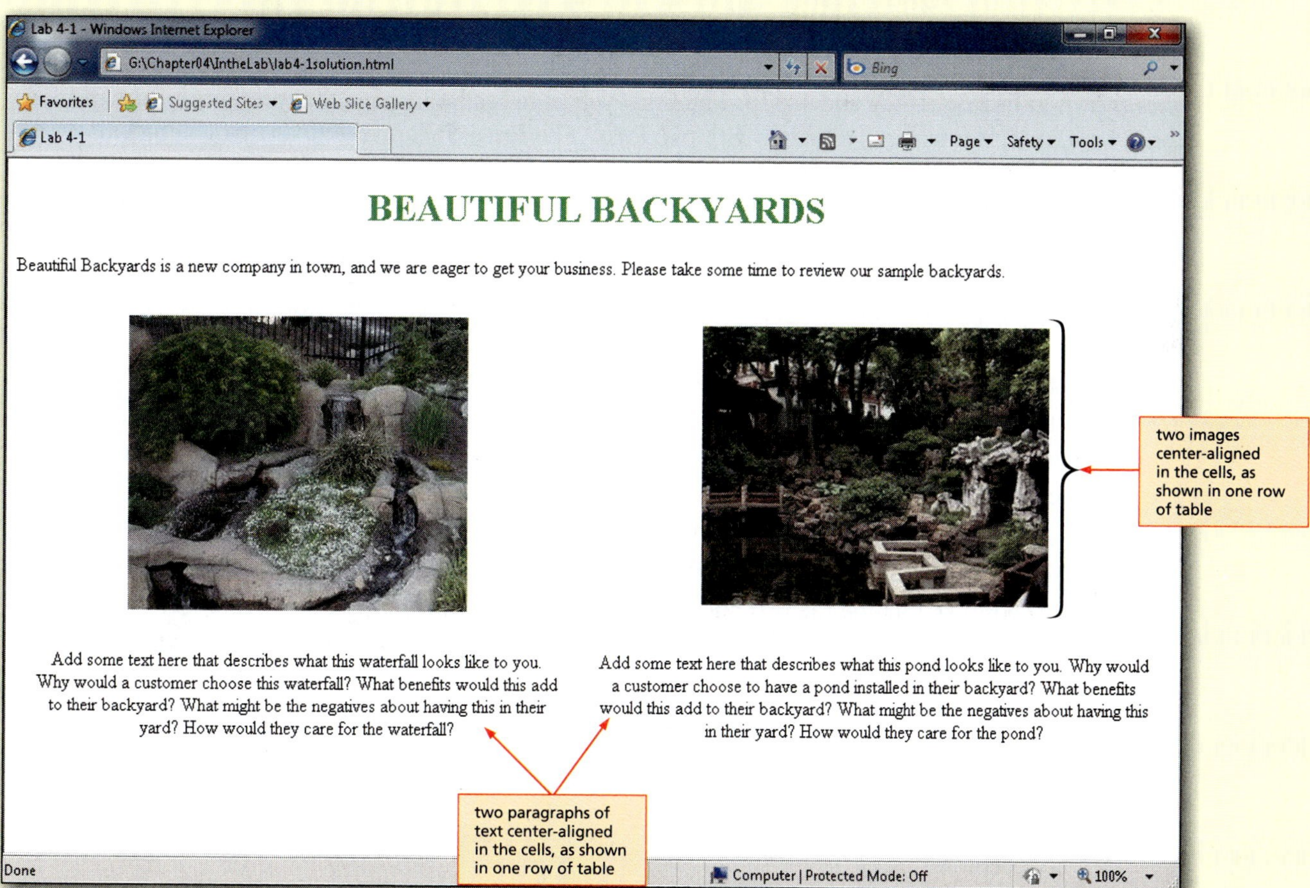

Figure 4–46

Instructions: Perform the following steps:

1. Start a new HTML file with the title Lab 4-1 in the main heading section.
2. Just as in Lab 3-2, the heading <h1> should be color #00934a.
3. Insert the text shown in the top lines of the Web page using a font size of large. (*Hint:* You can copy/paste the text from Lab 3-2.)
4. Add a centered borderless table with two columns and two rows and cellpadding of 15.
5. Insert the image largewaterfall.jpg in the first column of the first row. (*Hint:* You can use Microsoft Paint to determine the width and height of each image or right-click the image and select Properties.)
6. Add the second image pond.jpg to that same row in a second column.
7. Start a new row and add the text for each of the images.
8. Save the HTML file in the Chapter04\IntheLab folder using the file name lab4-1solution.html.
9. Validate the Web page using the W3C validator service.
10. Print the lab4-1solution.html file.
11. Open the lab4-1solution.html file in your browser to view it as a Web page.

Continued >

In the Lab *continued*

12. Print the Web page.
13. Submit the revised HTML file and Web page in the format specified by your instructor.

In the Lab

Lab 2: Creating Two Linked Pages

Problem: Your manager at Voytkovich Antiquities has asked you to create two Web pages, similar to the ones shown in Figures 4–47a and 4–47b. The first Web page is a home page that presents information about Voytkovich Antiquities, together with two links. The Prices link on the first page will be linked to a price list of items found at the antiquities store. The second link, called Links, should direct the Web page visitor to another Web page of your choosing that has to do with antiquities. You may select a museum or another similar site of your choosing. For this project, use a combination of inline style sheets, external (linked) style sheets, and formatting tag attributes in order to accomplish the tasks.

Instructions: Perform the following steps:

1. Start a new HTML file with the title Lab 4-2a in the main heading section.
2. Create a one-row, two-column borderless table with the image mask.jpg in the left-hand data cell and the words Voytkovich Antiquities (use the <br /> tag between those words) in an olive color and size xx-large in the right-hand data cell.
3. Create a second one-row, two-column borderless table. In the first column, include two text links named Prices (which links to lab4-2bsolution.html) and Links (which links to an antiquity Web site of your choosing). Include the text and an e-mail link, as shown in Figure 4–47a.
4. Create an external style sheet with the following styles. Save it as lab4-2styles.css. Link this external style sheet into the Web page.

```
body      {font-family: Arial, Verdana, Garamond;
          font-size: 11 pt}
a         {text-decoration: none;
          color: black}
table     {width: 65%;
          margin-left:auto;
          margin-right:auto}
.menu     {text-align: left;
          width: 20%}
.content  {width: 80%}
```

5. Save the HTML file using the file name lab4-2asolution.html in the Chapter04\IntheLab folder. Validate the file using the W3C validator service. Print the HTML file.
6. Start a new HTML file with the title Lab 4-2b in the main heading section. Link the external style sheet lab4-2styles.css into the file.
7. Create a five-row, two-column table with a five-pixel border, cellpadding of 15, and cellspacing of 5.
8. Span the first heading across both columns, as shown in Figure 4–47b, with olive text in size large.
9. Enter the headings, Item and Price, and additional information in the appropriate table cells, as shown in Figure 4–47b. Make sure to include a link (font size of small) back to the home page.
10. Save the HTML file in the Chapter04\IntheLab folder using the file name lab4-2bsolution.html. Validate the file using the W3C validator service. Print the HTML file.

11. Open the file lab4-2asolution.html in your browser and test the Prices link to verify it links to the lab4-2bsolution.html Web page.
12. Print both Web pages.
13. Submit the revised HTML file, .css file, and Web pages in the format specified by your instructor.

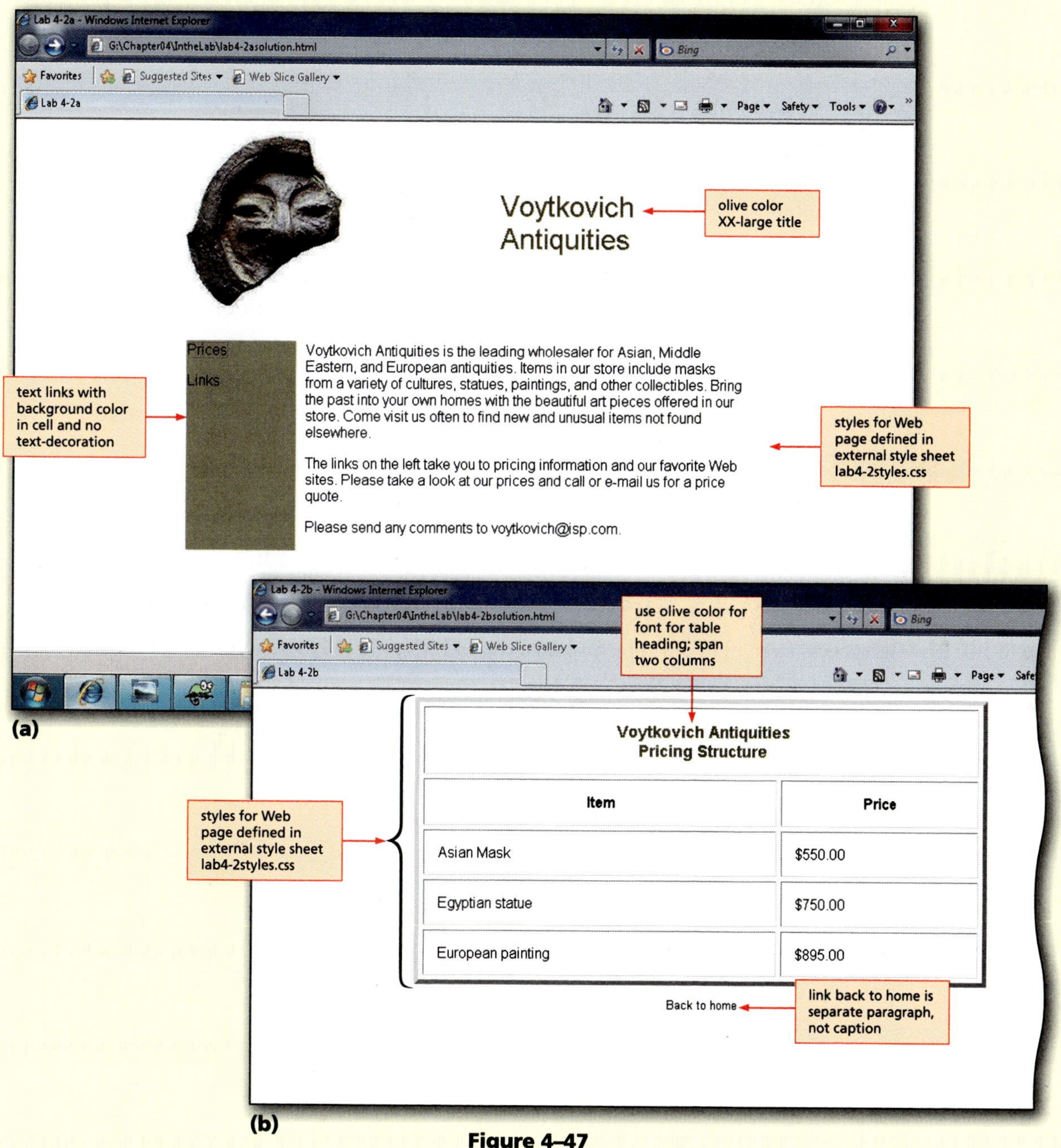

Figure 4–47

In the Lab

Lab 3: Creating Schedules

Problem: You want to create a Web page and an external style sheet that lists your piano practice and volunteer schedule, similar to the one shown in Figure 4–48. The Web page will use a table with images that span several rows and columns to organize the information.

Instructions: Perform the following steps:

1. Start a new HTML file with the title Lab 4-3 in the main heading section.
2. In the Web page, create a bordered table that displays in 90% of the browser in which only rows display, as shown in Figure 4–48. (*Hint:* See the rules attribute.)
3. Include the headings and data cells as shown, with valid information (i.e., real days and times as per a normal schedule of activities) in the data cells. The main headings should be center-aligned across three columns. The data other than the main headings should have an indent of 10 pixels.
4. Add two images, piano.jpg and volunteer.jpg, with all appropriate image attributes, each spanning five rows.
5. The external style sheet should contain the following styles and be saved as lab4-3styles.css:

   ```
   body         {font-family: Arial, Verdana, Garamond;
                 font-size: 11 pt}
   th.subtitle  {text-align: left; text-indent: 10px}
   td           {text-indent: 10px}
   ```

   (*Note:* The <th> element aligns text left. Where would you use that class named subtitle?)
6. Link lab4-3styles.css to the HTML file, and save the HTML file as lab4-3solution.html.
7. Validate the HTML file using the W3C validator service.
8. Print the HTML and CSS files.
9. Print the Web page from your browser.
10. Submit the HTML file, .css file, and Web page in the format specified by your instructor.

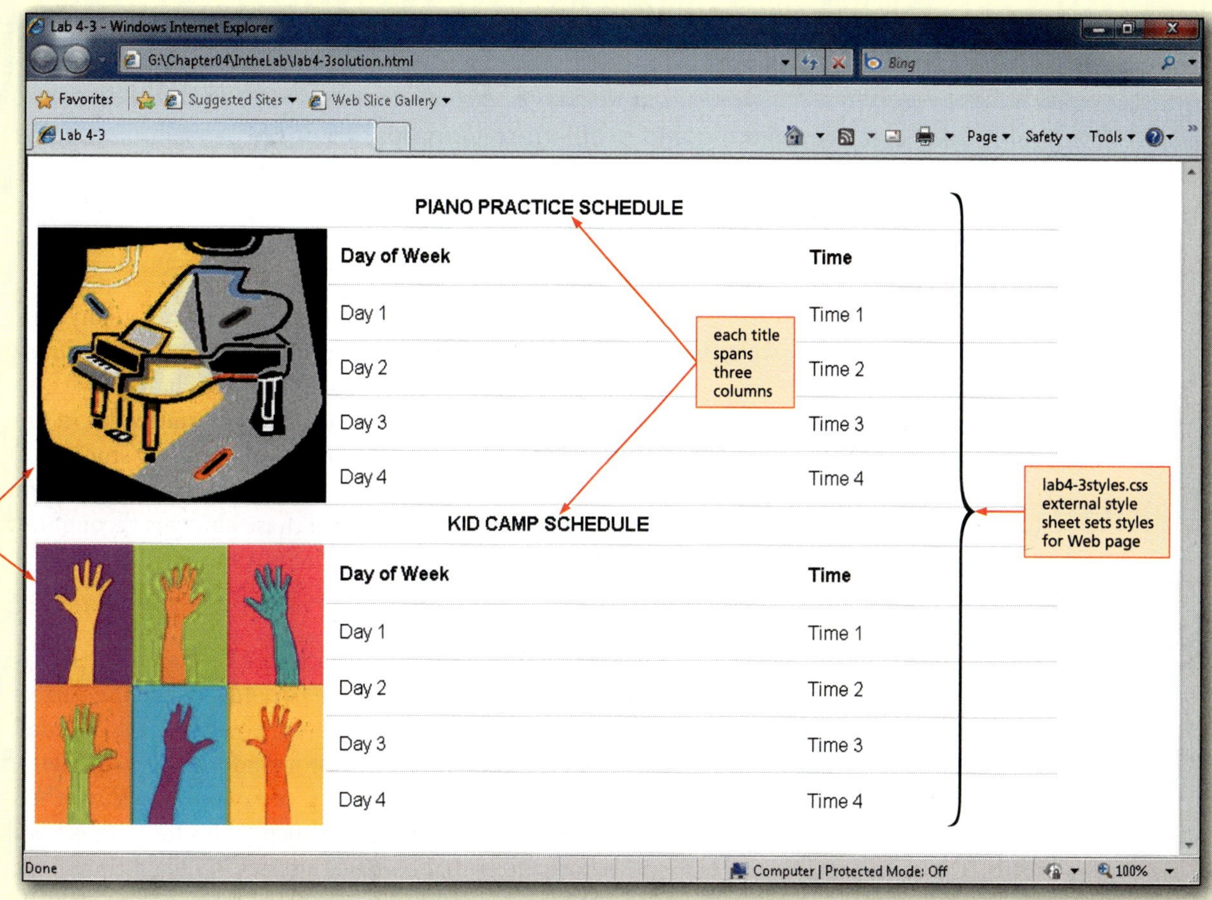
Lab 4-3 - Windows Internet Explorer
G:\Chapter04\IntheLab\lab4-3solution.html
PIANO PRACTICE SCHEDULE
Day of Week
Time
Day 1
Time 1
Day 2
Time 2
Day 3
Time 3
Day 4
Time 4
KID CAMP SCHEDULE
Day of Week
Time
Day 1
Time 1
Day 2
Time 2
Day 3
Time 3
Day 4
Time 4
each title spans three columns
each image spans five rows
lab4-3styles.css external style sheet sets styles for Web page

Figure 4–48

Cases and Places

Apply your creative thinking and problem-solving skills to design and implement a solution.

• Easier •• More Difficult

• 1: Adding to the Sabatina's Pizza Web Site

In the Sabatina's Pizza project, you created an external style sheet that contained many styles for different Web page elements. Analyze what styles might be good to change or add, and determine a design plan for the changes. Make changes to the style sheet and save the changes with another file name (remember to give the file name a .css extension). Revise the link statement in one of the Sabatina's Pizza Web pages to use the new external style sheet name. Have other students evaluate the page that uses the new external style sheet, comparing it with the same page using the original external style sheet. If you like your changes and decide you want to make these changes throughout all pages, modify the other Sabatina's Web pages to include the link to the new .css file.

• 2: Finding Tables on the Web

The Dean of your school wants to update the Web pages for the school's Web site. She has asked your help in doing this and wants to see a proposal. You think that tables would provide the perfect format for displaying the various academic programs available in your school, potential class schedules, and a calendar of events. Browse the Web to find examples of tables used for information such as what is needed on your school's Web site. Print those pages so that you have concrete examples to show the Dean. Prepare a document that explains to the Dean how you would use such tables for your school's particular needs. Try using a storyboard (a graphical organizer that contains a series of illustrations or images displayed in sequence and that visually depicts your ideas). Sketch a Web page design (see Figure 4–9 on page HTML nn and Figure 4–40 on page HTML nn) that incorporates tables for your purpose.

•• 3: Researching Style Sheet Classes

Your manager at WebSource wants you to prepare a brief presentation on the use of classes in style sheets, as described in this chapter. He asks you to find at least two Web sites that describe the use of classes in style sheets and then review how the techniques discussed in the Web sites compare to the style sheet methods described and used in this chapter. The presentation also should discuss how the use of classes can help make Web development more effective — both in developing a single Web page and in developing an entire Web site.

•• 4 Creating a Time Schedule

Make It Personal

Your computer club wants you to create a table that lists meeting, open lab, and lab class times for the computer labs. Sketch a basic table format to use for this purpose and ask a few friends (or classmates) what they think. Once you have determined a good design for the Web page, begin to code the table needed. As you begin to build the Web page, you start thinking about other table attributes that could make the Web pages look even better. Create a Web page with a basic five-row, two-column table with a one-pixel border. Review the additional table attributes listed in Appendix A, including the rules attribute. Find information on those attributes on other Web sites, including the W3C Web site (*www.w3.org*). Modify the basic table on your Web page to incorporate at least four of these attributes.

•• 5 Creating a Gift Shop Web Site

Working Together

Your design team at Triple-D Design has been asked to create a proposal for an existing customer to explain the value of using Cascading Style Sheets. Select a Web site with which you are familiar. Verify that the Web site does not utilize any of the three types of style sheets. Develop a graphic of the Web site hierarchy. Determine how the three types of style sheets could be used in this Web site and develop an outline explaining how they could enhance pages or sections of the site, add style consistency, or make the site easier to maintain. Write a proposal to the owners of the Web site that describes the features you could add with style sheets and the benefits of doing so, relative to the formatting techniques currently used in the Web site. As an example, you might want to address the number of times that a particular <font> tag is used in the site and contrast that with the ease of using one external style sheet and a link statement per page. Use other ideas as discussed in the chapter project to emphasize the other benefits of style sheets. Write the proposal in the form of a bid, giving time estimates and costs associated with the development effort. Include your hierarchy chart and style sheet outline as appendices to the proposal.

Special Feature 1

Attracting Visitors to Your Web Site

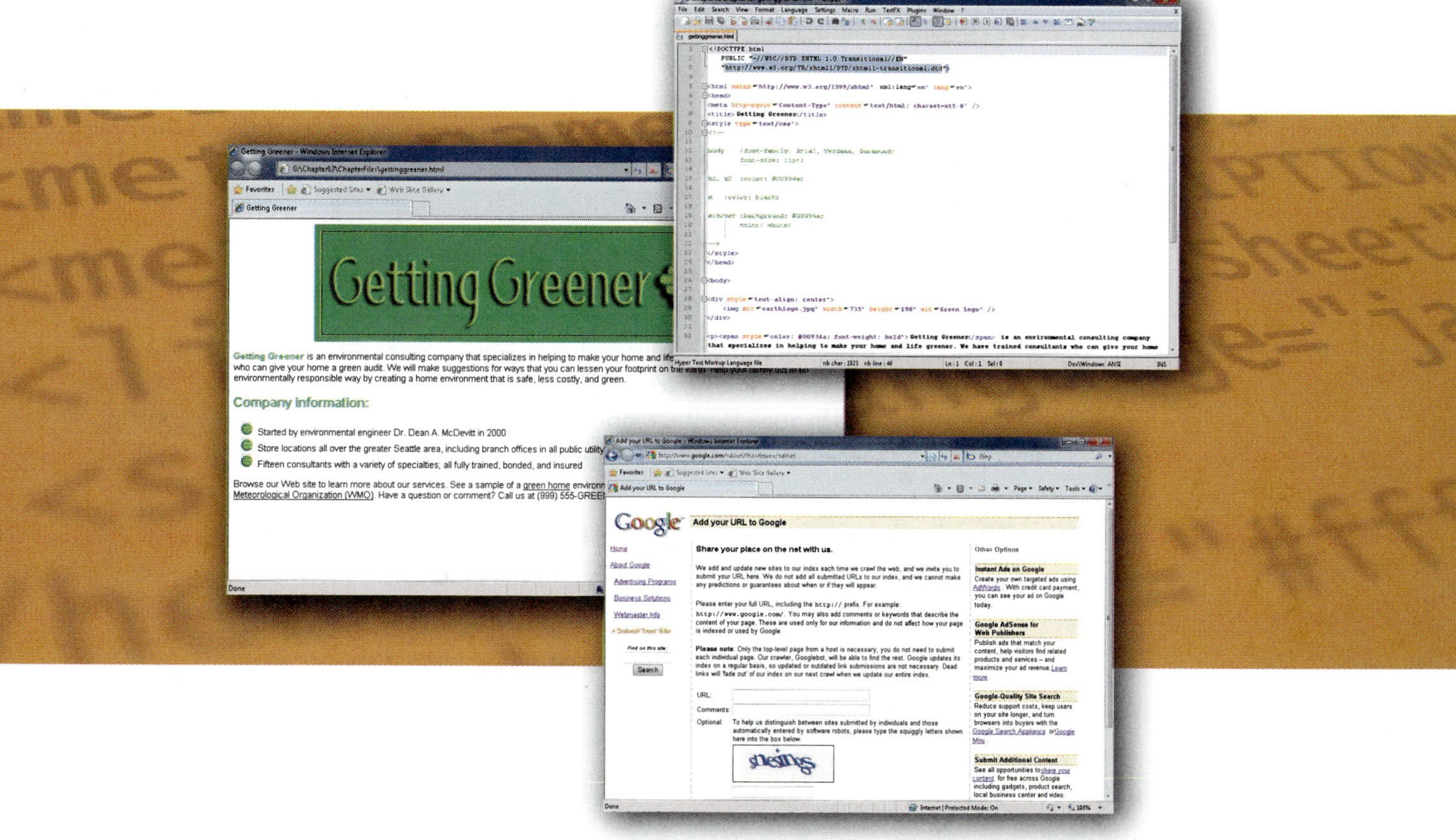

Objectives

You will have mastered the material in this special feature when you can:

- Add keywords and descriptions to your Web pages
- Find appropriate Web site servers
- Determine the availability of a domain name
- Discuss Web page publishing options
- Develop an advertising plan to get the word out about your Web site

Introduction

In Chapter 3, you developed the Getting Greener Web site, which consisted of two Web pages. In this special feature, you learn how to fine-tune that Web site to make sure that it will attract visitors. A Web site is a passive marketing tool; it serves no purpose if no one knows that it is there. It is not enough to just develop a Web site. You also have to make modifications to the Web pages to ensure that they will attract visitors.

Project — Attracting Visitors

Web sites have become an important means of worldwide communication. Businesses utilize Web sites to communicate with their customers and vendors. Teachers create Web sites to communicate with other teachers and their students, and private users create Web sites to share aspects of their personal life with family, friends, and others.

In Chapter 3, you created the Getting Greener home page, gettinggreener.html, as shown in Figure 1. The project in this feature shows you how to utilize <meta /> tags to add keywords and descriptions to this page to help Web site visitors looking for such topics find your Web page.

Overview

As you read through this feature, you will learn how to add keywords and descriptions to the meta tags that you previously developed (Figure 1a) to the Web page, as shown in Figure 1b. You also learn how to find a hosting site, determine a domain name, publish the Web pages, and determine an advertising plan by performing these general tasks:

- Decide what meta names (keywords and descriptions) you should use.
- Insert the keywords and descriptions into the meta tags.
- Identify available domain names.
- Determine an appropriate hosting situation for your Web site.
- Establish an advertising plan.

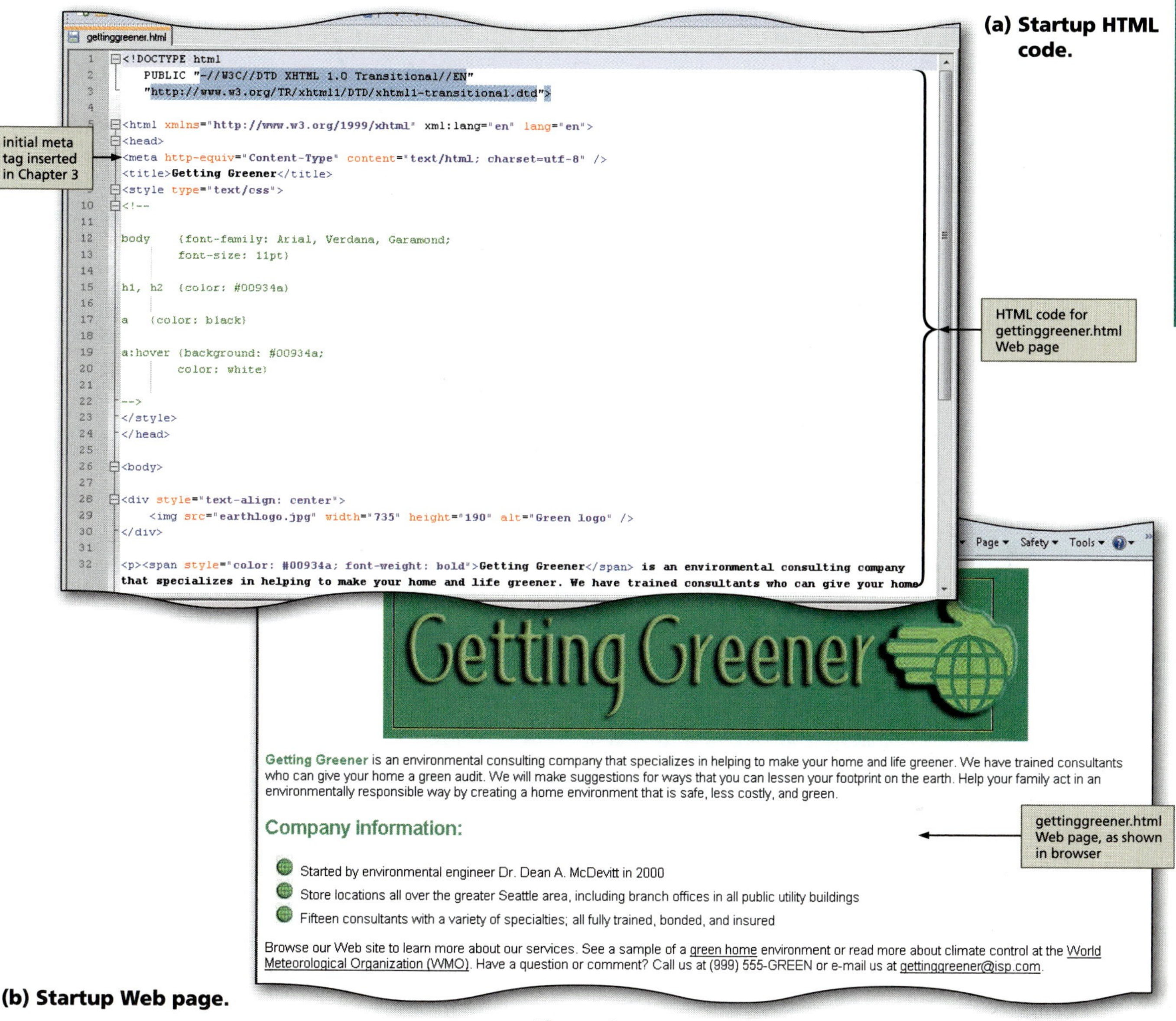

Figure 1

Plan Ahead

General Project Guidelines

In the Getting Greener home page in Chapter 3, you added a title, Getting Greener, that included the keyword "greener" in it. That word "greener" identifies the main subject matter for the Web site, but while your topic is clear, more must be done to your Web site. Once your Web page is complete, you need to publish it and attract visitors. There are several ways to attract visitors, which you will accomplish in the following project. In preparation for this project, you should follow these general guidelines:

1. **Identify the meta names you should use.** There are different meta names that you can use within the <meta /> tag, including keywords and description. In this step, you determine whether to use keywords or description or to use both keywords and description in different meta tags.
2. **Determine the keywords and descriptions that reflect the purpose of the Web site.** Before you add keywords and description to your meta tags, you need to determine the words and description that apply to the Web site. When Web users are searching for informative sites, they type those keywords or description into the search engine. You should put yourself in the role of a user looking for information relative to the theme of your Web site. This helps you come up with great ideas for the keywords that will work. These keywords/description are in addition to the relevant phrases already included in the Web page title or body content.

(continued)

Plan Ahead

(continued)

3. **Decide the available domain names.** A Web page address or URL is an important part of advertising your Web page. You can register your domain name, which will make it easier for Web users to find your site. You need to decide on a few possibilities and then determine if those domain names are already registered. If the name you choose is not registered, you can purchase and register it.
4. **Assess your Web hosting alternatives.** Many Web developers have access to their own corporate Web servers. If you do, then you do not have to consider other Web hosting options. If this is not an option, then you need to find a Web server on which to host your Web pages.
5. **Establish an advertising plan.** You have many choices for publicizing your Web pages. Most companies include the URL in all corporate correspondence, including letterheads, advertisements, and products. Sharing links with a related Web site also helps get visitors. You need to determine a plan that will incorporate the best techniques to effectively publicize your Web pages.

Adding Keywords

You have already created the HTML file that is used in this special feature. You use the file gettinggreener.html that you created in Chapter 3. The page includes a number of keywords: You added the word "greener" to the title on the Web page; you also used the phrases "environmental consulting company", "green audit", and "green home" in the Web page content. Any of these phrases might be used by visitors searching for companies that deal with environmental or "green" issues. You can explicitly identify the keywords that you want the search engine to find by adding additional keywords and phrases to your <meta /> tag.

As with other projects, you use Notepad++ to enhance this file by adding keywords and descriptions. To include additional information in your Web page, you will follow these general steps:

1. Open the gettinggreener.html file in Notepad++.
2. Add the keywords and description to new <meta /> tags.
3. Save and validate the file.

To Open the File

For this project, you will add keywords and a description to the gettinggreener.html Web page already created. The following steps show you how to add keywords.

1. Start Notepad++.
2. Open the gettinggreener.html file in the Chapter03\ChapterFiles folder that you stored on the G:\ drive (Figure 2).
3. If necessary, enable Word wrap in Notepad++.

Q&A What if I did not create the gettinggreener.html file from Chapter 3?
Your instructor should have a copy of the gettinggreener.html file.

Other Ways

1. Right-click the file name gettinggreener.html in Windows Explorer, select Edit with Notepad++

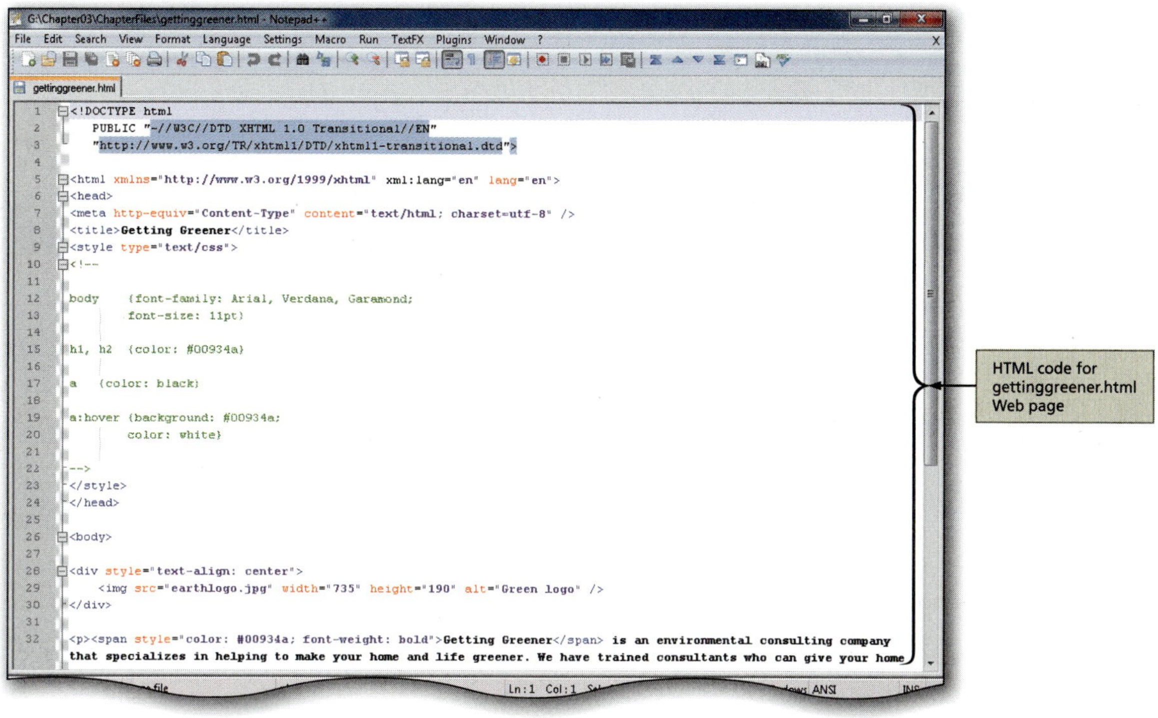

```
<!DOCTYPE html
    PUBLIC "-//W3C//DTD XHTML 1.0 Transitional//EN"
    "http://www.w3.org/TR/xhtml1/DTD/xhtml1-transitional.dtd">

<html xmlns="http://www.w3.org/1999/xhtml" xml:lang="en" lang="en">
<head>
<meta http-equiv="Content-Type" content="text/html; charset=utf-8" />
<title>Getting Greener</title>
<style type="text/css">
<!--

body    {font-family: Arial, Verdana, Garamond;
        font-size: 11pt}

h1, h2  {color: #00934a}

a    {color: black}

a:hover {background: #00934a;
        color: white}

-->
</style>
</head>

<body>

<div style="text-align: center">
    <img src="earthlogo.jpg" width="735" height="190" alt="Green logo" />
</div>

<p><span style="color: #00934a; font-weight: bold">Getting Greener</span> is an environmental consulting company
that specializes in helping to make your home and life greener. We have trained consultants who can give your home
```

HTML code for gettinggreener.html Web page

Figure 2

Meta Names

There are several meta names that you can use in the <meta /> tag, as shown in Table 1. You already included one meta tag in the initial HTML code that you inserted into every Web page created thus far. The

```
<meta http-equiv="Content-Type" content="text/html;
charset=utf-8" />
```

line has been included in all Web pages throughout the book. As mentioned earlier, this statement declares the character-encoding as UTF-8. The Unicode Transformation Format (UTF) is a compressed format that allows computers to display and manipulate text. When the browser encounters this meta tag, it will display the Web page properly, based on the particular UTF-8 encoding embedded in the tag. UTF-8 is the preferred encoding standard for Web pages, e-mail, and other applications.

Some of the more frequently used meta names are listed in Table 1. In this project, you use two of those meta names: description and keywords. The keywords are used by some search engines to find your Web pages. Other search engines use the keywords included in the content of your Web pages. The best plan includes putting keywords in both places. The description, on the other hand, is what some search engines add next to your Web page URL to describe the content of the Web page. Visitors often look at that description to determine whether they want to click that particular link (or URL) from the list of URLs that the search engine displays. The format that is used for each type of meta name is:

```
<meta name="keywords" content="green ideas, eco friendly" />
<meta name="description" content="Seattle area home or business
environmental consulting."
```

where name identifies the type of meta element that you use, and content identifies the specific phrases or words that are used.

BTW

SEO

SEO is an acronym for Search Engine Optimization or Search Engine Optimizer. SEO is the process of improving the amount of traffic that you get on your Web site. Optimizing a Web site involves editing the content and HTML in the Web page to increase its relevance to specific keywords and to remove barriers to the page indexing functions of search engines. To find more information, search for SEO on the Internet.

Table 1 Meta Names and Their Functions

Meta Name	Function
author	Supplies the name of the document author
description	Provides a description of the document
keywords	Provides a list of keywords that describe the document

To Add Keywords

The following step illustrates how to add keywords to the gettinggreener.html Web page.

- Click after the > at the end of line 7 and press the ENTER key to position the insertion point on line 8.
- Type <meta name="keywords" content="green ideas, eco friendly"/> and then press the ENTER key (Figure 3).

Figure 3

To Add a Description

The following step illustrates how to add a meta tag description to your Web page.

- If necessary, position the insertion point on line 9.
- Type <meta name="description" content="Seattle area home or business environmental consulting."/> but do not press the ENTER key (Figure 4).

Figure 4

Q&A

Is there a difference between keywords and description?

Yes. Search engines use keywords to find your Web pages, while they display descriptions next to the respective Web page URLs.

Q&A

If I have relevant keywords in the content of my Web page, why should I add other words to the <meta /> tags?

It always helps to have keywords identified in both places for those search engines that choose one method over the other.

To Save, Validate, and Print a Document

You are finished entering the meta tags. As with all Web development projects, you now need to save, validate, and print the file.

1. In Notepad++, click the Save icon on the toolbar to save the file with the new meta tags.
2. Validate the file using the w3.org validation service.
3. Once the file is successfully validated, print the file (Figure 5).

```
<!DOCTYPE html
   PUBLIC "-//W3C//DTD XHTML 1.0 Transitional//EN"
   "http://www.w3.org/TR/xhtml1/DTD/xhtml1-transitional.dtd">

<html xmlns="http://www.w3.org/1999/xhtml" xml:lang="en" lang="en">
<head>
<meta http-equiv="Content-Type" content="text/html; charset=utf-8" />
<meta name="keywords" content="green ideas, eco friendly" />
<meta name="description" content="Seattle area home or business environmental
consulting." />
<title>Getting Greener</title>
<style type="text/css">
<!--

body    {font-family: Arial, Verdana, Garamond;
        font-size: 11pt}

h1, h2  {color: #00934a}

a   {color: black}

a:hover {background: #00934a;
        color: white}

-->
</style>
</head>

<body>

<div style="text-align: center">
    <img src="earthlogo.jpg" width="735" height="190" alt="Green logo" />
</div>

<p><span style="color: #00934a; font-weight: bold">Getting Greener</span> is an
environmental consulting company that specializes in helping to make your home and life
greener. We have trained consultants who can give your home a green audit. We will make
suggestions for ways that you can lessen your footprint on the earth. Help your family
act in an environmentally responsible way by creating a home environment that is safe,
less costly, and green.</p>

<h2>Company information:</h2>

<ul style="list-style-image: url(earthbullet.jpg)">
<li>Started by environmental engineer Dr. Dean A. McDevitt in 2000</li>
<li>Store locations all over the greater Seattle area, including branch offices in all
public utility buildings</li>
<li>Fifteen consultants with a variety of specialties; all fully trained, bonded, and
insured</li>
</ul>

<p>Browse our Web site to learn more about our services. See a sample of a <a href=
"greenhome.html">green home</a> environment or read more about climate control at the <a

-1-
```

Figure 5

Determining a Domain Name

You may use the domain name of the server on which you publish your Web pages together with a path to your specific pages as an option for your Web page address or URL. A **domain name** is the server name portion of the URL. You are also able to register your own domain name on the Internet for about $10 per year. That sometimes makes it easier for visitors to find your Web pages. In the case of the gettinggreener.html file, you could register a domain name that is available for your Getting Greener Web site.

InterNIC
InterNIC contains trusted public information regarding Internet domain name registration services. The InterNIC Web site has a FAQs section, information about domain name registrars, as well as links for domain name disputes.

To determine if the domain name you are considering is available, you can start your search at InterNIC. InterNIC is a registered service mark of the U.S. Department of Commerce. The InterNIC Web site (*www.internic.net/alpha.html*) is operated by the Internet Corporation for Assigned Names and Numbers (ICANN) to provide information to the public regarding Internet domain name registration services. ICANN is responsible for managing and coordinating the Domain Name System (DNS) to ensure that every Internet address is unique, and that all users of the Internet can find all valid addresses.

Check Domain Name Availability

In order to check to see if a domain name is available, complete the following steps:

1

- Open Internet Explorer.
- Type `http://www.internic.net/alpha.html` into the address bar, as shown in Figure 6.
- Review the FAQ section of the Web site to better understand the domain naming process.
- Click the Whois link to see what domain names have previously been registered for gettinggreener. You can try .com, .net, or .org to see the results.

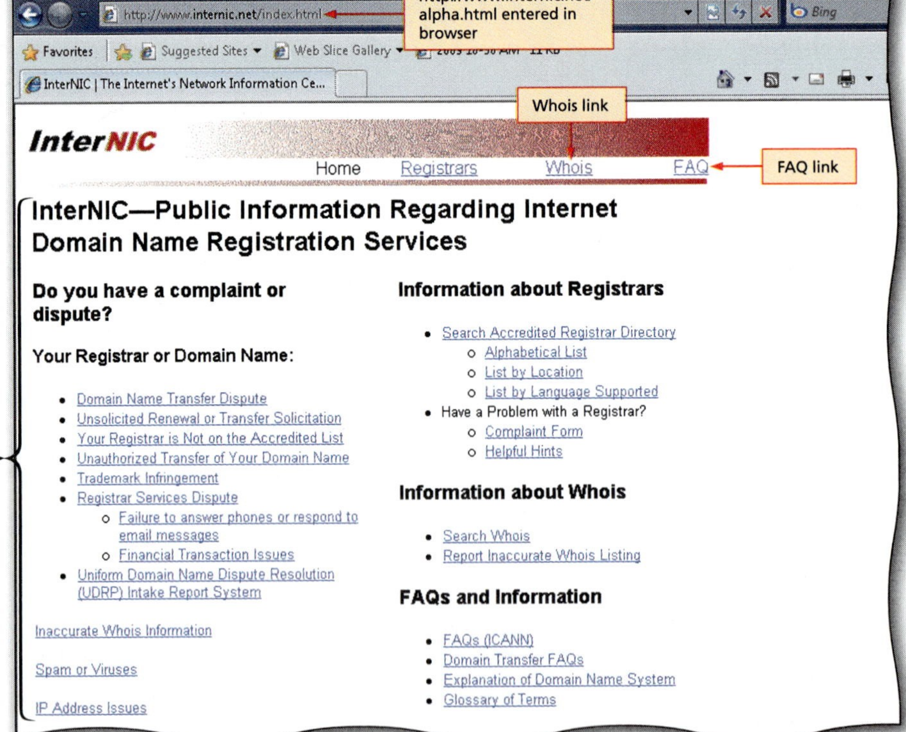

Figure 6

Finding a Web Hosting Site

The next step in the Web development process is to publish your Web pages so that visitors can see them. In order to publish your Web site, you need hosting services. There are many options available for Web hosting. You need access to a Web server onto which you can upload all of the Web pages in your Web site.

One option is to use the ISP that you use to connect to the Internet. ISPs sometimes provide space for their clients to host a Web site. If you registered your own domain name, you can even have your ISP set up a virtual domain, or shared Web hosting, on their server with your new domain name. Your ISP's server may be set up to allocate hosting services and bandwidth to more than one Web site by using a virtual domain. In other words, although you register the domain name gettinggreener.com, your ISP would host it on its own Web server. Virtual Web hosting is a much cheaper option because you do not have to pay for a dedicated server to host just your Web site. You can check with your ISP for details. A second option is to use a company that charges for Web site hosting. There are thousands of companies that provide Web hosting services. Most charge a monthly fee, but some offer free Web hosting in exchange for advertising on your Web site. A final option is for you to set up your own Web server. You would have to know enough about the technology to set it up and keep it running.

BTW

Web Site Hosting
There are a variety of Web site hosting options available today. To search for Web hosting services, use different search engines to find different alternatives. Make sure to use the checklist shown on this page to assess the hosting services and fees.

If you choose to utilize your own ISP or a Web hosting service, you need to consider a few things. These include:

- What is the total cost? Compare monthly or annual costs; the highest cost may not always provide the best service.
- How much space is available to you? You need to assess your current needs (i.e., file sizes, sizes of graphics) and also your future needs (i.e., how much more information you will create).
- How fast is the connection speed? The speed of the connection to the Internet is important to efficiently serve your visitors.
- How much total bandwidth transfer is available? The number and size of Web pages in your Web site together with the number and size of graphical images is important to consider.
- Do they provide technical support? You may occasionally need help, especially in the beginning.
- Do they offer tracking services? Many hosting companies allow you to see how visitors utilize your Web site by viewing a tracking log.

After you have selected a Web hosting service, you need to transfer your files to that server.

Publishing Your Web Site

Once you have determined a Web hosting strategy, the next step is to publish your Web pages so that visitors can see them. **Publishing** your Web site means transferring your files to the Web server. There are many options available for file transfers. You could use a File Transfer Protocol (FTP) program such as WS-FTP for Windows (Figure 7) or Fetch for Mac (for more information about FTP programs, see Appendix E). In addition, many Web page editors also provide publishing functionality. Once your Web pages are published, the last step is to advertise their location to attract visitors.

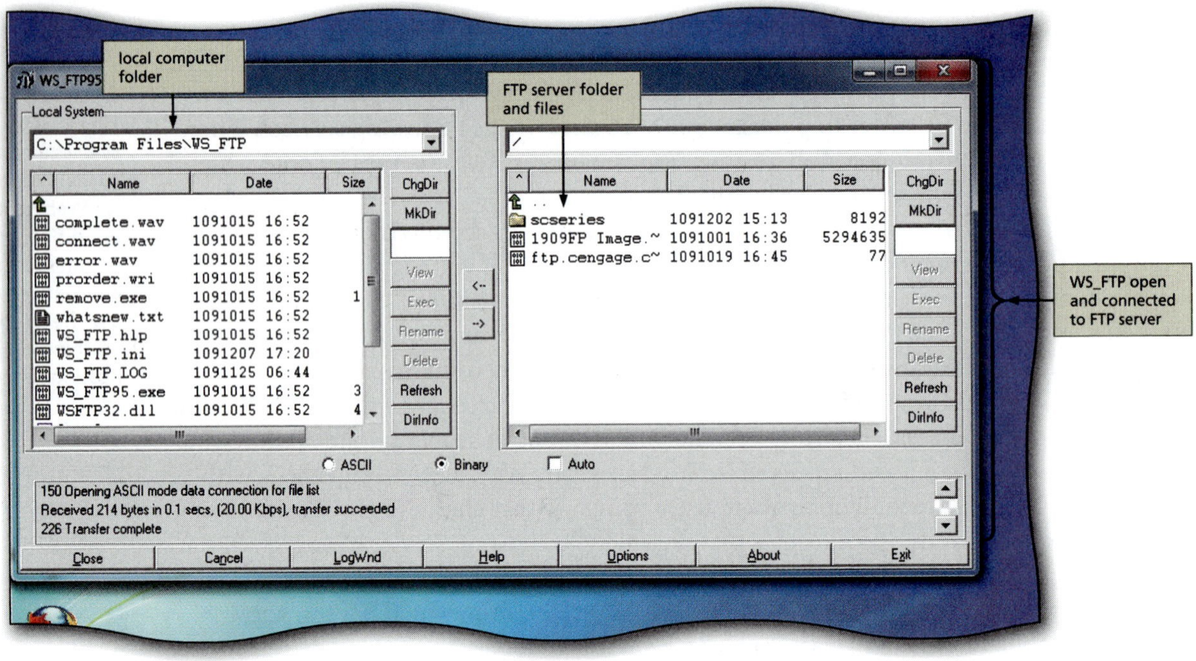

Figure 7

Advertising Your Web Site

Now that your Web pages are published, you need to get the word out to potential Web site visitors. You need to determine a comprehensive advertising plan. It serves no purpose for you to publish a Web site if no one visits it. There are several ways to start an advertising campaign:

- Put your URL on your business cards, company brochures, stationery, and e-mail signature.
- Advertise your URL in newsletters and print articles.
- Tell people verbally about your Web site.
- Find and get listed on targeted directories and search engines specific to your industry.
- Buy banner ads.
- Negotiate reciprocal links in which you agree to link to a Web site if they agree to link to your Web site.
- Utilize newsgroups specific to your industry.

BTW

Search Engines
Both Google and Yahoo! contain information about optimizing your Web sites. Review their Webmaster guidelines for great ideas on registering with their search engines. Google even provides a Google 101 section that explains how Google indexes and serves the Web.

Registering with Search Engines

You are finished entering the meta tags, publishing, and advertising your Web site. The next step is to register your Web site with the two most popular search engines, Google and Yahoo! It is also a good idea to register your site with search engines that specialize in subject matter related to your Web site.

To Register Your Web Site with Search Engines

The next step shows you how to register your Web pages with the Google and Yahoo! search engines.

- In Internet Explorer, type `http://www.google.com/addurl.html` in the address bar and press the ENTER key (Figure 8).
- Follow the directions to add your URL.

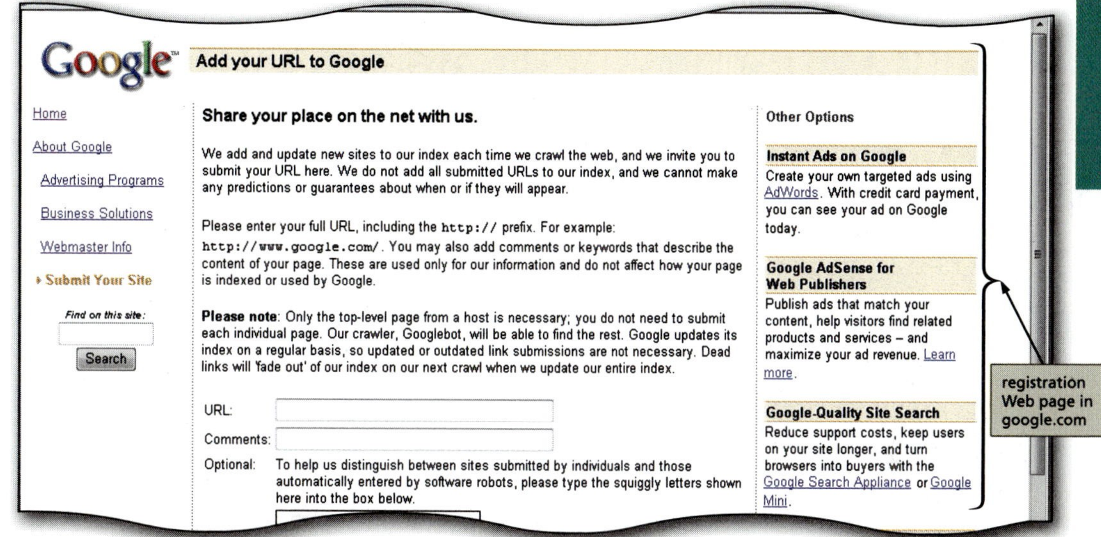

Figure 8

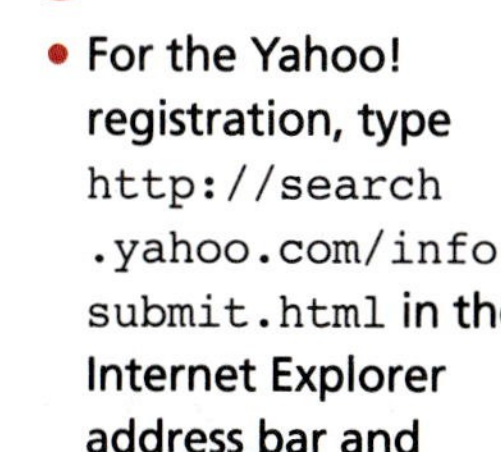

- For the Yahoo! registration, type `http://search.yahoo.com/info/submit.html` in the Internet Explorer address bar and press the ENTER key (Figure 9).
- Follow the directions to add your URL.

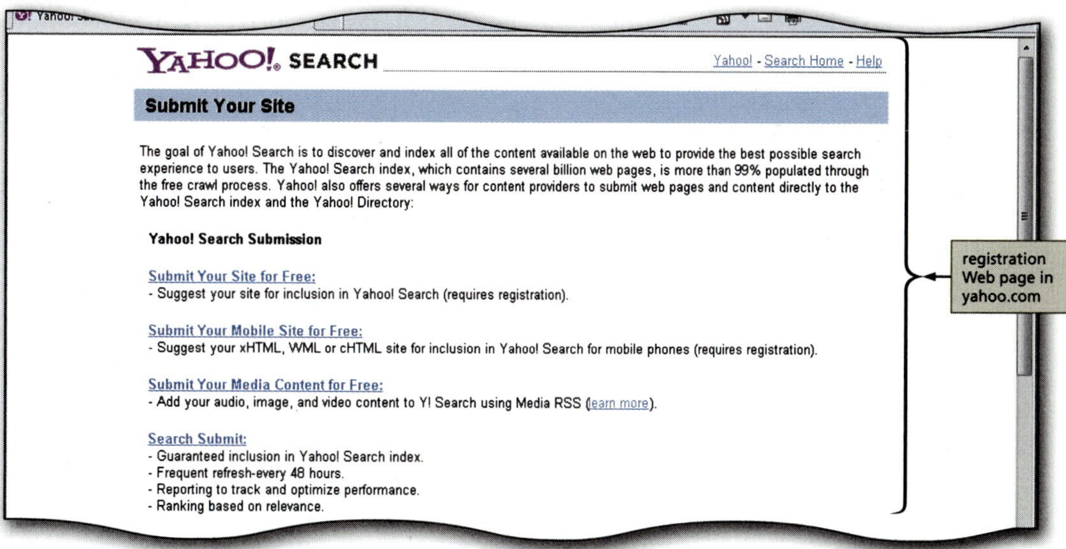

Figure 9

Feature Summary

In this feature, you have learned how to insert keywords and description meta tags into your Web page. You also learned about domain names, how to search for a Web host, publish your Web page, advertise your Web site, and register your site with search engines. The items listed below include all the new skills you have learned in this feature.

1. Add Keywords (HTML 226)
2. Add a Description (HTML 226)
3. Check Domain Name Availability (HTML 228)
4. Register Your Web Site with Search Engines (HTML 230)

In the Lab

Design and/or create a document using the guidelines, concepts, and skills presented in this chapter. Labs are listed in order of increasing difficulty.

Lab 1: Creating a Publishing and Advertising Plan

Problem: Your assignment is to apply the ideas and suggestions listed in this special feature to write a comprehensive publishing and advertising plan. This plan should all be noted in a Word file that can be submitted to your instructor.

Instructions:

1. Determine a domain name that is available to use for your Getting Greener Web site.
2. Research and identify several possible Web hosting options. Answer all six questions covered in this special feature section for each of your hosting options.
3. Research and identify the specifics about registering your Web site with both Google and Yahoo!.
4. Write an advertising plan that addresses specific ways that you can get the word out about your Web site. Specific plans should include:
   a. Locating targeted directories and search engines specific to the industry reflected in the Web site
   b. Investigating the pros and cons of buying banner ads
   c. Determining Web sites to which you could have possible reciprocal links
   d. Finding newsgroups specific to the industry reflected in the Web site
5. Save the file with the name Lab SF1-1 Advertising. Submit the file in the format specified by your instructor.

In the Lab

Lab 2: Attracting Visitors to Another Web Site

Problem: In this assignment, you are to assess another Web site to complete the same basic steps as taken in this feature to improve the site's visibility on the Internet.

Instructions:

1. Select a Web site that is of interest to you and open the site's home page.
2. Review the meta tags (if any) that are used on the home page. (*Hint:* View the page source to review those tags.) Determine how you can utilize additional meta tags for this Web page. What keywords and descriptions would be good to use? What keywords and descriptions do other related Web sites use?
3. Write an advertising plan that addresses specific ways that you can get the word out about this Web site. Specific plans should include:
   a. Locating targeted directories and search engines specific to the industry reflected in the Web site
   b. Determining Web sites to which you could have possible reciprocal links
   c. Finding newsgroups specific to the industry reflected in the Web site
4. Save the file with the name Lab SF1-2 Advertising. Submit the file in the format specified by your instructor.

5 Creating an Image Map

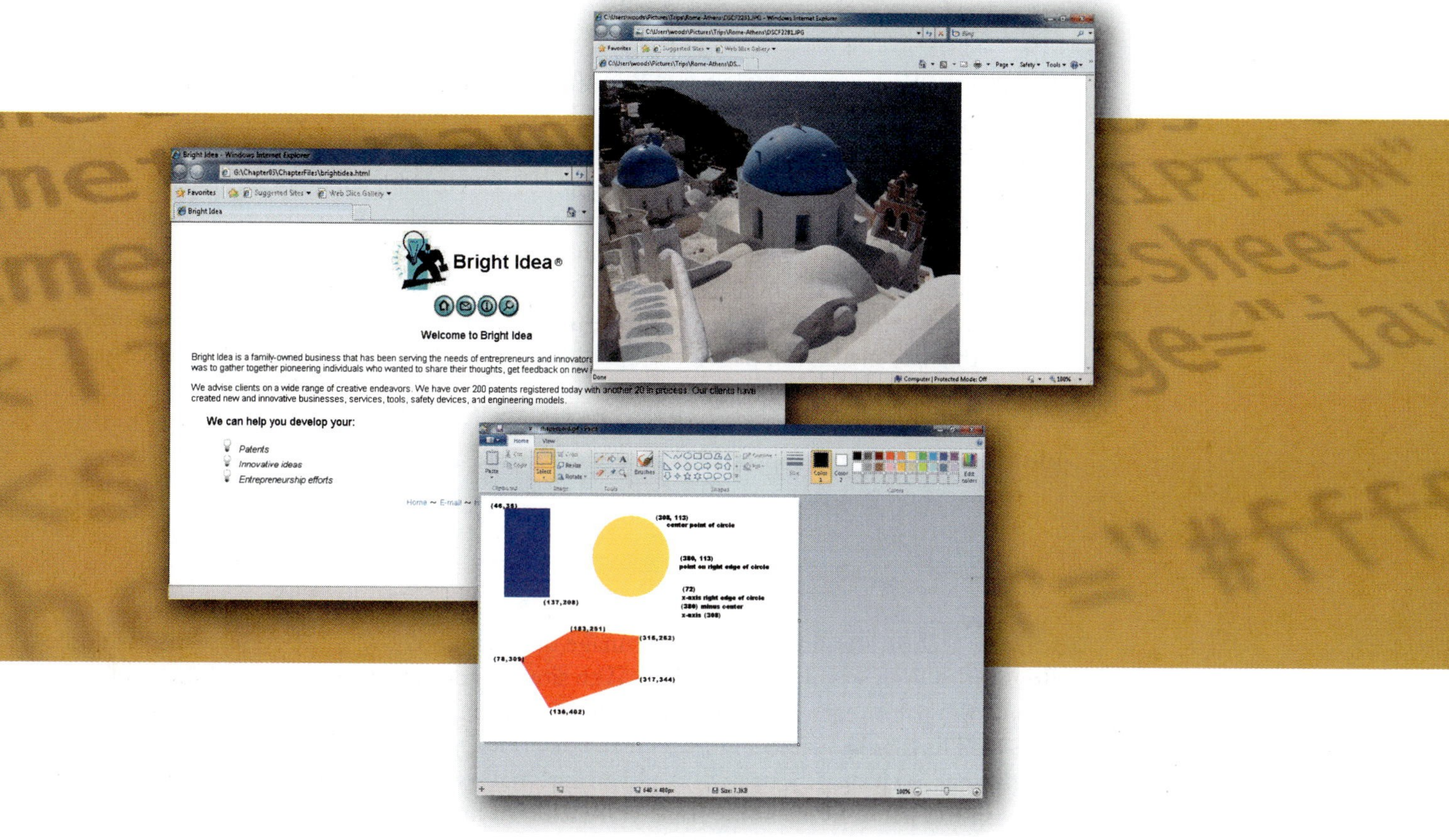

Objectives

You will have mastered the material in this chapter when you can:

- Define terms relating to image mapping
- List the differences between server-side and client-side image maps
- Name the two components of an image map and describe the steps to implement an image map
- Distinguish between appropriate and inappropriate images for mapping
- Sketch hotspots on an image
- Describe how the x- and y-coordinates relate to vertical and horizontal alignment
- Open an image in Paint and use Paint to locate the image map coordinates
- Create a home page
- Create a table, insert an image into a table, and use the usemap attribute to define an image map
- Insert special characters into a Web page
- Use the <map> </map> tags to start and end a map
- Use the <area> tag to indicate the shape, coordinates, and URL for a mapped area
- Create an external style sheet for styles used across the Web site

5 Creating an Image Map

Introduction

Many of the Web pages in Chapters 2 through 4 used the <img> tag to add images. In Chapter 3, an image also was used as a link back to the home page, by using the <a> </a> tags to define the image as the clickable element for the link. When an image is used as a link, as in Chapter 3, the entire image becomes the clickable element, or hotspot. With an image map, the entire image does not have to be clickable. Instead, one or more specific areas serve as hotspots. An image map is a special type of inline image in which you define one or more areas as hotspots. For example, each hotspot in an image map can link to another part of the same Web page or to a different Web page. Using an image map in this way gives Web page developers significant flexibility, as well as creative ways to include navigation options. Instead of using only text links, a Web page can include an image map that highlights key sections of a Web site and allows a user to navigate to that section by clicking the appropriate area of the image map.

Project — Bright Idea®

Chapter 5 illustrates how to create an image map with links to other Web pages within the Bright Idea Web site. The Bright Idea Web site includes the home page and three additional Web pages, each linked to the home page using an image map and text links, and an e-mail link, as shown in Figure 5–1. In Chapter 5, you will create the home page of the Bright Idea Web site (Figure 5–1a) and an external style sheet that is used with all Web pages in the site. On this home page, you include a link to the brightidea@isp.com e-mail address that opens an e-mail program, as shown in Figure 5–1b. The Web pages shown in Figures 5–1c and 5–1d are included in the Data Files for Students. (See the inside back cover of this book for instructions on downloading the Data Files for Students, or contact your instructor for information about accessing the required files.) HTML tags are used to create the image map that supports the four clickable areas in the image. One of the key features of the Web is its support for graphics, so Web visitors expect to view many images on the Web pages that they visit. Images make Web pages more exciting and interesting to view and, in the case of image maps, provide a creative navigational tool.

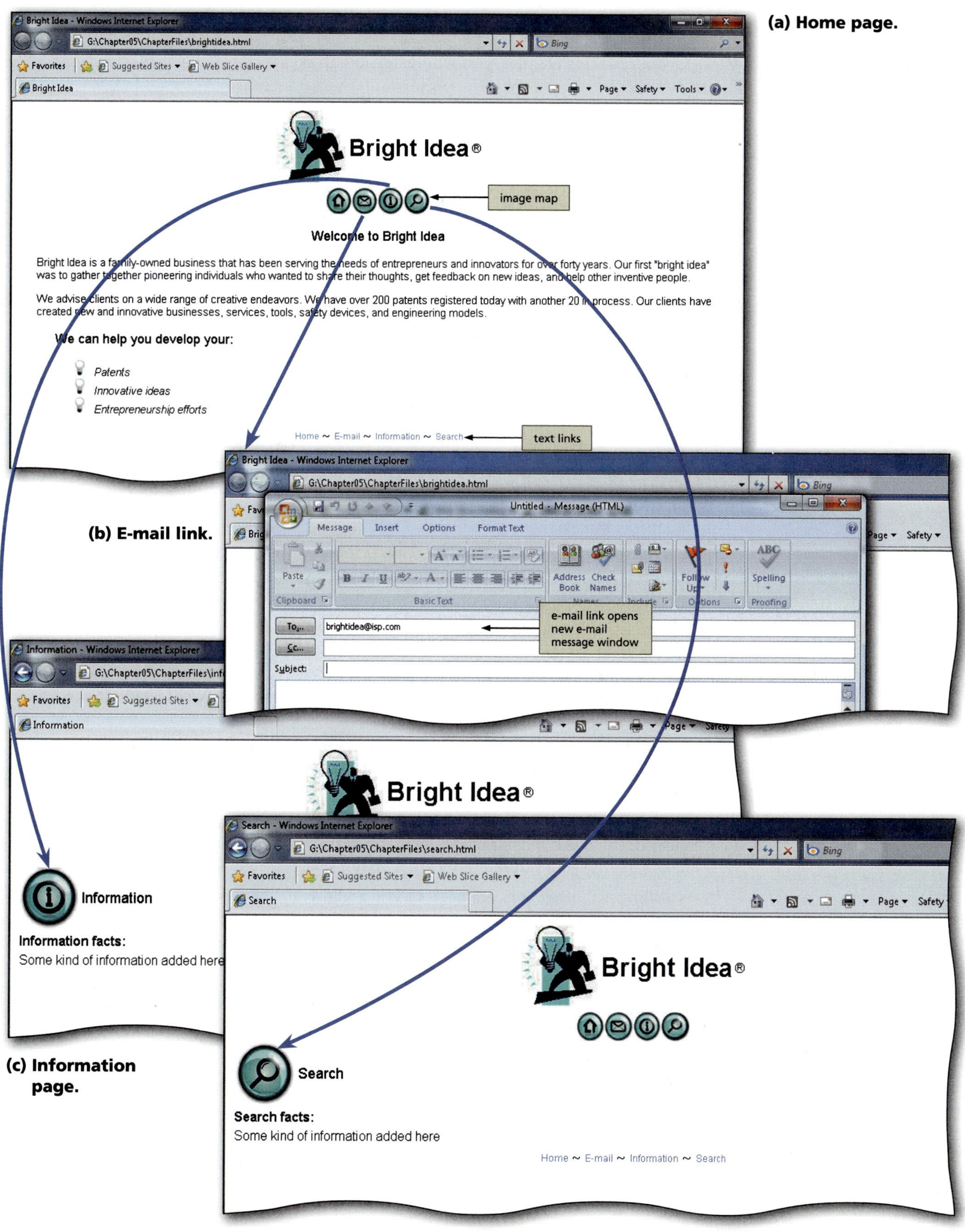

(a) Home page.
Bright Idea - Windows Internet Explorer
G:\Chapter05\ChapterFiles\brightidea.html
Bright Idea®
image map
Welcome to Bright Idea
Bright Idea is a family-owned business that has been serving the needs of entrepreneurs and innovators for over forty years. Our first "bright idea" was to gather together pioneering individuals who wanted to share their thoughts, get feedback on new ideas, and help other inventive people.
We advise clients on a wide range of creative endeavors. We have over 200 patents registered today with another 20 in process. Our clients have created new and innovative businesses, services, tools, safety devices, and engineering models.
We can help you develop your:
Patents
Innovative ideas
Entrepreneurship efforts
Home ~ E-mail ~ Information ~ Search
text links
(b) E-mail link.
Untitled - Message (HTML)
brightidea@isp.com
e-mail link opens new e-mail message window
Subject:
Information - Windows Internet Explorer
Information
Information facts:
Some kind of information added here
(c) Information page.
Search - Windows Internet Explorer
G:\Chapter05\ChapterFiles\search.html
Search
Search facts:
Some kind of information added here
Home ~ E-mail ~ Information ~ Search
(d) Search page.

Figure 5–1

Overview

As you read this chapter, you will learn how to create the Web pages shown in Figure 5–1 on the previous page by performing these general tasks:

- Enter HTML code into the Notepad++ window.
- Save the file as an HTML file.
- View an image in Microsoft Paint to see image map coordinates.
- Enter basic HTML tags and add text to the file.
- Insert an image to be used as an image map.
- Create an image map by mapping hotspots on the image.
- Create links to the other Web pages and to the home page with a horizontal menu bar.
- Add special characters to the home page.
- Create an external style sheet and insert the link into the home page.
- Save and print the HTML and CSS code.
- Validate, view, and print the Web pages.

Plan Ahead

General Project Guidelines

As you create Web pages, such as the project shown in Figure 5–1 on the previous page, you should follow these general guidelines:

1. **Plan the Web site.** As always with a multiple-page Web site, you should plan the site before you begin to write your HTML code. Refer to Table 1–4 on page HTML 15 for information on the planning phase of the Web Development Life Cycle.
2. **Analyze the need.** In the analysis phase of the Web Development Life Cycle, you should analyze what content to include on the Web page. The Web development project in Chapter 5 is different from the one completed in other chapters because it contains an image map. Part of the analysis phase then includes determining what image to use and where to put links within the image map.
3. **Choose the image.** You need to select an image that has distinguishable areas that can be used as links. Not all images are conducive to image mapping, as described in the chapter.
4. **Determine what areas of the image map to use as links.** Once an appropriate image is selected, you need to determine how to divide up the image map for links. You want to make sure that your hotspot (link) areas do not spill over into each other.
5. **Establish what other links are necessary.** In addition to links between the home page and secondary Web pages, you need an e-mail link on this Web site. It is a general standard for Web developers to provide an e-mail link on the home page of a Web site for visitor comments or questions. Additionally, you need to provide links to all other Web pages on the Web site (information.html and search.html).
6. **Create the Web page, image map, and links.** Once the analysis and design are complete, you create the Web pages. Good Web development standard practices should be followed, such as utilizing the initial HTML tags as shown in previous chapters, providing text links for all hotspots in the image map, and always identifying alt text for images.
7. **Test all Web pages within the Web site.** It is important to test your pages to assure that they follow XHTML standards. In this book, you use the World Wide Web Consortium (W3C) validator to validate your Web pages. Additionally, you should check all content for accuracy. Finally, all links (image map hotspots, text links, and page-to-page links within the same Web site) should be tested.

When necessary, details concerning the above guidelines are presented at appropriate points in the chapter. The chapter also will identify the actions performed and decisions made regarding these guidelines during the creation of the Web pages shown in Figure 5–1.

Introduction to Image Maps

In this chapter, you use an image map to create four clickable areas within a single menu bar image: a link to the home page, an e-mail link, a link to the Information page, and a link to the Search page. All four of the clickable areas have a circular shape. Figure 5–2 shows the four circular clickable areas, each of which encloses a specific area. A Web page visitor clicking one of the circular-shaped clickable areas will link to an e-mail window or to one of the associated Web pages (Home, Information, or Search).

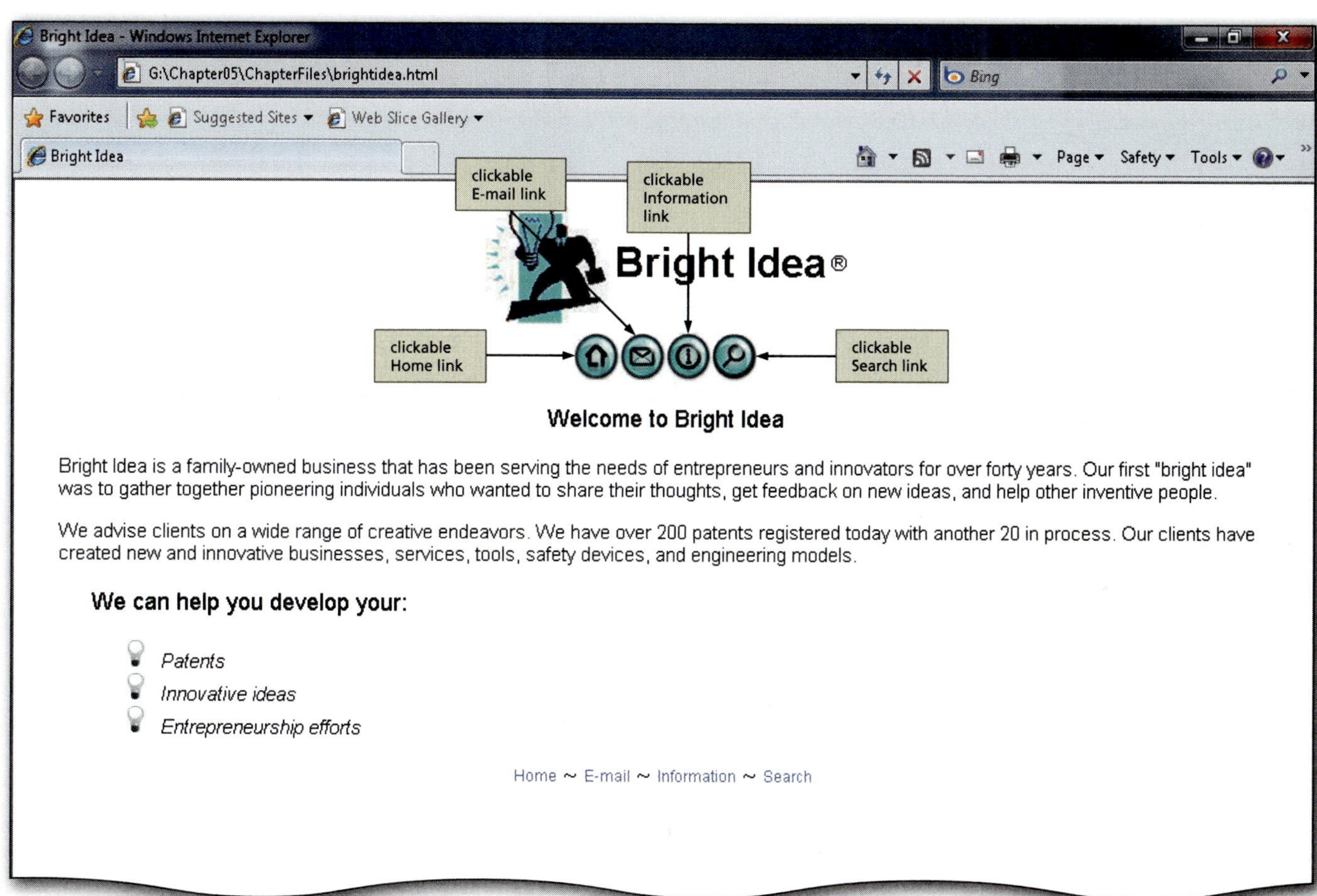

Figure 5–2

Using Image Maps

One of the risks in using image maps to provide navigational elements is that if the image does not load, a user will not have the ability to navigate to other linked Web pages. Another potential issue is that using a large image for an image map can increase the amount of time required for pages to download over lower-speed connections. To avoid such performance issues, some people turn off the viewing of images when they browse Web pages, electing to display only text in their browsers. These users, and users of text-based browsers, also will not be able to navigate a Web page that relies on an image map. For these reasons, a Web page that uses an image map for navigation also should include text links to the URLs and reflect these in the image map, as shown in Figure 5–3a on the next page. Using text links in conjunction with the image map ensures that if the image does not download or a Web page visitor has images turned off, as shown in Figure 5–3b, a user still can navigate to other Web pages using the text links.

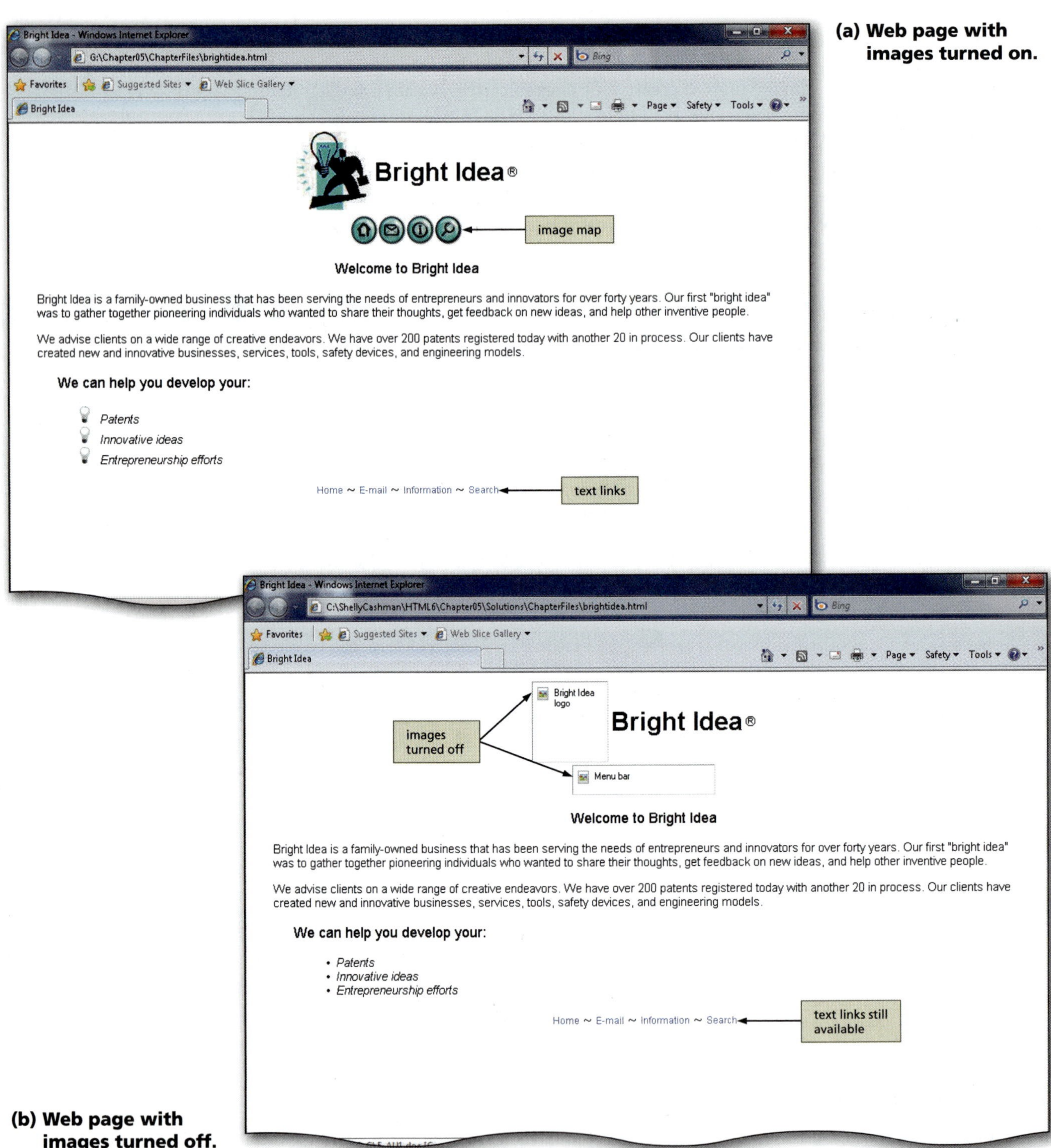

(a) Web page with images turned on.

(b) Web page with images turned off.

Figure 5–3

Image maps can enhance the functionality and appeal of Web pages in many ways. For example, an image map can be used as an **image map button bar**, which is a menu bar that uses graphical images, as shown in Figure 5–4 and in this chapter's project. This makes the menu bar a more attractive feature of the Web page.

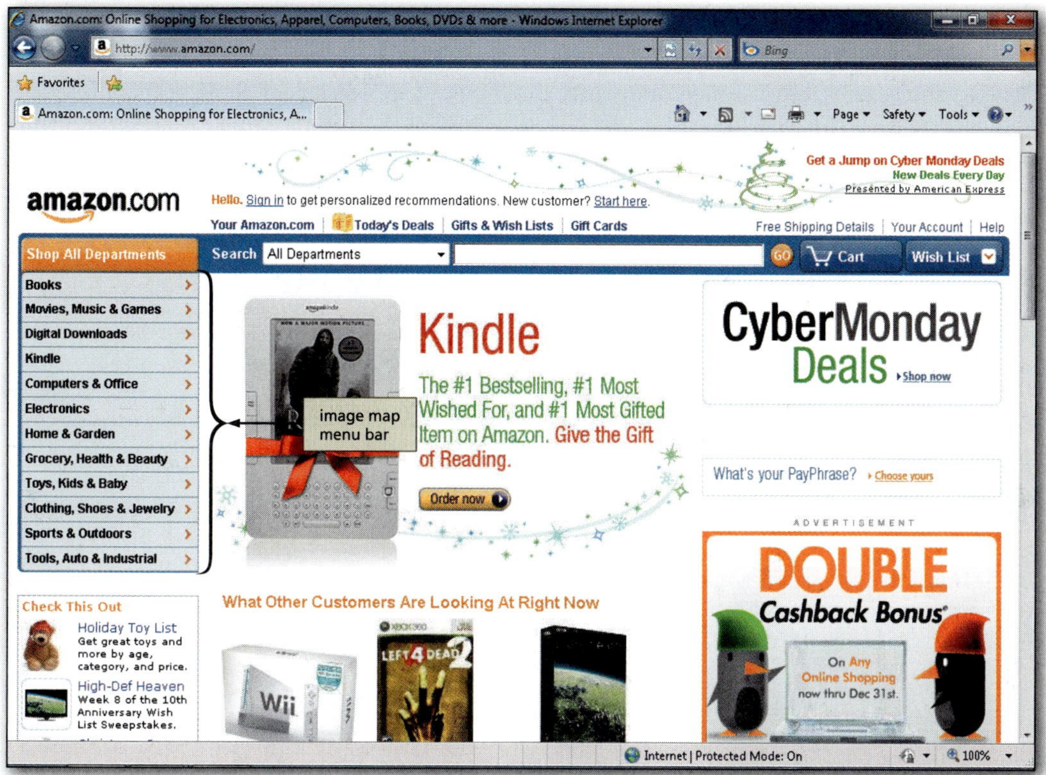

Figure 5–4 Image map menu bar.

Image maps are also utilized to divide a geographical map into hotspots, as shown in Figure 5–5. A Web page visitor can click a geographical area on the map and be linked to additional information about that location.

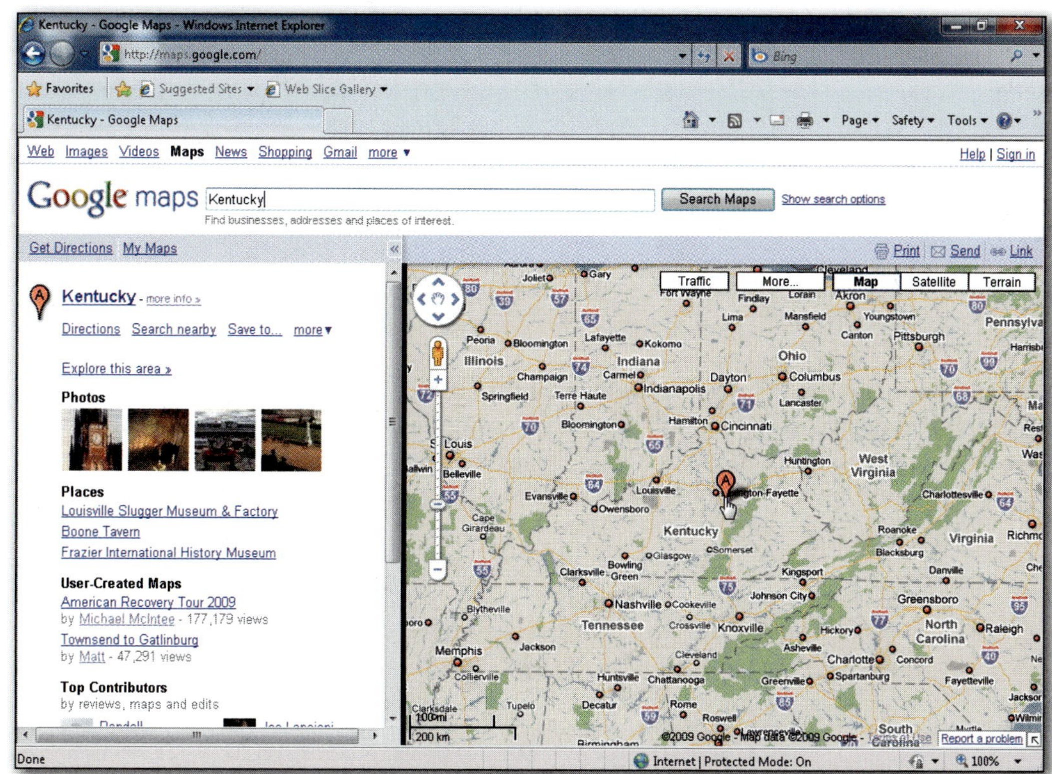

Figure 5–5 Image map on map Web page.

A theater may use an image map to show the seating chart of the facility (Figure 5–6). You could develop an application that links from the ticket purchase Web page to the seating chart image map and allow customers to select their seats. This map shows how the various tables are arranged, which helps customers understand the general layout of the theater.

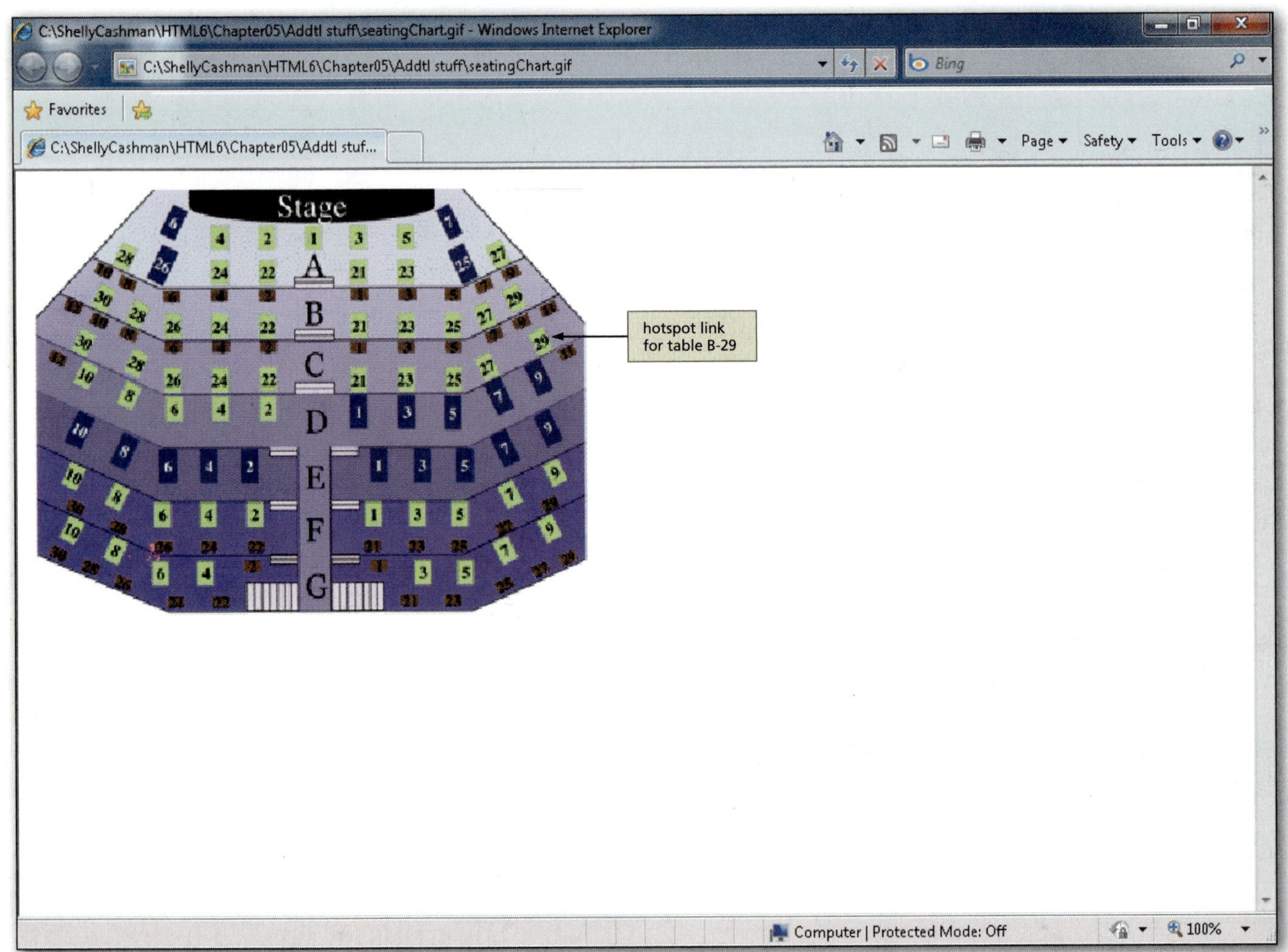

Figure 5–6 Image map of theater seating chart.

BTW

Image Maps
Image maps are used frequently for Web site navigation. Many online HTML sources address the purposes of image maps and give suggestions for their use. Review the w3schools section of the World Wide Web Consortium site (www.w3schools.com) for comprehensive image map information.

Image maps can be used for many applications. For instance, if you want to create a Web site that depicts your vacation travels, you could take a digital picture of your travel souvenirs (Figure 5–7a) and use that as an image map, linking personal souvenirs to photographs (Figure 5–7b) that you took in a particular country that you visited.

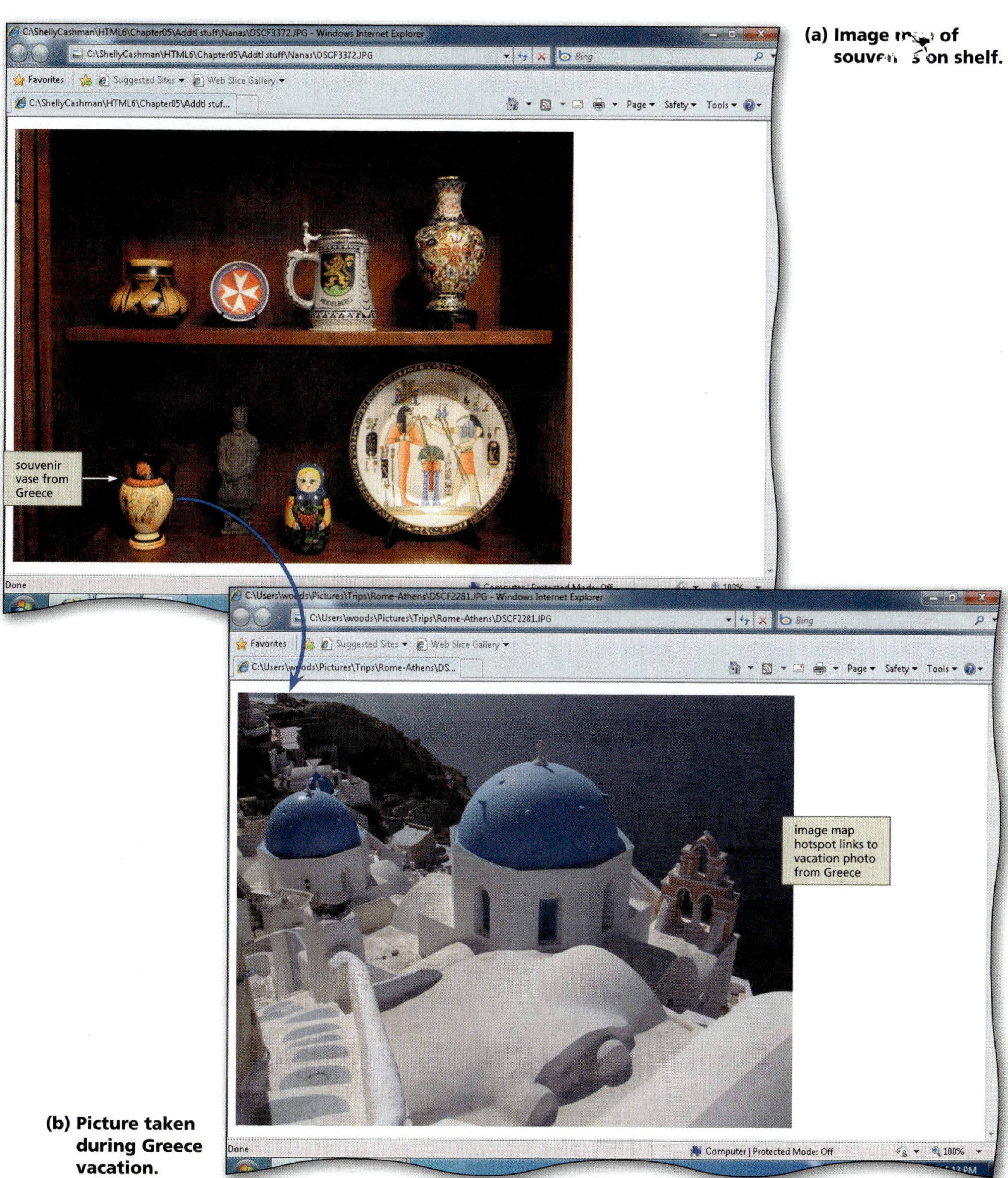

(a) Image map of souvenirs on shelf.

(b) Picture taken during Greece vacation.

Figure 5–7

There are real estate applications in which an image map of the house floor plan is used (Figure 5–8). This map allows a potential customer to click a hotspot of a particular room in the house in order to see pictures or get additional information about that room. Using an image map like this gives people the opportunity to view for sale houses online.

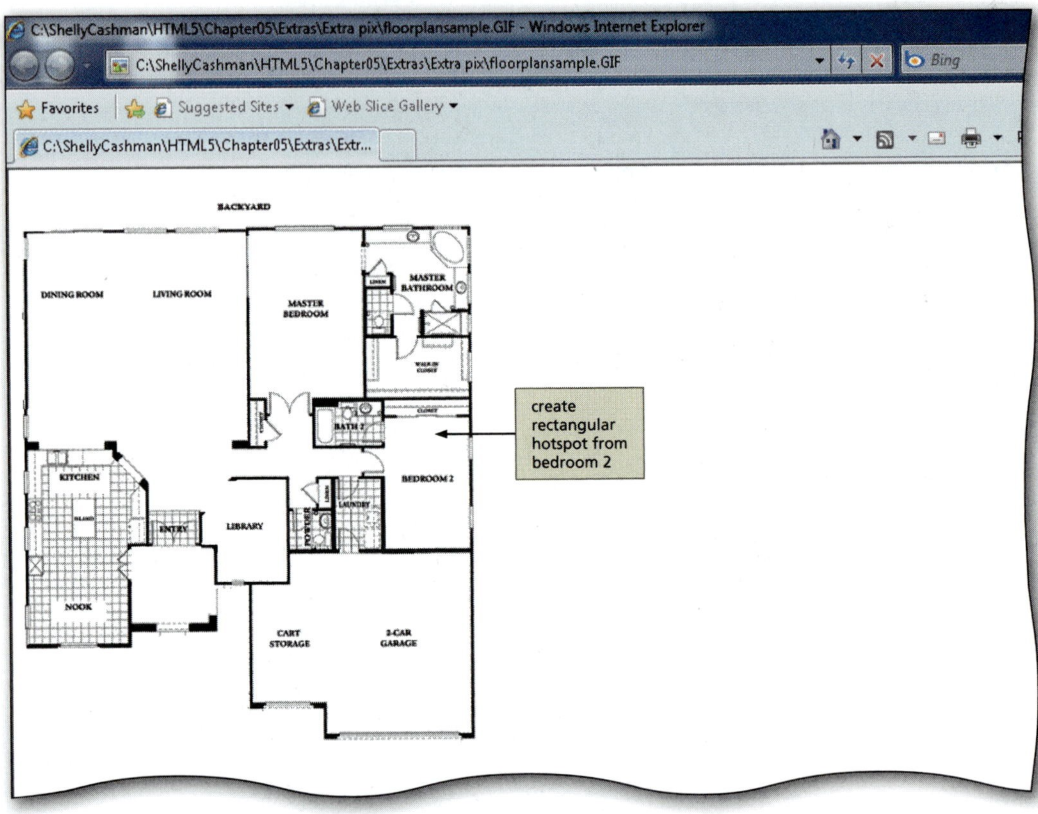

Figure 5–8 Floor plan can be used as image map.

BTW

Server-Side vs. Client-Side Image Maps
Web sites exist that provide information about server-side versus client-side image maps. To see an example of how image maps can be used for Web pages and which type is more efficient, use a search engine to search for the terms "server-side image maps" and "client-side image maps".

BTW

Server-Side Image Maps
When a hotspot on an image map is clicked, a special image map program that is stored on the Web server is run. In addition, the browser also sends the x- and y-coordinates to the Web server for the position of the link on the image map. Most, if not all, browsers support server-side image maps.

Server-Side vs. Client-Side Image Maps

Two types of image maps exist: server-side and client-side. In a **server-side image map**, the image is displayed by the client (browser) and implemented by a program that runs on the Web server. When a Web page visitor clicks a link on a server-side image map, the browser sends the x- and y-coordinates of the mouse click to the Web server, which interprets them and then links the visitor to the correct Web page based on those coordinates. Thus, with a server-side image map, the Web server does all the work.

With a **client-side image map**, the browser does all the work. Most Web developers prefer to work with client-side image mapping, which does not have to send the x- and y-coordinates of the mouse click to the Web server to be interpreted. Instead, the coordinates are included in the HTML file along with the URL to which to link. When a visitor to a Web page clicks within a client-side image map, the browser processes the data without interaction with the Web server.

One advantage of server-side image mapping is that most, if not all, browsers support server-side image maps, while some older browsers do not support client-side image maps. Server-side image maps have disadvantages, however. They require additional software in order to run on a Web server. This requires that the server administrator maintain and update the server software on a regular basis. Also, an image map available on a particular Web site's server must be registered to the server before it can be used. Although this process is simple, it must be done. Further, all changes to that registered image map must be coordinated on the Web server, which does not allow for quick updates. Client-side image maps help reduce the load on the Web server, generally download faster, and provide faster response when a user clicks a link. In this chapter's project, you will create a client-side image map with four links on the home page of the Bright Idea Web site. You will learn more about client- and server-side image maps later in the chapter.

Plan Ahead

Understand the image map process.

Before inserting the graphical and color elements on a Web page, you should plan how you want to format them. By effectively utilizing graphics and color, you can call attention to important topics on the Web page without overpowering it. Creating a client-side image map for a Web page is a four-step process:

1. **Select an image to use as an image map.** Not all images are appropriate for good image mapping. Those images without distinct boundaries are not easy to map. Besides causing difficulty to the Web developer to find the points to plot, nondistinct areas make it difficult for visitors to see where one link might end and another begins. When choosing an image to map, choose wisely.
2. **Sketch in the hotspots on the image.** It is sometimes good to print a copy of the image and draw the hotspot areas on top of the paper image. You can then take that hard copy and review it while working with the image in the image editing software. When sketching (either on paper or in the software), determine what shapes (i.e., circle, rectangle, or polygon) make sense for the specific area that you want to link. Based on this determination, start the next step of plotting those areas on the image.
3. **Map the image coordinates for each hotspot**. This chapter explains what x- and y-coordinates you need to provide for every linkable area. One thing to consider is making sure that the linkable areas do not run over one another. This overrun ends up confusing your Web site visitors because they think they will link to one area, and the coordinates take them somewhere else.
4. **Create the HTML code for the image map**. Writing HTML code for an image map is different from anything that you have done thus far in the book. When you create an image map, you first insert the image itself and then identify the name of the map that you use later in the HTML code. Further down in the code, you actually use that name and identify the map areas that form the boundaries around the hotspot.

Creating an Image Map

An image map consists of two components: an image and a map definition that defines the hotspots and the URLs to which they link.

Selecting Images

Not all images are appropriate candidates for image mapping. An appropriate image, and a good choice for an image map, is one that has obvious visual sections. The United States map image shown in Figure 5–9a on the next page, for example, has distinct, easy-to-see sections, which serve as ideal hotspots. A user easily could select an individual area on the map to link to more information about each region. The image in Figure 5–9b, however, would not be a good choice because the boundaries of the states are indistinct.

BTW

Images

Not all images are appropriate for image mapping. An appropriate image has obvious visual sections that can be easily divided into clickable areas. An inappropriate image does not have obvious visual sections and therefore is not a good choice as an image map.

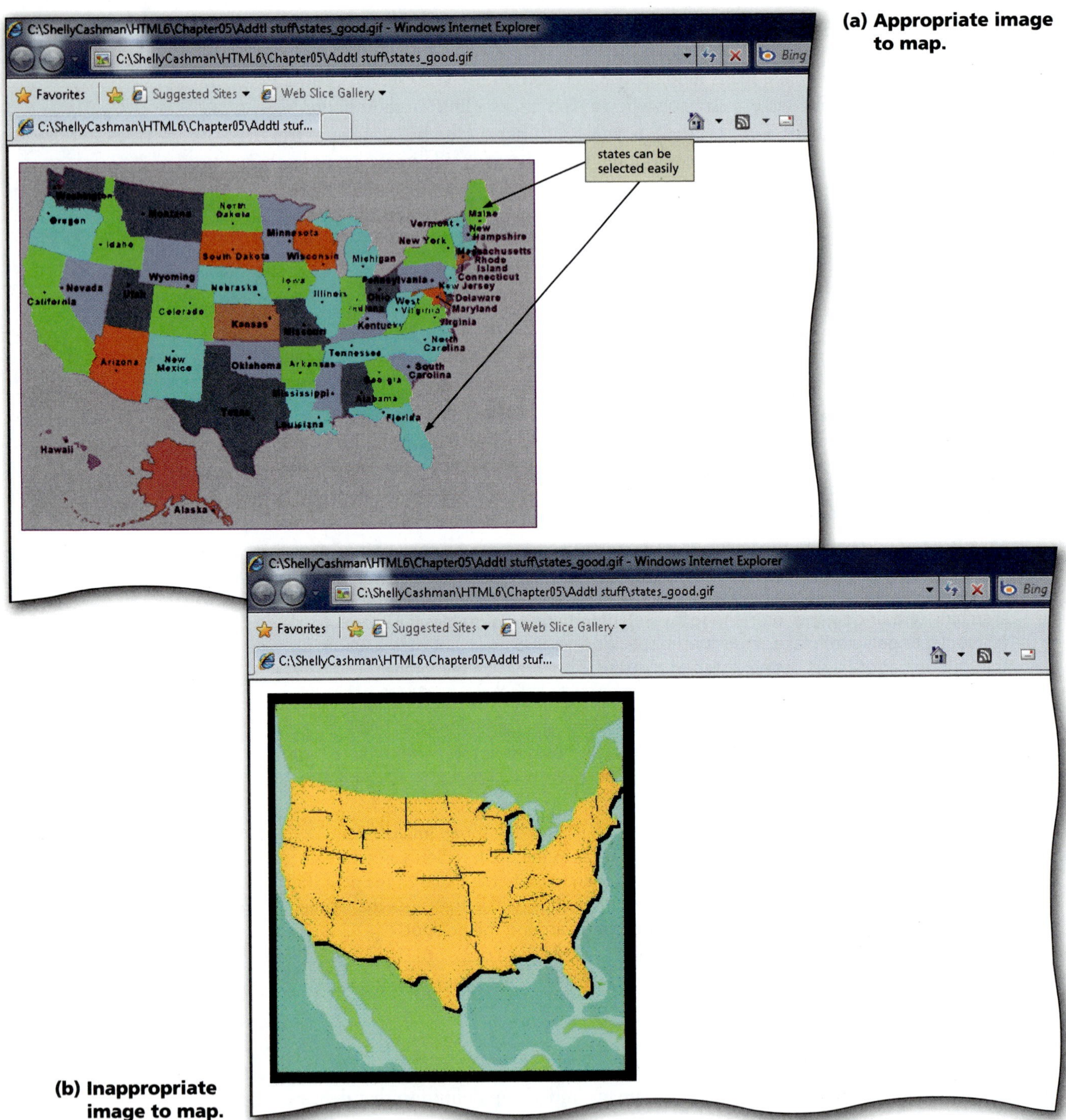

(a) Appropriate image to map.

(b) Inappropriate image to map.

Figure 5–9

Sketching the Borders of Hotspots

After an appropriate image is selected for the image map, the next step is to sketch the hotspots (clickable areas) within the image. Figure 5–10 shows an example of an image map with the borders of the hotspots sketched on the image. A map of Europe is used, with two countries (Spain and Sweden) defined as hotspots. The image map thus will include a hotspot for two countries, each of which can link to a different Web page.

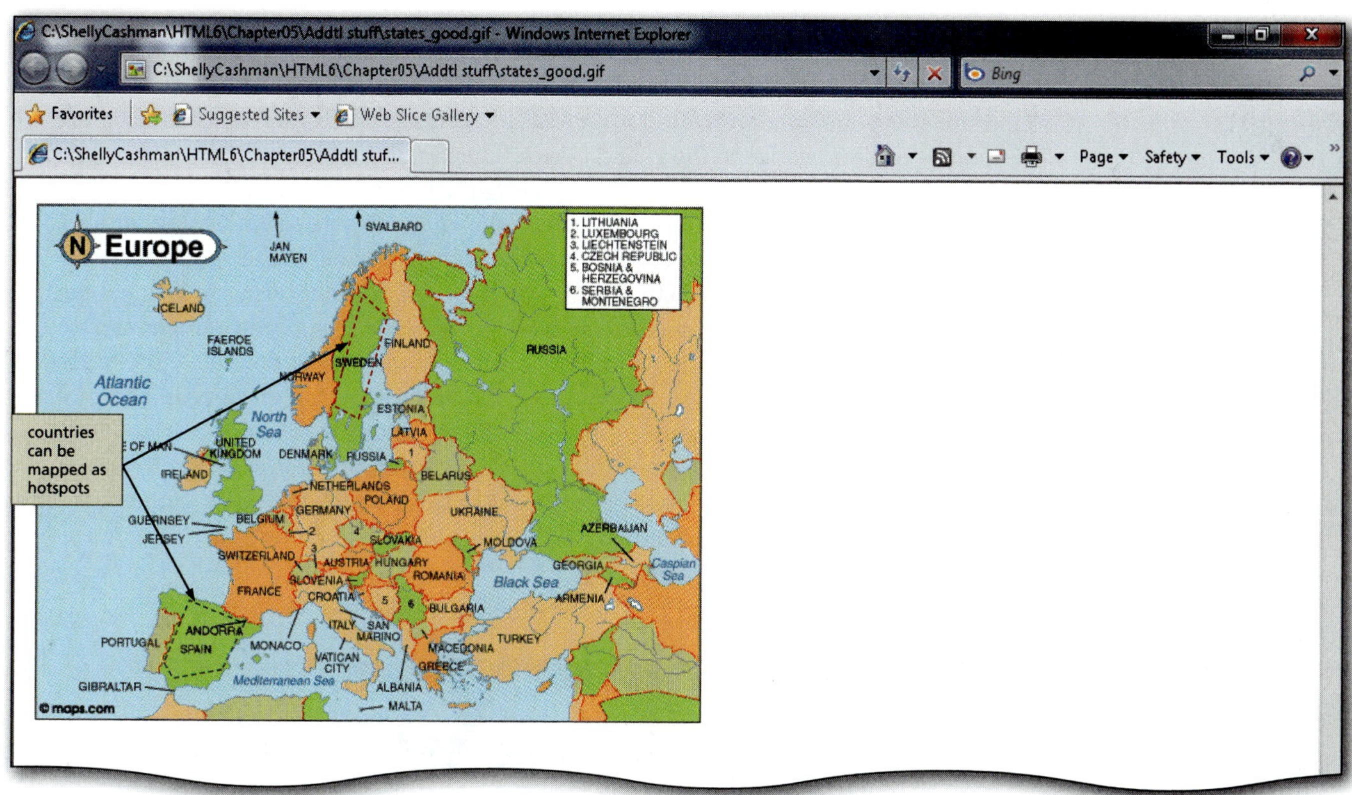

Figure 5–10 Sketched areas for image map hotspots.

Figure 5–11 shows an enlarged version of the Bright Idea menu bar image. It is made larger in this screenshot so that it is easier to show how you can sketch hotspots on this particular image. This menu bar image, menubar.jpg, is used as the image map in this chapter, and is shown here with the hotspots sketched in. The image is included in the Data Files for Students. Four circular shapes (labeled as Home, E-mail, Information, and Search) are defined as hotspots, which will link to an e-mail window or the Web pages that contain information about each option. The process of mapping the image coordinates for each hotspot is based on this initial sketch. The four icons used in this image menu bar are easily recognizable. The first link, Home, uses an icon that shows an outline of a house. This is commonly used for home page links on the Web. The second icon, an envelope, is also commonly used to depict an e-mail link. The third icon is a lowercase "i" which is often used for an Information link. The fourth icon is a magnifying glass, a symbol often used to depict a Search link.

Figure 5–11 Sketched circular areas to be used as hotspots.

Mapping Image Coordinates

After you have determined how to divide the image into hotspot areas, you must determine the x- and y-coordinates for each of the sections. The x- and y-coordinates are based on a position relative to the x- and y-axes. The **x-axis** runs horizontally along the base of the image, while the **y-axis** runs vertically along the left of the image. The top-left corner of an image thus is the coordinate point (0,0), as shown in Figure 5–12. The first number of a **coordinate pair** is the x-coordinate, and the second number is the y-coordinate. Figure 5–12 shows the starting (0,0) x- and y-coordinates in a Paint window that contains the image menubar.jpg. The y-coordinate numbers increase as you move the mouse pointer down the image, and the x-coordinate numbers increase as you move the mouse pointer to the right on the image. As you move the mouse pointer, the coordinates of its position as it relates to the image are displayed on the status bar.

You can use a simple or a sophisticated image editing or paint program to determine the x- and y-coordinates of various image points. In this project, the Paint program is used to find the x- and y-coordinates that you will use in the map definition that divides a single image into several areas.

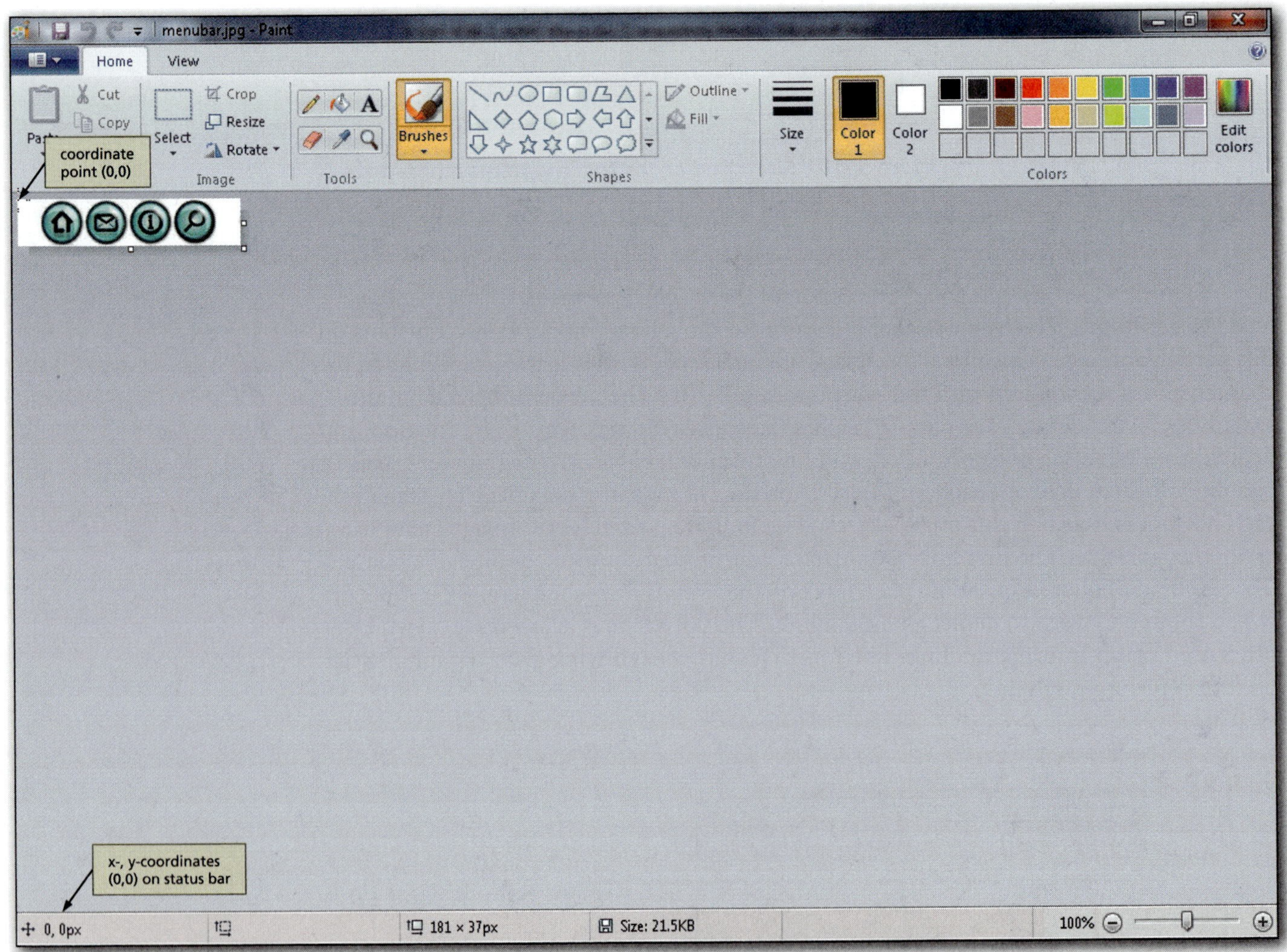

Figure 5–12

Map areas can use one of three shapes: rectangle, circle, or polygon. These shapes are shown in Figure 5–13. To define a map area of an image, you must determine the x- and y-coordinates for that shape and then insert the coordinates for the various map shapes in the HTML code.

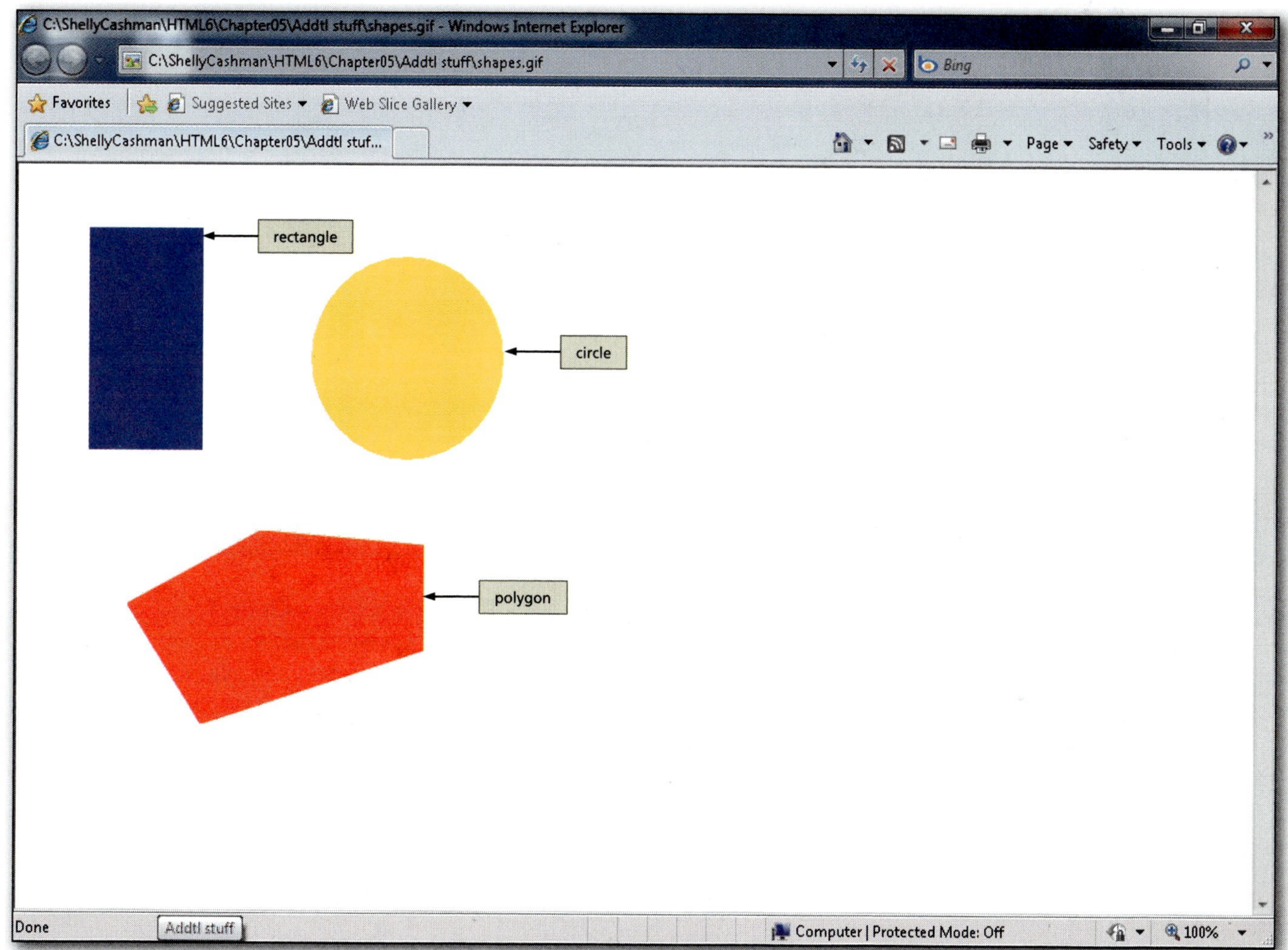

Figure 5–13

For a rectangular map area, you use the coordinates of the top-left and the bottom-right corners. For example, as shown in Figure 5–14a on the next page, the rectangle's x- and y-coordinates are (46,35) for the top-left corner and (137,208) for the bottom-right corner. You use "rect" as the value for the shape attribute for rectangles. For a circular map area, you use the center point and the radius as the coordinates. The x- and y-coordinates of the center point of the circle in Figure 5–14a are (308,113). If the mouse pointer is moved along the y-axis (113) to the border of the circle, the x-axis is 380. The radius can be calculated by subtracting the x-axis value of the center point (308) from the x-axis value of the circle's right border (380), which gives a radius of 72 (380 − 308). For circles, you use "circle" as the value for the shape attribute. For a polygonal map area, you must use the coordinates for each corner of the shape. For example, in Figure 5–14a, the polygon has five corners with the coordinates (78,309), (183,251), (316,262), (317,344), and (136,402). For polygonal shapes, you use "poly" as the value for the shape attribute. Figure 5–14b shows how you would use those x- and y-coordinates in the map statements needed to define these three shapes as clickable areas.

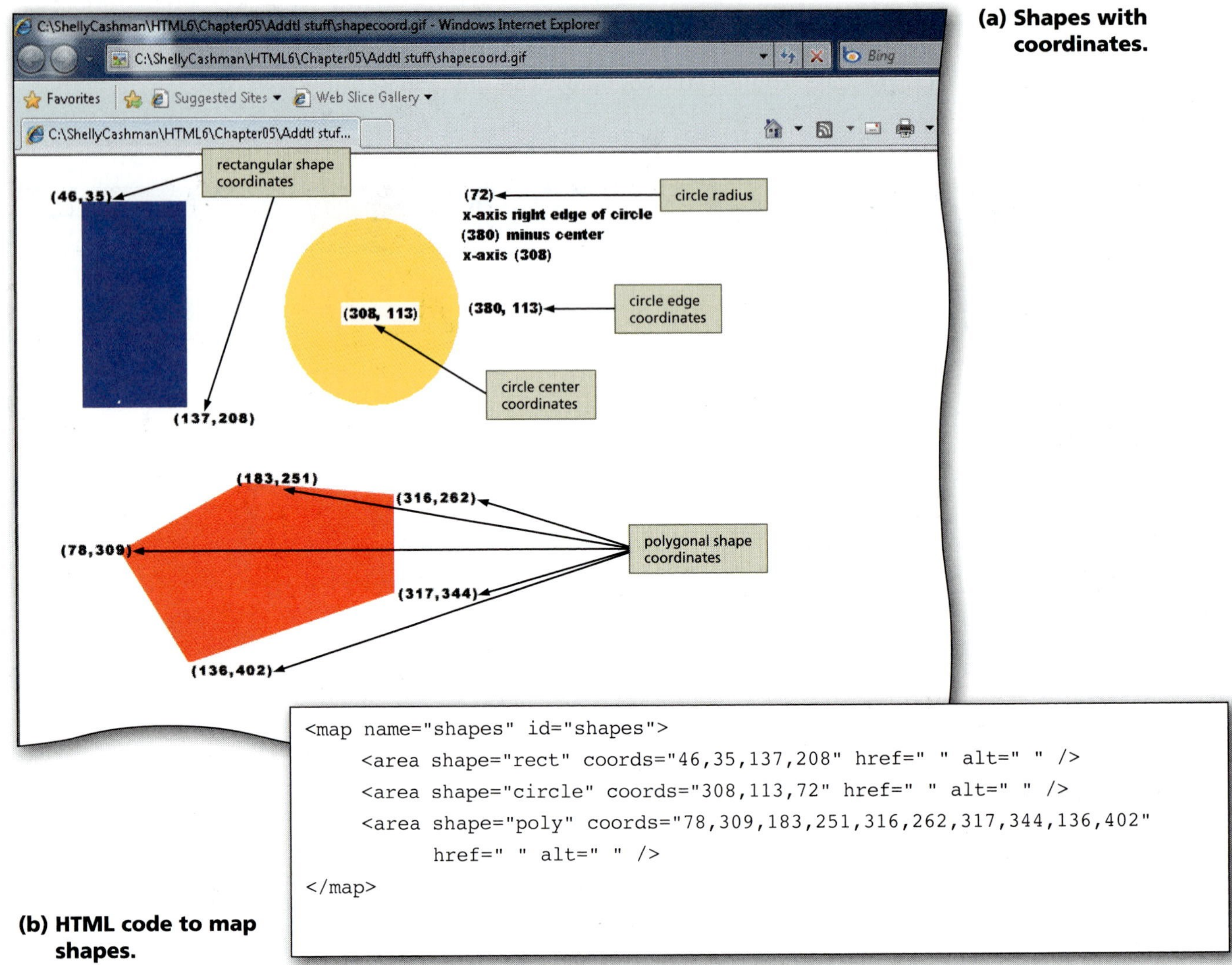


```
<map name="shapes" id="shapes">
     <area shape="rect" coords="46,35,137,208" href=" " alt=" " />
     <area shape="circle" coords="308,113,72" href=" " alt=" " />
     <area shape="poly" coords="78,309,183,251,316,262,317,344,136,402"
          href=" " alt=" " />
</map>
```

(a) Shapes with coordinates.

(b) HTML code to map shapes.

Figure 5–14

In the Bright Idea image (menubar.jpg), the image map will use four circular shapes for the four hotspots, as sketched in Figure 5–11 on page HTML 245. Clickable areas are mapped in circular shapes enclosing the following areas: Home, E-mail, Information, and Search.

Coding the Map

The final step in creating an image map is writing the HTML code for the map. To create a client-side image map, the tags <map> </map> and <area> are used. The map start tag (**<map>**) and map end tag (**</map>**) create the client-side image map. The **<area>** tag defines the specific areas of the map and the links and anchors for those areas. The x- and y-coordinates for each map area are inserted into the <area> tag with the **coords** attribute, within quotation marks and separated by commas. The HTML tags, attributes, and values needed to code the map are discussed later in this chapter.

Plan Ahead

Working with the image.
In order to determine the x- and y-coordinates for image map points, you need to open the image in the chosen software tool.

- **Select a software tool.** Computers running the Windows operating system already have an image editing tool available, Paint. This chapter shows you how to work with your image within Paint. For other suggested editing software products, see Table 5–2 on page HTML 254.
- **Edit the image.** It is sometimes necessary to alter the image before using it on the Web page (you may want to resize it or reposition it). Paint also gives you the image dimensions (i.e., width and height) you need for the <img> tag.
- **Make other changes to the image.** In Paint, you can make other changes to the image such as flipping the image horizontally or vertically, or altering the colors of the image. Other graphic editing software options provide a variety of tools to alter an image slightly or significantly.

Using Paint to Locate X- and Y-Coordinates

As you have learned, you can use a simple or a sophisticated image editing or paint program to determine the x- and y-coordinates of various points on an image. In this chapter, the Paint program is used to find the x- and y-coordinates used in the map definition that divides a single image into several areas.

To Start Paint

The following steps illustrate how to start Paint.

1

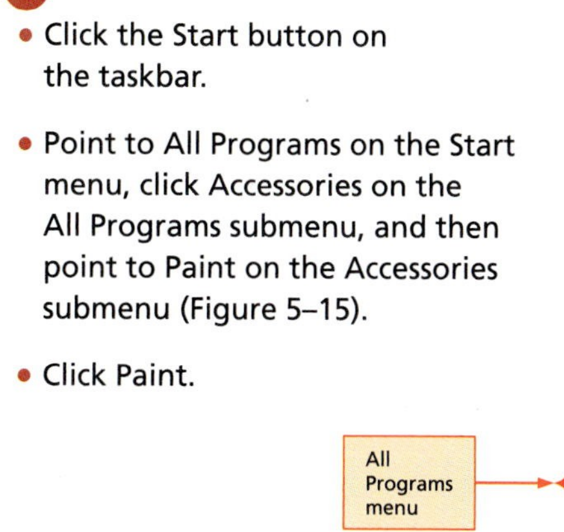

- Click the Start button on the taskbar.
- Point to All Programs on the Start menu, click Accessories on the All Programs submenu, and then point to Paint on the Accessories submenu (Figure 5–15).
- Click Paint.

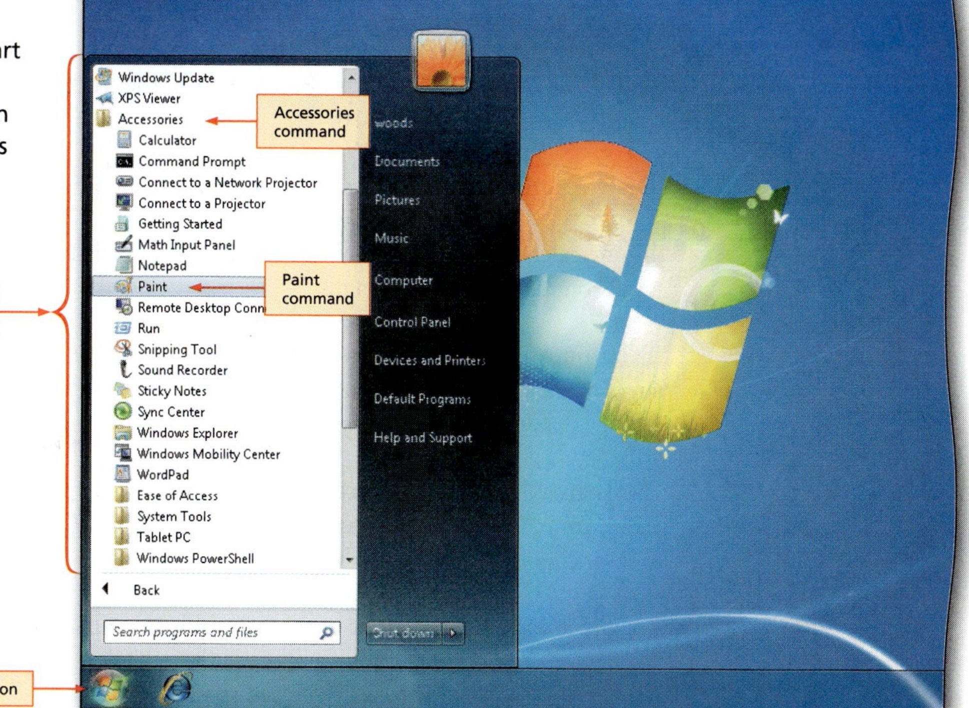

Figure 5–15

2

- If necessary, click the Maximize button on the right side of the title bar to maximize the window (Figure 5–16).

Q&A

Do all computers running Windows include Paint?

Yes, Paint should be included with all Windows operating systems.

Q&A

How can I find out more about using Paint?

The Paint Help utility is quite good. You can search for information using its Search option or Index. Paint Help gives step-by-step instructions for many tasks.

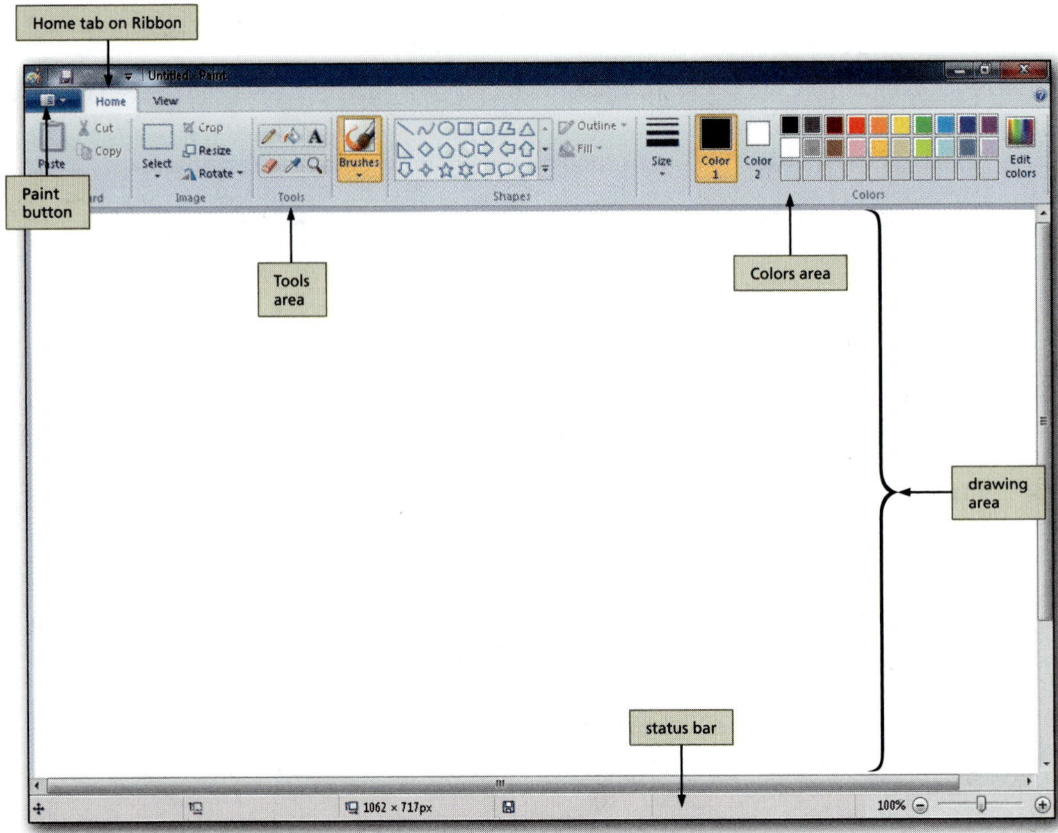

Figure 5–16

BTW

Paint Help
The Help feature of Paint can answer your questions about the use of this popular tool. Paint can be used to identify the x- and y-coordinates in an image used as an image map. It also can be used to create images that are used as image maps.

The Paint Window

The Paint window contains several elements similar to the document windows in other applications. The main elements of the Paint window are the drawing area, the Home tab on the Ribbon, the Paint button, the Tools area, the Colors area, and the status bar, as shown in Figure 5–16.

Drawing area — The **drawing area** is where the image is displayed.

Home tab — The **Home tab** on the Ribbon holds tools and commands most frequently used to create and edit images.

Paint button — The **Paint button** to the left of the Home tab contains a drop-down arrow to access functions such as Open, Save, and Print that were on the File menu in earlier versions of Windows.

Tools area — The **Tools area** on the Home tab displays tools that are used to edit or draw an image. In this project, the Pencil tool in the Tools area is used to find the x- and y-coordinates of the menu bar image.

Colors area — The **Colors area** on the Home tab displays a palette of colors that can be used to set the colors of the foreground, the background, or other elements in a drawing.

Status bar —The **status bar** displays the coordinates of the center of the mouse pointer at its current position on the image.

To Open an Image File in Paint

The image file (menubar.jpg) used for the image map in this chapter is stored in the Data Files for Students. This image is a menu bar that includes circular icons (from left to right) that are used for the following navigation functions: Home, E-mail, Information, and Search. The following step illustrates how to open an image file in Paint.

- With a USB drive plugged into your computer, click the Paint button arrow and then click Open.
- If Computer is not displayed in the left-hand navigation window, scroll until Computer is displayed.
- Click Computer to display a list of available drives.
- If necessary, scroll until UDISK 2.0 (G:) or your drive appears in the list of available drives.
- Double-click the drive, then double-click the Chapter05 folder, and then double-click the ChapterFiles folder in the list of available folders.
- Click the menubar.jpg image, and then click the Open button in the Open dialog box to display the image that will be used for image mapping in this chapter, as shown in Figure 5–17.

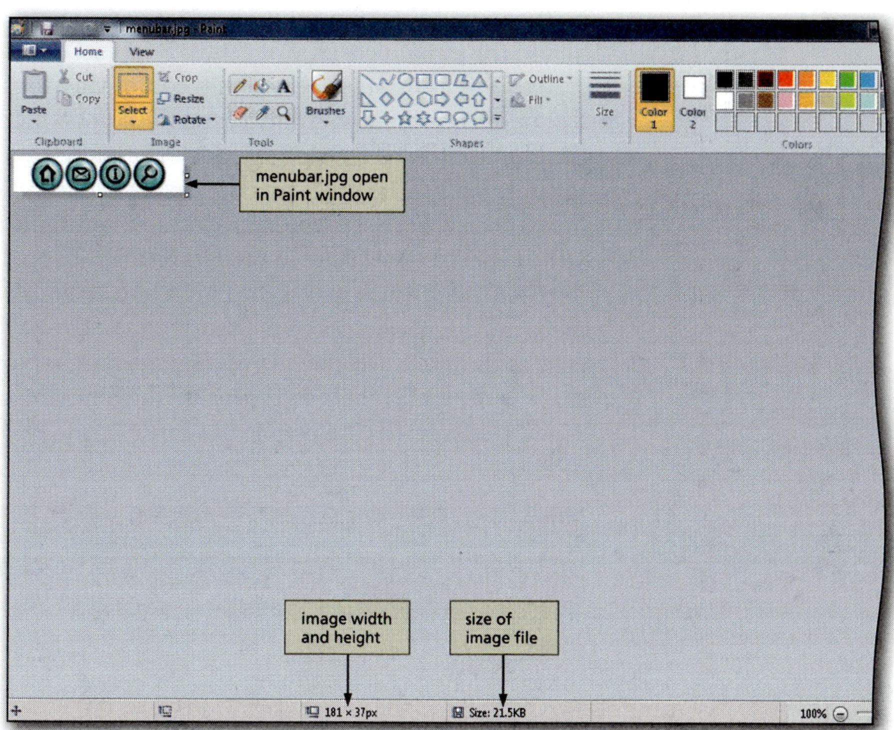

Figure 5–17

Locating X- and Y-Coordinates of an Image

The next step is to locate the x- and y-coordinates of the areas that should be mapped on the image. As shown in Figure 5–18, the image map should include four clickable circular areas that will link to other Web pages. For each of the four linkable map areas, the center x- and y-coordinate pair must be determined first. You then locate a point on the circumference of the circle to determine the circle radius.

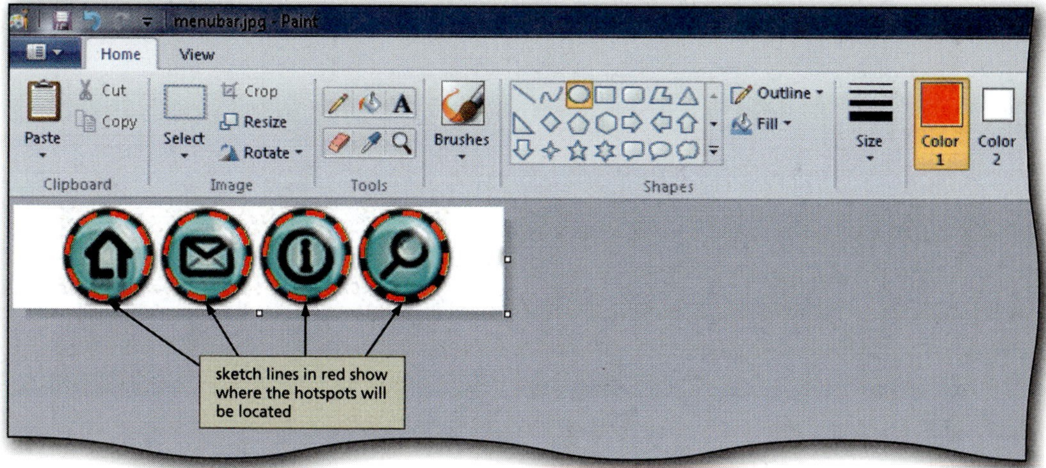

Figure 5–18

As you have learned, the x- and y-coordinates begin with (0,0) in the top-left corner of the image, as shown in Figure 5–12 on page HTML 246. As stated previously, moving the mouse pointer to the right (horizontally) increases the x-coordinate, and moving the mouse pointer down (vertically) increases the y-coordinate. Because the four clickable areas in the menu bar image sketched in red on the menubar.jpg image are circular, the map definition must include the x- and y-coordinate of the center of each circular shape. You then find a point on the edge of the circle and determine the radius of the circle. Those three numbers (x, y of center + radius) define the hotspot of the circular shape.

Table 5–1 shows the x- and y-coordinates for the four circular-shaped map areas. The first number is the x-coordinate, and the second number is the y-coordinate. For example, the Home circle consists of one pair of x- and y-coordinates in the center of the Home circle together with the number that depicts the circle radius. The first x-coordinate is 35 and the first y-coordinate is 18. You then find a point on the circumference of the circle, which gives you the next x-coordinate in the Home map shape. That x-coordinate point on the edge of the circle is 50, which makes the radius of that circle 15 (i.e., 50 − 35). For each circle, you find the x- and y-coordinates of the center of the circle. You then locate a point on the circumference of the circle, which will give you the radius. Notice that the radius (15) of each circular shape is the same (Table 5–1) because the four circular shapes are all the same size. These x- and y-coordinates are used in the <area> tag to create the map definition for the image map.

Table 5–1 Circle Center X- and Y-Coordinates and Circle Radius

Location	Coordinates and Radius
Home	35,18,15
E-mail	71,18,15
Information	107,18,15
Search	144,18,15

To Locate X- and Y-Coordinates of an Image

The following steps illustrate how to locate the x- and y-coordinates of the boundary points of each clickable circular area by moving the mouse pointer to the various points to see the x- and y-coordinates of those points. Although you do not need to record the coordinates for this project, you generally would do that. In this case though, you will compare the coordinates with those shown in Table 5–1, which lists the exact coordinates used in the <area> tags for this project.

- If necessary, click the Pencil button in the Tools area (Figure 5–19).

Figure 5–19

2

- Move the mouse pointer to the center of the Home icon circle and note the x- and y-coordinates for that point, as indicated in the status bar. Move the mouse until the coordinates read (35,18) (Figure 5–20a). (Do not click the mouse button.)
- Move the mouse pointer along the x-axis of the Home icon. The coordinates should read (50,18) (your coordinates may differ slightly), as indicated on the status bar (Figure 5–20b). (Do not click the mouse button.) Calculate the radius of the circle by subtracting the initial x-coordinate found in Figure 5–20a (35) from the x-coordinate found in Figure 5-20b (50). The radius is therefore 15. The three coordinates to be used for this circular hotspot are 35,18,15, as shown in Table 5–1.
- Move the mouse pointer to the center and edge of the three other circular shapes (E-mail, Information, and Search) hotspots on the menu bar image by following the x- and y-coordinates in Table 5–1 on page HTML 252.

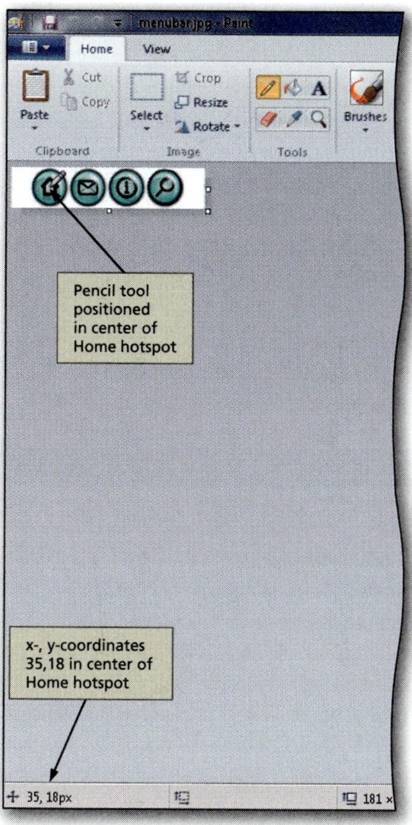

(a) Getting center coordinates.

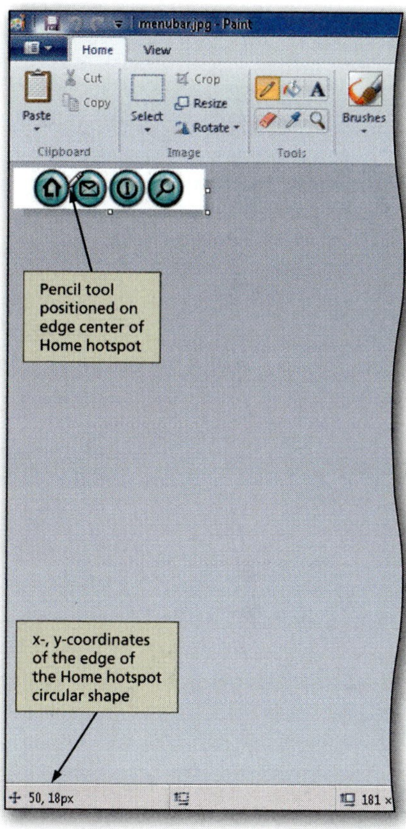

(b) Getting edge coordinate (radius).

Figure 5–20

- After you have finished, click the Close button on the right side of the title bar. If prompted, do not save any changes to the file.

Q&A I am not sure of the purpose of this exercise because the coordinates are already given to us for the project. Why am I doing these steps using Paint?

For the purpose of the project, the coordinates are given. The normal image mapping process, however, consists of: finding an appropriate image, sketching out where you think the boundaries will be, and finding the coordinates on your own using a software tool that shows that information. The purpose of this exercise is to become familiar with using Paint to find the coordinates.

Q&A I notice that in addition to the Pencil tool, I can use the Free-Form Select and the Select tools to show the x- and y-coordinates on the status bar. Is it okay to use them?

It is fine to use any of the three tools for this purpose. You are only trying to see the x- and y-coordinates for the hotspot areas.

Experiment

- Play with the Image and Colors areas on the Home tab. They give you many options to alter the image. Make sure to save the file with a different file name so that the image file included in the Data Files for Students folder remains untouched.

BTW

Graphics Software
Many graphics tools are available for advanced image creation and maintenance. One of the more popular tools is Adobe Photoshop. Photoshop allows you to create images that can be used as image maps or crop sections out of existing images.

Other Software Tools

Although Paint allows you to identify the coordinates for a map area manually, there are dedicated image map software tools that can simplify this process (see Table 5–2). These tools allow you to click the image to define the clickable areas of the image map and then automatically generate the x- and y-coordinates and HTML code needed for the image map. If possible, download one of the software tools listed in Table 5–2 and use that software to map the clickable areas in the menubar.jpg image. As further practice, open the file shapecoord.gif found in the Chapter05\ChapterFiles folder of the Data Files for Students in Paint (Figure 5–21) and use your mouse pointer to identify the coordinates to map the clickable areas in the shapecoord.gif image. You also could experiment with using one or more of the tools in Table 5–2 to map clickable areas in the image.

Table 5–2 Image Map Software Tools

Tool	Platform
Mapedit	Windows, UNIX, Mac OS
CoffeeCup Image Mapper	Windows
Imaptool	Linux/X-Window

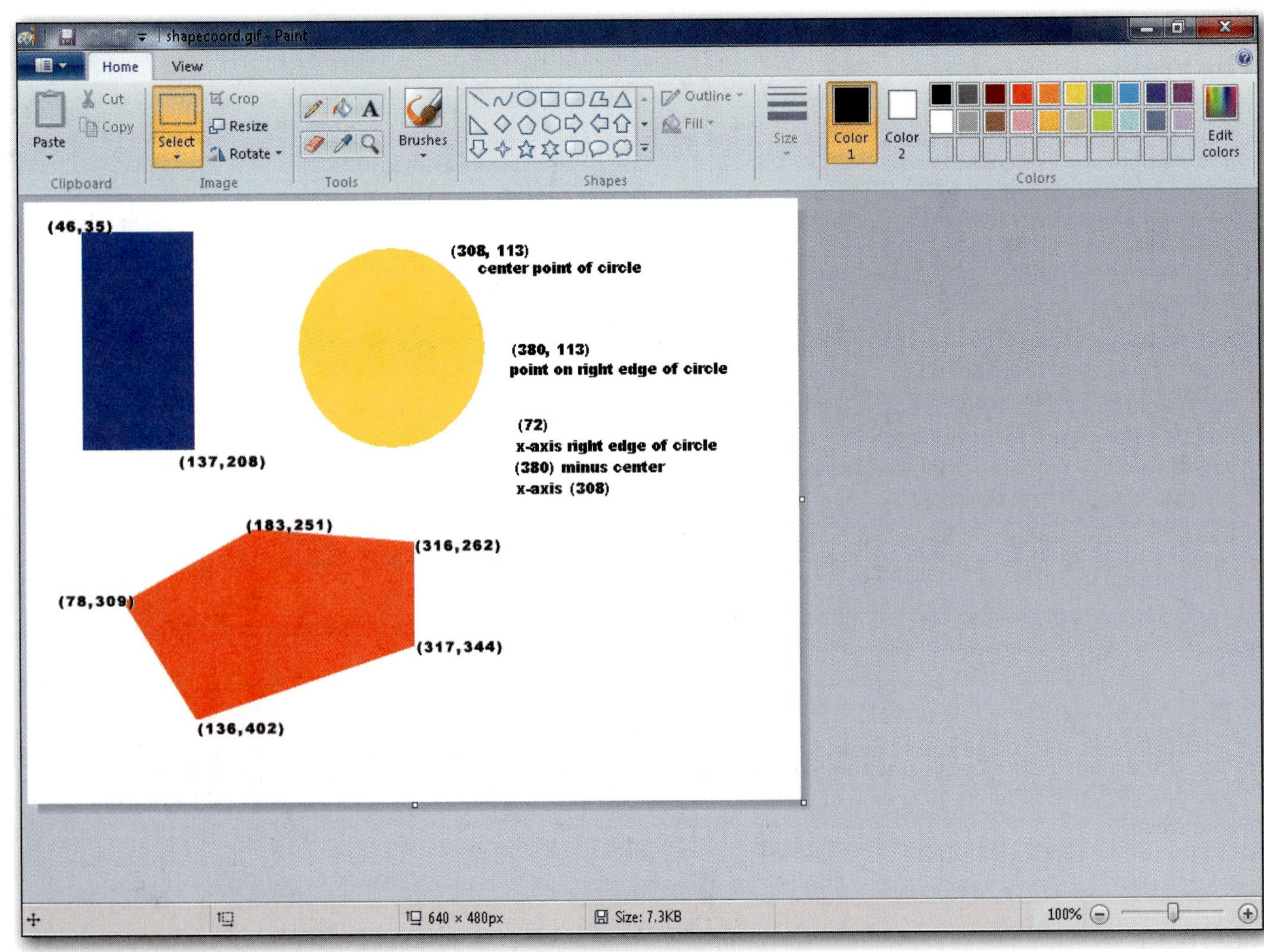

Figure 5–21

Plan Ahead

Starting the home page.
Just as with the other projects in previous chapters, you need to review good Web development standards before you start a new Web page.

- **Use the HTML structure tags required.** You will validate your Web pages for this project, so make sure that you use the HTML tags needed to make the page XHTML compliant. This includes using the <meta> tag and a DOCTYPE statement.
- **Copy what you can.** In earlier chapters, you copied HTML code from one completed page to another to make it easier. You should do the same in this project. Once a Web page is validated, you know that the initial HTML tags are correct. It makes sense then to copy/paste those lines of code to the next Web page file. If you are utilizing the same menu bar throughout a Web site, it also makes sense to copy that code from one Web page to another.

Creating the Home Page

Before the image map can be added to the home page of the Bright Idea Web site, the home page must be created. The home page includes a borderless table, a logo image, and paragraphs of text. At the bottom of the home page, a table of text links is inserted. The text links allow the Web page visitor to navigate to the home page, an e-mail link, the information.html Web page, and the search.html Web page.

To Start Notepad++

1. Click the Start button on the Windows taskbar to display the Start menu.
2. Click All Programs at the bottom of the left pane on the Start menu to display the All Programs list.
3. Click Notepad++ in the All Programs list.
4. Click Notepad++ in the list to display the Notepad++ window.
5. If the Notepad++ window is not maximized, click the Maximize button on the Notepad++ title bar to maximize it.
6. Click View on the menu bar.
7. If the Word wrap command does not have a check mark next to it, click Word wrap.

To Enter Initial HTML Tags to Define the Web Page Structure

To create the home page, you will start Notepad++ and enter the initial HTML tags to define the overall structure of the Web page, as shown in Table 5–3 on the next page. Notice that one additional line of code is added to this section of code. Line 10 is the link statement that links the external style sheet named styles5.css to the Web page. You will create the external style sheet later in this project.

Table 5–3 HTML Code to Define Web Page Structure

Line	HTML Tag and Text
1	`<!DOCTYPE html`
2	`PUBLIC "-//W3C//DTD XHTML 1.0 Transitional//EN"`
3	`"http://www.w3.org/TR/xhtml1/DTD/xhtml1-transitional.dtd">`
4	
5	`<html xmlns="http://www.w3.org/1999/xhtml" lang="en" xml:lang="en">`
6	`<head>`
7	`<meta http-equiv="Content-Type" content="text/html;charset=utf-8" />`
8	`<title>Bright Idea</title>`
9	
10	`<link rel="stylesheet" type="text/css" href="styles5.css" />`
11	
12	`</head>`
13	
14	`<body>`
15	
16	
17	`</body>`
18	`</html>`

1. Enter the HTML code shown in Table 5–3. Press ENTER at the end of each line. If you make an error as you are typing, use the BACKSPACE key to delete all the characters back to and including the incorrect characters, and then continue typing.
2. Position the insertion point on the blank line 16 (Figure 5–22).
3. Compare what you typed to Figure 5–22. If you notice errors, use your mouse pointer or ARROW keys to move the insertion point to the right of each error and use the BACKSPACE key to correct the error.

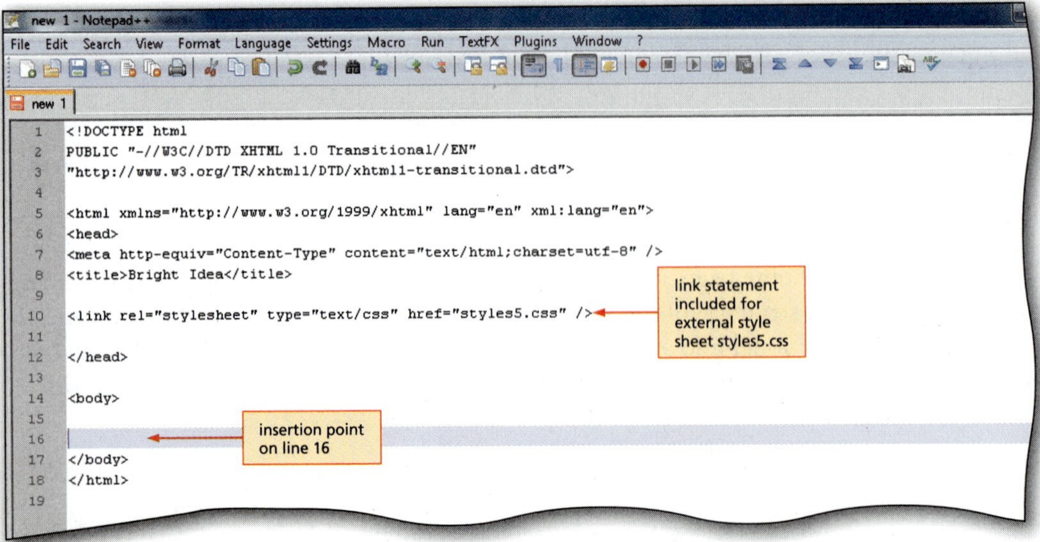

Figure 5–22

To Save an HTML File

With the initial HTML code for the Bright Idea home page entered, you should save the file. Saving the file frequently ensures you won't lose your work. Saving a file in Notepad++ also adds color to code that can help you identify different elements more easily.

1. With a USB flash drive connected to one of the computer's USB ports, click File on the Notepad++ menu bar and then click Save.
2. Type `brightidea.html` in the File name text box (do not press ENTER).
3. Click Computer in the left-hand navigation pane to display a list of available drives.
4. If necessary, scroll until UDISK 2.0 (G:) or the name of your storage device is displayed in the list of available drives.
5. Open the Chapter05\ChapterFiles folder.
6. Click the Save button in the Save As dialog box to save the file on the USB flash drive in the Chapter05\ChapterFiles folder with the name brightidea.html.

Creating a Table

The next task in developing the home page is to create a centered, borderless table with one row and three columns, as shown in Figure 5–23. The first data cell contains the image brightidealogo.jpg. The second data cell contains an <h1> heading with the company name Bright Idea. The third cell contains the special character that is the registered trademark symbol. You learn more about inserting special characters later in the chapter.

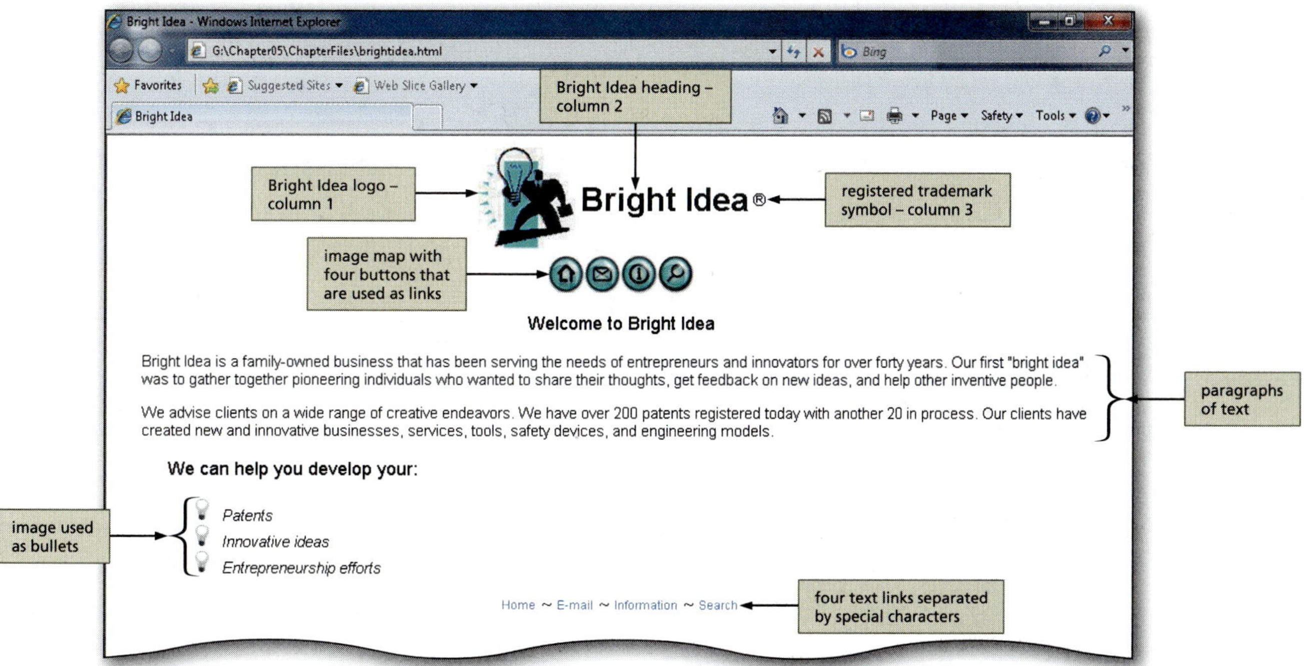

Figure 5–23

The three cells of the table are created using <td> tags that create table data cells. As you learned in Chapter 4, the <td> tag aligns the contents of a cell in the center of the cell vertically and to the left horizontally, by default. As shown in Figure 5–23, the table should use a vertical alignment so the contents of all cells are aligned with the top of the cell. The HTML code thus should use a <tr> tag with the valign="top" attribute to create a table row that uses vertical alignment. Using this tag eliminates the need to set each table data cell to use vertical alignment.

To Create a Table

Table 5–4 shows the code to insert a table to hold the company logo.

Table 5–4 HTML Code to Insert Company Logo

Line	HTML Tag and Text
16	`<table style="margin-left: auto; margin-right: auto">`
17	`<tr>`
18	`<td>`
19	`<img src="brightidealogo.jpg" width="97" height="100" alt="Bright Idea logo" />`
20	`</td>`
21	
22	`<td>`
23	`<h1>Bright Idea</h1>`
24	`</td>`

The following step creates a borderless table, with a table row that uses vertical alignment.

1. With the insertion point on line 16, enter the HTML code, aligning as shown in Table 5–4, and press the ENTER key twice to position the insertion point on line 26 (Figure 5–24).

Q&A What happens when you set the margin-left and margin-right properties to auto?
Setting these properties to auto is how you center a table.

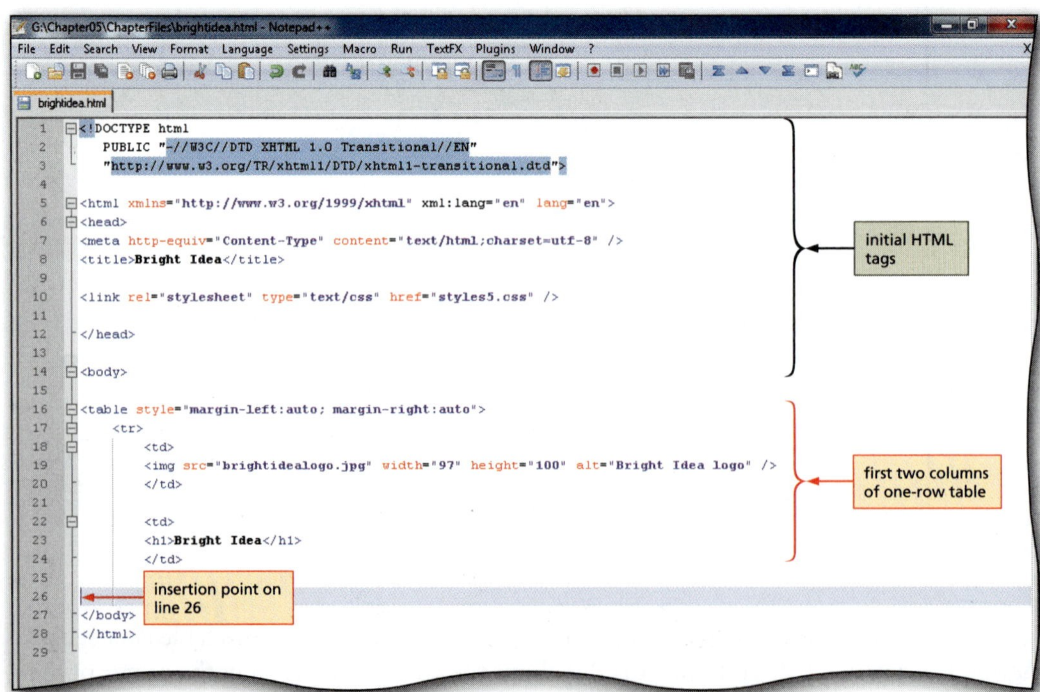

Figure 5–24

Inserting Special Characters

The next step in creating the home page is to add the registered trademark symbol, as shown in Figure 5–23 on page HTML 257. The registered trademark symbol (®) is one of the Special Characters found in Appendix F. You use the ® entity to display the registered trademark symbol. These predefined entity characters enhance the content on the Web pages that you create. A registered trademark symbol is a distinctive indicator used by an individual, a business organization, or another type of legal entity to identify that the products or services with which the trademark appears originate from a unique source. This symbol indicates that the trademark has been federally registered. This symbol differs from the ™ (trademark) symbol in that the ™ symbol is one in which the individual or business either has a pending federal trademark application or they are simply claiming the rights to the mark. The entity for the ™ symbol is &trade, as found in Appendix F.

You insert the ® entity in the third data cell of the table above. If you try to insert this symbol within the <h1> heading, the size of the symbol is the same as the heading size, which is too large (Figure 5–25a). If you try to insert the ® symbol just after the </h1> tag, it moves the symbol to a new line (Figure 5–25b). The best way is to insert this symbol in its own data cell in the table.

BTW

Using Special Characters

Some characters are reserved in HTML. If you want the browser to actually display these characters, you must insert the character entities in the HTML source. For example, you cannot use the greater than or less than signs within your text because the browser could mistake them for markup. You therefore use the special characters > (greater than) and < (less than) to display those characters.

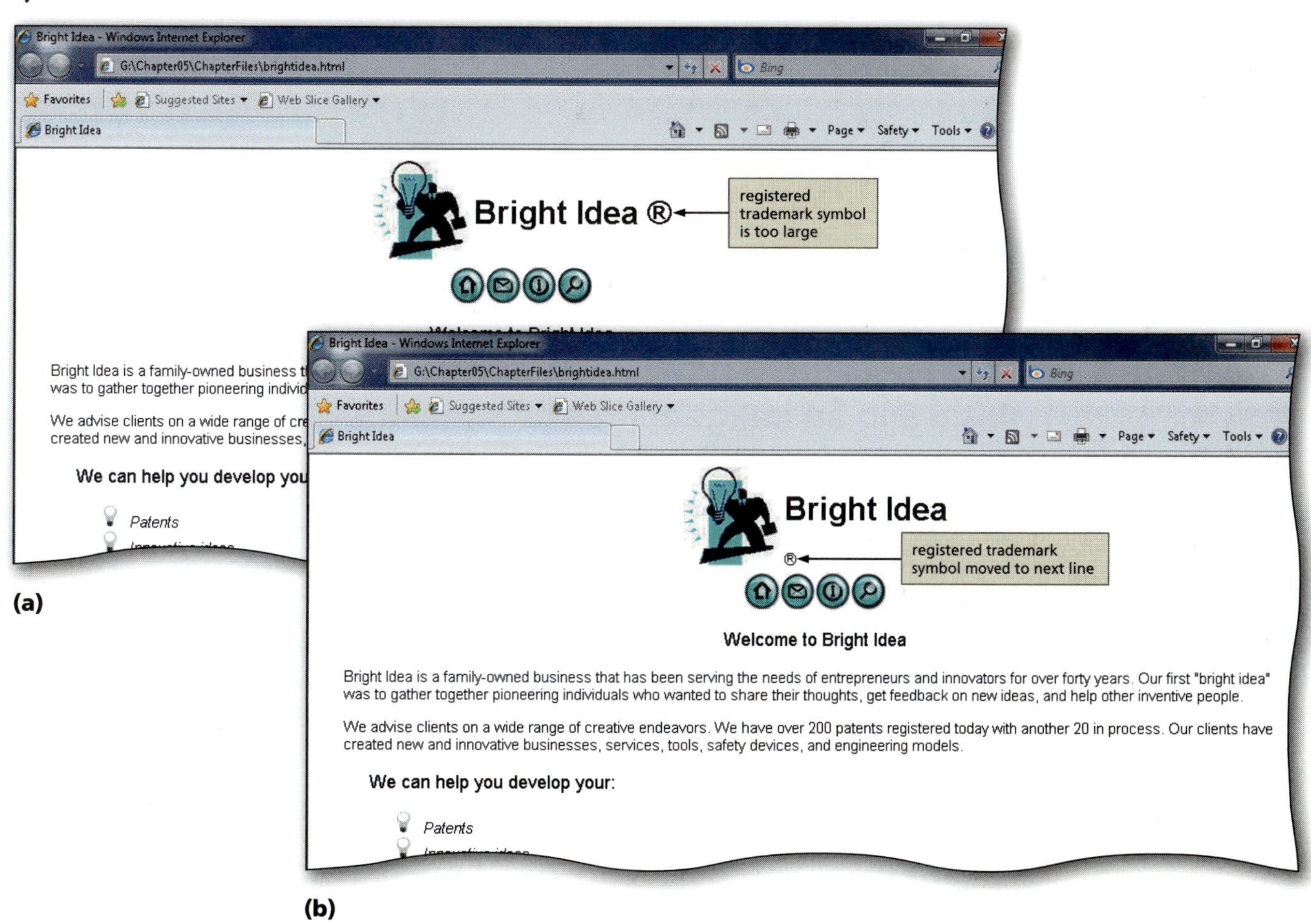

Figure 5–25

Also, in the first paragraph of text on the home page, you want to add quotation marks to your text by adding the " special character entity (see Appendix F). There are some browsers that may display the quotation marks if you insert the quotation marks themselves. In your Web development though, you need to account for browsers that would not display them unless you use the " symbol.

To Insert a Special Character

The following step inserts a registered trademark symbol.

1

- With the insertion point on line 26, press the TAB key twice and type `<td>®` and then press the ENTER key.
- Type `</td>` and then press the ENTER key.
- Press SHIFT-TAB once to move back a tab and type `</tr>` and then press the ENTER key.
- Press SHIFT-TAB to move back to the left margin and type `</table>` and press the ENTER key twice to position the cursor on line 31, as shown in Figure 5–26.

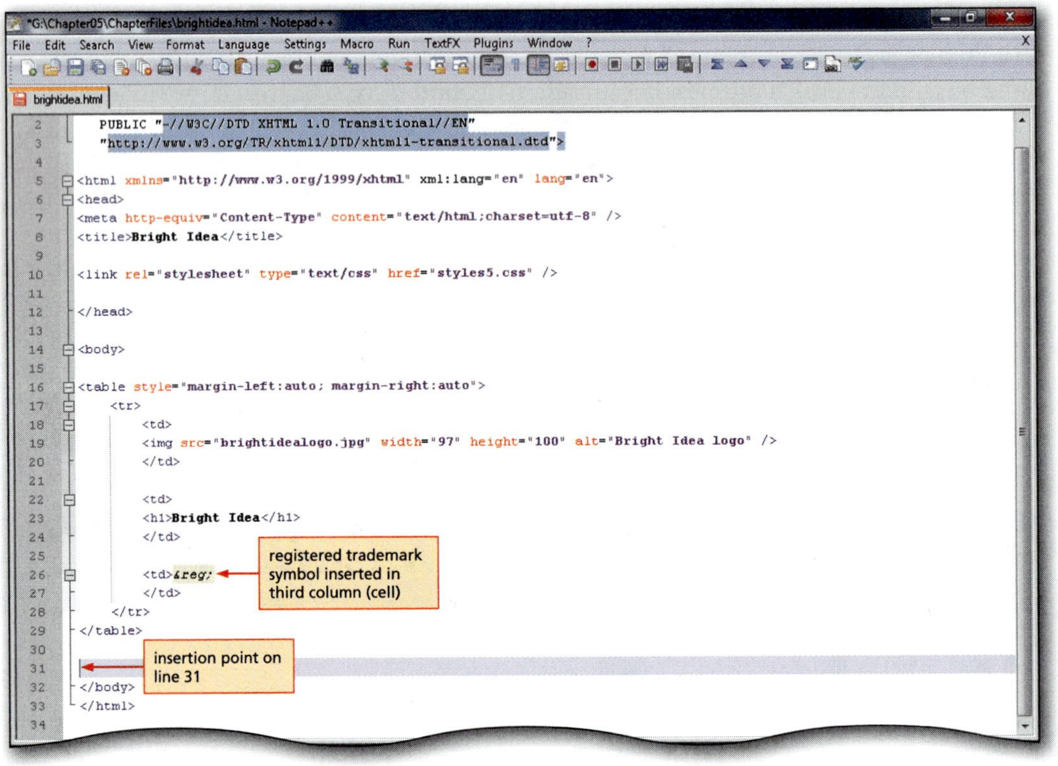

```
2      PUBLIC "-//W3C//DTD XHTML 1.0 Transitional//EN"
3      "http://www.w3.org/TR/xhtml1/DTD/xhtml1-transitional.dtd">
4
5   <html xmlns="http://www.w3.org/1999/xhtml" xml:lang="en" lang="en">
6   <head>
7   <meta http-equiv="Content-Type" content="text/html;charset=utf-8" />
8   <title>Bright Idea</title>
9
10  <link rel="stylesheet" type="text/css" href="styles5.css" />
11
12  </head>
13
14  <body>
15
16  <table style="margin-left:auto; margin-right:auto">
17      <tr>
18          <td>
19          <img src="brightidealogo.jpg" width="97" height="100" alt="Bright Idea logo" />
20          </td>
21
22          <td>
23          <h1>Bright Idea</h1>
24          </td>
25
26          <td>&reg;
27          </td>
28      </tr>
29  </table>
30
31
32  </body>
33  </html>
34
```

registered trademark symbol inserted in third column (cell)

insertion point on line 31

Figure 5–26

BTW

Image Map Tutorials
Many great resources are available on the Web that discuss image maps. For more information about tutorials, search for the term "image map tutorials" with any good search engine.

Inserting an Image to Use as an Image Map

The next step in creating the home page is to add the image, described in Table 5–5, which is used as the image map. The image, menubar.jpg, is stored in the Data Files for Students. This image consists of four circular icons that can be used as hotspots. Each icon has a picture of navigation function: Home, E-mail, Information, and Search. They are commonly used standards to identify navigation.

Table 5–5 shows the attributes associated with the <img> tag. The usemap attribute, a client-side image map, is what you use in this project. A **client-side image map** is an image map that is run by the browser (the client) rather than by a CGI script on the Web server. You provide all the information required to run the map, the image, and the hotspot coordinates in your HTML document. The map's functions are provided on the client's side, rather than on the server's side. When a visitor clicks a hotspot on the image map, the browser opens the corresponding URL.

A **server-side image map** uses CGI scripts to make the map work. The ismap attribute tells the browser to send the coordinates of the user mouse click directly to an associated map file on the server. If you look in Appendix C, Accessibility Standards and the Web, you will see that there is a reason to use client-side image maps instead of server-side image maps from a usability standpoint. The guideline in §1194.22(f) states, "Client-side image maps shall be provided instead of server-side image maps except where the regions cannot be defined with an available geometric shape." Also, the WAI Guidelines address this issue in guideline 9.1 where it says, "Provide client-side image maps instead of server-side image maps except where the regions cannot be defined with an available geometric shape."

Table 5–5 Tag Attributes Used to Create Image Maps

Tag	Attribute	Function
<img>	usemap ismap	• Indicates the URL of a client-side image map • Indicates a server-side image map

The Bright Idea home page will use a client-side image map. The HTML code to add the image thus will use attributes of the <img> tag — src, width, height, and usemap — as follows:

```
<img src="menubar.jpg" width="181" height="37" alt="Bright
        Idea menu" usemap="#menubar" />
```

where the src attribute identifies the image, and the width and height attributes define the image size.

The usemap attribute indicates to the browser which client-side image map will be used for that image. The client-side image map is placed within the <map> tag and defines the x- and y-coordinates of the areas on the image being used for the image map. When adding the image to use as an image map, the value of the usemap attribute — in this case, usemap="#menubar" — indicates that the browser should use the image map named menubar as its image map source.

BTW

Image Width and Height

As you have learned in earlier projects, specifying the width and height attributes helps improve page loading time. By identifying these attributes in the HTML code, the browser does not have to determine the width and height of the image.

To Insert an Image to Use as an Image Map

The following step shows how to insert an image to use for the image map.

1

- If necessary, click line 31.
- Type `<div style="text-align: center">` and then press the ENTER key.
- Press the TAB key once and type `<img src="menubar.jpg" width="181" height="37" alt="Menu bar" usemap="#menubar" />` and then press the ENTER key.

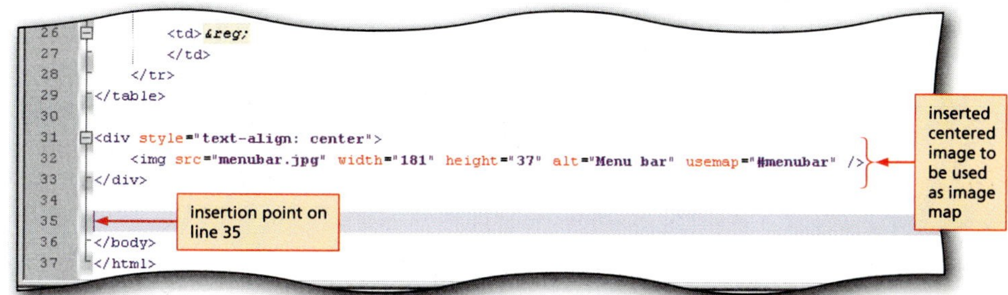

Figure 5–27

- Press SHIFT+TAB to move back to the left margin, type `</div>`, and then press the ENTER key twice (Figure 5–27).

Q&A I do not understand the purpose of the usemap attribute. Can you explain it?

The usemap attribute is what identifies the image with the map that will be inserted at the end of this Web page. The value (i.e., #menubar) in the usemap attribute tells the browser that this is an image map, and that it needs to look at the <map> tag name and id with that name (menubar) for the mapping.

Q&A If I want to speed up the download of a large image, can I change the dimensions of the image using the width and height attributes to make it smaller?

Although you can do this, you should not. Making a change to an image with these attributes still forces the browser to download the entire image and then display it as you indicate in the width and height attributes. If you want to speed up the download by making the image smaller, you should use Paint (or some other image editing software) to change the dimensions and then save the image. In Paint, use the Resize button in the Image group on the Home tab.

To Add a Header and Paragraphs of Text

Now you add the header and paragraphs of text for the home page. An h2 heading would be too large, so you use an inline style to set the text to large. You use the " special character entity to add quotation marks to your text. The HTML code for this text is shown in Table 5–6.

Table 5–6 HTML Code for a Header and Paragraphs

Line	HTML Tag and Text
35	`<p style="font-size: large; text-align: center">Welcome to Bright Idea</p>`
36	
37	`<p>Bright Idea is a family-owned business that has been serving the needs of entrepreneurs and innovators for over forty years. Our first "bright idea" was to gather together pioneering individuals who wanted to share their thoughts, get feedback on new ideas, and help other inventive people.</p>`
38	
39	`<p>We advise clients on a wide range of creative endeavors. We have over 200 patents registered today with another 20 in process. Our clients have created new and innovative businesses, services, tools, safety devices, and engineering models.</p>`

The following steps show how to enter the tags for the heading and paragraphs of text.

1. If necessary, click line 35.
2. Enter the HTML code shown in Table 5–6 and then press the ENTER key twice (Figure 5–28).

Experiment

- Take out the " in front of and after the words "bright idea" in the first paragraph and put in regular quotation marks and save the file. Open the file in your browser to see if the quotation marks display. Depending on your browser, this may or may not show quotation marks. That is why using the " entity is better.

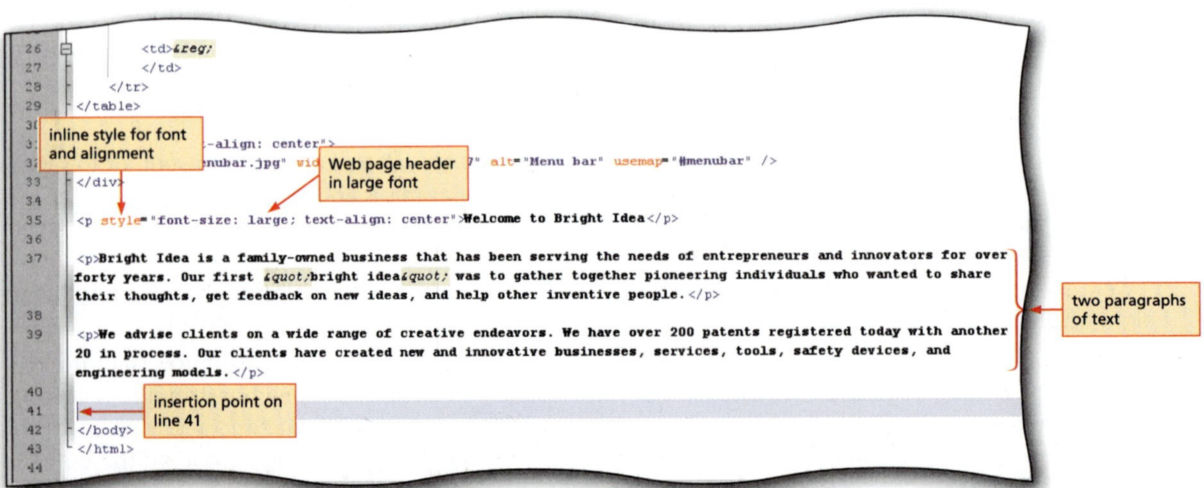

Figure 5–28

To Add a Title and an Unordered List

The home page also contains a section title and an unordered (bullet) list that identifies the company's special talents. Table 5–7 shows the code for this. You use an image (bulletbulb.png) for the bullets in the list. The font-size of the title is set to the same size (large) as the previous title for consistency. You also insert margin-left styles to bring the section title and the unordered list in to the right. You use more margin space on the unordered list to account for the image bullet.

Table 5–7 HTML Code for Inserting an Unordered List

Line	HTML Tag and Text
41	`<p style="font-size: large"><span style="margin-left: 20pt">We can help you develop your:</span></p>`
42	
43	`<div style="margin-left: 50pt">`
44	`<ul style="list-style-image: url(bulletbulb.png); font-size: 11pt; font-style: italic">`
45	`    <li>Patents</li>`
46	`    <li>Innovative ideas</li>`
47	`    <li>Entrepreneurship efforts</li>`
48	`</ul>`
49	`</div>`

The following steps show how to enter the tags for the unordered list.

1. If necessary, click line 41.
2. Enter the HTML code shown in Table 5–7 and then press the ENTER key twice (Figure 5–29).

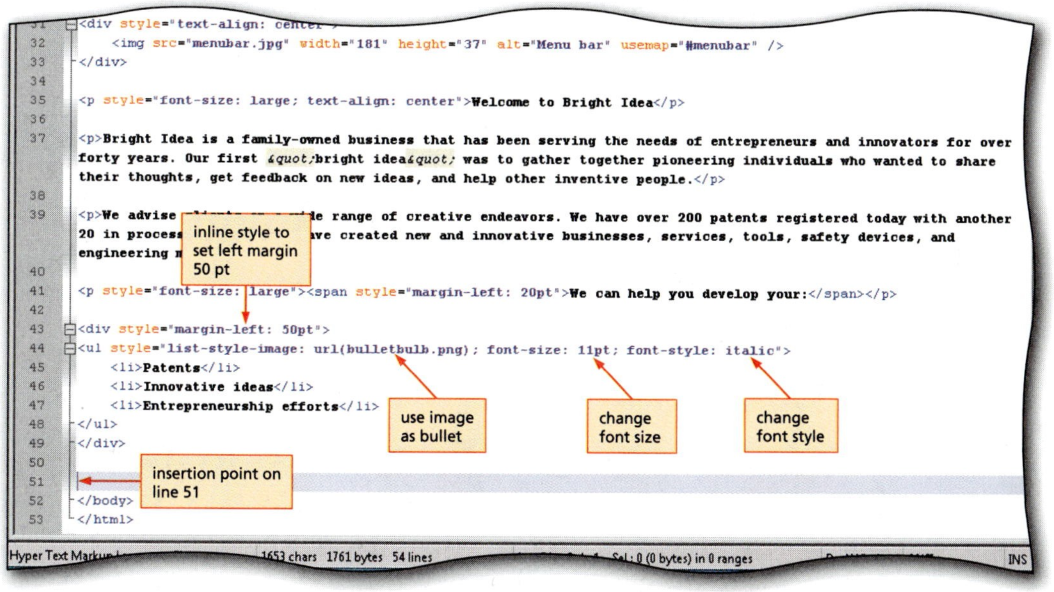

inline style to set left margin 50 pt

use image as bullet

change font size

change font style

insertion point on line 51

Figure 5–29

BTW

Text Links
It is very important to use text links on all Web pages in addition to using an image map for navigation. Some people turn graphics off while browsing the Web. If you did not have text links, those people could not access your other Web pages. In addition, you want to give your Web site visitors access to all Web pages in the Web site. Text links should provide that access.

BTW

Accessibility
Developers should utilize suggestions from accessibility guidelines when developing Web pages. It is important that the Web page content is understandable and navigable. The W3C gives some good suggestions for Web site accessibility issues that should be reviewed. For more information about accessibility, visit the W3C Web site, or refer to Appendix C, Accessibility Standards and the Web.

To Create a Horizontal Menu Bar with Text Links

The next step is to create a horizontal menu bar of text links at the bottom of the page that mirror the image map links. As previously discussed, it is important that a Web page include text links to all URLs in the image map, in the event the image does not download, a user is using a text reader of some sort, or a user's browser is set to not display images. Notice that you use another special character entity, the tilde (~), between the menu options, using the character entity ∼.

Table 5–8 shows the HTML code used to create the horizontal menu bar. As shown in lines 54 through 57, the HTML code adds the menu bar to a data cell in the table.

Table 5–8 HTML Code for Creating a Horizontal Menu Bar

Line	HTML Tag and Text
51	`<table style="margin-left: auto; margin-right: auto">`
52	`<tr>`
53	`<td>`
54	`<a href="brightidea.html">Home</a> ∼`
55	`<a href="mailto:brightidea@isp.com">E-mail</a> ∼`
56	`<a href="information.html">Information</a> ∼`
57	`<a href="search.html">Search</a>`
58	`</td>`
59	`</tr>`
60	`</table>`

The following steps show how to create the text links at the bottom of the home page.

1. If necessary, click line 51.
2. Enter the HTML code shown in Table 5–8 and then press the ENTER key twice (Figure 5–30).

Q&A

I notice that we use a horizontal menu bar for many projects in the book. Are there other ways to display a menu?

Many different ways exist to display your menu. The horizontal menu bar is used because it makes sense aesthetically in these projects. A great idea is to review other menu bar options on the Internet and view the HTML source. You can get a lot of ideas by looking at the Web pages and source code from other Web developers. Remember that the whole point of the menu bar is to provide easy navigation for your Web site visitors.

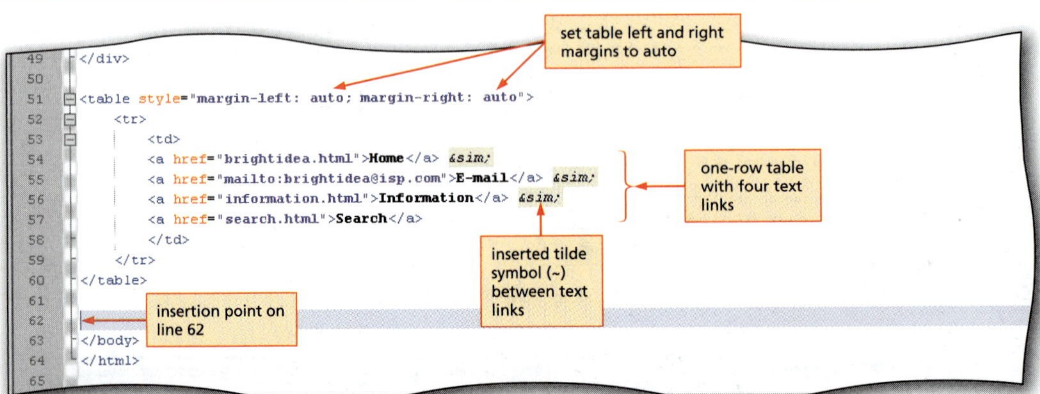

Figure 5–30

Plan Ahead

Creating an image map.

This is the final step in the four-step process of image mapping. The HTML code is very specific about what is required for image mapping. It only takes one coordinate that is not correct or one shape that is wrong for the image map not to work as intended.

- **Use the <map> tag.** The <map> tag identifies the name and ID for the image map. It is important that the name is spelled correctly, and that the same name is used in the usemap attribute in the <img> tag.
- **Use the <area> tag.** The <area> tag also is very important in image mapping. You identify the area shape and the x- and y-coordinates in this tag. Again, if even one number is typed incorrectly, it can make the image map nearly unusable. Image mapping software (described on page HTML 254) makes this a moot point because it inserts the coordinates for you into the HTML code.

Coding the Image Map Using HTML Tags and Attributes

Thus far, the chapter has addressed three of the four steps in creating an image map: the menubar.jpg image to use as an image map has been selected and added to the home page; the hotspots have been sketched on the menubar.jpg image; and Paint was used to locate the x- and y-coordinates for each map area on the image that serves as a hotspot. With these steps completed, the final step is to code the image map using HTML. Table 5–9 shows the two HTML tags used to create an image map, along with several key attributes of each.

Table 5–9 Tags and Tag Attributes Used to Create Image Maps

Tag	Attribute	Function
<map> </map>		• Creates a client-side image map
	name	• Defines the map's name
<area>		• Defines clickable areas within a <map> element, as well as links and anchors
	shape	• Indicates the shape of the map area; possible values are rect, poly, and circle
	coords	• Indicates the x- and y-coordinates of the points bounding the map area
	href	• Indicates the link (URL) used for a map area
	alt	• Indicates the alternate text for the image

The start <map> tag and end </map> tag define the section of code that includes the client-side image map. The <area> tag is used to define the clickable areas on the image map. An example of the <area> tag is:

```
<area shape="circle" coords="107,18,15" href="information.html"
             alt="Info" />brightidea.html
```

where the **shape** attribute with the **circle** value defines the clickable map area as a circle. Other possible values for the shape attribute are poly (polygon) and rect (rectangle). The alt attribute defines alternate text for the image. The **coords** attribute indicates the pairs of x- and y-coordinates of the center of the circle that serve as the starting point of the linkable area. In a circle, you next have to determine the radius of the circle. You do that by selecting a point on the circumference (edge) of the circle by moving along the x-axis to a point on the edge of the circle. You then subtract that x-axis coordinate from the x-axis coordinate in the center of the circle. Finally, the href attribute designates the URL of the link. In this example, a Web page visitor clicking anywhere within the circle bordered by the center x,y (107,18) and anywhere along the edge of the circle with the circle radius of 15 will link to the Web page information.html.

To insert the <area> tag for the circle, rectangle, and polygon shapes, such as those shown in Figure 5–14 on page HTML 248, the HTML code would be as follows:

```
<area shape="circle" coords="308,113,72" href="circle.html">
<area shape="rect" coords="46,35,137,208" href="rect.html">
<area shape= "poly" coords="78,309,183,251,316,262,317,344,
        136,402" href="poly.html">
```

To Create an Image Map

For the image map on the Bright Idea home page, four clickable areas are created: Home, E-mail, Information, and Search. All four clickable areas are circular in shape. Table 5–10 shows the HTML code used to create the image map for the menubar.jpg image on the home page. Line 62 defines the name of the image map as menubar, which is the name referenced in the usemap attribute of the <img> tag that added the menubar.jpg image. Lines 63 through 66 define the four circular map areas for the image map, based on the x- and y-coordinates listed in Table 5–1 on page HTML 252. Each circular map area links to one of the three other Web pages on the Web site or to the e-mail link.

Table 5–10 HTML Code for Creating an Image Map

Line	HTML Tag and Text
62	<map name="menubar" id="menubar">
63	<area shape="circle" coords="35,18,15" href="brightidea.html" alt="Home" />
64	<area shape="circle" coords="71,18,15" href="mailto:brightidea@isp.com" alt="Email" />
65	<area shape="circle" coords="107,18,15" href="information.html" alt="Info" />
66	<area shape="circle" coords="144,18,15" href="search.html" alt="Search" />
67	</map>

The following step illustrates how to enter the HTML code to create the image map for the menubar.jpg image.

1

- If necessary, click line 62.
- Enter the HTML code shown in Table 5–10 and press the ENTER key once (Figure 5–31).

image map named menubar

x- and y-coordinates for center + radius (15) of each circular shape

four links, one for each hotspot

Figure 5–31

Q&A For this project, I am using all circular shapes. Could I have used other shapes for these four clickable areas?

For these menu buttons, there really is no other shape that could be used. You may think to use a polygon shape for the Home link, for instance, but that would make the clickable area too small.

Q&A Could I have used other x- and y-coordinates for this image map?

Yes. This is a very subjective part of image mapping. You need to select the points in the boundaries that make sense to you. Just make sure that the points also will make sense to your Web page visitors. Also, take care not to overlap the points or you will end up with false results.

To Save the HTML File

With the HTML code for the Bright Idea home page complete, you should re-save the file.

1. Click the Save icon on the Notepad++ tool bar to save the most recent version of brightidea.html on the same storage device and in the same folder as the last time you saved it.

To Validate a Web Page

1. Open Internet Explorer and navigate to the Web site `validator.w3.org`.
2. Click the Validate by File Upload tab.
3. Click the Browse button.
4. Locate the brightidea.html file on your storage device and click the file name.
5. Click the Open button in the Choose File to Upload dialog box and the file name will be inserted into the File box.
6. Click the Check button.

Viewing the Web Page and Testing Links

After you save the HTML file for the Bright Idea home page, it should be viewed in a browser to confirm the Web page appears as desired. It also is important to test the four links on the Bright idea home page to verify they function as expected.

To View a Web Page

1. In Internet Explorer, click the Address bar to select the URL on the Address bar.
2. Type `g:\Chapter05\ChapterFiles\brightidea.html` on the Address bar of your browser and press ENTER to display the Web page (Figure 5–32 on the next page).

Q&A

Why do the Information and Search links work already?

These links work because the files information.html and search.html are stored in the Chapter05\ChapterFiles folder of the Data Files for Students.

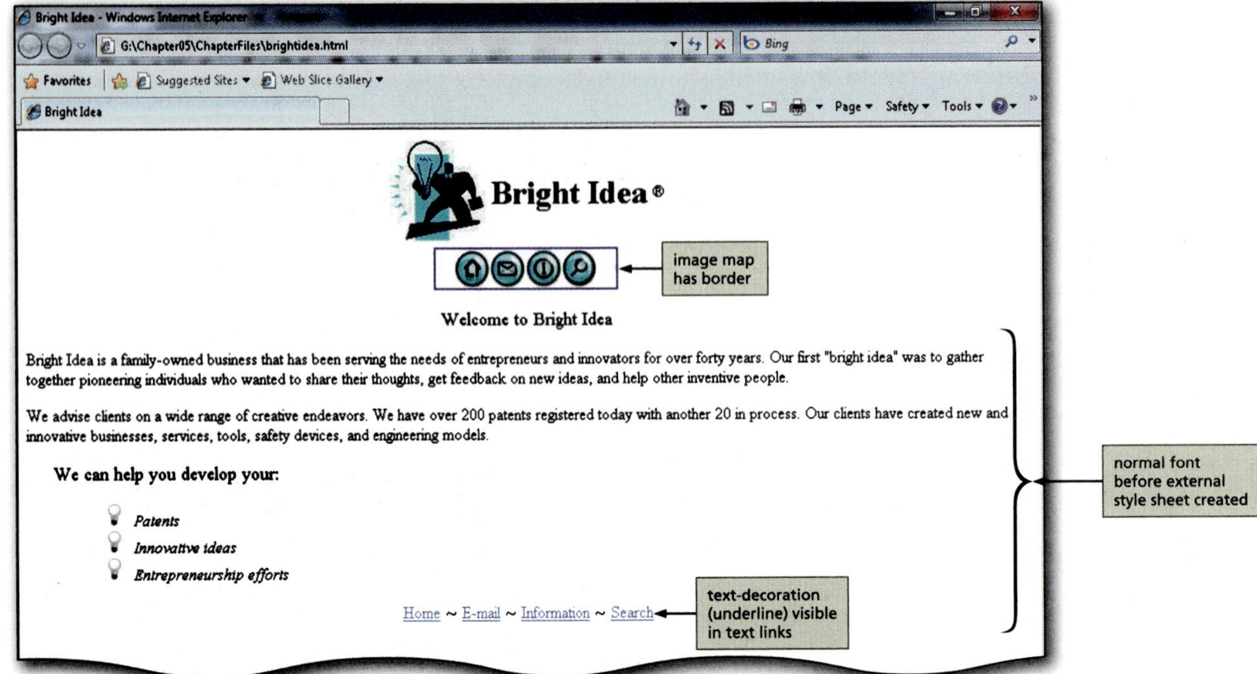

Figure 5–32

> **BTW**
> **Testing**
> Especially with image maps, it is important to test the Web page thoroughly in the browser. If one incorrect number is typed as an x- or y-coordinate, the entire image map can be wrong as a result. Make sure that the clickable area is exactly where you want it to be by testing your Web pages.

To Test Links on a Web Page

1. With the home page displayed in the browser, point to the e-mail link, brightidea@isp.com and click the link to open the default e-mail program with the address brightidea@isp.com in the To: text box.

2. Click the Close button in the New Message window. If a dialog box asks if you want to save changes, click No.

3. With the USB flash drive in drive G, click the Information link from the home page just created. Click back to the Home page from there, using either the image map or the text link. Next, click the other link to test the additional Web page provided in the Data Files for Students (search.html). Test the links back to the Home page from those Web pages.

To Print an HTML File

After your HTML code has passed validation, it is a good idea to make a hard copy printout of it.

1. Click the Notepad++ button on the taskbar to activate the Notepad++ window.

2. Click File on the menu bar and then click the Print command, and then click the Print button to print a hard copy of the HTML code (Figure 5–33).

```
<!DOCTYPE html
   PUBLIC "-//W3C//DTD XHTML 1.0 Transitional//EN"
   "http://www.w3.org/TR/xhtml1/DTD/xhtml1-transitional.dtd">

<html xmlns="http://www.w3.org/1999/xhtml" xml:lang="en" lang="en">
<head>
<meta http-equiv="Content-Type" content="text/html;charset=utf-8" />
<title>Bright Idea</title>

<link rel="stylesheet" type="text/css" href="styles5.css" />

</head>

<body>

<table style="margin-left:auto; margin-right:auto">
    <tr>
        <td>
        <img src="brightidealogo.jpg" width="97" height="100" alt="Bright Idea logo" />
        </td>

        <td>
        <h1>Bright Idea</h1>
        </td>

        <td>&reg;
        </td>
    </tr>
</table>

<div style="text-align: center">
    <img src="menubar.jpg" width="181" height="37" alt="Menu bar" usemap="#menubar" />
</div>

<p style="font-size: large; text-align: center">Welcome to Bright Idea</p>

<p>Bright Idea is a family-owned business that has been serving the needs of
entrepreneurs and innovators for over forty years. Our first &quot;bright idea&quot;
was to gather together pioneering individuals who wanted to share their thoughts, get
feedback on new ideas, and help other inventive people.</p>

<p>We advise clients on a wide range of creative endeavors. We have over 200 patents
registered today with another 20 in process. Our clients have created new and
innovative businesses, se

<p style="font-size: larg
your:</span></p>

<div style="margin-left:
<ul style="list-style-ima
    <li>Patents</li>
    <li>Innovative ideas<
    <li>Entrepreneurship
```

```
</ul>
</div>

<table style="margin-left: auto; margin-right: auto">
    <tr>
        <td>
        <a href="brightidea.html">Home</a> &sim;
        <a href="mailto:brightidea@isp.com">E-mail</a> &sim;
        <a href="information.html">Information</a> &sim;
        <a href="search.html">Search</a>
        </td>
    </tr>
</table>

<map name="menubar" id="menubar" style="text-decoration: none">
    <area shape="circle" coords="35,18,15" href="brightidea.html" alt="Home" />
    <area shape="circle" coords="71,18,15" href="mailto:brightidea@isp.com" alt="Email"
/>
    <area shape="circle" coords="107,18,15" href="information.html" alt="Info" />
    <area shape="circle" coords="144,18,15" href="search.html" alt="Search" />
</map>

</body>
</html>
```

Figure 5–33

Plan Ahead

Planning an external style sheet.
The home page is complete, but some style details are lacking. It is important to maintain a consistent look across a Web site. By creating an external style sheet, you can maintain that consistent look with great style.

- **Determine what styles you want to use.** As you have seen, there are many styles that you can use to enhance your Web site (see Appendix D). Some that you can utilize in this Web site are:
  - Font family – maintaining a consistent font family is very important because the style of font is what you see the most across a Web site.
  - Font size – for the same reason as above, you should maintain consistency in font size; there are exceptions to this, especially in titles on the Web page.
  - Margins – it is helpful to utilize margins to help define the structure of a Web page.
  - Borders around links – you do not always want to see borders around images that you use as links; setting the border to zero is sometimes better style.

Creating an External Style Sheet

With the home page complete, the next step is to create an external style sheet that is linked to all pages in the Web site. You already added the link statement into the HTML code in the brightidea.html file on line 10. This statement tells the browser to link to the external (linked) style sheet named styles5.css. If there is no styles5.css file available, as is the case at this time, then the styles used are the default styles, as shown in Figure 5–34a. Once you create the styles5.css external style sheet, your Web page looks like that shown in Figure 5–34b.

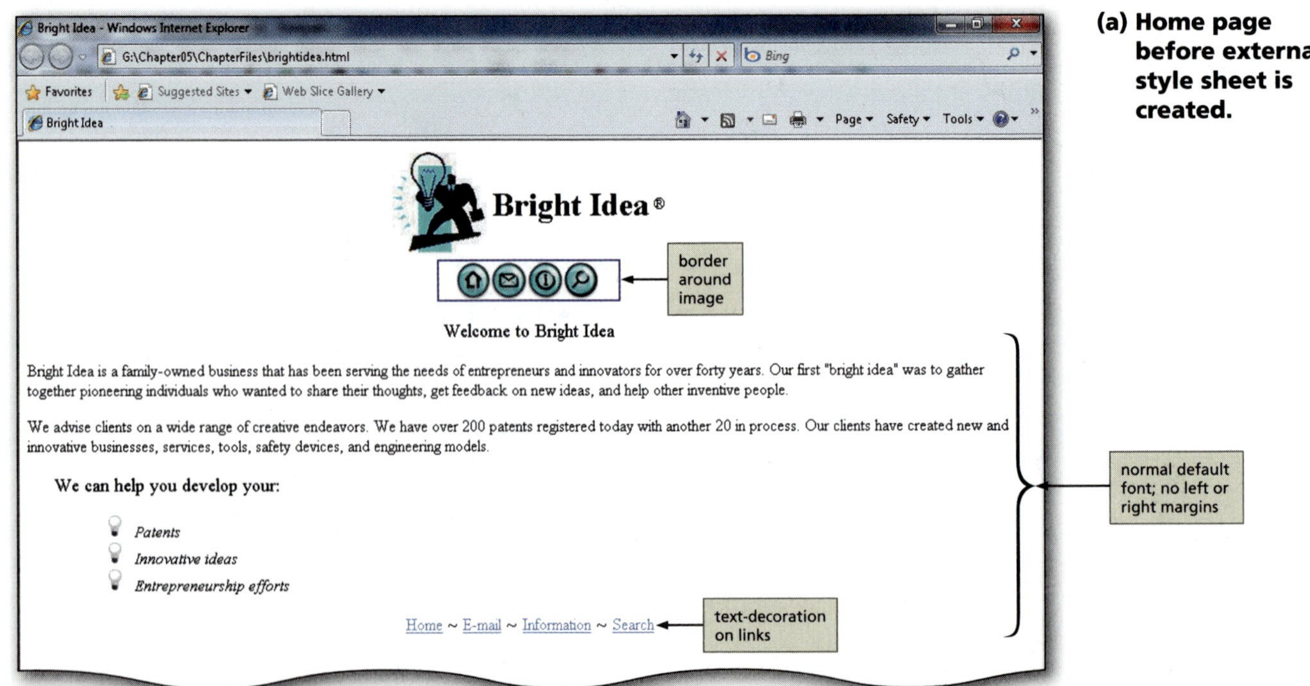

(a) Home page before external style sheet is created.

Figure 5–34

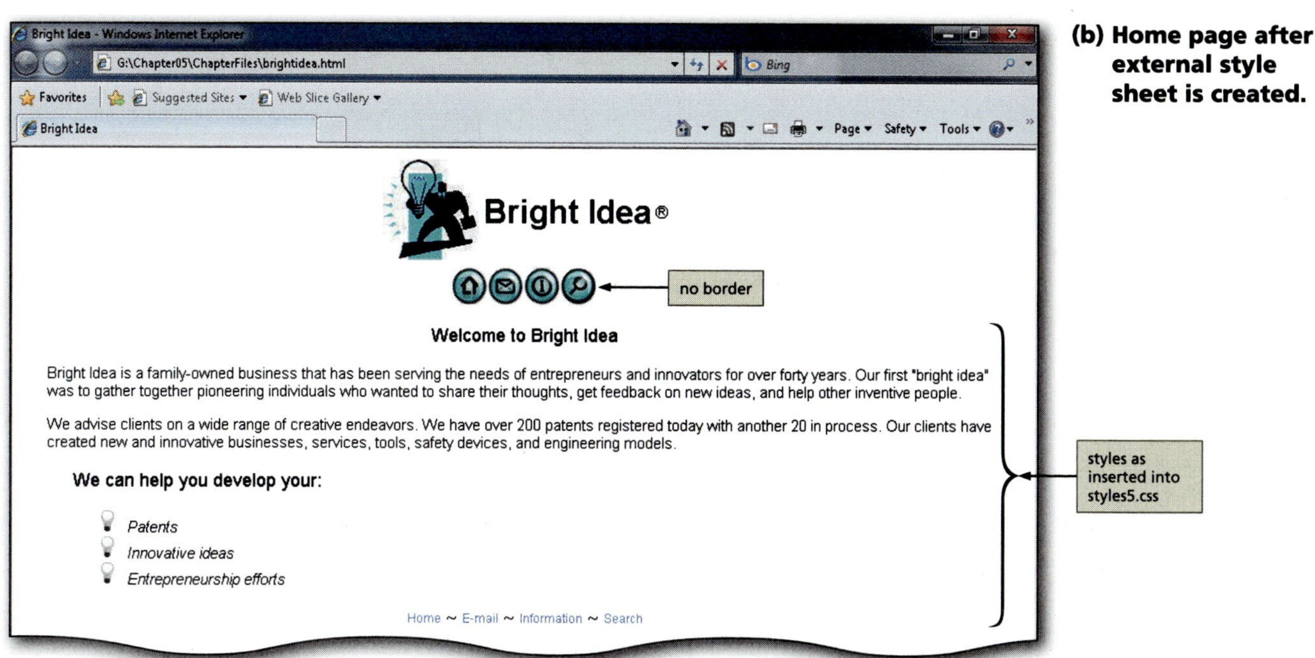

(b) Home page after external style sheet is created.

Figure 5–34 (continued)

To create an external style sheet, you first have to start a new file in Notepad++. Remember from Chapter 4 that an external style sheet does not need the initial HTML DOCTYPE tags that you use for all Web pages. The external style sheet contains only the code for the various styles that you want to use across a Web site.

To Create an External Style Sheet

Table 5–11 contains the CSS code for the external style sheet that is used in all Web pages. Lines 1 and 2 define the font- family and font-size for the Web page. Lines 4 and 5 set the right and left margins to 20 points. That will give 20 points of space from the edge of the Web page to the start of the text in a paragraph. Lines 8 and 11 set the font-size for links to nine point with no text-decoration (no underline). Line 13 sets the border around images to zero.

Table 5–11 Code for External Style Sheet

Line	CSS Properties and Values	
1	body	{font-family: Arial, Verdana, Garamond;
2		font-size: 11 pt}
3		
4	p	{margin-left: 20pt;
5		margin-right: 20pt;
6		font-size: 11pt}
7		
8	a	{font-size: 9pt;
9		margin-left: auto;
10		margin-right: auto;
11		text-decoration: none}
12		
13	img	{border: 0px}

The following step shows how to create an external style sheet.

1

- If necessary, click the Notepad++ button on the taskbar.
- Click the New button on the toolbar.
- Enter the HTML code shown in Table 5–11 (Figure 5–35).

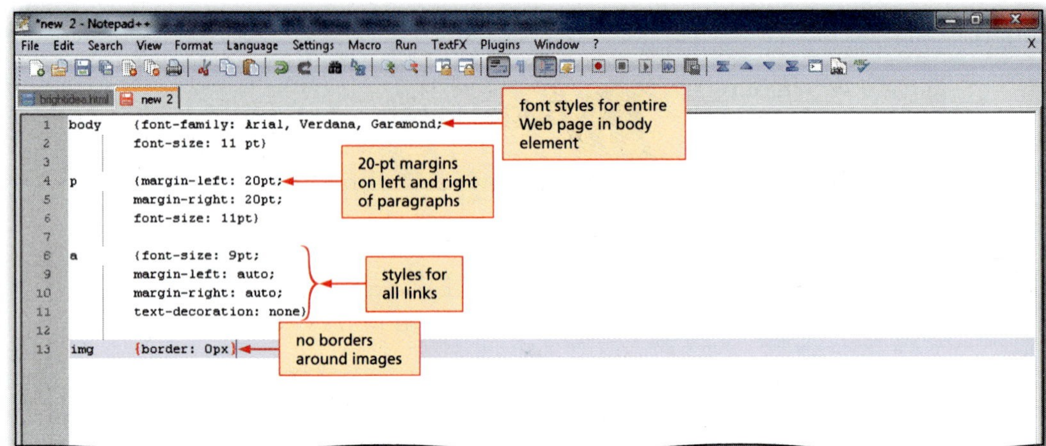

Figure 5–35

To Save and Print the CSS File

1. With a USB drive plugged into your computer, click File on the menu bar and then click Save As. Type `styles5.css` in the File name text box.
2. If necessary, click UDISK (G:) or your storage device in the Save in list. Click the Chapter05 folder and then double-click the ChapterFiles folder in the list of available folders. Click the Save button in the Save As dialog box.
3. Click File on the menu bar and then click Print Now on the File menu (Figure 5–36).

```
body {font-family: Arial, Verdana, Garamond;
      font-size: 11 pt}

p     {margin-left: 20pt;
      margin-right: 20pt;
      font-size: 11pt}

a     {font-size: 9pt;
      margin-left: auto;
      margin-right: auto;
      text-decoration: none}

img   {border: 0px}
```

Figure 5–36

To View the Web Page

1. Click the Internet Explorer button on the taskbar.
2. Click the Information area on the menu bar image map to display the Web page, as shown in Figure 5–37.

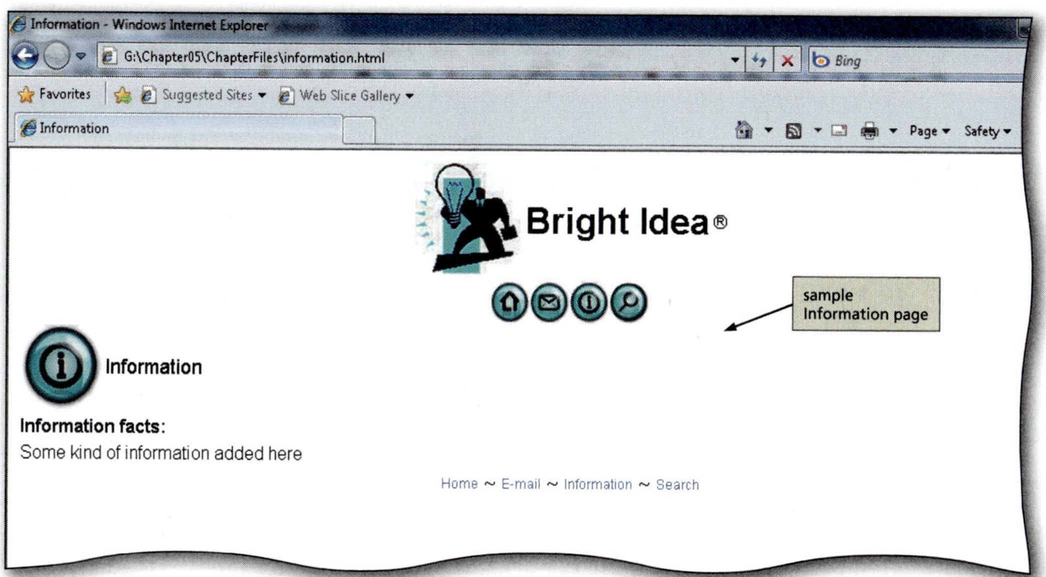

Figure 5–37

To Test and Print the Web Page

1. Click the Home link (either text or from the image map) on the Information Web page.
2. Click the Print button on the Command bar to print the Web page.
3. Click to test the other links, both text and those on the menu bar. If any of the links do not work correctly, return to Notepad++ to modify the HTML code, save the changes, and then retest the links in the browser.

To Quit Notepad++ and a Browser

1. In Notepad++, click the File menu, then Close All.
2. Click the Close button on the Notepad++ title bar.
3. Click the Close button on the browser title bar. If necessary, click the Close all tabs button.

Chapter Summary

BTW

Quick Reference
For a list of special characters, see the Symbols and Characters Quick Reference (Appendix F) at the back of this book, or visit the Quick Reference Web page for this book (scsite.com/HTML6e/qr).

In this chapter, you have learned how to develop a Web site that utilizes image mapping from the home page to create three clickable areas. The items listed below include all the new HTML skills you have learned in this chapter.

1. Start Paint (HTML 249)
2. Open an Image File in Paint (HTML 251)
3. Locate X- and Y-Coordinates of an Image (HTML 252)
4. Insert a Special Character (HTML 260)
5. Insert an Image to Use as an Image Map (HTML 261)
6. Create an Image Map (HTML 266)
7. Create an External Style Sheet (HTML 271)

Learn It Online

Test your knowledge of chapter content and key terms.

Instructions: To complete the Learn It Online exercises, start your browser, click the Address bar, and then enter the Web address `scsite.com/html6e/learn`. When the HTML Learn It Online page is displayed, click the link for the exercise you want to complete and read the instructions.

Chapter Reinforcement TF, MC, and SA
A series of true/false, multiple choice, and short answer questions that test your knowledge of the chapter content.

Flash Cards
An interactive learning environment where you identify chapter key terms associated with displayed definitions.

Practice Test
A series of multiple choice questions that test your knowledge of chapter content and key terms.

Who Wants To Be a Computer Genius?
An interactive game that challenges your knowledge of chapter content in the style of a television quiz show.

Wheel of Terms
An interactive game that challenges your knowledge of chapter key terms in the style of the television show, *Wheel of Fortune*.

Crossword Puzzle Challenge
A crossword puzzle that challenges your knowledge of key terms presented in the chapter.

Apply Your Knowledge

Reinforce the skills and apply the concepts you learned in this chapter.

Adding an Image Map to a Web Page

Problem: You decide to use your image mapping skills to create a Web page that describes your company's sales figures for the year. You plan to create a Web page similar to the one shown in Figure 5–38, with the file barchart.png (note the different image type) as an image map that links to four Web pages with information on the various sales for the four quarters of the year.

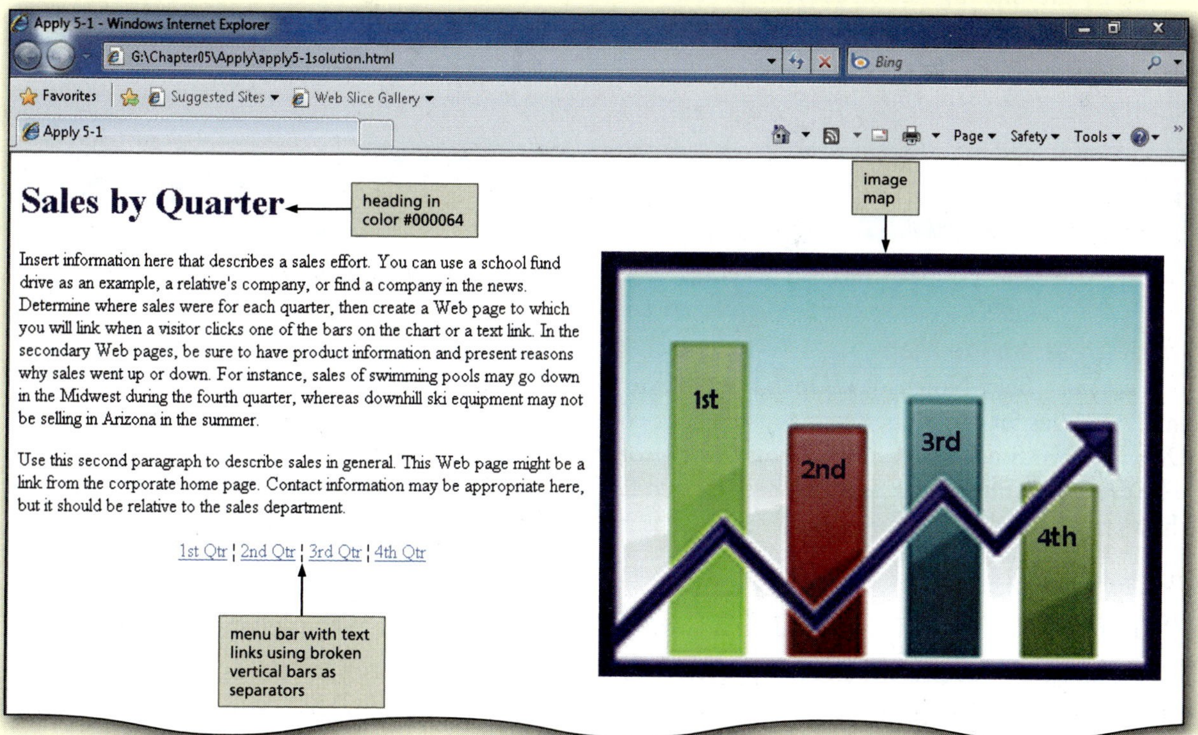

Figure 5–38

Instructions: Start Paint and Notepad++. Perform the following steps:

1. Using Paint, open the file barchart.png from the Chapter05\Apply folder of the Data Files for Students. See the inside back cover of this book for instructions on downloading the Data Files for Students, or contact your instructor for information about accessing the required files.
2. Each area on the bar chart image is a rectangular area. Use good judgment when planning the shapes of your image map, ensuring that no clickable areas overlap from one rectangular shape into another and that each shape makes sense for its respective area. Using Paint, estimate the x- and y-coordinates necessary to create four clickable areas on the barchart.png image. Write down these coordinates for later use.
3. Using Notepad++, create a new HTML file with the title Apply 5-1 in the title section. Add the heading and text, as shown in Figure 5–38. Use the broken vertical bar (see Appendix F) to separate the text links.
4. Begin the body section by adding a header with #000064 as the color. Use Paint to determine the dimensions of the image for the <img> tag. Align the image so that it is to the right of the text.

Continued >

Apply Your Knowledge *continued*

5. Use the usemap attribute usemap="#chart" in the <img> tag.
6. Enter the <map> </map> tags required to create the image map named chart.
7. Enter the <area> tags required to define four clickable areas on the image barchart.png. Use the x- and y-coordinates determined in Step 2 and set the href attribute to link to the sample.html file from the Data Files for Students or create your own secondary Web pages.
8. Save the HTML file in the Chapter05\Apply folder using the file name apply5-1solution.html Validate the Web page(s) using W3C. Print the HTML file.
9. Open the file apply 5-1solution.html in your browser and test the image map and text links to verify they link to the correct Web pages.
10. Print the main Web page and the three linked Web pages.
11. Submit the completed HTML files and Web pages in the format specified by your instructor.

Extend Your Knowledge

Extend the skills you learned in this chapter and experiment with new skills.

Creating an Image Map

Instructions: Start Notepad++. Open the file extend5-1.html from the Chapter05\Extend folder of the Data Files for Students. See the inside back cover of this book for instructions on downloading the Data Files for Students, or contact your instructor for information about accessing the required files. The extend5-1.html file is a partially completed HTML file that needs to be completed. Figure 5–39 shows the Extend Your Knowledge Web page as it should appear in your browser after it is completed.

Perform the following tasks:

1. Enter the URL G:\Chapter05\Extend\extend5-1.html to view the Web page in your browser.
2. Examine the HTML file and its appearance as a Web page in the browser.
3. Using Paint, open the file samerica.jpg from the Chapter05\Extend folder. Determine the x- and y-coordinates necessary to create three clickable areas on the map image, one each for Argentina, Brazil, and Peru. You may either use rectangle or polygon shapes for the three areas.
4. Add HTML code to the extend5-1.html file to create an image map that links each clickable area on the map image to an external Web page of your choice.
5. Create a Web page for one of the countries. Research information about the country and include some interesting facts. Include some images on the secondary Web page, but be aware of copyright laws governing their use.
6. Add code to create a horizontal menu bar, as shown in Figure 5–39.

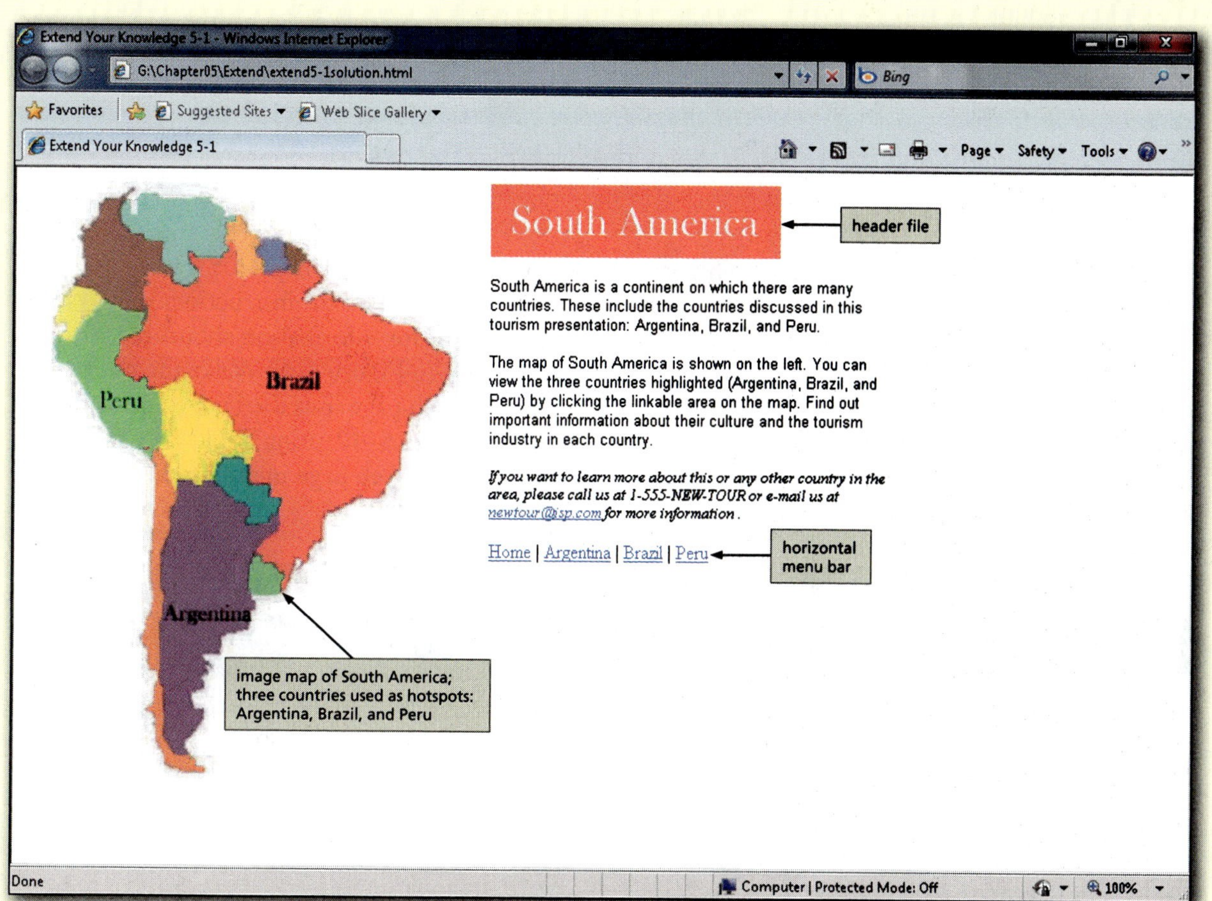

Figure 5–39

7. Save the revised file in the Chapter05\Extend folder using the file name extend5-1solution.html.
8. Validate the Web pages to assure that you are in compliance with current standards.
9. Test the links completely.
10. Print the revised HTML file.
11. Enter the URL G:\Chapter05\Extend\extend5-1solution.html to view the Web page in your browser.
12. Print the Web page.
13. Submit the completed HTML file and Web page in the format specified by your instructor.

Make It Right

Analyze a document and correct all errors and/or improve the design.

Correcting the Travel Agency Web Page

Instructions: Start Notepad++. Open the file makeitright5-1.html from the Chapter05\MakeItRight folder of the Data Files for Students. See the inside back cover of this book for instructions on downloading the Data Files for Students, or contact your instructor for information about accessing the required files. The Web page is a modified version of what you see in Figure 5–40. Make the necessary corrections to the Web page to make it look like the figure. The Web page uses the image getaway.gif. Add four text links at the bottom of the Web page, as shown in Figure 5–40, using Table 5–12 for link name suggestions and URLs. Submit the completed HTML file and Web page in the format specified by your instructor.

Table 5–12 Image Map Coordinates, URLs, and Text Links

Text Link	Image Map Coordinates	URL
Ski & Snow	55,96,253,134	http://www.coloradoski.com/
Surf & Sun	301,93,497,134	http://www.nationalgeographicexpeditions.com/
Golf & Spa	55,161,244,201	http://www.seasidegolf.com/
Adventure	283,158,498,195	http://www.abercrombiekent.com/index.cfm

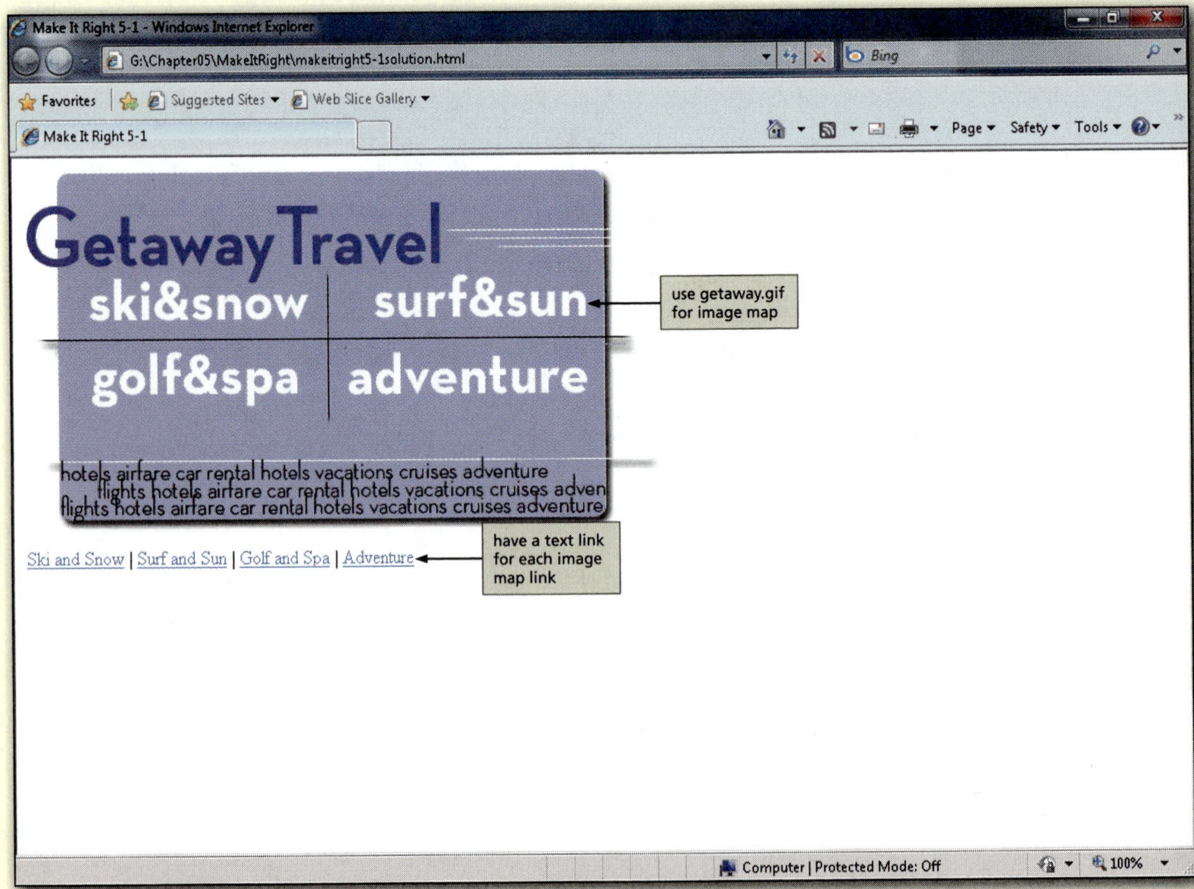

Figure 5–40

In the Lab

Lab 1: Creating an Earth-Friendly Web Page

Problem: You are very involved in making your home and school eco friendly. You decide to create a Web page similar to the Web page in Figure 5–41, with the file earthfriendly.jpg as an image map that links to six Web pages of your choosing.

Instructions: Start Paint and Notepad++. Perform the following steps:

1. Using Paint, open the file earthfriendly.jpg from the Chapter05\IntheLab folder.
2. Determine the x- and y-coordinates necessary to create six rectangular clickable areas on the graphical image, one for each of the six areas, including three recycle bags, two link bars (re-use and say no), and a trash can. Write down these coordinates for later use.
3. Using Notepad++, create a new HTML file with the title Lab 5-1 in the title section. Add the text links, as shown in Figure 5-41.
4. Insert the image earthfriendly.jpg. Use the usemap attribute usemap="#ecomenu" in the <img> tag.
5. Enter the <map> </map> tags required to create the image map named ecomenu.
6. Enter the <area> tags required to define six rectangular clickable areas on the earthfriendly.jpg image. Use the x- and y-coordinates determined in Step 2 and set the href attribute to display the sample.html Web page provided in the Data Files for Students.
7. For a bonus project, link the elements to relevant Web sites of your choosing.

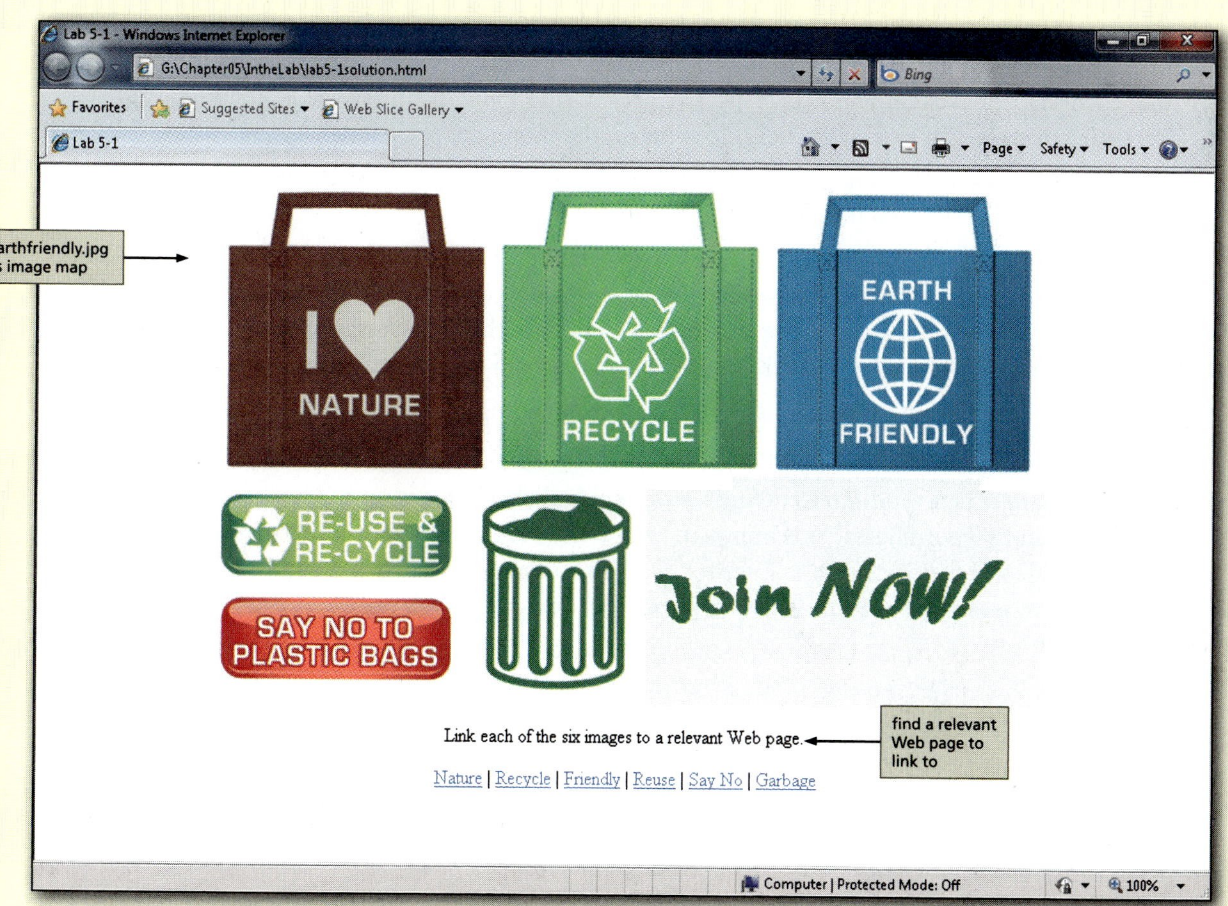

Figure 5–41

Continued >

STUDENT ASSIGNMENTS

In the Lab *continued*

8. Save the HTML file in the Chapter05\IntheLab folder using the file name lab5-1solution.html. Validate the Web page using W3C. Print the HTML file.
9. Open the file lab5-1solution.html in your browser and test the image map and text links to verify they link to the correct Web pages.
10. Print the main Web page and the three linked Web pages.
11. Submit the completed HTML files and Web pages in the format specified by your instructor.

In the Lab

Lab 2: Mapping Currency

Problem: You are learning about different denominations of money in your economics class. You decide to create a Web site that displays information about four different currencies (dollar, Euro, yen, and pound). Use your image mapping skills to create a Web page that has four circular links. You plan to create a Web page similar to the one shown in Figure 5–42, with the file moneymap.jpg as an image map that links to four Web pages (dollar.html, euro.html, yen.html, and pound.html) that contain one statement each of information about the selected currency.

Instructions: Start Paint and Notepad++. Perform the following steps:

1. Using Paint, open the file moneymap.jpg from the Chapter05\IntheLab folder.
2. Each area on the image is a circular shape. Use good judgment when planning the shapes of your image map, ensuring that no clickable areas overlap from one circular shape into another and that each shape makes sense for its respective area. Using Paint, estimate the x- and y-coordinates necessary to create four circular clickable areas on the moneymap.jpg image.
3. Using Notepad++, create a new HTML file with the title Lab 5-2 in the title section. Add the heading and text, as shown in Figure 5–42.
4. Begin the body section by adding a one-row, two-data-cell table. Center the text in the right-hand data cell. Make sure to include the special characters (see Appendix F) for the Euro, yen, and pound in the paragraph of text, as shown in Figure 5–42. (Why is there no special character needed for the dollar sign?) The e-mail text and link should be a paragraph below the table.
5. Use the usemap attribute usemap="#moneymap" in the <img> tag.
6. Enter the <map> </map> tags required to create the image map named moneymap.
7. Enter the <area> tags required to define four circular clickable areas on the image moneymap.jpg. Use the x- and y-coordinates determined in Step 2 and set the href attribute to link to the four Web pages provided as files in the Data Files for Students or create your own secondary Web page. For bonus points, insert relevant information in the four linked-to Web pages.
8. Save the HTML file in the Chapter05\IntheLab folder using the file name lab5-2solution.html. Validate the Web page(s) using W3C. Print the HTML file.
9. Open the file lab5-2solution.html in your browser and test the image map and text links to verify they link to the correct Web pages.
10. Print the main Web page and the four linked Web pages.
11. Submit the completed HTML files and Web pages in the format specified by your instructor.

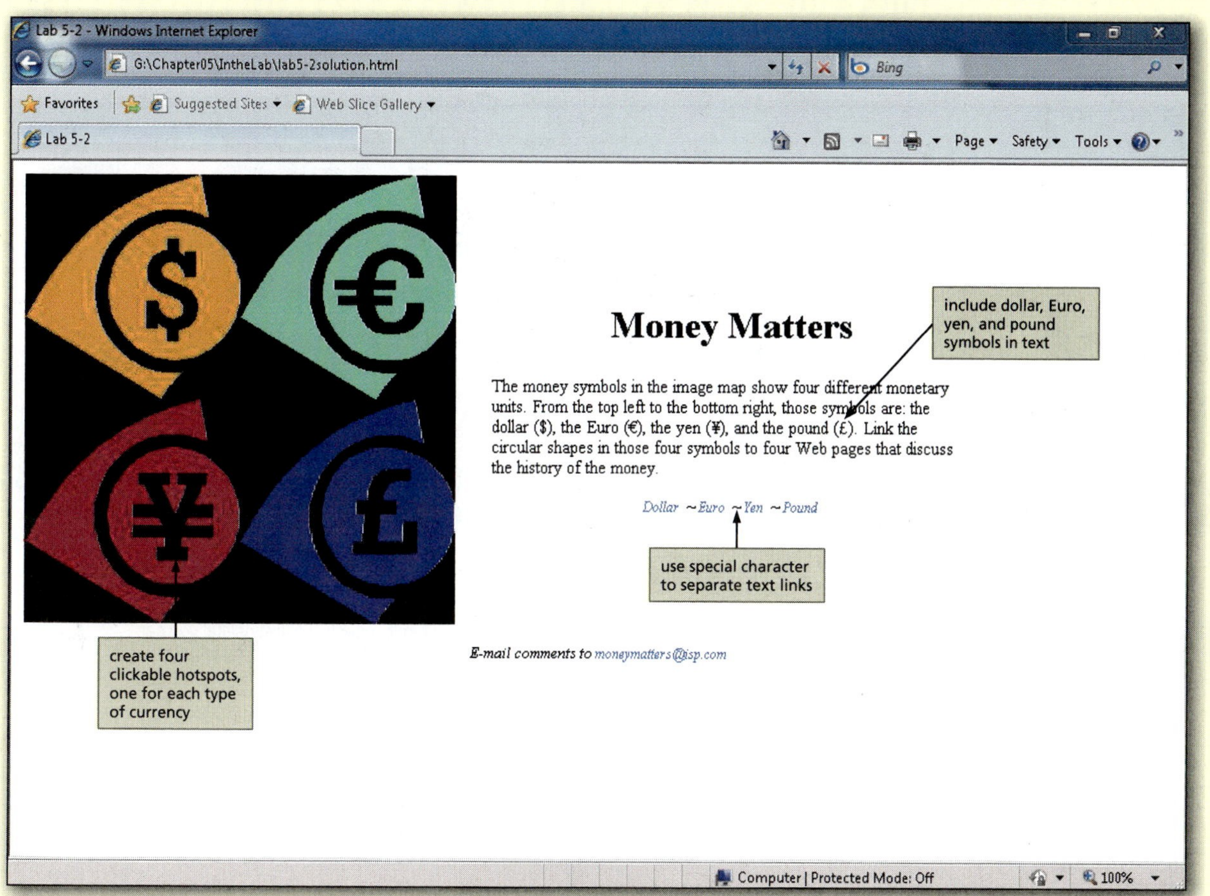

Figure 5–42

In the Lab

Lab 3: Creating an Exercise Web Page

Problem: You are trying to lead a healthier lifestyle, and have researched how many calories are burned for six different activities, based on a person's weight. To help others who are also interested in the benefits of exercise, you create a Web site with a home page similar to Figure 5–43 on the next page.

Instructions: Start Paint and Notepad++. Perform the following tasks:

1. Using Paint, open the file exercisemap.jpg from the Chapter05\IntheLab folder of the Data Files for Students.
2. Using Paint, determine the x- and y-coordinates necessary to create six clickable areas on the map image, using rectangular-shaped areas. Write down these coordinates for later use.
3. Using Notepad++, create a new HTML file with the title Lab 5-3 in the main heading section.
4. Begin the body section by adding the exercisemap.jpg image, as shown in Figure 5–43.
5. Use the usemap attribute usemap="#menubar" in the <img> tag.
6. Enter the <map> </map> tags required to create the image map named menubar.

Continued >

In the Lab *continued*

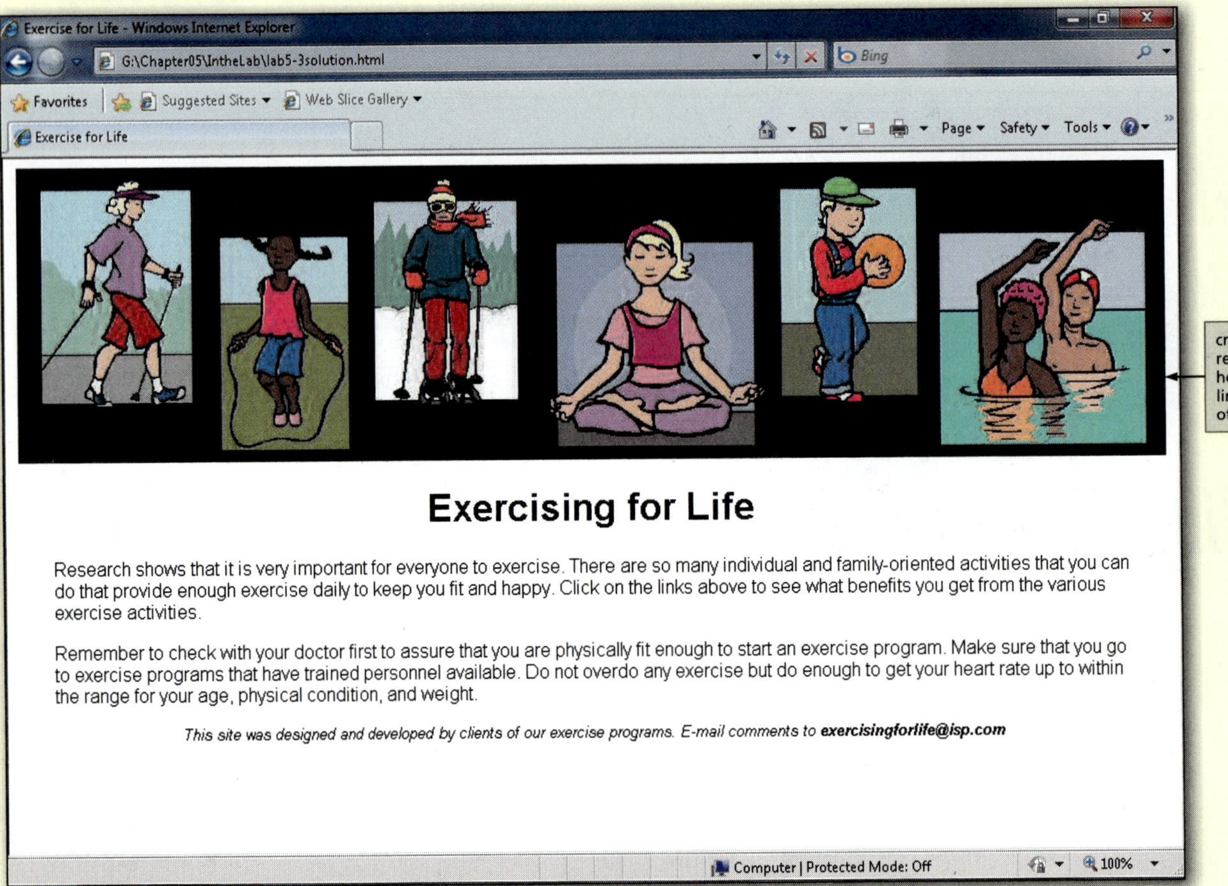

Figure 5–43

7. Enter the <area> tags required to define six clickable areas on the image exercisemap.jpg. Use the x- and y-coordinates determined in Step 2 and set the href attribute to use the URLs for the six exercise activity Web pages you have identified for the six different activities. Link the clickable areas to Web pages named: hiking.html, jumping.html, playingball.html, skiing.html, water.html, and yoga.html.
8. Save the HTML file in the Chapter05\IntheLab folder using the file name lab5-3solution.html. Validate the Web page. Print the HTML file.
9. Create the six Web pages to correspond with the links, naming them as shown above. Use the Word document lab5-3ActivityChart.doc from the Data Files for Students to find the calories burned by weight for each activity.
10. Open the file lab5-3solution.html in your browser and test the image map and text links to verify they link to the correct Web pages.
11. Print the main Web page and the six linked Web pages.
12. Submit the completed HTML files and Web pages in the format specified by your instructor.

Cases and Places

Apply your creative thinking and problem-solving skills to design and implement a solution.

• Easier •• More Difficult

• 1: Completing the Bright Ideas Web Site

The Board of Directors for the Bright Idea company likes the home page of the new Web site. They want you to create more final versions of the Information and Search pages. For the Information page, you should search for similar companies and add samples of what you found onto the Information page. Save and validate the Web page with the additional information. Submit it in the format specified by your instructor. For the Search page, you should review how to best handle a search function on a Web page. What resources are out there for companies to use for searches of their Web sites? (*Hint:* Try "powered by Google.") Note any information that you find in a paper and discuss what needs to be done to have an effective search function. Submit in the format specified by your instructor.

• 2: Promoting Library Services

The marketing director of your community library wants to create a new graphical home page that highlights the different services that the library provides, including: book reserve, video rentals, available meeting rooms, and computers with Internet access. Using the books.jpg image from the Chapter05\CasesandPlaces folder of the Data Files for Students, create a Web page. First, open the books.jpg image in Paint to determine hotspots that you can use as three or four links. For a higher level of difficulty, use the Text tool in Paint to add relevant words onto the books for those links. (*Hint:* Search the Paint Help utility for the word Text.) From those hotspots, create links to subsequent Web pages that describe the services. Be sure to include text links at the bottom of the page to mirror the links in the image map.

•• 3: Browsing with Images Turned Off

As discussed in this chapter, some Web site visitors turn graphics off while browsing. Find out how extensive this practice might be by researching statistics online that show the number of Web users who turn graphics off when they browse. With this information in hand, search the Web to find three Web sites that utilize image maps. Track the time that it takes to load the three Web pages with image maps. Turn off graphics in your browser (in Internet Explorer, click Tools on the Command bar and click Internet Options, and then click the Advanced tab; scroll down and click Show pictures under Multimedia to deselect it). Next, clear the browser's history (in Internet Explorer, click Tools on the Command bar and Internet Options, and then click the Delete button under Browsing history). Reload each of the three Web pages and again track the time it takes for the pages to load, this time without images. Determine if the Web pages load more quickly with images off. Review each Web page and determine if you can use all of the links despite having graphics turned off.

•• 4: Researching Image Mapping Software

Make It Personal

You are very interested in finding out more information about some of the image mapping software tools listed in Table 5–2 on page HTML 254. Review the information about each tool listed, including any associated costs, free trial version availability, platform(s) supported, and ease of use. If a free trial version is offered at any of the Web sites and you are using your own computer (or your instructor or lab coordinator allows it), download the software and use it to create an image map. Compare the technique of using these tools to the technique used in this chapter using Paint. Write a synopsis of the available products, including any associated costs, free trial version availability, platform(s) supported, and ease of use.

Continued >

Cases and Places *continued*

•• 5: Creating a Team Image Map

Working Together

Each member of your team should find an image that depicts the members of the team and can be used as an image map. The image could have areas that represent the different areas in which you are majoring, the sports or clubs of which you are members, or even personal interests. If you cannot find one image that suffices, you can use Paint (or another graphic editing tool) to combine relevant images that you found, making your own image map. Once you have an image map, sketch out the areas that you would use as hotspots. Use that image map to link these hotspots to your own personal Web pages.

6 Creating a Form on a Web Page

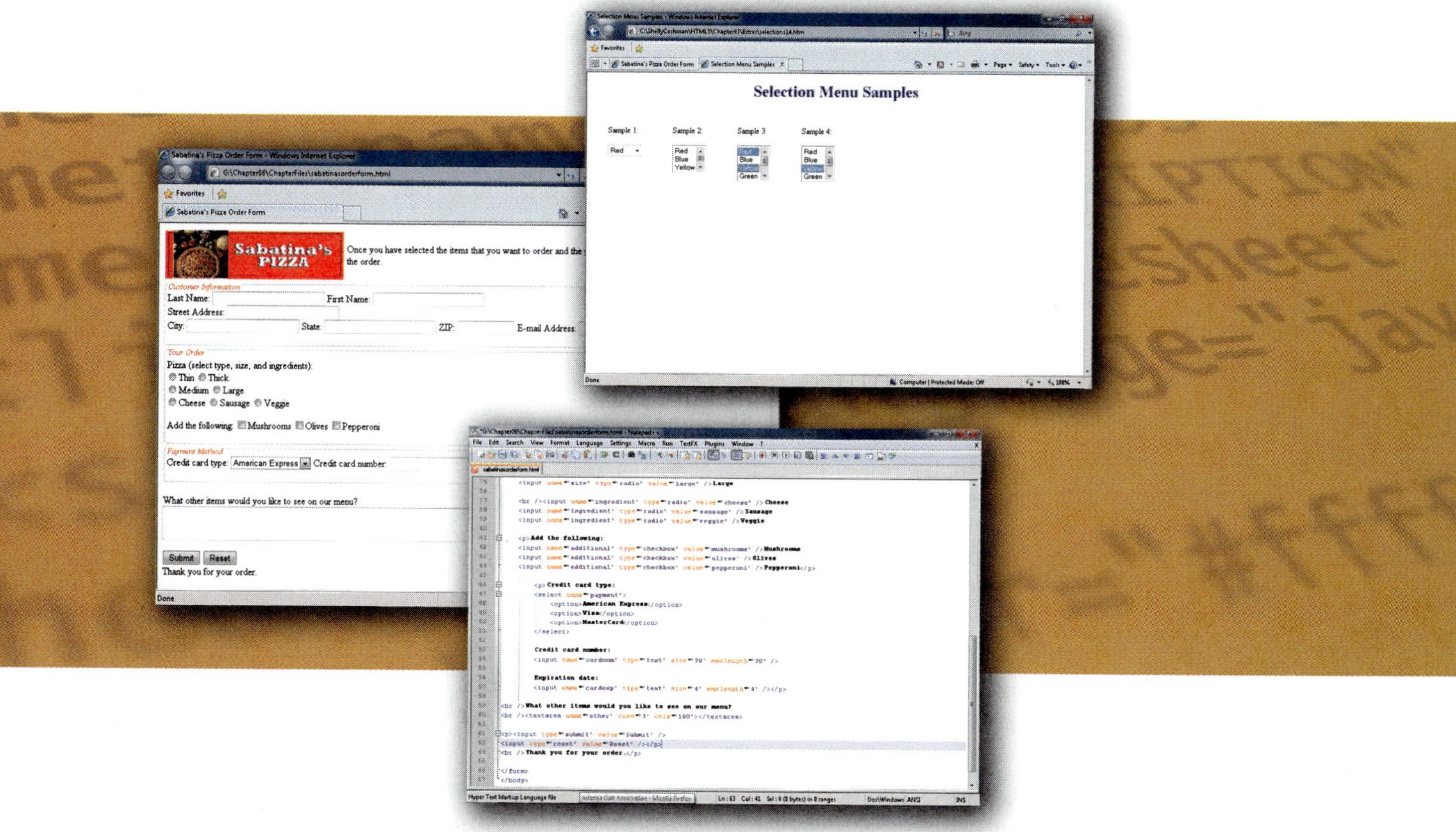

Objectives

You will have mastered the material in this chapter when you can:

- Define terms related to forms
- Describe the different form controls and their uses
- Use the <form> </form> tags
- Use the <input/> tag
- Create a text box
- Create check boxes
- Create a selection menu with multiple options
- Use the <select> tag
- Use the <option> tag
- Create radio buttons
- Create a textarea box
- Create a Submit button
- Create a Reset button
- Use the <fieldset> and <legend> tags to group form information

6 Creating a Form on a Web Page

Introduction

The goal of the projects completed thus far has been to present information *to* Web site visitors. In this chapter, you learn how to get information *from* Web site visitors by adding a form for user input.

Using a Web page form for user input reduces the potential for errors because customers enter data or select options from the form included directly on the Web page. A form has input fields to remind users to enter information and limits choices to valid options to avoid incorrect data entry. Forms provide an easy way to collect needed information from Web page visitors.

In this chapter, you will learn how to use HTML to create a form on a Web page. The form will include several controls, including check boxes, a drop-down list, radio buttons, and text boxes. You also will learn to add Submit and Reset buttons that customers can use to submit the completed form or clear the information previously entered into the form. Finally, you will learn to use the <fieldset> tag to group information on a form in a user-friendly way with the <legend> tag, which is used to add labels to the groups within the form.

Project — Creating Forms on a Web Page

The Sabatina's Pizza Web site (Chapter 4) has been a great success. Many customers have visited the Web site to review the menu choices. Sabatina's owners decided to add an online order form, but it has been cumbersome for the customers. They have to follow the instructions on the Order Form Web page, print out the form, fill in their menu item choices, and fax orders in. Although the orders are usually complete, sometimes they are missing key information, or the customers request options that are not available. Sabatina's owners ask you if an easier, less error-prone way exists for customers to order menu items online.

The Sabatina's Pizza Order Form Web page is provided in the Data Files for Students for this chapter. In this project, you enter HTML tags to modify the text-based Order Form Web page that the owner of Sabatina's Pizza originally created (Figure 6–1a) and from it, create a Web-based Order Form, as shown in Figure 6–1b. This page requests the same information as the text-based Web page, but is created with a Web-based form that allows users to enter data, select options, and then submit the form to the e-mail address indicated on the form.

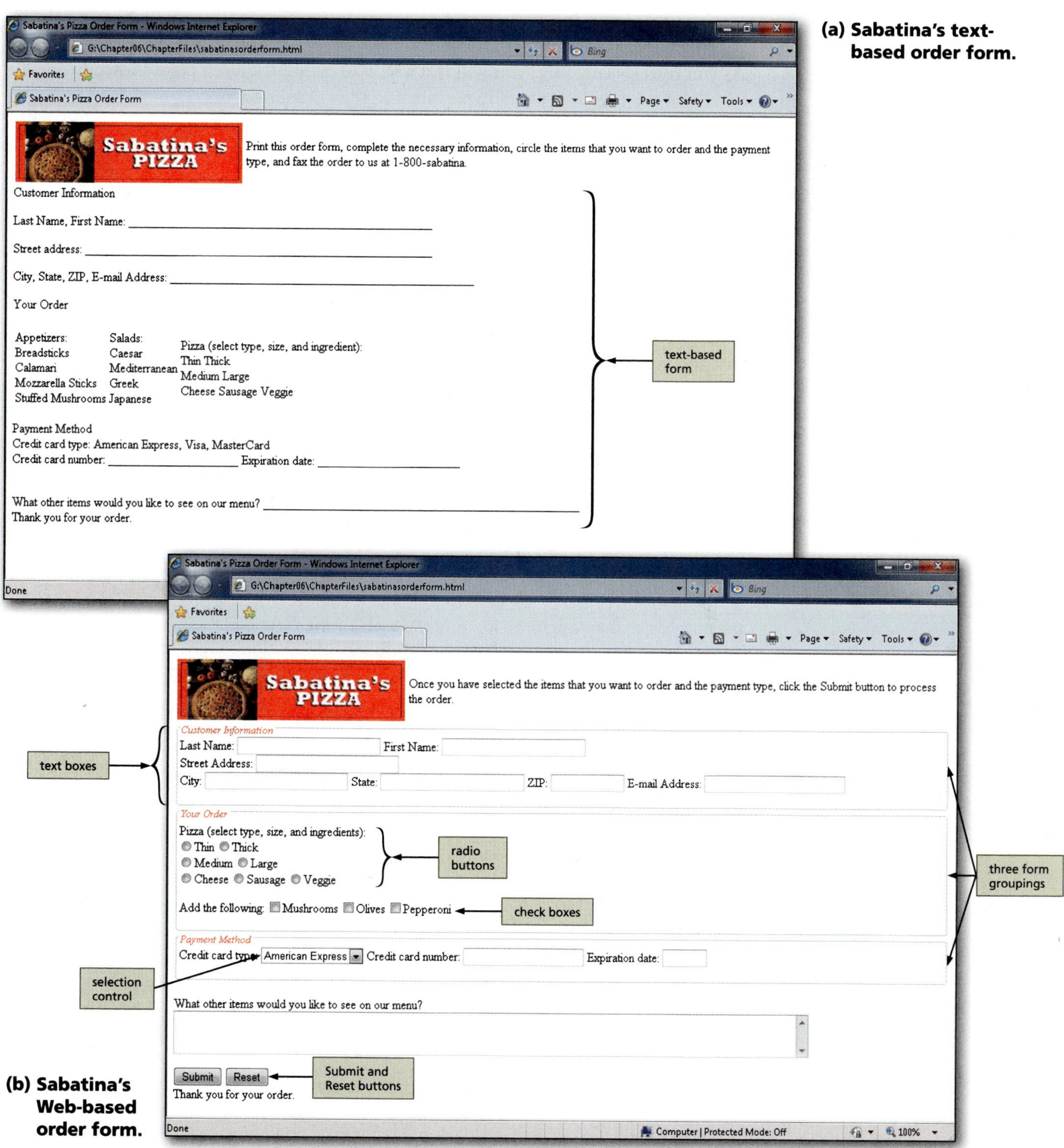

(a) Sabatina's text-based order form.

(b) Sabatina's Web-based order form.

Figure 6–1

Overview

As you read this chapter, you will learn how to create the Web page shown in Figure 6–1b on the previous page by performing these general tasks:

- Enter HTML code into the Notepad++ window.
- Save the file as an HTML file.
- Enter basic HTML tags and add text to the file.
- Insert tags to create a form with several input controls.
- Create Submit and Reset buttons on the form.
- Add interest and organization to the form using <fieldset> and <legend> tags.
- Add an embedded style sheet to format specific elements on a Web page.
- Save and print the HTML code.
- Validate, view, and print the Web pages.

Plan Ahead

General Project Guidelines

As you create Web pages, such as the project shown in Figure 6–1 on the previous page, you should follow these general guidelines:

1. **Plan the Web site.** You should plan the information that you hope to collect before you begin to write your HTML code. Refer to Table 1–4 on page HTML 15 for information on the planning phase of the Web Development Life Cycle. In this phase, you determine the purpose of the Web form, identify the users of the form and their computing environment, and decide how best to capture the information sought using a Web page.
2. **Analyze the need.** In the analysis phase of the Web Development Life Cycle, you should analyze what content to include in the Web page form. The Web development project in this chapter is different than the ones completed in other chapters because it contains a form. Part of the analysis phase then includes determining what information to collect and the best form input controls to use for this collection.
3. **Determine the types of controls to use.** The type of information a form is intended to gather dictates what controls are used in the form. For instance, in the case in which only one option from a list can be selected, you should use the radio button control. In the case in which more than one option can be selected, you can use check boxes or selection controls. If you want users to be able to add their own comments, you can use a textarea box. Most forms use a combination of controls, not just a single type.
4. **Establish what other form options are necessary.** Form organization is an important aspect of Web page form development. You want to be sure that the user understands what information to provide. You also want the form to be attractive and easy to use. Consider using fieldset and legend tags to divide the form attractively and segregate information into logical subsets.
5. **Create the Web page form and links.** Once the analysis and design is complete, the Web developer creates the Web page form using HTML. Good Web development standard practices should be followed in this step. Examples of good practices include utilizing the form controls that are appropriate for specific needs.
6. **Test the Web page form.** An important part of Web development is testing to assure that you are following XHTML standards. In this book, we use the World Wide Web Consortium (W3C) validator that allows you to test your Web page and clearly explains any errors you have. Additionally when testing, you should verify that all controls work as intended. Finally, both the Submit and the Reset buttons should be tested.

When necessary, more specific details concerning the above guidelines are presented at appropriate points in the chapter. The chapter also will identify the actions performed and decisions made regarding these guidelines during the creation of the Web page shown in Figure 6–1.

Web Page Forms

The Sabatina's Order Form Web page shown in Figure 6–1b on page HTML 287 shows an example of a Web page form designed to request specific information from the Web page visitor. A Web page form has three main components:

- Input controls
- A <form> tag, which contains the information necessary to process the form
- A Submit button, which sends the data to be processed

Input Controls

An **input control** is any type of input mechanism on a form. A form may contain several different input controls classified as data or text input controls. A **data input control** can be a radio button (radio), a check box (checkbox), a Submit button (submit), a Reset button (reset), or a selection menu (select). A **text input control** allows the user to enter text through the following:

- A **text box** (text), for small amounts of text
- A **textarea box** (textarea), for larger amounts of text
- A **password text box** (password), for entering a password

As shown in Figure 6–1b, the form developed in this chapter uses several different data and text input controls.

Of the available input controls, the eight listed in Table 6–1 are used most often in form creation.

BTW

Forms

Several HTML guides on the Internet discuss the use of forms on Web pages. Many of these sites are created and maintained at universities. The guides give practical tips on the purpose and use of HTML tags and attributes. To view an HTML guide, use a search engine to search for the phrase "HTML Guide" or a related phrase.

Table 6–1 Form Input Controls

Control	Function	Remarks
text	• Creates a single-line field for a relatively small amount of text	• Indicates both the size of the field and the total maximum length
password	• Identical to text boxes used for single-line data entry	• Echoes (or masks) the entered text as bullets
textarea	• Creates a multiple-line field for a relatively large amount of text	• Indicates the number of rows and columns for the area
select	• Creates a drop-down list or menu of choices from which a visitor can select an option or options	• Indicates the length of the list in number of rows
checkbox	• Creates a single item or a list of items	• Indicates a single item that can be checked • Indicates a list of more than one item that can be chosen
radio	• Creates a list item	• Indicates only one item in a list can be chosen
submit	• Submits a form for processing	• Tells the browser to send the data on the form to the server
reset	• Resets the form	• Returns all input controls to the default status

A **text control** creates a text box that is used for a single line of input (Figure 6–2 on the next page). The text control has two attributes:

- **size**, which determines the number of characters that are displayed on the form
- **maxlength**, which specifies the maximum length of the input field

The maximum length of the field may exceed the size of the field that appears on the form. For example, consider a field size of three characters and a maximum length of nine characters. If a Web page visitor types in more characters than the size of the text box (three characters), the characters scroll to the left, to a maximum of nine characters entered. For example, this code creates a text box to input the user's last name and password:

```
<p>Last Name: <input name="lastname" type="text" size="25" />
```

A **password control** also creates a text box used for a single line of input (Figure 6–2), except that the characters entered into the field can appear as asterisks or bullets. A password text box holds the password entered by a visitor. The password appears as a series of characters, asterisks, or bullets as determined by the Web developer, one per character for the password entered. This feature is designed to help protect the visitor's password from being observed by others as it is being entered.

Figure 6–2 Text and password text controls.

BTW

Radio Buttons

Old-time car radios were operated by a row of large black plastic buttons. Push one button, and you would get one preset radio station. You could push only one button at a time. Radio buttons on forms work the same way as the old-time radio buttons—one button at a time. With check boxes, more than one option can be selected at a time.

A **radio control** limits the Web page visitor to only one choice from a list of choices (Figure 6–3). Each choice is preceded by a **radio button**, or option button, which typically appears as an open circle. When the visitor selects one of the radio buttons, all other radio buttons in the list automatically are deselected. By default, all radio buttons are deselected. To set a particular button as the default, you use the checked value within the <input /> tag. Here is example code to create two radio controls:

```
<input name="ingredient" type="radio" value="sausage" />Sausage
<input name="ingredient" type="radio" value="veggie" />Veggie
Password: <input name="password" type="password" size="10" />
```

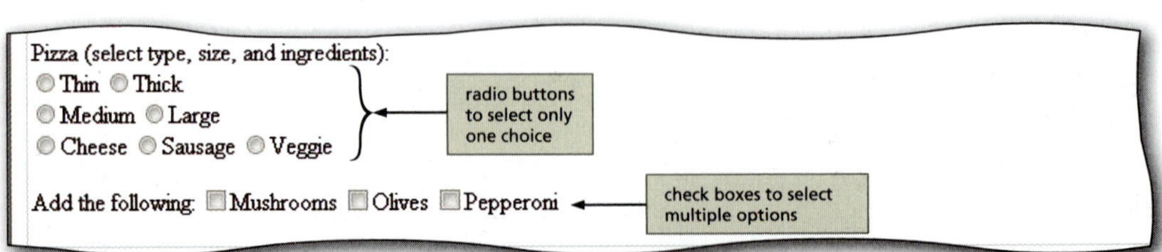

Figure 6–3 Radio and checkbox controls.

A **checkbox control** allows a Web page visitor to (a) select one item from a single-item list or (b) select more than one choice from a list of choices (Figure 6–3). Each choice in a check box list can be either on or off. By default, all check boxes are deselected.

The default can be changed so a particular check box is preselected as the default, by using the checked value within the <input /> tag. Here is sample code for a checkbox control:

```
<input name="additional" type="checkbox" value="mushrooms" />
Mushrooms
```

A **select control** creates a selection menu from which the visitor selects one or more choices (Figure 6–4). This prevents the visitor from having to type information into a text or textarea field. A select control is suitable when a limited number of choices are available. The user clicks the list arrow to view all the choices in the menu. When clicked, the default appears first and is highlighted to indicate that it is selected. Here is sample code for a select control:

```
<select name="payment">
<option>American Express</option>
<option>Visa</option>
<option>MasterCard</option>
</select>
```

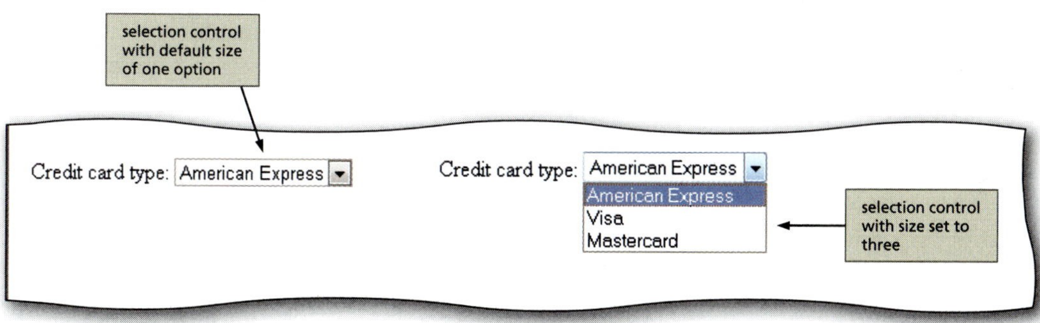

Figure 6–4 Different options for select controls.

A **textarea control** creates a field that allows multiple lines of input (Figure 6–5). Textarea fields are useful when an extensive amount of input is required from, or desired of, a Web page visitor. The textarea control has two primary attributes:

- **rows**, which specifies the number of rows in the textarea field
- **cols**, which specifies the number of columns in the textarea field

A textarea control is created with the following code:

```
What other items would you like to see on our menu?
<textarea name="other" rows="3" cols="100"></textarea>
```

BTW

Textareas
To create a textarea, the Web developer specifies the number of rows and columns in which the Web page visitor can enter information. The maximum number of characters for a textarea is 32,700. It is a good rule to keep the number of columns in a textarea to 50 or fewer. Using that as a limit, the textarea will fit on most screens.

The **fieldset control** (Figure 6–5 on the next page) helps to group related form elements together. This makes the form easier to read and complete. The form segment in Figure 6–5 shows two groupings: one with a left-aligned legend and the other with a right-aligned legend. Using fieldset tags to segregate information allows the Web page visitor immediately to see that two (or more) categories of information are included in the form. The easier that it is for a user to complete a form, the more likely it is that he or she will complete it. A fieldset control is created with the following code:

```
<fieldset><legend>Customer Information</legend></fieldset>
```

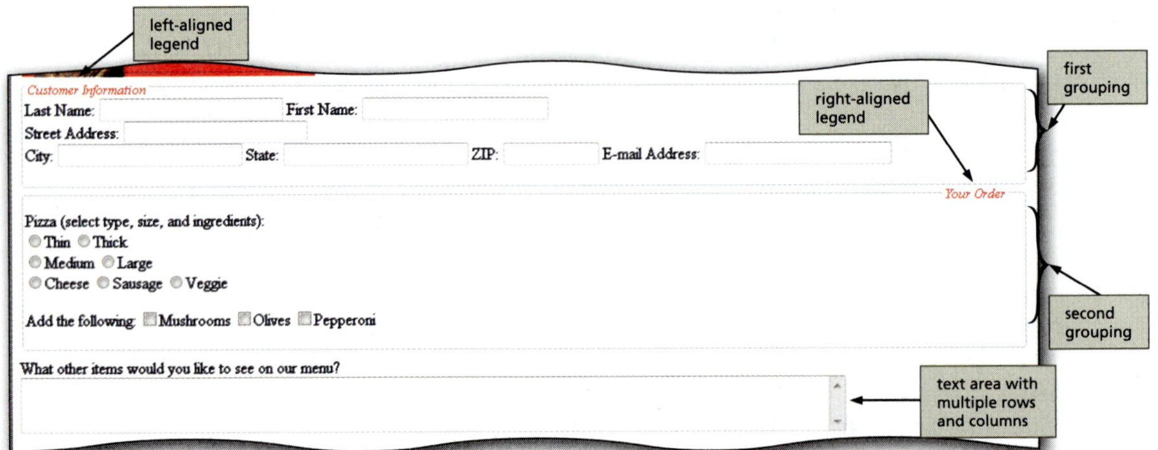

Figure 6–5 Fieldset and textarea controls.

The **submit control** and the **reset control** create the Submit and Reset buttons, respectively (Figure 6–6). The **Submit button** sends the information to the appropriate location for processing. The **Reset button** clears any input that was entered in the form, resetting the input controls back to the defaults. A Web page form must include a Submit button, and most also include a Reset button. The submit and reset controls are created with the following code:

```
<input type="submit" value="Submit" />
<input type="reset" value="Reset" />
```

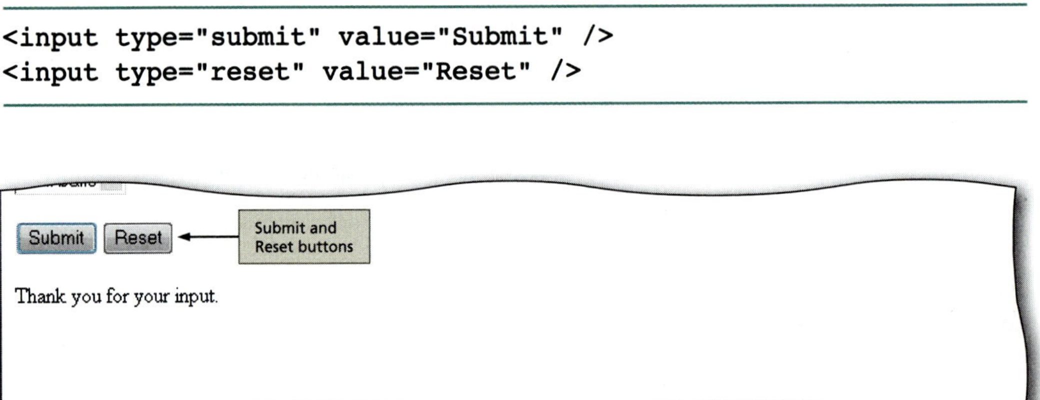

Figure 6–6 Submit and Reset button controls.

Regardless of the specific type, each input control has one or two attributes:

- **name**, which identifies the specific information that is being sent when the form is submitted for processing. All controls have a name.
- **value**, which is the type of data that is contained in the named input control (that is, the data that the Web page visitor enters). All controls except textarea also have a value attribute. For a textarea field, no value attribute is possible because of the variability of the input.

When a Web page visitor clicks the Submit button on the form, both the control name and the value of the data contained within that control are sent to the server to be processed.

HTML Tags Used to Create Forms

Form statements start with the <form> tag and end with the </form> tag. The input controls in a form are created using either HTML tags or attributes of HTML tags. For example, the select and textarea controls are created using the HTML tags <select> and <textarea>, respectively. Other input controls are created using attributes of HTML tags. For example, the text boxes, check boxes, radio buttons, and Submit and Reset buttons all are created using the type attribute of the <input /> tag. Table 6–2 lists the HTML tags used to create the order form in this chapter. Any combination of these elements can be used in a Web page form.

Table 6–2 HTML Tags Used to Create Forms

Tag	Function	Remarks
<fieldset> </fieldset>	Groups related controls on a form	Optionally used for readability
<form> </form>	Creates a form that allows user input	Required when creating forms
<input />	Defines the controls used in the form, using a variety of type attribute values	Required for input controls
<legend> </legend>	Defines the text that is displayed in the grouping borders	Optionally used when using <fieldset> tags
<select> </select>	Creates a menu of choices from which a visitor selects	Required for selection choices
<option> </option>	Specifies a choice in a <select> tag	Required, one per choice
<textarea> </textarea>	Creates a multiple-line text input area	Required for longer text inputs that appear on several lines

Attributes of HTML Tags Used to Create Forms

Many of the HTML tags used to create forms have several attributes. Table 6–3 lists some of the HTML tags used to create forms, along with their main attributes and functions.

BTW **Form Tutorial**
What better way to learn more about the HTML form tag than using a tutorial on the Web? Many Web sites have lessons grouped by topic, starting with initial HTML tags. An index is generally provided for ease of use. Most tutorials use illustrative examples to teach the important points of HTML to create Web pages. To find HTML tutorials, search the Web using a popular search engine.

Table 6–3 Attributes and Functions of HTML Tags Used to Create Forms

Tag	Attribute	Function
<form> </form>	action	• URL for action completed by the server
	method	• HTTP method (post)
	target	• Location at which the resource will be displayed
<input />	type	• Type of input control (text, password, checkbox, radio, submit, reset, file, hidden, image, button)
	name	• Name of the control
	value	• Value submitted if a control is selected (required for radio and checkbox controls)
	checked	• Sets a radio button to a checked state (only one can be checked)
	disabled	• Disables a control
	readonly	• Used for text passwords
	size	• Number of characters that appear on the form
	maxlength	• Maximum number of characters that can be entered
	src	• URL to the location of an image stored on the server
	alt	• Alternative text for an image control
	tabindex	• Sets tabbing order among control elements

Table 6–3 Attributes and Functions of HTML Tags Used to Create Forms (continued)

Tag	Attribute	Function
<legend> </legend>	align	• Indicates how a legend should be aligned
<select> </select>	name size multiple disabled tabindex	• Name of the element • Number of options visible when Web page is first opened • Allows for multiple selections in select list • Disables a control • Sets the tabbing order among control elements
<option> </option>	selected disabled value	• Specifies whether an option is selected • Disables a control • Value submitted if a control is selected
<textarea> </textarea>	name rows cols disabled readonly tabindex	• Name of the control • Height in number of rows • Width in number of columns • Disables a control • Used for text passwords • Sets the tabbing order among control elements

Creating a Form on a Web Page

In this chapter, you will modify the text-based Order Form Web page used in the Sabatina's Pizza Web site. The file, sabatinasorderform.html, currently contains only text and does not utilize a form or form controls (Figure 6–1a on page HTML 287). Using this text-based order form is inconvenient for the user, who must print the form, complete the required order information, and then fax that information to the phone number listed in the opening paragraph of text.

The file, sabatinasorderform.html, is stored in the Data Files for Students for this chapter. See the inside back cover of this book for instructions on downloading the Data Files for Students, or contact your instructor for information about accessing the required file. After opening this file in Notepad++, you will enter HTML code to convert this text-based Web page into the Web page form shown in Figure 6–1b on page HTML 287.

Plan Ahead

Processing form information.

One of the most important issues to determine when creating a Web page form is what to do with the information once it is entered. One way to process the information is to use a CGI script, which is code that has been previously written in a language other than HTML. The information collected from forms is often used to feed databases. A CGI script provides a much better way to process that information. For the scope of this book, we use the second method to process information, the post. The post can be used to send the information to an e-mail address.

- **Using a CGI script.** This action is beyond the scope of this book, but it is the more efficient way to handle the information input into the Web page form. A Web developer would have to find out what script capabilities reside on the server in order to utilize it.
- **Posting to an e-mail address.** Because we do not know what CGI scripts are available on the Web servers at your location, we will utilize the e-mail posting technique in this chapter. The information posted to an e-mail address is not readily usable, so other steps will have to be taken to utilize the data coming in via e-mail.

To Start Notepad++ and Open an HTML File

The following steps illustrate how to start Notepad++ and open the HTML file, sabatinasorderform.html.

1. Start Notepad++ and, if necessary, maximize the window.
2. With a USB drive plugged into your computer, click File on the menu bar and then click Open.
3. If necessary, navigate to the Chapter06\ChapterFiles folder on the USB drive.
4. Click sabatinasorderform.html in the list of files.
5. Click the Open button to open the sabatinasorderform.html file in Notepad++ (Figure 6–7).

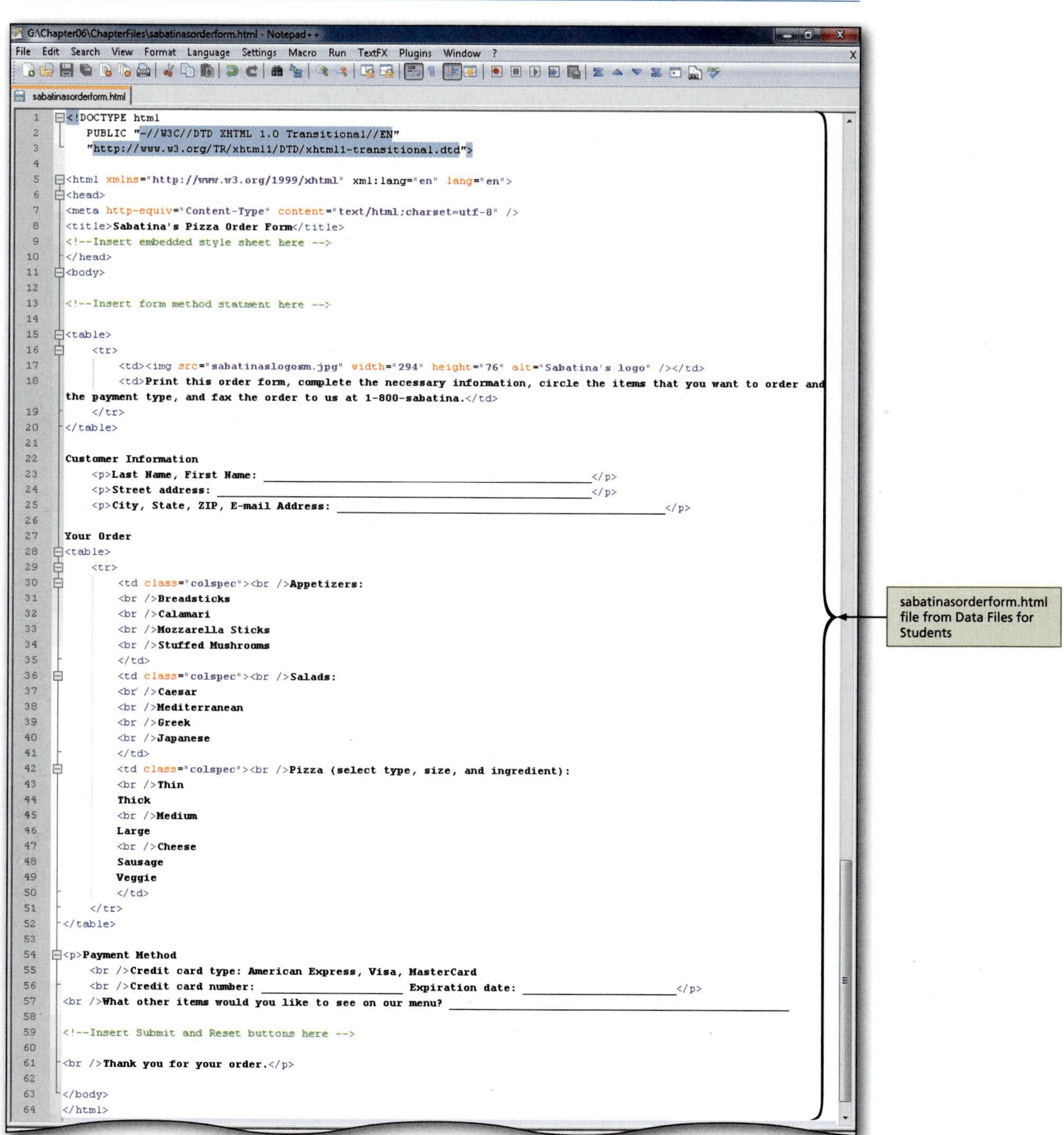


```
<!DOCTYPE html
   PUBLIC "-//W3C//DTD XHTML 1.0 Transitional//EN"
   "http://www.w3.org/TR/xhtml1/DTD/xhtml1-transitional.dtd">

<html xmlns="http://www.w3.org/1999/xhtml" xml:lang="en" lang="en">
<head>
<meta http-equiv="Content-Type" content="text/html;charset=utf-8" />
<title>Sabatina's Pizza Order Form</title>
<!--Insert embedded style sheet here -->
</head>
<body>

<!--Insert form method statment here -->

<table>
    <tr>
        <td><img src="sabatinaslogosm.jpg" width="294" height="76" alt="Sabatina's logo" /></td>
        <td>Print this order form, complete the necessary information, circle the items that you want to order and
the payment type, and fax the order to us at 1-800-sabatina.</td>
    </tr>
</table>

Customer Information
    <p>Last Name, First Name: ____________________________________________</p>
    <p>Street address: ____________________________________________</p>
    <p>City, State, ZIP, E-mail Address: ____________________________________________</p>

Your Order
<table>
    <tr>
        <td class="colspec"><br />Appetizers:
        <br />Breadsticks
        <br />Calamari
        <br />Mozzarella Sticks
        <br />Stuffed Mushrooms
        </td>
        <td class="colspec"><br />Salads:
        <br />Caesar
        <br />Mediterranean
        <br />Greek
        <br />Japanese
        </td>
        <td class="colspec"><br />Pizza (select type, size, and ingredient):
        <br />Thin
        Thick
        <br />Medium
        Large
        <br />Cheese
        Sausage
        Veggie
        </td>
    </tr>
</table>

<p>Payment Method
    <br />Credit card type: American Express, Visa, MasterCard
    <br />Credit card number: ____________________ Expiration date: ____________________</p>
<br />What other items would you like to see on our menu? ____________________________________________

<!--Insert Submit and Reset buttons here -->

<br />Thank you for your order.</p>

</body>
</html>
```

Figure 6–7

Creating a Form and Identifying the Form Process

When adding a form to a Web page, the first steps are creating the form and identifying how the form is processed when it is submitted. The start <form> and end </form> tags designate an area of a Web page as a form. Between the <form> and </form> tags, form controls can be added to request different types of information and allow the appropriate input responses. A form can include any number of controls.

The **action attribute** of the <form> tag specifies the action that is taken when the form is submitted. Information entered in forms can be sent by e-mail to an e-mail address or can be used to update a database. Although the e-mail option is functional, many Web sites process information from forms using Common Gateway Interface (CGI) scripting. A **CGI script** is a program written in a programming language (such as PHP or Perl) that communicates with the Web server. The CGI script sends the information input on the Web page form to the server for processing. Because this type of processing involves programming tasks that are beyond the scope of this book, the information entered in the order form created in this chapter will be submitted in a file to an e-mail address. The e-mail address will be specified as the action attribute value in the <form> tag.

> **BTW**
> **CGI Scripts**
> Using CGI scripts to process forms is a much more efficient way to handle the data that is sent from a form. Many Web sites have free sample CGI scripts for Web developers to use. Search the Web for relevant CGI information and free samples.

> **BTW**
> **Mailto Restrictions**
> Some schools and organizations restrict the use of the mailto action. This is something that you need to test in order to determine whether it will work in your situation.

The **method attribute** of the <form> tag specifies the manner in which the data entered in the form is sent to the server to be processed. Two primary ways are used in HTML: the get method and the post method. The **get method** sends the name-value pairs to the end of the URL indicated in the action attribute. The **post method** sends a separate data file with the name-value pairs to the URL (or e-mail address) indicated in the action attribute. Most Web developers prefer the post method because it is much more flexible. You need to be cautious when using the get method. Some Web servers limit a URL's size, so you run the risk of truncating relevant information when using the get method. The post method is used for the forms in this chapter.

The following HTML code creates a form using the post method and an action attribute to indicate that the form information should be sent to an e-mail address in an attached data file:

```
<form method="post" action="mailto: sabatinas@isp.com">
```

When the form is submitted, a file containing the input data is sent as an e-mail attachment to the e-mail address sabatinas@isp.com.

To Create a Form and Identify the Form Process

The following step shows how to enter HTML code to create a form and identify the form process.

- Highlight the words <!--Insert form method statement here --> on line 13.
- Type `<form method="post" action="mailto: sabatinas@isp.com">` to replace the highlighted words with the new tag.
- Click the blank line 62 and press the ENTER key.
- Type `</form>` but do not press the ENTER key (Figure 6–8).

```
54 <p>Payment Method
55     <br />Credit card type: American Express, Visa, MasterCard
56     <br />Credit card number: ____________________ Expiration date: ______________________</p>
57 <br />What other items would you like to see on our menu? ______________________________________________
58
59 <!--Insert Submit and Reset buttons here -->
60
61 <br />Thank you for your order.</p>
62
63 </form>
64 </body>
```

end form

Figure 6–8

To Change the Text Message

The next step in updating the text-based Order Form Web page is to modify the text that tells the user to submit the questionnaire by e-mail. Table 6–4 shows the new HTML code used to provide instructions to users on how to submit the information on the order form.

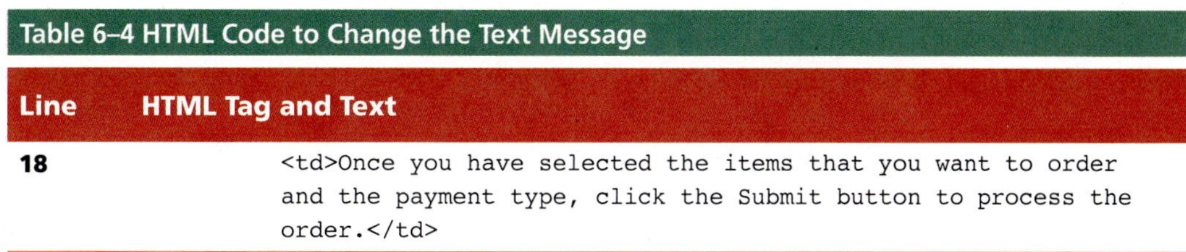

Table 6–4 HTML Code to Change the Text Message

Line	HTML Tag and Text
18	`<td>Once you have selected the items that you want to order and the payment type, click the Submit button to process the order.</td>`

The following step illustrates how to change the text message to provide instructions on how to use the order form.

- Highlight line 18.
- Enter the HTML code shown in Table 6–4, indenting as shown, but do not press the ENTER key (Figure 6–9).
- Highlight lines 22 through 57 (ending above the blank line 58) and then press the DELETE key (Figure 6–9).

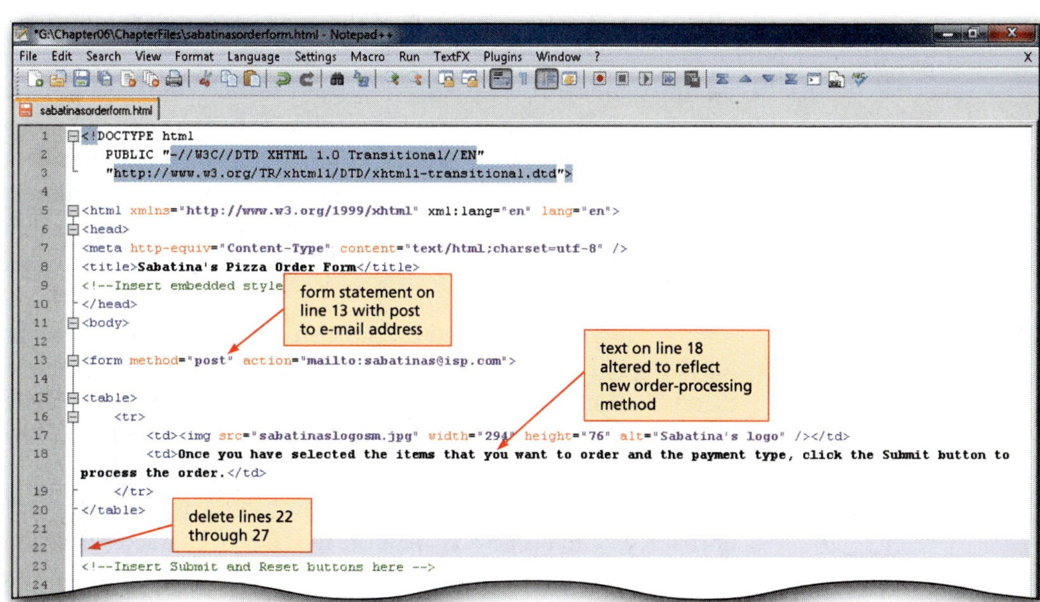

Figure 6–9

> **Form controls.**
> Before creating a Web page form, you should plan how you want to format it. By effectively utilizing input controls, you can call attention to important data-collection areas on the Web page without overpowering it. Creating an effective form includes:
>
> 1. **Determine what data to collect.** In the case of a form designed to sell a product, you need the visitor's name and address information. Make sure to provide enough space for each field so that you do not cut out important information. For instance, an address field only 10 characters long may cut out much of the street name.
> 2. **Determine what types of control to use.** For data such as name and address, you need text input areas. For data such as credit card type, there is a limited subset (i.e., American Express, Visa, and MasterCard), so a selection control is appropriate. When you ask what kind of pizza the visitor is interested in buying, you can use check boxes, which allow multiple selection. In the case of an answer with only two choices (i.e., Yes/No or Thick or Thin pizza?), a radio button is more appropriate.
>
> *(continued)*

Plan Ahead

(continued)

3. **Lay out the input areas effectively.** One of the first input items you may want is the visitor's name and address information. That should go to the top of the page. Also, you can group information together on the same line if it makes sense to make the Web page form short enough that visitors do not have to scroll much. Notice in our order form that the city/state/ZIP are on one line of the Web page. Another thing to consider is the use of e-mail addresses beyond the initial contact with a visitor or customer. An e-mail address is a great way to continue communication with visitors or customers. A company can e-mail newsletters, coupons, and general information to customers once they have their e-mail addresses.
4. **Use grouping techniques for clarity.** The last thing that you may want to do on a Web page form is group like input items together. Use the fieldset tag to segregate personal information from order information and from other comments that the visitor might make.

Adding Text Boxes

As previously discussed, a text box allows for a single line of input. The HTML code below shows an example of the code used to add a text box to a form:

```
<input name="address" type="text" size="25" maxlength="25" />
```

The <input /> tag creates an input control, while the attribute and value type="text" specifies that the input control is a text box. The name attribute of the input control is set to the value address, to describe the information to be entered in this text box. When the form is submitted, the name is used to distinguish the value associated with that field from other fields.

The size attribute indicates the size of the text box that appears on the form. In the following HTML code, size="25" sets the text field to 25 characters in length, which means that only 25 characters will appear in the text box. The maxlength attribute maxlength="25" limits the number of characters that can be entered in the text box to 25 characters. The maxlength attribute specifies the same number of characters (25) as the size attribute (25), so all characters entered by a user will appear in the text box. If you specify a maximum number of characters that is greater than the number of characters specified in the size attribute, the additional characters scroll to the right in the text box as the user enters them.

To Add Text Boxes

The next step in creating the order form is to add seven text boxes to the form for users to enter first name, last name, street address, city, state, ZIP, and e-mail address. Table 6–5 shows the HTML code to add seven text boxes to the form. Each text box has a size of 25 characters, except the ZIP text box, with only 10 characters. No maxlength attribute is specified, which means users can enter text items longer than 25 characters, but only 25 characters will display in the text box.

Table 6–5 HTML Code to Add Text Boxes

Line	HTML Tag and Text
22	<p>Last Name: <input name="lastname" type="text" size="25" />
23	First Name: <input name="firstname" type="text" size="25" />
24	 Street Address: <input name="address" type="text" size="25" />
25	 City: <input name="city" type="text" size="25" />
26	State: <input name="state" type="text" size="25" />
27	ZIP: <input name="zip" type="text" size="10" />
28	E-mail Address: <input name="email" type="text" size="25" /></p>

The following step illustrates how to add text boxes to the form.

1

- If necessary, click line 22.
- Enter the HTML code shown in Table 6–5 and then press the ENTER key twice (Figure 6–10).

Q&A How do I know what size to make each field?

Determine a reasonable field size for the various input areas. For instance, it would not be wise to allow only 10 characters for the last name, because many people now hyphenate their last names and last names can be more than 10 characters. To improve your judgment for field sizes, observe online and paper forms that you complete. Also, think of long street or city names and try those in the forms that you create.

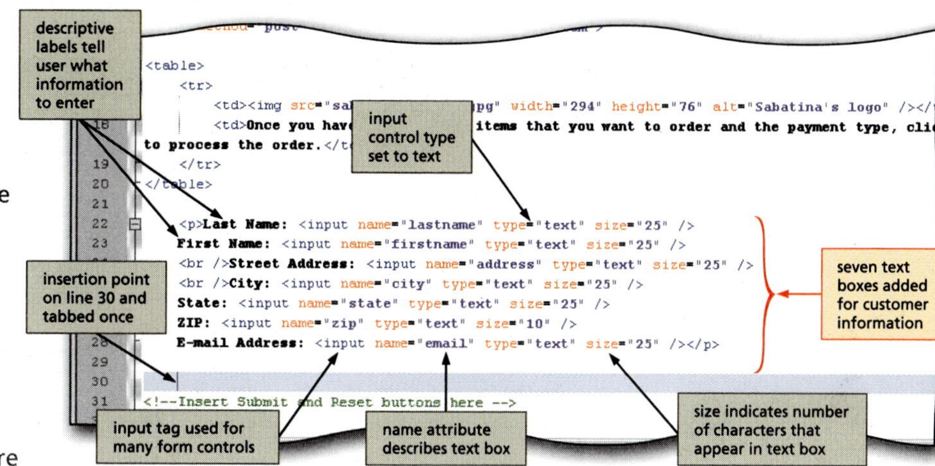

Figure 6–10

Q&A What is the default value if I do not specify the type in my <input /> tag?

The default type for the <input /> tag is a text box. Therefore, if the type attribute is not used in the <input /> tag, it creates a text box.

To Save an HTML File

Because you opened a file that was already created, you can press the CTRL+S keys to save what you have done so far. Do this frequently throughout your projects.

1 With the USB flash drive connected to one of the computer's USB ports, hold down the CTRL key and then press the S key.

Other Ways

1. Click File, then Save
2. Click Save icon on Notepad++ toolbar

Adding Radio Buttons

The next step is to add radio buttons to the form. Remember that radio buttons are appropriate to use when a user can select only one choice from a set of two or more choices. Questions with a Yes or No answer are perfect for the use of radio buttons. In the case of Thick or Thin (pizza) and Medium and Large, you have one of two choices to make. More than two options are possible with radio buttons also. In the case of Cheese, Sausage, or Veggie, you can only select one of the three choices. On the Order Form Web page, radio buttons allow users to select a one-choice answer to a question.

To Add Radio Buttons

Table 6–6 contains the HTML code to add a set of radio buttons to the Order Form Web page.

Table 6–6 HTML Code to Add Radio Buttons

Line	HTML Tag and Text
30	` Pizza (select type, size, and ingredients):`
31	` <input name="pizzatype" type="radio" value="thin" />Thin`
32	`<input name="pizzatype" type="radio" value="thick" />Thick`
33	
34	` <input name="size" type="radio" value="medium" />Medium`
35	`<input name="size" type="radio" value="large" />Large`
36	
37	` <input name="ingredient" type="radio" value="cheese" />Cheese`
38	`<input name="ingredient" type="radio" value="sausage" />Sausage`
39	`<input name="ingredient" type="radio" value="veggie" />Veggie`

The following step illustrates how to add three sets of radio buttons to the form.

1

- Check that the insertion point is on Line 30, indented one Tab stop.
- Enter the HTML code shown in Table 6–6 and then press the ENTER key twice (Figure 6–11).

Q&A

Could I have used check boxes for this control, rather than radio buttons?

You could have used check boxes, but it would not make sense for this information. In this case, this is a clear yes or no answer. With check boxes, you are assuming that they can make multiple selections. Again, look at the standards used in most Web development.

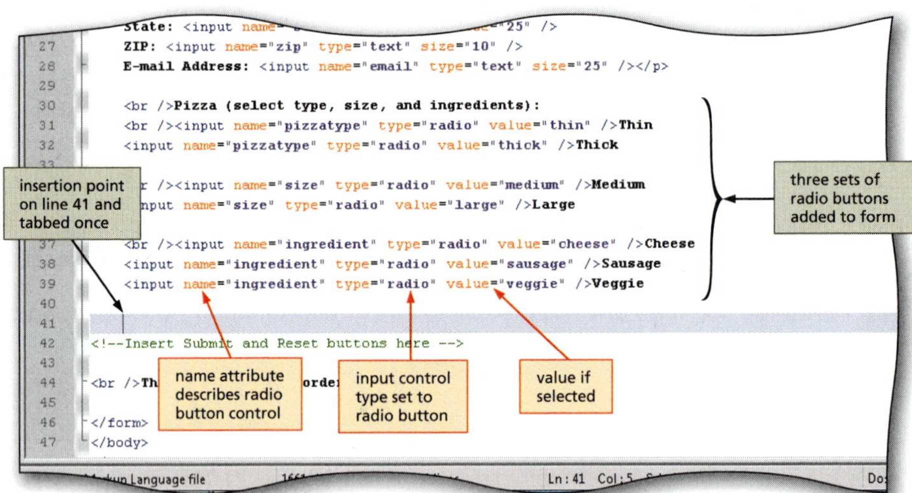

Figure 6–11

Adding Check Boxes

Check boxes are similar to radio buttons, except they allow multiple options to be selected. Radio buttons should be used when only one option can be selected, while check boxes should be used when the user can select more than one option.

The HTML code below shows an example of the code used to add a check box to a form:

```
<input name="additional" type="checkbox" value="mushrooms" />
Mushrooms
```

The <input /> tag creates an input control, while the attribute and value type="checkbox" specifies that the input control is a check box. The name attribute of the input control is set to the value additional. When the form is submitted, the name is used to distinguish the values associated with these checkbox fields from other fields. The value attribute "mushrooms" indicates the value submitted in the file, if this check box is selected.

To Add Check Boxes

In the Order Form Web page, three check boxes are used to allow the user to select one or more types of ingredients to add. Table 6–7 shows the HTML code to add three check boxes to the form.

Table 6–7 HTML Code to Add Check Boxes

Line	HTML Tag and Text
41	<p>Add the following:
42	<input name="additional" type="checkbox" value="mushrooms" />Mushrooms
43	<input name="additional" type="checkbox" value="olives" />Olives
44	<input name="additional" type="checkbox" value="pepperoni" />Pepperoni</p>

The step that follows illustrates how to enter HTML code to add check boxes to the form.

1

- Check that the insertion point is on Line 41, indented one Tab stop.
- Enter the HTML code shown in Table 6–7 and then press the ENTER key twice (Figure 6–12).

Q&A

How do I determine whether to list fields on the same line or use a line break or paragraph break between fields?

Consider the "real estate" (the amount of space available) of the Web page itself. If you have an especially long form that the visitor has to scroll down, consider positioning the fields across, rather than down the form. You do not want to crowd the information, but you also do not want to force the visitor to scroll excessively.

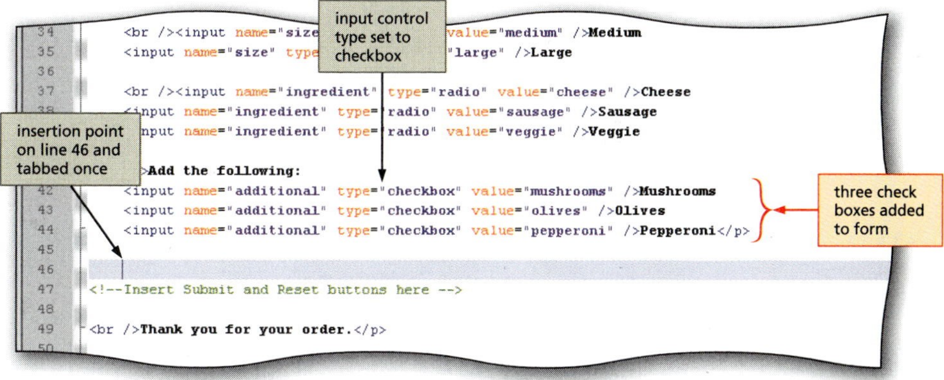

Figure 6–12

Adding a Selection Menu

A select control is used to create a selection menu from which the visitor selects one or more choices. A select control is suitable when a limited number of choices are available. Figure 6–13 on the next page. Shows the basic selection menu used in the order form, with three credit card types (Visa, MasterCard, and American Express) as the choices in the list. The topic of accepting credit cards via online forms is a serious one. See BTW on this page for more information.

BTW

Security

Security is an important issue to understand, especially when you are collecting credit card information on an online form. Search the Web for specific information concerning the usage of https SSL sites versus http sites. Also search for information regarding the vulnerability of sending unencrypted e-mail.

Figure 6–13 Select control.

If you do not specify a size attribute, only one option is displayed, along with a list arrow, as shown in Figure 6–13. When the list arrow is clicked, the selection menu displays all selection options. When the user selects an option, such as Visa, in the list, it appears as highlighted.

To Add a Selection Menu

Table 6–8 shows the HTML code used to create the selection menu shown in Figure 6–13.

Table 6–8 HTML Code to Add a Selection Menu

Line	HTML Tag and Text
46	`<p>Credit card type:`
47	`<select name="payment">`
48	`<option>American Express</option>`
49	`<option>Visa</option>`
50	`<option>MasterCard</option>`
51	`</select>`

The following step illustrates how to add a selection menu to the Web page form.

1

- Check that the insertion point is on Line 46, indented one Tab stop.
- Enter the HTML code shown in Table 6–8 and then press the ENTER key twice (Figure 6–14).

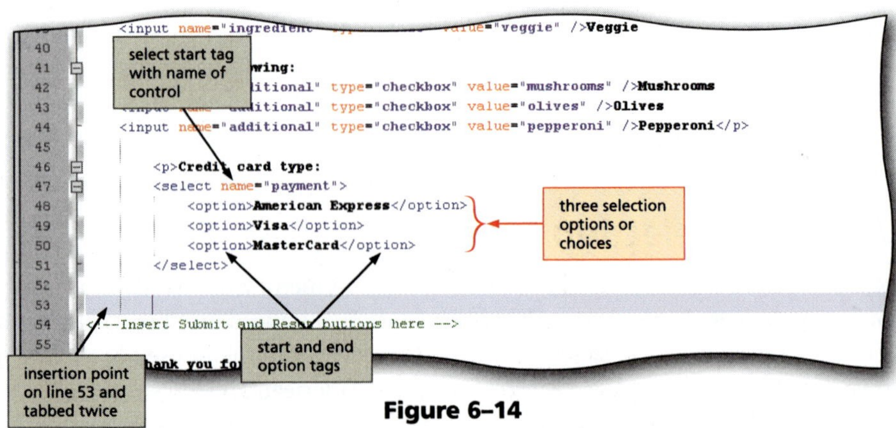

Figure 6–14

Q&A

How do I know what control type to use?

Consider the Web page "real estate," together with usability. If you have 20 options, it may not make sense to use a select control. With the three credit card options (American Express, Visa, MasterCard) it makes sense to use a select control, as users are familiar with this model. You can also look at the types of controls other Web developers use, and apply those that make sense for your situation.

Adding More Advanced Selection Menus

Selection menus have many variations beyond the simple selection menu used in the Order Form Web page. Table 6–3 on pages HTML 293 and HTML 294 lists several attributes for the <select> tag. Using these attributes, a selection menu can be set to display multiple choices or only one, with a drop-down list to allow a user to select another choice. A selection menu also can be defined to have one choice preselected as the default.

Figure 6–15 shows samples of selection menus. The HTML code used to create each selection menu is shown in Figure 6–16 on the next page.

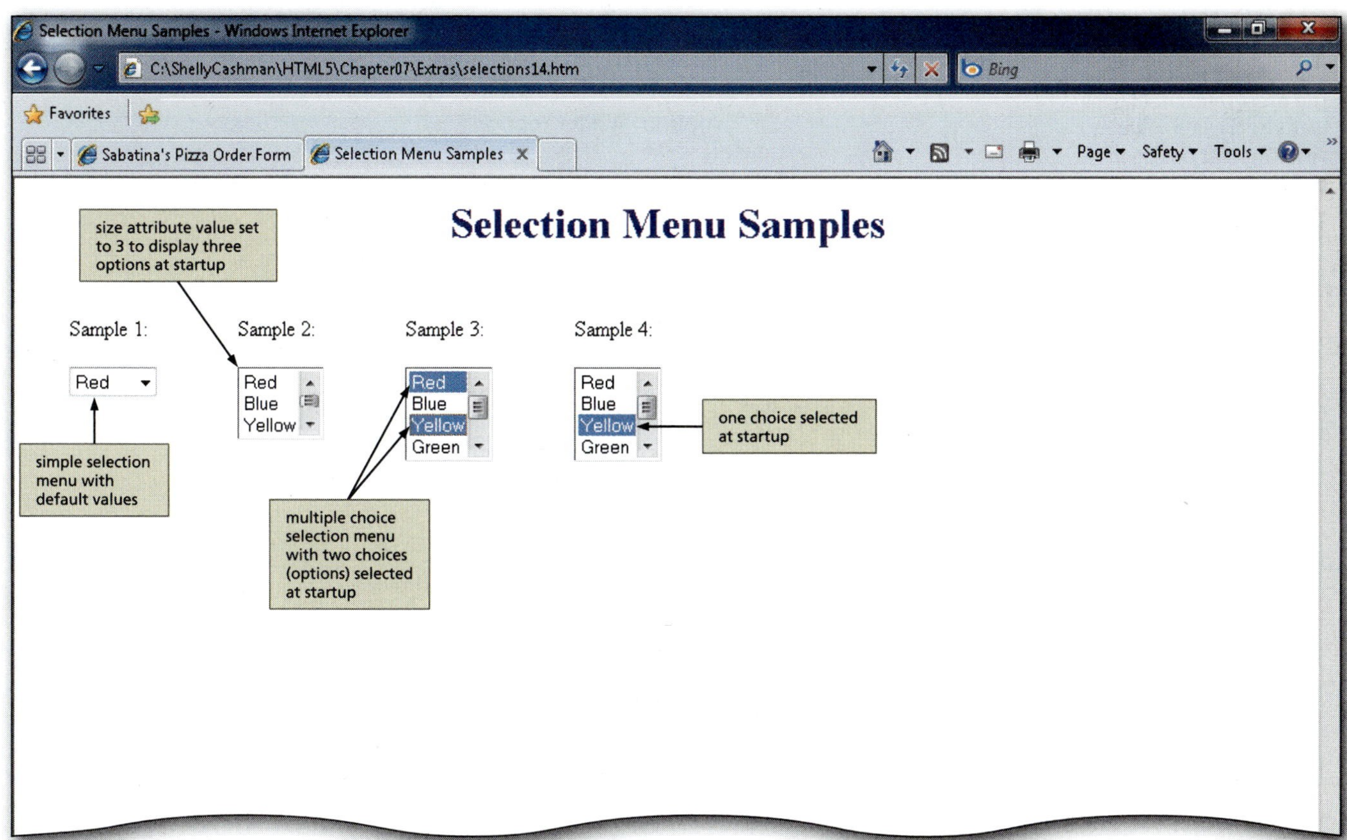

Figure 6–15 Sample selection controls with variations.

The selection menu in Sample 1 is a basic selection menu, with no attributes specified other than the name and the list options. This resulting selection menu uses a list menu that allows users to select one choice from the list. No choice is selected by default. The selection menu in Sample 2 uses a size attribute value of 3 to indicate that three choices should appear in the menu at startup. A user can use the up and down scroll arrows to view other choices in the list. The selection menu in Sample 3 uses the multiple attribute to allow a user to select more than one choice in the list. To select multiple choices, a user first must select one choice and then press and hold the CTRL key while clicking other choices in the list. If a user wants to select several consecutive choices, he or she can select the first choice and then press and hold the SHIFT key while selecting the last choice. All choices between the first choice and last choice automatically will be selected. The selection menu in Sample 4 also contains the multiple attribute, so one or more choices can be selected. In addition, Sample 4 provides an example of one choice (in this case, Yellow) being selected at startup. As shown in the HTML code in Figure 6–16, the selected attribute is included in the <option> tag for Yellow, to indicate that Yellow should be selected at startup.

BTW

Options

The <select> and <option> tags are useful when you have a limited number of choices from which a Web page visitor can select. If the number of options becomes too large, however, the list is difficult to read. A better idea might be to group together like options into submenus. You can use the <optgroup> tag before the first <option> tag in the first group that you want to use in a submenu. After the last option in that group, use the </optgroup> tag.

The purpose of the selection menu dictates the type of selection menu that should be used and the HTML code required to create that select control. Using the basic tags and attributes shown in Figure 6–16, you can create a wide variety of selection menus to suit almost any purpose.

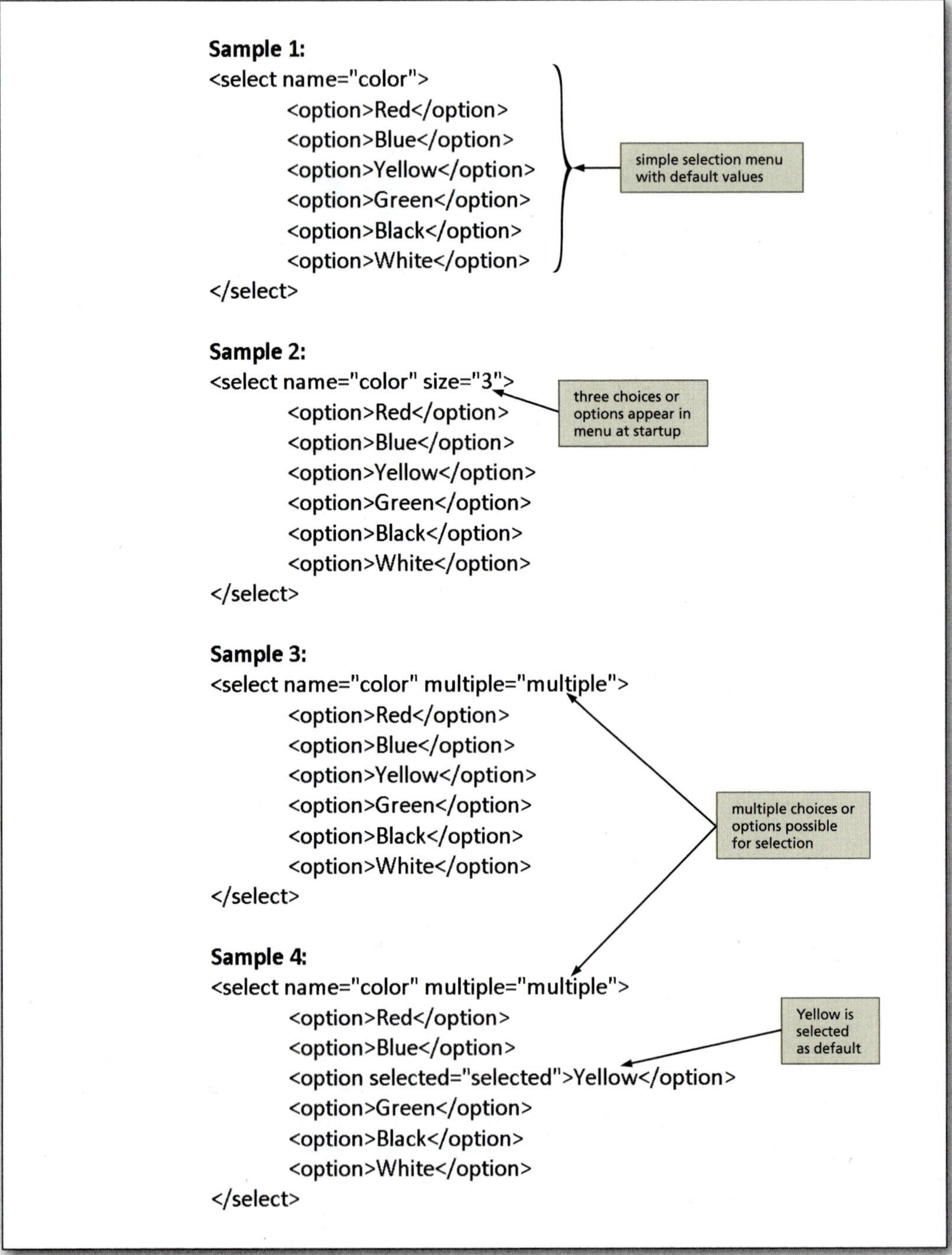

Figure 6–16 HTML code to create selection menus.

To Add Additional Text Boxes

The next step in creating the Order Form Web page is to add two more text boxes for credit card number and expiration date. Table 6–9 shows the HTML code used to add the additional text boxes. A text field is used rather than a textarea field because the user needs to enter only one row of characters.

Table 6–9 HTML Code to Add Additional Text Boxes

Line	HTML Tag and Text
53	Credit card number:
54	<input name="cardnum" type="text" size="20" maxlength="20" />
55	
56	Expiration date:
57	<input name="cardexp" type="text" size="4" maxlength="4" /></p>

The following steps illustrate how to add two additional text boxes to the Web page form.

1. Check that the insertion point is on Line 53, indented two Tab stops.
2. Enter the HTML code shown in Table 6–9 and then press the ENTER key twice (Figure 6–17). Use the BACKSPACE key, if necessary, to align the insertion point at the beginning of Line 59.

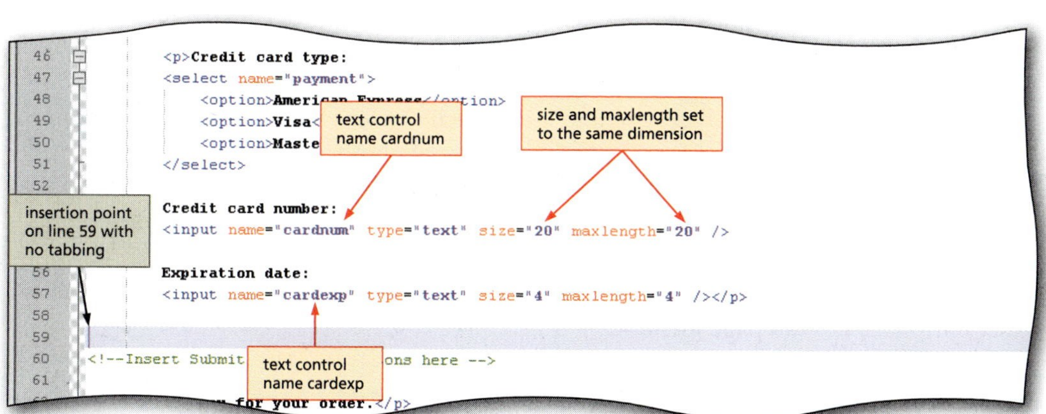
text control name cardnum
size and maxlength set to the same dimension
insertion point on line 59 with no tabbing
text control name cardexp
<p>Credit card type:
<select name="payment">
Credit card number:
<input name="cardnum" type="text" size="20" maxlength="20" />
Expiration date:
<input name="cardexp" type="text" size="4" maxlength="4" /></p>

Figure 6–17

Adding a Textarea Box

The next step is to add a textarea to the form. Remember that a textarea is used when you want a multiple-row input area. The text control only allows a user to input one row of information. For multiple rows, use the textarea control.

The order form includes a textarea that allows the user to add additional comments about what other items could be included on the menu. Because the response can be longer than just one line, a textarea control is used.

BTW

Feedback
One good use of forms is to get feedback from your visitors. Suggestions from visitors not only can help improve the Web site, but can give your visitors the sense that you care about their opinions. Taking visitor feedback into account provides for better customer satisfaction.

To Add a Textarea Box

The next step is to add a textarea to the form. You use a textarea because you want the user to be able to input more than one line. Table 6–10 contains the tags and text to specify a textarea for multiple-line input.

Table 6–10 HTML Code to Add a Textarea

Line	HTML Tag and Text
59	 What other items would you like to see on our menu?
60	 <textarea name="other" rows="3" cols="100"></textarea>

The following step illustrates how to add a textarea to the order form.

1

- If necessary, click line 59.
- Enter the HTML code shown in Table 6–10 and then press the ENTER key (Figure 6–18).

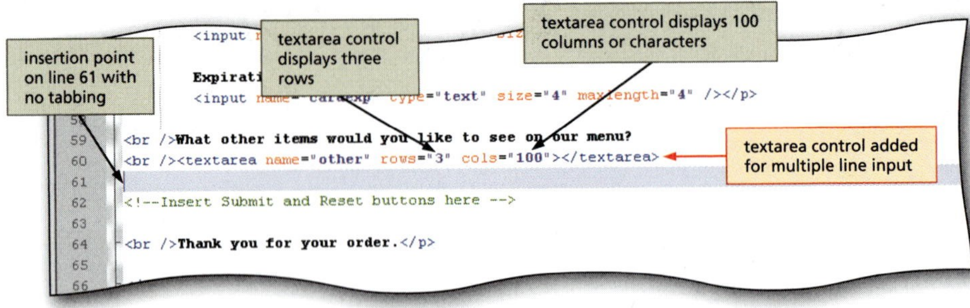

Figure 6–18

Q&A How do I know how big to make the textarea box?

Again, you need to look at the standards used in most Web development. You also have to view the textarea box in the browser to see how the size affects the Web page form. For instance, if we had made the number of rows 4, rather than 3, the Web page visitor would not have seen the "Thank you for your order." message on the bottom of the page. That is something that you want the visitor to see without scrolling.

BTW **Submit and Reset Buttons**

A simplistic, default button is created when you use the type="submit" attribute and value or the type="reset" attribute and value within the <input> tag. The <button> tag also can be used to create a submit button. The <button> tag gives you the option of using an image for the button, rather than using the default button style. The appearance of the button text can be changed with the <style> tag. These tags give you more flexibility when creating submit or reset buttons.

Adding Submit and Reset Buttons

The form controls are useless unless the information entered in the form can be submitted for processing. The next step in creating the order form is to add two buttons at the bottom of the Web page form. The first button, Submit, is for submitting the form. When the visitor clicks this button, the data entered into the form is sent to the appropriate location for processing. The second button, Reset, clears any data that was entered in the form.

The HTML code below shows the <input /> tags used to create the Submit and Reset buttons on a Web page form:

```
<p><input type="submit" value="Submit" />
<input type="reset" value="Reset" />
```

The first line of HTML code creates a Submit button on the Web page form. A Submit button is created by using the attribute type="submit" in an <input /> tag. The value attribute is used to indicate the text that should appear on the button face — in this case, Submit.

When a user clicks the Submit button, all data currently entered in the form is sent to the appropriate location for processing. The action taken when a form is submitted is based on the method and action attributes specified in the <form> tag. In the <form> tag at the start of this form, the HTML code set the form attributes to method="post" and action="mailto:sabatinas@isp.com". Thus, when a user clicks the Submit button, a data file that contains all the input data automatically is sent as an e-mail attachment to the e-mail address sabatinas@isp.com. By default, the data file is named Postdata.att.

The code below shows a sample of the data file that is sent to the e-mail address, when using the post method. In this sample, the user checked the radio button for a Thin crust, Sausage pizza, and is paying with an American Express card:

```
payment=American Express&pizzatype=thin&ingredient=sausage
```

The data entered in the form appears in the data file as name-value pairs — the name of the control as specified in the name attribute, followed by the value entered or selected in the control. In the above example, the user selected American Express in the selection menu, which is controlled by the field named payment, and clicked the Thin radio button, which is controlled by the field named pizzatype. The user also selected the Sausage radio button, which is controlled by the field named ingredient. An ampersand (&) strings together all of the name-value pairs to make them easier to read. The receiver of this e-mail could take the information in this format and decipher what is being requested. A simple program, written in a different programming language such as C++ or Java, could be developed that reads the information in the e-mail and transforms it into a more usable format. As mentioned earlier in the chapter, a CGI script is a better way to collect large amounts of information from forms, but that is beyond the scope of this book.

The Reset button also is an important part of any form. Resetting the form clears any information previously typed into a text box or textarea and resets radio buttons, check boxes, selection menus, and other controls to their initial values. As shown in the second line of the HTML code above, a Reset button is created by using the attribute type="reset" in an <input /> tag. The value attribute is used to indicate the text that should appear on the button face — in this case, Reset.

To Add Submit and Reset Buttons

The following step illustrates how to add a Submit button and a Reset button to the form.

1

- Highlight the statement <!--Insert Submit and Reset buttons here --> on line 62.
- Type `<p><input type="submit" value="Submit" />` to create the Submit button and then press the ENTER key.
- Type `<input type="reset" value="Reset" />` to create the Reset button. Do not press the ENTER key (Figure 6–19).

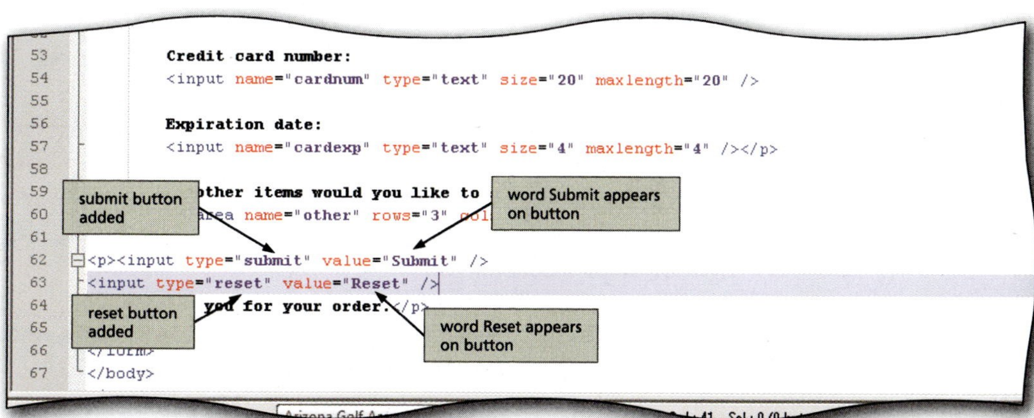

Figure 6–19

Q&A That submit option seems very easy to use. Do I need to do anything else in order to process the data?

No, the Submit button works in conjunction with the statements that you provided in your form tag in order to process the data entered.

Q&A Why do I need the Reset button?

It is best always to provide a Reset button next to the Submit button. This is useful to clear all of the data entered in case your visitors want to start over or if they change their minds or make mistakes.

Q&A If a visitor uses the Reset button, what does that do to default values that I have included in the tags?

Reset will set those default values back to the original values included in the tags. In other words, if you use a default value, Reset does not clear that value.

Plan Ahead

Organizing a form.
When using fieldset tags to separate and organize information on a form, consider the following:

- **Required vs. optional information.** You can group all required information into one section of the form and place all optional information into another grouping. By doing this, you call attention immediately to the required information on the form.
- **General organization.** It can be helpful to enhance the look and feel of the form with groupings. Especially in the case of a long form, using separators helps direct the visitors' attention.

BTW

Groupings
An important part of good Web design is to make a form easy to use. Your Web site visitors are more likely to complete a form if they readily understand the information that is being requested. You can use the <fieldset> tag to group like information together.

Organizing a Form Using Form Groupings

An important aspect of creating a Web page form is making the form easy for Web site visitors to understand. Grouping similar information on a form, for example, makes the information easier to read and understand — and, as a result, easier to complete. Grouping is especially helpful in cases where some information is required and some is optional. In the order form, for example, all the personal information is required (for example, name, address, and credit card number). The order information (i.e., pizza type, size, and ingredient) is also required. The final question on the form, however, (What other items would you like to see on our menu?) is optional. The form thus should be modified to group required and optional information.

A **fieldset** control is used to group similar information on a form. The HTML code below shows the <fieldset> tag used to add a fieldset control to a Web page form:

```
<fieldset><legend align="left">Left-aligned legend</legend>
</fieldset>
```

The <legend> tag within the fieldset tag is optional. Using the <legend> tag creates a legend for the fieldset, which is the text that appears in the grouping borders, as shown in the example in Figure 6–20. The align attribute is used to align the legend to the left or right of the fieldset control.

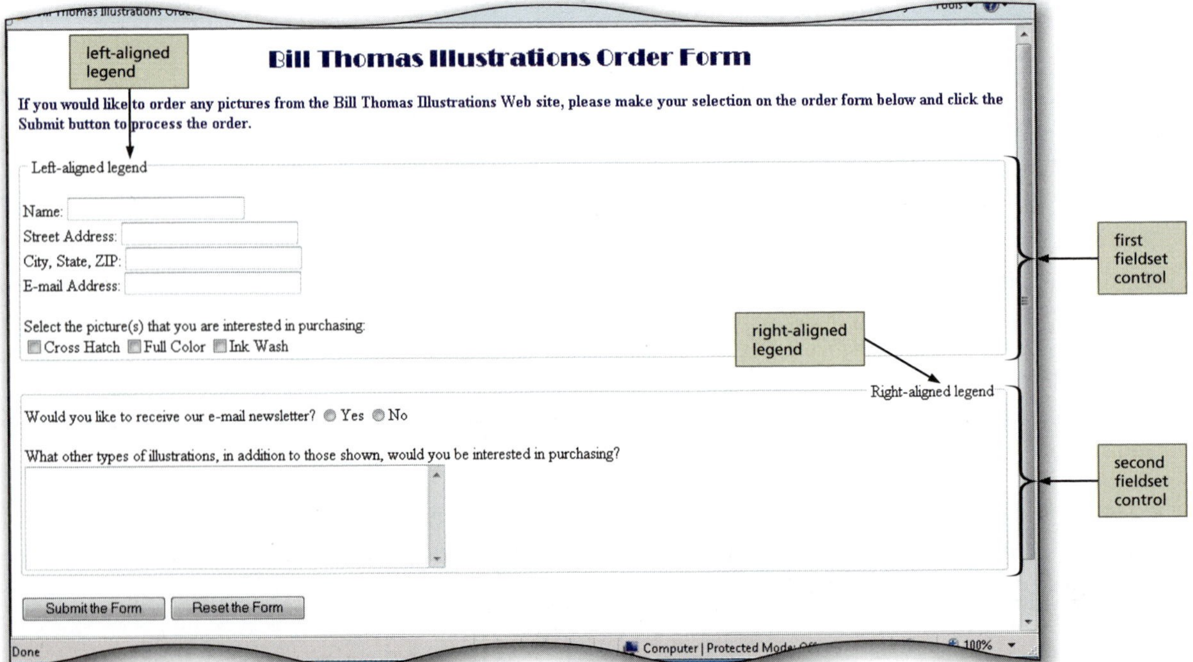

Figure 6–20 Fieldset controls on a form.

In the Order Form Web page that you will create, three fieldset controls are added to group similar information on the form. The first fieldset control is used to group customer information, as shown in Figure 6–21. The first fieldset control has the legend, Customer Information, aligned to the left. The second fieldset control is used to group order information. The second fieldset control has the legend, Your Order, aligned to the left. The third fieldset control, used to group the payment information, has the legend, Payment Method, aligned to the left. These groupings divide the form so it is more readable and clearly defines what information is required and what is optional.

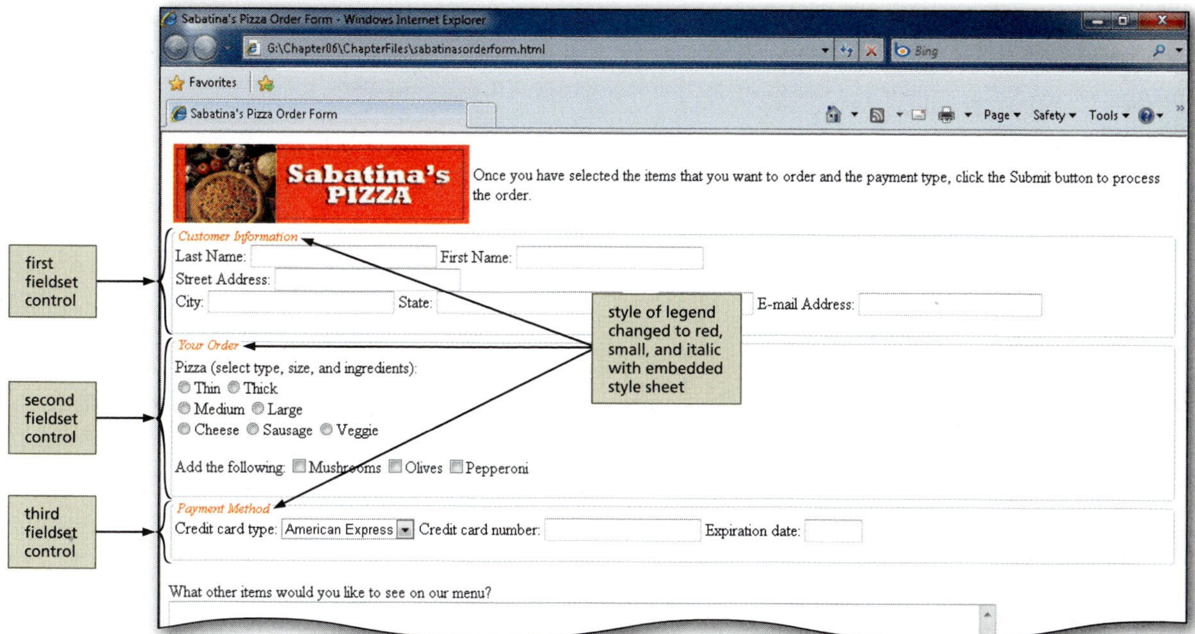

Figure 6–21

To Add Fieldset Controls to Create Form Groupings

The following step shows how to add three sets of fieldset tags to create information groupings on the Web page form.

- Click just before <p>Last Name at the beginning of line 22, and then press the ENTER key.
- Move the insertion point back up to line 22. If necessary, use the BACKSPACE key to move back to the left margin. Type `<fieldset><legend>Customer Information</legend>` as the tag to begin the first fieldset (Figure 6–22a).

Figure 6–22 (a)

- Click just after the </p> on line 29, and then press the ENTER key.
- If necessary, use the BACKSPACE key to move back to the left margin, type `</fieldset>` on line 30 to end the first fieldset, and then press the ENTER key.

2

- With the insertion point on line 32, type `<fieldset><legend>Your Order</legend>` to start the second fieldset.
- Click to the right of the </p> on line 47 (at the end of the Pepperoni</p> line), and then press the ENTER key.
- If necessary, use the BACKSPACE key to move back to the left margin, type `</fieldset>`, and then press the ENTER key.
- On line 50, type `<fieldset><legend>Payment Method</legend>` to start the third fieldset.

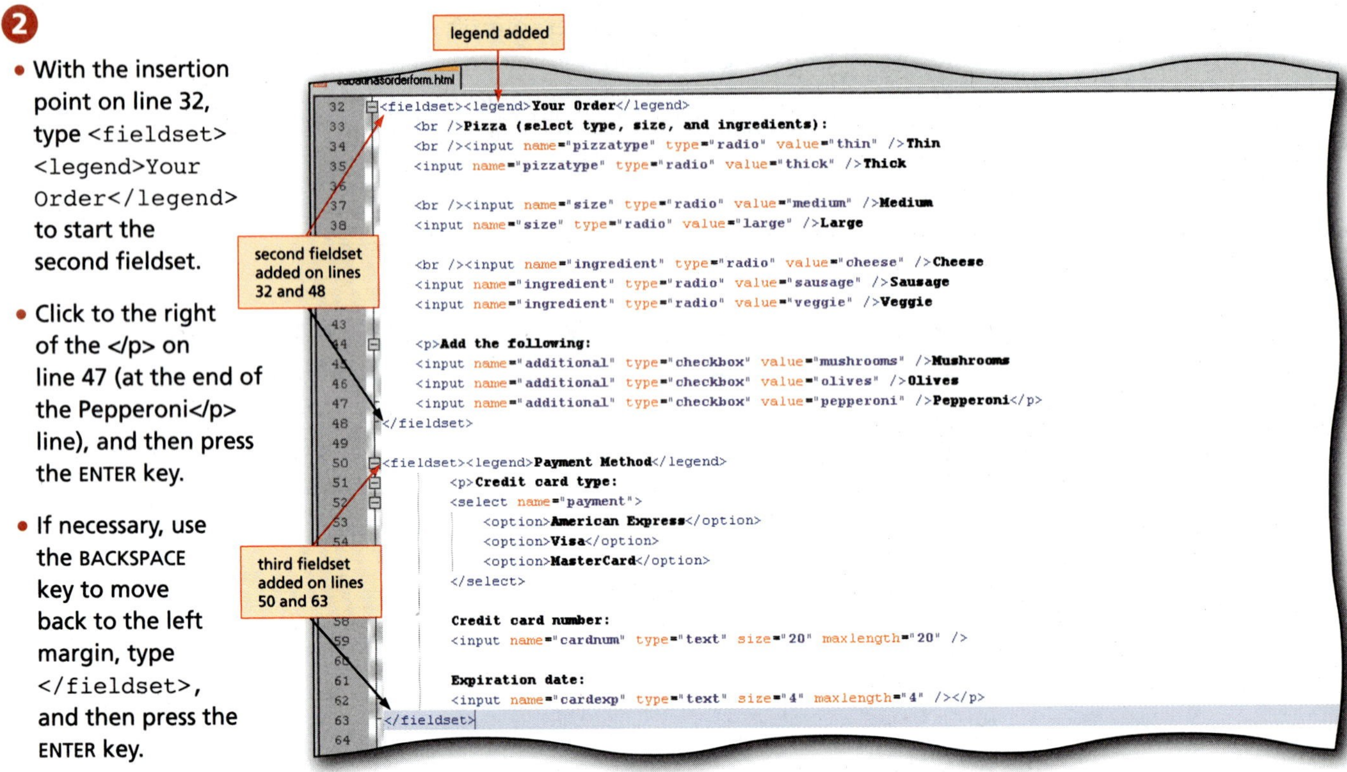
legend added
second fieldset added on lines 32 and 48
third fieldset added on lines 50 and 63
32 <fieldset><legend>Your Order</legend>
33
Pizza (select type, size, and ingredients):
34
<input name="pizzatype" type="radio" value="thin" />Thin
35 <input name="pizzatype" type="radio" value="thick" />Thick
37
<input name="size" type="radio" value="medium" />Medium
38 <input name="size" type="radio" value="large" />Large

<input name="ingredient" type="radio" value="cheese" />Cheese
<input name="ingredient" type="radio" value="sausage" />Sausage
<input name="ingredient" type="radio" value="veggie" />Veggie
44 <p>Add the following:
<input name="additional" type="checkbox" value="mushrooms" />Mushrooms
46 <input name="additional" type="checkbox" value="olives" />Olives
47 <input name="additional" type="checkbox" value="pepperoni" />Pepperoni</p>
48 </fieldset>
50 <fieldset><legend>Payment Method</legend>
51 <p>Credit card type:
<select name="payment">
<option>American Express</option>
<option>Visa</option>
<option>MasterCard</option>
</select>
Credit card number:
59 <input name="cardnum" type="text" size="20" maxlength="20" />
61 Expiration date:
62 <input name="cardexp" type="text" size="4" maxlength="4" /></p>
63 </fieldset>

Figure 6–22 (b)

- Click to the right of the </p> on line 62 (at the end of the <input name="cardexp" type="text" size="4" maxlength="4" /></p> line), and then press the ENTER key.
- If necessary, use the BACKSPACE key to move back to the left margin, and type `</fieldset>` to end the third fieldset (Figure 6–22b).

Q&A What is the default value for the <legend> alignment?

If you do not indicate otherwise, the legend will align left.

Q&A Are there other options such as colored borders that I can use with the <fieldset> tag?

Yes, you can set the margins, font, colors, etc. for the <fieldset> tag. You can use an inline, embedded, or external Cascading Style Sheet (CSS) for those options.

Adding an Embedded Style Sheet

The next step in creating the Order Form Web page is to add an embedded style sheet to improve the look of the legends in all three field groupings. Figure 6–23a shows the Web page as it displays currently without the change in legend style. Note that the default position for the legend is on the left, and the legend is the default color, black. Figure 6–23b shows the Web page with the new style for the legends as inserted in the embedded style sheet. Remember that an embedded style sheet changes the style for a single Web page. The embedded style sheet is inserted within the <style></style> container in the <head> section of the Web page.

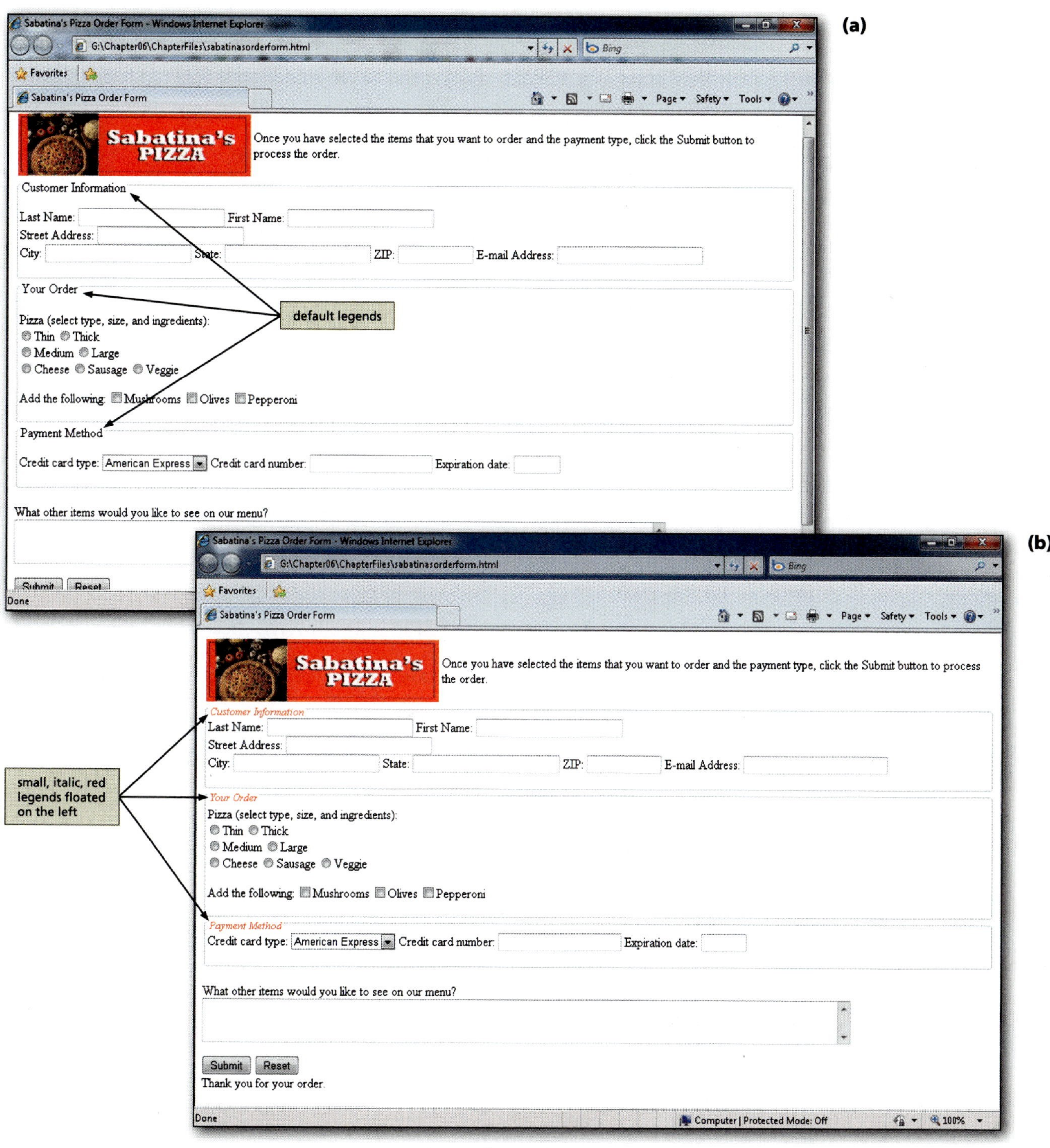

Figure 6–23

In this style sheet, you change the color, font-style, and font-size of the legend (lines 13 through 15), making it red (to match the Sabatina's logo) and smaller than the surrounding text. You also use the float property (line 12) to align the legend on the left. In Chapter 3, you used the float property to align images relative to the Web page text. The float property indicates in which direction (in this case left or right) to display (or float) an element (the legend) being inserted on a Web page. It can be an effective Web development practice to use an alignment element such as float so that you can easily change the alignment if you choose.

To Add an Embedded Style Sheet

Table 6–11 shows the HTML code to add an embedded style sheet to format the legends for the form fields.

Table 6–11 HTML Code to Add an External Style Sheet

Line	HTML Tag and Text
9	<style type="text/css">
10	<!--
11	
12	legend {float: left;
13	color: #ff1828;
14	font-style: italic;
15	font-size: small}
16	
17	-->
18	</style>

The following steps illustrate how to add an embedded style sheet to the Web page form.

1. Highlight the statement <!--Insert embedded style sheet here --> on line 9.
2. Enter the HTML code shown in Table 6–11 but do not press the ENTER key on line 18 (Figure 6–24).

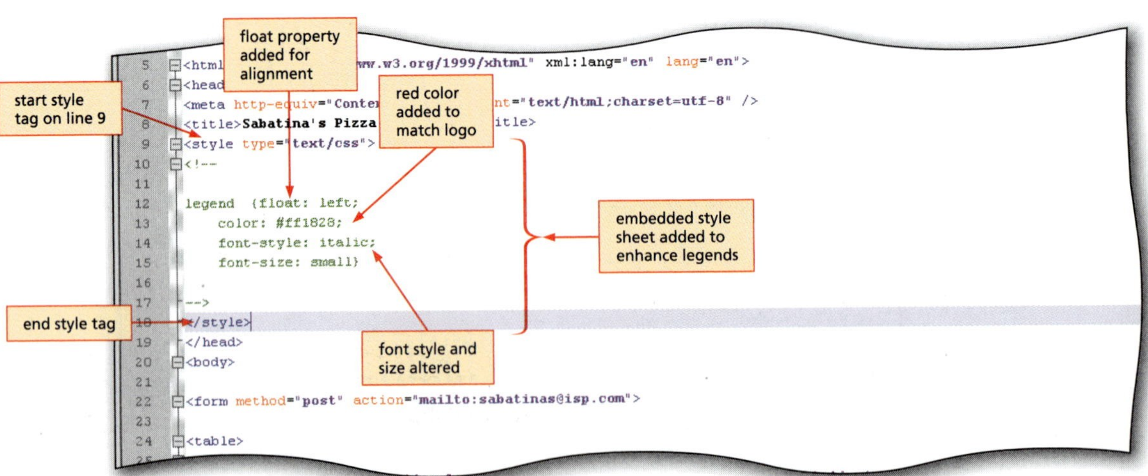

Figure 6–24

To Save the HTML File

With the Order Form Web page complete, the HTML file should be saved. The following step illustrates how to again save the sabatinasorderform.html file on the USB drive.

1. With a USB drive plugged into your computer, click File on the menu bar and then click Save to again save the sabatinasorderform.html file.

To Validate, View, and Test a Web Page

After completing the Sabatina's Order Form Web page, you should validate the code, and view and test it in a browser to confirm that the Web page appears as desired and that the controls function as expected. Note that you cannot test the Submit button because it automatically generates an e-mail message to sabatinas@isp.com, which is a nonexistent e-mail address. When you are collecting information from an online form, it is very important to test that the information is accurate. It is beyond the scope of this book to address validation issues related to server-side processing. After testing the controls, each Web page and the HTML code for each should be printed for future reference. The following steps illustrate how to validate, view, and test a Web page.

1. Validate the sabatinasorderform.html file by file upload at validator.w3.org.
2. In Internet Explorer, click the Address bar to select the URL on the Address bar, type `g:\Chapter06\ChapterFiles\sabatinasorderform.html` or the location of your file and then press the ENTER key to display the completed order form for Sabatina's Pizza (Figure 6–25 on the next page).
3. Review the form to make sure all spelling is correct and the controls are positioned appropriately.
4. Test all of the text boxes on the form. Try to type more than the maximum number of allowable characters in the cardnum and cardexp boxes.
5. Click the check boxes to test them. You should be able to choose one, two, or three of the boxes at the same time because check boxes are designed to select more than one option.
6. Test the selection control by clicking the list arrow and selecting one of the three options.
7. Click the radio buttons to test them. You should be able to make only one choice (Thick or Thin; Medium or Large; Cheese, Sausage, or Veggie).
8. Test the textarea by entering a paragraph of text. Verify that it allows more characters to be entered than are shown in the textarea.
9. Click the Reset button. It should clear and reset all controls to their original (default) state.

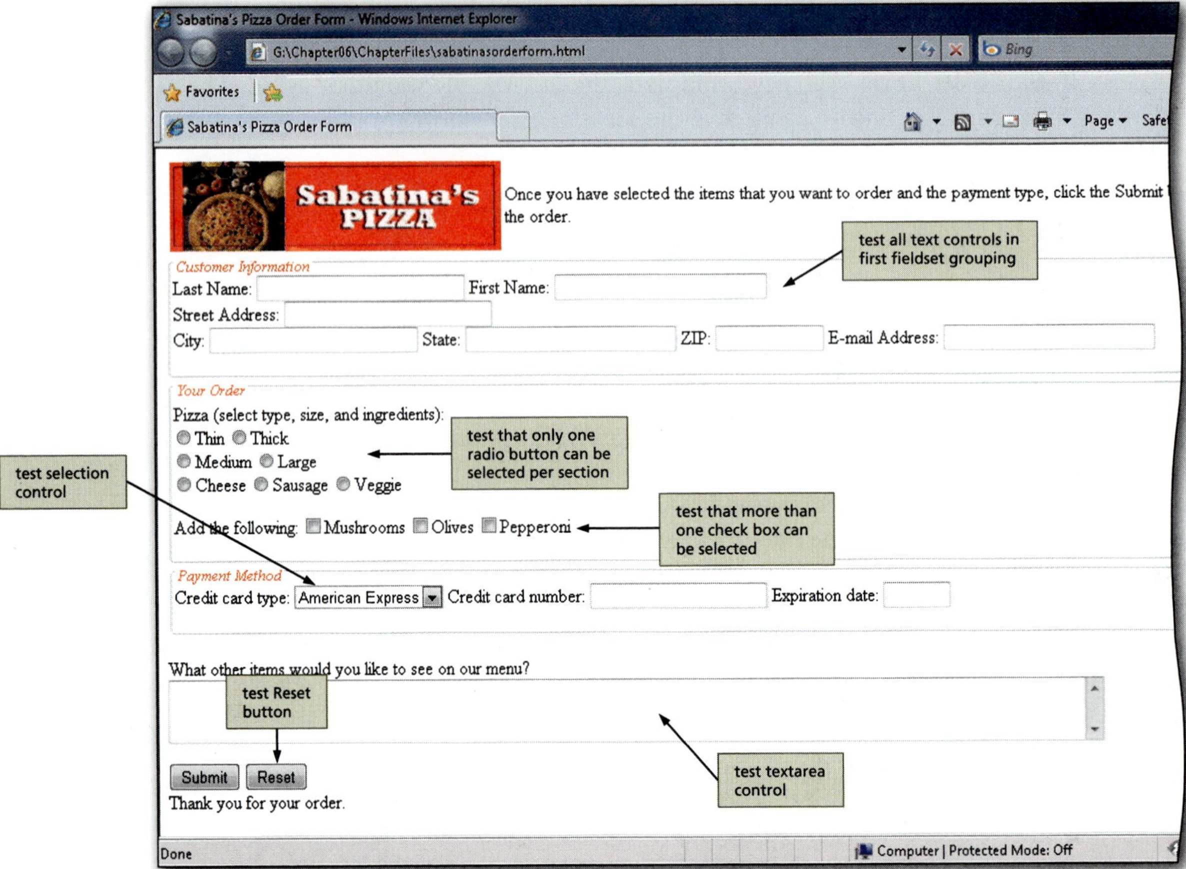

Figure 6–25

To Print a Web Page and HTML

1. Click the Print icon on the Command bar to print the Web page.
2. Click the Notepad++ button on the taskbar to activate sabatinasorderform.html.
3. Click File on the menu bar and then click Print. Click the Print button in the Print dialog box to print the HTML file (Figure 6–26).

```
<!DOCTYPE html
   PUBLIC "-//W3C//DTD XHTML 1.0 Transitional//EN"
   "http://www.w3.org/TR/xhtml1/DTD/xhtml1-transitional.dtd">

<html xmlns="http://www.w3.org/1999/xhtml" xml:lang="en" lang="en">
<head>
<meta http-equiv="Content-Type" content="text/html;charset=utf-8" />
<title>Sabatina's Pizza Order Form</title>
<style type="text/css">
<!--

legend {float: left;
    color: #ff1828;
    font-style: italic;
    font-size: small}

-->
</style>
</head>
<body>

<form method="post" action="mailto:sabatinas@isp.com">

<table>
    <tr>
        <td><img src="sabatinaslogosm.jpg" width="294" height="76" alt="Sabatina's logo"
 /></td>
        <td>Once you have selected the items that you want to order and the payment
type, click the Submit button to process the order.</td>
    </tr>
</table>

<fieldset><legend>Customer Information</legend>
    <p>Last Name: <input name="lastname" type="text" size="25" />
    First Name: <input name="firstname" type="text" size="25" />
    <br />Street Address: <input name="address" type="text" size="25" />
    <br />City: <input name="city" type="text" size="25" />
    State: <input name="state" type="text" size="25" />
    ZIP: <input name="zip" type="text" size="10" />
    E-mail Address: <input name="email" type="text" size="25" /></p>
</fieldset>

<fieldset><legend>Your Order</legend>
    <br />Pizza (select type, size, and ingredients):
    <br /><input name="pizzatype" type="radio" value="thin" />Thin
    <input name="pizzatype" type="radio" value="thick" />Thick

    <br /><input name="size" type="radio" value="medium" />Medium
    <input name="size" type="radio" value="large" />Large

    <br /><input name="ingredient" type="radio" value="cheese" />Ch
    <input name="ingredient" type="radio" value="sausage" />Sausage
    <input name="ingredient" type="radio" value="veggie" />Veggie
```

-1-

```
    <p>Add the following:
    <input name="additional" type="checkbox" value="mushrooms" />Mushrooms
    <input name="additional" type="checkbox" value="olives" />Olives
    <input name="additional" type="checkbox" value="pepperoni" />Pepperoni</p>
</fieldset>

<fieldset><legend>Payment Method</legend>
        <p>Credit card type:
        <select name="payment">
            <option>American Express</option>
            <option>Visa</option>
            <option>MasterCard</option>
        </select>

        Credit card number:
        <input name="cardnum" type="text" size="20" maxlength="20" />

        Expiration date:
        <input name="cardexp" type="text" size="4" maxlength="4" /></p>
</fieldset>

<br />What other items would you like to see on our menu?
<br /><textarea name="other" rows="3" cols="100"></textarea>

<p><input type="submit" value="Submit" />
<input type="reset" value="Reset" /></p>
<br />Thank you for your order.</p>

</form>
</body>
</html>
```

-2-

Figure 6–26

BTW

Quick Reference
For a list of HTML tags and their associated attributes, see Appendix A at the back of this book, or visit the HTML Quick Reference Web page (scsite.com/HTML6e/qr). For a list of CSS properties and values, see Appendix D at the back of this book, or visit the CSS Quick Reference Web page (scsite.com/HTML6e/qr).

To Quit Notepad++ and a Browser

1. In Notepad++, click the File menu, then Close All.
2. Click the Close button on the Notepad++ title bar.
3. Click the Close button on the browser title bar. If necessary, click the Close all tabs button.

Chapter Summary

In this chapter, you have learned how to convert a text-based Web page to a Web page form with various controls for user input. The items listed below include all the new HTML skills you have learned in this chapter.

1. Create a Form and Identify the Form Process (HTML 296)
2. Change the Text Message (HTML 297)
3. Add Text Boxes (HTML 298)
4. Add Radio Buttons (HTML 300)
5. Add Check Boxes (HTML 301)
6. Add a Selection Menu (HTML 302)
7. Add a Textarea Box (HTML 305)
8. Add Submit and Reset Buttons (HTML 307)
9. Add Fieldset Controls to Create Form Groupings (HTML 309)

Learn It Online

Test your knowledge of chapter content and key terms.

Instructions: To complete the Learn It Online exercises, start your browser, click the Address bar, and then enter the Web address `scsite.com/html6e/learn`. When the HTML Learn It Online page is displayed, click the link for the exercise you want to complete and read the instructions.

Chapter Reinforcement TF, MC, and SA
A series of true/false, multiple choice, and short answer questions that test your knowledge of the chapter content.

Flash Cards
An interactive learning environment where you identify chapter key terms associated with displayed definitions.

Practice Test
A series of multiple choice questions that test your knowledge of chapter content and key terms.

Who Wants To Be a Computer Genius?
An interactive game that challenges your knowledge of chapter content in the style of a television quiz show.

Wheel of Terms
An interactive game that challenges your knowledge of chapter key terms in the style of the television show, *Wheel of Fortune*.

Crossword Puzzle Challenge
A crossword puzzle that challenges your knowledge of key terms presented in the chapter.

Apply Your Knowledge

Reinforce the skills and apply the concepts you learned in this chapter.

Creating a Course Evaluation Web Page Form

Instructions: Start Notepad++. Open the file apply6-1.html from the Chapter06\Apply folder of the Data Files for Students. See the inside back cover of this book for instructions on downloading the Data Files for Students, or contact your instructor for information about accessing the required files. This sample HTML file contains all of the text for the Course Evaluation Survey Web page shown in Figure 6–27. You will add the necessary tags to make the Web page form, as shown in Figure 6–27.

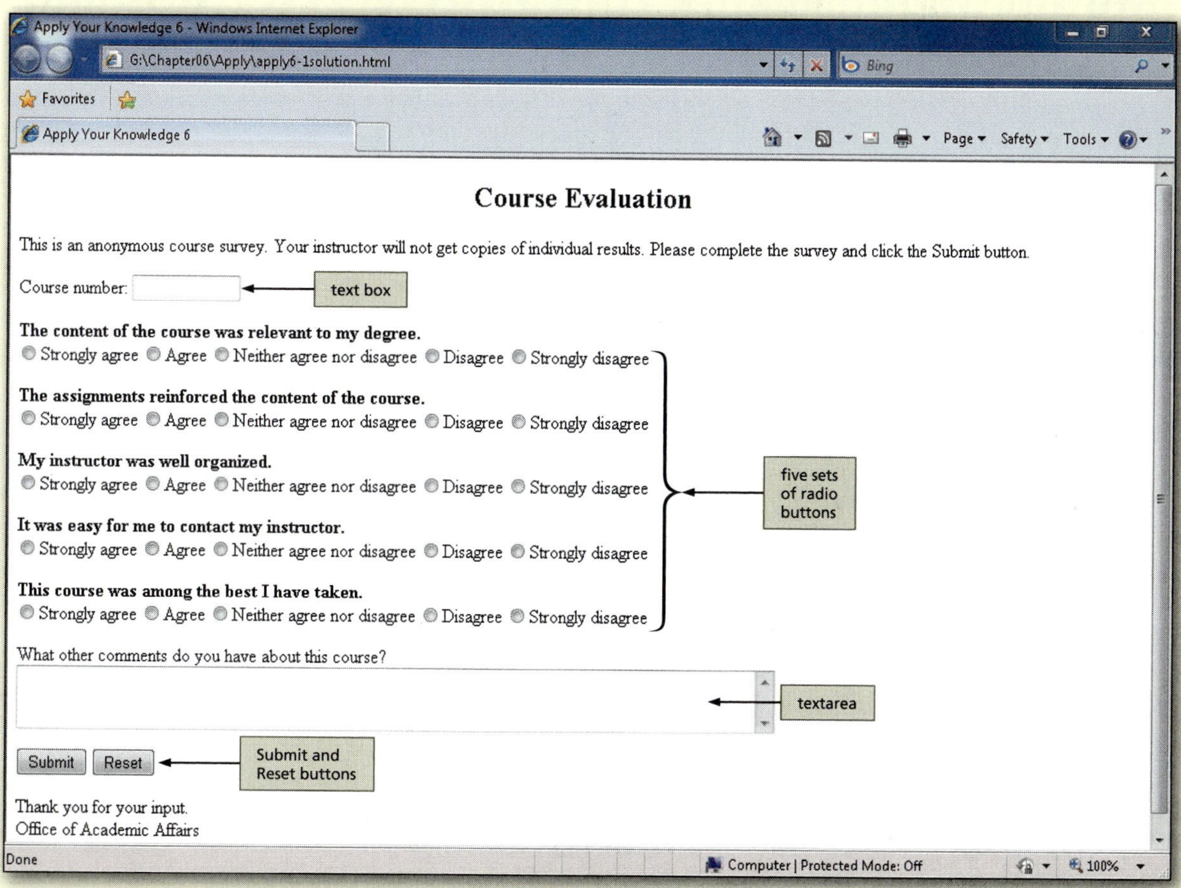

Figure 6–27

Perform the following tasks:

1. Using Notepad++, add the HTML code necessary to make the Web page look similar to the one shown in Figure 6–27. Controls used in the form include:
   a. One text box for Course number
   b. Five sets of radio buttons for course evaluation options
   c. A textarea box with 3 rows and 80 columns
2. Add the HTML code to add Submit and Reset buttons.
3. Use the post method to send an e-mail to email@isp.com.
4. Save the revised document as apply6-1solution.html.
5. Validate your HTML code and test all controls.
6. Print the Web page and HTML.
7. Submit the solution in the format specified by your instructor.

STUDENT ASSIGNMENTS

Extend Your Knowledge

Extend the skills you learned in this chapter and experiment with new skills.

Creating a Web Page Restaurant Questionnaire

Instructions: Start Notepad++. Create the form by adding the form controls and groupings, as shown in the Extend Your Knowledge Web page in Figure 6–28.

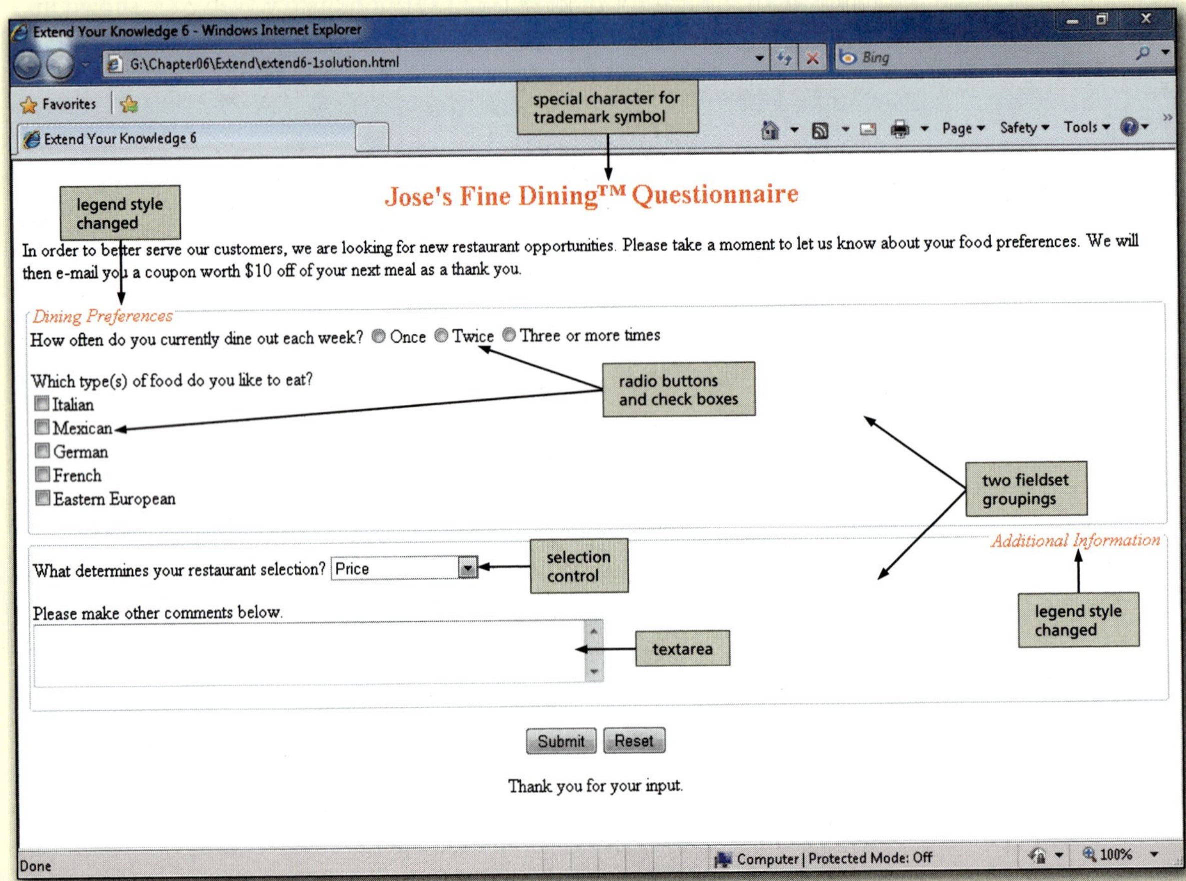

Figure 6–28

Perform the following steps:

1. Using Notepad++, create the Web page, adding any HTML code necessary to make the Web page look similar to the one shown in Figure 6–28. The code should include:
   a. An h2 heading that includes a special character (*Hint:* See Appendix F.)
   b. Three radio buttons for the number of times the visitor eats out
   c. Five check boxes for types of food the visitor eats
   d. A selection box with three options for factors that determine where they eat: Price, Proximity to home, Quality of food
   e. A textarea box with three rows and 60 columns
2. Add the HTML code necessary to add two groupings with the legends as shown. Use an embedded style sheet with classes or inline styles to change the legends to red and italics. Align the first legend to the left and the second to the right.

3. Add the HTML code necessary to add Submit and Reset buttons.
4. Save the revised file using the file name apply6-1solution.html.
5. Validate your HTML code and test all controls.
6. Print the revised HTML file.
7. View the Web page in your browser.
8. Print the Web page.
9. Submit the files in the format specified by your instructor.

Make It Right

Analyze a document and correct all errors and/or improve the design.

Correcting the Tennis Courts Survey Web Page

Instructions: Start Notepad++. Open the file makeitright6-1.html from the Chapter06\MakeItRight folder of the Data Files for Students. See the inside back cover of this book for instructions on downloading the Data Files for Students, or contact your instructor for information about accessing the required files. The Web page is a modified version of what you see in Figure 6–29. Make the necessary corrections to the Web page to make it look like the figure. Use the image tennis.png at the top of the Web page to the left of the h2 heading. Save the file as makeitright6-1solution.html.

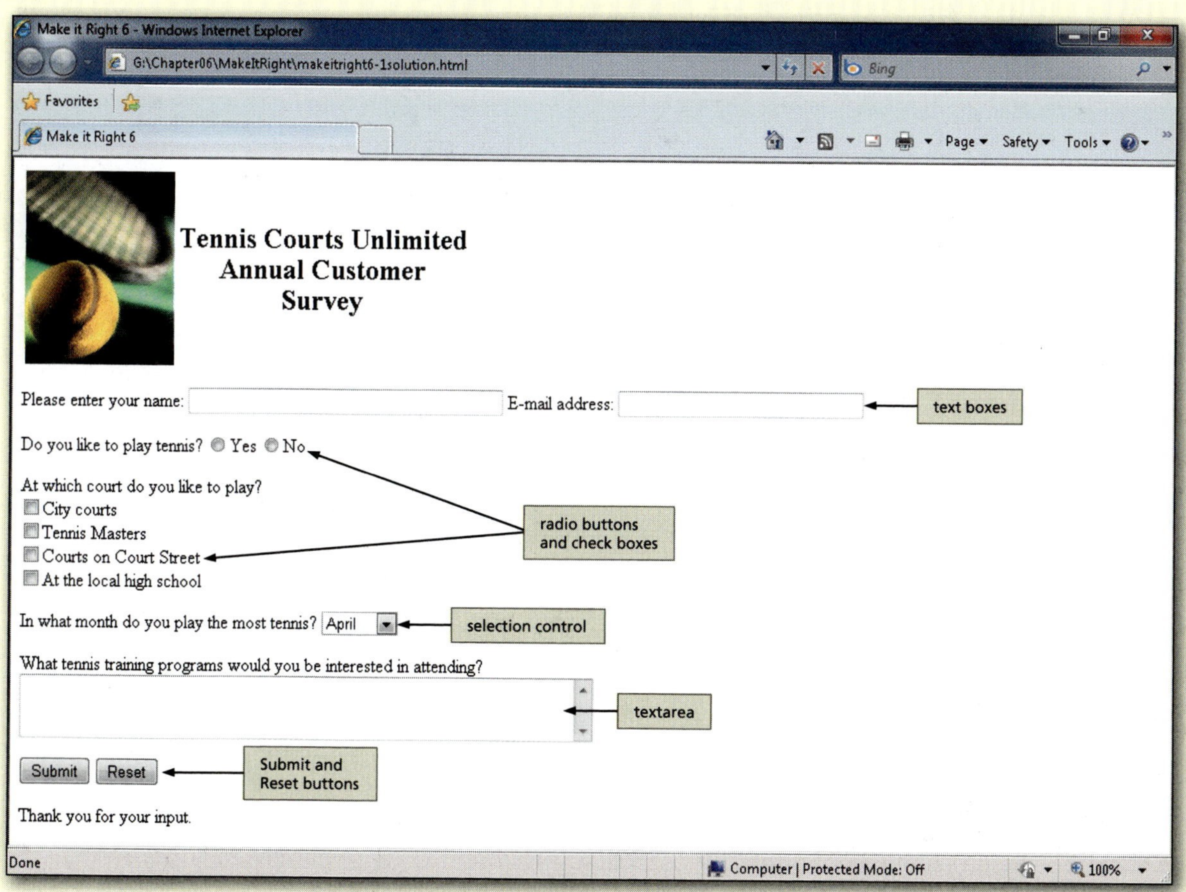

Figure 6–29

STUDENT ASSIGNMENTS

In the Lab

Lab 1: Creating a School Bookstore Survey

Problem: The staff of the school bookstore wants to survey students about their book-buying habits to determine where they purchase their books. The staff has asked you to create a Web page form that contains the questions shown in Figure 6–30.

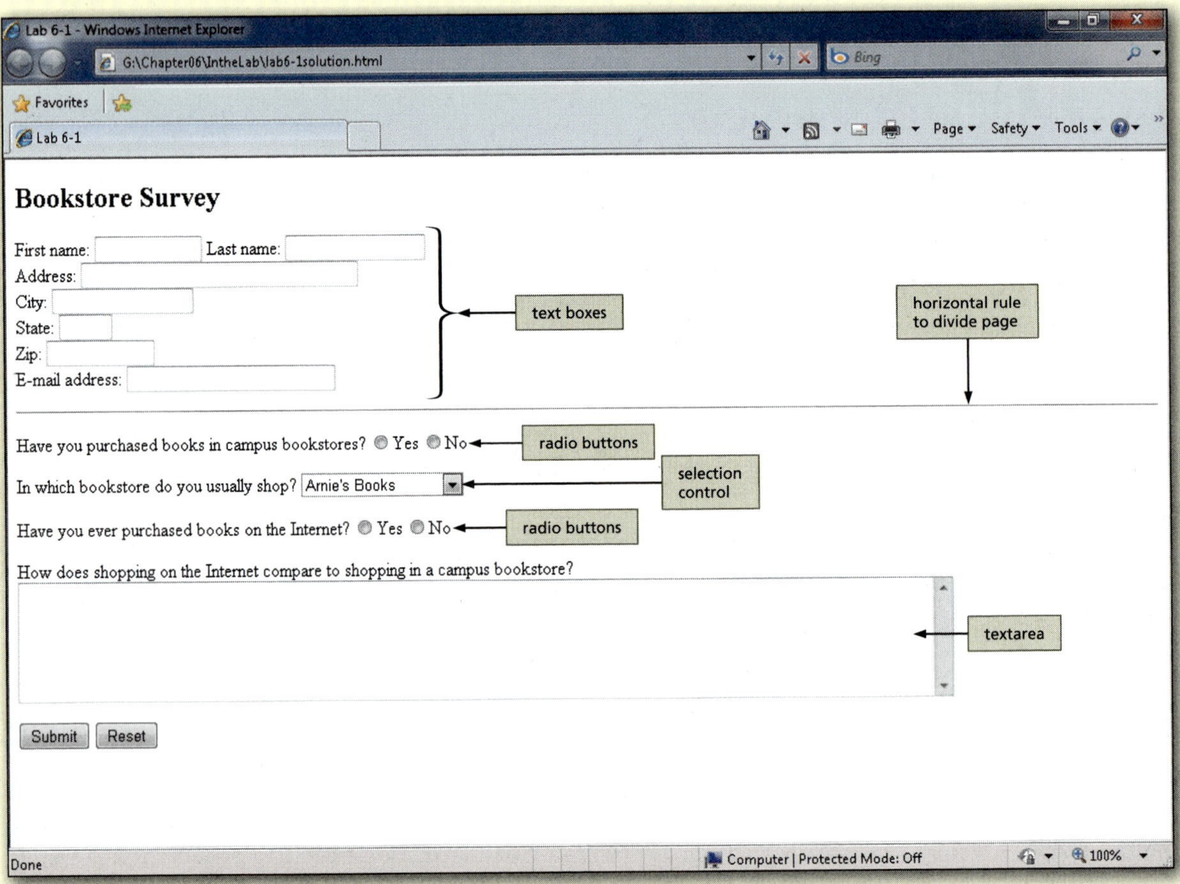

Figure 6–30

Instructions: Perform the following steps:

1. Using Notepad++, create a new HTML file with the title Lab 6-1 in the main heading section. Add the Web page heading Bookstore Survey at the top of the page.
2. Create a form and identify the form process using the post method with the action attribute set to mailto:email@isp.com.
3. Add seven text boxes for first name, last name, home or school address, city, state, ZIP, plus e-mail address.
4. Add two radio buttons for users to say whether or not they use the campus bookstore.
5. Add a selection menu with three options of your choosing (or use Arnie's Books, Lafollet Shops, and University Bookstore) for users to select the bookstore in which they shop, as shown in Figure 6–30.
6. Create a second set of radio buttons for users to say whether they have purchased books on the Internet, as shown in Figure 6–30.
7. Create a textarea for additional comments and set it to 6 rows and 100 columns.
8. Add Submit and Reset buttons at the bottom of the Web page form.

9. Save the HTML file in the Chapter06\IntheLab folder using the file name lab6-1solution.html. Validate the Web page. Print the HTML file.
10. Open the lab6-1solution.html file in your browser and test all controls except the Submit button.
11. Print the Web page.
12. Submit the files in the format specified by your instructor.

In the Lab

Lab 2: Recording Studio Survey

Problem: Abuizam Recording Studios is looking for information on their customers' musical tastes. They want to know what type of music and radio stations they listen to. The company has asked you to create the survey as a Web page form, as shown in Figure 6–31.

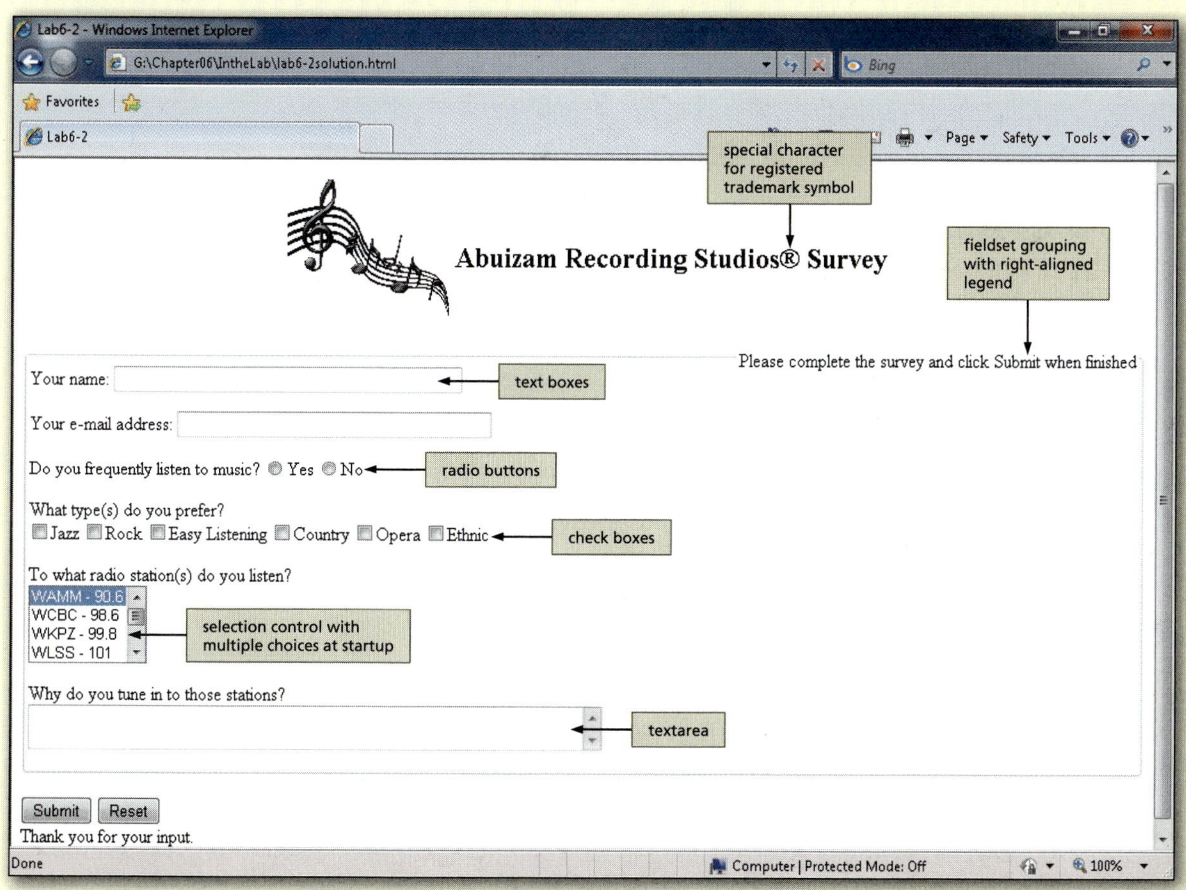

Figure 6–31

Instructions: Perform the following steps:

1. Using Notepad++, create a new HTML file with the title, Lab 6-2, in the main heading section.
2. Create a form and identify the form process using the post method with the action attribute set to mailto your e-mail address (if you do not have an e-mail address, use email@isp.com).
3. Add two text boxes for name and e-mail address, as shown in Figure 6–31.
4. Add a set of radio buttons and six check boxes for users to select their musical preferences.
5. Add a selection menu that initially displays four rows and allows multiple input. One of the menu options should be selected at startup. Use local radio stations' call letters and numbers as your options.

Continued >

In the Lab *continued*

6. Insert a 2-row, 60-column textarea for users to provide additional suggestions.
7. Add a Submit button and a Reset button at the bottom of the Web page form.
8. Add the music.png graphic and a registered trademark symbol in the heading, as shown in Figure 6–31 on the previous page.
9. Save the HTML file in the Chapter06\IntheLab folder using the file name lab6-2solution.html. Validate the Web page. Print the HTML file.
10. Open the lab6-2solution.html file in your browser and test all controls. Test the Submit button only if you used your own e-mail address as the value for the form action attribute.
11. Print the Web page.
12. Submit the files in the format specified by your instructor.

In the Lab

Lab 3: Using Fieldset Controls to Organize a Form

Problem: Your manager at Horizon Learning has asked you to create a Web page form that novice HTML developers can use as a model for a well-designed, user-friendly form. Having created forms for several different Web sites, you have learned that using fieldset controls to group form controls results in a well-organized, easily readable form. Create a Web page form that utilizes three fieldset controls, like the one shown in Figure 6–32.

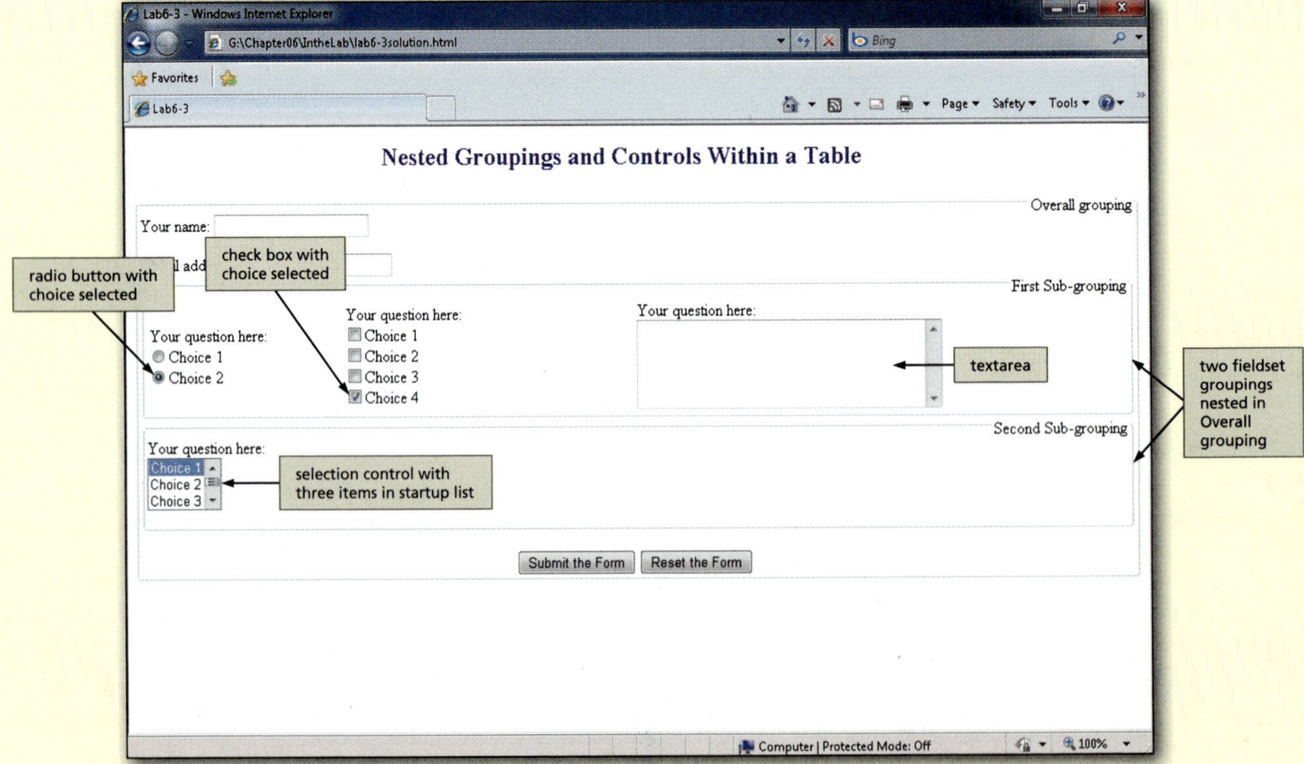

Figure 6–32

Instructions: Perform the following steps:

1. Using Notepad++, create a new HTML file with the title Lab 6-3 in the main heading section.
2. Add the Web page heading Nested Groupings and Controls Within a Table.
3. Create a form and identify the form process using the post method with the action attribute set to mailto your e-mail address (if you do not have an e-mail address, use email@isp.com).
4. Add two text boxes for name and e-mail address.
5. Add two radio buttons, with Choice 2 preselected, as shown in Figure 6–32, together with four check boxes with Choice 4 selected.
6. Add a 5-row, 35-column textarea, as shown in Figure 6–32.
7. Insert a selection menu with options of Choice 1 through Choice 4. Set the selection menu to display three rows and have Choice 1 preselected as the default option.
8. Add a Submit button that says Submit the Form and a Reset button that says Reset the Form at the bottom of the Web page form.
9. Add three fieldset controls to group the other form controls, as shown in Figure 6–32. Nest the two subgroupings within the main grouping.
10. Save the HTML file in the Chapter06\IntheLab folder using the file name lab6-3solution.html. Validate the Web page. Print the HTML file.
11. Open the lab6-3solution.html file in your browser and test all controls. Test the Submit button only if you used your own e-mail address as the value for the form action attribute.
12. Print the Web page.
13. Submit the files in the format specified by your instructor.

Cases and Places

Apply your creative thinking and problem-solving skills to design and implement a solution.

• Easier •• More Difficult

• 1: Creating a Travel Form

The marketing director at Getaway Travel asked you to create a Web page form to allow customers to request information on the four travel packages offered by the agency: ski & snow, surf & sun, golf & spa, and adventure. Using the techniques learned in this chapter, create a Web page form with input controls to allow customers to request information on one or more travel packages. By default, have all of the travel packages selected on the form. In addition, include input controls for customers to provide a mailing address, an e-mail address, and any suggestions for new travel packages. Include Submit and Reset buttons and use your e-mail address in the action attribute for the form. After creating the Web page, enter information and submit the form. Print the data file with the information and indicate which name-value pairs are related to which controls on the form.

• 2: Changing a Paper Form to an Online Form

As part of your Web development project, your instructor has asked you to find a text-based form that is currently in use by your school, a club, or another organization. Convert this text-based form to a Web page form. Start by designing the form on paper, taking into consideration the fields that are the most appropriate to use for each input area. Once your design is complete, use HTML to develop the Web page form. Test the form, and once testing is done, show the form to several people from the organization that controls the form. Explain to them why it is better to collect information using a Web page form, rather than a printed, text-based form.

Continued >

Cases and Places *continued*

•• 3: Collecting Information with a Form

The owners of Sabatina's Pizza were very excited about their new online order form. There are a few limitations to ordering on the form, however. As one example, the appetizers and salads (see Chapter 4) are not listed on the form, so no one can order them online. Also, the way the form is set up now, a customer can only order one of each item. A customer may want to order two or more of the same type of pizza. Analyze these requirements and begin a design that allows customers to order appetizers and salads and more than one of each item. Also, think of other ways the form could be improved. (*Hint:* Review other pizza restaurant order forms online.) Put all of your design ideas together and create a paper design. After showing this design to your instructor, add the new controls to the form you created in this chapter.

•• 4: Making a Form Easier to Use

Make It Personal

Your uncle's car club wants to collect information from club members. Search the Internet for two or three examples of Web page forms used to collect information from club members. Print the forms as examples. If you were the Web developer for these Web sites, how would you update the forms to gather more information or make the forms easier to use? Using the example Web pages that you have found, draw a sketch of a Web page form design for a car club. Develop the Web page form as an example to share with your uncle.

•• 5: Creating a Travel Journal

Working Together

Your team works in the Web development department for a small company in your community. You are interested in learning the latest programming techniques so you can stay current with the technology. In this chapter, data from a form was sent in a file to an e-mail address. The chapter mentioned CGI scripts and the PHP and Perl programming languages as better, more secure methods to use for processing the information submitted in a form. While CGI scripts and Perl programming are beyond the scope of this book, they are important topics to study. Search the Web to find additional information about CGI scripts, PHP, and Perl used in conjunction with forms. Try to find online tutorials that explain how to use these techniques. What other options are available for collecting information online? Develop a Web page that lists links to various Web sites that discuss these topics. Under each link, write a brief paragraph explaining the purpose of each Web site and why it is important to review.

7 Using Advanced Cascading Style Sheets

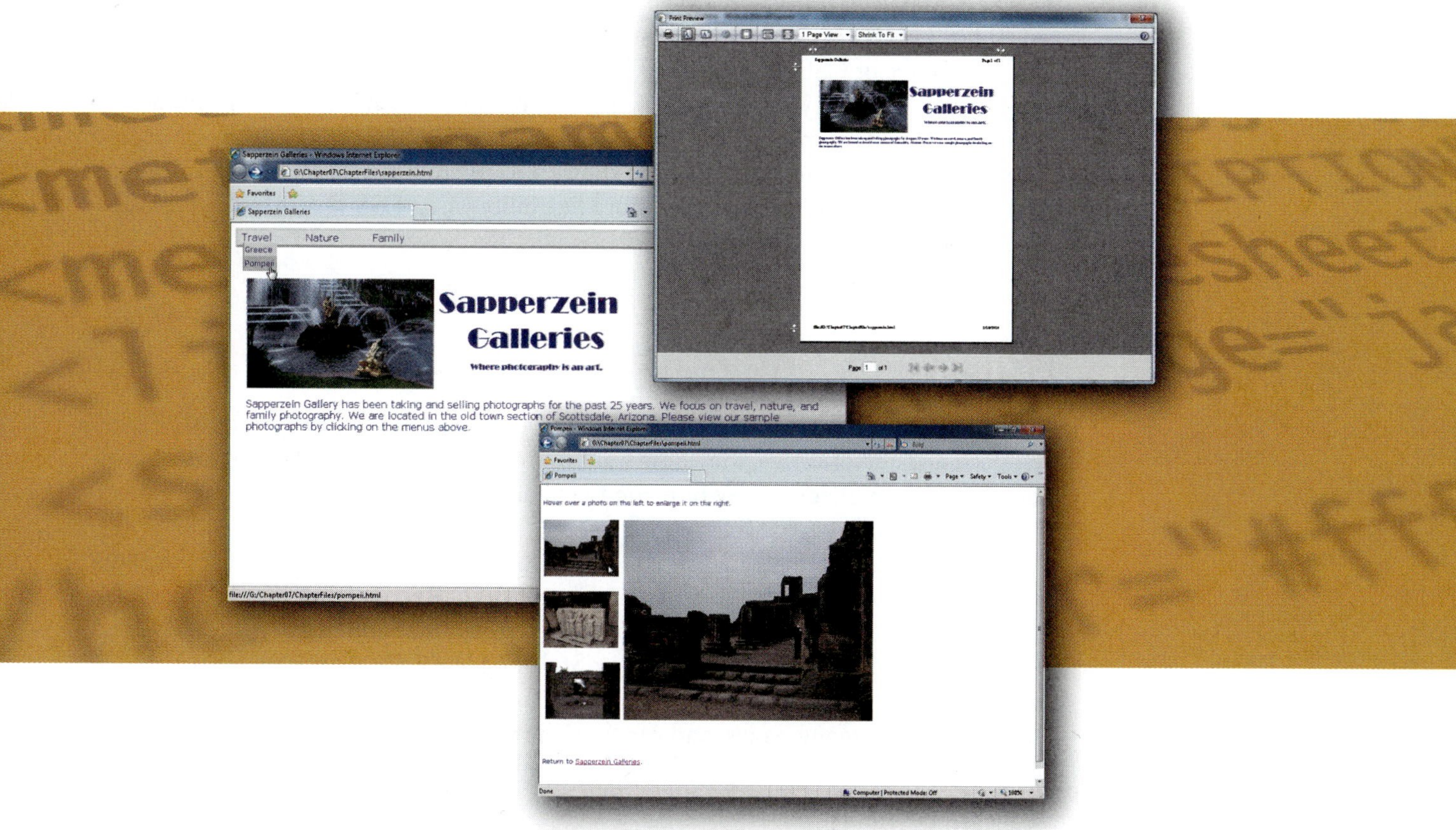

Objectives

You will have mastered the material in this chapter when you can:

- Add an embedded style sheet to a Web page
- Change the body and link styles using an embedded style sheet
- Create a drop-down menu bar using an embedded style sheet
- Change the color and font styles of the drop-down menus
- Create an external style sheet
- Change the paragraph margins and font styles using an external style sheet
- Create a hover pop-up using an external style sheet
- Use classes, pseudoclasses, and divisions for the pop-up function
- Use the <link> tag to insert a link to an external style sheet
- Add an external style sheet for printing Web pages

7 Using Advanced Cascading Style Sheets

Introduction

In previous chapters, you used HTML tags and Cascading Style Sheets (CSS) to change the way a Web page appears in a Web browser, such as adding italic, bold, colors, headings, and tables. This is also known as the style of the Web page. In this chapter, you expand your knowledge of CSS to give added functionality to your Web pages. You insert drop-down menus for your Web site visitors to use for navigation. This advanced technique is done with more complex CSS code. You also add pop-up image effects using an advanced CSS technique. This method shows you a better way to format your Web pages as opposed to using tables. You have more flexibility using CSS versus tables for Web page structure.

Project — Using Advanced Cascading Style Sheets

Sapperzein Galleries had a Web site created several years ago. Although the Web site is well-designed and effective, they now want to improve their Web site with drop-down menus and image effects. They hire you to enhance their Web site using advanced Cascading Style Sheets (CSS).

At Mr. Sapperzein's request, you use advanced Cascading Style Sheets to add a drop-down menu structure, as shown in Figure 7–1b. Recognizing that the Sapperzein Galleries Web site will continue to grow, you suggest that you modify the Web site to use embedded and external Cascading Style Sheets (CSS). You explain to him that Cascading Style Sheets maintain a consistent look across a Web site — especially Web sites that contain many pages, and can give the pages a more polished look. You suggest that you create an external style sheet that is linked to the other Web pages. This style sheet, which can be easily linked into all pages in the Web site, is used to give the images on the Web page a pop-up effect (Figure 7–1b). Additionally, you would like to create a second external style sheet that can be used to print only the content of a Web page and not the menu bar. Mr. Sapperzein is supportive of the plan and encourages you to start as soon as possible.

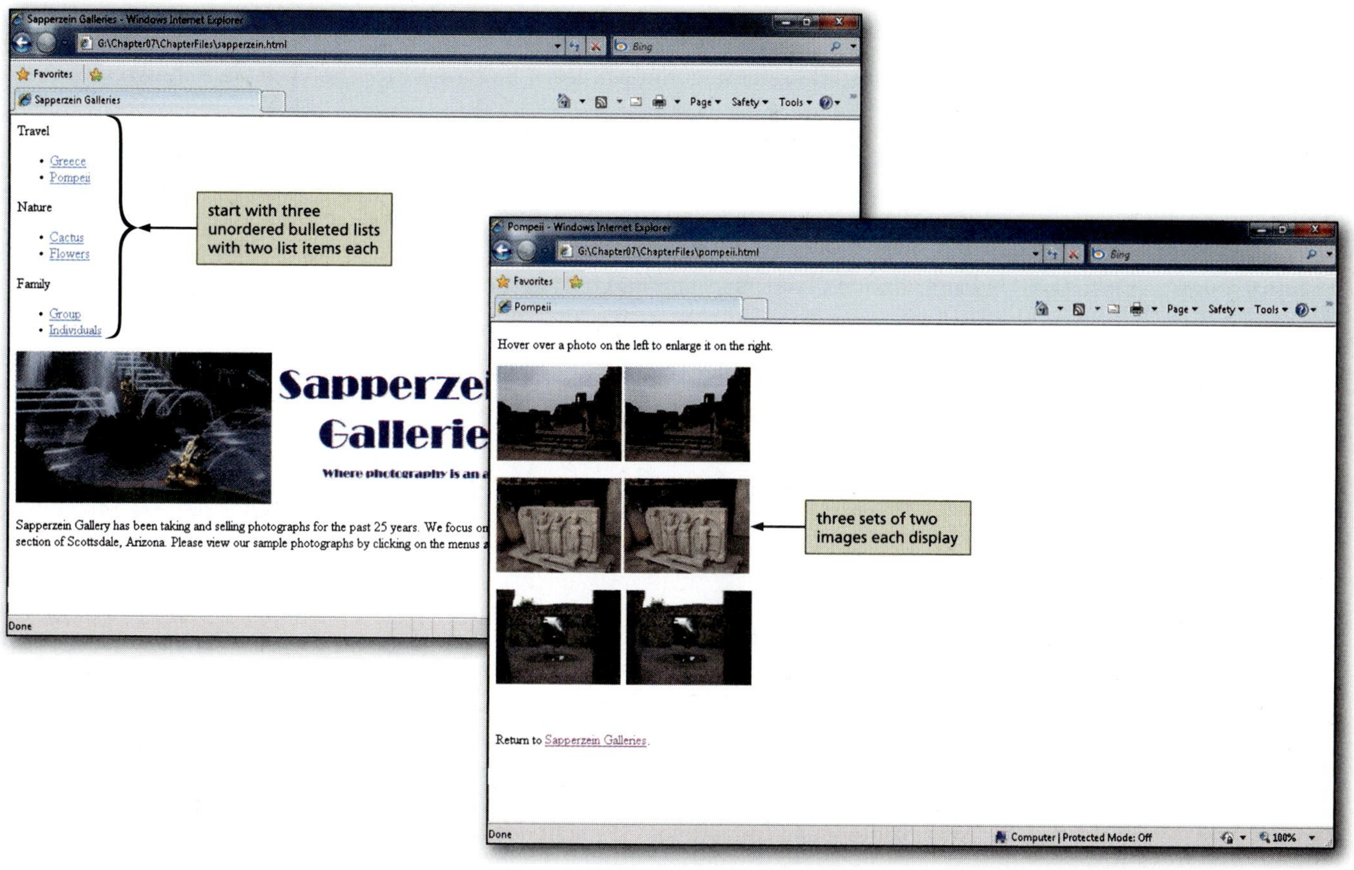

start with three unordered bulleted lists with two list items each

three sets of two images each display

(a) Web pages without style sheets.

(b) Web pages with style sheets.

Figure 7–1

Overview

As you read this chapter, you will learn how to create the Web page shown in Figure 7–1 on the previous page by performing these general tasks:

- Plan the CSS structure.
- Enter HTML code into the Notepad++ window.
- Save the file as an HTML file.
- Enter basic HTML tags and add text to the file.
- Use the <style> tag in an embedded style sheet.
- Create external CSS files that are linked into Web pages with a <link /> tag.
- View the Web pages and HTML code in your browser.
- Validate the Web pages.
- Test and print the Web pages.

Plan Ahead

General Project Guidelines

As you create Web pages, such as the project shown in Figure 7–1 on page HTML 327, you should follow these general guidelines:

1. **Plan the Web site.** First, you should determine if using Cascading Style Sheets (CSS) is appropriate for your Web site. If you have several Web pages and need a consistent style that can be easily updated, CSS is a good choice. If you have a single page with mostly static content and formatting, CSS might not be needed.
2. **Analyze the need.** In the analysis phase of the Web Development Life Cycle, you should analyze what content to include in the Web page. Chapter 7 introduces advanced CSS techniques that can be used for Web development. Using style sheets can eliminate the need to edit multiple Web pages for simple changes. An external style sheet can be edited to make changes across a Web site. Part of the analysis phase includes determining how the multiple Web pages work together using CSS. In this chapter, you create both embedded and external style sheets.
3. **Choose the content for the Web page.** With a multiple-page Web site, you can distribute the content as needed throughout the Web site.
4. **Determine the type of style sheets to use for the pages and their precedence.** If you determine that CSS is appropriate, then you must decide which type(s) of style sheet is best. For Web sites with many Web pages that have a common look, an external style sheet may be the best option. For Web sites with few common looks to the pages, using embedded or inline style sheets may be a better option. Also, knowing style sheet precedence helps you to understand how each style interacts with the others.
5. **Create the style sheets.** Once the analysis and design is complete, the Web developer creates the Web page using CSS. Good Web development standard practices should be followed in this step. Embedded and inline style sheets are used within particular Web pages. An external style sheet must first be created and saved as a .css file. Then a link statement must be inserted into all Web pages in which you want to use the external style sheet.

(continued)

6. **Test all Web pages within the Web site.** An important part of Web development is testing to assure that you are following XHTML standards. In this book, you use the World Wide Web Consortium (W3C) validator that allows you to test your Web page and clearly explains any errors you have. When testing, you should check all content for accuracy. Finally, all of the Web pages with style sheets (external as well as embedded) should be validated as per the standard set throughout this book.

When necessary, more specific details concerning the above guidelines are presented at appropriate points in the chapter. The chapter also will identify the actions performed and decisions made regarding these guidelines during the creation of the Web page shown in Figure 7–1 on page HTML 327.

Plan Ahead

Using Style Sheets

As you learned in earlier chapters, although HTML allows Web developers to make changes to the structure, design, and content of a Web page, HTML is limited in its ability to define the appearance, or style, across one or more Web pages. As a result, Cascading Style Sheets (CSS) were created. With CSS, you can establish a standard look for all Web pages in a Web site. Using CSS, you avoid the tedious steps of adding repetitive codes to format the same types of information. For example, instead of making all paragraphs of text 10pt Verdana in individual <p> tags, you can define that style in an external style sheet (.css file) and link that external file to all Web pages. CSS is also perfect for formatting Web pages with tabular material, but without using HTML table tags.

A style is a rule that defines the appearance of an element on a Web page, and a style sheet is a series of rules that defines the style for a Web page or an entire Web site. There are three types of CSS: inline, embedded, and external. In previous chapter projects, you have used all three types to alter the appearance of a Web page or pages by changing characteristics such as font family, font size, margins, and link specifications. In this chapter, you learn to use more advanced CSS features to add functionality to Web pages.

First, an embedded style sheet is used to add a drop-down menu to the home page of the Web site (Figure 7–2a). You use an embedded style sheet in this case because the menu appears only on the home page. An external style sheet (Figure 7–2b) is created for printing and is linked into the home page, sapperzein.html. With these style sheets added, the Sapperzein Galleries home page is more attractive, polished, and professional looking (Figure 7–2c). An external style sheet is then created to add a pop-up function in the other Web pages in the Web site (Figure 7–2d). You use an external style sheet because the style will be the same across several Web pages. That external style sheet is linked into the other Greece and Pompeii pages to give the pop-up effect shown in Figure 7–2e.

BTW

CSS
The World Wide Web Consortium (W3C) has a wealth of information about Cascading Style Sheets (CSS). You can find out what is new with CSS, access CSS testing suites, and find links to CSS authoring tools from this Web site. For more information, visit the W3C Web site and search for CSS.

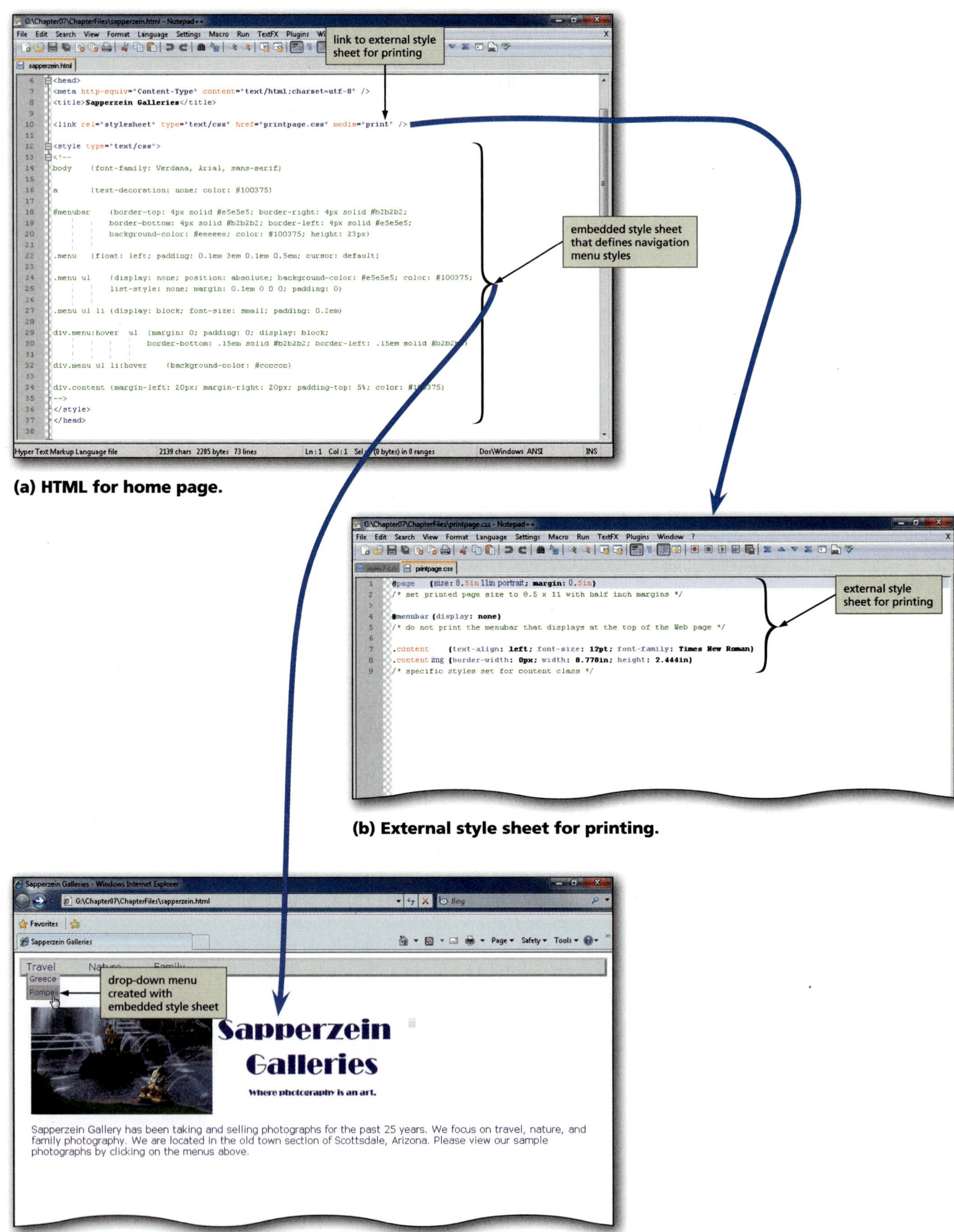

(a) HTML for home page.

(b) External style sheet for printing.

(c) Home page with embedded and external style sheets.

Figure 7–2

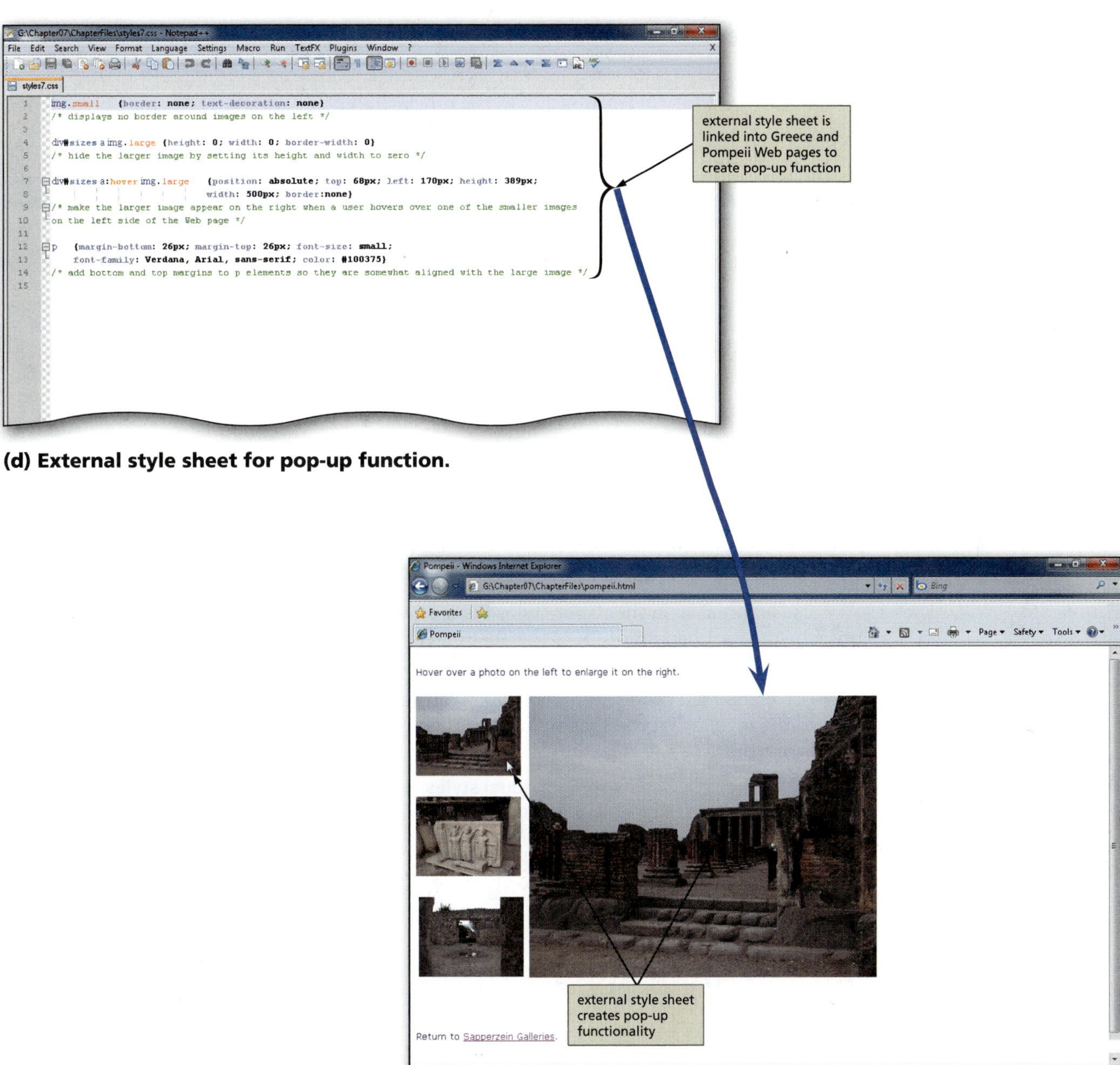

(d) External style sheet for pop-up function.

(e) Secondary Web page with link to external style sheet.

Figure 7–2 (continued)

Style Sheet Precedence Review

As discussed in previous chapters, each style sheet type has a different level of precedence or priority in relationship to the others. Table 7–1 reviews style sheet precedence.

Table 7–1 Style Sheet Precedence

Type	Level and Precedence
Inline	• To change the style within an individual HTML tag • Overrides embedded and external style sheets
Embedded	• To change the style of one Web page • Overrides external style sheets
External	• To change the style of multiple pages in a Web site

Plan Ahead

Identify what style sheets to use.
The first step to consider when using style sheets is to lay out a plan that takes style sheet precedence into account. This project uses only embedded and external style sheets.

- **Use external style sheets for styles that you want across the Web site.** As mentioned, the greatest benefit of CSS is the ability to identify a style across a Web site. For Web pages in which you want a common look, use external style sheets.
- **Use embedded style sheets for single Web page styles.** This type of style sheet is good to use if you want the style to just affect one (or a few) Web pages, and not all pages across the Web site.
- **Use inline style sheets for individual styles.** If you want to change the style of one or a few sections of one Web page, then using inline style sheets is the most appropriate. If the style is intended for most (or all) of the Web pages, you may want to switch to embedded or external style sheets.

Adding Style Sheets to the Sapperzein Galleries Site

The Sapperzein Galleries Web site for this chapter consists of nine files, as shown in Table 7–2. The first Web page, sapperzein.html, is the home page of the Web site. The sapperzein.html file contains the navigation menu at the top of the Web page. It also contains the company logo and the home page content.

Table 7–2 Files Used for the Chapter 7 Project

File Name	Purpose and Display Specifics at Startup	Changes Made in Chapter 7
sapperzein.html	• Home page of the Web site • Contains an unordered list of menu options, an image logo, and a paragraph of text	• Add an embedded style sheet that creates a drop-down menu
greece.html	• Contains the text and images that are needed for the pop-up function	• Add a link to an external style sheet that displays a large pop-up image when a user hovers over the smaller image

Table 7–2 Files Used for the Chapter 7 Project (continued)

File Name	Purpose and Display Specifics at Startup	Changes Made in Chapter 7
pompeii.html	• Contains the text and images that are needed for the pop-up function	• Add a link to an external style sheet that displays a large pop-up image when a user hovers over the smaller image
styles7.css	• Nothing at startup; created from scratch	• Create an external style sheet • Save as a .css file
printpage.css	• Nothing at startup; created from scratch	• Create an external style sheet • Save as a .css file
cactus.html flowers.html group.html individuals.html	• Dummy Web pages that contain initial HTML code and link statement to external style sheet	• Nothing is done to any of these Web pages in the chapter; you can use them as starting points for additional Web pages

In this project, you will add different types of style sheets to the Web pages in the Sapperzein Galleries Web site. To add the style sheets, you will make changes to three of the Web pages stored in the Chapter07/ChapterFiles folder of the Data Files for Students: sapperzein.html, greece.html, and pompeii.html. You also will create two external style sheet files, styles7.css and printpage.css. In addition to the files listed in Table 7–2, all image files needed for the chapter project are stored in the Data Files for Students. See the inside back cover of this book for instructions on downloading the Data Files for Students, or contact your instructor for information about accessing the required files.

Plan Ahead

Creating an Embedded Style Sheet.

You would use an embedded style sheet if you want to set the styles within a Web page. In the case of this Web site, you want to create a drop-down navigation menu on the home page only. You design that menu on the home page by creating an embedded style sheet.

- **Determine which Web pages vary enough that an embedded style sheet makes sense.** You may have only one or even just a few Web pages in a Web site that will vary slightly from all other pages. In this case, an embedded style sheet makes sense. If there are styles that are to be repeated in that one Web page (or in a few pages), you would be better off using an embedded style sheet rather than a series of inline style sheets. For instance, if you want all paragraphs of text to have the same style within one Web page, then it makes more sense to embed that style rather than add the style to each paragraph tag within the Web page.
- **Copy an embedded style sheet into other Web pages.** If you have a few Web pages that should have the same style, insert the embedded sheet in one Web page, save, validate, and test it. Once you have verified that it works as you intend, then you can copy/paste the embedded style sheet into the other Web pages.
- **Change to an external style sheet when necessary.** If you find that the style from the embedded style sheet is used on more Web pages as time goes on, you should create an external style sheet and link it into all Web pages in which you had previously inserted an embedded style sheet. For instance, if you decide that you want to have the drop-down menu on all Web pages in the Web site, you should move the code in the embedded style sheet to an external style sheet and link that external style sheet into all Web pages in the Web site.

Adding a Navigation Menu with an Embedded Style Sheet

The first step in adding style sheets to the Sapperzein Galleries Web site is to add an embedded style sheet to the home page of the Web site, sapperzein.html. First, the HTML file sapperzein.html must be opened in Notepad++. Then you enter the code for the embedded style sheet. Figure 7–3a shows the home page in the default style (without a style sheet) as provided in the Data Files for Students, and Figure 7–3b shows the same Web page after the embedded style sheet has been added.

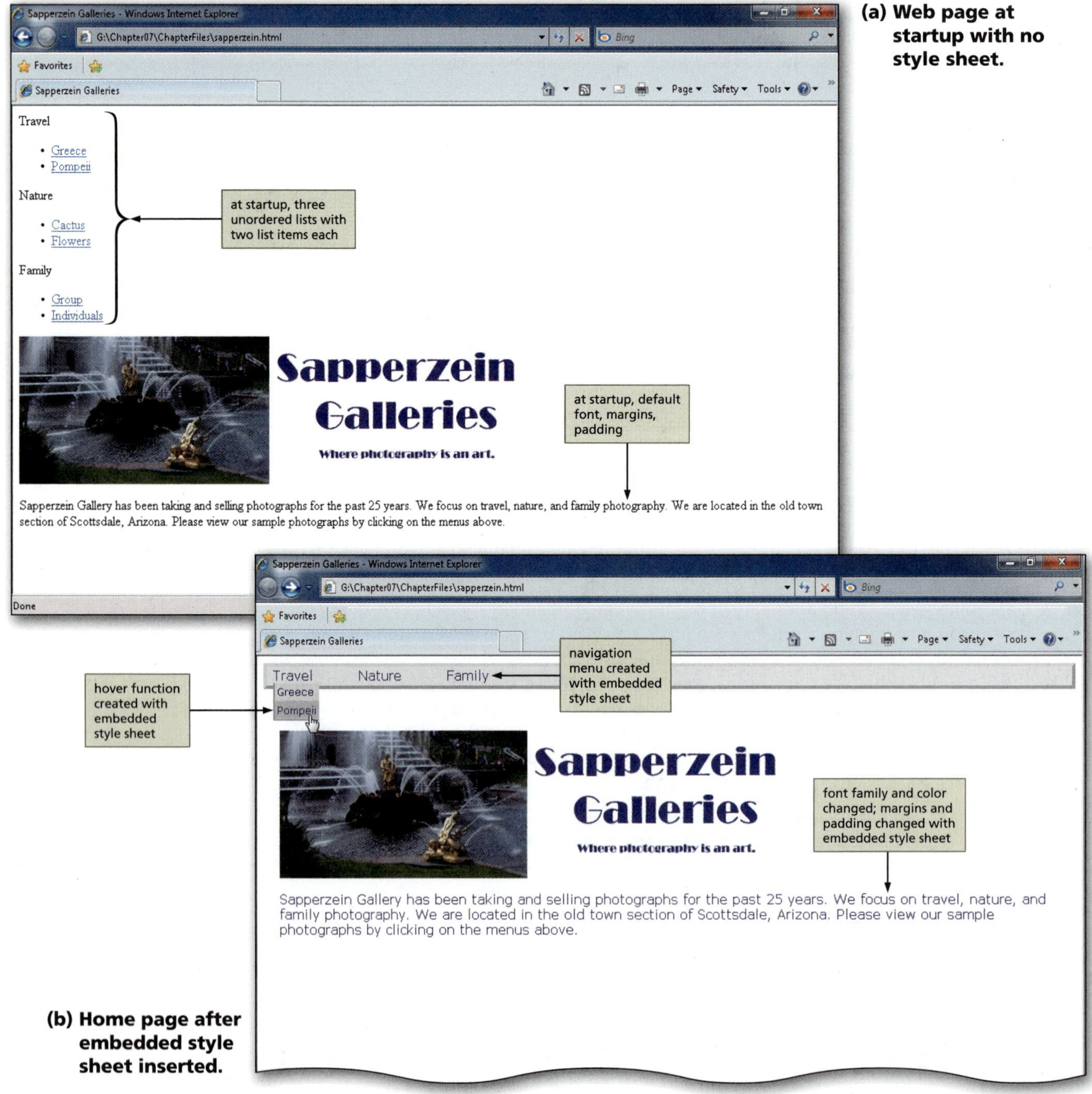

Figure 7–3

To Start Notepad++ and Open an HTML File

1. Start Notepad++ and, if necessary, maximize the window.
2. With the USB drive plugged into your computer, click File on the menu bar and then click Open.
3. If necessary, navigate to the Chapter07\ChapterFiles folder on the USB drive.
4. Double-click sapperzein.html in the list of files to open the file shown in Figure 7–4.

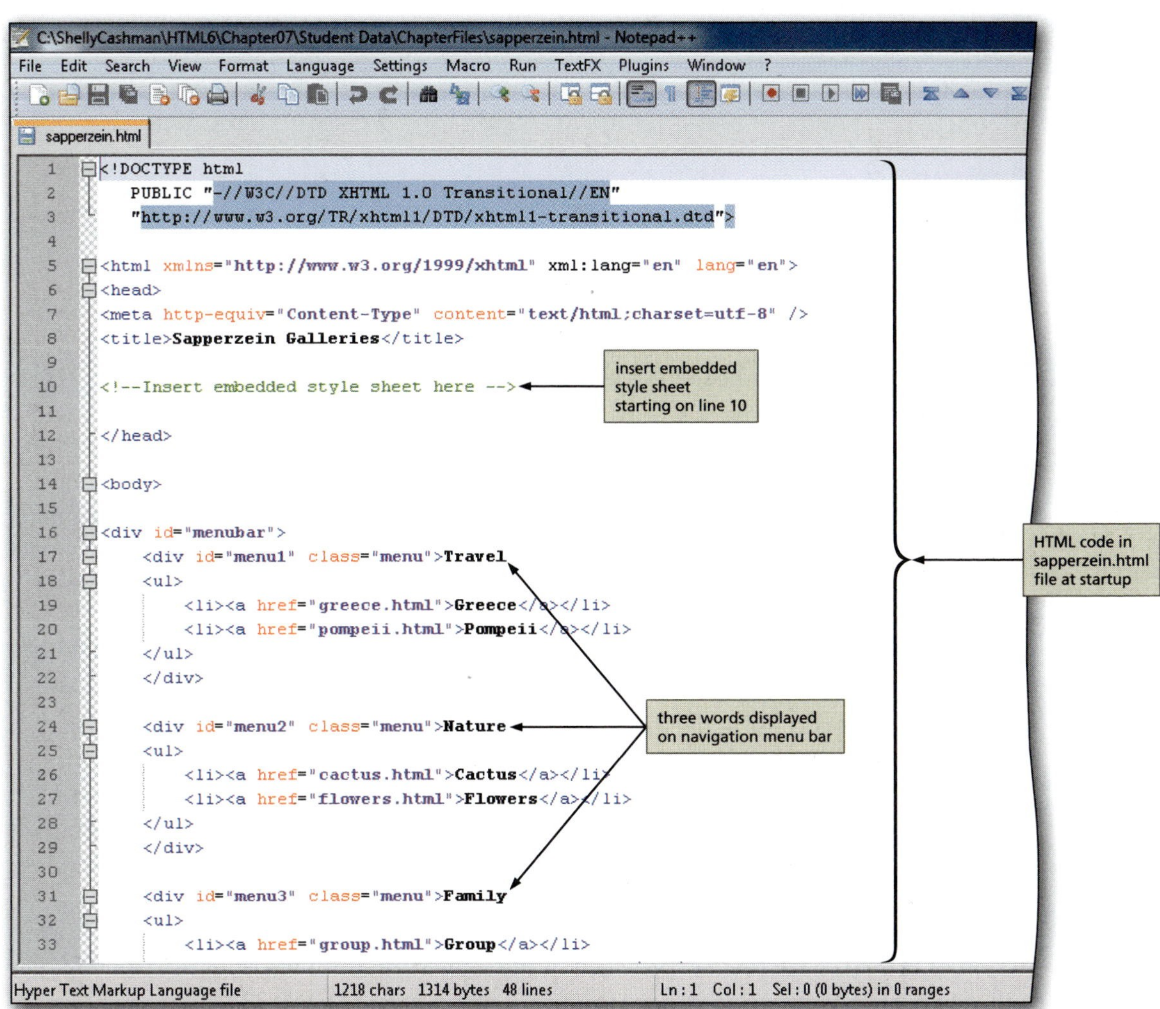

Figure 7–4

Setting the Body Style and Link Style, and Adding a Drop-down Menu

The code you will be entering for the embedded style sheet is shown in Figure 7–5 on the next page. Before entering the code, however, you should understand a little more about the styles you are setting.

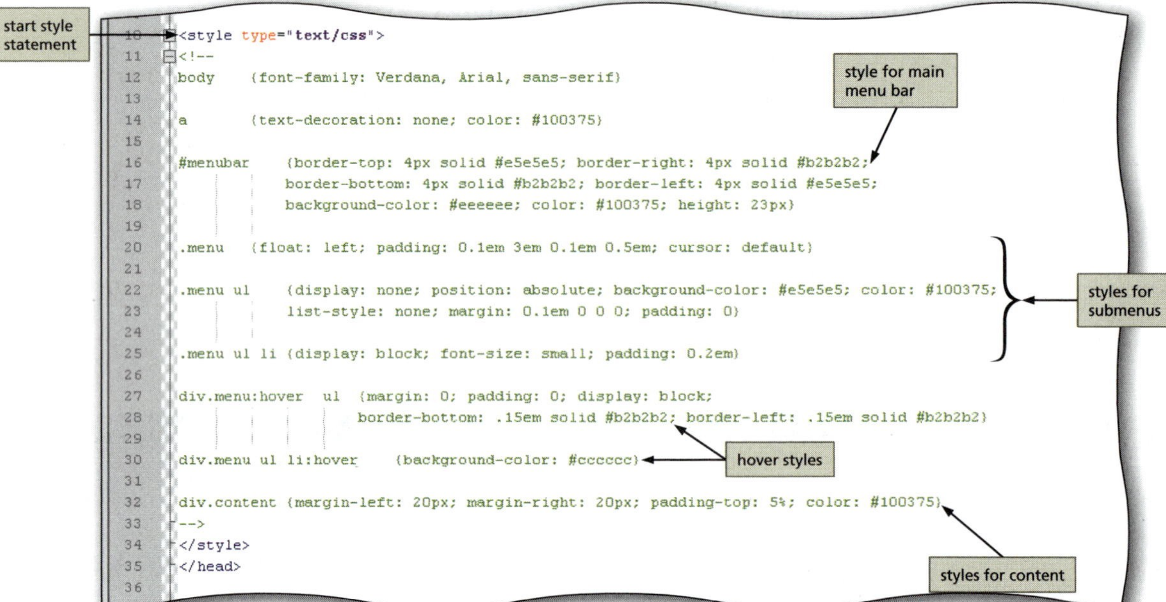
start style statement
style for main menu bar
styles for submenus
hover styles
styles for content
10 <style type="text/css">
11 <!--
12 body {font-family: Verdana, Arial, sans-serif}
14 a {text-decoration: none; color: #100375}
16 #menubar {border-top: 4px solid #e5e5e5; border-right: 4px solid #b2b2b2;
17 border-bottom: 4px solid #b2b2b2; border-left: 4px solid #e5e5e5;
18 background-color: #eeeeee; color: #100375; height: 23px}
20 .menu {float: left; padding: 0.1em 3em 0.1em 0.5em; cursor: default}
22 .menu ul {display: none; position: absolute; background-color: #e5e5e5; color: #100375;
23 list-style: none; margin: 0.1em 0 0 0; padding: 0}
25 .menu ul li {display: block; font-size: small; padding: 0.2em}
27 div.menu:hover ul {margin: 0; padding: 0; display: block;
28 border-bottom: .15em solid #b2b2b2; border-left: .15em solid #b2b2b2}
30 div.menu ul li:hover {background-color: #cccccc}
32 div.content {margin-left: 20px; margin-right: 20px; padding-top: 5%; color: #100375}
33 -->
34 </style>
35 </head>

Figure 7–5

> **BTW**
> **Word Spacing**
> The word-spacing property is a good way to add additional space between words. You can use any of the length units including: inches, centimeters, millimeters, points, picas, ems, x-height, and pixels.

The code for an embedded style sheet must be inserted between a start <style> tag (line 10) and an end </style> tag (line 34), which are positioned within the head element. Within the style tag container, Web developers generally follow the coding practice to add an HTML start comment code <!-- (line 11) and end comment code --> (line 33). The beginning and ending HTML comment lines hide any script language that an older browser cannot interpret.

Let's first take a look at what the CSS code in Figure 7–5 will create on the home page of Sapperzein Galleries. This code will enhance the three unordered lists displayed at the top of the Web page by creating a navigation menu bar (see Figure 7–3b on page HTML 334) with the words Travel, Nature, and Family. It will also improve the appearance of the two list items within each unordered list that are used as submenus. Figure 7–3b on page HTML 334 shows the two list items, Greece and Pompeii. Notice the different background colors on the menu bar and the submenu. This technique utilizes CSS to give the appearance of a menu and submenu system. You could use graphical images such as menu bars here as well. For instance, you could utilize the menubar.jpg image that you used in Chapter 5 to give this same menu and submenu effect.

It may help for you to compare the uses of these menu styles (in Figure 7–5) to the section of HTML code (below) provided in the sapperzein.html file (Figure 7–4), together with viewing the resulting Web page (Figure 7–3b on page HTML 334). The structure of the divisions and unordered lists used in the sapperzein.html file at start-up are as follows (line numbers have been added):

```
16   <div id="menubar">
17        <div id="menu1" class="menu">Travel
18        <ul>
19             <li><a href="greece.html">Greece</a></li>
20             <li><a href="pompeii.html">Pompeii</a></li>
21        </ul>
22        </div>
23
```

```
24        <div id="menu2" class="menu">Nature
25        <ul>
26            <li><a href="cactus.html">Cactus</a></li>
27            <li><a href="flowers.html">Flowers</a></li>
28        </ul>
29        </div>
30
31        <div id="menu3" class="menu">Family
32        <ul>
33            <li><a href="group.html">Group</a></li>
34            <li><a href="individuals.html">Individuals</a></li>
35        </ul>
36        </div>
37    </div>
```

Notice that all three menu bar options (Travel, Nature, Family) are within a division (section) of the Web page, as indicated on lines 16 <div> and 37 </div> above. This division is given the id name menubar. Note in Figure 7–5 that lines 16 through 18 define the styles that are to be used for id="menubar" in the CSS code. There are also three unordered lists within this same division (for Travel, Nature, and Family), each containing two list items. Those unordered lists each use the class="menu" (see lines 20, 22, and 25 in Figure 7–5). Therefore, the styles defined in the CSS code lines 20 through 30 are reflected in the submenu list items from the three unordered lists.

This menu structure is further discussed here per lines of CSS code. Refer to Figure 7–5, lines 11 through 33 of HTML code in the file sapperzein.html, and Figures 7–7a and 7–7b on page HTML 339 as you review this information.

Line 12 in the embedded style sheet (Figure 7–5) sets the font family throughout the Web page by use of the body element. Line 14 sets the link color and turns text-decoration (i.e., underline) off. Lines 16 through 30 set the styles for the drop-down menu bar that will display at the top of the Web page, as shown in Figure 7–7a on page HTML 339. In lines 16 through 18, you set the borders (top, right, bottom, and left) of an element named menubar that will used be used in a <div> tag. All of the borders are set to 4px solid style. The top and left borders are set to the same color, while the bottom and right are set to another color. The background color is set to #eeeeee, while the text color is set to #100375. This portion of the statement on line 18:

```
height: 23px
```

sets the height of the area to 23 pixels. This is something that you adjust as you develop the Web page. You need to determine how much space you want relative to the default font size.

Line 20 (Figure 7–5) sets the styles for a class named menu. The statement:

```
.menu {float: left; padding: 0.1em 3em 0.1em 0.5em; cursor: default}
```

floats the text to the left. The padding property uses the "shorthand property" code. The **shorthand property** allows a Web developer to shorten the code. Instead of using padding-top, padding-bottom, padding-right, and padding-left, you can specify all the padding values in one property as line 20.

BTW

Line Height

The CSS property line-height property gives you the ability to control line height. With this property, you can control the vertical spacing between lines of text. There are three different ways to add the line-height value: by number, by length unit, and by percentage. If you specify by number, the browser uses the font-size property to determine the space. You also can use em and pt to set the height by unit. Finally, you can determine the line spacing by a percentage.

BTW

Em Units

The em is a very useful unit in CSS, because it adapts automatically to the font size that the Web page visitor uses.

BTW

Shorthand Properties
Shorthand properties are great to use and make your CSS code very efficient. You can use shorthand properties with many different elements, including padding, borders, margins, and fonts. See the w3.org Web site for helpful information about shorthand properties.

The padding property can have from one to four values. Table 7–3 shows the shorthand statement together with the resulting values.

Table 7–3 Shorthand Properties

Padding Property Statement	Resulting Values
`padding: 25px 50px 75px 100px;`	top padding is 25px right padding is 50px bottom padding is 75px left padding is 100px
`padding: 25px 50px 75px;`	top padding is 25px right and left paddings are 50px bottom padding is 75px
`padding: 25px 50px;`	top and bottom paddings are 25px right and left paddings are 50px
`padding: 25px;`	all four paddings are 25px

Line 20 also sets the cursor to the default value using cursor: default as the statement. If you do not have this statement, then you would not see a cursor as shown in Figure 7–6a. With this cursor code statement inserted, you see the cursor as shown in Figure 7–6b. Notice also that you are setting the padding in the statement to an "em" measurement value. Table 7–4 describes the units that can be used by Web developers.

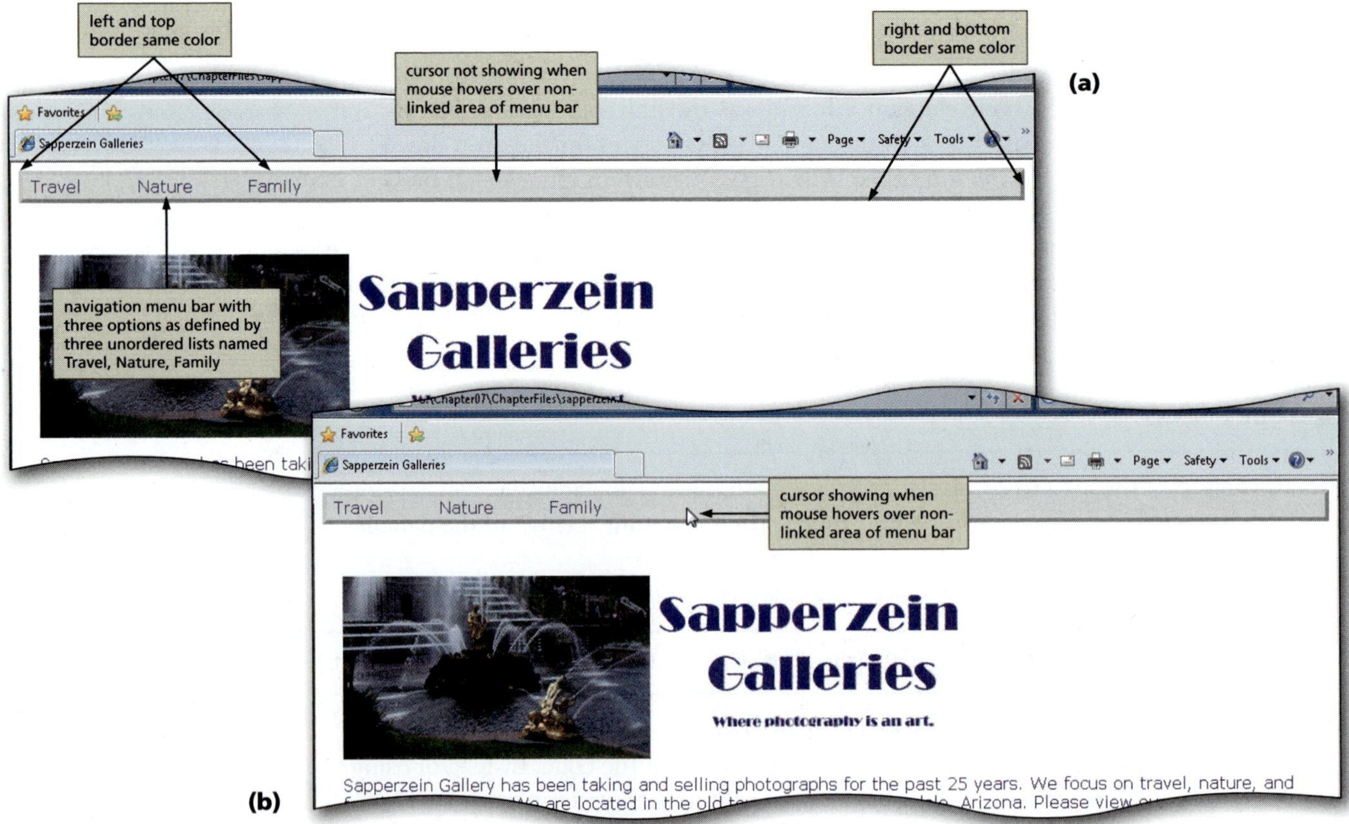

Figure 7–6

Table 7–4 Measurement Values

Unit	Description
%	percentage
in	inch
cm	centimeter
mm	millimeter
em	1em is equal to the current font size; 2em means 2 times the size of the current font. For example, if an element is displayed with a font of 12 pt, then 2em is 24 pt
ex	one ex is the x-height of a font (x-height is usually about half the font size)
pt	point (1 pt = 1/72 inch)
pc	pica (1 pc = 12 points)
px	pixels (a dot on the computer screen)

The next section of code in the embedded style sheet (lines 22 through 30 in Figure 7–5 on page HTML 336) specifies additional styles for the menu bar and submenus. Figure 7–6b shows the menu bar at startup. Figure 7–7a shows the menu bar when the pointer is on one of the three main menu options (Travel, Nature, Family). This is defined with the style statements on lines 22 and 23 in the CSS code. Figure 7–7b shows the menu bar when a Web site visitor hovers over one of the two list items in each of three unordered lists. This style is defined on lines 27 and 30 where the hover pseudoclass is used.

BTW

CSS Pseudoclasses
To expand the possibilities of CSS, you can use pseudoclasses (e.g., the link hover). When used effectively, CSS pseudoclasses are used to add special effects to some selectors.

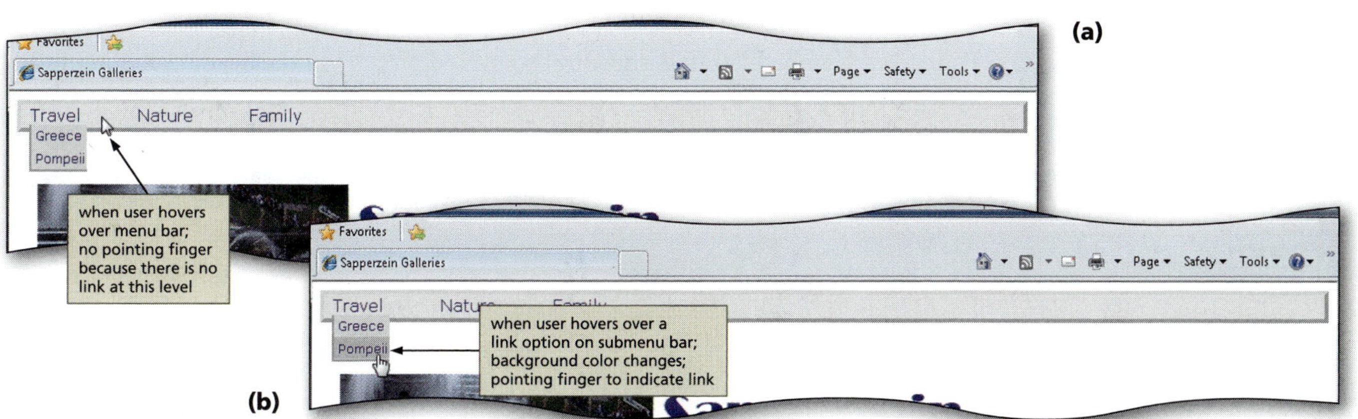

Figure 7–7

Next, there are some properties with which you are not yet familiar. Line 22 in the CSS code sets a style for the unordered lists (ul) in the menu class. It starts by setting display to none. That means at Web page startup (i.e., before the user hovers over the menu), the unordered lists will not display (Figure 7–7a). The position property is used to position an element on the Web page. If you do not use the position property, the elements display on the Web page in the order in which they appear. For example, if you have a line of text entered in your HTML code, and then you insert an image in the code, the text appears on the Web page before the image. The position: absolute code sets the style so that the menu text remains constant and does not move. Table 7–5 lists the available property values for position.

Table 7–5 Position Property Values

Property Values	Value Description
absolute	Generates an absolutely positioned element, positioned relative to the first parent element that has a position other than static
fixed	Generates an absolutely positioned element, positioned relative to the browser window
relative	Generates a relatively positioned element, positioned relative to its normal position, so "left: 10" adds 10 pixels to the element's left position
static	Default; no position; the element occurs in the normal flow
inherit	Specifies that the value of the position property should be inherited from the parent element

BTW

Measurement Values
When is it best to use the "em" measurement versus using the "pt" measurement? There are many advanced Web page design resources available that discuss this topic. The main goal with any measurement value is to design a Web page so that it is legible.

When you add the list-style: none code in line 23, you turn off the display of the disc that is the default bullet for an unordered list. The margin: 0.1em 0 0 0 code is a shorthand property statement for margins. When you set the style display: block on lines 25 and 27, the ul element will generate a block box (line break) before and after the element.

Finally, line 32 sets a new division id name called content. This division is used in the sapperzein.html file that begins with the <div> tag on line 39. This will be the style just for the paragraph of text on the Sapperzein Galleries home page. Again, review this material while looking at Figure 7–5 together with the open sapperzein.html file and Figure 7–7 for a comprehensive view of this embedded style sheet.

To Add an Embedded Style Sheet

Table 7–6 shows the CSS code for the embedded style sheet to be entered directly in the header section of the HTML code for the home page, sapperzein.html.

Table 7–6 Code for an Embedded Style Sheet

Line	CSS Code	
10	`<style type="text/css">`	
11	`<!--`	
12	body	{font-family: Verdana, Arial, sans-serif}
13		
14	a	{text-decoration: none; color: #100375}
15		
16	#menubar	{border-top: 4px solid #e5e5e5; border-right: 4px solid #b2b2b2;
17		border-bottom: 4px solid #b2b2b2; border-left: 4px solid #e5e5e5;
18		background-color: #eeeeee; color: #100375; height: 23px}
19		
20	.menu	{float: left; padding: 0.1em 3em 0.1em 0.5em; cursor: default}
21		
22	.menu ul	{display: none; position: absolute; background-color: #e5e5e5; color: #100375;
23		list-style: none; margin: 0.1em 0 0 0; padding: 0}
24		

Table 7–6 Code for an Embedded Style Sheet (continued)

Line	CSS Code		
25	.menu ul li	{display: block; font-size: small; padding: 0.2em}	
26			
27	div.menu:hover	ul	{margin: 0; padding: 0; display: block;
28			border-bottom: .15em solid #b2b2b2; border-left: .15em solid #b2b2b2}
29			
30	div.menu ul li:hover		{background-color: #cccccc}
31			
32	div.content	{margin-left: 20px; margin-right: 20px; padding-top: 5%; color: #100375}	
33	-->		
34	</style>		

The following step illustrates how to add an embedded style sheet to the Web page sapperzein.html.

1

- Highlight the comment <!--Insert embedded style sheet here -->, on line 10.
- Enter the CSS code shown in Table 7–6 (Figure 7–8).

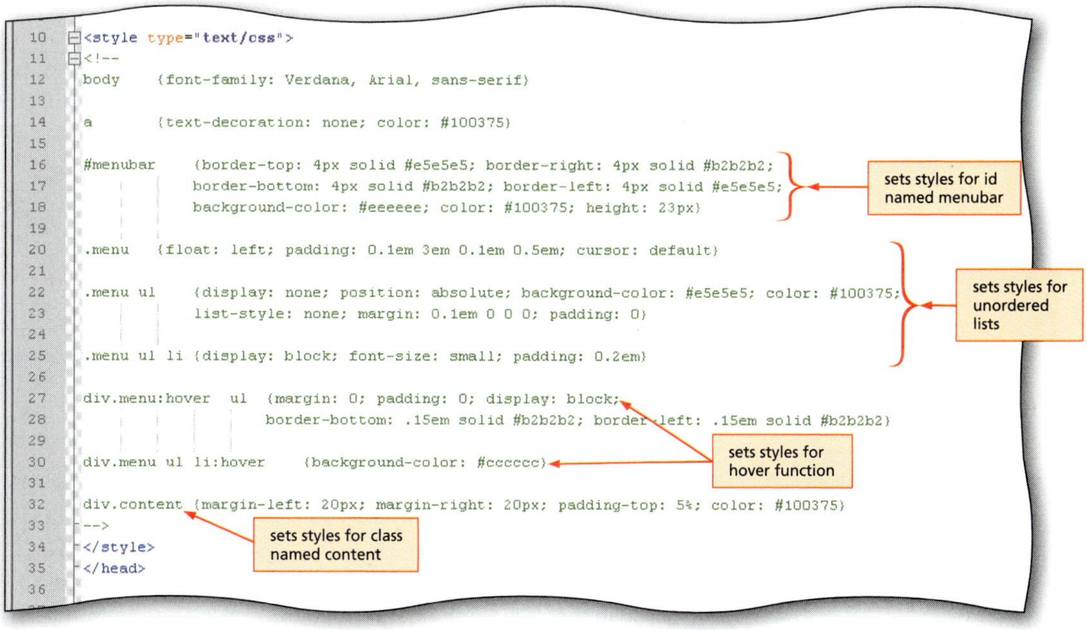

```
10 <style type="text/css">
11 <!--
12 body    {font-family: Verdana, Arial, sans-serif}
13
14 a       {text-decoration: none; color: #100375}
15
16 #menubar    {border-top: 4px solid #e5e5e5; border-right: 4px solid #b2b2b2;
17             border-bottom: 4px solid #b2b2b2; border-left: 4px solid #e5e5e5;
18             background-color: #eeeeee; color: #100375; height: 23px}
19
20 .menu    {float: left; padding: 0.1em 3em 0.1em 0.5em; cursor: default}
21
22 .menu ul    {display: none; position: absolute; background-color: #e5e5e5; color: #100375;
23             list-style: none; margin: 0.1em 0 0 0; padding: 0}
24
25 .menu ul li {display: block; font-size: small; padding: 0.2em}
26
27 div.menu:hover  ul  {margin: 0; padding: 0; display: block;
28                 border-bottom: .15em solid #b2b2b2; border-left: .15em solid #b2b2b2}
29
30 div.menu ul li:hover     {background-color: #cccccc}
31
32 div.content {margin-left: 20px; margin-right: 20px; padding-top: 5%; color: #100375}
33 -->
34 </style>
35 </head>
36
```

sets styles for id named menubar

sets styles for unordered lists

sets styles for hover function

sets styles for class named content

Figure 7–8

Q&A What is an easy way to find out what fonts are supported on your computer system?

One way is to review the font names and examples as they appear in an application such as in the Font menu in Microsoft Word. You may want to try different fonts and sizes in an application such as Word to see what they look like. You can save a document as a Web page from Word and view it in the browser as well.

Q&A Why would I want to use the "hover" technique for links?

It adds a bit of interactivity and in this case helps to highlight the menu and submenu structure for the user.

Experiment

- Remove the position: absolute statement in line 22 and see what it does to the words Nature and Family when you hover over the word Travel. Put the statement back in.

BTW

Font Families
You also can specify font-weight using numerical values from 100 to 900. Normal text that is not bold has a value of 400. Each larger number is at least as bold as the one above it, and 900 is the boldest option of the font. The browser determines how bold each value is as it is displaying the Web page.

To Save, Validate, and View an HTML File

After you have added the embedded style sheet to the sapperzein.html Web page, you should save the HTML file, and view the Web page to review the style changes.

1. With the USB drive plugged into your computer, click File on the menu bar and then click Save.
2. Validate the Web page using the W3C validation service.
3. Open the sapperzein.html file in the Web browser to show the completed navigation menu, as shown at the top of the sapperzein.html Web page (Figure 7–9).

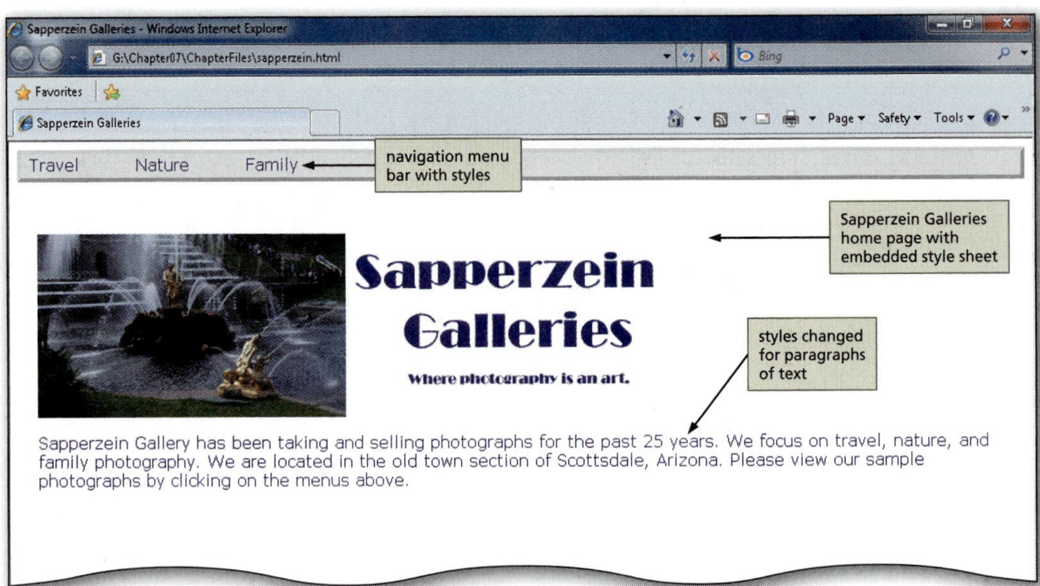

Figure 7–9

Plan Ahead

Creating an External Style Sheet
The external style sheet is the most powerful and lowest precedence style sheet. With this style sheet, you can easily create a common look across a Web site by creating the external (.css) style sheet and linking it into all other Web pages. In this chapter project, you have two list items per main category (Travel, Nature, Family), or six Web pages that you want to have a common look.

- **Create the external style sheet.** The first step is to create the file itself. This file, which contains all of the style statements that you want, has to be saved with a file name extension of .css. Make sure to store this file in the same folder as the other Web pages.
- **Link the external style sheet into the Web pages.** The second step is to link the external style sheet (.css file) into the Web pages where you want it. The link statement is placed between the <head> and </head> tags.
- **Add comments to your code as needed.** The CSS code added to this external style sheet is complex. Comments help you remember and explain what you have done. The comments will not display on the Web page, but they will stay in the file with the CSS code.

Adding Pop-ups with an External Style Sheet

As you learned in previous chapters, an external style sheet is a separate text file that contains the style statements that define how the Web page elements will appear across multiple pages. After you create the text file with all of the desired style statements and comments, you save the file with the file extension .css to identify it as a CSS file. You then use a <link> tag to link the external style sheet to the Web pages to which you want to apply the style.

Structuring the Web Page

It is useful to understand how you can structure your Web page by dividing it into logical sections. In previous chapters, you used the <div> </div> tags for structure. Specifically, you aligned images by placing the image element within the <div> </div> container. You also set specific styles using the <div> </div> tags. When you use the <div> </div> tags, you are able to design a layout that uses CSS, including inserting images.

When structuring your Web pages, it is also useful to understand the concept of the box model. The **box model** describes the structure of the elements that are displayed on the Web page. Once you have positioned the box on the Web page, you can control its appearance by manipulating its padding, borders, and margins, as shown in Figure 7–10. The **margin** specifies the space between the element and other content on the Web page. The **border** is what surrounds the element content. The **padding** is the space between the content of the element and the box border. These four elements (content, padding, border, and margin) determine how the element content is displayed in the browser.

> **BTW**
> **The Box Model**
> The box model is an important concept to understand. Determining an effective structure of your Web pages involves correctly determining the box model controls. Search the Web for the term "box model" to find numerous resources that discuss box model control principles.

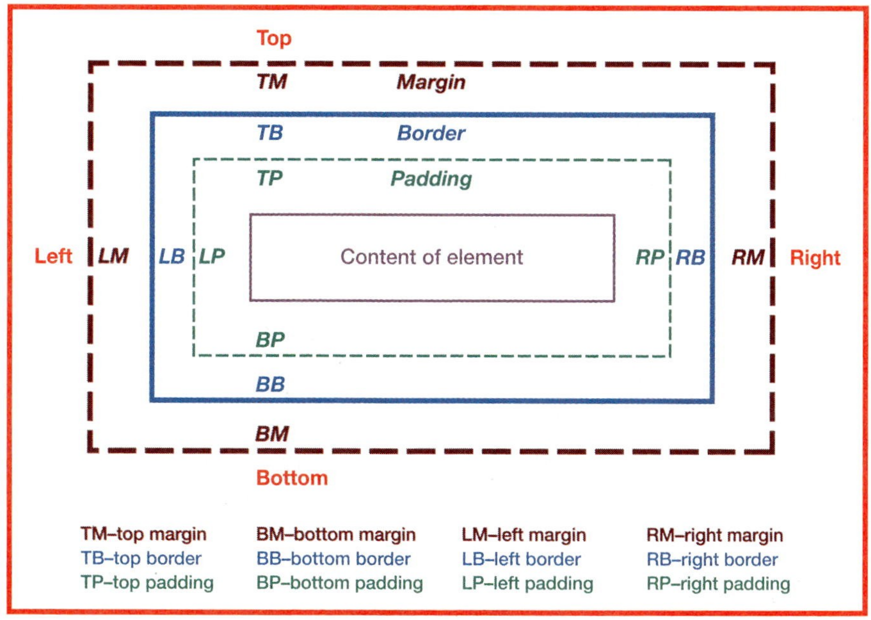

Figure 7–10

You will manipulate some of these characteristics (border, margin-bottom, margin-top) in the external style sheet completed in this section of the chapter. You also use the <div> </div> tags to divide the Web page to allow the pop-up effect.

> **BTW**
> **Box Model Troubleshooting**
> You can also find an abundance of information on the Box model troubleshooting tools like those in Firebug or Google Chrome's Developer Tools.

Creating a Pop-up Using Cascading Style Sheets

The CSS code for the external style sheet defines a new style that provides a pop-up capability on a Web page. In this case, you add link and hover functionality that allows a Web site visitor to hover (i.e., move the mouse pointer) over an image and display a larger version of the image.

The two files used for the pop-up function, greece.html and pompeii.html, are stored in the Data Files for Students. These files are all ready to use for the pop-ups but need to have the link statements inserted after the external style sheet is created and saved. It helps to look at the code in one of those files (greece.html) to see how the CSS code you will enter is used in the HTML file. The HTML code from greece.html follows:

```
<div id="sizes">
<p><a>
    <img class="small" src="greece1.jpg" width="150"
    height="110" alt="Greece 1" />
    <img class="large" src="greece1.jpg" width="150"
    height="110" alt="Greece 1" />
</a></p>
<p><a>
    <img class="small" src="greece2.jpg" width="150"
    height="110" alt="Greece 2" />
    <img class="large" src="greece2.jpg" width="150"
    height="110" alt="Greece 2" />
</a></p>
<p><a>
    <img class="small" src="greece3.jpg" width="150"
    height="110" alt="Greece 3" />
    <img class="large" src="greece3.jpg" width="150"
    height="110" alt="Greece 3" />
</a></p>
</div>
```

BTW **External Style Sheet Validator**
For the external style sheet, be sure to use the CSS validator found at the w3.org validation service at http://jigsaw.w3.org/css-validator/#validate_by_upload.

There are two areas that need to be discussed to understand how the CSS code applies to the HTML code. Table 7–7 contains the CSS code that you will input into an external style sheet named styles7.css. The HTML code above from greece.html shows a division with an id named sizes and three sets of images for the three images, as shown in Figure 7–1b on page HTML 327.

Lines 4 and 7–8 in Table 7–7 define the styles for the id named "sizes" as used in the greece.html code. The <div> statement at the start of this code identifies an id named "sizes" at the start of the HTML code. Line 1 in Table 7–7 creates a class named "small" that is used with the image element. Lines 4 and 7 identify a class named "large" to be used as shown in the greece.html code above. Note that line 4 identifies the styles for a link of an image for a class named large (a img.large), as used in the division with id sizes. Line 4 also tells the browser to set the large image size to height of zero and width of zero. The net effect of this is that the large image does not display at startup.

Line 7 targets the same elements (a and img) and the same class (large), but this time it sets styles for the hover pseudoclass (a:hover). This style statement tells the browser to enlarge the image with class name large when a user hovers over the small image.

The "large" version of the image is set to an absolute position 68 pixels from the top of the browser window and 170 pixels from the left of the window. The height of the image when enlarged is 389 pixels, while the width is 500 pixels. This CSS code enlarges an image, but you can also display text or other elements using this same basic code structure.

To Create and Print an External Style Sheet

To create an external style sheet, you open a new text file and enter CSS code shown in Table 7-7. After coding the style statements, you save the file with the file extension .css to identify it as a CSS file.

Table 7–7 Code for an External Style Sheet

Line	CSS Code
1	`img.small {border: none; text-decoration: none}`
2	`/* displays no border around images on the left */`
3	
4	`div#sizes a img.large {height: 0; width: 0; border-width: 0}`
5	`/* hide the larger image by setting its height and width to zero */`
6	
7	`div#sizes a:hover img.large {position: absolute; top: 68px; left: 170px; height: 389px;`
8	`width: 500px; border:none}`
9	`/* make the larger image appear in the same space as the frame on the right when a user hovers over`
10	`one of the smaller images on the left side of the Web page */`
11	
12	`p {margin-bottom: 26px; margin-top: 26px; font-size: small;`
13	`font-family: Verdana, Arial, sans-serif; color: #100375}`
14	`/* add bottom and top margins to p elements so they are somewhat aligned with the large image */`

The following step illustrates how to create an external style sheet to define Web page style.

- If necessary, click the Notepad++ button on the taskbar. Click File on the menu bar and then click New.
- Enter the CSS code as shown in Table 7–7.
- With the USB drive plugged into your computer, click File on the menu bar and then click Save As. Type `styles7.css` in the File name text box. If necessary, navigate to the Chapter07\Chapterfiles folder on your USB drive. Click the Save button in the Save As dialog box to save the file as styles7.css (Figure 7–11).
- Click the File menu, click Print on the File menu, and click the Print button in the Print dialog box.

comment lines

styles for image class named small

styles for image class named large

styles set for paragraphs of text

Figure 7–11

Linking to an External Style Sheet

You now want to add this pop-up capability to two Web pages in the Sapperzein Galleries Web site: greece.html and pompeii.html. Linking the external style sheet to each of these Web pages gives you the capability to enlarge images in a pop-up format.

To link to the external style sheet, a <link> tag must be inserted into each of these two Web pages. The <link> tag used to link an external style sheet is added within the <head> tag of the Web page HTML. The general format of the <link> tag is:

```
<link rel="stylesheet" type="text/css" href="styles7.css" />
```

where rel="stylesheet" establishes that the linked document is a style sheet, type="text/css" indicates that the CSS language is used in the text file containing the style sheet, and href="styles7.css" provides the name and location (URL) of the linked style sheet. To link a style sheet to a Web page, the <link> tag must use "stylesheet" as the value for the rel property and text/css as the value for the type property. The URL used as the value for the href property varies, based on the name and location of the file used as the external style sheet. The URL used here indicates that the external style sheet, styles7.css, is located in the main or root directory of the Web site.

To Link to an External Style Sheet

The following steps illustrate how to add a link to an external style sheet using a <link> tag and then save the HTML file.

- If necessary, click the Notepad++ button on the taskbar.
- With the USB drive plugged into your computer, click File on the menu bar and then click Open on the File menu.
- If necessary, navigate to the G:\Chapter07\ChapterFiles folder. Click the greece.html file.
- Click the Open button in the Open dialog box.
- Highlight the text, <!--Insert external style sheet link statement here -->on line 10.
- Type `<link rel="stylesheet" type="text/css" href="styles7.css" />` to enter the link to the external style sheet (Figure 7–12).

link statement to external style sheet styles7.css

Figure 7–12

Q&A Will the styles from the styles7.css take effect for all menus within the Web site?

As long as you insert the style sheet link statement into the Web page, then the menu styles will take effect. Remember that you can override those styles with either an embedded or an inline style sheet. You would do this if there is content that you want to vary from the styles used in the external style sheet.

2

- Click File on the menu bar and then click Save on the File menu.
- Validate the Web page using the W3C service.
- Return to the browser window and use the menu bar to click Travel and then click Greece. Hover over each image shown on the Web page (Figure 7–13) to see the changes in the Web page.

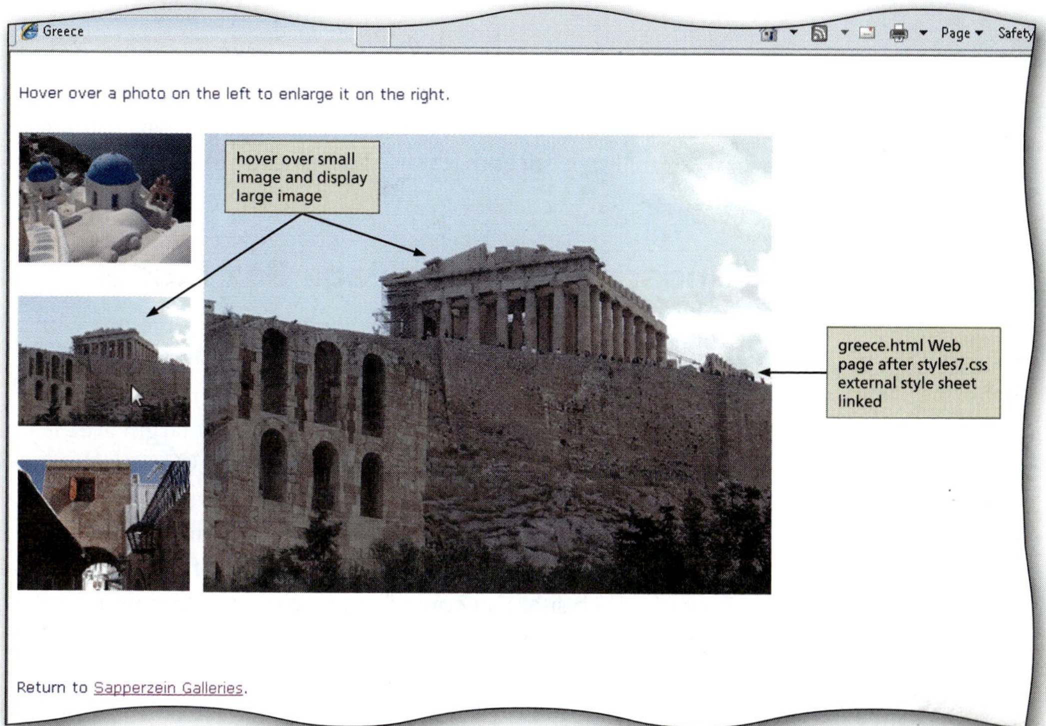

Figure 7–13

To Link the Remaining HTML File to an External Style Sheet

You have linked the greece.html page to the external style sheet styles7.css. Now you need to link the pompeii.html Web page to the same style sheet. The following steps show how to add a <link> tag to the Pompeii Web page and then save the file.

1. If necessary, click the Notepad++ button on the taskbar.
2. With the USB drive plugged into your computer, click File on the menu bar and then click Open on the File menu.
3. If necessary, navigate to the G:\Chapter07\ChapterFiles folder. Click the pompeii.html file.
4. Click the Open button in the Open dialog box.
5. Highlight the text, <!--Insert external style sheet link statement here --> on line 10.
6. Type `<link rel="stylesheet" type="text/css" href="styles7.css" />` to enter the link to the external style sheet.

To Save, Validate, and Test the Web Page

1. Click File on the menu bar and then click Save on the File menu.
2. Validate the Web page. For the external style sheet, make sure to use the CSS validator found at http://jigsaw.w3.org/css-validator/#validate_by_upload.
3. Open pompeii.html in a Web browser and test to see that the pop-up styles are implemented.

Creating an External Style Sheet for Printing

You next create an external style sheet that will be used for printing a Web page. When Web site visitors print a Web page, they generally want to print the content of the Web page, which does not include the navigation menu bar. You can limit what prints by creating an external style sheet that is used specifically to set the styles for a printed Web page.

Understanding the Page Box Model

BTW

@page Rule
There are many ways to control the printing of a Web page. Paged media (paper or transparencies) differ from continuous media in that the content of the document is split into one or more discrete pages. Using the @page rule gives you the flexibility that you need.

In this external style sheet, you will add a page box with an @page rule to format the printed page. A **page box** is a rectangular region that contains two areas: the page area and the margin area. The page area includes the elements (or boxes) laid out on the page. The margin area surrounds the page area; the page margin area is transparent. Web developers can specify the margins of a page box inside an @page rule. An **@page rule** contains the keyword @page, followed by an optional page selector, followed by a block of declarations. Page selectors give a Web developer the flexibility to designate the first page, all left pages, or all right pages. For instance, you could specify different margins for the first printed page of a Web site. You could therefore use the first pseudoclass in your @page rule by using the statement:

```
@page :first { }
```

The printing external style sheet does not use any optional page selectors. It does include a declaration in the @page rule with the statement:

```
@page {margin: 0.5in}
```

As with other external style sheets, you must first create the external style sheet, and then you must link that style sheet into the Web page(s) for which you want to use it using the <link /> statement.

To Create and Print an External Style Sheet for Printing

Table 7–8 shows the code for the external style sheet for printing.

Table 7–8 Code for a Print Style Sheet

Line / CSS Code

```
@page       {margin: 0.5in}
/* set printed page with half-inch margins */

#menubar {display: none}
/* do not print the menubar that displays at the top of the Web page */

.content    {text-align: left; font-size: 12pt; font-family: sans-serif}
.content img      {border-width: 0px; width: 8.778in; height: 2.444in}
/* specific styles set for content class */
```

1

- If necessary, click the Notepad++ button on the taskbar. Click File on the menu bar and then click New.
- Enter the CSS code as shown in Table 7–8.
- With the USB drive plugged into your computer, click File on the menu bar and then click Save As. Type `printpage.css` in the File name text box. If necessary, navigate to the Chapter07\ChapterFiles folder on your USB drive. Click the Save button in the Save As dialog box to save the file as printpage.css (Figure 7–14).

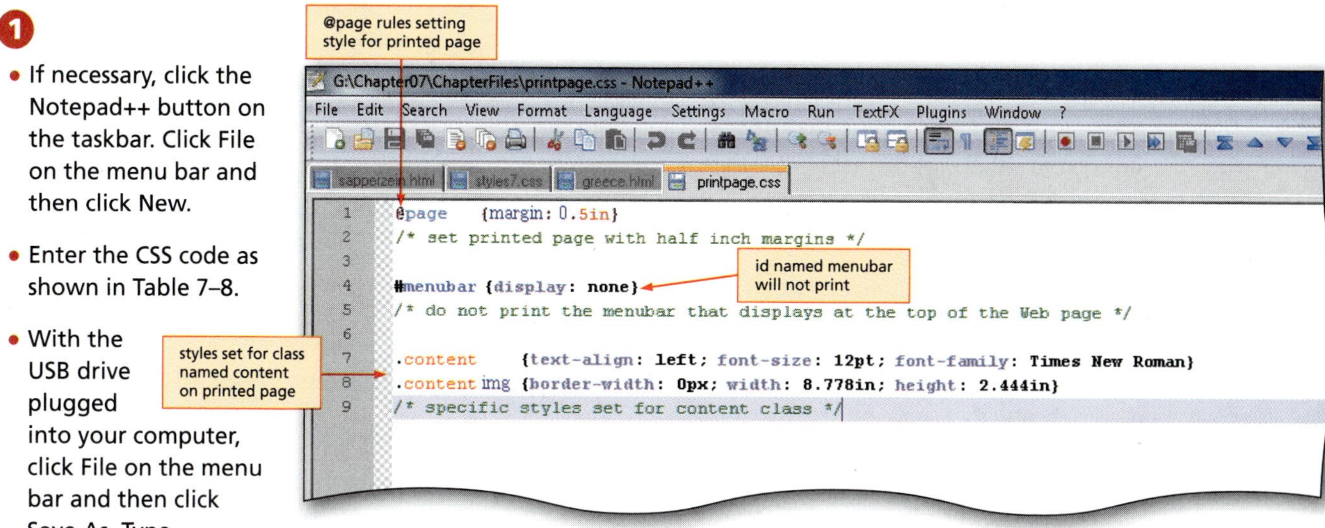

Figure 7–14

- Click the File menu, click Print on the File menu, and click the Print button in the Print dialog box to print the CSS code.

To Link to an External Style Sheet

The following steps illustrate how to add a link to an external style sheet using a <link> tag and then save the HTML file.

1 Click the sapperzein.html tab in Notepad++.

2 Click to the right of the > at the end of </title> in line 8 and press the ENTER key twice.

3 Type `<link rel="stylesheet" type="text/css" href="printpage.css" media="print" />` to enter the link to the external style sheet (Figure 7–15).

4 Click File on the menu bar and then click Save on the File menu.

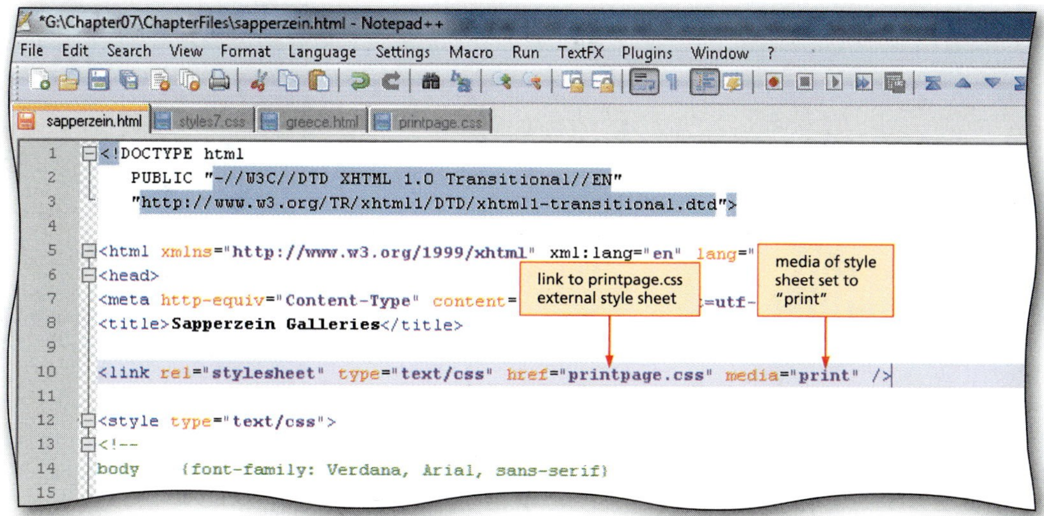

Figure 7–15

To Print an HTML File

1. Click Print on the File menu and then click the Print button in the Print dialog box to print the sapperzein.html code.

To Test the External Style Sheet

The following steps illustrate how to test the printpage.css external style sheet.

1. Click the Internet Explorer button in the taskbar and then click the Return to Sapperzein Galleries link at the bottom of the Web page.
2. Click the Refresh button.
3. Click the Print icon arrow in the Command bar and then click Print Preview (Figure 7–16) to verify that the menu bar will not print.

Q&A

What other styles might be appropriate for printing?

As mentioned above, Web site visitors generally want to print the content of a Web page, not necessarily the format. You therefore might want to change the way that headings (h1 through h6) print. You could add a style to the printpage.css that prints all headings in one particular size (perhaps slightly larger than the general content of the Web page). You also might want to vary the margins from the Web page as displayed in the browser versus the margins on a printed page.

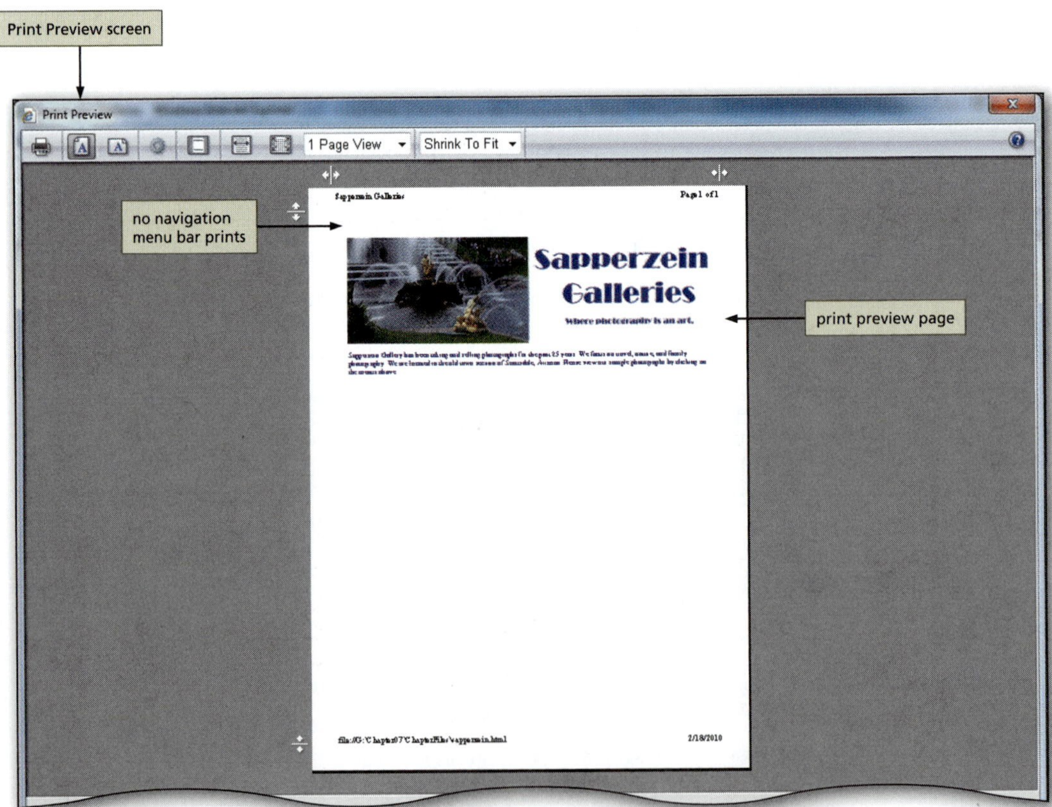

Figure 7–16

To Quit Notepad++ and a Browser

After you have viewed and printed the HTML and CSS files, the project is complete.

1. Close all open browser windows.
2. Click File on the Notepad++ menu bar and then click Close All.
3. Click the Close button on the Notepad++ window title bar.

BTW

Quick Reference
For a list of CSS properties and values, see the CSS Quick Reference (Appendix D) at the back of this book, or visit the CSS Quick Reference Web page (scsite.com/HTML6e/qr).

Chapter Summary

In this chapter, you have learned how to add advanced CSS features in embedded and external style sheets to give your Web pages a consistent and polished look and to add functionality. The items listed below include all the new HTML and CSS skills you have learned in this chapter.

1. Add an Embedded Style Sheet (HTML 340)
2. Create and Print an External Style Sheet (HTML 345)
3. Link to an External Style Sheet (HTML 346)
4. Create and Print an External Style Sheet for Printing (HTML 348)

Learn It Online

Test your knowledge of chapter content and key terms.

Instructions: To complete the Learn It Online exercises, start your browser, click the Address bar, and then enter the Web address `scsite.com/html6e/learn`. When the HTML Learn It Online page is displayed, click the link for the exercise you want to complete and read the instructions.

Chapter Reinforcement TF, MC, and SA

A series of true/false, multiple choice, and short answer questions that test your knowledge of the chapter content.

Flash Cards

An interactive learning environment where you identify chapter key terms associated with displayed definitions.

Practice Test

A series of multiple choice questions that test your knowledge of chapter content and key terms.

Who Wants To Be a Computer Genius?

An interactive game that challenges your knowledge of chapter content in the style of a television quiz show.

Wheel of Terms

An interactive game that challenges your knowledge of chapter key terms in the style of the television show, *Wheel of Fortune*.

Crossword Puzzle Challenge

A crossword puzzle that challenges your knowledge of key terms presented in the chapter.

Apply Your Knowledge

Reinforce the skills and apply the concepts you learned in this chapter.

Creating an Egyptian Web Site

Instructions: Start Notepad++ and a browser. Using your browser, open the apply7-1.html file from the Chapter07\Apply folder of the Data Files for Students. See the inside back cover of this book for instructions on downloading the Data Files for Students, or contact your instructor for information about accessing the required files. The apply7-1.html file is the partially completed HTML file needed for this exercise. Figure 7–17 shows the Apply Your Knowledge Web page as it should appear in the browser after the necessary code is added.

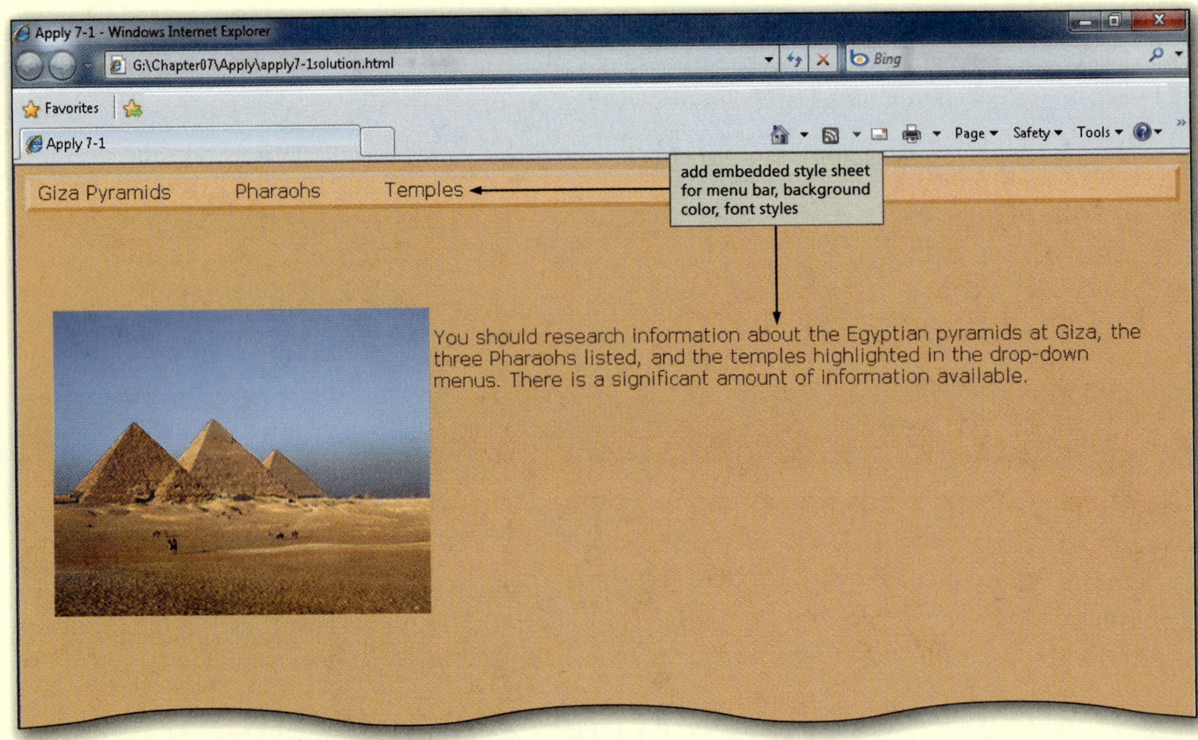

Figure 7–17

Perform the following tasks.

1. Examine the HTML file and its appearance in the browser.
2. Embed the following style sheet into the apply7-1.html file:

```
body        {font-family: Verdana, Arial, sans-serif;
            background: #edbf79}
a           {text-decoration: none; color: #5a3702}
#menubar    {border-top: 4px solid #f4dab2; border-right: 4px
            solid #e0a140; border-bottom: 4px solid #e0a140;
            border-left: 4px solid #f4dab2; background-color:
            #f5cb8a; color: #5a3702; height: 23px}
.menu       {float: left; padding: 0.1em 3em 0.1em 0.5em;
            cursor: default}
```

```
.menu ul               {display: none; position: absolute;
                       background-color: #f4dab2; color: #5a3702;
                       list-style: none; margin: 0.1em 0 0 0; padding: 0}
.menu ul li            {display: block; font-size: small; padding: 0.2em}
div.menu:hover ul      {margin: 0; padding: 0; display: block;
                       border-bottom: .15em solid #e0a140; border-left:
                       .15em solid #e0a140}
div.menu ul li:hover   {background-color: #e0a140}
div.content            {margin-left: 20px; margin-right: 20px;
                       padding-top: 8%; color: #5a3702}
```

3. Insert the necessary HTML in the body of the Web page to utilize the classes within the embedded style sheet. (*Hint:* Refer to the chapter project to help you determine where these classes should be inserted.)
4. Save the file as apply7-1solution.html, validate the code, and print the file.
5. View the Web page in your browser.
6. Print the Web page as laid out on the screen.
7. Submit the solution in the format specified by your instructor.

Extend Your Knowledge

Extend the skills you learned in this chapter and experiment with new skills.

Creating an External Style Sheet

Instructions: You will create and save an external style sheet, and then link it to the file extend7-1.html from the Chapter07\Extend folder of the Data Files for Students. See the inside back cover of this book for instructions on downloading the Data Files for Students, or contact your instructor for information about accessing the required files. This HTML file contains all of the text for the Web page shown in Figure 7–18.

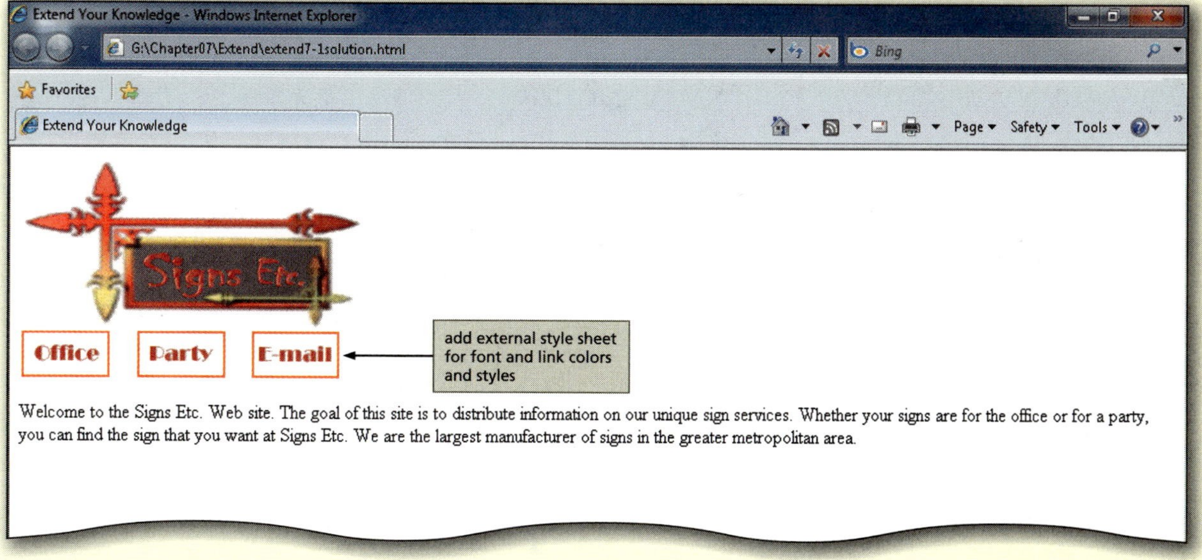

Figure 7–18

Continued >

Extend Your Knowledge *continued*

Perform the following tasks:

1. Start a new file in Notepad++, and add the following CSS code to create a new external style sheet that specifies the following:
   a. all links red in color, bolder weight, and no text-decoration
   b. table left margin of 10, color of red, and 14pt font size
   c. hover color yellow with a red background
2. Save the file as extend7-1styles.css and print the file.
3. Open the extend7-1.html file from the Data Files for Students and add a link statement to the external style sheet extend7-1styles.css.
4. Save the file as extend7-1solution.html, validate the code, and then print the file.
5. Open the extend7-1solution.html file in the browser and print the Web page.
6. Submit the solution in the format specified by your instructor.

Make It Right

Analyze a document and correct all errors and/or improve the design.

Correcting the Valentine's Day Dinner and Dance Web Page

Instructions: Start Notepad++. Open the file makeitright7-1.html from the Chapter07\MakeItRight folder of the Data Files for Students. See the inside back cover of this book for instructions on downloading the Data Files for Students, or contact your instructor for information about accessing the required files. The Web page is a modified version of what you see in Figure 7–19, but it contains some errors. Although the code in the embedded style sheet has the styles that you want, the CSS code is incorrect. Make the necessary corrections to the Web page to make it look like the figure.

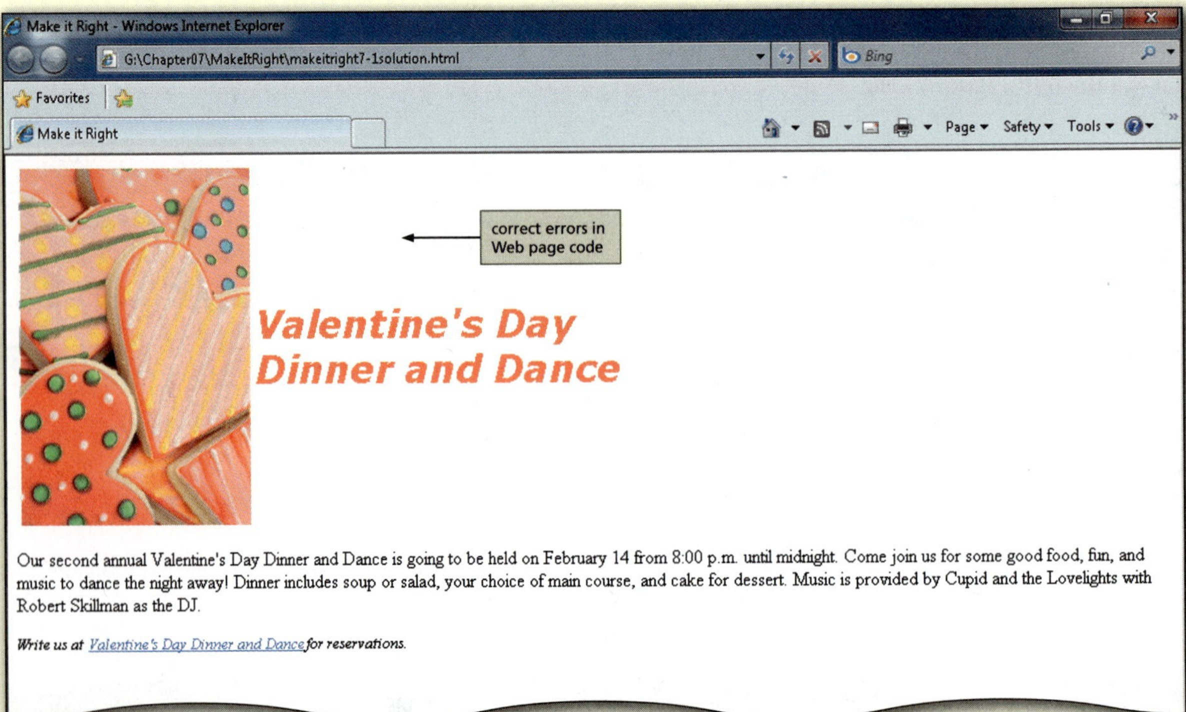

Figure 7–19

In the Lab

Lab 1: Creating an External Style Sheet for Printing

Problem: You have been asked to create a style sheet that can be used for printing across a number of people's personal Web pages. You decide to set the printing styles in an external style sheet so that it can easily be linked to any number of Web page files. You use the lab7-1.html file for this exercise. The HTML code is completed for the Web page, as shown in Figure 7–20a. You should create the external style sheet that results in Figure 7–20b.

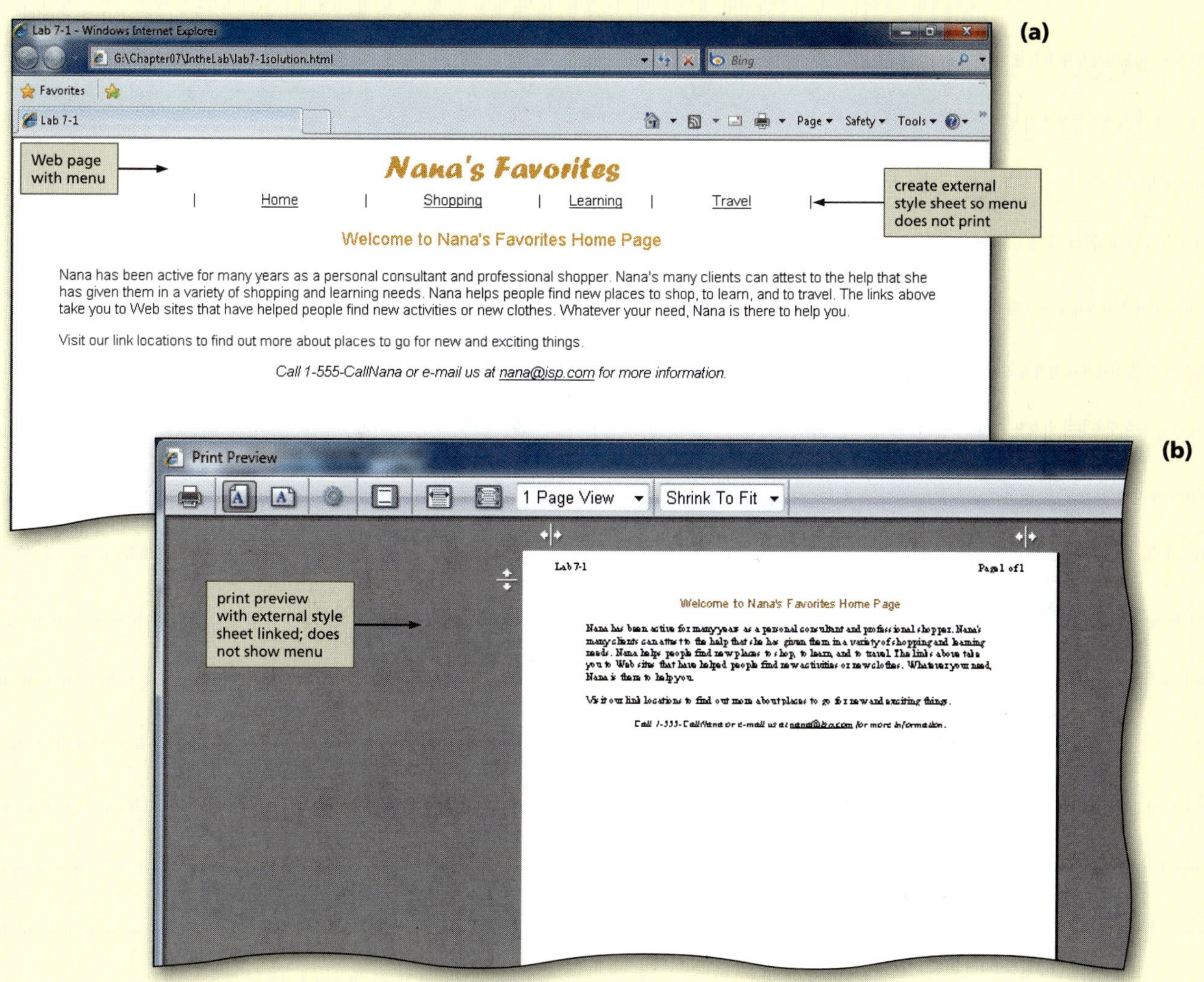

Figure 7–20

Instructions: Perform the following steps to create an external style sheet and link it to an HTML file from the Data Files for Students.

1. Using Notepad++, create a new file for an external style sheet that is used for printing.
2. Using CSS, create the style structure so that the menu bar on the Web page is not printed. (*Hint:* Use the menubar class.) Also, align the content of the Web page on the left with a font size of 12 points in Times New Roman font for the printed page. (*Hint:* Use the content class.)
3. Save the file as lab7-1print.css.

Continued >

In the Lab *continued*

4. Open the HTML file lab7-1.html in the Chapter07\IntheLab folder of the Data Files for Students. Add a link to the external style sheet, lab7-1print.css.
5. Save the HTML file in the Chapter07\IntheLab folder as lab7-1solution.html. Validate the file and then print it.
6. Open the file, lab7-1solution.html in the browser. Use Print Preview to test if your printing external style sheet works correctly.
7. Print the Print Preview view of the Web page.
8. Submit the solution in the format specified by your instructor.

In the Lab

Lab 2: Adding External and Inline Style Sheets

Problem: Your father's business, Bold Ones Painting, is participating in the Home and Garden Show and wants to create a Web page to notify people about the event. The event coordinator asks you to create a Web page that contains information about the business and an e-mail address link, as shown in Figure 7–21. The Web page should have a link to the external style sheet, lab7-2styles.css, which is in the Chapter07\IntheLab folder of the Data Files for Students. The external style sheet is not complete, so you must add some selectors and declarations to complete it.

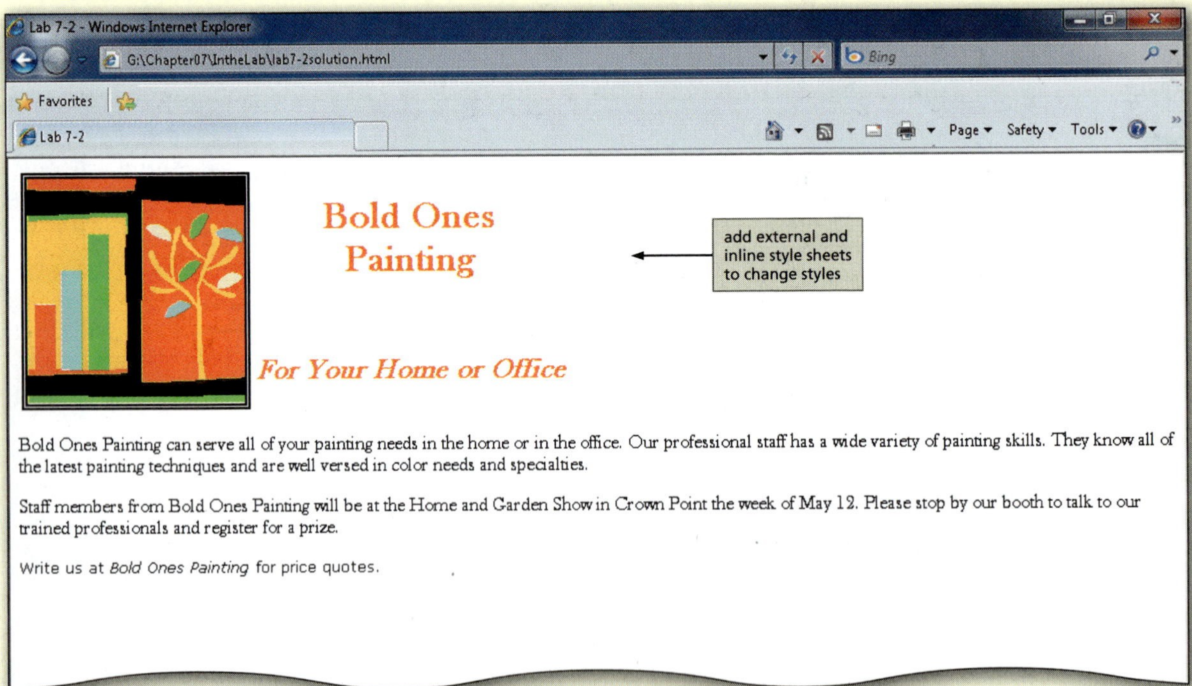

Figure 7–21

Instructions: Perform the following steps.

1. Using Notepad++, open the HTML file lab7-2styles.css in the Chapter07\IntheLab folder of the Data Files for Students.
2. Add the following styles to the external style sheet:
   a. h1 and h2: "Baskerville Old Face", "Calligrapher", "Arial" font in a bolder weight and color #ff3300
   b. paragraphs: "Sans Serif", "Baskerville Old Face" font, color of black, with 10 pt left margin
3. Save the file using the same file name.

4. Using Notepad++, open the HTML file Chapter07\IntheLab\lab7-2.html in the Data Files for Students.
5. Add the link necessary to apply the styles from the lab7-2styles.css external style sheet.
6. Add an inline style sheet to the last paragraph of text that sets the font to Verdana and size 10pt.
7. Within the borderless table provided, add the image boldones.jpg in the top data cell of the Web page. Insert an <h1> heading tag next to the image that contains the words Bold Ones Painting with a line break as indicated. Also add an <h2> heading with the words For Your Home or Office in italic font. (*Hint:* Use an inline style.)
8. Save the file as lab7-2solution.html, validate the file, and print it.
9. Open the Chapter07\IntheLab\lab7-2solution.html file in your browser.
10. Print the Web page.
11. Submit the solution in the format specified by your instructor.

In the Lab

Lab 3: Developing an External Style Sheet for Pop-ups

Problem: The owners of Sabatina's Pizza want to continue enhancing their Web site. They would like to include a pop-up that displays the ingredients and nutrition information for some of their pasta dishes, as shown in Figure 7–22. The file lab7-3.html is an HTML file that contains some of the structure of the Web page. The file, lab7-3.html, is included in the Chapter07\IntheLab folder of the Data Files for Students. In this exercise, you will create an embedded style sheet that pops up the text under the pasta image when a user hovers over the image. Research the three pasta dishes (fettuccine, lasagna, and ravioli) to get an idea of ingredients and nutrition information that you will use in your pop-up text.

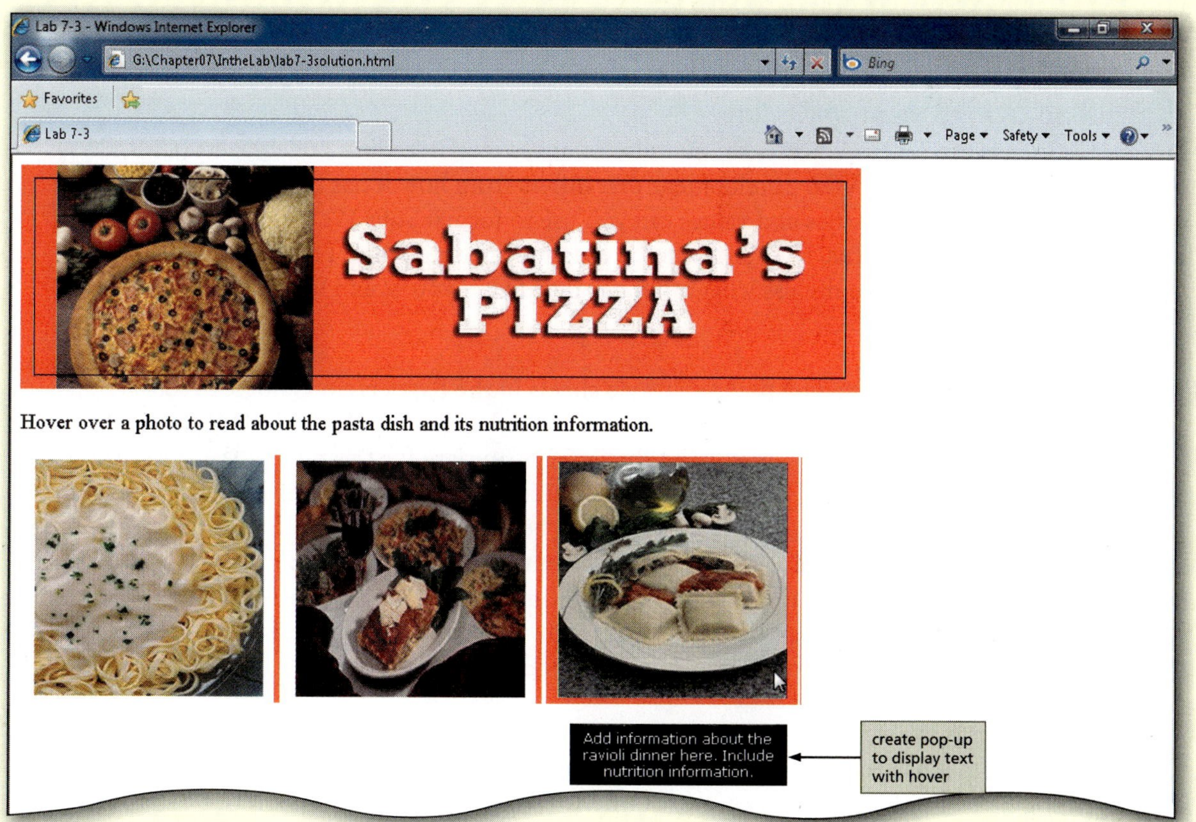

Figure 7–22

Continued >

STUDENT ASSIGNMENTS

In the Lab *continued*

Instructions: Perform the following steps.

1. Open the lab7-3.html file in Notepad++ and add an embedded style sheet that includes the styles shown in Figure 7–22.
2. Add an embedded style sheet to set the following:
   a. links should be 1em sans-serif font with padding of 5 and 10 pixels and margins of 0 0 1 pixels (*Hint:* Use shorthand properties); the right border should be 5 pixels and color #ff1828
   b. when a user hovers over a link, the right border should be style double with 5 pixels in white
   c. at startup, there should be no display of text beneath any of the three images of pasta; use the <span> </span> tags to control the display of text pop-up upon hovering; position the block of text as absolute with a top margin of 220 pixels and left margin of 550 pixels; the width of the block should be 180 pixels at a minimum, depending on how much text you find in your research; use padding of 5 pixels and margins of 10 pixels; the text should be white on a black background.
3. Add the ingredient/nutrition information to your HTML file.
4. Save the file as lab7-3solution.html, validate it, and then print the HTML code.
5. Open the Web page in your browser to test that the pop-ups display when you hover over each pasta image, as shown in Figure 7–22. Print the Web page.
6. Submit the solution in the format specified by your instructor.

Cases and Places

Apply your creative thinking and problem-solving skills to design and implement a solution.

• Easier •• More Difficult

• 1: Finding CSS Information Online

Browse the Internet to find two Web sites that discuss advanced Cascading Style Sheets (CSS). How else can CSS be used in your Web development that differs from how it has been used in Chapters 2 through 7? What other properties and values can you use to format your Web pages? What are other ways that you can create external style sheets to be used for printing only? Think about these other techniques and be prepared to discuss what other advanced CSS you would like to utilize.

• 2: Trying More Styles

Mr. Sapperzein is very impressed by the use of style sheets in the Sapperzein Galleries Web site and would like to explore additional styles that can be applied. Using Appendix D, find three CSS properties that were not used in Chapter 7 and that are appropriate for this type of Web site. Make sure to do a thorough analysis on this; i.e., do not just find three properties, but determine through your analysis and design process what three properties would be beneficial to the Web site. Then modify the styles7.css style sheet that you used in the chapter project to include these properties and values. Save the style sheet as styles7new.css in the Chapter07\CasesandPlaces folder. Update the link in the Web page, sapperzein.html, and then view the Web page in the browser using the new style sheet. How did the use of these new properties improve the appearance of the Web page?

•• 3: Applying Pop-up Text

Create a Web site that utilizes several pictures. Use the basic pop-up techniques covered in this chapter to pop up text rather than larger images when a Web site visitor hovers over one of the images. Determine how you could use this text pop-up function and why it might be helpful in your own Web development. Write a one-page paper explaining your thoughts on text pop-ups created using CSS.

•• 4: Determining How CSS Could Be Used on a Web Site

Make It Personal

Select a Web site with which you are familiar. Verify that the Web site does not utilize any of the three types of style sheets. Develop a graphic of the Web site hierarchy. Determine how the three types of style sheets could be utilized in this Web site and develop an outline explaining how they would help enhance pages or sections of the site, add style consistency, or make the site easier to maintain. Write a proposal to the owners of the Web site that describes the features you could add with style sheets and the benefits of doing so, relative to the formatting techniques currently used in the Web site. As an example, you might want to address the number of times that a particular <font> tag is used in the site and contrast that with the ease of using one external style sheet and a link statement per page. Use other ideas as discussed in the project to stress the other benefits of style sheets. Write the proposal in the form of a bid, giving time estimates and costs associated with the development effort. Include your hierarchy chart and style sheet outline as appendices to the proposal.

•• 5: Completing the Sapperzein Galleries Web Site

Working Together

In this team exercise, you will complete the Sapperzein Galleries Web site. There are four additional dummy Web pages provided in the Data Files for Students in the Chapter7\ChapterFiles folder. The four remaining Web pages are called cactus.html and flowers.html that drop down from the Nature menu selection and group.html and individuals.html that drop down from the Family menu selection. As a first step, determine in your team if the Nature menu item is of interest to the members of the team. If it is not, determine another category to replace Nature and two drop-down submenu categories to replace Cactus and Flowers. All teams should complete this project using the Family category. Once you determine the third category, you need to take the pictures relative to these four final drop-down items and complete the Web pages provided.

8 Adding Multimedia Content to Web Pages

Objectives

You will have mastered the material in this chapter when you can:

- Describe the benefits and limitations of multimedia in Web sites
- Identify audio and video formats
- Describe parameters for embedded multimedia
- Add an audio clip to a Web page
- Add a video clip to a Web page

8 Adding Multimedia Content to Web Pages

Introduction

In previous chapters, you used HTML tags and CSS code to change the way a Web page is displayed in a Web browser. You learned how to collect data from Web site visitors using Web page forms. You also learned advanced CSS techniques to create drop-down menus and pop-ups. In this chapter, you learn how to insert multimedia content in the form of audio and video clips.

Project — Adding Multimedia to a History Class Web Site

In your U.S. History class, you are studying the Berlin Wall. Several U.S. Presidents made famous speeches at the Brandenburg Gate of the Berlin Wall. Your class created a Web site that describes the historical significance of two of these speeches, one by President Kennedy, and one by President Reagan. Your instructor, Ms. Amy Sirko, would like you to enhance that Web site to make these speeches as "real" as possible.

The history class Web site consists of a home page (Figure 8–1a) and two linked Web pages (Figures 8–1b and 8–1c). The home page contains a picture of the Berlin Wall that is used as an image map for navigation. The other two pages use part of that image for navigation to speeches by Presidents Kennedy and Reagan, together with text that explains the most significant line in each speech. You feel that the addition of multimedia files (one audio and one video) might help make Ms. Sirko's history class Web site more engaging for the students. It is one thing for a student to read a historically significant line from a speech, but it may have greater impact to see or hear the line being delivered. Multimedia content can provide that valuable experience. Because the use of multimedia content is complex, you must first research how to add multimedia to Web pages. Ms. Sirko is supportive of the plan and encourages you to start as soon as possible.

Overview

As you read this chapter, you will learn how to add the multimedia content to the two Web pages shown in Figures 8–1b and 8–1c by performing these general tasks:

- Plan the use of multimedia in the Web site
- Enter the HTML code to insert an audio clip
- Enter the HTML code to insert a video clip
- Save the files as HTML files
- View the Web pages and HTML code in your browser
- Validate the Web pages
- Test and print the Web pages

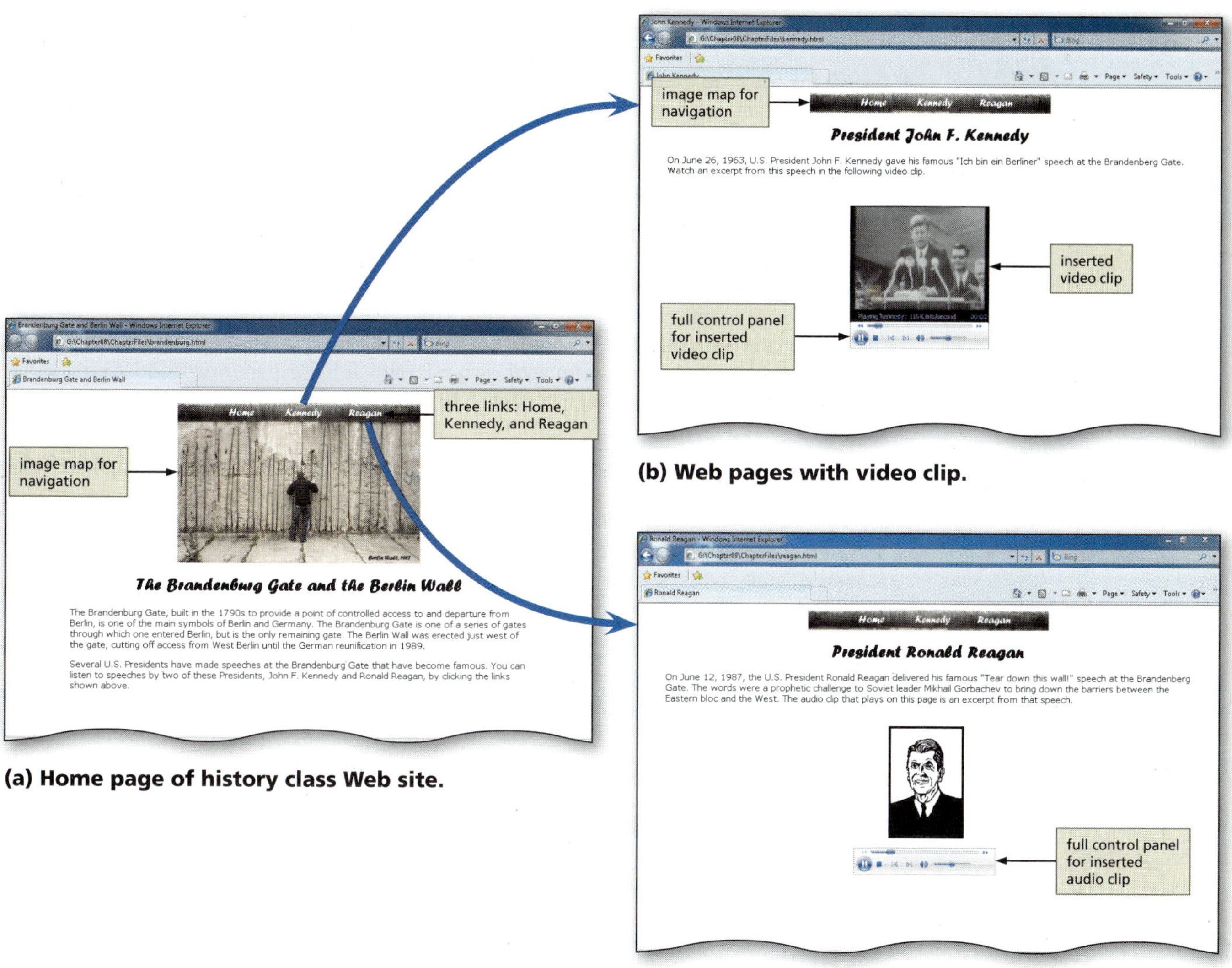

(a) Home page of history class Web site.

(b) Web pages with video clip.

(c) Web page with audio clip.

Figure 8–1

Plan Ahead

General Project Guidelines

As you create Web pages, such as the chapter project shown in Figure 8–1, you should follow these general guidelines:

1. **Plan the Web site**. First, you should determine if using multimedia content is appropriate for your Web site. If your subject matter is such that audio or video would enhance the visitors' experience, multimedia is a good choice.
2. **Analyze the need**. In the analysis phase of the Web Development Life Cycle, you should analyze what content to include on the Web page. Chapter 8 introduces a new Web development technique, adding multimedia content to your Web page; this technique can enhance the text and graphics content that you have developed in other chapters.
3. **Choose the content for the Web page**. You always want your content to add positively to your Web site visitors' experience. You therefore have to assess multimedia content just as you would text or graphics content. Many sources of content are available for Web sites. You can create your own video and audio clips easily and insert those into the appropriate Web pages. You can also take advantage of free use audio and video clips available online.

Plan Ahead

(continued)

4. **Determine the type of multimedia to incorporate into your Web pages.** The type of multimedia that you select is based on the purpose of the content. If you want to provide background music, an audio clip is fine; there would be no need for a video clip in this instance. For more complex topics though, a video clip might be more effective. As an example, if you are explaining to someone where middle C is on the piano, a video clip is more appropriate. If you want to give someone the experience of hearing a speech that does not explain things in a "how to" approach, then an audio clip is acceptable.
5. **Create or find the multimedia content and insert it into the Web site.** Once the analysis and design are complete, the Web developer creates or finds the appropriate multimedia content for the Web site. Again, consider free use content sources. Otherwise, developing multimedia content on your own might be a fun experience. Good Web development standard practices should be followed in the steps that you take to insert the multimedia.
6. **Test all Web pages within the Web site.** An important part of Web development is testing to assure that you are following XHTML standards. In this book, you use the World Wide Web Consortium (W3C) validator that allows you to test your Web page and clearly explains any errors you have. When testing, you should check all content for accuracy. Finally, all of the Web pages with multimedia content should be validated per the standard set throughout this book.

When necessary, more specific details concerning the above guidelines are presented at appropriate points in the chapter. The chapter also will identify the actions performed and decisions made regarding these guidelines during the creation of the Web page shown in Figure 8–1 on the previous page.

Using Multimedia

The popularity of the World Wide Web (the Web) is due in part to the ability to view Web pages that include graphic images, audio, and video. These additions can be wonderful for a Web site and give the users more enhanced and effective browsing experiences. Sometimes, however, the addition of multimedia can distract from the Web site message. Always remember the purpose of the Web site. If the multimedia content enhances that purpose, it should be included. If the multimedia content distracts from the purpose of the Web site, then you should reconsider using it.

Multimedia is defined as the combination of text, sound, and video to express an idea or convey a message. In the past, it was somewhat prohibitive to use multimedia on the Web. Most people dialed up to connect to the Internet, so the bandwidth (i.e., the capacity for data transfer) was not there to accommodate the large files required for audio, video, and even some graphic images. The Web of yesterday was mostly text-based with a few background colors and small graphic images. Today, most people have broadband Internet connections with a much greater capacity for data transfer. Multimedia Web pages that include large graphics, audio, and video are therefore common today.

Multimedia is used widely on Web pages. Many companies utilize videos to show potential customers new products or how to use their existing products. You may be able to review a medical procedure online before having the procedure done yourself. You can view clips of movies or hear segments of audio recordings from Web pages that provide content in those formats. **Podcasts**, a series of audio or video clips that are released in a sequence, are becoming more prevalent in both academic and corporate settings. Additionally, some instructors rely on multimedia content to stress important aspects of a class. It is important to determine where multimedia content may enhance the learning or viewing experience. You do not want to divert your Web site visitors with distracting multimedia. The Web site enhanced in this chapter is one based on historical information. To improve the user experience, you insert an audio clip and a video clip on two different Web pages. These clips enhance the content of each Web page nicely; they do not distract from the message.

This chapter provides an introduction to the use of multimedia in Web development. The chapter focuses on two different forms of multimedia: audio and video. Other multimedia formats exist, but are not covered in this chapter, including Java applets, Flash, and automated slideshows. The finished Web pages (Figure 8–2a and 8–2b) are more useful for the Web site visitors because they contain relevant audio and video clips that provide valuable multimedia content.

BTW

Slideshows, Java, and Flash

You can easily create a slideshow from your pictures using most movie editing software. A Java applet is a program written in the Java programming language that can be included in a Web page. Adobe Flash is a popular multimedia platform not discussed in this chapter. Search the Web for more information on these formats.

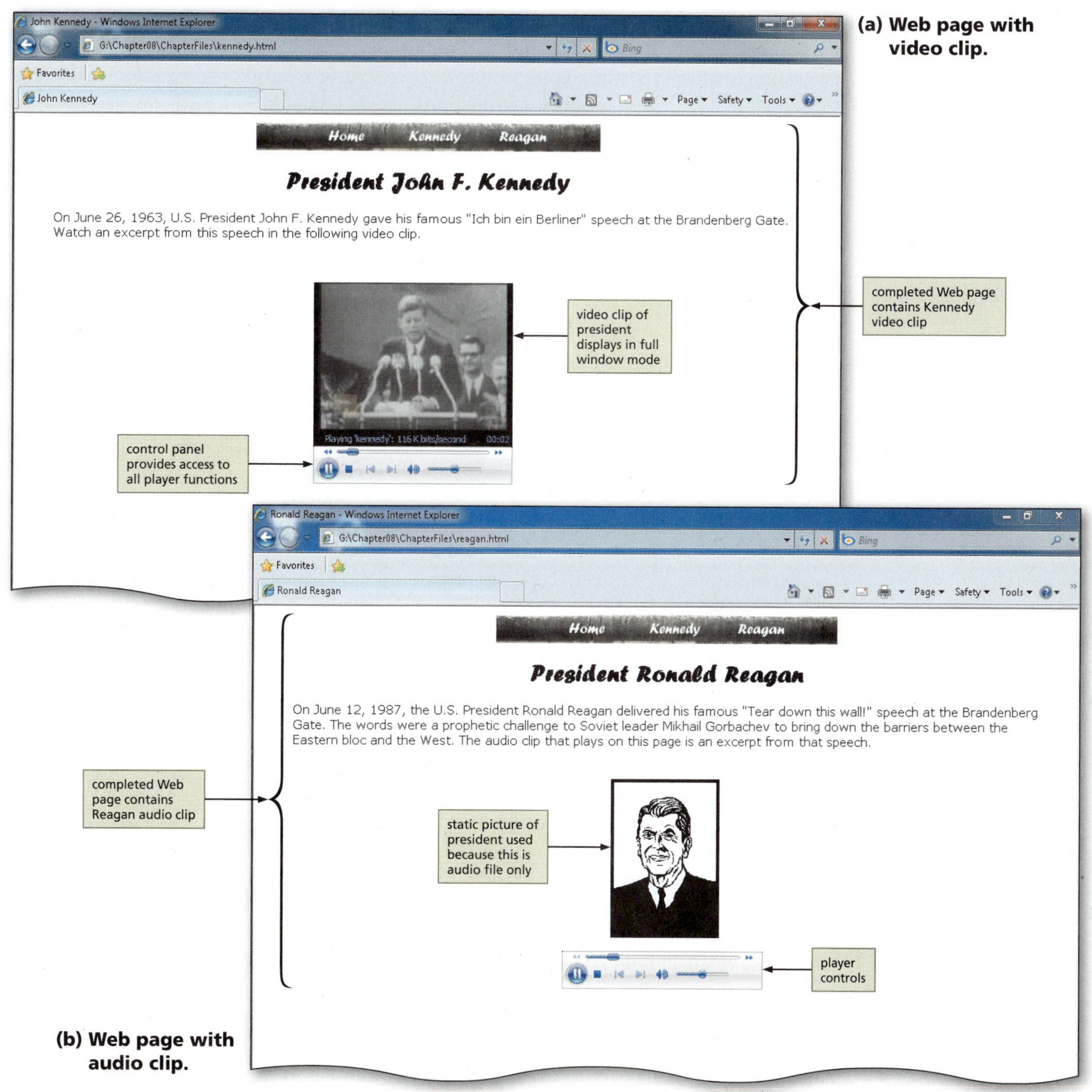

(a) Web page with video clip.

(b) Web page with audio clip.

Figure 8–2

BTW

Multimedia Sources
Search the Web for sources that you can use to download free use audio and video clips. Determine a way to keep track of the site, the specific licensing language, and the clips that you download. This is a great way to make sure that you follow the guidelines required by that Web site.

Creating or Finding Multimedia Files

You can obtain multimedia files by creating them yourself or finding files that are already available. The good thing about creating your own multimedia files is that you do not have to be concerned with licensing agreements. The bad thing about creating your own multimedia files is that they may not be the same quality as those that are created professionally. You can create your own audio files using a microphone and software designed to edit digital files. Many software options are available today for audio creation and editing. If you do use any portion of files that have been professionally developed, be certain that you understand and apply all licensing requirements.

For video files, a digital camcorder allows you to create clips that can be used on a Web page. This is what has made video Web sites such as YouTube so popular. For the Windows environment, Windows Movie Maker is available on many new computers. MAGIX Movie Edit Pro software is another option that provides online support, blogs, newsletters, and access to free downloads of a variety of software. Corel VideoStudio has simple and more advanced menu system options that novice movie editors and professionals alike can utilize comfortably. Roxio Creator is another software option that allows you to create professional-quality videos. Many other software options for Windows offer free trial versions that can be used for several days or weeks.

BTW

Multimedia Software
Many software products are available to make and edit audio and video content. Search for the names of products that you can use. Price levels vary, but you may be able to find free trials that you can download.

For Mac users, iMovie is installed on most new computers and is an excellent option. DVD Studio Pro is another Mac option that provides support for all professional audio formats. Final Cut Studio gives you the flexibility that you need for movie project work that you do individually or in collaboration with a team. Final Cut Studio allows you to have technical control together with creative options. Many other multimedia software products are available for the Mac operating system as well.

Adobe Premiere Elements is another highly rated software solution for movie editing that can be used on either the Mac or Windows operating systems. Adobe provides a frequently updated online library of templates and effects. As with many multimedia software products, Premier Elements provides the capability to edit as a novice or as a professional.

You might try downloading a free trial of the software, if available, and using it to edit a movie that you have made. You could even try a few different programs to see how they work. Most multimedia software operates in a similar fashion and has a user-friendly help utility that you can use to guide you through the process of editing. Most products also provide templates and effects that you can use to enhance the creative aspects of presenting multimedia.

To find multimedia resources on the Web, search for "free audio or video." Many Web sites contain these types of multimedia files. Again, be certain to understand and apply the license agreements that accompany any multimedia content that you find on the Web.

Embedded vs. External Multimedia

Embedding media is a similar in concept to inserting inline images. The embedded media files appear within the Web page and users have access to the audio or video player controls right on the page. Because the media file is embedded directly into the Web page, you can complement the audio or video clip resource with surrounding text or graphical images. The <object> tag is used to insert embedded content. Figure 8–3 shows how the embedded video clip of President Kennedy's speech is supplemented with a heading, text, and a menu bar.

External media files are accessed through a link that your Web site visitor clicks. This gives your visitors the option of downloading or not downloading the file. Unlike embedded media, the external media is displayed out of context with the Web page that calls it. The <embed> tag is used to define external interactive content or plug-ins. Using external links is a Web development practice that is used often in Web sites such as YouTube. Although external media files are frequently used, the <embed> tag is not XHTML compliant, so this text will not cover that tag.

> **BTW**
> **The <embed> tag**
> The <embed> tag is not XHTML compliant, so it is not used in this chapter. However, many people do use the <embed> tag. Search the Web for more information on this tag.

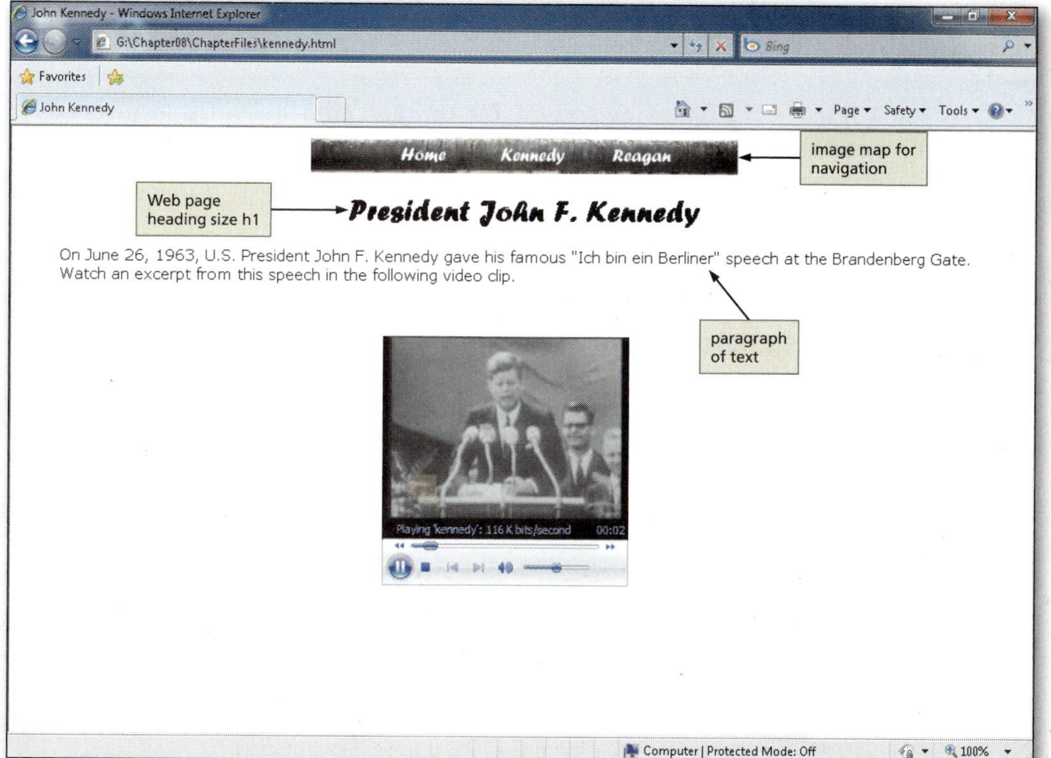

Figure 8–3 Completed Web page at startup with video clip.

Media Players and Plug-Ins

The functionality of a browser includes the ability to display text and the graphics formats discussed in earlier chapters. In order to play an audio or video file, a browser needs the help of an application called a player or a plug-in. A **media player** is computer software that is used to play multimedia files. Most software media players support an array of media formats, including both audio and video files. Windows Media Player, used in this chapter, plays both audio and video. Some media players work only with audio files, known as audio players, while others work only with video files, known as video players. The producers of these players focus on providing a better user experience as they are specifically tailored toward the media type. Windows Media Player is included with Microsoft Windows. Mac operating systems are preloaded with QuickTime Player for playing movies and iTunes for playing a variety of media formats.

A **plug-in** (also called an add-in or add-on) is extra software that is added to the browser (or other program) to provide a capability that is not inherent to the program (the browser in this case). In other words, for an embedded media file to work in a browser, the Web site visitor needs to have the correct plug-in. Most browsers do have a variety of plug-ins installed, but the Web site visitor can also download and install necessary plug-ins from the browsers' manufacturers. Common plug-ins are Windows Media Player, Apple QuickTime Player, Adobe Flash and Shockwave, Microsoft Silverlight, and Adobe Acrobat.

> **BTW**
> **Players and Plug-ins**
> Investigate what plug-ins are available for the version of browser that you use. (In Internet Explorer, click on the Tools menu, then select Manage Add-Ons.) Search the Web for information about the listed plug-ins and determine if there are other plug-ins that would be helpful that you can download.

BTW

Updating or Installing Plug-ins

Your Web site visitors may not have the plug-ins that are required to play the multimedia content on your Web site. Many Web sites discuss how to best provide users with access to such software.

Internet Explorer (used in this book) utilizes proprietary ActiveX controls. When IE encounters a multimedia file, it searches for the appropriate ActiveX control. If it cannot find it, users are most often asked if they want to install that control. Some browsers direct users to the Web site from which they can download the required plug-in. A suggestion to Web developers is to utilize common formats, such as .wmv, .mp4, .m4u, .flv, and .mp3. It is also a good idea to let your users know what format is being used. If the plug-in is not installed, IE generally provides the capability to install it. Many Web sites today also provide a link to the appropriate manufacturer for an ActiveX control needed to play the file.

As you will see in the following section, the various audio and video formats can be played on a variety of players. For embedded multimedia, it is good to use a format supported by multiple players.

Audio and Video File Formats

A variety of audio and video formats can be used on the Web. Table 8–1 lists the most commonly used audio file formats, and Table 8–2 lists common video file formats. Audio files that are used on the Web often utilize file compression techniques. This reduces the size of the file, but it can also diminish the sound quality. Uncompressed audio formats included in Table 8–1 are: AIFF, AU, and WAV. In this project, you insert an .mp3 file.

Table 8–1 Common Audio File Formats

Format	File Extension	Description
AIFF	.aiff	• The standard audio file format used by Apple • Limited to synthesizers and music files • Can be much smaller in size than other formats
AU	.au	• The standard audio file format used by Sun, UNIX, and Java • Can be compressed
MIDI	.mid .rmi	• Musical Instrument Digital Interface (MIDI) • Limited to synthesizers and music files • Can be much smaller in size than other formats
MP3	.mp3	• One of the most popular formats for music storage • Compresses files to approximately 1/10 the size of uncompressed files
MP4	.mp4	• Created on basis of the QuickTime format; used for audio and video • Is a quicker, faster, high-quality media • Can be used with QuickTime Player, Adobe Flash Player, or RealPlayer
RealAudio	.ra .ram	• Designed for streaming audio over the Internet • Sound quality not as good as other formats
WAV	.wav	• Standard audio format for Windows • Commonly used for storing uncompressed CD-quality sound files • Compression is available to reduce file size

The video format that you choose depends on the visitors you expect to visit your Web site. Are most of your Web site visitors users of Macs or PCs? What is the level of computer (e.g., amount of RAM or cache) and connection speed (e.g., broadband) for your average user? In this project, you insert a .wmv file.

Table 8–2 Common Video File Formats

Format	File Extension	Description
AVI	.avi	• Audio/Video Interleaved • Developed by Microsoft to use with Windows • Can contain both audio and video data • Requires Windows Media Player
Flash Video	.flv	• Developed by Adobe • Format of choice for embedded video on the Web • Used by Google and YouTube
MPEG	.mpg .mpeg .mp3	• Moving Pictures Group • Can be highly compressed resulting in small file size • Requires QuickTime Player, RealPlayer, or Windows Media Player, which are easily downloaded
MP4	.mp4	• Created on basis of QuickTime format; used for audio and video • Is a quicker, faster, high-quality media • Can be used with QuickTime Player, Adobe Flash Player, or RealPlayer
QuickTime	.mov	• Developed by Apple Computer for both Windows and Apple computers • File compression can result in smaller file size • Requires QuickTime Player or Adobe Flash Player, which are easily downloaded
RealVideo	.rm .rv	• Proprietary video format developed by RealNetworks • Requires RealPlayer
Shockwave Flash	.swf	• Small Web Format • Can contain audio, video, or animations • Requires Adobe Flash Player
Windows Media	.wmv	• Developed by Microsoft • Originally designed for Internet streaming applications • Requires Windows Media Player

Adding an Audio File to a Web Page

Ms. Amy Sirko's history class Web site consists of three files. The first Web page, brandenburg.html, is the home page, which contains an image map for Web site navigation together with two paragraphs of text. This Web page will not change. The next Web page, reagan.html, is the file into which you will insert an audio file, reagan-audio.mp3. The third page, kennedy.html, will contain a video clip. All Web pages in this Web site are linked to the external style sheet, styles8.css. The external style sheet file is also not changed. Please review the file, however, so that you are familiar with the styles used in the Web site. Pay special attention to the classes that are named in the external style sheet and review how those classes are used in the kennedy.html and reagan.html files.

BTW

Audio Clips
Many good Web design sites discuss the use of audio clips in Web development. Search for ideas of how you can most effectively utilize an audio clip.

BTW

Multimedia <object> Tag
The World Wide Web Consortium (W3C) has a wealth of information about the use of the <object> tag. For more information about attributes that can be used with this tag, visit the W3C Web site and search for <object> tag.

The Object Tag

The object element supports many different media types, including: pictures, sounds, videos, as well as other objects. The term **object** is used to describe the things that people want to place in HTML documents. Appendix A lists the attributes that can be used with the <object> tag.

To insert the audio clip, you will use the same classid (the Windows Media Player) that you will use for the video clip. The <object> statement used for the audio clip insertion is as follows:

```
<object classid="clsid:6BF52A52-394A-11D3-B153-00C04F79FAA6"
        height="45" width="250">
        <param name="URL" value="reagan-audio.mp3" />
</object>
```

The **classid** is an attribute that specifies which ActiveX control is being used. Table 8–3 shows the classids for the available ActiveX controls. For the insertion of an audio clip, you use the classid for Windows Media Player. It is imperative that you specify the classid correctly, or the multimedia content may not work correctly or at all. The classid is not case sensitive, so you can type the classid string as shown in Table 8–3 or use all lowercase letters. This information can also be found at each manufacturer's Web site.

Table 8–3 Class IDs for ActiveX Controls

ActiveX Control	Class ID
Flash Shockwave Player	D27CDB6E-AE6D-11cf-96B8-444553540000
Java Applet	8AD9C840-044E-11D1-B3E9-00805F499D93
QuickTime Player	02BF25D5-8C17-4B23-BC80-D3488ABDDC6B
RealAudio Player	CFCDAA03-8BE4-11cf-B84B-0020AFBBCCFA
Windows Media Player	6BF52A52-394A-11d3-B153-00C04F79FAA6

The object statement also includes the **height** and **width** attributes — that is, the height and width of the object in pixels. You include the height and width for the audio file to identify the view of the player control panel that you want to display. Table 8–4 shows the resulting control panel when you specify different widths. In all cases in Table 8–4, the height of the object is 45 pixels, which provides enough room to view the player control horizontally. These are not exact numbers, but suggestions for a width that displays the image in the right column. You can experiment with the width and height to see what might best fit your application.

Table 8–4 Control Panel Views for Windows Media Player

Width Setting	Resulting Control Display	Image
42 pixels	Displays the fast forward and play/pause buttons	
66 pixels	Displays the rewind, fast forward, play/pause, and stop buttons	
118 pixels	Adds the previous and next buttons	
250 pixels	Adds a volume control (full control panel)	

Figure 8–4 shows how the various width dimensions display the player control relative to the Web page. In the styles8.css external style sheet, the left margin of the class="audio" is set to 375 pixels. That means the object displays 375 pixels from the left margin, regardless of what control width is set. Figures 8–4a through 8–4d illustrate how the controls shown in Table 8–4 display, with each control starting 375 pixels from the left. Certainly, you would want to adjust the left margin in the external style sheet if you decided to use various widths of the control. As for most Web development decisions, the application purpose would dictate why you would select various widths. For instance, if you wanted to allow Web site visitors to only play and stop the audio clip and not allow them to vary the volume, you would set width to 42 pixels.

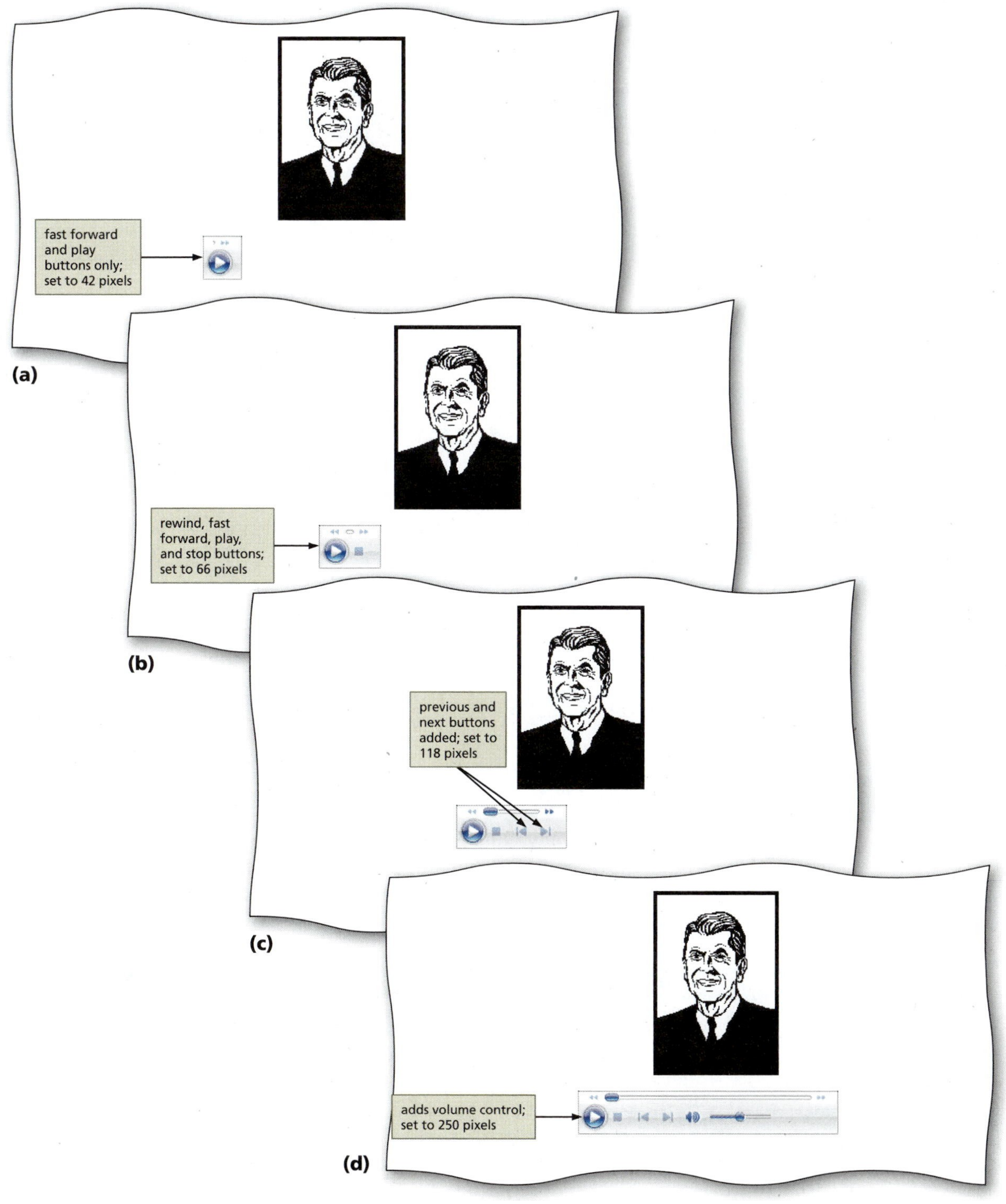

Figure 8–4

BTW

Parameters
Many other object parameters are available that are not discussed in this chapter. The various ActiveX controls have different parameters that can be used with that control. Review online what other parameters might be effective for you to use in your Web development.

Object Tag Parameters

Each type of player has various <object> tag parameters that can be used. A **parameter** identifies the behavior and appearance of the object to which you assign the parameters. Table 8–5 lists the most commonly used parameters for Windows Media Player.

Table 8–5 Commonly Used Parameters for Windows Media Player

Parameter	Default	Description
autostart	true	Specifies whether the current media item begins playing automatically
balance	0	Specifies the current stereo balance; values range from –100 to 100
baseURL	[no default]	Specifies the base URL used for relative path resolution with URL script commands that are embedded in media items
enabled	false	Specifies whether the Windows Media Player control is enabled
fullscreen	false	Specifies whether video content is played back in full-screen mode
mute	false	Specifies if audio is muted
playcount	1	Specifies the number of times a media item will play; minimum value of one
rate	1.0	Specifies the playback rate; 0.5 equates to half the normal playback speed, 2 equates to twice
showaudiocontrols	true	Sets if the audio controls should show
showcontrols	true	Sets if the player controls should show
showdisplay	false	Sets if the display should show
showstatusbar	false	Sets if status bar should show
stretchtofit	false	Specifies whether video displayed by the control automatically sizes to fit the video window, when the video window is larger than the dimensions of the video image
uimode	full	Specifies which controls are shown in the user interface; possible values: invisible, none, mini, full
URL		Specifies the name of the media item to play; you can specify a local filename or a URL
volume	[last setting; 0–100]	Zero specifies no volume and 100 specifies full volume
windowlessvideo	false	Specifies or retrieves a value indicating whether the Windows Media Player control renders video in windowless mode; when windowlessvideo is set to true, the player control renders video directly in the client area, so you can apply special effects or layer the video with text

Although you do not add any QuickTime (QT) video clips to any Web pages in this chapter, Table 8–6 lists the most commonly used parameters for another popular player, Apple QuickTime. To see complete parameters for any player, review them online at the manufacturers' Web sites.

Table 8–6 Commonly Used Parameters for Apple QuickTime

Parameter	Default	Description
autoplay	true	Specifies whether the current media item begins playing automatically
bgcolor	[no default]	Sets the background color for the object
controller	true	Specifies if the player controls should show
endtime	[no default]	Specifies the time in the clip at which the video ends

Table 8–6 Commonly Used Parameters for Apple QuickTime (continued)

Parameter	Default	Description
loop	true	Plays the clip in a continuous loop
mute	false	Specifies if audio is muted
src	[no default]	Specifies the source of the clip
starttime	[no default]	Specifies the time in the clip at which the video begins
volume	[last setting]	Sets the initial audio volume

You add one parameter in the <object></object> container for the audio clip, as shown in the code below.

```
<object classid="clsid:6BF52A52-394A-11D3-B153-00C04F79FAA6"
        height="45" width="250">
        <param name="URL" value="reagan-audio.mp3" />
</object>
```

The URL parameter, as shown in Table 8–5, identifies what audio clip is to be played. In this case, you are inserting an MPEG (.mp3) file. This is a short audio clip of President Reagan speaking his famous line at the Brandenburg Gate. As soon as you open the Web page with this <object> statement, the reagan-audio.mp3 audio clip starts immediately (note the autostart default in Table 8–5). This Web page includes a picture of President Reagan, so it could be appropriate to start the audio immediately. As stated before, the purpose of the Web site dictates what parameters you use. Think about yourself as a Web site visitor. How do you feel when a loud audio clip plays as soon as you enter a Web site? What do you think if you have no option to pause or stop the clip? Always consider your own browsing habits, likes, and dislikes when you design Web sites. If you did not want to start the .mp3 file automatically, you would add a <param name="autostart" value="false" /> statement within the <object></object> container. With this audio clip insertion, you do provide the player control panel that gives the user the opportunity to pause or stop the audio clip.

Plan Ahead

Inserting an audio file.

You would insert an audio file into a Web page if you want your Web site visitors to be able to hear content or background music. In the case of this Web site, you will insert an audio clip of President Reagan's famous line, "Mr. Gorbachev, tear down this wall!"

- **Determine the area on the Web page into which you want to insert the audio clip.** This was a simple task for the Web site under development. There is a reagan.html Web page that discusses the speech made by that president. A picture of President Reagan is already inserted into the Web page. Because this is an audio clip, and only the player control bar will display, you insert the audio clip directly under the picture of the president.
- **Decide which parameters (if any) that you should use.** For this audio clip, you just want to play it with the default settings, so you will not set any parameters. The audio clip will start automatically when the Web page is opened. The Web site visitors will have the ability to pause, stop, or replay the audio clip using the default player control panel provided.

To Start Notepad++ and Open an HTML File

1. Start Notepad++ and, if necessary, maximize the window.
2. With the USB drive plugged into your computer, navigate to the Chapter08\ChapterFiles folder.
3. Double-click reagan.html in the list of files to open the file shown in Figure 8–5.

Q&A What is the purpose for the "audio" class on line 28?

This is a class identified in the external style sheet, styles8.css, to which you link on line 10. If you have not already done so, you should review that external style sheet. All classes (on lines 21, 25, and 28) are created in that external style sheet.

Q&A Why is the map container (lines 32 through 36) in this file?

Notice that line 16 contains an image file that includes the usemap="#menubar" statement. Line 32 identifies that map as the menubar, which is an image map used for navigation.

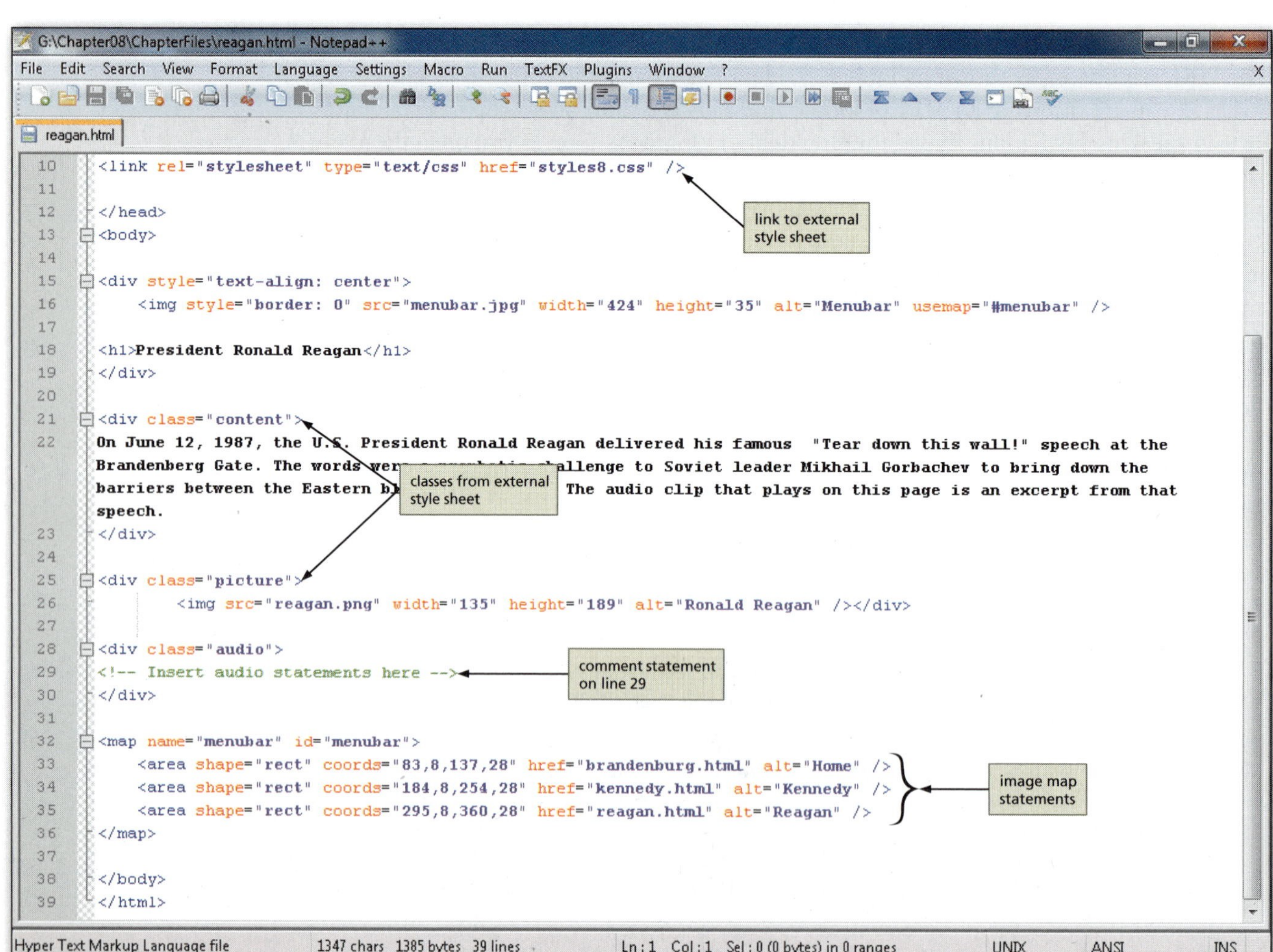

Figure 8–5

To Add an Audio Clip to a Web Page

The reagan.html Web page file is complete except for the <object> statement which will be added next. Table 8–7 shows the HTML code for this statement.

Table 8–7 HTML Code to Add Audio Clip Object Statement

Line	HTML Code
29	`<object classid="clsid:6BF52A52-394A-11D3-B153-00C04F79FAA6" height="45" width="250">`
30	
31	`   <param name="URL" value="reagan-audio.mp3" />`
32	
33	`</object>`

The following step shows how to add an audio clip to the President Reagan Web page.

1

- Highlight the words <!-- Insert audio statements here --> on line 29.
- Enter the HTML code in Table 8–7, indenting as shown.
- Click File on the menu bar and then click Save to save the reagan.html file (Figure 8–6).

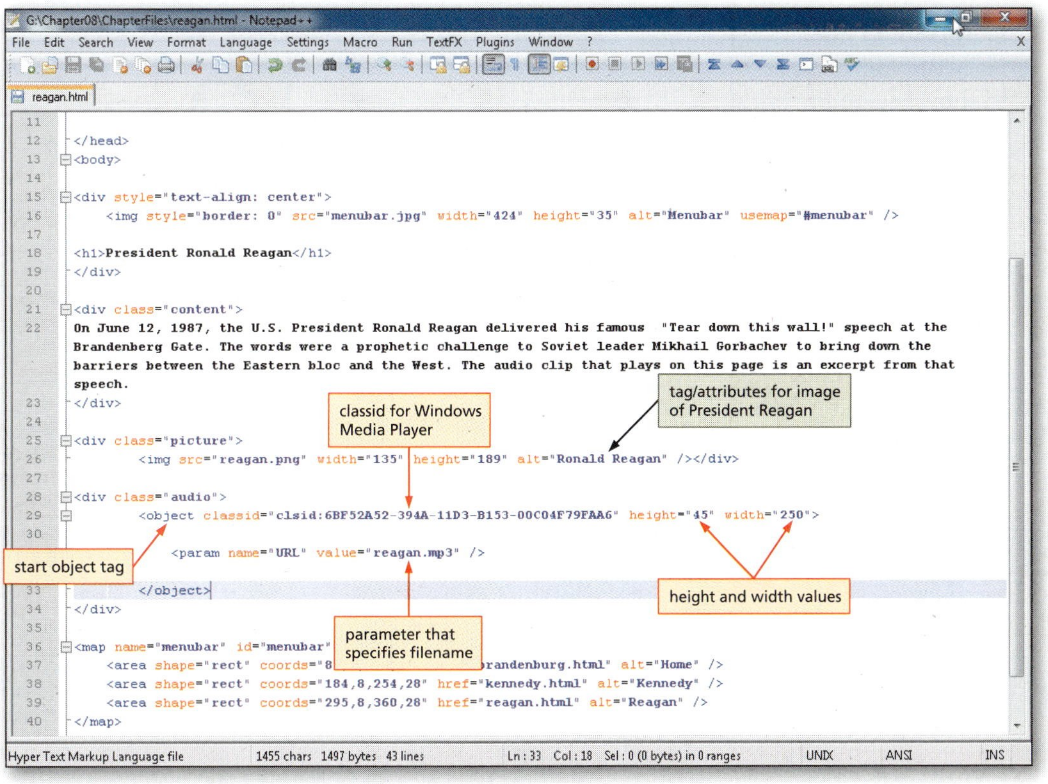

Q&A

How will I know what classid to use for various ActiveX controls?

Table 8–3 on page HTML 370 lists the classids for the most commonly used ActiveX controls. If there are other controls that you use, you can find their classids online on the manufacturer's Web site or by doing a Web search for that information.

Figure 8–6

Experiment

- Change the width and height attribute values and save the file with each change. Open the Web page in the browser to see how the changes affect the display of the control panel.

To Validate and View a Web Page Using ActiveX Controls

As always, you should validate and then view your pages. When you try to link to the Reagan Web page, it is likely that your browser will block the page's ActiveX content and display a security notification. Internet Explorer sets security to high by default. This prohibits ActiveX controls from running without your intervention. The following steps illustrate how to validate the Web page, and then respond to the security notification in Internet Explorer to view the Web page.

- Validate the reagan.html Web page using the W3C validation service.
- With the USB drive plugged in to your computer, navigate to the Chapter08\ChapterFiles folder and open the brandenburg.html file in the Web browser to show the home page of this Web site. Click the Reagan link to navigate to the newly saved file.
- Because of Internet Explorer's high level of security, you get a notification in the gold bar at the top of the browser, as shown in Figure 8–7.

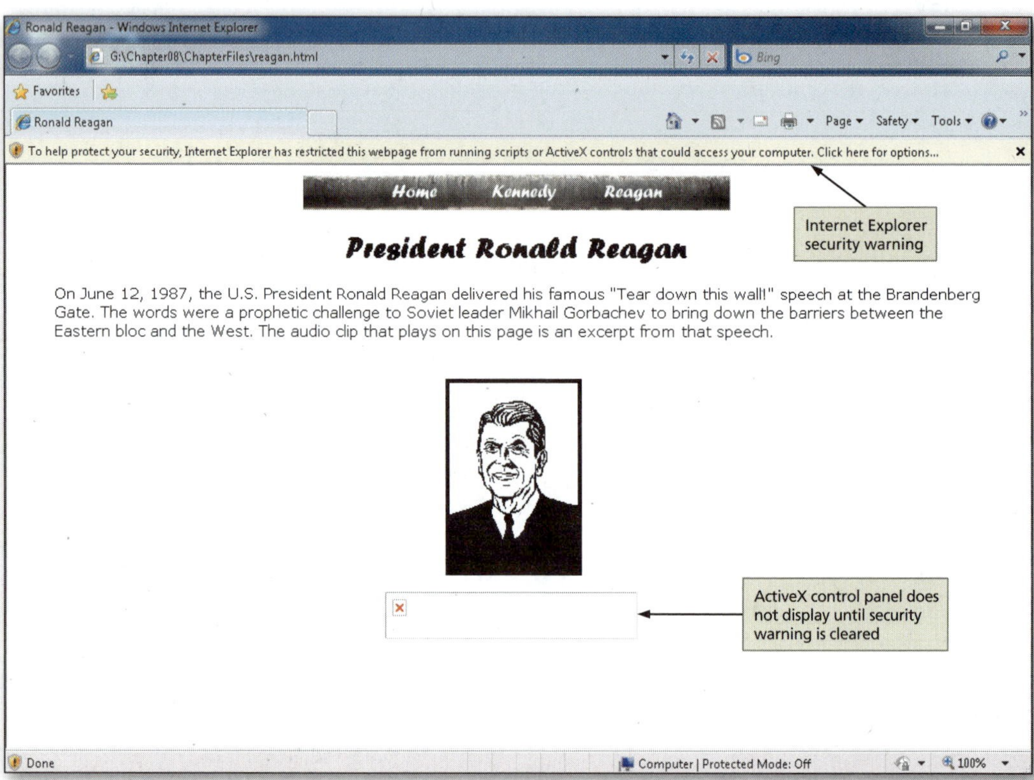

Figure 8–7

Q&A Will the ActiveX controls and security notification appear if I use a browser other than Internet Explorer?

No. ActiveX controls only display in the Internet Explorer Web browser. If you display this page in another browser, the multimedia control panel will not appear and the audio file will not play.

2

- Click anywhere in the gold bar at the top of the browser window to view the options (Figure 8–8).

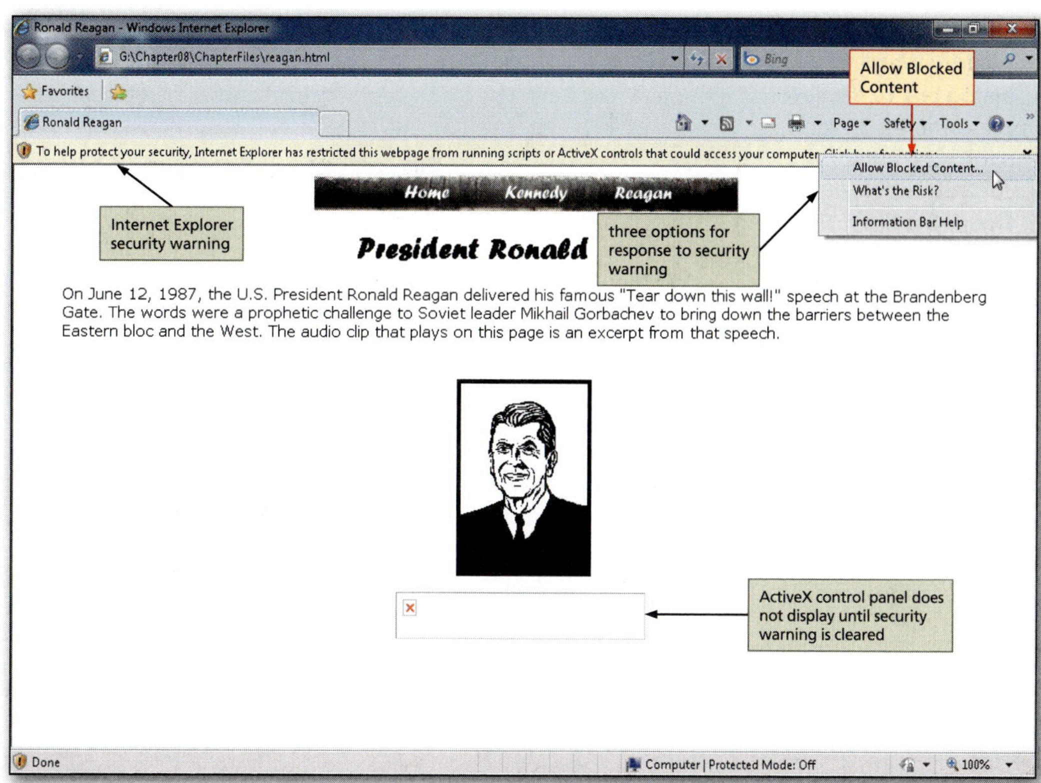

Figure 8–8

3

- Click the Allow Blocked Content option to display the dialog box shown in Figure 8–9.

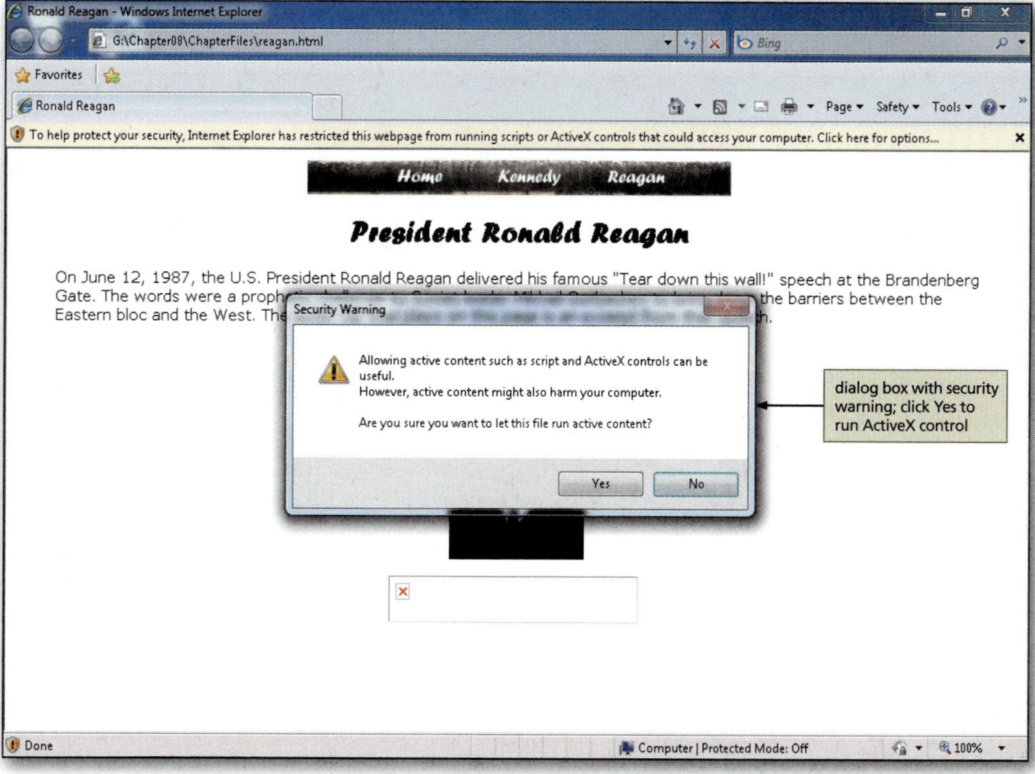

Figure 8–9

- Click Yes in the Security Warning dialog box to display the completed Web page with audio controls shown in Figure 8–10.

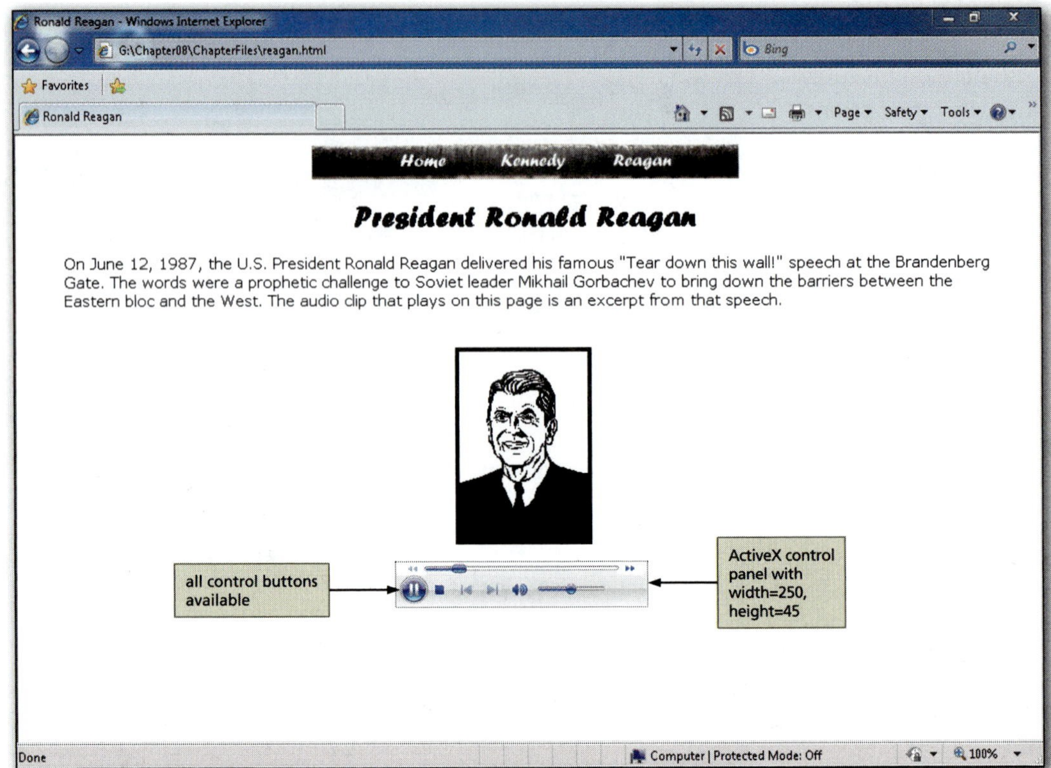

Figure 8–10

Q&A Do I have to respond to the security questions for each page in a Web site?

No, you are asked to respond just once within a given Web site. For example, if you were to open the kennedy.html Web page next (once the video clip is inserted), you would not be asked those security questions.

Q&A Can I change the security level in IE?

Yes, but you need to consider what that means. If you disable the high security in IE, then you are allowing all ActiveX controls to run automatically. It might be best to leave the security as it is and respond to the prompts as shown here.

To Print a Web Page and an HTML File

1. Print the Reagan Web page from the browser.
2. Click the Notepad++ button on the taskbar.
3. Print the Reagan.html file from Notepad++.

Plan Ahead

Creating a video clip.
Video clips can add valuable content to a Web page. There are many uses for video clips. Companies use clips for training or to convey messages from the CEO. Instructors use videos to help students better understand complex topics in online classes. Many people use video clips just for fun on their personal Web sites or on YouTube.

- **Utilize video clips that enhance the content of the Web page.** In the chapter project, a video clip of a live speech adds value to the Web page.
- **Determine whether to utilize the autostart parameter.** Sometimes you want to force the user to read some material on the Web page first and then view the corresponding video clip. In this case, you want to turn autostart off and force the user to click play in order to watch the video.
- **Use uimode and screen stretching parameters as needed.** There are many ways to show a video. Sometimes you want the video to be a small part of a Web page; at other times, you want it to be the entire message or full screen. Sometimes you want a control panel to display; at other times you need no control panel. You need to determine what values to use with the various parameters that add to the viewing experience.

Adding a Video Clip to a Web Page

The next step is to add a video file, kennedy-video.wmv, to the kennedy.html file. You use the <object></object> container for this, just as you did for the audio clip. You continue to use the Windows Media Player (WMP) ActiveX control, so the classid is the same. You add different parameters for this video insertion.

The following section of HTML code shows the statements that you add for this video clip addition.

```
<object classid="clsid:6BF52A52-394A-11D3-B153-00C04F79FAA6">
    <param name="URL" value="kennedy-video.wmv" />
    <param name="autostart" value="false" />
    <param name="uimode" value="full" />
    <param name="stretchtofit" value="true" />
</object>
```

Note that the classid is specific to the Windows Media Player ActiveX control (see Table 8–3 on page HTML 370). The parameters can be found in Table 8–5 on page HTML 372. You do not enter the width and height attributes this time so that you can see what this movie clip looks like at its default size. You can, however, add width and height attributes in the <object> tag. This is something that you can experiment with. Because you insert the stretchtofit parameter within the <object></object> container, the movie clip will stretch regardless of the sizes that you specify in the width and height attributes. Remember that you have a link to an external style sheet, styles8.css, so if you do change the width and height, you will probably need to change the left margin dimension as well.

The four parameters used for the video clip insertion are: URL, autostart, uimode, and stretchtofit. The URL parameter is used in the same way for a video clip as it was for an audio clip. It tells the name of the object that you want to insert. The default for the autostart parameter is "true", which means that a clip will automatically start unless you set autostart to "false" by entering <param name="autostart" value="false" /> as the command. With autostart turned off, your Web site visitor has to click the play button on the ActiveX control panel to start the video clip. Just as with other decisions that are made

BTW

Video Clips
Video clips can have a large file size depending on the length of the clip together with the quality of the clip. Search for information about rules-of-thumb for file sizes when video clips are incorporated into a Web site.

during the analysis phase of the Web development life cycle, you have to decide what is best for your application. Do you want the audio or video clip to start as soon as the Web page is opened, or is it best to force your user to start them?

The next parameter statement <param name="uimode" value="full" /> specifies which controls are shown. For this project, the uimode is set to full. Figure 8–11a shows the media player window when the uimode is set to full. Figure 8–11b shows the Web page when uimode is set to none. Note that this is an unusable situation. You have set the uimode to none together with no autostart. Your Web site visitor therefore has no access to the controls to start the video. The video is also not going to autostart because of the autostart="false" statement. Figure 8–11c shows the Web page with uimode set to mini. Compare the Web page in Figure 8–11c to Figure 8–11a. Although users have access to some controls, they do not have access to all of the controls. Finally, Figure 8–11d is the Web page displayed when uimode is set to invisible. Again, because you have the autostart set to false, you display nothing and you also see and hear nothing. For video clips, this is unusable. For audio clips, this might be effective. If you wanted to hear background sounds but not see the controls, you could set an invisible uimode along with autostart set to true (the default).

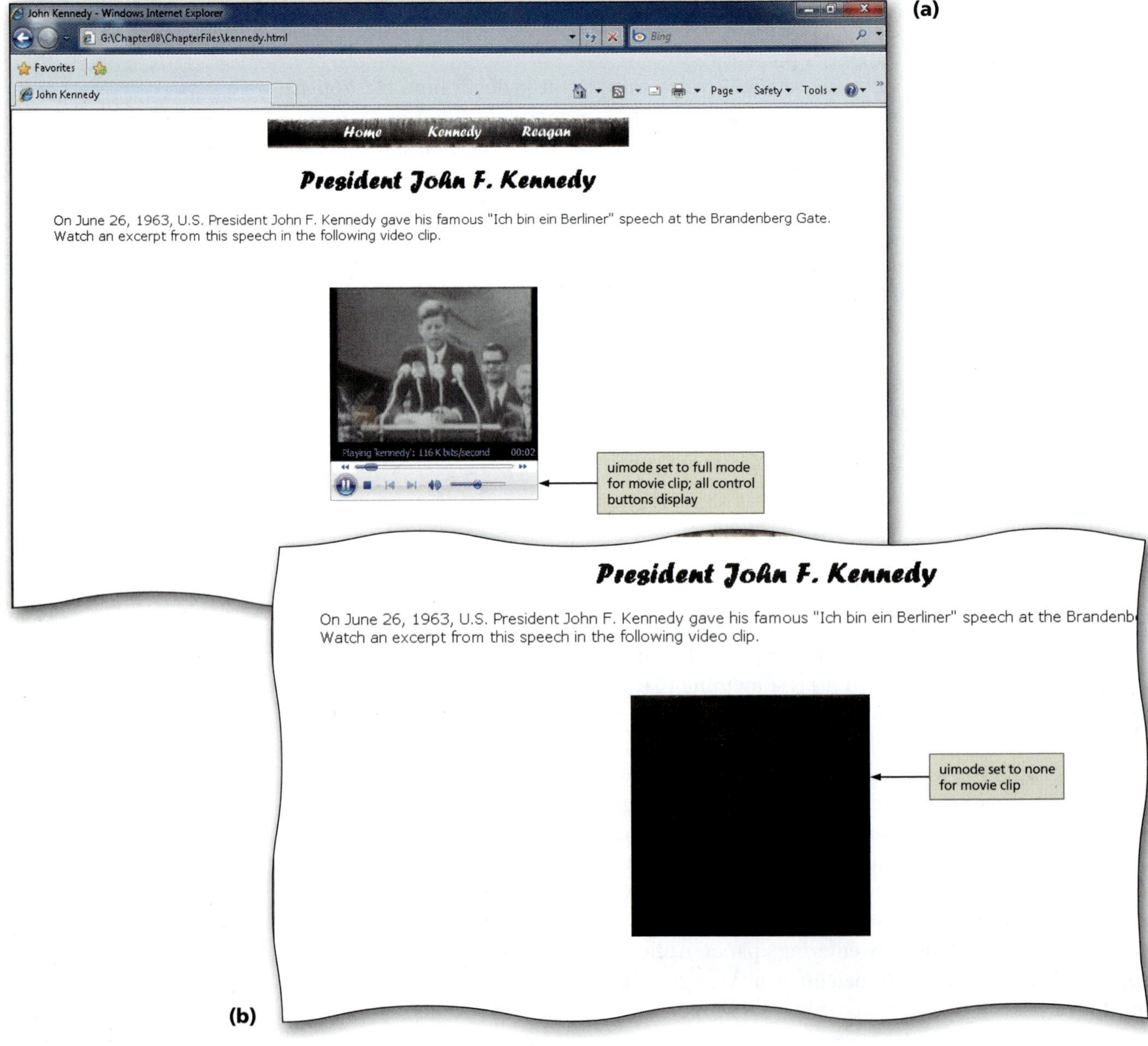

Figure 8–11

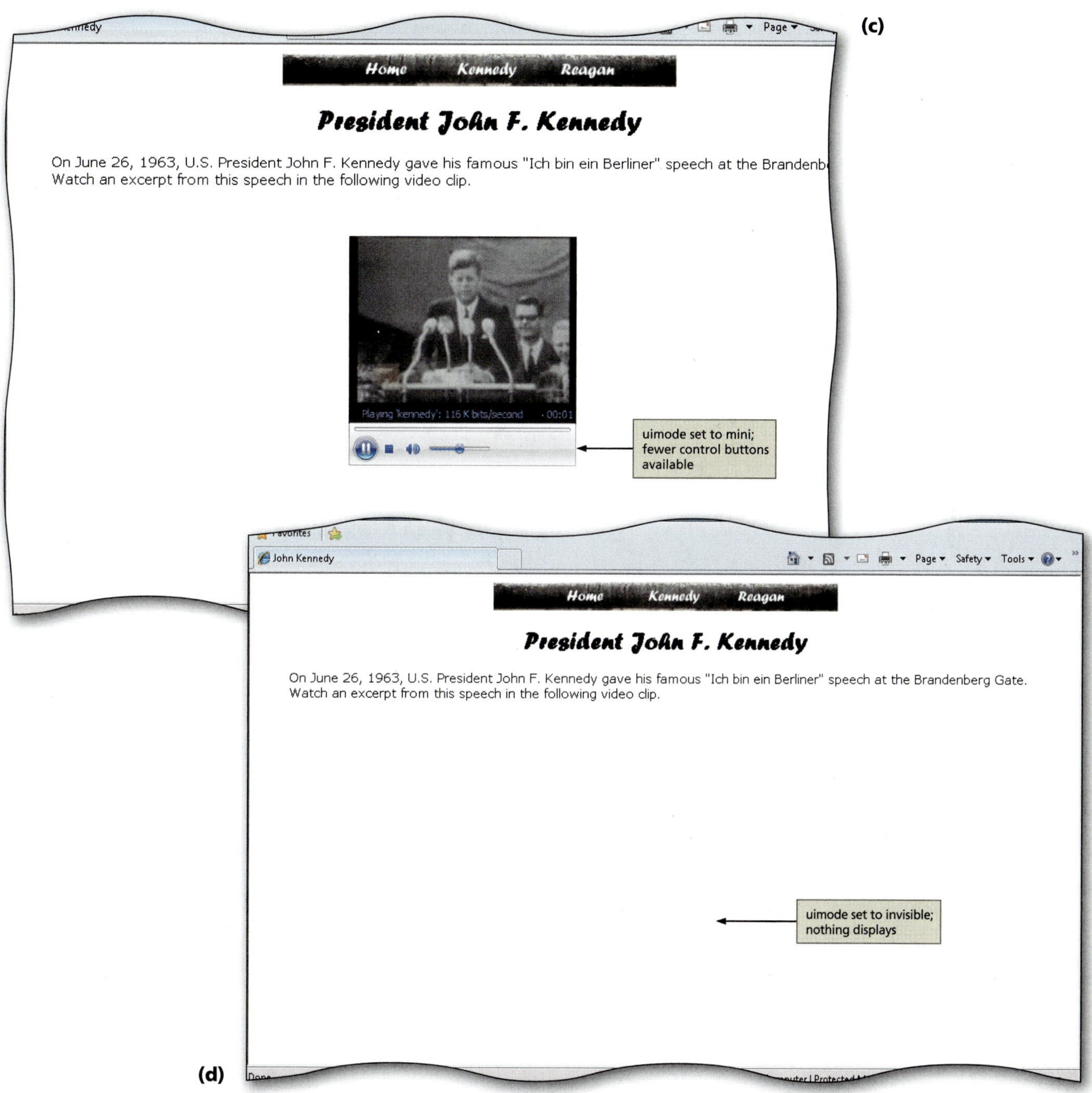

Figure 8–11 (continued)

The last parameter used in this container is stretchtofit. The stretchtofit parameter sizes the video to fit the video window, when the video window is larger than the dimensions of the video image. In the case of this video, it is smaller than the video window in Windows Media Player. The default for this option is false, so the effect on the Web page looks like the video clip shown in Figure 8–12a on the next page. Figure 8–12b shows the Web page with stretchtofit set to true.

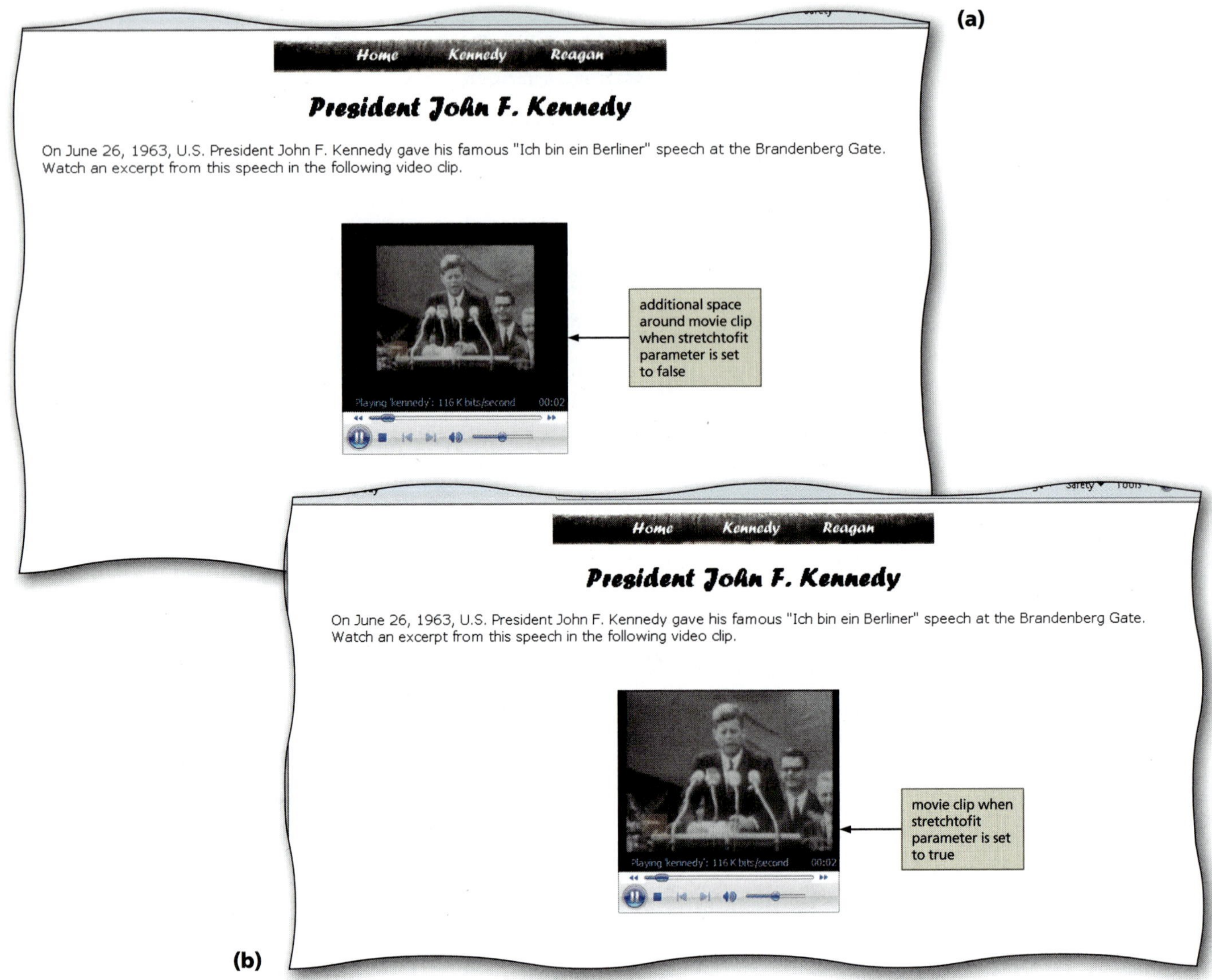

Figure 8–12

To Add a Video Clip to a Web Page

To add the video file, kennedy-video.wmv, to the kennedy.html file, you use the <object></object> container, just as you did for the audio clip, but with different parameters. Table 8–8 shows the code to add the video clip.

Table 8–8 HTML Code to Add Video Clip

```
<object classid="clsid:6BF52A52-394A-11D3-B153-00C04F79FAA6">
        <param name="URL" value="kennedy-video.wmv" />
        <param name="autostart" value="false" />
        <param name="uimode" value="full" />
        <param name="stretchtofit" value="true" />
</object>
```

1

- If necessary, click the Notepad++ button on the taskbar.
- With the USB drive plugged in to your computer, open the kennedy.html file from the Chapter08\ChapterFiles folder (Figure 8–13).

```
5  <html xmlns="http://www.w3.org/1999/xhtml" xml:lang="en" lang="en">
6  <head>
7  <meta http-equiv="Content-Type" content="text/html;charset=utf-8" />
8  <title>John Kennedy</title>
9
10 <link rel="stylesheet" type="text/css" href="styles8.css" />
11
12 </head>
13 <body>
14
15 <div style="text-align: center">
16     <img style="border: 0" src="menubar.jpg" width="424" height="35" alt="Menubar" usemap="#menubar" />
17
18     <h1>President John F. Kennedy</h1>
19 </div>
20
21 <div class="content">
22 On June 26, 1963, U.S. President John F. Kennedy gave his famous "Ich bin ein Berliner" speech at the Brandenberg
   Gate. Watch an excerpt from this speech in the following video clip.
23 </div>
24
25 <div class="movie">
26 <!-- Insert video statements here -->
27 </div>
28
29 <map name="menubar" id="menubar">
30     <area shape="rect" coords="83,8,137,28" href="brandenburg.html" alt="Home" />
31     <area shape="rect" coords="184,8,254,28" href="kennedy.html" alt="Kennedy" />
32     <area shape="rect" coords="295,8,360,28" href="reagan.html" alt="Reagan" />
33 </map>
34
35 </body>
36 </html>
```

HTML code in kennedy.html file at start-up

comment on line 26 where object tag is inserted

Figure 8–13

2

- Highlight the words <!—Insert the video statements here --> on line 26.
- Enter the HTML code shown in Table 8–8 (Figure 8–14).
- Save the file.

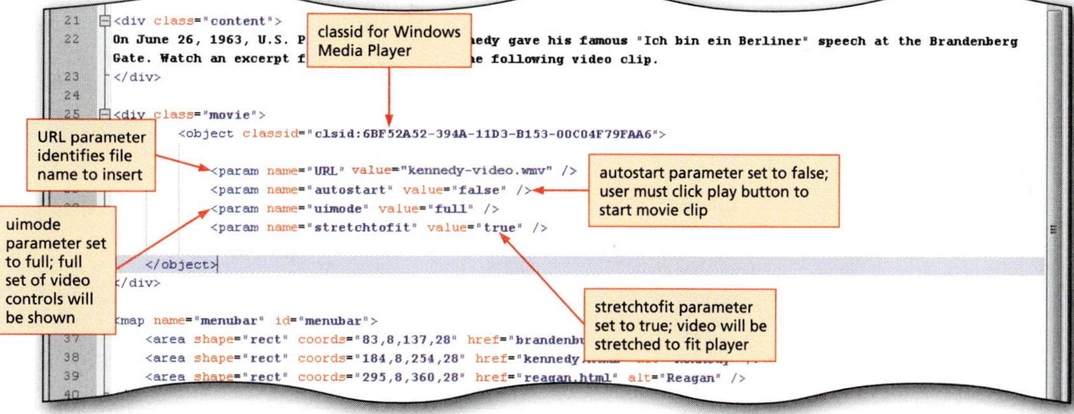

Figure 8–14

Q&A What determines whether or not you should automatically start the video clip when the Web page is opened?

Your specific Web page purpose determines this option. If you want your Web site visitors to read some text beforehand, as is the case here, you should set autostart to false, forcing visitors to click the play button when they want to view the video.

Q&A I like leaving a lot of space around the video clip. Do I have to stretch the video to fit the screen?

No. The default is to not stretch the video; that is why you had to turn that off with the stretchtofit="true" parameter. This is something with which you should experiment.

Experiment

- Add the width and height attributes to the <object> statement. Change the values of the width and height and save the file with each change. Open the Web page in the browser to see how the changes affect the display of the video. Remove the width and height attributes.

To Validate and View a Web Page

After you have added the video clip to the kennedy.html Web page file, you need to validate the file and view the Web page to review the style changes.

1. Validate the Web page using the W3C validation service.
2. Return to the Web site home page and click the navigation link for the kennedy.html file in the browser to view the changes (Figure 8–15).

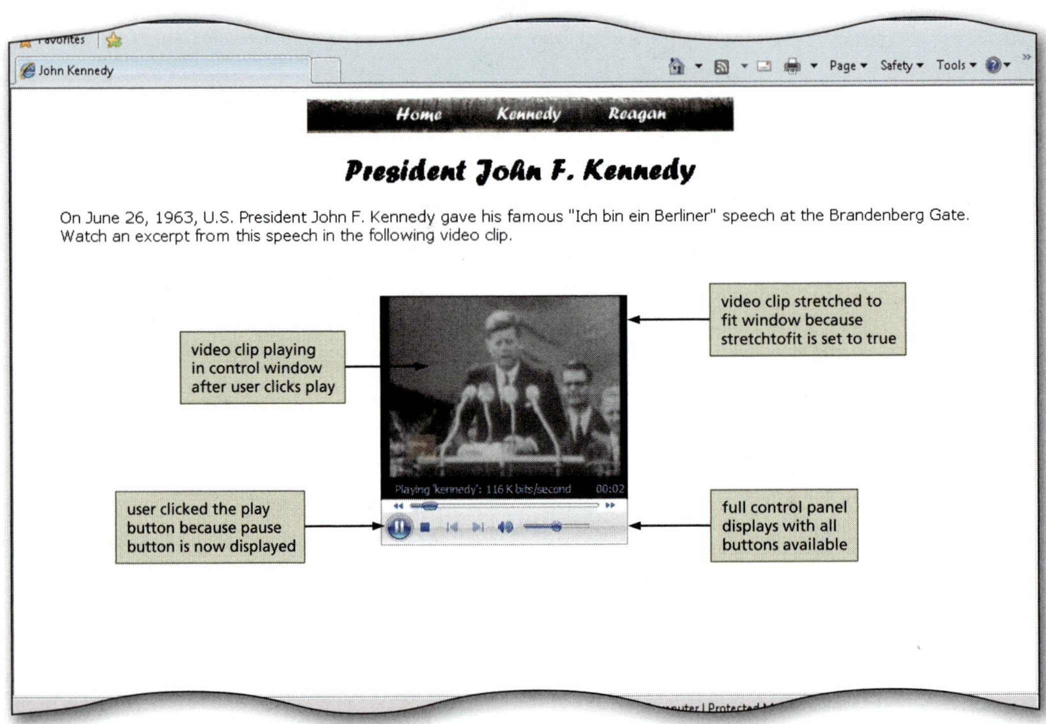

Figure 8–15

> **BTW**
> **Quick Reference**
> For a list of HTML tags and attributes, see the HTML Quick Reference (Appendix A) at the back of this book, or visit the HTML Quick Reference Web page (scsite.com/HTML6e/qr).

To Print a Web Page and HTML File

1. Print the Kennedy Web page from the browser.
2. Print the Notepad++ kennedy.html file.

Chapter Summary

In this chapter, you have learned how to embed audio and video files in your Web pages. The items listed below include all the new HTML skills you have learned in this chapter.

1. Add an Audio Clip to a Web Page (HTML 375)
2. Validate and View a Web Page Using ActiveX Controls (HTML 376)
3. Add a Video Clip to a Web Page (HTML 382)

Learn It Online

Test your knowledge of chapter content and key terms.

Instructions: To complete the Learn It Online exercises, start your browser, click the Address bar, and then enter the Web address `scsite.com/html6e/learn`. When the HTML Learn It Online page is displayed, click the link for the exercise you want to complete and read the instructions.

Chapter Reinforcement TF, MC, and SA

A series of true/false, multiple choice, and short answer questions that test your knowledge of the chapter content.

Flash Cards

An interactive learning environment where you identify chapter key terms associated with displayed definitions.

Practice Test

A series of multiple choice questions that test your knowledge of chapter content and key terms.

Who Wants To Be a Computer Genius?

An interactive game that challenges your knowledge of chapter content in the style of a television quiz show.

Wheel of Terms

An interactive game that challenges your knowledge of chapter key terms in the style of the television show *Wheel of Fortune*.

Crossword Puzzle Challenge

A crossword puzzle that challenges your knowledge of key terms presented in the chapter.

Apply Your Knowledge

Reinforce the skills and apply the concepts you learned in this chapter.

Adding a Background Sound

Instructions: Start Notepad++ and a browser. Using your browser, open the apply8-1.html file from the Chapter08\Apply folder of the Data Files for Students. See the inside back cover of this book for instructions on downloading the Data Files for Students, or contact your instructor for information about accessing the required files. Figure 8–16 shows the Apply Your Knowledge Web page as it should appear in the browser after the necessary code is added.

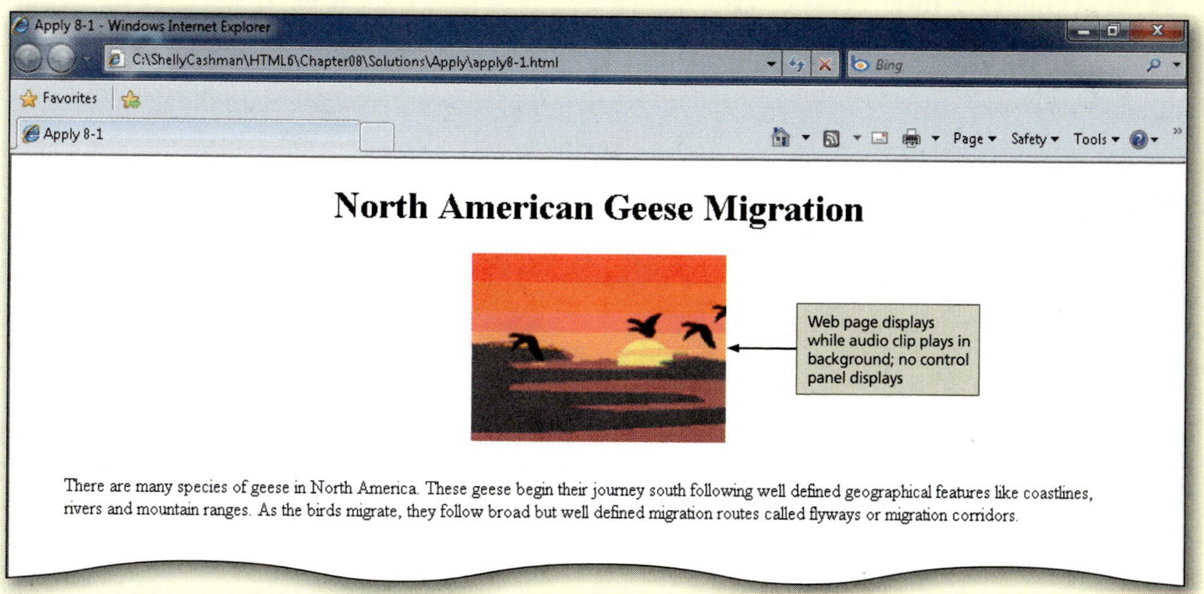

Figure 8–16

Continued >

Apply Your Knowledge *continued*

Perform the following tasks:

1. With the apply8-1.html file open in Notepad++, add the 04geeseflyhonk.mp3 audio clip with the following options:
   a. Insert the audio clip in such a way that no control panel displays. (*Hint:* Refer to Table 8–4 on page HTML 370.)
   b. Repeat the audio clip three times. (*Hint:* Refer to Table 8–5 on page HTML 372.)
2. Save the file as apply8-1solution.html. Validate the code and print the file.
3. Submit the solution in the format specified by your instructor.

Extend Your Knowledge

Extend the skills you learned in this chapter and experiment with new skills.

Combining Audio and Video Files

Instructions: Start Notepad++. Open the file extend8-1.html from the Chapter08\Extend folder of the Data Files for Students. See the inside back cover of this book for instructions on downloading the Data Files for Students, or contact your instructor for information about accessing the required files. Save the file as extend8-1solution.html. This file contains the Web page shown in Figure 8–17.

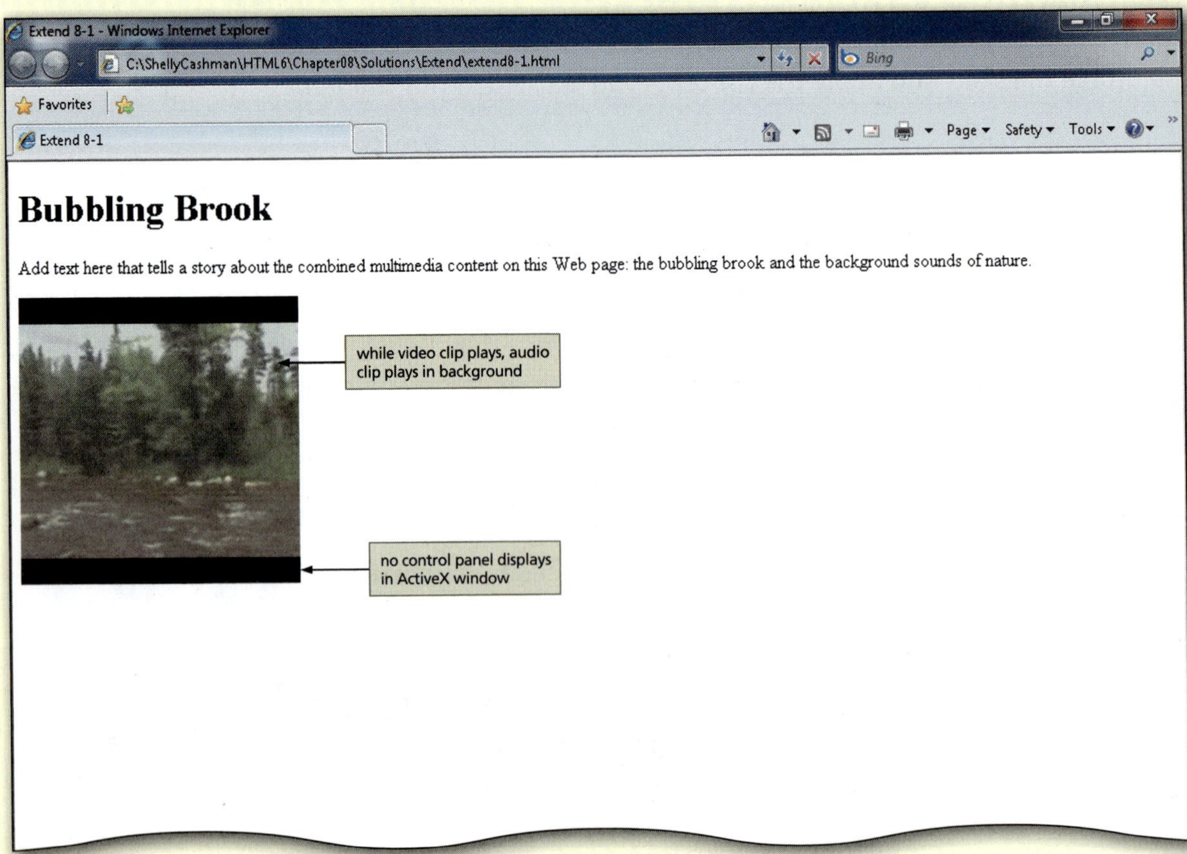

Figure 8–17

Perform the following tasks:

1. With the extend8-1solution.html file open in Notepad++, add the bkgrndnature.mp3 audio clip with the following options:
   a. Insert the audio clip in such a way that no control panel displays.
   b. Do not display the audio clip.
2. Add the video clip brook.wmv with the following options:
   a. Stretch the video to fit the window.
   b. Do not display the control panel.
3. Save the file; validate the code; print the file.
4. Submit the solution in the format specified by your instructor.

Make It Right

Analyze a document, and correct all errors and/or improve the design.

Correcting the Dog Tricks Web Page

Instructions: Start Notepad++. Open the file makeitright8-1.html from the Chapter08\MakeItRight folder of the Data Files for Students and save it as makeitright8-1solution.html. See the inside back cover of this book for instructions on downloading the Data Files for Students, or contact your instructor for information about accessing the required files. The Web page is a modified version of what you see in Figure 8–18, but it contains some errors. The dogtricks.wmv video should not autostart and should display in the default size with the control panel. Make the necessary corrections to the Web page to make it look like the figure.

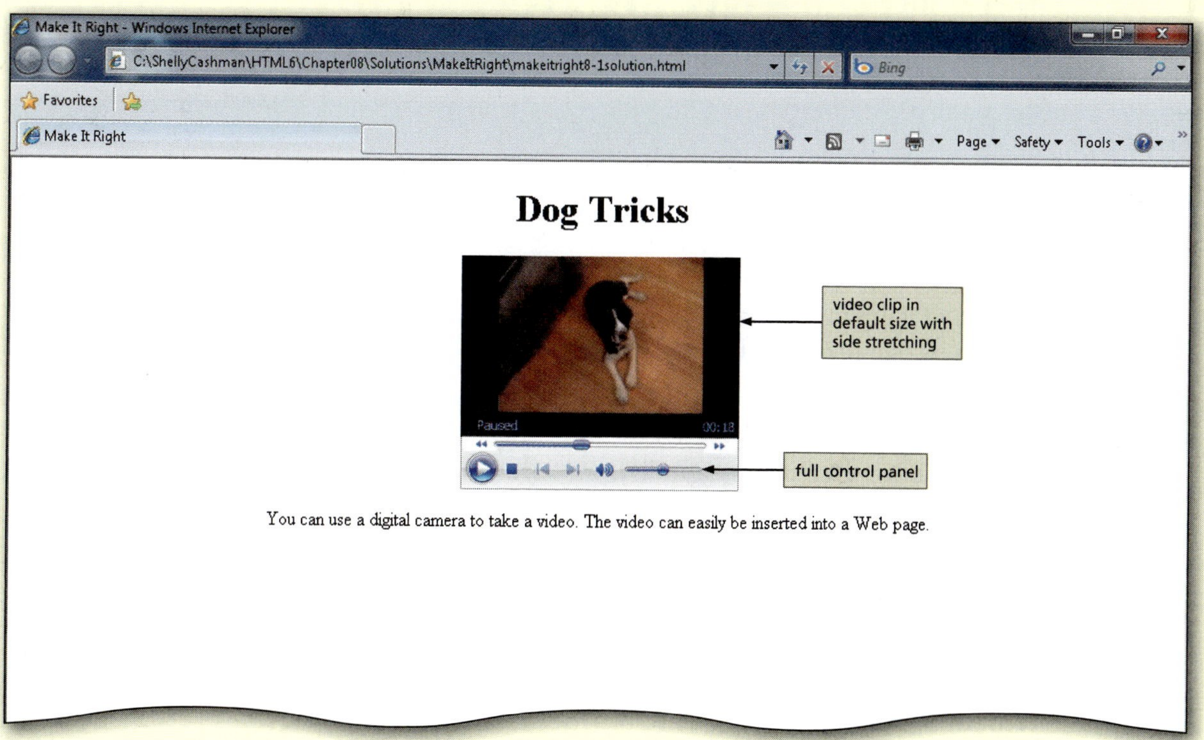

Figure 8–18

In the Lab

Lab 1: Creating Beautiful Music

Problem: Your piano teacher would like to see an example of how an audio clip of piano playing would look on a Web page. She wants to be able to pause, stop, and replay the audio clip. She also wants to see visual images of the sound waves as the clip is playing, as shown in Figure 8–19.

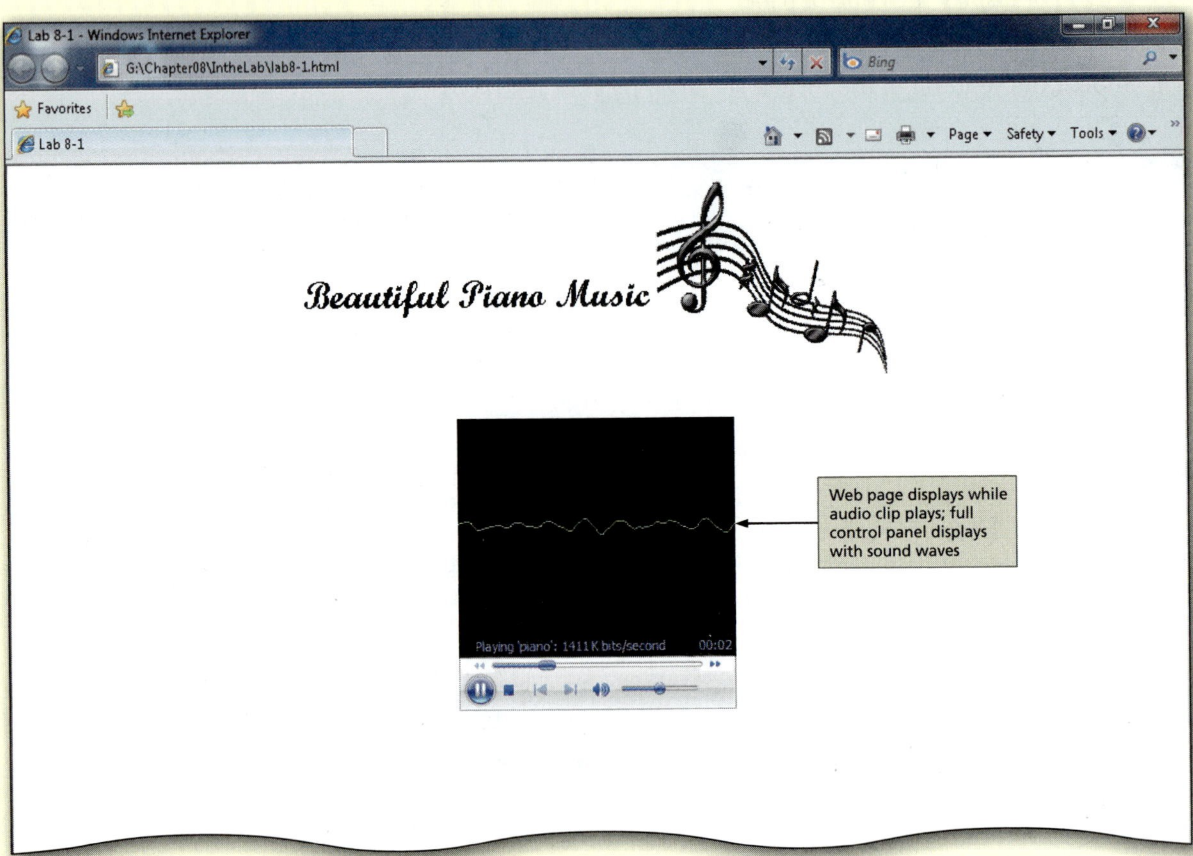

Figure 8–19

Instructions: Perform the following steps.

1. Using Notepad++, open the HTML file lab8-1.html in the Chapter08\IntheLab folder of the Data Files for Students.
2. Add the audio clip, piano.wav, to the Web page.
3. Do not allow this video to start automatically.
4. Add the parameter needed to display this audio clip so that you can see the sound waves as the music plays, as shown in Figure 8–19. (*Hint:* Review the uimode parameter.)
5. Add the parameter needed to display the control panel for the ActiveX control.
6. Save the HTML file in the Chapter08\IntheLab folder as lab8-1solution.html. Validate the file and then print it.
7. Test the Web page in Internet Explorer.
8. Submit the solution in the format specified by your instructor.

In the Lab

Lab 2: Video on a Full Screen

Problem: Your biology class is learning about bird migration. You have read about how some researchers are attempting to reintroduce whooping cranes in the U.S. and help whooping cranes raised in captivity participate in migration. You have found a video clip that shows these efforts in progress. You decide to create a Web page that will show this video. You want the video to display on the full screen of the monitor, as shown in Figure 8–20.

Figure 8–20

Instructions: Perform the following steps.

1. Using Notepad++, open the HTML file lab8-2.html in the Chapter08\IntheLab folder of the Data Files for Students.
2. Add the video clip whooper.wmv to the Web page.
3. Do not allow this video to start automatically.
4. Add the parameters needed to display this video on a full screen with the full control panel, as shown in Figure 8–20.
5. Save the HTML file in the Chapter08\IntheLab folder as lab8-2solution.html. Validate the file and then print it.
6. Test the Web page in Internet Explorer.
7. Submit the solution in the format specified by your instructor.

In the Lab

Lab 3: Adding Audio and Video Clips That Play Simultaneously

Problem: You want to create a Web page for your magic show that uses audio and video that come from two different sources, as shown in Figure 8–21. With the Kennedy video clip, the audio and video are together in one file. Using two media files (magicshow.wmv and magicmusic.mp3) gives the same effect (audio + video) with two separate files. As an example, you might use this technique when you shoot a video yourself but want to combine it with appropriate audio that you either create or find. This lab shows you how to combine separate audio and video files to play at the same time. The file lab8-3.html is a file that is complete other than the statements needed to insert the two multimedia objects. The file lab8-3.html is included in the Chapter08\IntheLab folder of the Data Files for Students.

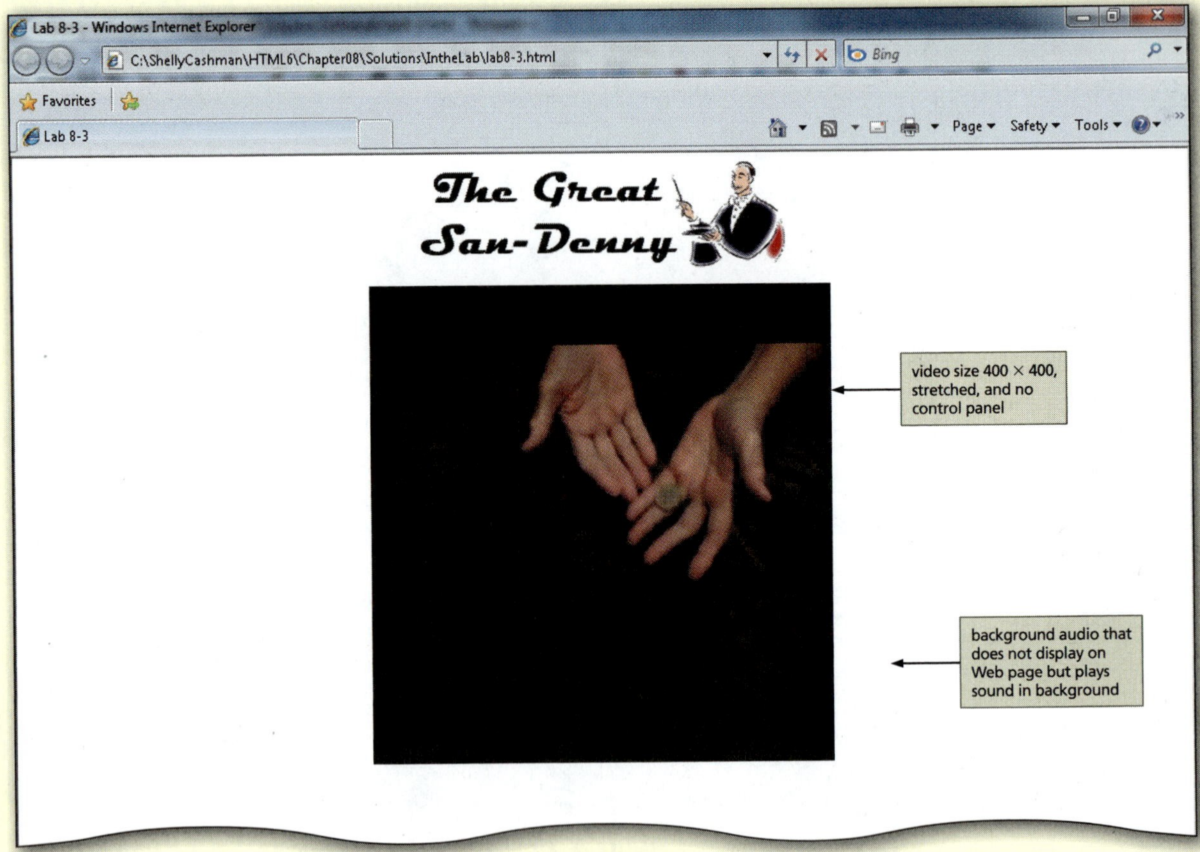

Figure 8–21

Instructions: Perform the following steps.

1. Open the file lab8-3.html in Notepad++. Save the file as lab8-3solution.html.
2. Insert the magicshow.wmv file as the video. Make sure it fills the Windows Media Player window as much as possible, but not the full monitor screen. The video should start automatically. There should not be any control panel on the WMP window, as shown in Figure 8–21.
3. Insert the magicmusic.mp3 file. This audio clip should not display at all, but it should start automatically.
4. Save the file, validate it, and then print it.

5. Test the Web page in Internet Explorer.
6. Submit the solution in the format specified by your instructor.
7. Bonus: If you have downloaded video editing software, try to combine these two files into one video file. How would this change the code that you inserted in Steps 2 and 3?

Cases and Places

Apply your creative thinking and problem-solving skills to design and implement a solution.

• Easier •• More Difficult

• 1: Finding Multimedia Information Online

Search on the Internet for an ActiveX control other than those discussed in this chapter (see Table 8–3 on page HTML 370 for ideas). Why would you use Flash in lieu of Windows Media Player or QuickTime? Is the functionality of Java Applets different from or similar to the functionality of Windows Media Player or QuickTime? How does RealAudio differ from its competition? Determine when you would use ActiveX controls other than the ones used in the exercises you have completed in this chapter.

• 2: Other Multimedia Formats

Review the audio and video formats listed in Tables 8–1 and 8–2 on pages HTML 368 and HTML 369. In this chapter, you used only two types of files: .mp3 and .wmv. What are the benefits of these other formats? How are these formats better or worse than the formats used in the chapter? Why would you use one format over the other? How prevalent is one media format over the others? Search online for free audio or video clips in at least three of the other formats.

•• 3: Movie-Making Software

Search for software that you can use to make or edit movie and audio clips. Most software that can be used to edit or make movies can also be used with audio files. Find software that has a free trial period. Download that software and play with it, using the video and audio clips provided in the Data Files for Students. Make sure to copy the file that you plan to use and save the original, just in case something happens. As you work with the software, use the Help utility if you have any problems. Demonstrate the software to the class.

•• 4: Adding to the Chapter 8 Web Site

Make It Personal

Who is your favorite U.S. President? Has that president ever given a speech or visited the Berlin Wall? If you cannot find information on that president speaking there, what speech is that president famous for? Find an audio or video clip of that U.S. President and add the clip to the Chapter 8 Web site. If the president served at a time prior to the availability of audio or video clips, what else can you look for? Is there a “reenactment” clip of someone dressed as that president speaking? Can you record the audio for a famous speech and use a picture of the president? What will you have to do to the image map in order to accommodate a new clip? How can you restructure the Web site if you use a speech other than one at the Berlin Wall?

Continued >

Cases and Places *continued*

•• 5: Creating a Video

Working Together

Work with your team to analyze and design a video that you can use in a Web site of your creation. You might want to storyboard the scenes (i.e., to graphically organize a process with a series of illustrations or images displayed in sequence for the purpose of visualizing the motion) so that it is fully designed. Use a digital camera to film the video. Using the software evaluated in Cases and Places 3, edit the video so that it is a reasonable file size (if necessary). Create a Web site in which this video can be inserted. Share your Web site and video with the class.

Special Feature 2

Converting Frames on Your Web Site

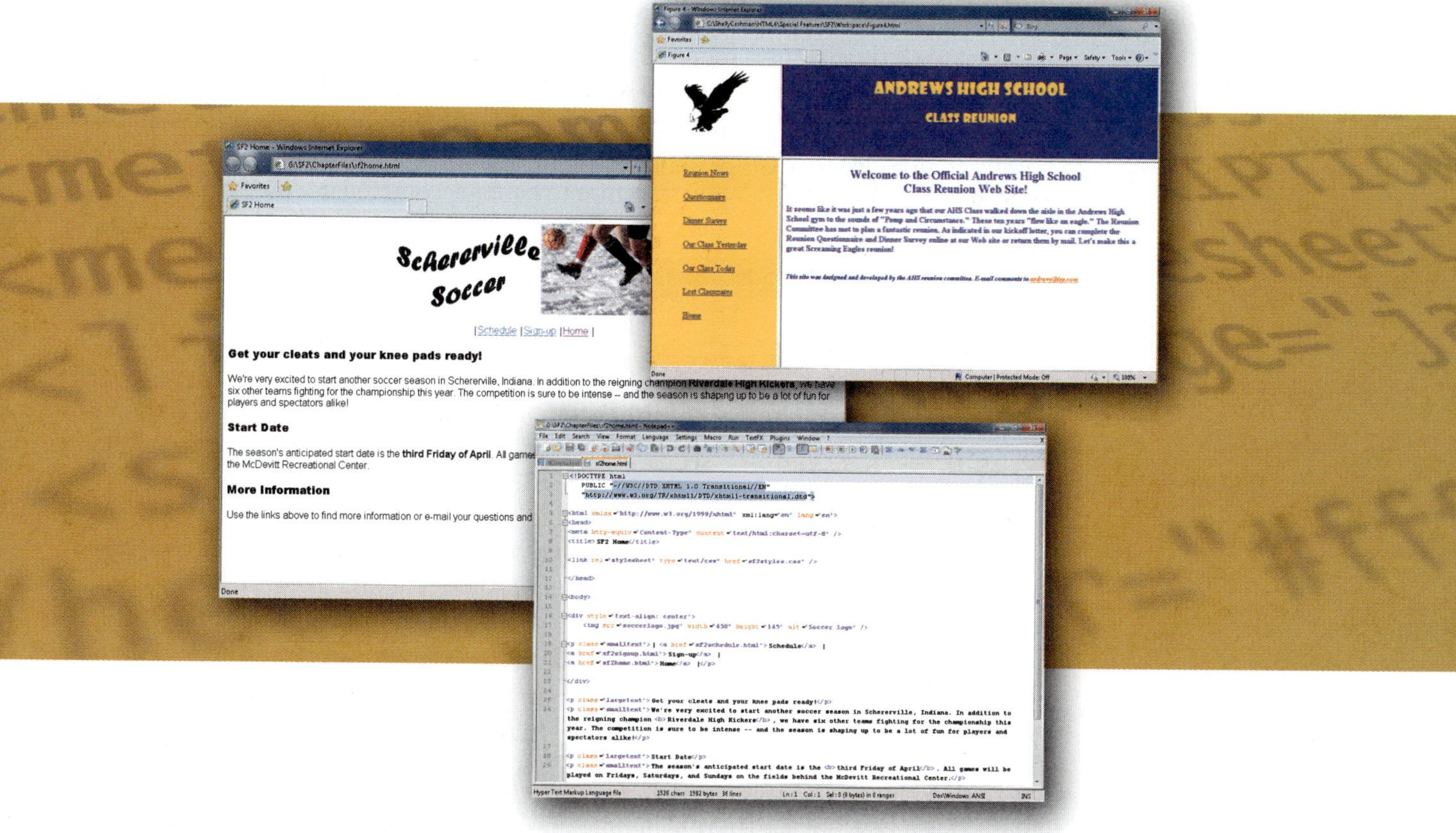

Objectives

You will have mastered the material in this special feature when you can:

- Define terms related to frames
- Identify all parts of a framed Web site structure
- Discuss the purpose and design of a frame definition file
- Determine a structure to replace frames on a Web site
- Develop a Web site to replace frames

Introduction

A **frame** is a rectangular area of a Web page — essentially, a window — in which a separate Web page can be displayed. Frames allow a user to display several Web pages at one time in a single browser window. Each frame displays a different, individual Web page, each of which is capable of interacting with other Web pages. Web pages that include frames look and act differently from Web pages created in previous projects. Frames are not used in the projects in this book because many screen readers, such as those used by visually impaired people, have difficulty displaying a Web site that uses frames. The Americans with Disabilities Act (ADA) standards recommend that frames not be used for Web sites. In addition to problems with devices for the disabled, there are other potential problems with the use of frames for Web development. Frames can cause problems when people bookmark or add the Web page as a favorite. It is the frame definition that is stored, and that may not be the page that the user wants to save. Search engines also may have problems indexing a Web site that uses frames. Finally, when users print a Web page with frames, they may not get what they see on the screen. However, many Web sites do utilize a frame structure, and as a Web developer, you may be responsible for maintaining Web sites based on frames. This Special Feature explains frames and how they are used, and shows you how to convert Web sites from a frame structure to better accommodate ADA standards and to address other frame-related issues.

BTW **Americans with Disabilities Act**
Review the Web site dedicated to this act, www.ada.org. It contains a wealth of information on the standards related to this act, including information about Web site functionality.

Project — Converting Frames

The Web site presented in this Special Feature is based on a frame structure. In order to understand the frame structure, you have to know what the frame definition is and how it works. You also have to understand how the other Web pages in a Web site are related to the frame definition file.

In this Special Feature, you review frame-based Web pages provided in the Data Files for Students. See the inside back cover of this book for instructions on downloading the Data Files for Students, or contact your instructor for information about accessing the required files. Figure 1a shows the initial Web site using frames. A red dashed line indicates where the Web page is divided into frames. You see that the top frame (the section of the Web page above the red dashed line) contains an image of soccer players and a menu bar that is used for navigation. The bottom frame (the section of the Web page beneath the red dashed line) contains the Web page content. You look at the frame definition file (Figure 1b) and see how it works with the other files in the Web site. You are then introduced to options that can take the place of a frame structure. Finally, you redesign the Web site to look similar but remove the frames (Figures 1c and 1d).

Overview

As you read through this feature, you will learn how to assess the frame definition file that creates the Web site shown in Figure 1a. You then convert the Web site structured with frames (Figure 1b) to a Web site structured without frames, using techniques that you have previously studied (Figures 1c and 1d). You complete this by performing these general tasks:

- Determine the use of a frame definition file to structure a Web site.
- Identify what other Web design methods could be used to restructure the Web site.
- Make the changes necessary to the Web pages provided to restructure the Web site.
- Validate and test the Web pages.

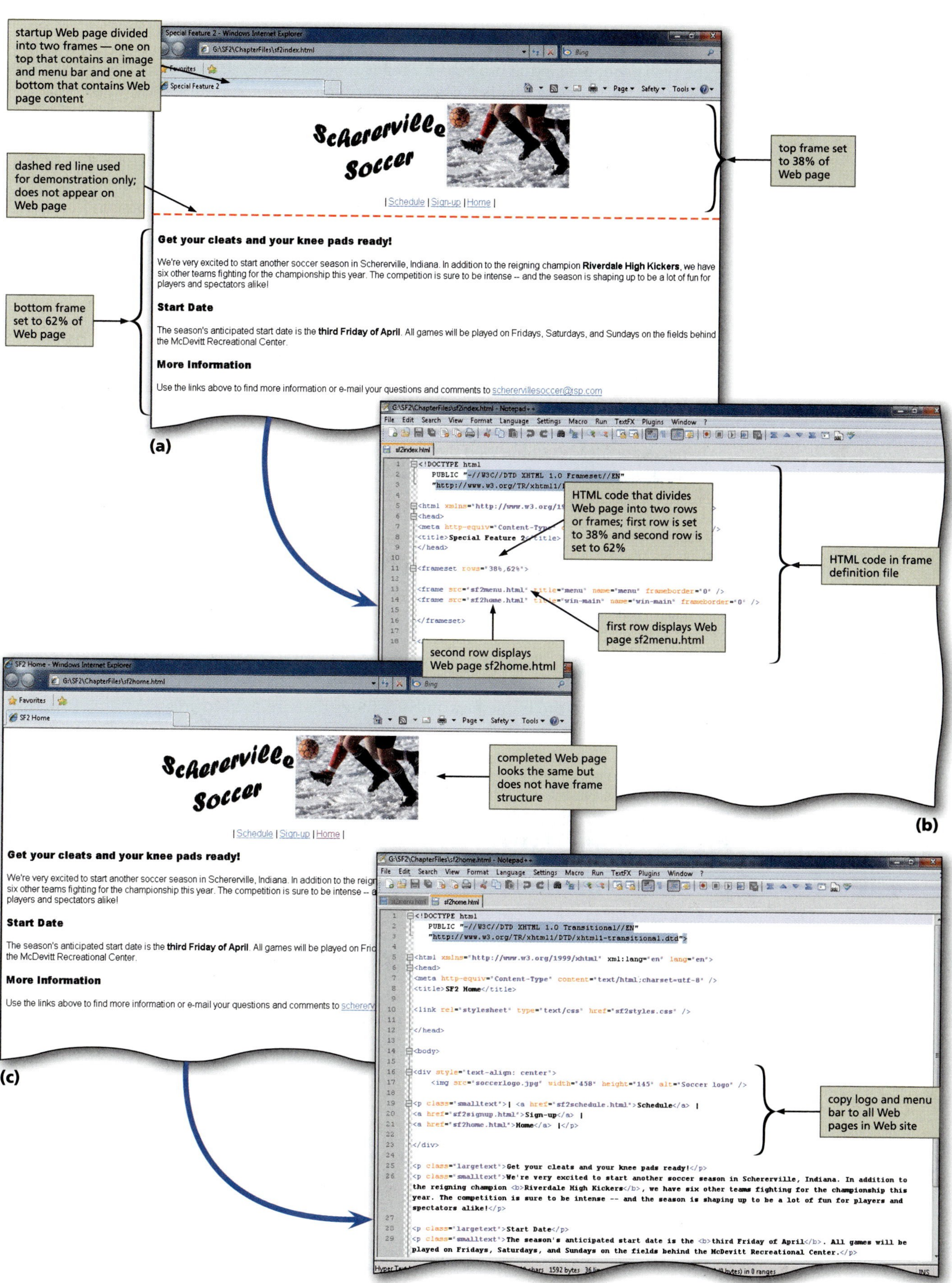
startup Web page divided into two frames — one on top that contains an image and menu bar and one at bottom that contains Web page content
dashed red line used for demonstration only; does not appear on Web page
top frame set to 38% of Web page
bottom frame set to 62% of Web page
Get your cleats and your knee pads ready!
Start Date
More Information
(a)
HTML code that divides Web page into two rows or frames; first row is set to 38% and second row is set to 62%
HTML code in frame definition file
first row displays Web page sf2menu.html
second row displays Web page sf2home.html
completed Web page looks the same but does not have frame structure
(b)
(c)
copy logo and menu bar to all Web pages in Web site
(d)

Figure 1

Plan Ahead

General Project Guidelines

The Web pages used in this project are already completed with a frame structure. In order to change the structure, you first need to understand how the current frame structure works. Then you can determine techniques that can be used to change the structure. In preparation for this project, you should follow these general guidelines:

1. **Review the layout of the frame structure.** Frames can assume different layouts. You could have a two-frame layout in which there is a menu bar across the top or left side of the Web page or a three- or four-frame layout. You must first assess the existing frame structure.
2. **Identify the purpose and structure of the frame definition file.** Once you have determined the structure, you need to review the frame definition file to see how it applies to the layout. This must be done so that you can convert the Web site appropriately.
3. **Determine a conversion strategy that can be used to restructure the Web site.** A Web site needs to be converted effectively. There are different techniques that you can use, but each technique needs to be assessed for effectiveness and efficiency.
4. **Make the changes necessary.** Once your technique is determined, you need to make the necessary changes to the Web site to convert it from a frame structure to a new structure (as developed in all chapters of this book).

BTW

Frames

Frames represent an older technology that is still in use today. Research the terms "frames" or "HTML frames" on the Internet to determine how prevalent they are in current Web development.

The Frame Definition File

The frame definition file tells the browser what frames to display and structures the frame layout. This is the file that you open in the browser in order to view the Web site. The frame definition file contains the names of the two, three, or four Web pages that are opened in frames at startup.

Table 1 shows the frame tags and attributes that are used to create a frame structure.

Table 1 Frame Tag Attributes

Tag	Attribute	Function
`<frameset>`	cols rows	• Indicates the number of columns • Indicates the number of rows
`<frame>`	frameborder marginwidth marginheight noresize name scrolling src	• Turns frame borders on or off (1 or 0) • Adjusts the margin on the left and right of a frame • Adjusts the margin above and below a document within a frame • Locks the borders of a frame to prohibit resizing • Defines the name of a frame that is used as a target • Indicates whether a scroll bar is present • Indicates the Web page or other file to be displayed in the frame

The HTML code that creates this frame structure for the Web page shown in Figure 1a on page HTML 395 is contained in the sf2index.html frame definition file, and is as follows (line numbers have been added):

```
1    <!DOCTYPE html
2       PUBLIC "-//W3C//DTD XHTML 1.0 Frameset//EN"
3       "http://www.w3.org/TR/xhtml1/DTD/xhtml1-frameset.dtd">
4    <html xmlns="http://www.w3.org/1999/xhtml" xml:lang="en"
     lang="en">
5    <head>
6    <meta http-equiv="Content-Type" content="text/
     html;charset=utf-8" />
7    <title>Special Feature 2</title>
8    </head>
9    <frameset rows="38%,62%">
10   <frame src="sf2menu.html" title="menu" name="menu"
     frameborder="0" />
11   <frame src="sf2home.html" title="win-main" name="win-main"
     frameborder="0" />
12   </frameset>
13   </html>
```

Note that in lines 2 and 3 of the code, the word "Transitional" that you have used in all chapter projects is replaced with "Frameset." This is because the document type to use frames is Frameset.

In the code above, also notice that one frameset (line 9) is inserted that contains two rows (top and bottom) that create two sections (or frames) of 38% and 62% of the Web page, respectively. (If you wanted to structure the frames with the menu frame on the left and the content frame on the right, you would change the attribute "rows" in the frameset line of code to "cols" instead and adjust the percentages as needed.) There will always be one frame for each <frame /> tag that is used. That is, the <frame /> tag defines one particular window (or frame) within a frameset. Each frame in a frameset can have different attributes, such as border, scrolling, the ability to resize, etc., but each frame contains only one Web page at a time as described below.

At startup (on lines 10 and 11 of the code), you see that the sf2menu.html file opens in the first (top) frame, and the sf2home.html file opens in the second (bottom) frame (or row). In other words, the top frame (sf2menu.html, that contains the logo and menu bar) displays in the top 38% of the Web page, while the content frame (or section) named sf2home.html displays in the bottom 62% of the Web page. Also note that line 11 gives that frame the target name "win-main" as an identifier. The name "win-main" is used by the sf2menu.html file (shown later) as the target frame in which all content is displayed.

BTW

Framesets

A frameset can be thought of as a window with various windowpanes. Within each pane is a separate Web page. The frame definition file is the HTML file that defines the Web pages that are displayed in the individual panes. Every Web page used in a frameset can be viewed independently in the browser as well as within the frameset.

To View a Web Site with Frames

To view the Web site with frames used in this project, you open the sf2index.html frame definition file in the browser. Then you open the HTML file and compare this Web site to the code shown in the frame definition file.

1

- With a USB drive plugged into your computer, start your browser.
- Open the sf2index .html file in the SF2\ ChapterFiles folder of the Data Files for Students (Figure 2a).
- Click the menu options (Schedule, Sign-up, and Home) to view the entire Web site.

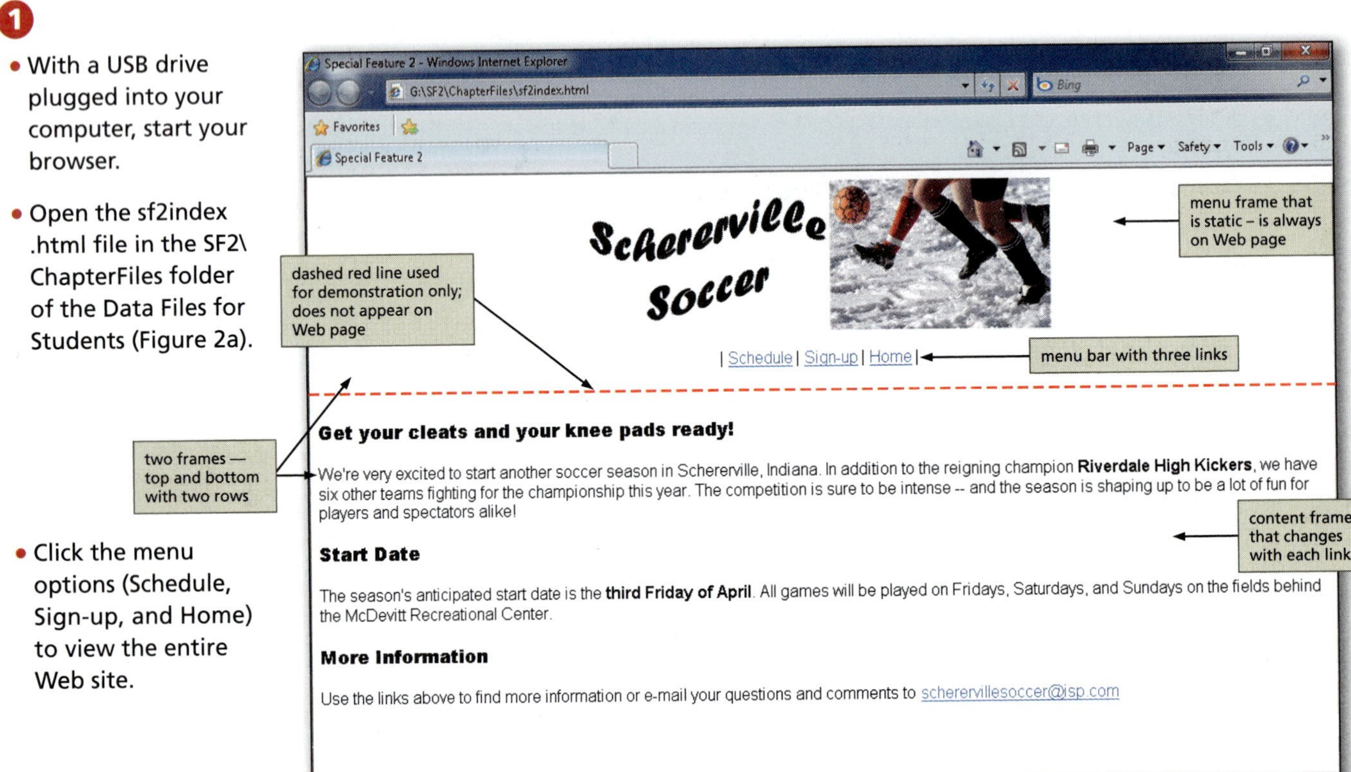

Figure 2 (a)

2

- Start Notepad++ and open the sf2index .html frame definition file in the SF2\ChapterFiles folder of the Data Files for Students (Figure 2b).

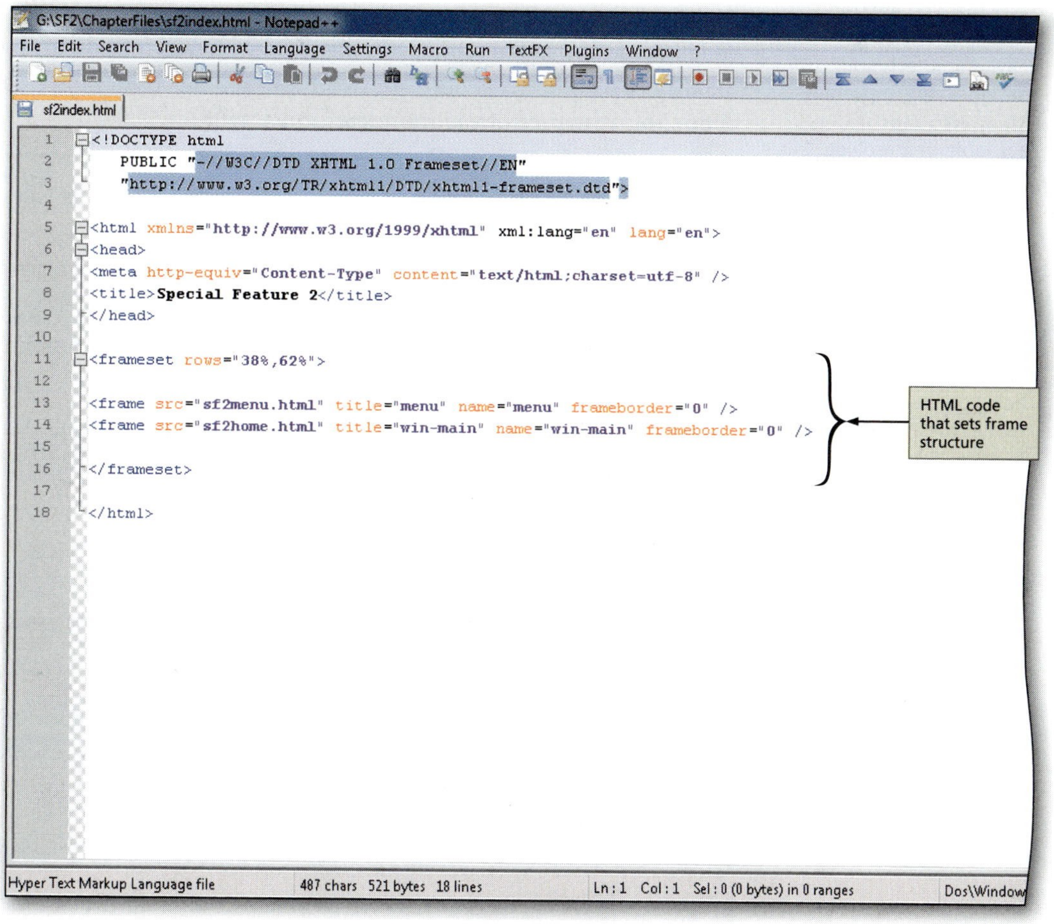

Q&A

How can you tell that this Web site uses frames?

The only way to be completely sure that the structure uses frames is to open the Web page source code. You immediately see that the structure of the Web page (shown in Figure 2b) is developed in frames. In this Web site, the soccer logo and the menu bar are always present on the top section (or frame) of the Web page, and this section is static (i.e., it remains the same always). The content from the sf2home.html file displays in the bottom frame (the target named "win-main"). A Web site visitor can click any of the three menu items (Schedule, Sign-up, Home), and the content from those Web pages displays in the dynamic (i.e., changing) target "win-main" (the bottom frame) of the Web page.

G:\SF2\ChapterFiles\sf2index.html - Notepad++

File Edit Search View Format Language Settings Macro Run TextFX Plugins Window ?

sf2index.html

```
<!DOCTYPE html
    PUBLIC "-//W3C//DTD XHTML 1.0 Frameset//EN"
    "http://www.w3.org/TR/xhtml1/DTD/xhtml1-frameset.dtd">

<html xmlns="http://www.w3.org/1999/xhtml" xml:lang="en" lang="en">
<head>
<meta http-equiv="Content-Type" content="text/html;charset=utf-8" />
<title>Special Feature 2</title>
</head>

<frameset rows="38%,62%">

<frame src="sf2menu.html" title="menu" name="menu" frameborder="0" />
<frame src="sf2home.html" title="win-main" name="win-main" frameborder="0" />

</frameset>

</html>
```

HTML code that sets frame structure

Hyper Text Markup Language file 487 chars 521 bytes 18 lines Ln : 1 Col : 1 Sel : 0 (0 bytes) in 0 ranges Dos\Window

Figure 2 (b)

Frame Layouts

Frame layouts can be designed in a variety of ways. The goal and purpose of the Web site determine which layout is appropriate. For example, the Schererville Soccer Web site uses a basic two-frame structure, as shown in Figures 2a and 2b. The menu on the top remains constant, and the content frame on the bottom changes.

BTW

Web Page Design
Whether you are using frames or any other navigation technique, design is very important. Many Web sites are available that provide information about the use of frames and other Web design techniques. These sites include links to sample Web sites that demonstrate advanced Web design topics. Many design tips also are available that can help you create a Web site that is informative as well as attractive.

Figure 3 shows a three-frame structure, often used to display a company logo (top) in the third frame. To create a three-frame structure as shown in Figure 3, the HTML code is as follows. This time, you identify two rows first. Within the second row, you identify two columns. There are two frameset tags used in the code because these tags define the structure of the frames within a window.

```
<frameset cols="25%,75%">
<frameset rows="20%,80%">
<frame src="header.html" title="header" name="header"
scrolling="no" />
<frame src="menu.html" title="menu" name="menu" />
</frameset>
<frame src="home.html" title="win-main" name="win-main" />
</frameset>
```

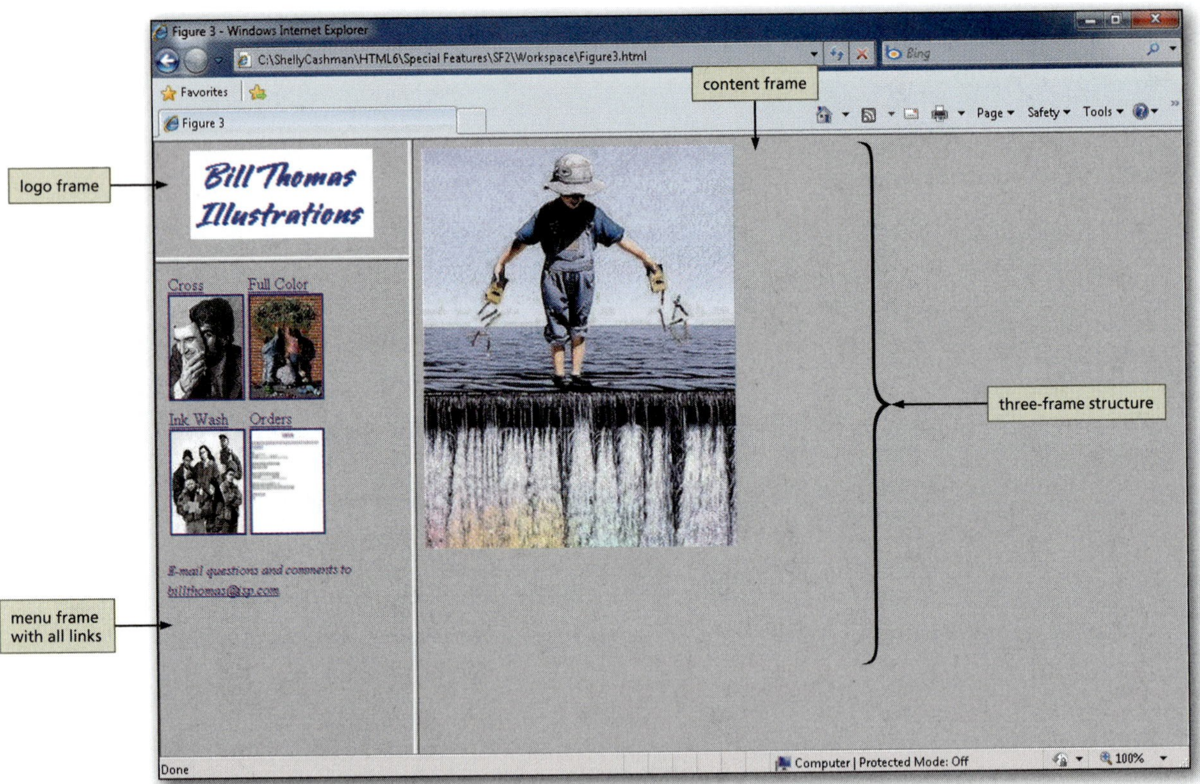

Figure 3

A four-frame structure, as shown in Figure 4, can be used to split a header image from the header text. The HTML code needed to create the four-frame structure shown in Figure 4 is as follows. This time, you identify two rows first with two columns in each row.

```
<frameset rows="30%,70%">
<frameset cols="25%,75%">
<frame src="logo.html" title="logo" name="logo" />
<frame src="header.html" title="header" name="header" />
</frameset>
<frameset cols="25%,75%">
<frame src="menu.html" title="menu" name="menu" />
<frame src="home.html" title="win-main" name="win-main"/>
</frameset>
</frameset>
```

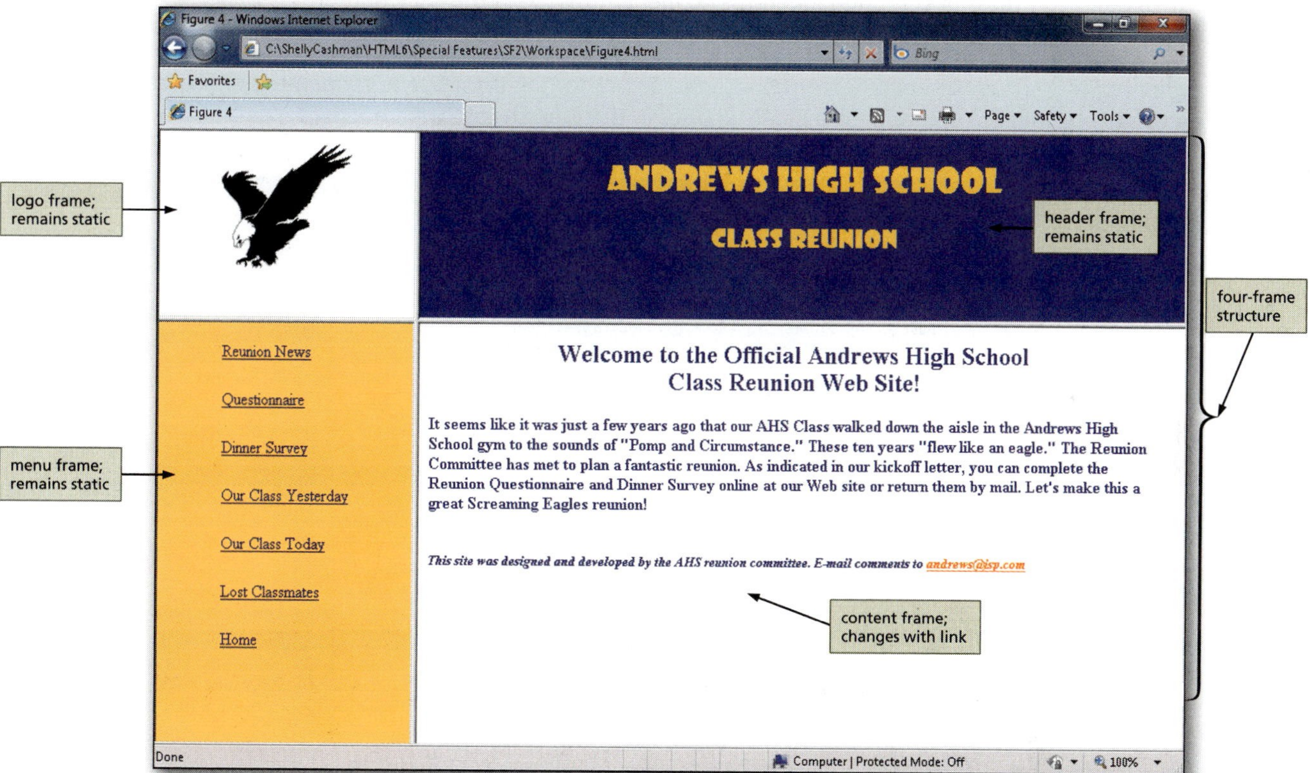

Figure 4

Determining a Conversion Strategy

Now that you understand the purpose and organization of the frame definition file, you must decide how to convert the Web site from a frame structure to an ADA-compliant structure. You have several methods to choose from to accomplish this conversion. One way is similar to what you did in the Chapter 7 project, using the <div> </div> tags to provide a pop-up window when a user hovers over an image. Here, however, you want the content of a second Web page to remain visible all the time, not just when a user hovers over it. Using the division tag, you can lay out a Web page so that a menu remains constant in one division (or section), and the content displays in a second division (or section) of the Web page. That is fine, but it means that you must have all content in one Web page. That is not an efficient way to convert from frames for this project.

A second way to convert from a frame structure is to copy the static portion of the Web page (the image and the menu bar) to all pages in the Web site. The sf2menu.html file contains the logo and the menu bar for this Web site. You will open this file and copy the logo and menu bar code and paste it into the sf2home.html, sf2schedule.html, and sf2signup.html Web pages.

To Copy HTML Code for a Menu Bar

The following step illustrates how to copy the necessary menu bar code from the sf2menu.html file.

- If necessary, start Notepad++.
- With a USB drive plugged into your computer, open the sf2menu.html file in the SF2\ChapterFiles folder.

Q&A Why open this file and not the frame definition file, sf2index.html?

The frame definition file, sf2index.html, only contains the structure for the frames. The sf2menu.html contains the logo and menu bar that you want to copy to the other Web pages in the Web site.

- Highlight lines 16 through 23 (Figure 5).
- Click Edit on the menu bar and then click Copy.

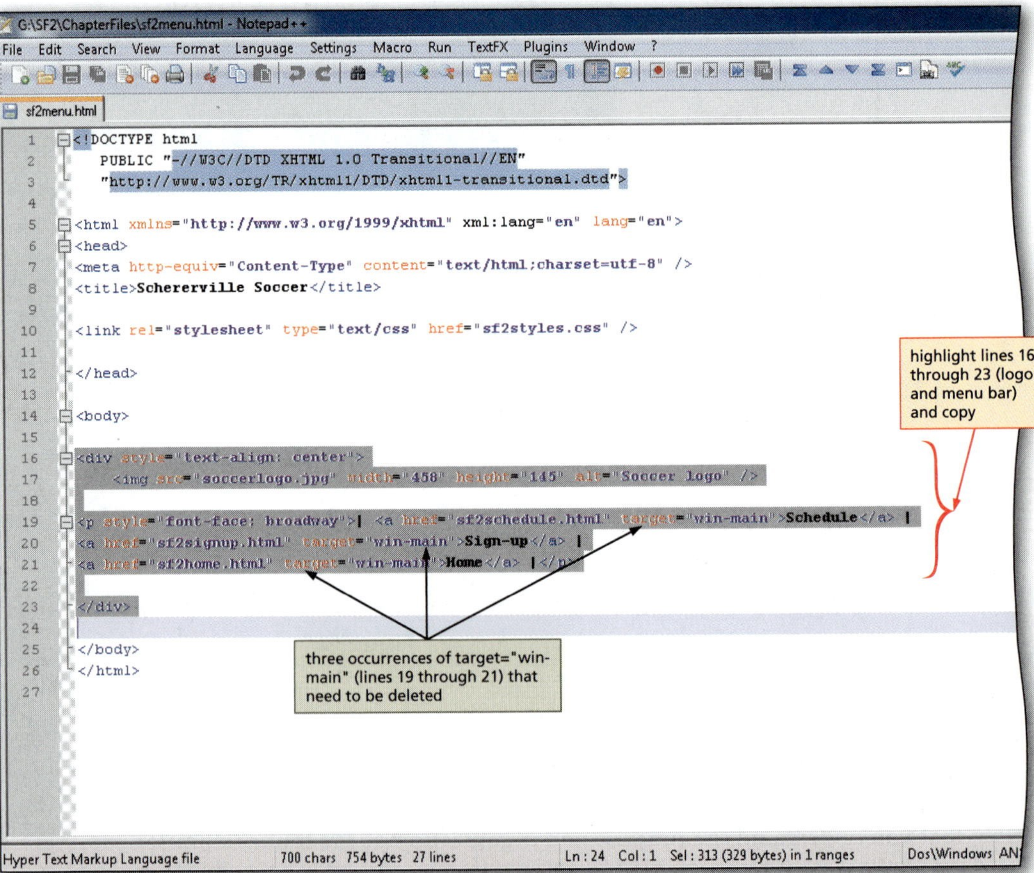

Figure 5

To Paste Code into the Home Page and Edit the Code

The following step illustrates how to paste the code copied above into the home page and edit the code to remove the target property.

- In Notepad++, open the sf2home.html file in the SF2\ChapterFiles folder on the USB drive.
- Click after the > in the <body> tag on line 14 and press the ENTER key twice.
- Click Edit on the menu bar and then click Paste.
- Delete the code target="win-main" on lines 19, 20, and 21 (Figure 6).
- Click the Save icon on the toolbar to save the sf2home.html file with the new code.

G:\SF2\ChapterFiles\sf2home.html - Notepad++

File Edit Search View Format Language Settings Macro Run TextFX Plugins Window ?

sf2menu.html | sf2home.html

```
1  <!DOCTYPE html
2      PUBLIC "-//W3C//DTD XHTML 1.0 Transitional//EN"
3      "http://www.w3.org/TR/xhtml1/DTD/xhtml1-transitional.dtd">
4
5  <html xmlns="http://www.w3.org/1999/xhtml" xml:lang="en" lang="en">
6  <head>
7  <meta http-equiv="Content-Type" content="text/html;charset=utf-8" />
8  <title>SF2 Home</title>
9
10 <link rel="stylesheet" type="text/css" href="sf2styles.css" />
11
12 </head>
13
14 <body>
15
16 <div style="text-align: center">
17     <img src="soccerlogo.jpg" width="458" height="145" alt="Soccer logo" />
18
19 <p class="smalltext">| <a href="sf2schedule.html">Schedule</a> |
20 <a href="sf2signup.html">Sign-up</a> |
21 <a href="sf2home.html">Home</a> |</p>
22
23 </div>
24
25 <p class="largetext">Get you          knee pads ready!</p>
26 <p class="smalltext">We're very excited to start another soccer season in Schererville, Indiana. In addi
   the reigning champion <b>Riverdale High Kickers</b>, we have six other teams fighting for the championsh
   year. The competition is sure to be intense -- and the season is shaping up to be a lot of fun for playe
   spectators alike!</p>
27
28 <p class="largetext">Start Date</p>
29 <p class="smalltext">The season's anticipated start date is the <b>third Friday of April</b>. All games
   played on Fridays, Saturdays, and Sundays on the fields behind the McDevitt Recreational Center.</p>
```

Hyper Text Markup Language file | 1520 chars 1592 bytes 36 lines | Ln : 1 Col : 1 Sel : 0 (0 bytes) in 0 ranges | Dos\Windows AN

Figure 6

Q&A

By copying/pasting this code, I can provide the same look to my Web site visitors as a frame structure, right?

Yes, your Web site will operate in the same manner without the frame structure, with the image and the menu bar across the top of the Web page and the content changing on the bottom part.

Q&A

Why do I have to remove the target="win-main" code?

The target is named to support the dynamic (i.e., changing) frame within the frame structure. Because there is now only one Web page and no frame structure, you do not need to identify the target frame.

To Copy and Paste Code into Other Web Pages

The following steps illustrate how to copy and paste the menu bar code into the Schedule and Signup Web pages.

- Copy lines 16 through 23 in the newly saved sf2home.html file (the code target ="win-main" on lines 19 through 21 should be deleted).
- In Notepad ++, open the sf2schedule.html file. Click the beginning of line 16 and press ENTER once. Move the insertion point back to line 16 and paste the copied eight lines of code.
- Click the Save icon on the toolbar to save the sf2schedule.html file with the new code (Figure 7).

G:\SF2\ChapterFiles\sf2index.html - Notepad++

File Edit Search View Format Language Settings Macro Run TextFX Plugins Window ?

sf2schedule.html

```
1  <!DOCTYPE html
2     PUBLIC "-//W3C//DTD XHTML 1.0 Transitional//EN"
3     "http://www.w3.org/TR/xhtml1/DTD/xhtml1-transitional.dtd">
4
5  <html xmlns="http://www.w3.org/1999/xhtml" xml:lang="en" lang="en">
6  <head>
7  <meta http-equiv="Content-Type" content="text/html; charset=utf-8" />
8  <title>SF2 Schedule</title>
9
10 <link rel="stylesheet" type="text/css" href="sf2styles.css" />
11
12 </head>
13
14 <body>
15
16 <div style="text-align: center">
17    <img src="soccerlogo.jpg" width="458" height="145" alt="Soccer logo" />
18
19 <p style="font-face: broadway">| <a href="sf2schedule.html">Schedule</a> |
20 <a href="sf2signup.html">Sign-up</a> |
21 <a href="sf2home.html">Home</a> |</p>
22
23 </div>
24
25 <table border="5" cellpadding="5" cellspacing="10">
26    <tr>
27       <th colspan="3">April Games</th>
28    </tr>
29
30    <tr>
31       <th>Teams</th>
32       <th>Day</th>
33       <th>Time</th>
```

Hyper Text Markup Language file 487 chars 521 bytes 18 lines Ln : 1 Col : 1 Sel : 0 (0 bytes) in 0 ranges Dos\Windows AN

code that was copied and then pasted

Figure 7

- Open the sf2signup.html file. Click the beginning of line 16 and press ENTER once. Move the insertion point back to line 16 and paste the same eight lines of code.
- Click the Save icon on the toolbar to save the sf2signup.html file with the new code.

To Validate and Print a Document

You are finished entering the lines of code needed for the logo and menu bar. As with all Web development projects, you now need to save, validate, and print the files.

1. Validate sf2home.html, sf2schedule.html, and sf2signup.html using the w3.org validation service.
2. Once the files are all successfully validated, print the files.

To View the Web Site in the Browser

As with all other projects, it is important to view the Web pages in the browser and test all links. After converting the Web site structure, you open the sf2home.html file as your starting point rather than the frame definition file sf2index.html.

1. If necessary, start your browser. Open the file sf2home.html in the browser (Figure 8).
2. Test all links by clicking the menu bar items Schedule, Sign-up, and Home.

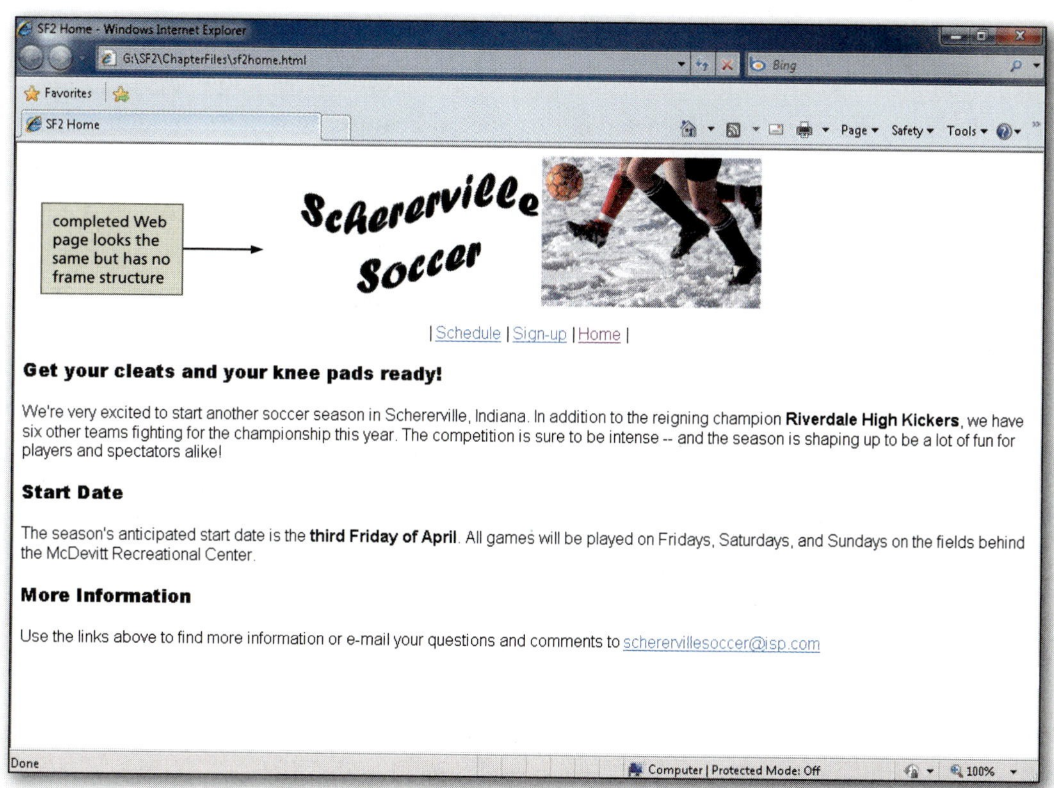

Figure 8

Feature Summary

In this feature, you have learned how to convert a frame-structured Web site to one in which frames are not used. This is an important aspect of Web development because of the ADA compliance standards that do not fully support frames. The items listed below include all the new Web development skills you have learned in this feature.

1. View a Web Site with Frames (HTML 398)
2. Copy HTML Code for a Menu Bar (HTML 402)
3. Paste Code into the Home Page and Edit the Code (HTML 403)
4. Copy and Paste Code into Other Web Pages (HTML 404)

In the Lab

Design and/or create a document using the guidelines, concepts, and skills presented in this chapter. Labs are listed in order of increasing difficulty.

Lab 1: Determining Another Way to Convert from Frames

Problem: Your assignment is to research frame conversion strategies and determine another way to convert a Web site from a frame structure to a non-frame structure.

Instructions:

1. Search online for additional information about ADA compliance issues related to frames.
2. Review other techniques that can be used to convert a Web site structured with frames.
3. Write a paper that addresses the topics discussed in this Special Feature. Your paper should:
   a. Specify reasons frames may not be an effective Web site structure
   b. Identify techniques that could be used to restructure a Web site
   c. Determine how you could utilize these techniques in your own Web development.
4. Save the paper with the name Lab SF2-1 Conversion Strategies. Submit the file in the format specified by your instructor.

In the Lab

Lab 2: Convert a Second Web Site

Problem: In this assignment, you convert a Web site that is based on the frame structure to a non-frame structure, as shown in Figure 9.

Instructions:

1. In your browser, open the LabSF2-2.html file found in the Data Files for Students.
2. Review the structure and functionality of the Web site highlighted in this file.
3. Determine how you can restructure the Web site by converting from its current frame structure. Your conversion strategy can be that which is used in this Special Feature or another strategy that you found in your research in Lab 1.
4. Make the changes to the Web pages in the Web site. Save the new file as LabSF2-2solution.html, validate all files, test the site, and print the pages of the modified site.
5. Submit the files in the format specified by your instructor.

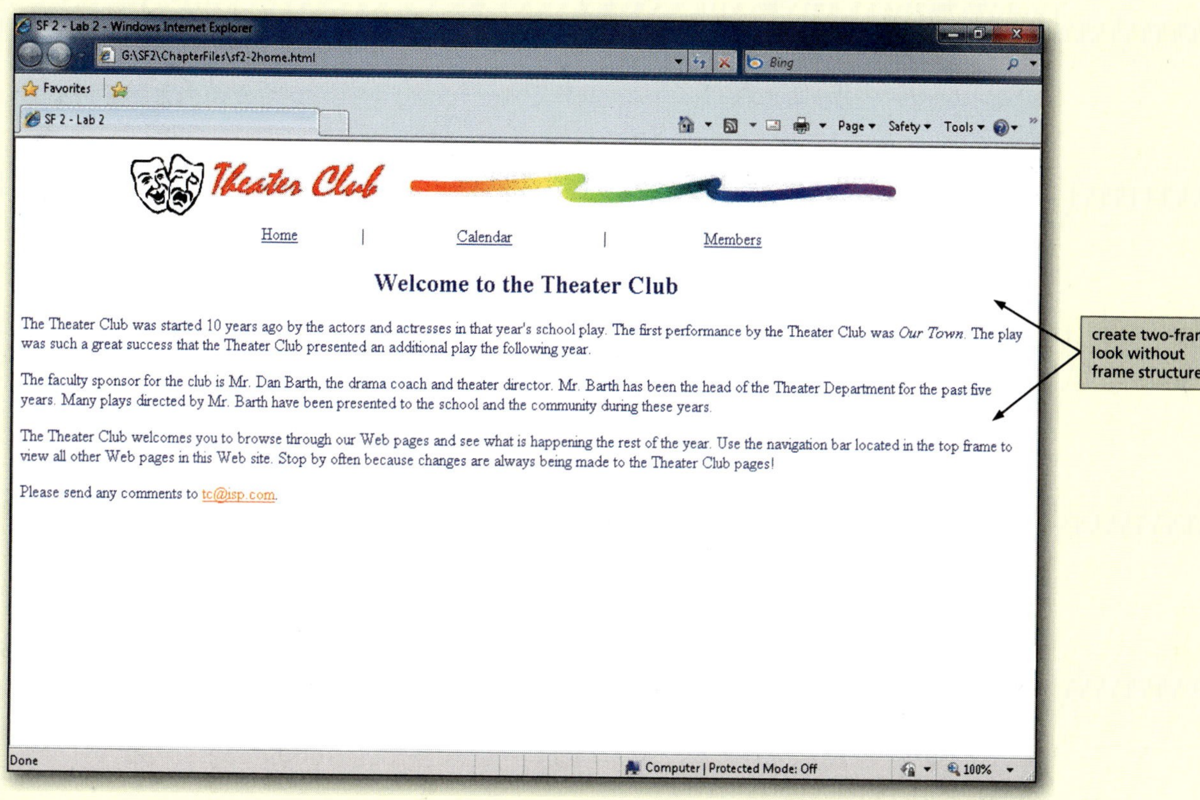
SF 2 - Lab 2 - Windows Internet Explorer
G:\SF2\ChapterFiles\sf2-2home.html
Theater Club
Home | Calendar | Members
Welcome to the Theater Club
The Theater Club was started 10 years ago by the actors and actresses in that year's school play. The first performance by the Theater Club was Our Town. The play was such a great success that the Theater Club presented an additional play the following year.
The faculty sponsor for the club is Mr. Dan Barth, the drama coach and theater director. Mr. Barth has been the head of the Theater Department for the past five years. Many plays directed by Mr. Barth have been presented to the school and the community during these years.
The Theater Club welcomes you to browse through our Web pages and see what is happening the rest of the year. Use the navigation bar located in the top frame to view all other Web pages in this Web site. Stop by often because changes are always being made to the Theater Club pages!
Please send any comments to tc@isp.com.
create two-frame look without frame structure

Figure 9

9 Integrating JavaScript and HTML

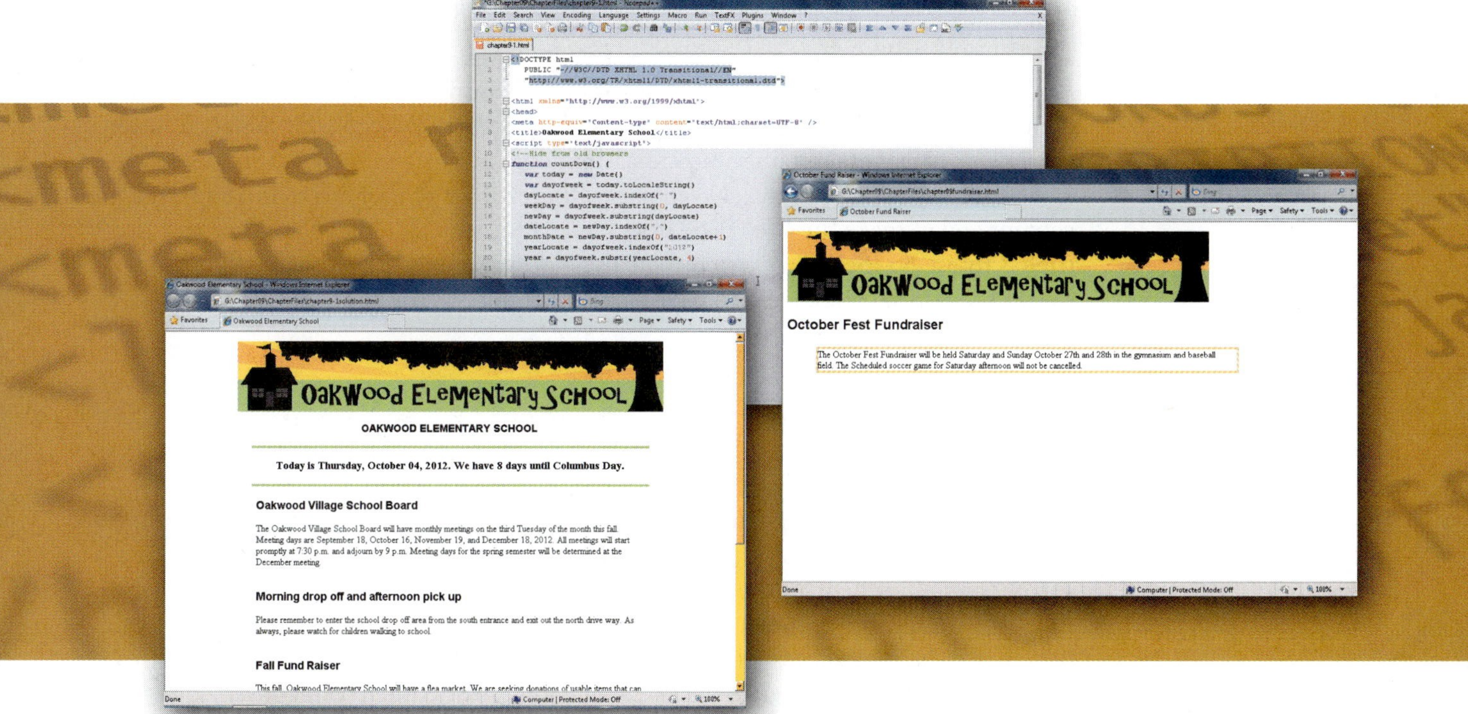

Objectives

You will have mastered the material in this chapter when you can:

- Describe JavaScript and how it can be integrated with HTML
- Describe how the <div> tag container is used to display text
- Describe a valid JavaScript user-defined function
- Write the code to create a <script> section on a Web page
- Define and describe JavaScript variable
- Extract the current system date
- Calculate the number of days from the current date to a future date
- Use the innerHTML property to display a dynamic message to a Web page
- Write a user-defined JavaScript function that changes the color of the browser's scroll bar
- Write a user-defined JavaScript to open a Web page from a <select> tag <option> value
- Use the lastModified property to display the date the document was last modified.
- Use an event handler to invoke a JavaScript user-defined function when a Web page is loaded

9 Integrating JavaScript and HTML

Introduction

Many individuals, organizations, and companies rely on their Web sites as a key vehicle to communicate with friends, members, and current and future customers. Web pages often announce upcoming events, provide updated information, or act as a sales tool or catalog. Regardless of the content, Web page features should spark visitors' interests and entice them to return to the Web site. As with an advertisement, a Web page has six to seven seconds to attract and retain someone's attention.

An effective way to make Web pages interesting and useful is to include dynamic content and to make the Web page interactive. One way to add dynamic content to a Web page is to use JavaScript code to display dynamic messages. This chapter shows you how to add JavaScript code to a Web page to make it more dynamic and attractive.

Project — Oakwood Elementary School Web Page

Oakwood Elementary School wants you to update their Web page with a dynamic message, a drop-down menu to navigate to other Web pages, and to make the Web page more colorful. You suggest a dynamic message that can be easily modified to address current announcements, such as the number of days to a specific date or event; using a drop-down list or jump menu for navigation to other Web pages, and changing scroll bar color to help balance the look of the page with the margin and banner colors. You also suggest including the date the Web page was last modified so that users know the Web page content is current. Chapter 9 shows the JavaScript code to add these dynamic features to create the Web pages shown in Figure 9–1.

Overview

As you read through this chapter, you will learn how to integrate JavaScript onto a Web page, as shown in Figure 9–1, by performing these general tasks:

- Write a JavaScript function to display a dynamic message in a <div> container
- Write a JavaScript function to change the color of the scroll bar
- Write a JavaScript function to use a drop-down list to link to new Web pages
- Write a JavaScript function to display the date the Web page was last modified and a copyright message in a <div> container

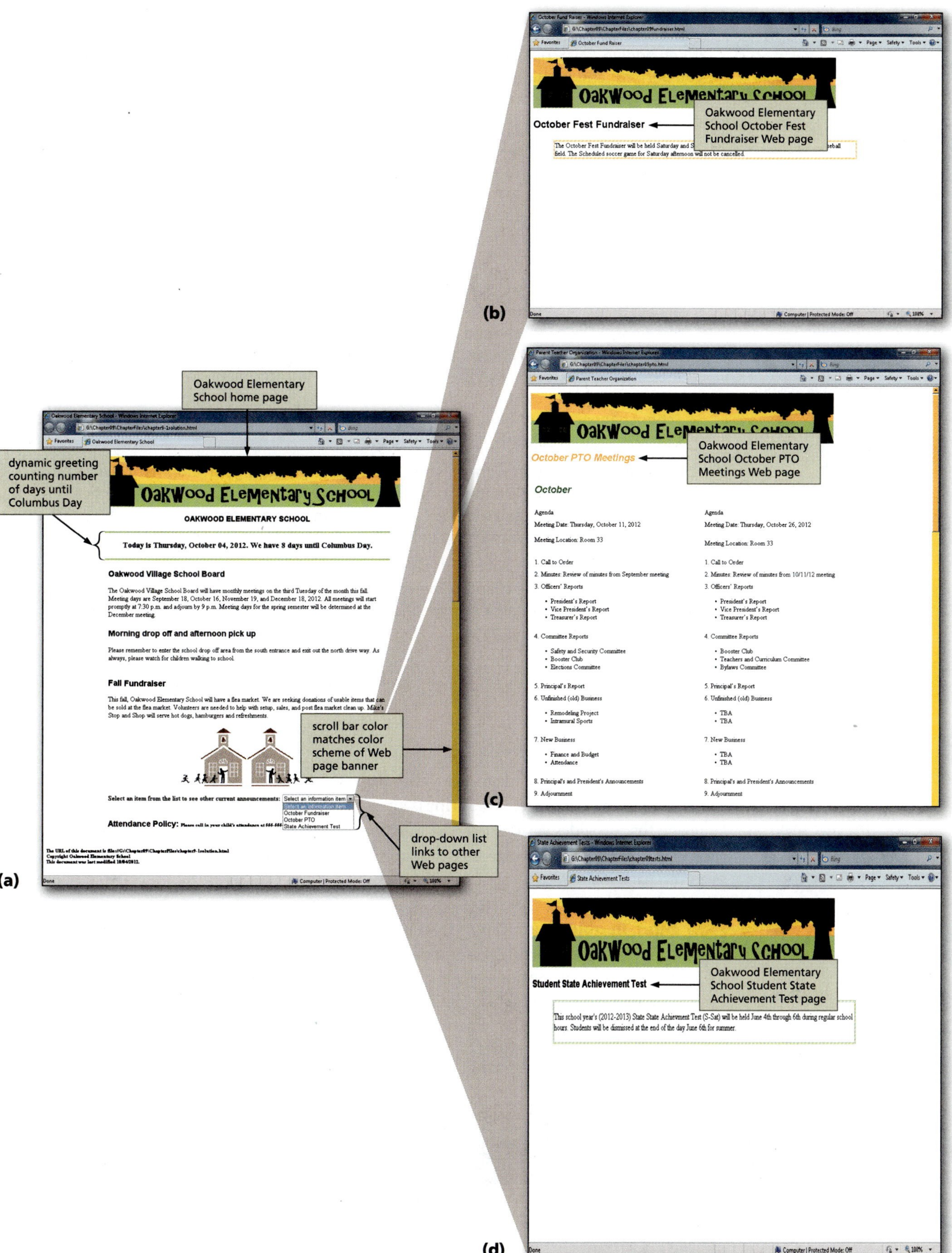
Oakwood Elementary School October Fest Fundraiser Web page
October Fest Fundraiser
Oakwood Elementary School home page
dynamic greeting counting number of days until Columbus Day
OAKWOOD ELEMENTARY SCHOOL
Today is Thursday, October 04, 2012. We have 8 days until Columbus Day.
Oakwood Village School Board
Morning drop off and afternoon pick up
Fall Fundraiser
scroll bar color matches color scheme of Web page banner
drop-down list links to other Web pages
Oakwood Elementary School October PTO Meetings Web page
October PTO Meetings
October
Oakwood Elementary School Student State Achievement Test page
Student State Achievement Test
(a)
(b)
(c)
(d)

Figure 9–1

Plan Ahead

General Project Guidelines

When adding JavaScript or any scripting language to a Web page document, the actions you perform and decisions you make will affect the appearance and characteristics of the finished Web page. Before you write the JavaScript code, you should follow these general guidelines:

1. **Determine what you want the code to accomplish.** The JavaScript tasks in this chapter calculate the number of days to a future date and display a dynamic message that includes the current date and number of days until another date, change the color of the scroll bar, use a drop-down menu (HTML <select/options>) to link to other Web pages, and display a copyright notice and date the Web page was last modified at the bottom of the Web page.
2. **Determine where on the Web page you want the code to appear.** JavaScript code should always be placed in the <head> section of the HTML code. To display messages at specific locations, JavaScript can send text to a <div> container tag. By using a <div> container and the innerHTML property, a JavaScript user-defined function can display dynamic messages at any location in the <body> of the HTML document. In this project, <div> container tags are used to display a dynamic message beneath the Oakwood Elementary School banner, and to display the date last modified and copyright information at the bottom of the Web page.
3. **Determine where you want to store the Web page during development.** The storage location of HTML code and associated images is very important. A best practice is to create folders to organize HTML files and graphics in a specific location. This practice makes finding and maintaining links to graphics and other Web site pages easy.

When necessary, more specific details concerning the above guidelines are presented at appropriate points in the chapter. The chapter also will identify the actions performed and decisions made regarding these guidelines during the creation of the Web page shown in Figure 9–1 on the previous page.

BTW

JavaScript Advantages and Disadvantages
JavaScript allows for faster response in client pages to requests such as form validation. JavaScript code downloads faster than other kinds of applets, like Java or Flash, and no extra plug-in is needed to execute the JavaScript code. The main disadvantage to JavaScript is that diverse browser versions may not execute JavaScript as intended.

JavaScript

Before adding JavaScript code to your Web page, you should understand some basics about the programming language. **JavaScript** is an event-driven, object-based programming language that provides various types of functionality to Web pages, such as the ability to interact with the user. An **event-driven** programming language is one that responds to events, such as a Web page loading or a user clicking a Submit button. JavaScript is **object-based** because it is a scripting language that uses built-in objects that belong to the browser.

Built-in objects are values that are common to a browser (arrays, dates, strings, etc.), which neither depend on nor belong to another object. Table 9–1 contains a general list of the built-in JavaScript objects common to many browsers. JavaScript developers can create new objects based on the built-in objects, and the new objects inherit properties from the original objects. For more information about these objects, see the JavaScript Quick Reference in Appendix G.

BTW

Object-oriented Programming (OOP)
Object-oriented programming is an approach to programming in which the code that operates on the data is packaged into a single unit called an object.

BTW

Event-driven Programming
Code in event-driven programs executes only when a certain event, such as clicking a button, triggers the code to execute.

Table 9–1 Built-In JavaScript Objects

Object	Description
Array	Returns an ordered set of values
Boolean	Converts objects to Boolean values
Date	Accesses the system time and date
Document	Represents the content of a browser's window

Table 9–1 Built-In JavaScript Objects (continued)

Object	Description
Form	Represents forms created with the <form> tag
Function	Accesses information about specific functions
History	Keeps track of Web pages visited
Image	Represents images created with the <img> tag
Location	Switches to a new Web page
Math	Performs calculations
Navigator	Obtains information about the current Web browser
Number	Supports special constants
RegExp	Describes patterns of characters
Screen	Gives platform-specific information about the user's screen
String	Represents a set of characters
Window and Frame	Represents a browser window or every frame within a browser window; every frame is a window and uses the same properties and methods as the window object

JavaScript objects have properties and methods. **Properties** are attributes that describe an object's characteristics. As shown in Table 9–2, an object and its property are written by separating the object from its property with a period. A specific value can be assigned to a property, as shown in the following example:

```
cat.breed="American curl"
```

where the cat is the object, breed is the property, and American curl is the value assigned to the property.

BTW

Other Scripting Languages
Although JavaScript and VBScript are the two main client-side script languages used today, there are over a dozen other scripting languages that work on specific platforms or operating systems. For example, PHP Perl. Perl stands for Practical Extraction and Report Language, and was developed by NASA's Jet Propulsion Laboratory.

Table 9–2 Object and Property

General form:	object.property
Comment:	where the object is stated first, then a period, then the descriptive property. A value can be assigned to the property, or the property can return a value, as shown in the examples below.
Examples:	document.bgColor="lightblue" browser=navigator.appName

Methods are actions that an object can perform. For example, methods associated with the cat object might be eat, play, and sleep. An object and one of its methods would be written as:

```
cat.play()
```

where cat is the object and play is a method of the cat object. Methods are followed by parentheses, which may be empty, or may contain an argument.

An **argument** is a value given to a method. Some methods require arguments, and others do not. For example, given a cat object and the play() method, the argument "ball" describes a toy a cat may play with and would be written as:

```
cat.play("ball")
```

where the argument "ball" describes the toy the cat plays with.

BTW

Object Inheritance
Once a built-in object has been converted to a new object, the new object inherits all the properties and methods available to the original object.

As shown in Table 9–3, the general form of writing an object with its method is similar to writing objects and properties.

BTW **JavaScript Methods and Arguments**
Not all JavaScript methods require an argument. In fact, with some methods, if an argument is used, it generates an error.

Table 9–3 Object and Method

General form:	objectname.method(argument values)
Comment:	where objectname is the object, method is the action, and argument values are optional items or instructions the method should use. A period separates the object name from the method.
Examples:	window.open(Url, "", "toolbar=no,width=500,height=400,status=no,resize=yes") window.alert("This is a message") var ToDayDate=Date.toString( )

BTW **JavaScript Help**
Many Web sites provide help for JavaScript developers. To find such Web sites, search for keywords such as "JavaScript Tutorials" or "JavaScript Help" in any good search engine.

User-Defined Functions

A **function** is JavaScript code that is written to perform certain tasks repeatedly. A **user-defined function** is JavaScript code written by a Web developer to perform a particular task. The function can be used whenever that task is needed, eliminating the need to repeat the code several times throughout an application. Functions replace large sets of JavaScript code that are too large to fit within an HTML attribute. Functions are placed in a JavaScript section within the <head> section of the HTML code.

JavaScript also contains a number of built-in functions called **global functions**, such as close() to close a window, open() to open a window, and print() to print the contents of a window. Most of these functions actually belong to the window object, but because the window object is assumed, they are called built-in functions. For a complete list of built-in functions, see the JavaScript Quick Reference in Appendix G.

In this project, one of the user-defined functions uses a <div> tag container. A **container** is an HTML tag that identifies a section of HTML code using the id attribute. The <div> tag container defines a division or section of code that groups similar elements together. To uniquely identify this <div> container, use an id attribute, with a unique id value not used by any other tag. In this project, the id value will be used by JavaScript to assign text to that container. Because an empty division contains no other tags or text, it can be used to dynamically display text at a particular location within a Web page.

Most JavaScript user-defined functions are called or invoked using event handlers. An event is the result of an action, such as a mouse click or a Web page loading into the browser. An **event handler** is JavaScript's way to associate an action with a function. In this project, you first write the functions, and then the event handlers that will associate the functions with specific events, such as loading the Web page.

Plan Ahead

Create a <div> tag container to display a dynamic message.
To display a dynamic message on a Web page, you must:

- **Identify the location within the Web page in which a dynamic message displays.** In this Web page, you determine to place the dynamic message between the two horizontal lines beneath the banner.
- **Create a <div> tag container for your message.** You need to create a <div> tag container with an id attribute, which will identify that division as separate from any other <div> tag and act as a holding location for the message. This container, working in conjunction with the innerHTML property, will display the dynamic message.

To Open an Existing HTML File

The following steps show how to open the chapter9-1.html file included in the Data Files for Students, in which you will place the <div> tag container.

1. Start Notepad++, and, if necessary, maximize the window.
2. Click View on the menu bar. If the Word wrap command does not have a check mark next to it, click Word wrap.
3. With a USB flash drive plugged in to your computer, click File on the menu bar and then click Open on the File menu.
4. Navigate to the Chapter09\ChapterFiles folder on the USB drive.
5. Double-click chapter9-1.html in the list of files to display the HTML code for the chapter9-1.html Web page, as shown in Figure 9–2.

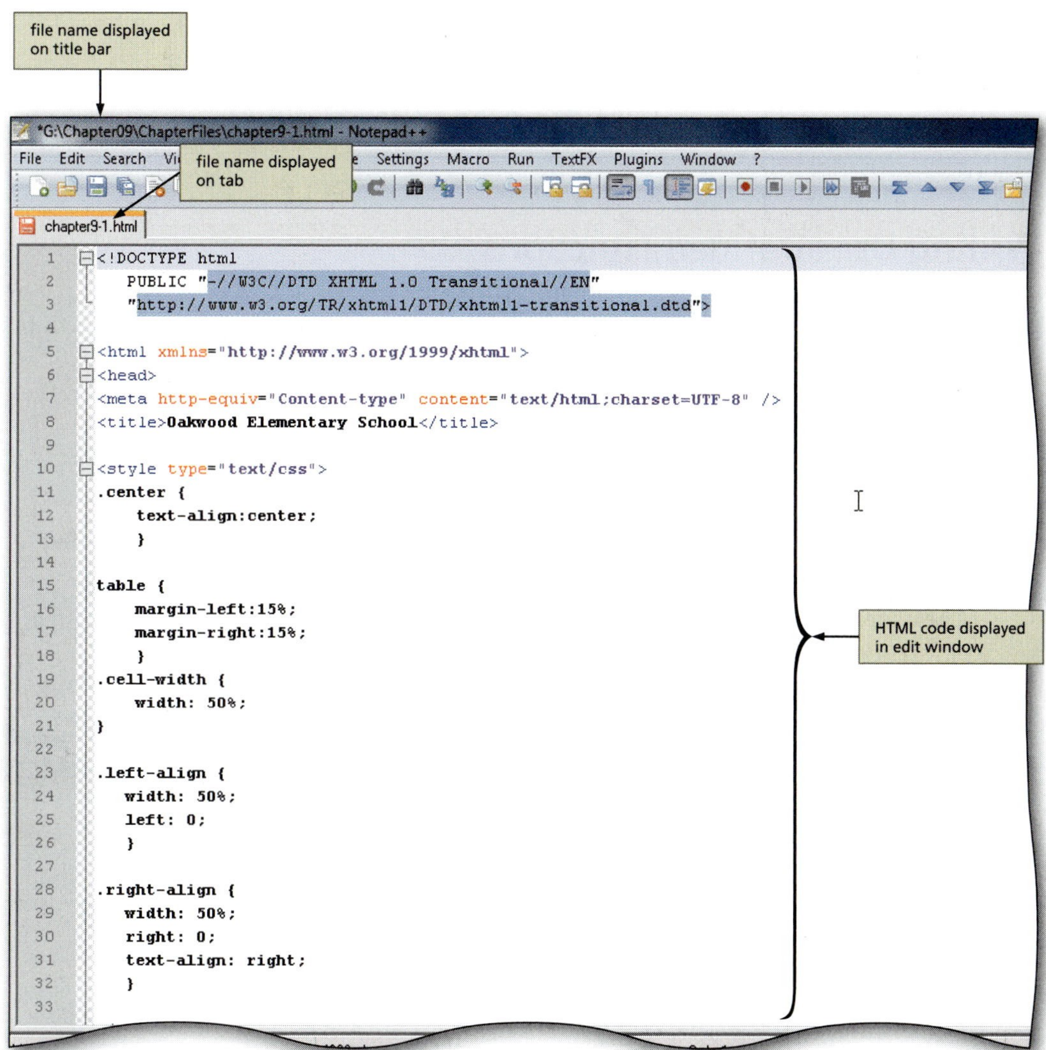

Figure 9–2

To Enter a <div> Tag Container

The following step illustrates how to enter the <div> tag with the id attribute. No other tags or text are needed between the beginning <div> and the closing </div> tag.

1

- Click the blank line at line 41 and type `<div id="displayDate">` and press ENTER.
- Type `</div>` and do not press ENTER (Figure 9–3).

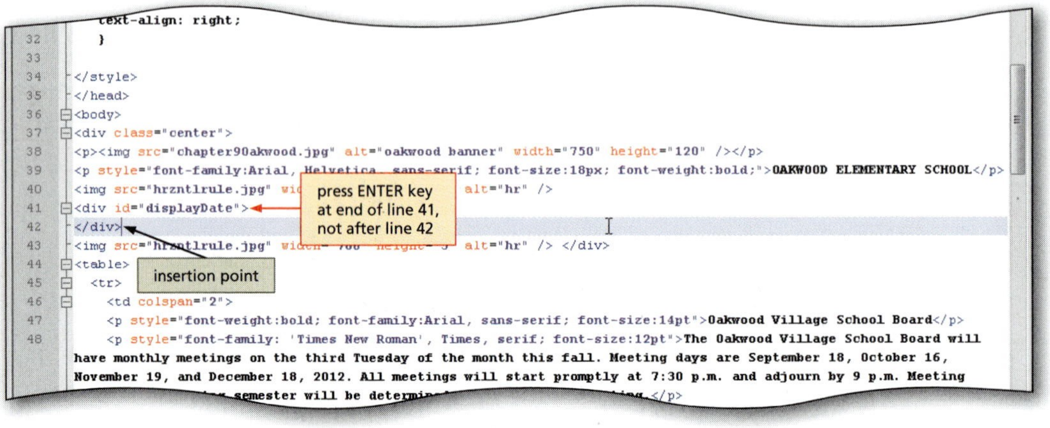

```
    text-align: right;
32      }
33
34  </style>
35  </head>
36  <body>
37  <div class="center">
38  <p><img src="chapter9Oakwood.jpg" alt="oakwood banner" width="750" height="120" /></p>
39  <p style="font-family:Arial, Helvetica, sans-serif; font-size:18px; font-weight:bold;">OAKWOOD ELEMENTARY SCHOOL</p>
40  <img src="hrzntlrule.jpg" wi                alt="hr" />
41  <div id="displayDate">
42  </div>
43  <img src="hrzntlrule.jpg" wi                alt="hr" /> </div>
44  <table>
45    <tr>
46      <td colspan="2">
47      <p style="font-weight:bold; font-family:Arial, sans-serif; font-size:14pt">Oakwood Village School Board</p>
48      <p style="font-family: 'Times New Roman', Times, serif; font-size:12pt">The Oakwood Village School Board will
have monthly meetings on the third Tuesday of the month this fall. Meeting days are September 18, October 16,
November 19, and December 18, 2012. All meetings will start promptly at 7:30 p.m. and adjourn by 9 p.m. Meeting
... semester will be determi... </p>
```

press ENTER key at end of line 41, not after line 42

insertion point

Figure 9–3

> **BTW**
> **Placing JavaScript Functions in the <head> Section**
> Always place your JavaScript functions in the <head> section to ensure they are loaded completely before they are called.

Writing User-Defined Functions

User-defined functions are normally written in the <head> section so that this code is loaded before the remainder of the Web page. The user-defined functions in the Oakwood Elementary School Web page do the following:

- Calculate and display the number of days until Columbus Day.
- Change the color of the scroll bar to match the Web page colors.
- Display the date the Web page was last modified.
- Use the <option> tag values in a <select> list as a drop-down menu linking to other Web pages.

The code in the user-defined function in the <head> section is not executed until a JavaScript statement calls or invokes the function. To call a function means to invoke or execute the function. The general form of a user-defined function is shown in Table 9–4.

Table 9–4 User-Defined Functions

General form:	function functionName(optional parameters) {
	JavaScript Code
	}

Comment:	where functionName is the name of the user-defined function, the optional parameters represent values or properties passed to the function that will be used by the function in the JavaScript code. JavaScript Code is the statements that execute.

Examples:	function showBrowserName() {
	alert("You are using" +navigator.appname)
	}
	function getSum(myform) {
	var sum= document.Calculator.Amount1.value+document.Calculator.Amount2.value
	}

Table 9–5 shows the naming conventions for a function name with valid and invalid examples. A function name must begin with a letter or an underscore; it may contain numerals, but may not contain any spaces, punctuation (such as periods or commas), or reserved words. Values or parameters are passed to the function by placing a variable name between the parentheses.

Table 9–5 Valid Function Names

Rule	Valid Function Names	Invalid Function Names
Must Start with a letter or underscore	verifyForm() _3Ddisplay()	3Ddisplay()
No periods allowed or other punctuation allowed	get_Cookie()	make.cookie() valid,form()
No spaces allowed	calcPayment()	calc payment()
No hyphens allowed	popWind() pop_Wind()	pop-upWindow()

Plan Ahead

To display a message with the current date and the number of days until a specific future date, you must:

- **Create the <script> section in the <head> section**. In this project, the <script> sections will be placed in the <head> section.
- **Define variables**. A set of variables must be defined to work with the system date to calculate the number of days from today to Columbus Day.
- **Calculate the number of days until Columbus Day**. To calculate the number of days to Columbus Day, you write code to subtract the current date from the future date.
- **Display a message string**. Use the innerHTML property to place the message to the Web page.
- **Close the <script> section**. All HTML tags must have a closing tag. If you fail to close the <script> section, you will have undesired results.
- Add the event handlers to call the function to display a dynamic message when the Web page loads.

Inserting <script> Tags in the <head> Section

Although JavaScript code can be placed anywhere in the HTML code in a <script> section, developers follow the coding practice and place user-defined functions and variables in the <head> section. Placing the JavaScript code in the <head> section ensures that all the JavaScript is loaded and interpreted before the user can begin using the Web page.

In this chapter, you use only JavaScript features that work in the latest versions of Microsoft Internet Explorer. JavaScript sections always start with a <script> tag, which indicates the language being used. Similar to other HTML tags, the JavaScript <script> tag has a start <script> tag and an end </script> tag.

The general form of the script tag is shown in Table 9–6 on the next page. The <script> tag supports several attributes, including src, type, and defer. In the past, the start <script> tag was written as <script language="JavaScript">, but, as noted in the Table 9–6 example, the preferred style is to use the type attribute. If the type or language attribute is omitted, most browsers default to JavaScript.

The <!-- HTML comment line after the <script> tag is used to hide the JavaScript code in the event a browser does not recognize the JavaScript code. Like all other HTML tags, it must be closed.

BTW

Script Sections
Many Web developers recommend inserting the start <script> tag and the end </script> tag immediately as the Web page is modified or constructed. The important rule to remember is that a complete set of <script> tags must be included, both <script> and </script>.

BTW

HTML Comments within JavaScript
Within a <script> section, an HTML comment often is added to hide the JavaScript from old browsers. The HTML comment is a tag that begins with <!-- and ends with -->. If you fail to close the HTML comment properly in the <script> section, it could hide the remainder of your Web page and it will not be visible in the browser.

Table 9–6 JavaScript Section

General form:	<script src="url" type="content-type" language="language" defer>
Comments:	where script is the script tag, src specifies the location of an external script URL, type indicates the content-type or specific scripting language, language is a deprecated attribute, and defer is a Boolean attribute that indicates whether the script is going to generate any document content. The type attribute is supported by the XHTML and XML standards. The src, language, and defer attributes are optional.
Example:	<script type="text/javascript"> <!- -Hide from old browsers miscellaneous JavaScript code //--> </script>

To Enter the Start <script> and Comment Tags

The following step illustrates how to enter the <script> and HTML comment tags.

- In the Notepad++ file chapter9-1.html, click line 9 (a blank line).
- Type `<script type="text/javascript">` as the beginning of the script and then press the ENTER key.
- Type `<!--Hide from old browsers` and then press the ENTER key to put the insertion point on line 11 (Figure 9–4).

```
3       "http://www.w3.org/TR/xhtml1/DTD/xhtml1-transitional.dtd">
4
5   <html xmlns="http://www.w3.org/1999/xhtml">
6   <head>
7   <meta http-equiv="Content-type" content
8   <title>Oakwood Elementary School</title
9   <script type="text/javascript">
10  <!--Hide from old browsers
11
12  <style
13  .center {
14      text-align:center;
15      }
16
17  table {
18      margin-left:15%;
19      margin-right:15%;
20      }
21  .cell-width {
```

code to begin JavaScript section embedded in body of HTML code and end </script> and comment tags will be entered when script section code is completed
insertion point

Figure 9–4

Q&A

Why is a > character not included on the HTML comment line?

Because the comment does not actually end until after the JavaScript code that you do not want to display in an older browser. The end comment tag (//-->) follows the JavaScript code. When the browser sees the > character, it treats that character as the end of the comment.

BTW

JavaScript Comments
Comments can be added to JavaScript in two ways. The double slash [//] is used to indicate a comment for a single line. To comment multiple lines with a script, begin the comment with a slash and asterisk [/*] and place an asterisk and slash [*/] to end the comment lines.

Using JavaScript Variables

As in other programming languages, JavaScript uses variables to store values temporarily in internal memory. A variable's value can change, depending on the results of an expression or data entered by a user from a form. Variables must have a unique name, and must follow the same naming conventions as user-defined functions. JavaScript variable names are case sensitive, which means the variable name months is different from the variable name Months. Table 9–7 shows the rules with valid and invalid variable name examples.

Table 9–7 Naming Conventions for JavaScript Variables

Rule	Valid Name Examples	Invalid Name Examples
Name must begin with a letter or underscore	menu	$menu
Rest of name must be letters, numerals, or underscores	Last_Name	Last-name
Name may not use spaces, hyphens, or punctuation	ZipCode	zip.code or zip code
Name may not contain JavaScript objects, properties, and reserved words	xNow	Date

JavaScript variables are considered global, unless the variable is defined within a user-defined function, in which case it is considered a local variable. **Global** means that the variable value is available for use anywhere inside the HTML file Web page. To define a variable as global, it must be declared in the <script> section before any of the user-defined functions. **Local** means that the variable's value is available only in the function in which it is defined.

A variable's **data type**, the type of data it stores, such as text or numbers, must be known so the computer knows how to store and manipulate the data. JavaScript has four data types: numeric, string, date, or Boolean. **Numeric data types** hold numbers. **String data types** are variables that hold characters or a combination of letters, numbers, or symbols. **Date data types** contain a date and time. **Boolean data types** contain logical data that can be one of two values, such as True/False or Yes/No.

BTW

Undefined Variables
If a variable's value, which has not been defined or declared previously, is used or displayed on the Web page, JavaScript assigns the value "undefined" to that variable. An undefined variable can cause errors in mathematical calculations.

JavaScript variables are **loosely typed**, which means they do not have to be assigned an initial specific data type as in other programming languages. Instead, JavaScript defines the data type by declaring the variable with an initial value. This feature allows variables to be flexible and store any data type. Web developers, however, do not recommend changing a variable's data type in the middle of JavaScript code. This action may create an error, which can be very difficult to find. Table 9–8 shows the general form of declaring a variable and assigning a value to it.

Table 9–8 Assigning Values to Variables

General form:	var variableName=value
Comment:	where var is an optional keyword to designate a variable; variableName is a valid variable name; and value is the string, numeric, date, or Boolean value being assigned to the variable
Examples:	var NickName="Jasper" // This variable is a string data type var lineCnt=1 // This variable is a numeric data type var Continue=false // This variable is a Boolean data type

In the examples in Table 9–8, the keyword var, meaning variable, appears before the variable name. A **keyword**, or **reserved word**, is a word with special meaning in a programming language. The JavaScript var keyword is optional for global variables; however, it is good programming practice to precede the variable name with the var keyword the first time it is defined. In addition, the var keyword is required for local variables defined within a function.

Plan Ahead

For the dynamic greeting on the home page, you need to calculate the number of days between two dates. First, you must extract information about the current date using the following steps:

- Obtain the current system date with the Date() object and create a new object instance.
- Use the toLocaleString() method to convert the date to a string to be manipulated.
- Use the indexOf() method to find the space between the month and the day of the week to extract the month.
- Use the substring() method to extract the day of the week from the string.
- Use the substring() method to extract the remainder of the date from the string.
- Use the indexOf() method to locate the position of the year in the string.
- Use the substring() method to extract the day of the week.
- Use the substring() method to extract the current year.
- Use the substr() method to extract the year from the string.

Extracting the Current System Date

The built-in Date() object accesses the current system date and time. On the Oakwood Elementary School Web page, the Date() object and several of its methods are used to extract the current system date and then display it on the Web page as part of the greeting.

To manipulate the Date() object, a new object instance must be created. Table 9–9 shows the general form of the JavaScript statement to create a new object instance, which uses the new keyword and assigns the built-in object to a variable. This variable is referred to as an **object instance variable**.

BTW — Date() Object
The Date() object can use three other methods to build a string for a current date: getDate(), getMonth(), or getFullYear(). The getDate() method returns the date in the month; getMonth() returns the value of the month as a number from 0 to 11 with 0 representing January; and the getFullYear() method returns the four digit year. Because the getMonth() method returns an integer that represents the month, the developer must add 1 to the result to get the current month.

Table 9–9 Creating a New Object Instance

General form:	var variableName=new Builtin_Object
Comments:	where variableName is the name of the new object instance, new is the required keyword, and Builtin_Object is the name of the object from which the new object instance is to be created
Examples:	var sysDate=new Date() var sysDate=new Date("October 8, 2012")

The Date() object allows developers to enter a specific date and time other than the current system date and time. The first example shown in Table 9–9 has no specific date value provided, thus the current system date and time from the computer is stored in the variable sysDate. The second example in Table 9–9 has a specific date value enclosed within quotation marks inside the parentheses. That value, October 8, 2012, is assigned to the object instance variable sysDate.

BTW — Extracting the System Date
The results in extracting the Date are based upon the how the system date is stored. Individual users and other countries may use different computer settings. The default display is: Day Month Date, Year HH:MM:SS AM/PM.

Converting the System Date to a String To use the date and time value stored in the variable sysDate, the variable first must be converted to a string using the toLocaleString() method. Table 9–10 shows the general form of the toLocaleString() method.

Table 9–10 toLocaleString() Method

General form:	var variable=dateString.toLocaleString()
Comment:	where dateString is an object instance and the toLocaleString() method converts an object instance of the Date() to a string using the default display format used on the client computer
Example:	var curDate=sysDate.toLocaleString()
Result:	curDate contains the date and time stored as: Day of the Week, Month, Date, Year HH:MM:SS

Once the current system date has been converted to a string, the JavaScript indexOf(), substring(), and substr() methods can be used to extract the day of the week, the month, date, the year, and the hours (HH), minutes (MM), and seconds (SS) to be displayed on the Web page.

Using the indexOf() Method Table 9–11 explains how the indexOf() method searches a string for a particular value, which is enclosed within the quotation marks, and then returns the relative location of the parameter value within the string. If the search finds the value in the search string object, the indexOf() method returns the relative position of the value within the string object. If the search value is not found, the indexOf() method returns a negative one (–1).

BTW

IndexOf() Method
Using the IndexOf() method, items in a select list are indexed in the order in which they appear in the list. The first item is indexed as 0 (zero). Set the selectedIndex property to 0 (zero) to clear any existing selected items.

Table 9–11 indexOf() Method

General form:	var position=stringValue.indexOf("x")
Comment:	where stringValue is a string in which a search is conducted, x is the value to be searched for within the stringValue, and position is the location of x in the string. The value x must be a literal value.
Examples:	curDate="October 8, 2012" dateLocate=curDate.indexOf(",")
Result:	returns the relative position of the comma found in the string value of curDate: 9

BTW

Using the Current Year in IndexOf()
When extracting the system date and comparing it to another day, the date you search for in the system Date in the IndexOf() method must match the current year, or you will received incorrect results.

Using the substring() Method to Extract the Month from a String The substring() method uses two parameters (x,y), where x is the starting point of the string and y is the location of the last character needed. If only an x parameter is given, the substring() method returns all the characters starting at that position through the end of the string. Table 9–12 describes the general form of the substring() method.

Table 9–12 substring() Method

General form:	var variable=string.substring(x,y)
Comment:	where string is any string object. The substring method extracts a portion of a string, starting at location x and ending at location y. x and y may be constants or variables.
Example:	weekDay=dayofweek.substring(0, dateLocate)
Result:	the variable weekDay contains the substring

Using the substr() Method Table 9–13 on the next page describes the substr() method. The substr() method is similar to the substring() method, in that it extracts part of a string. Although the methods perform similar functions in JavaScript, they differ in how they use parameter values. The substring() method uses the exact byte locations in a string to extract part of the string between the x and y locations, whereas the substr() method uses a length value to extract y number of characters starting at x location.

Table 9–13 substr() Method

General form:	var variable=string.substr(x,y)
Comment:	where string is any string object instance. This method extracts a portion of a string, starting at location x for a length of y. x and y may be constants or variables.

Example:	var dayofweek = today.toLocaleString() //Converts date into string as: Day, Month Date, Year HH:MM:SS AM/PM
	year=dayofweek.substr(yearLocate, 4)

Result:	the variable year contains the four-digit year

Both the substring() and substr() methods use relative addressing as a means of locating characters in a string. A **relative address** is the location of a byte in a string of bytes, as defined by its position relative to the first byte in that string. As an example, assume the data in Table 9–14 is a string value stored in the variable birthDay. The address of the first byte in a string of characters is zero (0). To extract the year 2012 from the string using the substring() method, the JavaScript code would be written as:

```
birthDay.substring(17,20)
```

Table 9–14 Relative Addressing

F	r	i	d	a	y	,		M	a	r	c	h		9	,		2	0	1	2
0	1	2	3	4	5	6	7	8	9	10	11	12	13	14	15	16	17	18	19	20

Table 9–15 shows the JavaScript code used to extract the system date for the Oakwood Elementary School Web page. The JavaScript code uses the toLocaleString(), substr(), substring(), and indexOf() methods of the Date() object to obtain the current system date and then extract the weekday, the date, the month, and the year. Once these values have been extracted and assigned to variables, they can be displayed on the Web page.

Table 9–15 Code to Extract the System Date

Line	Code
11	`function countDown() {`
12	`    var today = new Date()`
13	`    var dayofweek = today.toLocaleString()`
14	`    dayLocate = dayofweek.indexOf(" ")`
15	`    weekDay = dayofweek.substring(0, dayLocate)`
16	`    newDay = dayofweek.substring(dayLocate)`
17	`    dateLocate = newDay.indexOf(",")`
18	`    monthDate = newDay.substring(0, dateLocate+1)`
19	`    yearLocate = dayofweek.indexOf("2012")`
20	`    year = dayofweek.substr(yearLocate, 4)`

Line 11 starts the JavaScript function, countDown(). The function must include the open brace. Line 12 creates the new date object instance variable, today, and assigns the current system date and time to the variable. Line 13 converts the date and time value stored in the today variable to a string, using the toLocaleString() method and assigns it to the dayofweek variable. To find the day of the week in the string, the indexOf() method in line 14 looks for the first blank space in the string. Line 15 uses the substring() method to extract the day of the week, while line 16 extracts the remainder of the string, which includes the month, day, year, and time. Line 17 looks for the comma that separates the date from the year using the indexOf() method. Using the address of the comma, the substring() method in line 18 extracts the date. To find the year, line 19 uses the indexOf() method and the current year to determine the starting address of the year. When inserting the date at line 19, you must use the current year. Line 20 uses the substr() method, using the starting address from the indexOf() method and length of the year, which is four characters long.

To Extract the Current System Date Using the Date() Object

This step illustrates how to write JavaScript code that uses the Date() object and its methods to extract the current system date.

- If necessary, activate the Notepad++ window.
- If necessary, click line 11 below the <!--Hide from old browsers statement.
- Enter the JavaScript code shown in Table 9–15, indenting as shown. Press ENTER at the end of each complete line of code. If the current year is different from 2012, replace 2012 with the current year in the indexOf() method on line 19.
- After typing the last line in Table 9–15, press the ENTER key twice to leave space for additional JavaScript code.

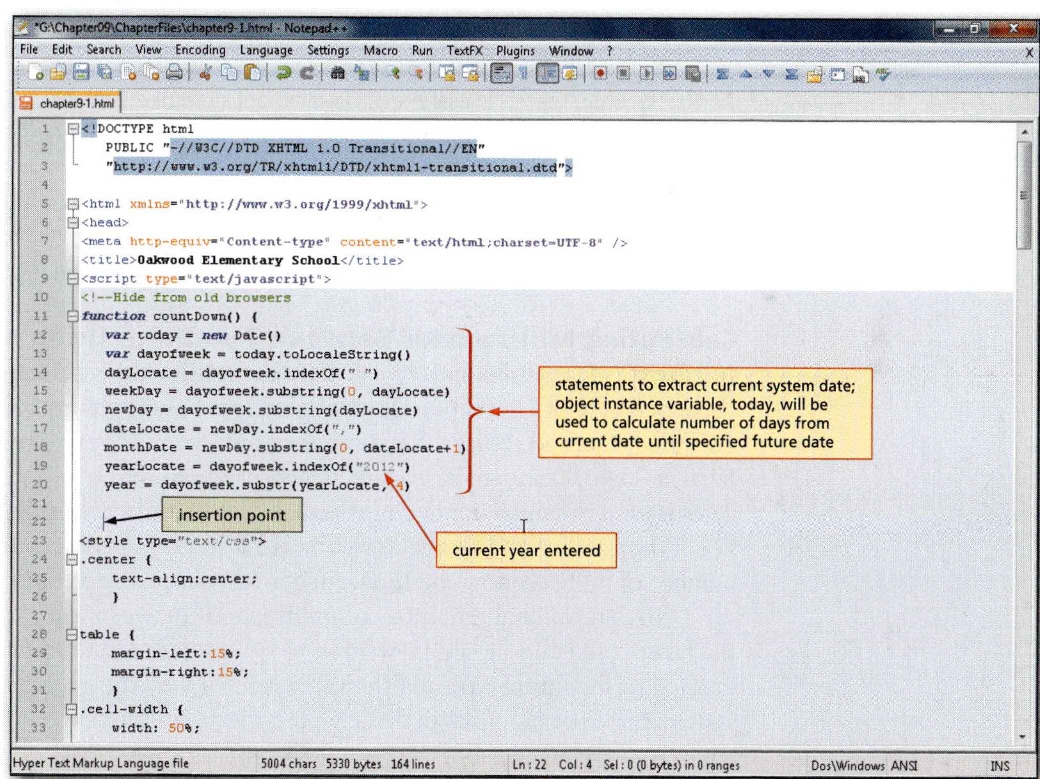

Figure 9–5

- Compare what you typed to Figure 9–5. Correct any errors before proceeding.

Q&A

Why is some of the code in Figure 9–5 indented?

The code is indented with the SPACEBAR for ease of reading. It does not affect the execution of the code. You may want to indent sections of code to make it easier to identify.

Q&A

What happens if a different year is entered in the indexOf() method than what is in the system?

The year will never match and JavaScript returns unknown results, but not as an error message.

Plan Ahead

The steps required to calculate a future date for a dynamic greeting include:

- Create a Date() object instance with the future date and the current date.
- Use the getTime() method on the current and future date, calculate the milliseconds between the current date and the future date by subtracting the current getTime() date from the future getTime() date.
- Convert the number of milliseconds to days using the Math.ceil() method to round up to the next integer.

Calculating the Number of Days Until a Future Event

Calculating the number of days until a future date can be useful for a dynamic greeting. With the Oakwood Elementary School Web page, each time users view the Web page in a browser, the Web page displays a greeting that notifies them of the number of days until Columbus Day.

Creating a Date() Object Instance to Store a Future Date To calculate the number of days until a future date, an object instance of the Date() object must be created using the future date. As previously discussed, the Date() object can have a specific literal date as a value, which is assigned to an object instance variable. For example, the JavaScript code to set the date to Columbus Day, which is October 8, 2012, is written as follows:

```
var ColumbusDay = new Date("October 8, 2012")
```

The object instance variable ColumbusDay now will contain the future date of October 8, 2012.

Calculating Milliseconds Between Two Dates Using the getTime() Method The next step is to calculate the milliseconds between the current date and the actual date of Columbus Day using the getTime() method of the Date() object. The getTime() method returns the number of milliseconds that have elapsed since January 1, 1970 at 00:00:00 and another date. Calculating the number of milliseconds between two dates is easier than trying to count actual days because each month has a different number of days and it may be necessary to take leap years into account. After determining the number of milliseconds, you then can convert that value to days.

To determine the number of milliseconds between a current date and another date, the JavaScript code should be written to subtract the value returned by the getTime() method of the future date and the value returned by the getTime() method of the current system date. For example, in this chapter, the JavaScript code is written as follows:

```
var daysToGo = ColumbusDay.getTime()-today.getTime()
```

where the variable daysToGo will contain the number of milliseconds between the future date and the current system date.

Converting Milliseconds to Days and Rounding Up Using the ceil() Method After calculating the number of milliseconds between the current date and Columbus Day, the next step is to convert the milliseconds to days. To convert milliseconds to days, the JavaScript code is written to divide the number of milliseconds stored in the daysToGo variable by the product of 1000*60*60*24. This expression represents the 1,000 milliseconds in a second, the 60 seconds in a minute, the 60 minutes in an hour, and the 24 hours in a day.

The value returned from the calculation daysToGo/(1000*60*60*24) probably will contain a decimal value. The Oakwood Elementary School Web page, however, should display the number of days to Columbus Day as an integer value. The ceil() method of the Math object is used to round up to the nearest integer (for example, if the result is 12.843 days, 13 will display because of the ceil() method). The general form of the ceil() method is shown in Table 9–16.

Table 9–16 Math ceil() Method

General form:	var variable=ceil(value)
Comment:	where value may be the result of any calculation. The ceil() method returns a value that rounds the value up to the next highest integer.
Examples:	var myResult=ceil(–3.8) var myNumber=ceil(4.179)
Result:	myResult is –3 myNumber is 5

The JavaScript code for the Oakwood Elementary School Web page is written as follows:

```
var daysToColumbusDay = Math.ceil(daysToGo/(1000*60*60*24))
```

which first finds the product of 1000*60*60*24, then divides the value stored in the daysToGo variable by this product, and then raises the result (rounds up) to the next highest integer.

To Calculate the Number of Days to a Future Date

The code to calculate the number of days to a future date is shown in Table 9–17. Line 22 creates the ColumbusDay object from the future date of Columbus Day in 2012. Line 23 subtracts the number of milliseconds of the current date (today.getTime()) from the future date (ColumbusDay.getTime()). Line 24 converts the number of milliseconds to days.

Table 9–17 Code to Calculate the Number of Days to Columbus Day

Line	Code
22	`var ColumbusDay = new Date("October 8, 2012")`
23	`var daysToGo = ColumbusDay.getTime()-today.getTime()`
24	`var daysToColumbusDay = Math.ceil(daysToGo/(1000*60*60*24))`

The step on the next page illustrates how to enter the code to calculate the number of days to Columbus Day.

1

- If necessary, click line 22.
- Enter the JavaScript code shown in Table 9–17 on the previous page. Enter the current year's Columbus Day date in line 22, if necessary. Press ENTER at the end of each complete line of code.

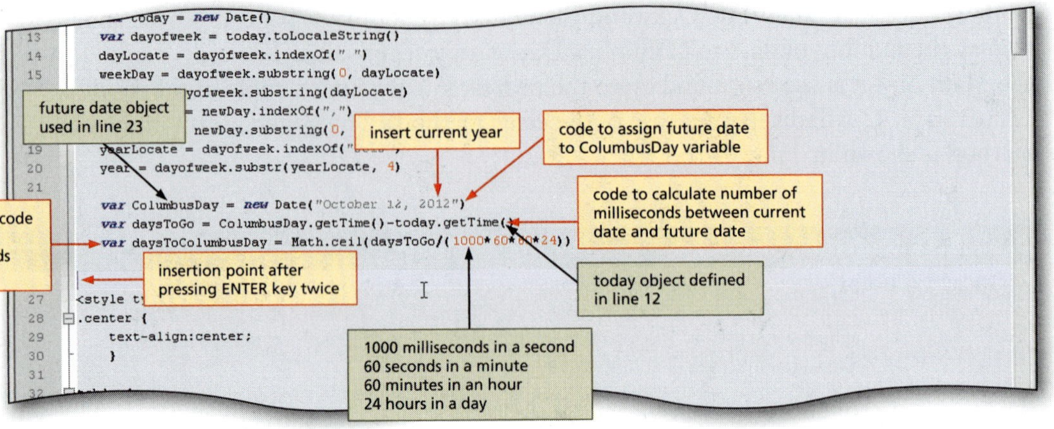

Figure 9–6

- After typing the last line in Table 9–17, press the ENTER key twice (Figure 9–6).
- Compare what you typed to Figure 9–6. Correct any errors before proceeding.

Q&A

Can a date only be entered as "October 8, 2012" in the Date() object?

The date can be entered as 2012, 9, 8 in the Date object. Because the Date() object starts numbering the months with 0, that means October is 9.

Plan Ahead

Using JavaScript to write dynamic text to a Web page.
Before writing dynamic text to a Web page, you need to determine what your message will say and how you will format it for display. Most messages will be a combination of text strings and variables. Text can be formatted using standard HTML tags or using embedded styles. Embedded styles can be placed in <p> or <span> tags to format text.

BTW

JavaScript Strings
The recommended maximum length of a string is 256 characters or bytes. This limit is based on a limit of older browsers.

Displaying Text and Variable Values to a Web Page with innerHTML

After the number of days until Columbus Day has been calculated, this data can be written on the Web page using JavaScript. To write data directly to the Web page, JavaScript can use the write() or writeln() methods of the document object. These methods, however, will not be useful in user-defined functions located in the <head> section. Instead, to display text at a specific location, developers use the innerHTML property in association with the id value of a <div> tag container. Table 9–18 shows the general form of the innerHTML property.

BTW

JavaScript writeln() Method
The writeln() method works only in HTML tags that either are sensitive to the new line character ("/n") or the carriage return, line feed, such as the <textarea> tag.

Table 9–18 innerHTML Property

General form:	tag_id.innerHTML="text string"
Comment:	where tag_id Is the Id attribute of a designated container tag, and text string is any combination of HTML tags, text, and variables
Examples:	displayDate.innerHTML = "Today is "+weekDay+" "+monthDate+" "+year+". We have "+daysToColumbusDay+" days until Columbus Day."

To display the contents of a variable as part of a text string, JavaScript can concatenate text and variables to create a seamless string of characters. Concatenate means to join or link together. The symbol for concatenation is the plus sign (+).

To Display Text and Variable Values to a Web Page Using innerHTML

Table 9–19 shows the code to write a simple welcome message that concatenates text with the values stored in several variables. In line 26, the innerHTML property is used to place data directly to a Web page in the <div> tag container. The text message string encloses the HTML tags in quotation marks within the text message string. The plus sign (+) concatenates the three variables weekDay, monthDate, and year together, along with the text message and variable daysToColumbusDay. Placement of quotation marks is important and you must include closing HTML tags. Line 27 is the closing brace for the countDown() user-defined function.

Table 9–19 Code to Write a Message to the Web Page

Line	Code
26	`displayDate.innerHTML = "<h3>Today is "+weekDay+" "+monthDate+" "+year+". We have "+daysToColumbusDay+" days until Columbus Day.</h3>"`
27	`}`

The following step illustrates how to display text and variables using the innerHTML property.

1

- Click line 26, if necessary.
- Enter the JavaScript code shown in Table 9–19 to create the message text with the stored values. Press the ENTER key only at the end of each complete line of code.
- Press the ENTER key once more after the last } in Table 9–19 to leave a blank line between user-defined functions (Figure 9–7).

Figure 9–7

Q&A Can the innerHTML property be used for anything else?

The innerHTML property can retrieve the contents of any tag that has an id attribute. The id attribute values must be unique for each tag.

Q&A How does JavaScript know to concatenate instead of add when it sees the plus sign (+)?

When the JavaScript interpreter identifies the values surrounding a plus sign (+) and they are not numeric values, it will attempt to join them together.

Plan Ahead

Changing the color of the browser scroll bar.

The scroll bar color can be changed with a JavaScript user-defined function. To change the scroll bar color, follow these guidelines:

- JavaScript must have access to the object (the scroll bar). Use the getElementsByTagName() method of the document object to assign the "HTML" object to a variable. The getElementsByTagName() method returns an array of elements belonging to the identified object and all associated properties to that object.
- Using the variable as an object, JavaScript can set values to the various scroll bar properties: FaceColor, ArrowColor, HighlightColor, 3DlightColor, DarkshadowColor, TrackColor, and ShadowColor.
- Assign a color that matches or complements the colors on the Web page to at least the FaceColor and TrackColor.

BTW

Color Values

For the most flexibility in using colors, Web developers suggest using either the hexadecimal version or the rgb() method version to assign a color. Be careful in using a standard color name. Color names like "lightblueaqua" may not be recognized by the style property.

Changing the Color of the Browser Scroll Bar

Currently, cascading style sheets (CSS) do not have an official standard style for changing colors of the browser scroll bar that is recognized by all browsers. To modify the scroll bar, JavaScript needs to know the object so it can assign new style values. The getElementsByTagName() method will identify the scroll bar object for JavaScript. Table 9–20 shows the general form of the getElementsByTagName() method.

Table 9–20 getElementsByTagName() Method

General form:	document.getElementsByTagName('html')
Comments:	where getElementsByTagName() is a method of the document object and 'html' is the object to be returned. Tag element must be entered as a string in single quotation marks and is case sensitive. The returning values are returned in an array format, so that each element can be referenced individually by an array value. The returned value also can use any properties associated with that value. The example shows the method to create an object of the html tag styles named styleObject.
Example:	styleObject=document.getElementsByTagName('html')[0].style

BTW

CSS and Scroll Bars

Not all browsers support the CSS scroll bar color attributes. Internet Explorer, however, will modify the scroll bar properties using JavaScript and the getElementsByTag method associated with the <html> tag.

To modify the colors of the scroll bar, use the styleObject object name with the standard scroll bar properties: FaceColor, ArrowColor, HighlightColor, 3DlightColor, DarkshadowColor, TrackColor, and ShadowColor. For example, to change the FaceColor of the scroll bar write

```
styleObject.scrollbarFaceColor="#006600"
```

where the color must be written as a standard color name, a hexadecimal value, or defined by using the rgb() values method.

On the Oakwood Elementary School Web page, the scroll bar colors should be changed so the scroll bar is orange and the scroll bar track is yellow.

To Enter the User-Defined Function to Change the Browser Scroll Bar Color

Table 9–21 shows the code to change the scroll bar colors. Line 29 defines the function as scrollColor(). Line 30 defines the style property of the <html> tag and assigns it to an object, so face color and track color can be changed in lines 31 and 32. Line 31 changes the color of the scroll bar face to orange using a hexadecimal value. Line 32 changes the scroll bar track color to yellow using a hexadecimal value. Line 33 closes the scrollColor() function.

Table 9–21 Code to Change the Browser Scroll Bar Color

Line	Code
29	`function scrollColor() {`
30	`  styleObject=document.getElementsByTagName('html')[0].style`
31	`  styleObject.scrollbarFaceColor="#fbb040"`
32	`  styleObject.scrollbarTrackColor="#ffe700"`
33	`}`

The following step illustrates how to enter the user-defined function to change the browser scroll bar color in the <head> section.

- If necessary, click blank line 29.
- Enter the JavaScript code shown in Table 9–21.
- Press the ENTER key twice after the last } to leave a blank line between user-defined functions (Figure 9–8).

Figure 9–8

Plan Ahead

Using the select list as a drop-down menu.

To use a <select> list as a drop-down menu, a user-defined function must make use of the following:

- The window's location property (window.location), to which a URL can be assigned, and which changes the location of the Web page in the browser.
- The selectedIndex property to identify which item was selected in the drop-down menu list.

Using the Location Object and selectedIndex Property to Link to a New URL

As shown in Figure 9–1 on page HTML 411, the Oakwood Elementary School Web page also includes a drop-down list that allows users to select items from a drop-down menu. Depending on the item selected in the select list, the code will link users to one of three Web pages containing information about the October fundraiser, the October PTO meeting, or the state achievement test.

When a user selects an item in the select list, the selectedIndex property of the select list returns the value of the selected item. The selectedIndex values of the items in a select list are considered to be numbered, starting with zero for the first item. The second

BTW

The selectedIndex Property

The selectedIndex property cannot be used alone; it must be used in full reference to the particular select list, the form it belongs to, and its options.

item is number one, and so on. The value returned by the selectedIndex property is an integer, starting with zero for the first item in the list. Table 9–22 shows the general form of the selectedIndex property.

Table 9–22 selectedIndex Property

General form:	var varname=formName.SelectListName.selectedIndex
Comments:	where varname is a variable, formName is the identifier of the form that holds the select list, SelectListName is the name of the select list, and selectedIndex is a property that returns an integer corresponding to the position of the item in the list
Example:	var menuSelect=myForm.Menu.selectedIndex

As you learned in earlier chapters, the text that appears for each item in a select list is enclosed in <option> tags. The option tag also supports a value attribute, as shown in the code in Figure 9–9. The value in the value attribute describes the item and can be assigned to a variable.

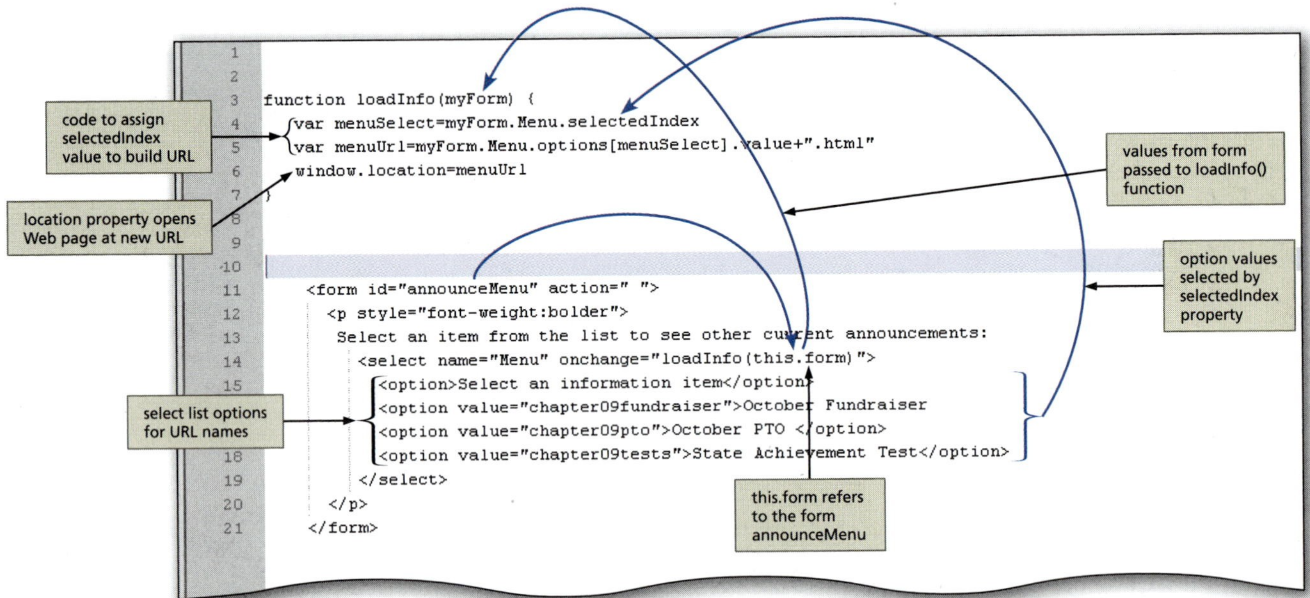

Figure 9–9

This variable can then be used to assign the new Web page location to the window's location property. This statement will load a new URL into the browser. Table 9–23 shows the general form of the location property.

Table 9–23 Location Property

General form:	object=window.location or window.location=URL
Comments:	where object is a variable or some other object that can display the URL of the current window, and URL is the address of the Web page to display. The use of the window object is optional.
Examples:	myform.textbox.value=window.location window.location="http://www.scsite.com"

Table 9–24 shows the JavaScript code for a loadInfo() function that uses the selected Index value to determine which item in a list was selected, assigns the value attribute for that item, and then uses that variable to create a URL.

Table 9–24 Code to Change Location

Line	Code
35	`function loadInfo(myForm) {`
36	`var menuSelect=myForm.Menu.selectedIndex`
37	`var menuUrl=myForm.Menu.options[menuSelect].value+".html"`
38	`window.location=menuUrl`
39	`}`

The selectedIndex property then is used on the object name of the select list and the form. Line 35 defines the function name. The form object, myForm, is passed to the function from the select list name attribute. In line 36, the selectedIndex statement assigns the numerical value of the item selected from the list to the variable menuSelect. In this line, menuSelect is a variable name, myForm is the identifier of the form that holds the select list, and Menu is the name of the select list. The options property of Menu refers to the <option> tag in the select list, while selectedIndex indicates the integer value of the item selected in the select list. Line 37 concatenates the value attribute of the selected item (menuSelect) with the file extension .html to create a URL. The URL name is concatenated to the .html file name extension using the plus sign (+). Line 38 uses that URL to load that Web page into the browser window. Line 39 closes the function.

To Enter the User-Defined Function to Link to a New URL Using the Drop-Down Menu List

The following step illustrates how to enter the user-defined function to link to a new URL using the drop-down menu.

1

- Click line 35 if necessary.
- Enter the JavaScript code shown in Table 9–24 to enter the options and links for the drop-down menu list.
- Press the ENTER key twice after line 39 (Figure 9–10).

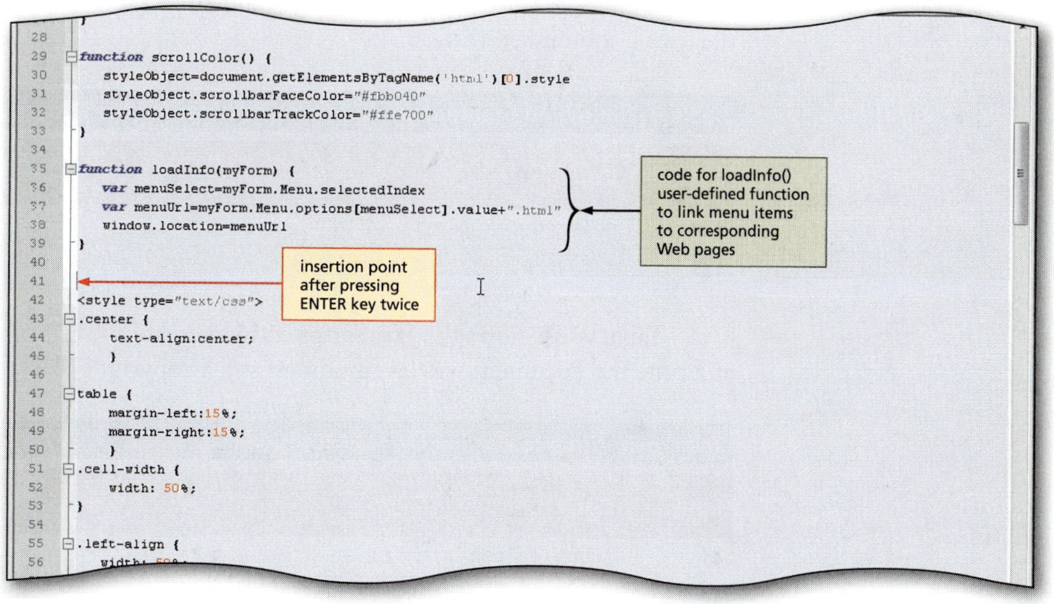

code for loadInfo() user-defined function to link menu items to corresponding Web pages

insertion point after pressing ENTER key twice

Figure 9–10

Plan Ahead

Writing the date last modified on the Web page.

The date the Web page was last modified indicates how current the information is. When writing this content, you should follow these guidelines:

- Determine what your message will be. Many Web pages display a copyright notice with the date last modified.
- Create a <div> tag container with the id displayCopyRight.
- Create a text message string enclosed in quotation marks and include the document.lastModified property with the text string.
- Use the innerHTML property to assign the message to the <div> tag container.

BTW

The .lastModified Property
The .lastModified property may return different values than expected with older browsers and unknown Web servers.

Displaying the Date the Document Was Last Modified

Most Web developers agree that a Web page should display the date the Web page was last modified, so visitors are aware of how current the Web page content is. For the Oakwood Elementary School Web page, the date last modified should appear at the bottom of the page in a smaller font to keep the message from distracting the user (see Figure 9–1 on page HTML 411).

JavaScript provides an easy way to display the date by using the lastModified property of the document object. The lastModified property displays the date in the form of mm/dd/yyyy followed by the time in the form of hh:mm:ss. Table 9–25 shows the general form of the lastModified property of the document.

Table 9–25 lastModified Property

General form:	document.lastModified
Comment:	where lastModified is a property of the document object that returns the date the document was last saved
Example:	var lastDateModified= document.lastModified

Table 9–26 shows the code to place the <div> tag container for the copyright and the date last modified text.

Table 9–26 Code to Create the <div> Tag Container for the Copyright and Date Last Modified

```
<div id="displayCopyRight">
</div>
```

Table 9–27 shows the JavaScript code to create a <script> section to display the date and time the document was last modified and a copyright message.

Table 9–27 Code to Display the lastModified Date

```
function copyRight() {
   var lastModDate = document.lastModified
   var lastModDate = lastModDate.substring(0,10)
   displayCopyRight.innerHTML = "<h6>The URL of this document is
   "+document.URL+"<br />Copyright Oakwood Elementary School"+"<br />
   This document was last modified "+lastModDate+".</h6>"
}
```

Line 41 defines the copyRight() function. Line 42 assigns the date the Web page was last modified and assigns it to a temporary variable, lastModDate. Line 43 uses the substring() method to extract the date portion only. Line 44 uses the innerHTML property to assign the message string to the <div> tag container. The document.URL displays the Web address of this document. Line 45 closes the function.

To Include the Date Last Modified and a Copyright Message in a Text String

The following steps show how to enter JavaScript code to include the date last modified and a copyright message in a text string.

- Scroll down and click line 124.
- Enter the JavaScript code In Table 9–26. Do not press the ENTER key after the last line.

```
108             <option value="chapter09fundraiser">October Fundraiser</option>
109             <option value="chapter09pto">October PTO </option>
110             <option value="chapter09tests">State Achievement Test</option>
111           </select>
112        </p>
113      </form></td>
114    </tr>
115    <tr>
116      <td colspan="2">
117      <p style="font-weight:bold; font-family:Arial, sans-serif; font-size:14pt">Attendance Policy:
118      <span style="font-family: 'Times New Roman', Times, serif; font-size:8pt">Please call in your child's
attendance at 555-555-5555 x2205.</span>
119      </p>
120      </td>
121    </tr>
122  </table>
123  <p></p>
124  <div id="displayCopyRight">
125  </div>
126  </body>
127  </html>
```


Figure 9–11

2

- Scroll up and click line 41.
- Enter the JavaScript code shown in Table 9–27.
- Press the ENTER key after each line, and press the ENTER key twice after the } in line 45 (Figure 9–12).

```
37      var menuUrl=myForm.Menu.options[menuSelect].value+".html"
38      window.location=menuUrl
39   }
40
41   function copyRight() {
42      var lastModDate = document.lastModified
43      var lastModDate = lastModDate.substring(0,10)
44      displayCopyRight.innerHTML = "<h6>The URL of this document is "+document.URL+"<br />Copyright Oakwood
Elementary School"+"<br />This document was last modified "+lastModDate+".</h6>"
45   }
46
47
48   <style type="text/css">
49   .center {
50      text-align:center;
51      }
52
53   table {
54      margin-left:15%;
55      margin-right:15%;
56      }
```


Figure 9–12

Completing the JavaScript Section

As you know, all HTML tags must have start and end tags to separate them from other page elements. To complete this section of JavaScript code, it is necessary to add the end comment tag and the end </script> tag.

To Enter the End Comment and End </script> Tags

Table 9–28 shows the code used to close the start <script> tag on line 9 and the start comment tag on line 10, as entered in Figure 9–4 on page HTML 418.

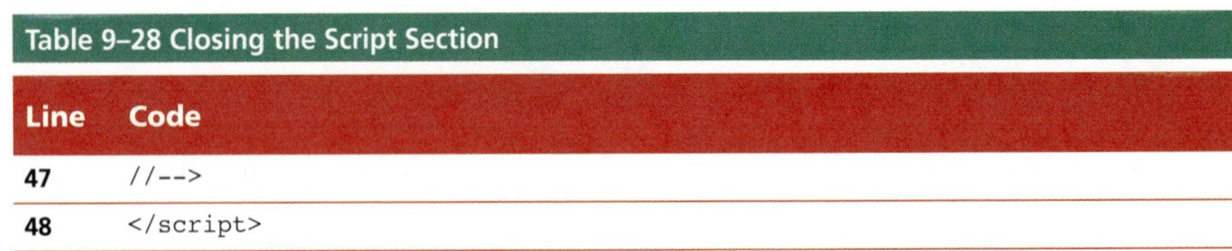

Table 9–28 Closing the Script Section

Line	Code
47	`//-->`
48	`</script>`

Line 47 ends the comment, <!--Hide from old browsers, that was started on line 10. If the HTML comment line is used and it is not closed properly, it will read the rest of the Web page document as part of the comment. The end </script> tag on line 48 ends the JavaScript code section and prevents the HTML code that follows from being interpreted as JavaScript code.

The following step shows how to enter the end comment tag and the end </script> tag.

- If necessary, click blank line 47.
- Enter the JavaScript code shown in Table 9–28 and do not press the ENTER key after the last line (Figure 9–13).

```
40
41 function copyRight() {
42    var lastModDate = document.lastModified
43    var lastModDate = lastModDate.substring(0,10)
44    displayCopyRight.innerHTML = "<h6>The URL of this document is "+document.URL+"<br />Copyright Oakwood
Elementary School"+"<br />This document was last modified "+lastModDate+".</h6>"
45 }
46
47 //-->
48 </script>
49 <style type="text/css">
50 .center {
51     text-align:center;
52     }
53
54 table {
55     margin-left:15%;
56     margin-right:15%;
57     }
```


Figure 9–13

Q&A What happens if a <script> section is not closed properly?

If the HTML comment line is used and it is not closed properly, the rest of the Web page document will be treated as a comment. When the user attempts to view the Web page, nothing will appear after that comment line.

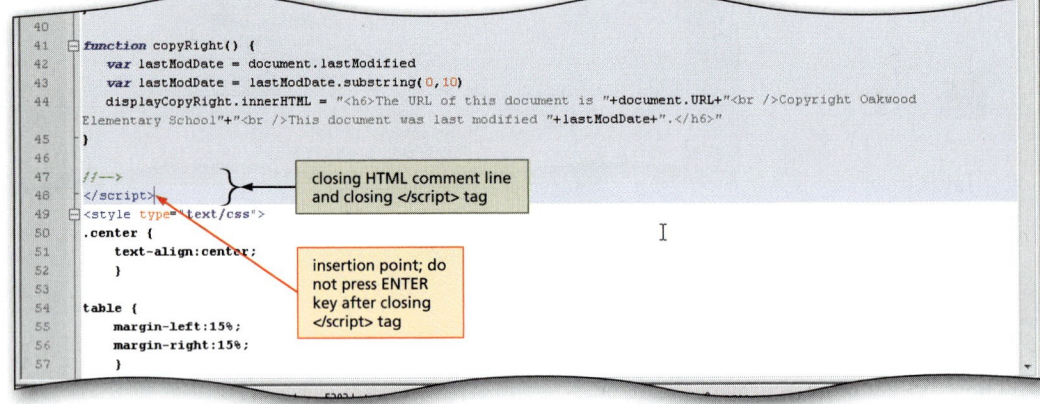

Q&A Why is the comment needed in <script> sections?

Some browsers or mobile Web devices do not interpret JavaScript code correctly, so the comment hides the JavaScript code. If the comment line is not closed properly, the Web page may not display from the point of the comment forward, thus giving the impression the Web page is blank. If this occurs, always check to ensure the end comment tag was included.

Plan Ahead

Using event handlers to call user-defined functions.
Event handlers must be placed with the object (such as a button, drop-down list, or HTML tag) that controls the event. In this chapter, the events are load and change, so you use the event handlers onload and onchange to call the user-defined functions. In this chapter, you will:

- Place the onload event handler in the <body> tag.
- Place the onchange event handler in the <select> tag that starts the drop-down menu list.

Calling JavaScript Functions Using Event Handlers

Now that you have added user-defined functions to count down to a certain date, changed the scroll bar color, created a drop-down menu list, and added the date last modified at the bottom of the page, you need to add code that calls these functions when the Web page is loaded. JavaScript has two basic methods to call functions. One method to call a function is to use event handlers and object methods. The other method is to code the function name in a JavaScript section at the logical point of execution. The user-defined functions written in this chapter execute using event handlers.

As you have learned, an event is the result of an action, such as a mouse click or a window loading. An event handler is a way to associate that action with a function. For example, when a user clicks a button or a check box, a JavaScript user-defined function may be associated with that event. The associated function will execute if the event is captured and then triggers, or calls, the JavaScript user-defined function. The general form of an event handler is shown in Table 9–29.

Table 9–29 Event Handlers

General form:	<tag attribute eventhandler="JavaScript code">
Comment:	where tag is the HTML tag; attribute is a property of the tag that can have a value assigned to it, eventhandler is the name of the JavaScript event handler, and JavaScript code is the instruction to execute, usually in the form of a function name
Example:	<body onload="scrollColor()">

JavaScript event handlers make Web pages more dynamic and interactive by allowing JavaScript code to execute only in response to a user action, such as a mouse click or selection of an item in a list. For a complete list of event handlers, see the JavaScript Quick Reference in Appendix G. You use the onload and onchange event handlers in the Oakwood Elementary School Web page.

To have a JavaScript user-defined function execute automatically when a page loads, use the onload event. The onload event handler triggers the associated function when the Web page has completed loading into the browser. The onchange event handler triggers when the value of an object changes. For example, when the user selects a list item in the select list, the value of the select list is changed.

To Associate User-Defined Functions with the onload Event

The following steps illustrate how to enter JavaScript code to associate the countDown(), scrollColor(), and copyRight() user-defined functions with the onload event.

- Click to the right of the y in the <body> tag in line 75, as shown in Figure 9–14.

```
69     right: 0;
70     text-align: ri
71     }
72
73  </style>
74  </head>
75  <body>
76  <div class="center">
77  <p><img src="chapter9Oakwood.jpg" alt="oakwood banner" width="750" height="120" /></p>
78  <p style="font-family:Arial, Helvetica, sans-serif; font-size:18px; font-weight:bold;">OAKWOOD ELEMENTARY SCHOOL</p>
79  <img src="hrzntlrule.jpg" width="700" height="5" alt="hr" />
80  <div id="displayDate">
81  </div>
82  <img src="hrzntlrule.jpg" width="700" height="5" alt="hr" /> </div>
83  <table>
84    <tr>
```

insertion point in <body> tag; press SPACEBAR once to begin adding onload event handler

Figure 9–14

- Press the SPACEBAR once and then type `onload="scrollColor(); countDown(); copyRight()"` within the <body> tag. Do not press the ENTER key (Figure 9–15).

onload event handler to call scrollColor(), countDown(), and copyRight() user-defined functions

do not press ENTER key after onload event handler

Figure 9–15

To Associate a User-Defined Function with the onchange Event

When the user selects an item in the select list (changes the value of the select list), this change triggers the associated user-defined function loadInfo(). The this.form parameter in the function call sends the values of the <option> tags to the function. The following step illustrates how to associate the user-defined function loadInfo() with the onchange event.

- Scroll to line 113 and click to the right of "Menu".
- Press the SPACEBAR once and then type `onchange="loadInfo(this.form)"` within the <select> tag. Do not press the ENTER key (Figure 9–16).

position insertion point after Menu and press SPACEBAR once

do not press ENTER key after entering event handler

enter onchange event handler to call loadInfo() user-defined function

Figure 9–16

To Save an HTML File

With the first section of JavaScript code for the Oakwood Elementary School Web page complete, you should save the file.

1. With a USB drive plugged into your computer, click File on the menu bar and then click Save As to display the Save As dialog box.
2. Type `chapter9-1solution.html` in the File name text box (do not press the ENTER key).
3. Click Computer in the left-hand side of the dialog box to display a list of available drives.
4. If necessary, scroll until your USB drive, such as UDISK 2.0 (G:), appears in the list of available drives.

5. If necessary, open the Chapter09\ChapterFiles folder.

6. Click the Save button in the Save As dialog box to save the file on the USB flash drive with the name chapter9-1solution.html (Figure 9–17).

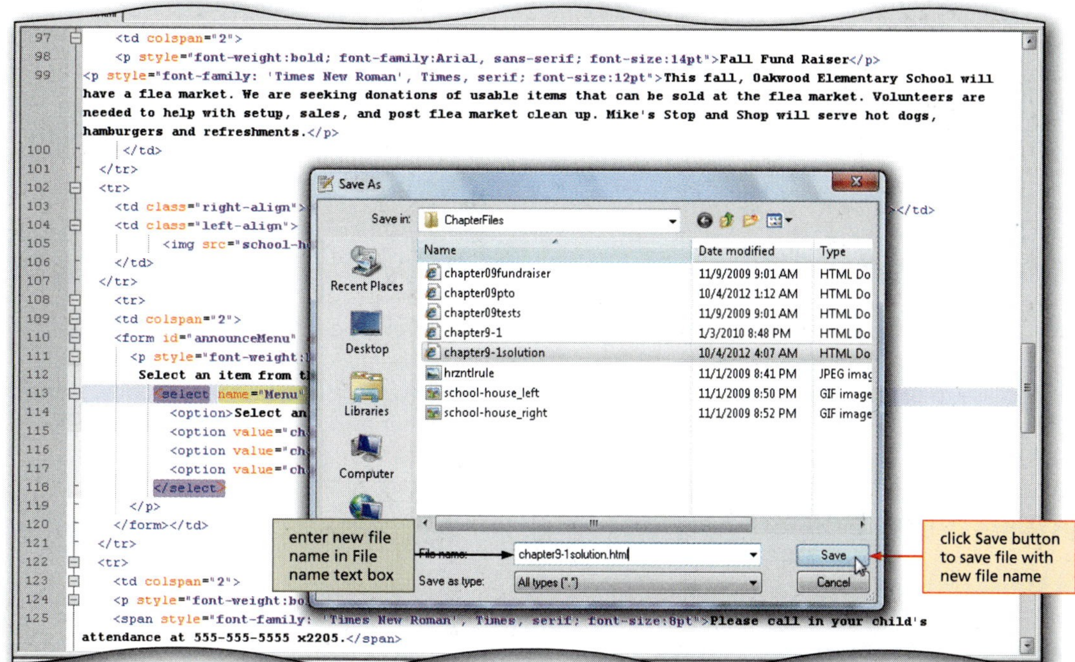

Figure 9–17

To Test the Completed Web Page

Once you complete your JavaScript code, you should test the code in a browser. The following steps illustrate how to open a browser, such as Internet Explorer, and load the chapter9-1solution.html Web page to test if the JavaScript works correctly.

1. Open Internet Explorer and type `g:\Chapter09\ChapterFiles\chapter9-1solution.html` in the Address box.

2. Press ENTER to display the Web page (Figure 9–18a). If a security message appears, click that bar, click the Allow Blocked Content option that displays, and then click Yes in the confirmation dialog box.

3. Select October PTO in the drop-down menu list to display the October PTO Web page.

4. Click the Back button on the Standard Buttons toolbar to return to the Oakwood Elementary School home page.

5. Select State Achievement Test in the drop-down menu list (Figure 9–18b) to display the State Achievement Test Web page.

6. Click the Back button on the Standard Buttons toolbar to return to the Oakwood Elementary School home page, and select October Fundraiser from the drop-down menu list to display the October Fest Fundraiser Web page.

7. Click the Back button on the Standard Buttons toolbar to return to the Oakwood Elementary School home page.

Q&A Should I always allow a Web page running an ActiveX control to load?

For the Web page you just created, or one you are familiar with, you can let the ActiveX control execute. If you are not familiar with a Web site, however, it is not advisable to let them run.

Q&A What should I do if the Web page is not displaying properly?

If your Web page is not displaying correctly, close any error message and then click the Notepad++ button on the taskbar. Check your JavaScript code according to Figures 9–3 through 9–17 on pages HTML 416 through HTML 437. Correct any errors, save the file, click the Internet Explorer taskbar button to activate the browser, and then click the Refresh button on the Standard Buttons toolbar.

Q&A Is there any way to display all the errors on a Web page at once?

Internet Explorer does not offer this feature. If the JavaScript code is missing periods, is missing quotation marks, or has misspelled words, the Web page displays with errors. To continue loading the Web page, click the OK button in the dialog box. The browser will cease to process any more JavaScript code, but will load what it can of the Web page. After you fix the errors, refresh the Web page to see if any other errors are found.

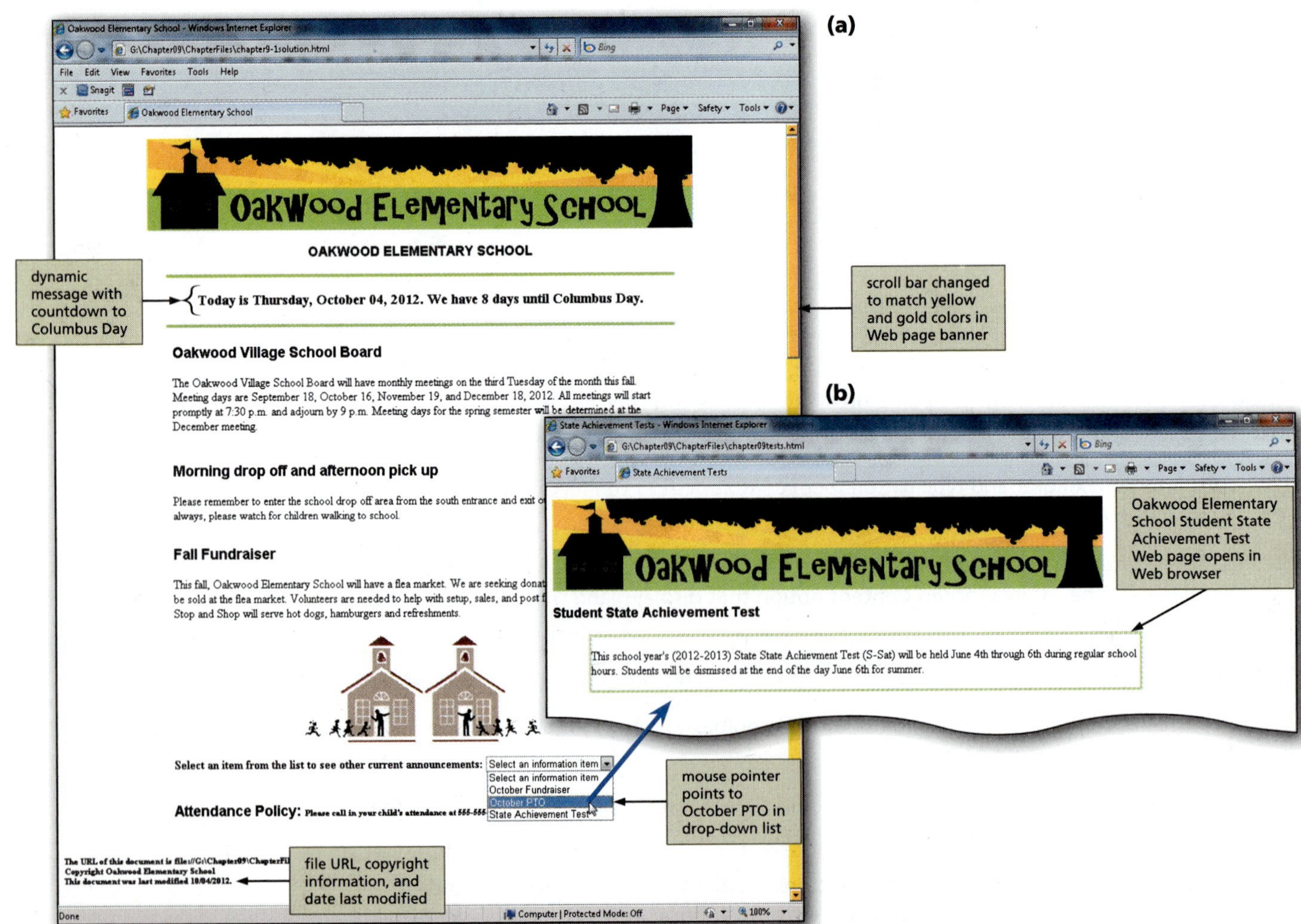

Figure 9–18

To Validate a Web Page

Now that you have tested the Web page and made sure the JavaScript works as desired, you should validate the page at the w3.org Web site.

1. Open Internet Explorer and navigate to the Web site `validator.w3.org`.
2. Click the Validate by File Upload tab.
3. Click the Browse button.
4. Locate the chapter9-1solution.html file on your storage device and click the file name.
5. Click the Open button on the Choose File to Upload dialog box and the file name will be inserted into the File box.
6. Click the Check button.

To Print an HTML File

After completing and testing the Web page, you should print the HTML file using Notepad++ for future reference.

1. Click the Notepad++ icon on the taskbar and click the chapter9-1solution.html tab to activate the file.
2. Click File on the menu bar and then click Print. Click the Print button in the Print dialog box.

To Quit Notepad++ and a Browser

1. In Notepad++, click the File menu, then Close All.
2. Click the Close button on the Notepad++ window title bar.
3. Click the Close button on all open browser windows.

BTW **Quick Reference**
For a list of JavaScript statements and their associated attributes, see the JavaScript Quick Reference (Appendix G) at the back of this book, or visit the HTML Quick Reference Web page (scsite.com/HTML6e/qr).

Chapter Summary

In this chapter, you learned basic JavaScript concepts and how to write and insert JavaScript code to make your Web page more dynamic and interactive. The items listed below include all the new HTML and JavaScript skills you have learned in this chapter.

1. Enter a <div> Tag Container (HTML 416)
2. Enter the Start <script> and Comment Tags (HTML 418)
3. Extract the Current System Date Using the Date() Object (HTML 423)
4. Calculate the Number of Days to a Future Date (HTML 425)
5. Display Text and Variable Values to a Web Page Using innerHTML (HTML 427)
6. Enter the User-Defined Function to Change the Browser Scroll Bar Color (HTML 428)
7. Enter the User-Defined Function to Link to a New URL Using the Drop-Down Menu List (HTML 431)
8. Include the Date Last Modified and a Copyright Message in a Text String (HTML 433)
9. Enter the End Comment and End </script> Tags (HTML 434)
10. Associate User-Defined Functions with the onload Event (HTML 435)
11. Associate a User-Defined Function with the onchange Event (HTML 436)

Learn It Online

Test your knowledge of chapter content and key terms.

Instructions: To complete the Learn It Online exercises, start your browser, click the Address bar, and then enter the Web address `scsite.com/html6e/learn`. When the HTML Learn It Online page is displayed, click the link for the exercise you want to complete and read the instructions.

Chapter Reinforcement TF, MC, and SA
A series of true/false, multiple choice, and short answer questions that test your knowledge of the chapter content.

Flash Cards
An interactive learning environment where you identify chapter key terms associated with displayed definitions.

Practice Test
A series of multiple choice questions that test your knowledge of chapter content and key terms.

Who Wants To Be a Computer Genius?
An interactive game that challenges your knowledge of chapter content in the style of a television quiz show.

Wheel of Terms
An interactive game that challenges your knowledge of chapter key terms in the style of the television show, *Wheel of Fortune*.

Crossword Puzzle Challenge
A crossword puzzle that challenges your knowledge of key terms presented in the chapter.

Apply Your Knowledge

Reinforce the skills and apply the concepts you learned in this chapter.

Adding User-Defined Functions

Instructions: Start Notepad++. Open the file apply9-1.html from the Chapter09\Apply folder of the Data Files for Students. See the inside back cover of this book for instructions on downloading the Data Files for Students, or contact your instructor for information about accessing the required files.

The apply9-1.html file is a partially completed HTML file that you will use for this exercise. Figure 9–19 shows the Apply Your Knowledge Web page as it should be displayed in a browser after the JavaScript has been added. This problem requires using JavaScript to change the scroll bar color, to display a dynamic message, and display copyright information and the date the Web page was last modified. The problem also requires adding event handlers in the <body> tag to invoke the JavaScript user-defined functions.

Perform the following tasks:

1. Using Figure 9–3 on page HTML 416 as a guide, enter a <div> tag with an id name of displayDate between the two green divider images at line 47.
2. Enter the beginning of a JavaScript code section for a user-defined function in the <head> section of the Web page before the <style> tag. Be sure to include a comment line to hide the JavaScript from old browsers.
3. Using the code in Tables 9–15, 9–17, and 9–19 on pages HTML 422, 425, and 427 as a guide, write a JavaScript user-defined function to display the countdown message shown in Figure 9–19. Use your own current and future dates for this Web page.

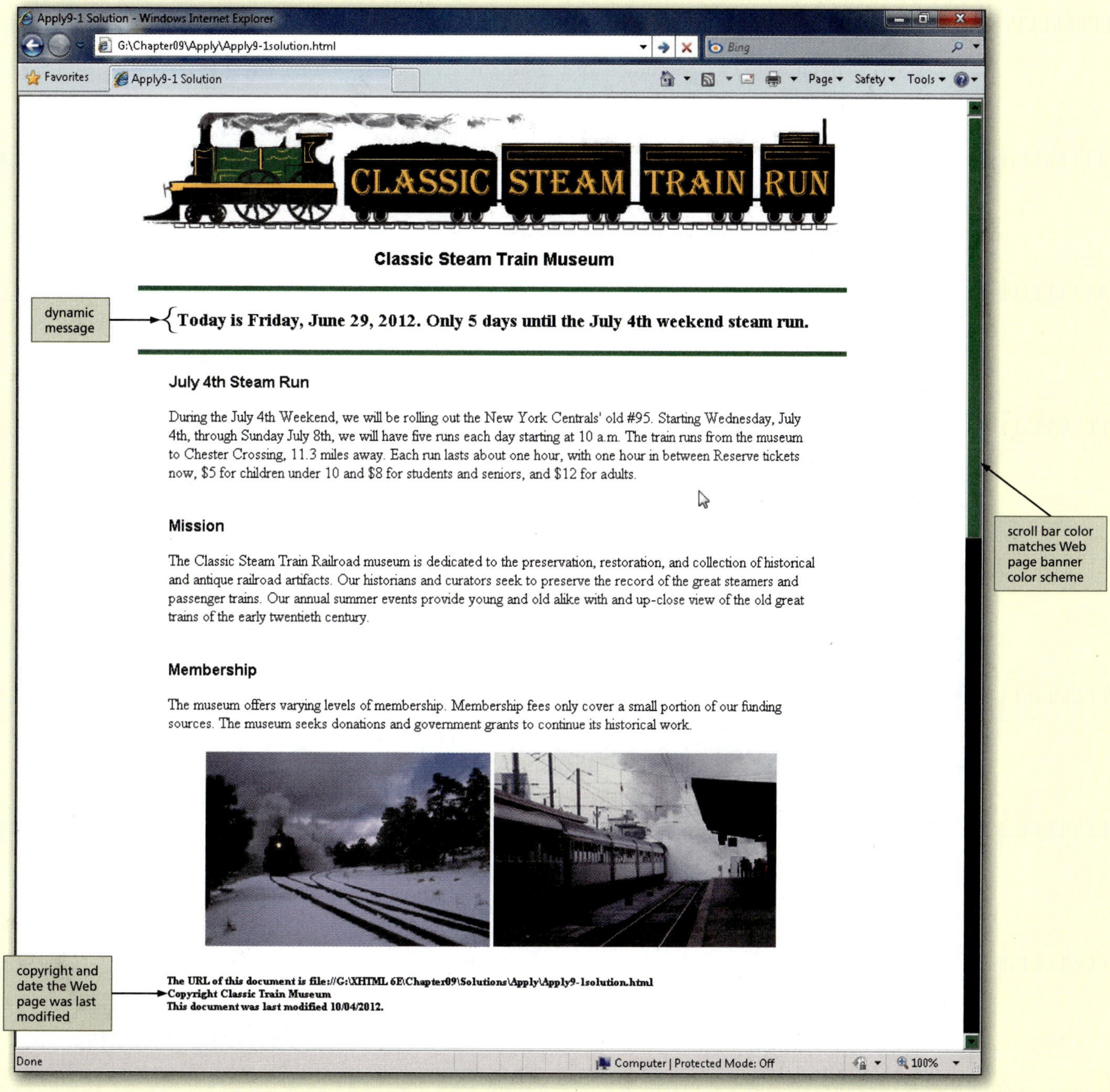

Figure 9–19

4. Using the code in Table 9–21 on page HTML 429 as a guide, enter the code for a user-defined function called scrollColor() to change the scroll bar face color and scroll bar track color to the hexadecimal values shown in Table 9–28.

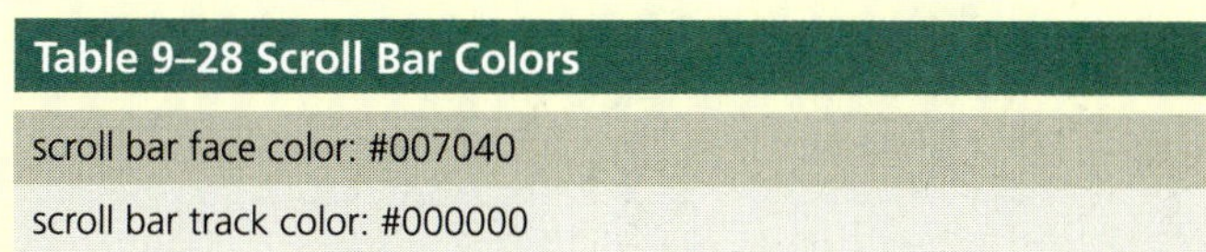

Table 9–28 Scroll Bar Colors
scroll bar face color: #007040
scroll bar track color: #000000

Continued >

Apply Your Knowledge *continued*

5. Make sure to enter the closing brace for the function, followed by the closing HTML tags to close the <script> section.
6. Using the code in Table 9–26 on page HTML 432 as a guide, enter the code to create a <div> tag container with an id attribute of copyright in the last table row with a column span of 2.
7. Using the code in Table 9–27 on page HTML 432 as a guide, write a user-defined function using the <div> tag container and the innerHTML property to display the document URL, a copyright message, and the date the document was last modified at the bottom of the Web page, as shown in Figure 9–19 on the previous page.
8. Enter the onload event handler in the <body> tag to call the three user-defined functions when the Web page loads.
9. Save the revised file in the Chapter09\Apply folder using the file name apply9-1solution.html.
10. Validate the file using the w3.org validator.
11. View and test the Web page in your browser.
12. If any errors occur, check the code against Steps 1 through 8, make any required changes, save the file using the same file name, and then refresh the Web page in the browser.
13. Submit the revised HTML file and Web page in the format specified by your instructor.

Extend Your Knowledge

Extend the skills you learned in this chapter and experiment with new skills. You will need to search the Internet to complete the assignment.

Learning More about Displaying Messages

Instructions: Start Notepad++ and your browser. Open the file extend9-1.html from the Chapter09\Extend folder of the Data Files for Students. See the inside back cover of this book for instructions on downloading the Data Files for Students, or contact your instructor for information about accessing the required files.

Perform the following tasks:

1. Search the Internet for the JavaScript instructions on how to display a message on the status bar of your browser. (*Hint:* Look for properties of the Windows object.)
2. In a <script> section, write the code for a user-defined function, called statusMsg(), that assigns the message "The Allen County Fair Grounds are open every day except Thanksgiving and Christmas." on the status bar.
3. Search the Internet for the proper scroll bar names for the arrow and shadow color. Using the code in Table 9–21 on page HTML 429 as a guide, enter the code for a user-defined function called newScroll() to change the scroll bar colors to the hexadecimal values shown in Table 9–29.

Table 9–29 Scroll Bar Colors
scroll bar face color: #000000
scroll bar arrow color: #ffffff
scroll bar track color: #999999
scroll bar shadow color: #ffffff

4. Locate the blank line between the black divider line images, enter the <div> tag container for the dynamic message.

5. Using the code from Tables 9–15, 9–17, and 9–19, write the user-defined function to display the dynamic message shown in Figure 9–20. Pick a date about 30 days from the current date to use in the calculation.
6. The <div> tag is not the only container tag. What other tag can be used to contain items? In the last row of the table, beneath the two car images, enter a container tag with an id attribute of dateMsg.
7. Write the JavaScript user-defined function to display the copyright and the date last modified using the substring() method, as shown in Table 9–12 on page HTML 421, to display only the year portion of the date last modified.
8. Add the onload event handler to the <body> tag to call all the user-defined functions when the Web page loads.
9. Save the revised file in the Chapter09\Extend folder using the file name extend9-1solution.html.
10. Validate the file using the w3.org validation Web page.
11. View and test the Web page in your browser.
12. If any errors occur, check the code against Steps 1 through 8, make any required changes, save the file using the same file name, and then refresh the Web page in the browser.
13. Submit the revised HTML file and Web page in the format specified by your instructor.

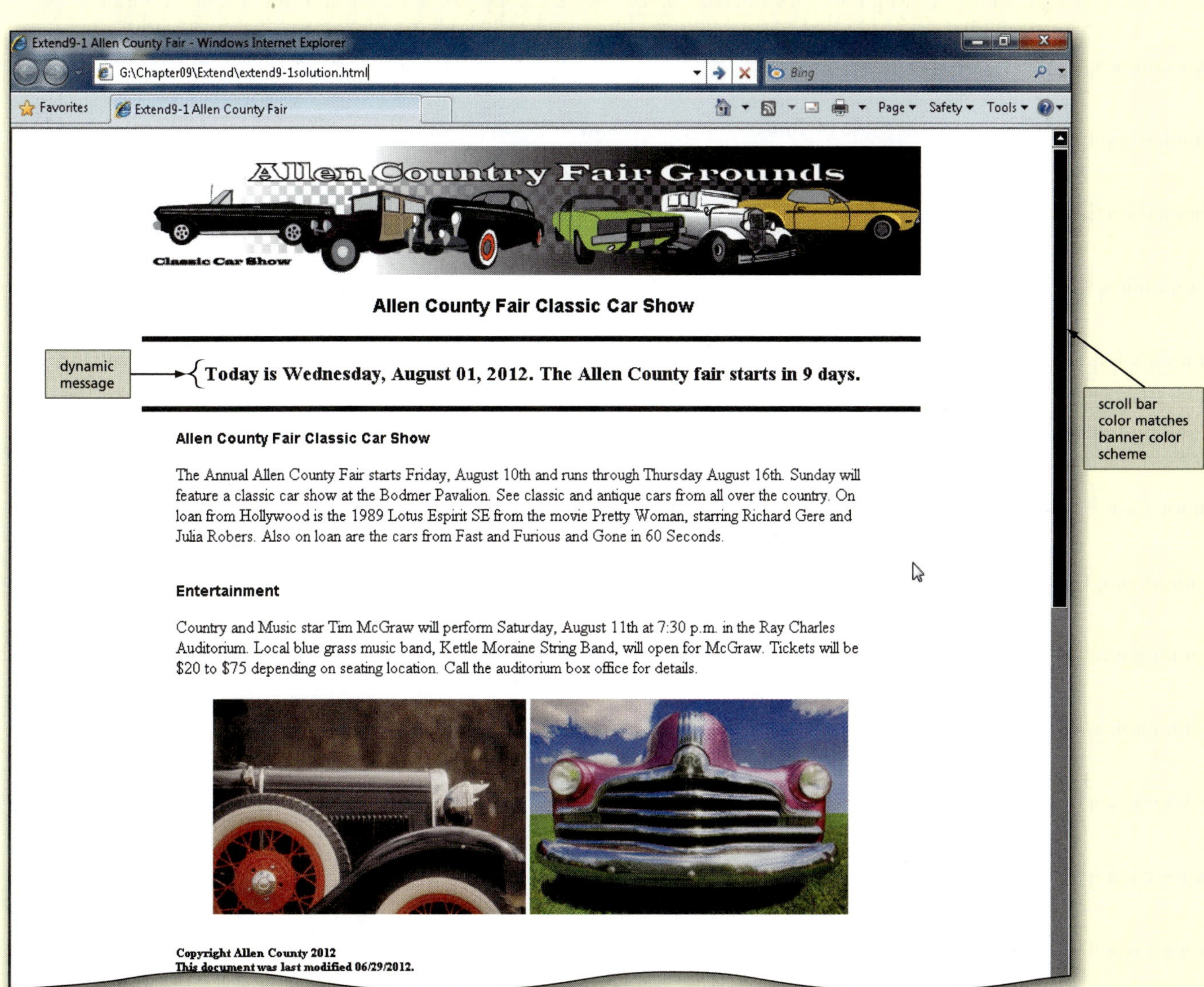

Figure 9–20

Make It Right

Analyze the JavaScript code on a Web page and correct all errors.

Correcting Syntax Errors and Inserting Missing Code

Instructions: Start your browser. Open the file makeitright9-1.html from the Chapter09\MakeItRight folder of the Data Files for Students. See the inside back cover of this book for instructions for downloading the Data Files for Students, or see your instructor for information on accessing the files required in this book.

The Web page shown in Figure 9–21 is an announcement for a sorority Ice Cream Social. This Web page has four errors that you are to find and correct.

Perform the following tasks:

1. When you open the makeitright9-1.html file in the browser, you will notice that the scroll bar did not change color, the dynamic message did not display between the horizontal lines, and the copyright and date last modified did not display.
2. Start Notepad++. Open the makeitright9-1.html file. Save the HTML file in the Chapter09\MakeItRight folder using the file name makeitright9-1solution.html.
3. Compare the code in the user-defined function to the code to change the scroll bar color in Table 9–21 on page HTML 429. Make the changes necessary to change the scroll bar color in the Phi Beta Alpha Ice Cream Social Web page.
4. Compare the code in Tables 9–15, 9–17, and 9–19 on pages HTML 422, 425, and 427, to the code in the dynamic message in the Phi Beta Alpha Ice Cream Social Web page, and make corrections as necessary.
5. Make sure the user-defined functions are called properly by the correct event handlers, and that they are in the correct locations.
6. Save the corrected HTML file and test it using your browser. If errors occur, check your code and save again. Your Web page should look similar to Figure 9–21.
7. Submit the revised HTML file and Web page in the format specified by your instructor.

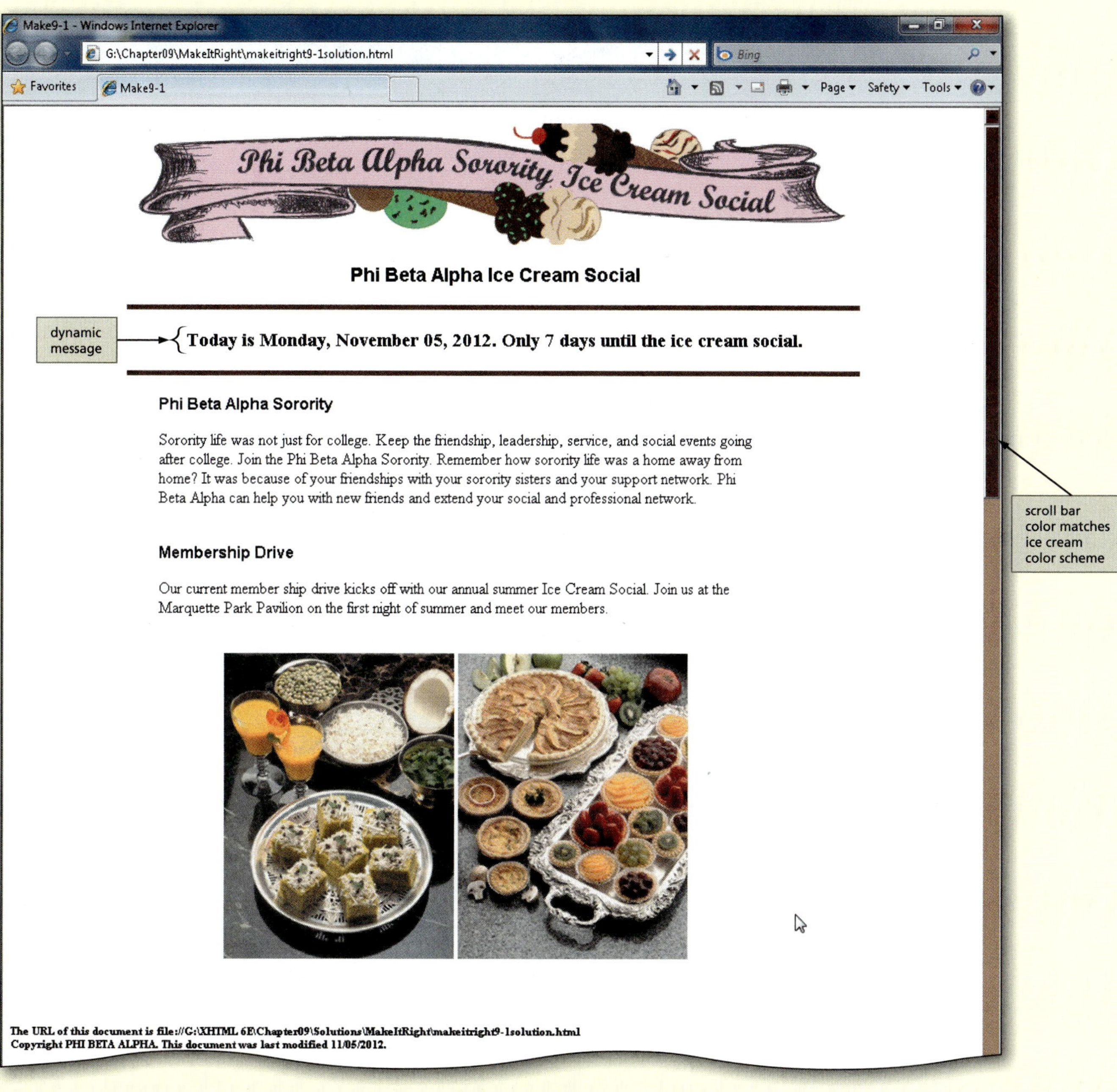
Make9-1 - Windows Internet Explorer
G:\Chapter09\MakeItRight\makeitright9-1solution.html
Phi Beta Alpha Sorority Ice Cream Social
Phi Beta Alpha Ice Cream Social
dynamic message
Today is Monday, November 05, 2012. Only 7 days until the ice cream social.
Phi Beta Alpha Sorority
Sorority life was not just for college. Keep the friendship, leadership, service, and social events going after college. Join the Phi Beta Alpha Sorority. Remember how sorority life was a home away from home? It was because of your friendships with your sorority sisters and your support network. Phi Beta Alpha can help you with new friends and extend your social and professional network.
Membership Drive
Our current member ship drive kicks off with our annual summer Ice Cream Social. Join us at the Marquette Park Pavilion on the first night of summer and meet our members.
scroll bar color matches ice cream color scheme
The URL of this document is file://G:\XHTML 6E\Chapter09\Solutions\MakeItRight\makeitright9-1solution.html
Copyright PHI BETA ALPHA. This document was last modified 11/05/2012.

Figure 9–21

STUDENT ASSIGNMENTS

In the Lab

Design and/or create a Web page using the guidelines, concepts, and skills presented in this chapter. Labs are listed in order of increasing difficulty.

Lab 1: Creating a Web Page for the St. Michael's Hospital Health Care Fair

Problem: You work for St. Michael's Hospital IT Department and have been asked to create a Web site to promote the Health Care Fair. You create the Web page shown in Figure 9–22, which includes changing the color of the scroll bar, using a drop-down menu to link to related Web pages, and add the copyright and date last modified at the bottom of the Web page.

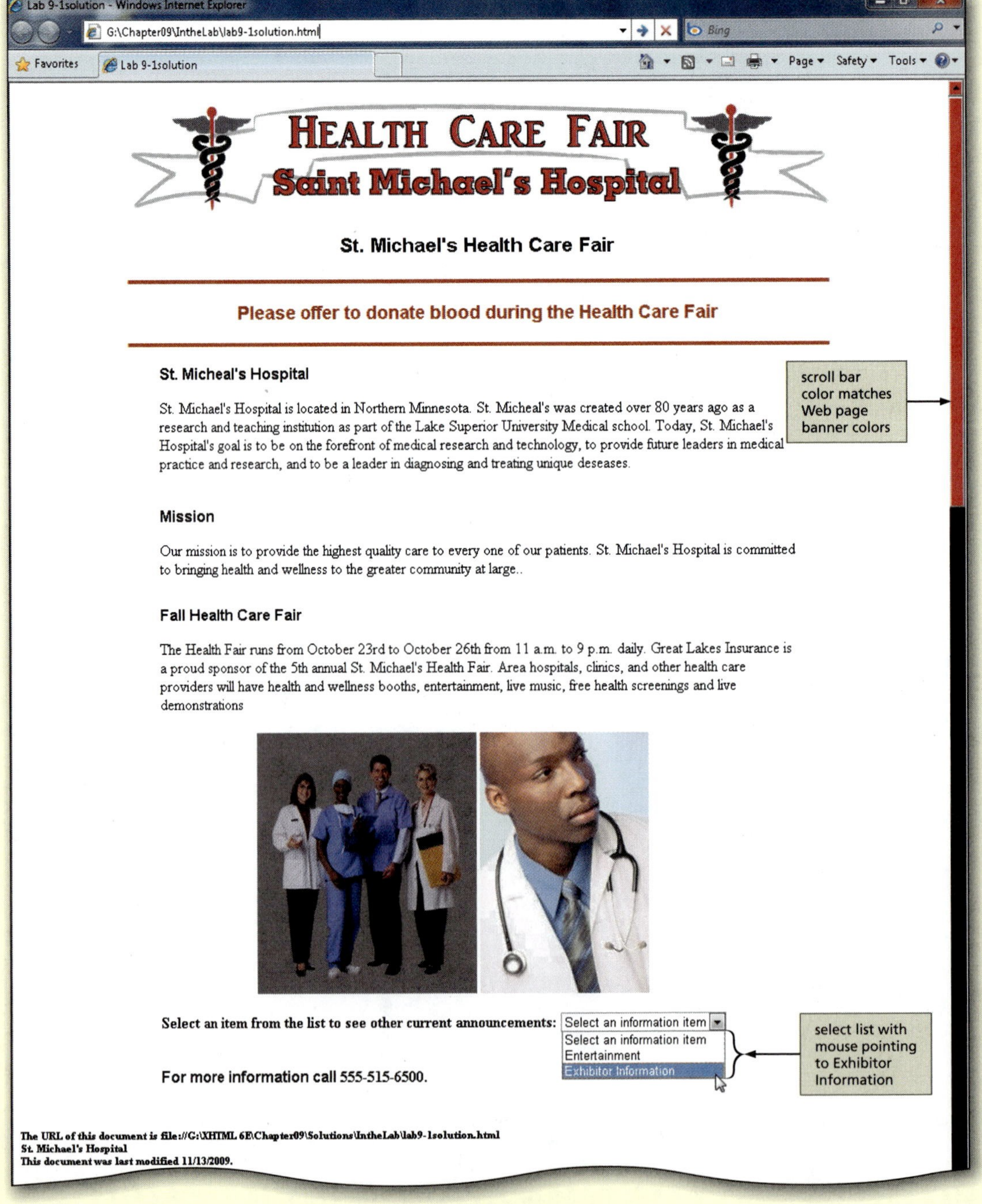

Figure 9–22

Instructions: Perform the following tasks:

1. Start Notepad++ and open the lab9-1.html file from the Chapter09\IntheLab folder of the Data Files for Students.
2. Save the file as lab9-1solution.html.
3. Start a new <script> section in the <head> section under the <title> tag.
4. Write JavaScript user-defined function to change the scroll bar colors called scrollColor(). Use the code in Table 9–21 on page HTML 429 as a guide, and use the following color values for the scroll bar face and track colors:

   face color: #be1e20

   track color: #000000
5. Write a JavaScript user-defined function called loadInfo() that uses the selectedIndex value of the Menu <select> list in the announceMenu <form>. Use the code in Table 9–24 on page HTML 431 as a guide.
6. Enter the HTML code to create a <div> tag with the id attribute of displayCopyRight after the <p> tag and the closing </table> tag but before the closing </body> tag.
7. Write a JavaScript user-defined function, called copyRight(), to display the copyright and date-last-modified message, as shown in Figure 9–22. The date the document was last modified should display only the date, not the time, using a substring() method on the lastModified property.
8. Add the onchange event handler in the <select> tag to call the loadInfo() function. Then, add the proper event handler to the <body> tag to call the scrollColor() and copyRight() user-defined functions when the Web page loads.
9. Save the completed HTML file, validate it, and test it using your browser. If an error occurs, check your code and save and test again.
10. Submit the completed HTML file and Web page in the format specified by your instructor.

In the Lab

Lab 2: Tri-State Job Fair

Problem: You are an intern at Tri-State Employment Services. Your supervisor knows of your Web page development experience and asks you to create a Web page announcing an upcoming job fair. The Web page should include links to other pages of information using a drop-down menu. In addition, your supervisor wants to add a dynamic announcement with a countdown to when the job fair will occur. You suggest adding some color to the scroll bar, and copyright information with the date-last-modified at the bottom of the Web page. You add the JavaScript to make the Web page appear as in Figure 9–23 on the next page.

Continued >

In the Lab *continued*

Figure 9–23

Instructions: Perform the following tasks:

1. Start Notepad++ and open the lab9-2.html file from the Chapter09\IntheLab folder of the Data Files for Students.
2. Save the file as lab9-2solution.html.
3. Start a new <script> section in the <head> section, on the line following the <title> tag, for four user-defined functions.
4. Write a JavaScript function to change the scroll bar colors called jobfairScroll(). Use the code in Table 9–21 as a guide, and use the following color values for the scroll bar face and track colors:

   face color: #00aef0

   track color: #999999
5. Write a JavaScript function called menuLinks() that uses the selectedIndex value of the Menu <select> list in the infoMenu <form>. Use the code in Table 9–24 on page HTML 431 as a guide.
6. Enter the HTML code to create a <div> tag with an id attribute of displayDate between the two blue divider line images.
7. Write a JavaScript user-defined function called countDown() to take the current date and calculate the number of days until the job fair. Use a future date associated with the current date in your code. The script code should display a dynamic message, as shown in Figure 9–23.
8. Before the closing </body> tag, enter the HTML code to create a <div> tag with an id attribute of displayCopyRight.
9. Using the code in Table 9–27 on page HTML 432, write the JavaScript user-defined function to display a copyright message and the date the Web page was last modified.
10. Add the event handler to call the jobfairScroll(), countDown(), and copyRight() functions when the Web page loads, and the event handler to call the menuLinks() function when the user selects an item from the drop-down list. Place these event handlers in the appropriate HTML tags.
11. Save the completed HTML file, validate it, and test it using your browser. If an error occurs, check your code and save and test again.
12. Submit the completed HTML file and Web page in the format specified by your instructor.

In the Lab

Lab 3: Miller High School Band Web Page

Problem: You are a member of the Miller High School Band Board. Because of your experience as a Web master, the board has asked you to create a Web page that announces upcoming events (Figure 9–24).

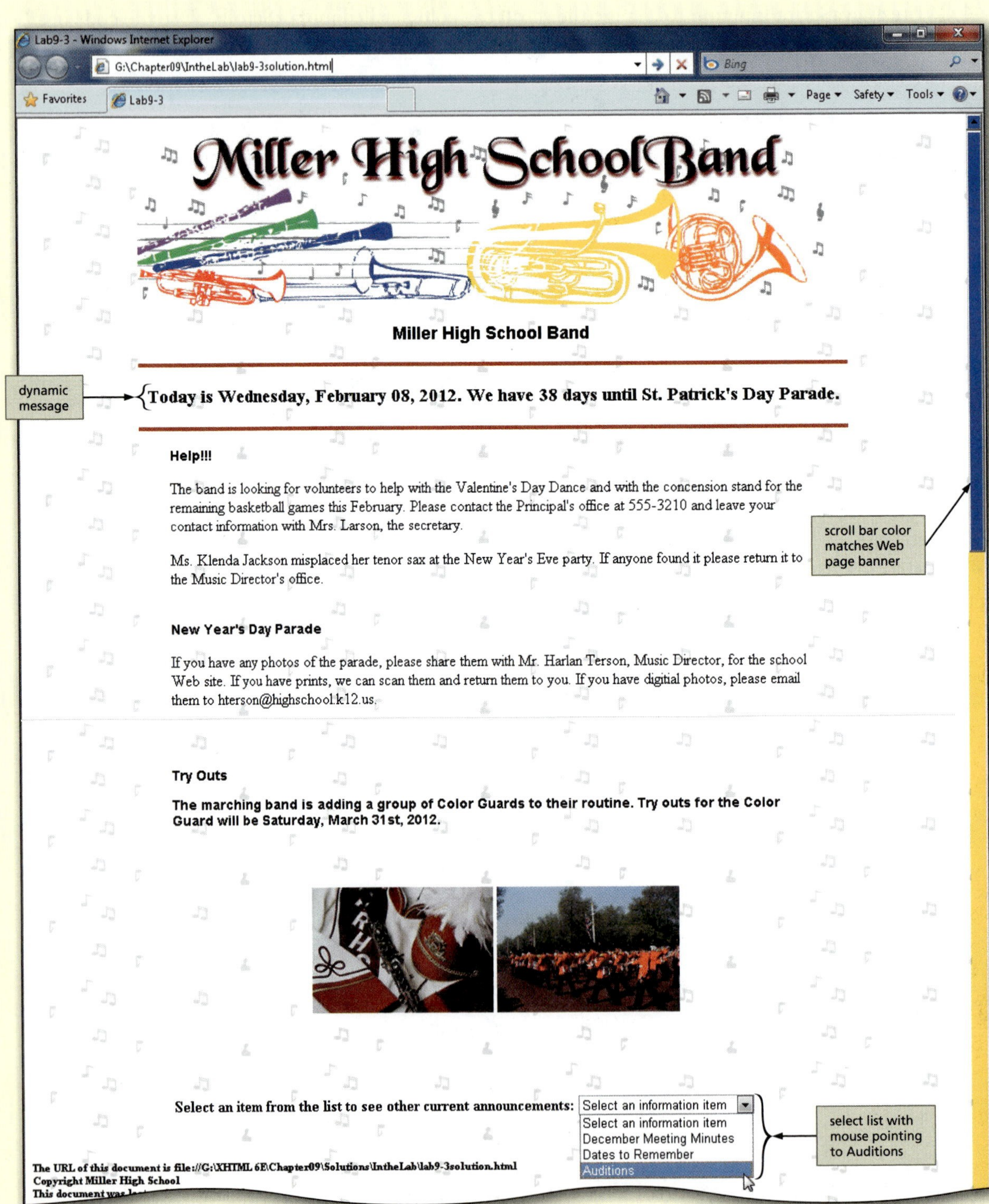

Figure 9–24

Instructions: Perform the following tasks:

1. Start Notepad++ and open the lab9-3.html file from the Chapter09\IntheLab folder. Save the file as lab9-3solution.html.
2. Using the techniques learned in this chapter, write the JavaScript code to create a dynamic message with a countdown, change the scroll bar color, and use the selectedIndex in the <select> tag to link to new Web pages. The menu links are December Meeting Minutes, Dates to Remember, and Auditions. In addition, add a copyright notice and the date the Web page was last modified. Use a future date near the current date for this lab. Use #20409a for the scroll bar face color, and #ffde20 for the scroll bar track color.
3. Save the completed HTML file, validate it, and test it using your browser. If an error occurs, check your code, and save and test again.
4. Submit the completed HTML file and Web page in the format specified by your instructor.

Cases and Places

Apply your creative thinking and problem-solving skills to design and implement a solution.

• Easier •• More Difficult

• 1: Create the Fix-It Hardware Web Site

Your uncle who owns a local hardware store has asked you to create a Web page to launch his new online presence. Use the file case9-1.html in the Cases and Places folder of the Data Files for Students and create a dynamic greeting announcing the number of days until the Independence Day sale, change the color of the scroll bar, and add the document URL and date-last-modified information in the last data cell of the table. Save as case9-1solution.html.

•• 2: Create the City of Ashland Centennial Home Page

As a summer intern for the city of Ashland, you have been asked to create the online announcement for the city's centennial celebration of 150 years of existence. The page should have a drop-down menu list with links to block parties, park department activities, and parades Web pages. The home page should change the scroll bar face color to #6575ae and the track color to #ffffff. Make up information about holding block parties to celebrate the founding of the city. Create a dynamic message indicating the number of days to the main celebration on March 9. Be sure to add the document URL and the date last modified at the end of the home page.

•• 3: Create the Allen Travel Agency Web Site

As the newly hired Webmaster for Allen Travel Agency, you are going to redesign its Web site. You want to add a dynamic message to announce the number of days until the upcoming cruise: "We have X days until the Star Liner Alaskan Cruise," where X is the days until the Alaskan Cruise. You use a drop-down menu to link to Cruise Planning, Honeymoon Planning, and a Cruise Meeting and write a JavaScript user-defined function to change the URL location.

Because CSS does not have a standard for changing scroll bar colors, you add a JavaScript user-defined function to change the face color to #f7901e, and the track color to #ffff00. At the bottom of the Web page, you display the copyright information and the date the Web page was last modified. Display only the date, not the time, with the lastModified property. Be sure to add the proper event handlers in the correct locations to call the user-defined functions. Use files from the Chapter09\ CasesandPlaces folder of the Data Files for Students to help build your Web site.

Continued >

Cases and Places *continued*

•• 4: Create a Family Web Page

Make It Personal

Many families have begun sharing information via the Internet. Many people use Facebook® or MySpace® to share photos and other information. Carefully consider your own family and friends, and then use the concepts and techniques presented in this chapter to create a Web page that announces a birthday, wedding, anniversary, or some other special family event. Use a dynamic message to display the current date and the number of days to the event. Make your page long enough (perhaps add several photos) so that the scroll bar is active and write the JavaScript user-defined function to change the scroll bar color. Create a drop-down menu list to link to other Web pages that you have created or that already exist, such as links to family or friends who have Web pages or FaceBook sites. Add a copyright notice and add the date the page was last modified at the bottom in small print. Be sure to check spelling and grammar on the Web pages that you create.

•• 5: Critique an Existing Web Site

Working Together

Many organizations in your community have Web pages. Each team member should search for these organizations' Web pages. Your team should find at least eight to ten Web sites. Print the Web pages and critique the layout and information presented on the page. Try to determine if the Web site has used JavaScript or some other scripting method (you can look at the source code). As a group, list four to five features that you like on each page, and four to five features you think could be improved on each page. If you find that a page used JavaScript, make note of how JavaScript was used for future reference in this book. Write up your evaluation and critique as a team and hand in the printed Web pages with the critique report.

10 Creating Pop-Up Windows, Adding Scrolling Messages, and Validating Forms

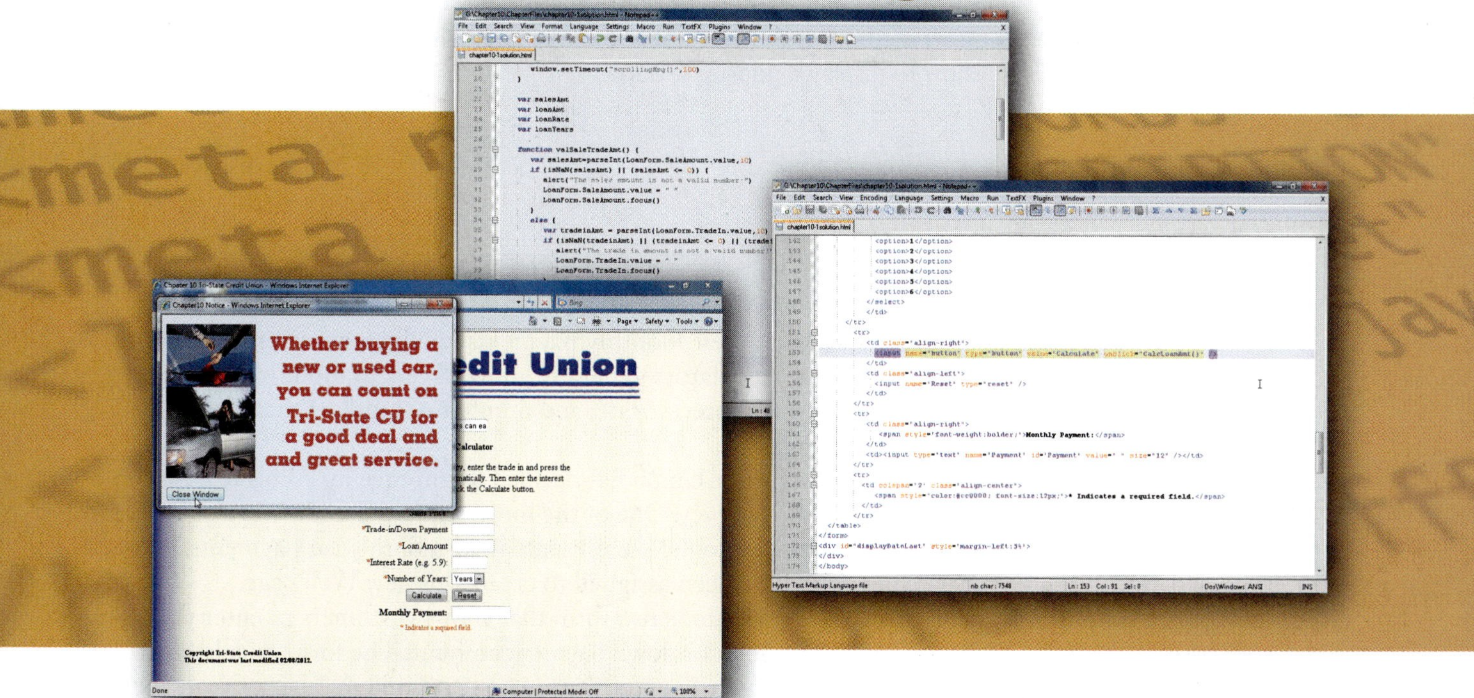

Objectives

You will have mastered the material in this chapter when you can:

- Write a JavaScript user-defined function to display a scrolling message
- Write a JavaScript user-defined function to validate form data
- Write a JavaScript user-defined function to calculate a total loan amount
- Write a JavaScript user-defined function to calculate monthly loan payments
- Define if and if...else statements, conditionals, and operands
- Write a JavaScript user-defined function to format output in a text field
- Describe how to open a pop-up window

10 Creating Pop-Up Windows, Adding Scrolling Messages, and Validating Forms

Introduction

In Chapter 9, you learned how to integrate JavaScript into an HTML document using variables and objects, and how to write JavaScript user-defined functions called by event handlers. This chapter reinforces these skills and shows you how to create a scrolling message that displays a text message in a form text field, and use JavaScript to validate the data users enter into forms. The validation techniques discussed in this chapter use the if…else statement; parseInt(), parseFloat(), and isNaN() built-in functions; the Math object's pow() method; and the Number object's toFixed() method. Finally, the chapter discusses how to display a pop-up window.

Project — Tri-State Credit Union Loan Calculator

Many bank and real estate Web sites include monthly payment calculators that help buyers determine what their monthly payments will be for a car, mortgage, or other type of loan. These calculators generally allow buyers to input basic loan information — loan amount, interest rate, and number of years — that is used to estimate the monthly payment.

Recently, Tri-State Credit Union has decided to improve its Web site based on a recent customer-satisfaction survey. One of the most-requested items was a simple loan calculator that would allow customers to estimate their monthly car payments. As one of the Web developers, you have been assigned to create this new Web page.

You decide to create an interactive form that allows customers to enter the selling price of the car and the trade-in or down payment amount. The form calculates the loan amount and then allows the user to enter the interest rate, and number of years for the loan. When the user clicks the Calculate button, the monthly car loan payment displays. A Reset button allows the user to restart and try different values. You suggest adding a simple scrolling message, in which the credit union wants to mention a cash-back Visa offer. You also suggest adding a pop-up window to promote Tri-State's other services. Figure 10–1 shows the pop-up window, the scrolling message, and the user input form for the loan calculator.

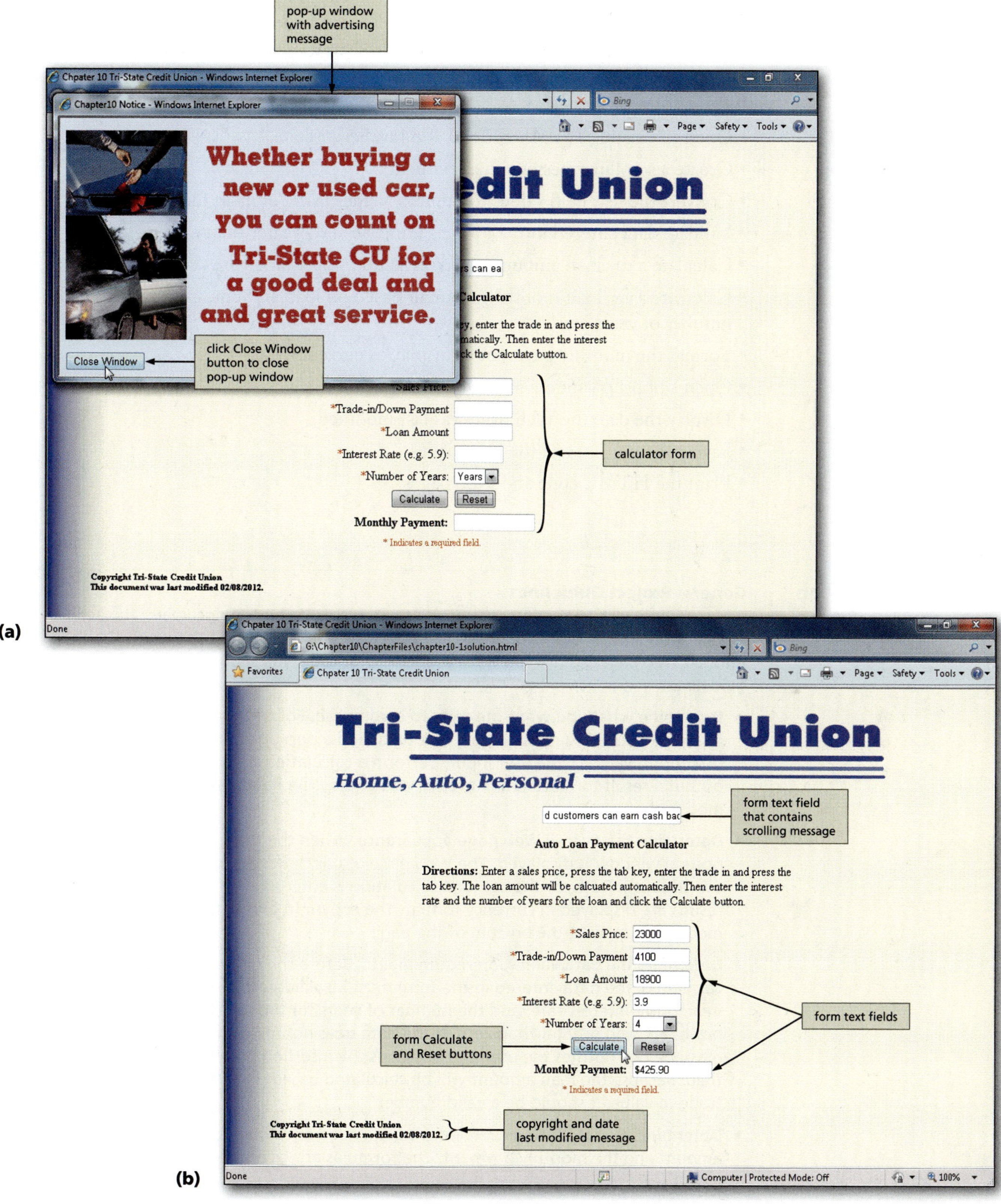
pop-up window with advertising message
Chpater 10 Tri-State Credit Union - Windows Internet Explorer
Chapter10 Notice - Windows Internet Explorer
Whether buying a new or used car, you can count on Tri-State CU for a good deal and great service.
Close Window
click Close Window button to close pop-up window
calculator form
Copyright Tri-State Credit Union
This document was last modified 02/08/2012.
(a)
G:\Chapter10\ChapterFiles\chapter10-1solution.html
Tri-State Credit Union
Home, Auto, Personal
d customers can earn cash bac
form text field that contains scrolling message
Auto Loan Payment Calculator
Directions: Enter a sales price, press the tab key, enter the trade in and press the tab key. The loan amount will be calcuated automatically. Then enter the interest rate and the number of years for the loan and click the Calculate button.
*Sales Price: 23000
*Trade-in/Down Payment 4100
*Loan Amount 18900
*Interest Rate (e.g. 5.9): 3.9
*Number of Years: 4
form text fields
form Calculate and Reset buttons
Calculate
Reset
Monthly Payment: $425.90
* Indicates a required field.
Copyright Tri-State Credit Union
This document was last modified 02/08/2012.
copyright and date last modified message
(b)

Figure 10–1

Overview

As you read this chapter, you will learn how to write embedded JavaScript code to create the Web pages shown in Figures 10–1a and 10–1b on the previous page by performing these general tasks:

- Open an existing HTML file and add JavaScript code.
- Create a scrolling message in a text field.
- Convert the text field values to numeric values using built-in functions.
- Validate data entered into a form as numeric and greater than zero.
- Calculate a car loan amount based on selling price minus the trade-in value.
- Calculate a car loan monthly payment based on loan amount, interest rate, and number of years.
- Format the monthly payment to display as currency.
- Open a pop-up window when the Web page initially loads.
- Display the date the Web page was last modified.
- Save, validate, and test the Web pages.
- Print the HTML code and Web pages.

Plan Ahead

General Project Guidelines

When adding JavaScript or any scripting language to a Web page document, the actions you perform and decisions you make will affect the appearance and characteristics of the finished Web page. Before you write the JavaScript code, you should follow these general guidelines:

- **Determine what you want the code to accomplish.** For this chapter's project, you want to create a scrolling message in a text field, add a pop-up window, create a form for user input, validate the user input, perform a calculation based on the user input, output a result formatted as currency, and display the date the Web page was last modified.
- **Determine the overall Web page appearance.** When the Web page first loads, a pop-up window is displayed. The Web page also includes a text message that scrolls continuously. Data for the car loan calculation is entered in a form, validated, and the results are displayed in currency format. The copyright and date the page was last modified display at the bottom of the page.
- **Determine the data validation requirements.** Before the monthly payment can be calculated, the data entered in the form must be validated. The selling price, trade-in amount, interest rate, and the number of years for the loan must be numeric, not blank, and greater than zero. If the data does not meet these criteria, an alert message box notifies the user and positions the insertion point in the appropriate text field. Because the loan amount will be calculated based on the selling price minus the trade-in value, it should be a valid number.
- **Determine the calculations needed.** You will need a formula for calculating the loan amount and the monthly payment. The formulas are given later in the chapter.

When necessary, more specific details concerning the above guidelines are presented at appropriate points in the chapter. The chapter also will identify the actions performed and decisions made regarding these guidelines during the creation of the Web page shown in Figure 10–1.

Inserting a Scrolling Message on a Web Page

A simple way to provide a Web site visitor with information is to add a scrolling text message to a Web page. Companies often use scrolling messages on their Web sites to highlight breaking news, key products, or special promotions. A scrolling text message can appear either in a text field within the Web page or on the status bar in the browser window. Because visitors to a Web page often do not look at the status bar, most Web developers agree that a scrolling message in a text field on the Web page is a better location.

A scrolling message has four basic components:

- The display object (a form text field)
- The text message to scroll in the text field
- The position of the next character in the text message
- A time delay

The **display object** identifies where the scrolling message is displayed, which, in this project, is in a form text field. The scrolling **message** is a text string assigned to a variable. The text string is what the user sees when the message is displayed. The **position** is the location of the next character in the text string. The **delay** regulates the speed in which the characters display in the text field.

The first step in creating the scrolling message for the Tri-State Credit Union Web page is to create the object that will display the scrolling message. The most common object to display a scrolling message is a text field. The text field must be part of a form object. In the Tri-State Credit Union Web page, you place the form and text field below the banner.

Although the <marquee> tag can be used to scroll text, it works only in Internet Explorer and not in other browsers. A text field can be used by all browsers, and like the <marquee> tag, a text field can be set to a specific size.

You must name the form using the id attribute and the text field using the name attribute. These attribute names serve as the object and properties used in the JavaScript code to assign the message string to the text field. The size attribute of the text field indicates the display width of the text field. Table 10–1 shows the HTML code to create the form and a text field for the scrolling message.

Table 10–1 Code to Create a Form and a Text Field

Line	Code
44	<form id="msgForm" action="">
45	<p style="text-align:center"><input type="text" name="scrollingMsg" size="25" /></p>
46	</form>

Line 44 starts the form and uses the id attribute to give the form the unique name, msgForm. The action attribute is blank because no action should be taken with this form object. Line 45 starts with a <p> tag and an inline style that centers the text field. The input box is a text type, which means it can receive data. The text field is named scrollingMsg and is set to a size of 25. Line 46 is the closing </form> tag.

To Open an Existing HTML File

As in Chapter 9, you will integrate JavaScript into an existing HTML document. The chapter10-1.html file has an already completed embedded CSS. The following steps show how to open the chapter10-1.html file included in the Data Files for Students.

1. Start Notepad++, and, if necessary, maximize the window.
2. Click View on the menu bar. If the Word wrap command does not have a check mark next to it, click Word wrap.
3. With a USB flash drive plugged in to your computer, click File on the menu bar and then click Open on the File menu.
4. Navigate to the Chapter10\ChapterFiles folder on the USB drive.
5. Double-click chapter10-1.html in the list of files to display the HTML code for the chapter10-1.html Web page, as shown in Figure 10–2.

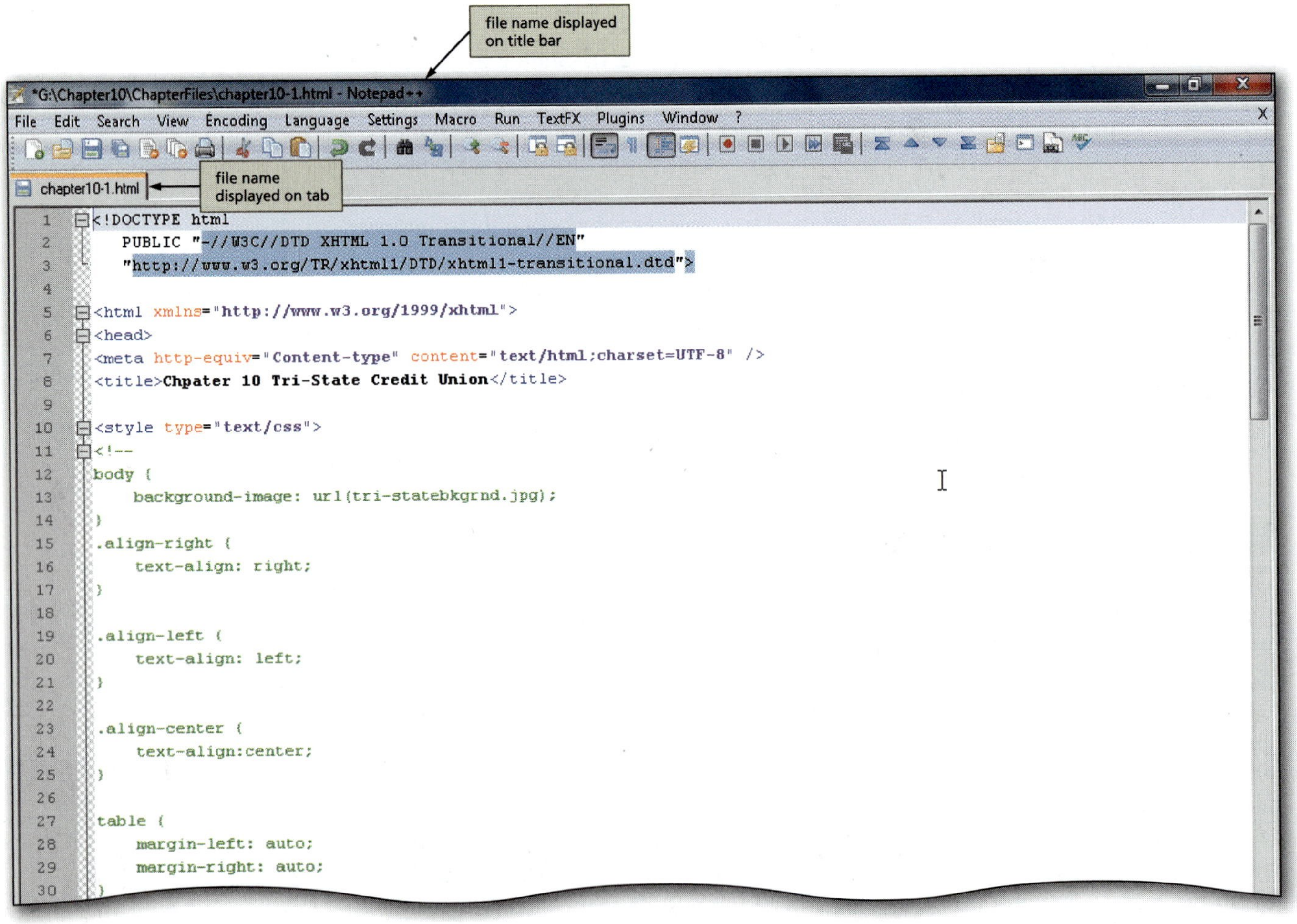

file name displayed on title bar

*G:\Chapter10\ChapterFiles\chapter10-1.html - Notepad++

File Edit Search View Encoding Language Settings Macro Run TextFX Plugins Window ?

chapter10-1.html

file name displayed on tab

```
<!DOCTYPE html
   PUBLIC "-//W3C//DTD XHTML 1.0 Transitional//EN"
   "http://www.w3.org/TR/xhtml1/DTD/xhtml1-transitional.dtd">

<html xmlns="http://www.w3.org/1999/xhtml">
<head>
<meta http-equiv="Content-type" content="text/html;charset=UTF-8" />
<title>Chpater 10 Tri-State Credit Union</title>

<style type="text/css">
<!--
body {
    background-image: url(tri-statebkgrnd.jpg);
}
.align-right {
    text-align: right;
}

.align-left {
    text-align: left;
}

.align-center {
    text-align:center;
}

table {
    margin-left: auto;
    margin-right: auto;
}
```

Figure 10–2

To Create a Form Text Field to Display a Scrolling Message

The following step illustrates how to create a form and a form text field to display a scrolling message.

1

- Click the blank line 44 below the </p> tag.
- Enter the JavaScript code shown in Table 10–1 on page HTML 457 to create the form and text field (Figure 10–3).

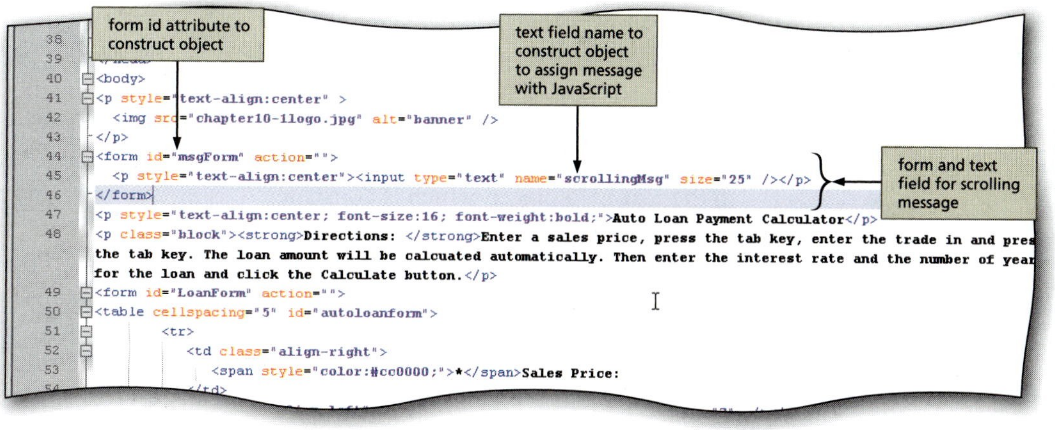

form id attribute to construct object

text field name to construct object to assign message with JavaScript

form and text field for scrolling message

```
38
39
40  <body>
41  <p style="text-align:center" >
42    <img src="chapter10-1logo.jpg" alt="banner" />
43  </p>
44  <form id="msgForm" action="">
45    <p style="text-align:center"><input type="text" name="scrollingMsg" size="25" /></p>
46  </form>
47  <p style="text-align:center; font-size:16; font-weight:bold;">Auto Loan Payment Calculator</p>
48  <p class="block"><strong>Directions: </strong>Enter a sales price, press the tab key, enter the trade in and pres
the tab key. The loan amount will be calcuated automatically. Then enter the interest rate and the number of year
for the loan and click the Calculate button.</p>
49  <form id="LoanForm" action="">
50  <table cellspacing="5" id="autoloanform">
51          <tr>
52             <td class="align-right">
53                <span style="color:#cc0000;">*</span>Sales Price:
```

Figure 10–3

Q&A

Can a scrolling message be placed in other Web elements in addition to text fields?

Besides a text field, any object that can have values assigned to it, such as a button, the status bar, or a title bar, can be used to display a scrolling text message.

Creating the scrollingMsg() User-Defined Function

The scrollingMsg() function requires two variables and performs five tasks. The two variables are:

- The scrollMsg variable represents the message.
- The beginPos variable represents the current character in the text message.

The five tasks the scrollingMsg() function performs are:

- Assigns the string message to the display object (which, in this project, is the text field)
- Increments the beginPos variable by 1 to place the next character in the text message in the display object
- Uses an if statement to test for the end of the message
- If the text has scrolled to the end of the message, starts over with the first character
- Makes the display continuous and regulates the speed of the display using the setTimeout() method set to 200 milliseconds

Table 10–2 shows the code to begin the JavaScript section, declare and initialize the scrollMsg and beginPos variables, declare the scrollingMsg() function, and assign the first characters of the message to the text field.

BTW

Placement of Scrolling Text

Although scrolling text can be assigned to a <div> tag container using the innerHTML property, it does not allow for as much control as a form object like a text field or button.

BTW

Marquee <marquee> Tag

To make it easier to build scrolling messages, Microsoft developed the <marquee> tag. The direction attribute in the <marquee> tag controls scrolling up, down, left, or right. While Internet Explorer recognizes the <marquee> tag, other browsers do not. To create a scrolling message that works with Internet Explorer and other browsers, use a form text field, as discussed in this chapter.

Table 10–2 Code to Begin the scrollingMsg() Function

Line	Code
9	`<script type="text/javascript">`
10	`<!--Hide from old browsers`
11	`var scrollMsg=" ** Qualified customers can earn cash back with a Tri-State Visa card **  "`
12	`var beginPos=0`
13	`function scrollingMsg() {`
14	`msgForm.scrollingMsg.value=scrollMsg.substring(beginPos, scrollMsg.length)+ scrollMsg.substring(0,beginPos)`

Lines 9 and 10 start the <script> section of the Web page file. Line 11 declares the scrollMsg variable and assigns the message string, "** Qualified customers can earn cash back with a Tri-State Visa card **" to it. The spaces at the beginning and end of the message string ensure that spaces appear at both ends of the message. Line 12 declares the beginPos variable, used to indicate the beginning position of the text string, and initializes it to zero. Line 13 declares the function scrollingMsg(). Line 14 assigns the message string to the text field object, which is constructed using the form (msgForm), the text field object (scrollingMsg) as an attribute of the msgForm form object, and the value property. The value property is used to assign text to the contents of the text field. Figure 10–4 illustrates the relationship between these objects and how the statement is derived.

form text field object constructed from form name using id attribute and text field using name attribute

text field name scrollingMsg is property of msgForm

```
msgForm.scrollingMsg.value = scrollMsg.substring(beginPos,scrollMsg.length)+scrollMsg.substring(0,beginPos)

<form id="msgForm" action="">
  <p style="text-align:center"><input type="text" name="scrollingMsg" size="25" /></p>
</form>
```

form name

text field object named with name attribute

text field size attribute

Figure 10–4

The rest of the assignment statement in line 14 uses the substring() method and concatenates the remainder of the scrollMsg variable to the beginning of the scrollMsg variable. As you learned in Chapter 9, the substring() method needs two parameters (x,y), where x is the starting point of the string and y is the location of the last character needed. This statement tells the scrollingMsg() function to assign the next character in the string message to the text field, to make the message appear as if it is scrolling.

To Create the scrollingMsg() User-Defined Function

The following step shows how to create the scrollingMsg() user-defined function and define its variables.

1

- Click line 9, the blank line below the <title> tag.
- Enter the JavaScript code shown in Table 10–2 on the previous page to enter the beginning script tags and define the variables used in the scrolling message, indenting as shown. Press the ENTER key to position the insertion point on line 15 (Figure 10–5).

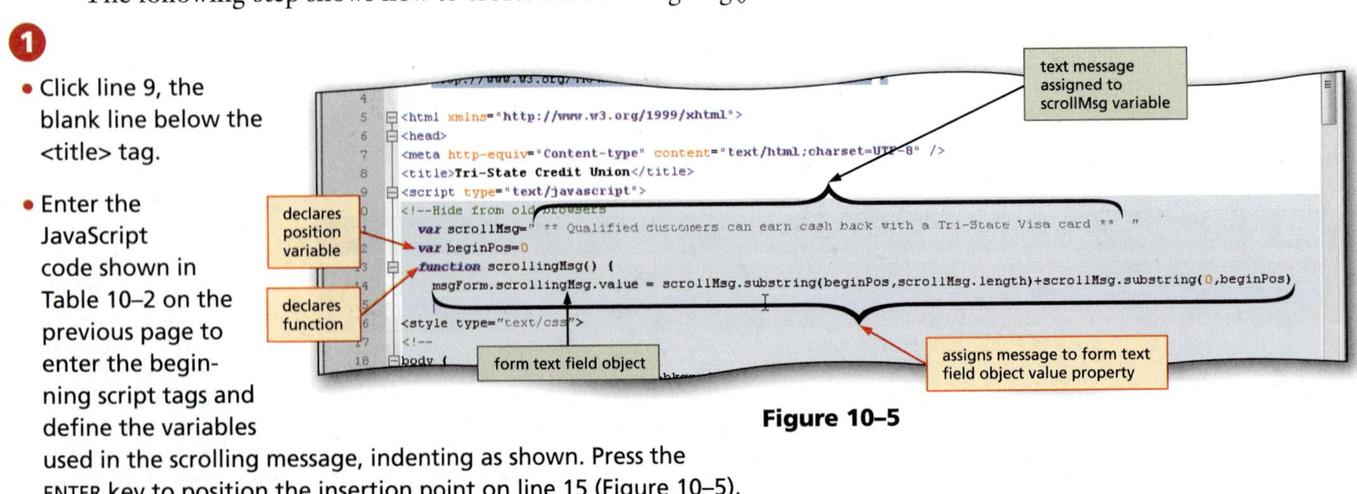

Figure 10–5

Q&A How can the scrolling message be formatted?

The best way to format a scrolling message in a <div> tag is to use an embedded style as you learned in earlier chapters.

Incrementing the Position Locator Variable After declaring the scrollingMsg() function, the next step is to increment the beginPos variable and append the next character from the message string to the text field. To cause the message to scroll in the text field, the position locator variable (beginPos) must be incremented by one. Table 10–3 describes the various ways JavaScript statements can be used to increment variables.

Table 10–3 Incrementing a Variable

Statement	Explanation
`variable=variable+1`	Executes the expression on the right side of the equal sign and assigns the result to a variable on the left side
`variable+=1`	Adds the number after the equal sign to a variable
`variable++`	Adds 1 to a variable; increments after the assignment
`++variable`	Adds 1 to a variable before the assignment

Once incremented, the new value of the position locator variable, beginPos, allows the substring() method in line 14 to extract the next character in the message string and append it to the end of the message in the text field.

To Enter the Code to Increment the Position Locator Variable

The following step illustrates how to enter the code to increment the position counter.

1

- If necessary, click line 15 and indent under the previous line.
- Type `beginPos=beginPos+1` to increment the position locator by one, and then press the ENTER key (Figure 10–6).

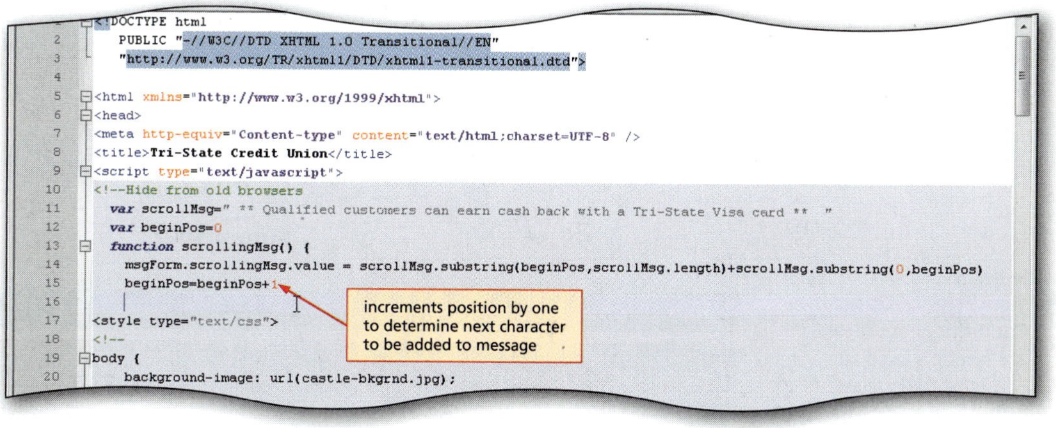

```
1  <!DOCTYPE html
2     PUBLIC "-//W3C//DTD XHTML 1.0 Transitional//EN"
3     "http://www.w3.org/TR/xhtml1/DTD/xhtml1-transitional.dtd">
4
5  <html xmlns="http://www.w3.org/1999/xhtml">
6  <head>
7  <meta http-equiv="Content-type" content="text/html;charset=UTF-8" />
8  <title>Tri-State Credit Union</title>
9  <script type="text/javascript">
10 <!--Hide from old browsers
11   var scrollMsg=" ** Qualified customers can earn cash back with a Tri-State Visa card **  "
12   var beginPos=0
13   function scrollingMsg() {
14     msgForm.scrollingMsg.value = scrollMsg.substring(beginPos,scrollMsg.length)+scrollMsg.substring(0,beginPos)
15     beginPos=beginPos+1
16     
17 <style type="text/css">
18 <!--
19 body {
20     background-image: url(castle-bkgrnd.jpg);
```

increments position by one to determine next character to be added to message

Figure 10–6

Q&A Why did we write the increment statement this way instead of using one of the other methods?

This method is the most common and easiest for beginners to understand. In addition, developers should use a format that can be recognized by anyone who might have to modify their code after the initial implementation.

Entering an if Statement After incrementing the position location variable (beginPos) by one, the JavaScript code must determine if the current value of beginPos exceeds the length of the message string. An **if statement** is used to test a condition and then take one or more actions, based on the results of the test. The general form of the if statement is shown in Table 10–4. The if statement tests a **condition**, which is any comparison of values that evaluates to true or false. If the result of the comparison is true, the JavaScript code within the braces is executed. If the result of the comparison is false, the code after the closing brace is executed. Figure 10–7 shows the flowchart that corresponds

BTW **Operands in a Conditional Evaluation**
An operand is a numerical, string, logical, or object data type or value. Operands must be of the same data type, or you will not get a true comparison result.

to an if statement. The if statement determines if the current value of the beginPos variable is greater than the length of the message.

BTW

Spaces Between Operators and Operands

Spaces between an operand and operator are optional. It may be easier to read an expression if spaces are used, but they are not necessary.

Table 10–4 if Statement

General form:	`if (condition) {`
	`JavaScript statements if condition true`
	`}`

Comment:	where condition is the comparison of values. All conditions must be placed in parentheses. If the result of the comparison is true, JavaScript executes the statements between the curly braces. If the result of the comparison is false, the JavaScript statements after the closing brace are executed.

Example:	`if (beginPos>scrollMsg.length) {`
	`beginPos=0`
	`}`

As shown in the example in Table 10–4, the conditions use symbols called operators to indicate what type of comparisons should be made between the values. Table 10–5 shows the conditional operators used for comparisons. For more information about conditional operators, see the JavaScript Quick Reference in Appendix G.

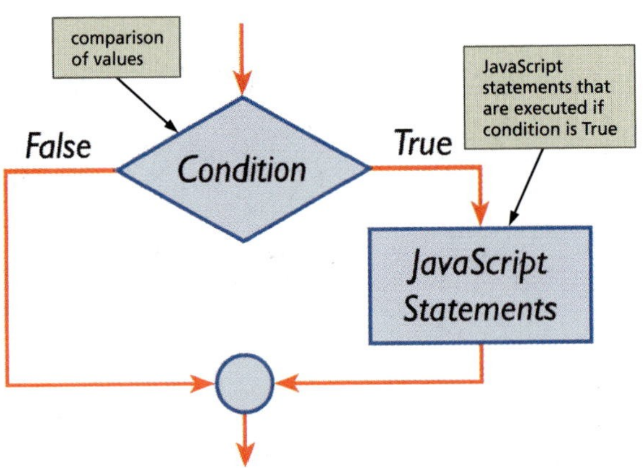

Figure 10–7

BTW

Conditional Operators

Conditional operators are symbols used to compare two values, called operands. The operator compares the two operands and returns a logical value based on whether the comparison is true.

Table 10–5 Conditional Operators

Operators	Example	Results
==	(a==b)	True if a equals b
===	(a=== b)	True if a equals b and the data are of the same type
!=	(a!=b)	True if a does not equal b
!==	(a!==b)	True if a does not equal b and/or the data are not of the same type
>	(a>b)	True if a is greater than b
<	(a<b)	True if a is less than b
>=	(a>=b)	True if a is greater than or equal to b
<=	(a<=b)	True if a is less than or equal to b
&&	(a==b) && (x<y)	True if both conditions are true (a equals b and x is less than y)
||	(a!=b) || (x>=a)	True if either condition is true (a does not equal b or x is greater than or equal to a)

The flowchart and sample code shown in Figure 10–8 illustrate how the if statement compares the beginning position variable (beginPos) with the overall length of the message (scrollMsg.length).

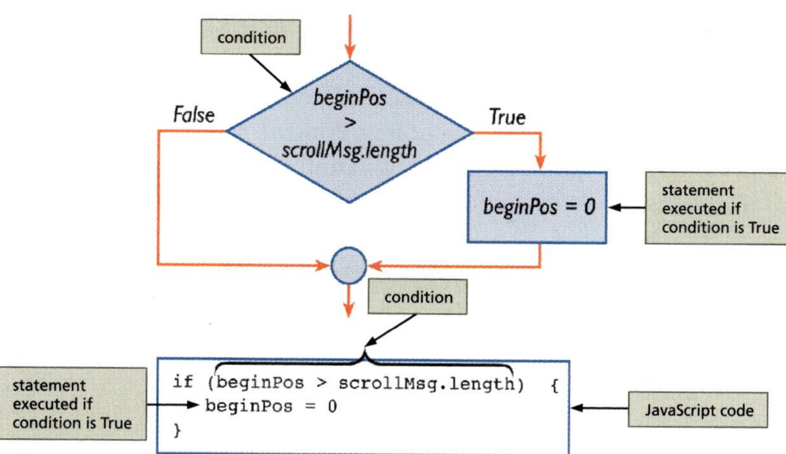

Figure 10–8

If the current value of the beginPos variable exceeds the length of the scrollMsg variable, the statement assigns the value zero to the beginPos variable. By setting beginPos to zero, the JavaScript code starts over assigning the first character of the string message to the text field, which gives the illusion the text is scrolling in the text field.

To Enter an if Statement

Table 10–6 shows the code to enter an if statement.

Table 10–6 Code to Enter an if Statement

Line	Code
16	`if (beginPos > scrollMsg.length) {`
17	`    beginPos=0`
18	`}`

The following step illustrates how to enter an if statement.

1

- If necessary, click line 16 and indent under the previous line.
- Enter the code in Table 10–6, indenting as shown, to add the if statement to test the beginPos value, and press the ENTER key (Figure 10–9).

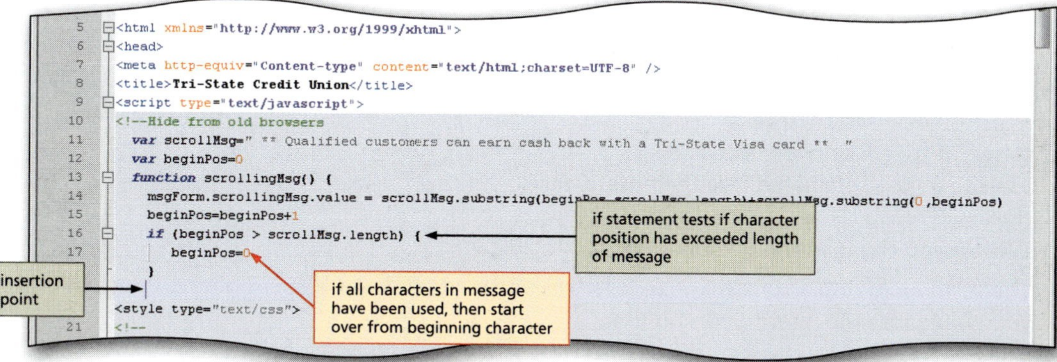

Figure 10–9

Q&A

Do all JavaScript if statements have to be written in this format?

When only one statement follows the condition, like in this example, the statement could have been written as follows: `if (beginPos > scrollMsg.length) beginPos=0`. Note that the braces have been dropped for just one statement to be executed if the condition is true. If more than one statement needs to be executed, then the braces must be used to create the block of statements.

BTW

Recursion
In this chapter's project, recursion is used to keep a routine going indefinitely or until some other function is called to stop it. Normally, a recursive function should have a mechanism that terminates the function when it completes its task.

Using the setTimeout() Method to Create a Recursive Call To have the message text scroll continuously in the text field, you use a programming technique called **recursion**, in which a function is called within itself, creating an "endless loop." The setTimeout() method is used to call a function or evaluate an expression after a specified amount of time has elapsed, which is measured in milliseconds. The general form of the setTimeout() method is shown in Table 10–7.

Table 10–7 setTimeout() Method	
General form:	`setTimeout("instruction", time delay in milliseconds)`
Comment:	where instruction is any valid JavaScript statement and time delay is expressed in number of milliseconds
Example:	`window.setTimeout("scrollingMsg()",200)`

The recursive call of the scrollingMsg() user-defined function by the setTimeout() method continuously displays characters and regulates the speed of the characters displaying in the text field.

To Add the setTimeout() Method to Create a Recursive Call

The following step illustrates how to add the setTimeout() method to create a recursive call to the scrollingMsg() function.

- If necessary, click line 19 and indent under the previous line of code, then type `window.setTimeout ("scrollingMsg()",200)` to call scrollingMsg() from within itself and then press the ENTER key.
- Align the insertion point under the function statement, then type } on line 20 to close the function and then press the ENTER key two times (Figure 10–10).

```
7  <meta http-equiv="Content-type" content="text/html;charset=UTF-8" />
8  <title>Tri-State Credit Union</title>
9  <script type="text/javascript">
10 <!--Hide from old browsers
11   var scrollMsg=" ** Qualified customers can earn cash back with a Tri-State Visa card **  "
12   var beginPos=0
13   function scrollingMsg() {
14     msgForm.scrollingMsg.value = scrollMsg.substring(beginPos,scrollMsg.length)+scrollMsg.substri
15     beginPos=beginPos+1
16     if (beginPos > scrollMsg.length) {
17       beginPos=0
18     }
19     window.setTimeout("scrollingMsg()",200)
20   }
21
22
23 <style type="text/css">
24 <!--
25 body {
26   background-image: url(castle-bkgrnd.jpg);
```

setTimeout recursive call every 200 milliseconds

end of function

Figure 10–10

Q&A

How do you know how fast to make the scrolling?

The best way is to try several different speeds and ask potential users to look at it and indicate their preference.

Q&A

What if you changed the number from 200 to 2000?

The text would display one character every two seconds and would be so boring to watch, you would lose the interest of your user.

To Complete a JavaScript Section

The following steps show how to enter the JavaScript code to complete the <script> section.

1. If necessary, click line 22.
2. If necessary, position the insertion point to line up under the <script> tag.
3. Type `//-->` to close the comment to hide the JavaScript and then press the ENTER key.
4. Type `</script>` to close the <script> section but do not press the ENTER key (Figure 10–11).

Q&A Can I use one hyphen and the greater than sign to end the comment?

No, it must be two hyphens and the greater than sign to close the comment.

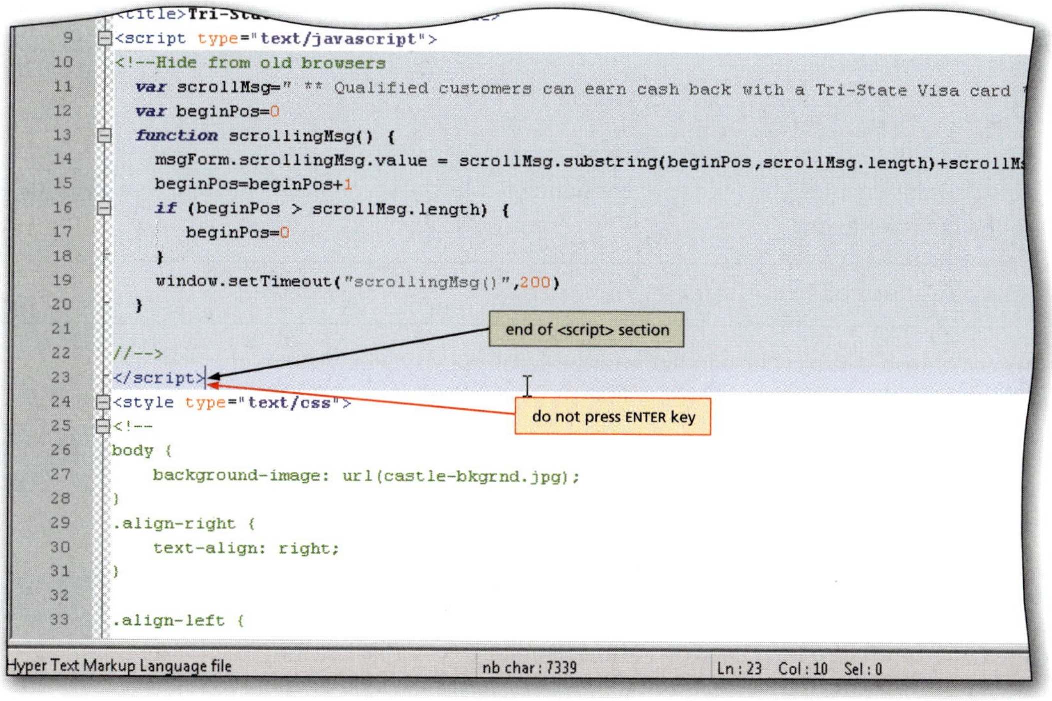

```
9  <script type="text/javascript">
10 <!--Hide from old browsers
11   var scrollMsg=" ** Qualified customers can earn cash back with a Tri-State Visa card
12   var beginPos=0
13   function scrollingMsg() {
14     msgForm.scrollingMsg.value = scrollMsg.substring(beginPos,scrollMsg.length)+scrollM
15     beginPos=beginPos+1
16     if (beginPos > scrollMsg.length) {
17        beginPos=0
18     }
19     window.setTimeout("scrollingMsg()",200)
20   }
21
22 //-->
23 </script>
24 <style type="text/css">
25 <!--
26 body {
27     background-image: url(castle-bkgrnd.jpg);
28 }
29 .align-right {
30     text-align: right;
31 }
32
33 .align-left {
```


Figure 10–11

Adding an Onload Event Handler

The last step in adding a scrolling message to a Web page is to add an event handler to start the scrolling message when the Web page loads. As discussed in Chapter 9, an **event** is an action, such as a mouse click or a window loading. An **event handler** is a way to associate that action with a function. The event handler that starts the scrolling message is the onload event handler and is placed in the <body> tag.

The JavaScript standard uses both uppercase and lowercase in spelling event handlers, as shown in Table 10–8 on the next page. To be XHTML-compliant and to pass XML validation, this text follows the XHTML standards. Because XHTML treats event handlers as tag attributes, the XHTML standard requires all tag attributes to be lowercase.

Table 10–8 shows some of the event handlers and the associated objects. As the table indicates, event handlers can be used only with certain objects. For example, the onclick event handler is used to trigger JavaScript code when a user clicks a button or link, while the onload event handler is used to trigger JavaScript code when a document is loaded into the browser window. For more information about event handlers, see the JavaScript Quick Reference in Appendix G.

Table 10–8 Objects and Associated Event Handlers

Object	Event Handler
button	`onClick, onDblClick`
document	`onLoad, onUnload`
form	`onSubmit, onReset, onBlur, onKeydown, onKeypress, onKeyup`
hyperlink	`onClick, onMouseover, onMouseout, onDblClick, onMousemove, onMousedown`
image	`onLoad, onAbort, onError, onMousemove, onMousedown`
input box	`onBlur, onChange, onFocus, onKeypress, onKeyup, onKeydown`
Submit button	`onClick`
window	`onLoad, onUnload, onBlur, onFocus`

In this chapter, the onload event handler calls the scrollingMsg() function, using the following statement:

```
onload="scrollingMsg()"
```

where onload is the event handler and the scrollingMsg() function is the code that is executed as the result of the event. The statement is entered in the <body> tag to indicate that the onload event handler should call the scrollingMsg() function when the Web page loads.

To Enter the onload Event Handler to Call the scrollingMsg() Function

The following step illustrates how to enter the onload event handler to call the scrollingMsg() function.

- Click to the right of the y in body in line 54.
- Press the SPACEBAR once.
- Type `onload="scrollingMsg()"` to add the event handler and do not press the ENTER key (Figure 10–12).

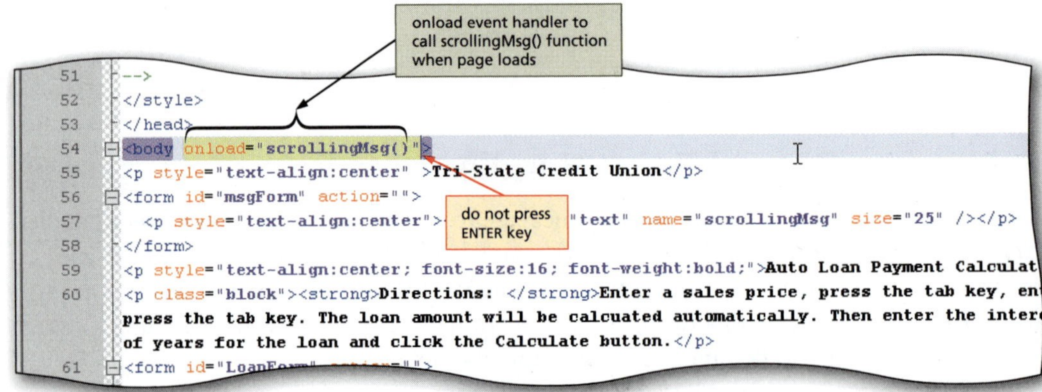

Figure 10–12

To Save an HTML File and Test a Web Page

After completing a section of JavaScript code, you should test your Web page to ensure the code works. You should not continue with the next section until you are sure the scrolling message works correctly. With the code for the scrollingMsg() function complete and the onload event handler added to call the function when the Web page loads, you should save the HTML file and test the Web page. The following steps illustrate how to save the HTML file and then test the Web page.

1. With a USB drive plugged into your computer, click File on the menu bar, and then click Save As to display the Save As dialog box.
2. Type `chapter10-1solution.html` in the File name text box (do not press the ENTER key).
3. Click Computer in the left-hand side of the dialog box to display a list of available drives.
4. If necessary, scroll until your USB drive, such as UDISK 2.0 (G:), appears in the list of available drives.
5. If necessary, open the Chapter10\ChapterFiles folder.
6. Click the Save button in the Save As dialog box to save the file on the USB flash drive with the name chapter10-1solution.html.
7. Open Internet Explorer and type `g:\Chapter10\ChapterFiles\chapter10-1solution.html` in the Address box.
8. Press ENTER to display the Web page. If a security message appears, click that bar, click the Allow Blocked Content option that displays, and then click Yes in the confirmation dialog box. The message should start scrolling in the form text field (Figure 10–13).
9. Before proceeding to the next section, verify that this code works. If you have errors, check your code against Figures 10–3, 10–11, and 10–12. Correct any mistakes, save your Web page file, and refresh the browser.

Q&A

What if I do not see a security bar?

That simply means that tight restrictions and security are not set on your browser.

Figure 10–13

Plan Ahead

Validating form input.

The validations and calculations in this project require two separate user-defined functions. In order to calculate the monthly payment, the values entered into the text fields must be valid numbers. A user-defined function called valSaleTradeAmt() performs the following steps to validate the text field entries and calculate the loanAmt:

- Convert the text field value to a numeric value using the parseInt() or parseFloat() function
- Use the isNaN (is Not a Number) function to verify the value is numeric and then verify the value is greater than zero
- Use an if statement to test if the value is not a number or is zero or less, display an error message, clear the text field, and position the insertion point in that text field
- Subtract the trade-in amount from the sales amount to calculate the loan amount

To call the valSaleTradeAmt() validation function, an onblur event handler is added to the form.

Once the loan amount is calculated, the user must enter the loan interest rate and the number of years to pay the loan off. The number of years is obtained from a <select> drop-down list to help reduce user input error. A user-defined function called CalcLoanAmt() follows these steps to validate the text field and <select> drop-down list entries and calculate the monthly payment:

- For the loan rate, convert the loan rate text field value to a numeric value using the parseInt() or parseFloat() function
- For the loan years, use the selectedIndex property of the <select> drop-down list to determine the number years for the loan
- Use the isNaN (is Not a Number) function to verify the value is numeric and then verify the value is greater than zero
- If the value is not a number or is zero or less, display an error message, clear the text field, and position the insertion point in that text field.

BTW

Validating Web Form Data

Web developers use multiple techniques to validate Web forms using JavaScript. Some developers choose to validate each item as it is entered by using a combination of onchange event handlers and user-defined functions. It is important to validate Web forms because some Web databases are sensitive to invalid data and may crash, or mathematical formulas may cease to function when using invalid data.

Adding a Loan Calculator with Validation

The car loan payment calculator form shown in Figure 10–14 requests user input. The form, which is named LoanForm, already has been created in the HTML file. JavaScript code must be added to validate the input, calculate the loan amount, and display the results in the LoanForm form. In order for the calculator to work, each text field must have a valid data entry. You will write two user-defined functions, one called valSaleTradeAmt() and the other CalcLoanAmt(), to perform these three tasks. Other JavaScript user-defined functions will calculate the monthly payment and display the formatted results.

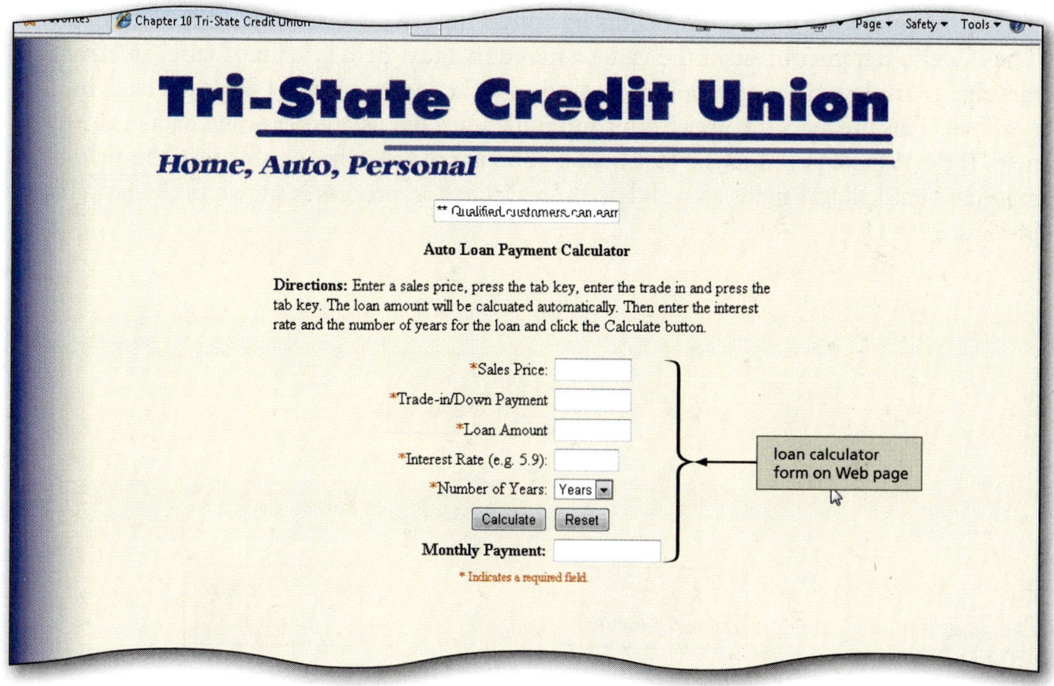

Figure 10–14

Validating Forms Using Nested if...else Statements

You can use different techniques to validate forms. This chapter uses a series of nested if…else statements. The if…else statement is like the if statement except that it specifies statements to execute if the condition is false, as shown in the flowchart in Figure 10–15. Much like the if statement, an if…else statement tests a condition. If the condition is true, the statements between the curly braces after the if statement execute. If the condition is false, the statements between the braces after the else statement execute.

BTW

if and if...else Statements
JavaScript if and if…else statements are an integral part of the programming language. These statements control the flow of logic or execution of expressions based on the result of a conditional test.

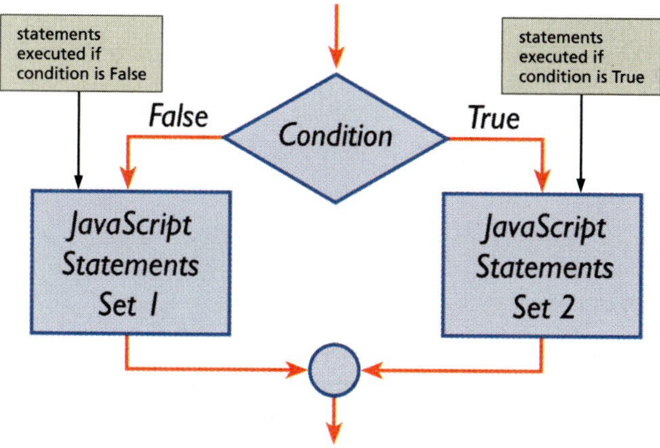

Figure 10–15

The validation algorithm begins by converting the text field value to a number. The if...else statement tests if the value entered in a text field is valid. If false, an error message is displayed, the text field is cleared, and the insertion point is placed back in the text field. This prevents the user from continuing until the user enters valid data in the text field. If the value entered in the text field is valid (a true condition), the next text field is examined until all text fields are validated. The validation process is shown in the flowchart in Figure 10–16.

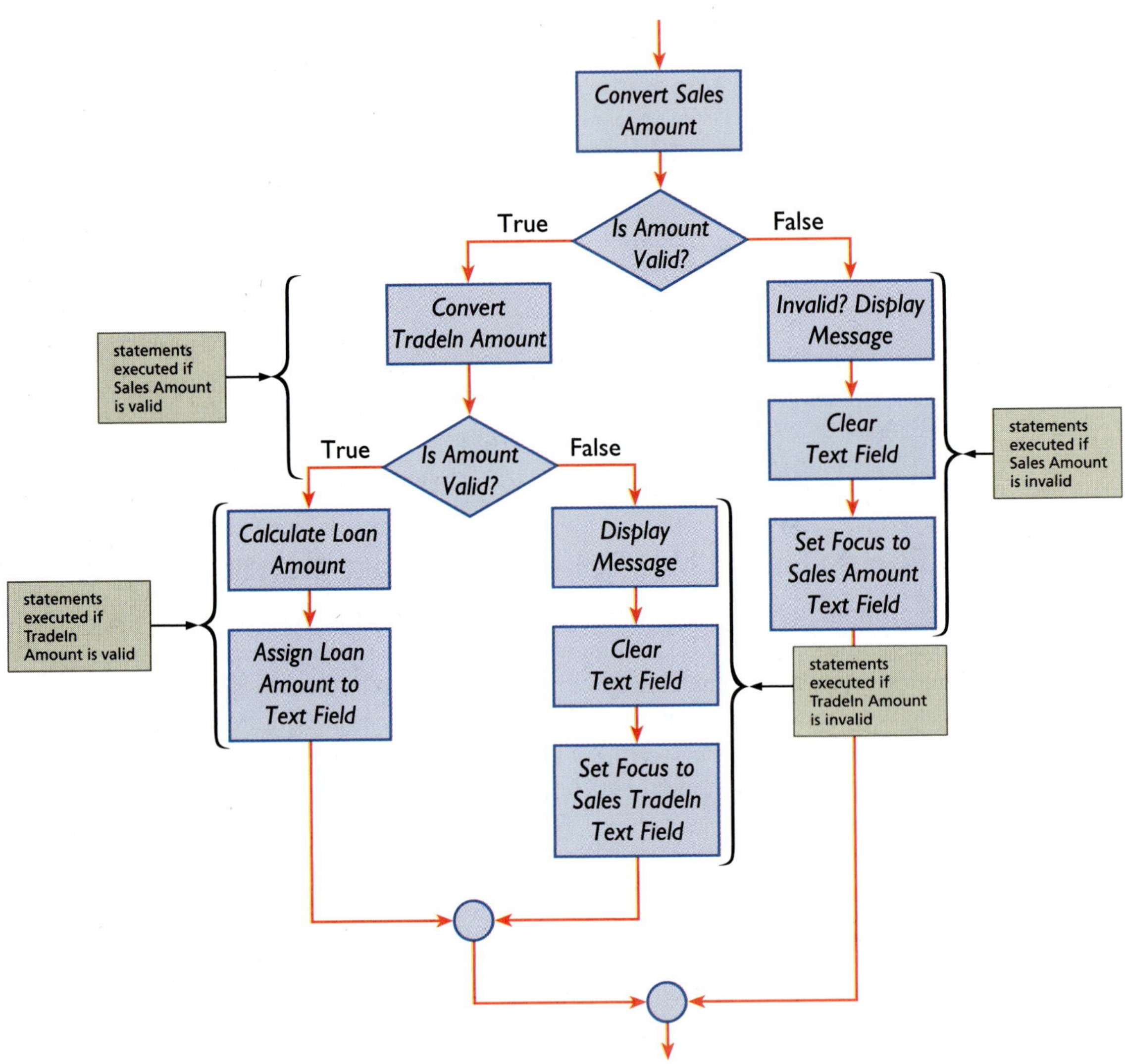

Figure 10–16

This validation design is necessary because of the event-driven nature of JavaScript. When a user triggers an event that calls a function, processing stays within that function until all statements execute. Because all the statements execute in a function, the form validation routine uses nested if...else statements to ensure each text field is validated correctly. By nesting if...else statements, you can place an if...else statement inside another, as shown in Figure 10–17.

```
if (condition) {
   if (condition) {
      JavaScript statements if true
   }
   else {
        if (condition) {
            JavaScript statements if true
        }
        else {
             JavaScript statements if false
        }
   }
}
```

statements executed if first If statement is True

statements executed if second If statement is False

Figure 10–17

Using Built-In Functions to Validate Data

When validating data, the JavaScript code may have to evaluate several criteria — for example, to ensure that a text field is not blank or that it contains numeric data (not text or characters). HTML forms accept data entered into a text field as text character data, which means that the values must be converted to a number before they can be tested or validated. Table 10–9 describes the two built-in functions, parseInt() and parseFloat(), used to convert values and one function, isNaN(), used to test if the converted value is a number.

BTW

Radix or Number Base
Radix is the number base to which the integer value should be converted. The use of the numeral 2 represents binary, 8 represents octal, and 16 represents hexadecimal.

BTW

parseFloat() and parseInt() Built-in Functions
The parseFloat() function is a built-in function. parseFloat()parses a string argument and converts the value into a decimal floating-point number. If the first character cannot be converted to a number, the result is NaN, which means "not a number." The parseInt() built-in function converts a value to an integer. If a value of 12Wre is entered, parseInt() will convert to 12.

Table 10–9 Built-In Functions: parseInt(), parseFloat(), isNaN()

General form:	`variable = parseInt(value, base)`
Comment:	converts to an integer. Value is any string, which can be a variable or literal; base is the number base to which you want the string converted. A base of 2 means binary base number, an 8 means octal, and a 10 means decimal. The function returns an integer value, stripping the value after the decimal point.
Example:	`parseInt(loanAmount,10)`
General form:	`variable = parseFloat(value)`
Comment:	converts to a floating point number. Value is any string, which can be a variable or literal, representing a floating-point number. A floating-point number is one with a fractional or decimal value (including percentages). The function returns the value as a floating-point number.
Example:	`parseFloat(loanAmount)`
General form:	`isNaN(value)`
Comment:	isNaN means is Not a Number. Value is any value, which can be a variable or literal. The function returns a Boolean condition of true or false.
Example:	`isNaN(loanAmount)`

Figure 10–18 on the next page shows how the values of the form are passed to the valSaleTradeAmt() user-defined function. Table 10–10 on the next page shows the general form of the JavaScript statement used to assign a null, or other, value to a text field object within a form.

BTW

isNaN() Built-in Function

The isNaN() built-in function to test whether a value is not a number is the only function that tests a numeric value as the argument. The test uses the NOT operator and returns a Boolean value of true or false.

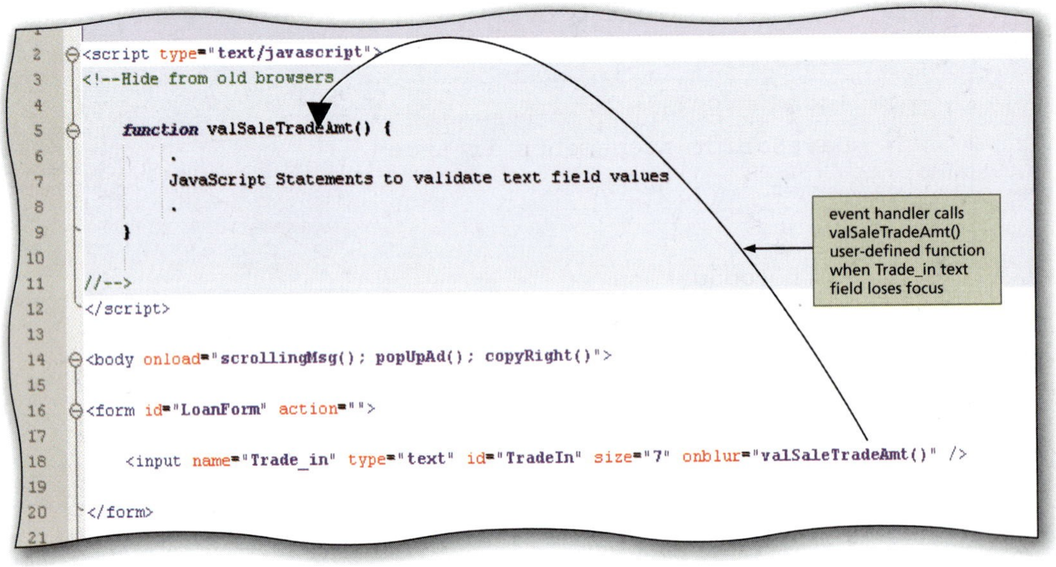

```
<script type="text/javascript">
<!--Hide from old browsers

    function valSaleTradeAmt() {
        .
        JavaScript Statements to validate text field values
        .
    }

//-->
</script>

<body onload="scrollingMsg(); popUpAd(); copyRight()">

<form id="LoanForm" action="">

    <input name="Trade_in" type="text" id="TradeIn" size="7" onblur="valSaleTradeAmt()" />

</form>
```

event handler calls valSaleTradeAmt() user-defined function when Trade_in text field loses focus

Figure 10–18

Table 10–10 Assignment Statement

General form:	`document.formname.textfieldname.value=variable_or_literal`
Comment:	where formname is the name of the form; textfieldname is the name of a text field in the form; value is the attribute; and the variable_or_literal is the value assigned to the text field.

Examples:	`document.LoanForm.Amount.value=LoanAmt`
	`document.LoanForm.Amount.value="12500"`
	`document.LoanForm.Amount.value=""`

To place the insertion point back in a specific text field in the form, the focus must be set for that text field. Setting the focus means giving attention to an object. JavaScript uses the **focus() method** to give attention to an object. When the focus is set to an object, such as the Amount text field, the JavaScript statement automatically positions the insertion point in the text field. Table 10–11 shows the general form of the focus() method.

Table 10–11 focus() Method

General form:	`document.formname.objectname.focus()`
Comment:	where formname is the name of the form that contains the object; and objectname identifies the object to which focus should be set.
Examples:	`document.LoanForm.Amount.focus()`

The first step in creating this validation function is to define the variables that will be needed. Table 10–12 shows the code to define the variables for the valSaleTradeAmt() and CalcLoanAmt() user-defined functions.

Table 10–12 Code for valSaleTradeAmt() Function to Validate the Loan Amount

Line	Code
22	`var salesAmt`
23	`var loanAmt`
24	`var loanRate`
25	`var loanYears`

Lines 22 through 25 declare the variables that will be used in the two user-defined functions. Table 10–13 shows the code to enter the valSaleTradeAmt() user-defined function and the statements necessary to validate and calculate the car loan amount based on the sales amount minus the trade-in amount using the parseInt() and isNaN() functions.

Table 10–13 Code for valSaleTradeAmt() Function to Validate and Calculate the Loan Amount

```
Line  Code
27    function valSaleTradeAmt() {
28       var salesAmt=parseInt(LoanForm.SaleAmount.value,10)
29       if (isNaN(salesAmt) || (salesAmt <= 0)) {
30          alert("The sales amount is not a valid number!")
31          LoanForm.SaleAmount.value = ""
32          LoanForm.SaleAmount.focus()
33       }
34       else {
35          var tradeinAmt = parseInt(LoanForm.TradeIn.value,10)
36          if (isNaN(tradeinAmt) || (tradeinAmt <= 0) ||
                (tradeinAmt > salesAmt)) {
37             alert("The trade-in amount is not a valid number!")
38             LoanForm.TradeIn.value = " "
39             LoanForm.TradeIn.focus()
40          }
41          else {
42             loanAmt = salesAmt-tradeinAmt
43             LoanForm.LoanAmount.value = loanAmt
44             LoanForm.Rate.focus()
45          }
46       }
47    }
```

Line 27 declares the valSaleTradeAmt() function and uses the values entered or selected in the LoanForm. Line 28 assigns the data entered in the SaleAmount text field to the salesAmt variable and the parseInt() function converts that value to an integer. The if statement beginning on line 29 tests if the value for the salesAmt variable is not a number or if the value entered is less than or equal to zero. If the result of the condition is true (that is, the value entered is not a number or it is a negative number), the function notifies the user with an alert message (line 30) that the sales amount is not valid, clears the data entered in the SaleAmount text field (line 31), and then sets the focus back to the SaleAmount text field (line 32). The brace in line 33 closes the if statement.

Because an event must be executed until completion, the valSaleTradeAmt() function validates all the entered values. Line 34 continues with the else statement to validate the trade-in amount. Line 35 converts the TradeIn value to an integer assigned the tradeinAmt variable. The if statement at line 36 tests if the tradeinAmt is a number and greater than zero but less than or equal to the sales amount. The compound condition using the OR operator requires all three conditions must be true. If the tradeinAmt does not meet the conditions, line 37 displays an alert message. Line 38 clears the input text field, and line 39 sets the focus back to the TradeIn input text field. Line 40 closes the if statement. Line 41 starts the else statement block, which processes the valid data. Line 42 calculates the loan amount by subtracting the trade-in value from the sales amount. Line 43 assigns the loan amount to the LoanAmount input text field to display on the form. Line 44 sets the focus to the interest rate input text field to continue processing the form.

To Add the valSaleTradeAmt() Function with Nested if...else Statements to Validate Form Data

The following step illustrates how to enter the valSaleTradeAmt() user-defined function and the if...else statements that validate the amounts entered in the SaleAmount and TradeIn text fields and calculates the loan amount.

- If necessary, click the Notepad++ button on the taskbar to display chapter10-1solution .html in the Notepad++ window.
- Click line 21.
- Press the ENTER key once to create a blank line, and position the insertion point on line 22.
- Enter the JavaScript code shown in Table 10–12 on page HTML 472, indenting as shown to enter the code to define the variables for the user-defined functions.

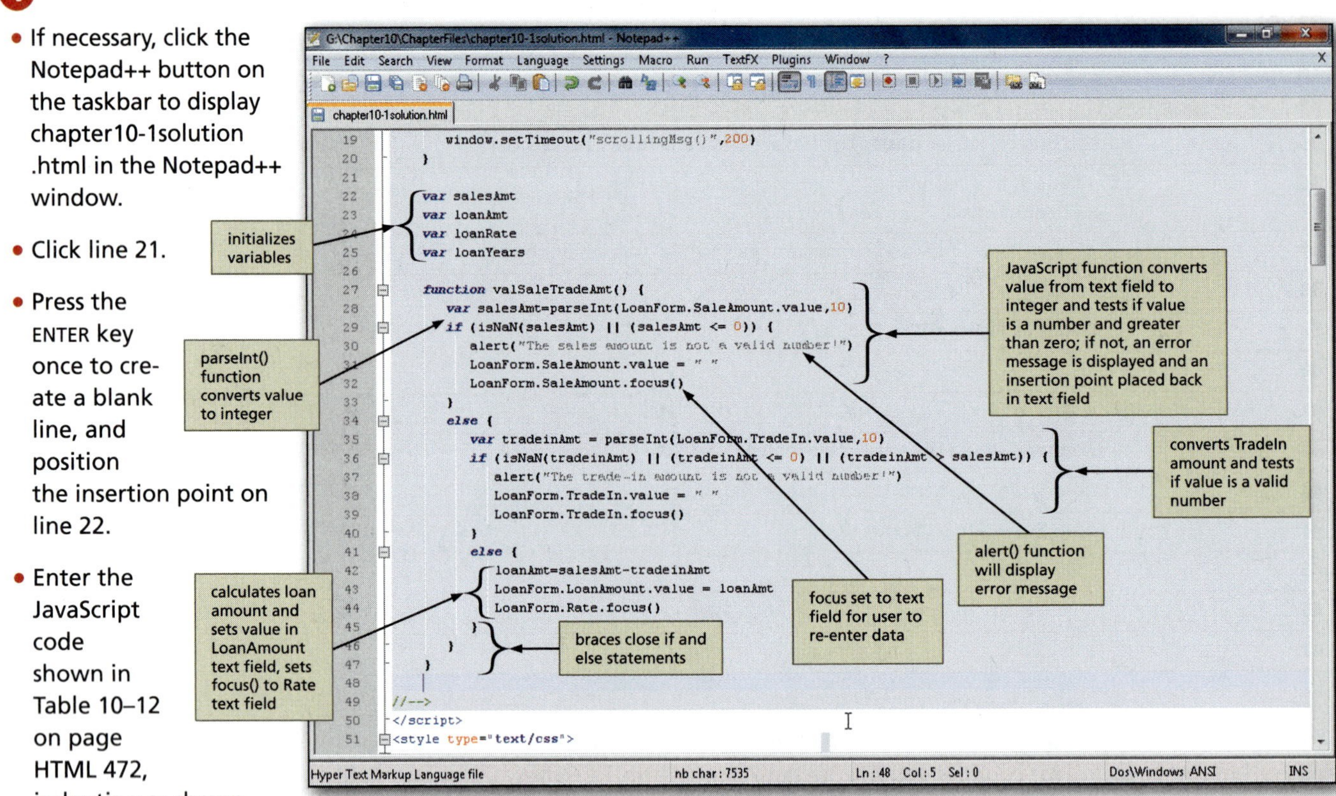

Figure 10–19

- Press the ENTER key twice after line 25.
- Enter the JavaScript code shown in Table 10–13 on the previous page, indenting as shown to enter the code for the user-defined function valSaleTradeAmt(), which validates the data entered and calculates the loan amount based on the sales amount minus the trade-in value.
- Press the ENTER key once after line 47 (Figure 10–19).

Q&A

Are spaces necessary around equal signs in JavaScript statements?

No, spaces are not required. You can write one line of code with spaces around the equal signs and another without spaces and it will not make any difference.

To Enter the onblur Event Handler to Call the valSaleTradeAmt() Function

After adding the user-defined function to validate the sales price and the trade-in values and calculate the loan amount, you need to add an event handler to invoke the valSaleTradeAmt() function when the user presses the Tab key or clicks the Interest Rate text field. Moving the insertion point to another form field or object after the Trade-in value is entered means the text field no longer has the focus, which is called blur. The following step shows how to enter the onblur event handler to call the valSaleTradeAmt() function.

- Scroll down to the HTML code for the form and then click line 102 right after the closing quote in the size="7" attribute and before the rightmost /> bracket.
- Press the SPACEBAR once.

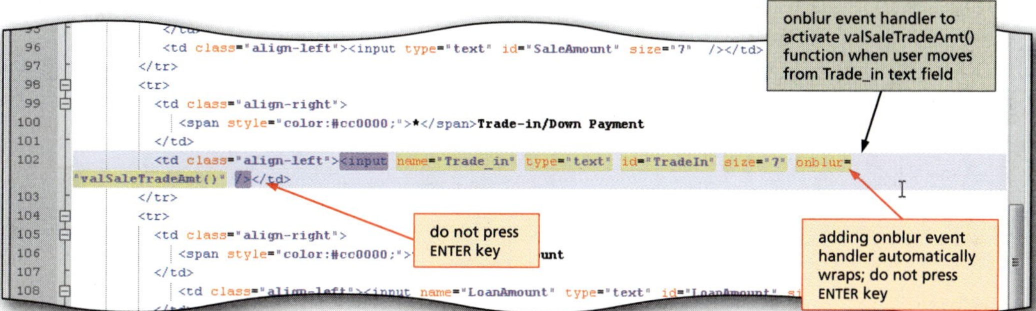

Figure 10–20

- Type `onblur="valSaleTradeAmt()"` to add the event handler to the Trade_in text field, but do not press the ENTER key (Figure 10–20).

Validating the Interest Rate and the Number of Years for the Loan

Table 10–14 shows the code in the CalcLoanAmt() user-defined function to validate the interest rate and number of years of the loan. This function is called after the user enters the interest and selects the number of years from the drop-down list, and then clicks the Calculate button.

Table 10–14 Code to Validate the Interest Rate

Line	Code
49	`function CalcLoanAmt() {`
50	`loanRate=parseFloat(LoanForm.Rate.value)`
51	`if (isNaN(loanRate) || (loanRate <= 0)) {`
52	`alert("The interest rate is not a valid number!")`
53	`LoanForm.Rate.value = ""`
54	`LoanForm.Rate.focus()`
55	`}`

Line 49 declares the user-defined function CalcLoanAmt. This function is called when the user clicks the Calculate button. Line 50 passes the value in the Interest Rate (e.g. 5.9) text field to the loanRate variable, and converts it to a floating-point number using the parseFloat() function. Because the interest rate is a floating-point number, you must use the parseFloat() function to keep the interest rate a floating-point number.

The if statement in line 51 tests the loanRate variable to determine if it is a number or if the value is less than or equal to zero. If the result of the condition is true, an alert message (line 52) notifies the user that the interest rate is not valid. Line 53 clears the data entered in the Interest Rate as % text field, and then line 54 sets the focus back to the

> **BTW**
> **Domain**
> A domain is a range of acceptable values for a field or column in a database. Using an HTML select list can ensure that accurate values are entered.

Interest Rate text field. The brace in line 55 closes the if statement. If the loanRate data is valid, the function then proceeds to validate the number of years.

Table 10–15 shows the code used to validate the value selected in the Years drop-down list.

Table 10–15 Code to Convert and Validate the Years Entered Value

Line	Code
56	`else {`
57	`loanYears=parseInt(LoanForm.Years.selectedIndex)`
58	`if (isNaN(loanYears) || (loanYears < 1)) {`
59	`alert("Please select a valid number of years from the list!")`
60	`LoanForm.Years.selectedIndex = "0"`
61	`LoanForm.Years.focus()`
62	`}`
63	`}`
64	`}`

Line 56 is an else statement that executes the statements if the if condition on line 51 is false. Line 57 converts years to an integer, using the parseInt() function. The if statement beginning in line 58 checks the condition to determine if the loanYears value entered is a number or is less than one. If the number of years is not valid, line 59 displays a message and line 60 sets the <select> drop-down list to 0. Line 61 places the focus back in the Years drop-down list. The braces in lines 62 through 64 close the nested if...else statements and the function.

To Enter the CalcLoanAmt() User-Defined Function

The following step shows how to enter the CalcLoanAmt() function to validate the Interest Rate (e.g. 5.9) text field and the Number of Years from the drop-down list.

- If necessary, click line 48 and then press the ENTER key once.
- Enter the JavaScript code shown in Table 10–14 on page HTML 475 starting on line 49 to validate the interest rate, indenting the code as shown in Figure 10–21.
- Continue on line 56 and enter the JavaScript code shown in Table 10–15 to validate the number of years for the loan, indenting to align the code as shown in Figure 10–21.
- Press the ENTER key to finish the else portions of the nested if...else statements (Figure 10–21).

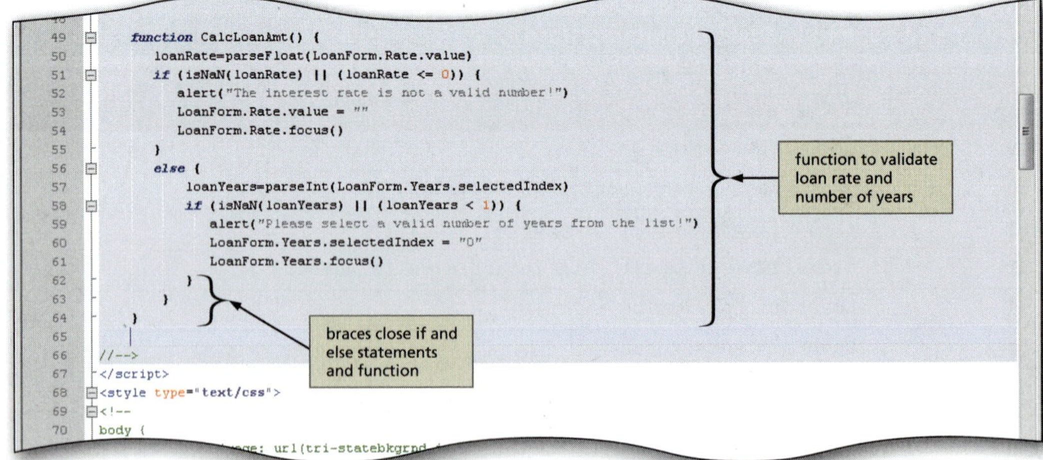

Figure 10–21

> **Q&A**
> Why is the year not converted to a floating point number?
> Most loans, especially mortgage loans, are NOT made on part of a year, so the number of years should be an integer.

To Enter an onclick Event Handler to Call the CalcLoanAmt() Function

The last step in validating the car loan payment calculator is to add an event handler to invoke the CalcLoanAmt() function when the user clicks the Calculate button. After entering all the data in the form, a user clicks the Calculate button, which triggers the CalcLoanAmt() function to validate the interest rate and number of years data entered in the form. The following step shows how to enter the onclick event handler to call the CalcLoanAmt() function.

1

- Scroll down to the HTML code for the form and then click line 153 right after the closing quote in "Calculate" and before the right-most /> bracket.
- Press the SPACEBAR once.
- Type `onclick= "CalcLoanAmt()"` to add the event handler to the Calculate button, but do not press the ENTER key (Figure 10–22).

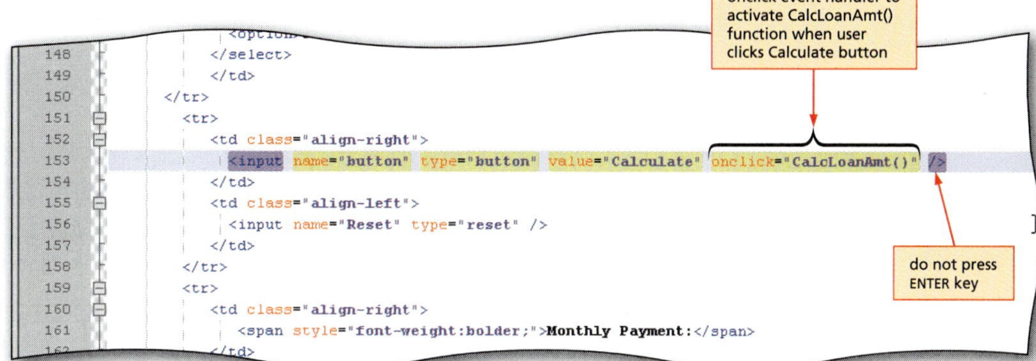

onclick event handler to activate CalcLoanAmt() function when user clicks Calculate button
do not press ENTER key

Figure 10–22

To Save an HTML File and Test a Web Page

With the JavaScript code for the form validation entered, the Web page can be saved and tested in a browser. The CalcLoanAmt() function will validate the text field entries, but will not yet calculate the monthly payment. The following steps show how to save the HTML file and test the Web page. Do not continue until this code is working properly.

1. With the USB drive plugged into your computer, click File on the menu bar, and then click Save.
2. Click the browser button on the taskbar.
3. Click the Refresh button on the browser toolbar.
4. When the Web page is displayed, click the Sales Price text field.
5. Enter test data set 1, as shown in Table 10–16 on the next page, pressing the TAB key to move to the next text field.
6. When an error message appears, click the OK button, and enter a valid number for the missing data.
7. When you have entered test data set 1, click the Calculate button at the bottom of the form.
8. After completing a set of data, click the Reset button at the bottom of the form.
9. Repeat Steps 5 through 8, using test data sets 2, 3, and 4, as shown in Table 10–16, and respond to any error messages. Figure 10–23 on the next page shows the fourth data set with the error message.

Table 10–16 Test Data Set

Data Set	Sales Amount	Trade-In	Interest Rate %	Years	Comment
1		3000	4.75	3	The sales amount is not a valid number!
2	23900	6500	A	4	The interest rate is not a valid number!
3	19000	4500	3.9	3	No error messages
4	31000	19000	5.9		Please select a valid number of years from the list!

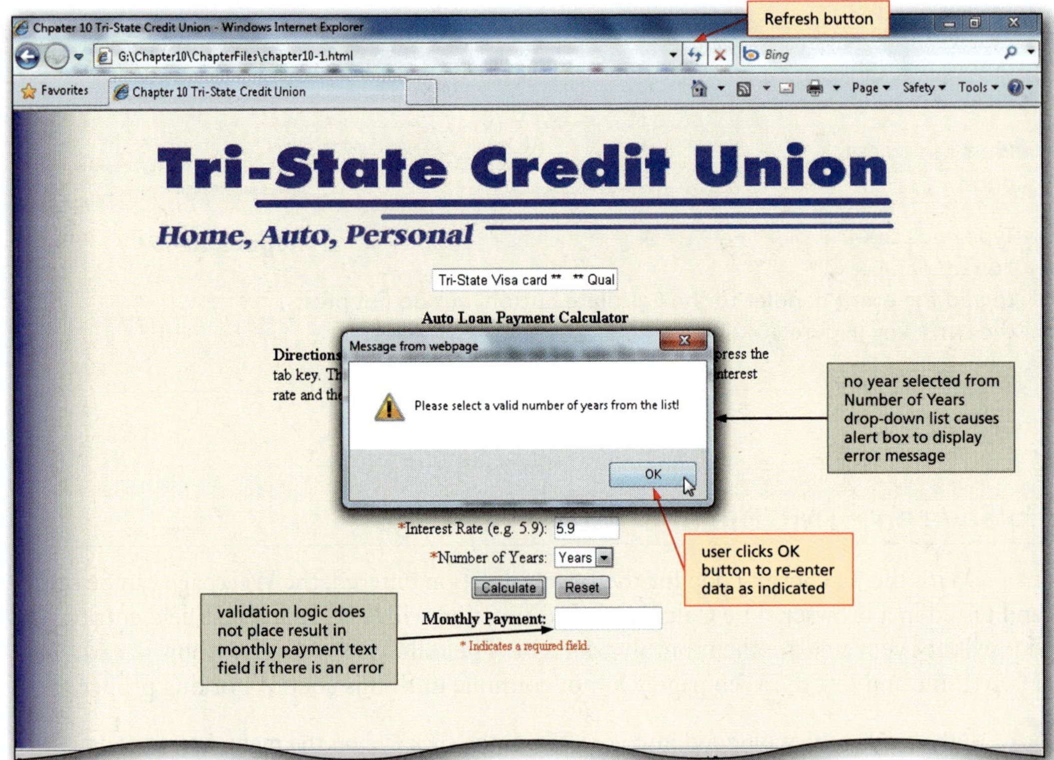

Figure 10–23

Plan Ahead

Calculating the monthly payment.

The monthly() function requires three parameters: the loan amount (loanAmt), the interest rate (loanRate), and the number of years that the payments will be made (loanYears). These values are passed from the CalcLoanAmt() user-defined function to the monthly() function. The steps to calculate the monthly payment are as follows:

- Pass the three variables — loanAmt, loanRate, and loanYears — to the monthly() function.
- Convert the monthly interest rate to Irate by dividing loanRate by 1200
- Convert the number of years to Pmts by multiplying loanYears by 12
- Calculate the monthly payment with the following formula:
- loanAmt * (Irate / (1 - (1 / Math.pow(1+Irate,Pmts))))
- Return the monthly payment as a fixed decimal value to two decimal places using the toFixed(2) method.

Adding the Monthly Payment Calculation

With the JavaScript code for the form validation complete, the next step is to add code to the CalcLoanAmt() function to calculate the monthly payment. First, a statement must be added to the CalcLoanAmt() function to call a user-defined function named monthly(), which calculates the monthly payment. The monthly() function uses the valid data in the form and calculates the monthly payment. The result is the monthly payment, which is returned as a floating-point value.

The placement of the monthly() function within the CalcLoanAmt() function is important so that, if a value in a text field is invalid, the function does not attempt to process invalid data and return an undefined result. To place this function properly, one more else statement must be added to the CalcLoanAmt() function, as shown in Table 10–17.

Table 10–17 Code to Call the monthly() Function

Line	Code
63	`else {`
64	`    var monthlyPmt = monthly(loanAmt,loanRate,loanYears)`
65	`    LoanForm.Payment.value=monthlyPmt.toString()`
66	`}`

Line 63 adds an additional else statement to the nested if…else statements. Line 64 calls the monthly() function and passes the loan amount, interest rate, and number of years for the loan as variables: loanAmt, loanRate, and loanYears. The result is stored in a temporary variable named monthlyPmt. Line 65 assigns the result to the Monthly Payment text field on the form using the toString() method to convert the value to a string for display in the text field and for use in the formatting user-defined function, which will be written later. Line 66 is the closing brace for the additional else statement.

To Enter Code to Call the monthly() Function

The following step illustrates how to enter the final else statement and the function call that passes the required values to the monthly() function.

- Click the beginning of line 63 and then press the ENTER key to insert a blank line.
- Click the blank line just inserted (line 63).
- Press the SPACEBAR to indent under the closing brace in line 62, then enter the JavaScript code shown in Table 10–17 to call the monthly user-defined function and assign the result to the payment text field, but do not press the ENTER key (Figure 10–24).

Figure 10–24

Q&A If I try to execute this Web page now, will an error occur?

Yes, because the monthly() user-defined function has not been written and entered.

Creating the monthly() User-Defined Function The monthly() function is a user-defined function that calculates the monthly payment amount. The JavaScript code for the monthly() function is shown in Table 10–18.

Table 10–18 Code for monthly() User-Defined Function

Line	Code
70	`function monthly(loanAmt,loanRate,loanYears) {`
71	`  var Irate = loanRate/1200`
72	`  var Pmts = loanYears*12`
73	`  var Amnt = loanAmt * (Irate / (1 - (1 / Math.pow(1+Irate,Pmts))))`
74	`  return Amnt.toFixed(2)`
75	`}`

BTW

Math Object

The Math object cannot be used to create other objects. Most of the properties of the Math object return preset values. Other properties of the Math object really are methods and act as functions.

Line 70 declares the monthly() function. Line 71 determines the monthly interest rate percentage by dividing the annual rate by 1200. The result is assigned to the Irate (interest rate) variable. Line 72 determines the number of monthly payments on the loan, by multiplying the number of years in the loan by 12. The resulting value is assigned to the Pmts variable.

Line 73 is the formula for calculating a monthly payment based on the amount of the loan, the monthly interest percentage, and the number of monthly payments. The mathematical representation of the formula is:

$$\texttt{loan amount * (monthly interest rate / (1 - (1 /(1 + monthly interest rate)}^{\texttt{number of payments}}\texttt{)))}$$

JavaScript, however, does not use typical programming language symbols to represent exponentiation in code. Instead, to calculate the expression (1 + monthly interest rate)$^{\text{number of payments}}$, JavaScript uses the pow() method associated with the Math object. Table 10–19 shows the general form of the pow() method.

Table 10–19 Math.pow() Method

General form:	`Math.pow(number, exponent)`
Comment:	where number is the value raised to the power of the exponent value. The pow() method accepts variables (X,n), constants (2,3), or both (Sidelength,2).

Examples:	`Math.pow(2,3)`
	`Math.pow(X,n)`
	`Math.pow(Sidelength,2)`

The return statement in line 74 tells the function to send the results of the expression back as a fixed decimal value with a length of two. The Number object's toFixed() method returns a value set to a specific decimal length, as shown in Table 10–20.

Table 10–20 Number.toFixed() Method

General form:	`Number.toFixed(digits)`		
Comment:	where digits is the exact number of digits after the decimal point. The number is rounded or padded with zeros if necessary.		
Examples:	Pmt = 234.8932	`Pmt.toFixed(3)`	Result: 234.893
	Amt = 843.6778	`Amt.toFixed(2)`	Result: 843.68

To Create the monthly() Function

The following step illustrates how to enter the monthly() user-defined function to calculate the monthly payment on a auto loan.

1

- Click the beginning of line 70 and press the ENTER key once.
- Position the insertion point on the blank line 70 just created.
- Enter the JavaScript code shown in Table 10–18 to write the code to calculate the monthly payment and then press the ENTER key once (Figure 10–25).

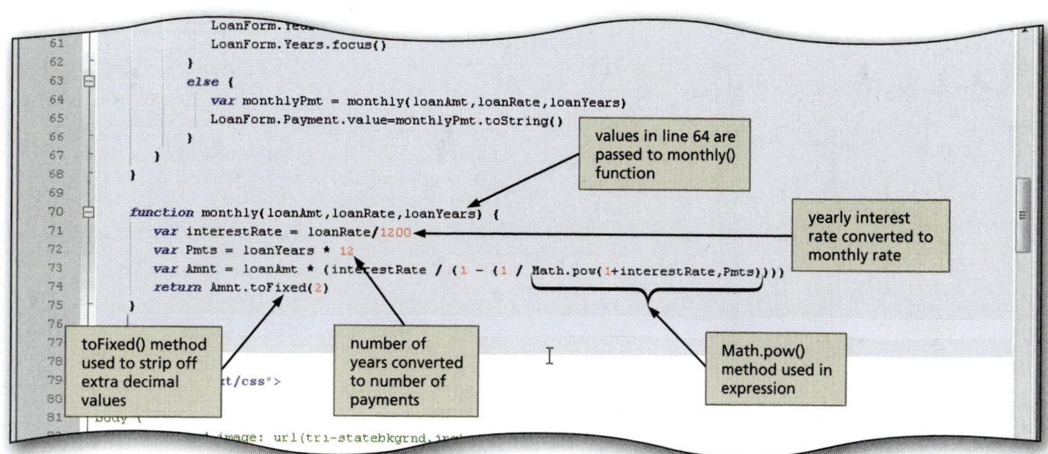
LoanForm.Years.focus()
else {
var monthlyPmt = monthly(loanAmt,loanRate,loanYears)
LoanForm.Payment.value=monthlyPmt.toString()
function monthly(loanAmt,loanRate,loanYears) {
var interestRate = loanRate/1200
var Pmts = loanYears * 12
var Amnt = loanAmt * (interestRate / (1 - (1 / Math.pow(1+interestRate,Pmts))))
return Amnt.toFixed(2)
values in line 64 are passed to monthly() function
yearly interest rate converted to monthly rate
toFixed() method used to strip off extra decimal values
number of years converted to number of payments
Math.pow() method used in expression

Figure 10–25

To Save an HTML File and Test a Web Page

Now that the monthly payment can be calculated, this is a good place to test the Web page. You should not continue to the next section until this code is working properly. The following steps show how to save the HTML file and test the Web page.

1. With the USB drive plugged into the computer, click File on the menu bar, and then click Save.
2. Click the browser button on the taskbar.
3. Click the Refresh button next to the Address box.
4. Click the Reset button on the form.
5. If necessary, click the Sales Price text field to place the insertion point in the text field.
6. Type 33000 in the Sales Price text field, and then press the TAB key.
7. Type 13000 in the Trade-in/Down Payment text field, and then press the TAB key.
8. Type 5.5 in the Interest Rate (e.g., 5.9) text field, and then press the TAB key.
9. Select 4 in the Number of Years drop-down list field, and then click the Calculate button (Figure 10–26 on the next page).

Q&A

What if my result was slightly different? Did I do something wrong?

If your result is only a few pennies different, it is probably just a difference in the math processor on your computer. If the value is hundreds or even thousands of dollars off, check your formula code on lines 71 through 73.

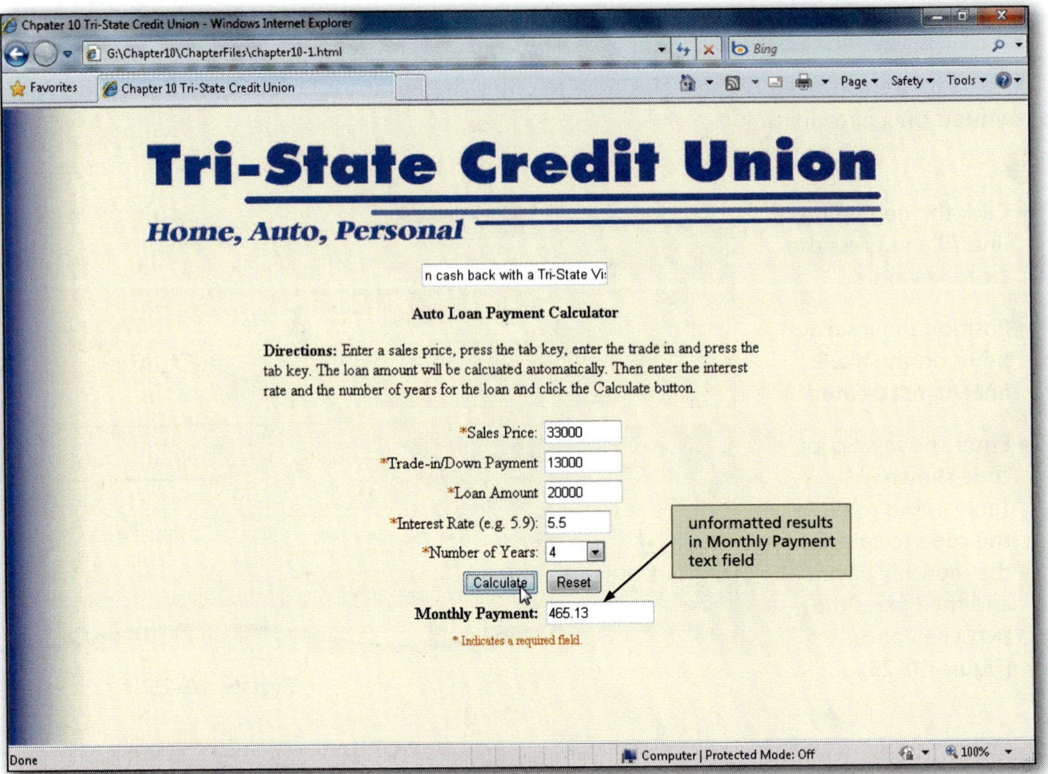

Figure 10–26

Plan Ahead

Formatting output results.

To format the result, the dollarFormat() function performs these seven basic steps:

1. Use the string value passed to the function, which separates the dollars from the cents based on the position of the decimal point
2. Separate the dollars portion from the cents portion by using the split() method
3. Separate the value to the left of the decimal point as the dollar amount and the value to the right of the decimal point as the cents amount
4. Insert commas every three positions in dollar amounts exceeding 999
5. Reconstruct the result string value with two decimal places
6. Insert a dollar sign immediately to the left of the first digit without spaces
7. Return the completed formatted value

The value is assigned to the Monthly Payment text field in the form.

Formatting the Monthly Payment Output as Currency

As shown in Figure 10–26, the loan payment calculator currently displays the monthly payment amount as a value with two decimal places. To set the form to display the monthly payment amount in a currency format with a dollar sign, the dollarFormat() function is used. First, you must enter a statement that passes the resulting string object of the monthly payment CalcLoanAmt() function to the dollarFormat() function. The dollarFormat() function then analyzes the string, adds commas, and returns the number with a dollar sign and two decimal places.

Using the split() Method of the String Object The split() method is used to split a string based on an identified separator and a desired number of "sub" strings. The split() method searches the string object for the separator, which is enclosed within the quotation marks, and for every separator creates a separate sub string. These values are stored in an array. An array is a JavaScript object that stores multiple values in one variable name. Arrays are discussed in detail in Chapter 11. Table 10–21 shows the general form of the split() method.

Table 10–21 split() Method

General form:	`var newValue = stringname.split (separator, how many)`
Comment:	where newValue Is a variable holding the results of the split; stringname is any string object; separator is a string value such as a space, comma, or period that can separate a string, and how many is the value that indicates how many items will result from the split.
Example:	`formatAmt=valuein.split(".",2)` split places valuein into an array with 2 elements. Dollars in element 0, pennies in element 1

In this chapter, the split() method is used to separate the dollars from the pennies at the decimal point in the monthly payment amount. Figure 10–27 provides an example of how the split() method works.

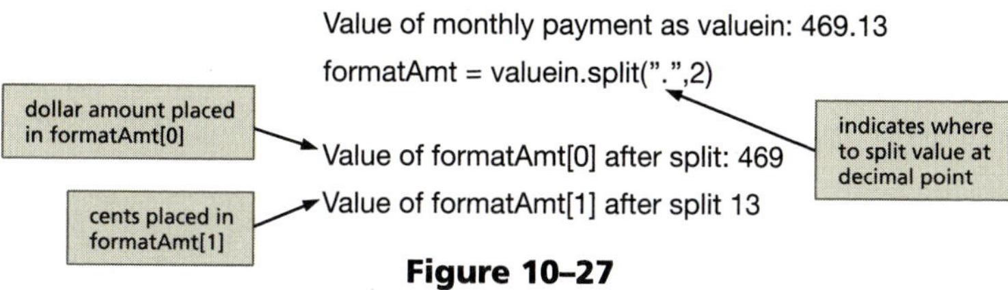
Value of monthly payment as valuein: 469.13
formatAmt = valuein.split(".",2)
dollar amount placed in formatAmt[0]
Value of formatAmt[0] after split: 469
indicates where to split value at decimal point
cents placed in formatAmt[1]
Value of formatAmt[1] after split 13

Figure 10–27

Beginning the dollarFormat() Function and Formatting the Dollars Portion The dollarFormat() function initializes the variables that will be used to format value as currency. Most programmers agree it is a good programming practice to clear and initialize variables to ensure the data is valid. Table 10–22 shows the JavaScript code used to add the dollarFormat() function.

Table 10–22 Code for the dollarFormat() Function

Line	Code
77	`function dollarFormat(valuein) {`
78	`    var formatValue = ""`
79	`    var formatDollars = ""`
80	`    formatAmt = valuein.split(".",2)`
81	`    var dollars = formatAmt[0]`

Line 77 declares the dollarFormat() function and the valuein variable. Lines 78 and 79 clear the variables used to assemble the formatted output by assigning null (or empty) values. The split() method in line 80 returns the dollar portion of the value and the cents portion into an array called formatAmt. As an array, formatAmt[0] contains the dollar amount, and formatAmt[1] contains the cents. Line 81 assigns the dollar amount to the dollars variable.

To Enter the dollarFormat() Function

The following step shows how to enter the dollarFormat() function and initialize the variables.

- Click line 76 and press the ENTER key once.
- On line 77, enter the JavaScript code from Table 10–22 on the previous page to begin the dollarFormat() function and then press the ENTER key (Figure 10–28).

```
70  function monthly(loanAmt,loanRate,loanYears) {
71      var interestRate = loanRate/1200
72      var Pmts = loanYears * 12
73      var Amnt = loanAmt * (interestRate / (1 - (1 / Math.pow(1+interestRate,Pmts))))
74      return Amnt.toFixed(2)
75  }
76
77  function dollarFormat(valuein) {
78      var formatValue = ""
79      var formatDollars = ""
80      formatAmt = valuein.split(".",2)
        lars = formatAmt[0]
```

split () used to find decimal point in value by searching for period; 2 indicates into how many items string should be split;items stored in array

dollar amount is stored in element zero [0]

Figure 10–28

Plan Ahead

Using a while loop to insert commas every three digits in a number.
To place a comma every three digits, use a while loop. The following steps describe the logic of the while loop:

1. Extract three digits from the dollar value, starting from the right by subtracting 3 from the length of the dollar value (dollarLen)
2. Verify three digits have been subtracted and then insert a comma in the output string
3. Decrement the length of the dollar value to look for the next group of three digits
4. The process (loop) is complete when no more groups of three digits exist and the length of dollarLen is zero

Using a while Loop and if...else Statement to Extract the Dollars Portion and Insert Commas A **loop** is a series of statements that executes repeatedly until it satisfies a condition. JavaScript has two types of loops: for loops and while loops. Both types of loops use the logic illustrated by the flowchart in Figure 10–29. Both loops first test a condition to determine if the instructions in the loop are to be executed.

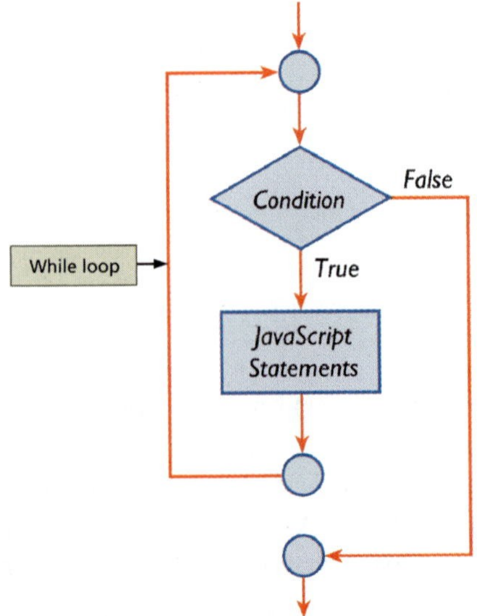

Figure 10–29

The **for loop** relies on a conditional statement using numeric values and thus often is referred to as a counter-controlled loop. Table 10–23 shows the general form of the for loop.

Table 10–23 for Loop

General form:	`for (start; stop; counter-control) {`
	`        JavaScript statements`
	`}`

Comment:	where start is a variable initialized to a beginning value; stop is an expression indicating the condition at which the loop should terminate; and the counter-control is an expression indicating how to increment or decrement the counter. Semicolons separate the three variables.

Examples:	`for (j=1; j<5; j++) {`
	`for (ctr=6; ctr>0; ctr--) {`
	`for (itemx=1; itemx<10; itemx=itemx+2) {`

The while loop relies on a conditional statement that either can use a numeric value or a string. Table 10–24 shows the general form of the while loop.

Table 10–24 while Loop

General form:	`while (condition) {`
	`        JavaScript statements`
	`}`

Comment:	where condition is either a numeric value or a string; and the JavaScript statements execute while the result of the condition is true.

Examples:	`while (ctr < 6) {`
	`while (isNaN(temp)) {`
	`while (Response != "Done") {`

In this chapter, the while loop is used in formatting the dollar value of the Monthly Payment value. The dollars portion is represented by the digits to the left of the decimal point. If the dollars portion of the auto loan payment contains more than three digits, commas need to be inserted. Table 10–25 shows the JavaScript statements used to determine the length of the dollar value and placement of the commas.

Table 10–25 Code for Determining the Length of the Dollar Value and Comma Placement

```
var dollarLen = dollars.length
if (dollarLen > 3) {
   while (dollarLen > 0) {
      tempDollars = dollars.substring(dollarLen - 3,dollarLen)
         if (tempDollars.length == 3) {
            formatDollars = "," + tempDollars + formatDollars
            dollarLen = dollarLen - 3
         }  else {
               formatDollars = tempDollars + formatDollars
                dollarLen = 0
            }
   }
```

Table 10–25 (continued)

Line	Code
94	`if (formatDollars.substring(0,1) == ",")`
95	`   dollars = formatDollars.substring(1,formatDollars.length)`
96	`else`
97	`   dollars = formatDollars`
98	`}`

Because the dollar portion of the value is still a string, line 82 uses the length property to determine how many digits are in the dollar portion. The if statement at line 83 determines if the dollar portion of the value is longer than three digits. If that is true, then a while loop routine (lines 84 through 93) places a comma every three digits. Line 85 extracts three digits starting from the right by subtracting 3 from the length of the dollar value (dollarLen). The if statement at Line 86 verifies three digits and line 87 inserts a comma in the output string. Line 88 decrements the length of the dollar value to look for the next group of three digits. When no more groups of three digits exist, the length of dollarLen is set to zero (line 91) and the loop terminates at line 93. The statements in lines 94 through 98 prevent the code from inserting a comma if only three digits are to the left of the decimal point.

To Enter an if...else Statement and while Loop to Extract the Dollar Portion of the Output and Insert Commas

The following step illustrates how to enter the if...else statement and while loop to extract the dollar portion of the output and insert commas into the output if needed.

- If necessary, click line 82.
- Enter the JavaScript code as shown in Table 10–25 starting on the previous page, indenting as shown to extract the dollar portion of the output, and insert the appropriate commas and then press the ENTER key (Figure 10–30).

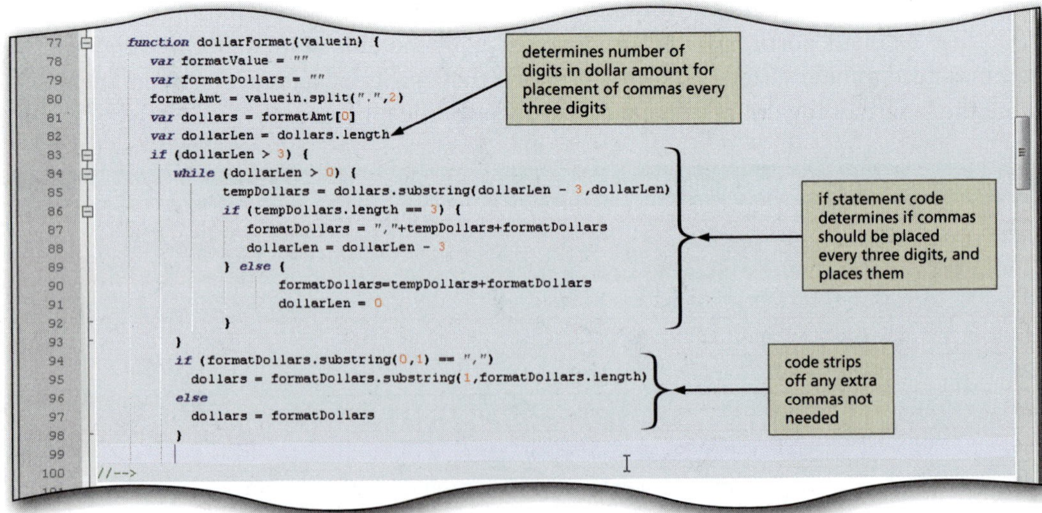

Figure 10–30

Reconstructing the Formatted Output and Returning the Formatted Value Next, the JavaScript statements must be written to reconstruct (concatenate) the formatted dollars and cents output into a formatted payment amount value, store the payment amount value in the formatValue variable, and return the formatValue variable. Table 10–26 shows the statements needed to complete this task.

Table 10–26 Code for Reconstructing the Formatted Output and Returning the Formatted Value

Line	Code
99	`var cents = formatAmt[1]`
100	`var formatValue="$"+dollars+"."+cents`
101	`return formatValue`
102	`}`

Line 99 assigns two decimal values to the cents variable from the formatAmt[1] array. Line 100 reconstructs the values, concatenating a dollar sign ($) and the dollars, and the cents. Line 101 returns the formatted value to the CalcLoanAmt() function. Line 102 closes the function.

To Reconstruct the Formatted Output and Return the Formatted Value

The following step illustrates how to reconstruct the formatted output and return the formatted value to the calling function.

- If necessary, click line 99.
- Enter the JavaScript code from Table 10–26, indenting as shown to reconstruct the formatted output and return the formatted value, and then press the ENTER key (Figure 10–31).

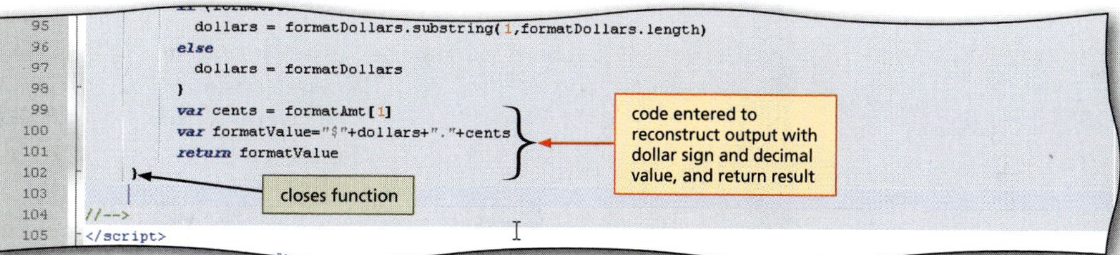

Figure 10–31

To Pass the Monthly Payment Value to the dollarFormat() Function

To have the monthly payment value appear in the Monthly Payment text field formatted as currency, it must be passed to the dollarFormat() function. Because the dollarFormat() function manipulates a string value, the monthly payment result first must be converted to a string using the toString() method. In Chapter 9, the toString() method was used to convert a date value to a string. In this chapter, the toString() method is used to convert the monthly payment to a string that the dollarFormat() function can manipulate.

The following step shows how to enter the JavaScript statements needed to pass the monthly payment as a string object to the dollarFormat() function.

- Scroll up to and click line 65 (the line that starts LoanForm .Payment.value.
- Position the insertion point before monthlyPmt .toString(), then type `dollarFormat(` without a space.

```
else {
    var monthlyPmt = monthly(loanAmt,loanRate,loanYears)
    LoanForm.Payment.value = dollarFormat(monthlyPmt.toString())
  }
}

function monthly(loanAmt,loanRate,loanYears) {
  var interestRate = loanRate/1200
```

do not press ENTER key

modify line 65 to pass monthly payment value as a string to the dollarFormat() user-defined function

Figure 10–32

- Position the insertion point after dollarFormat (monthlyPmt.toString() and type) but do not press the ENTER key (Figure 10–32).

To Save an HTML File and Test a Web Page

The following steps show how to save the HTML file and test the Web page.

1. With the USB drive plugged into your computer, click File on the menu bar, and then click Save.
2. Click the browser button on the taskbar.
3. Click the Refresh button.
4. Enter the test data as follows: Sales Price: 23000, Trade-in: 4100, Interest Rate: 3.9, and Number of Years: 4.
5. Click the Calculate button. The result should be formatted as shown in Figure 10–33.

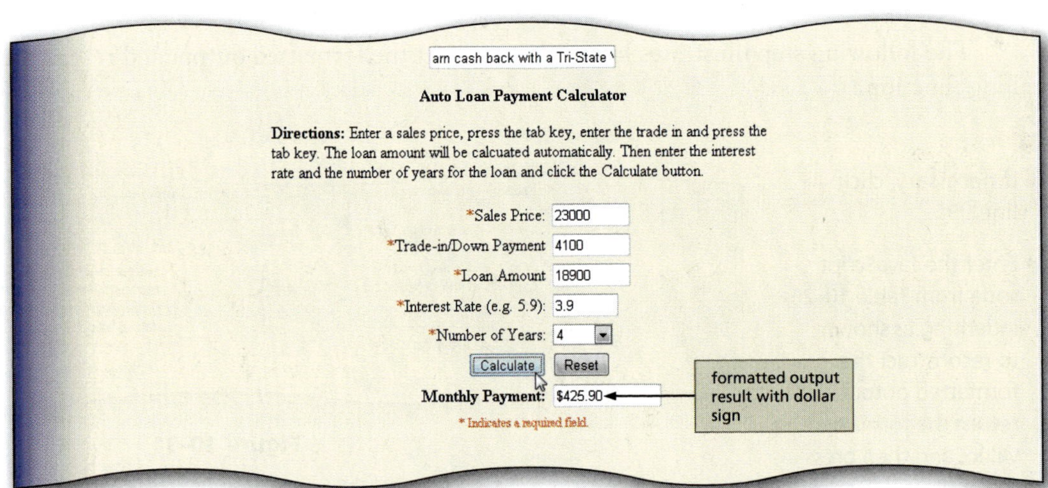

Figure 10–33

Plan Ahead

Planning pop-up windows.
A pop-up window is used to add additional information to a Web page. You must decide what features you want the pop-up window to utilize. Ask yourself these questions:

- Do you want to include the status bar, title bar, address bar, scroll bars, toolbars, and menu bar?
- Do you want the user to be able to resize the window?
- What width and height should the window be?

Each of these properties can be set as properties in the open() method, creating a customized look for that particular pop-up window.

BTW

Pop-up Windows
In addition to alert() message boxes, Web developers use pop-up windows to display more information to gain attention. Use pop-up windows sparingly because having many pop-up windows can annoy visitors.

Adding a Pop-Up Window

As you have learned in this chapter, the alert() method is one way to display messages to a user. These message boxes, however, only display text on a gray background. To create more visually interesting messages, you can use JavaScript to open and display another HTML file in a separate window that displays colors, graphics, animations, and other media. Such a window is called a **pop-up window** because it appears over the previously opened browser window.

The **open() method** is used to create a pop-up window. Table 10–27 shows the general form of the open() method.

Table 10–27 open() Method

General form:	`var windowname=open("window file name(URL)", "object name", "features")`
Comment:	where windowname is an optional name of a window object (required only if you need to refer to the pop-up window in any other Web page); window file name is the name of the HTML file; and features describe how the window should appear.
Examples:	`open("Adwindow.htm", "AdWin", "resize=off,titlebar=false")`

As shown in Table 10–27, when adding the open() method to create a pop-up window, all of the pop-up window features must be enclosed within one set of quotation marks. Table 10–28 describes the more commonly used attributes of the open() method, which are used to define pop-up window features. For more information about the open() method, see the JavaScript Quick Reference in Appendix G.

Table 10–28 open() Method Attributes

Feature	Description	Written As
location	Includes address bar	"location=yes"
menubar	Includes menu bar	"menubar=yes"
resize	Allows user to resize	"resizeable=yes"
scrollbars	Includes scroll bars	"scrollbars=yes"
status	Includes status bar	"status=yes"
titlebar	Removes title bar	"titlebar=yes"
toolbar	Includes toolbar	"toolbar=yes"
width	States width in pixels	"width=220"
height	States height in pixels	"height=450"

In this chapter, the open() method is used to open a pop-up window that will display information about Tri-State Credit Union services. You insert code for the popUpAd function and open() method, and then add an event handler to call the popUpAd() function when the page is loaded. Earlier in the chapter, the onload event handler was associated with the scrollingMsg() function. You also will use the onload event handler for the popUpAd() function. Multiple functions can be associated with the same event handler.

Table 10–29 shows the code to create the user-defined function popUpAd(). The chapter10-1notice.html file already has been created and is stored in the Chapter10\ ChapterFiles folder of the Data Files for Students.

Table 10–29 Code to Open chapter10-1notice.html Pop-Up Window

```
function popUpAd() {
     open("chapter10-1notice.html","noticeWin","width=520,height=330")
}
```

Line 104 declares the popUpAd() function. The statement in line 105 opens the chapter10-1notice.html Web page as a pop-up window that is 520 pixels wide and 330 pixels high. Line 106 closes the function.

To Enter the popUpAd() Function to Open a Pop-Up Window

The following step illustrates how to enter the popUpAd() user-defined function that contains the open() method to open the chapter10-1notice.html file in a pop-up window.

- Activate the Notepad++ chapter10-1solution .html window.
- Click line 103, the line directly above the //--> tag and press the ENTER key once.
- On line 104, enter the JavaScript code from Table 10–29 on the previous page, indenting as shown, and press the ENTER key after line 106 to open a pop-up window (Figure 10–34).

```
94          if (formatDollars.substring(0,1) == ",")
95            dollars = formatDollars.substring(1,formatDollars.length)
96          else
97            dollars = formatDollars
98          }
99          var cents = formatAmt[1]
100         var formatValue = "$"+dollars+"."+cents
101         return formatValue
102       }
103
104   function popUpAd() {
105     open("chapter10-1notice.html","noticeWin","width=520,height=330")
106   }
107
108 //-->
109 </script>
110 <style type="text/css">
111 <!--
```

JavaScript statement to open pop-up window
no spaces in window dimension attributes

Figure 10–34

To Add the Event Handler to Call the popUpAd()Function

Now you need to add the onload event handler to open the pop-up window when the Web page loads. Each function name is enclosed in one set of quotation marks and separated by a semicolon. The following steps illustrate how to add the second function call to the onload() event handler.

- Position the insertion point in front of the "> at the end of line 140 (the line that begins <body onload=) (Figure 10–35).

```
        margin-right: auto;
130 }
131 .block {
132     width: 50%;
133     margin-right: auto;
134     margin-left: auto;
135 }
136
137 -->
138 </style>
139 </head>
140 <body onload="scrollingMsg()">
141 <p style="text-align:center">
142   <img src="chapter10-1logo.jpg" alt="b
143 </p>
144 <form id="msgForm" action="">
145   <p style="text-align:center"><input type="text" name="scrollingMsg" size="25" /></p>
146 </form>
147 <p style="text-align:center; font-size:16; font-weight:bold;">Auto Loan Payment Calculator</p>
148 <p class="block"><strong>Directions: </strong>Enter a sales price, press the tab key, enter the trade
```

click before quotation marks and do not press SPACEBAR before typing

Figure 10–35

2

- Type `; popUpAd()` to add the call to the popUpAd() user-defined function to the left of the second quotation mark, but do not press the ENTER key (Figure 10–36).

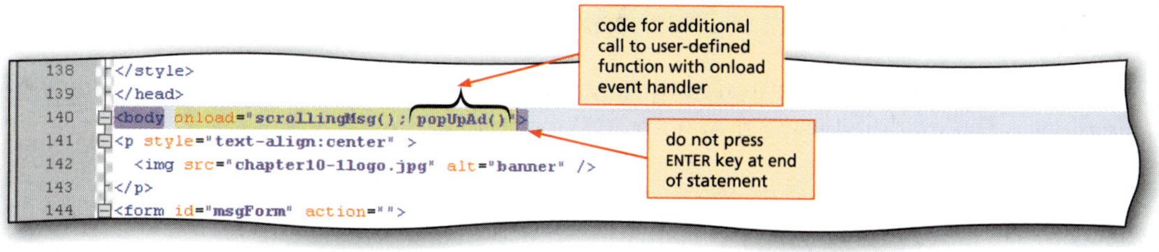

```
</style>
</head>
<body onload="scrollingMsg(); popUpAd()">
<p style="text-align:center" >
  <img src="chapter10-1logo.jpg" alt="banner" />
</p>
<form id="msgForm" action="">
```

code for additional call to user-defined function with onload event handler

do not press ENTER key at end of statement

Figure 10–36

Q&A

Is this the only way to open a pop-up window?

An open() method can be placed anywhere in the <script> section in the <head> section. Once the <head> section loads in the browser, it will execute the “stand-alone” open() method, opening a pop-up window. The code must be in the <head> section, however, for this to work properly.

Adding Copyright and the Date Last Modified

As you learned in Chapter 9, the purpose of displaying the date a Web page was last modified is to make sure the user knows how current the information is contained on the Web page. You added JavaScript code to the Oakwood Elementary School Web page to display the URL, a copyright notice, and the date the file was last modified. The Tri-State Credit Union Web page should include similar JavaScript code to display just the date the Web page was modified, not the time.

To display the footer message of the copyright and date the Web page was last modified, you need to insert a <div> tag at the bottom of the Web page. Table 10–30 shows the code for creating the <div> tag container.

Table 10–30 Code to Create a <div> Tag Container

Line	Code
214	<div id="displayDateLast" style="margin-left:5%">
215	</div>

To display just the date, the code in Table 10–31 uses the substring() method to grab just the date and display copyright information. The parameters used in the substring() method only return the date for Microsoft Internet Explorer properly.

Table 10–31 Code to Display the Date Last Modified Using the substring() Method

Line	Code
108	function copyRight() {
109	var lastModDate = document.lastModified
110	var lastModDate = lastModDate.substring(0,10)
111	displayDateLast.innerHTML = "<h6>Copyright Tri-State Credit Union"+" This document was last modified "+lastModDate+".</h6>"
112	}

Line 108 declares the copyRight() user-defined function. Line 109 assigns the date last modified from the document lastModified property. The substring(0,10) method in line 110 extracts the first 10 characters of the date and time — mm/dd/yyyy — so only the date is displayed, not the time. Line 111 assigns the message string to the <div> tag container using the id attribute, displayDateLast, and the innerHTML property.

To Display the Date Last Modified Using the substring() Method

The following steps illustrate how to enter the JavaScript code to add a <div> container and display the date the file was last modified using the substring() method.

- Click line 214 (the blank line just above the </body> tag).
- Enter the HTML <div> tag code from Table 10–30, but do not press the ENTER key after line 215 (Figure 10–37).

```
212       </table>
213    </form>
214    <div id="displayDateLast" style="margin-left:5%">
215    </div>
216    </body>
217    </html>
218
219
```

<div> tag division container to display date last modified

do not press ENTER key

Figure 10–37

2

- Click line 108.
- Enter the JavaScript code from Table 10–31 on the previous page to enter copyright and date-last-modified code, pressing the ENTER key only at the end of each complete line (Figure 10–38).

```
107
108       function copyRight() {
109          var lastModDate = document.lastModified
110          var lastModDate = lastModDate.substring(0,10)
111          displayDateLast.innerHTML = "<h6>Copyright Tri-State Credit Union"+"<br />This document was last modified "
     +lastModDate+"</h6>"
112       }
113
114    //-->
115    </script>
116    <style type="text/css">
```

code to insert copyright and date last modified on Web page

Figure 10–38

3

- Position the insertion point in front of the "> at the end of line 146 (the line that contains the <body> tag).

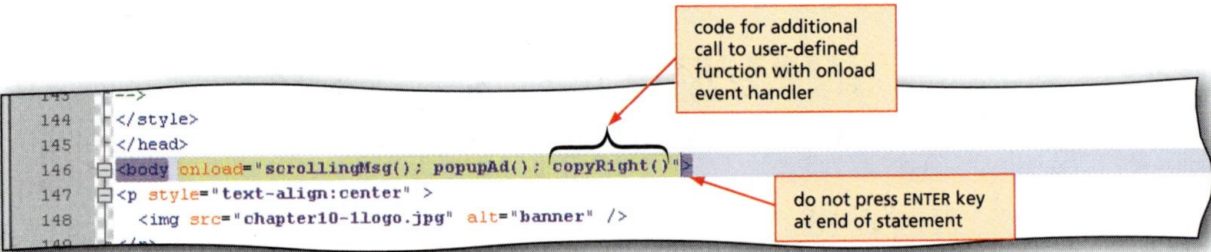
code for additional call to user-defined function with onload event handler
144 </style>
145 </head>
146 <body onload="scrollingMsg(); popupAd(); copyRight()">
147 <p style="text-align:center" >
148 <img src="chapter10-1logo.jpg" alt="banner" />
do not press ENTER key at end of statement

Figure 10–39

- Type `; copyRight()` after popUpAd() to add the call to the copyRight() user-defined function to the <body> tag, and do not press the ENTER key (Figure 10–39).

To Save an HTML File, Test a Web Page, and Print the HTML File

The code for the Tri-State Credit Union Web page with a loan payment calculator and pop-up window is complete. Now you should save the HTML file, test the JavaScript code using a Web browser, and then print the HTML file.

1. With the USB drive plugged into your computer, click File on the menu bar, and then click Save.
2. Click the browser button on the taskbar.
3. Click the Refresh button on the browser toolbar.
4. If necessary, click the security bar in the pop-up Window, click Allow Blocked Content..., and, if necessary, click Yes in the Security Warning dialog box to display the scrolling message.

5. Click the Close Window button to close the pop-up window.
6. If necessary, scroll down to verify that the bottom of the Web page displays the date the page was last modified (the date the file was saved), as shown in Figure 10–40.
7. Click the Notepad++ button on the taskbar to activate the chapter10-1solution.html document.
8. Click Print on the File menu to print the HTML file.

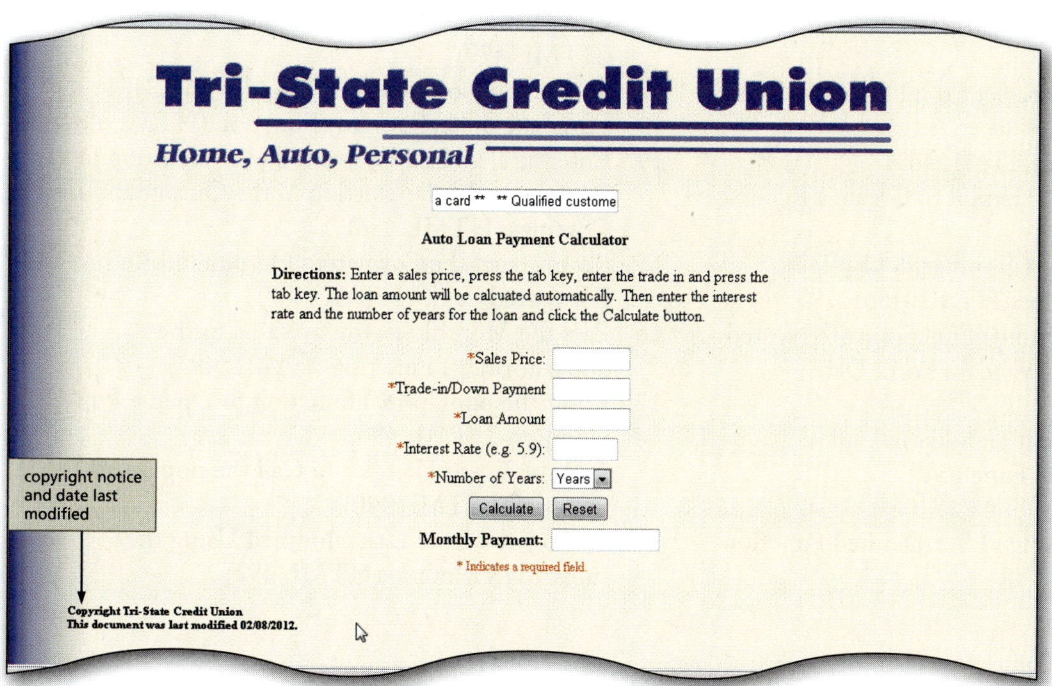

Figure 10–40

To Validate a Web Page

1. Open Internet Explorer and navigate to the Web site validator.w3.org.
2. Click the Validate by File Upload tab.
3. Click the Browse button.
4. Locate the chapter10-1solution.html file on your storage device and click the file name.
5. Click the Open button in the Choose File to Upload dialog box and the file name will be inserted into the File box.
6. Click the Check button.

To Quit Notepad++ and a Browser

1. In Notepad++, click the File menu, then Close All.
2. Click the Close button on the Notepad++ title bar.
3. Click the Close button on the browser title bar. If necessary, click the Close all tabs button.

BTW

Quick Reference
For a list of JavaScript statements and their associated attributes, see the JavaScript Quick Reference (Appendix G) at the back of this book, or visit the HTML Quick Reference Web page (scsite.com/HTML6e/qr).

Chapter Summary

This chapter described how to write JavaScript to create a scrolling message, a pop-up window, and if and if...else statements; how to pass values to a user-defined function; how to validate the data entered into a form and convert text to numeric values using the parseInt(), parseFloat(), and isNaN() built-in functions; and how to format string output results to display as currency. The items listed below include all the new JavaScript skills you have learned in this chapter.

1. Create a Form Text Field to Display a Scrolling Message (HTML 458)
2. Create the scrollingMsg() User-Defined Function (HTML 460)
3. Enter the Code to Increment the Position Locator Variable (HTML 461)
4. Enter an if Statement (HTML 463)
5. Add the setTimeout() Method to Create a Recursive Call (HTML 464)
6. Enter the onload Event Handler to Call the scrollingMsg() Function (HTML 466)
7. Add the valSaleTradeAmt() Function with Nested if...else Statements to Validate Form Data (HTML 474)
8. Enter an onblur() Event Handler to Call the valSaleTradeAmt() Function (HTML 475)
9. Enter the CalcLoanAmt() User-Defined Function (HTML 476)
10. Enter an onclick() Event Handler to Call the CalcLoanAmt() Function (HTML 477)
11. Enter Code to Call the monthly() Function (HTML 479)
12. Create the monthly() Function (HTML 481)
13. Enter the dollarFormat() Function (HTML 484)
14. Enter an if...else Statement and while Loop to Extract the Dollar Portion of the Output and Insert Commas (HTML 486)
15. Reconstruct the Formatted Output and Return the Formatted Value (HTML 487)
16. Pass the Monthly Payment Value to the dollarFormat() Function (HTML 487)
17. Enter the popUpAd() Function to Open a Pop-Up Window (HTML 490)
18. Add the Event Handler to Call the popUpAd() Function (HTML 490)
19. Display the Date Last Modified Using the substring() Method (HTML 492)

Learn It Online

Test your knowledge of chapter content and key terms.

Instructions: To complete the Learn It Online exercises, start your browser, click the address bar, and then enter the Web address `scsite.com/html6e/learn`. When the HTML Learn It Online page is displayed, click the link for the exercise you want to complete and read the instructions.

Chapter Reinforcement TF, MC, and SA

A series of true/false, multiple choice, and short answer questions that test your knowledge of the chapter content.

Flash Cards

An interactive learning environment where you identify chapter key terms associated with displayed definitions.

Practice Test

A series of multiple choice questions that test your knowledge of chapter content and key terms.

Who Wants To Be a Computer Genius?

An interactive game that challenges your knowledge of chapter content in the style of a television quiz show.

Wheel of Terms

An interactive game that challenges your knowledge of chapter key terms in the style of the television show, *Wheel of Fortune*.

Crossword Puzzle Challenge

A crossword puzzle that challenges your knowledge of key terms presented in the chapter.

Apply Your Knowledge

Reinforce the skills and apply the concepts you learned in this chapter.

Instructions: Start Notepad++. Open the file apply10-1.html from the Chapter10\Apply folder of the Data Files for Students. See the inside back cover of this book for instructions on downloading the Data Files for Students, or contact your instructor for information about accessing the required files.

The apply10-1.html file is a partially completed HTML file for the California Wine Country Growers Association that you will use for this exercise. You will use JavaScript to create a scrolling message and validate a text field entry for an e-mail address. You must add the event handler in the <body> tag to call the scrolling message function and the event handler in the Submit button to call the validate function. Figure 10–41 shows the Apply Your Knowledge Web page as it should be displayed in a browser after the JavaScript has been added.

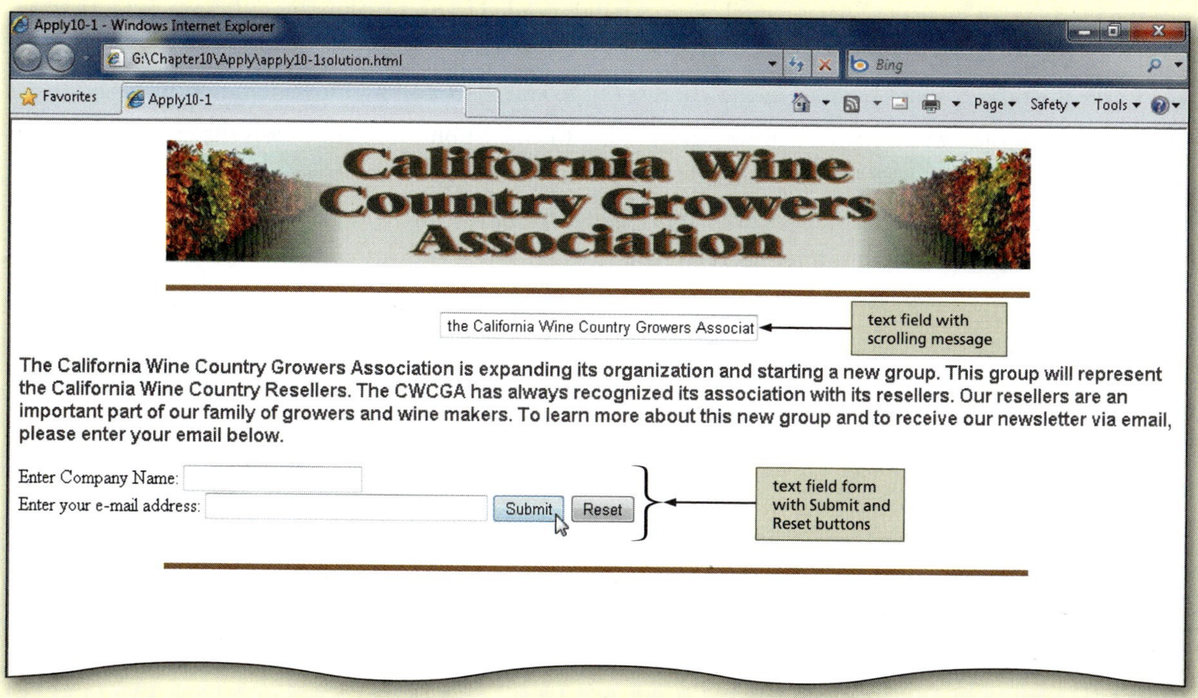

Figure 10–41

Perform the following tasks:

1. Enter the beginning of a JavaScript code section for a user-defined function in the <head> section of the Web page.
2. Using the code presented in Table 10–1 on page HTML 457 as a guide, enter a form for the input text field beneath the first divider.
3. Using the code in Tables 10–2, 10–6, and Figure 10–10 on pages HTML 459, 463, and 464, as a guide, write a JavaScript user defined function called scrollingMsg() to display the following text string, "Join the California Wine Country Growers Association Resellers Group." Be sure to leave a space before and after the text string message.
4. Assign this text string to a variable named Msg.
5. Use the variable name startAt as the position locator for the message.

Continued >

STUDENT ASSIGNMENTS

Apply Your Knowledge *continued*

6. Use Message as the name of the form and msgBox as the name of the text field.
7. In the setTimeout() method used to call the scrollingMsg() function, use 300 milliseconds as the time delay.
8. Declare a new user-defined function named emailValidate(emailForm).
9. Use an if statement to verify that the company name text field (company_name) is not blank by testing if the length of the text field is less than 1. If the field is blank, use an alert to notify the user with the message, "Please enter a company name."
10. Use the indexOf() method to determine if an @ sign is in the e-mail text field. Assign the result of the indexOf() method to a variable named atSign.
11. Enter an if statement to test the value of atSign. If atSign is less than 0, then use an alert() method to display the message, "Sorry, that e-mail address is not valid. Please re-enter your e-mail address."
12. Enter the else statement so that, if the e-mail address is in proper form, an alert() method will display the message, "Thank you. Your e-mail address will be added to our mailing list." Be sure to close the JavaScript <script> section properly.
13. Enter the proper event handler in the <body> tag to call the scrolling message function.
14. Enter the proper event handler in the <input> tag for the Submit button to call the emailValidate() user-defined function in the <head> section.
15. Save the revised file in the Chapter10\Apply folder using the file name apply10-1solution.html.
16. Validate using the w3.org validation Web page.
17. Start your browser. Enter the URL g:\Chapter10\Apply\apply10-1solution.html to view and test the Web page in your browser.
18. If any errors occur, check the code against Steps 1 through 14, make any required changes, save the file using the same file name, and then refresh the Web page in the browser.
19. Submit the revised HTML file and Web page in the format specified by your instructor.

Extend Your Knowledge

Extend the skills you learned in this chapter and experiment with new skills. You will need to search the Internet to complete the assignment.

Learning More About Displaying Messages

Instructions: Start Notepad++ and your browser. Open the file extend10-1.html from the Chapter10\Extend folder of the Data Files for Students. See the inside back cover of this book for instructions on downloading the Data Files for Students, or contact your instructor for information about accessing the required files.

The extend10-1.html file is a partially completed HTML file that you will use for this exercise. Figure 10–42 shows the Extend Your Knowledge Web page as it should be displayed in a browser after the JavaScript has been added.

Search the Internet for information on how to change the color of a text field. Use that code to change the text field color to red if there is an invalid choice. Also, search for information on the getElementById property. You will use this property in Step 9. In addition, search the Internet for current exchange rates, and update the <select> list option values. (*Hint:* a good site for current values to use in this exercise is http://www.bloomberg.com/invest/calculators/currency.html)

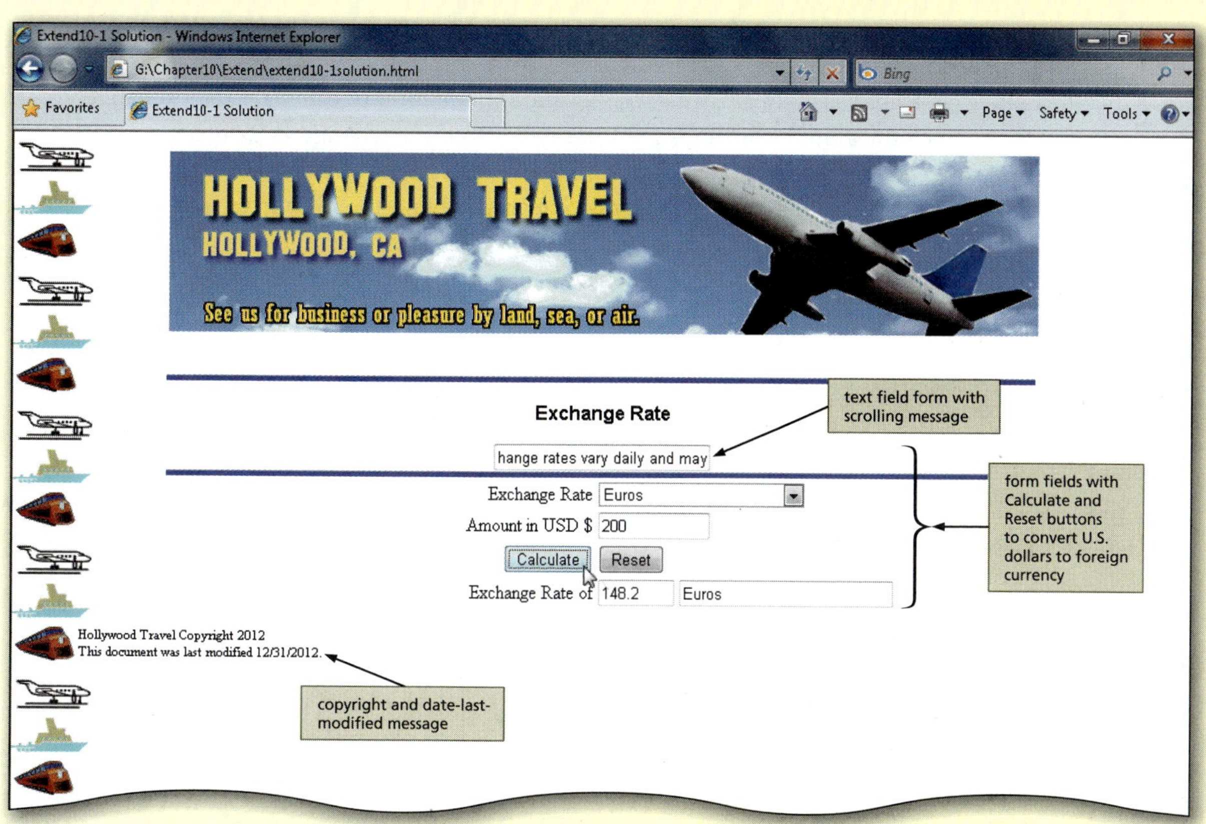

Figure 10–42

Instructions: Perform the following steps:

1. Save the file extend10-1.html as extend10-1solution.html.
2. Create a <script> section in the <head> section for the user-defined functions.
3. Using the code presented in Figures 10–5 through 10–11 on pages HTML 460 through HTML 465 as a guide, write the user-defined function called textMsg(). Use the message string "** Exchange rates vary daily and may not be the same in the country you visit. **" for the scrolling message.

   Enter the form for the text field for the scrolling message using the name msgForm for the form, and the name scrollingMsg for the text field for the scrolling message. Use these names when creating your user-defined function, textMsg().
4. Use 200 for the setTimeout() method to recursively call the textMsg() function.
5. Enter the appropriate event handler in the <body> tag to call the textMsg() function when the Web page is loaded.
6. Using the code in Table 10–13 on page HTML 473 as a guide, write the JavaScript user-defined function exchangeit() to validate the data entered into the form as numeric. Be sure to enter the appropriate event handler to call the exchangeit() function when the user clicks the Calculate button on the form.
7. In validating the values, assign the selectedIndex value from the drop-down list to a variable called rateSelect. Validate the <option> value by using the parseFloat() function. Use the code you found on the Internet to change the rate field to red if a rate is not chosen.
8. Assign the U.S. dollar amount from the eAmount text field to a variable named exAmount. Validate this text field and value using the parseFloat function. Use the code you found on the Internet to change the text field to red if the field is not valid.

Continued >

Extend Your Knowledge *continued*

9. Once the data is validated as numeric, write the JavaScript equation to calculate the exchange rate result and assign the amount of the U.S. dollar result to the ExchangeValue text field and the exchRate from the <select> tag drop-down list to the foreignCurrency text field. Use the getElementById and the selectedIndex value (rateSelect) to obtain the foreign currency from the <select> tag drop-down list. (*Hint:* depending on how the foreign currency is represented, you may have to multiply or divide to calculate the conversion.) Test your results with existing Web calculators.
10. Using the code from Table 10–30 on page HTML 491 as a guide, enter a <div> tag with an id of copyright before the closing </body> tag and use the code from Table 10–31 on page HTML 491 as a guide to write a JavaScript function to display a copyright message and the date last modified, as shown in Figure 10–42.
11. Enter the necessary event handlers in the <body> tag and the form to invoke the JavaScript user-defined functions.
12. Save the completed HTML file and test it using your browser. If an error occurs, check your code from Steps 3 through 11 and save and test again.
13. Validate using the w3.org validation Web page.
14. Submit the completed HTML file and Web page in the format specified by your instructor.

Make It Right

Analyze the JavaScript code on a Web page and correct all errors.

Correcting Syntax Errors and Inserting Missing Code

Instructions: Start your browser. Open the file make10-1.html from the Chapter10\MakeItRight folder of the Data Files for Students. See the inside back cover of this book for instructions for downloading the Data Files for Students, or contact your instructor for information about accessing the required files.

The make10-1.html Web page is a home mortgage calculator. Not all errors are necessarily typos or syntax errors. Some are logic errors, which means a statement may be executed out of order, is missing, or, in the case of JavaScript, is using an incorrect property or method.

This page contains four errors. Use the following information as background for your corrections. The sale price is $174,500, the down payment is 20%, the interest rate is 5.75%, and the number of years is 30. The correct loan amount should be $139,600.00 and the monthly payment should be $814.67. The corrected Web page is shown in Figure 10–43.

Perform the following tasks:

1. Refresh the Web page in the browser and look at the error messages.
2. Correct any misspelled variable names, function, and object names. Search for any logic errors that may be in the JavaScript code that produce incorrect results.
3. Insert the missing <div> tag for the date-last-modified message to display.
4. Add the missing event handler to display the date-last-modified message.
5. Save the corrected HTML file as make10-1solution.html, test using your browser, and then validate the Web page. If an error still occurs, check your code from Steps 1 through 4 and save again.
6. Submit the revised HTML file and Web page in the format specified by your instructor.

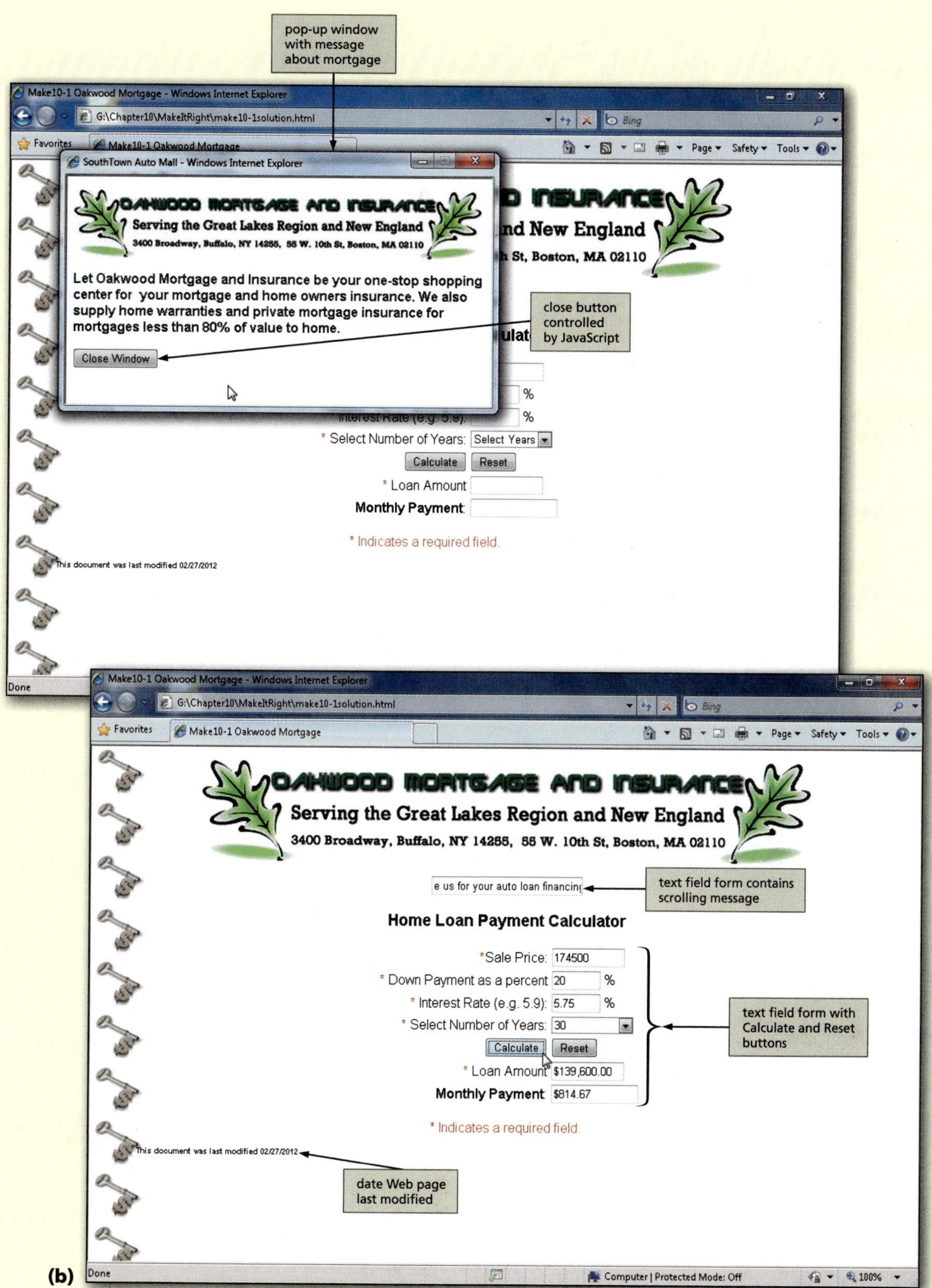
pop-up window with message about mortgage
Make10-1 Oakwood Mortgage - Windows Internet Explorer
SouthTown Auto Mall - Windows Internet Explorer
Serving the Great Lakes Region and New England
3400 Broadway, Buffalo, NY 14255, 55 W. 10th St, Boston, MA 02110
Let Oakwood Mortgage and Insurance be your one-stop shopping center for your mortgage and home owners insurance. We also supply home warranties and private mortgage insurance for mortgages less than 80% of value to home.
Close Window
close button controlled by JavaScript
(a)
(b)
text field form contains scrolling message
e us for your auto loan financing
Home Loan Payment Calculator
*Sale Price: 174500
* Down Payment as a percent 20 %
* Interest Rate (e.g. 5.9): 5.75 %
* Select Number of Years: 30
Calculate
Reset
* Loan Amount $139,600.00
Monthly Payment $814.67
* Indicates a required field.
text field form with Calculate and Reset buttons
This document was last modified 02/27/2012
date Web page last modified

Figure 10–43

STUDENT ASSIGNMENTS

In the Lab

Design and/or create a Web page using the guidelines, concepts, and skills presented in this chapter. Labs are listed in order of increasing difficulty.

Lab 1: Galaxy Investments

Problem: You have an internship with Galaxy Investments as a Web developer. The manager asks you to create an interactive Web page that would allow users to enter Years to Retirement, an estimated interest rate, and a retirement goal. When the users click the Calculate button, the values entered are validated and the amount that must be saved each month to reach the retirement goal is shown in a text field. A sample solution is shown in Figure 10–44.

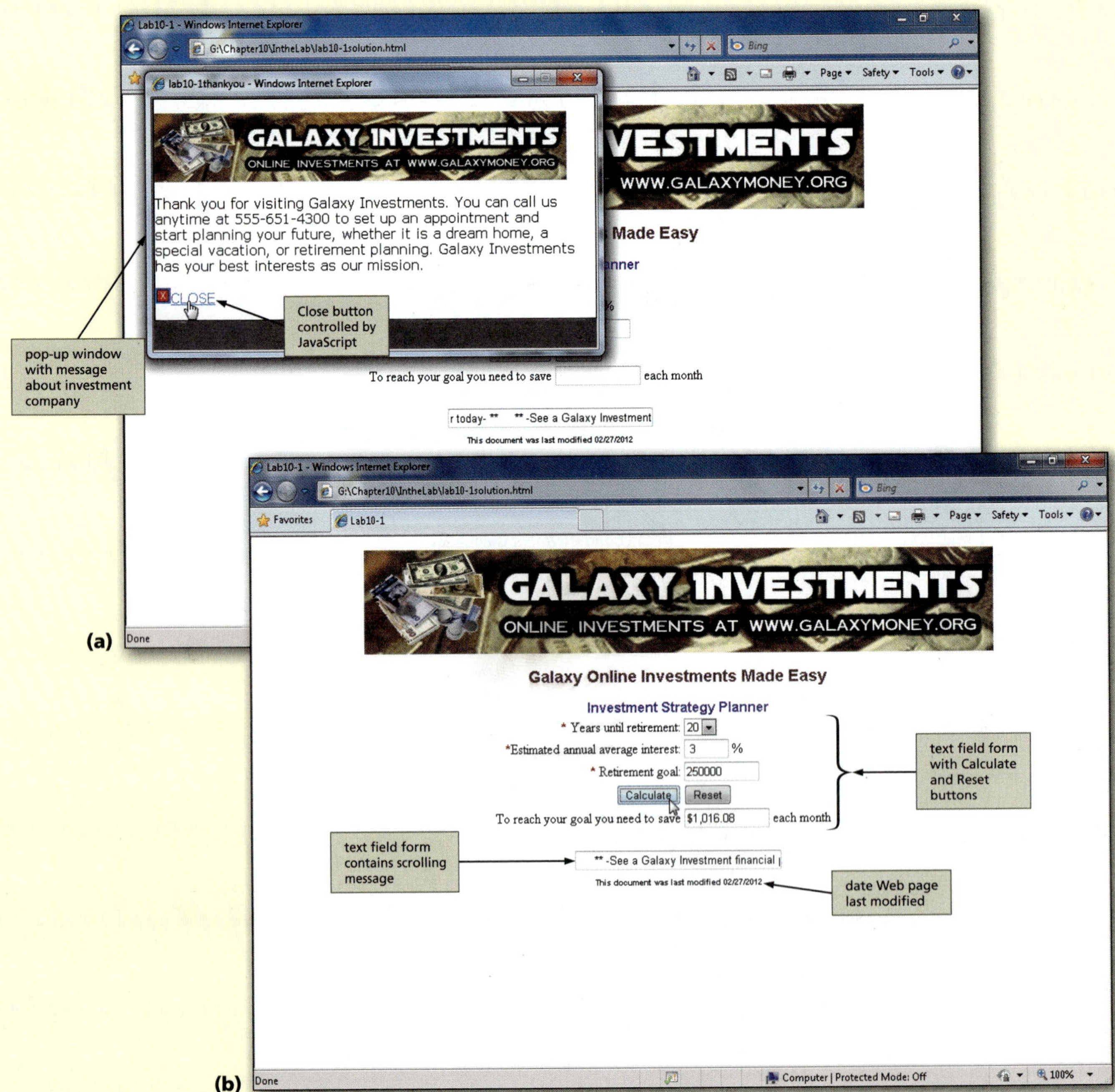

Figure 10–44

Perform the following tasks:

1. Start Notepad++ and open the lab10-1.html file from the Chapter10\IntheLab folder of the Data Files for Students.
2. Save the file as lab10-1solution.html.
3. Create a <script> section in the <head> section for user-defined functions.
4. Create a form for a scrolling message. Use the text ** -See a Galaxy Investment financial planner today- ** as the message.
5. Place the form at the bottom of the Web page using "msgBox" for the form name, and "Message" for the input box name. Make the size 35.
6. Using the form named Invest, write the JavaScript code to validate the text field values in the form. Use a series of nested if statements to validate that the Years, Irate (Interest Rate), and Goal are valid numeric values.
7. Display a message if the values are not numeric, clear the text field, set the background color of the text field to red, and use the focus() method to position the insertion point back in that text field. (*Hint:* To change the background color to red, set the object's style.backgroundColor properties to #ff0000.)
8. If the values are valid, compute the amount of monthly savings required to reach a specific goal using the formula $P = iF / [(1+i)^N - 1]$. (*Hint:* F is future value, i is interest, and N is number of years.)
9. Assign the result in the Monthly text field.
10. Use the code in Tables 10–22, 10–25, and 10–26 on pages HTML 483 through HTML 487 as a guide to display the result in currency format.
11. Add a function called adWindow to display the pop-up window, lab10-1thankyou.html.
12. Add a function called footerMsg to display the date the document was last modified. Display only the date portion.
13. Be sure to add the appropriate event handlers where required.
14. Save the revised lab10-1solution.html file.
15. Start your browser. Enter the URL g:\Chapter10\IntheLab\lab10-1solution.html to view and test the Web page in your browser.
16. Validate the Web page using the w3.org validation Web page.
17. If any errors occur, check the code against Steps 1 through 14, make any required changes, save the file using the same file name, and then refresh the Web page in the browser.
18. Submit the revised HTML file and Web page in the format specified by your instructor.

In the Lab

Lab 2: Edgewood Milling Bowling

Problem: You are the Webmaster for Edgewood Milling. The bowling team is in first place again this year, and you have been asked to create an interactive Web page that will allow team members and other employees to input bowling scores and calculate an average. The Web page has a scrolling message and validates the data entered into the form as numeric. The calculated average is rounded and displayed in the text field named Avg. Add the JavaScript to make the Web page appear as in Figure 10–45.

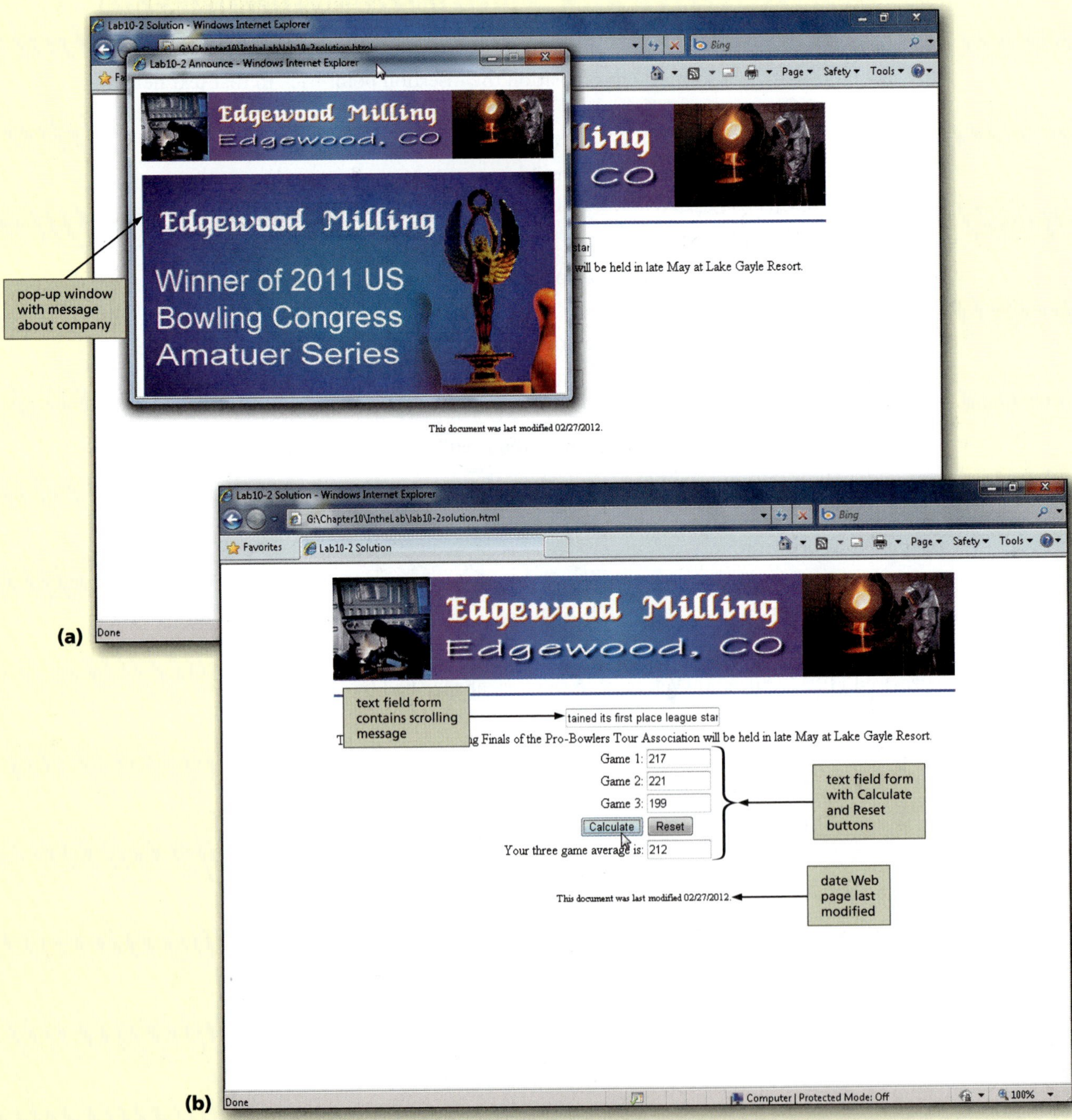

Figure 10–45

Instructions: Perform the following steps:

1. Start Notepad++ and open the file lab10-2.html from the Chapter10\IntheLab folder of the Data Files for Students.
2. Save the file as lab10-2solution.html.
3. Using the code from Table 10–1 on page HTML 457 as a guide, create a form with one text field for a scrolling message. Name the form msgForm, the input text field messageBox, and make the size 25. Enter the form below the second <div class="centerit"> tag.
4. Create a <script> section in the <head> section for the user-defined functions.
5. Using the code presented in Figures 10–4 through 10–10 on pages HTML 460 through HTML 464 as a guide, write the user-defined function called textMsg(). Assign the message string "** The Edgewood Five Bowling Team has maintained its first place league standing **" to a variable named bowlingMsg.
6. Use 200 for the setTimeout() method to recursively call the textMsg() function.
7. Using the code in Tables 10–14 and 10–15 on pages HTML 475 and HTML 476 as a guide, write the JavaScript user-defined function avergCalc() to validate the data entered into the form as numeric, and not less than 0 or greater than 300.
8. Assign the first game value to gameOne, the second game value to gameTwo, and the third game value to gameThree.
9. Once the data is validated as numeric, calculate the average score and assign it to a variable called avgGame. Use the Math.round() method to round the average and assign it to the Avg text field.
10. If an error occurs, check your code from Steps 3 through 9 and save and test again. Do not continue unless there are no errors.
11. Using the code in Table 10–29 on page HTML 489, write a user-defined function that opens a pop-up window using the file lab10-2announce.html. Set the window size to 520 pixels wide by 370 pixels high.
12. Use the code in Table 10–30 on page HTML 491 as a guide to enter a <div> tag with an id displayDateLast.
13. Use the code in Table 10–31 on page HTML 491 as a guide to enter the user-defined function to display the date the Web page was last modified, as shown in Figure 10–45.
14. Be sure to enter the event handlers as needed in the form and the <body> tag.
15. Save the completed HTML file, validate, and test the Web page using your browser using the scores shown in Figure 10–45.
16. If an error occurs, check your code from Steps 11 through 14, save, and test again.
17. Submit the completed HTML file and Web page in the format specified by your instructor.

In the Lab

Lab 3: Wabash River College Alumni Association

Problem: You are a summer intern for the Wabash River College Alumni Association. The Alumni Association is sponsoring a cruise. Your assignment is to create a Web page that allows alumni to calculate monthly payments on the cruise (Figure 10–46). This Web page has a scrolling message, "*** A minimum deposit of $500 is required to hold a cruise reservation. **". When the Web page loads, a pop-up window displays providing instructions on how to use the interactive form. Validate the form for numeric values. No value may be blank. Display the monthly payment formatted as currency.

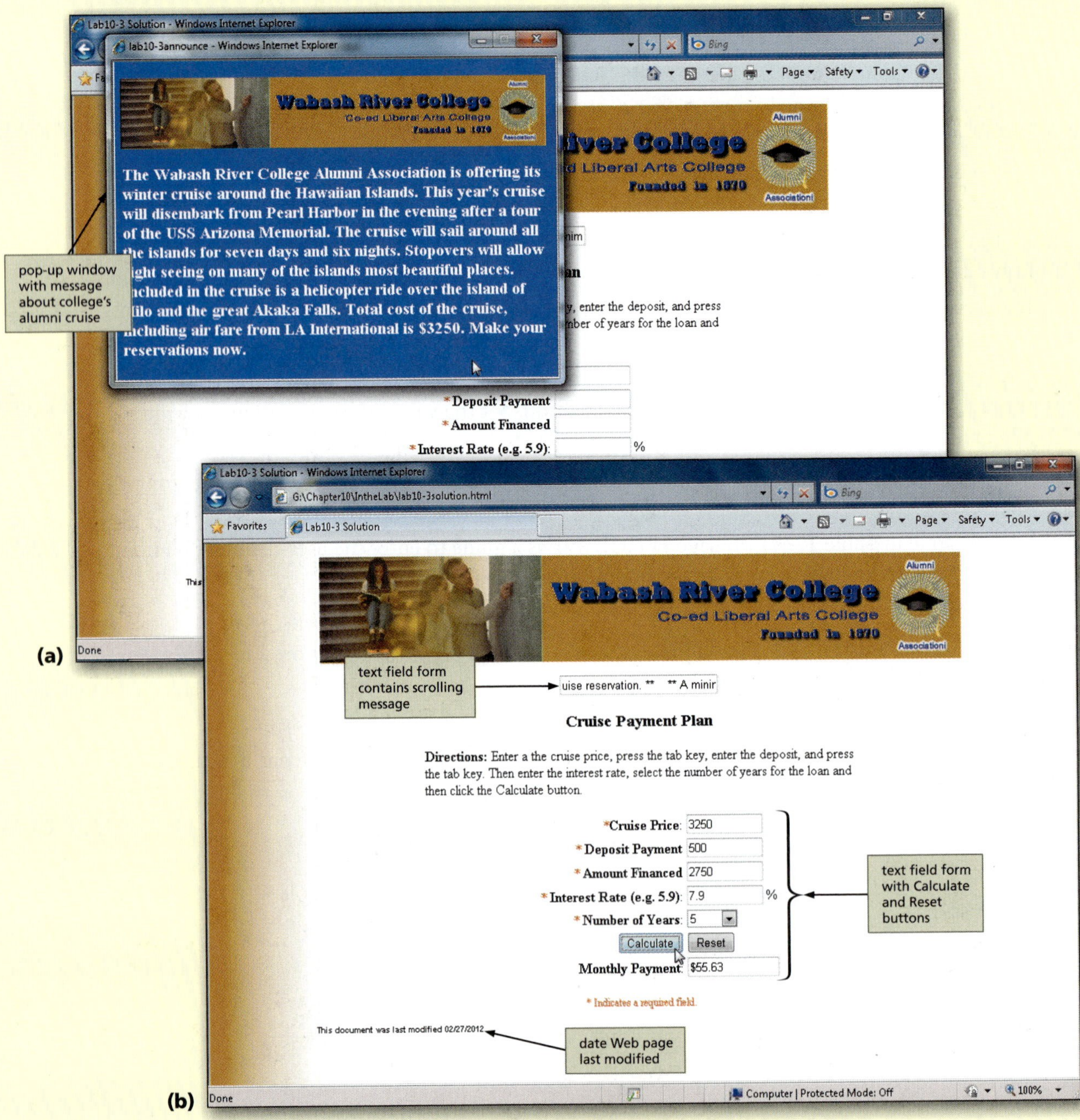

Figure 10–46

Instructions: Perform the following steps:

1. Start Notepad++ and open the lab10-3.html file from the Chapter10\IntheLab folder of the Data Files for Students. Save immediately as lab10-3solution.html.
2. Using the techniques learned in this chapter, write the JavaScript code to create a scrolling message, validate the data entered into the form, and calculate the monthly payment on a loan. Place the scrolling message form text field in the blank line after the banner image. Add the date the Web page was last modified in the blank before the </div> tag before the closing </body> tag. A pop-up window should display with a message as indicated in Figure 10–46a. The pop-up window size is 520 pixels wide by 360 pixels high. The pop-up file name is lab10-3announce.html.
3. Save the completed HTML file, validate, and test it using your browser. If an error occurs, check your code, save, and test again.
4. Submit the completed HTML file and Web page in the format specified by your instructor.

Cases and Places

Apply your creative thinking and problem-solving skills to design and implement a solution.

• Easier •• More Difficult

• 1: E-mail Validation and Adding a Widget

DuneLand Investments has received numerous questions about tracking stock activities. Clients want to have current stock quotes sent to their e-mail. Include a scrolling message function. Name the function instructionMsg() and assign the message " ** Sign up with Duneland Investments for current stock quotes direct to email. ** " to a variable named instructions. Set the setTimeout() function to 200 milliseconds. Write a user-defined function called validateEmail() that validates the e-mail address entered, looking for an "@" sign. In addition, search the Internet for a stock quote widget that can be embedded beneath the e-mail form. Cut and paste this HTML or JavaScript code beneath the form.

• 2: Create the Globe Cinema Ticket Page

The Globe Cinema is a local theater that runs classic, foreign, and art films. The owner has asked you to develop a Web page for the theater so patrons can purchase tickets online. In addition, he wants a message advising patrons about prepaid tickets. Assign the following message " ** You must present the credit card used when picking up prepaid tickets. ** " to a variable named scrollMsg. Create a user-defined function named calcTickets() to validate the form and calculate the ticket prices. Regular price of tickets is $9.75 and the matinee charge is $6.00.

•• 3: Create the Tri-State Credit Union Mortgage Calculator

As one of the Web developers for Tri-State Credit Union, you are asked to create a Web page to allow patrons to calculate monthly payments on a home mortgage. The Web page contains a scrolling message assigned to a variable called mortgageMsg. The message " ** Don't miss out on our low, fixed-rate mortgages! ** " scrolls at 200 milliseconds. The form allows the user to enter the selling price and the percent down, and then calculates a loan amount. The user enters in the interest rate and number of years for the mortgage. A user-defined function named CalcMortgage() should validate the values entered as numeric and determine if Private Mortgage Insurance (PMI) is required. If the percent down is less than 20%, the monthly PMI amount is calculated by multiplying the loan amount by one

Continued >

Cases and Places *continued*

half of one percent and then dividing by 12 for the monthly PMI amount. The monthly PMI is added to the monthly mortgage payment and displayed in the monthly payment text field. The Web page has a pop-up window ad (case10-3notice.html) that should display when the Web page is loaded. Be sure to add the proper event handlers in the correct locations to call the user-defined functions and to display the pop-up window provided.

•• 4: Exploring Alternative Form and Calculator Validation Methods

Make It Personal

Search the Internet to find one or more Web sites for various JavaScript routines that validate forms. Cut and paste the code into a Word document, indicating the Web site from which you copied the code. Write a paragraph or two describing how this validation method is different from or similar to the method presented in the chapter project.

•• 5: Financial Calculators on the Web

Working Together

As a team, search the Web for various financial calculators and formulas. Calculators are used for taxes, loans, savings plans, student financial aid, insurance, and many other applications as well. Each member should find at least two that are different from the others on the team. Determine which calculators can be created in a similar style to the ones in this chapter. Create a complete Web site for the Tri-State Credit Union that has links to the various calculator forms that your team has found and created as Web pages.

11 Using DOM to Enhance Web Pages

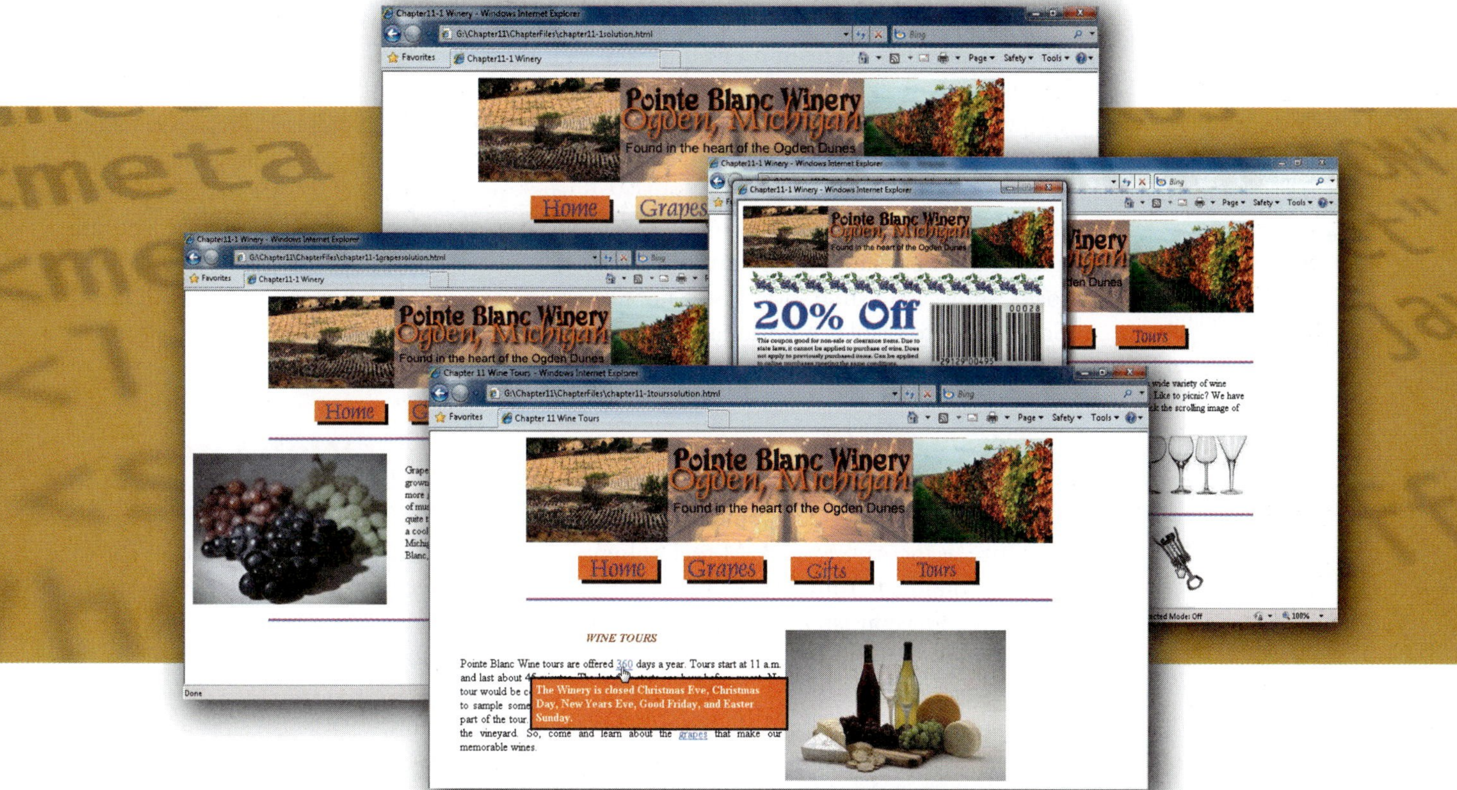

Objectives

You will have mastered the material in this chapter when you can:

- Define the Document Object Model (DOM)
- Use the Math.random() method to display a different image on a Web page every time the Web page is loaded
- Describe how mouse event handlers control image rollovers
- Integrate Cascading Style Sheets (CSS) with JavaScript statements to position elements on a Web page
- Use the JavaScript setTimeout() and clearTimeout() methods to control a floating image on a page
- Call JavaScript functions directly using the JavaScript command
- Use onmouseover and onmouseout event handlers to control ScreenTips
- Integrate the <span> tag in JavaScript statements for ScreenTips
- Define an array and describe how to create an array instance
- Create a slide show using image objects

11 Using DOM to Enhance Web Pages

Introduction

BTW

The Document Object Model (DOM)
The DOM is an application programming interface (API) that identifies interfaces, semantics, and relationships, which allow JavaScript and other languages to manipulate the structure of the underlying document. The DOM is a simple, hierarchical naming system that makes certain objects on a Web page, such as images, forms, and layers, accessible to scripting languages. The core parts of the DOM are the scripting language, the markup language, and style sheets.

In Chapter 10, you learned to write JavaScript user-defined functions to add scrolling messages and pop-up windows to your Web site, to validate user entries on Web forms, to make calculations from user input, and to format output to a text field. This chapter builds on those skills and others you have learned so far by introducing the **Document Object Model** (**DOM**), a combination of technologies that includes HTML, Cascading Style Sheets (CSS), and a scripting language, such as JavaScript, often referred to as DHTML. The DOM will make your Web pages more dynamic. In this chapter, you will use DOM to manipulate image objects. You will create four Web pages that incorporate a navigation bar menu using image rollovers, display a random image when a Web page loads, showcase a slide show, use a floating image as a link to a pop-up screen, and use ScreenTips to display additional information.

Project — The Pointe Blanc Winery Web Site

You are on the Web development team for Pointe Blanc Winery, which is redesigning its Web site to incorporate DOM technology. The new design includes a navigation bar that uses button image rollovers as links to three different Web pages about grapes, a gift shop, and tours. For consistency, every Web page uses the same navigation bar. The home page uses a random number generator to display a different image every time the user goes to or reloads the page.

To make the Winery Web site more interesting, you will have the Grapes Web page automatically start a slide show displaying different grape images. You will have the Gifts Web page use a floating image to add animation to the page, which stops when the user places the mouse over the image and starts up again when the user moves the mouse off the image. If the user clicks the floating image, a pop-up window displays with a coupon. For the Tours Web page, you will add ScreenTips providing more information about certain aspects of the tours. A **ScreenTip** is text that appears in a small pop-up box when you hover the mouse pointer over an item on the screen; the text provides additional information about the item.

Figure 11–1 shows the completed Pointe Blanc Winery home page and the three supporting Web pages with dynamic elements.

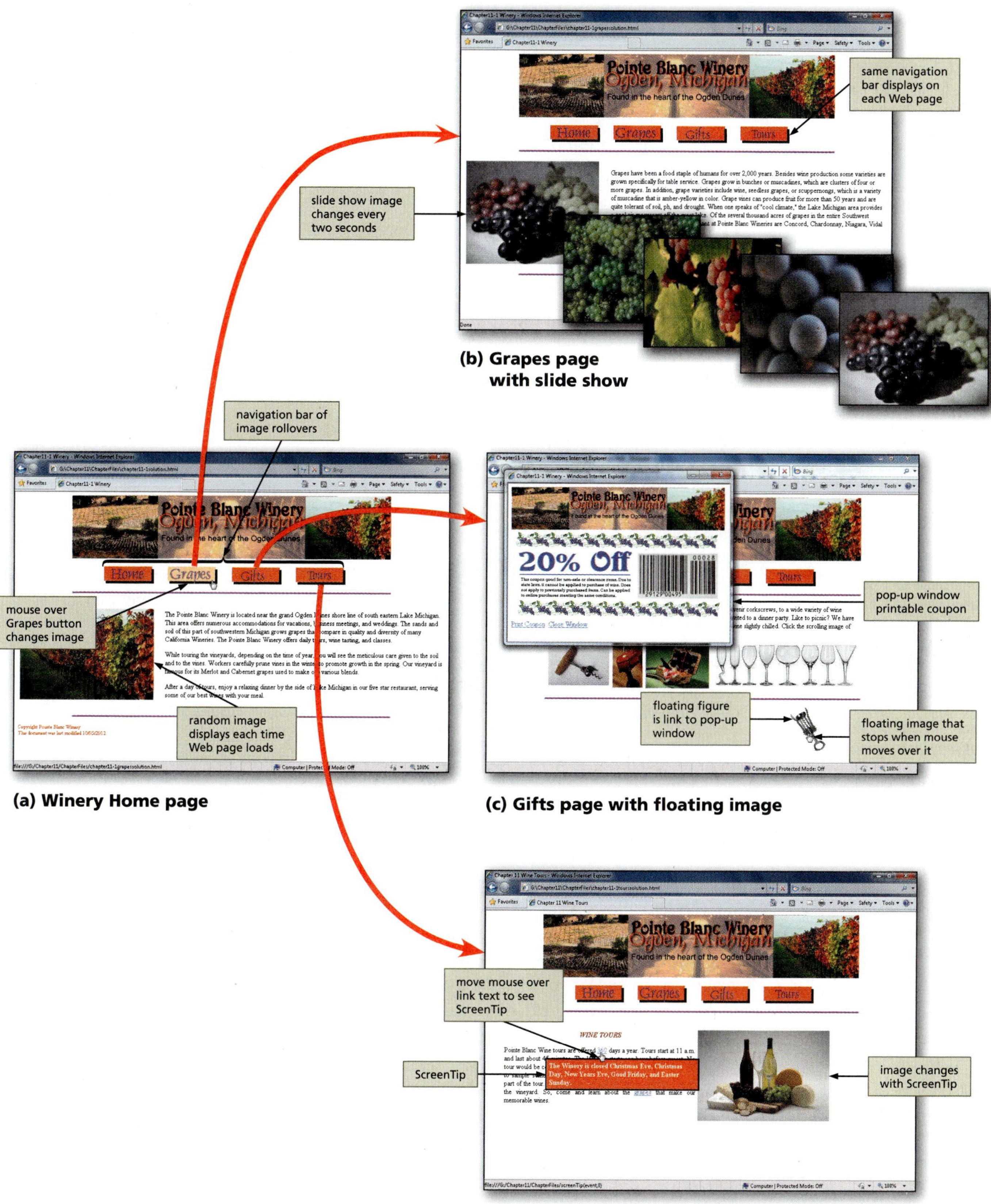
same navigation bar displays on each Web page
slide show image changes every two seconds
navigation bar of image rollovers
mouse over Grapes button changes image
random image displays each time Web page loads
pop-up window printable coupon
floating figure is link to pop-up window
floating image that stops when mouse moves over it
move mouse over link text to see ScreenTip
ScreenTip
image changes with ScreenTip
Pointe Blanc Winery
Ogden, Michigan
Found in the heart of the Ogden Dunes
Home
Grapes
Gifts
Tours
20% Off
WINE TOURS
The Winery is closed Christmas Eve, Christmas Day, New Years Eve, Good Friday, and Easter Sunday.

(b) Grapes page with slide show

(a) Winery Home page

(c) Gifts page with floating image

(d) Tours page with ScreenTips

Figure 11–1

Overview

As you read through this chapter, you will learn how to use DOM with JavaScript to create dynamic pages as shown in Figure 11–1 on the previous page by performing these general tasks:

- Create a navigation bar using image rollovers for all Web pages.
- Create a Home page that displays a different random image each time the Web page is loaded.
- Create a slide show on the Grapes Web page showing different types of grapes.
- Create a floating image on the Gifts Web page that also serves as a link to launch a pop-up window.
- Create ScreenTips on the Tours Web page to provide additional information about selected terms.

Plan Ahead

General Project Guidelines
In creating a complex Web site with multiple Web pages, you should determine what pages will be created and what content each page will contain. In addition, you should determine the links to other pages. The Pointe Blanc Winery Web site contains four Web pages. The main Home page has links to three other pages: Grapes, Gifts, and Tours. Each Web page uses the same navigation bar with image rollovers as buttons. The Home page uses a random number generator to display a different image each time the Web page is loaded. The Grapes Web page has a slide show. The Gifts Web page has a floating image and uses a pop-up window that displays a coupon for the winery's gift shop. The Tours Web page uses ScreenTips to provide more information about tour elements. When necessary, more specific instruction concerning the above guidelines is presented at appropriate points in the chapter. The chapter also will identify the actions performed and decisions made regarding these guidelines during the creation of the Web pages shown in Figure 11–1.

BTW

Document Object Model Techniques
The DOM techniques used to create these Web pages are designed for use in Microsoft Internet Explorer 8. Because not all browsers recognize objects in the same way, these techniques may not work or may yield unexpected results in other browsers. The DOM hierarchical naming system makes objects on a Web page, such as images, form components, layers, and so on, accessible to scripting languages. Because style sheets control position or location of objects, they allow a scripting language even greater control over these objects. The DOM naming system uses these objects to create a tree-like hierarchy of parent and child relationships. In this hierarchy, each object is a node.

The Document Object Model (DOM)

Each section and component on a Web page is an object, and the Document Object Model (DOM) allows scripting languages such as JavaScript to access and manipulate those objects. DOM, sometimes referred to by the older term DHTML, uses a combination of HTML objects, tags and attributes, style sheet properties, and scripting languages to create Web pages that are more animated and more responsive to visitor interaction than basic HTML Web pages.

With DOM, a developer is able to identify objects, such as graphics, and position, replace, or move them anywhere on a Web page. **Positioning** specifies the placement of elements, such as text and graphics, on a Web page. Dynamic positioning of elements is a key feature of modern Web pages and makes the Web pages more appealing and interactive.

To Open an Existing HTML File in Notepad++

In this chapter, the partially completed HTML code for the Home Web page is provided in the Data Files for Students in the file chapter11-1.html. You begin by opening this file in a new Notepad++ window.

1. Start Notepad++, and, if necessary, maximize the window.
2. Click View on the menu bar. If the Word wrap command does not have a check mark next to it, click Word wrap.
3. With a USB flash drive plugged in to your computer, click File on the menu bar and then click Open on the File menu.
4. Navigate to the Chapter11\ChapterFiles folder on the USB drive.
5. Double-click chapter11-1home.html in the list of files to display the HTML code for the chapter11-1home.html Web page, as shown in Figure 11–2.

BTW

Document Object Model Hierarchy Nodes

The DOM naming system uses a tree-like hierarchy of parent and child relationshipswhere each object is a node. A **node** is a point in a tree-like structure that indicates the relationship between objects. The <html> tag is the root node, and the <body> tag is a child to the <html> tag node. These relationships allow an object to become a child of another object, and the relationship between the document object and the objects within a Web page is what gives Web developers access to every aspect of the Web page.

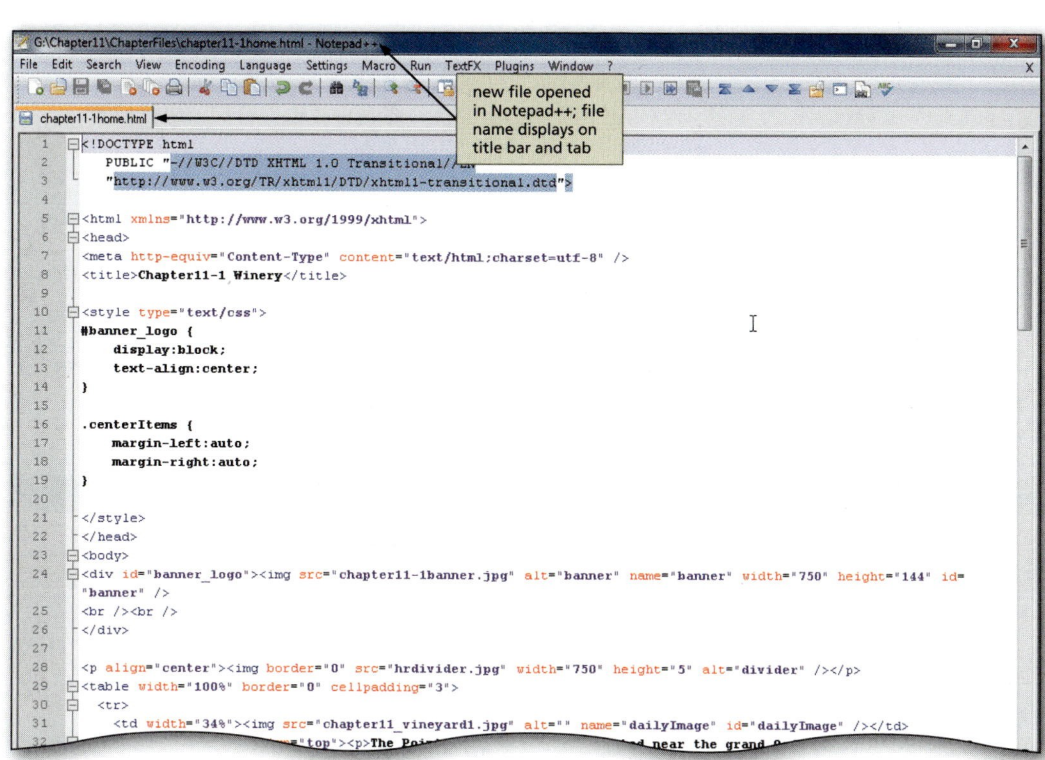

Figure 11–2

Creating the navigation bar with image rollovers.

To create and utilize the navigation bar on the Pointe Blanc Winery Web page, create the following items:

- A set of images used as buttons, to represent the mouse state: up-state, over-state, and down-state
- A table with one row and as many data table cells as needed for each button
- JavaScript user-defined functions associated with each mouse event handler

The buttons should be named the same way and include the state (up, over, down) as part of the name. The name will be used to select the correct button to match the event handler calling the image rollover user-defined function.

Plan Ahead

Creating the Navigation Bar

BTW

Making Web Pages Dynamic with DOM
Using JavaScript takes away the dependence on the server to produce interesting effects and animation on a Web page. As the content of the Web page grows or changes, so does the appearance and presentation of the Web page.

The first step in updating the Pointe Blanc Winery Web site is to create the graphics needed for the buttons. In this case, a graphic artist has created the buttons and supplied the images. The button image names should relate to the mouse state: up, down, or over. The navigation bar is an HTML table with one table row (<tr>), and four table data cells (<td>) that will contain the images (<img>) and event handlers to call a user-defined function to change the button depending on the action of the mouse. In addition, in each table data cell, an anchor tag (<a href>) makes the image a link to another Web page.

Within each table data cell the <img> tag contains a name and id attribute to identify that image as an object. The name value will be used to help construct the file name in the user-defined function to display the correct image. Table 11–1 reviews the general form of the <img> tag.

Table 11–1 General Form of <img> Tag to Create Image Object

General form:	<img src="img_Filename" name="Object_Name" id="Object_name" border="0" alt="alternative text" />
Comment:	where the source (img_Filename) represents the file name of the image that initially is displayed at the location where the tag appears. The name and id attributes identify the object for JavaScript. In some cases, a browser may place a border around an image; to remove that border, use the border attribute of "0." To be XHTML compliant, <img> tags need an alt attribute, which is alternative text that appears if the graphic does not load. In addition, all tags must have a closing tag. Empty tags like <img> may place the closing / symbol within the tag.
Example:	<img src="chapter11-1home_up.jpg" border="0" name="home" id="home" alt="Home button" />

Table 11–2 shows the code to enter the HTML table to create the image objects for the image rollover navigation bar.

Table 11–2 HTML Code to Create the Table to Contain a Navigation Bar

Line	Code
27	`<table width="60%" border="0" cellpadding="0" cellspacing="0" class="centerItems">`
28	`<tr>`
29	`<td>`
30	`<a href="#">`
31	`<img src="chapter11-1home_up.jpg" border="0" name="home" id="home" width="120" height="40" alt="home"/></a>`
32	`</td>`
33	`<td>`
34	`<a href="chapter11-1grapessolution.html">`
35	`<img src="chapter11-1grapes_up.jpg" border="0" name="grapes" id="grapes" width="120" height="40" alt="grapes"/></a>`
36	`</td>`
37	`<td>`
38	`<a href="chapter11-1giftssolution.html">`
39	`<img src="chapter11-1gifts_up.jpg" border="0" name="gifts" id="gifts" width="120" height="40" alt="gifts"/></a>`
40	`</td>`

Table 11–2 HTML Code to Create the Table to Contain a Navigation Bar (continued)

Line	Code
41	`<td>`
42	`<a href="chapter11-1tourssolution.html">`
43	`<img src="chapter11-1tours_up.jpg" border="0" name="tours" id="tours" width="120" height="40" alt="tours" /></a>`
44	`</td>`
45	`</tr>`
46	`</table>`

Line 27 starts the table that holds the navigation bar. The class attribute centerItems will center the table on the page based on a style sheet selector and rule. Line 28 starts the only table row. Lines 29, 33, 37, and 41 start a new column or data cell tag (<td>) to hold each image. Lines 32, 36, 40, and 44 close the data cell </td> tag. Lines 30, 34, 38, and 42 include an <a href> tag to link to each of the four Web pages. Lines 31, 35, 39, and 43 contain the <img> tag with the image of the button in its "up state." Line 45 closes the row </tr> tag and line 46 closes the </table>.

To Create an HTML Table to Contain the Navigation Bar

The following step illustrates how to enter the HTML code to create the navigation bar.

1

- Click line 27 (the blank line after the </div> tag).
- Enter the HTML code shown in Table 11–2 to create the HTML table for the navigation bar, indenting as shown. Do not press the ENTER key after the </table> tag on line 46 (Figure 11–3).

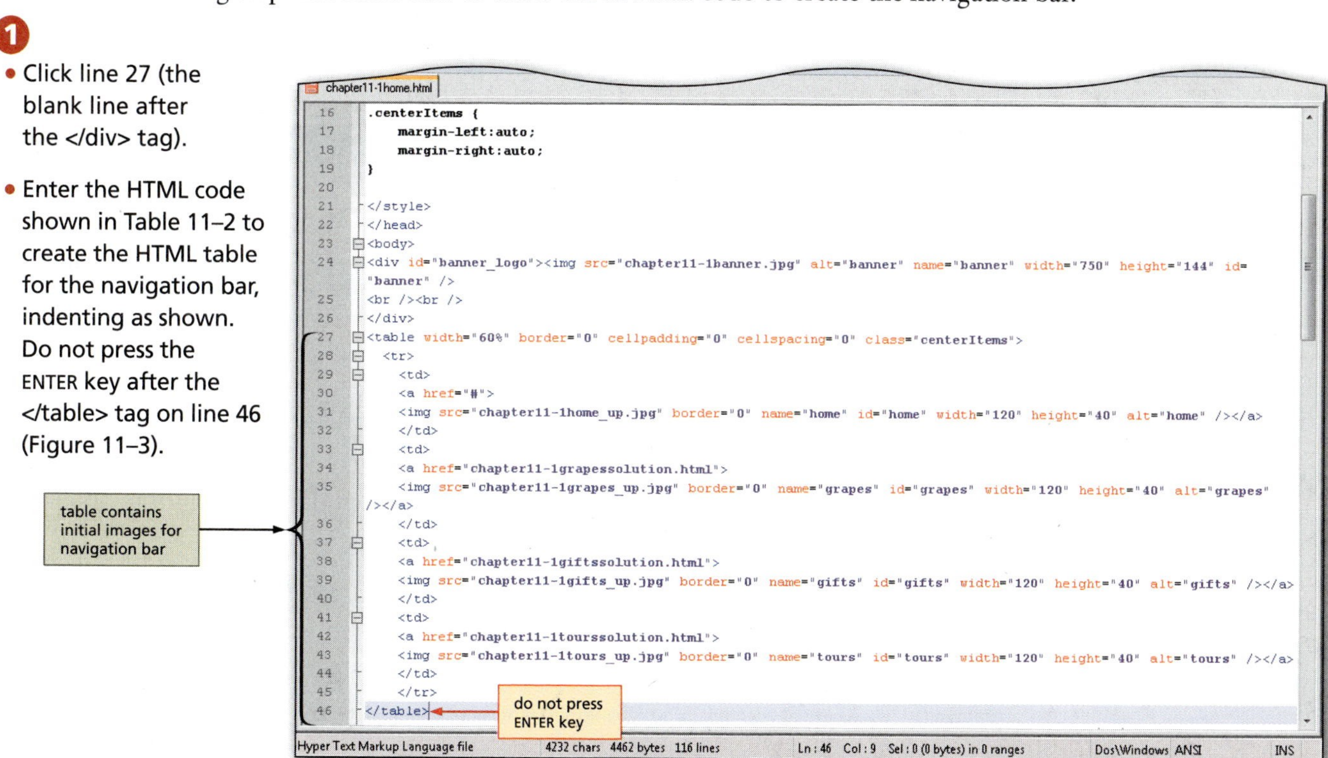

Figure 11–3

Plan Ahead

Creating the user-defined functions for the image rollovers.

To make the navigation bar on the Pointe Blanc Winery Web site work, three user-defined functions must be written for the mouse events, one for each state of the navigation button. The mouse event handlers you will use are onmouseover, onmousedown, onmouseup, and onmouseout. The same function will be used for onmouseup and onmouseout. Each function will do the following:

- Use the state of the mouse (over, down, up, and out) associated with the event handler to construct the associated graphic file name for that state
- Use the getElementById() method to assign the file name to the correct image location

The id attribute with the <img> tag is used by the getElementById() method to identify the correct button. When the function code is complete, the mouse event handlers are added to the <img> tags to invoke the appropriate image rollover function.

Creating the JavaScript User-Defined Functions for the Image Rollovers

You will write a user-defined function for each of the three states (up, over, and down) of the button associated with a particular mouse event: a function named overButton() for when the mouse is hovering over the button, which is invoked by the onmouseover event handler; a function named downButton() for when the user clicks the button, which is invoked by the onmousedown event handler; and a function named upButton() for when the user releases the mouse button, which is invoked by the onmouseup event handler. If the user decides not to click that button, and moves the mouse off the button, the onmouseout event handler will also invoke the upButton() user-defined function.

Table 11–3 shows the general form of the JavaScript statement to assign a new image to the defined location, using the <img> id attribute as part of the object.

Table 11–3 Assign Image to Defined Location

General form:	document.objectname.src="new-img_filename"
Comment:	where the new image appears in the same location as the original by assigning a new file name to the image object source (src) property. The objectname in the JavaScript code must match the object name in the id attribute of the image tag.
Example:	document.Rotate.src="chapter11-1home_down.jpg "

To make the user-defined functions generic enough to work with all the possible images for one button, getElementById() can be used to identify the button graphic file and placeholder. Table 11–4 shows the general form of the getElementById() method.

Table 11–4 getElementById() Method

General form:	getElementById('id_value') getElementById(variable)
Comments:	where getElementById() is a method that returns the object with that specific id. The Id element value must be entered in quotation marks or as a valid variable name. As a string in quotation marks, it is case-sensitive and must match exactly the tag id property value. The returned value also can use any properties associated with that value. The example below shows the method to assign a new graphic file to an image placeholder, using a variable name (img) in the method.
Example:	buttonImg="chapter11-1"+img+"_over.jpg" document.getElementById(img).src=buttonImg

The code for each of the functions is shown in Table 11–5. The functions will be associated with mouse event handlers, so when the user places the mouse over a button image, clicks a button, releases a button, or moves the mouse off an image, the image changes to the appropriate button.

Table 11–5 JavaScript Code for User-Defined Functions

Line	Code
9	<script type="text/javascript">
10	<!-- Hide from old browsers
11	
12	function overButton(img) {
13	buttonImg="chapter11-1"+img+"_over.jpg"
14	document.getElementById(img).src=buttonImg
15	}
16	
17	function downButton(img) {
18	buttonImg="chapter11-1"+img+"_down.jpg"
19	document.getElementById(img).src=buttonImg
20	}
21	
22	function upButton(img) {
23	buttonImg="chapter11-1"+img+"_up.jpg"
24	document.getElementById(img).src=buttonImg
25	}
26	
27	//-->
28	</script>

Line 9 starts a JavaScript section. Line 10 is a standard HTML comment to hide the JavaScript code from older browsers. Line 12 defines the user-defined function, overButton() with the parameter img. Img is passed to the function to create the name of the image file needed for that event. Line 13 constructs the image file name using the parameter, and line 14 uses the getElementById to assign the new file image to the <img> tag using the src property. Lines 17 and 22 define the downButton() and upButton() functions. Lines 18 and 23 construct the appropriate image file name, and lines 19 and 24 assign the new image to the <img> tag. Line 25 closes the function, and lines 27 and 28 close the JavaScript section.

To Create User-Defined Functions for Image Rollovers

The following step shows how to enter the code to create the user-defined functions for the image rollovers.

1

- Click line 9 (the blank line after the title code).
- Enter the code from Table 11–5 on the previous page to create the JavaScript user-defined functions for each button, indenting as shown. Do not press the ENTER key after the closing </script> tag (Figure 11–4).

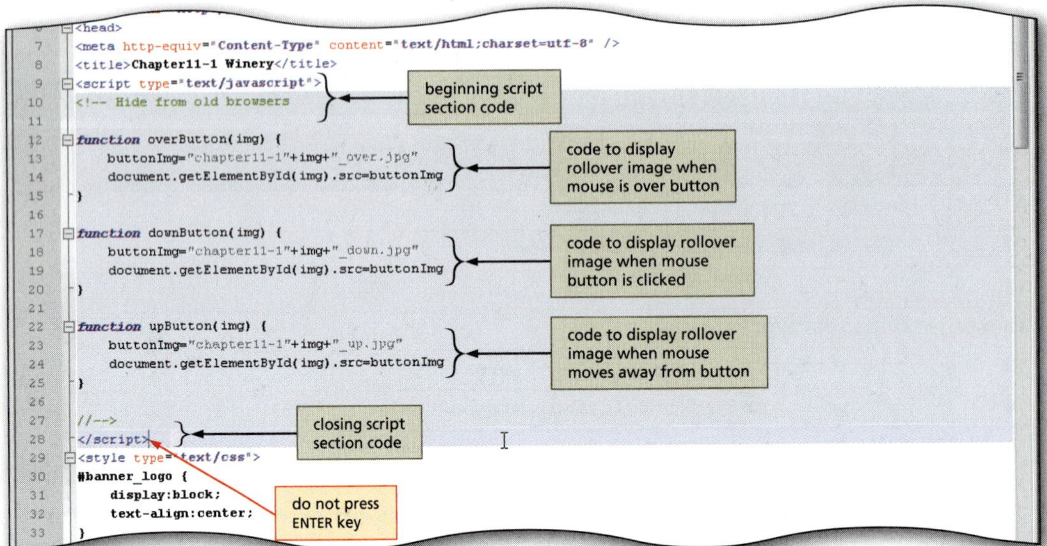
<head>
7 <meta http-equiv="Content-Type" content="text/html;charset=utf-8" />
8 <title>Chapter11-1 Winery</title>
9 <script type="text/javascript">
10 <!-- Hide from old browsers
12 function overButton(img) {
13 buttonImg="chapter11-1"+img+"_over.jpg"
14 document.getElementById(img).src=buttonImg
15 }
17 function downButton(img) {
18 buttonImg="chapter11-1"+img+"_down.jpg"
19 document.getElementById(img).src=buttonImg
20 }
22 function upButton(img) {
23 buttonImg="chapter11-1"+img+"_up.jpg"
24 document.getElementById(img).src=buttonImg
25 }
27 //-->
28 </script>
29 <style type="text/css">
30 #banner_logo {
31 display:block;
32 text-align:center;
33 }
beginning script section code
code to display rollover image when mouse is over button
code to display rollover image when mouse button is clicked
code to display rollover image when mouse moves away from button
closing script section code
do not press ENTER key

Figure 11–4

Adding the Mouse Event Handlers for the Image Rollovers

The next step is to enter the mouse event handlers in the <img> tags. Table 11–6 shows the code to add the mouse event handlers to the <img> tags.

Table 11–6 Code to Enter the Mouse Event Handlers in the <img> Tags

Line	Code
50	onmouseover="overButton('home')" onmousedown="downButton('home')" onmouseout="upButton('home')" onmouseup="upButton('home')"
...	
54	onmouseover="overButton('grapes')" onmousedown="downButton('grapes')" onmouseout="upButton('grapes')" onmouseup="upButton('grapes')"
...	
58	onmouseover="overButton('gifts')" onmousedown="downButton('gifts')" onmouseout="upButton('gifts')" onmouseup="upButton('gifts')"
...	
62	onmouseover="overButton('tours')" onmousedown="downButton('tours')" onmouseout="upButton('tours')" onmouseup="upButton('tours')"

Line 50 adds the mouse event handler for the Home button. Line 54 adds the mouse event handler for the Grapes button. Line 58 adds the mouse event handler for the Gifts button. Line 62 adds the mouse event handler for the Tours button.

To Enter Mouse Event Handlers to Invoke User-Defined Functions

The following steps illustrate how to enter the code for the mouse event handlers to invoke the associated user-defined functions for the image rollovers. Note that each line of code may wrap to a second line in Notepad++.

- Click line 50 and position the insertion point after the alt="home" attribute.
- Press the SPACEBAR and enter the code shown in Table 11–6 for line 50 to enter all the mouse event handlers associated with image rollovers for the Home button. Do not press the ENTER key when finished.

- Click line 54 and position the insertion point after the alt="grapes" attribute.
- Press the SPACEBAR and enter the code shown in Table 11–6 for line 54 to enter all the mouse event handlers associated with image rollovers for the Grapes button. Do not press the ENTER key when finished.

3

- Click line 58 and position the insertion point after the alt="gifts" attribute.
- Press the SPACEBAR and enter the code shown in Table 11–6 for line 58 to enter all the mouse event handlers associated with image rollovers for the Gifts button. Do not press the ENTER key when finished.

4

- Click line 62 and position the insertion point after the alt="tours" attribute.
- Press the SPACEBAR and enter the code shown in Table 11–6 for line 62 to enter all the mouse event handlers associated with image rollovers for the Tours button. Do not press the ENTER key when finished (Figure 11–5).

Figure 11–5

To Save and Test the Pointe Blanc Winery Web Page Navigation Bar

The code for the Pointe Blanc Winery Web page navigation bar is complete. Now you should save the HTML file and then test the JavaScript code using a Web browser. The following steps show how to save and test the Pointe Blanc Winery Web page.

1

- With a USB drive plugged into your computer, click File on the Notepad++ menu bar and then click Save As. Type `chapter11-1homesolution.html` in the File name text box (do not press the ENTER key).
- If necessary, browse to the USB drive and open the Chapter11\ChapterFiles folder.
- Save the file on the USB drive with the name chapter11-1homesolution.html.
- Start your browser. If necessary, click the Maximize button.
- Type `g:\chapter11\ChapterFiles\chapter11-1homesolution.html` in the Address box and then press the ENTER key.
- If necessary, click the security bar under the tabs, click Allow Blocked Content, and then click Yes in the confirmation dialog box (Figure 11–6).

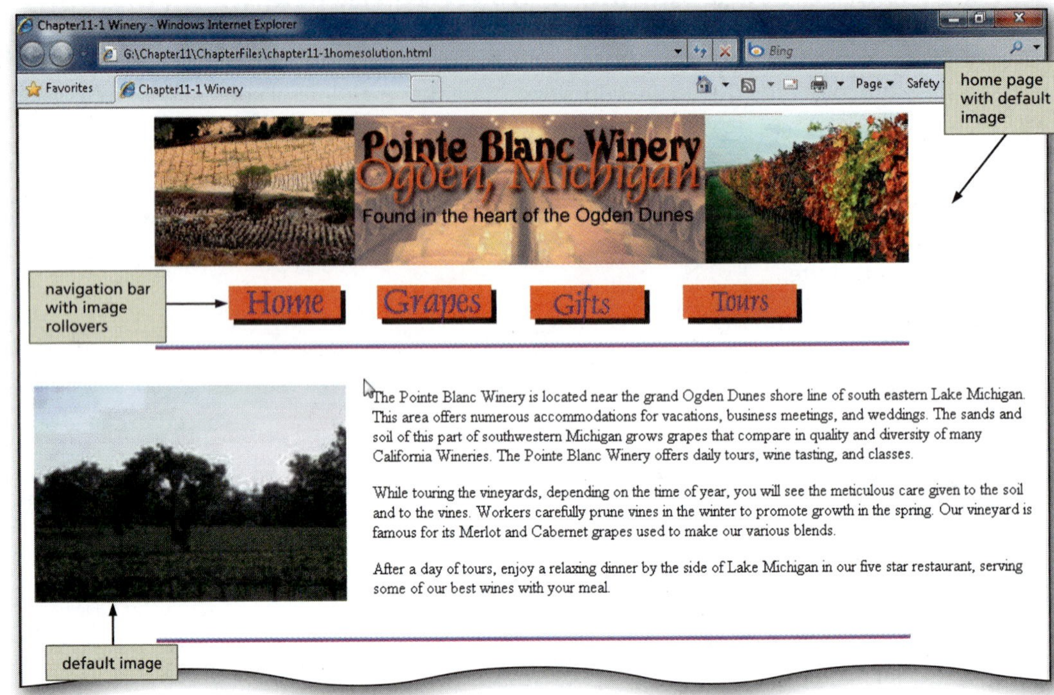
Chapter11-1 Winery - Windows Internet Explorer
G:\Chapter11\ChapterFiles\chapter11-1homesolution.html
Favorites
Chapter11-1 Winery
home page with default image
Pointe Blanc Winery
Ogden, Michigan
Found in the heart of the Ogden Dunes
navigation bar with image rollovers
Home
Grapes
Gifts
Tours
The Pointe Blanc Winery is located near the grand Ogden Dunes shore line of south eastern Lake Michigan. This area offers numerous accommodations for vacations, business meetings, and weddings. The sands and soil of this part of southwestern Michigan grows grapes that compare in quality and diversity of many California Wineries. The Pointe Blanc Winery offers daily tours, wine tasting, and classes.
While touring the vineyards, depending on the time of year, you will see the meticulous care given to the soil and to the vines. Workers carefully prune vines in the winter to promote growth in the spring. Our vineyard is famous for its Merlot and Cabernet grapes used to make our various blends.
After a day of tours, enjoy a relaxing dinner by the side of Lake Michigan in our five star restaurant, serving some of our best wines with your meal.
default image

Figure 11–6

2

- Position the mouse pointer over the Home button. The button image should change color, as in Figure 11–7.

Chapter11-1 Winery
Pointe Blanc Winery
Ogden, Michigan
Found in the heart of the Ogden Dunes
Home button image changes when mouse is over button
Home
Grapes
Gifts
Tours

Figure 11–7

3

- Click the mouse on the Home button. The button image should change to appear as if it is being physically pressed down (Figure 11–8).

Chapter11-1 Winery
Pointe Blanc Winery
Ogden, Michigan
Found in the heart of the Ogden Dunes
Home button image appears pressed down when user clicks mouse button
Home
Grapes
Gifts
Tours

Figure 11–8

Plan Ahead

Creating a random image generator with a user-defined function.
A random image generator will display a new image in the image placeholder every time the Web page is loaded. To create a user-defined function to display random images, the following steps and programming logic must be followed.

- Determine the location for an image object
- Determine the image to be used as the default image
- Make sure each image is the same size
- Write the user-defined JavaScript function using the following logic:
  1. Define a list of images in an array object making the first element blank or null
  2. Determine the maximum random number size by subtracting 1 from the array length
  3. Use the Math.ceil() and Math.random() methods to create the random number
  4. Assign the array value using the random number as a subscript to the image placeholder
  5. Add the onload event handler to the <body> tag to invoke the user-defined function when the Web page is loaded

In the Home Web page, the first element in the array is blank or null because it is element zero, and the Math.ceil() method will never return a zero with the Math.random() method. Thus, that image would never be used or displayed.

Creating the User-Defined Function Random Number Generator

The first step in creating the random image on the Home Web page is to create a list in which to store the file names of the images that will be selected by the random number generator: chapter11_vineyard1.jpg, chapter11_vineyard2.jpg, and chapter11_vineyard3.jpg, chapter11_vineyard4.jpg, chapter11_vineyard5.jpg, and chapter11_vineyard6.jpg. (These files can be found in the Data Files for Students.) JavaScript, like other programming languages, uses a data structure called an array to work with lists of data. An **array** is a collection of data items, represented by one variable name. This variable is called the **array name**. Each of the individual data items is called an element, and a subscript references the individual data items in the array. A **subscript** is a number that designates a single occurrence of an array element.

Arrays are built-in objects. To create an array and fill that array with data, create an object instance of the Array object. Recall from Chapter 9 that an **object instance** is a new JavaScript object created from a built-in object. Table 11–7 shows the general form for creating an array object instance from the Array object.

BTW

Arrays
JavaScript arrays are not a fixed length like in other programming languages. New elements can be added to the array without having to redefine the structure. Remember, also, that JavaScript is a loosely typed language and does not require variables to be declared as a data type. Thus, you can store string, numeric, or Boolean values to the same array.

Table 11–7 Create an Array

General form:	var myarrayname=new Array()
Comment:	where Array is a built-in object and the new command creates a new object instance of the array. Data items may fill an array in one of two ways: (1) by placing the data directly in the array object; or (2) by assigning the items separately.
Examples:	var randomImage = new Array ("", "chapter11_vineyard1.jpg", "chapter11_vineyard2.jpg", "chapter11_vineyard3.jpg","chapter11_vineyard4.jpg") or var randomImage=new Array() randomImage[0]="" randomImage[1]="chapter11_vineyard1.jpg" randomImage[2]="chapter11_vineyard2.jpg" randomImage[3]="chapter11_vineyard3.jpg" randomImage[4]="chapter11_vineyard4.jpg"

Subscripts are placed after the array name in square [ ] brackets, as shown in the examples in Table 11–7. A subscript must be any valid JavaScript variable or numeric literal value. The first element in a JavaScript array is element zero [0].

After the data elements are assigned to the array, the JavaScript code can retrieve or use the data by referencing the array name with the subscript. As shown in Figure 11–9, the data in an array is stored sequentially. For example, to reference the second element (chapter11_vineyard1.jpg), the JavaScript code uses the contents of randomImage[1]. To reference the third element in the array, the JavaScript code uses the contents of randomImage[2].

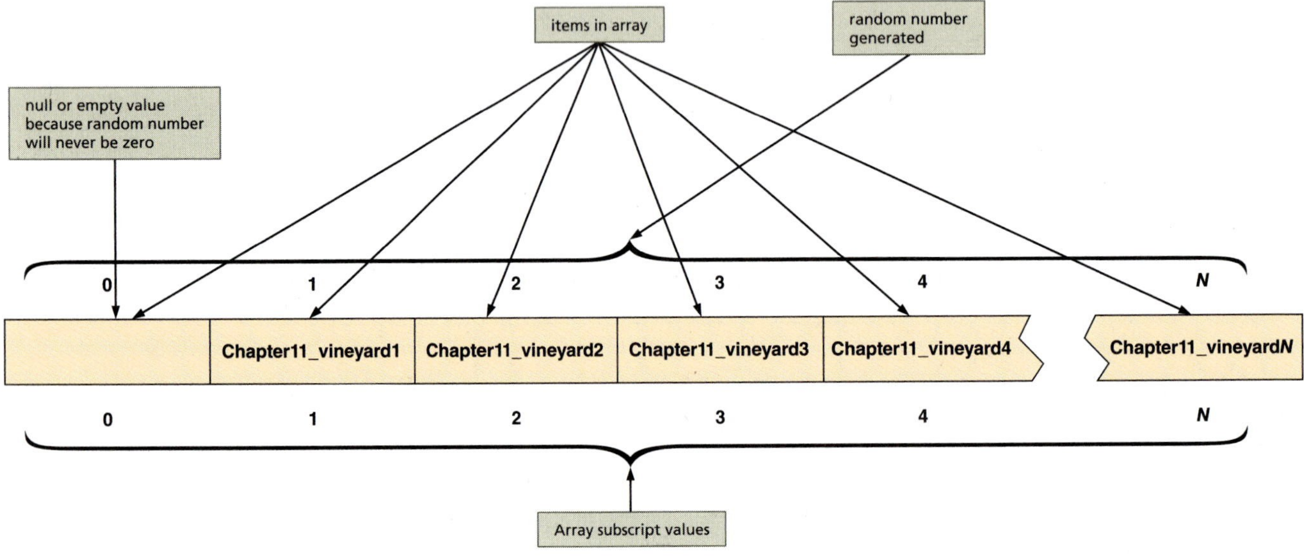

Figure 11–9

The next step in updating the Pointe Blanc Winery home page is to create the user-defined function to display an image from an array using a random number generator. With this function, the Web page will show a different main image every time the page is loaded. Table 11–8 shows the code for the creating the array object, generating the random number, and assigning the new image to the image placeholder.

Table 11–8 Code for User-Defined Functions to Create a Randomly Displayed Image

Line	Code
27	`var randomImage = new Array ("", "chapter11_vineyard1.jpg", "chapter11_vineyard2.jpg", "chapter11_vineyard3.jpg","chapter11_vineyard4.jpg", "chapter11_vineyard5.jpg", "chapter11_vineyard6.jpg")`
28	`function rndimage() {`
29	`rndnumsize=randomImage.length-1`
30	`var randomnumber=Math.ceil(Math.random()*rndnumsize)`
31	`document.dailyImage.src=randomImage[randomnumber]`
32	`}`

Line 27 creates the Array object, randomImage, with one null element and six image file names. The null element is created by an empty set of quotation marks (""). Line 28 declares the user-defined function, rndimage(). Line 29 determines the maximum value of the random number by taking the size of the array (randomImage.length) and subtracting 1 from that size. This subtraction is necessary because an array's first element is identified as element zero. Line 30 generates the random number using the Math.ceil() method and Math.random() methods. The Math.random() method generates a number between 0 and 1. The result is multiplied by the array size minus one (rndnumsize), which in this case is six.

The multiplication by the array size provides a number between 1 and 6, and the Math.ceil() method will round the value to the next integer, which is assigned to the variable randomnumber. The randomnumber value is used in line 31 to assign an array element to the image placeholder. Line 32 closes the function.

To Enter a Random Number Generator User-Defined Function

The following step shows how to enter the user-defined function, rndimage(), to randomly assign an image to the image placeholder.

1

- Click line 26 and press the ENTER key once.
- On line 27, enter the JavaScript code shown in Table 11–8 to create the user-defined function to randomly assign an image to the image placeholder, as shown in Figure 11–10.
- Press the ENTER key twice.

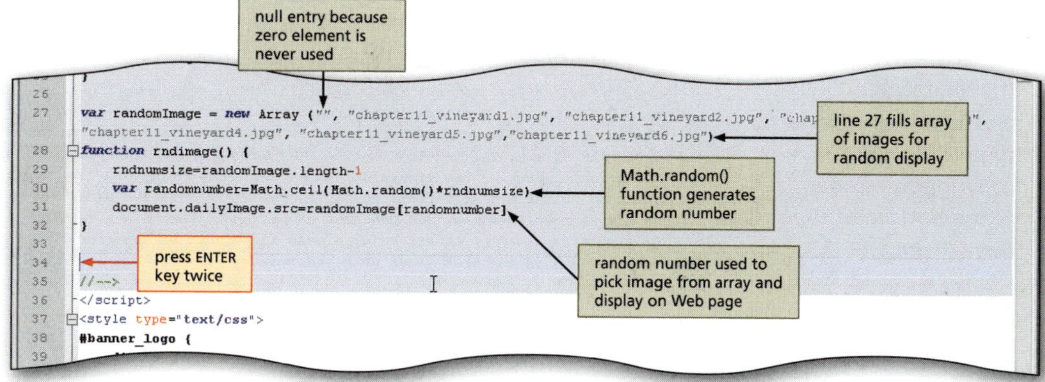

Figure 11–10

To Enter Code to Show Copyright Information and Date Last Modified

As shown in Figure 11–1a on page HTML 509, the Pointe Blanc Winery Web page displays copyright information and the date the file was last modified at the bottom of the Web page. To show just the date, without the time, the JavaScript code uses the substring() method, which was introduced in Chapter 10. First, however, a <div> tag with an id attribute must be inserted in the HTML code where the message is to display. Table 11–9 shows the HTML code for the <div> tag with the id attribute.

Table 11–9 Code for <div> Tag with the id Attribute

Line	Code
84	`<div id="copyright">`
85	`</div>`

Table 11–10 on the next page shows the JavaScript code for the <script> section to show the copyright information and date the Web page was last modified.

Table 11–10 Code to Show the Date Last Modified

Line	Code
34	function copyRight() {
35	var lastModDate = document.lastModified.substring(0,10)
36	copyright.innerHTML = "<p style='font-size:8pt; color:#cc0000;'>Copyright Pointe Blanc Winery"+" This document was last modified "+lastModDate+".</p>"
37	}

The following steps illustrate how to enter the HTML <div> tag and the JavaScript user-defined function to show copyright information and the date the file was last modified using the substring() method so it is displayed at the bottom of the Web page.

- Click line 84.
- Enter the HTML code shown in Table 11–9 on the previous page to position the copyright message at the bottom of the page (Figure 11–11).

division created to display copyright and date Web page last modified

do not press ENTER key

Figure 11–11

- Click line 34.
- Enter the JavaScript code shown in Table 11–10 to show the copyright information and date last modified and press the ENTER key (Figure 11–12).

code to display copyright and date Web page last modified

insertion point

Figure 11–12

To Enter Onload Event Handlers in the <body> Tag

With the code for the user-defined functions entered to display the random pictures, the copyright information, and the date last modified, the final step is to add the onload event handlers in the <body> tag to invoke the rndimage() and copyRight() user-defined functions. The following step illustrates how to enter the event handlers in the <body> tag.

1

- In line 54, click after the y in the word body.
- Press the SPACEBAR once and type `onload="rndimage(); copyRight()"` before the >.
- Do not press the ENTER key at the end (Figure 11–13).

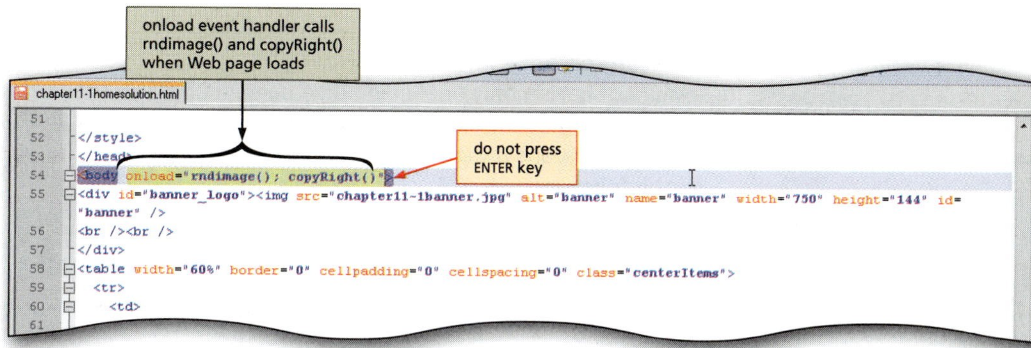
onload event handler calls rndimage() and copyRight() when Web page loads
do not press ENTER key
chapter11-1homesolution.html

Figure 11–13

To Save an HTML File and Test a Web Page

With the code for the user-defined functions and the JavaScript section for the copyright information and the date last modified complete, you should save the HTML file and test the Web page. The following steps illustrate how to save the HTML file and then test the Pointe Blanc Winery Web page.

1. With a USB drive plugged into your computer, click File on the menu bar and then click Save to save the Chapter11-1homesolution.html file.
2. Activate the browser from the status bar and click the Refresh button on the browser window.
3. If necessary, scroll down to the see the bottom of the Web page and the copyright information.
4. Move the mouse over the Grapes button, but do not click the mouse. Note that the image changes.
5. Click the Refresh button to see a different vineyard image generated by the random number generator user-defined function (Figure 11–14).

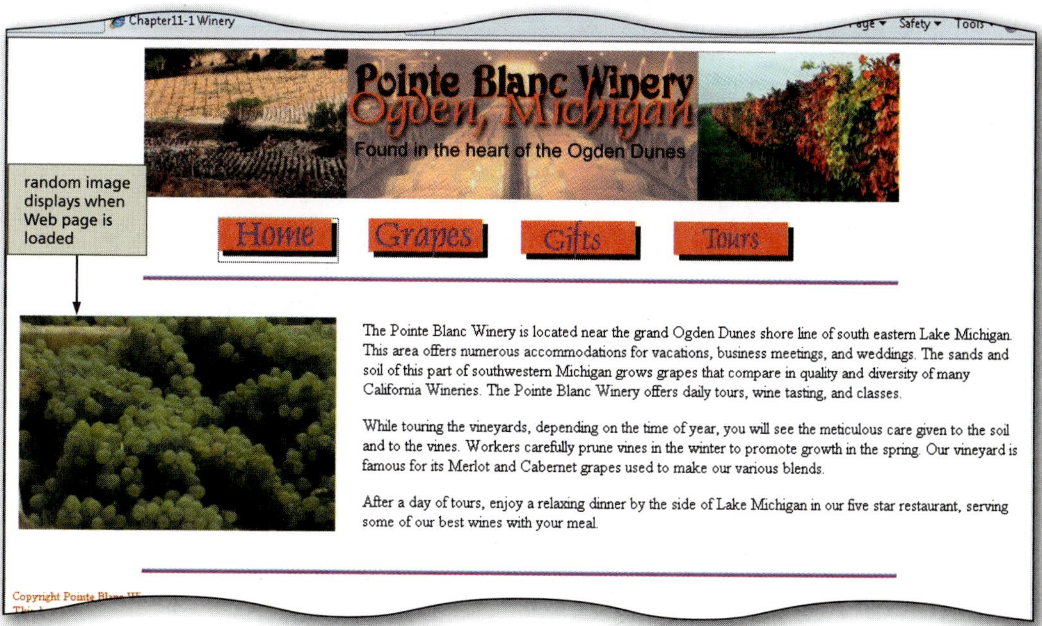
Chapter11-1 Winery
Safety
Tools
Pointe Blanc Winery
Ogden, Michigan
Found in the heart of the Ogden Dunes
random image displays when Web page is loaded
Home
Grapes
Gifts
Tours
The Pointe Blanc Winery is located near the grand Ogden Dunes shore line of south eastern Lake Michigan. This area offers numerous accommodations for vacations, business meetings, and weddings. The sands and soil of this part of southwestern Michigan grows grapes that compare in quality and diversity of many California Wineries. The Pointe Blanc Winery offers daily tours, wine tasting, and classes.
While touring the vineyards, depending on the time of year, you will see the meticulous care given to the soil and to the vines. Workers carefully prune vines in the winter to promote growth in the spring. Our vineyard is famous for its Merlot and Cabernet grapes used to make our various blends.
After a day of tours, enjoy a relaxing dinner by the side of Lake Michigan in our five star restaurant, serving some of our best wines with your meal.

Figure 11–14

Plan Ahead

Creating an automatic slide show.
Instead of having only one image on a page, many Web sites include slide shows to display multiple images. The intent is to grab the visitors' attention and keep them on the page. To include a slide show that will start automatically when the Grapes page opens, you need to do the following:

- Determine the location for an image object
- Determine the images to be used
- Write the user-defined JavaScript function using the following logic:
  1. Define a list of images in an array object
  2. Establish a counter
  3. Increment the counter by 1
  4. Test the counter against the number of items in the list
  5. Assign the list element, based on the current counter value, to the image object
  6. Call the function again using the setTimeout() method
- Add the event handler to call the function

Creating a Slide Show on the Grapes Web Page

As shown in Figure 11–1b on page HTML 509, the Grapes Web page contains a slide show. A **slide show** is a set of images, all the same size, that are displayed in the same location for a few seconds, one after the other, to create the appearance that the images are rotating. The slide show in this chapter continuously runs, with no controls.

To Open an Existing HTML File in Notepad++

In this chapter, the partially completed HTML code for the Grapes Web page is provided in the Data Files for Students. To modify this Web page, the file chapter11-1grapes.html must be opened in a new Notepad++ window.

1. If necessary, start Notepad++.
2. Open the chapter11-1grapes.html file in the Chapter11\ChapterFiles folder.

To Copy and Paste the Navigation Bar, Event Handlers, and Image Rollover Functions

To maintain consistency in looks among all the Web pages, the Grapes Web page should use the same navigation bar created for the Winery Home page.

1. If necessary, open the chapter11-1homesolution.html file in Notepad++ in the Chapter11\ChapterFiles folder.
2. Copy the HTML <table> code from lines 58 through 77 to enter the HTML code and mouse event handlers for the navigation bar.
3. Click line 27 in the chapter11-1grapes.html file and paste the code to insert the navigation bar from Table 11–2 on page HTML 512 into the Grapes Web page file.

4. In the chapter11-1grapes.html file, modify line 30 to replace the # symbol with `chapter11-1homesolution.html`.

5. In the chapter11-1homesolution.html file, copy the JavaScript code from lines 9 through 26. Return to the chapter11-1grapes.html file and insert the copied code for the navigation bar image rollovers on line 9. Add the closing HTML comment (//-->) and the closing `</script>` tags on lines 27 and 28 (Figure 11–15).

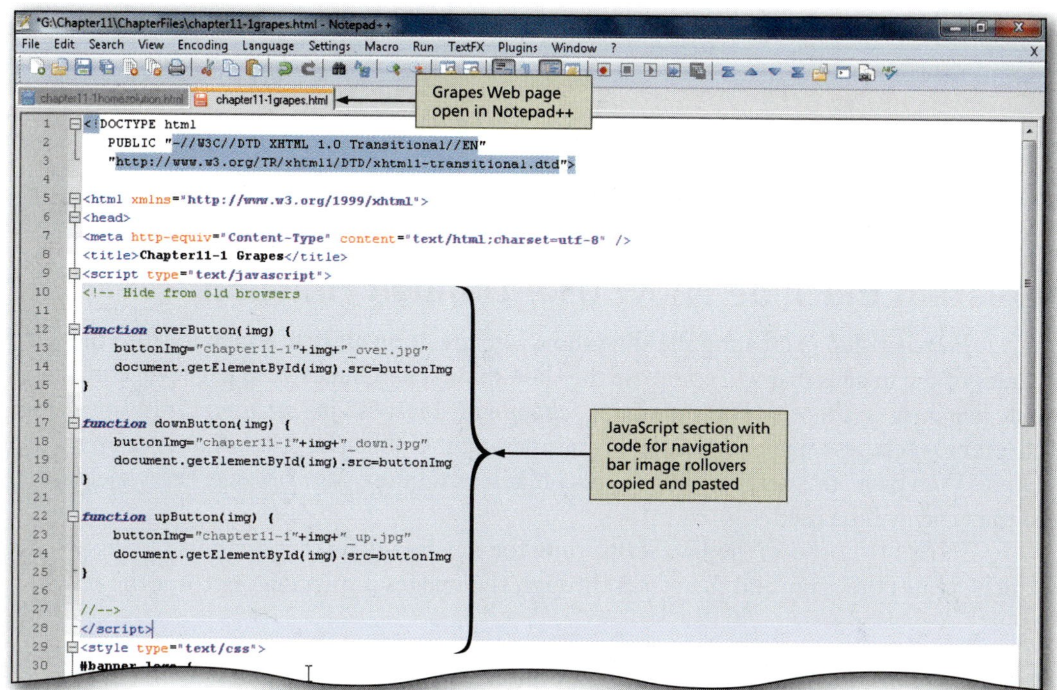

Figure 11–15

Creating and Placing an Image Object

The first step in creating a slide show is to determine the location of the slide show images. To define the image for the user-defined function, you must add the name attribute and value. The name attribute allows JavaScript to assign a new graphic image to the same location as the original image. This technique is the same as in Table 11–1 on page HTML 512. A new graphic file is assigned the image placeholder as described in Table 11–3 on page HTML 514.

To Create an Image Object

The initial image is placed in a data table cell with text in the next data cell describing grapes. Table 11–11 shows the HTML code to place the image object in the data cell in the Web page.

Table 11–11 Code to Enter the <img> Object for the Slide Show

Line	Code
70	`<img src="chapter11-1grapes1.jpg" alt="grape slide show" name="slideHolder" width="312" height="235" id="slideHolder"/>`

The following step shows how to create an image object at a specific location on a Web page.

1

- Position the insertion point on line 70.
- Indenting as shown, enter the code in Table 11–11 on the previous page to define and place the initial image and do not press the ENTER key at the end of the line (Figure 11–16).

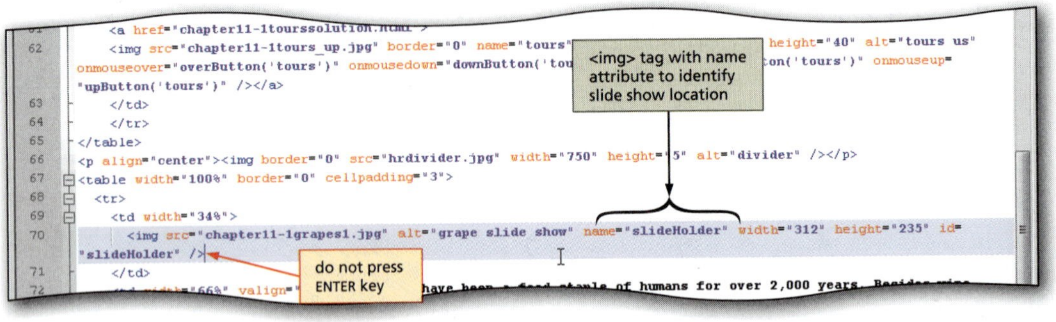

Figure 11–16

Creating the Slide Show User-Defined Function

The first step in creating the slide show is to create an array in which to store the file names of the images that will comprise the slide show. The Grapes Web page will contain only five images: chapter11-1grapes1.jpg, chapter11-1grapes2.jpg, chapter11-1grapes3.jpg, chapter11-1grapes4.jpg, and chapter11-1grapes5.jpg. Unlike the random images on the Home Web page, this array will not need a blank or dummy page because every element of the array will be used.

Table 11–12 shows the JavaScript code for the user-defined function slideShow(), which creates the array and the cycles through the images displaying one after the other.

Table 11–12 Code to Create the slideShow() Function

Line	Code
11	`var slides=new Array("chapter11-1grapes1.jpg", "chapter11-1grapes2.jpg", "chapter11-1grapes3.jpg", "chapter11-1grapes4.jpg", "chapter11-1grapes5 .jpg")`
12	
13	`var slideCntr=slides.length-1`
14	`function slideShow() {`
15	`slideCntr+=1`
16	`if (slideCntr==slides.length) slideCntr=0`
17	`document.slideHolder.src = slides[slideCntr]`
18	`setTimeout("slideShow()",2000)`
19	`}`

Line 11 begins by creating an array named slides, with five image file names set as the data elements. Line 13 initializes the counter variable named slideCntr to the number of elements in the table using the length property slides.length. One is subtracted from the length so the counter does not exceed the number of elements in the array on line 15. Line 14 declares the user-defined function slideShow(). Line 15 increments the slideCntr by one, and line 16 tests the counter against the number of items in the array, using the slides.length property. If slideCntr is equal to the number of elements in the array, line 16 assigns a zero (0) to slideCntr, which reinitializes the counter to the first element of the array. Using the length property allows a developer to add or subtract images in the array without having to change other lines of code. Line 17 assigns the contents of slides[slideCntr] to the image object, so the new image is displayed. The function then uses the setTimeout() method on line 18 to make a recursive call to itself after a two-second delay. The brace (}) on line 19 completes the slideShow() function.

To Create a User-Defined Function to Add a Slide Show

The following step illustrates how to enter the slideShow() function to create a slide show on the Grapes page.

- Click blank line 11, and then enter the JavaScript code shown in Table 11–12 to create the slideShow() user-defined function, indenting as shown (Figure 11–17).
- Press the ENTER key once after the closing brace to complete the user-defined function.

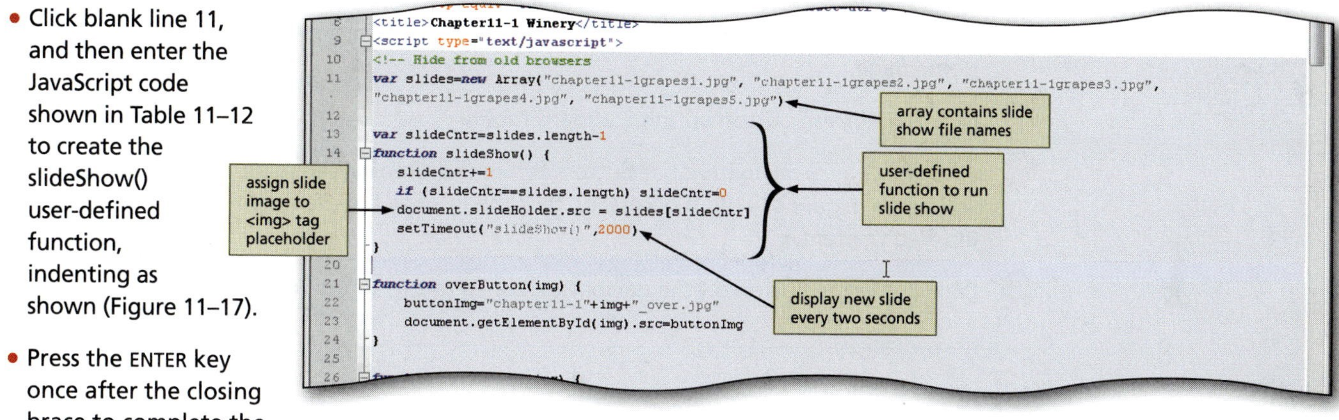

Figure 11–17

Q&A Why is this function placed before the image rollover functions for the navigation menu in the <script> section?

This placement allows this function to be loaded and executed first, which will start the slide show.

To Enter an Onload Event Handler to Call a Function

The next step is to enter the onload event handler that calls the slideShow() function when the Grapes Web page loads. To call the slideShow() user-defined function initially, an onload event handler is placed in the <body> tag. The following steps show how to enter the onload event handler to call the slideShow() function.

1. Position the insertion point between the y and the > symbol in the <body> tag on line 51.
2. Press the SPACEBAR once.
3. Type `onload="slideShow()"` to enter the onload event handler in the <body> tag, and then do not press the ENTER key (Figure 11–18).

```
49 </style>
50 </head>
51 <body onload="slideShow()">
52 <div id="banner_logo">
53    <img src="chapter11-1banner.jpg" name="banner" width="750" height="144" id="banner" />
54    <br />
55    <br />
56 </div>
57 <table width="60%" border="0" cellpadding="0" cellspacing="0" class="centerItems">
58    <tr>
59       <td>
60       <a href="chapter11-1solution.html">
```

onload event handler to start slide show

do not press ENTER key

Figure 11–18

To Save an HTML File and Test a Web Page

With the code for the Grapes Web page complete, the HTML file should be saved and the Web page should be viewed in a browser to confirm the Web page appears and functions as desired.

1. With a USB drive plugged into your computer, click File on the menu bar and then click Save As on the File menu.
2. Type `chapter11-1grapessolution.html` in the File name text box to save the file with a new name, and then click the Save button in the Save As dialog box.
3. Click the Internet Explorer button on the taskbar and display the Pointe Blanc Winery Home page.
4. Click the Refresh button on the Standard toolbar.
5. Click the Grapes navigation bar button. When the Grapes Web page loads, the slide show will begin (Figure 11–19). If necessary, click the Information Bar and then click Allow Blocked Content.
6. Click the Home button on the navigation bar to return to the Home Web page.

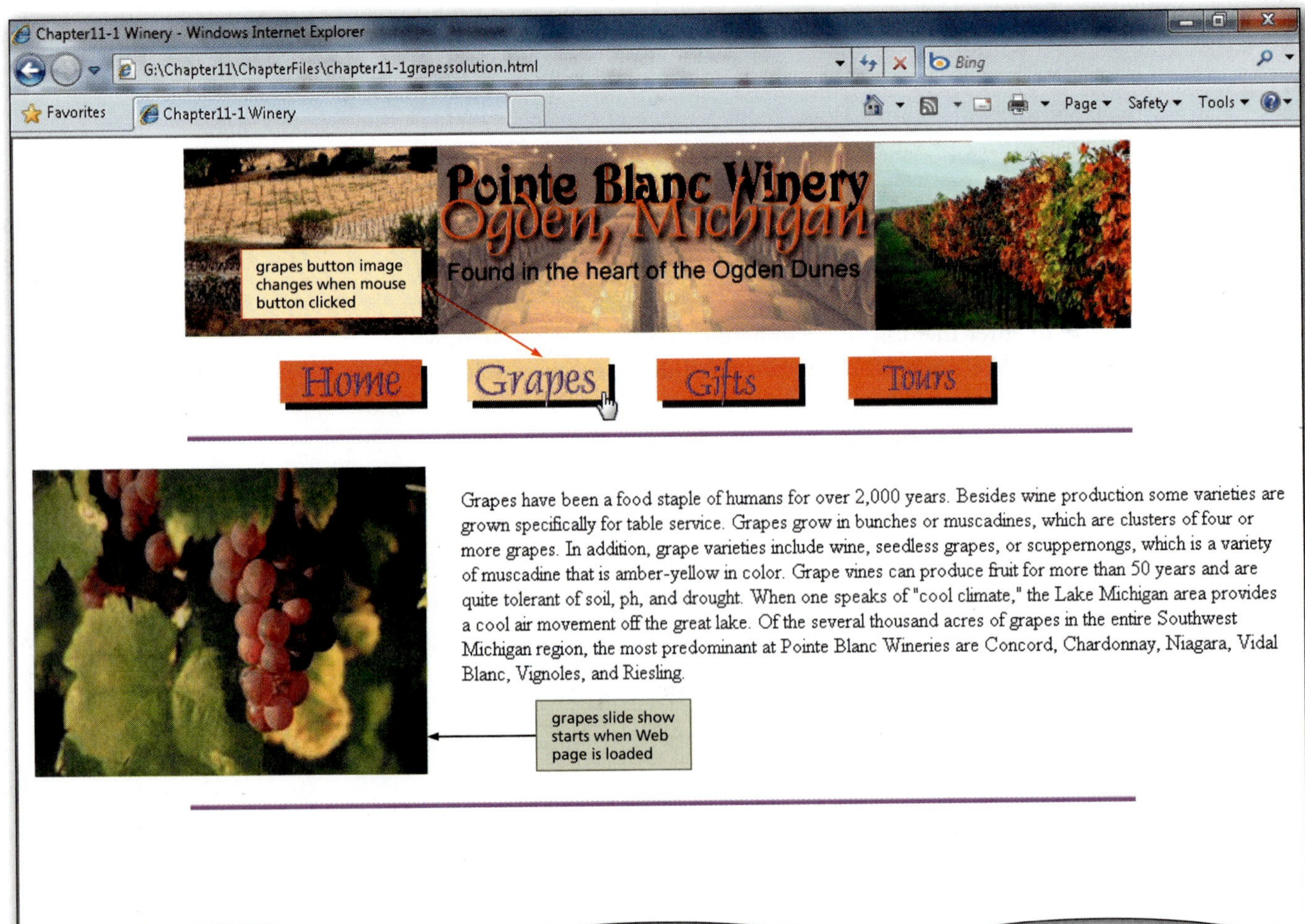

Figure 11–19

Plan Ahead

Creating a floating image.
The position of the image on the Web page is based on a screen resolution of 1024 × 768. Different screen resolutions will need to adjust the positioning values. In this chapter, the JavaScript code used to create a floating image includes four user-defined functions that do the following:

- Have an image float from right to left (floatingImage() function)

  The following steps detail the programming logic for the floatingImage() function:

  1. Decrement the left pixel position by 10
  2. Test left pixel position to determine if it is off the screen
  3. If left pixel < 250, reset to the right side of the screen (950) based on the screen resolution of 1024 by 768
  4. Use the id selector for the <div> tag to assign the calculated value of the left pixel to the pixelLeft property of the image object
  5. Assign the setTimeout() method used to call the floatingImage() function to a variable so the clearTimeout() method can be used to stop the scrolling
- Stop the image from scrolling (stopFloat() function) with the clearTimeout() method
- Restart the image scrolling (restartFloat() function) using the setTimeout() method
- Open a pop-up window for the coupon offer (coupon() function) using the open() method

Adding a Floating Image to the Gifts Web Page

The Gifts Web page (Figure 11–1c on page HTML 509) highlights the gift shop at the Pointe Blanc Winery. The Web page has an image that scrolls from right to left, and if the user clicks the image, a pop-up window displays with a coupon. When a visitor places the mouse over the image, it stops scrolling. When the mouse is moved off the floating image, it starts scrolling again. The image stops by using the clearTimeout() method and the mouse pointer becomes a hand by using an embedded style in the <img> tag. The floating image is a link to the Coupon Web page that is displayed as a pop-up window.

To Open an Existing HTML File in Notepad++

To move or float an image, it is placed in a <div> tag layer that is referenced by the user-defined functions. The floating image is positioned after images on the page to fill some of the blank space and to avoid overlaying any other text. To begin, the Gifts Web page must be opened.

1. If necessary, start Notepad++.
2. Open the chapter11-1gifts.html file in the Chapter11\ChapterFiles folder.

To Copy and Paste the Navigation Bar, Event Handlers, and Image Rollover Functions

To maintain consistency in looks among all the Web pages, the Gifts Web page should use the same navigation bar, event handlers, and image rollover functions created for the Winery Home page.

1. Open the chapter11-1homesolution.html file in Notepad++ in the Chapter11\ChapterFiles folder.
2. Copy the HTML <table> code from lines 58 through 77 (the HTML code and mouse event handlers for the navigation bar).
3. In the chapter11-1gifts.html file, click line 31 and paste the code to create the navigation bar.
4. Modify line 34 to replace the # symbol with `chapter11-1homesolution.html`.
5. In the chapter11-1homesolution.html file, copy the JavaScript code from lines 9 through 26. Return to the chapter11-1gifts.html file and insert the copied code for the navigation bar image rollovers on line 9. Add the closing HTML comment (//-->) and the closing `</script>` tags on lines 27 and 28 (Figure 11–20).

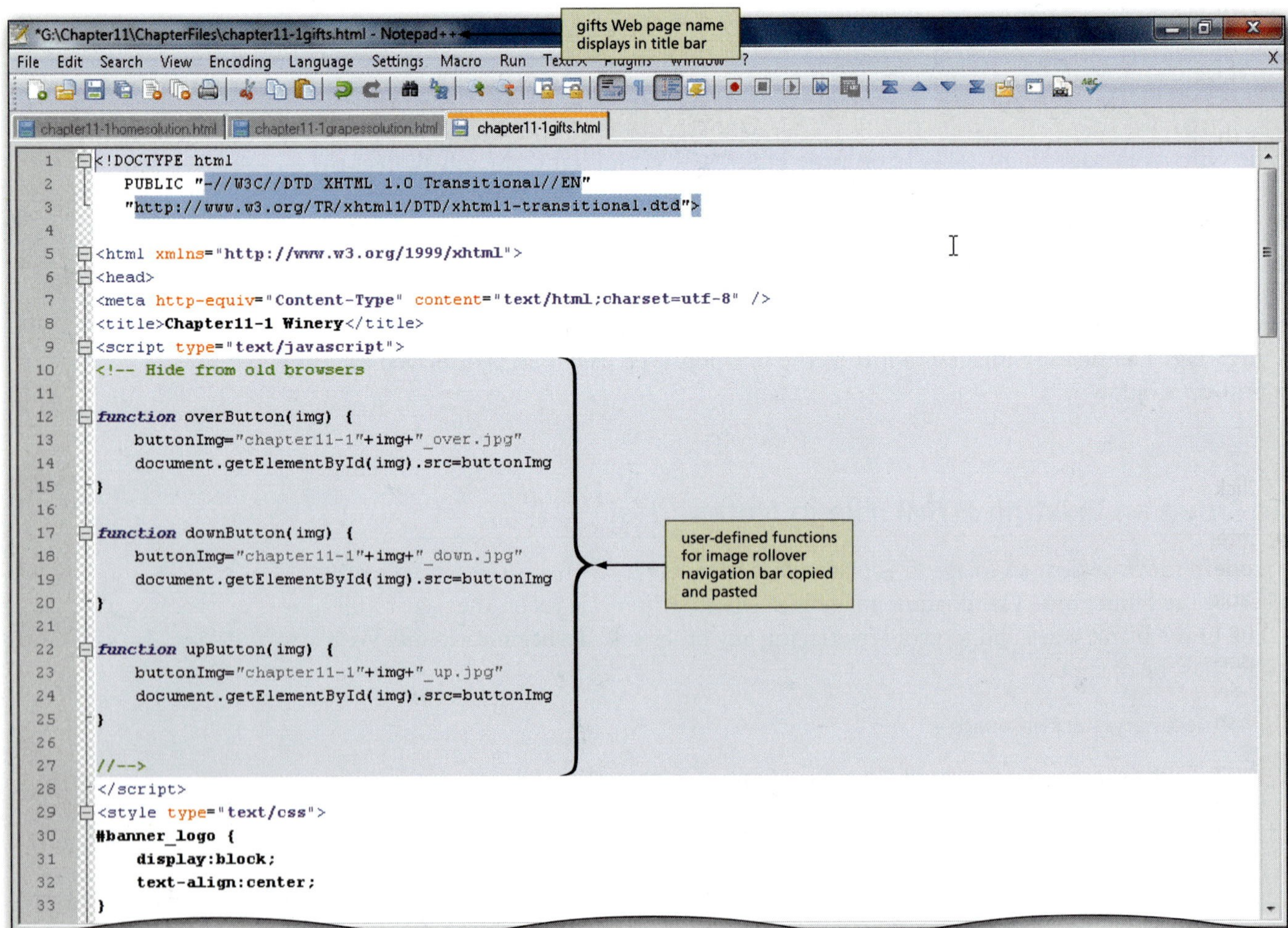

Figure 11–20

Entering the floatingImage(), stopFloat(), and restartFloat()Functions

The next step is to enter the code to have the image float across the screen on the Gifts Web page from right to left, to stop floating when the mouse is over the image, and to restart floating when the mouse moves off the image. Table 11–13 shows the code for the floatingImage() function.

Table 11–13 Code for the floatingImage() Function

Line	Code
11	`var leftPX=950`
12	`function floatingImage() {`
13	`        leftPX-=10`
14	`        if (leftPX<-150) leftPX=950`
15	`        document.all['floatImg'].style.pixelLeft=leftPX`
16	`        imager=setTimeout("floatingImage()",100)`
17	`}`

Line 11 assigns 950 to the variable leftPX to represent the right side of the screen for the screen resolution 1024 by 768. Line 12 declares the function, floatingImage(). Line 13 decrements the leftPX variable by 10 pixels. Line 14 tests the value of leftPX to see if it has extended past the end of the screen. The value −150 was chosen to allow the image to scroll completely off the screen before starting over at the right. If the value is less than −150, leftPX is assigned 950 so the image can start from the right again.

Line 15 assigns the value of leftPX to the pixelLeft property of the image object, identified by the Img1 name. Line 16 assigns the recursive call of the setTimeout() method to a variable so the floating image can be stopped with an onmouseover event handler calling a different function. Line 17 closes the function code.

BTW

Simple Animation on a Web Page with JavaScript
Animation can be created by moving objects associated with a division (layer). By repeatedly changing the position and placement of the division in a recursive user-defined function, the object moves.

To Enter the floatingImage() Function

The following step illustrates how to enter the floatingImage() function.

1

- Click line 11.
- Enter the JavaScript code as shown in Table 11–13 to enter the floatingImage() user-defined function, indenting as shown.
- Press the ENTER key twice to place the insertion point on line 19 (Figure 11–21).

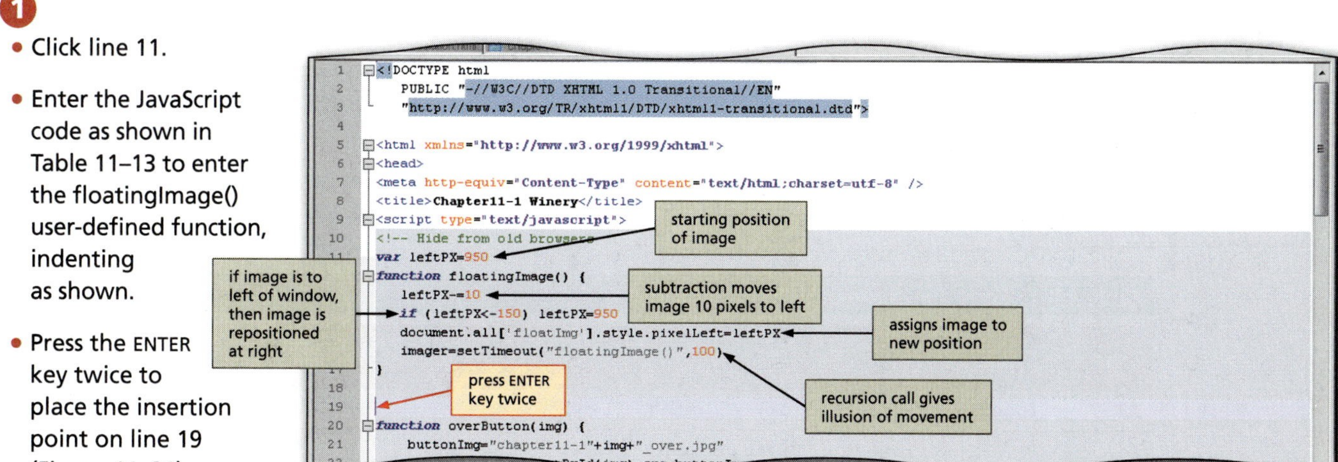

Figure 11–21

To Enter the stopFloat() Function

The stopFloat() function stops the image from floating when the visitor moves the mouse over the image. The function, stopFloat(), responds to an onmouseover event handler. Table 11–14 shows the JavaScript code for the stopFloat() function.

Table 11–14 Code for the stopFloat() Function

Line	Code
19	`function stopFloat() {`
20	`        clearTimeout(imager)`
21	`}`

Line 19 defines the stopFloat() user-defined function. The clearTimeout() method on line 20 stops the floating image by clearing the imager variable used in the recursive call made by the setTimeout() method on line 16 in Table 11–13. Line 21 closes the stopFloat() function.

The following step illustrates how to enter the stopFloat() user-defined function.

- If necessary, click line 19.
- Enter the code shown in Table 11–14 to create the stopFloat() user-defined function, indenting as shown.
- Press the ENTER key twice to position the insertion point on line 23 (Figure 11–22).

```
11  var leftPX=950
12  function floatingImage() {
13     leftPX-=10
14     if (leftPX<-150) leftPX=950
15     document.all['floatImg'].style.pixelLeft=leftPX
16     imager=setTimeout("floatingImage()",100)
17  }
18
19  function stopFloat() {
20     clearTimeout(imager)
21  }
22
23
24  function overButton(img) {
25     buttonImg="chapter11-1"+img+"_over.jpg"
26     document.getElementById(img).src=buttonImg
27  }
28
29  function downButton(img) {
```


Figure 11–22

To Enter the restartFloat() Function

The restartFloat() function restarts the image scrolling when the visitor moves the mouse off the floating image. This function, restartFloat(), responds to an onmouseout event handler. Table 11–15 shows the code for the restartFloat() user-defined function.

Table 11–15 Code for the restartFloat() Function

Line	Code
23	`function restartFloat() {`
24	`        setTimeout("floatingImage()",100)`
25	`}`

Line 23 declares the function. Line 24 uses the setTimeout() method to call the floatingImage() user-defined function. Line 25 closes the restartFloat() function code.

The following step shows how to enter the user-defined function restartFloat().

1

- If necessary, click line 23.
- Enter the code shown in Table 11–15 to create the restartFloat() user-defined function, indenting as shown.
- Press the ENTER key once to place the insertion point on line 26 (Figure 11–23).

Figure 11–23

Entering the coupon() Function on the Gifts Web Page

The fourth user-defined function added to the Gifts Web page is the coupon() function, which opens the coupon pop-up window when the user clicks the floating image. Table 11–16 shows the code for the coupon() function.

Table 11–16 Code for the coupon() Function

Line	Code
42	`function coupon() {`
43	`window.open("chapter11-1coupon.html", "coupon", "width=525,height=360")`
44	`}`

Line 42 declares the function. Line 43 uses the open() method to open the Coupon Web page as a pop-up window. The attributes settings size the window to a width of 525 pixels and a height of 360 pixels. This window does not need any menu or scroll bars. Line 44 closes the function.

To Enter the coupon() Function

The following step shows how to enter the coupon() user-defined function.

- Click line 42 and then press the ENTER key once.
- Click line 42 again and enter the code shown in Table 11–16 to create the coupon() user-defined function, indenting as shown.
- Press the Enter key once after line 44 to position the insertion point on line 45 (Figure 11–24).

Figure 11–24

Adding an id Selector to the Style Sheet for the Floating Image

The next step is to add an id selector to the embedded CSS to place the floating image. The style sheet uses the id selector, floatImg, which later will be associated with the <div> tag container to position the image. The embedded style sheet sets the position to absolute, and 950 pixels from the left side of the screen.

To Enter an Embedded Style Sheet to Format the Floating Image

The following step shows how to enter the id selector in the embedded style sheet used to position the floating image on the Gifts Web page.

- Click line 63 and press the ENTER key to insert a blank line. Click the blank line 63.
- Type `#floatImg {` to create the id selector and then press the ENTER key.
- Indent as shown, then type `position: absolute; left=950;` to define the initial position of the image, and then press the ENTER key.
- Move to the left margin and type `}` to close the #floatImg id selector, and then press the ENTER key (Figure 11–25).

```
59 .rightalign {
60     text-align:right;
61 }
62 
63 #floatImg {
64    position: absolute; left=950;
65 }
66 
67 </style>
68 </head>
69 <body>
70 <div id="banner_logo"><img src="chapter11-1banner.jpg" alt="banner" name="banner" width="750" height="1
```


Figure 11–25

> **BTW**
> **The Purpose of the <div> Tag**
> The <div> tag is called a container, and is used to format the layout of sections or divisions of text needing the same style. Web developers often describe divisions as layers because they can be placed on top of each other and revealed dynamically as needed.

> **BTW**
> **Moving Objects**
> Object positions can be dynamically modified within a division <div> or a span <span> tag using a scripting language. Differences in browsers may cause a division to appear slightly lower or higher than originally intended by the developer.

Entering an Image Object for the Floating Image Using the <div> and <img> Tags

The next step is to add the floating image. First, a <div> tag container must be added on the Web page. The <div> tag uses the id selector, #floatImg, to indicate where the image should be initially positioned. The <div> tag layer becomes the image object whose pixelLeft property is modified to change the position of the image to float across the page. Table 11–17 shows the HTML code for the <div> tag and image tags that must be added to the Web page table.

Table 11–17 Code to Add the Floating Image <div> Tag

Line	Code
106	`<div id="floatImg">`
107	`<img src="chapter11-1corkscrew1_sm.gif" alt="scrolling banner" style="cursor:hand" onmouseover="stopFloat()" onmouseout="restartFloat()" onclick="coupon()" />`
108	`</div>`

Line 106 starts the <div> tag with the floatImg id selector attribute (id="floatImg"). Line 107 is the <img> image tag with three event handlers. This line must be typed without any line breaks. The onmouseover event handler calls the stopFloat() user-defined function to stop the movement. When the visitor takes the mouse off the image, the onmouseout event handler calls the restartFloat() user-defined function. The onclick event handler calls the coupon() user-defined function, which displays a pop-up window with a coupon. The style attribute will cause the mouse pointer to change to a hand when the mouse is over the image.

To Enter <div> and <img> Tags for the Floating Image

The following step illustrates how to enter the <div> and <img> tags.

- Click line 106 to position the insertion point on the blank line before the </body> tag.
- Enter the HTML code shown in Table 11–17 to create the <div> and <img> tags for the floating image at this position on the Web page (Figure 11–26).

<div> container with <img> tag and mouse event handlers for floating image

do not press ENTER key

Figure 11–26

To Add an Onload Event Handler to Call the floatingImage() Function

The final step in modifying the Gifts Web page is to enter the onload event handler to call the floatingImage() user-defined function as soon as the Web page is loaded. The following step shows how to add the onload event handler to the <body> tag.

- Click line 69.
- Position the insertion point between the y in body and the > symbol and press the SPACEBAR once.
- Type `onload="floatingImage()"` and do not press the ENTER key (Figure 11–27).

onload event handler to start floating image

do not press ENTER key

Figure 11–27

To Save an HTML File and Test a Web Page

With the code for the Gifts Web page complete, the HTML file should be saved and the Web page should be viewed in a browser to confirm the Web page appears and functions as desired. The following steps show how to save an HTML file and then view and test the Web page in a browser.

1. With a USB drive plugged into your computer, click File on the menu bar, and then click Save As on the File menu.
2. Type `chapter11-1giftssolution.html` in the File name text box to save the file with a new name, and then click the Save button in the Save As dialog box.
3. Click the Internet Explorer button on the taskbar.
4. Type `g:\chapter11\ChapterFiles\chapter11-1giftssolution.html` in the Address box, and then press the ENTER key. If necessary, allow blocked content.
5. When the Gifts Web page loads, a corkscrew image begins to float across the page from right to left.
6. Place your mouse over the floating image. The image will stop floating (Figure 11–28a).
7. Click the floating image. The coupon pop-up window appears (Figure 11–28b).

(a) Floating Image of Cork Screw

(b) Pop-up Window with Coupon

Figure 11–28

Plan Ahead

Creating ScreenTips

Creating a ScreenTip requires four steps:

1. Entering the JavaScript code for the user-defined function, screenTip(), that is associated with a particular image

   The following steps detail the programming logic for the screenTip() function:

   a. Define the image file using the element id

   b. Construct the pop-up object and determine the state (hidden or visible)

   c. If visible, hide the ScreenTip and restore the original image

   d. If hidden, show the ScreenTip with the new image

2. Entering the embedded style sheet
3. Entering the <a> tags and event handlers for each of the three terms
4. Entering the <span> tags containing the ScreenTip text and style sheet attributes that format the appearance of the ScreenTip text

Creating ScreenTips on the Tours Web Page

The Tours Web page includes three tour elements that appear as hyperlinks on the Web page: 360, tickets, and grapes. When the user places the mouse over these hyperlinks, ScreenTips will display with more information about these elements. Figure 11–1d on page HTML 509 shows an example of a ScreenTip.

The three words appear as hyperlinks by using the anchor tag <a> embedded with JavaScript statements and event handlers to call the user-defined function screenTip(). The screenTip() user-defined function uses a combination of JavaScript objects and properties, in conjunction with associated style sheet definitions, to show the ScreenTip text. Each ScreenTip is defined by <span> tags that work in conjunction with the style sheet.

To Open an Existing HTML File in Notepad++

Now you will open the Tours HTML file in Notepad++ to enter the JavaScript user-defined function, the style sheet information, the <a> tag, the event handlers to call the JavaScript function, and the <span> tags containing the ScreenTip text. The following steps show how to open the chapter11-1tours.html file in Notepad++.

1. If necessary, start Notepad++.
2. Open the chapter11-1tours.html file in the Chapter11\ChapterFiles folder.

To Copy and Paste the Navigation Bar, Event Handlers, and Image Rollover Functions

To maintain consistency in looks among all the Web pages, the Tours Web page should use the same the navigation created for the Winery Home page.

1. If necessary, open the chapter11-1homesolution.html in Notepad++ in the Chapter11\ChapterFiles folder.
2. Copy the HTML <table> code from lines 58 through 77 for the HTML code and mouse event handlers for the navigation bar.

3. In the chapter11-1tours.html file, click line 27 and paste the code to create the navigation bar.

4. Modify line 30 to replace the # symbol with `chapter11-1homesolution.html`.

5. In the chapter11-1homesolution.html file, copy the JavaScript code from lines 9 through 26. Return to the chapter11-1tours.html file and insert the copied code on line 9. Add the closing HTML comment (`//-->`) and the closing `</script>` tags on lines 27 and 28 (Figure 11–29).

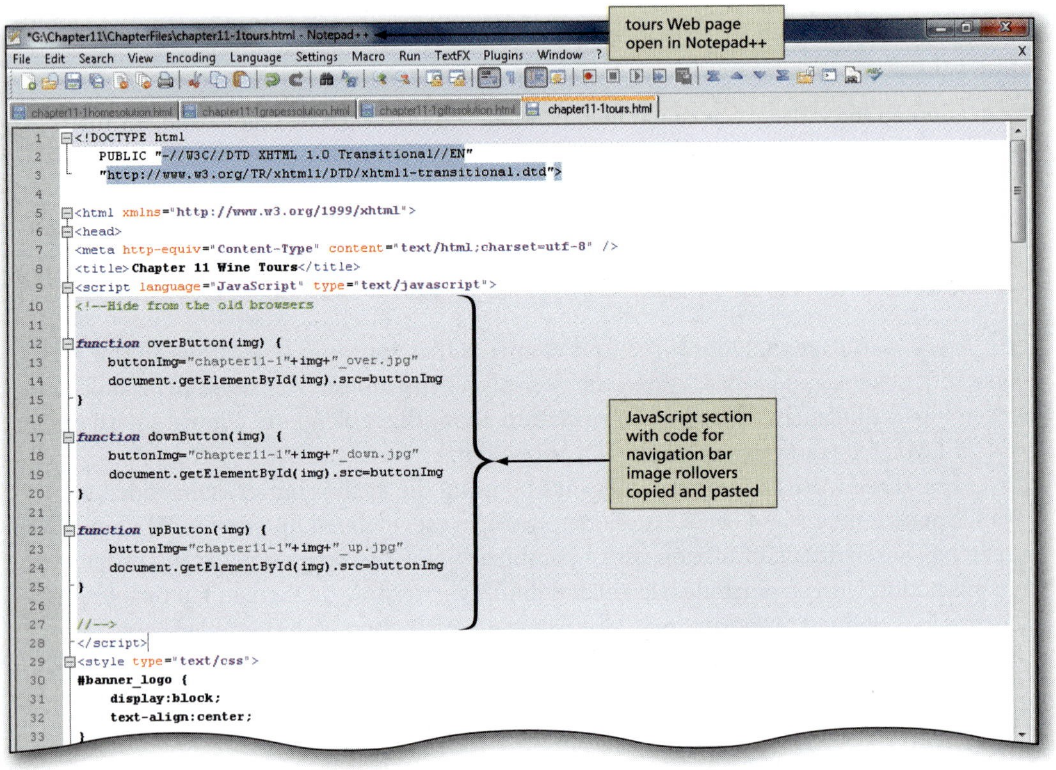

*G:\Chapter11\ChapterFiles\chapter11-1tours.html - Notepad++

File Edit Search View Encoding Language Settings Macro Run TextFX Plugins Window ?

chapter11-1homesolution.html | chapter11-1grapessolution.html | chapter11-1giftssolution.html | chapter11-1tours.html

tours Web page open in Notepad++

```
1  <!DOCTYPE html
2     PUBLIC "-//W3C//DTD XHTML 1.0 Transitional//EN"
3     "http://www.w3.org/TR/xhtml1/DTD/xhtml1-transitional.dtd">
4
5  <html xmlns="http://www.w3.org/1999/xhtml">
6  <head>
7  <meta http-equiv="Content-Type" content="text/html;charset=utf-8" />
8  <title>Chapter 11 Wine Tours</title>
9  <script language="JavaScript" type="text/javascript">
10 <!--Hide from the old browsers
11
12 function overButton(img) {
13      buttonImg="chapter11-1"+img+"_over.jpg"
14      document.getElementById(img).src=buttonImg
15 }
16
17 function downButton(img) {
18      buttonImg="chapter11-1"+img+"_down.jpg"
19      document.getElementById(img).src=buttonImg
20 }
21
22 function upButton(img) {
23      buttonImg="chapter11-1"+img+"_up.jpg"
24      document.getElementById(img).src=buttonImg
25 }
26
27 //-->
28 </script>
29 <style type="text/css">
30 #banner_logo {
31      display:block;
32      text-align:center;
33 }
```

JavaScript section with code for navigation bar image rollovers copied and pasted

Figure 11–29

Creating the screenTip() User-Defined Function

The JavaScript code for the screenTip() user-defined function is written in such a way that it can be used for all ScreenTips. The function will accept two parameters from the event handlers and display the appropriate ScreenTip. Table 11–18 shows the JavaScript code used to create the screenTip() function.

BTW

The eval() Statement

The eval() statement, short for evaluator, executes an expression as if it were originally written as language code. The eval() statement is useful in executing JavaScript statements using data whose value is not known at the time the Web page loads, such as the size of a window.

Table 11–18 Code to Create screenTip() Function

Line	Code
27	`function screenTip(evnt,currElement) {`
28	`var imgShow="chapter11-1popup"+currElement+".jpg"`
29	`var documentObj="document.all"`
30	`var styleObj=".style"`
31	`if (currElement!=0) {`
32	`var tipObject=eval(documentObj+'.'+currElement+styleObj)`

Table 11–18 Code to Create screenTip() Function (continued)

<table>
<tr><th>Line</th><th>Code</th></tr>
<tr><td>33</td><td><code>var state=tipObject.visibility</code></td></tr>
<tr><td>34</td><td><code>if (state=="visible" || state=="show") {</code></td></tr>
<tr><td>35</td><td><code>tipObject.visibility="hidden"</code></td></tr>
<tr><td>36</td><td><code>document.popupImage.src="chapter11-1tours.jpg"</code></td></tr>
<tr><td>37</td><td><code>}</code></td></tr>
<tr><td>38</td><td><code>else {</code></td></tr>
<tr><td>39</td><td><code>topVal=eval(event.y+10)</code></td></tr>
<tr><td>40</td><td><code>leftVal=eval(event.x-125)</code></td></tr>
<tr><td>41</td><td><code>if (leftVal<2) leftVal=2</code></td></tr>
<tr><td>42</td><td><code>tipObject.top=topVal</code></td></tr>
<tr><td>43</td><td><code>tipObject.left=leftVal</code></td></tr>
<tr><td>44</td><td><code>tipObject.visibility="visible"</code></td></tr>
<tr><td>45</td><td><code>document.popupImage.src=imgShow</code></td></tr>
<tr><td>46</td><td><code>}</code></td></tr>
<tr><td>47</td><td><code>}</code></td></tr>
<tr><td>48</td><td><code>}</code></td></tr>
</table>

Line 27 declares the screenTip() user-defined function and assigns two parameter values: the event value (evnt), and the element name or id (currElement). Later in the chapter, the code for the onmouseover and onmouseout event handlers, which pass values to the function for these parameters, will be entered. The event value indicates if the mouse pointer is moved over or off the hyperlink or if the hyperlink is clicked. If the visitor clicks the mouse, the function receives the null parameter as the event value, which does not trigger an event. The name or id parameter passed to the function indicates the style sheet selector to be used with the associated text in the <span> tags.

Line 28 uses currElement and constructs a graphic file name associated with the ScreenTip, and is used to replace the image the ScreenTip displays. Lines 29 and 30 define two local variables — documentObj and styleObj — that will be used to create statements using the eval() function in the screenTip() user-defined function. The **eval() function** is a global function that accepts a string or command and returns the result of an executed statement. Line 31 tests the value of currElement to determine which ScreenTip to show. If the value is greater than 0, lines 32 and 33 construct the strings to show the correct ScreenTip using the document.all object, the currElement, and style properties. The **document.all object** is used to reference elements by their id, which is necessary when multiple <div> or <span> containers exist. Line 32 assigns the result of the eval() method, which combines and executes the constructed statement, to the tipObject variable. The tipObject variable can be used with the visibility property on line 33 to assign the current state of the object. Line 34 tests the state of the object to determine if another ScreenTip already is showing. If the test is true, line 35 hides any ScreenTips already visible, so the new ScreenTip can be displayed. Line 36 restores the original image in the image placeholder.

Lines 37 through 44 cause the ScreenTip to appear and ensure that the ScreenTip does not appear too far to the left. Line 38 begins the else portion of the if statement (for lines 39 through 44), which calculates the display position of ScreenTip. Lines 39 and 40 set the topVal position and the leftVal position of the ScreenTip. These position values are set using the eval() function and the x and y properties of the event object. The x and y properties are the x- and y-axis coordinates defined by Microsoft Internet Explorer.

The if statement on line 41 tests the value of leftVal to determine whether the ScreenTip is too close to the left edge of the browser window; if so, it sets leftVal to 2. Lines 42, 43, and 44 set the top, left, and visibility properties of the tipObject to define where the ScreenTip is displayed. Line 45 now displays the new graphic file image associated with this ScreenTip.

The braces on lines 46 and 47 close the if and else statements, and the brace on line 48 closes the function.

To Enter the screenTip() Function

The following step shows how to enter the code for the screenTip() user-defined function.

1

- Click line 27 and press the ENTER key once. Click the blank line 27.
- Enter the code shown in Table 11–18 on pages HTML 538 and HTML 539 to create the screenTip() function, indenting as shown, and then press the ENTER key once to place the insertion point on line 49 (Figure 11–30).

chapter11-1homesolution.html | chapter11-1grapessolution.html | chapter11-1giftssolution.html | chapter11-1tours.html

```
26
27 function screenTip(evnt,currElement) {
28     var imgShow="chapter11-1popup"+currElement+".jpg"
29     var documentObj="document.all"
30     var styleObj=".style"
31       if (currElement!=0) {
32         var tipObject=eval(documentObj+'.'+currElement+styleObj)
33         var state=tipObject.visibility
34         if (state=="visible" || state=="show") {
35           tipObject.visibility="hidden"
36           document.popupImage.src="chapter11-1tours.jpg"
37         }
38         else {
39             topVal=eval(event.y+10)
40             leftVal=eval(event.x-125)
41             if (leftVal<2) leftVal=2
42             tipObject.top=topVal
43             tipObject.left=leftVal
44             tipObject.visibility="visible"
45             document.popupImage.src=imgShow
46         }
47     }
48 }
49
50 //-->
51 </script>
52 <style type="text/css">
53 #banner_logo {
54
```

eval() method assembles objects for mouse event handlers

determines state of ScreenTip; if visible, hides and displays default image

positions and displays ScreenTip and associated image

press ENTER key once

Figure 11–30

Adding an Embedded Style Sheet Using id and Class Properties

> **BTW**
> **id and class Selectors**
> An id selector is used to identify one element, and the class can be used to identify more than one. The class selector must be notated by the class attribute in the HTML tag. In the normal hierarchy of cascading selectors, the id selector has a higher priority than attribute selectors. When used with XML documents, however, id selectors are discouraged to prevent confusion.

The embedded style sheets used on the Tours Web page employ the id and class selectors to define the style for each of the three ScreenTips. Each ScreenTip is identified uniquely using an id attribute and value, so the screenTip() function can ensure that only one ScreenTip appears at a time. An id selector is used in a style sheet much like a class selector — except that the id selector is entered with a preceding pound sign (#).

In the Tours Web page, the <span> tag is used to enclose the text that appears in the ScreenTips. In this use, the <span> tag is referred to as a container. A **container** means that the text is grouped together. Text enclosed within the <span> tag is referred to as **inline**. The id and class attributes are used in the <span> tag to associate the selectors in the embedded style sheet with each of the three ScreenTips.

The screenTip() user-defined function needs two parameters: evnt and currElement. For each ScreenTip, the evnt parameter indicates the type of event, using an onmouseover or onmouseout event handler, and the currElement parameter passes the style sheet id selector. Figure 11–31 illustrates the relationship between the event handler function call, the associated selector in the style sheet, and the text in the <span> tag. The <span> tag

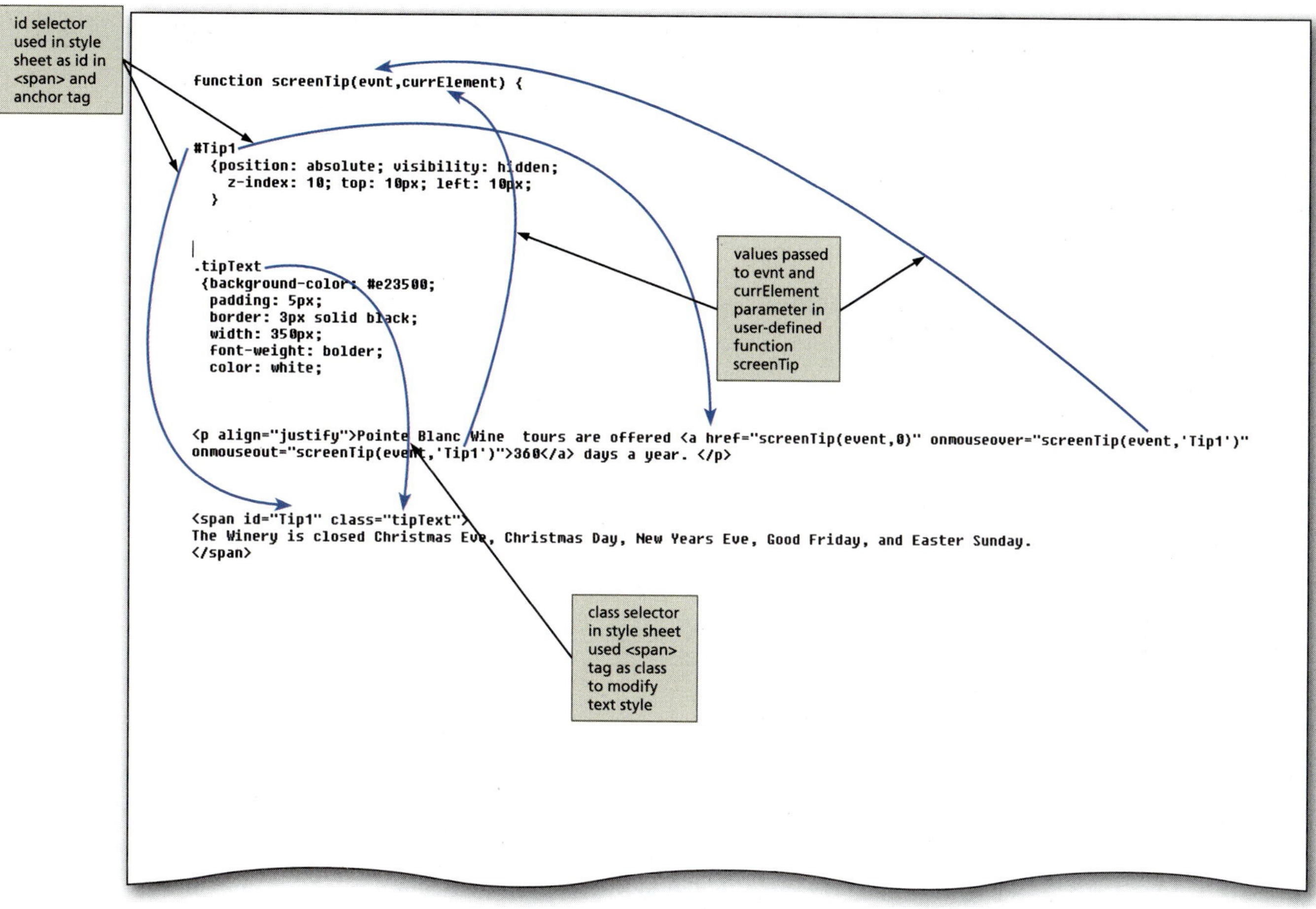

Figure 11–31

contains an id attribute, which is the style sheet selector, and the style sheet class, which indicates how to format the displayed ScreenTip text. To apply a style to the ScreenTips, the embedded style sheet thus uses the id attribute value as the selector.

The screenTip() function code uses these values to show the ScreenTip at the position defined by the Tip1 selector in the style sheet. The embedded style sheet on the Tours Web page has three id selectors — Tip1 through Tip3 — to set the position at which each ScreenTip appears. It also defines a style for the class tipText, which defines the format of the ScreenTip text. Table 11–19 shows the embedded style sheet code used to set the position of the ScreenTips and format the ScreenTip text.

Table 11–19 Code to Use Selectors in a Style Sheet

Line	Code
63	`#Tip1`
64	`  {position: absolute; visibility: hidden;`
65	`   z-index: 10; top: 10px; left: 10;`
66	`  }`
67	
68	`#Tip2`
69	`  {position: absolute; visibility: hidden;`

BTW

When to use <div> and <span> Container Tags

The <div> tag groups items as a block, and the <span> tag groups items inline. Inline refers to the fact that the <span> tag does not do any formatting of its own. For example, the <div> tag will cause a paragraph break, and the <span> tag will not. Using the <span> tag allows changing styles within a division or paragraph.

Table 11–19 Code to Use Selectors in a Style Sheet (continued)

Line	Code
70	z-index: 10; top: 10px; left: 10;
71	}
72	
73	#Tip3
74	{position: absolute; visibility: hidden;
75	z-index: 10; top: 10px; left: 10;
76	}
77	
78	.tipText
79	{background-color: #e23500;
80	padding: 5px;
81	border: 3px solid black;
82	width: 350px;
83	font-weight: bolder;
84	color: white;
85	}

Line 63 is the first style statement with the id selector, Tip1. The declarations on lines 64 and 65 define the positioning for the Tip1 style. Line 66 closes the declaration for Tip1. Lines 68 through 76 define the remaining selectors for Tip2 and Tip3.

Line 78 starts the style statement with the class selector, tipText. The declarations on lines 79 through 84 define the style of the ScreenTips text. The background color and layer background are the same red in the banner. The padding declaration sets 5 pixels around the text in the ScreenTip. The border declaration sets the border thickness to 3 pixels, the line type to solid, and the color to black. The width of the ScreenTip is 350 pixels, and the color of the text font is white. Line 85 closes the declarations.

To Enter Cascading Style Sheet id and Class Selectors for the ScreenTips

The following steps illustrate how to enter the Cascading Style Sheet id and class selectors for the ScreenTips.

- Click line 63 and press the ENTER key. Click the blank line 63.
- Enter the code shown in Table 11–19 starting on the previous page from lines 63 to 76 to enter the class id and selectors for the ScreenTip style sheet, indenting as shown. Press the ENTER key twice to position the insertion point on line 78 (Figure 11–32).
- Press the ENTER key twice to position the insertion point on line 78 (Figure 11–32).

```
63 #Tip1
64   {position: absolute; visibility: hidden;
65     z-index: 10; top: 10px; left: 10px;
66   }
67
68 #Tip2
69  {position: absolute; visibility: hidden;
70   z-index: 10; top: 10px; left: 10px;
71 }
72
73 #Tip3
74   {position: absolute; visibility: hidden;
75     z-index: 10; top: 10px; left: 10px;
76 }
77
78
79 </style>
   </head>
```

style sheet Tip selectors are IDs connected to text in <span> tags for each ScreenTip

press ENTER key twice

Figure 11–32

- Continuing on line 78, enter the code shown in Table 11–19 from lines 78 through 85 to enter the format style for the ScreenTip text, indenting as shown, and then press the ENTER key to position the insertion point on line 86 (Figure 11–33).

```
74    {position: absolute; visibility: hidden;
75      z-index: 10; top: 10px; left: 10px;
76    }
77
78    .tipText
79     {background-color: #e23500;
80      padding: 5px;
81      border: 3px solid black;
82      width: 350px;
83      font-weight: bolder;
84      color: white;
85    }
86
87   </style>
88   </head>
89   <body>
90   <div id="banner_logo"><img src="chapter11-1banner.jpg" alt="logo" width="750" height="
```

selector for ScreenTip text so all text has same formatting

press ENTER key once

Figure 11–33

Q&A In this code for the style sheet, actual color names are used. Why not use the hex representations? What is the difference?

No difference exists. Most browsers will recognize the standard Web-safe colors by name. Non-Web-safe colors must be entered using the hex value. Using Web-safe color names makes it easier for others to maintain the Web site.

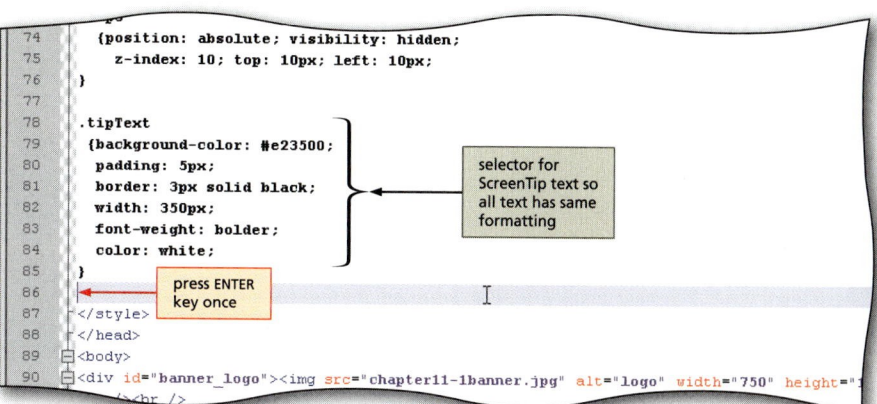

Adding Links and Event Handlers to Call the screenTip() Function

The three linked terms in the Tours Web page must have onmouseover and onmouseout event handlers code associated with these links to call the screenTip() user-defined function to make the ScreenTips and images display when the visitor places the mouse over the hyperlink.

Normally, a link is associated with a URL, so when the visitor clicks the hyperlink, the browser shows a new Web page. This Web page uses links associated with the onmouseover and onmouseout event handlers to show a ScreenTip when a user points to the link. The element zero (0) is used so the browser will not show a new Web page if a user accidentally clicks the link.

To Add Links and Event Handlers to Call the screenTip() Function

The following steps describe how to enter the ScreenTip links and the onmouseover and onmouseout event handlers to call the screenTip() function.

- In line 121, position the insertion point before the word 360 in the first sentence.
- Type `<a href="screenTip(event,0)" onmouseover="screenTip(event,'Tip1')" onmouseout="screenTip(event,'Tip1')">` to enter the link for the 360 ScreenTip. Do not press the ENTER key.
- Click immediately to the right of the number 360, and type </a> to close the <a> anchor tag. Do not press the ENTER key (Figure 11–34).

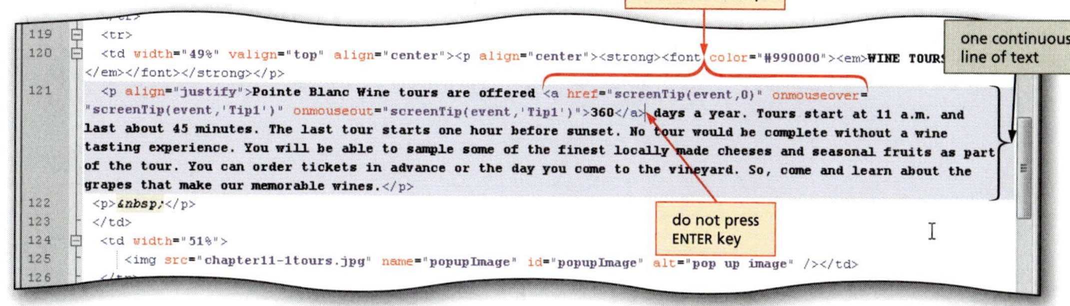

Figure 11–34

- Farther in the same line and paragraph, position the insertion point just before the word tickets in the next-to-last sentence.
- Type `<a href="screenTip(event,0)" onmouseover="screenTip(event,'Tip2')" onmouseout="screenTip(event,'Tip2')">` to enter the link for the tickets ScreenTip. Do not press the ENTER key.

```
onmouseover="overButton('tours')" onmousedown="downButton('tours')" onmouseout="upButton('tours')" onmouseup=
"upButton('tours')" /></a>
    </td>
    </tr>
</table>
<p align="center"><img src="hrdivider.jpg" width="750" height="5" alt="divider" /></p>
<table width="94%" border="0" align="center" cellpadding="0" cellspacing="5">
  <tr>
  <td colspan="2">
  </td>
  </tr>
  <tr>
  <td width="49%" valign="top" align="center"><p align="center"><strong><font color="#990000"><em>WINE TOURS
</em></font></strong></p>
   <p align="justify">Pointe Blanc Wine tours are offered <a href="screenTip(event,0)" onmouseover=
"screenTip(event,'Tip1')" onmouseout="screenTip(event,'Tip1')">360</a> days a year. Tours start at 11 a.m. and
last about 45 minutes. The last tour starts one hour before sunset. No tour would be complete without a wine
tasting experience. You will be able to sample some of the finest locally made cheeses and seasonal fruits as part
of the tour. You can order <a href="screenTip(event,0)" onmouseover="screenTip(event,'Tip2')" onmouseout=
"screenTip(event,'Tip2')">tickets</a> in advance or the day you come to the vineyard. So, come and learn about the
grapes that make our memorable wines.</p>
  <p> </p>
  </td>
  <td width="51%">
    <img src="chapter11-1tours.jpg" name="popupImage" id="popupImage" alt="pop up image" /></td>
```

anchor tag for mouseover events for tickets ScreenTip

do not press ENTER key

Figure 11–35

- Click to the right of the word tickets and type </a> to close the <a> anchor tag. Do not press the ENTER key (Figure 11–35).

3

- Farther in the same paragraph in the last sentence, position the insertion point before the word grapes.
- Type `<a href="screenTip(event,0)" onmouseover="screenTip(event,'Tip3')" onmouseout="screenTip(event,'Tip3')">` to enter the link for the grapes ScreenTip. Do not press the ENTER key.

```
  </td>
  </tr>
  <tr>
  <td width="49%" valign="top" align="center"><p align="center"><strong><font color="#990000"><em>WINE TOURS
</em></font></strong></p>
   <p align="justify">Pointe Blanc Wine tours are offered <a href="screenTip(event,0)" onmouseover=
"screenTip(event,'Tip1')" onmouseout="screenTip(event,'Tip1')">360</a> days a year. Tours start at 11 a.m. and
last about 45 minutes. The last tour starts one hour before sunset. No tour would be complete without a wine
tasting experience. You will be able to sample some of the finest locally made cheeses and seasonal fruits as part
of the tour. You can order <a href="screenTip(event,0)" onmouseover="screenTip(event,'Tip2')" onmouseout=
"screenTip(event,'Tip2')">tickets</a> in advance or the day you come to the vineyard. So, come and learn about the
<a href="screenTip(event,0)" onmouseover="screenTip(event,'Tip3')" onmouseout="screenTip(event,'Tip3')">grapes</a>
that make our memorable wines.</p>
  <p> </p>
  </td>
  <td width="51%">
    <img src="chapter11-1tours.jpg" name="popupImage" id="popupImage" alt="pop up image" /></td>
  </tr>
</table>

</body>
</html>
```

anchor tag for mouseover events for grapes ScreenTip

do not press ENTER key

Figure 11–36

- Click to the right of the word grapes and type </a> to close the <a> anchor tag. Do not press the ENTER key (Figure 11–36).

Q&A The Tip selectors all have the same features. Why must we use so many?

Each ScreenTip must have its own selector to be identified by the ScreenTip code and to match the text in the <span> containers.

Entering the <span> Tags Containing ScreenTip Text

The text then appears in each of the four ScreenTips on the Tours Web page enclosed in <span> tags. The <span> tags use the id and class attributes to associate the ScreenTips with the embedded style sheet declarations that control the appearance of the text in the ScreenTip. Table 11–20 shows the HTML code used to enter the <span> tags that define the ScreenTip text.

Table 11–20 Code for <span> Tags Containing ScreenTip Text

Line	Code
128	`<span id="Tip1" class="tipText">`
129	`The Winery is closed Christmas Eve, Christmas Day, New Year's Eve, Good Friday, and Easter Sunday.`
130	`</span>`
131	`<span id="Tip2" class="tipText">`
132	`Tickets are $12 for adults, $8 for seniors (over 62), and $6 for children under 12.`
133	`</span>`
134	`<span id="Tip3" class="tipText">`
135	`Pointe Blanc grows primarily vinifera, the highest quality grapes. Of course, we grow the American favorite, concord, to make juices and jam.`
136	`</span>`

Line 128 contains the ScreenTip text that appears when the mouse pointer points to the link for the word 360. The id property value, Tip1, associates the ScreenTip text with the 360 link defined on line 121 in Figure 11–34 on page HTML 543, which sets Tip1 as a parameter of the screenTip() function. The id property value, Tip1, also sets the ScreenTip text to appear using the position defined by the style statements for the id. The class property value, tipText, sets the ScreenTip text to appear using the background, font colors, borders, and width defined by the style statements in the embedded style sheet.

The <span> tag on line 131 associates the ScreenTip text with the tickets link. The <span> tag on line 134 associates the ScreenTip with the grapes link.

To Enter <span> Tags Containing ScreenTip Text

The following step shows how to enter the <span> tags containing the ScreenTip text.

1

- Click line 128, between the closing < /table> tag and the closing </body> tag.
- Enter the code shown in Table 11–20 to create <span> containers for the ScreenTip text. Do not press ENTER after the </span> tag on the last line (Figure 11–37).

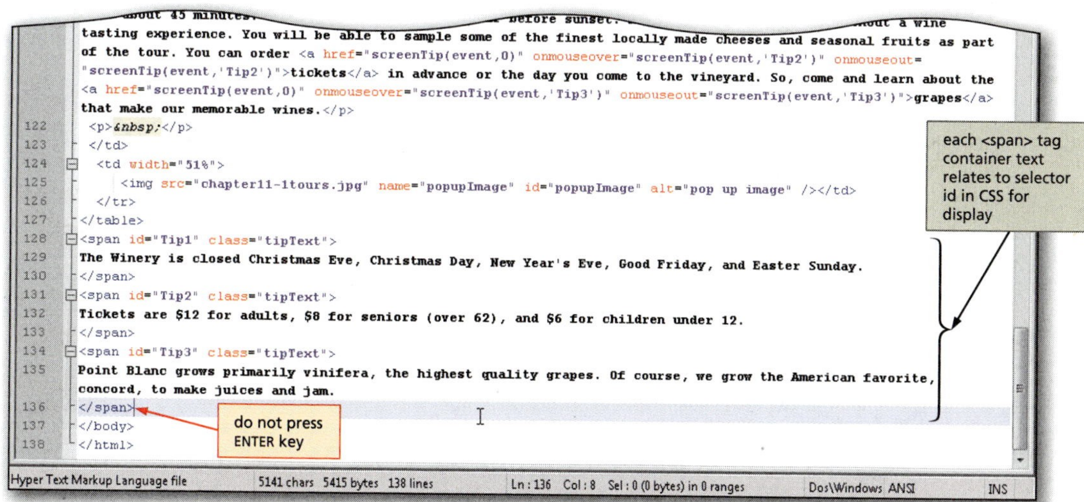

Figure 11–37

To Save an HTML File and Test the Tours Web Page

After the JavaScript code for the Tours Web page is complete, the HTML file should be saved and the Web page should be viewed in a browser to confirm the Web page appears as desired and that ScreenTip text is displayed correctly. The following steps show how to save and test the Tours Web page.

1. With a USB drive plugged into your computer, click File on the menu bar and then click Save As.
2. Type `chapter11-1tourssolution.html` in the File name text box and then click the Save button.
3. Click the Internet Explorer button on the status bar.
4. Type `g:\chapter11\ChapterFiles\chapter11-1tourssolution.html` in the Address box and then press the ENTER key.
5. When the Tours Web page is displayed, move the mouse pointer over the link 360 to view the ScreenTip. If necessary, allow blocked content.
6. Next, move the mouse pointer over the word tickets to view the ScreenTip.
7. Next, move the mouse pointer over the word grapes to view the ScreenTip, as shown in Figure 11–38.

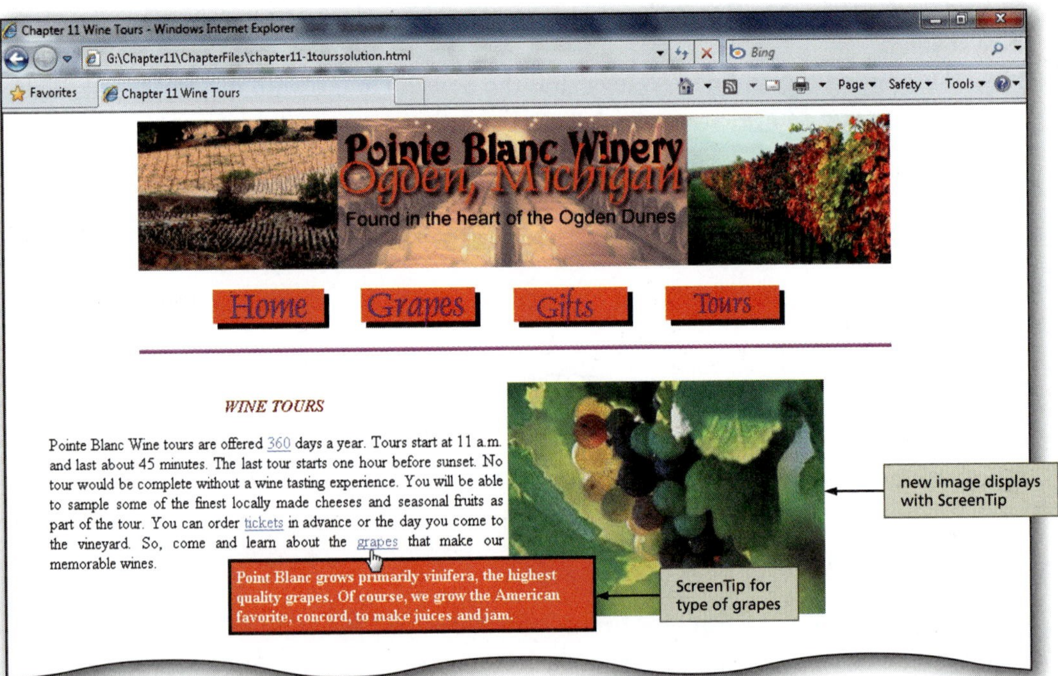

Figure 11–38

To Test and Validate the Pointe Blanc Winery Web Pages

The final task in developing a Web site is to test and validate all the Web pages and links. The following steps illustrate how to test the Pointe Blanc Winery Web pages.

1. Click the address box and type `g:\chapter11\chapter11-1homesolution.html` and press the ENTER key. If necessary, click the Information Bar and Allow Blocked Content.

2 Position the mouse over the Grapes, Gifts, or Tours image rollover buttons to make sure they function properly.

3 Click the Gifts button. Check to see that the floating image moves across the screen of the Gifts page.

4 Move the mouse over the floating image to ensure it stops, and then click the image to display the coupon pop-up window.

5 Click the Print link in the pop-up coupon window, and then click the Cancel button in the Print dialog box. Click Close to close the pop-up window.

6 Click the Grapes button. After the slide show plays, click the Tours button.

7 Drag the mouse over the underlined terms to verify the ScreenTips are displayed, and then click the Home link.

8 Validate the Chapter 11 Pointe Blanc Winery Web pages using validator.w3.org.

To Quit Notepad++ and a Browser

1 In Notepad++, click the File menu, and then Close All.

2 Click the Close button on the Notepad++ title bar.

3 Click the Close button on the browser title bar. If necessary, click the Close all tabs button.

BTW

Quick Reference
For a list of JavaScript statements and their associated attributes, see the JavaScript Quick Reference (Appendix G) at the back of this book, or visit the HTML Quick Reference Web page (scsite.com/HTML6e/qr).

Chapter Summary

Chapter 11 introduced the concepts of the Document Object Model (DOM), a combination of technologies that include HTML, Cascading Style Sheets (CSS), and a scripting language, such as JavaScript. Using the DOM, you learned how to create a navigation bar with image rollovers, display a random image from an array of images, create and display a slide show that automatically starts when a Web page is loaded, create a floating image that also serves as a link to a pop-up window, and how to use ScreenTips to add more information about a term on a Web page. The items listed below include all the new skills you have learned in this chapter.

1. Create an HTML Table to Contain the Navigation Bar (HTML 513)
2. Create User-Defined Functions for Image Rollovers (HTML 516)
3. Enter Mouse Event Handlers to Invoke User-Defined Functions (HTML 517)
4. Save and Test the Pointe Blanc Winery Web Page Navigation Bar (HTML 517)
5. Enter a Random Number Generator User-Defined Function (HTML 521)
6. Enter Code to Show Copyright Information and Date Last Modified (HTML 521)
7. Enter Onload Event Handlers in the <body> Tag (HTML 522)
8. Create an Image Object (HTML 525)
9. Create a User-Defined Function to Add a Slide Show (HTML 527)
10. Enter the floatingImage() Function (HTML 531)
11. Enter the stopFloat() Function (HTML 532)
12. Enter the coupon() Function (HTML 533)
13. Enter an Embedded Style Sheet to Format the Floating Image (HTML 534)
14. Enter <div> and <img> Tags for the Floating Image (HTML 535)
15. Add an Onload Event Handler to Call the floatingImage() Function (HTML 535)
16. Enter the screenTip() Function (HTML 540)
17. Enter Cascading Style Sheet id and Class Selectors for the ScreenTips (HTML 542)
18. Add Links and Event Handlers to Call the screenTip() Function (HTML 543)
19. Enter <span> Tags Containing ScreenTip Text (HTML 545)

Learn It Online

Test your knowledge of chapter content and key terms.

Instructions: To complete the Learn It Online exercises, start your browser, click the Address bar, and then enter the Web address `scsite.com/html6e/learn`. When the HTML Learn It Online page is displayed, click the link for the exercise you want to complete and read the instructions.

Chapter Reinforcement TF, MC, and SA

A series of true/false, multiple choice, and short answer questions that test your knowledge of the chapter content.

Flash Cards

An interactive learning environment where you identify chapter key terms associated with displayed definitions.

Practice Test

A series of multiple choice questions that tests your knowledge of chapter content and key terms.

Who Wants To Be a Computer Genius?

An interactive game that challenges your knowledge of chapter content in the style of a television quiz show.

Wheel of Terms

An interactive game that challenges your knowledge of chapter key terms in the style of the television show, *Wheel of Fortune*.

Crossword Puzzle Challenge

A crossword puzzle that challenges your knowledge of key terms presented in the chapter.

Apply Your Knowledge

Reinforce the skills and apply the concepts you learned in this chapter.

Instructions: Start Notepad++. Open the file apply11-1.html from the Chapter11\Apply folder of the Data Files for Students. See the inside back cover of this book for instructions on downloading the Data Files for Students, or contact your instructor for information about accessing the required files.

The apply11-1.html file is a partially completed HTML file that you will use for this exercise. Figure 11–39 shows the Apply Your Knowledge Web page as it should be displayed in a browser after the JavaScript code has been added.

Perform the following tasks:

1. Using the JavaScript code in Tables 11–7 and 11–8 on pages HTML 519 and HTML 520 as a guide, and the names of the .jpg photo files in the Apply data folder of baseball teams and players, create an array named randomPic.
2. Using the JavaScript code logic presented in Table 11–8, enter a JavaScript function called rndPhoto(). Determine the maximum number of random photos by assigning the size (length) of the randomPic array minus 1 to rndnumsize. Use the Math.ceil() and Math.random() methods to generate a random number. Use the random number as the subscript for the array to assign that associated photo to the leaguePhoto <img> tag placeholder. Be sure to add the onload event handler to call this function.
3. Using the code in Table 11–18 on pages HTML 538 and HTML 539 and the step for Figure 11–30 on page HTML 540, enter the code for the JavaScript user-defined function to display a ScreenTip.
4. Find the words *five different divisions* in the paragraph (indicated as a link in Figure 11–39).

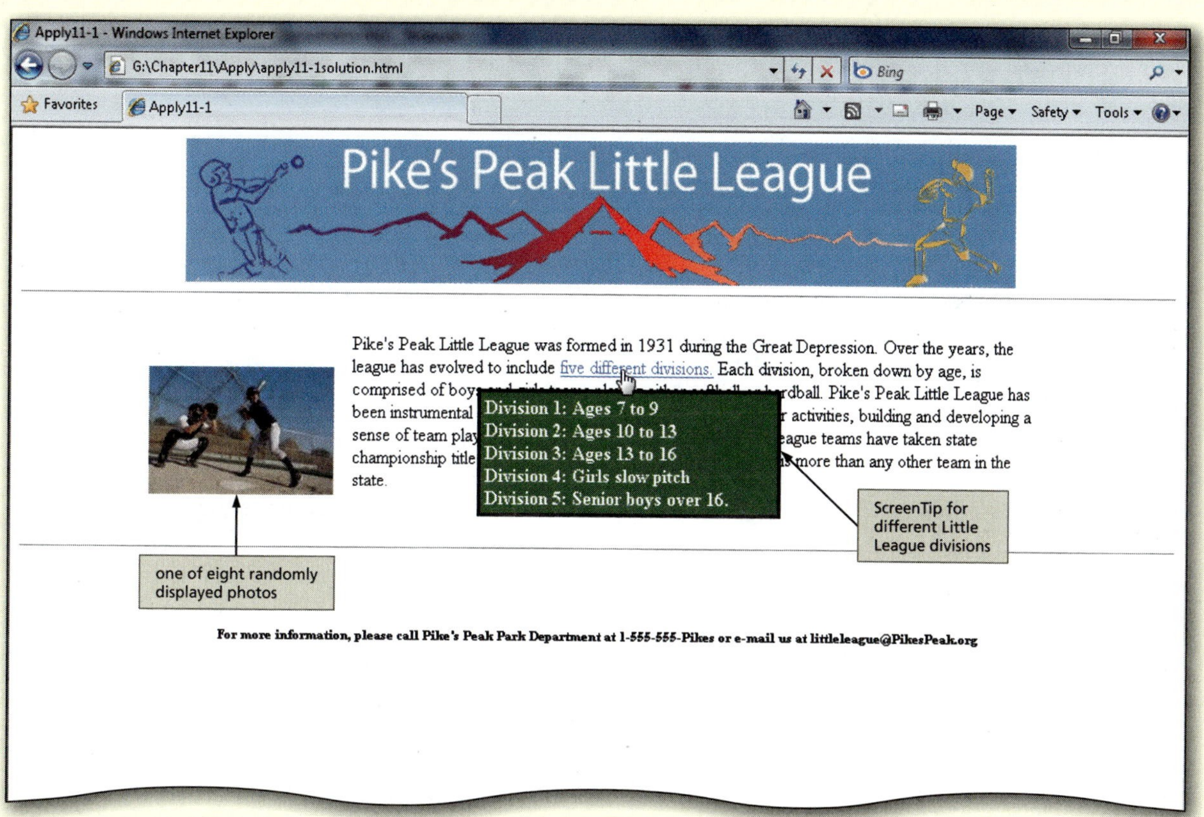

Figure 11–39

5. Using the code described in the steps for Figure 11–34 on page HTML 543 as a guide, enter the HTML <a href> tag with the JavaScript event handlers to show the ScreenTip text for the five different divisions. Use the id selector Tip1 in the event handlers. Be sure to close the <a href> tag after the word divisions.
6. Using the code in Table 11–19 on pages HTML 541 and HTML 542 as a guide, enter the code for the Cascading Style Sheet selectors and rules for the ScreenTips. Use the id selector Tip1 and the class selector TipText.
7. For the #Tip1 id selector, use the following attribute values: position: absolute; visibility: hidden; z-index: 10px; top: 10px; left: 10px. For the TipText class selector, use the following attribute values: background-color#006600; padding: 3px; border: 3px solid black; width: 250px; font-weight: bolder; color: white;.
8. Using the code in Table 11–20 on page HTML 545 as a guide, write the <span> tag and place it in the blank line after the HTML comment <!-- span tag for ScreenTip -->. Be sure to close the <span> tag.
9. The ScreenTip message should read: Division 1: Ages 7 to 9
Division 2: Ages 10 to 13
Division 3: Ages 13 to 16
Division 4: Girls slow pitch
Division 5: Senior boys over 16.
10. Save the revised file in the Chapter11\Apply folder using the file name apply11-1solution.html.
11. Start your browser. Enter the URL g:\Chapter11\Apply\apply11-1solution.html to view and test the Web page in your browser. Validate the Web page.
12. If any errors occur, check the code against Steps 1 through 9, make any required changes, save the file using the same file name, and then refresh the Web page in the browser.
13. Submit the revised HTML file and Web page in the format specified by your instructor.

STUDENT ASSIGNMENTS

Extend Your Knowledge

Extend the skills you learned in this chapter and experiment with new skills. You will need to search the Internet to complete the assignment.

Learning More About Moving or Floating Objects

Instructions: Start Notepad++ and your browser. Open the file extend11-1.html from the Chapter11\Extend folder of the Data Files for Students. See the inside back cover of this book for instructions on downloading the Data Files for Students, or contact your instructor for information about accessing the required files.

Search the Internet at JavaScript sites and find some code that explains how to scroll an object down the page as one drags the scroll bar with the mouse or uses the mouse wheel. The object for this Web page is a <div> container, which is one column and four rows, and serves as the menu. Name the <div> moveMenu using an id attribute. The technique for moving objects is to use the positioning of the object with Cascading Style Sheets and then use the document object with the style property to change the screenTop properties. The scroll wheel on the mouse is captured by the event .wheelDelta property. As the user scrolls down the Web page window, the <div> object should move down also (Figure 11–40). The additional supplied Web pages may use the Latin Lorem Ipsum for text filler.

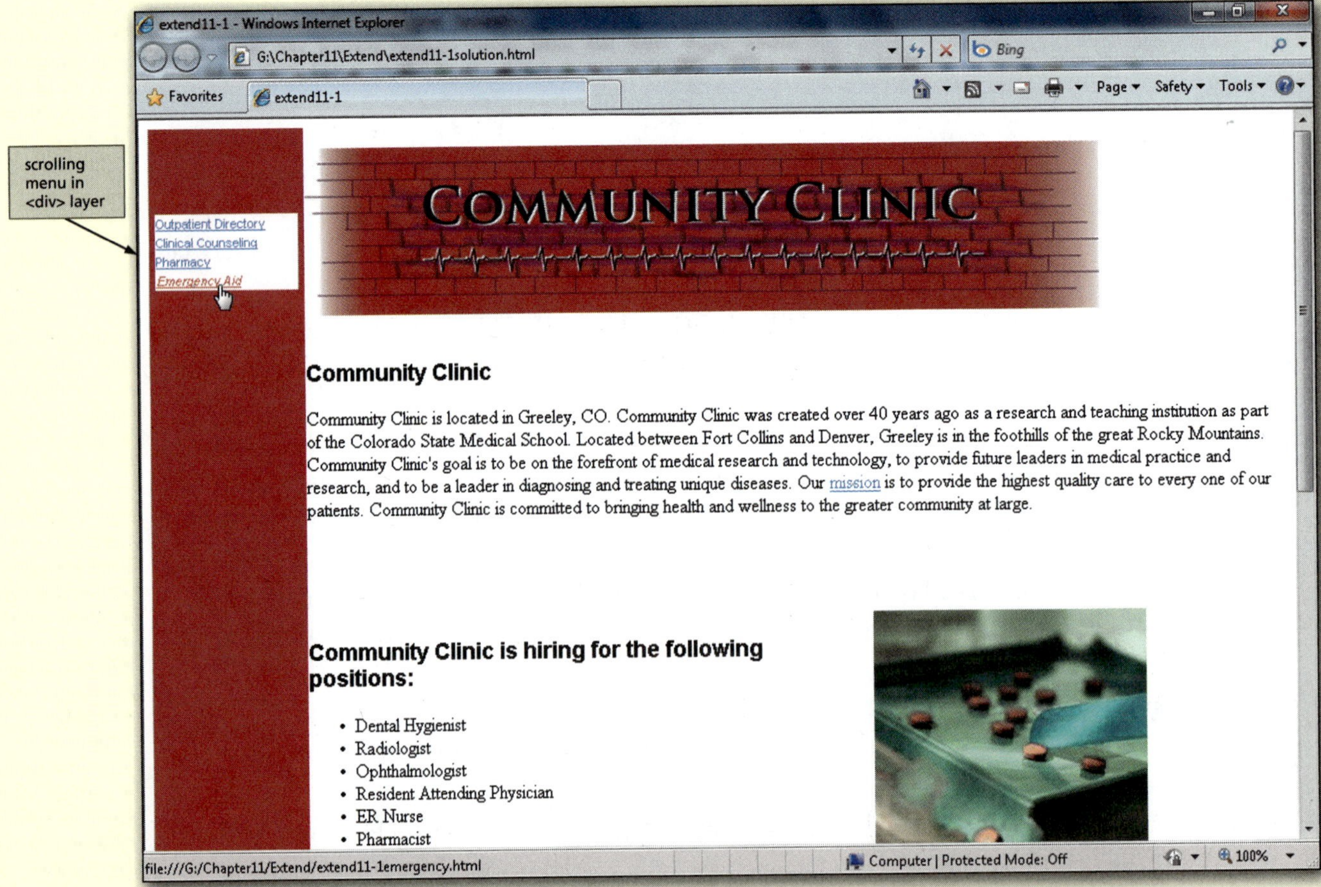

Figure 11–40

Perform the following tasks:

1. Save the extend11-1.html file as extend11-1solution.html.
2. Enter the moveMenu <div> tag and HTML table as shown in Table 11–21 after the <body> tag to create the menu object.

Table 11–21

```
<div id="moveMenu" style="left: 13px; width: 125px; position: absolute; top: 0px; z-index: 0;
background-color: #ffffff; border: 1px none #000000;">
<table width="100%" border="0" style="border-collapse: collapse;">
  <tr>
    <td class="menubg" width="20%">
      <a href="extend11-1outpatientsolution.html">Outpatient Directory</a></td>
  </tr>
  <tr>
    <td class="menubg" width="20%">
      <a href="extend11-1counselingsolution.html">Clinical Counseling</a>
  </td>
  </tr>
  <tr>
    <td class="menubg" width="20%">
       <a href="extend11-1pharmacysolution.html">Pharmacy</a></td>
  </tr>
  <tr>
    <td class="menubg" width="20%">
      <a href="extend11-1emergencysolution.html">Emergency Aid</a>
    </td>
</tr>
</table>
</div>
```

3. Using the code found on the Internet, write a JavaScript function called checkLocation(delta) that checks if the mouse wheel has been used to scroll through the Web page for moving an object up or down a screen.
4. Add an id selector in the embedded CSS called menubg. Set the properties as follows: font-size: 8pt; font-family: arial, helvetica, sans-serif; color: #000000.
5. Using the code in Table 11–16 on page HTML 533 as a guide, write a JavaScript function that opens a pop-up window to display the mission statement. The mission statement Web page file name is extend11-1mission.html, the title is missionstatement, the width is 525px, and the height is 440px.
6. Use the javascript:command in the <a href> tag to call this function (the link is currently a #).
7. Add the appropriate event handler to the <body> tag to invoke the checkLocation() user-defined function.
8. Save the revised file in the Chapter11\Extend folder using the file name extend11-1solution.html.
9. Open the file extend11-1pharmacy.html. Copy and paste the <div> tag and the HTML table for the scrolling menu from extend11-1solution.html to this file. Copy and paste the JavaScript code for the checkLocation() user-defined function from extend11-1solution.html to this file. Add the event handler to the <body> tag. Save the file as extend11-1pharmacysolution.html.

Continued >

Extend Your Knowledge *continued*

10. Open the file extend11-1counseling.html. Copy and paste the <div> tag and the HTML table for the scrolling menu from extend11-1solution.html to this file. Copy and paste the JavaScript code for the checkLocation() user-defined function from extend11-1solution.html to this file. Add the event handler to the <body> tag. Save the file as extend11-1counselingsolution.html.
11. Open the file extend11-1emergency.html. Copy and paste the <div> tag and the HTML table for the scrolling menu from extend11-1solution.html to this file. Copy and paste the JavaScript code for the checkLocation() user-defined function from extend11-1solution.html to this file. Add the event handler to the <body> tag. Save the file as extend11-1emergencysolution.html.
12. Open the file extend11-1outpatient.html. Copy and paste the <div> tag and the HTML table for the scrolling menu from extend11-1solution.html to this file. Copy and paste the JavaScript code for the checkLocation() user-defined function from extend11-1solution.html to this file. Add the event handler to the <body> tag. Save the file as extend11-1outpatientsolution.html.
13. Start your browser. Enter the URL g:\Chapter11\Extend\extend11-1solution.html to view and test the Web page in your browser.
14. If any errors occur, check the code against Steps 1 through 12, make any required changes, save the file using the same file name, and then refresh the Web page in the browser. (*Note:* the onmousewheel event handler will not validate in the <body> tag as an attribute, so validation will generate one error.)
15. Submit the revised HTML file and Web page in the format specified by your instructor.

Make It Right

Analyze the JavaScript code on a Web page and correct all errors.

Correcting Syntax Errors and Inserting Missing Code

Instructions: Start your browser, and open the file make11-1.html from the Chapter11\MakeItRight folder of the Data Files for Students in the browser. See the inside back cover of this book for instructions on downloading the Data Files for Students, or contact your instructor for information about accessing the required files. The file is a Web page for Erin's Pet Palace FAQ Web page that contains three errors. The errors can be in the form of syntax, logic, or missing code. The corrected page appears as shown in Figure 11–41.

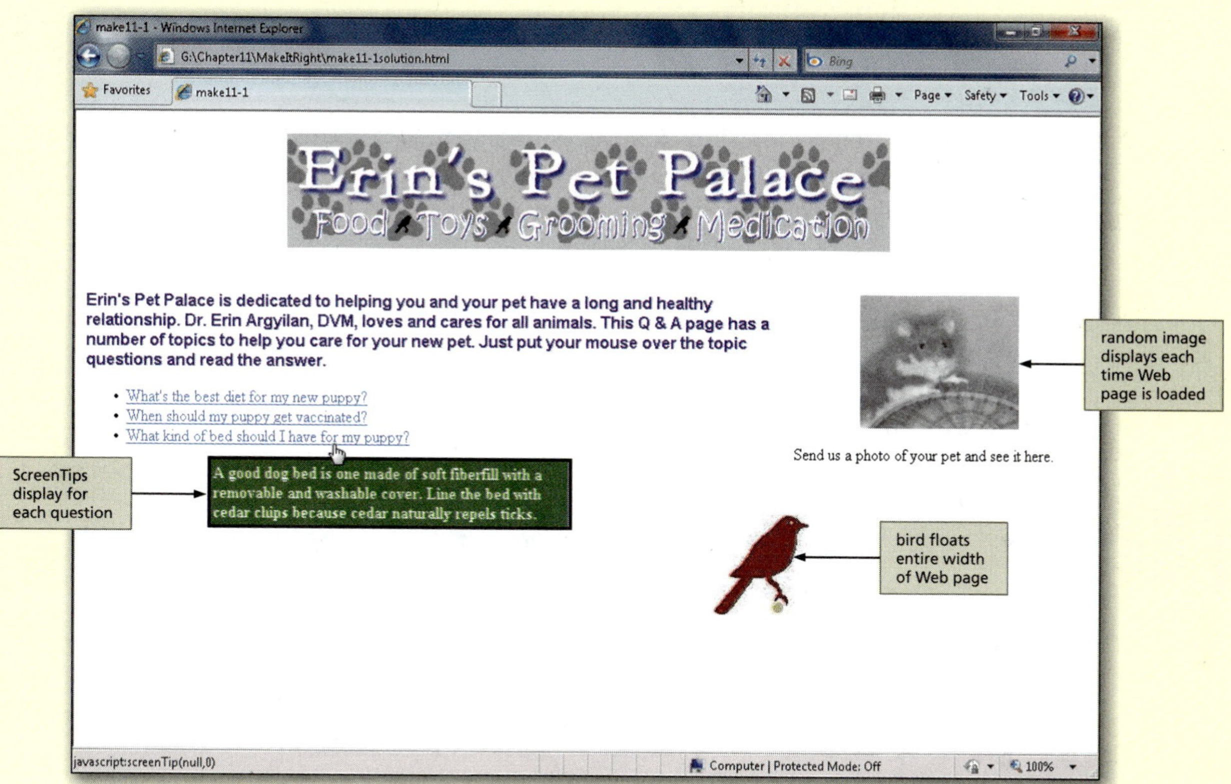

Figure 11–41

Perform the following tasks:

1. Start Notepad++. Open the make11-1.html file and save the file as make11-1solution.html.
2. The floatImage() user-defined function has one error. The image on the left should scroll the entire width of the Web page. Find the error in the floatImage() function so that the image scrolls the entire width of the Web page.
3. One of the ScreenTips for the FAQs is the same ScreenTip as another. Find the error in the <a href> tags for the ScreenTips and correct it so the correct ScreenTip is displayed when the onmouseover event handler is used.
4. The random picture user-defined function does not display any of the photos from the array. Every time the Web page is loaded, it shows the same image.
5. Correct these errors, and then save the corrected HTML file. Test the corrected Web page using your browser. If you still have an error, check your code, save, and test again.
6. Submit the revised HTML file and Web page in the format specified by your instructor.

In the Lab

Design and/or create a Web page using the guidelines, concepts, and skills presented in this chapter. Labs are listed in order of increasing difficulty.

Lab 1: Finn's Catering

Problem: Your Aunt Felicia runs a successful catering business called Finn's Catering because she specializes in seafood preparation. She wants to update her Web page to make it more dynamic. You tell her you can create a photo slide show of various catered meals. In addition, you tell her you can create ScreenTips that display when the user places the mouse over a particular item. Finally, you can create an image floating across the screen that opens a pop-up window with a message about specials when it is clicked (Figure 11–42).

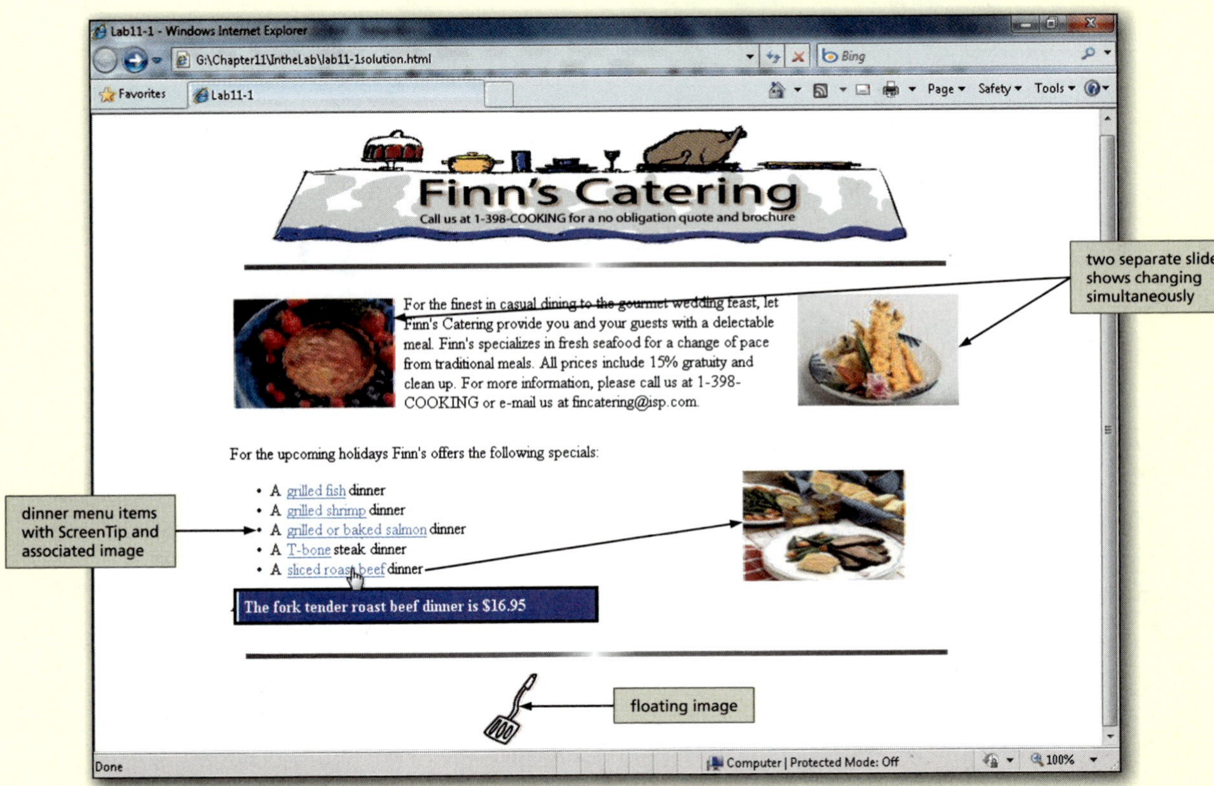

Figure 11–42

Instructions: Perform the following steps:

1. Start Notepad++ and open the file lab11-1.html from the Chapter11\IntheLab folder of the Data Files for Students.
2. Save the file as lab11-1solution.html.
3. Start a <script> section in the <head> section below the <title> tag on line 8.
4. Using the code in Table 11–12 on page HTML 526 as a guide, write two JavaScript functions called RotateIt1() and RotateIt2() to have two slide shows of various catered foods display on either side of the central Web page paragraph. Use the odd-numbered food image files in the Chapter11\IntheLab folder (lab11-1food*n*.jpg, where *n* is an even or odd number) in an array for the left slide show, and the even-numbered food image files in the Chapter11\IntheLab folder in an array for the right slide show. Use rotateCntr1 as the variable name for the counter in the RotateIt1() user-defined function, and use rotateCntr2 as the variable name for the counter in the RotateIt2() user-defined function.

5. Using the code in Table 11–18 on pages HTML 538 and HTML 539 as a guide, write a JavaScript function called popUp() to show a ScreenTip.
6. When the user places the mouse over a dinner item, change the photo in the user-defined function associated with the ScreenTip id. For example, the ScreenTip associated with id dinner1 should display lab11-1dinner1.jpg.
7. Using the code in Table 11–19 on pages HTML 541 and HTML 542 as a guide to enter the embedded CSS rules dinner1, dinner2, dinner3, dinner4, and dinner5 and class selector priceText. For the five id selectors, use the following attributes: position: absolute; visibility: hidden; z-index: 10; top: 10px; left: 10px. For the class selector priceText, use the following attributes: background-color: #cccccc; padding: 5px; border: 3px solid black; width: 350px; font-weight: bolder; color: white;.
8. Use the text in Table 11–22 to create the <span> tags for the screenTip text.

Table 11–22
`<span id="dinner1" class="priceText">`
`The grilled fish is $19.95 per person`
`</span>`
`<span id="dinner2" class="priceText">`
`The grilled shrimp dinner on a bed of greens is $21.95 per person`
`</span>`
`<span id="dinner3" class="priceText">`
`The grilled or baked salmon is served with a green vegetable for $16.95 per person`
`</span>`
`<span id="dinner4" class="priceText">`
`The prime T-bone steak dinner is $22.95 per person`
`</span>`
`<span id="dinner5" class="priceText">`
`The fork-tender roast beef dinner is $16.95`
`</span>`

9. Add the <a href> anchor tags to the unordered list of the dinner items (A grilled fish dinner, A grilled shrimp dinner, A grilled or baked salmon dinner, A T-bone steak dinner, A sliced roast beef dinner) for the mouseover and mouseout event handlers to call the popUp() function written in Step 5.
10. Use the code in Tables 11–13, 11–14, and 11–15 on pages HTML 531 through HTML 532 as a guide to write a user-defined function to make the lab11-1spatula.gif image float from left to right across the bottom of the Web page. Name the function scrollImage(). Using the names stopScroll() and restartScroll(), write user-defined functions to stop and restart the floating image. Initialize the leftPX variable to 10.
11. Use the code in Table 11-16 on page HTML 533 as a guide to write a use defined function called specialsPage() to open a pop-up window to display lab11-1specials.html.
12. Add an id selector to the embedded CSS named #catering with the following attribute values: position: absolute; top: 520px; and left: 10px.
13. Enter the <div> tag with the catering id attribute beneath the divider image at the bottom of the page. In the division, enter the <img> tag with the following mouse event and the inline style: <img src="lab11-1spatula.gif" onmouseover="stopScroll()" onmouseout="restartScroll()" onclick="specialsPage()" style="cursor:hand" />. Be sure to add the closing </div> tag.
14. Add the necessary event handlers to the <body> tag to launch the slide show and the floating image user-defined functions.
15. Save the completed HTML file and test it using your browser. If an error occurs, check your code from Steps 3 through 13, save, and test again.
16. Validate your Web page, and submit the completed HTML file and Web page in the format specified by your instructor.

STUDENT ASSIGNMENTS

In the Lab

Lab 2: Stem's Floral and Landscaping Web Site

Problem: Your neighbor owns and operates a local floral shop and landscaping business. He has been wanting to expand his Web site to include a page about flowers, using rocks in landscaping, and some basic landscape design principles for "do-it-yourself" landscapers. Your neighbor wants to use image rollovers for a navigation bar on all Web pages. In addition, on the Flowers Web page, he would like random images to display, and on the Design page, he wants to use ScreenTips. You are to add the JavaScript code to make these Web pages appear as shown in Figure 11–43.

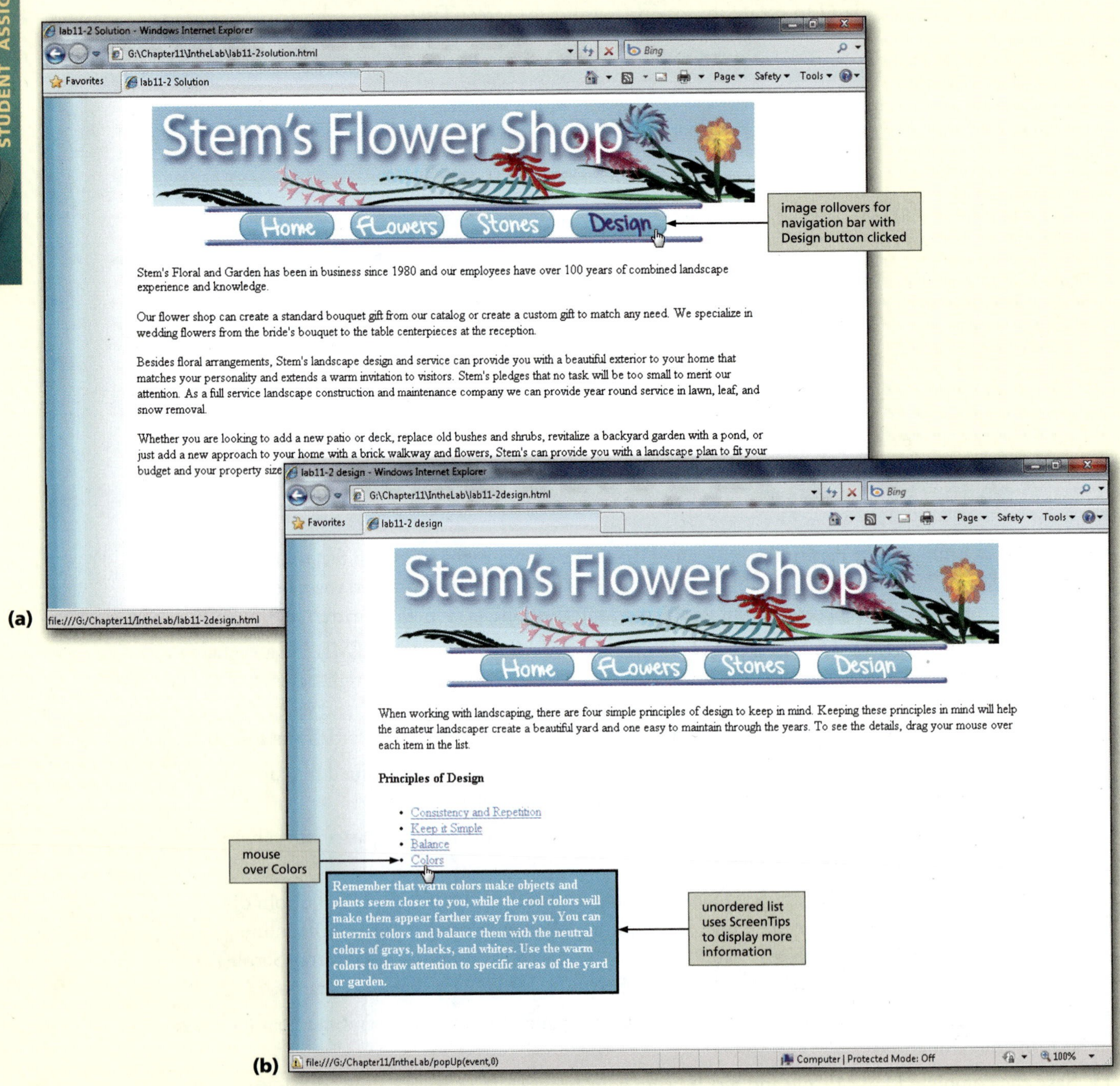

Figure 11–43

Instructions: Perform the following steps:

1. Start Notepad++ and open the file lab11-2.html from the Chapter11\IntheLab folder of the Data Files for Students.
2. Save the file as lab11-2solution.html.
3. Use the code in Table 11–2 on pages HTML 512 and HTML 513 and Table 11-6 on page HTML 516 as a guide to create the HTML code for the image rollovers with the <a href> tags starting on line 35. Use the user-defined function names of overBtn(), downBtn() and upBtn() in the mouse event handlers.
4. Start a <script> section in the <head> section below the <title> tag.
5. Use the code in Table 11–5 on page HTML 515 as a guide to write three JavaScript user-defined functions: overBtn(img), downBtn(img), and upBtn(img).
6. In each function, use the img parameter to construct a file name and assign to a variable named buttonImg. Use that variable name to replace the button image using the getElementById for the appropriate state (over, down, or up) of the button based on the mouse event.
7. Save lab11-2solution.html.
8. Open lab11-2flowers.html. Copy and paste the HTML table containing the navigation bar, and the JavaScript user-defined functions to lab11-2flowers.html. Make sure the appropriate mouse event handlers are in the table with the button images. Change the # in the home button <ahref> to lab11-2solution.html.
9. Use Table 11–8 on page HTML 520 to create an array called randomImage using the flower image files lab11-2flower1.jpg, lab11-2flower2.jpg, lab11-2flower3.jpg, lab11-2flower4.jpg, lab11-2flower5.jpg, lab11-2flower6.jpg, lab11-2flower7.jpg, and lab11-2flower8.jpg. Remember to use a null image for the zero element.
10. Use Table 11–8 on page HTML 520 to write a JavaScript user-defined function named rndimage(), which uses the length of the array and Math.ceil and Math.random to generate a random number. Use this number to assign that element to the flowerleft image placeholder. Then generate another random number and assign that element to the flowerright image placeholder. Add the appropriate onload event handler to the <body> tag.
11. Save the file as lab11-2flowersolution.html.
12. Open the lab11-2design.html file. Copy and paste the navigation bar HTML table from lab11-2solution.html and the JavaScript user-defined functions for the image rollovers to the lab11-2design.html file. Change the # in the home button <ahref> to lab11-2solution.html.
13. Use the code in Table 11–18 on pages HTML 538 and HTML 539 as guide to write the JavaScript user-defined function popUp(). Do not include the code for displaying a new image, as no image should be displayed.
14. Use the code in Table 11–19 on pages HTML 541 and HTML 542 as a guide to add the id selectors CandP, KIS, Bal, and Color using the same attributes and values.
15. For the class selector popupText use the following attributes: background-color: #5bb1e0; padding: 5px; border: 3px solid black; width: 350px; font-weight: bolder; color: white;.
16. Use the code presented in Figures 11–34 through 11–36 on pages HTML 543 and HTML 544 as a guide to enter the correct <a href> tag mouse event handlers before the words in the unordered list: Consistency and Repetition, Keep it Simple, Balance, and Colors. Use the corresponding Cascading Style Sheet selector for each mouse event: CandP, KIS, Bal, and Color.
17. Enter the <span> tags in Table 11–23 for the ScreenTip text.

Continued >

In the Lab *continued*

Table 11–23 ScreenTip Text

`<span class="popupText" id="CandP">Create unity in your design by focusing on a single theme. A theme should represent something you are interested in expressing about your landscape. For example, if you wish to attract birds, use different kinds of structures and ornaments that birds can use for homes or resting. </span>`
`<span class="popupText" id="KIS">When picking plants, boulders, or other items, pick two or three colors and repeat. Keep items to a minimum for starters; you can always add more later as the need arises.</span>`
`<span class="popupText" id="Bal">Try to keep things balanced through symmetrical or asymmetrical design. Contrast items so they complement each other, not compete for your attention. Use of lines and other geometric shapes can create the kind of balance and harmony you want to achieve. Also, as you pick your plants, keep in mind different maturity levels throughout the yard, so some plants are in bloom, while others are just beginning to bloom. </span>`
`<span class="popupText" id="Color">Remember that warm colors make objects and plants seem closer to you, while the cool colors will make them appear farther away from you. You can intermix colors and balance them with the neutral colors of grays, blacks, and whites. Use the warm colors to draw attention to specific areas of the yard or garden. </span>`

18. Save the completed HTML file as lab11-2designsolution.html.
19. Open the lab11-2stones.html file. Copy and paste the HTML table for the navigation bar and the menu image rollover JavaScript user-defined functions from the lab11-2solution.html file to lab11-2stones.html. Change the # in the home button <ahref> to lab11-2solution.html.
20. Save the file as lab11-2stonessolution.html.
21. Test the completed Web page by loading the lab11-2solution.html in your browser. Click the navigation bar buttons, and then test the random images in the Flowers Web page and the ScreenTips in the Design Web page. If an error occurs, check your code from Steps 3 through 19, save, and test again.
22. Validate your Web pages, and submit the completed HTML files and Web pages in the format specified by your instructor.

In the Lab

Lab 3: Dreambuilders Construction and Remodeling Web Page

Problem: Your father owns a construction and remodeling company and has asked you to create a Web page that showcases the company. He wants a total of four Web pages, including a Home page, Build page, Remodel page, and Plan page. He wants to use image rollovers for a navigation bar. The Build Web page showcases the materials he uses in construction. To do this, he wants to use ScreenTips and have an image associated with the ScreenTip display in the image placeholder on the page. He wants the Remodel page to have a slide show that displays examples of their remodeling jobs. The Plan Web page introduces the company's architects, who can help a customer plan and design a renovation or build new home. To make the Web page more animated, you add an image of a hammer that scrolls across the bottom of the page (Figure 11–44).

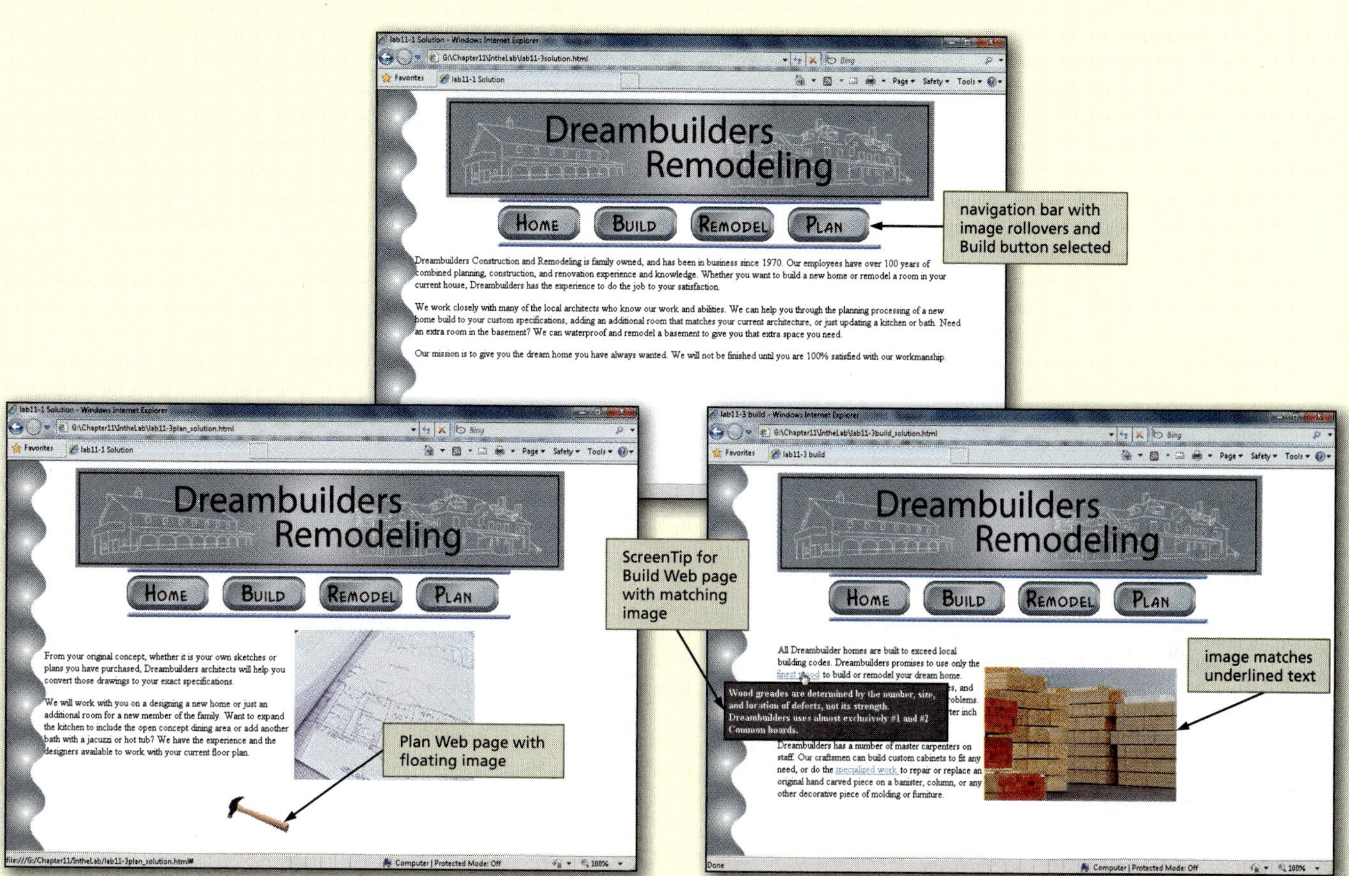

Figure 11–44

Instructions: Perform the following steps:

1. Start Notepad++ and open the lab11-3.html file. Save it immediately as lab11-3solution.html.
2. Using the techniques learned in this chapter, create the table to create a navigation bar using the images provided to create the navigation bar for the home page (lab11-3solution.html). The images are for the Home, Build, Remodel, and Plan Web pages.
3. Using the techniques learned in this chapter, write the JavaScript code to change the image for a mouse down event handler and for the mouse up and out event handlers for the navigation bar. For the onmousedown event handler, link to the appropriate Home, Build, Remodel, and Plan Web pages.
4. Save the file as lab11-3solution.html to be used as the Home page.
5. Open the lab11-3build.html and add the table, the JavaScript code, and mouse event handlers to create a navigation bar.
6. Write the JavaScript code to display ScreenTips for each of the building materials. Use the image file lab11-3build.jpg as the default image, and use lab11-3lumber.jpg for the finest wood link, use lab11-3build2.jpg for the oriented strand board link, and use lab11-3craftsman.jpb for the specialized work link. Use the text in Table 11–24 on the next page for the ScreenTips and the CSS id and class selectors.
7. Save the Web page as lab11-3build_solution.html.

Continued >

In the Lab *continued*

Table 11–24 ScreenTip Text

`class: buildText`
`id: lumber`
`Text: Wood grades are determined by the number, size, and location of defects, not by strength. Dreambuilders uses almost exclusively #1 and #2 Common boards.`

`class: buildText`
`id: build2`
`Text: OSB or oriented strand board is made of chips of wood instead of a continuous veneer. The chips are lined up in different layers to create a strong wood. Though OSB is about half the cost of veneer plywood, it is less attractive.`

`class: buildText`
`id: craftsman`
`Text: Our craftsmen are master woodworkers. They have extensive training and experience in duplicating pieces that may have been damaged by weather or fire.`

8. Open the lab11-3remodel.html file and add the table, the JavaScript code, and mouse event handlers to create the image rollover navigation bar.
9. Write the JavaScript code to create a slide show using the five lab11-3remodelX.jpg images. Use the following attributes to complete the <img> tag for the slide show image placeholder: name=slideHolder, id=slideHolder, width=235, height=235, and alt=remodeled rooms.
10. Save the HTML file as lab11-3remodel_solution.html.
11. Open the lab11-3plan.html file and add the table, the JavaScript code, and mouse event handlers to create the navigation bar.
12. Write the JavaScript code to display a random image in the <img> placeholder tag. Assign the file lab11-3plan1.jpg as the initial image. Use the following values for the remaining attributes: name=planImg, id=planImg, width=290, height=235, and alt=working with plans.
13. Write the JavaScript code to make an image float across the page from right to left. Use the hammer image lab11-3hammer.gif. Place the image in a <div> tag container with an id of scrollImg. Add the CSS selector scrollImg with a position as absolute, top at 510px, and left at 950px.
14. Be sure to add the appropriate event handlers to invoke the user-defined functions to all the Web pages.
15. Save the completed HTML file as lab11-3plan_solution.html.
16. With all the Web pages saved, test them using your browser. If an error occurs, check your code, save, and test again.
17. Validate your Web pages, and submit the completed HTML files and Web pages in the format specified by your instructor.

Cases and Places

Apply your creative thinking and problem solving skills to design and implement a solution.

• Easier •• More Difficult

•• 1: S and C Air Charters

As a summer intern for S and C Air Charters, you have been asked to update a Web page for the company. The owners want to have a slide show and two floating images: one image of a helicopter (case11-1helicopter.gif) flying right to left, and the other a jet (case11-1jet.gif) flying left to right. Use the images supplied in the Chapter11\CasesandPlaces folder of the Data Files for Students to make the rotating slide show and floating images.

•• 2: Computer Corner

Your older sister, Carrie, has started a technology store called the Computer Corner. She sells computers, cell phones, software, and games. She asks you to create a Web site to showcase her store. On her home page (case11-2.html), she wants a slide show and ScreenTips for her items. Using the images (case11-2custom.jpg, case11-2cellphone.jpg, case11-2games.jpg, case11-2software1.jpg, and case11-2computer.jpg), create an array and a user-defined function to display these images in the image placeholder with the id computerSlides.

Use the text in Table 11–25 for the ScreenTips.

Table 11–25 ScreenTips
id: custom class: popupText Are you an avid gamer and want to build your own powerhouse, or just someone ready to try building your dream computer from scratch with the custom parts to meet your individual needs? We will explain and help you put together that dream computer.
id: cellphone class: popupText We have a complete stock of "pay as you go" cell phones, and are an authorized dealer for American Cell Company (AC&C).
id: games class: popupText Looking for a game console for your children... or maybe your spouse? We carry all the top game consoles at competitive prices.
id: software class: popupText We carry a complete line of home and office production software, plus games for PCs, Sony, and Nintendo. We also rent game software and carry used games. Ask about our Game Exchange Club.
id: namebrand class: popupText Just want to get a ready-to-go computer? We carry the top brands and can do in-store customizing to upgrade RAM or video needs.

Continued >

Cases and Places *continued*

•• 3: Expanding the Chapter Web Page

The case11-3.html file in the Chapter11\CasesandPlaces folder of the Data Files for Students is a start of a Recipe Web page that contains the same image rollover navigation bar as the files in the Chapter11\ChapterFiles folder. The Chapter11\CasesandPlaces folder has three additional button files for recipes. The case11-3recipe.html file has three bullet items: Native Wild Grapes, Native Wine Grapes, and European Wild Grapes. Using the techniques discussed in this chapter, add a JavaScript user-defined function to add a ScreenTip for each item. Search the Internet for information about each of these wines and use that information as the text for the ScreenTips.

Along with each ScreenTip, display the similarly named graphic image placeholder (wineImg). Be sure to add the CSS id selectors (wine1, wine2, and wine3) and class selector (grapeText) for the ScreenTips. Use the same attribute properties as in the chapter. In addition, do not forget to add the appropriate event handlers for the ScreenTips. If necessary, rename files as indicated by your instructor.

•• 4: Create a Family Event Web Page

Make It Personal

Using a family event like a wedding, christening, bar mitzvah, or reunion, create one or more Web pages that detail events. Create at least one rotating image slide show with at least five photos from the event. Also, list the names of people being honored at the event. For each name, create a ScreenTip with a short comment about that person. The comment can be something from their life, or something that was amusing that happened at the family event.

•• 5: Creating Student Clubs and Organization Web Pages

Working Together

At your school there are many student clubs and organizations that hold or sponsor different events. Depending on the number of members in your team, each one should take one club and meet with them. Ask permission to make a Web page about their group. Collect some information, photos, or other images they may have. Construct a home page that showcases the various clubs using a scrolling vertical menu or a navigation bar with image rollovers similar to the text. Each menu item should link to the club Web pages that each team member created. Each team member's Web page should have a rotating slide show of images, and at least one ScreenTip highlighting some feature of the club.

12 Creating and Using XML Documents

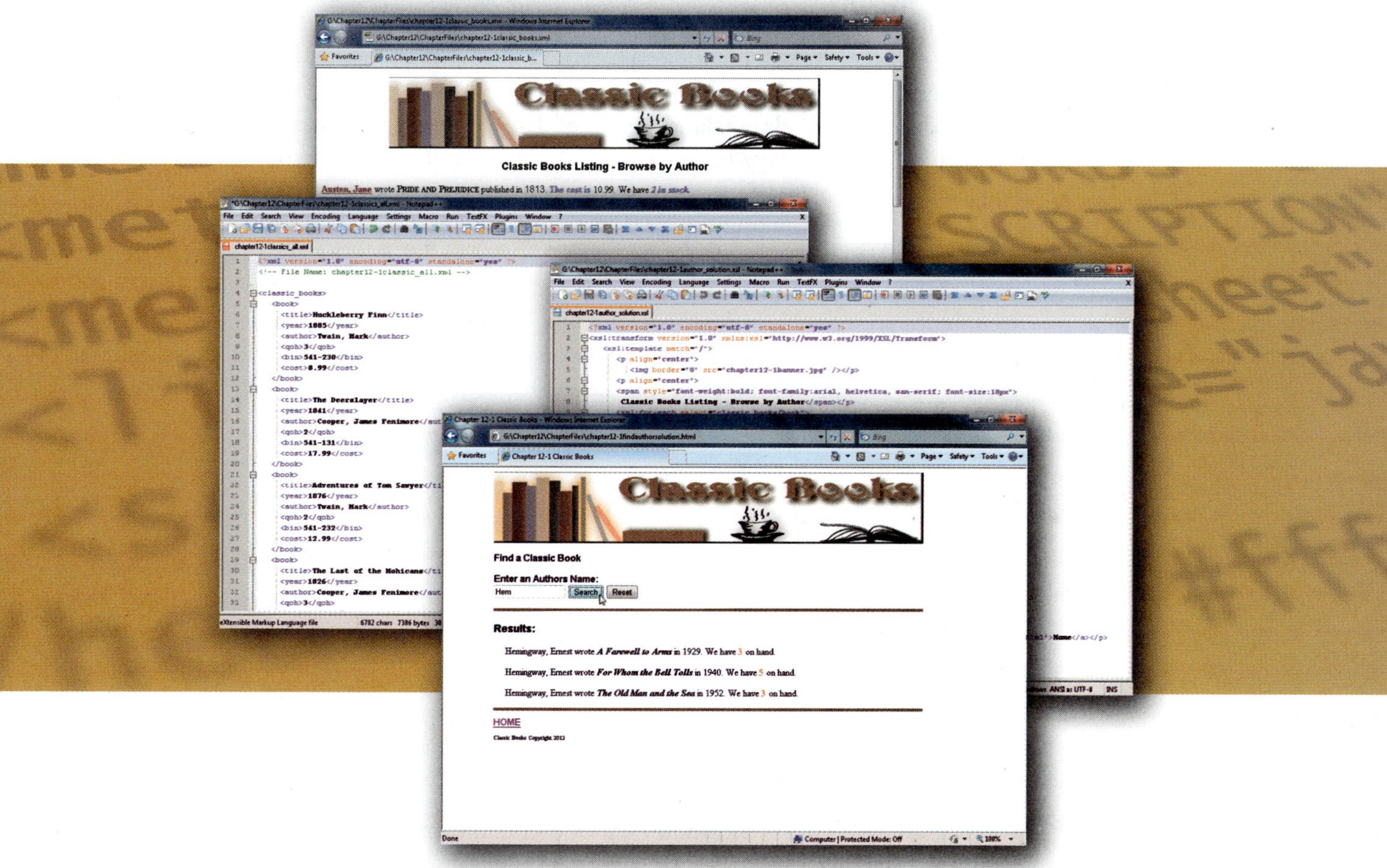

Objectives

You will have mastered the material in this chapter when you can:

- Describe how XML differs from HTML
- Describe an XML document instance, and rules for creating a well-formed and valid XML document
- Define the purpose of the processing instruction, the document prolog, and the document instance
- Describe an XML Schema Definition (XSD) language file
- Create and bind an XSL style sheet file to an XML document
- Discuss the uses of an XML data island
- Discuss the built-in table element methods for displaying an XML document in a table
- Create a JavaScript user-defined function to search an XML document

12 Creating and Using XML Documents

Introduction

In this chapter, you learn how to create XML data files for use as stand-alone Web pages, format files using an XSL style sheet, and bind XML files to HTML Web pages. In some cases, the XML data will display in HTML tables, and in other cases, the XML data will display in other formats. In particular, you create and use an XML document as a database or data island. A **data island** is a set of data elements separate from the main HTML Web page. The advantage to using an XML data island is the reduction of DBMS activity needed just to display data.

By binding or linking the XML data to an HTML Web page using the <xml> tag, the HTML objects can be manipulated to enhance usability. The <xml> tag, which is particular only to Microsoft Internet Explorer (IE), was first introduced with IE5. The techniques presented in this chapter work best with Microsoft Internet Explorer 8. In particular, the HMTL code is used to display the data island in a table and to search for specific books using a JavaScript user-defined function.

BTW

XML as a Data Island

A data island has the capability of embedding XML documents in HTML pages. The process uses data source object (dso) technology. The disadvantage to using an XML data island is that the XML documents are static. Client-side processing does not allow real-time updates to the XML document on the server.

Project — Creating an XML Document

Classic Books' Web site with its book list has been a great success. Customers, however, have been asking for other ways to browse or search the book offerings. You recently have learned about Extensible Markup Language (XML), which offers some flexibility not found with traditional HTML pages. You suggest the Web site offer clients various ways to view the book lists, including using the Extensible Stylesheet Language (XSL) to transform an XML document into a readable format displayed by author. Next, you suggest using an HTML table in which the user can browse the book offerings in order by title. Finally, you suggest using JavaScript to allow a user to search for books by a specific author.

The Web pages shown in Figure 12–1 demonstrate three different applications of the same XML document. Figure 12–1a shows Classic Books' Web home page containing three links: one link opens an XML page in a browser displaying a table of all the available books formatted by an XSL style sheet in author order (Figure 12–1b). The next link displays the XML data in a table in title order (Figure 12–1c). The last link displays a Web page to search for books by any part of the author's name (Figure 12–1d).

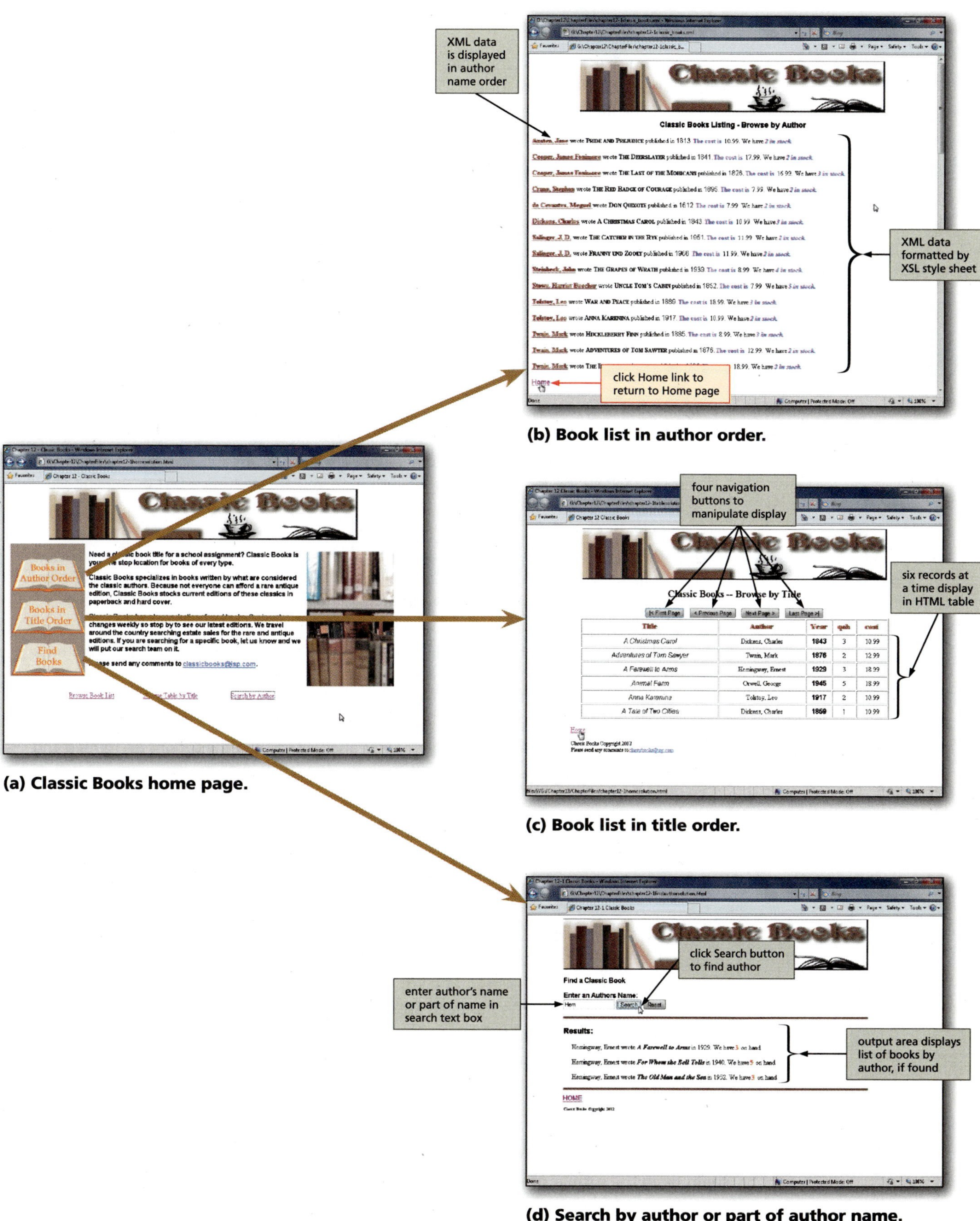

(a) Classic Books home page.

(b) Book list in author order.

(c) Book list in title order.

(d) Search by author or part of author name.

Figure 12–1

Overview

As you read through this chapter, you will learn how to create well-formed and valid XML documents (creating an XML Schema Definition), format and display XML documents using an XSL style sheet, display an XML document in a Web page table, and search for books by performing these general tasks:

- Create an XML Schema Definition (XSD) file.
- Create an XSL style sheet to format the output of an XML document.
- Bind an XSL style sheet to an XML document.
- Bind an XML document to an HTML document and display XML data in an HTML table.
- Create a JavaScript function to search for items in an XML document data island.

Plan Ahead

General Project Guidelines
When creating an XML document, you should follow these general guidelines:

1. **Determine what type of XML document you are going to create.** An XML document should follow the form of the desired output. If you are creating a text document, like a memo or a database of inventory items, the XML document should conform to the general form of that type of document.
2. **Determine the contents of the document.** The contents may be created from an existing document or database. Many applications can create XML documents automatically, or the XML document may have to be created manually. In either case, the type of data must be defined with an XML Schema Definition file.
3. **Determine how the document will be displayed.** If the document will be displayed on a Web page, you must think about how to format its contents for display. For example, the document may be formatted with an XSL style sheet or displayed using an HTML table.

When necessary, more specific details concerning the above guidelines are presented at appropriate points in the chapter. The chapter also will identify the actions performed and decisions made regarding these guidelines during the creation of the Web pages shown in Figure 12–1 on the previous page.

XML vs. HTML

The first Web pages developed with HTML presented static information and allowed linking to other Web pages with additional information. In early Web development, data was converted into forms used in HTML documents. If the data changed, the Web documents had to be changed. As the need arose for more dynamic Web pages that would present current data and allow users to interact with that data, Web developers began relying on various database management systems (DBMSs) to store and retrieve data. Some popular DBMS systems include Oracle, Microsoft SQL Server, MySQL, Objectstore, and Postgres SQL. Each DBMS uses various programming language interfaces within HTML documents to access data.

Formatting that data in an HTML document, however, could be problematic. Data could be in the format of simple text, a table of rows and columns, or a hierarchical structure with complex relationships. It could be in the form of tables, e-mails, and reports. The **Extensible Markup Language (XML)** was developed to provide a way to share all various types of data in one clear and efficient method. XML provides a common format for all types of data that can be used by anyone using software than can read XML, such as a Web browser. XML also provides a way to separate the data from the HTML document, so that when the data is updated, the HTML document simply displays the new data, allowing for dynamic Web pages that change as the data changes.

Designing XML Documents

XML uses tags to describe the structure of a document and its contents. XML tags do not format the display of text as with an HTML document. XML provides a flexible way for organizations to share common data and to integrate data with Web pages. The main XML document created in this chapter is a list of books available at Classic Books, which will serve as a database (or data island) formatted by XSL or bound to an HTML Web page for display in a table or used to search using JavaScript.

Formatting XML documents for display on a Web page requires binding or linking a style sheet to the XML document, which formats the elements of the XML document as they appear in a browser. An XML document can be formatted with Cascading Style Sheets (CSS) or an Extensible Stylesheet Language (XSL) style sheet. **Extensible Stylesheet Language (XSL)** is used to create style sheets for formatting structured XML data. XSL style sheets provide more flexibility and control over XML documents than CSS. While CSS can format individual XML elements, XSL can control the order of elements or add other information. Most developers prefer XSL style sheets over CSS for formatting XML documents.

BTW

XML

Like HTML, XML is a subset of Standard Generalized Markup Language (SGML). SGML gives developers the ability to create their own elements. XML inherits this ability from SGML. XML does not replace HTML, but it provides a means to extend and enhance the use and appearance of a document. Developers can create XML documents manually using any editor, or generate an XML document using existing tables in a Microsoft SQL Server or Microsoft Access database, and then bind them to their Web pages.

XML Standards

As you learned in Chapter 1, the World Wide Web Consortium (W3C) oversees and develops standards for Web development. To help ensure consistency among the discipline-specific tags created in XML, the W3C has defined a set of standards, or goals, for XML, shown in Table 12–1. The goals provide a framework for all future XML development and XML-related, discipline-specific markup languages.

Table 12–1 Design Goals for XML

1.	XML shall be straightforwardly usable over the Internet.
2.	XML shall support a wide variety of applications.
3.	XML shall be compatible with SGML.
4.	It shall be easy to write programs which process XML documents.
5.	The number of optional features in XML is to be kept to the absolute minimum, ideally zero.
6.	XML documents should be human-legible and reasonably clear.
7.	The XML design should be prepared quickly.
8.	The design of XML shall be formal and concise.
9.	XML documents shall be easy to create.
10.	Terseness in XML markup is of minimal importance.

Using XML documents as databases is just one of the many ways Web developers use XML. The creation and use of these databases is the central focus of this chapter. As the W3C group continues to develop XML standards, businesses and organizations find numerous new uses for XML. An important goal of XML is to allow the creation of discipline-specific markup language tags. Table 12–2 on the next page is a partial list of uses and extended markup languages created using XML.

BTW

Uses of XML

XML is not limited to use in Web databases. There are over a hundred industries using some form of XML, ranging from accounting and finance to weather.

Table 12–2 Real-World Uses of XML

Use	Description of Extended Markup Languages
Define databases	Use labels and fields to store and display data in a variety of ways
Give structure to documents	Provide structure to elements in books and plays, such as indexes or scene directions
Provide Web services	Execute Web services (functions) over a network with the Simple Object Access Protocol (SOAP) and Web Services Description Language (WSDL)
Exchange financial information	Exchange information among various applications using Open Financial Exchange (OFX)
Store voice scripts	Store voice mail messages or regular daily messages
Annotate maps	Add place marks, shapes, and paths to a map using Keyhole Markup Language (KML), an XML markup language
Format mathematical formulas	Format math and science content markup with MathML
Define standard document format for businesses	Allow business partners to share a standard library of XML business documents, such as purchase orders and invoices; identify the documents exchanged in a particular context using Universal Business Language (UBL)
Create HTML pages that are valid XML	Transition to XHTML following XML standards and tools
Edit open source documents	Open Document Format (ODF) and Office Open XML (OOXML) are file formats for word processing, spreadsheets, and presentation software
Display electronic texts	Use XHTML and XML to display contents of eBooks and ePub devices

BTW

Purpose of the XML Parser

The XML parser is necessary to create, read, update, or manipulate an XML document. Most modern Web browsers contain various parsers for scripting languages and XML.

Syntax Rules

XML documents must be well-formed to be processed by an application. For an XML document to be **well-formed**, it must adhere to the basic syntax rules for XML, as listed in Table 12–3. Before an XML document is displayed in an application, the document must be parsed. A **parser** is an XML processor that verifies the document follows the syntax rules for a well-formed document and converts the document into a tree of elements. Most modern Web browsers contain XML parsers. For more information on XML syntax, see the XML Quick Reference in Appendix H.

BTW

Generic Identifier

An element consists of tags based on names that a developer provides or defines. The name that a developer provides for the tags is called the **generic identifier (GI)**. When choosing generic identifiers to name document elements, a developer must follow two simple rules: (1) The name must begin with a letter or underscore (_) and may contain letters, numbers, periods, hyphens, or underscores, and (2) A prefix of XML or the use of colons is reserved for future, anticipated standardization.

Table 12–3 XML Syntax Rules

Rule	Comment	Example
XML is case sensitive.	Use any case — uppercase, lowercase, or mixed — but be consistent.	Correct: <Root></Root> or <root></root> or <ROOT></ROOT> Incorrect: <Root></ROOT>
All tags must have a closing tag.	All tags, including empty tags, must have a closing tag. Empty tags are allowed a special form. Empty tags have no content, such as and <img> tags.	<p>This is a paragraph</p> <name>Susan</name>
All documents must have a root element.	Include the root or start tag that begins a document.	<root> <child></child> </root>
Elements must be nested.	Elements cannot stand alone unless they are the only root element.	<club> <name>Spanish</name> </club>
Attribute values must be enclosed in quotation marks.	Use single or double quotation marks, but be consistent.	<Image picture="icon.jpg" />
With XML, white space is preserved.	Spaces between words within tags are preserved.	No need for ASCII characters ( ) to add spaces

This chapter shows how to create well-formed documents manually. Figure 12–2a shows a simple XML document created in Notepad ++. When displayed in or parsed by a browser or application (Figure 12–2b), this XML document may have little meaning to a user. Linking the XML document to an XSL style sheet (Figure 12–2c) enables the browser to display the document in a more readable format (Figure 12–2d).

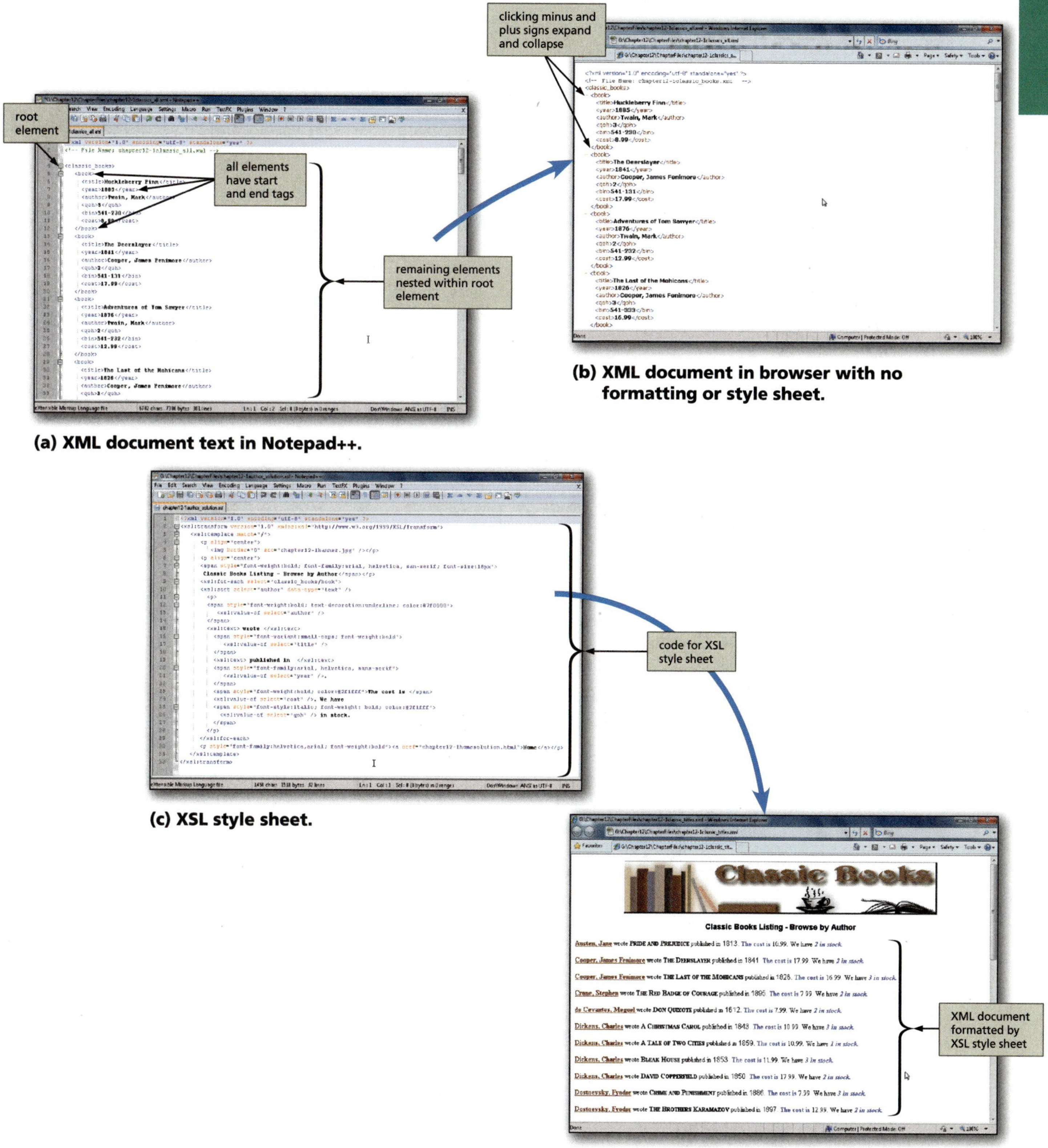

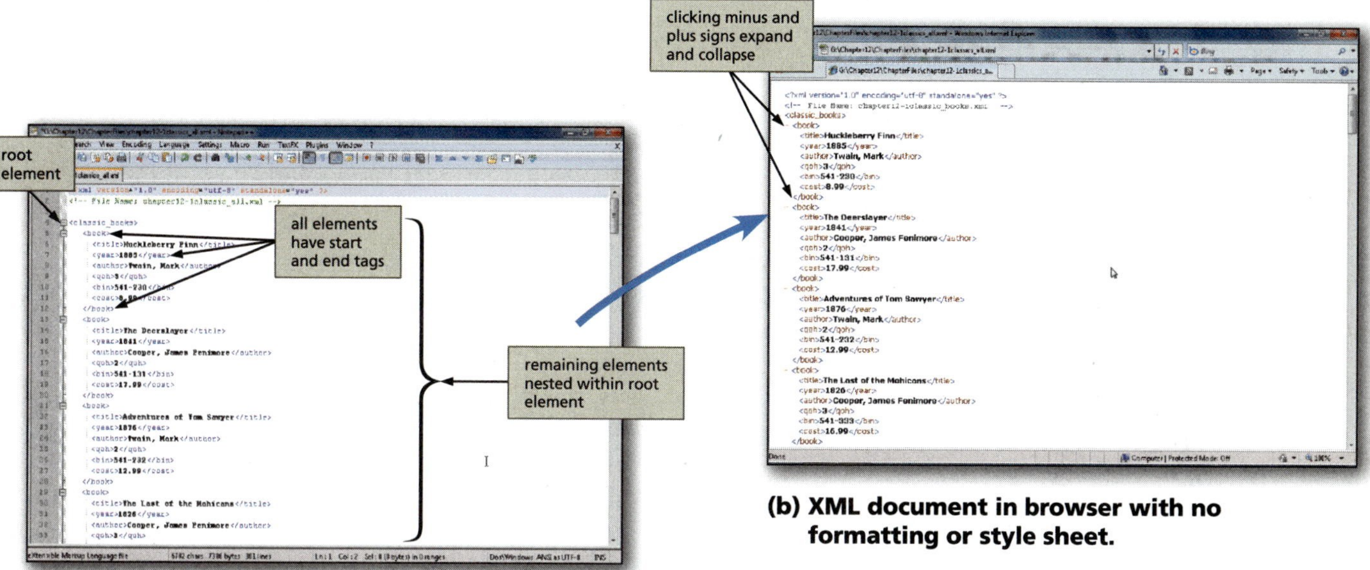

(b) XML document in browser with no formatting or style sheet.

(a) XML document text in Notepad++.

code for XSL style sheet

(c) XSL style sheet.

XML document formatted by XSL style sheet

(d) XSL formatted document.

Figure 12–2

Plan Ahead

Creating a well-formed XML document.
The following tasks are necessary to create a well-formed XML document, as described in the next section:

1. Identify the tags to describe the document content and create the Document Type Definition (DTD) or XML Schema Definition (XSD).
2. Create the prolog.
3. Create the document instances.

BTW

Well-Formed Documents
A well-formed document meets certain criteria: the document must have at least one root element, and it must nest child elements in the root; every tag must have a beginning and closing tag, including empty tags; and all attribute values must be enclosed in quotation marks, either single or double, but they must be consistent.

Creating a Well-Formed XML Document

Database analysts refer to a collection of data as a **relation**. To represent the attributes or fields in a relation, database analysts use a simple notation, called a schema. A database **schema** is a logical design to show relationships, and is written as the relation name followed by a list of attributes or fields in parentheses, in the form:

```
Relation_Name (attribute1, attribute2..., attributen)
```

The Relation_Name indicates the name of the collection of data, and *n* represents the total number of attributes. After data analysis, a relation for the Classic Books book store is developed, and using the notation style above, the logical schema design for the XML document is written as

```
book (title, year, author, qoh, bin, cost)
```

The name of the relation is book; the attributes within the parentheses describe things about the each book.

BTW

The XML Prolog
Every XML document must have a prolog. The prolog must contain at least one line — a declaration statement — identifying the document as an XML document: <?xml version="1.0"?>.

A well-formed XML document consists of two main parts: the prolog and the document instance or elements (Figure 12–3). The **prolog** contains the processing instruction statements and any additional comments necessary to provide information about the document's content and structure such as an optional Document Type Definition (DTD) or a link to a DTD. The **document instance** contains the main content or elements of the XML document. The **root element** of a document instance contains the link to the XML Schema Definition file. Because the XML Schema Definition is the preferred method for forming an XML document, this chapter discusses how to create and link an XML Schema Definition (XSD) file to an XML file.

The prolog may contain processing instruction statements, declaration statements, or comments. A **processing instruction** is one or more instructions passed to the application using the XML document. The **XML declaration** is a processing instruction statement identifying the version of XML used in the document. The prolog shown in Figure 12–3 contains an XML declaration, a processing instruction on line 1, a comment on line 2 identifying the file.

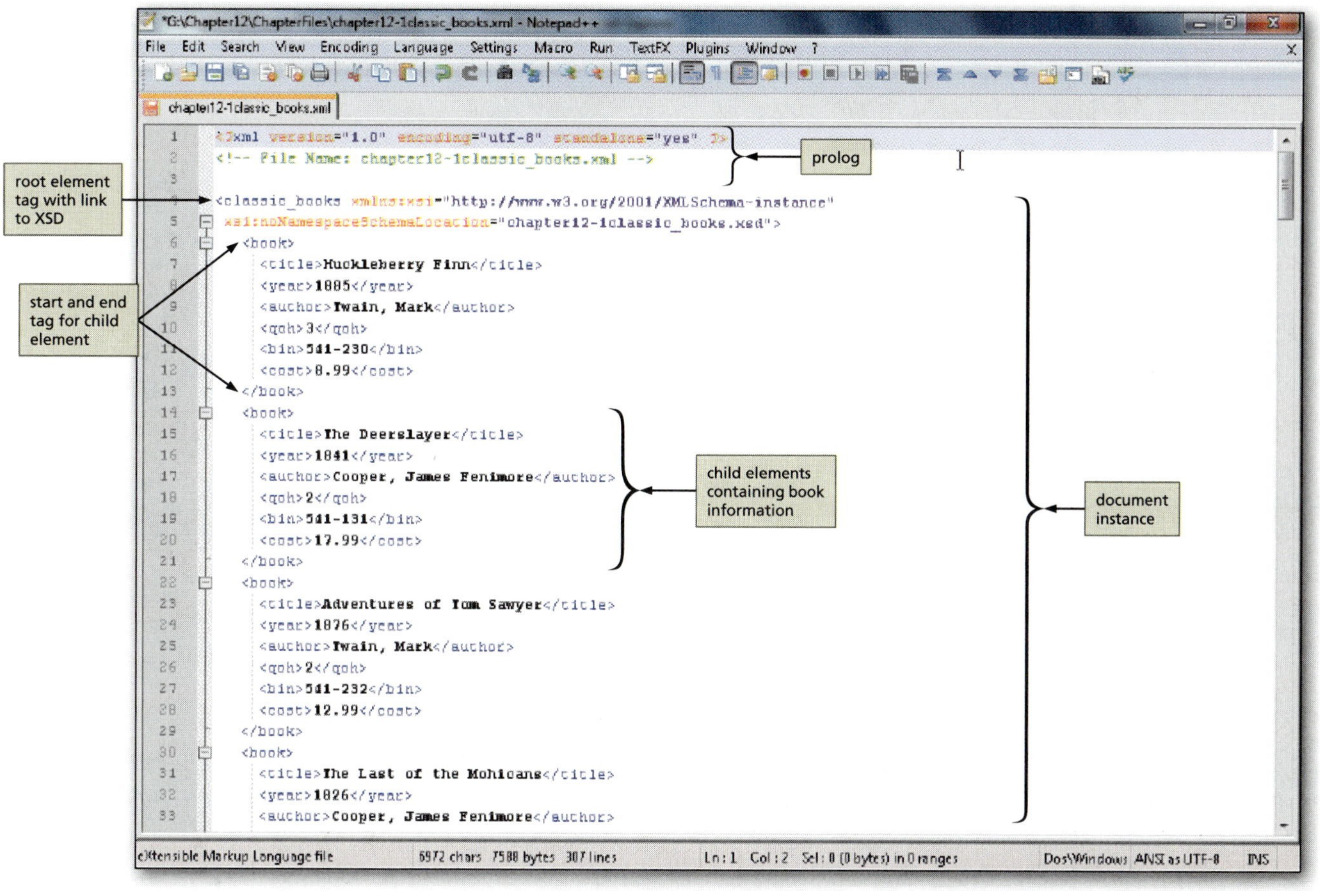

*G:\Chapter12\ChapterFiles\chapter12-1classic_books.xml - Notepad++

File Edit Search View Encoding Language Settings Macro Run TextFX Plugins Window ?

chapter12-1classic_books.xml

```
<?xml version="1.0" encoding="utf-8" standalone="yes" ?>
<!-- File Name: chapter12-1classic_books.xml -->

<classic_books xmlns:xsi="http://www.w3.org/2001/XMLSchema-instance"
 xsi:noNamespaceSchemaLocation="chapter12-1classic_books.xsd">
  <book>
    <title>Huckleberry Finn</title>
    <year>1885</year>
    <author>Twain, Mark</author>
    <qoh>3</qoh>
    <bin>5d1-230</bin>
    <cost>8.99</cost>
  </book>
  <book>
    <title>The Deerslayer</title>
    <year>1841</year>
    <author>Cooper, James Fenimore</author>
    <qoh>2</qoh>
    <bin>5d1-131</bin>
    <cost>17.99</cost>
  </book>
  <book>
    <title>Adventures of Tom Sawyer</title>
    <year>1876</year>
    <author>Twain, Mark</author>
    <qoh>2</qoh>
    <bin>5d1-232</bin>
    <cost>12.99</cost>
  </book>
  <book>
    <title>The Last of the Mohicans</title>
    <year>1826</year>
    <author>Cooper, James Fenimore</author>
```

eXtensible Markup Language file 6972 chars 7588 bytes 307 lines Ln : 1 Col : 2 Sel : 0 (0 bytes) in 0 ranges Dos\Windows ANSI as UTF-8 INS

prolog

root element tag with link to XSD

start and end tag for child element

child elements containing book information

document instance

Figure 12–3

The document instance contains the main content or elements of the XML document and provides a logical structure for the document. An **instance** is an occurrence of XML elements. The XML document must include at least one instance, or occurrence, of an element. The main element is the root element and may contain one or more subelements or **child elements**. This parent-child relationship between elements gives XML its hierarchical, treelike structure, as shown in Figure 12–4.

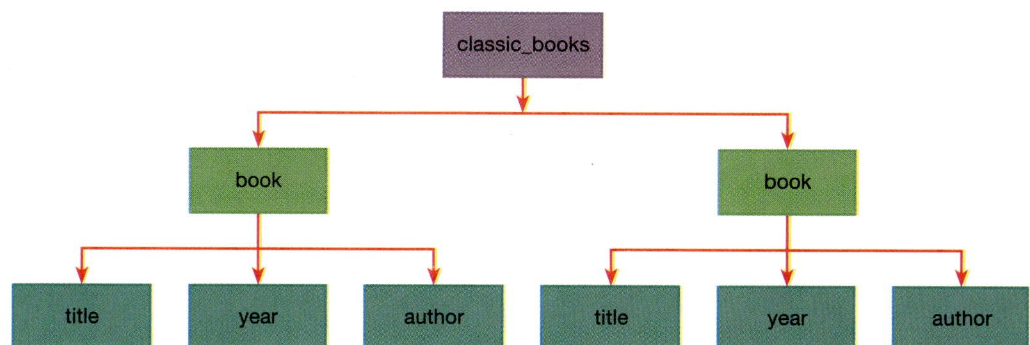

Figure 12–4

To Start Notepad++ and Create a New XML Document

The following step illustrates how to use Notepad++ to create a new XML document.

- Start Notepad++, and, if necessary, maximize the Notepad++ window. If the Word wrap feature is not enabled, enable it.
- With the USB drive plugged into your computer, click File on the menu bar, and then click Save As on the File menu.
- If necessary, navigate to the Chapter12\ChapterFiles folder on your storage device.
- Type `chapter12-1classic_books.xsd` in the File name text box.
- Click the Save button in the Save As dialog box to save the Schema Definition file (Figure 12–5).

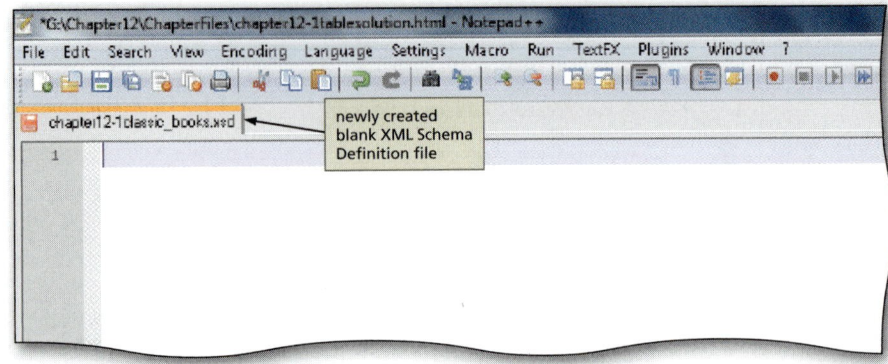

Figure 12–5

Creating an XML Schema Definition

An **XML Schema Definition** describes the structure of an XML document, which includes the data types. An XML Schema Definition is more useful than a Document Type Definition (DTD), because DTDs do not describe the data types. In addition, the DTD is not able to enforce that a specific data type, such as a date, is being implemented. Because of these limitations, XML standards prefer the use of an XML Schema Definition to describe an XML file.

XML Schema Definitions are XML files, and as such, they must conform to the same rules that any XML document must follow. Tags must have a beginning and end tag, though many XML Schema Definitions will use an empty tag with attributes. The rules for attributes must be followed: they must be lowercase and values must be enclosed in quotation marks. The basic component of an XML Schema Definition is the element. Table 12–4 shows the basic format of an XML Schema Definition <element> tag.

Table 12–4 General Form of an XML Schema Definition Element

General form:	<xs:element name="field name" type="data type" />
Comment:	xs: is a namespace, to differentiate this element from any other element that may have the same name. The name is an attribute to define the field name; type is an attribute to state one of the valid data types. Simple elements may have an optional default or fixed attributes to assign a default value to a field. The default value is assigned if no other value is assigned; the fixed value does not allow any other value to be assigned. Most developers use xs or xsd as a default namespace. This text uses xs.
Examples:	<xs:element name="qoh" type="xs:integer" default="0" />

Elements in an XML Schema Definition can be either simple type or complex type. A **simple type** element is one that contains only text. A **complex type** element is one that contains sub or child elements and/or attributes, which themselves contain data. Table 12–5 compares simple type and complex type elements.

Table 12–5 XML Simple Type and Complex Type Elements

Type	Description and XML Element	XML Schema
Simple	an XML element that contains only text <first_name>Bill</first_name>	<xs:element name="first_name" type="string" />
Complex	an XML element that contains child elements or attributes <schedule_item> <course_no>CSCI-C340</course_no> <course_title>Web programming</course_title> </schedule_item>	<xs:element name="schedule item"> <xs:complexType> <xs:sequence> <xs:element name="course_no" type="string" /> <xs:element name="course_title" type="string" /> </ xs:sequence> </ xs:complexType> </ xs:element>

The definition of elements in the schema must include the data type. XML Schema Definition has several built-in data types shown in Table 12–6. From this list of simple data types, a developer can build custom data types. Custom data types begin with a base data type and include restrictions in the form of domain (range of valid values), length, or number of characters or digits (patterns).

Table 12–6 XML Schema Definition Data Types

Data Types	Description
String	data is any set of characters
Integer	data is any whole number not a fraction
Decimal	data is any number that contains a decimal fraction
Date	represent the date as YYYY-MM-DD
Boolean	binary logic of true or false, yes or no, on or off
Binary	a set of binary codes in groups of eight
AnyURI	a valid URI Internet address

Custom data types are quite common in database systems. These data types help in validating data fields, to reduce erroneous data entry. Table 12–7 shows an example custom data type. The example shows a simple type field called age_range, which has a domain between 18 and 70. A **domain** is a set of valid values for a database field.

Table 12–7 XML Custom Data Types

Custom Data Type Example
<xs:simpleType name="age_range"> <xs:restriction base=xs:integer"> <xs:minInclusive value="18" /> <xs:maxInclusive value="70" /> </xs:restriction> </xs:simpleType> <xs:element name="employee"> <xs:complexType> <xs:sequence> <xs:element name="employment_age" type="age_range" /> </xs:sequence> </xs:complexType> </xs:element name="employee">

An XML Schema Definition is an XML file and starts with an XML processing statement. The general form of the XML processing instruction is shown in Table 12–8.

Table 12–8 General Form of a Processing Instruction	
General form:	<?target attribute1="value" attribute2="value"?>
Comment:	The ? identifies this as a processing instruction. The target is the name of the application. The attributes and values tell the processor how to handle the statement. The values assigned to the attributes can be enclosed in single or double quotation marks, as long as they are consistent.
Examples:	<?xml?> <?xml version="1.0"?> <?xml version="1.0" encoding="UTF-8" standalone="yes"?>

The next statement in the XML Schema Definition is the <xs:schema> root element. This statement contains a namespace declaration. Table 12–9 shows a simple root element with namespace declaration for a single XML file.

Table 12–9 General Form of a Root Element	
Root element:	<xs:schema xmlns:xs="http://www.w3.org/2001/XMLSchema" [targetNamespace="URI" xmlns="URI" elementFormDefault="qualified"] >
Comment:	The xs is the namespace. The xmlns is XML namespace location and associates the xs to the schema of all schemas at the w3.org Web site. The most commonly used namespaces are xs or xsd. The optional elements within the brackets include targetNamespace that associates other namespace items with the designated URI. The xmlns defines the default namespace location and the elementFormDefault indicates the definition must be a qualified namespace.
Example	<xs:schema xmlns:xs="http://www.w3.org/2001/XMLSchema">

Developers add documentation to their XML Schema Definition files using the <annotation> and <documentation> tags. Documentation should include descriptions of all changes made to files by whom and when. In the XML Schema Definition, <annotation> and <documentation> tags are used. Table 12–10 describes the general format of the <annotation> and <documentation> tags in an XML Schema Definition file.

Table 12–10 General Form of annotation and Documentation Elements	
General form:	<namespace:annotation [id="value" | other attributes]> <namespace:documentation [source=URI | xml:lang="language"> Descriptive text </namespace:documentation> </namespace:annotation>
Comment:	The <annotation> element is the top-level tag for descriptive documentation. The <annotation> element may have an optional id or other non schema attributes. The <documentation> element tag denotes that the text within the opening and closing tags is non schema data. The <documentation> element may have an optional Web source of information. The xml:lang attribute identifies the language of the documentation content.
Examples:	<xs:annotation> <xs:documentation> This XSD describes the data structure of Classic Books created March 9, 2012 by SWD. </xs:documentation> </xs:annotation>

To Enter the Code for the Prolog, Root, Annotation, and Documentation Elements

Table 12–11 shows the code to begin a new XML Schema Definition with a prolog, root, annotation, and documentation tags.

Table 12–11 Code for the Prolog, Root, Annotation, and Documentation Elements

Line	Code
1	<?xml version="1.0" encoding="utf-8" standalone="yes" ?>
2	
3	<xs:schema xmlns:xs="http://www.w3.org/2001/XMLSchema">
4	
5	<xs:annotation>
6	<xs:documentation>
7	This XSD describes the data structure of Classic Books created March 9, 2012 by SWD.
8	</xs:documentation>
9	</xs:annotation>
10	
11	</xs:schema>

Line 1 is a standard XML processing statement. Line 3 is the <schema> root element and assigns namespace declaration from the w3.org Web site. Line 5 is the beginning <annotation> tag for documentation. Line 6 is the <documentation> tag. Line 7 is the description of this file. Lines 8 and 9 close the tags started on lines 5 and 6. Line 11 is the closing <schema> element tag.

The following step illustrates how to enter the code for the prolog, root, annotation, and documentation elements.

- Click line 1.
- Enter the XML code shown in Table 12–11 to create the beginning of the XML Schema Definition with the prolog, root, annotation, and documentation elements, as shown in Figure 12–6.

Q&A Why is the closing root tag included?

It is included so you do not forget to add it at the end of the schema, thus causing an error when the schema is validated.

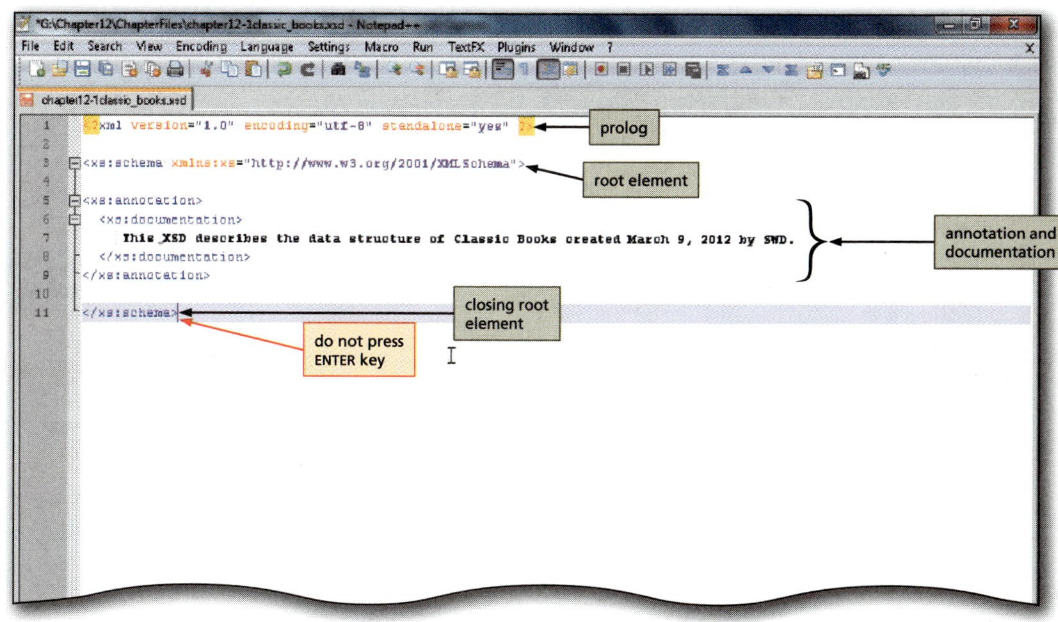

Figure 12–6

Defining the Parent Element

The next part of the schema defines the parent element, <classic_books>. This element is a complex type because it contains a child element, <book>. The attributes of minOccurs and maxOccurs indicate the cardinality. **Cardinality** is the number of relationships between a parent and child element. The minOccurs attribute indicates that at least one book must exist, and the maxOccurs attribute of unbounded indicates there can be an infinite number of books.

To Enter Code for the <classic_books> Element

Table 12–12 shows the code for inserting the parent element.

Table 12–12 Code for Inserting the <classic_books> Element

Line	Code
11	<xs:element name="classic_books">
12	<xs:complexType>
13	<xs:sequence>
14	<xs:element name="book" type="childType" minOccurs="1" maxOccurs="unbounded" />
15	</xs:sequence>
16	</xs:complexType>
17	</xs:element>

Line 11 is an element tag that defines the classic_books element in the XML document. Line 12 indicates this is a complex data type element with children. The <sequence> tag at line 13 indicates the following elements must appear in sequence. Only one element is identified in line 14, and that is book with the minOccurs and maxOccurs attributes, used to define cardinality. Lines 15, 16, and 17 close the element tags in 13, 12, and 11, in order.

The following step illustrates how to enter the code for the parent element.

- Click line 10 and press the ENTER key once to place the insertion point on a blank line 11.
- Enter the XML code shown in Table 12–12 to add the classic_books element tags.
- Press the ENTER key twice after line 17 (Figure 12–7).

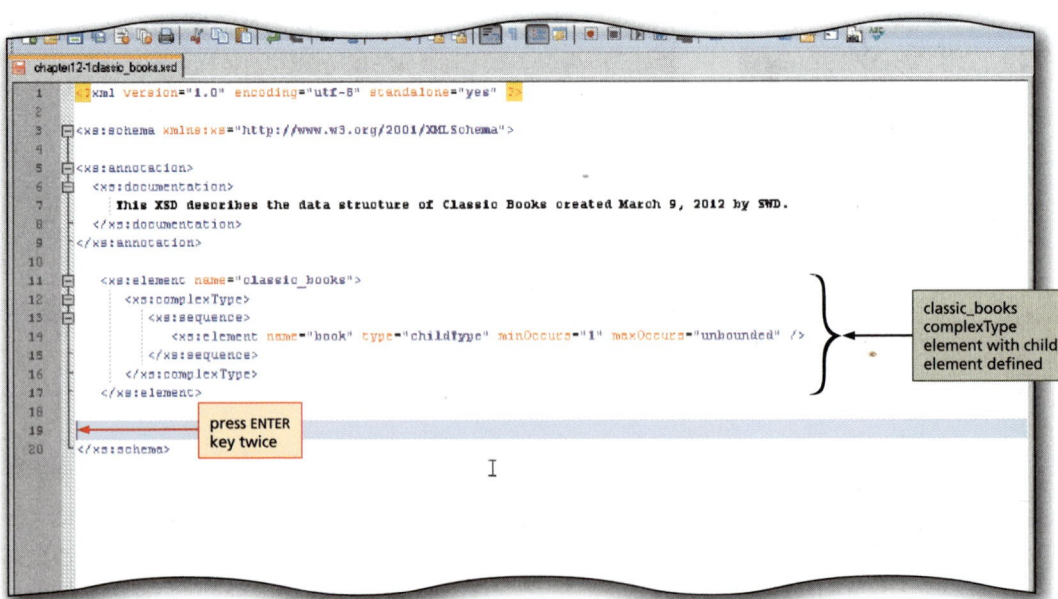

Figure 12–7

Defining and Inserting the Child Elements

The next part of the schema defines the child elements, which are defined as <complexType> elements using a group element. Table 12–13 describes the basic form of a <group> element.

Table 12–13 General Form of a Group Element

Group element:	<namespace:group [id=ID name=Name ref=referencedName maxOccurs=positive Integer minOccurs=zero or any positive Integer any attributes] >
Comment:	The group element indicates a series of elements are part of a larger group element. The id is a unique name. The name specifies the name for the group and is used only when the element is the parent of the group. Ref relates this group to another group element. The name and ref attributes cannot be used together. The minOccurs and maxOccurs indicate a valid range of values that can occur with a minimum of zero (minOccurs) to infinity as defined by unbounded in maxOccurs. The any attributes are any non-XML attributes.
Example	<xs:group ref="childElements" />

To Enter Code for the <complexType> Element

The code in Table 12–14 shows the XML Schema Definition element tags to define the group elements.

Table 12–14 Code for Inserting the <complexType> Elements

Line	Code
19	`<xs:complexType name="childType">`
20	`   <xs:group ref="childElements" />`
21	`</xs:complexType>`

Line 19 is a <complexType> element that indicates the following element is a child element. Line 20 expands this definition by indicating with a <group> element tag that the group elements belong to a child element, which is <book>. Line 21 closes the <complexType> element. The following step illustrates how to enter the code for the <complexType> element.

1

- If necessary, click line 19.
- Enter the XML code shown in Table 12–14 to enter the <complexType> element to define the group elements.
- Press the ENTER key twice after line 21 and position the insertion point at the beginning of line 23 (Figure 12–8).

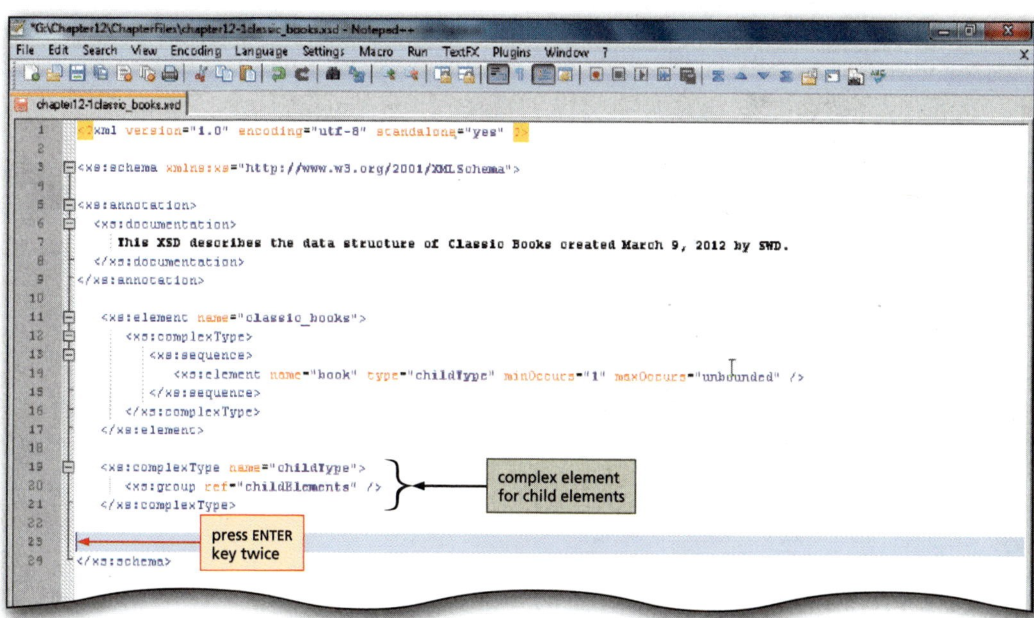

Figure 12–8

To Enter Code for the Child Group Elements

The last <group> element lists the individual elements that belong to the <book> element. The <book> element is a child of the <classic_books> element, and each book instance has elements that describe the book. These descriptive (or <sequence>) elements are child elements of the <book> element. The code in Table 12–15 contains the group element and the <sequence> elements for each individual book and that item's data type.

Table 12–15 Code for Inserting the <group> Element

Line	Code
23	`<xs:group name="childElements">`
24	`    <xs:sequence>`
25	`        <xs:element name="title" type="xs:string" />`
26	`        <xs:element name="year" type="xs:string" />`
27	`        <xs:element name="author" type="xs:string" />`
28	`        <xs:element name="qoh" type="xs:integer" />`
29	`        <xs:element name="bin" type="xs:string" />`
30	`        <xs:element name="cost" type="xs:decimal" />`
31	`    </xs:sequence>`
32	`</xs:group>`

Line 23 is the <group> element that relates the <sequence> items to the child element (book), which is referenced by the name childElements on line 20. Line 24 starts the <sequence> elements. Recall that elements after a <sequence> element must be in order as they exist in the XML file. Lines 25 through 30 are element tags that name the individual fields and define their data type. Line 31 closes the <sequence> element tag and line 32 closes the <group> element tag. The closing </xs:schema> element (line 34) was entered with the prolog in Table 12–11 so it would not be forgotten.

The following step illustrates how to enter the code for the <group> element to define the childElements that belong to the <book> element.

- If necessary, click line 23.
- Enter the XML code shown in Table 12–15 to enter the <group> element to define the childElements, pressing the ENTER key once after line 32 (Figure 12–9).

```
<xs:schema xmlns:xs="http://www.w3.org/2001/XMLSchema">

<xs:annotation>
  <xs:documentation>
    This XSD describes the data structure of Classic Books created March 9, 2012 by SWD.
  </xs:documentation>
</xs:annotation>

   <xs:element name="classic_books">
      <xs:complexType>
         <xs:sequence>
            <xs:element name="book" type="childType" minOccurs="1" maxOccurs="unbounded" />
         </xs:sequence>
      </xs:complexType>
   </xs:element>

   <xs:complexType name="childType">
      <xs:group ref="childElements" />
   </xs:complexType>

   <xs:group name="childElements">
      <xs:sequence>
         <xs:element name="title" type="xs:string" />
         <xs:element name="year" type="xs:string" />
         <xs:element name="author" type="xs:string" />
         <xs:element name="qoh" type="xs:integer" />
         <xs:element name="bin" type="xs:string" />
         <xs:element name="cost" type="xs:decimal" />
      </xs:sequence>
   </xs:group>

</xs:schema>
```

child element with data types

press ENTER key once

Figure 12–9

To Save and Validate an XML Schema Definition File

The following steps illustrate how to re-save the XML Schema Definition file and check that it is a valid XML document.

- With the USB drive plugged into your computer, click the Save icon on the Notepad++ toolbar to re-save the chapter12-1classic_books.xsd file.
- Close the chapter12-1classic_books.xsd file, but don't close Notepad++.
- Start your browser and type `www.w3.org/2001/03/webdata/xsv` in the Address box and press the ENTER key.
- Scroll down to find the section that begins with "Use this form only if you are behind a firewall or have a schema to check which is not accessible via the Web" as shown in Figure 12–10.

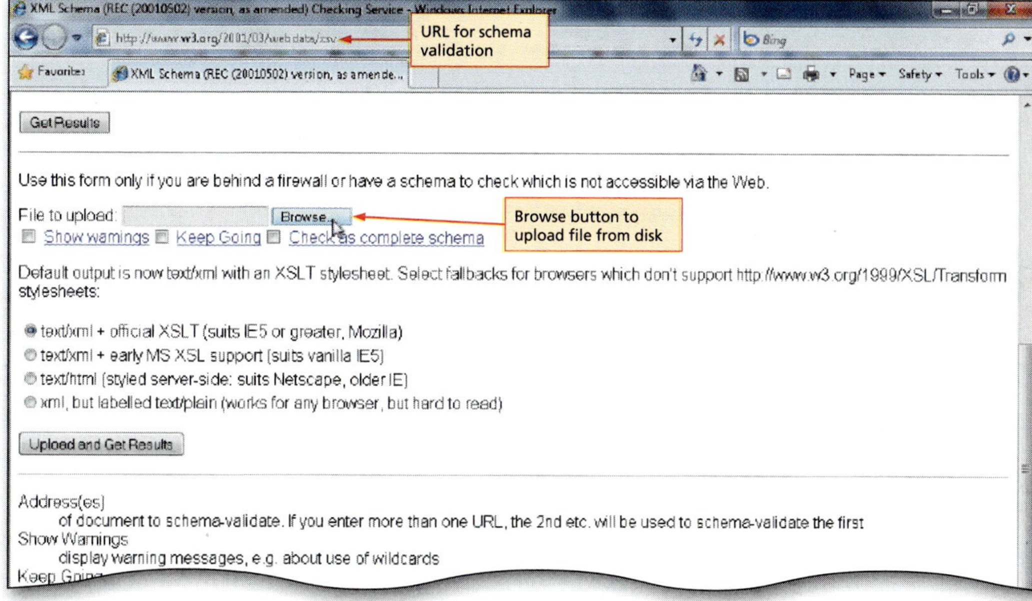

Figure 12–10

2

- Click the Browse button and navigate to your USB drive.
- Double-click the chapter12-1classic_books.xsd file to select the XML Schema definition file for the validation Web page.
- Click the Show warnings and Keep Going check boxes, but not the Check as complete schema check box (Figure 12–11).

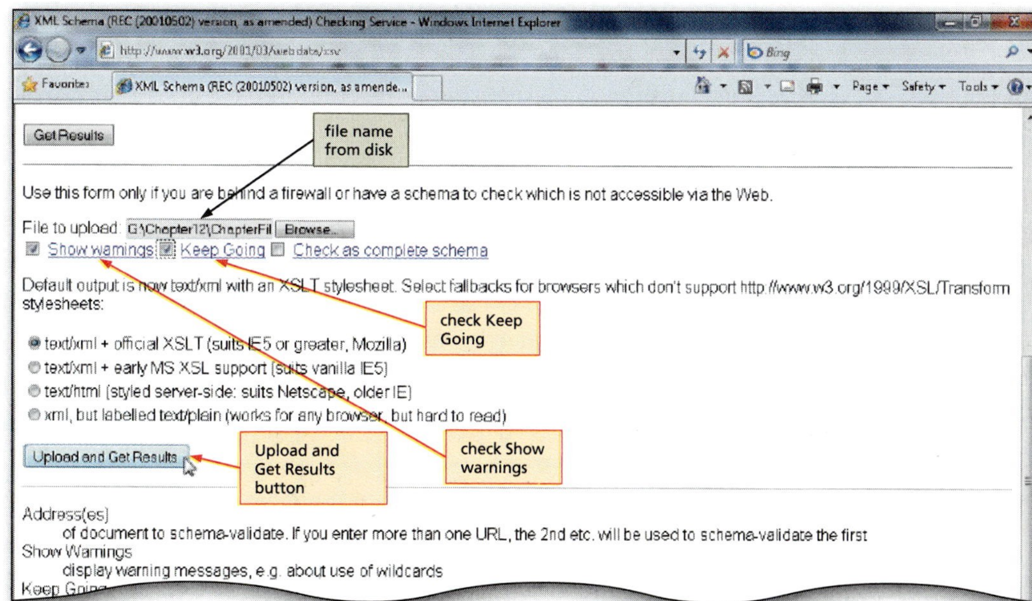

Figure 12–11

Q&A Why didn't we click the Check as complete schema check box?

This should be checked if the schema and the XML file are going to be validated together. We have not yet completed the XML file.

- Click the Upload and Get Results button. A valid XML Schema Definition will have no error messages (Figure 12–12).

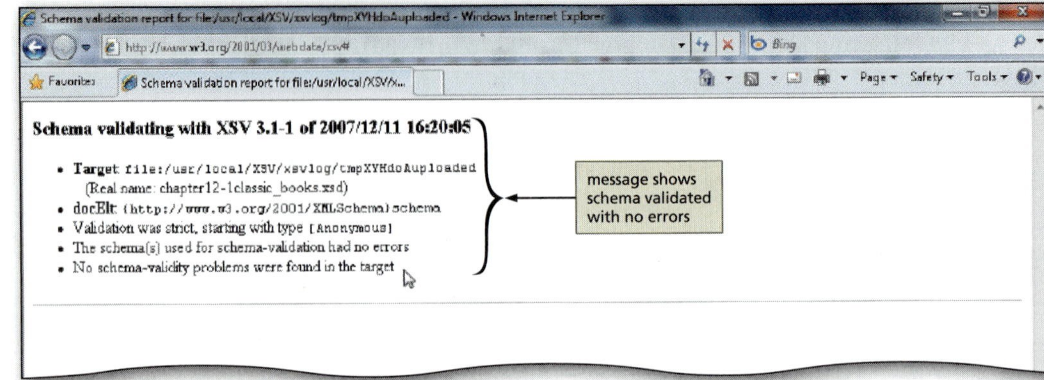

Figure 12–12

Q&A I have an error; it did not validate. What do I do?

You need to check your code and make sure everything is spelled and formatted as indicated in the tables. Check for missing tags or tags not closed properly.

Plan Ahead

Creating the XML document file.
The first step in creating an XML document is to create the prolog. The following tasks are necessary to create the prolog and begin a well-formed XML document:

1. Enter the XML declaration.
2. Enter an XML comment (HTML comment tag) to identify the name of the XML file as documentation.

Creating the Prolog in an XML Document

The first statement in an XML prolog is the XML declaration. The **XML declaration** is a processing instruction in the prolog that provides additional information to the application that will process the XML document. Although optional, the first processing instruction in most XML document prologs is the XML declaration. This processing statement is the same as described in Table 12–8 on page HTML 574.

The prolog also can contain comments that provide a user or developer with information about the document. XML comments are very similar in form to HTML comments. As with HTML comments, the browser or parser ignores the XML comments. Table 12–16 presents the general form of an XML comment.

Table 12–16 General Form of an XML Comment

General form:	<!- - comment statements -->
Comment:	Comments are optional and can be placed anywhere between tags, but not within a tag. Comments must begin with the left angle bracket (<), an exclamation point (!), and double hyphens (--). The comment must terminate with the double hyphens (--) and the right angle bracket (>).
Valid example:	<!- - File Name: chapter12-1classic_titles.xml - -> <Tag><!- - Comment about tag --></Tag>
Invalid example:	<Tag <!- - This tag is new -->>Data</Tag>

To Create a New XML Document and Enter the Prolog Code

The code in Table 12–17 contains the code for the prolog in the XML file.

Table 12–17 Code for the Prolog

Line	Code
1	`<?xml version="1.0" encoding="utf-8" standalone="yes" ?>`
2	`<!-- File Name: chapter12-1classics.xml -->`

Line 1 is the XML declaration that identifies this as an XML document using XML version 1.0, uses the utf-8 coding standard, and identifies that this is a stand-alone file. Line 2 is a comment stating the name of the XML file. Prior to the recommendation by W3C, a Document Type Definition (DTD) would follow. Because this text follows the current recommendation to use the XML Schema Definition, the XSD file created previously will be attached in the document instance code. The following step illustrates how to use Notepad++ to create a new XML document and enter the prolog code.

- If necessary, activate the Notepad++ window.
- Click File on the menu bar, then click New to create a new Notepad++ document.
- With the USB drive plugged into your computer, click File on the menu bar, and then click Save As on the File menu.
- If necessary, navigate to the Chapter12\ChapterFiles folder on UDISK (G:).
- Type `chapter12-1classics.xml` in the File name text box.
- Click the Save button in the Save As dialog box (Figure 12–13).

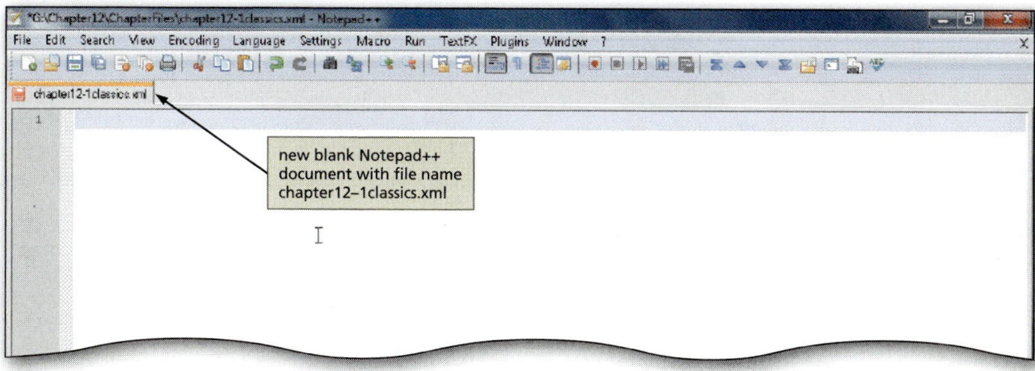

Figure 12–13

2

- If necessary, click line 1.
- Enter the XML code shown in Table 12–17 to create the prolog and press the ENTER key twice (Figure 12–14).

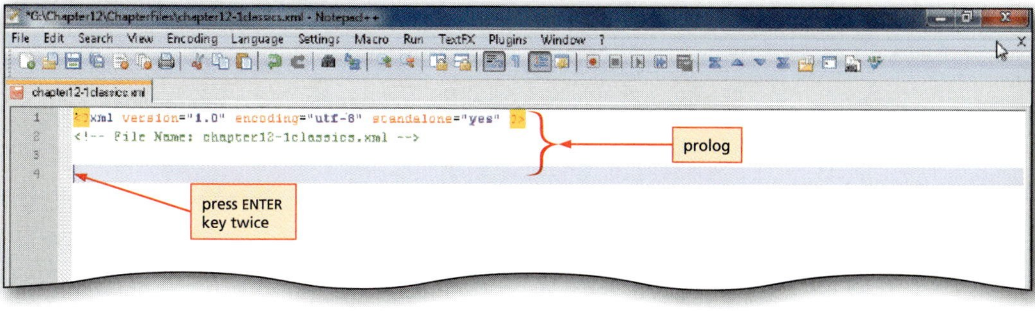

Figure 12–14

Q&A

Why isn't the link to the XSD file in the prolog?

It will be entered as part of the root element of the document instance.

Plan Ahead

Creating a document instance.

The main data of an XML document is the document instance. The document instance is all the components of the document, whether the document is free-form text or a database. When creating the document instance, a designer should complete the following tasks:

- Use the relation or logical schema with attributes created in the XML Schema Definition.
- Determine if namespaces are necessary if duplicate identifier names are used.
- Identify the data values for the various XML elements.

Creating the Document Instance in an XML Document

The second part of an XML document is the document instance, or elements. The document instance section contains the document elements and actual content or data. There must be one root element with all other elements nested inside the root. This format creates a hierarchical, treelike structure. This structure defines the XML document as a well-formed document. Table 12–18 shows the general form of an element tag.

Table 12–18 General Form of an Element Tag

General form:	<element start tag>element contents</element end tag>
Comment:	XML documents require start and end element tags. The element tag name must be a valid name. The tag describes the type of content represented by the element (for example, Title, Year). Start and end tags must match exactly in spelling and case. The element contents or data are the text entered between the tags.
Examples:	<NAME>Konner Ridge</NAME> <ADDRESS>23 Monroe St.</ADDRESS> <PHONE>256-5533</PHONE>

To Start Entering a Document Instance in an XML Document

As shown in Table 12–19, title, year, author, qoh, bin, and cost are all child elements within the book element. The book element is a child element nested within the <classic_books> root element.

Table 12–19 Code for Inserting the Document Instance

```
<classic_books xmlns:xsi="http://www.w3.org/2001/XMLSchema-instance"
xsi:noNamespaceSchemaLocation="chapter12-1classicbooks.xsd">
   <book>
      <title>Huckleberry Finn</title>
      <year>1885</year>
      <author>Twain, Mark</author>
      <qoh>3</qoh>
      <bin>541-230</bin>
      <cost>8.99</cost>
   </book>
```

Line 4 represents the root element of the XML document, with the start <classic_books> tag. Line 5 is a continuation of the root element that identifies and binds the XML Schema Definition file to this XML document. Line 6 defines the <book> element. Lines 7 through 12 are the child elements of the <book> element, with one instance for each occurrence of a data item. Line 13 is the </book> element end tag. The following step shows how to start entering the document instance in the XML document, chapter12-1classics.xml.

1

- If necessary, click line 4.
- Enter the XML code shown in Table 12–19 to create the root and first document instance. Press the ENTER key after line 13 (Figure 12–15).

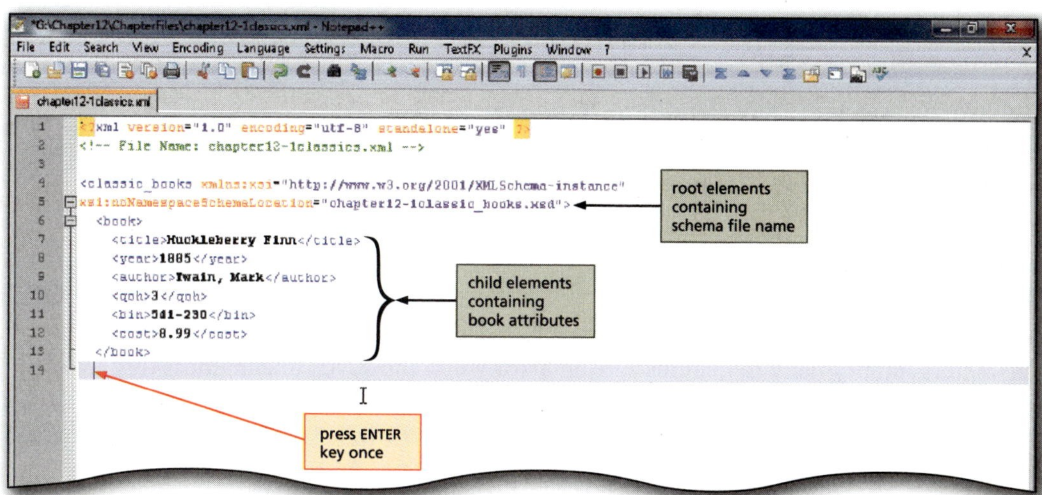

Figure 12–15

To Finish Entering a Document Instance in an XML Document

To complete the document instance, the remaining elements for each book record in the list are entered using the same format, as shown in Table 12–20.

Table 12–20 Code for Completing the Document Instance

Line	Code
14	`<book>`
15	`    <title>The Deerslayer</title>`
16	`    <year>1841</year>`
17	`    <author>Cooper, James Fenimore</author>`
18	`    <qoh>2</qoh>`
19	`    <bin>541-131</bin>`
20	`    <cost>17.99</cost>`
21	`  </book>`
22	`  <book>`
23	`    <title>Adventures of Tom Sawyer</title>`
24	`    <year>1876</year>`
25	`    <author>Twain, Mark</author>`
26	`    <qoh>2</qoh>`
27	`    <bin>541-232</bin>`
28	`    <cost>12.99</cost>`
29	`  </BOOK>`

Table 12–20 Code for Completing the Document Instance (continued)

Line	Code
30	`<book>`
31	`<title>The Last of the Mohicans</title>`
32	`<year>1826</year>`
33	`<author>Cooper, James Fenimore</author>`
34	`<qoh>3</qoh>`
35	`<bin>541-333</bin>`
36	`<cost>16.99</cost>`
37	`</book>`
38	`</classic_books>`

Lines 14 through 37 repeat elements for each book. The end </BOOK > tag on line 29 is entered in uppercase characters intentionally to demonstrate an error when the XML document is displayed in the browser. Line 38 is the end tag for the root element, </classic_books>.

The following step illustrates how to enter the remainder of the document instance for the XML document, chapter12-1classics.xml.

1

- If necessary, click line 14, indented as shown in Figure 12–15.
- Enter the XML code shown in Table 12–20 with the error on line 29 to finish creating the document instance and do not press the ENTER key (Figure 12–16).

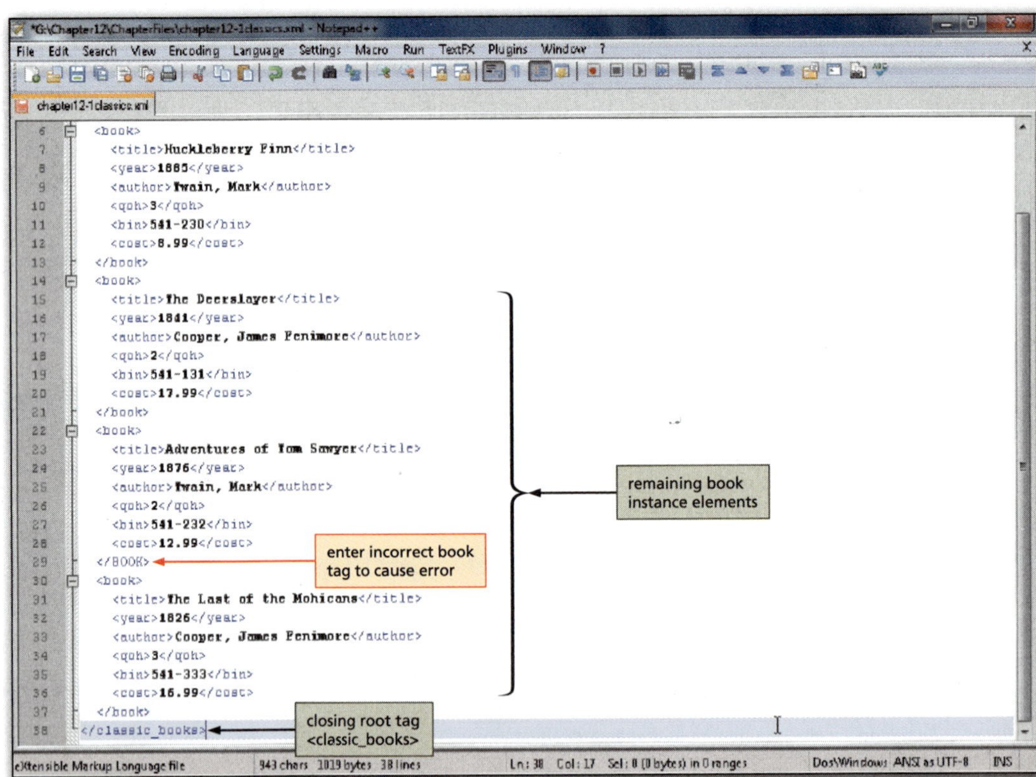

Figure 12–16

To Save and Test an XML Document in a Browser

The following steps show how to save and test the XML document.

1. With a USB drive plugged into your computer, click the Save Icon on the Notepad++ toolbar to save the completed chapter12-1classics.xml document.
2. Start your browser. If necessary, click the Maximize button.
3. Click the Address bar.
4. Type `g:\Chapter12\ChapterFiles\chapter12-1classics.xml` and then press the ENTER key to display the completed document (Figure 12–17).

Q&A An error message occurred and the document did not display. What happened?

The tag on line 29 is not correct and generates an error. The error message indicates that the </BOOK> tag did not match a starting <book> tag.

Q&A This error was made on purpose, so we know the line number. How do I find the line number of an accidental error?

Double-click the triangular warning shield in the lower-left corner of the browser next to Done. If necessary, click OK, and an error dialog box will display with the line number.

Q&A Will the browser show all the errors at one time?

Unfortunately, you will have to correct each error as it is found by the browser; the browser parser stops processing when it finds the first error.

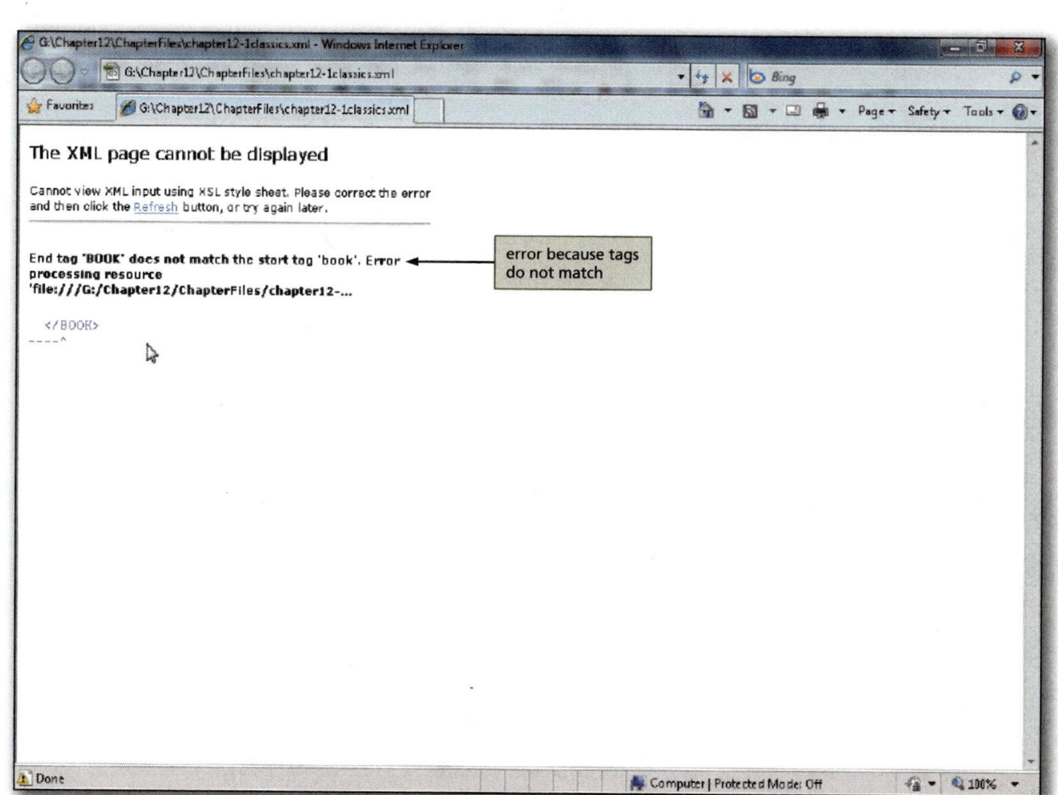

Figure 12–17

To Correct a Tag Error and Retest an XML Document

The following steps show how to correct the tag error and retest the XML document.

1

- Click the Notepad++ button on the taskbar.
- Click line 29.
- Delete the uppercase </BOOK> tag.
- Type `</book>` as the new tag in place of the deleted tag to correct the closing book tag (Figure 12–18).

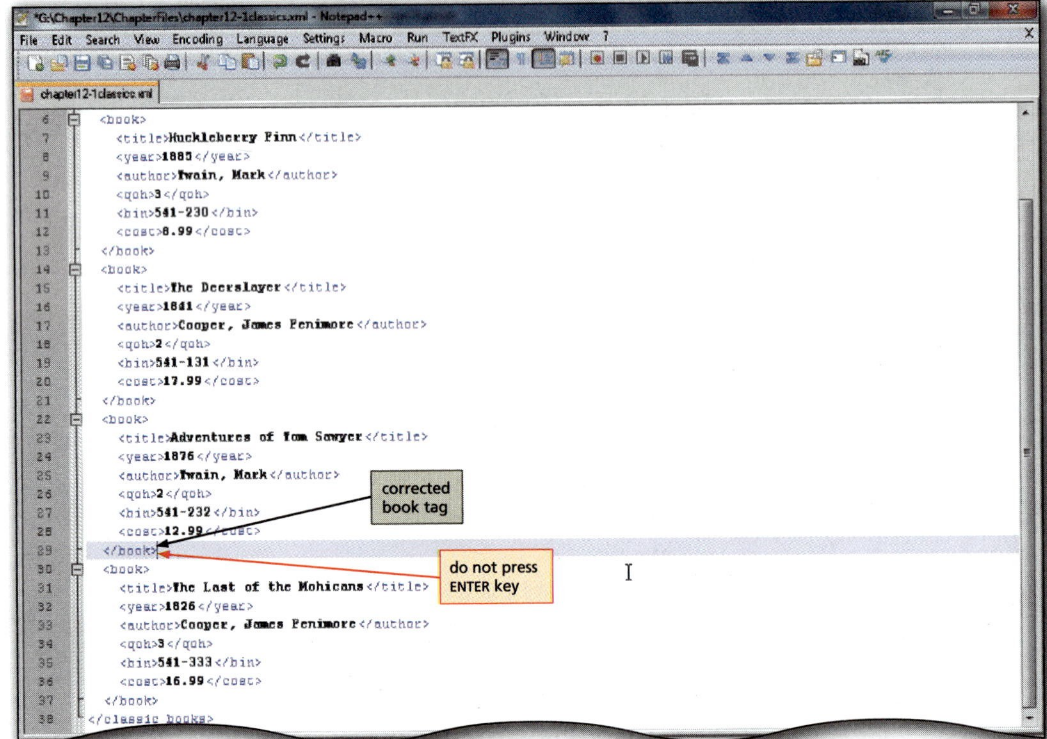

Figure 12–18

2

- Click the Save icon on the Notepad++ toolbar to save the corrected file.
- Activate the browser.
- Click the Refresh button on the browser toolbar to display the corrected page (Figure 12–19).
- If necessary, click the security bar under the tabs, and then click Allow Blocked Content on the shortcut menu.
- If necessary, click Yes in the Security Warning dialog box.

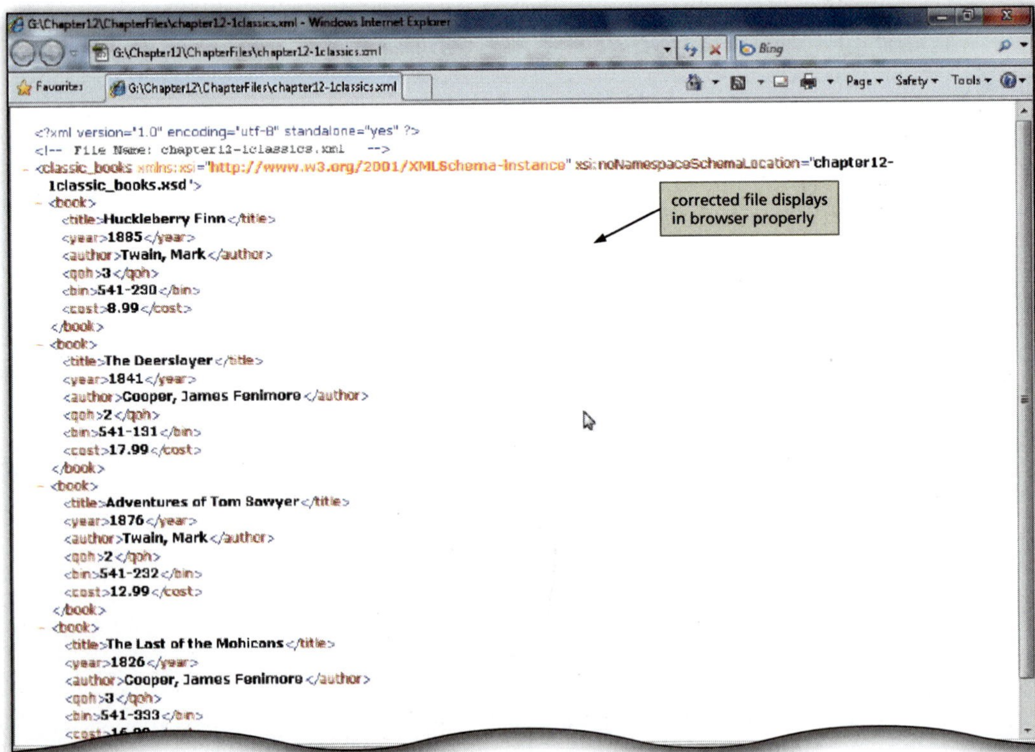

Figure 12–19

Q&A What are the minus signs by the <classic_books> and <book> tags?

The minus signs preceding the tags <classic_books> and <book> indicate the level or node (root or child) of the data. A user can collapse or expand the levels of the document by clicking a plus sign to expand or a minus sign to collapse. An XML document, however, can be quite difficult to read as an unformatted Web page.

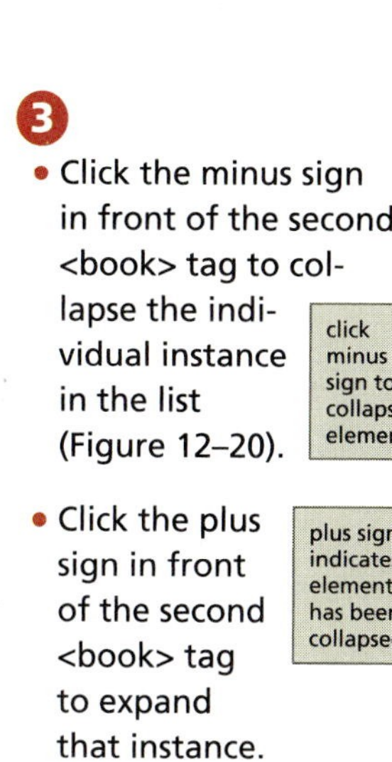

3

- Click the minus sign in front of the second <book> tag to collapse the individual instance in the list (Figure 12–20).
- Click the plus sign in front of the second <book> tag to expand that instance.

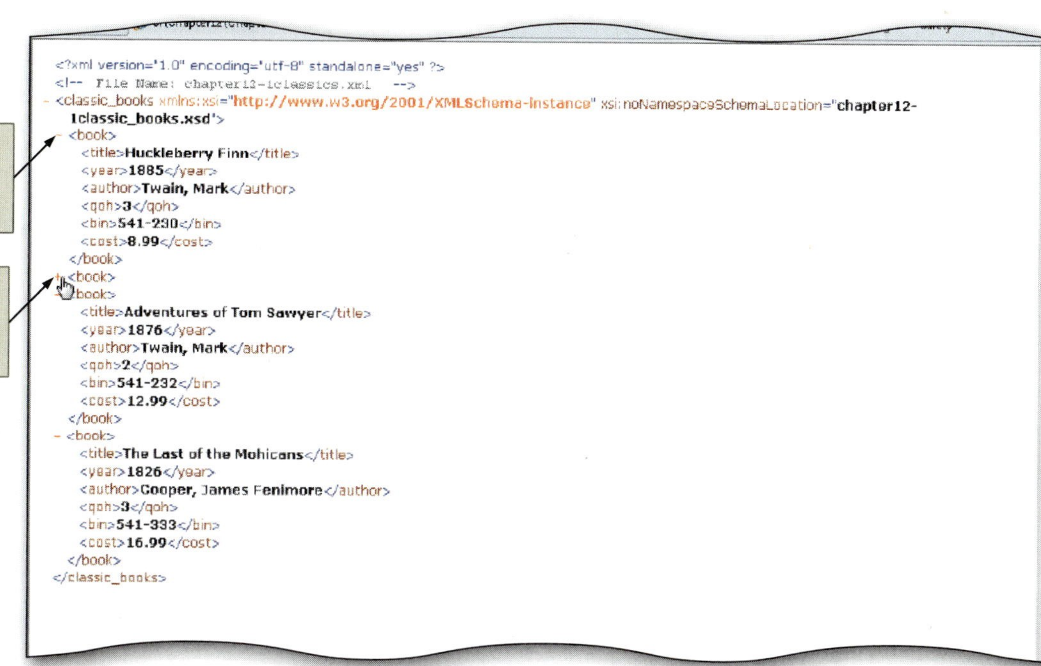

Figure 12–20

Q&A

What would happen if I clicked the minus sign in front of the first <classic_books> tag?

The entire list of instances would collapse and none of the child <book> tags would be visible.

To Validate XML and XSD Files

Once the XSD and XML files are created and bound together with the <xml> tag you should validate that the XSD does define the XML instance. The following steps show how to validate the XSD and XML files using a Web site that offers this service.

1

- If necessary, activate your browser.
- Click the Address bar.
- Type `tools.decisionsoft.com/schemaValidate/index.jsp` and then press the ENTER key to load the Web page (Figure 12–21).

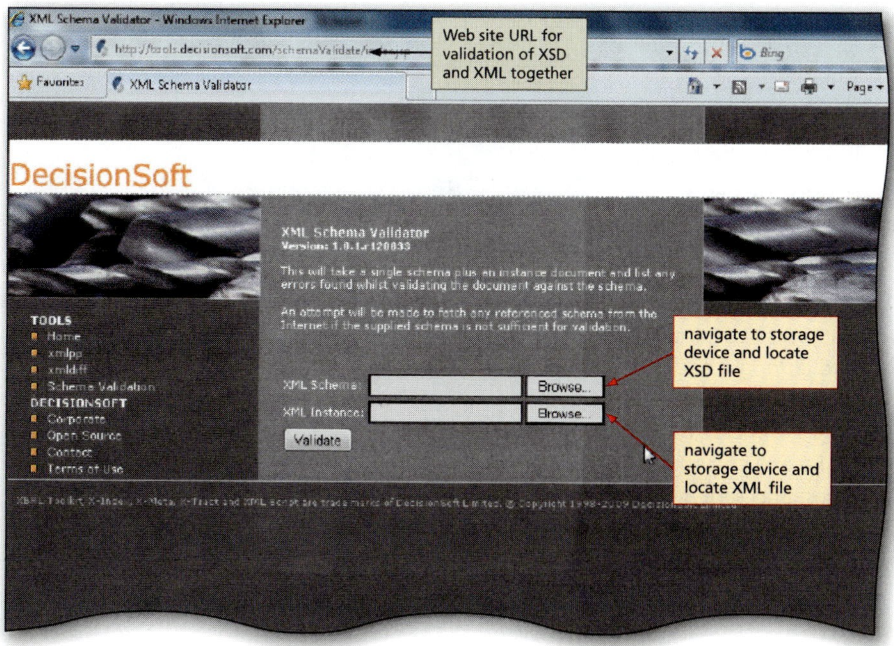

Figure 12–21

2

- Click the Browse button next to the XML Schema text box.
- Navigate to your storage device and locate the XML Schema Definition file, chapter12-1classic_books.xsd.
- Click the Open button on the Choose File to Upload dialog box.
- Click the Browse button next to the XML Instance text box.
- Navigate to your storage device and locate the XML document instance file, chapter12-1classics .xml.
- Click the Open button on the Choose File to Upload dialog box.

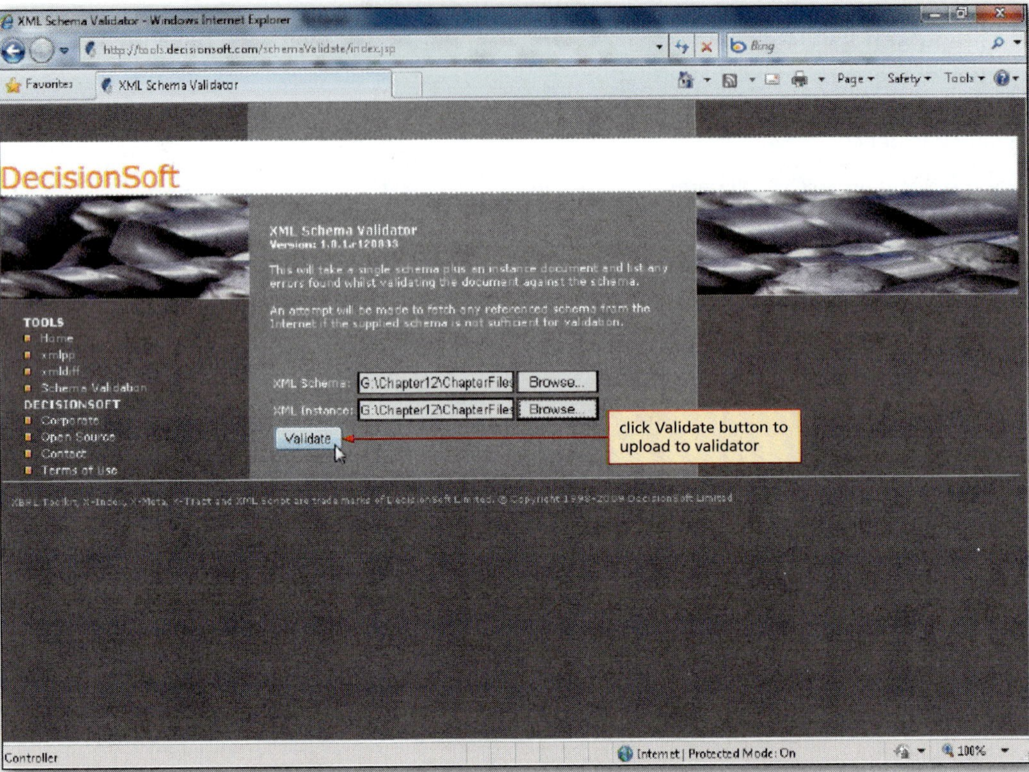

Figure 12–22

3

- Click the Validate button on the XML Schema Validator to upload the files.
- When the Web page indicates the XML instance and XML schema are present, click the Click here link to see the results (Figure 12–23).

Q&A

What do I do if it returns errors?

Look at the line numbers indicated, and compare the code in Figures 12–9, 12–15, and 12–16, make any corrections, and repeat Steps 1 through 3.

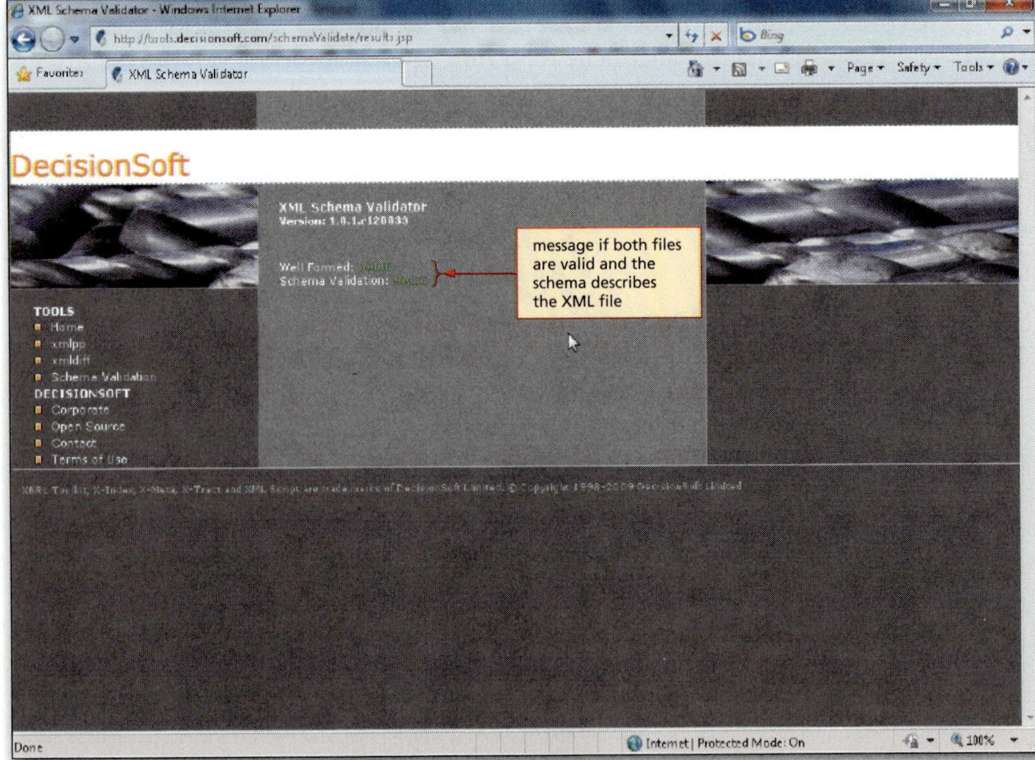

Figure 12–23

Plan Ahead

Formatting and linking an XSL style sheet to an XML document.
XSL style sheets are used to transform an XML document into a more stylized document. To create an XSL document, perform these tasks:

1. Determine the XML document elements that will be displayed and how you want them to appear.
2. Determine the XSL elements:
   a. Determine if the <template> element will use all or only some elements.
   b. Determine the for-each elements.
   c. Determine the style for each XSL value-of element and format with <span> tags and inline styles.
   d. Determine if sorting is required and which XML element to use as a sort key.
   e. Determine any descriptive text that is needed.
3. Link the XSL style sheet to the XML document.

Formatting an XML Document Using an XSL Style Sheet

This section outlines the techniques needed to format the display of an XML document using the Extensible Stylesheet Language (XSL) and to bind the XML document to the XSL style sheet. Recall that the Browse by Author link on the Classic Books home page links to an XML document that will display the books in ascending order by author name (Figure 12–1b on page HTML 565). The output and display of this XML document are defined using an XSL style sheet that sets each record to be displayed in a list, sorted in ascending order by the <author> element.

Instead of the .xml file you started, you will continue with a file supplied in the Data Files for Students that is similar but contains additional books. The next steps are to open that document, save it with a new name, and then create the XSL style sheet to format and place the book listing in the desired order.

BTW

XSL
XSL is three languages: one to transform XML (XSLT), one to define XML parts or patterns (XPath), and one to format objects and define the XML display (XSL). An XSL style sheet assumes that the associated XML document uses a hierarchical structure, which contains a root element, child elements, and any optional attributes, namespaces, processing statements, or comments. An XSL style sheet cannot transform any other type of document, such as Word, PDF, or PostScript files, into HTML documents.

To Open an XML Document and Save It with a New Name

Next, you open the XML document, chapter12-1classic_more.xml, supplied in the Data Files for Students. See the inside back cover of this book for instructions on downloading the Data Files for Students, or contact your instructor for information about accessing the required files. Because you will modify this file, you will save it with a new name.

The following steps illustrate how to open the XML document, chapter12-1classic_more.xml, and save it as chapter12-1classic_books.xml.

1. Click the Notepad++ button on the status bar to activate the Notepad++ window.
2. With the USB drive plugged into your computer, click File on the menu bar, and then click Open on the File menu.
3. If necessary, navigate to the Chapter12\ChapterFiles folder on the USB drive. Click All types (*,*) in the Save as type: drop-down list.
4. Double-click chapter12-1classic_more.xml in the list of files.
5. Click File on the menu bar, and then click Save As on the File menu.
6. If necessary, navigate to the Chapter12\ChapterFiles folder on UDISK (G:).

7 Type `chapter12-1classic_books.xml` in the File name text box.

8 Click the Save button in the Save As dialog box.

BTW

The XSL stylesheet Element

The xsl:stylesheet or xsl:transform element must have a version number and should be written as follows: <xsl:stylesheet version="1.0" xmlns:xsl="http://www.w3.org/1999/XSL/Transform"> or <xsl:transform version="1.0" xmlns:xsl="http://www.w3.org/1999/XSL/Transform">. The version number is required because the namespace code, xmlns:xsl="http://www.w3.org/1999/XSL/Transform", indicates the use of the official W3C specification.

Creating an XSL Style Sheet

As previously stated, an XML document can be formatted with CSS or XSL style sheets. Most Web developers agree that formatting with CSS is impractical and prefer to use XSL style sheets. An XSL style sheet performs two actions: it formats and transforms XML documents. An XSL style sheet can **transform** an XML document by instructing the browser or parser to output the XML document in a completely different form. XSL takes the XML document, called a **source**, and produces completely different output, called a **result tree**.

An XSL style sheet uses syntax similar to the syntax used for XML documents and has the same hierarchical, treelike structure as other XML documents. Each of the style sheet elements in an XSL style sheet must use the namespace prefix, **xsl**, to distinguish the XSL elements from XML elements. The general form of the stylesheet element in an XSL style sheet is shown in Table 12–21. For a complete list of XSL style sheet elements, see the XML Quick Reference in Appendix H.

Table 12–21 General Form of the stylesheet Element in an XSL Style Sheet

General form:	<xsl:stylesheet xmlns:prefix="URL" language="language"> ... *(other stylesheet code)* </xsl:stylesheet> or <xsl:transform version="v.x" xmlns:prefix="URL" language="language"> ... *(other stylesheet code)* </xsl:transform>
Comment:	The stylesheet element is the root element of an XSL style sheet. The prefix defines the xml namespace (xmlns). The namespace allows duplicate names to be used in a document. The URL indicates the official XSL specification as recommended by the W3C. The language attribute is optional. The stylesheet element must be closed at the end of the document by the end tag, </xsl:stylesheet>.
Examples:	(1) <xsl:stylesheet xmlns:xsl="http://www.w3.org/TR/WD-xsl"> (2) <xsl:transform version="1.0" xmlns:xsl="http://www.w3.org/1999/XSL/Transform">

BTW

The XSL template Element

The XSL template element associates each output with an input. The match="/" attribute defines the entire document.

The **stylesheet element** establishes a namespace, so the remaining elements, such as the template, can use names that will not be confused with other elements. A **template** is an instruction that identifies the elements in a document that should be transformed or converted and then specifies how the element should be transformed. The browser refers to the template when displaying a particular element in the XML document. The template is the most important part of the XSL style sheet, and the XSL style sheet must include at least one template element. Table 12–22 shows the general form of the template element.

Table 12–22 General Form of the template Element

General form:	<xsl:template match="pattern" language="language"> ... *(other stylesheet code)* </xsl:template>
Comment:	The pattern indicates the XML element or node. A pattern of "/" indicates that the entire document will be displayed. The template element needs an end element.
Example:	<xsl:template match="/"> ... *(other stylesheet code)* </xsl:template>

To Start Creating an XSL Style Sheet

This XSL style sheet will display the books in order by author name, using the <author> tag element in the XML file. Table 12–23 shows the code for the processing instruction, an XML declaration, a stylesheet element, and a template element in an XSL style sheet.

Table 12–23 Code for Creating an XSL Style Sheet

Line	Code
1	<?xml version="1.0" encoding="utf-8" standalone="yes" ?>
2	<xsl:transform version="1.0" xmlns:xsl="http://www.w3.org/1999/XSL/Transform">
3	<xsl:template match="/">

Line 1 is the XML declaration that identifies this as an XML document using XML version 1.0. Line 2 is the XSL stylesheet element used to define the namespace, xsl, for the remaining elements. Line 3 defines the template pattern, using a "/" to indicate that the template applies to the entire XML document. The following step illustrates how to start creating an XSL style sheet.

1

- If necessary, activate the Notepad++ window.
- Click File on the menu bar, and then New to start a new Notepad++ document.
- With your USB drive plugged into your computer, click File on the menu bar, and then click Save As.
- If necessary, navigate to the Chapter12\ChapterFiles folder on UDISK (G:).

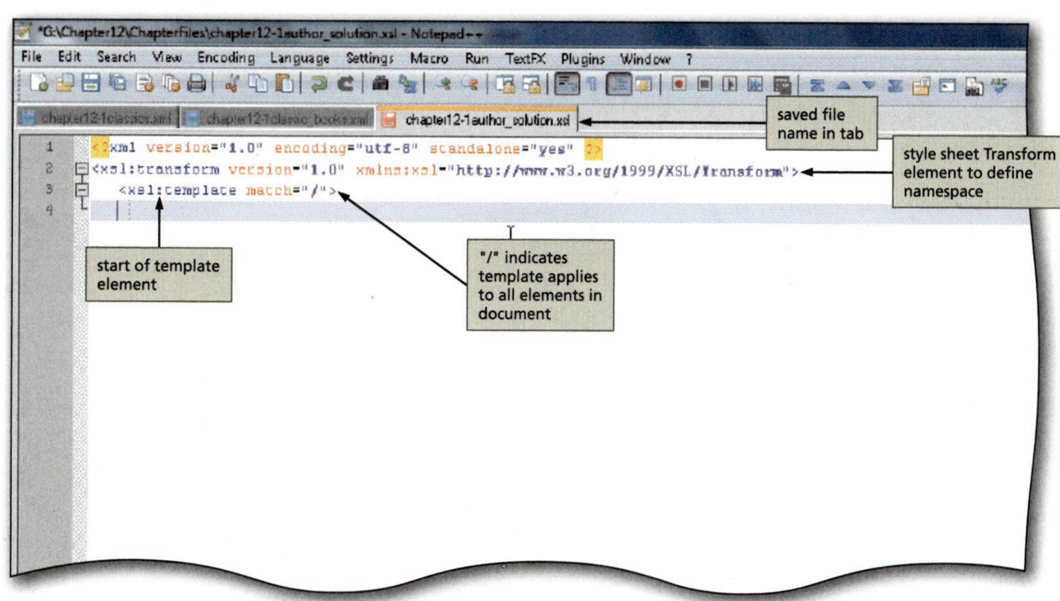

Figure 12–24

- Type `chapter12-1author_solution.xsl` in the File name text box.
- Click the Save button in the Save As dialog box to save the chapter12-1author_solution.xsl style sheet.
- Enter the code shown in Table 12–23 to start the XSL style sheet, and then press the ENTER key once after line 3 (Figure 12–24).

Q&A What happens if more than one XSL style sheet is linked to an XML document?

If more than one XSL style sheet is linked to an XML document, the first XSL style sheet the browser reads is used and the others are ignored.

Q&A Can an XSL style sheet and Cascading Style Sheet both be linked to an XML document?

If an XSL style sheet and a Cascading Style Sheet both are linked to an XML document, the XSL style sheet is used and the Cascading Style Sheet is ignored.

To Enter HTML Code to Display the Banner and Text Title in a Web Page

The next step is to enter the HTML tags that will display the banner and text title in the browser. The <p> and <span> tags will use inline CSS styles to format and center the banner and text on the Web page. This code must be placed after the <template> tag and is shown in Table 12–24.

Table 12–24 Code for the HTML Tags to Center the Banner and Title Text

Line	Code
4	<p align="center">
5	<img border="0" src="chapter12-1banner.jpg" /></p>
6	<p align="center">
7	<span style="font-weight:bold; font-family:arial, helvetica, sans-serif; font-size:14pt">
8	Classic Books Listing - Browse by Author</span></p>

Line 4 is a paragraph tag with an align attribute to center the banner <img> in line 5. The closing </p> tag is after the <img> tag. Line 6 is a new <p> tag with an align attribute to center the Web page title text. The <span> tag in line 7 contains the inline style to format the title text as bold, Arial font, and size 14. Line 8 contains the text title and the closing </span> and </p> tags. The following step illustrates how to enter the HTML tags to center the banner and center and format the title text.

- Click line 4.
- Enter the code shown in Table 12–24 to enter the HTML tags to center the banner and format the title text. Press the ENTER key after line 8 (Figure 12–25).

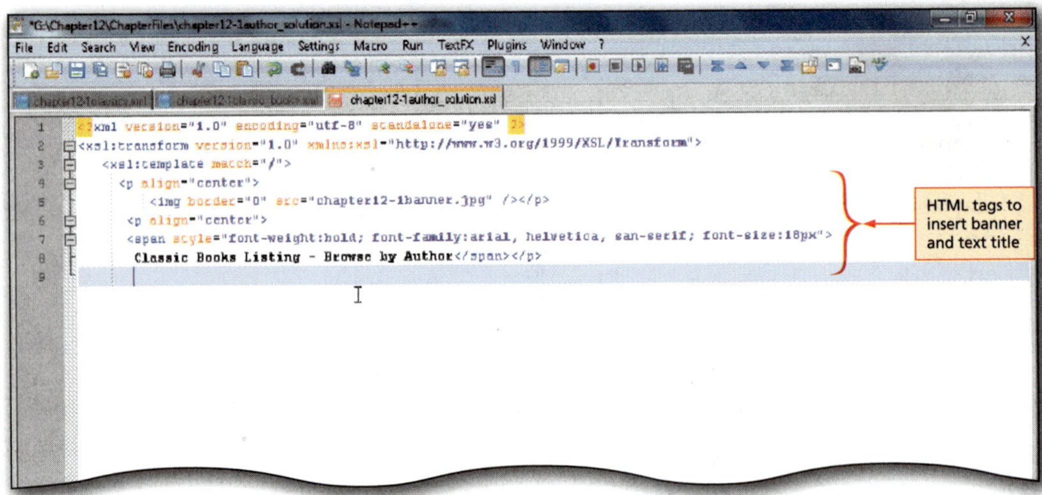

Figure 12–25

Using XSL Style Sheet Tags

By combining the XSL elements and XML markup tags, an XSL style sheet tells the browser how to transform and format the XML document to display records in paragraph mode on the Web page. In this project, you will use the for-each, sort, text, and value-of XSL style sheet tags. The **for-each** element makes each element appear in the list, and associates each child element <book> related with the <classic_books>. This association identifies the XML elements that should appear in the books list on the Web page. Table 12–25 shows the general form of the for-each element.

Table 12–25 General Form of the for-each Element

General form:	<xsl:for-each select="pattern">
Comment:	The for-each element returns the associated child element's data identified by the select attribute pattern. As the for-each cycles through the data, each of the child nodes contained in the pattern name becomes the current node element or record.
Example:	<xsl:for-each select="classic_books/book">

BTW

The XSL for-each Element
The for-each element allows a developer to "loop" through a set of XML data. The use of the for-each selects every item in a set of nodes. In the event of multiple items, the first value is used.

XSL style sheets allow for a more free-form, yet organized, display of data. To display the books in order by author name, use the sort element as shown in Table 12–26.

Table 12–26 General Form of the sort Element

General form:	<xsl:sort [select="value" lang="token" data-type="value" order="ascending|descending" case-order="upper-first|lower-first"] />
Comment:	The sort element has five optional attributes: select, lang, data-type, order, and case-order. The select attribute value indicates on which element to sort; lang indicates the language of the sort keys. The system default language is assumed. Data-type is used to indicate the data type of the select value (alphabetic or numeric). In an alphabetic sort, numbers are sorted alphabetically, meaning 100 comes before 99. Numeric data types sort numbers in their correct numeric order. Order indicates ascending (default) or descending. Case-order indicates if uppercase or lowercase order should be first.
Example:	<xsl:sort select="author" data-type="text" />

BTW

The XSL sort Element
If the select attribute is omitted, the XSLT processor sorts on all the elements as a string as the sort key.

In conjunction with the for-each element, to display text on a page, XSL uses the <xsl:text> tag. Any text placed between the <xsl:text> and closing </xsl:text> tags will display based on the formatting of any HTML tags. Recall that spaces in XML documents are kept, unlike in HTML documents where special codes must be used to insert a space.

To display any element values from the XML document, the XSL style sheet uses the XSL value-of element to display each instance within the books list. Table 12–27 shows the general form of the XSL value-of element.

Table 12–27 General Form of the value-of Element

General form:	<xsl:value-of select="pattern" />
Comment:	The value-of element indicates that the page should display the value for the specified element. The pattern value of the select attribute identifies the name of the specific element used in the output.
Example:	<xsl:value-of select="title" />

BTW

The XSL value-of Element
The value-of element transfers the value of the designated XML tag (field) to the output document.

To Add XSL Style Sheet Tags

Table 12–28 on the next page shows the code for the remainder of the XSL to sort the data by author in ascending order and display the author, title, year, cost, and qoh in a sentence format on the Web page.

Table 12–28 Code for Adding the for-each, sort, text, and value-of XSL Style Sheet Tags

Line	Code
9	`<xsl:for-each select="classic_books/book">`
10	`<xsl:sort select="author" data-type="text" />`
11	`<p>`
12	`<span style="font-weight:bold; text-decoration:underline; color:#7f0000">`
13	`<xsl:value-of select="author" />`
14	`</span>`
15	`<xsl:text> wrote </xsl:text>`
16	`<span style="font-variant:small-caps; font-weight:bold">`
17	`<xsl:value-of select="title" />`
18	`</span>`
19	`<xsl:text> published in  </xsl:text>`
20	`<span style="font-family:arial, helvetica, sans-serif">`
21	`<xsl:value-of select="year" />.`
22	`</span>`
23	`<span style="font-weight:bold; color:#2f1fff">The cost is </span>`
24	`<xsl:value-of select="cost" />. We have`
25	`<span style="font-style:italic; font-weight: bold; color:#2f1fff">`
26	`<xsl:value-of select="qoh" /> in stock.`
27	`</span>`
28	`</p>`
29	`</xsl:for-each>`
30	`<p style="font-family:helvetica,arial; font-weight:bold">` `<a href="chapter12homesolution.html">Home</a></p>`
31	`</xsl:template>`
32	`</xsl:transform>`

Line 9 is the <for-each> tag that cycles through the XML file displaying each individual instance. Line 10 is the <sort> that directs the elements to be displayed in sorted order on the author's name using the <author> element. The paragraph <p> tag on line 11 displays each record on a separate line. Line 12 is a <span> tag with an embedded style sheet used to set the font weight to bold. Line 13 uses the value-of select attribute to display the value for the author element. Line 14 closes the <span> tag started on line 12, so the next text displayed does not use the same style.

Line 15 uses the text attribute to insert the text "wrote" between the author's name and the title of the book displayed by line 17. The style in line 16 displays the title in small caps and bold text. Line 19 inserts the text "published in" and the <span> tag on line 20 uses an embedded style sheet to set the font of the year, which is displayed with the <value-of> tag in line 21. Line 22 closes the <span>. Line 23 starts a new <span> to format the text "The cost is". Line 24 uses the value-of select attribute to display the cost of the book, and the text "We have". Line 25 is a <span> tag with an embedded style to format the <value-of> tag for the quantity on hand (qoh) element followed by the text "in stock". Line 27 closes the <span> tag on line 25.

Line 28 closes the <p> on line 11. Line 29 closes the <for-each>. Line 30 is a <p> tag with an embedded style followed by an <a href> tag to create a link back to the home page. Line 31 closes the <xsl:template> tag on line 3. Line 32 closes the <xsl:transform> tag on line 2, which began the XSL markup tag elements.

The following step shows how to enter the remaining code to complete the XSL style sheet.

1

- If necessary, click line 9.
- Enter the code shown in Table 12–28, indenting as shown, to complete the XSL style sheet (Figure 12–26).

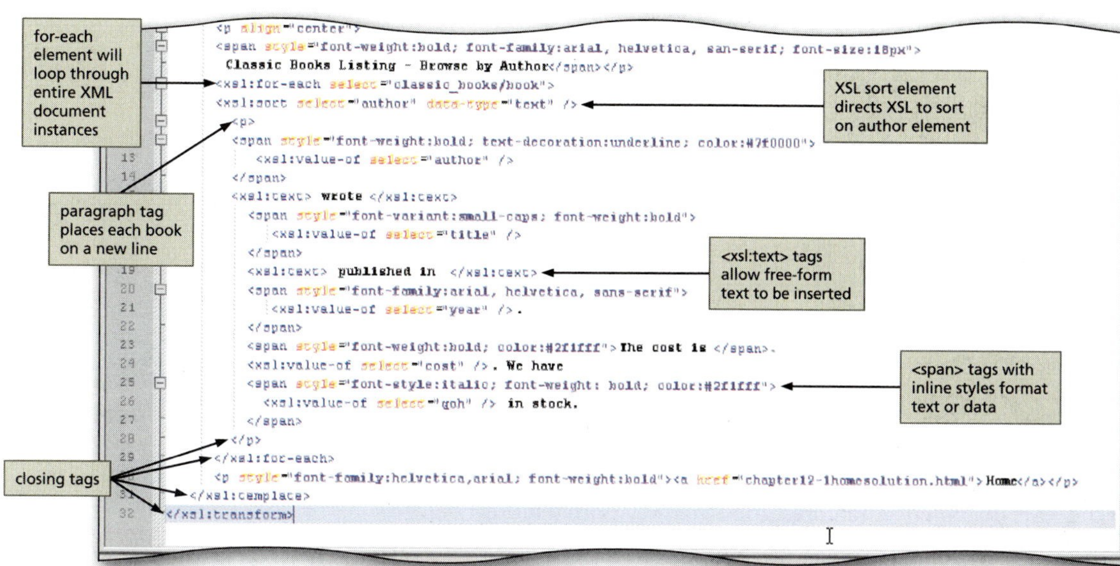
for-each element will loop through entire XML document instances
paragraph tag places each book on a new line
closing tags
XSL sort element directs XSL to sort on author element
<xsl:text> tags allow free-form text to be inserted
<span> tags with inline styles format text or data
<p align="center">
<span style="font-weight:bold; font-family:arial, helvetica, san-serif; font-size:18px">
Classic Books Listing - Browse by Author</span></p>
<xsl:for-each select="classic_books/book">
<xsl:sort select="author" data-type="text" />
<p>
<span style="font-weight:bold; text-decoration:underline; color:#7f0000">
<xsl:value-of select="author" />
</span>
<xsl:text> wrote </xsl:text>
<span style="font-variant:small-caps; font-weight:bold">
<xsl:value-of select="title" />
</span>
<xsl:text> published in </xsl:text>
<span style="font-family:arial, helvetica, sans-serif">
<xsl:value-of select="year" />.
</span>
<span style="font-weight:bold; color:#2f1fff">The cost is </span>.
<xsl:value-of select="cost" />. We have
<span style="font-style:italic; font-weight: bold; color:#2f1fff">
<xsl:value-of select="qoh" /> in stock.
</span>
</p>
</xsl:for-each>
<p style="font-family:helvetica,arial; font-weight:bold"><a href="chapter12-1homesolution.html">Home</a></p>
</xsl:template>
</xsl:transform>

Figure 12–26

To Save an XSL Style Sheet

Once the XSL style sheet is complete, the file should be saved.

1 With your USB drive plugged into your computer, click the Save icon on the Notepad++ toolbar to re-save the XSL style sheet chapter12-1author_solution.xsl.

Linking an XSL Style Sheet to an XML Document

With the XSL file saved, the next step is to link the XSL style sheet to the XML document. For this part of the project, you will link the chapter12-1author_solution.xsl style sheet to the chapter12-1classic_books.xml file that you previously completed. Linking an XSL style sheet to an XML document requires an xml-stylesheet processing instruction. Table 12–29 shows the general form of this xml-stylesheet processing instruction.

Table 12–29 General Form of the xml-stylesheet Processing Instruction

General form:	<?xml-stylesheet type="text/xsl" href="file path"?>
Comment:	The processing instruction used to link an XSL style sheet contains the xml-stylesheet type attribute. The value, text/xsl, indicates that this is an XSL file. The href attribute indicates the external path or URI of the XSL file.
Example:	<?xml-stylesheet type="text/xsl" href="chapter12-1author_solution.xsl"?>

XSL style sheet processing instructions usually are entered in the prolog of the XML document.

To Link an XSL Style Sheet to an XML Document

The following step illustrates how to add an XSL style sheet processing instruction to link the XSL style sheet to the XML document, chapter12-1classic_books.xml.

- Click the chapter12-1classic_books.xml tab in Notepad++.
- Click at the beginning of line 3, then press the ENTER key once.
- On line 4, type <?xml-stylesheet type="text/xsl" href="chapter12-1author_solution.xsl"?> to enter the code to link the XSL style sheet to the XML document, then press the ENTER key once (Figure 12–27).

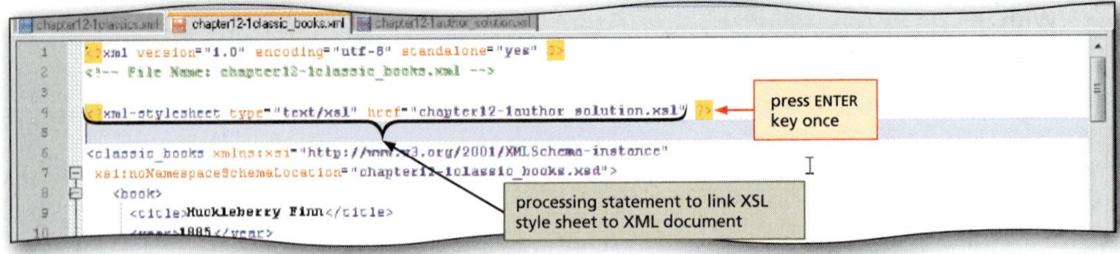

Figure 12–27

To Save and Test an XML Document Formatted Using an XSL Style Sheet

Once the XSL style sheet is complete and the processing instruction is added to the XML document, you should save and test the XML document in a browser. The following step shows how to save and test the XML document formatted using an XSL style sheet.

- With the USB drive plugged into your computer, click the Save icon on the Notepad++ toolbar to save the chapter12-1classic_books.xml file.
- Activate the browser.
- Click the Address bar.
- Type g:\Chapter12\ChapterFiles\chapter12-1classic_books.xml, and then press the ENTER key to display the XML document formatted by the XSL style sheet in author order (Figure 12–28).

Q&A What should I do if there is an error?

Check your code against Figures 12–25 and 12–26, save the XSL file, and then refresh the browser display.

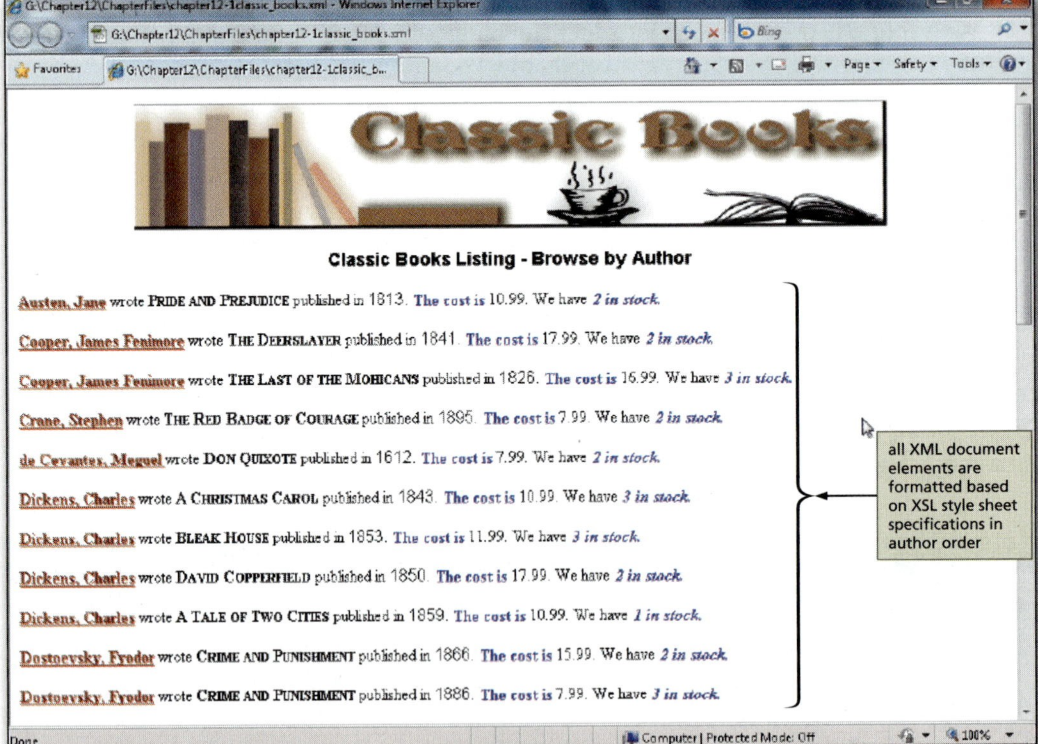

Figure 12–28

To Close the XML and XSL Files in Notepad++

Once the XSL style sheet is complete and the XML file displays properly, you should close the XSL and the XML files in Notepad++. The following steps show how to close the open files in Notepad++.

1. With the Notepad++ window active, right-click the chapter12-1classic_books.xml file tab, and click Close on the shortcut menu.
2. Right-click the chapter12-1classics.xml file tab and click Close on the shortcut menu.
3. Right-click the chapter12-1author_solution.xsl file tab, and click Close on the shortcut menu.

Plan Ahead

Displaying XML data in an HTML table.
Long lists of data can be tedious to look at. Dividing a list into manageable pages using a table can make the data easier to read. To plan a table:

- Determine the number of rows to display on each Web page.
- Determine the ID names to associate the objects properly with the table.
- Create the navigation control buttons for the table.
- Determine any style formatting for the data in the table.

Using an HTML Table with Paging to Display XML Data

The second hyperlink on the Classic Books home page (Figure 12–1c on page HTML 565) is Browse by Title. This Web page displays a list of available books in a table in title order (Figure 12–29) using the XML file as a data island. Recall that a data island is a set of data elements separate from the HTML Web page. The HTML Web page binds with the XML document and displays each record element in an HTML table. In Internet Explorer, the <table> tag has a nonstandard attribute, datapagesize, which dictates the number of rows that can be displayed. This attribute works only in Internet Explorer. The Web page has four buttons that use built-in browser functions, allowing users to navigate forward and backward through the table rows or to move to the first or last page.

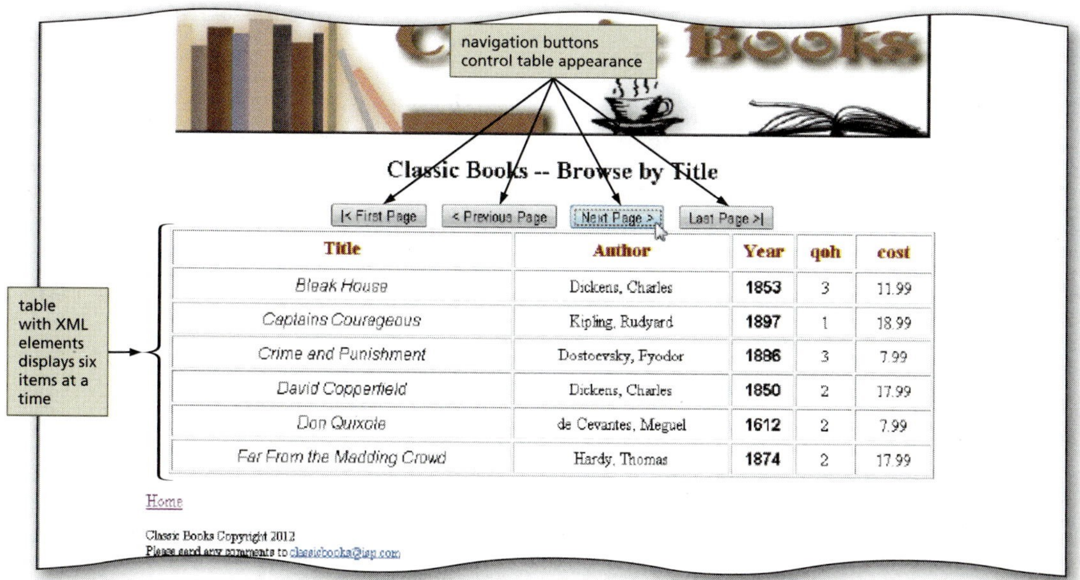

Title	Author	Year	qoh	cost
Bleak House	Dickens, Charles	1853	3	11.99
Captains Courageous	Kipling, Rudyard	1897	1	18.99
Crime and Punishment	Dostoevsky, Fyodor	1886	3	7.99
David Copperfield	Dickens, Charles	1850	2	17.99
Don Quixote	de Cevantes, Meguel	1612	2	7.99
Far From the Madding Crowd	Hardy, Thomas	1874	2	17.99

Figure 12–29

BTW

Data Binding

Data binding consists of four major pieces: the data source object (DSO), data consumers, the binding agent, and the table repetition agent.

Linking an XML document to an HTML Web page requires the use of the HTML element <xml> to create a data island. The <xml> tag also works only in Internet Explorer. A unique name represents the data island in the XML element, called a **data source object (dso)**. Table 12–30 shows the general form of the <xml> element. Because the <xml> tag is unique to Internet Explorer, this HTML Web page will not validate properly from the w3.org validation page.

Table 12–30 General Form of the HTML <xml> Element

General form:	<xml id="name" src="URL"></xml>
Comment:	The <xml> element is a Microsoft extension and may not be recognized by browsers other than Internet Explorer. The id attribute value, name, must be a unique name, and it must represent the data source. Web developers use the prefix dso before any name value to indicate that it is the data source object. The URL is the location and name of the XML data file. The <xml> element must have an end element.
Example:	<xml id="dsoBooks" src="chapter12-classic_books.xml"></xml>

BTW

The <xml> Tag and Validation

The <xml> tag is unique to Microsoft Internet Explorer. This tag is what links or binds an XML document to the Web page. This tag is not recognized by other browsers, so when validating the HTML pages, this tag will be identified as invalid.

When the browser opens the HTML Web page, the XML parser reads and parses the XML data. The browser then creates a data island or data source object (dso), which handles and manipulates the XML data as a recordset. A **recordset** is a collection of data records and their fields. The Internet Explorer browser also contains several built-in methods, properties, and events that are automatically associated with the recordset.

To Create an HTML Document to Display XML Data in a Table

The following steps illustrate how to create the HTML document to display the XML data in a table.

1. Activate the open Notepad++ window.
2. With a USB drive plugged into your computer, open the file chapter12-1table.html from the Chapter12\ChapterFiles folder.
3. Click File on the menu bar, and then click Save As.
4. Type `chapter12-1tablesolution.html` in the File name text box.
5. Click the Save button in the Save As dialog box to save the file with a new name (Figure 12–30).

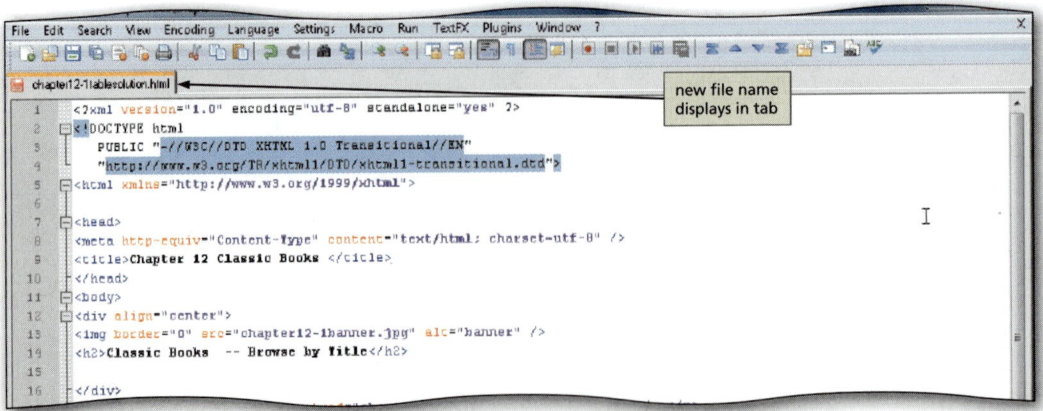

Figure 12–30

To Enter Code to Link an XML Document with an HTML Web Page

Because embedding the binding tags for an XSD or XSL file prevents the HTML table from reading the XML file, this section will use a different XML file provided in the Data Files for Students, chapter12-1classic_titles.xml. This file is in book title order. The following step illustrates how to bind this XML file with an HTML Web page.

1

- With the chapter12-1tablesolution.html Notepad++ window active, click line 6.
- Type <xml id="dsoBooks" src="chapter12-1classic_titles.xml"></xml> to link the XML document to the HTML Web page. Do not press the ENTER key (Figure 12–31).

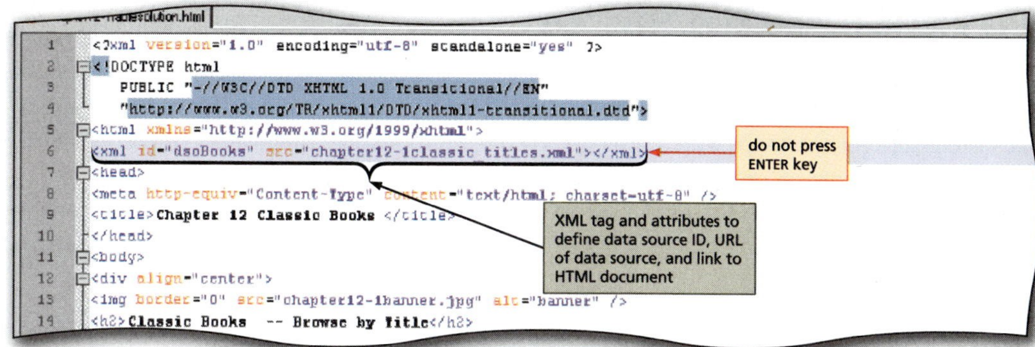

Figure 12–31

Adding Navigation Controls

The next step is to enter code to add the four navigation buttons that allow a user to manipulate the table appearance on the HTML Web page. Each of the four buttons calls an element method that will display the records in the table. Table 12–31 lists four table element methods.

Table 12–31 Table Element Methods

Method	Action	Example Code
firstPage	Displays the first page of records	TableName.firstPage()
previousPage	Displays the previous page of records	TableName.previousPage()
nextPage	Displays the next page of records	TableName.nextPage()
lastPage	Displays the last page of records	TableName.lastPage()

To Enter Code to Add Navigation Buttons

The buttons used to navigate through the records are standard HTML <form> buttons, but are entered without a form. When a user clicks a button, the onclick event handler calls the associated built-in method. Table 12–32 shows the code to add the navigation buttons to the HTML Web page.

Table 12–32 Code for Adding Navigation Buttons

Line	Code
15	<button onclick="bookTable.firstPage()">|< First Page </button>
16	<button onclick="bookTable.previousPage()">< Previous Page </button>
17	<button onclick="bookTable.nextPage()"> Next Page > </button>
18	<button onclick="bookTable.lastPage()"> Last Page >| </button>

The bookTable object in each line associates the onclick event handlers for each button to the <table> tag, which will have an id attribute bookTable that will be entered in a later step.

Line 15 creates the First Page button with the caption |< First Page. The code < is an ASCII character set that creates a less-than symbol (<), or angle bracket, on the button caption. The First Page button calls the firstPage() method, which tells the Web page to display the first set of records in the table. The code,   , is an ASCII character set to represent two spaces that separate the buttons. Line 16 creates the Previous Page button with the caption, < Previous Page. The Previous Page button calls the previousPage() method, which tells the Web page to display the previous set of records in the table. Line 17 creates the Next Page button with the caption, Next Page >. The > code is an ASCII character set that creates a greater than symbol (>), or angle bracket, on the button caption. The Next Page button calls the nextPage() method, which tells the Web page to display the next set of records in the table. Line 18 creates the Last Page button with the caption, Last Page >|. The Last Page button calls the lastPage() method, which tells the Web page to display the last set of records in the table. Each button uses the ASCII character set code,   , to place spaces between the buttons.

The following step illustrates how to enter the code to add the navigation buttons to the HTML Web page.

- Click line 15.
- Enter the code shown in Table 12–32 on the previous page and press the ENTER key twice after line 18 (Figure 12–32).

code for navigation buttons with built-in methods

press ENTER key twice

Figure 12–32

To Enter <table> Table Header and Row Tags

Table 12–33 shows the <table> tag and the attributes needed to indicate the width of the table, indicate the number of rows to be displayed, and bind the data source object. The code in Table 12–33 includes the table heading <thead> and the individual column heading names. An inline style attribute formats the text of the column headings.

Table 12–33 Code for <table> and Table Header and Row Tags

Line	Code
20	<table width="760" border="1" cellpadding="5" datapagesize="6" id="bookTable" datasrc="#dsoBooks">
21	<thead style="color:darkred; font-size:14pt; font-weight:900">
22	<tr>
23	<th width="290">Title</th>

Table 12–33 Code for <table> and Table Header and Row Tags (continued)

Line	Code
24	<th width="180">Author</th>
25	<th width="44">Year</th>
26	<th width="38">qoh</th>
27	<th width="57">cost</th>
28	</tr>
29	</thead>

Line 20 starts the table definition with the <table> tag and includes an id attribute to name the table, bookTable, which relates to the onclick event handler for the buttons and built-in functions. The datasrc attribute must match the name of the data source object defined in the <xml> element on line 6 and be preceded by a pound sign (#) to read: #dsoBooks. The datapagesize attribute sets the size of the page to 6, so the table will displayed six records or rows at a time. The border and cellpadding attributes define the look of the HTML table. Line 22 is a single table row <tr> tag. Lines 23 through 27 use the <thead> tag to create column headings. Line 28 is the closing </tr> tag, and line 29 is the closing </thead> tag. The following step shows how to enter the code to start the HTML table.

- If necessary, click line 20.
- Enter the code shown in Table 12–33 to create the table header and press the ENTER key once after line 29 (Figure 12–33).

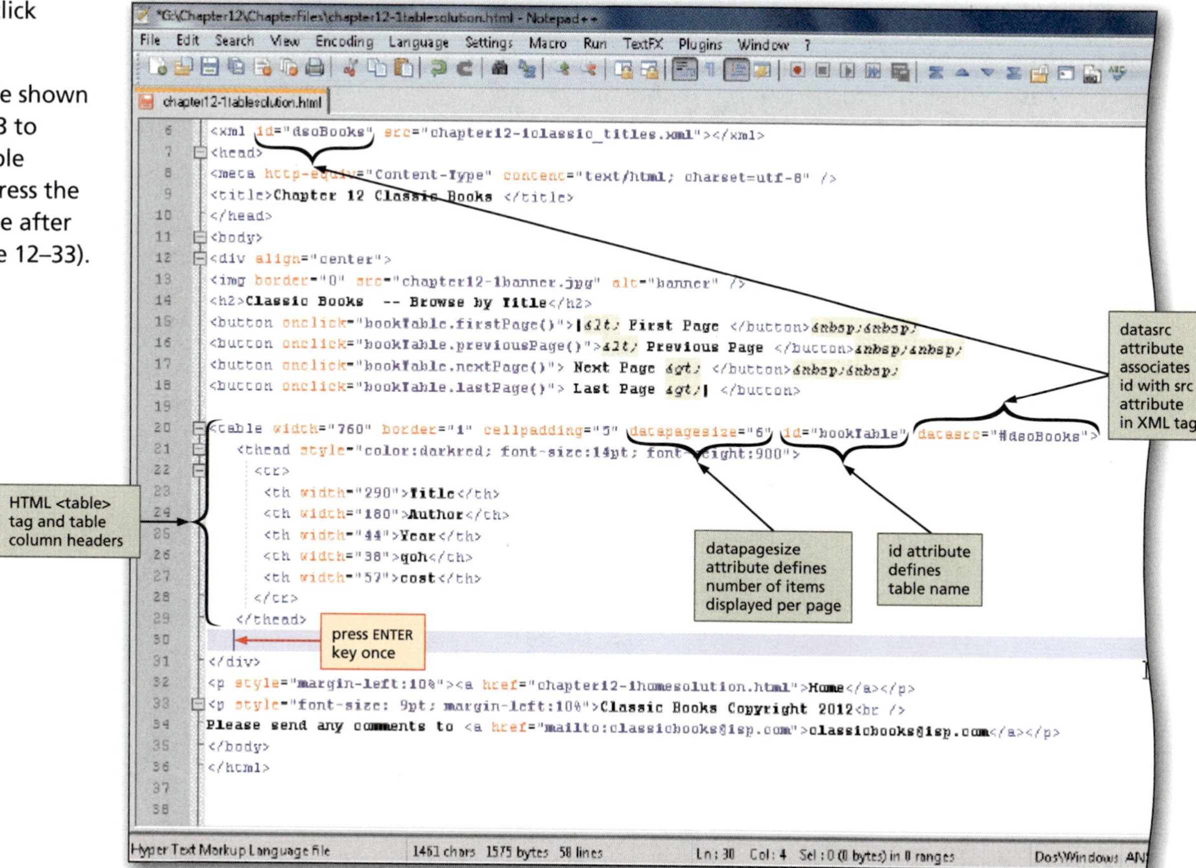

Figure 12–33

To Enter <tr> Tags and Attribute Values to Bind XML Elements to a Table

Table 12–34 shows the code to complete the table that will display each row of data. The table contains one row and five cells of data. The <span> tag and the datafld attribute identify the XML element value to be displayed in each cell. Inline styles format the contents of the cells.

Table 12–34 Code for <tr> Tags and Attributes to Bind the XML Elements to the HTML Table

Line	Code
30	`<tr>`
31	`<td><span datafld="title" style="font-family:arial; font-style:italic"></span></td>`
32	`<td><span datafld="author"></span></td>`
33	`<td><span datafld="year" style="font-family:arial; font-weight:900"></span></td>`
34	`<td><span datafld="qoh"></span></td>`
35	`<td><span datafld="cost"></span></td>`
36	`</tr>`
37	`</table>`

Line 30 creates a table row with the <tr> tag. Because the table automatically cycles through the data and is controlled by the datapagesize attribute, only one HTML table row is needed. Lines 31 through 35 create table data cells (<td> tags) using the <span> tags and the datafld attribute to define the specific XML element data value that appears in that cell. The <span> tags on line 31 and 33 also use an inline style to format the displayed values. Line 36 is the closing </tr> tag, and line 37 is the closing </table> tag. The following step illustrates how to enter the code to complete the table.

- If necessary, click line 30.
- Enter the code shown in Table 12–34 to bind the XML elements to the table rows. Do not press the ENTER key (Figure 12–34).

table data cell tags <td> and <span> tags with datafld attribute to define XML elements to display in each table cell

do not press ENTER key

Figure 12–34

To Save the HTML File and Test the Web Page

With the Web page code complete, you should save and test the HTML Web page.

1

- With the USB drive plugged into your computer, click the Save icon on the Notepad++ toolbar.
- Activate your browser. If necessary, maximize the window.
- Click the Address bar.
- Type `g:\Chapter12\ChapterFiles\chapter12-1tablesolution.html` and then press the ENTER key so the Web page is displayed in the browser.
- If necessary, click the security bar under the tabs, click Allow Blocked Content, then click Yes in the Security Warning dialog box.

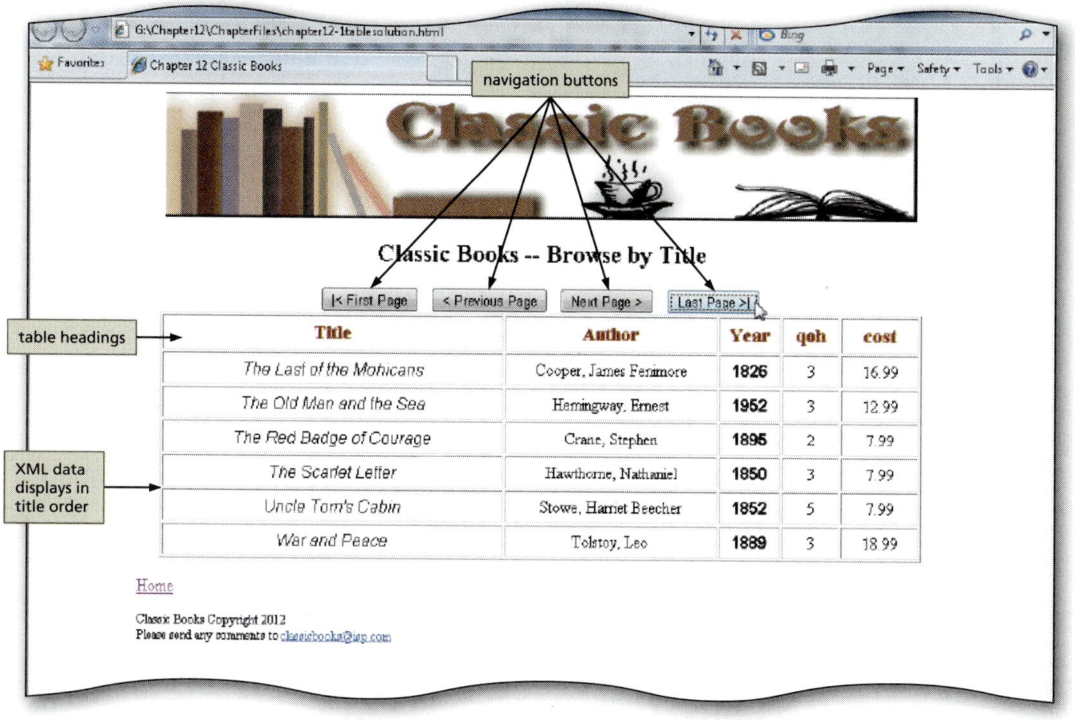

navigation buttons
table headings
XML data displays in title order
Classic Books -- Browse by Title
|< First Page
< Previous Page
Next Page >
Last Page >|
Title
Author
Year
qoh
cost
The Last of the Mohicans
Cooper, James Fenimore
1826
3
16.99
The Old Man and the Sea
Hemingway, Ernest
1952
3
12.99
The Red Badge of Courage
Crane, Stephen
1895
2
7.99
The Scarlet Letter
Hawthorne, Nathaniel
1850
3
7.99
Uncle Tom's Cabin
Stowe, Harriet Beecher
1852
5
7.99
War and Peace
Tolstoy, Leo
1889
3
18.99
Home
Classic Books Copyright 2012
Please send any comments to classicbooks@isp.com

Figure 12–35

- Click the Next Page button.
- Click the First Page button and then click the Last Page button to scroll through the table (Figure 12–35).

Q&A

No JavaScript was actually entered into this HTML code. Where is the function that is associated with the buttons?

The firstPage(), nextPage(), previousPage(), and lastPage() functions are built into the Internet Explorer browser. These codes will not work with other browsers such as Firefox.

Plan Ahead

Creating an HTML document to search an XML document and display results.
The JavaScript code to find books written by a particular author has four key components that you will create:

- The HTML element <xml> to create a data island
- An input text box and Search command button
- A <div> tag with an id attribute to identify the output area on the Web page
- A JavaScript function to search through the recordset until it finds a match between the text box input value and the corresponding XML data element

After adding the four key elements, you will need to do the following:

- Bind the XML document to the HTML so the JavaScript user-defined function can find the data.
- Add a form text field for input.
- Add a button to activate the search.
- Determine the output display area and format.

Using JavaScript to Search an XML Document and Display Results on a Web Page

A common use for an XML data island is providing a mechanism for users to search for specific data items. The third hyperlink on the Classic Books home page, Search by Author, is a link to a Web page that allows users to search for books by a particular author (Figure 12–36). By creating data islands that bind with a Web page, a user can view records without conflicting with other database processes. This Web page allows users to enter an author's name or part of a name, and then press the ENTER key or click the Search button. If the input text field is not blank, a JavaScript function searches the data island for matches. If matches are found, the Web page displays all the books matching that author's name.

The Find Author HTML Web page (found in the Data Files for Students) is bound to the XML document, chapter12-1classic_titles.xml, and uses a JavaScript function to search the XML recordsets for a match. The JavaScript code uses data source object properties and methods that are built-in functions of the Internet Explorer browser. Because the search is sequential, the order of the XML is immaterial; however, as with the HTML table Web page, the XML file cannot have the XSD or XSL files bound to it.

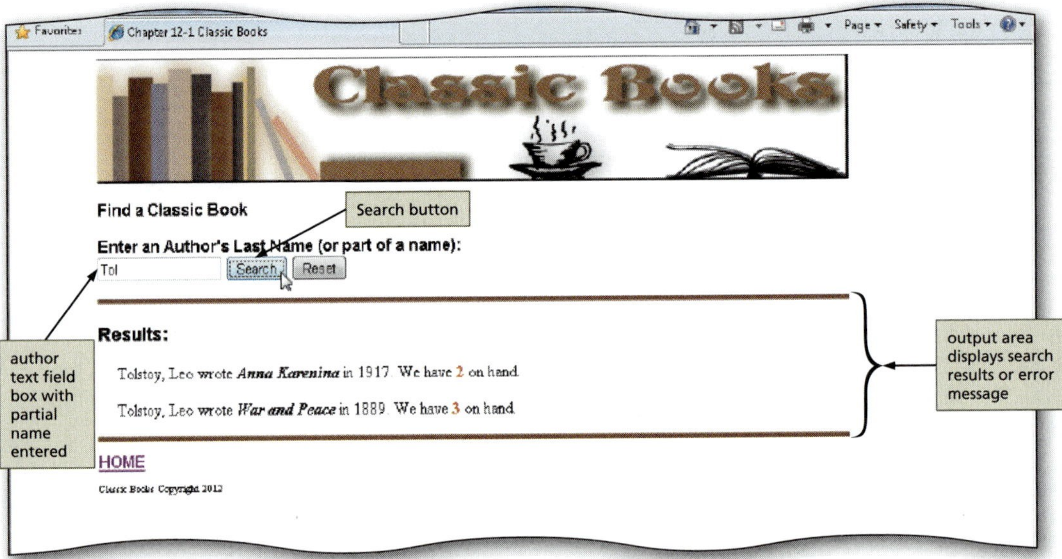

Figure 12–36

To Open an HTML Document and Save It with a New Name

The following steps illustrate how to open the HTML Web page that allows users to search an XML document and view the results, and save the document with a new name.

1. If necessary, click the Notepad++ button on the taskbar to activate the Notepad++ window.
2. Close the chapter12-1tablesolution.html document window.
3. With the USB drive plugged into your computer, open chapter12-1findauthor.html, from the Chapter12\ChapterFiles folder.
4. Save the file as `chapter12-1findauthorsolution.html`.

To Enter Code to Bind an XML Document with an HTML Web Page

To allow a user to search the XML document using the search function on this Web page, the XML document chapter12-1classic_titles.xml must be bound to the HTML Web page by first linking the XML document to the HTML Web page and then binding the XML document with the HTML Web page. The following step shows how to enter the code that links the XML document, chapter12-1classic_titles.xml, with the HTML Web page.

1

- With the chapter12findauthorsolution.html Notepad++ window active, click line 6.
- Type `<xml id="dsoBooks" src="chapter12-1classic_titles.xml"></xml>`, but do not press the ENTER key, to bind the XML document with the HTML code (Figure 12–37).

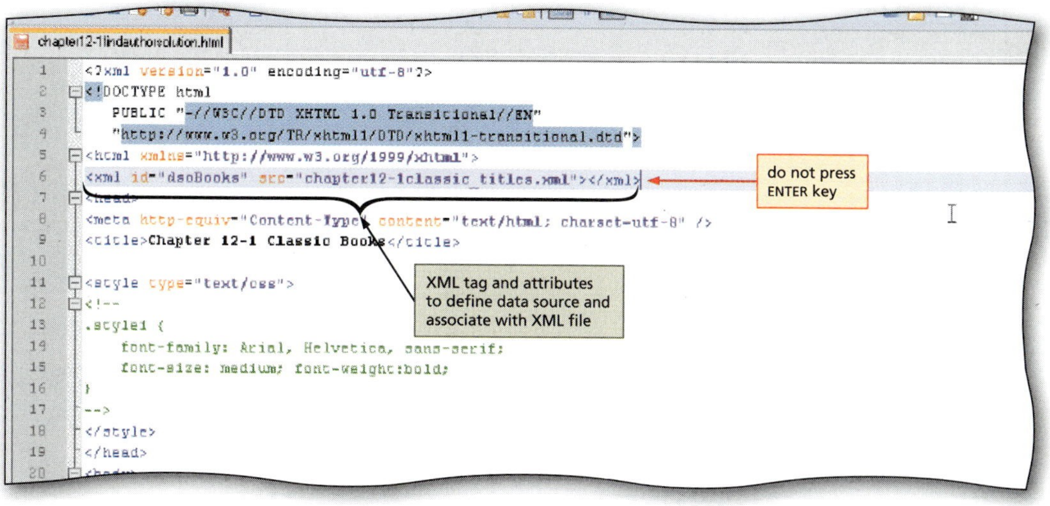

chapter12-1findauthorsolution.html

```
1  <?xml version="1.0" encoding="utf-8"?>
2  <!DOCTYPE html
3     PUBLIC "-//W3C//DTD XHTML 1.0 Transitional//EN"
4     "http://www.w3.org/TR/xhtml1/DTD/xhtml1-transitional.dtd">
5  <html xmlns="http://www.w3.org/1999/xhtml">
6  <xml id="dsoBooks" src="chapter12-1classic_titles.xml"></xml>
7  <head>
8  <meta http-equiv="Content-Type" content="text/html; charset=utf-8" />
9  <title>Chapter 12-1 Classic Books</title>
10
11 <style type="text/css">
12 <!--
13 .style1 {
14    font-family: Arial, Helvetica, sans-serif;
15    font-size: medium; font-weight:bold;
16 }
17 -->
18 </style>
19 </head>
20 <body>
```

do not press ENTER key

XML tag and attributes to define data source and associate with XML file

Figure 12–37

Adding the <input> and <button> Elements

The next step is to add the HTML <input> and <button> elements to create the input text box and Search and Reset command buttons. The code for the <input> and <button> element is shown in Table 12–35.

Table 12–35 Code for <input> and <button> Elements with onkeypress and onclick Event Handlers

Line	Code
27	`<input type="text" id="SearchText" size="15" onkeypress="keyPressed()"/>`
28	`<button onclick="findAuthor()">Search</button>`
29	`<button onclick="clearField()">Reset</button></p>`

Line 27 defines an <input> object. The type attribute defines the object as a text field. The id attribute names the text box as SearchText, which becomes an object that the user-defined JavaScript function uses to access the input characters. The size attribute sets the width of the text field to 15 characters. The onkeypress event handler calls the keyPressed() user-defined function every time a user presses a key. The keyPressed() user-defined function calls the findAuthor() user-defined function if the ENTER key has been pressed.

Line 28 defines a button with a caption of Search. The onclick event handler calls the user-defined JavaScript function findAuthor() if the user clicks the Search button. Line 29 defines a button with a caption of Reset. This button is not a normal <form> Reset button and needs the onclick event handler that calls the user-defined JavaScript function clearField() when the user clicks the button. This function clears the text field and the output area of any listings or error messages.

To Enter Code for the <input> and <button> Elements

The following step shows how to enter the code for the <input> and <button> elements to the Web page.

- Click line 27.
- Enter the code in Table 12–35 on the previous page. Do not press the ENTER key after line 29 (Figure 12–38).

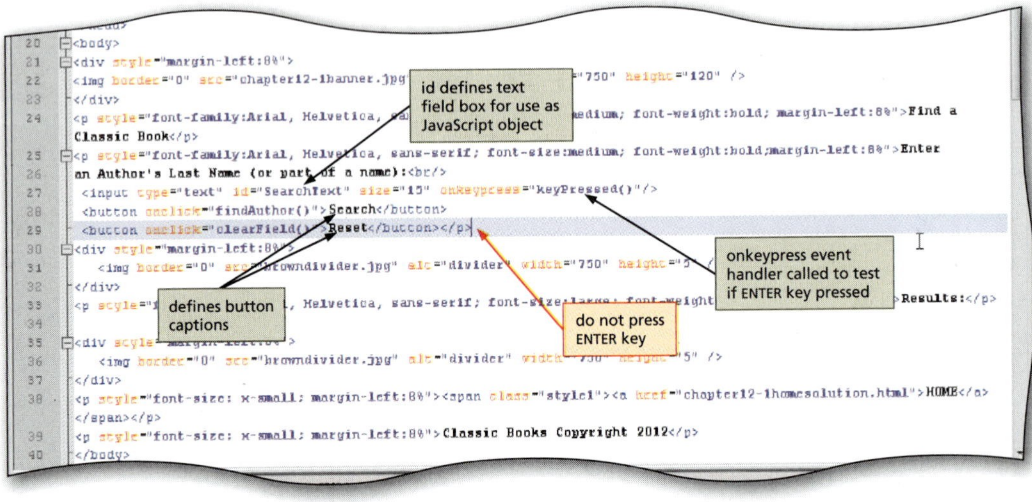

id defines text field box for use as JavaScript object

onkeypress event handler called to test if ENTER key pressed

defines button captions

do not press ENTER key

Figure 12–38

To Enter an HTML <div> Tag Container

The next step is to add the <div> tag container to define an output area of the Web page where search results will appear. Recall from Chapter 9 the use of the <div> tag container and the innerHTML property. To create the dynamic output area for the search results, the <div> tag uses the id attribute and value, SearchResult, to indicate that search results will be displayed in that area. The JavaScript user-defined function uses that id value to assign the search results to the output area of the Web page. An inline style attribute sets the left margin at a relative distance of 10% of the screen width, so the results are aligned with the input text field. The following step illustrates how to enter the <div> element to define the output area of the Web page.

- Click line 34.
- Type `<div id="SearchResult" style="margin-left:10%">` and press the ENTER key.
- On line 35, type `</div>` and do not press the ENTER key (Figure 12–39).

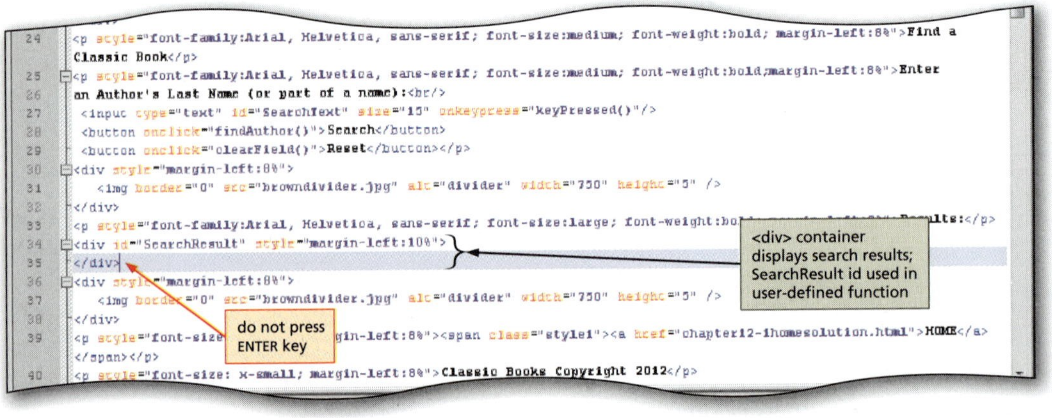

<div> container displays search results; SearchResult id used in user-defined function

do not press ENTER key

Figure 12–39

Q&A Why is the margin-left set to 10% and not a specific number of pixels?

By using a percent value, the left margin will always be 10% from the left regardless of the screen resolution. If it was set to a specific number of pixels, it might look too small or too large at different resolutions.

Plan Ahead

Writing the user-defined function findAuthor().

The user-defined function, findAuthor(), uses a combination of standard document object model (DOM) objects, properties, and methods and Internet Explorer's built-in XML parser methods to find books by author name in the XML document. The findAuthor() function will accomplish the following activities to complete this action:

1. Convert the text field (search) input value character data to uppercase characters.
2. Validate that the input value is not blank or a non-character value.
3. Move to the first record in the XML document.
4. Compare each element in the XML document with the text box value until a match is found.
5. Construct an output text string with search results.

Creating the JavaScript User-defined Functions, findAuthor() and keyPressed()

The next step is to create the JavaScript user-defined function that takes a target value from the input search text box and compares it with the <author> elements in the XML document, chapter12-1classic_titles.xml.

With the XML document linked to the chapter12findauthorsolution.html Web page, the next step is to add the JavaScript user-defined functions, findAuthor() and keyPressed(), to the HTML document. The findAuthor() function is called when a user clicks the Submit button. The keyPressed() function is called with every key pressed by the user and tests if the user pressed the ENTER key on the keyboard by comparing the key to ASCII value 13, which represents the ENTER key. If the ENTER key was pressed, the findAuthor() function is called.

To Enter Code for the findAuthor() User-defined Function

The code to begin the JavaScript section and create the findAuthor() user-defined function is shown in Table 12–36.

Table 12–36 Code to Begin the JavaScript Section and Create the findAuthor() Function

Line	Code

```
10  <script type="text/javascript">
11  <!--Hide from old browsers
12  function findAuthor() {
13     SearchString = SearchText.value.toUpperCase()
14     if ((SearchString == "") || (SearchString == " ")) {
15        SearchResult.innerHTML = "&ltPlease enter a valid author name.&gt"
16        return
17     }
```

Lines 10 and 11 start the JavaScript <script> section. Line 12 defines the findAuthor() user-defined function. Line 13 converts the SearchText text field value to uppercase characters using the toUpperCase() method. Line 14 is a standard if statement to determine if the resulting SearchString value is blank or null. If the string is blank or null, the code on line 15 assigns a message to the contents to <div> area innerHTML property. The return statement on line 16 stops the search and displays the error message. The brace on line 17 closes the if statement.

The following step shows how to enter the statements to convert the text field to uppercase characters and test for blank or null values in the findAuthor() user-defined function.

- Click line 10.
- Enter the code shown in Table 12–36 on the previous page and then press the ENTER key after line 17 to enter the findAuthor() user-defined function (Figure 12–40).

```
<meta http-equiv="Content-Type" content="text/html; charset=utf-8" />
<title>Chapter 12-1 Classic Books</title>
<script type="text/javascript">
<!--Hide from old browsers
function findAuthor() {
  SearchString = SearchText.value.toUpperCase()
    if ((SearchString == "") || (SearchString == " ")) {
      SearchResult.innerHTML = "&lt;Please enter a valid author name.&gt;"
      return
    }

<style type="text/css">
<!--
.style1 {
    font-family: Arial, Helvetica, sans-serif;
    font-size: medium; font-weight:bold;
```

beginning of findAuthor() user-defined function and code to validate data entered in text field box

Figure 12–40

Searching the Recordset Values and Outputting Results

After testing that the SearchText text field input value is not blank or null, the findAuthor() user-defined function sequentially searches through the data in the linked XML document, chapter12-1classic_titles.xml, to find a match for the text box input value. The search uses the data source object, dsoBooks, and Internet Explorer's built-in methods to move through the records in the XML document. If a match is found, the function creates a results message that incorporates specific XML elements in the HTML string. Table 12–37 shows the JavaScript code that sequentially searches the XML document and creates the results message to be displayed in the output area.

Table 12–37 Code for Searching the Recordset Values and Building the Output String

Line	Code
18	`dsoBooks.recordset.moveFirst()`
19	`var outputResult=""`
20	`while (!dsoBooks.recordset.EOF) {`
21	`  authorString = dsoBooks.recordset("author").value.toUpperCase()`
22	`  if (authorString.indexOf(SearchString)>=0)`
23	`    outputResult += dsoBooks.recordset("author")`
24	`    + " wrote <span style='font-style:italic; font-weight:bold;'>" + dsoBooks.recordset("title")`
25	`    + " </span> in "`
26	`    + dsoBooks.recordset("year")`
27	`    + ". We have <span style='font-weight:bold; color:#cc0000;'>"`
28	`    + dsoBooks.recordset("qoh") + " </span>on hand.<p></p>"`
29	`  dsoBooks.recordset.moveNext();`
30	`}`

Recall that a recordset is a collection of data records. The built-in moveFirst() method on line 18 positions an internal pointer to the first record in the recordset of the data source object, dsoBooks. Line 19 initializes an output variable, outputResult, to a null value. Line 20 starts a while processing loop. As you learned in Chapter 10, the while loop relies on a conditional statement to terminate. In this function, the while loop processes each record until the EOF property is true. **EOF** means end of file and signals that all XML document records have been read.

Line 21 assigns the values of the <author> element to the authorString variable of the current record. To determine if the value in the SearchString matches any part of the search text, the if statement in line 22 uses the indexOf() method to look for SearchString value in authorString. Recall from Chapter 10 that the indexOf() method returns the relative location of the value found. If the returned value is greater than or equal to 0, indicating a match was found, lines 23 through 28 construct an output value concatenating the various elements and descriptive text together. This method is used to allow this script to be changed easily and adapt to searching any text string.

The <p></p> tags at the end of line 28 ensure that each outputResult string will appear on a separate line in the output area of the Web page. To read each of the records in the recordset, line 29 uses the built-in moveNext() method to tell the function to read the next record in the XML document. Line 30 closes the while loop.

To Enter Code to Search the Recordset Values and Build the Output String

The following step shows how to enter the code to search the chapter12-1classic_titles XML file for books by a particular author.

1

- If necessary, click line 18.
- Enter the code shown in Table 12–37 to search the recordset values and build the output string. Press the ENTER key after line 30 (Figure 12–41).

Q&A Why isn't there a bracket ({) after the if statement on line 22?

Normally, in JavaScript you cannot break statements in the middle of a line. The expression at line 23 is one exception because an expression statement can be broken at places like operands. Recall that if an if statement has only one statement after the condition, no brace is needed to set a block of code. In this case lines from 23 to 28 are treated as one JavaScript expression.

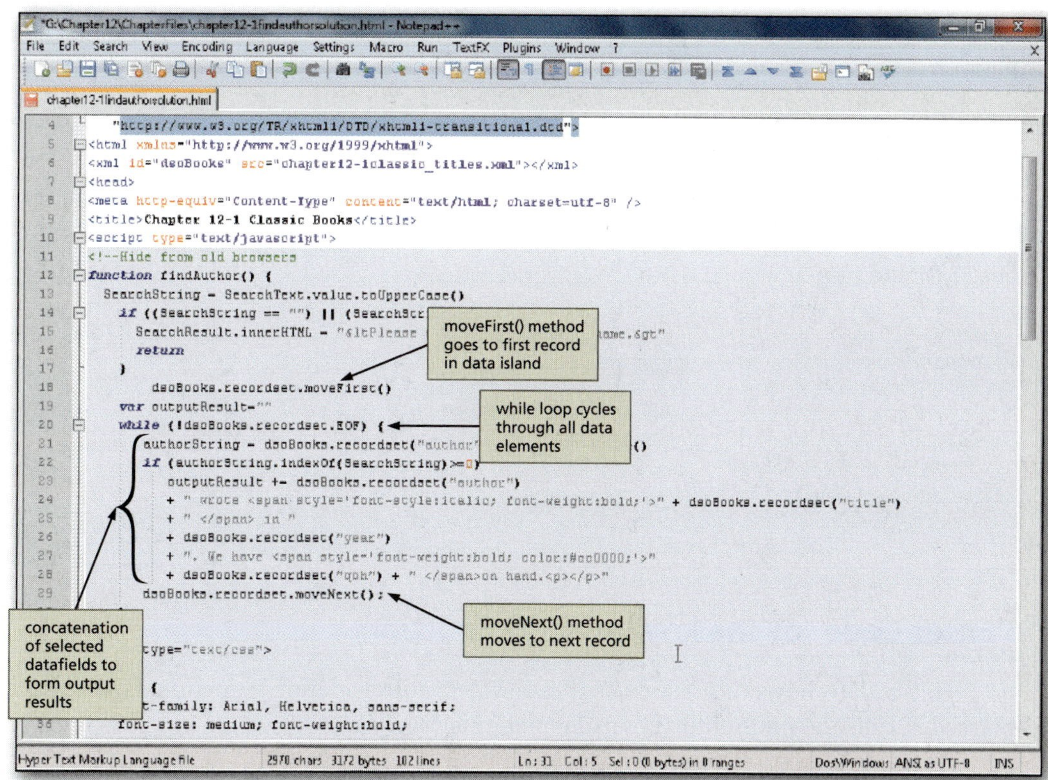

Figure 12–41

To Enter Code to Complete the findAuthor() Function

The next step is to test if the outputResult string has any content. If not, then a message to tell the users no results were found is assigned to the SearchResult.innerHTML object. Table 12–38 shows the code for building the no result found message.

Table 12–38 Completing the findAuthor() Function

Line	Code
31	`if (outputResult=="")`
32	`SearchResult.innerHTML = "<Sorry, we have no books by that author now. Call us for more information>";`
33	`else`
34	`SearchResult.innerHTML = outputResult`
35	`}`

Line 31 tests the outputResult variable. If the outputResult is blank because no match was found on line 22, then line 32 assigns a message to the SearchResult.innerHTML property that no record was found. If a match is found, the else portion of the if...else statement on line 34 displays the outputResult results message constructed on lines 23 through 28 using the innerHTML property. Line 35 ends the user-defined function. The following step shows how to enter the code to complete the findAuthor() function.

1

- If necessary, click line 31.
- Enter the code shown in Table 12–38 to complete the findAuthor() function and then press the ENTER key twice at line 35 (Figure 12–42).

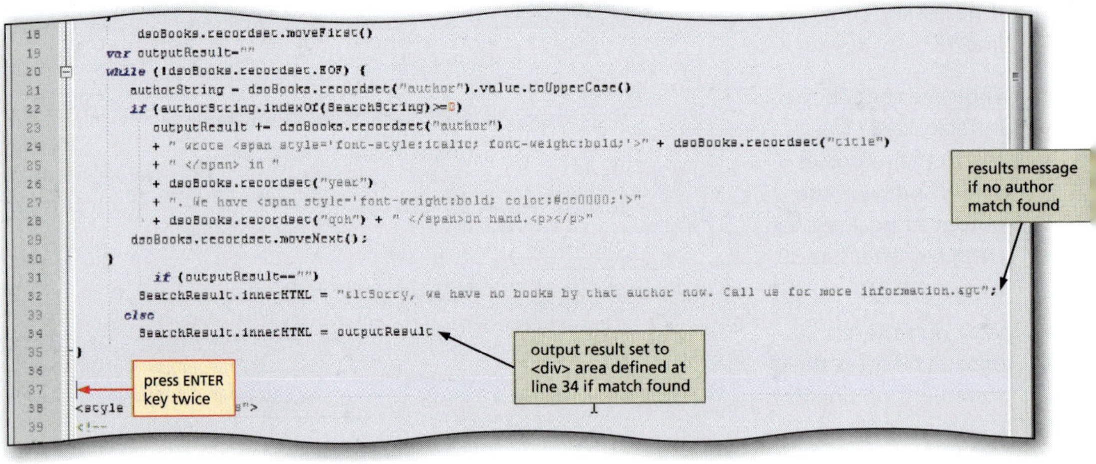

results message if no author match found

output result set to <div> area defined at line 34 if match found

press ENTER key twice

Figure 12–42

To Enter Code for the keyPressed() Function

Table 12–39 shows the code to create a JavaScript user-defined function, keyPressed(), so that if the ENTER key is pressed, it calls the findAuthor() user-defined function.

Table 12–39 Code for the keyPressed() User-defined Function

Line	Code
37	`function keyPressed(k) {`
38	`var hitEnter=event.keyCode`
39	`if (hitEnter==13) findAuthor()`
40	`}`

Line 37 declares the keyPressed() user-defined function and accepts a parameter value k, which represents the key pressed. Line 38 assigns the value of the keyCode property of the key pressed to a decimal value stored in the variable, hitEnter. The if statement on line 39 tests if the value of hitEnter is equal to an ASCII 13, which is the equivalent of the ENTER key. If hitEnter is equal to 13, meaning the ENTER key has been pressed, then the findAuthor() user-defined function is called. The keyPressed() function is called with every press of a key until the ENTER key is pressed. Line 40 closes the JavaScript function.

The following step shows how to enter the keyPressed() user-defined function.

- If necessary, click line 37.
- Enter the code shown in Table 12–39 to create the keyPressed() function. Press the ENTER key twice after line 40 (Figure 12–43).

keyPressed() user-defined function

press ENTER key twice

Figure 12–43

To Enter Code for the clearField() Function

The Reset button does not automatically clear the input text field as in a normal HTML form, nor does it clear the output area of the <div> container. Table 12–40 shows the code to create a JavaScript user-defined function called clearField() that clears the input text field, clears the <div> container area, and sets the focus back in the text field.

Table 12–40 Code for the clearField() User-defined Function

Line	Code
42	`function clearField() {`
43	`    SearchText.value = ""`
44	`    SearchResult.innerHTML = ""`
45	`    SearchText.focus()`
46	`}`
47	
48	`//-->`
49	`</script>`

Line 42 defines the clearField() user-defined function. Line 43 clears the SearchText text field. Line 44 uses the innerHTML to clear the SearchResult <div> container. Line 45 sets the focus and places the insertion point back in the SearchText text field for the next entry. Lines 48 and 49 close the HTML comment and close the </script> section.

The following step shows how to enter the clearField() user-defined function.

1

- If necessary, click line 42.
- Enter the code shown in Table 12–40 on the previous page to create the clearField() function. Do not press the ENTER key after line 49 (Figure 12–44).

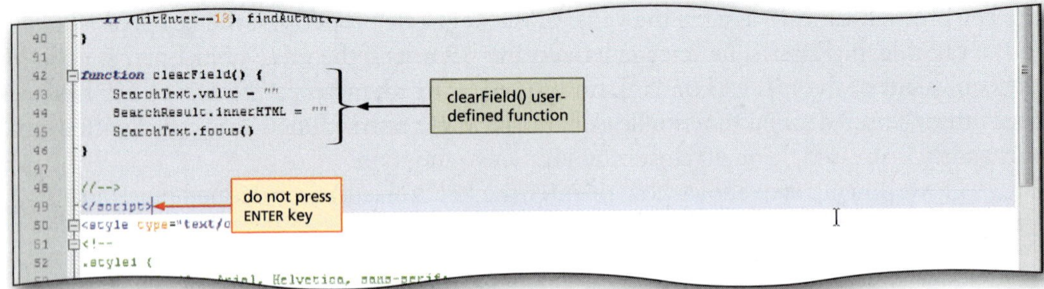

Figure 12–44

To Save and Test the HTML Document in the Browser

1

- With your USB drive plugged into your computer, click the Save icon on the Notepad++ toolbar.
- Click the browser button on the taskbar to activate the browser.
- Click the Address bar. Type `g:\Chapter12\ChapterFiles\chapter12-1findauthorsolution.html`, and then press the ENTER key so the Web page is displayed in the browser.

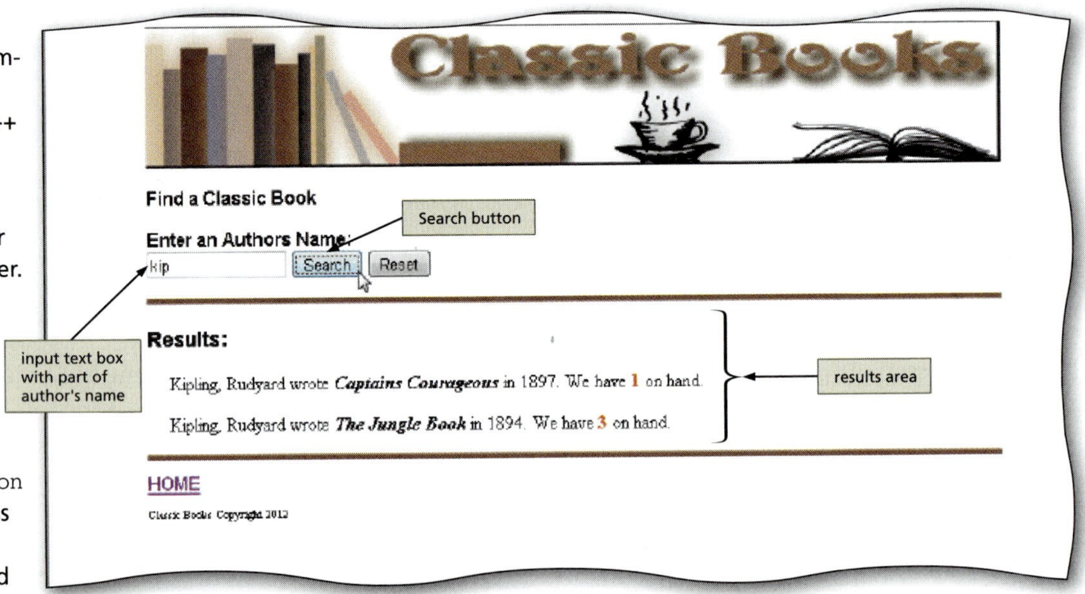

Figure 12–45

- If necessary, click the security bar under the tabs, click Allow Blocked Content, then click Yes in the Security Warning dialog box.
- Enter the data values in the Author's Name column in Table 12–41 in the input text box, and then click the Search button to test this Web page. Figure 12–45 shows how the lowercase kip entered for the author's name returns the books by Rudyard Kipling.

Table 12–41 Search Test Data

Test Data Set	Author's Name	Results Message
1	Hem	Three books by Hemingway should display.
2	blank	<Please enter a valid author name.>
3	Milton	<Sorry, we have no books by that author now. Call us for more information.>
4	kip	Two books by Rudyard Kipling should display.

To Verify the Links on the Classic Books Home Page

The Classics Books home page has already been created and is included in the Data Files for Students. A final test is necessary to verify that the links in the home page function correctly. The following step illustrates how to verify that the links on the Classic Books Web page are correct.

- Click the Address bar. Type `g:\Chapter12\ChapterFiles\chapter12-1homesolution.html`, and then press the ENTER key to display the Web page in the browser.
- Click the Books in Author Order image hot spot link (Figure 12–46a).
- After viewing the Web page, click the Back button on the browser toolbar to return to the Classic Books Web home page.
- Click the Books in Title Order image hot spot link (Figure 12–46b).
- After viewing the Web page, click the Back button on the browser toolbar or click the Home link to return to the Classic Books Web page.
- Click the Find Books image link.
- Type `dickens` in the search text field, and then click Search to search for books written by Charles Dickens (Figure 12–46c).

Q&A What if the browser does not display the Web pages correctly?

Close any error message windows. Make sure the file names match the hyperlinks, and check the code associated with that Web page.

Q&A Why don't we validate the Web page at this point?

The <xml> tag is unique to Internet Explorer and therefore when you submit the HTML file to the w3.org validator, that tag will not validate. The validator also does not recognize many of the attributes associated with the <xml> tag, such as the datafld attribute in the <span> tag, resulting in numerous "errors" from the validator.

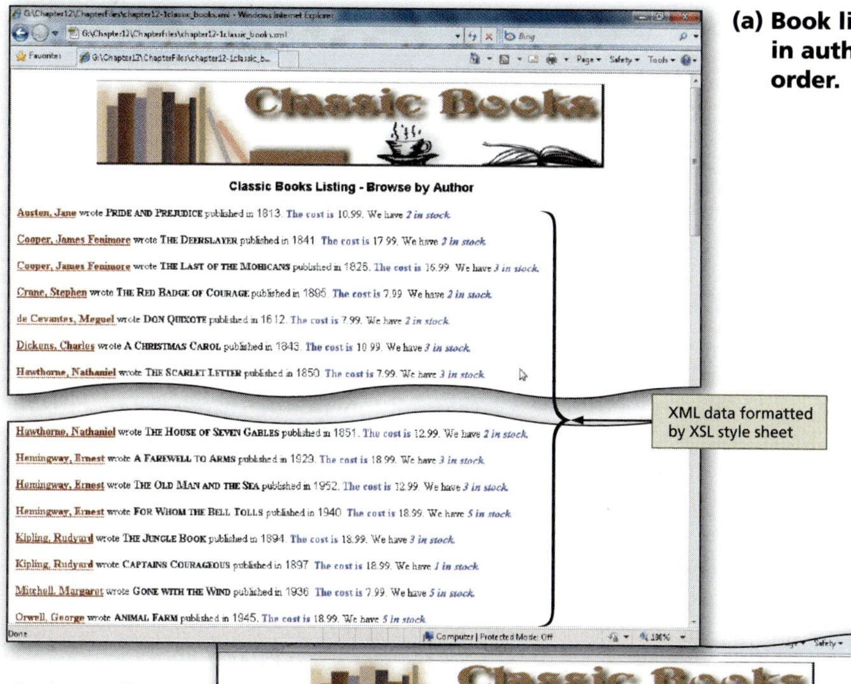

(a) Book list in author order.

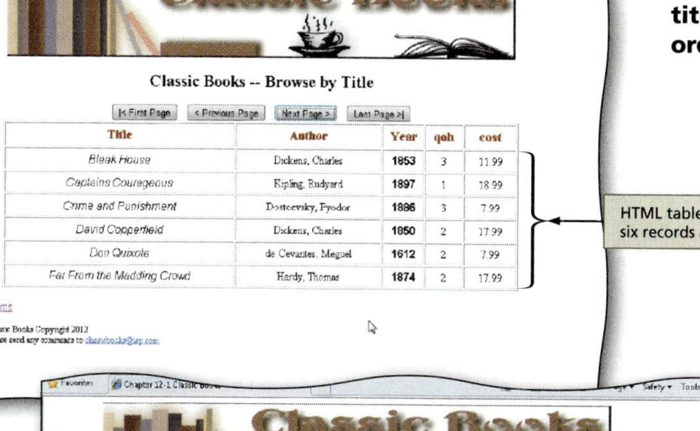

(b) Book list in title order.

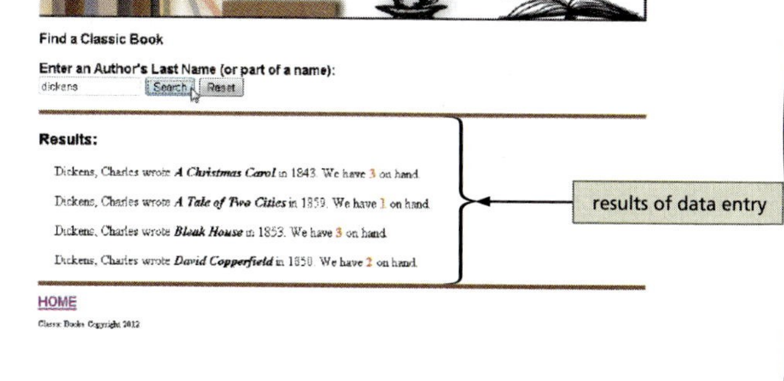

(c) Search by author name.

Figure 12–46

BTW

Quick Reference
For more information on XML and XSL, see the XML Quick Reference (Appendix H) at the back of this book, or visit the HTML Quick Reference Web page (scsite.com/HTML6e/qr).

To Quit Notepad++ and the Browser

After verifying the links on the main Classic Books Web page are correct and that the Web page is valid, close Notepad++ and your browser.

1. In Notepad++, click the File menu, then Close All.
2. Click the Close button on the Notepad++ title bar.
3. Click the Close button on the browser title bar. If necessary, click the Close all tabs button.

Chapter Summary

In Chapter 12, you learned how to create and use XML documents. You created a well-formed and valid XML Schema Definition and XML document instance. You created an XSL style sheet to format and display an XML document. By binding an XML document with an HTML Web page, you created Web pages that displayed XML data in a table and you learned to code a JavaScript function to search for records in an XML document. The items listed below include all the new skills you have learned in this chapter.

1. Start Notepad++ and Create a New XML Document (HTML 572)
2. Enter Code for the Prolog, Root, Annotation, and Documentation Elements (HTML 575)
3. Enter Code for the <classic_books> Element (HTML 576)
4. Enter Code for the <complexType> Element (HTML 577)
5. Enter Code for the Child Group Elements (HTML 578)
6. Save and Validate an XML Schema Definition File (HTML 579)
7. Create a New XML Document and Enter the Prolog Code (HTML 581)
8. Start Entering a Document Instance in an XML Document (HTML 582)
9. Finish Entering a Document Instance in an XML Document (HTML 583)
10. Correct a Tag Error and Retest an XML Document (HTML 586)
11. Validate XML and XSD Files (HTML 587)
12. Start Creating an XSL Style Sheet (HTML 591)
13. Enter HTML Code to Display the Banner and Text Title in a Web Page (HTML 592)
14. Add XSL Style Sheet Tags (HTML 593)
15. Link an XSL Style Sheet to an XML Document (HTML 596)
16. Save and Test an XML Document Formatted Using an XSL Style Sheet (HTML 596)
17. Enter Code to Link an XML Document with an HTML Web Page (HTML 599)
18. Enter Code to Add Navigation Buttons (HTML 599)
19. Enter <table> Table Header and Row Tags (HTML 600)
20. Enter <tr> Tags and Attribute Values to Bind XML Elements to a Table (HTML 602)
21. Save the HTML File and Test the Web Page (HTML 603)
22. Enter Code to Bind an XML Document with an HTML Web Page (HTML 605)
23. Enter Code for the <input> and <button> Elements (HTML 606)
24. Enter an HTML <div> Tag Container (HTML 606)
25. Enter Code for the findAuthor() User-defined Function (HTML 607)
26. Enter Code to Search the Recordset Values and Build the Output String (HTML 609)
27. Enter Code to Complete the findAuthor() Function (HTML 610)
28. Enter Code for the keyPressed() Function (HTML 610)
29. Enter Code for the clearField() Function (HTML 611)
30. Save and Test the HTML Document in the Browser (HTML 612)
31. Verify the Links on the Classic Books Home Page (HTML 613)

Learn It Online

Test your knowledge of chapter content and key terms.

Instructions: To complete the Learn It Online exercises, start your browser, click the Address bar, and then enter the Web address, `scsite.com/html6e/learn`. When the HTML Learn It Online page is displayed, click the link for the exercise you want to complete and read the instructions.

Chapter Reinforcement TF, MC, and SA

A series of true/false, multiple choice, and short answer questions that test your knowledge of the chapter content.

Flash Cards

An interactive learning environment where you identify chapter key terms associated with displayed definitions.

Practice Test

A series of multiple choice questions that test your knowledge of chapter content and key terms.

Who Wants To Be a Computer Genius?

An interactive game that challenges your knowledge of chapter content in the style of a television quiz show.

Wheel of Terms

An interactive game that challenges your knowledge of chapter key terms in the style of the television show, *Wheel of Fortune*.

Crossword Puzzle Challenge

A crossword puzzle that challenges your knowledge of key terms presented in the chapter.

Apply Your Knowledge

Reinforce the skills and apply the concepts you learned in this chapter.

Instructions: Start Notepad++. Open the file apply12-1trainschedule.txt from the Chapter12\Apply folder of the Data Files for Students. See the inside back cover of this book for instructions on downloading the Data Files for Students, or contact your instructor for information about accessing the required files. Create an XML document and an associated XML Schema Definition file for the Chicago-Milwaukee Commuter Railroad. The root level of the XML file should be Chicago-Milwaukee. The remaining values for the XML instance have the following schema: Eveningsched(Station, Train3, Train7, Train11, Train15, Train17, Train21, Train27, Train29) as indicated by the title row in the text file. Figure 12–47 shows the Apply Your Knowledge XML page as it would be displayed in a browser.

Continued >

Apply Your Knowledge *continued*

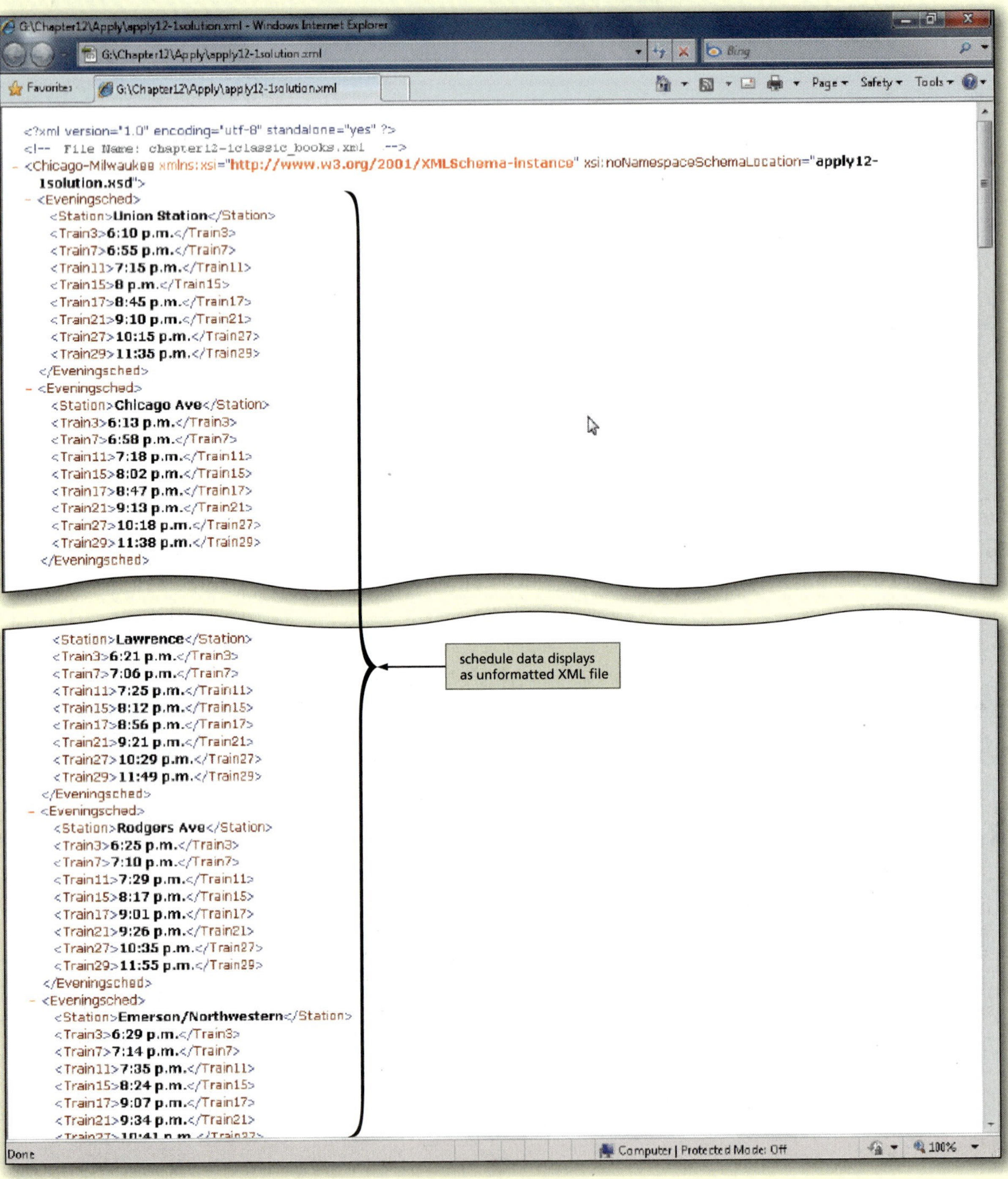

```
<?xml version="1.0" encoding="utf-8" standalone="yes" ?>
<!-- File Name: chapter12-1classic_books.xml -->
- <Chicago-Milwaukee xmlns:xsi="http://www.w3.org/2001/XMLSchema-instance" xsi:noNamespaceSchemaLocation="apply12-1solution.xsd">
  - <Eveningsched>
      <Station>Union Station</Station>
      <Train3>6:10 p.m.</Train3>
      <Train7>6:55 p.m.</Train7>
      <Train11>7:15 p.m.</Train11>
      <Train15>8 p.m.</Train15>
      <Train17>8:45 p.m.</Train17>
      <Train21>9:10 p.m.</Train21>
      <Train27>10:15 p.m.</Train27>
      <Train29>11:35 p.m.</Train29>
    </Eveningsched>
  - <Eveningsched>
      <Station>Chicago Ave</Station>
      <Train3>6:13 p.m.</Train3>
      <Train7>6:58 p.m.</Train7>
      <Train11>7:18 p.m.</Train11>
      <Train15>8:02 p.m.</Train15>
      <Train17>8:47 p.m.</Train17>
      <Train21>9:13 p.m.</Train21>
      <Train27>10:18 p.m.</Train27>
      <Train29>11:38 p.m.</Train29>
    </Eveningsched>

      <Station>Lawrence</Station>
      <Train3>6:21 p.m.</Train3>
      <Train7>7:06 p.m.</Train7>
      <Train11>7:25 p.m.</Train11>
      <Train15>8:12 p.m.</Train15>
      <Train17>8:56 p.m.</Train17>
      <Train21>9:21 p.m.</Train21>
      <Train27>10:29 p.m.</Train27>
      <Train29>11:49 p.m.</Train29>
    </Eveningsched>
  - <Eveningsched>
      <Station>Rodgers Ave</Station>
      <Train3>6:25 p.m.</Train3>
      <Train7>7:10 p.m.</Train7>
      <Train11>7:29 p.m.</Train11>
      <Train15>8:17 p.m.</Train15>
      <Train17>9:01 p.m.</Train17>
      <Train21>9:26 p.m.</Train21>
      <Train27>10:35 p.m.</Train27>
      <Train29>11:55 p.m.</Train29>
    </Eveningsched>
  - <Eveningsched>
      <Station>Emerson/Northwestern</Station>
      <Train3>6:29 p.m.</Train3>
      <Train7>7:14 p.m.</Train7>
      <Train11>7:35 p.m.</Train11>
      <Train15>8:24 p.m.</Train15>
      <Train17>9:07 p.m.</Train17>
      <Train21>9:34 p.m.</Train21>
```


Figure 12–47

Perform the following tasks:

1. Using the code in Tables 12–11, 12–12, 12–14, and 12–15 on pages HTML 575 to HTML 578 as a guide, create the XML Schema Definition file for the Chicago-Milwaukee Railroad.
2. Save the XSD file in the Chapter12\Apply folder using the file name apply12-1solution.xsd.
3. Using the code in Tables 12–17 and 12–19 on pages HTML 581 and HTML 582 as a guide, enter the XML document instance elements using the item data in the apply12-1trainschedule.txt file.
4. Save the XML document in the Chapter12\Apply folder using the file name apply12-1solution.xml.
5. Start your browser. Enter http://tools.decisionsoft.com/schemaValidate/ in the Address box to view the Decision Soft Web page in your browser.

6. Click the Browse button next to the XML Schema input text field. Navigate to your storage device and select the apply12-1solution.xsd file.
7. Click the Browse button next to the XML Instance text field. Navigate to your storage device and select the apply12-1solution.xml file.
8. Click the Validate button. When the Your results are ready page displays, click the Click here link to see if your XML and XSD files are valid.
9. If an error occurs, check your code against the instructions in Steps 1 through 3 and then save and test the XML and XSD document files again.
10. Submit the revised XSD and XML files in the format specified by your instructor.

Extend Your Knowledge

Extend the skills you learned in this chapter and experiment with new skills. You will need to search the Internet to complete the assignment.

Learning More about Displaying XML Data Islands

Instructions: Start Notepad++ and your browser. Open the file extend12-1.html from the Chapter12\Extend folder of the Data Files for Students. See the inside back cover of this book for instructions on downloading the Data Files for Students, or contact your instructor for information about accessing the required files.

Images do not display in XML files. To display images along with XML data, you need the help of HTML. Search the Internet for instructions on how to display an image in an HTML table. You may have to modify this code slightly. Using the concepts presented in the chapter, you will create an XML document instance and modify an HMTL document to display images of pets in the HTML table. The images are in the Data Files for Students Chapter 12\Extend folder. Figure 12–48 shows the completed first page of the Web site.

Figure 12–48

Continued >

Extend Your Knowledge *continued*

Perform the following tasks:

1. Start a new Notepad++ document and, using the data found in extend12-1data.txt, create an XML instance document. Save the completed document file as extend12-1solution.xml.
2. With the extend12-1.html file open in Notepad++, save it as extend12-1solution.html.
3. With the extend12-1solution.html Notepad++ window active, use the steps described for Figure 12–31 on page HTML 599 as a guide, and add the <xml> tag to identify the source file extend12-1solution.xml.
4. Using the code in Table 12–32 on page HTML 599 as a guide, enter the code beneath the HTML comment line <!-- Button code goes here --> to create buttons with the following text values: First Page, Previous Page, Next Page, and Last Page.
5. Using the code in Table 12–33 on pages HTML 600 and 601 and Table 12–34 on page HTML 602 as a guide, enter the code to create HTML heading and table cells beneath the comment line <!--Table header goes here-- > to display the XML contents in the table. Set the <table> tag attributes as follows: id="petlist" datasrc="#dsoPetlist" datapagesize="3" border="1" cellpadding="5". Modify the last <td> cell to display pet image.
6. Save the completed HTML document in the Chapter12\Extend folder.
7. Start your browser. Enter g:\Chapter12\Extend\extend12-1solution.html in the Address box to view the XML document in a table in your browser. If an error occurs, check your code against the instructions in Steps 1 through 6 and then save and test the XML page again.
8. Submit the revised XML file and HTML Web page in the format specified by your instructor.

Make It Right

Analyze the XML code on a Web page and correct all errors.

Correcting Syntax Errors

Instructions: Start your browser. You will use the file make12-1error.xml from the Chapter12\MakeItRight folder of the Data Files for Students. See the inside back cover of this book for instructions on downloading the Data Files for Students, or contact your instructor for information about accessing the required file.

The Twentieth Century Cinema Web page displays its movie schedule in an HTML table. If you attempt to open the XML instance document in Internet Explorer, it will not display because it has two errors. If you attempt to validate the XML Schema Definition (XSD) file, it will have two errors. Even after the errors are fixed in the XSD file and XML instance document, the show-times will not display in the HTML table because there is one error in the HTML file. You are to find the errors in each page and correct them. The corrected Web page will show one of the movie times as shown in Figure 12–49.

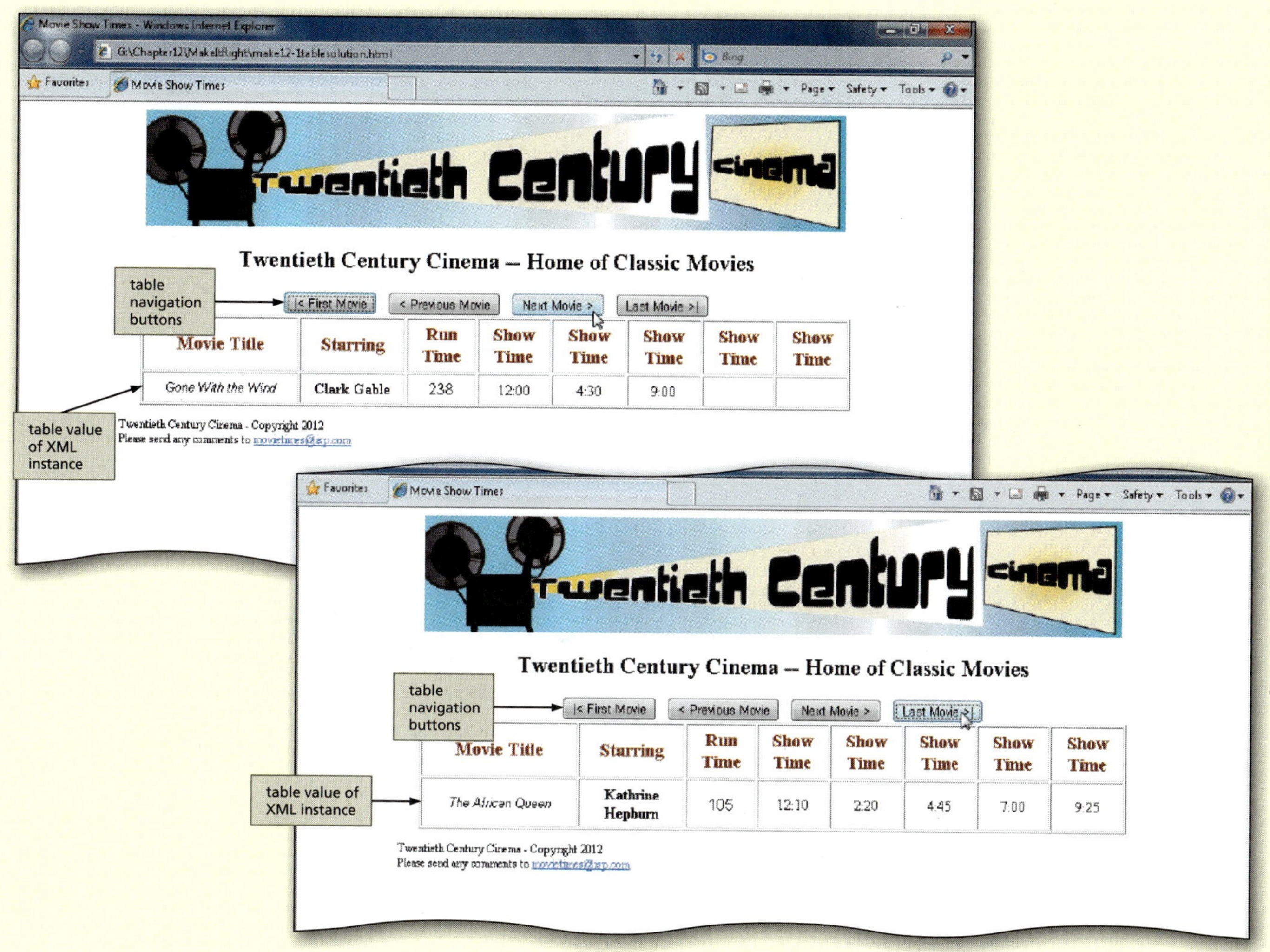

Figure 12–49

Perform the following tasks:

1. Open make12-1error.xml in Notepad++ and save it as make12-1solution.xml.
2. Click the browser button on the taskbar. Enter g:\Chapter12\MakeItRight\make12-1solution.xml in the Address box to view the XML document in your browser. Make note of the error message that appears.
3. Correct the error and save the XML file. Activate the browser and refresh the Web page. A second error message should display. Correct the error and save the XML file. Activate the browser and refresh the Web page. Make sure the XML file is error-free before continuing.
4. Open make12-1schema.xsd in Notepad++ and save it as make12-1schemasolution.xsd.
5. Start your browser. Enter http://tools.decisionsoft.com/schemaValidate/ in the Address box to view the Decision Soft Web page in your browser.
6. Click the Browse button next to the XML Schema input text field. Navigate to your storage device and select the make12-1schema.xsd file (this file has the errors).
7. Click the Browse button next to the XML Instance text field. Navigate to your storage device and select the make12-1solution.xml file (this is your corrected XML instance document).
8. Click the Validate button. When the Your results are ready page displays, click the Click here link to see an error message regarding the invalid XSD file. Note that one error in the XSD will not be found by the validation. You will need to compare the XSD file with the XML file to find the error.

Continued >

STUDENT ASSIGNMENTS

Make It Right *continued*

9. Correct both XSD file errors, save the file, and revalidate the file using the Decision Soft Web page. Do not continue until both the XSD and XML documents are error-free.
10. Open the make12-1table.html file and save it as make12-1tablesolution.html.
11. Activate your browser, and enter g:\Chapter12\MakeItRight\make12-1tablesolution.html in the Address box to view the HTML table. Nothing displays because there is an error in the data source name.
12. Open make12-1tablesolution.html in Notepad++. Find and correct the error in the data source name. Save the make12-1tablesolution.html file.
13. Activate the browser and click the Refresh button.
14. If an error still occurs, check the spelling of the data source name, save the file, and test again in the browser.
15. Submit the revised XML, HTML, and XSD files in the format specified by your instructor.

In the Lab

Design and/or create a Web page using the guidelines, concepts, and skills presented in this chapter. Labs are listed in order of increasing difficulty.

Lab 1: Searching for the Record High Temperature in a Weather Data Island

Problem: You are one of the Web page developers for National WeatherWatch, an Internet weather station. The organization is gradually putting historical data on its Web site. You have been assigned to create a Web page using an XML data island to allow users to search for the record high temperature in any state (Figure 12–50). You are given the XML document instance, lab12-1temp_solution.xml, found in the Chapter12\IntheLab folder in the Data Files for Students. To verify that the data in the XML instance document is well formed, you will create an XML Schema Definition and validate the XML Schema Definition and the XML instance document together.

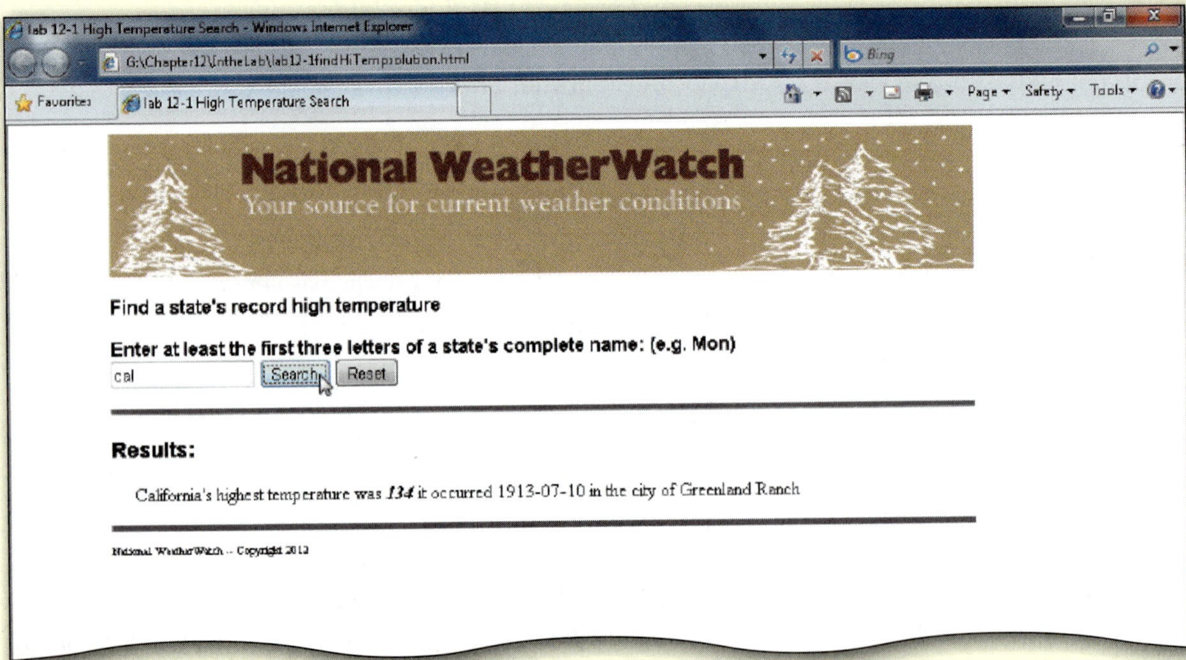

Figure 12–50

Instructions: Perform the following steps:

1. Start a new Notepad++ file.
2. Using the code in Tables 12–11, 12–12, 12–14, and 12–15 on pages HTML 575 through HTML 578 as a guide, create an XML Schema Definition file and save it as lab12-1tempsolution.xsd. Note the format of the date in the XML instance document.
3. Start your browser. Enter http://tools.decisionsoft.com/schemaValidate/ in the Address box to view the Decision Soft Web page in your browser.
4. Click the Browse button next to the XML Schema input text field. Navigate to your storage device and select the lab12-1tempsolution.xsd file.
5. Click the Browse button next to the XML Instance text field. Navigate to your storage device and select the lab12-1temp_solution.xml file.
6. Click the Validate button. When the Your results are ready page displays, click the Click here link to see if any error messages display.
7. If errors exist, correct your XSD file, save it, and revalidate at the Decision Soft Web page. Do not continue until both the XSD and XML documents are error-free.
8. Open the file lab12-1findHiTemp.html from the Chapter12\IntheLab folder of the Data Files for Students and save it immediately as lab12-1findHiTempsolution.html.
9. Use the code presented in Figure 12–31 on page HTML 599 to add the <xml> tag. Use the id of dsoHiTemp to identify the data island in the remainder of the HTML page.
10. Using the steps presented in Figure 12–39 on page HTML 610 as a guide, add the code for the results area using a <div> tag with an id of SearchResult. Add an embedded style to set the left margin at 10%.
11. Using the code presented in Table 12–35 on page HTML 605 as a guide, complete the code for entering the text field and buttons for Search and Reset. Use the id of SearchText for the input text field. Call the findState() user-defined function using the onclick event handler associated with the Search button. Call the clearField() user-defined function using the onclick event handler associated with the Reset button.
12. Using the code presented in Tables 12–35 through 12–37 on pages HTML 605 through HTML 608 as a guide, enter the JavaScript code to create a user-defined function called findState(). The findState() user-defined function should check for blank entries in the input text field before proceeding with the search. When a state is found, a concatenated string message should be assigned to the outputResult variable to display in the <div> container using the innerHTML property.
13. If no state is found, assign the message "Sorry, There is no state like that listed. Please check your spelling." to the innerHTML property of the <div> tag that has the id attribute of SearchResult.
14. Using the code presented in Table 12–39 on page HTML 610 as a guide, enter the JavaScript code to create a user-defined function called keyPressed(). The keyPressed() user-defined function is called on every key pressed; however, if the user presses the ENTER key, the keyPressed() user-defined function will call the findState() user-defined function.
15. Using the code presented in Table 12–40 on page HTML 611 as a guide, enter the JavaScript code to create a user-defined function called clearField(). The clearField() user-defined function clears the input text field, clears the SearchResult division, and uses the focus() method to place the insertion pointer in the input text field.
16. Save the completed HTML file and test it using your browser. If an error occurs, check your code from Steps 9 through 15, and then save and test again.
17. Submit the completed XML file, XSD file, and HTML Web page in the format specified by your instructor.

In the Lab

Lab 2: Creating the Madison Ave Mall XML Data Island

Problem: You are a summer intern for the IT Department of Madison Ave Mall. Management wants to develop a database of mall clients to be used for the accounting and billing office. The Webmaster, Evonn Woods, assigns you the task of converting the text file version of the clients to an XML data island. She wants you to create two versions of the Web page that display the clients. One version is a list sorted in alphabetic order by job name, and the other is a table that displays all the clients, four at a time. You determine the sorted list can be displayed with an XSL style sheet and the search can be done with a simple HTML table using built-in table functions. You add the XSL code and HTML code to make the Web pages appear as shown in Figure 12–51.

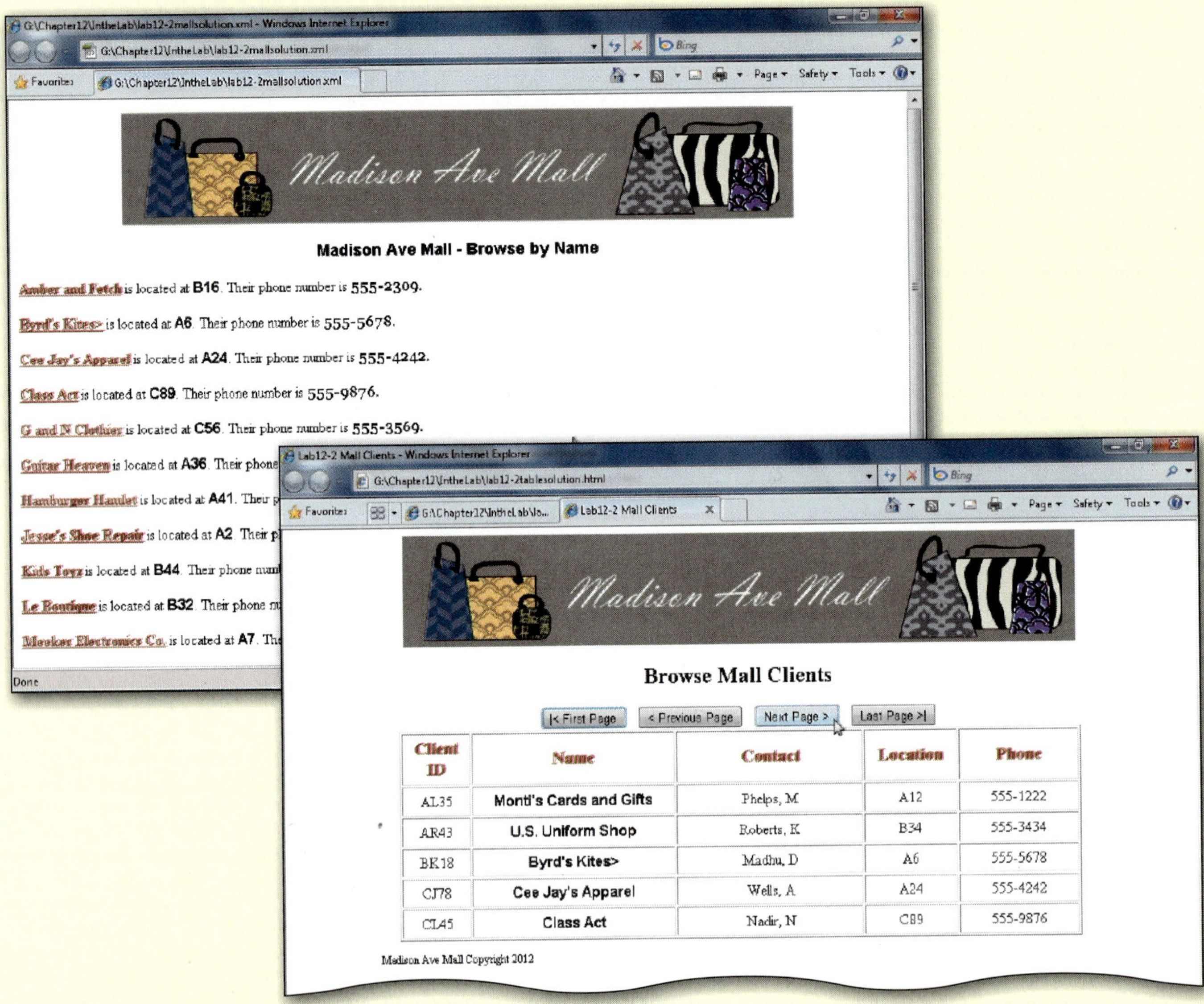

Figure 12–51

Instructions: Perform the following steps:

1. Use Notepad++ and open the lab12-2mall_clients-data.txt file from the Chapter12\IntheLab folder of the Data Files for Students.
2. Create an XML data file using this data and save the file as lab12-2mallsolution.xml.
3. Create an associated XML Schema Definition file and save the file as lab12-2mallsolution.xsd.

4. Start your browser. Enter http://tools.decisionsoft.com/schemaValidate/ in the Address box to view the Decision Soft Web page in your browser. Validate the XML Schema Definition and the XML instance document.
5. If any errors exist, correct your XML and XSD files, save them, and revalidate at the Decision Soft Web page. Do not continue until both the XSD and XML documents are error-free.
6. Start a new Notepad++ document, and save it as lab12-2mallsolution.xsl.
7. Use the code in Tables 12–23, 12–24, and 12–28 on pages HTML 591, HTML 592, and HTML 594 as a guide to complete the XSL style sheet to display the list in alphabetic order by store name. Display the store name, location, and phone number using the style definitions in Table 12–42, as shown in Figure 12–51.

Table 12–42 Style Definitions

Text/Element Items	Style
Name	font-weight:bold; text-decoration:underline; color:#7f0000
value-of select="MallLocation"	font-family:arial, helvetica, sans-serif; font-weight:bold
value-of select="TelePhone"	font-family: Georgia, 'Times New Roman', Times, serif; font-weight:bold

8. Activate the lab12-2mallsolution.xml Notepad++ file and add the XML processing statement to link the XSL file with the XML data.
9. Start your browser and display your lab12-2mallsolution.xml file in the browser to make sure it displays correctly.
10. Start another new Notepad++ session, open the lab12-2table.html file, and save it as lab12-2tablesolution.html.
11. Use the code presented in Figures 12–32 through 12–34 on pages HTML 600 through HTML 602 as a guide to write the HTML code to display the mall clients in a table. Set the attributes to display five rows at a time in the table. Do not forget to add the <xml> tag to bind the XML file as a data island.
12. Save the completed HTML file and test it using your browser. If an error occurs, check your code from Step 11 and save and test again.
13. Submit the completed XSD, XML, XSL, and the HTML Web page in the format specified by your instructor.

In the Lab

Lab 3: Creating the Texas Gulf Coast College Web Site

Problem: You work for Texas Gulf Cost College in Campus Advancement and Marketing. Part of your job is to work with the registrar's office to create and maintain the Schedule Web site. You recently converted the schedule data to an XML data island to allow students to browse or search the schedule for classes. Your assignment is to create the Web pages depicted in Figure 12–52 on the next page. The Web pages include an XML instance document displayed using an XSL style sheet, and the ability to search for specific departments by department code. In addition, to help promote the new Internet radio station, the radio schedule is displayed in an HTML table format.

The lab12-3homesolution.html home page is provided in the Data Files for Students. This page has links to the three pages. You will create the lab12-3fall_class_sched.xml and lab12-3sched_solution.xsl to display the schedule in a formatted list. You will create lab12-3findclasssolution.html to allow users to search for open classes by department code. For the KTGC Internet radio station you will create the lab12-3radio_sched.xml and lab12-3tablesolution.html to display the radio schedule in an HTML table.

Continued >

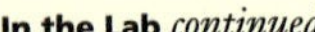

In the Lab *continued*

(a) Home page.

(b) Class schedule by department.

(c) Search by department code.

(d) Radio schedule by day.

Figure 12–52

Instructions: *Perform the following steps:*

1. Using the techniques learned in this chapter, create an XML data island from the lab12-3fall_sched_data.txt file found in the Data Files for Students. The data in this file is in random order. Test the XML file to make sure it is error-free and well formed.
2. Using the techniques learned in this chapter, write XSL code to create an XSL style sheet that will display the schedule data island in department code order. Use the style definitions in Table 12–43 to create the XSL style sheet. Save this file as lab12-3sched_solution.xsl. In addition, add the proper XML processing statement to link the XSL style sheet to the lab12-3fall_class_sched.xml file created in Step 1.

Table 12–43 Style Definitions

Text/Element Items	Style
dept_code	font-variant:small-caps; font-weight:bold
value-of select="course_number"	font-weight:bold; text-decoration:underline
value-of select="course_name"	font-family:arial, helvetica, sans-serif
Credit Hours	font-weight:bold; color:#660099
value-of select="start_time" and value-of select="end_time"	font-style:italic; font-weight: bold; color:#660099
value-of select="seats_avail"	font-family:arial, helvetica, sans-serif; font-weight: bold; color:#990033

3. Starting with lab12-3findclass.html, use the techniques learned in this chapter to create an HTML Web page that allows the students to search the XML data file on department code. As in the chapter project, the user should be able to click the Search button or press the ENTER key to activate the search. Save this file as lab12-3findclasssolution.html. Use lab12-3fall_class_sched.xml as the XML data island for the JavaScript search function.
4. Use lab12-3radio_data.txt to create an XML instance document. Save the XML file as lab12-3radio_sched.xml. Start with lab12-3table.html and use the techniques learned in this chapter to create an HTML Web page that will display the radio schedule data island in a table. Show only one weekday at a time. Save this file as lab12-3tablesolution.html.
5. Make sure you save the completed XML, XSL, and HTML files. The lab12-3homesolution.html file has been provided in the Data Files for Students. The HTML lab12-3homesolution.html Web page has links to each of these files. Start your browser and test the files. If an error occurs, check your code, save, and test again. The HTML Web page will not validate at the http://validator.w3.org/ site because the Microsoft <xml> tag and the special <table> tag attributes (datasrc and datapagesize) are not recognized by the validator.
6. Submit the completed XML, XSL, and HTML Web page files in the format specified by your instructor.

Cases and Places

Apply your creative thinking and problem solving skills to design and implement a solution.

• Easier •• More Difficult

• 1: Write an E-Mail to Request Authorization to Return Damaged Goods

You work in IT at the Dishes-r-Us store. Many of your suppliers prefer to use e-mail for correspondence. Your company wants to keep a database of this correspondence and has asked you to create an XML instance document, XML Schema Definition, and the XSL style sheet for typical e-mails.

Using the case12-1email_text.txt file in the Chapter12\CasesandPlaces folder of the Data Files for Students, create an XML instance. Save the XML instance document as case12-1email_solution.xml. To enter the date correctly, be sure to use the form yyyy-mm-dd so that when you create the schema, you can use the date data type for the e-mail date.

Create an XML Schema Definition and save it as case12-1email_schema.xsd. Create the XSL style sheet to display the e-mail without the element tags in a typical memo/e-mail layout form. Place the to, cc, bcc, reply-to, date, and subject identifiers in XSL <xsl:text> tags. Place each identifier in a <p> tag to display on a separate line. Format the body identifier as small caps and underlined. Format the contents of each element as follows: font-family:arial, helvetica, sans-serif; font-style:italic; font-weight: bold; color: #000099.

Save the style sheet as case12-1email_style.xsl. Link the XSL style to the XML instance document. Test and validate the files.

•• 2: Create the Record Low Temps Web Page

As a summer intern for the National WeatherWatch, you are given the task to create an XML document instance of record low temperatures to go along with the record high temperatures Web page created in In the Lab 1. Using the file called case12-2data.txt in the Chapter12\CasesandPlaces folder of the Data Files for Students, create an XML data island. Save the XML instance document as case12-2lowtemps.xml. Create an XML Schema Definition file and verify that the XSD and XML files are valid using the tools.decisionsoft.com/schemaValidate/index.jsp Web page.

Use the images provided for a banner and buttons as needed. Copy the lab12-1findHiTempsolution HTML file you created from In the Lab 1 or ask your instructor for the file. Rename the file to case12-2findHiTempsolution.html. Using the lab12-1findHiTempsolution.html as a guide, create an HTML Web page that searches for the record low temps in the state XML data island. Save this file as case12-2findLowTempsolution.html. Create a simple Web page called case12-2homesolution.html with two links, one to the find record low temps Web page (case12-2findLowTempsolution.html) and the other link to the find record high temps Web page (lab12-1findHiTempsolution.html; you may need to ask your instructor for this file).

•• 3: Create the Phoenix Fire Web Site

You work for the Phoenix Fire, a Single A, semi professional baseball team, as part of the team's public relations group. Part of your job is collecting and recording team statistics and creating and maintaining the team Web site. You recently converted the team's stats to an XML data island to allow fans to browse or search information about the team or individual team members. Your assignment is to create a Web site that allows fans to browse the database in batting average order, to browse a table of team players in player number order, and to search for individual team members by last name.

The team data is supplied with the file case12-3playersdata.txt in Chapter12\CasesandPlaces folder of the Data Files for Students. You are to create an XML Schema Definition and an XML instance document. Name the schema file case12-3player_solution.xsd, and the document instance file case12-3players_solution.xml. Save case12-3players_solution.xml as case12-3players_xsl-solution.xml so you have two versions of the same file, One will be used to display the data sorted using an XSL style sheet and the other will be used in HTML Web pages as a data island.

Create an XSL file that will sort and display the players in batting average order. Bind this XSL style sheet to the file case12-3players_xsl-solution.xml. Using the case12-3table.html file, create an HTML page to display the XML document instance in an HTML table using navigation buttons you learned in the chapter. Name this Web page case12-3tablesolution.html. Use the case12-3players_solution.xml file to bind the XML file to the HTML Web page.

Using case12-3search.html, create an HTML Web page (save as case12-3searchsolution.html) that allows users to search for a player by name and displays basic statistics: at bats, hits, and home runs using the JavaScript techniques learned in the chapter for search, clear, and key-pressed user-defined functions. Use the case12-3players_solution.xml file to bind the XML file to the search Web page. Use the home page case12-3homesolution.html file to launch and test each of the XML and HTML files created. Check the links on the home page to verify that they call the files you created.

•• 4: Create a Searchable List of Music Downloads

Make It Personal

Create an XML data island that contains your iPod/iTunes, Napster, or Rhapsody music downloads. Include song title, artist, length, album source, and any other information of interest. Display the list in a Web page using an XSL style sheet sorted by song title. Display the list using an HTML table. Create the Web pages to search for songs by artist.

•• 5: Create XML Files from Existing Database or Spreadsheet Files

Working Together

Each group member should find at least one Microsoft Access database file and one Microsoft Excel file (or you can create your own). Using Office 2007 or Office 2010, use the Help system to learn how to export these files to an XML file. Create the XML files with and without the schemas. If possible, the group members should use both versions of Office to create the XML files. As a group, write the instructions for each piece of software on how to export the files to XML. Finally, create a main index Web page that displays the XML files based on what you discovered.

Credits

All of the following artwork was created by Diana Allen.

Chapter 9:

Figure 9-1a, 9-18a+b: Oakwood Elementary School art
Figure 9-19: Classic Steam Train Run banner
Figure 9-20a: Allen Country Fair Grounds art
Figure 9-21: Phi Beta logo
Figure 9-22: Heath Care Fair art
Figure 9-23: Job Fair art
Figure 9-24: Miller High School Band art
Cases and Places 3, Chapter 9 data file art

Chapter 11:

Figure 11-39: Pike's Peak Little League banner
Figure 11-42: Finn's Catering banner
Figure 11-43: Stem's Flower Shop banner
Cases and Places 1, Chapter 11 data file art
Cases and Places 2, Chapter 11 data file art
Cases and Places 3, Chapter 11 data file art

Chapter 12:

Figure 12-1: Classic Books banner
Figure 12-2d: Classic Books banner
Figure 12-28: Classic Books banner
Figure 12-29: Classic Books banner
Figure 12-35: Classic Books banner
Figure 12-36: Classic Books banner
Figure 12-45: Classic Books banner
Figure 12-46: Classic Books banner
Figure 12-48: Palmer Pet House banner
Figure 12-49: Twentieth Century Cinema banner
Figure 12-50: National Weather Watch banner
Figure 12-51: Madison Ave Mall banner
Figure 12-52: Texas Gulf Coast College banner
Cases and Places 2, Chapter 12 data file art
Cases and Places 3, Chapter 12 data file art

NOTES

NOTES

NOTES

Appendix A
HTML Quick Reference

HTML and XHTML Coding Standards

HTML is the original language used for publishing hypertext on the World Wide Web. It is a nonproprietary format based on Standard Generalized Markup Language (SGML). HTML documents can be created with a wide variety of tools, from simple text editors such as Notepad and Notepad++, to sophisticated WYSIWYG authoring tools such as Adobe Dreamweaver. Extensible Markup Language (XML) is a markup language that uses tags to describe the structure and content of a document, not just the format.

Extensible Hypertext Markup Language (XHTML) is a reformulation of HTML so it conforms to XML structure and content rules. By combining HTML and XML, XHTML provides the display features of HTML and the stricter coding standards required by XML.

Table A–1 lists some important XHTML coding practices that Web developers should follow to ensure that their HTML code conforms to XHTML standards as defined by the World Wide Web Consortium (W3). The projects in this book follow XHTML standards and adhere to the rules outlined in Table A–1. This information is also shown in Table 1–3 in Chapter 1.

Table A–1 XHTML Coding Practices

Practice	Invalid Example	Valid Example
HTML file must include a DOCTYPE statement	<html> <head><title>sample Web page</title>	<!DOCTYPE html PUBLIC "-//W3C//DTD XHTML 1.0 Transitional//EN" "http://www.w3.org/TR/xhtml1/DTD/xhtml1-transitional.dtd"> <html> <head><title>sample Web page</title></head>
All tags and attributes must be written in lowercase	<TABLE WIDTH="100%">	<table width="100%">
All attribute values must be enclosed by single or double quotation marks	<table width=100%>	<table width="100%">
All tags must be closed, including tags such as img, hr, and br, which do not have end tags, but which must be closed as a matter of practice	 <hr> <p>This is another paragraph	 <hr /> <p>This is another paragraph</p>
All elements must be nested properly	<p><strong>This is a bold paragraph</p></strong>	<p><strong>This is a bold paragraph</strong></p>

HTML Tags and Attributes

HTML uses tags such as <h1> and <p> to structure text into headings, paragraphs, lists, hypertext links, and so on. Many HTML tags have attributes that can be defined in different ways to further modify the look of the Web page. Table A–2 lists HTML tags and their associated attributes. The list provides a brief description of each tag and its attributes. The default value for each attribute is indicated by bold text in the Description column. For a comprehensive list, more thorough descriptions, examples of all HTML tags, and XHTML coding standards, visit the World Wide Web Consortium Web site at *www.w3.org*.

As the World Wide Web Consortium continually updates the HTML specifications, HTML tags are added to, deleted, and replaced by newer tags. In the list in Table A–2, deprecated elements—tags that can be replaced with newer elements—are indicated with an asterisk. Deprecated elements still are available for use, and most browsers still support them. Browsers will probably continue to support deprecated tags and attributes in the near future, but eventually these tags may become obsolete, so future support cannot be guaranteed. It is therefore a best practice to not use deprecated tags. Obsolete elements are no longer in use and are not supported by common browsers. This appendix does not list obsolete elements.

Table A–2 HTML Tags and Attributes

HTML Tag and Attributes	Description
<!DOCTYPE>	Indicates the version of XHTML used
<!--Text here-->	Inserts invisible comments
<a>....</a>	Anchor; creates a hyperlink or fragment identifier
charset=*character set*	Specifies the character encoding of the linked resource
href=*url*	Hyperlink reference that specifies the target URL
name=*text*	Specifies a name for enclosed text, allowing it to be the target of a hyperlink
rel=*relationship*	Indicates the relationship going from the current page to the target
rev=*relationship*	Indicates the relationship going from the target to the current page
target=*name* *	Defines the name of the window or frame in which the linked resource will appear
<address>....</address>	Used for information such as authorship, e-mail addresses, or addresses; enclosed text appears italicized and indented in some browsers
No attributes	
<area>....</area>	Creates a clickable area, or hotspot, on a client-side image map
coords=*value1, value2*	Specifies the coordinates that define the edges of the hotspot; a comma-delimited list of values
href=*url*	Hyperlink reference that specifies the target URL
Nohref	Indicates that no link is associated with the area
shape=*shape*	Identifies the shape of the area (poly, rect, circle)
target=*name* *	Defines the name of the window or frame in which the linked resource will appear
<b>....</b>	Specifies text to appear in bold
No attributes	
<base />	Identifies the base in all relative URLs in the document
href=*url*	Specifies the absolute URL used to resolve all relative URLs in the document
target=*name* *	Defines the name for the default window or frame in which the hyperlinked pages are displayed

Table A–2 HTML Tags and Attributes *(continued)*

HTML Tag and Attributes	Description
<big>....</big>	Increases the size of the enclosed text to a type size bigger than the surrounding text; exact display size depends on the browser and default font
No attributes	
<blockquote>....</blockquote>	Sets enclosed text to appear as a quotation, indented on the right and left
No attributes	
<body>....</body>	Defines the start and end of a Web page's content
alink=*color* *	Defines the color of an active link
background=*url* *	Identifies the image to be used as a background
bgcolor=*color* *	Sets the document's background color
link=*color* *	Defines the color of links not yet visited
vlink=*color* *	Defines the color of visited links
<b>....</b>	Sets enclosed text to appear in bold
No attributes	
** **	Inserts a line break
clear=*margin* *	Sets the next line to start in a spot where the requested margin is clear (left, right, all, none); used to stop text wrap
<caption>....</caption>	Creates a caption for a table
align=*position* *	Sets caption position (top, bottom, left, right)
<center>....</center> *	Centers the enclosed text horizontally on the page
No attributes	
<cite>....</cite>	Indicates that the enclosed text is a citation; text usually is displayed in italics
No attributes	
<code>....</code>	Indicates that the enclosed text is a code sample from a program; text usually is displayed in fixed width font such as Courier
No attributes	
<col>....</col>	Organizes columns in a table into column groups to share attribute values
align=*position*	Sets horizontal alignment of text within the column (char, center, top, bottom, left, right)
span=*value*	Sets the number of columns that span the <col> element
valign=*position*	Specifies vertical alignment of text within the column (top, middle, bottom)
width=*value*	Sets the width of each column in the column group
<colgroup>....</colgroup>	Encloses a group of <col> tags and groups the columns to set properties
align=*position*	Specifies horizontal alignment of text within the column (char, center, top, bottom, left, right)
char=*character*	Specifies a character on which to align column values (for example, a period is used to align monetary values)
charoff=*value*	Specifies a number of characters to offset data aligned with the character specified in the char property
span=*number*	Sets the number of columns the <col> element spans
valign=*position*	Specifies vertical alignment of text within the column (top, middle, bottom)
width=*value*	Sets the width of each column spanned by the colgroup statement

Table A–2 HTML Tags and Attributes *(continued)*

HTML Tag and Attributes	Description
<dd>....</dd>	Indicates that the enclosed text is a definition in the definition list
No attributes	
<div>....</div>	Defines block-level structure or division in the HTML document
align=*position* *	Specifies alignment of the content block (center, left, right)
class=*name*	Assigns the class name to each class of divisions
id=*name*	Assigns a unique name to a specific content block
<dl>....</dl>	Creates a definition list
No attributes	
<dt>....</dt>	Indicates that the enclosed text is a term in the definition list
No attributes	
<em>....</em>	Indicates that the enclosed text should be emphasized; usually appears in italics
No attributes	
<fieldset>....</fieldset>	Groups related form controls and labels
align=*position*	Specifies alignment of a legend as related to the fieldset (top, bottom, middle, left, right)
<font>....</font> *	Defines the appearance of enclosed text
size=*value* *	Sets the font size in absolute terms (1 through 7) or as a relative value (for example, +2)
color=*color* *	Sets the font color; can be a hexadecimal value (#rrggbb) or a word for a predefined color value (for example, navy)
face=*list* *	Identifies the font face; multiple entries should be separated by commas
point-size=*value* *	Sets the point size of text for downloaded fonts
weight=*value* *	Sets the weight of the font, ranging from 100 (lightest) to 900 (heaviest)
<form>....</form>	Marks the start and end of a Web page form
action=*url*	Specifies the URL of the application that will process the form; required attribute
enctype=*encoding*	Specifies how the form element values will be encoded
method=*method*	Specifies the method used to pass form parameters (data) to the server
target=*text*	Specifies the frame or window that displays the form's results
<frame>....</frame>	Delimits a frame within a frameset
frameborder=*option*	Specifies whether the frame border is displayed (yes, no)
marginheight=*value*	Adds *n* pixels of space above and below the frame contents
marginwidth=*value*	Adds *n* pixels of space to the left and the right of the frame contents
name=*text*	Specifies the name of the frame
noresize	Prevents the user from resizing the frame
scrolling=*option*	Adds scroll bars or not—always (yes), never (no), or add when needed (**auto**)
src=*url*	Defines the URL of the source document that is displayed in the frame
<frameset>....</frameset>	Defines a collection of frames in a frameset
cols=*value1*, *value2*,...	Defines the number and width of frames within a frameset
rows= *value1*, *value2*,...	Defines the number and height of frames within a frameset
frameborder=*option*	Specifies whether the frame border is displayed (yes, no)

Table A–2 HTML Tags and Attributes *(continued)*

HTML Tag and Attributes	Description
<hn>....</hn>	Defines a header level *n*, ranging from the largest (h1) to the smallest (h6)
align=*position* *	Specifies the header alignment (**left**, center, right)
<head>....</head>	Delimits the start and end of the HTML document's head
No attributes	
<hr />	Inserts a horizontal rule
align=*type* *	Specifies the alignment of the horizontal rule (left, **center**, right)
noshade *	Specifies to not use 3D shading and to round the ends of the rule
size=*value* *	Sets the thickness of the rule to a value in pixels
width=*value or %* *	Sets the width of the rule to a value in pixels or a percentage of the page width; percentage is preferred
<html>....</html>	Indicates the start and the end of the HTML document
version=*data*	Indicates the HTML version used; not usually used
<i>....</i>	Sets enclosed text to appear in italics
No attributes	
<iframe>....</iframe> *	Creates an inline frame, also called a floating frame or subwindow, within an HTML document
align=*position* *	Aligns the frame with respect to context (top, middle, **bottom**, left, right)
frameborder=*option* *	Specifies whether a frame border is displayed (1=yes; 0=no)
height=*value* *	Sets the frame height to a value in pixels
marginheight=*value* *	Sets the margin between the contents of the frame and its top and bottom borders to a value in pixels
marginwidth=*value* *	Sets the margin between the contents of the frame and its left and right borders to a value in pixels
name=*text* *	Assigns a name to the current frame
noresize *	Prevents the user from resizing the frame
src=*url* *	Defines the URL of the source document that is displayed in the frame
width=*value* *	Sets the frame width to a value in pixels
scrolling=*option* *	Adds scroll bars or not—always (yes), never (no), or add when needed (**auto**)
<img>....</img>	Inserts an image into the current Web page
align=*type* *	Defines image alignment in relation to the text or the page margin (top, middle, bottom, right, left)
alt=*text*	Provides a text description of an image if the browser cannot display the image; always should be used
border=*value* *	Sets the thickness of the border around the image to a value in pixels; default size is 3
height=*value*	Sets the height of the image to a value in pixels; always should be used
src=*url*	Specifies the URL of the image to be displayed; required
usemap=*url*	Specifies the map of coordinates and links that defines the href within this image
width=*value*	Sets the width of the image to a value in pixels; always should be used
<input>....</input>	Defines controls used in forms
alt=*text*	Provides a short description of the control or image button; for browsers that do not support inline images

Table A–2 HTML Tags and Attributes *(continued)*	
HTML Tag and Attributes	**Description**
<input>....</input> *(continued)*	
checked	Sets radio buttons and check boxes to the checked state
disabled	Disables the control
maxlength=*value*	Sets a value for the maximum number of characters allowed as input for a text or password control
name=*text*	Assigns a name to the control
readonly	Prevents changes to the control
size=*value*	Sets the initial size of the control to a value in characters
src=*url*	Identifies the location of the image if the control is set to an image
tabindex=*value*	Specifies the tab order between elements in the form, with 1 as the first element
type=*type*	Defines the type of control (**text**, password, check box, radio, submit, reset, file, hidden, image, button)
usemap=*url*	Associates an image map as defined by the <map> element
value=*data*	Sets the initial value of the control
<ins>....</ins>	Identifies and displays text as having been inserted in the document in relation to a previous version
cite=*url*	Specifies the URL of a document that has more information on the inserted text
datetime=*datetime*	Date and time of a change
<kbd>....</kbd>	Sets enclosed text to display as keyboard-like input
No attributes	
<label>....</label>	Creates a label for a form control
for=*data*	Indicates the name or ID of the element to which the label is applied
<legend>....</legend>	Assigns a caption to a fieldset element, as defined by the <fieldset> tags
No attributes	
<li>....</li>	Defines the enclosed text as a list item in a list
value=*value1* *****	Inserts or restarts counting with value1
<link />	Establishes a link between the HTML document and another document, such as an external style sheet
charset=*character set*	Specifies the character encoding of the linked resource
href=*url*	Defines the URL of the linked document
name=*text*	Names the current anchor so that it can be the destination for other links
rel=*relationship*	Indicates the relationship going from the current page to the target
rev=*relationship*	Indicates the relationship going from the target to the current page
target=*name*	Defines the name of the frame into which the linked resource will appear
type=*mime-type*	Indicates the data or media type of the linked document (for example, text/css for linked style sheets)
<map>....</map>	Specifies a client-side image map; must enclose <area> tags
name=*text*	Assigns a name to the image map
<meta />	Provides additional data (metadata) about an HTML document
content=*text*	Specifies the value for the <meta> information; required
http-equiv=*text*	Specifies the HTTP-equivalent name for metadata; tells the server to include that name and content in the HTTP header when the HTML document is sent to the client

Table A–2 HTML Tags and Attributes *(continued)*

HTML Tag and Attributes	Description
<meta /> *(continued)*	
name=*text*	Assigns a name to metadata
scheme=*text*	Provides additional context for interpreting the information in the content attribute
<noframes>....</noframes>	Defines content to be displayed in browsers that do not support frames; very important to include
No attributes	
<object>....</object>	Includes an external object in the HTML document such as an image, a Java applet, or other external object, not well-supported by most browsers
archive=*url*	Specifies the URL of the archive containing classes and other resources that will be preloaded for use by the object
classid=*url*	Specifies the URL of the embedded object
codebase=*url*	Sets the base URL for the object; helps resolve relative references
codetype=*type*	Identifies the content type of the data in the object
data=*url*	Identifies the location of the object's data
Declare	Indicates the object will be declared only, not installed in the page
height=*value*	Sets the height of the object to a value in pixels
name=*text*	Assigns a control name to the object for use in forms
standby=*text*	Defines the message to display while the object loads
tabindex=*value*	Specifies the tab order between elements, with 1 as the first element
type=*type*	Specifies the content or media type of the object
usemap=*url*	Associates an image map as defined by the <map> element
width=*value*	Sets the width of the object to a value in pixels
<ol>....</ol>	Defines an ordered list that contains numbered list item elements (<li>)
type=*option* *****	Sets or resets the numbering format for the list; options include: A=capital letters, a=lowercase letters, I=capital Roman numerals, i=lowercase Roman numerals, or **1**=Arabic numerals
<option>....</option>	Defines individual options in a selection list, as defined by the <select> element
label=*text*	Provides a shorter label for the option than that specified in its content
Selected	Sets the option to be the default or the selected option in a list
value=*value*	Sets a value returned to the server when the user selects the option
Disabled	Disables the option items
<p>....</p>	Delimits a paragraph; automatically inserts a blank line between text
align=*position* *****	Aligns text within the paragraph (left, center, right)
<param>....</param>	Passes a parameter to an object or applet, as defined by the <object> or <applet> element
id=*text*	Assigns an identifier to the element
name=*text*	Defines the name of the parameter required by an object
type=*type*	Specifies the content or media type of the object
value=*data*	Sets the value of the parameter
valuetype=*data*	Identifies the type of parameter used in the value attribute (data, ref, object)

Table A–2 HTML Tags and Attributes *(continued)*

HTML Tag and Attributes	Description
<pre>....</pre>	Preserves the original format of the enclosed text; keeps line breaks and spacing the same as the original
No attributes	
<q>....</q>	Sets enclosed text as a short quotation
lang=*option*	Defines the language in which the quotation will appear
<samp>....</samp>	Sets enclosed text to appear as sample output from a computer program or script; usually appears in a monospace font
No attributes	
<script>....</script>	Inserts a client-side script into an HTML document
defer	Indicates that the browser should defer executing the script
src=*url*	Identifies the location of an external script
type=*mime-type*	Indicates the data or media type of the script language (for example, text/javascript for JavaScript commands)
<select>....</select>	Defines a form control to create a multiple-choice menu or scrolling list; encloses a set of <option> tags to define one or more options
name=*text*	Assigns a name to the selection list
multiple	Sets the list to allow multiple selections
size=*value*	Sets the number of visible options in the list
disabled	Disables the selection list
tabindex=*value*	Specifies the tab order between list items, with 1 as the first element
<small>....</small>	Sets enclosed text to appear in a smaller typeface
No attributes	
<span>....</span>	Creates a user-defined container to add inline structure to the HTML document
No attributes	
<strike>....</strike> *	Sets enclosed text to appear with strong emphasis; usually displayed as bold text
No attributes	
<strong>....</strong>	Sets enclosed text to appear with strong emphasis; usually displayed as bold text
No attributes	
<style>....</style>	Encloses embedded style sheet rules for use in the HTML document
media=*data*	Identifies the intended medium of the style (**screen**, tty, tv, projection, handheld, print, braille, aural, all)
title=*data*	Indicates the title of the style sheet
type=*data*	Specifies the content or media type of the style language (for example, text/css for linked style sheets)
_{....}	Sets enclosed text to appear in subscript
No attributes	
^{....}	Sets enclosed text to appear in superscript
No attributes	
<table>....</table>	Marks the start and end of a table
align=*position* *	Aligns the table text (left, right, center, justify, char)
border=*value*	Sets the border around a table to a value in pixels
cellpadding=*value*	Sets padding around each cell's contents to a value in pixels

Table A–2 HTML Tags and Attributes *(continued)*

HTML Tag and Attributes	Description
<table>....</table> *(continued)*	
cellspacing=*value*	Sets spacing between cells to a value in pixels
summary=*text*	Provides a summary of the table's purpose and structure
width=*value or %*	Sets table width in pixels or a percentage of the window
frame=*option*	Defines which parts of the outer border (frame) to display (void, above, below, hsides, lhs, rhs, vsides, box, border)
rules=*option*	Specifies which inner borders are to appear between the table cells (none, groups, rows, cols, all)
<tbody>....</tbody>	Defines a groups of rows in a table body
align=*option*	Aligns text (left, center, right, justify, char)
char=*character*	Specifies a character on which to align column values (for example, a period is used to align monetary values)
charoff=*value*	Specifies a number of characters to offset data aligned with the character specified in the char property
valign=*position*	Sets vertical alignment of cells in a group (top, middle, bottom, baseline)
<td>....</td>	Defines a data cell in a table; contents are left-aligned and normal text by default
bgcolor=*color* *	Defines the background color for the cell
colspan=*value*	Defines the number of adjacent columns spanned by the cell
rowspan=*value*	Defines the number of adjacent rows spanned by the cell
width=*n* or % *	Sets the width of the table in either pixels or a percentage of the whole table width
headers=*idrefs*	Defines the list of header cells for the current cell
abbr=*text*	Provides an abbreviated version of the cell's contents that browsers can use if space is limited
scope=*option*	Specifies cells for which the element defines header cells (row, col, rowgroup, colgroup)
align=*position*	Specifies horizontal alignment (left, center, right, justify, char)
char=*character*	Specifies a character on which to align column values (for example, a period is used to align monetary values)
charoff=*value*	Specifies a number of characters to offset data aligned with the character specified in the char property
valign=*position*	Sets vertical alignment of cells in the group (top, middle, bottom, baseline)
<textarea>....</textarea>	Creates a multiline text input area within a form
cols=*value*	Defines the number of columns in the text input area
name=*data*	Assigns a name to the text area
rows=*value*	Defines the number of rows in the text input area
disabled	Disables the element
readonly	Prevents the user from editing content in the text area
tabindex=*value*	Specifies the tab order between elements, with 1 as the first element
<tfoot>....</tfoot>	Identifies and groups rows into a table footer
align=*position*	Specifies horizontal alignment (left, center, right, justify, char)
char=*character*	Specifies a character on which to align column values (for example, a period is used to align monetary values)
charoff=*value*	Specifies a number of characters to offset data aligned with the character specified in the char property

Table A–2 HTML Tags and Attributes *(continued)*

HTML Tag and Attributes	Description
<tfoot>....</tfoot> *(continued)*	
valign=*position*	Sets vertical alignment of cells in a group (top, middle, bottom, baseline)
<th>....</th>	Defines a table header cell; contents are bold and center-aligned by default
bgcolor=*color* *	Defines the background color for the cell
colspan=*value*	Defines the number of adjacent columns spanned by the cell
rowspan=*value*	Defines the number of adjacent rows spanned by the cell
width=*n* or % *	Sets the width of the table in either pixels or a percentage of the whole table width
<thead>....</thead>	Identifies and groups rows into a table header
align=*position* *	Specifies horizontal alignment (left, center, right, justify, char)
char=*character*	Specifies a character on which to align column values (for example, a period is used to align monetary values)
charoff=*value*	Specifies a number of characters to offset data aligned with the character specified in the char property
valign=*position*	Sets vertical alignment of cells in a group (top, middle, bottom, baseline)
<title>....</title>	Defines the title for the HTML document; always should be used
No attributes	
<tr>....</tr>	Defines a row of cells within a table
bgcolor=*color* *	Defines the background color for the cell
align=*position* *	Specifies horizontal alignment (left, center, right, justify, char)
char=*character*	Specifies a character on which to align column values (for example, a period is used to align monetary values)
charoff=*value*	Specifies a number of characters to offset data aligned with the character specified in the char property
valign=*position*	Sets vertical alignment of cells in a group (top, middle, bottom, baseline)
<tt>....</tt>	Formats the enclosed text in teletype- or computer-style monospace font
No attributes	
<u>....</u> *	Sets enclosed text to appear with an underline
No attributes	
<ul>....</ul>	Defines an unordered list that contains bulleted list item elements (<li>)
type=*option* *	Sets or resets the bullet format for the list; options include: circle, **disc**, square
<var>....</var>	Indicates the enclosed text is a variable's name; used to mark up variables or program arguments
No attributes	

Appendix B

Browser-Safe Color Palette

Browser-Safe Colors

Three hardware components help deliver color to a computer user: the processor, the video card, and the monitor. Because of the wide variety of components that exist, the color quality that users see varies greatly. The software on a user's computer, specifically the Web browser, also affects the way that color is displayed on a monitor. For Web developers, it is the browser that limits color significantly. It is very difficult, if not impossible, to plan for all possible color variations created by a Web browser. Using browser-safe colors allows for the browser variations, but it also limits the number of colors used on the Web page.

A total of 216 browser-safe colors appear well on different monitors, operating systems, and browsers—including both Windows and Macintosh operating systems and Internet Explorer and Mozilla Firefox browsers. When using color on your Web site, keep in mind that using only the 216 browser-safe colors can be very restrictive, especially for the approximately 10% of Web visitors who have 256-color monitors. On those monitors, only the browser-safe colors will be displayed. If you decide to use a non-browser-safe color, the visitor's browser will try to create the color by combining (a process called dithering) any number of the 216 acceptable colors. The resulting color could be slightly different from the color you had intended.

For a complete list of the 216 browser-safe colors, see Table B–1 on the next page or visit the Shelly-Cashman Series HTML Web page (*scsite.com/html6e*) and click Color Chart. Links to other Web sites with information about browser-safe colors also are available.

Note that you can use the color name as well as the color number when identifying a particular color to use. For instance, you can use the number #000099 (see color sample on the following page) or the word "navy" to specify the same color. Also note that to comply with XHTML standards, color names such as "navy" or "silver" must be all lowercase letters.

Table B–1 Browser-Safe Colors

#ffffff	#ffffcc	#ffff99	#ffff66	#ffff33	#ffff00
#ffccff	#ffcccc	#ffcc99	#ffcc66	#ffcc33	#ffcc00
#ff99ff	#ff99cc	#ff9999	#ff9966	#ff9933	#ff9900
#ff66ff	#ff66cc	#ff6699	#ff6666	#ff6633	#ff6600
#ff33ff	#ff33cc	#ff3399	#ff3366	#ff3333	#ff3300
#ff00ff	#ff00cc	#ff0099	#ff0066	#ff0033	#ff0000
#ccffff	#ccffcc	#ccff99	#ccff66	#ccff33	#ccff00
#ccccff	#cccccc	#cccc99	#cccc66	#cccc33	#cccc00
#cc99ff	#cc99cc	#cc9999	#cc9966	#cc9933	#cc9900
#cc66ff	#cc66cc	#cc6699	#cc6666	#cc6633	#cc6600
#cc33ff	#cc33cc	#cc3399	#cc3366	#cc3333	#cc3300
#cc00ff	#cc00cc	#cc0099	#cc0066	#cc0033	#cc0000
#99ffff	#99ffcc	#99ff99	#99ff66	#99ff33	#99ff00
#99ccff	#99cccc	#99cc99	#99cc66	#99cc33	#99cc00
#9999ff	#9999cc	#999999	#999966	#999933	#999900
#9966ff	#9966cc	#996699	#996666	#996633	#996600
#9933ff	#9933cc	#993399	#993366	#993333	#993300
#9900ff	#9900cc	#990099	#990066	#990033	#990000
#66ffff	#66ffcc	#66ff99	#66ff66	#66ff33	#66ff00
#66ccff	#66cccc	#66cc99	#66cc66	#66cc33	#66cc00
#6699ff	#6699cc	#669999	#669966	#669933	#669900
#6666ff	#6666cc	#666699	#666666	#666633	#666600
#6633ff	#6633cc	#663399	#663366	#663333	#663300
#6600ff	#6600cc	#660099	#660066	#660033	#660000
#33ffff	#33ffcc	#33ff99	#33ff66	#33ff33	#33ff00
#33ccff	#33cccc	#33cc99	#33cc66	#33cc33	#33cc00
#3399ff	#3399cc	#339999	#339966	#339933	#339900
#3366ff	#3366cc	#336699	#336666	#336633	#336600
#3333ff	#3333cc	#333399	#333366	#333333	#333300
#3300ff	#3300cc	#330099	#330066	#330033	#330000
#00ffff	#00ffcc	#00ff99	#00ff66	#00ff33	#00ff00
#00ccff	#00cccc	#00cc99	#00cc66	#00cc33	#00cc00
#0099ff	#0099cc	#009999	#009966	#009933	#009900
#0066ff	#0066cc	#006699	#006666	#006633	#006600
#0033ff	#0033cc	#003399	#003366	#003333	#003300
#0000ff	#0000cc	#000099	#000066	#000033	#000000

Appendix C

Accessibility Standards and the Web

Making the Web Accessible

Nearly 20% of the world population has some sort of disability, a physical condition that limits the individual's ability to perform certain tasks. The U.S. Congress passed the Rehabilitation Act in 1973, which promotes economic independence for those with disabilities. In 1998, Congress amended this act to reflect the latest changes in information technology. Section 508 requires that any electronic information developed, procured, maintained, or used by the federal government be accessible to people with disabilities. Disabilities that inhibit a person's ability to use the Web fall into four main categories: visual, hearing, motor, and cognitive. This amendment has had a profound effect on how Web pages are designed and developed.

Although Section 508 is specific to Web sites created and maintained by the federal government, all competent Web developers adhere to the Section 508 guidelines. It is important to include everyone as a potential user of your Web site, including those with disabilities. To ignore the needs of nearly 20% of our population is just poor practice.

The World Wide Web Consortium (W3C) developed its own set of guidelines, called the Web Accessibility Initiative (WAI), for accessibility standards. These guidelines cover many of the same issues defined in the Section 508 rules and expand on them relative to superior Web site design.

Section 508 Guidelines Examples

The 13 parts of the Section 508 guidelines are as follows:

- Subpart A—General
  - 1194.1 Purpose.
  - 1194.2 Application.
  - 1194.3 General exceptions.
  - 1194.4 Definitions.
  - 1194.5 Equivalent facilitation.

- Subpart B—Technical Standards
  - 1194.21 Software applications and operating systems.
  - 1194.22 Web-based intranet and Internet information and applications. 16 rules.
  - 1194.23 Telecommunications products.
  - 1194.24 Video and multimedia products.
  - 1194.25 Self contained, closed products.
  - 1194.26 Desktop and portable computers.
- Subpart C—Functional Performance Criteria
  - 1194.31 Functional performance criteria.
- Subpart D—Information, Documentation, and Support
  - 1194.41 Information, documentation, and support.

Web developers should review these guidelines thoroughly. We focus on the specific guidelines for intranet and Internet development in the following sections.

Sub-section **§ 1194.22** of Section 508, **Web-based intranet and Internet information and applications**, is the segment of the amendment that impacts Web design. There are 16 paragraphs within § 1194.22, which are lettered (a) through (p). These 16 paragraphs describe how each component of a Web site should be designed to ensure accessibility. The following is a list of the 16 paragraphs:

§ 1194.22 (a) A text equivalent for every non-text element shall be provided (e.g., via "alt", "longdesc", or in element content).

Graphical images that contain Web page content should include a text alternative (for example, using the alt or longdesc attributes). For good Web development practice, all images should include the alt attribute to describe that image, as shown in Project 2.

§ 1194.22 (b) Equivalent alternatives for any multimedia presentation shall be synchronized with the presentation.

Audio clips should contain a transcript of the content; video clips need closed captioning.

§ 1194.22 (c) Web pages shall be designed so that all information conveyed with color is also available without color, for example from context or markup.

Although color is an important component of most Web pages, you need to consider those site visitors with forms of color blindness if the color contributes significantly to the Web site content.

§ 1194.22 (d) Documents shall be organized so they are readable without requiring an associated style sheet.

Style sheets have an important role in Web development. Some browsers, however, allow users to create their own customized style sheets, which could alter the style sheets that you have designated. When developing a Web site using style sheets, ensure that the site maintains its functionality, even if your specified style sheets have been turned off.

§ 1194.22 (e) Redundant text links shall be provided for each active region of a server-side image map.

and

§ 1194.22 (f) Client-side image maps shall be provided instead of server-side image maps except where the regions cannot be defined with an available geometric shape.

This means that it is preferable for the Web developer to use client-side image maps unless the map uses a shape that the client-side will not allow. If the Web developer chooses to use server-side image maps, the developer should provide text alternatives for each link on the image map.

§ 1194.22 (g) Row and column headers shall be identified for data tables.
and

§ 1194.22 (h) Markup shall be used to associate data cells and header cells for data tables that have two or more logical levels of row or column headers.

You should structure your tables so that they appear in a linear fashion. In other words, the table content should be displayed one cell at a time, working from left to right across each row before moving to the next row.

§ 1194.22 (i) Frames shall be titled with text that facilitates frame identification and navigation.

Nonvisual browsers open frame sites one frame at a time. It is therefore important that the Web developer gives a name to each frame, and that the name reflects the contents of that frame. You can use either the title or the name attribute, but because nonvisual browsers differ in which attribute they use, the Web developer should use both attributes.

§ 1194.22 (j) Pages shall be designed to avoid causing the screen to flicker with a frequency greater than 2 Hz and lower than 55 Hz.

Animations on a Web page can be irritating to many people. However, they also can be quite harmful to people who have certain cognitive or visual disabilities or seizure disorders. You should therefore ensure that animations fall within the ranges stated, and you should limit the use of animations when possible. You also should make certain that necessary page content is available without the animations.

§ 1194.22 (k) A text-only page, with equivalent information or functionality, shall be provided to make a Web site comply with the provisions of this part, when compliance cannot be accomplished in any other way. The content of the text-only pages shall be updated whenever the primary page changes.

If you cannot comply with the other 15 guidelines, you should provide a text-only page to display the content of the page. You should also provide an easily accessible link to that text-only Web page.

§ 1194.22 (l) When pages utilize scripting languages to display content, or to create interface elements, the information provided by the script shall be identified with functional text that can be read by adaptive technology.

Scripts are often used to create a more interesting and dynamic Web page. You should ensure that the functionality of the script is still available for any person using nonvisual browsers.

§ 1194.22 (m) When a Web page requires that an applet, plug-in, or other application be present on the client system to interpret page content, the page must provide a link to a plug-in or applet that complies with 1994.21 (a) through (i).

Any applet or plug-in that is used on your Web pages should also comply with Section 508. The Web developer should provide a link to the applet or plug-in that is compliant with Section 508.

§ 1194.22 (n) When electronic forms are designed to be completed on-line, the form shall allow people using assistive technology to access the information, field elements, and functionality required for completion and submission of the form, including all directions and cues.

Forms need to be accessible to anyone, including those using nonvisual browsers. You should therefore include value attributes or alternative text for buttons, input boxes, and text area boxes on any form included on your Web page.

§ 1194.22 (o) A method shall be provided that permits users to skip repetitive navigation links.

It can be helpful to provide text links at the very top of a Web page so that users of nonvisual browsers can quickly link to the content of the Web site. Some Web developers use a link that allows users to skip to the main content of the Web page immediately by using a transparent image.

§ 1194.22 (p) When a timed response is required, the user shall be alerted and given sufficient time to indicate that more time is required.

Users need to be given sufficient time to react to a time-out from inactivity by notifying users that the process will soon time out. The user should then be given a way to easily request additional time.

WAI Guidelines

The WAI identifies 14 guidelines for Web developers. Within each guideline is a collection of checkpoints that identifies how to apply the guideline to specific Web site features. Each checkpoint is given a priority score that shows how much importance the WAI places on that guideline. All Web developers should review the information at the official Web site at *www.w3c.org/WAI* for complete information on these guidelines, and should apply the guidelines, together with the following suggestions on the application of the guidelines, to their Web page development.

The three WAI priorities are:

Priority 1: A Web content developer **must** satisfy this checkpoint. Otherwise, one or more groups will find it impossible to access information in the document. Satisfying this checkpoint is a basic requirement for some groups to be able to use Web documents.

Priority 2: A Web content developer **should** satisfy this checkpoint. Otherwise, one or more groups will find it difficult to access information in the document. Satisfying this checkpoint will remove significant barriers to accessing Web documents.

Priority 3: A Web content developer **may** address this checkpoint. Otherwise, one or more groups will find it somewhat difficult to access information in the document. Satisfying this checkpoint will improve access to Web documents.

Table C–1 contains the WAI guidelines together with the checkpoints and corresponding priority value.

Table C–1

WAI Guidelines and Checkpoints	Priority
1. Provide equivalent alternatives to auditory and visual content.	
1.1 Provide a text equivalent for every non-text element (e.g., via "alt", "longdesc", or in element content). *This includes*: images, graphical representations of text (including symbols), image map regions, animations (e.g., animated GIFs), applets and programmatic objects, ASCII art, frames, scripts, images used as list bullets, spacers, graphical buttons, sounds (played with or without user interaction), standalone audio files, audio tracks of video, and video.	1
1.2 Provide redundant text links for each active region of a server-side image map.	1
1.3 Until user agents can automatically read aloud the text equivalent of a visual track, provide an auditory description of the important information of the visual track of a multimedia presentation.	1
1.4 For any time-based multimedia presentation (e.g., a movie or animation), synchronize equivalent alternatives (e.g., captions or auditory descriptions of the visual track) with the presentation.	1
1.5 Until user agents render text equivalents for client-side image map links, provide redundant text links for each active region of a client-side image map.	3
2. Don't rely on color alone.	
2.1 Ensure that all information conveyed with color is also available without color; for example, from context or markup.	1
2.2 Ensure that foreground and background color combinations provide sufficient contrast when viewed by someone having color deficits or when viewed on a black and white screen.	2
3. Use markup and style sheets and do so properly.	
3.1 When an appropriate markup language exists, use markup rather than images to convey information.	2
3.2 Create documents that validate to published formal grammars.	2
3.3 Use style sheets to control layout and presentation.	2
3.4 Use relative rather than absolute units in markup language attribute values and style sheet property values.	2
3.5 Use header elements to convey document structure and use them according to specification.	2
3.6 Mark up lists and list items properly.	2
3.7 Mark up quotations. Do not use quotation markup for formatting effects such as indentation.	2
4. Clarify natural language usage.	
4.1 Clearly identify changes in the natural language of a document's text and any text equivalents (e.g., captions).	1
4.2 Specify the expansion of each abbreviation or acronym in a document where it first occurs.	3
4.3 Identify the primary natural language of a document.	3

Table C–1 *(continued)*

WAI Guidelines and Checkpoints	Priority
5. Create tables that transform gracefully.	
5.1 For data tables, identify row and column headers.	1
5.2 For data tables that have two or more logical levels of row or column headers, use markup to associate data cells and header cells.	1
5.3 Do not use tables for layout unless the table makes sense when linearized. Otherwise, if the table does not make sense, provide an alternative equivalent (which may be a linearized version).	2
5.4 If a table is used for layout, do not use any structural markup for the purpose of visual formatting.	2
5.5 Provide summaries for tables.	3
5.6 Provide abbreviations for header labels.	3
6. Ensure that pages featuring new technologies transform gracefully.	
6.1 Organize documents so they may be read without style sheets. For example, when an HTML document is rendered without associated style sheets, it must still be possible to read the document.	1
6.2 Ensure that equivalents for dynamic content are updated when the dynamic content changes.	1
6.3 Ensure that pages are usable when scripts, applets, or other programmatic objects are turned off or not supported. If this is not possible, provide equivalent information on an alternative accessible page.	1
6.4 For scripts and applets, ensure that event handlers are input-device-independent.	2
6.5 Ensure that dynamic content is accessible or provide an alternative presentation or page.	2
7. Ensure user control of time-sensitive content changes.	
7.1 Until user agents allow users to control flickering, avoid causing the screen to flicker.	1
7.2 Until user agents allow users to control blinking, avoid causing content to blink (i.e., change presentation at a regular rate, such as turning on and off).	2
7.3 Until user agents allow users to freeze moving content, avoid movement in pages.	2
7.4 Until user agents provide the ability to stop the refresh, do not create periodically auto-refreshing pages.	2
7.5 Until user agents provide the ability to stop auto-redirect, do not use markup to redirect pages automatically. Instead, configure the server to perform redirects.	2
8. Ensure direct accessibility of embedded user interfaces.	
8.1 Make programmatic elements such as scripts and applets directly accessible or compatible with assistive technologies (Priority 1 if functionality is important and not presented elsewhere, otherwise Priority 2).	2
9. Design for device-independence.	
9.1 Provide client-side image maps instead of server-side image maps except where the regions cannot be defined with an available geometric shape.	1
9.2 Ensure that any element that has its own interface can be operated in a device-independent manner.	2
9.3 For scripts, specify logical event handlers rather than device-dependent event handlers.	2
9.4 Create a logical tab order through links, form controls, and objects.	3
9.5 Provide keyboard shortcuts to important links (including those in client-side image maps), form controls, and groups of form controls.	3

Table C–1 *(continued)*

WAI Guidelines and Checkpoints	Priority
10. Use interim solutions.	
10.1 Until user agents allow users to turn off spawned windows, do not cause pop-ups or other windows to appear and do not change the current window without informing the user.	2
10.2 Until user agents support explicit associations between labels and form controls, for all form controls with implicitly associated labels, ensure that the label is properly positioned.	2
10.3 Until user agents (including assistive technologies) render side-by-side text correctly, provide a linear text alternative (on the current page or some other) for *all* tables that lay out text in parallel, word-wrapped columns.	3
10.4 Until user agents handle empty controls correctly, include default, place-holding characters in edit boxes and text areas.	3
10.5 Until user agents (including assistive technologies) render adjacent links distinctly, include non-link, printable characters (surrounded by spaces) between adjacent links.	3
11. Use W3C technologies and guidelines.	
11.1 Use W3C technologies when they are available and appropriate for a task and use the latest versions when supported.	2
11.2 Avoid deprecated features of W3C technologies.	2
11.3 Provide information so that users may receive documents according to their preferences (e.g., language, content type, etc.).	3
11.4 If, after best efforts, you cannot create an accessible page, provide a link to an alternative page that uses W3C technologies, is accessible, has equivalent information (or functionality), and is updated as often as the inaccessible (original) page.	1
12. Provide context and orientation information.	
12.1 Title each frame to facilitate frame identification and navigation.	1
12.2 Describe the purpose of frames and how frames relate to each other if it is not obvious by frame titles alone.	2
12.3 Divide large blocks of information into more manageable groups where natural and appropriate.	2
12.4 Associate labels explicitly with their controls.	2
13. Provide clear navigation mechanisms.	
13.1 Clearly identify the target of each link.	2
13.2 Provide metadata to add semantic information to pages and sites.	2
13.3 Provide information about the general layout of a site (e.g., a site map or table of contents).	2
13.4 Use navigation mechanisms in a consistent manner.	2
13.5 Provide navigation bars to highlight and give access to the navigation mechanism.	3
13.6 Group related links, identify the group (for user agents), and, until user agents do so, provide a way to bypass the group.	3
13.7 If search functions are provided, enable different types of searches for different skill levels and preferences.	3
13.8 Place distinguishing information at the beginning of headings, paragraphs, lists, etc.	3
13.9 Provide information about document collections (i.e., documents comprising multiple pages).	3
13.10 Provide a means to skip over multi-line ASCII art.	3

Table C–1 *(continued)*

WAI Guidelines and Checkpoints	Priority
14. Ensure that documents are clear and simple.	
14.1 Use the clearest and simplest language appropriate for a site's content.	1
14.2 Supplement text with graphic or auditory presentations where they will facilitate comprehension of the page.	3
14.3 Create a style of presentation that is consistent across pages.	3

Appendix D
CSS Properties and Values

This appendix provides a brief review of Cascading Style Sheets (CSS) concepts and terminology, and lists CSS level 1 and 2 properties and values supported by most browsers.

CSS Concepts and Terminology

CSS supports three types of style sheets: inline, embedded, and external (or linked). A **style** is a rule that defines the appearance of an element on a Web page. Inline styles are used to change the appearance (or style) for individual elements, such as a heading or a paragraph. A **style sheet** is a series of rules that defines the style for a Web page or an entire Web site. The **style statement** changes that specific element, but does not affect other elements in the document. With an embedded style sheet, you add the style sheet within the <style></style> container between the <head></head> tags of the HTML document. An embedded style sheet allows you to define the style for an entire Web page. With a linked, or external, style sheet, you create a text file that contains all of the styles that you want to apply, and save the text file with the file extension .css. You then add a link to this external style sheet on any Web page in the Web site in which you want to use those styles. External style sheets give you the most flexibility and are ideal to apply the same formats to all of the Web pages in a Web site. External style sheets also make it easy to change formats quickly across Web pages.

The part of the style statement that identifies the page element that you want to change is called the selector. In the example below, the selector is the h1 (heading size 1) element. The part of the style statement that identifies how the element(s) should appear is called the declaration. In this example, the declaration is everything between the curly brackets {color: red}. This includes the property named color and the value named red. You could use the statement below in both an embedded and an external style sheet. With an external (linked) style sheet, you save the file with the selectors and declarations as a .css file. You then link that file into any Web page into which you want those styles to apply.

```
h1    {color: red}
```

To add the same style statement into an embedded style sheet, you have to put the selector and declaration within the <style></style> container as shown below. This code would be inserted within the <head></head> container.

```
<style type="text/css">
h1    {color: red}
</style>
```

These two style sheets (embedded and external) give you the most flexibility. For instance, if you want all h1 and h2 headings to be the color red, you would simply add the code below:

```
h1, h2      {color: red}
```

You also could make the style change to the h1 heading as an inline style. You insert that code within the body of the Web page in the following format:

```
<h1 style="color: red">
```

Although this can be very useful, understand that you would have to insert the same declaration for every h1 (or h2 or h3) heading within the Web page. That makes the inline style less flexible than the other style sheets.

As shown in Table D–1, the three style sheets supported by CSS control the appearance of a Web page at different levels. Each style sheet type also has a different level of precedence or priority in relationship to the others. An external style sheet, for example, is used to define styles for multiple pages in a Web site. An embedded style sheet is used to change the style of one Web page, but overrides or takes precedence over any styles defined in an external style sheet. An inline style sheet is used to control the style within an individual HTML tag and takes precedence over the styles defined in both embedded and external style sheets.

Table D–1 CSS Precedence

Type	Level and Precedence
Inline	• To change the style within an individual HTML tag • Overrides embedded and external style sheets
Embedded	• To change the style of one Web page • Overrides external style sheets
External	• To change the style of multiple pages in a Web site

Because style sheets have different levels of precedence, all three types of style sheets can be used on a single Web page. For example, you may want some elements of a Web page to match the other Web pages in the Web site, but you also may want to vary the look of certain sections of that Web page. You can do this by using the three types of style sheets.

A newer version of Cascading Style Sheets, CSS3, is currently being defined, but is not covered in this appendix. CSS3 utilizes a modularized approach to style sheets, which allows CSS to be updated in a more timely and flexible manner.

For a more comprehensive list of CSS properties and values, see the *www.w3.org* Web site. In addition to an abundance of information about CSS levels 1 and 2, the w3 site also has extensive information about CSS3, from its history to its use with browsers today. The Web site also includes many online tutorials for learning CSS levels 1 and 2 as well as CSS3.

CSS Properties

Tables D–2 through D–10 show the property names, descriptions, and valid values for various categories of CSS properties. Values listed in bold are the default.

Acceptable Units of Measure

Many of the properties below use units of measure for their attribute values. Table D–2 lists the acceptable units of measure that can be used.

Table D–2 Units of Measure

Property Name	Description	Values
color	A color is either a keyword or a numerical RGB specification	[keyword – aqua, black, blue, fuchsia, gray, green, lime, maroon, navy, olive, purple, red, silver, teal, white, and yellow] [#rrggbb]
length	Indicates both relative (em, ex, px) and absolute (in, cm, mm, pt, pc) lengths	em – relative to size of capital M of browser default font ex – relative to small x of browser default font px – represents one pixel, smallest unit of measure in – one inch cm – one centimeter mm – one millimeter pt – 1/72 of an inch pc – 1/12 of an inch
percentage	Values are always relative to another value; default if not defined	percentage of width or height of parent element

Background and Color Styles

Colors and subtle backgrounds can enhance the style of a Web page significantly. You can set the background or color of an element using these style sheet properties. Not all browser versions support these style attributes, however, so be aware that not all users will be able to see the background and color styles set by these properties. Table D–3 provides a list of background and color properties.

Table D–3 Background and Color Properties

Property Name	Description	Values
background	The background property is a shorthand property for setting the individual background properties (i.e., background-color, background-image, 'background-repeat, 'background-attachment, and background-position) at the same place in the style sheet.	
background-attachment	Sets the background image to fixed, or scrolls with the page	scroll fixed
background-color	Sets the background color of an element	**transparent** [color]
background-image	Sets an image as the background	**none** [url]
background-position	Sets the starting position of a background image	[length] [percentage] bottom center left right top
background-repeat	Sets if/how a background image will be repeated	**repeat** repeat-x repeat-y no-repeat
color	Sets the foreground color of an element	[color] transparent

Border Styles

Many changes can be made to the style, color, and width of any or all sides of a border using the border properties listed in Table D–4. Using the border-color, border-width, or border-style border properties allows you to set the style for all sides of a border. Using style properties such as border-top-width, border-right-color, or border-bottom-style gives you the option to set the width, color, or style for only the top, right, bottom, or left border of a table cell. If you do not make changes to the border style using style sheet properties, the default border will be displayed.

Table D–4 Border Properties

Property Name	Description	Values
border-color	Sets the color of the four borders; can have from one to four colors	[color] transparent
border-top-color border-right-color border-bottom-color border-left-color	Sets the respective color of the top, right, bottom, and left borders individually	[color]
border-style	Sets the style of the four borders; can have from one to four styles	**none** dashed dotted double groove inset outset ridge solid
border-top-style border-right-style border-bottom-style border-left-style	Sets the respective style of the top, right, bottom, and left borders individually	**none** dashed dotted double groove inset outset ridge solid
border-width	Shorthand property for setting the width of the four borders in one declaration; can have from one to four values	**medium** [length] thick thin
border-top-width border-right-width border-bottom-width border-left-width	Sets the respective width of the top, right, bottom, and left borders individually	**medium** [length] thick thin

Classification Styles

These properties classify elements into categories more than they set specific visual parameters. Table D–5 lists common classification properties that can be used.

Table D–5 Classification Properties

Property Name	Description	Values
display	Describes how/if an element is displayed on the canvas, which may be on a printed page, a computer monitor, etc.	**block** inline list-item none
white-space	Declares how whitespace inside the element is handled: the 'normal' way (where whitespace is collapsed), as *pre* (which behaves like the <pre> element in HTML) or as *nowrap* (where wrapping is done only through elements)	**normal** pre nowrap

Font Styles

An element's font can be changed using the font attribute and various font properties. When you set the font family for an element, you can set one or more fonts or font families by using a comma-delimited list. Each font family generally includes several font definitions. For example, the Arial font family includes Arial Black and Arial Narrow. If you specify more than one font, the browser assesses the user's system and uses the first font family installed on the system. If the system has none of the font families specified in the style sheet, the browser uses the default system font. Table D–6 lists common font properties.

Table D–6 Font Properties

Property Name	Description	Values
font	Shorthand property for setting font-style, font-variant, font-weight, font-size, line-height, and font-family at the same place in the style sheet	
font-family	A prioritized list of font-family names and/or generic family names for an element	[family-name] cursive fantasy monospace sans-serif serif
font-size	Sets the size of a font	[length] [percentage] large medium small x-large x-small xx-large xx-small
font-style	Sets the style of a font	**normal** italic oblique
font-variant	Displays text in a small-caps font or a normal font	**normal** small-caps
font-weight	Sets the weight of a font	**normal** bold bolder lighter

List Styles

Using the properties associated with list styles allows you to set the kind of marker that identifies a list item. An unnumbered list marker, for example, can be a filled disc, an empty circle, or a square. A numbered list marker can be a decimal, lower-alpha, lower-Roman numeral, upper-alpha, or upper-Roman numeral. Table D–7 provides compatible browser list properties.

Table D–7 List Properties

Property Name	Description	Values
list-style-image	Sets an image as the list-item marker	**none** url
list-style-position	Indents or extends a list-item marker with respect to the item's content	**outside** inside
list-style-type	Sets the type of list-item marker	**disc** circle square decimal lower-alpha lower-Roman upper-alpha upper-Roman

Margin and Padding Styles

Many changes can be made to the width and spacing around an element using the margin and padding properties listed in Table D–8. Padding is the space that occurs between the edge of an element and the beginning of its border. If you increase padding around an element, you add space inside its border. The border, therefore, has a larger area to cover.

You can use the margin or padding property to set the widths of margins and padding amounts along all four sides of an element. Using margin and padding properties such as margin-top, margin-right, padding-left, or padding-bottom gives you the option to set the margin or padding for only the top, right, bottom, or left side of an element.

Table D–8 Margin and Padding Properties

Property Name	Description	Values
margin	Shorthand property for setting margin-top, margin-right, margin-bottom, and margin-left at the same place in the style sheet.	
margin-top margin-right margin-bottom margin-left	Sets the top, right, bottom, and left margin of an element individually	[length] [percentage] auto
padding	Shorthand property for setting padding properties in one declaration	
padding-top padding-right padding-bottom padding-left	Sets the top, right, bottom, and left padding of an element individually	[length] [percentage]

Miscellaneous Formatting Styles

Other changes can be made to the width and spacing around elements using the properties listed in Table D–9. These properties can be applied to text elements. They are most useful, however, with elements such as images.

You can use the width or height property to set the widths or heights of images or text, or the size of the box. The float and clear properties alter the position of the element on a Web page. You can float images on a Web page and clear the sides where floating elements are not accepted.

Table D–9 Miscellaneous Formatting Properties

Property Name	Description	Values
width	Can be applied to text elements, but it is most useful with elements such as images	[length] [percentage] **auto**
height	Can be applied to text elements, but it is most useful with elements such as images	[length] **auto**
float	With the value none, the element will be displayed where it appears in the text; with a value of left (right) the element will be moved to the left (right) and the text will wrap on the right (left) side of the element	left right **none**
clear	Specifies if an element allows floating elements on its sides	**none** left right both

Text Styles

Text styles can be used to change the letter-spacing, alignment, line-height (not recommended), and text decoration, along with other text properties. The text-transform property can change text into all uppercase, all lowercase, or be used to change the first letter of each word to uppercase. With text-align, you can align text left, right, center, or justify the text. The text style properties are listed in Table D–10.

Table D–10 Text Properties

Property Name	Description	Values
letter-spacing	Increases or decreases the space between characters	**normal** [length]
line-height	Sets the spacing between text baselines	**normal** [length] [number] [percentage]
text-align	Aligns the text in an element	left right center justify
text-decoration	Adds decoration to text	**none** blink line-through overline underline

Table D–10 Text Properties (*Continued*)

Property Name	Description	Values
text-indent	Indents the first line of text in an element	[length] [percentage]
text-transform	Controls text capitalization	**none** capitalize lowercase uppercase
vertical-align	Sets the vertical positioning of text	**baseline** [length] [percentage] bottom middle sub super text-bottom text-top top
word-spacing	Increases or decreases the space between words	**normal** [length]

Appendix E

Publishing Web Pages to a Web Server

Publishing your Web site means transferring your files to a Web server (Web host) that will make your pages available 24/7 on the Web. Publishing involves two basic steps: choosing a Web host and uploading your Web site files (usually via FTP) to that host.

Choosing a Web Host

There are many options available for Web hosting, as detailed in the "Finding a Web Hosting Site" section of the Special Feature on "Attracting Visitors to Your Web Site." Common options are to use the ISP that you use to connect to the Internet or to use a Web hosting service.

Your Internet service provider (ISP) may provide space for its clients to host a Web site. If it does, you should contact your network system administrator or technical support staff at your ISP to determine if their Web server supports FTP, and to obtain necessary permissions to access the Web server. There are other options for hosting Web sites as well. You can search for free Web hosts using any browser. Whatever Web host you choose, you must secure a username and password in order to gain access to the host.

Uploading Files to the Host

Once you have chosen a Web host, you'll need a program to transfer your files to the Web server. The most common file transfer program is called FTP. **File Transfer Protocol (FTP)** is an Internet standard that allows computers to exchange files with other computers on the Internet. FTP was developed to promote sharing files across a variety of computers reliably and efficiently. FTP programs that run on PCs are sometimes called FTP clients.

There are many FTP programs available for free on the Internet. Search for FTP in any browser and you will find a variety of programs. Read the documentation to assure that the program works with your computer and operating system. Then download and install the FTP program of your choice.

Now you can use your FTP program to upload your Web pages to the server. Be sure to include all HTML files, CSS files, and any graphic files that make up your Web site. Table E–1 shows the steps to use FTP to upload your files. All of the necessary information (e.g., username) should be provided to you by the network administrator for the Web host. Specific keystrokes or mouse clicks to accomplish each step may vary among FTP clients.

Table E–1 Using FTP to Upload Your Web Files
1. Start your FTP program.
2. Type in the host name/address as provided by the network administrator.
3. Select the host type.
4. Enter the user ID and password that you were given and then click the OK button.
5. You should see both a local system (your computer) as well as the remote system (the Web host) in the FTP dialog box.
6. Use the up arrow to find the folders in which you stored your files; use the up arrow to locate the folders on the remote system also.
7. Highlight the files that you want to upload and click the right arrow to move the files to the remote system.

Appendix F

Symbols and Characters Quick Reference

Using Symbols and Special Characters

There is a way to insert special characters into your HTML and XHTML code by using the entity character reference. Tables F–1 through F–3 contain the most commonly used entity characters, mathematical and technical characters, and arrow characters. Several projects in the book use the predefined entity characters to enhance content on the Web pages that you create.

You can find a complete list of characters at www.unicode.org.

Table F–1 Most Commonly Used Predefined Entity Characters

Symbol	Entity	Description
&	&	Ampersand
¦	¦	Broken vertical bar
¢	¢	Cent sign
©	©	Copyright sign
¤	¤	Currency sign
†	†	Dagger
‡	‡	Double dagger
€	€	Euro
>	>	Greater-than sign
«	«	Left-pointing double angle quotation mark
<	<	Less-than sign
—	—	Em dash
[Tab]		Non-breaking space (can be used for tabbing on a Web page)
–	–	En dash
¬	¬	Not sign
¶	¶	Paragraph sign
£	£	Pound
"	"	Quotation mark = APL quote
®	®	Registered mark sign
»	»	Right-pointing double angle quotation mark
§	§	Section sign
™	™	Trademark sign
¥	¥	Yen

Table F–2 Mathematical and Technical Characters

Symbol	Entity	Description
∧	∧	Logical and
∠	∠	Angle
≈	≈	Almost equal to
∩	∩	Intersection
∪	∪	Union
°	°	Degree sign
÷	÷	Division sign
≡	≡	Identical to
∃	∃	There exists
ƒ	ƒ	Function
∀	∀	For all
½	&fract12;	Fraction one half
¼	&fract14;	Fraction one quarter
¾	&fract34;	Fraction three quarters
≥	≥	Greater-than or equal to
∞	∞	Infinity
∫	∫	Integral
∈	∈	Element of
≤	≤	Less-than or equal to
µ	µ	Micro sign
∇	∇	Backward difference
≠	≠	Not equal to
∋	∋	Contains as a member
∂	∂	Partial differential
⊥	⊥	Perpendicular
±	±	Plus-minus sign
∏	∏	n-ary product
∝	∝	Proportional to
√	√	Square root
∼	∼	Tilde
∑	∑	n-ary summation
∴	∴	Therefore

Table F–3 Arrow Characters

Symbol	Entity	Description
↓	↓	Downward arrow
↔	↔	Left right arrow
←	←	Leftward arrow
→	→	Rightward arrow
↑	↑	Upward arrow

Appendix G

JavaScript Quick Reference

JavaScript Introduction

Webster's dictionary defines **script** in several ways: first, as a style of handwriting or font style, such as cursive; second, as a document; and third, as text for stage, film, or a radio or television show. A stage, movie, or television script also contains stage directions for actors. Computers, however, also use scripts, which are a set of instructions used by a program to perform a specific task or set of tasks. A **scripting language** follows a set of rules and has its own syntax. Scripting languages generally need to be interpreted by the program or utility using the script.

Scripting languages like JavaScript extend the power of **HTML** (Hypertext Markup Language) and allow Web pages to be interactive. Whereas HTML tells your browser how to display text and images, set up lists and option buttons, and establish hyperlinks, JavaScript brings Web pages to life by adding dynamic content and interactive elements. Using JavaScript, a Web page developer enhances a Web page by adding features such as:

- Scrolling messages
- Animation and dynamic images
- Pop-up windows
- Dynamic messages
- Data validation

JavaScript is a product of a joint venture between Sun Microsystems and Netscape. Netscape developed a script language called LiveScript, and Sun Microsystems was trying to simplify its Java programming language. The cooperation of those two efforts brought about JavaScript. The following reference guide applies to the JavaScript model version 1.5 standardized in 1999 and still in effect for all cross-browser applications. Later versions of JavaScript are browser-specific and are not detailed. For more detailed information about JavaScript 1.5, see *http://developer.mozilla.org/En/Core_JavaScript_1.5_Reference.*

JavaScript standards are created and developed by the European Computer Manufacturers Association (ECMA) and the language is also referred to as ECMAScript. The current edition of ECMAScript is edition five, which was finalized in December of 2009. JavaScript version 1.5 was based on ECMAScript edition three. Edition four was never released due to disagreement among members, who include Yahoo!, Microsoft, Mozilla, and Google. This disagreement led to the development of JavaScript extensions beyond version 1.5 based on individual browser engines. For a list of engines and ECMAScript editions and JavaScript versions associated with particular browser engines, visit one of the following Web sites: *http://en.wikipedia.org/wiki/List_of_web_browsers*, *http://en.wikipedia.org/wiki/ECMAScript*, or *http://en.wikipedia.org/wiki/Comparison_of_layout_engines_(ECMAScript)*.

Why Use JavaScript?

Using JavaScript enhances your Web page by adding interactivity to it. Users can receive instant feedback, without complicated Common Gateway Interference (**CGI**) scripts and languages. A CGI script is any program that runs on a Web server for the purpose of processing data. The Web page sends the data to the server that processes the data and may return a result to the Web page. Along with server-side scripts and programs, many Web sites use CGI for searching databases or processing purchase orders on a server.

The disadvantage of using CGI scripts is that they waste resources when the needed task can be processed on the user's computer. For example, with JavaScript you can validate a data-entry form, such as a purchase request, immediately on the user's computer. The need to send the data back to the server for validation is eliminated. The user receives feedback instantly and does not have to wait for a response during heavy Internet traffic times.

Reserved Words

Reserved words (also called **keywords**) are words with special meaning to a programming language. Most reserved words are used in program statements or in defining data. A reserved word cannot be used as a JavaScript variable, function, method, or object name. The JavaScript reserved word list is summarized in Table G–1.

Table G–1 Reserved Words

abstract	double	import	this
boolean	else	in	throw
break	enum	instanceof	throws
byte	export	int	transient
case	extends	label	true
catch	false	long	try
char	final	native	typeof
class	finally	new	var
const	float	null	void
continue	for	return	volatile
debugger	function	short	while
default	goto	super	with
delete	if	switch	
do	implements	synchronized	

Some of the reserved words have special meaning to JavaScript; some are reserved for future use with JavaScript extensions. Table G-2 lists these future reserved words.

Table G–2 Future Reserved Words

implements	package	public
interface	private	static
let	protected	yield

Data Types

Data type refers to the category of data held by a variable. JavaScript supports several data types, including primitive data types (numbers, strings, and boolean values), compound types (objects and arrays), special types (null and undefined), regular expressions, and functions. Table G–3 summarizes the primitive and special data types.

Table G–3 Primitive and Special Data Types

Data Type	Form	Description	Example	Range
Boolean	True/False	Can represent yes or no, on or off, true or false	check_pt = true test_2 = false	true or false
Null	No value	Empty	val_hold = null	null
Numeric	Integer	Positive or negative numbers with no decimal places	count = 4	–253 to 253
	Floating-point	Positive or negative numbers, with decimal places, or numbers written using exponential notation	accum = 4.678 amt = –67.126 distance = 2e11	Approximately +1.79769e308 to –1.7e308
	Special numbers	NaN	ValType = NaN	NaN means Not a Number
		Infinity (or MAX_VALUE or POSITIVE_INFINITY)	highNum = Infinity	MAX_VALUE: +1.7976931348623157e308
		–Infinity (or MIN_VALUE or NEGATIVE_INFINITY)	highNegNum = –Infinity	MIN_VALUE: +5e-324
String	Text and nonnumeric characters	A set of continuous characters surrounded by quotation marks	productName = "Router" phone = "555-1212"	zero or more characters
Undefined	No value	A variable that has been declared but not yet assigned a value	var i	undefined

Variable Names

A **variable name** (also called an **identifier**) must begin with a letter, dollar sign ($), or an underscore and cannot be a reserved word shown in Table G–1 on the previous page. Variable names are case sensitive and may not contain a space. Variables can be declared with the var statement, where they also can be initialized.

Although the dollar sign ($) is a valid variable name character, most developers avoid using it because the dollar sign also can indicate machine-generated code to the interpreter. In addition, the number of characters in a variable is not subject to any specific limitation. Older browsers, however, do have a limitation of 255 characters for an entire statement.

A variable name cannot use a period because periods separate objects, properties, and methods. See Table G–4 on the next page for examples of valid and invalid variable names. In addition, you must remember that, in JavaScript, variable names are case sensitive. If you create a form and use mixed-case spelling, such as State, as a variable name, and later use the uppercase spelling, STATE, as a variable name, JavaScript will treat these spellings as two different variable names.

Table G–4 Valid and Invalid Variable Names

Valid Variable Names	Invalid Variable Names
cust_id	cust.id
Cust_Id	%Cust_Id
_cust_id	+cust_identifier
cust_id_number	Cust id number
CustIdNumber	9custIDNumber
Custid1	Cust ID
_case	case

Variables are declared the first time they are used by inserting the word **var**, then the variable name, followed by an equal sign (=), and then the value. For example, if you declare a variable named gpa by typing `var gpa`, this variable would be assigned no value. To assign a variable an initial value of zero, type `var gpa=0`. Current versions of Mozilla Firefox and Microsoft Internet Explorer indicate that a variable is **undefined** if the variable has not been assigned a value. In addition, a variable can have a **null** value.

Literals

While a variable is used to store data or values, a **literal** is a constant value that does not change. A literal is an actual number or text, rather than a calculated result or value input from a keyboard. If the literal is a number, it is called a numeric literal; if it is a character or text value, it is called a string literal.

A **string literal** is text enclosed in quotation marks. With string literals, you must place the text inside a pair of quotation marks. If numeric digits are enclosed within quotation marks, they will be treated as a string, not as a number. Think of the characters between quotation marks as a sequential group of characters, one after the other, forming a continuous string.

Escape Sequences in Strings

The **escape character** (\) indicates that the character that follows in a string has a special meaning. The escape character and its following character form an **escape sequence**. The escape sequences are summarized in Table G–5.

Table G–5 Escape Sequences

Escape Sequence	Meaning	Escape Sequence	Meaning
\'	Single quotation mark	\r	Carriage return
\"	Double quotation mark	\t	Horizontal tab
\\	Backslash	\ddd	Octal sequence (deprecated)
\b	Backspace	\xdd	Hexadecimal sequence
\f	Form feed	\udddd	Unicode sequence
\n	New line		

Operators

Operators are symbols used to manipulate operands in an expression.

Operator Types

Table G–6 summarizes the JavaScript operator types.

Table G–6 Operator Types

Type	Operator	Name	Description	Example
Arithmetic	+	Addition	Adds two operands	rtn = amt + 5.6
	–	Subtraction	Subtracts one operand from another	rtn = amt – disc
	*	Multiplication	Multiplies one operand by another	rtn = amt * .5
	/	Division	Divides one operand by another	rtn = amt / 4
	%	Modulo	Returns the remainder of a division operation	rtn = amt % 3
	++	Increment	Increases an operand by one	newAmt = ++oldAmt newAmt = oldAmt++
	--	Decrement	Decreases an operand by one	newAmt = --oldAmt newAmt = oldAmt--
	–	Negation	Returns the opposite value of an operand	newAmt = –oldAmt
Assignment	=	Assigns	Assigns the value of the right operand to the left operand	discRate = 4
	+=	Combines	Adds the value of the right operand to the value of the left operand and assigns a new value to the left operand	discRate += 13
	-=	Subtracts	Subtracts the value of the right operand from the value of the left operand and assigns a new value to the left operand	discRate -= 3
	*=	Multiplies	Multiplies the value of the right operand by the value of the left operand and assigns a new value to the left operand	discRate *= .2
	/=	Divides	Divides the value of the left operand by the value of the right operand and assigns a new value to the left operand	discRate /= 10
	%=	Modulus	Divides the value of the left operand by the value of the right operand and assigns a remainder to the left operand	discRate %= 5
Bitwise	~	Complement	Performs a binary NOT	secur = ~rights
	<<	Shift left	Performs a binary shift left of the bits of an integer	Op = 15 << 1
	>>	Shift right	Performs a binary shift right of the bits of an integer	Op = 15 >> 1
	>>>	Shift right with zero extension	Performs a binary unsigned shift right on an integer	Op = 15 >>> 1
	&	AND	Performs a bitwise AND on an integer	Op = 01111 & 11111
	^	XOR	Performs a bitwise XOR on an integer	Op = 01111 ^ 11111
	|	OR	Performs a bitwise OR on an integer	Op = 01111 | 11111

Table G–6 Operator Types (continued)

Type	Operator	Name	Description	Example
Comparison	= =	Equal	Returns true if operands are equal	if (a = = b) {
	!=	Not Equal	Returns true if operands are not equal	if (a != b) {
	>	Greater Than	Returns true if the left operand is greater than the right operand	if (a > b) {
	<	Less Than	Returns true if the left operand is less than the right operand	if (a < b) {
	>=	Greater Than or Equal	Returns true if the left operand is greater than or equal to the right operand	if (a >= b) {
	<=	Less Than or Equal	Returns true if the left operand is less than or equal to the right operand	if (a <= b) {
	= = =	Equal (no type conversion done)	Returns true if operands are equal and their types are the same	if (a = = = b) {
	! = =	Not Equal (no type conversion done)	Returns true if operands are not equal or their types are the same	if (a ! = = b) {
	in	in	Returns true if the property is found as a property member of the object	(property in object)
	instanceof	instanceof	Returns true if the datatype matches the object	(datatype instanceof object)
Conditional	?:	If?then:else	Performs an inline if-then-else and assigns one of two possible values	Ret = (test = = true) ? "Its true" : "Its false"
Expression Control	void	Return a void	Sets a variable to an undefined state	ret = void
Logical	&&	And	Returns true if both the left operand and the right operand return a value of true, otherwise it returns a value of false	if ((a < b) && (c > d)) {
	||	Or	Returns true if either the left operand or the right operand returns a value of true; if neither operand returns a value of true, then the expression containing the || (or) operator returns a value of false	if ((a < b) || (c > d)) {
	!	Not	Returns true if an expression is false and returns false if an expression is true	if (!(a < b)) {
Multiple Evaluation	,	Evaluate/Return right+	Evaluates two expressions and returns the second one	Ret = (x- -, z) * (y- -, q)
Object	new	New object	Creates a new object	CD = new Album
	delete	Remove an object property	Removes a single property of an object	delete CD
String	+	Concatenation	Combines two strings	lang = "Java" + "Script"
	+=	Concatenates	Concatenates the value of the right operand to the value of the left operand and assigns a new value to the left operand	Lang += "Script"
Type Identification	typeof	Return type	Returns the data type of the operand	ret = typeof(CD)

Order of Precedence

Unless parentheses/brackets/dots dictate otherwise, reading from left to right in an expression, all negation/increment/misc are performed first, then all multiply/divide/modulo, then all addition/subtraction, then all comparison, then all equality/identity, then all logical and, then all logical or, and then all assignment operators. The **order of precedence** is summarized in Table G–7.

Table G–7 Order Of Precedence

Operator	Symbol	Precedence
Parentheses/brackets/dot	( ) [ ] .	highest
Negation/increment/misc	! – ++ – – ~ delete new type of void	
Multiply/divide/modulo	* / %	
Addition/subtraction	+ –	
Shift	<< >> >>>	
Comparison	< <= > >=	
Equality/Identity	= = != = = ! = = != ===	
Bitwise AND	&	
Bitwise XOR	^	
Bitwise OR	|	
Logical and	&&	
Logical or	||	
Conditional	?:	
Assignment operators	= += –= *= /= %=	
Multiple evaluation	,	lowest

JavaScript Statements

Statements are used to write JavaScript instructions. Table G–8 summarizes the JavaScript statements.

Table G–8 JavaScript Statements

Statement	Description
block	A block of JavaScript statements delimited by a pair of braces { }.
break	Exits switch statements and loops. Transfers program control to the statement line following the switch statement or following the terminated loop .
comment	Notations that explain what a script does. Comments are ignored by the interpreter. Single-line comments begin with //. Multiple-line comments begin with /* and end with */.
continue	Halts execution of a block of statements in a while or for loop and continues execution of the loop with the next iteration.
do...while	Executes the block of statements in a loop until the test condition evaluates to false. Statements in a loop execute at least once.
debugger ;	Will cause a breakpoint to occur when code is run in a debugger, otherwise it has no effect.
export	Makes functions and properties available to other windows (Navigator 4 and up). Statement not supported in version 1.5.
;	An empty statement that returns normal.
finally	Executes a block of statements after the try and catch block of statements execute. The finally block of statements executes whether or not an exception is thrown. A good use for the finally block of statements is to allow a graceful failure.
for	Creates a loop that consists of three optional expressions, enclosed in parentheses and separated by semicolons, followed by a block of statements executed in the loop. The test to terminate a loop is done before the block of statements in the loop executes.
for...in	Iterates a specified variable over all the properties of an object. For each distinct property, JavaScript executes the specified statements.

Table G–8 JavaScript Statements (continued)

Statement	Description
function	Defines a new function. Acceptable parameters include strings, numbers, and objects. For example, function myfunc() {.
if...else	Executes one block of statements if the condition is true. Executes another block of statements if the condition is false.
import	Allows use of other objects available at run-time (Navigator 4 and up). Not supported in version 1.5.
label	Provides an identifier that can be used with break or continue to indicate where the program should continue execution.
return	Causes the current function to halt and possibly returns a value to the caller. For example, return endingval.
switch	Allows a program to evaluate an expression and attempts to match the expression's value to a case label.
throw	Throws or sends an exception. The exception can be an expression or an object.
try...catch	Executes a block of statements to try, and the statements to execute if an error occurs. Implemented in IE 5 and later versions of Navigator.
var	Declares and possibly initializes new variables. For example, var retval.
while	Creates a loop that evaluates an expression, and if it is true, executes a block of statements. The loop then repeats, as long as the specified condition is true.
with	Establishes the default object for a block of statements.

Event Handlers

JavaScript makes HTML documents dynamic through events. An **event** is an action that a user makes, such as clicking a button. Usually, when an event occurs, JavaScript code executes. Event handler names always begin with "on." In standard HTML, event handler names are in mixed case; the first letter after the word "on" is in uppercase. In XML, because all attributes must be in lowercase, they are spelled in all lowercase characters. Table G–9 summarizes the JavaScript event handlers.

Table G–9 Event Handlers

Event Handler	Triggered When	Handler For	Used in HTML Statement
onabort	The loading of an image is interrupted	Image	<img>
onafterprint	After page has printed	Window (IE 5+ only)	<body>
onbeforeprint	Fires just before a page is printed or examined for Print Preview	Window (IE 5+ only)	<body>
onbeforeunload	Displays message just before a page is unloaded	Window	<iframe>
onblur	An element becomes inactive	Button, Checkbox, FileUpload, Layer, Password, Radio, Reset, Select, Submit, Text, Textarea, Window	<body> ... </body> <frameset> ... </frameset> <frame> ... </frame> <input type="text" /> <textarea> ... </textarea> <select> ... </select>
onchange	The value of an element changes	FileUpload, Select, Text, Textarea	<input type="text" /> <textarea> ... </textarea> <select> ... </select>

Table G–9 Event Handlers (continued)

Event Handler	Triggered When	Handler For	Used in HTML Statement
onclick	An element is clicked once	Button, Checkbox, Document, Link, Radio, Reset, Submit	<a> ... </a> <input type="submit" /> <input type="reset" /> <input type="radio" /> <input type="checkbox" /> <input type="text" />
oncut	Text is being cut to be placed on Clipboard	Return of false disables cutting of text	<textarea> ... </textarea> <input type="text" /> <select> ... </select>
onclose	Current window is being closed		Window elements
oncontextmenu	Right-click to fire context menu	Return of false prevents context menu from displaying	All elements
oncopy	Text is being copied to be placed on Clipboard	Return of false prevents text from being copied	<textarea> ... </textarea> <input type="text" /> <select> ... </select>
ondblclick	An element is double-clicked	Document, Link	<a> ... </a> <input type="submit" /> <input type="reset" /> <input type="radio" /> <input type="checkbox" /> <input type="text" />
ondragdrop	An object is dragged and dropped into a window	Window (may not be available on all platforms)	<body> ... </body> <frameset> ... </frameset>
onerror	An error occurs when loading a document or image	Image, Window	<img /> <body> ... </body> <frameset> ... </frameset>
onfocus	An element becomes active	Button, Checkbox, FileUpload, Layer, Password, Radio, Reset, Select, Submit, Text, Textarea, Window (may not be available on all platforms)	<body> ... </body> <frameset> ... </frameset> <frame> ... </frame> <input type="text" /> <textarea> ... </textarea> <select> ... </select>
onkeydown	A designated key is pressed	Document, Image, Link, Textarea	<body> ... </body> <frameset> ... </frameset> <img /> <a> ... </a> <textarea> ... </textarea>
onkeypress	A designated key is pressed and released	Document, Image, Link, Textarea	<body> ... </body> <frameset> ... </frameset> <img /> <a> ... </a> <textarea> ... </textarea>
onkeyup	A designated key is released	Document, Image, Link, Textarea	<body> ... </body> <frameset> ... </frameset> <img /> <a> ... </a> <textarea> ... </textarea>
onload	A document or image loads	Image, Layer, Window	<img /> <body> ... </body> <frameset> ... </frameset>

Table G–9 Event Handlers (continued)

Event Handler	Triggered When	Handler For	Used in HTML Statement
onmousedown	A mouse button is pressed	Button, Document, Link	<a> ... </a> <input type="submit" /> <input type="reset" /> <body> ... </body> <frameset> ... </frameset>
onmousemove	The mouse moves	Not associated with any particular object because the mouse moves so frequently; must be specifically associated with a particular object	<body> ... </body>
onmouseout	The mouse moves off an element	Layer, Link	<a> ... </a> <area> ... </area>
onmouseover	The mouse moves over an element	Layer, Link	<a> ... </a> <area> ... </area>
onmouseup	A button is released	Button, Document, Link	<a> ... </a> <input type="submit" /> <input type="reset" /> <body> ... </body> <frameset> ... </frameset>
onmousewheel	User scrolls with mouse wheel (IE 6+, Opera, Safari) FF uses DOMMouseScroll	wheelDelta property to determine direction and amount of scroll	All elements
onmouseenter (IE 5+ only)	For use when mouse first enters element and does not continue to fire for all inner elements, unlike onmouseover		All elements
onmouseleave (IE 5+ only)	For use when mouse leaves element		All elements
onmove	A window or frame is moved	Window	<body> ... </body> <frameset> ... </frameset>
onoffline	Browser is working offline		Browser
ononline	Browser is working online		Browser
onpaste	When user attempts to paste from Clipboard	Return of false prevents paste	All <form> elements
onreset	A form resets	Form	<form> ... </form>
onresize	A window or frame is resized	Window	<body> ... </body> <frameset> ... </frameset>
onselect	A user selects a field in a form	Text, Textarea	<input type="text" /> <textarea> ... </textarea>
onsubmit	A user submits a form	Form	<form> ... </form>
onunload	A document unloads	Window	<body> ... </body> <frameset> ... </frameset>

Objects

This section lists the properties, methods, and events of the major JavaScript objects.

Date Object

The **Date object** is used to access the system time and date. The Date object methods are summarized in Table G–10.

Table G–10 Date Object

Method	Returns	Method	Sets
getDate()	Date of Date object	setDate()	Date of Date object
getDay()	Day of Date object	setFullYear()	Four-digit year of Date object
getFullYear()	Year of Date object (four-digit format)	setHours()	Hours of Date object
getHours()	Hour of Date object	setMilliseconds()	Milliseconds of Date object
getMilliseconds()	Milliseconds of Date object	setMinutes()	Minutes of Date object
getMinutes()	Minutes of Date object	setMonth()	Month of Date object
getMonth()	Month of Date object	setSeconds()	Seconds of Date object
getSeconds()	Seconds of Date object	setTime()	Time of Date object
getTime()	Time of Date object	setUTCDate()	Date of Date object in universal time
getTimezoneOffset()	Local time zone offset in minutes from the current date and GMT	setUTCFullYear()	Four-digit year of Date object in universal time
getUTCDate()	Date of Date object in universal time	setUTCHours()	Hours of Date object in universal time
getUTCDay()	Day of week of Date object in universal time	setUTCMilliseconds()	Milliseconds of Date object in universal time
getUTCFullYear()	Four-digit year of Date object in universal time	setUTCMinutes()	Minutes of Date object in universal time
getUTCHours()	Hours of Date object in universal time	setUTCMonth()	Month of Date object in universal time
getUTCMilliseconds()	Milliseconds of Date object in universal time	setUTCSeconds()	Seconds of Date object in universal time
getUTCMinutes()	Minutes of Date object in universal time	setYear()	Year of Date object (best to use setFullYear() instead)
getUTCMonth()	Month of Date object in universal time	toDateString()	Returns a date as a string in current time zone
getUTCSeconds()	Seconds of Date object in universal time	toLocaleDateString()	Date as string value in current time zone
getYear()	Year of Date object (best to use getFullYear() instead)	toLocaleTimeString()	Time as string value in current time zone
parse()	Parses a date into component pieces	toTimeString()	Time as string value in current time zone
UTC()	Converts a date to milliseconds		
Method	**Converts**		
toGMTString()	Date object to string, set to the GMT time zone		
toLocaleString()	Date object to string, set to the current time zone		
toString()	Date object to string		
toUTCString()	Date object to string, set to universal time		
valueOf()	Date object to millisecond format		

Document Object

The **Document object** represents the content of a browser's window. Table G–11 summarizes the Document object properties and methods. Note that all properties and methods may not work with all browsers, especially older versions.

Table G–11 Document Object

Property	Description
activeElement	Element that currently has focus
alinkColor	Color of an active link specified by the alink attribute of the <body> tag; recommend using style sheet in place of property
all[]	Array referring to all HTML elements in a document
anchors[]	Array referring to the document's anchors
applets[]	Array referring to the document's applets
bgColor	Background color of the document as specified by the bgColor attribute of the <body> tag; recommend using style sheet in place of property
charset	Character set currently in use
children[]	Array referring to child elements of the document
classes	Defines classes for style
cookie	Specifies a cookie for the current document
defaultCharset	Default character set of the document
domain	Domain name of the server where the current document is located
embeds[]	Array referring to the document's ActiveX controls and plug-ins
expando	Do not allow creation of new properties
fgColor	Foreground text color of the document as specified by the fgColor attribute of the <body> tag; recommend using style sheet in place of property
forms[]	Array referring to multiple forms within a document
height	Document height
ids	Styles for individual tags
images[]	Array referring to the document's images
lastModified	Date the document was last modified
layers[]	DHTML layers in a document; not supported in Navigator 6.x
linkColor	Color of the document's unvisited links as specified by the link attribute of the <body> tag; recommend using style sheet in place of property
links[]	Array referring to the document's links
location	URL of the document
parentWindow	Refers to the document's window
plugins[]	Array referring to objects used in the document, synonym for embeds[] array
readyState	State of the document as it loads
referrer	URL of the document that provided a link to the current document
tags	Styles for HTML tags
title	Title of the document as specified by the <title> ... </title> tag pair in the document's HEAD section
URL	URL of the current document
vlinkColor	Color of the document's visited links as specified by the vlink attribute of the <body> tag (deprecated)
width	Document width

Table G–11 Document Object (continued)	
Method	**Description**
captureEvents()	Names event types to be captured
clear()	Clears a document
close()	Notifies the Web browser you are finished writing to a window or frame and that the document should be displayed
contextual()	Defines the contextual style
elementFromPoint()	Specifies which HTML element is at a point
getElementByID()	Refers to an object by its specified id; id attribute values may be enclosed in single or double quotation marks
getElementByName()	Refers to an object by its name value; name attribute values may be enclosed in single or double quotation marks
getElementByTagName()	Refers to an object by its tag name; tag attribute values may be enclosed in single or double quotation marks
getSelection()	Returns selected text
open()	Opens a window or frame, other than the current window or frame, and is used to update its contents with the write() and writeln() methods
releaseEvents()	Stops the capturing of events
routeEvent()	Passes the captured events to the next event handler
write()	Creates new text on a Web page
writeln()	Creates new text on a Web page followed by a line break

Assigning Color to an Object

When assigning color to an object, like foreground or background, the color should be follow the red, green, blue (rgb) color scheme. The color can be written as a standard color name, red, orange, green and so on; or the color can be represented by its hexadecimal value of r, g, b. The color red would be written as #ff0000, where ff means full red, and 0000 means no green or blue. Color may be written as an rgb() method, where green would be written as rgb(0,255,0).

Form Object

The **Form object** represents forms created with the <form> ... </form> tag pair. Table G–12 summarizes the Form object properties and methods.

Table G–12 Form Object	
Property	**Description**
action	URL to which a form's data will be submitted
method	Method in which a form's data will be submitted (GET or POST)
encoding	Format of data being submitted
target	Window in which any results returned from the server are displayed
name	Name of a form
elements[]	Array representing a form's elements
elements.length	Number of elements on a form
Method	**Function**
reset()	Clears any data entered into a form
submit()	Submits a form to a Web server

History Object

The **History object** keeps track of the pages that have been visited. Table G–13 summarizes the History object property and methods.

Table G–13 History Object

Property	Description
current	URL of the current document
length	Contains the specific number of documents that have been opened during the current browser session
next	URL of the next document in the history array
previous	URL of the previous document in the history array
Method	**Function**
back()	Equivalent to clicking a Web browser's Back button
forward()	Equivalent to clicking a Web browser's Forward button
go(n)	Opens a specific document in the history list indicated by n
toString()	Browsing history in the HTML format

Image Object

The **Image object** represents images created using the <img> tag. Table G–14 summarizes the Image object properties and events.

Table G–14 Image Object

Property	Description
border	Read-only property containing border width, in pixels, as specified by border attribute of <img> tag, including if an error occurs during loading
complete	Boolean value that returns true when an image is completely loaded
height	Read-only property containing height of image as specified by height attribute of <img> tag
hspace	Read-only property containing amount of horizontal space, in pixels, to left and right of image, as specified by hspace attribute of <img> tag
lowsrc	URL of alternate image to display at low resolution
name	Name assigned to tag
src	URL of displayed image
vspace	Read-only property containing amount of vertical space, in pixels, above and below image, as specified by vspace attribute of <img> tag
width	Read-only property containing width of image as specified by width attribute of <img> tag
Event	**Description**
onLoad	Image finishes loading
onAbort	User cancels the loading of an image, usually by clicking the Stop button
onError	Error occurs while loading image

JSON Object

The **JSON object** (JavaScript Object Notation) provides the capability of inserting data in a script without using XML. Table G-15 shows two examples of how to represent JSON data, and Table G-16 summarizes JSON methods.

Table G–15 JSON Example

Examples	Rules
{ "author": "Mark Twain", "title": "Tom Sawyer", "year": 1876 }	All string values must be in double quotation marks. The identifier (field name) must be in double quotation marks and followed by a semicolon. A value cannot be a function or property.
var jsonBooks={ "author": "Mark Twain", "title": "Tom Sawyer", "year": 1876 }	

Table G–16 JSON Methods

Method	Description
stringify(obj, [replacer, space])	Converts an object into a string. Replacer and Space are optional. Replacer is a user-defined function used to replace one value with another. Space is an integer used to place spaces in front of data elements.
parse(string [reviver])	Converts a JSON string into an object. Reviver is optional. Reviver is a user-defined function used to modify any data further.
toJSON()	Dictates how JSON.stringify will serialize data.

Math Object

The **Math object** provides the capability of performing calculations. Table G–17 summarizes the Math object properties and methods.

Table G–17 Math Object

Property	Description
E	Base of a natural logarithm
LN10	Natural logarithm of 10
LN2	Natural logarithm of 2
LOG2E	Base-2 logarithm of e
LOG10E	Base-10 logarithm of e
PI	Ratio of the circumference of a circle to its diameter
SQRT1_2	1 divided by the square root of 2
SQRT2	The square root of 2
Method	**Function**
abs(x)	Absolute value of x
acos(x)	Arc cosine of x
asin(x)	Arc sine of x
atan(x)	Arc tangent of x
atan2(y,x)	Angle from the x-axis
ceil(x)	Value of x rounded to the next highest integer
cos(x)	Cosine of x
exp(x)	Exponent of x
floor(x)	x rounded to the next lowest integer
log(x)	Natural logarithm of x

Table G–17 Math Object (continued)	
Property	**Description**
max(x,y)	Larger of two numbers
min(x,y)	Smaller of two numbers
pow(x,y)	x raised to the y power
random()	Random number between 0.0 and 1.0
round(x)	x rounded to the nearest integer
sin(x)	Sine of x
sqrt(x)	Square root of x
tan(x)	Tangent of x

Location Object

The **Location object** allows you to switch to a new Web page. Table G–18 summarizes the Location object properties and methods.

Table G–18 Location Object	
Property	**Description**
hash	URL's anchor
host	Combination of URL's host name and port sections
hostname	URL's host name
href	Full URL address
pathname	URL's path
port	URL's port
protocol	URL's protocol
search	URL's search or query portion
Method	**Function**
reload()	Causes the page currently displayed in the Web browser to open again
replace()	Replaces the currently loaded URL with a different one

Navigator Object

The **Navigator object** is used to get information about the current Web browser. Table G–19 summarizes the Navigator object properties and methods.

Table G–19 Navigator Object	
Property	**Description**
appCodeName	Web browser code name
appName	Web browser name
appVersion	Web browser version
cookieEnabled	Boolean result to indicate if cookies are enabled
language	Language used by the Web browser
mimeTypes[]	Array containing MIME types supported by the client browser
platform	Operating system in use
plugins[]	Array containing installed plugins

Table G–19 Navigator Object (continued)	
Property	**Description**
systemLanguage	Default language of the client system
userAgent	User agent
userLanguage	Language currently in use on the client
Method	**Function**
javaEnabled()	Determines whether Java is enabled in the current browser
plugins.refresh()	Enables newly installed plugins on the client
preference()	Gets or sets a user preference
savePreferences()	Saves all user preferences
taintEnabled()	Boolean that determines whether data tainting is enabled

Window and Frame Objects

The **Window object** represents a browser's window or an individual frame within a window. Thus, every **Frame object** is a window object, and uses all the methods and properties of the Window object. Table G–20 summarizes the Window and Frame objects' properties, methods, and events.

Table G–20 Window and Frame Objects	
Property	**Description**
closed	Boolean value to determine if window has been closed
defaultStatus	Default text that is written to the status bar
document	Reference to the Document object
frames[]	Array listing the Frame objects in the window
history	Reference to the History object
length	Number of frames in a window
location	Reference to the Location object
name	Name of a window
navigator	Points to the Navigator object for the browser
offscreenBuffering	Boolean to determine if updates for the window are buffered
opener	Window object that opens another window
parent	Parent frame that contains the current frame
screen	Screen information where the browser is running
self	Self-reference to the Window object
status	Temporary text that is written to the status bar
top	Topmost Window object that contains the current frame
window	Self-reference to the Window object
Method	**Function**
alert()	Displays a message dialog box with an OK button
blur()	Removes the focus from the window
clearTimeout()	Cancels a set timeout
close()	Closes the window
confirm()	Displays a confirmation dialog box with OK and Cancel buttons
focus()	Makes the Window object the active window

Table G–20 Window and Frame Objects (continued)

Method	Function
moveBy(x,y)	The moveBy() method moves the window horizontally or vertically by the number of pixels; positive numbers move right and down, negative move the opposite direction
moveTo(x,y)	The moveTo() method moves the window to the location specified by the numeric values
open()	Opens a new window
prompt()	Displays a dialog box prompting a user to enter information
setTimeout()	Executes a function after a specified number of milliseconds has elapsed
Event	**Triggered When**
onblur	Window becomes inactive
onerror	Error occurs when the window loads
onfocus	Window becomes active
onload	Document is completely loaded in the window
onresize	Window is resized
onunload	Current document in the window is unloaded

The Window object open() method has many possible parameters. Table G-21 shows the features and values for the open() method.

Table G–21 open() Method

Feature	Description	Written As
location	Includes address bar	"location=yes"
menubar	Includes menu bar	"menubar=yes"
resize	Allows user to resize	"resizeable=yes"
scrollbars	Includes scroll bars	"scrollbars=yes"
status	Includes status bar	"status=yes"
titlebar	Removes title bar	"titlebar=false"
toolbar	Includes toolbar	"toolbar=yes"
width	States width in pixels	"width=220"
height	States height in pixels	"height=450"

Number Object

The **Number object** gives support for special constants that may be platform specific and exposes one conversion method. Table G–22 summarizes the Number object properties and methods.

Table G–22 Number Object

Property	Description
MAX_VALUE	Maximum numeric value
MIN_VALUE	Minimum numeric value
NaN	Not a number value
NEGATIVE_INFINITY	Value for negative infinity
POSITIVE_INFINITY	Value for positive infinity

Table G–22 Number Object (continued)

Method	Description
toExponential()	Returns a string representing the number in exponential notation
toFixed()	Returns a string representing the number in fixed-point notation
toLocaleString()	Returns a string representation of the number based on system setting
toPrecision()	Returns a string representing the number to a specified precision in fixed-point notation
toString()	Converts a numeric value to a string value

Function Object

The **Function object** gives the programmer access to information about specific functions. Table G–23 summarizes the Function object properties and methods.

Table G–23 Function Object

Property	Description
arguments[]	Array containing arguments passed to the function
arity	Number of arguments declared for the function
caller	Name of the function that called the current one
length	Number of arguments declared for the function
prototype	Prototype for a class of objects
Method	**Description**
apply()	Uses a function as a method for an object
call()	Allows you to call (execute) a method of another object in the context of a different object (the calling object)
toSource()	Returns a string representing the source code of the function; overrides the Object .toSource method
toString()	Converts a function to a string value

Screen Object

The **Screen object** gives platform-specific information about the user's screen. Table G–24 summarizes the Screen object properties.

Table G–24 Screen Object

Property	Description
availHeight	Available height of the screen
availLeft	First horizontal pixel available
availTop	First vertical pixel available
availWidth	Available width of the screen
colorDepth	Depth of the client browser's color palette
height	Height of the client screen
pixelDepth	Depth of the client browser's screen
width	Width of the client screen

Boolean Object

The **Boolean object** converts other objects to Boolean values. A value of False is returned for values of undefined, null, 0, -0, false, NaN, or an empty string (""). All other values return a value of True. Table G–25 summarizes the methods for the Boolean object.

Table G–25 Boolean Object

Method	Function
toSource	Returns an object literal representing the specified Boolean object; you can use this value to create a new object. It overrides the Object.toSource method.
toString	Returns a string representing the specified object. It overrides the Object.toString method.

Array Object

An **array** is an ordered set of values associated with a single variable name. Table G–26 summarizes the properties and methods for the Array object.

Table G–26 Array Object

Property	Description
index	For an array created by a regular expression match, the zero-based index of the match in the string
input	For an array created by a regular expression match, reflects the original string against which the regular expression was matched
length	Reflects the number of elements in an array; can be changed to truncate or extend array
Method	**Function**
concat()	Joins two arrays and returns a new array
join()	Joins all elements of an array into a string
pop()	Removes the last element from an array and returns that element
push()	Adds one or more elements to the end of an array and returns the new length of the array
reverse()	Transposes the elements of an array; first array element becomes the last and the last becomes the first
shift()	Removes the first element from an array and returns that element
slice()	Extracts a section of an array and returns a new array
splice()	Adds and/or removes elements from an array
sort()	Sorts the elements of an array
toSource()	Returns an array literal representing the specified array; use this value to create a new array as it overrides the Object.toSource method
toLocaleString()	Returns a string representing the array and its elements
toString()	Returns a string representing the array and its elements; overrides the Object.toString method
unshift()	Adds one or more elements to the front of an array and returns the new length of the array

String Object

The **String object** represents a set of characters. Any object converted to the String object can use any of the string methods. Table G–27 summarizes the property and methods for the String object.

Table G–27 String Object

Property	Description
length	Specifies the length of the string
Method	**Function**
anchor()	Creates a hypertext target
big()	Displays text in a big font as if it were in a <big> … </big> tag
blink()	Blinks text as if it were in a <blink> … </blink> tag
bold()	Displays text as if it were in a <b> … </b> tag
charAt()	Returns the character at the specified location (relative index)
charCodeAt()	Returns a number indicating the Unicode value of the character at the given location (relative index)
concat()	Combines the text of two strings
fixed()	Displays text in a fixed-pitch font as if it were in a <tt> … </tt> tag
fontcolor()	Displays text in the specified color as if it were in a <font> … </font> tag
fontsize()	Displays text in the specified font size as if it were in a <font> … </font> tag
fromCharCode()	Creates a string by using the specified sequence of Unicode values
indexOf()	Returns the index within the calling String object of the first occurrence of the specified value, or –1 if not found
italics()	Displays a string to be italic as if it were in an <i> … </i> tag
lastIndexOf()	Returns the index within the calling String object of the last occurrence of the specified value, or –1 if not found
link()	Creates an HTML hypertext link that requests another URL
match()	Matches a regular expression against a string
replace()	Matches a regular expression and a string, and replaces the matched substring with a new substring
search()	Searches for a match between a regular expression and a specified string
slice()	Returns a new string from an existing string
small()	Displays text in a small font as if it were in a <small> … </small> tag
split()	Splits a String object into an array of substrings
strike()	Displays text as struck-out text as if it were in a <strike> … </strike> tag
sub()	Displays text as a subscript as if it were in a _… tag
substr()	Returns the characters in a string starting at a specific location for a specific length
substring()	Returns a substring of a string
sup()	Displays text as a superscript as if it were in a […] tag
toLowerCase()	Displays a string value converted to lowercase
toSource()	Returns the source of the instance created; overrides the Object.toSource method
toString()	Returns the object type or name of the constructor that created the object; overrides the Object.toString method
toUpperCase()	Displays a string value converted to uppercase

Regular Expression

A Regular Expression (RegExp) is used for pattern matching. The special characters used for the patterns are described in Table G–28.

Table G–28 RegExp

Character	Description
/	Every pattern must begin with a slash
\d	Match any digit
\s	Match any space, newline, tab, return
\w	Match any alphanumeric character
^	Beginning of a string
$	End of a string
?	First of all characters (?xy) means x or xy
*	Multiple of characters (*xy) means x or xy or xyy
+	Multiple of all characters (xy+) means xy, or xyy, or xyyy
[xx]	Used in brackets for alternatives; (Adobe CS[234]) means Adobe CS2, Adobe CS3, or Adobe CS4
[x–x]	Used in brackets for sequence; (JavaScript 1.[1–5]) means JavaScript 1.1 or JavaScript 1.2, etc.
[^x–x]	Used in brackets to match anything BUT the selected characters; ([^w–y]) means any letter but w through y.
(x)	Subpattern
.	The dot means any character
{min, max}	The minimum or maximum number of sequences; (x{1,3}) means x or xx or xxx

Global Functions

Table G–29 summarizes the **global functions** that always are available in JavaScript.

Table G–29 Global Functions

Function	Description
decodeURI()	Decodes or replaces an escape sequence in the encoded URI with the character that it represents; cannot decode escape sequence not coded by encoded URI
decodeURI	Decodes or replaces each escape sequence in the encoded URI Component() component with the character that it represents
escape()	Returns the hexadecimal code
eval()	Evaluates a string of JavaScript code without reference to a particular object
isFinite()	Evaluates an argument to determine whether it is a finite number
isNaN()	Evaluates an argument to determine if it is not a number
number()	Converts an object to a number
parseFloat()	Parses a string argument and returns a floating-point number
parseInt()	Parses a string argument and returns an integer
string()	Converts an object to a string
encodeURI()	Replaces all characters, except those with special meaning in a URI, with the appropriate UTF-8 escape sequences
encodeURI	Assumes that the URI is not complete, and does not treat reserved Component() characters as if they have special meaning and encodes them
unescape()	Returns the ASCII string for the specified hexadecimal encoding value

Appendix H

XML Quick Reference

What Is XML?

Extensible Markup Language (XML) is a subset of the Standard Generalized Markup Language (SGML). XML allows developers to create their own document elements or tags. The World Wide Web Consortium (W3C, *www.w3.org*) develops the standards for XML and other Web languages.

An XML document consists of two main parts: the **prolog** and the **document instance**. The prolog contains processing instructions and any additional comments necessary to provide information about the document's content and structure. An XML prolog can include any of the following:

- XML declaration statements and comments
- Document type declaration with an optional Document Type Definition (DTD) to define elements, attributes, and logical relationships of data
- Optional link to either a CSS or XSL style sheet

The document instance contains the main content or elements of the XML document and provides a logical structure for the document.

Well-Formed and Valid XML Documents

XML documents must be well formed to be processed by an application. A valid XML document is one that adheres to the rules and structure specified in a DTD or an XML Schema Definition (XSD). The element is the basic building block of any XML file. Table H–1 shows the syntax rules that define well-formed and valid XML documents. An XML document must be at least well formed. Besides the Web site shown in Chapter 12, *http://tools.decisionsoft.com/schemaValidate/index.jsp*, you can check the syntax of your XML document at *http://www.w3schools.com/dom/dom_validate.asp* or check for a valid DTD at *http://www.xmlvalidation.com/*. See the Web sites for instructions on how to use and validate XML documents.

Table H–1 Rules for Well-Formed and Valid XML Documents

Rule Number	Rules
1	XML is case sensitive.
2	Element tags must be nested correctly; the document must contain at least one root element and nest the child elements within the root.
3	All elements include a start tag and end tag.
4	Element attribute values must be enclosed in quotation marks.
5	Elements can be empty; empty elements must be formatted correctly to include a / (forward slash) before the end tag.
6	Entity references use < and & characters, which must be used in entity references.

XML Processing Instructions

Table H–2 shows the basic form of the declarations, statements, and comments found in the prolog section of an XML document.

Table H–2 XML Instructions

Instruction	General Form	Example	Comment
XML declaration	<?xml version="#" [encoding="encoding" standalone="yes|no"]?>	<?xml version="1.0" standalone="yes"?>	Defines version, character encoding, and if DTD is required to parse XML document
Document type declaration	<!DOCTYPE ROOT-ELEMENT PUBLIC/SYSTEM="URL-DTD.DTD">	<!DOCTYPE PHONELIST SYSTEM="PHONELIST.DTD">	PUBLIC indicates location of public DTD; SYSTEM indicates location of private DTD
Processing Instruction	<?target attribute="value" ?>	<?xml-stylesheet type="text/xsl" href="xslalphaclublist.xsl"?>	Gives instruction to the application to access a document or file outside the application (in this example, a style sheet); can include one or more attributes
Comment	<!--Comments -->	<!-- File Name: studentclubs.xml -->	Provides a user or developer with information about the document; comments are ignored by application
Character Data Type	<![CDATA [text]]>	<![CDATA [The <b> tag should always have an end </b> tag.]]	Special section of character data not interpreted as markup, as opposed to parsed character data (PCDATA), to which the XML syntax rules apply; CDATA sections often used to show XML or HTML syntax examples

XML Element and Attribute Rules

Elements must be bound by start and end tags or be an empty element. Elements may contain other elements, but they must be nested in the proper order. Table H–3 lists the syntax rules for creating valid XML elements. Table H–4 contains a list of element rules. Table H–5 shows examples of valid, invalid, and empty XML elements.

Table H–3 XML Element Syntax Rules

Rule Number	Rules
1	Must begin with a letter or an underscore
2	May contain letters, numbers, hyphens, periods, or underscores
3	May not contain spaces, commas, or symbols (@#$%^&*!)
4	May not begin with XML, which is reserved for future use
5	Names are case sensitive; start and end tags must use same case
6	Colons are acceptable only for declaring namespaces
7	Empty elements have no text or values, but may contain attributes

Table H–4 XML Element Rules

Symbol	Meaning
#PCDATA	Element contains parsed character data or text and conforms to XML constraints (CDATA attributes are non-parsed character data.)
element name (by itself)	Element name may be used one time only
element name ?	Element is used either once or not at all
element name +	Element has a one-to-many (1:n) relationship
element name *	Element has a zero, or one-to-many (1:n) relationship
, (comma)	Used between elements to indicate order
| (bar)	Used between elements to indicate either or
( )	Used to group related elements together; may be nested

Table H–5 Valid and Invalid Examples of XML Elements

Example	Comment
<FirstName></FirstName>	Valid
<45Degree></45Degree>	Invalid (starts with a numeral)
<_Project></_Project>	Valid
<First-Name></First-Name>	Valid
<Hanger_41></Hanger_41>	Valid
<Java Script></Java Script>	Invalid (contains a space)
<xmlproject></xmlproject>	Invalid (may not begin with xml)
<Para></PARA>	Invalid (start and end tags use different case)
<Picture SRC="mypic.jpg" />	Valid empty element

Element attributes describe additional information about the element. Attribute values must be enclosed in quotation marks (either single or double quotation marks are acceptable). Attribute names follow the same rules as elements. Table H–6 shows the reserved attributes.

Table H–6 Reserved Attributes

Attribute	Comment	Example
xml:lang="code"	where code indicates language of element body	<Greet xml:lang="en">Hey</Greet>
xml:space="action"	where action is either default or preserve; preserve means preserve white space, default means treat white space based on default settings	<Lines xml:space="preserve">This is one line </Lines>
xml:link="type"	where type is simple, extended, locator, group, or document	<a xml:link="simple" href=http://www.w3.org>W3C</A>

XML Schema Definition (XSD)

An **XML Schema Definition** (**XSD**) describes in more exact detail the structure of an XML document. Because the XML document can be used as a database, its structure must be defined. The XSD describes the fields, the data types, and the values that can be stored in a field. XSD files are external documents to the XML document instance and are linked to the XML file in the root xml tag.

The **Document Type Definition (DTD)** is a precursor to the XSD and defines the elements and attributes in an XML document. While the DTD was used to validate the structure of an XML file, it has been abandoned because the XSD provides more detail about the XML structure because it can define specific data types to enforce data validity. A DTD defines an XML document using one data type. In an XSD, you must define the content by its particular type of data. For example, a DTD cannot define a field as a date, whereas an XSD can. Moreover, a DTD cannot create and define complex data types in the same way an XSD can. In an XSD, an element defined as a date must conform to the format of a date.

An XML Schema Definition is an XML file in itself. It must conform to the same rules of any XML document to be valid and well formed. An XSD file contains the primary components of simple type definitions, complex type definitions, attributes declarations, and elements. **Simple type** definitions do not contain child elements nor do they contain attributes. **Complex type** definitions contain other elements and attributes. **Attributes** are values that appear in start or empty elements. **Elements** define the contents of an XML file and the relationship to other elements.

The <schema> element is the root element of every XSD. The <schema> contains information to identify and associate the namespace to the schema definitions. The xmlns attribute points to the URI to define the namespace. A **namespace** is used to prevent confusion over multiple elements being used by different sources. These elements may have the same name but have data types. Table H–7 shows the general form of the <schema> root element of the XSD defining the namespace.

Table H–7 The Root <schema> Element

Root element:	<xs:schema xmlns:xs="http://www.w3.org/2001/XMLSchema" [targetNamespace="URI " xmlns="URI " elementFormDefault="qualified"] >
Comment:	The xs is the namespace. The xmlns is the XML namespace location and associates the xs to the schema of all schemas at the *www.w3.org* Web site. The most used namespaces are xs or xsd. The optional elements within brackets are targetNamespace that associates other namespace items with the designated URI. The xmlns defines the default namespace location and the elementFormDefault Indicates the definition must be namespace qualified.
Example	<xs:schema xmlns:xs="http://www.w3.org/2001/XMLSchema">

To define an XML element, the XSD <element> tag names the element and data type. Table H–8 shows the general form of the XSD <element> tag.

Table H–8 The <element> Tag Element

General form:	<xs:element name="field name" type="data type" />
Comment:	xs: is a namespace, to differentiate this element from any other element that may have the same name. The name is an attribute to define the field name; type is an attribute to state one of the valid data types. Simple elements may have an optional default or fix attributes to assign a default value to a field. The default value is assigned if no other value is assigned; the fixed value does not allow any other value to be assigned. Most developers use xs or xsd as a default namespace. This book uses xs.
Examples:	<xs:element name="qoh" type="xs:integer" default="0" />

Table H–9 defines the remaining XSD elements that define the structure of any XML document.

Table H–9 XSD Elements

Element Name	Description
all	Indicates child elements can appear in any order (See sequence below.)
annotation	Indicates the element for schema comments
any	Allows extension of the XML document with elements not defined by the schema
anyAttribute	Allows extension of the XML document with attributes not defined by the schema
appInfo	Contained within the annotation with information to be used by the application
attribute	Defines an attribute
attributeGroup	Defines an attribute group to be used in complex type definitions
choice	Within a group, choice, sequence, complexType, or restriction elements, only one of the elements may be present within the element
complexContent	Indicates whether mixed content is allowed; an element of xs:extension allows mixed, whereas xs:restriction does not allow mixed content
complexType	Defines a complex type element
documentation	Contained with the annotation for comments about the schema
element	Defines an element
extension	Combined with complexContent to allow existing simpleType or complexType element mixed content
field	An XPath expression used by unique, key, or keyref
group	Defines a group of elements used in a complex type definition
import	References schemas for namespace for additional namespace definitions
include	Used to break large schemas into smaller parts
key	Indicates an attribute or element value as a key that must be unique
keyref	Defines constraints on specified key or unique element
list	Available only in a simple type element to specify a list of values to be used in content
notation	Allows the format of non-XML data
redefine	Redefines simple, complex types, and groups (see include)
restriction	Defines restrictions on a simpleType, simpleContent, or a complexContent to clarify domains (valid ranges)
schema	Defines the root element of a schema
selector	Selects a set of elements for an identity constraint (see key, unique, keyref)
sequence	Indicates that the child elements must appear in a sequence.
simpleContent	Used in complexType elements to define simple content such as text and attributes
simpleType	Defines a simple type and specifies the constraints and information about the values of attributes or text-only elements
union	Allows creation of simple type as a collection (union) of more than one type of data
unique	Indicates an element or an attribute value must be unique within the document

Simple Types

A simple element is an XML element that does not contain any other elements or attributes. In the XSD, the <element> tag declares the name of the element and its data type. A sample simple XML element and its associated schema is shown in Table H–10.

Table H–10 Simple Type Element

Simple XML Element	XML Schema
an XML element that contain only text <first_name>Bill</first_name>	<xs:element name="first_name" type="string" />

The <element> in the XSD must have a data type. Table H–11 shows the most common data types.

Table H–11 XSD Data Types

Data Types	Description
String	Data is any set of characters
Integer	Data is any whole number not a fraction
Decimal	Data is any number that contains a decimal fraction
Date	Represent the date as YYYY-MM-DD
Boolean	Binary logic of true or false, yes or no, or on or off
Binary	A set of binary codes in groups of eight
AnyURI	A valid URI Internet address

Data types can have constraints or facets. These values further define restrictions or validations for the data contained within an XML element beyond whether it is a string or a numeric value. For example, to specifically define acceptable values in an element, enumeration constraint is used to list acceptable values. Table H–12 shows the common constraints or facets.

Table H–12 Constraints or Facets

Data Type Constraints	Description
enumeration	A list of acceptable values
fractionDigits	Defines the maximum number of decimal places and value must be equal to or greater than zero
length	Explicitly states the number of characters or list items allowed and must be equal to or greater than zero
maxExclusive	The numeric values for the upper bound for a domain
maxInclusive	Defines the upper bounds for numeric values
maxLength	Defines the maximum number of characters or list items allowed and the value must be equal to or greater than zero
minExclusive	The numeric values for the lower bounds
minInclusive	Defines the lower bounds for numeric values
minLength	Defines the minimum number of characters or list items allowed and the value must be equal to or greater than zero
pattern	Defines the exact sequence of characters that are acceptable
totalDigits	Defines the number of digits allowed and must be greater than zero
whiteSpace	Defines line feeds, tabs, spaces, and carriage returns

Complex Types

A complex element is an XML element that contains other elements or attributes. In the XSD, the <element> tag declares the name of the element and its data type. A sample complex element and its associated schema is shown in Table H–13.

Table H–13 Complex Type Element

Complex XML Element	XML Schema
an XML element that contains child elements or attributes <schedule_item> <course_no>CSCI-C340</course_no> <course_title>Web programming</course_title> </schedule_item>	<xs:element name="schedule item"> <xs:completeType> <xs:sequence> <xs:element name="course_no" type="string" /> <xs:element name="course_title" type="string" /> </ xs:sequence> </ xs:complexType> </ xs:element>

XSL Style Sheets

Extensible Stylesheet Language (**XSL**), which is a language for expressing style sheets, incorporates three technologies:

- XSL Transformations (**XSLT**), a language for transforming XML documents into other types of documents.
- XML Path Language (**XPath**), a language used by XSLT to access or refer to parts of an XML document.
- **XSL Formatting Objects**, a language that defines XML formatting and display.

Table H–14 shows the XSLT elements specified by the W3C.

Table H–14 XSLT Elements

Element Name	Description	Attributes
xsl:apply-imports	Applies template rule from an imported style sheet	N/A
xsl:apply-templates	Applies a template to the current element	order-by="+|−pattern" select="pattern"
xsl:attribute	Adds a new attribute to the current output element	name="attribute-name"
xsl:attribute-set	Defines a named set of attributes	N/A
xsl:call-template	Provides a way to call a named template	name="template-name"
xsl:choose	Provides a selection mechanism based on conditions	N/A
xsl:comment	Adds a comment node to the output	N/A
xsl:copy	Copies the current node to the output	N/A
xsl:copy-of	Creates a copy of the current node	N/A
xsl:decimal-format	Defines the characters and symbols to be used when converting numbers into strings in conjunction with the format-number() function	N/A
xsl:element	Adds a new element node to the output	name="name"
xsl:fallback	Indicates code to execute if the processor does not support an XSLT element	N/A
xsl:for-each	Provides a mechanism to create a loop in the output stream	select="pattern" order-by="−|+ pattern"
xsl:if	Provides a conditional branch mechanism based on a condition	match="pattern"
xsl:import and xsl:include	Merges rules from different style sheets	N/A
xsl:key	Declares a named key that can be used in the style sheet with the key() function	N/A
xsl:message	Writes error message to the output	N/A

Table H–14 XSLT Elements (continued)

Element Name	Description	Attributes
xsl:namespace-alias	Replaces namespaces in the style sheet with different namespaces in the output	N/A
xsl:number	Determines the integer position of the current node and formats a number	N/A
xsl:otherwise	Is part of the choose mechanism (see xsl:choose)	N/A
xsl:output	Defines the format of the output document	N/A
xsl:param	Declares a local or global parameter	N/A
xsl:preserve-space	Indicates elements to preserve white space	N/A
xsl:processing-instruction	Adds a processing statement or instruction to the output	name="name"
xsl:sort	Reorders input before copying to output	N/A
xsl:strip-space	Indicates elements to remove white space	N/A
xsl:stylesheet	Defines the root element of the style sheet	xmlns:xml="namespace" language="language" indent-result="yes|no"
xsl:template	Defines a template	match="pattern" language="language"
xsl:text	Writes literal text or spaces to the output	N/A
xsl:transform	The root element of a style sheet	N/A
xsl:value-of	Defines a node to insert into the output	select="pattern"
xsl:variable	Defines constants	N/A
xsl:when	Is part of the choose mechanism (see xsl:choose)	test="expression"
xsl:with-param	Defines the value of a parameter to be passed into a template	N/A

Document Type Definition (DTD)

A **document type declaration** is a processing instruction that tells the processor where to locate the Document Type Definition. A **Document Type Definition** (**DTD**) defines the elements and attributes in an XML document. A DTD also defines the order in which the elements and attributes appear. The DTD can be embedded within a document type declaration, or linked as an external document. Using a DTD allows the developer to confirm that an XML document is **valid**, meaning it conforms to the specified structure in the DTD. The DTD, however, has been largely replaced by developers in favor of the more succinct definition of the XML Schema Definition. It is included here strictly for reference only.

The prolog also can contain a document type declaration that tells the processor where to locate the DTD. The DTD can be an external file or embedded within the XML document. The DTD has two elements that indicate a relationship between the parent (CLASSIC_BOOKS) and the child (BOOK). Table H–15 shows the general form of a document type declaration identifying an embedded DTD.

Table H–15 General Form of a Document Type Declaration and an Embedded Document Type Definition	
General form:	<!DOCTYPE Name [<!ELEMENT Parent Definition (Child Definition * | + | ?)> <!ELEMENT Child Definition (child element list) <!ELEMENT Child element Definition ANY|(#PCDATA)>] >
Comment:	!DOCTYPE is a reserved word that indicates the start of a document type declaration. Name is any valid name of an element and defines the name of the embedded DTD. The square bracket on line 2 indicates the beginning of the DTD. !ELEMENT is a reserved word that defines the type of elements in the document. The child definition qualifiers are an asterisk (*), a plus sign (+), or a question mark (?). The asterisk means zero to many, the plus sign means one to many, and the question mark means zero or one only. Definition is one or more valid element definitions. ANY indicates that any type of data may be associated with the element. (#PCDATA) indicates that the element contains parsed character data, which is text data. The square bracket in line 6 ends the DTD, and the right angle bracket on line 7 ends the document type declaration.
Example:	<!DOCTYPE [<!ELEMENT CLASSIC_BOOKS (BOOK*)> <!ELEMENT BOOK (TITLE, YEAR, AUTHOR, QOH, BIN, COST)> <!ELEMENT TITLE (#PCDATA)> <!ELEMENT YEAR (#PCDATA)> <!ELEMENT AUTHOR (#PCDATA)> <!ELEMENT QOH (#PCDATA)> <!ELEMENT BIN (#PCDATA)> <!ELEMENT COST (#PCDATA)>] >

A **Document Type Definition (DTD)** is similar to a database schema and defines the elements and attributes in an XML document. A DTD indicates how elements of an XML document relate to each other. A DTD provides the grammar rules of a document. When an XML document adheres to a DTD, it is considered valid.

A DTD can include element declarations, attribute list declarations, entity declarations, and notation declarations. An element declaration defines the type of content contained in an element. Table H–16 describes the basic form of an element declaration.

Table H–16 General Form of an Element Declaration	
General form:	<!ELEMENT element-name (rule)>
Comment:	!ELEMENT is the declaration element-name; is any valid XML element name (see rules in Table H–3 on page APP 58); rule is a keyword, such as ANY or #PCDATA. The ANY keyword means other valid tags and data can be displayed; #PCDATA means only parsed character data can be displayed.
Example:	<!ELEMENT SONG (Title, Singer)> <!ELEMENT Title (#PCDATA)> <!ELEMENT Singer (#PCDATA)>

Attribute List Declarations

A DTD also can contain an attribute list declaration. The items in the attribute list must correspond to any attributes declared within XML elements. Table H–17 shows the general form of an attribute list declaration.

Table H–17 General Form of an Attribute List Declaration

General form:	<!ATTLIST element-name attribute-name data-type default-value>
Comment:	The element-name is the name of the XML element. The attribute-name is the name of the attribute. The data-type is the data type of the attribute. The default-value is any default value of the attribute. In the example, width is an attribute, with a CDATA (character data) type and default value of 10.
Example:	<!ATTLIST txtBox width CDATA "10">

The data type in an attribute list declaration can be one of 10 different kinds of data type attributes, as shown in Table H–18.

Table H–18 DTD Data Type Attributes

Type	Description
CDATA	Character data; can include any character string as well as special symbols for ampersand (&), less than and greater than symbols or angle brackets (< or >), or quotation marks (")
Enumerated	List of possible values for an attribute; only one can be used
ENTITY	Single entity; either external data or declared DTD entity
ENTITIES	Multiple entities; either external data or declared in DTD
ID	Unique element identifier for an attribute that distinguishes one element from others
IDREF	Identifies the value of an attribute of a unique ID
IDREFS	Identifies multiple values for an attribute, separated by white space
NMTOKEN	XML name token; restricts the attribute value to any valid XML name (letters, number, hyphens, underscores, and periods)
NMTOKENS	Allows the attribute value to include multiple XML tokens, separated by white space
NOTATION	Allows the attribute value to be a value specified in a DTD notation declaration

The default value in an attribute list declaration must match the data type. If a specific value is noted, the value must be enclosed within quotation marks. A default value consists of one of the four options shown in Table H–19.

Table H–19 DTD Data Type Attributes

Modifier	Description
#REQUIRED	Attribute value must be specified with the element
#IMPLIED	Attribute value is optional; if used in an element type, no default value is supplied
#FIXED "value"	Attribute value is fixed and must always take the default value assigned
"value"	Specific value set at the default attribute value

Entity Declarations

As just discussed, a DTD also can include entity declarations, which assign a name to a block of text or other characters that can be interpreted as markup language and substituted in a document. The replacement text must begin with an ampersand (&) and end with a semicolon (;). Entity declarations can be internal or external. Table H–20 shows the general form of an internal entity declaration. Table H–21 shows the predefined symbols that can be used in an entity declaration.

Table H–20 General Form of Internal Entity Declaration

General form:	<!ENTITY name "replacement;"> <ELEMENT>text "&replacement;"</ELEMENT>
Comment:	The attribute name is a valid element name and the replacement is the entity characters to be substituted within the string. Circular references are not allowed.
Example:	<!ENTITY copyright "©"> <PUBLISHED>2010, Course Technology ©right;</PUBLISHED>

Table H–21 Predefined Entity Symbols

Entity	Symbol	Explanation
&	&	Cannot be used in processing instructions
<	<	Use with attributes beginning with quotation marks
>	>	Use after]] in normal text and processing instructions
"	"	Use in attributes within double quotation marks
'	'	Use in attributes within single quotation marks
&#xhex		To use a hexadecimal value for a character, such as A9 for the copyright symbol (©)

XML allows the use of external entities to refer to the contents of another file. An external entity exists at a specified location or URL. The content of the external file is inserted at the point of reference and parsed as part of the referring document. Table H–22 shows the general form of an external entity.

Table H–22 General Form of an External Entity

General form:	<!ENTITY name PUBLIC/SYSTEM "identifier"> <ELEMENT>text "&replacement;" </ELEMENT>
Comment:	The attribute name is a valid element name; identifier is an identifier that points to a file on that system or a public file available via URL. ENTITY must be declared first.
Example:	<!ENTITY stockquotes SYSTEM "http://www.stockquotes.com/dowjones.xml"> <finances> <dowjones>Dow Jones Industrial Averages</dowjones> &stockquotes; </finances>

Unparsed Entities and Notation Declarations

A notation declaration tells a processor that an entity refers to non-XML content that should not be parsed. Unparsed entities are used most frequently on XML elements that incorporate graphics into a document.

A notation also has to be declared in an entity. An unparsed entity is indicated by the NDATA keyword. Ampersands and semicolons are not used with unparsed data. Table H–23 shows an example.

Table H–23 Unparsed Entity Example

<!ENTITY imageA SYSTEM http://www.mysite.com/myimage.gif NDATA GIF89a><image src="imageA" />

Index

C

E

F

G

H

I

J

K

L

M

N

O

T

U

V

W

X

Y